FRONT PAGE
VIETNAM

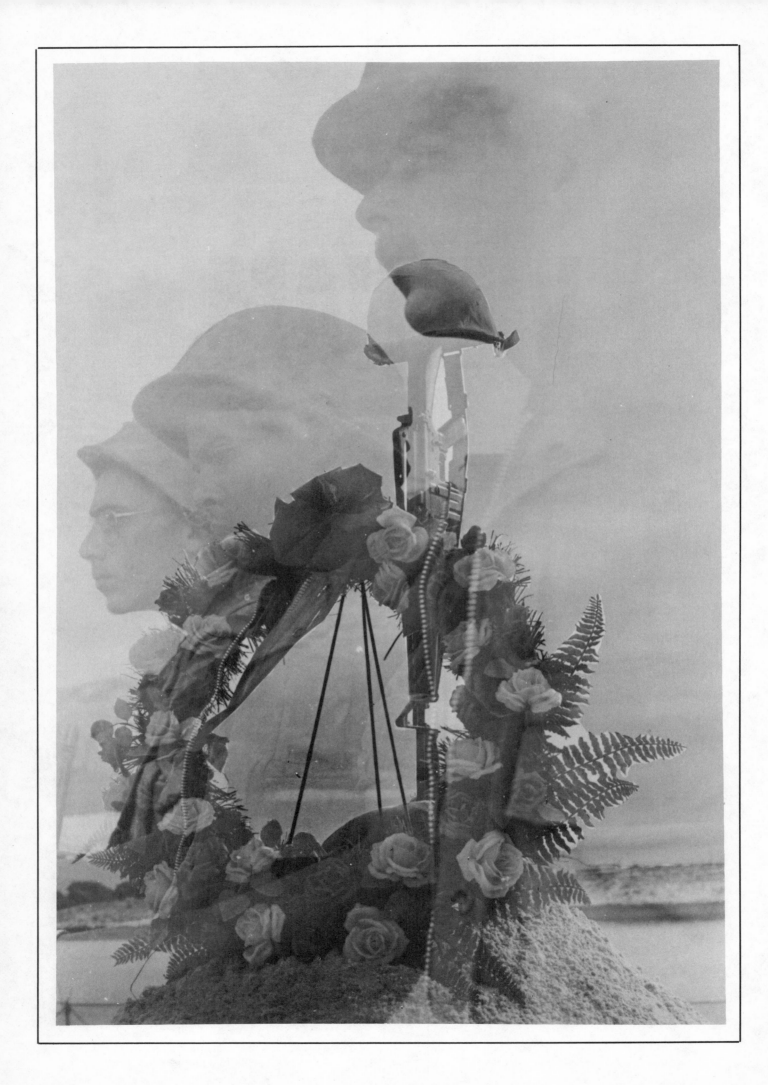

FRONT PAGE
VIETNAM

As Reported By
The New York Times

**Edited By
Arleen Keylin
and
Suri Boiangiu**

Introduction By Drew Middleton

Arno Press
New York 1979

Copyright © 1950, 1954, 1955, 1961, 1962, 1963, 1964,
1965, 1966, 1967, 1968, 1969, 1970, 1971, 1972, 1973
1974, 1975, 1976, 1977, 1978 by The New York Times Company.

Copyright © 1979 by The New York Times Company.

Library of Congress Cataloging in Publication Data

Main entry under title:

Front page Vietnam.

 SUMMARY: Text and photographs trace the conflict
and American involvement in Vietnam as reported by the
New York Times.
 1. Vietnamese Conflict, 1961–1975--United States.
2. United States--History--1945-   3. Vietnam
--History--1945-1975. [1. Vietnamese Conflict, 1961-
1975. 2. United States--History--1945-   3. Vietnam
--History--1945-1975] I. Keylin, Arleen. II. Boiangiu,
Suri. III. New York times.
DS558.F76   959.704'3373   79-17462
ISBN 0-405-12492-9

Book design by Stephanie Rhodes
Editorial Assistant: Jonathan Cohen

Manufactured in the United States of America

Contents

VIETNAM

Introduction

The story told by this collection of front pages from *The New York Times* must be accounted one of the most important in the history of the Republic. It tells how a great power, acting—its leaders and its people originally believed—for the highest moral and political motives, enmired itself in a war halfway around the world. The war was one which could never have been won completely because victory of the battlefield, although possible, would have been incompatible with the convictions of a great mass of Americans. This, of course, is the major lesson of the war. The military side can not be separated from the political side; the two are interdependent. History has taught the lesson repeatedly, but, unhappily, it must be learned by every great power.

The tale told by these front pages is much else. Courage and cowardice, arrogance and humility, insight and blunders march across the pages. Names that once seemed so important, Diem and Calley, Taylor and Lodge, Lynd and Bunker, appear again. And this, the raw material of history, reminds us that wars can never be neatly packaged. They compound the primitive and the sophisticated; jungle ambush and the advent of "smart bombs." Battles, even the most complete victories like Waterloo, are a sloppy, bloody business.

The relation between what was happening in Vietnam, and to a lesser extent in Laos and Cambodia, and in the United States gives this book a special significance.

At the outset nothing foreshadowed the storm that was to break. The United States offered to train troops fighting the Communists in Indochina and that indefatigable anti-Communist, John Foster Dulles, appealed for unity to block "Red Rule" in Southeast Asia. The notion that the People's Republic of China would enter the war, a mirage that endured for 20 years, made its appearance in 1955. But Dienbienphu fell, the brave, mismanaged French intervention ended and the western powers moved to Geneva to pick up the pieces.

In July of 1954 an armistice was signed and Vietnam was divided at the 17th parallel. In the next year the pace quickened, the American stake increased. While the Americans began to train the Vietnamese, an interminable process, the internal political rivalries in Saigon increased, complicating the task of successive administrations in Washington and, ultimately, reinforcing the arguments of those who argued that the governments of the South were unrepresentative and corrupt. There was a good deal of truth in this, although the same could have been said about a half dozen other governments in East Asia, some of them reliable allies of the United States.

The perceptive reader may see 1964 as the year in which United States involvement moved beyond training and logistical support to active military participation. By August North Vietnamese torpedo boats had fired on an American destroyer and two days later American bombers attacked bases in the north in what was termed "limited retaliation." As the war expanded, these front pages demonstrate, it penetrated areas and raised issues undreamed of in the Fifties. Increasing American political involvement went hand in hand with the growth of the military effort. It is worth noting, too, that the United States' quest for a peaceful solution began early in the conflict. In April of 1965 President Johnson offered to begin peace talks "unconditionally" and proposed $1 billion in aid for Asia.

But by the end of that month heavy bombers from Guam were attacking targets in North Vietnam. And in July the President ordered 50,000 more men to Southeast Asia and raised the draft quotas. The drama was being played in three different theaters that year; in the steaming, treacherous jungles of Vietnam, at the presidential palace in Saigon and at the White House. The world knew precious little about events in Hanoi but now the war moved to another level closely related to the North Vietnamese and their policies. Early in 1966, at the time when American troops were launching a major attack, Staughton Lynd emerged as one of the most persuasive leaders of the nascent anti-war movement.

Four months later Mr. Johnson was appealing for "unity" in the war. From that point until the end of hostilities, Hanoi, sometimes by chance, sometimes by design, used the activities of the anti-war movement in the United States to discredit America around the world. The movement went beyond America, touching countries with no military, economic or political interests in Vietnam. At home and abroad it played a major role.

This book also will remind the reader that the Johnson Administration did try, however unsuccessfully, to bring the war to a close. In October 1966 the administration pledged itself to leave Vietnam six months after Hanoi abandoned the war. The next year the peace effort continued. But it made little impression on the anti-war movement. By April of 1967, 100,000 anti-war demonstrators had rallied at the United Nations. By August the administration announced a goal of 525,000 troops in Vietnam. Remorselessly, the headlines sweep slowly toward the bitter climax: the Tet offensive and a new offer of peace terms to Hanoi. Tet, we can see now, was a military defeat for the North Vietnamese; one that, with consummate skill, they turned into a resounding political and propaganda triumph.

Now the American tide begins to ebb. In April of 1968 Mr. Johnson announces that he will not run again for the presidency and halts raids on North Vietnam. Almost desperately he asks again that Hanoi join in moves toward peace. That autumn Richard Nixon is elected president and, as the protests against the war expand, the new administration begins its search for a peace formula. In November the President appeals for popular support for a "secret" military withdrawal timetable. That month a quarter of a million rallied in Washington to protest the continuation of the war. And the war expands into Cambodia and Laos instead of contracting. The headlines of the last years of the American involvement portray a country uncertain of its direction, increasingly distrustful of its leaders; an Army of doubtful morale, a people shaken by the revelations in *The New York Times'* report on the Pentagon Papers. The war has begun to unravel.

By August of 1972 the last ground combat troops have left Vietnam. But the B-52's make their heaviest attack on North Vietnam. In September Henry Kissinger announces that "peace is at hand." The curtain fell, temporarily, in 1973. On January 24 after Mr. Nixon had halted all bombing, a peace formula was achieved. By August American bombing had halted generally and the American military effort in Southeast Asia was over.

There was an epilogue. In March of 1975 the North Vietnamese fell on the southern armies. By May 1 the Communists took Saigon and almost all of those who had fought beside the Americans, believed in the United States, and sought independence, were left to the tender mercies of their new masters. It is not a happy story, from beginning to end. One regret is that these are only the front pages of *The New York Times.* Inside the newspaper throughout the war years were stories of gallantry and enterprise on the part of both the Americans and their allies. These were shafts of sunlight in the gathering gloom.

Finally, this book would not have been possible had it not been for the work of *New York Times* correspondents in Saigon, the battle areas, Washington and a half dozen foreign capitals. Throughout a war that was more confusing than most and that made great demands on intellectual integrity, these correspondents retained their objectivity. Others did not.

Drew Middleton

The New York Times.

LATE CITY EDITION
Fair and cold today and tonight.
Cloudy, not so cold tomorrow.
Temperature Range Today—Max., 32; Min., 22
Temperatures Yesterday—Max., 41; Min., 22
Full U. S. Weather Bureau Report, Page 23

Copyright, 1950, by The New York Times Company.

VOL. XCIX...No. 33,618.   Entered as Second-Class Matter, Postoffice, New York, N. Y.   NEW YORK, WEDNESDAY, FEBRUARY 8, 1950.   Times Square, New York 18, N. Y. Telephone LAckawanna 4-1000   FIVE CENTS

$1,100,000 BACK PAY WON BY 3D AVE. MEN; LINE ASKS 10C FARE

Bus Concern Says Award Ends Benefits of August Increase —Will Ask P. S. C. for Rise

3,800 IN UNION AFFECTED

Some Get 3-Week Vacations— Severance and Change in Pension Plan Denied

By JAMES P. McCAFFREY

The Third Avenue Transit System announced yesterday afternoon, shortly after an arbitrator had granted $1,100,000 in back pay to its 3,800 union employes, that it would seek a 10-cent fare.

The employes, members of Local 100, Transport Workers Union, CIO, received other concessions including three-week annual vacations for some.

James Hodes, the company's operating director, said the company would have to raise its fare 2 cents if the riding public was to be served properly. The company is now going through a reorganization proceeding in the Federal Court.

Meanwhile, in its dispute with the Board of Transportation the union pressed its demands yesterday on behalf of the city's 43,000 transit workers. It is seeking an increase of 21 cents an hour, a reduction in the work week from forty-eight to forty hours, the establishment of grievance machinery and the abolition of an alleged spy system. The demands were laid before the Mayor's fact-finding board on the second day of its hearings.

Court Must Approve Terms

Prof. Emanuel Stein of New York University, was named by Mayor O'Dwyer to arbitrate the dispute between the employes and the bankrupt company, made public the terms of the settlement. The professor had been taking testimony for three months. The agreement is binding on both sides, but it must bear the final approval of Federal Judge Samuel H. Kaufman.

Under the terms of the award the employes will get a wage increase of 6 cents an hour as of July 1, 1949; three-week annual vacations for those with ten years' service, and the distribution of retroactive pay on a $20-a-month basis. But the men will not get severance pay, a change in pension plan, payments for rain clothes, a guarantee for extra men, paid lunch periods, or the establishment of a night differential.

As soon as the details of the award were made public Michael J. Quill, international president of the union, and Matthew Guinan, president of Local 100, said:

"The granting of the 6-cent increase and the three-week vacation provision is definite evidence that receivership or no receivership, workers must be paid a living wage and be granted decent conditions of work."

Fare Rise to Be Asked Soon

Mr. Hodes, who is one of the three trustees appointed by the Federal Court in the reorganization proceeding, said an increased fare would be proposed to the Public Service Commission even before he had a financial analysis from the system's auditors.

"This award erases all the financial benefits expected from the 8-cent fare established in August," Mr. Hodes said. "The cost of the higher wages and other working advantages will result in operating deficits which can only be overcome by increasing the fare to 10 cents.

"The Third Avenue Transit System is beset by the same problems as all other private and municipal transit services, including those of the city of New York—constant deficits. The plight of our company is aggravated by the fact that a substantial proportion of our annual gross income must be turned over to the city of New York as franchise payments."

Professor Stein took cognizance of the 1,500,000 passengers who ride the buses and trolley cars of the transit system in Manhattan, the Bronx and lower Westchester. He said it was obvious that the trustees had "a legal duty to furnish adequate service."

"Sound business judgment dictates that the trustees should have sufficient authority in the matter of schedules so that they can provide

Continued on Page 16, Column 4

FACT-FINDING COAL BOARD OUTLINES ITS PLANS

Dr. John T. Dunlop, left, and Prof. William Willard Wirtz, right, at their first meeting with Chairman David L. Cole in Washington yesterday.

The New York Times (by Bruce Hoertel)

Senators Hear F. B. I. Chief, Favor Plea for More Agents

By WILLIAM S. WHITE
Special to The New York Times.

WASHINGTON, Feb. 7—A Senate appropriations subcommittee was understood tonight to be ready to recommend an expansion of the staff of the Federal Bureau of Investigation.

J. Edgar Hoover, director of the bureau, which carries a heavy load of investigative work in the atomic-hydrogen bomb programs, appeared before the subcommittee for more than two hours in closed session in the afternoon.

Mr. Hoover declined any comment as he emerged. He was said on Senatorial authority to have told his hearers that Dr. Klaus Fuchs, the naturalized British scientist held in London as an accused spy, had systematic "contacts" with Russian agents both in this country and Great Britain.

Mr. Hoover, according to this informant, told the subcommittee that Dr. Fuchs, who had access to the highest American secrets in the atomic and hydrogen fields, was in communication with Soviet agents in Britain twice a month during one period as a paid spy. His liaison with Russian agents in the United States, it was added, was less frequent.

On the point of the general work of the Federal Bureau of Investigation, a subcommittee member said, its director asserted that there were 54,000 card-holding members of the Communist party in the United States, and roughly ten times that number of fellow-travelers or Communist sympathizers.

Mr. Hoover, it was said, appealed strongly—and successfully, although a formal subcommittee vote will not be taken until later—for an addition of 700 persons to his staff, of whom about half would be investigative agents and the rest clerical workers.

In the Congressional stir still persisting over the Fuchs case, the Joint Congressional Atomic Energy Committee scheduled a meeting for tomorrow, on what were described as "intelligence matters." Rear Admiral R. H. Hillenkoetter, Director of the Central Intelligence Agency, will be heard in private.

Continued on Page 13, Column 1

STRAUSS RESIGNS FROM ATOM BOARD

Former Banker, Who Backed Hydrogen Bomb Production, Praised by President

Special to The New York Times.

WASHINGTON, Feb. 7—Rear Admiral Lewis L. Strauss, one of those who counseled President Truman to order production of the hydrogen bomb, submitted his resignation as a member of the Atomic Energy Commission today and the President accepted it in a letter of high praise for his service.

The former New York banker, who had a key role in the Navy's wartime ordnance procurement program, will not step out until April 15. Thus he will stay on the job two months longer than David E. Lilienthal, the commission chairman, whose resignation is set for Feb. 15. Mr. Truman is expected to appoint Mr. Lilienthal's successor in the near future.

Mr. Truman's eulogistic letter to one of the founding civilian commissioners of the atomic program was quickly echoed on Capitol Hill by Republicans and Democrats alike.

In ending nine years of public service, three and a half of them in the AEC, Admiral Strauss said the moment had come for his return to private affairs. Mr. Truman said he could understand this and added:

"Your service with the commission has been during a critical and formative period and your counsels have been invaluable. From your experience in military and business affairs you have made a contribution of utmost value in the development of the atomic energy program."

Continued on Page 13, Column 3

Carol Paight Acquitted as Insane At Time She Killed Ailing Father

By HAROLD FABER
Special to The New York Times.

BRIDGEPORT, Conn., Feb. 7.— Carol Paight was acquitted tonight of a charge that she murdered her father when she shot and killed him last Sept. 23 as he lay fatally ill of cancer in Stamford Hospital.

The jury of nine mothers and three fathers returned its verdict at 8:07 P. M., less than five hours after it began its deliberations.

The 21-year-old girl broke down and cried as the foreman of the jury, Mrs. Judith A. Menhard, announced, "We of the jury find her not guilty."

Despite a warning by the judge, there was an outburst of cheers from the spectators. The noise continued despite the efforts of deputy sheriffs to maintain order.

Miss Paight smiled on the shoulder of the matron and then leaned from the courtroom as the technical procedures of receiving the jury's verdict went on.

Her mother, the widow of Police Sgt. Carl Paight, sobbed on the shoulders of a friend.

Judge John A. Cornell ordered the verdict recorded. David Goldstein, the defense attorney, asked that the defendant be discharged. The motion was immediately granted. Judge Cornell discharged the jury.

While the uproar in the courtroom continued Miss Paight came back. Her eyes were red from crying. She first saw a friend, Mrs. Josephine Smith. Her only words were "Oh, Josie!"

She then saw her mother. She cried, "Oh, Mommie." Her mother said only "Oh, Carol," as they embraced.

The blonde girl then walked into the jury room and shook hands with members of the panel that had freed her. They declined to say how many ballots had been

Continued on Page 24, Column 5

LEWIS AND OWNERS MEET COAL BOARD; TO TESTIFY TODAY

Cooperation Reported Pledged to Panel in Informal Talk on Eve of Open Hearings

THESE WILL LAST 2 DAYS

Fact - Finding Body Plunges Into Work, Hoping to Beat Truman's Monday Deadline

By JOSEPH A. LOFTUS
Special to The New York Times.

WASHINGTON, Feb. 7 — The board of inquiry appointed by President Truman began its hunt for the facts in the soft-coal dispute today by conferring informally with John L. Lewis and three of the mine operators.

The board, composed of David L. Cole, Prof. William Willard Wirtz and Dr. John T. Dunlop, earlier had sent invitations to both Mr. Lewis and the operators to attend public hearings beginning at 10 A. M. tomorrow. The talks late today were reportedly of a preliminary nature.

[The railroads started Tuesday to take emergency measures to meet the coal shortage. The Baltimore & Ohio seized thirty-odd cars of coal as its supplies dwindled, and the New York Central dropped forty-eight trains.

[The nation's coal stocks were reported to be down to eighteen or nineteen days' supply.]

Coal operators who conferred with the Presidential board of inquiry were George H. Love of the Pittsburgh Consolidation Coal Company, Joseph E. Moody of the Southern Coal Producers Association, and Harry M. Moses of the H. C. Frick Coke Company, coal mining subsidiary of the United States Steel Corporation.

Lewis Refuses to Comment

None of those meeting with the board would discuss what transpired.

However, it was stated on good authority that both sides assured the board of willingness to cooperate. It was not clear, though, whether this meant Mr. Lewis, as head of the striking United Mine Workers, would respond to the board's invitation by appearing in person at the hearing tomorrow.

Emerging from the hotel used as headquarters by members of the board, Mr. Lewis tonight said he was "disinclined" to comment on anything and would not say whether he had already met with

Continued on Page 18, Column 6

TELEPHONE STRIKE POSTPONED 16 DAYS

Proposal by Federal Mediator Is Accepted but Union Men Assail Company Methods

By STANLEY LEVEY

A national telephone strike, set for 6 o'clock this morning, was postponed yesterday for sixteen days at the request of the Federal Government.

Both sides in the dispute agreed to the proposal, which came from Cyrus S. Ching, chief of the Federal Mediation and Conciliation Service, and turned their attention to new peace-making efforts. The strike deadline is now Feb. 24.

The union, the Communications Workers of America, CIO, announced its acceptance of the plan through Joseph A. Beirne, national president, after polling the nine members of the organization's executive board across the country. In Washington, Mr. Beirne said:

"Mr. Ching through his personal intervention and his grave concern for the interest of the public may be successful in getting the Bell System to do some real collective bargaining.

"We, too, have grave concern for the interests of the public. We think we have demonstrated that

Continued on Page 17, Column 2

World News Summarized

WEDNESDAY, FEBRUARY 8, 1950

The dollar shortage remains a most critical problem and can be solved only by cooperation between the United States and Western Europe over a period of years, the European Marshall Plan Council said. In a report issued yesterday the Council declared the Marshall Plan had helped restore Europe's output and foreign trade to near pre-war levels. The document goes to the ECA and Congress. [1:8.]

Administrator Hoffman, expressing "grave disappointment" over the attitude of the Europeans, indicated the ECA might adopt a "get tough" policy. The ECA, he also indicated, will ask less funds than were requested in President Truman's budget. [2:3.] In this city, former Secretary of State Marshall said the next two years would be crucial for the European Recovery Program. [3:4-5.]

This country's objective in Germany, the State Department stated in a directive to High Commissioner McCloy, is the development of a peaceful, self-supporting, democratic state that can support an adequate living standard and contribute to an integrated economy in Europe. The directive, sent last Nov. 17, instructed Mr. McCloy to help the Germans enter "the common structure of a free Europe," but to see that they were "deprived of the means of waging war." The Germans, he was told, must be allowed freedom to make their own decisions under adequate security safeguards. [4:4-5.]

Western Germans were stunned and pained by Mr. McCloy's blunt speech in Stuttgart. Some sources expected the net result to be good, but the Bonn Government was plainly embarrassed. [4:2.]

Premier Bidault barely won a confidence vote for his new Cabinet from the French Assembly. Many members, including the Socialists, abstained. [1:6-7.]

The United States and Britain recognized the Viet Nam Government of Bao Dai in French Indo-China. Russia has recognized the Communist-led regime of Ho Chi Minh. [1:6-7.]

President Truman's fact-finding board in the soft-coal dispute called union and operator leaders to hearings today and tomorrow. Railroads have curtailed eighteen or nineteen days' supply. [1:5.] Railroads commandeered coal in transit and industries prepared to lay off workers. [17:1.] The New York Central dropped forty-eight coal-burning trains in eleven states. [17:2-3.]

The nation-wide telephone strike set for this morning was postponed until Feb. 24 at Federal request. [1:4.]

Shortly after an arbitrator had awarded Third Avenue bus employes $1,100,000 in back pay the company said it would seek a 10-cent fare. [1:1.]

The Treasury asked Congress to require labor unions, charitable and educational bodies to pay income taxes on unrelated business activities. The exemption on religious groups would be continued. [19:1.]

Rear Admiral Strauss has resigned from the Atomic Energy Commission as of April 15. [1:2.]

The State Insurance Department asked that the required liability insurance on private automobiles be doubled. [1:6-7.]

Carol Paight, who shot her father as he lay hopelessly ill with cancer in a Stamford, Conn., hospital, was acquitted of murder. [1:2-3.]

Index to other news appears on Page 28.

U. S. Recognizes Viet Nam, Two Other Indo-China States

Diplomatic Ties With Bao Dai Regime, Laos and Cambodia Based on Fundamental American Policy, Washington Says

WASHINGTON, Feb. 7—The United States extended full recognition today to the independent states of Viet Nam, Laos and Cambodia in French Indo-China. The Government's action, following a similar move taken earlier today by Britain, was based, according to the State Department, on the formal establishment of the state of Viet Nam and the kingdoms of Laos and Cambodia as individual states within the French union.

"This recognition," the department continued, "is consistent with our fundamental policy of giving support to the peaceful and democratic evolution of dependent peoples toward self-government and independence."

Recognition of the regime headed by Bao Dai in Viet Nam, which is backed by the French Government, nevertheless places the United States and Britain squarely in opposition to the Soviet Union in that area. Russia has formally recognized the Viet Minh regime

Continued on Page 7, Column 5

of Ho Chi Minh, long a leader of the extreme "Nationalists."

The initial result of today's development will be an elevation in the status of the United States diplomatic mission in Saigon from a consulate general to a legation. Although he has not yet been named, the minister to head the Saigon mission will be responsible for relations with all of the three new states.

President Truman, in instructing the Consul General at Saigon to notify the heads of the three states, said that the United States looked forward to an exchange of diplomatic representatives with their three governments.

United States interest in the growth of autonomy for the three states was expressed as lately as last June, when the Government expressed its gratification at the signing of the French-Viet Nam agreements of March 8. This agreement

Bidault's New Cabinet Wins Precarious Confidence Vote

By LANSING WARREN
Special to The New York Times.

PARIS, Wednesday, Feb. 8—By a vote of 225 to 185, Premier Georges Bidault early today obtained the confidence of the National Assembly for his newly reorganized Cabinet. The majority was a precarious one, as the 185 votes against the Government, there were fully 150 members of the Assembly who abstained. These included the Socialist Deputies, whose withdrawal from the Government coalition over the cost-of-living bonus had forced the Premier to fill a half-dozen vacant posts.

After the session, it was learned that the Premier, despite the weakening of prestige resulting from a tenuous endorsement of this kind, intended to continue in office and that he would resume his efforts in the Assembly to obtain passage of the bill removing Government wage controls.

M. Bidault lost the previously proffered support of the Socialists because he had published before the debate a decree instituting the bonus as it had been passed by the Cabinet and in the terms that the Socialists had rejected. He did not gain compensatory support in the Assembly by this move, as the Socialists refrained from voting for him for the Socialist defection.

The Cabinet was saved by the fact that the Socialists and a large part of the center, instead of voting against the Government, expressed passive disapproval by abstaining.

The Cabinet, perhaps, was saved also by the gravity of the situation as outlined by M. Bidault and by Paul Reynaud. They both referred to the situation in foreign affairs, to the discord with the Soviet Union, to the trouble in Germany and Indo-China and to the probable effects on public opinion in Britain and the United States of another French Cabinet fall. There also was obviously some sympathy for the Premier, who was regarded as a victim of French internal party disputes.

The Premier did not ask, as he

Continued on Page 5, Column 3

STAMP FRAUDS LAID TO HIGH POSTAL AIDE

Donaldson Ousts Assistant as Scheme for Fake Sales of Rare Issues Is Bared

By The United Press.

WASHINGTON, Feb. 7—Postmaster General Jesse M. Donaldson disclosed tonight that he had discharged his $10,000-a-year special assistant, Harold F. Ambrose, for perpetrating a scheme that took large sums from "speculators" in fake deals in United States stamps.

Mr. Donaldson told the United Press that he asked Ambrose for his resignation Jan. 11 and it was accepted "with prejudice, which is tantamount to removal."

He said postoffice inspectors have been working on the case since Jan. 11, but disclaimed knowledge of reports that the Federal Bureau of Investigation was also acting.

He declared that no Postoffice Department funds or actual stamps were involved in the scheme, under which Ambrose paid off his first credulous "investors" with sums received from later "clients."

He was "quite confident" that the mails were not used to defraud in the case, he stated, and "I don't know that there has been any violation of a Federal law."

He asserted, however, that he thought there might have been some violation of state laws, such as obtaining money under false pretenses, but did not know whether

Continued on Page 24, Column 6

Doubled Auto Liability Is Urged By State Insurance Department

By LEO EGAN
Special to The New York Times.

ALBANY, Feb. 7—The State Insurance Department has recommended that the Legislature double the required liability insurance coverage of New York automobiles.

Under the existing financial responsibility law, car owners are required, after they have been involved in one accident, to carry insurance sufficient to pay $5,000 to any one person injured in an accident and to pay $10,000 if more than one is injured in the same accident.

If the proposal advanced by Robert E. Dineen, State Insurance Superintendent, is accepted, the required coverage would be $10,000 and $20,000. The recommendation is based on higher jury verdicts in recent years, the increased cost of medical and hospital care and other factors.

The State Insurance Department also recommended that taxicabs be required to carry as much liability

coverage as private car owners. Under existing law they are required to carry only half as much. Bills to raise taxi coverage have been introduced by Senator Pliny W. Williamson and Assemblyman Samuel Falk, Westchester Republicans.

The cost of the additional coverage to private car owners, according to Insurance Department estimates, would be roughly 20 per cent more than they are paying for existing policies. But less than half of all car owners in New York would be affected since 51 per cent of those carrying insurance now have $10,000 and $20,000 policies.

Mr. Dineen's proposal came to light today as the Senate debated charges that insurance companies were discriminating against Negroes and against thickly-populated areas in writing fire, casualty and life policies.

In the discussion, it was revealed

Continued on Page 20, Column 4

EUROPEANS REPORT OUTPUT AT '38 RATE MIDWAY IN E. R. P.

Marshall Plan Nations Inform Congress and E. C. A. Dollar Deficit Has Been Halved

BUT IT IS DUE TO PERSIST

Hoffman Hints to Senators He Will Ask New Cut in Aid— Tells of 'Disappointment'

Summary of Marshall Plan Council report is on Page 3.

By HAROLD CALLENDER
Special to The New York Times.

PARIS, Feb. 7 — Western Europe's production and foreign trade have rapidly regained approximately their pre-war volume and the dollar deficit in its balance of payments has been about halved in two years, it was pointed out in the annual report of the European Marshall Plan Council issued here today, to be submitted to ECA and Congress.

Nevertheless, Western Europe's dollar shortage, now running at about $4,000,000,000 a year and estimated to be about $2,250,000,000 annually at the end of the Marshall Plan, is expected to persist as a major international problem for years to come.

[In Washington Paul G. Hoffman, Economic Cooperation Administrator, intimated before the Senate Foreign Relations Committee on Tuesday that the appropriation he would request for the third year of the Marshall Plan would be less than the $3,-100,000,000 proposed by President Truman.

[Mr. Hoffman told the Senators of his "grave disappointment" with some of the results of the recent conference of the Marshall Plan countries in Paris.]

Marshall Aid Gets Credit

The report makes it clear that the Marshall Plan has succeeded brilliantly in restoring Western Europe's economic activity as a whole, although living standards still lag some 10 per cent below pre-war levels. It also makes clear that the Marshall Plan, while making notable headway in reducing the dollar shortage, will not solve and could not hope to solve this problem in the allotted four years of operation.

The Marshall Plan could not restore the pattern of world trade that existed in 1939, which may never be restored. Nor could it entirely replace that pattern with a new pattern and a new equilibrium. New social factors such as the demand for full employment, ruled out drastic adjustments that might have cut the dollar shortage further by lowering living standards.

Consequently the report insists there is no sure cure for the dollar shortage, least of all one that Europe alone could apply. It is seen as an American as well as a European problem since the world trade picture will long be dominated by the state of the United States balance of payments."

This means that with world trade at about the same volume as before the war, United States exports are more than twice their pre-war volume. The report calls this an unstable situation. The distorted pattern of world trade may be viewed as typified by the huge excess of United States exports over imports, or by the excess of European dollar imports over dollar exports. These are merely two ways of describing the same problem of the dollar shortage.

Trade With U. S. to Shrink

"Until United States trade is nearer to a balance, there will be a contraction in United States exports," says the report. Being short of dollars, the rest of the world must cut its buying of United States goods at the same time that it tries to earn more dollars to pay for them.

The authors of the report hesitate to guess precisely how far these inevitable measures will reduce Western Europe's dollar deficit. But they suggest that with luck this deficit might be brought within manageable limits in the first year after the Marshall Plan, 1952-53.

One favorable element necessary to make this possible is a high level of economic activity in the United States meanwhile—a level equal to that of the latter half of the year 1949. Another is dollar aid for the next two years— in the form of Marshall Plan aid and dollar aid allotted separately to Western Europe—at the expected amounts of $3,072,000,000 for the

Continued on Page 3, Column 1

1

Ho Chi Minh, the prime mover of revolution in Vietnam for almost half a century shown here in May 1941 when he founded the Viet Minh, his Communist guerrilla army.

U.S. military and economic aid to the anti-Communist countries in Southeast Asia began in 1950. Here, French and Vietnamese soldiers are shown manning U.S.-built armored cars.

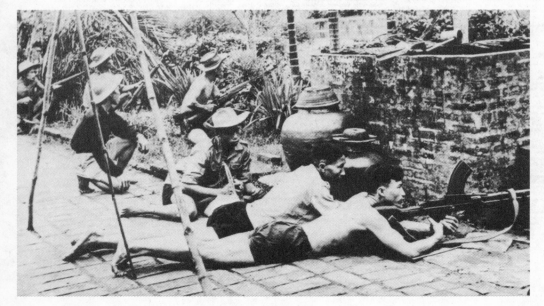

A citizen militia force in a village near Hanoi prepares itself to defend its combat post against the Viet Minh demonstrating that all Vietnamese did not support the Communist guerrillas.

"All the News That's Fit to Print"

The New York Times.

LATE CITY EDITION
Rain and colder today; clearing, colder tonight. Fair tomorrow.
Temperature Range Today—Max., 45; Min., 36
Temperature Yesterday—Max., 68.4; Min., 54
Full U. S. Weather Bureau Report, Page 35

Copyright, 1954, by The New York Times Company.

VOL. CIII..No. 35,088.

Entered as Second-Class Matter,
Post Office, New York, N. Y.

NEW YORK, WEDNESDAY, FEBRUARY 17, 1954.

Times Square, New York 36, N. Y.
Telephone Lackawanna 4-1000

FIVE CENTS

CONGRESS FINDING EISENHOWER BUDGET IS DIFFICULT TO CUT

$3,300,000,000 for Treasury and Post Office Trimmed $5,000,000 by House Unit

CONCERN IS EXPRESSED

Group Questions Whether Requests Submitted by President Are Too Lean

By C. P. TRUSSELL
Special to The New York Times.

WASHINGTON, Feb. 16—The House Appropriations Committee took its first action on President Eisenhower's new budget today.

It cut about $5,000,000, or less than two-tenths of 1 per cent, from budget estimates totaling $3,333,241,600, to run the Treasury and Post Office Departments through the fiscal year starting July 1.

Ten or more similar appropriations problems must go before Congress to complete the $65,000,000,000 budget.

The first bill raised in Congress a picture of a rough job ahead if the predicted $3,000,000,000 national budget deficit is to be reduced materially through appropriations cuts.

This picture was accentuated by indications that the Appropriations subcommittee handling the measure reported that at some key points it seemed the budget estimates themselves were too lean for prudence.

As the Appropriations Committee reported an almost negative scratching into estimates, Arthur E. Summerfield, Postmaster General, appeared before another House group to urge pay rises totaling $80,000,000 a year for more than 400,000 employes in the postal field service.

Deficit Is Estimated

The Post Office Department's deficit for the coming fiscal year, estimated at $329,000,000, is well designed to help cut this deficit by $240,000,000 through increases in postal rates is awaiting floor action.

The Treasury-Post Office measure was the first appropriation bill to clear the House committee that was built wholly on estimates made by the Eisenhower Administration. Last year's money measures constituted largely revised estimates made earlier by the Truman Administration.

Intensive hearings on the Treasury and Post Office Departments were held behind closed doors by a subcommittee headed by Representative Gordon Canfield, Republican of New Jersey. The full Appropriations Committee of thirty Republicans and twenty Democrats approved this afternoon every recommendation it made.

The bill allocated $2,755,386,000 to the postal service and $577,855,600 to the Treasury. This represented $80,491,150 less than the appropriations for the present fiscal year. The reduction, however, was made in the budget estimates rather than in committee-recommended cuts.

In the Treasury there also are about $7,000,000,000 of steadily outgoing funds that must be made available annually without any Congressional authority to increase or cut them. They represent obligations and fixed charges, such as the payment of

Continued on Page 24, Column 2

15% of City Thefts Solved; U. S. Police Average Is 23%

Bruce Smith Urges Change in Department to End Splitting of the Authority of Top Officers Into Four 'Slivers'

By PETER KIHSS

The city's police appear to be doing a one-third poorer job than the national average in solving burglaries, robberies and thefts. While the Federal Bureau of Investigation reports 23 per cent of the nation's property crimes as cleared by arrests in 1952, city data indicate that the police here solved only 15 per cent of such cases last year.

Bruce Smith, director of the 1952 police study for the former Mayor's Committee on Management Survey, said yesterday that the situation reinforced his group's call to reorganize the department's structure. The "basic solution," he said, is to give captains and inspectors larger powers and flexibility, in stead of splitting up field authority into four separate "slivers"—patrols, crime investigations, traffic control and juvenile programs.

The picture of law enforcement emerges from taking the Police Department's Feb. 1 report of rates of clearance by arrest in major crimes in 1952 and 1953 and comparing this with the F. B. I. reports for 1952. The national rates remain relatively stable from one year to the next.

A case is considered cleared when at least one of the perpetrators is arrested and arraigned in court. The arrest of a lone bandit may clear up five armed robberies if he is charged with each one.

The F. B. I. provides a national average for 1,706 cities with a 1950 population of 61,592,916 persons, as well as an average for the nation's thirty-one largest cities—those over 250,000 population, with 27,861,794 inhabitants.

Mr. Smith applauded Commissioner Francis W. H. Adams and

Continued on Page 39, Column 4

LEGISLATURE GETS BILLS TO ELIMINATE CHARITY 'RACKETS'

Dewey, in Special Message, Supports Action That Would Initiate State Control

Text of Dewey's message is on the Legislature is on Page 20.

Special to The New York Times.

ALBANY, Feb. 16—Bills designed to curb fraudulent fund-raising activities were introduced in the Legislature today with its partisan backing. The fraudulent activities were believed to cost residents of the state $25,000,000 a year.

Sponsored by the Joint Legislature Committee that has been investigating charitable organizations for the last year, the legislation would give the state power for the first time to deal with rackets carried on in the name of charity.

As the bills were introduced, Governor Dewey sent a special message to the Legislature urging favorable action on them to protect "the immensely useful, honest and competently administered charitable and philanthropic agencies of the state and nation."

Steps Are Proposed

The Joint Legislative Committee, headed by Senator Bernard Tompkins, Republican of Queens, proposed that these steps be taken by the Legislature:

¶That all agencies soliciting funds from the public, with the exception of religious, educational, fraternal and social organizations, be required to register with the State Department of Social Welfare and to submit annual statements showing income and expenses which would be available for public inspection.

¶That professional fund raisers be required to register annually, paying a $50 annual fee and posting a $5,000 bond.

¶That the unauthorized use of a name in connection with the solicitation of funds be made a misdemeanor.

¶That the Attorney General be empowered to prosecute violations of the proposed laws.

¶That nonresident charitable organizations seeking to solicit funds in the state be required to designate the Secretary of State as the agent for the service of process.

These recommendations, which were contained in a report filed with the Legislature by the Tompkins Committee today, were incorporated in three bills introduced in both houses by members of the committee.

¶The bill requiring the registration of professional fund raisers would exempt bona fide officers or employes of charitable organizations. Its purpose is to eliminate practices that make for excessive costs in the raising of funds.

A professional fund raiser is defined in the bill as a person who for pay conducts or manages a campaign for the solicitation of funds for a charitable organization. The bill also requires annual registration for "professional solicitors," who are defined as paid employes of professional fund

Continued on Page 20, Column 3

TOUGH FISCAL JOB IS SEEN FOR STATE FOR NEXT 10 YEARS

Report to Dewey Says Costs for Programs Must Rise— New Urgent Needs Noted

By DOUGLAS DALES
Special to The New York Times.

ALBANY, Feb. 16—State and local governments face difficult but not insuperable problems in making ends meet financially in the next ten years, but they will rise and see revenues level off even if there is no depression or recession.

This was the major finding of the State's Temporary Commission on the Fiscal Affairs of State Government in a seventy eight-page preliminary report submitted today to Governor Dewey and the Legislature.

Without any change in economic conditions, state expenditures under programs now authorized by law will increase a minimum of $261,000,000 during the next ten years, the commission reported. If new programs for which there are strong pressures are undertaken, costs would rise an additional $169,000,000, it found.

If economic conditions remain substantially as they now are state revenues will go up $296,000,000 in the same period, the commission estimated. Alternative computations, based on a slight decline in the level of economic activity within the state, put the probable revenue increase at either $264,000,000 or $176,000,000.

Cite Urgent Requirements

The cost estimate is based on continuing appropriations from the general fund for capital construction purposes at the present rate of about $74,000,000 a year. But the commission emphasized that this would not be enough to meet the urgent construction needs of the state during the ten-year period.

It estimated urgent construction requirements, principally for highways and mental hospitals, at $2,700,000,000 to $3,400,000,000, assuming no great change in building costs. Thus the present rate of appropriations for capital construction would fall $2,000,000,000 to $2,700,000,000 short of needs, the commission found.

During the next year, the commission said it would give careful study to means that could be employed to bridge the gap between expected cost increases and prospective revenue. These studies will concern themselves with making the present revenue structure more productive by reducing evasion and improving compliance; improved budgetary controls and management, tax increases or resort to borrowings.

The commission reported that a review of state-Federal and state-local financial relationships was urgently needed.

¶The bill requiring the registration of state-Federal and state-local financial relationships between the state's corporate franchise taxes and the Federal Government's corporate income taxes.

The greatest problem in state-local financial relationships is listed as meeting the needs of "urbanized areas" that include a number of political subdivisions—the metropolitan area of New

Continued on Page 25, Column 4

U. S. Offers to Train Troops Fighting Reds in Indo-China

O'Daniel to Head Enlarged Military Mission to Aid Native Vietnam Army

By JAMES RESTON
Special to The New York Times.

WASHINGTON, Feb. 16—The United States has offered to help train the Vietnamese and other native troops in Indo-China in an effort to gain a military victory over the Communist rebels.

It is also understood that Lieut. Gen. John Wilson O'Daniel will be sent to Indo-China to head an expanded United States military mission in that country. General O'Daniel, a training expert who knows Indo-China, will replace Maj. Gen. Thomas J. H. Trapnell, a hero of the Battle of the Philippines.

The Acting Secretary of State, Gen. Walter Bedell Smith, and the Chairman of the Joint Chiefs of Staff, Admiral Arthur W. Radford, told the Senate Foreign Relations Committee today that reports of Communist gains in Indo-China had been exaggerated. They emphasized, however, that

Lieut. Gen. John W. O'Daniel

the future of the war there depended not on greater military efforts by the United States or France but on the development of the native troops in that country. Admiral Radford was reported

Continued on Page 2, Column 4

Supporters of Treaty Curb Moving Nearer an Alliance

By WILLIAM S. WHITE
Special to The New York Times.

WASHINGTON, Feb. 16—Conservative bipartisan forces seeking some constitutional amendment to limit the President's treaty-making powers drew closer toward an alliance today. As they did so, the Senate worked on at the fringes of the whole issue in preparation for a series of decisive tests. These are likely to begin tomorrow and continue the rest of the week.

The Senate provisionally adopted by vote of 72 to 16 a proposition that Senatorial consent to the ratification of future treaties should always be a recorded roll-call as distinguished from less formal balloting.

All factions conceded that no question of great substance was involved here and some who voted for the proviso had publicly ridiculed it.

In the first place, the Eisenhower Administration, while it is resisting any sort of proposed constitutional amendment that would do more than simply reaffirm the Constitution's supremacy to any treaty, had no objection to the roll-call stipulation.

Secondly, it was approved by the Senate only as a part of any complete proposed constitutional amendment that might ultimately win by the two-thirds majority necessary in the final test.

Some who are against any alteration at all voted "aye" today on the conviction that no amendment would be approved.

To amend the Constitution requires first the approval of two-thirds of those voting in both the Senate and House of Representatives and then of the legislatures of three-fourths of the states.

Bricker and George Confer

Outside the Senate chamber, Senator John W. Bricker, Republican of Ohio, the initiator of the proposed amendment, was in a series of meetings with Senator Walter F. George of Georgia, dean of the conservative Southern Democratic delegation in the Senate.

Both propose substantial restrictions on the President's power. Separating the two at present is only one big difference.

Mr. George wants to require that executive agreements with other nations—that is, non-treaty Presidential arrangements with another head of state—shall be valid as law within the United States only if approved by Congress.

Mr. Bricker wants all this and one other feature; he wants to put treaties under the same limitations.

Bricker to Push Proposal

An added Bricker provision would be that a treaty (but not an executive agreement) could become internal law without the action of all of Congress if the Senate should so ordain by a two-thirds vote.

President Eisenhower's spokesmen have rejected both the Bricker and George plans.

Senator George said he would not willingly accept now an expansion of his proposal to bring treaties under the same limitation that he seeks for executive agreements. He added, however, that if Senator Bricker's supporters were able in floor action to put limitations on treaties as well in his document, he would then not turn against that plan now

Continued on Page 2, Column 2

SEOUL THREATENS TO HOLD INDIANS

Transfer of 76 South Koreans to New Delhi Called Breach of Prisoner Unit's Power

By LINDESAY PARROTT

TOKYO, Wednesday, Feb. 17—South Korea protested yesterday against the shipment to India of seventy-six former South Korean war prisoners who had asked to be sent to neutral countries.

The South Korean Army Provost Marshal, Lieut. Gen. Won Yung Duk, threatened to hold the Indian custodial troops still on the peninsula until the Government's demands in the matter had been satisfied.

The protest was made in a note to Lieut. Gen. K. S. Thimayya, head of the Neutral Nations Repatriation Commission, at whose order the prisoners had been sent to India to await resettlement in other countries. While under Indian detention in the neutral zone the men had refused to go either to North or South Korea and had expressed a desire for resettlement in various neutral nations, including Poland and Czechoslovakia.

General Won, who was principally responsible for carrying out the liberation before the armistice of 27,000 anti-Communist North Korean captives held in South Korea, told General Thimayya the neutral commission had exceeded its powers in transferring the prisoners. Until they are returned or until satisfactory assurances are given regarding their fate, he added, "the remaining Indian troops will not leave here."

Approximately 3,000 Indians

Continued on Page 4, Column 4

MOLOTOV MODIFIES TERMS ON AUSTRIA BUT MEETS REBUFF

West Rejects Plan to Maintain Occupation Until 1955 and Then Restudy Exit Date

FULL FREEDOM DEMANDED

Dulles Calls Russian's Move 'Just Another Excuse' for Delaying Troop Removal

By CLIFTON DANIEL
Special to The New York Times.

BERLIN, Feb. 16—Under steady pressure from the West, Vyacheslav M. Molotov modified today his demand for the indefinite military occupation of Austria, but the modification did not satisfy either the Western powers or the Vienna Government. They continued to insist on a clear and unequivocal declaration of Austria's independence.

The Soviet Foreign Minister's proposal, made at this afternoon's session of the Big Four foreign ministers' conference, was this: That while the four powers might leave their troops in Austria after the signing of an Austrian independence treaty, they would be obliged to reconsider "not later than in 1955" the date for their withdrawal.

John Foster Dulles, United States Secretary of State, spoke for the whole Western contingent when he replied that Mr. Molotov's modification "means nothing," and that it was "just another pretext, just another excuse."

The Secretary of State declared the Soviet "concession" would merely postpone the end of the military occupation of Austria by eighteen months and gave no assurance that Soviet troops would be withdrawn even then.

Molotov Rejects Pleas

He and the two other Western ministers and Leopold Figl, Austrian Foreign Minister, who was at the conference table again, appealed to Mr. Molotov to abandon his amendments and allow the Austrian treaty to be signed. But Mr. Molotov was adamant.

Finally Georges Bidault, French Foreign Minister, who was presiding, said he was obliged to note that agreement on an Austrian treaty had not been reached.

However, the Soviet Foreign Minister was still calling for further discussion as the session ended. He professed surprise that the Austrian Government was not interested in having a treaty on his terms and asked Herr Figl to reconsider. He withheld comment on some observations made by Anthony Eden, British Foreign Secretary, and proposed that the discussion continue tomorrow.

Finally the four ministers agreed that they would return to the question of European security tomorrow and try to "find time" for further argument about Austria Thursday, the agreed last day of the conference. In a restricted and secret session tomorrow morning they will make a last effort to agree on the terms for calling a larger conference, to include Communist China.

Today's session was probably the dullest and most futile of all the dull and futile meetings here since Jan. 25. No progress whatsoever was made.

The unhappy Herr Figl was put in the unenviable position of saying "no" repeatedly to a powerful government that keeps

Continued on Page 6, Column 3

Tax-Filing Date of April 15 Approved by House Group

By JOHN D. MORRIS
Special to The New York Times.

WASHINGTON, Feb. 16—The country's 55,000,000 individual income taxpayers will have an extra month in which to prepare their annual returns starting next year if a proposal approved today by the House Ways and Means Committee becomes law.

The committee agreed to move the present deadline of March 15 to April 15, as recommended by President Eisenhower in his Budget Message Jan. 21. Such a provision is written into a general tax-reform bill now being drafted by the House group.

In another development affecting taxpayers, the House Appropriations Committee approved a proposed setup of enforcement activities by the Internal Revenue Service. It voted funds for an increase of 1,500 in front-line enforcement personnel, now numbering about 26,000, and approved plans for a $400,000 training program.

Aim Is to Ease Task

The new deadline for filing returns will "make taxpaying easier for millions of Americans," according to the Ways and Means Committee. "In addition," he said, "the change will ease the burden of those who assist in the preparation of returns."

Tax lawyers and accountants have complained that too much of their work is now confined to the period Jan. 1 to March 15.

There is no apparent opposition to the change, which seems likely to be written into law at this session of Congress. It would affect this year's deadline, which remains March 15.

Under the provision, taxpayers would also have until April 15 to file their first estimate and pay their first quarterly installment on income in the current year that is not covered by withholding. No changes were made in the present dates of June 15, Sept. 15 and Jan. 15 for the other three quarterly payments and amended estimates.

Some May Get Relief

Under present law, anyone with wages of more than $4,500 after personal exemptions of $600 each for the tax payer and his dependents, is supposed to make such estimates and quarterly payments, since his taxes are not likely to be fully covered by the 18 per cent withholding rate. The requirements also apply to anyone who receives $100 or more than $100 from sources other than wages subject to withholding, provided his total income is $600 or more.

Farmers are not required to file declarations of estimated tax until Jan. 15 of the year after their income is received. As an alternative, they can file their final returns by Jan. 31. The committee voted to give them until Feb. 15 to file returns under the alternative procedure. It extended the definition of farming to include raising of fish for market and the raising of oysters.

No change was voted in the March 15 filing date for corporations except that tax-free cooperatives would be given until Sept. 15 to make their returns.

NEW COUNT RAISES JOBLESS BY 728,000

Wider Sample in Test Totals 3,087,000—Slump Called Sharper Than Foreseen

By JOSEPH A. LOFTUS
Special to The New York Times.

WASHINGTON, Feb. 16—Government estimates of unemployment apparently have been too low.

By spreading its sampling over a larger area, the Census Bureau of the Department of Commerce has found tentatively that unemployment passed the 3,000,000 mark in January. This is 728,000 higher than the figure originally announced for the month.

The Secretary of Commerce, Sinclair Weeks, announced the revised figures late today. He said they represented the first complete enumeration of improved sampling but were subject to further evaluation by Census Bureau experts.

The new sample is based on the same period, Jan. 3 to 9, and the same number of households, 25,000, as the old. But the households were distributed more widely. The old check covered sixty-eight areas in 123 counties; the new one, 230 areas in 450 counties.

The new estimate was 3,087,000 unemployed instead of 2,359,000.

That put unemployment at nearly 5 per cent of the civilian labor force, instead of the original estimate of 3.8 per cent. The total does not include about 275,000 persons who were on temporary lay-off from their jobs with definite instructions to return to work within thirty days.

Meanwhile, a Federal Reserve

Continued on Page 39, Column 2

It Was a Record 68.4° Yesterday, But Winter Reclaims City Today

Heat reached a historic visit to New York last night after giving the city its warmest climate for the date in eighty-three years of official readings.

At 1:40 P. M. yesterday the mercury reached 68.4 degrees, offering this area a second-day preview of spring, 1954. Throughout the city and the suburbs it was a matter of everybody talking about the weather and everybody doing something about it.

Windows were wide open in sudden surrender to the sun, children needed at least two coats more than the usual three to five to come into the house, coats that were left unbuttoned in Monday's warmth were left in the closet yesterday, and stenographers seemed to their bosses to be slower even than usual with that last important letter.

Some rain fell last night, and temperatures today are due to go back to the forties. But the two-day look-see at spring, which is not due until 5:01 P. M. on March 20, made a solid impact on Weather Bureau statistics. In addition to the high for the date, yesterday also broke the highest mean temperature record for the date (the

average of the day's high and low marks). This was 61 degrees, a considerable increase in the 48-degree figure previously recorded as a high in 1921.

The previous high temperature mark for Feb. 16 was 62.8, which also was set thirty-three years ago. For New Yorkers here, the day was a happy postscript to Monday's 68-degree climate, and compared pleasantly with the wind-whipped snow that fell in parts of northern New York.

From all reports there was an impressive turnout for the spring preview. In White Plains residents were already taking out their brassies and drivers and mashie-niblicks. In the city penthouse gardeners were confidently turning over box soil and removing winter rust from terrace settees preparatory to painting.

Sixty starlings took a noisy swim in a puddle at Times Square, a scene of the wildest confusion and many shops in the vicinity were pillaged. Among those seriously injured by bullets were six staff members of the British-owned newspaper Statesman who gathered outside the office to watch the riots.

Many sections of the city were in complete darkness tonight as

Continued on Page 13, Column 4

Court Allows Heiress to Defy Will, Wed Outside Faith, Get Legacy

The Appellate Division ruled yesterday that despite the will of her great-grandfather, Miss Lane L. Tanburn, a Park Avenue debutante, could marry outside the Jewish faith without forfeiting her inheritance.

The 3-to-2 decision of the court reversed a ruling made last May by Surrogate William T. Collins. The surrogate had upheld the validity of the great-grandfather's will, which stipulated that should any of his descendants marry outside the Jewish faith, they would have to lose their rights to the family legacy.

The surrogate's decision said in effect that if Miss Tanburn, who lives at 1160 Park Avenue, married Donelson Morrison Kelley Jr., to whom she became engaged fifteen months ago, she would lose $6,500 in annual income from a trust fund totaling $675,000 and a $10,000 legacy on her twenty-first birthday last

May 24. Miss Tanburn would also have been forced to yield whatever interest she might have in the principal of the trust fund upon its termination.

The case first reached the courts on a petition filed by the executors and trustees of the estate of Miss Tanburn's great-grandfather, Abraham S. Rosenbaum, a silk importer, who died on May 7, 1938.

The Appellate Division's majority decision was written by Justice Bernard Botein. It held that Miss Tanburn, who is the daughter of Mrs. Stephen Tanburn, also of 1160 Park Avenue, and the late Mr. Tanburn, was not a direct heir of Mr. Rosenbaum and that an appointee under the will of her father.

"There is no reason," the majority said, "why the court should read into the power of appointment a prohibition broader than

Continued on Page 6, Column 5

Calcutta Police Fire on Rioters; 4 Die as Reds Fan Teacher Strike

Special to The New York Times.

CALCUTTA, India, Feb. 16—The police fired on rioters today following open Communist participation in a strike of school teachers. The police attacked the mobs with tear gas and guns.

[Four persons were killed and sixty-five injured in the rioting, Reuters reported.]

At least five streetcars and several buses and police trucks were set ablaze or the rioters, Chowringhee, Calcutta's Times Square, was a scene of the wildest confusion and many shops in the vicinity were pillaged. Among those seriously injured by bullets were six staff members of the British-owned newspaper Statesman who gathered outside the office to watch the riots.

Many sections of the city were in complete darkness tonight as engines were kept busy dealing with incendiarism.

[The rioters smashed the windows of the United States information offices, Reuters said.]

In the afternoon, the police tried to break up a demonstration outside the Legislative Assembly, which was in session. They threw tear-gas bombs at the crowd that attempted to break the police cordon around the building.

Earlier, a crowd had held a meeting to press the demands of the West Bengal teachers who are on strike for higher pay and cost-of-living allowances.

The teachers are asking for a monthly cost-of-living allowance of 35 rupees ($7.35). The Government recently conceded 10 rupees ($2.10) conditional on the school management's paying an

Continued on Page 2, Column 6

3

Before the Vietnamese conflict had escalated into a full-blown war involving the United States, the Kennedy administration had hoped that providing advisers and materiél would preclude sending a U.S. combat force. Here, an American sergeant discusses tactics with Vietnamese infantrymen.

Religious riots swept South Vietnam when General Khanh resisted Buddhist demands. Here, Catholic youths challenge Buddhists to recover the body of a comrade killed in an attack on a Catholic high school.

As part of the U.S. program of the early Sixties to train South Vietnam's military, troops of the Vietnamese 100th Airborne Division make practice drops in the area around Vung Tau, 80 miles south of Saigon.

"All the News That's Fit to Print"

The New York Times.

LATE CITY EDITION

Chance of showers and warmer today. Clearing and warm tomorrow.
Temperature Range Today-Max., 65; Min., 40
Temperatures Yesterday-Max., 43; Min., 33
Full U. S. Weather Bureau Report, Page 59

VOL. CIII..No. 35,136. Entered as Second-Class Matter, Post Office, New York, N. Y. NEW YORK, TUESDAY, APRIL 6, 1954. Times Square, New York 36, N. Y. Telephone LAckawanna 4-1000 FIVE CENTS

DULLES WARNS RED CHINA NEARS OPEN AGGRESSION IN INDO-CHINA; PRESIDENT CAUTIONS ON 'JITTERS'

14,000 IN 2 UNIONS TOIL TO RID PIERS OF PILES OF CARGO

Market Glut Cuts Vegetable and Fruit Prices—Losses of Importers Are High

DAY'S WORK IS PEACEFUL

I. L. A. Head Charges Rival Is Favored in Hiring—Men Get No Pay Concession

By A. H. RASKIN

Fourteen thousand members of rival dock unions worked side by side yesterday to clear the piers of cargo that had piled up during the port's worst strike.

Fruit and vegetable importers, hard hit by the twenty-nine-day tie-up, found that their losses did not end with the return to work. Such a glut of grapes, garlic, wild onions and similar items was brought up from ships' holds that market prices tumbled.

One importer estimated that New York merchants had lost $500,000 on the produce unloaded yesterday. He said total losses for the strike period ran to "many times" that amount.

A check-up by the Waterfront Commission showed 14,041 men at work on 133 ships. There are 31,000 longshoremen registered with the commission, but the actual work total seldom goes above 20,000 on any single day.

Industry officials said yesterday's turnout was "excellent." They noted that it would require several days to reroute all diverted ships back to New York, and create full work opportunities.

The most heartening sign of the strike's end was the docking last night of the giant Cunarder Queen Elizabeth. Last week a sympathy strike of tug workers forced her sister ship, the Queen Mary, to berth at Halifax, N. S.

I. L. A. Charges 'Lockout'

The old International Longshoremen's Association remained disconsolate over the outcome of its walkout. Capt. William V. Bradley, the union's president, charged that I. L. A. members were being "locked out" at a dozen Brooklyn and Manhattan piers. He warned that discrimination in putting men back to work might lead to a new strike, but other I. L. A. officials expressed confidence that the hiring mix-up would be unscrambled in a day or two.

The old union had sought to force the New York Shipping Association to give it a new contract making it exclusive bargaining agent for the harbor's 24,000 longshoremen. Instead, the union was obliged to send its members back to work without a contract or concessions of any kind. If it had failed to call off the strike, the I. L. A. would have forfeited its right to compete against the American Federation of Labor in a new National Labor Relations Board election here.

By putting off its back-to-work order until Friday afternoon, the I. L. A. killed an offer by the shipping association to put into effect a "package" wage increase of 10 cents an hour. This offer expired at 8 A. M. last Thursday. At a meeting yesterday, the 170 members of the association voted not to revive it but to pay the men at the rates that prevailed before the strike began last March 5.

This means that longshoremen will get $2.27 an hour, instead of

Continued on Page 25, Column 5

Roosevelt Raceway Sells Yonkers Stock

By EMANUEL PERLMUTTER

Roosevelt Raceway has sold its majority voting stock in Yonkers Raceway for $1,750,000.

The sale is subject to approval by Harness Racing Commissioner George P. Monaghan. Mr. Monaghan was officially informed of the deal yesterday. He reserved decision on the transaction.

Involved in the provisional purchase are 26,000 voting shares and 66,000 non-voting shares in the Algam Corporation. The shares are owned by Old Country Trotting Association, owner of Roosevelt Raceway in Westbury, L. I. Algam owns the Yonkers track. There are 50,000 shares of voting stock in the corporation.

The Moreland Act Commission that investigated harness

Continued on Page 40, Column 7

HIGH COURT BACKS GIVE-AWAY SHOWS

Justices Say F. C. C. Exceeds Rule-Making Power in Move to Ban Such Programs

By LUTHER A. HUSTON
Special to The New York Times.

WASHINGTON, April 5—The Supreme Court ruled today, 8 to 0, that "give-away" programs on radio and television did not violate the lottery laws.

The Federal Communications Commission, in prescribing regulations that would have banned such programs, "overstepped the boundaries of interpretation," the court said, "and exceeded its rule-making power."

The ruling affirmed a decision of a three-judge Federal court for the Southern District of New York enjoining the commission from enforcing its regulations.

Chief Justice Earl Warren delivered the court's opinion. Justice William O. Douglas did not participate in the case.

Returning to the bench after a recess since March 15, the high court handed down ten opinions and a number of orders. Three of the opinions were written by Justice Robert H. Jackson, who suffered a mild heart attack last week. He was not present, and Justices Felix Frankfurter and Stanley F. Reed read the opinions for him.

Pupil Bias Ruling Awaited

After handing down opinions next Monday, the court will again recess until April 26. There were no indications as to when the tribunal would hand down its long-awaited ruling in the school segregation cases. The prevailing belief is that this momentous decision still is several weeks away.

Among the opinions announced today were the following:

¶A provision of the New York State banking law that prohibited national banks from using the term "savings" in soliciting or receiving deposits was held to be in conflict with Federal law and therefore invalid.

¶The Interstate Commerce Commission was held to be without power to order the involuntary merger of one railroad with another. The decision reversed a lower court ruling that would have compelled a merger of the Florida East Coast Railway with the Atlantic Coast Line.

¶The disbarment from practice in Federal courts of Harry

Continued on Page 24, Column 4

DEMOCRATS IMPLY THEY DOUBT SEARS IS SUITED FOR JOB

McCarthy Inquiry Unit Slated to Rule on Counsel Today—Senator Goes to Arizona

By W. H. LAWRENCE
Special to The New York Times.

WASHINGTON, April 5—Key Democrats questioned today whether it was suitable for Samuel P. Sears, Boston lawyer, to remain as chief counsel investigating the Army dispute with Senator Joseph R. McCarthy.

The question of whether Mr. Sears is to be retained in the light of his numerous pro-McCarthy statements in the past is slated for settlement tomorrow before six members of the Senate Permanent Subcommittee on Investigations.

[Senator McCarthy left New York by plane for Arizona Monday for a brief rest on a ranch. He left behind the question of who would pay a reported $7,500 cost for the filming of an address he made for Edward R. Murrow's television program.]

The counsel issue, as the Democrats see it, is not so much that Mr. Sears has spoken favorably of Senator McCarthy—but that he had withheld this information from the subcommittee members who voted last Thursday to employ him.

"Mr. Sears was not as candid to me as I would have liked to have had him to be," said Senator John L. McClellan, Arkansas Democrat.

McClellan Has 'Reservations'

Senator McClellan is the key man in this inquiry, as the leader of the three Democratic subcommittee members.

Senator Karl E. Mundt, Republican of South Dakota and temporary chairman of the subcommittee, left little doubt that Mr. Sears would have to satisfy Senator McClellan and the other Democrats if he was to keep his job. Senator McCarthy has disqualified himself from voting, and Senator Mundt said the three Democrats and three Republicans had sought unanimity on all issues of the Army-McCarthy dispute.

"I certainly have some reservations as to his [Mr. Sears] suitableness to serve," Senator McClellan said in a radio interview tonight.

Mr. Sears arrived at the Senate Office Building this morning for a brief conference with Senators Mundt, McClellan and Stuart Symington, Missouri Democrat. Mr. McClellan said he purposely postponed any discussion of Mr. Sears' continuance in office until the full subcommittee could be present.

Senator Everett M. Dirksen, Republican of Illinois, was in Tennessee awaiting the birth of a grandchild, but promised to return to Washington immediately.

Sears Defers Comment

Mr. Sears told reporters he would not begin work at least until after tomorrow's session with the subcommittee.

Talking with news men outside Senator Mundt's office, the lawyer told them that "I'm not going to say anything about anything today.

"Nothing is settled."

Senator Mundt said that the session with Mr. Sears lasted only about three minutes.

"We told him we wanted him in to discuss all the developments," said Senator Mundt. "He told us he very much wanted to discuss them, too."

Meanwhile, on the Senate floor, Senator Pat McCarran, Nevada Democrat, asserted that the "real issue" in the current controversy was not the veracity of Senator McCarthy and his chief counsel, Roy M. Cohn, or of Robert T. Stevens, Secretary of the Army, and his counsel John G. Adams.

The Army charged that Senator McCarthy and Mr. Cohn threatened it in an effort to get special preferential treatment for Pvt. G. David Schine, former unpaid subcommittee consultant. Senator McCarthy, in turn, accused the Army officials of seeking to "blackmail" him into calling off his investigation of Communists in the service.

Senator McCarran, a powerful leader of his party's Right Wing, indicated at one point he agreed with Senator McCarthy.

"I do not believe quite all the American people have lost sight of the basic question that started this entire controversy," Senator McCarran said. "That question is 'who in the United States Army promoted and permitted the hon-

Continued on Page 20, Column 3

BRITISH ASK TALKS

Big 3 Parley on Arms Urged by Commons—Churchill Heckled

Excerpts from Churchill, Attlee speeches are on Page 12.

By DREW MIDDLETON
Special to The New York Times.

LONDON, April 5—Foreign Secretary Anthony Eden pledged the British Government tonight to use every influence in its power to bring about "fruitful" high-level talks with the Soviet Union on control of the hydrogen bomb and easing of international tension.

Encouraged by this assurance, the House of Commons agreed without a vote to support a Laborite motion asking for "immediate" Government initiative to bring about a meeting of Prime Minister Churchill, President Eisenhower and Premier Malenkov on reduction and control of armaments.

The Foreign Secretary's affirmation of the Government's desire to ease international tension and his plea that it be allowed to pick its time to propose high-level talks salvaged something from the day's debate for the Conservatives, especially for Sir Winston Churchill.

1943 Pact Disclosed

The revelation by the Prime Minister of a 1943 agreement with President Roosevelt, signed at Quebec, which stipulated that the atomic bomb would not be used against a third party save by mutual consent, failed to satisfy the Labor Opposition.

The Laborites guessed—correctly, as a White House announcement later revealed—that the agreement was no longer in force.

When Sir Winston criticized the post-war Labor Government's handling of atomic affairs he provoked the fiercest criticism and abuse that the present Parliament has seen. Some observers agreed that not since the late Prime Minister Neville Chamberlain tried to defend his war policy in the critical debate of May, 1940, had a Prime Minister met such violent condemnation in the House.

At one point Sir Winston stood with hands outstretched declaring, "I have a right to be heard," while the Labor side of the House shouted "Resign!" and his own supporters sat silent.

The debate began at 3:30 o'clock this afternoon and lasted for about seven hours. It was notable for two reasons. It emphasized the intention of the present Government, in the face

Continued on Page 12, Column 5

EISENHOWER SPEAKS

Asks Unity—Declares Soviet Courts Ruin if It Ventures War

The text of Eisenhower speech is printed on Page 16.

By ANTHONY LEVIERO
Special to The New York Times.

WASHINGTON, April 5—President Eisenhower declared tonight that communism could not prevail against the spiritual and material might of the United States.

He urged his countrymen to put an end to their internal strife, not to yield to "jitters" and to face the future resolutely.

The Soviet Union contains the seeds of its own destruction and will disintegrate if it ventures into war, the President said in a television and radio speech broadcast to the nation and the world. Therefore, he said, he does not believe Russia will precipitate a war except through some fit of madness or miscalculation.

Moreover, the United States holds the advantage of a capacity for massive retaliation with its superiority in hydrogen bombs, the President asserted. This counter-threat, he reasoned, is the greatest deterrent to an aggressive move by Moscow.

Against this overshadowing background of a troubled world, General Eisenhower calmly discussed domestic and international problems and pleaded for unity at home. He asked the American people not to "fall prey to hysterical thinking" as a result of the controversy over Communist subversion.

Shuns 'Any Kind of Panic'

"The greater any of these apprehensions," he said, "the greater is the need that we look at them clearly, face to face, without fear, like honest straightforward Americans so we do not develop the jitters or any kind of panic."

He also argued against the abuse of power by Congressional investigating committees and spoke out against the "very grave offenses" that could be committed against the innocent by those enjoying Congressional immunity.

The President obviously was referring to the methods of Senator Joseph R. McCarthy, Republican of Wisconsin, and his Permanent Subcommittee on Investigations, now tied up in a bitter quarrel between Mr. McCarthy and the Army. But he did not name the Senator.

While speaking out against Congressional abuses, the President did not propose that Congress or the Executive Branch

Continued on Page 17, Column 1

Associated Press Wirephoto

CALLS FOR 'COURAGE AND FAITH': The President in White House broadcast room prior to start of his speech.

PEIPING ROLE CITED

Secretary Reveals That Chinese Are in Action—Retaliation Hinted

Text of the statement by Dulles is printed on Page 4.

By WILLIAM S. WHITE
Special to The New York Times.

WASHINGTON, April 5—The United States warned the Chinese Communists today that they were approaching a form of undisguised aggression in Indo-China that might bring major retaliation.

John Foster Dulles, Secretary of State, emphasized again and again the Administration's grave view concerning the position in Asia. He appeared before the House Foreign Affairs Committee to support the new Mutual Security Program.

Mr. Dulles made public a fresh, top-secret United States intelligence report that Chinese Communists had been identified in actual combat alongside the Communist-led Vietminh in Indo-China.

He made it plain that the United States was in urgent consultation with other free peoples in the Indo-China theatre in an effort to draw up, if need be, a free-nation front against the fall of Indo-China.

He spoke of "united action" and declared that, as of now, he could only "deprecate" suggestions that the United States would intervene, alone if all else failed, to hold Southeast Asia from Communist imperialism.

Nowhere did he totally and finally exclude such intervention if it came to that as the only way to save the free world's position in Asia.

Secretary Accuses Peiping

In a statement that combined a world review and an appeal for Congressional approval of continued military and economic aid to the free world, Mr. Dulles accused Communist China of "intensifying Communist aggression in Indo-China."

In the questioning period that followed he read off in support of this charge a document that, as he put it, told "an ominous story." The document presumably had just been cleared through this country's highest strategic body, the National Security Council, of which President Eisenhower is chairman. It follows:

"Most recent advices with respect to extent of Communist Chinese participation in the fighting at Dienbienphu [the presently vital position in Indo-China] indicate the following:

"1. A Chinese Communist general, Li Chen-hou, is stationed at the Diebienphu headquarters of General [Vo Nguyen] Giap, the Vietminh commander.

"2. Under him there are nearly a score of Chinese Communist technical military advisers at headquarters of General Giap. Also, there are numerous other Chinese Communist military advisers at division level.

"3. There are special telephone

Continued on Page 5, Column 1

PALESTINE SESSION SET IN U. N. COUNCIL

Vishinsky Calls for Meeting Thursday—Israel Charges Jordan Violates Accord

By THOMAS J. HAMILTON
Special to The New York Times.

UNITED NATIONS, N. Y., April 5—The United Nations Security Council will meet Thursday to take up the latest round of charges and counter-charges exchanged by Israel and her Arab neighbors.

The meeting was called late today by Andrei Y. Vishinsky, Soviet representative and Council president for April, after Israel had accused Jordan of the "repudiation" of several provisions of the Israeli-Jordanian armistice agreement.

Abba Eban, Israeli representative, emphasized the refusal of Jordan to agree to direct negotiations with Israel, as provided under the armistice. He asked the Council to give "urgent consideration" to these and other charges.

Mr. Vishinsky bracketed with the Israeli allegations Lebanon's complaint against Israel for the slaying of nine persons at Nahhalin, a Jordanian frontier village. He placed the latter at the top of the agenda.

Effect of Soviet Stand

Since Mr. Vishinsky has twice vetoed resolutions supporting Israel in the Palestine dispute but has allowed an Arab-endorsed resolution to go through, there is not much likelihood that he will permit the Council to do anything positive about Israel's complaint.

On the other hand, he said a few days ago, before vetoing a resolution upholding Israel's complaint against Egypt's restrictions on Suez Canal traffic, that such issues ought to be settled by direct negotiation instead of by Security Council resolutions.

Israel is expected to argue that since this is the Soviet position, Mr. Vishinsky certainly should be in favor of direct talks between Israel and Jordan. These are mandatory under Article 12 of the Israeli-Jordanian armistice. The article, which was invoked by Israel last November, provides that if one side refuses to negotiate, the other can appeal to the Council.

Article 12 also directs Secretary General Dag Hammarskjold to convene the talks, but he never did so because he kept on waiting

Continued on Page 10, Column 4

VIETMINH ATTACK BARS MERCY PLANE

Fierce New Blow at Airfield of Dienbienphu Prevents Removal of Wounded

By TILLMAN DURDIN
Special to The New York Times.

HANOI, Vietnam, April 5—One of the bloodiest battles in the fight for Dienbienphu resulted from a new attack by Communist-led Vietminh forces last night against a French defense point at the northern end of the main Dienbienphu airfield.

After ten hours of bitter fighting lasting until morning, the Vietminh troops were pushed back and victorious French Union troops counted 1,000 enemy dead in the tangle of barbed wire and blasted entrenchments that marked the area of conflict.

[According to a dispatch from Paris, a Vietminh column of 20,000 fresh troops was heading toward Dienbienphu to strengthen the battered attacking force.]

It is believed here that the Vietminh attack was specially mounted to strike at the main Dienbienphu airstrip and prevent the evacuation of French wounded. Gen. Henri-Eugene Navarre, French commander in chief, advised the Vietminh command the night before last that the evacua-

Continued on Page 2, Column 2

Coffee Prices Jump Again 6 Cents; May Go to $1.50, Roaster Asserts

By The Associated Press.

WASHINGTON, April 5—Coffee prices jumped again today and one roaster said the day might not be far off when housewives would be paying $1.50 a pound for the bean in the grocery.

Maxwell House increased its wholesale price 6 cents a pound to $1.22. The Great Atlantic and Pacific Tea Company, made a 5-cent increase on its own brands. Its new prices will range from $1.09 to $1.17. Other concerns are expected to follow suit.

The prediction of $1.50-a-pound coffee came from a New York roaster, whose coffee now sells wholesale at more than $1.20. He declined use of his name.

"Our price must go up another 15 cents at least to get it in line with the green coffee market," he said, adding:

"When you figure in the retailer's mark-up, that means $1.50 coffee."

Meanwhile, a Senate Banking subcommittee pushed ahead with its hunt for the cause of the increases. Brazilian coffee growers have attributed the price rises to a heavy frost that hurt millions of coffee trees.

John K. Evans, general manager of the Maxwell House division of the General Foods Corporation, told the Senators his company's sales were stil ahead of sales in previous years but "there can be no doubt that high prices ultimately will result in consumer resistance."

Actually, Mr. Evans said, coffee consumption in general was down 12 per cent in February compared with the same month of 1953.

Mr. Evans and other witnesses assured the Senators that American wholesalers and retailers were not making huge profits in coffee.

"Wholesalers and retailers gen-

Continued on Page 41, Column 2

Duke U. Denies Degree to Nixon; He Cancels Commencement Talk

Special to The New York Times.

DURHAM, N. C., April 5—The faculty of Duke University has voted against awarding an honorary degree to one of the university's most distinguished graduates, Vice President Richard M. Nixon.

The Vice President, in turn, has decided that the pressure of business in Washington will make it impossible for him to deliver the university's commencement address in June.

Mr. Nixon had accepted the invitation earlier this year, when a secret committee of members of the faculty and the board of trustees recommended that he be the recipient of an honorary Doctor of Laws degree. He had earned his Bachelor of Laws degree at the university in 1937.

He apparently reconsidered, however, after a faculty meeting a month ago voted down the recommendation. His office announced two weeks ago that he was canceling the engagement.

The faculty vote, according to one of the top officials of the university, was 61 to 42 against giving the degree to the Vice President. The meeting was secret, and it was not until tonight that the report was officially confirmed. No reasons for the action were made public.

The university announced today that the replacement commencement speaker would be Dr. Reuben G. Gustavson, president of Resources for the Future, Inc., a Ford Foundation subsidiary. Dr. Gustavson, a former member of the Board of Governors of the Argonne National Laboratory for Atomic Energy, was previously chancellor of the University of Nebraska.

The names of those who will receive honorary degrees will not be announced until commencement morning, June 7. Dr. Charles Jordan, vice president of the University, said tonight that although the degrees were conferred by the board of trustees, the choice of the board was limited to a list approved by the faculty.

All suggestions for honorary degrees, he said, were submitted to a secret panel comprised of members of the Board of Trustees and of the faculty. Other members of the board or the faculty did not know who was on this committee. The recommendations of the committee were then submitted to the faculty to be approved or rejected.

The university spokesman who confirmed that the faculty had rejected the name of Vice President Nixon declared tonight that only about a sixth of the faculty had attended the meeting. Duke has a teaching staff of 606.

Air Unity in Hemisphere Lagging Over Difficulty in Buying U.S. Jets

By PAUL P. KENNEDY
Special to The New York Times.

BOGOTA, Colombia, April 5—Inter-American air defense is becoming more complicated. Little or no attempt is being made to attain unification of equipment.

Colombia has an order for June delivery of six T-33 Lockheed jet fighter planes. She will thus be the first Latin-American air force to have jets. Brazil, Venezuela and Argentina have British jet fighters. At last report, Peru and Chile were wavering between United States and British jets.

Ecuador has been casting about for months for jet planes and finally has received encouragement from a United States manufacturer. Still other countries are in the market for jet fighters and would prefer United States equipment, but the Latin Americans are finding it difficult to acquire this equipment.

The United States is providing Latin-American air forces with millions of dollars worth of World War II equipment, either free or at extremely low prices, but the Latin Americans say it is hard to deal with their northern neighbor when modern equipment is sought at market prices.

Colombia is a case in point. If the United States did not know that the Colombian Air Force was in the market for jet planes, it apparently was the only jet-manufacturing country so much in the dark.

Britain, Sweden and France were eager to sell Colombia the planes, and had submitted elaborate sales prospectuses. One undoubtedly would have won a contract had not a Colombian Air Force official pleaded with the United States Embassy to obtain the planes for Colombia.

In each country where British jets have been purchased, the

Continued on Page 17, Column 3

"All the News That's Fit to Print"

The New York Times.

LATE CITY EDITION

Rain ending late today. Fair and mild tomorrow.

Temperature Range Today—Max., 60; Min., 46
Temperature Yesterday—Max., 57; Min., 41
Full U. S. Weather Bureau Report, Page 73

Copyright, 1954, by The New York Times Company.

VOL. CIII..No. 35,147.   Entered as Second-Class Matter, Post Office, New York, N. Y.   NEW YORK, SATURDAY, APRIL 17, 1954.   Times Square, New York 36, N. Y. Telephone LAckawanna 4-1000   FIVE CENTS

M'CARTHY PRESSED BY MUNDT TO QUIT INQUIRY ENTIRELY

Panel Chairman Says Senator Might Submit Questions but Not Cross-Examine

DISCOUNTS NEWS 'LEAK'

Still Believes Investigation Will Start on Time With the Wisconsinian There

By W. H. LAWRENCE
Special to The New York Times.

WASHINGTON, April 16—The chairman of the Senate subcommittee investigating the dispute between the Army and Senator Joseph R. McCarthy, suggested publicly today that the Wisconsin Republican remove himself entirely from the investigation.

The chairman said Mr. McCarthy could submit in writing any questions he might have for witnesses.

Senator Karl E. Mundt, South Dakota Republican who replaced Senator McCarthy as chairman of the Senate Permanent Subcommittee on Investigations for this case, took his stand at a news conference on Senator McCarthy's demand for the right of unrestricted cross-examination.

At the same time, Senator Mundt discounted as diversionary the threat of Senator McCarthy and his chief counsel, Roy M. Cohn, to boycott the subcommittee until it conducted an investigation of "news leaks."

He said he still hoped and expected to receive on Monday, as promised, the answer of the McCarthy group to charges that they had used "improper means" to seek preferential treatment from the military for Pvt. G. David Schine. Private Schine was an unpaid committee consultant before he was drafted.

Senator Mundt continued to be optimistic that the televised public hearings into this dispute would start Thursday morning, as scheduled, barring a plea of ill health by Senator McCarthy. Mr. McCarthy was well enough today to go fishing in the Gulf of Mexico off Galveston, Tex., where he is vacationing and recuperating from a severe attack of virus laryngitis.

Relies on Promise

Senator Mundt said he still was relying on Senator McCarthy's promise that he would return here over the week-end to discuss with subcommittee members the ground rules and procedure for the inquiry. He said he would summon the subcommittee into extraordinary session Easter Sunday if Senator McCarthy arrived in time, but otherwise the meeting would be held at 10 A. M. Monday.

While Senator Mundt said he spoke for only himself, his public suggestion that Senator McCarthy resign temporarily from the subcommittee and surrender his rights to examine witnesses was believed to represent the consensus of his investigating group.

He said the suggestion had been conveyed directly to Senator McCarthy and that while Mr. McCarthy's initial reaction was not favorable, he had not as yet finally and formally turned the proposal down—pending a conference with the group. If he refuses the issue may have to go to the floor of the Senate for a final decision. This eventually

Continued on Page 5, Column 4

Thruway to Charge Autos 1¼c a Mile

By WARREN WEAVER Jr.
Special to The New York Times.

ALBANY, April 16—A motorist driving from New York to Buffalo on the State Thruway will have to pay a minimum of $5.25 in tolls.

Under a fee schedule announced today, the Thruway Authority set a 1¼ cent-a-mile toll for all passenger cars. Other rates range from 1¾ to 5 cents a mile for truck and bus travel, depending on the size of the vehicle.

These tolls will be charged beginning June 24 on a 120-mile section of the expressway that will be opened then between Rochester and Westmoreland, Oneida County. Most of the main route, between Buffalo and Spring Valley, in Rockland County, is scheduled to be finished late this year. There will be thirty-seven toll booths over this section.

The authority listed these sam-

Continued on Page 16, Column 6

Associated Press Wirephoto
AN ORCHID FOR THE SENATOR: Mrs. Eva Bowring receives an orchid from Gov. Robert Crosby of Nebraska. Mr. Crosby appointed her to the United States Senate to fill the vacancy created by the death of Dwight P. Griswold.

Nebraska Woman Named To Griswold Senate Seat

Special to The New York Times.

LINCOLN, Neb., April 16—Mrs. Eva Bowring, 62-year-old ranch operator and vice chairman of the Republican party in Nebraska, was named today to the United States Senate by Gov. Robert Crosby.

Mrs. Bowring will serve until the November general election, but will not run for the full term thereafter. Governor Crosby filed yesterday as a Republican candidate for the full six-year term. Mrs. Bowring will fill the post vacated by the death Monday of Senator Dwight P. Griswold, Republican.

Others who have filed for the nomination as Republican State Chairman David T. Martin of Kearney, State Senator Terry Carpenter of Scotts Bluff and Walter A. Nielsen of Omaha. Mrs. Bowring's interim appointment leaves the Senate line-up at forty-seven Republicans, forty-eight Democrats and one Independent.

Reported to be one of the state's wealthiest women, Mrs. Bowring will be the first woman to represent Nebraska in Congress. Since the death of her second husband, Arthur Bowring, in 1944 she has managed her 10,000-acre Bar 99 Ranch near Merriman.

A Baptist of Scotch-Irish descent, she described her philosophy of life thus: "I've not been one who thought the Lord should make life easy; I've just asked Him to make me strong."

Mrs. Bowring pledged support

Continued on Page 6, Column 2

NEW HAVEN R. R. WON BY M'GINNIS

He Ousts Dumaine by Gaining 11 of 21 Directorships— Victor in Plea for Unity

By The Associated Press.

NEW HAVEN, April 16—Control of the $500,000,000 New York, New Haven and Hartford Railroad passed today to Patrick B. McGinnis and his supporters.

A proxy count that started at 2 P. M. Wednesday wound up here at 7:30 o'clock this morning.

On a cold, dismal morning in a room cluttered with cigarette butts, a board of tellers told reporters, railroad men and other curious persons the fate of Frederic C. Dumaine, who has been president of the line for three years.

The vote was 10,260,702 for the eleven elected on the McGinnis slate of directors to 10,107,343 for the ten elected on the Dumaine slate.

The votes were spread among twenty-six of the forty-two nominees. A substantial difference was that the Dumaine vote was spread among fifteen nominees while the McGinnis vote was held to the eleven successful nominees.

Dumaine Remains on Board

Each stockholder had twenty-one votes at his disposal for each share he held. He could divide those votes any way he wished. Under provision of the railroad's charter, however, each of the three southern New England states had to be represented on the board and that was done.

Mr. Dumaine, who had come into the presidency in 1951 upon the death of his father, remains on the board. He and his wife, incidentally, were in the meeting room when the news was broken this morning, as were Mr. McGinnis and his wife.

The 49-year-old McGinnis, who probably will be elected to the presidency next Tuesday or Wednesday, extended the verbal olive branch, saying:

"It's a victory but I hope to get the support of 'Buck' (Dumaine) and his directors. The railroad needs a united board."

He said that John E. Slater of New York, president of the American Export Line, would succeed Morgan B. Brainard of Hartford, president of the Aetna Life Insurance Company, as chairman of the board. Mr. Brainard, however, a Dumaine man, was re-elected to board membership.

Mr. McGinnis, a nationally known railroad expert who has figured in many important rail reorganizations, is no stranger to the New York, New Haven and Hartford.

He was associated for many years with the New Haven when it was in bankruptcy and had, in fact, helped Mr. Dumaine's father

Continued on Page 26, Column 5

GAMBLING LOSSES OF $5,000 IN NIGHT LAID TO F.H.A. AIDE

Report to F. B. I. on Official Said to Have Set Off Inquiry Into Housing Scandals

By C. P. TRUSSELL

WASHINGTON, April 16—The Administration's investigation into alleged housing frauds was inspired by a report to the Federal Bureau of Investigation of heavy gambling losses by an official of the Federal Housing Administration.

Albert M. Cole, Administrator of the Housing and Home Finance Agency, parent of the F. H. A., made the disclosure tonight after it had been reported here that one official had lost up to $5,000 in a single session at the gaming table. That was more than half of his annual salary.

Mr. Cole said he had not heard that, but he added:

"I do know one official is known to be a gambler. He is in a responsible position. I had his situation in mind when I began the investigation."

This development came a few hours after Mr. Cole outlined steps taken for an investigation that was expected to lead to prosecutions.

He had called for the help of the Department of Justice, the F. B. I. and the Bureau of Internal Revenue. He also welcomed investigations by two committees of the Senate, which already have stepped in.

F. H. A Counsel 'On Leave'

While stating these plans, Mr. Cole announced that the general counsel of the F. H. A., Burton C. Bovard, had been "put on leave" after he had refused to "resign by request."

This development followed by four days the suddenly requested resignation of Guy T. O. Hollyday, F. H. A. Commissioner, head of that agency. Concurrently the White House authorized Mr. Cole to seize the F. H A files.

A week previously, Clyde D. Powell, Assistant Commissioner for multiple-family housing, had resigned, but his resignation was rescinded. Mr. Bovard appeared to have been held in a similar position for further investigation.

Mr. Cole said today that other officials would be removed within a few days. This would be necessary, he said, to insure "a free, swift, uninhibited investigation of all relevant matters."

Today President Eisenhower ordered all agencies of the Government to give complete cooperation to Congressional committees as they went into the scandal. The President did not detail what specific cooperation

Continued on Page 6, Column 4

HIGH U. S. OFFICIAL SAYS OPPENHEIMER IS A LOYAL CITIZEN

Declines Use of Name, but States Expert Should Stay if Cleared of Any Risk

By The Associated Press.

WASHINGTON, April 16—A high Administration official today expressed the opinion that Dr. J. Robert Oppenheimer "is a loyal American" and should not be barred from Government work if he was not a security risk.

"If the man is not a security risk, if he is not subject to blackmail," the official said, "he should have a right to work for the Government."

The official, who talked to newsmen with the stipulation that his identity not be disclosed, declared that it was up to a special panel to decide whether Dr. Oppenheimer was a security risk.

The famed nuclear physicist, who is credited with having played a leading role in developing the atomic bomb, was barred from further access to atomic reports last December pending a review of his case. The Atomic Energy Commission said it had received information that he was a security risk.

Dr. Oppenheimer denied he was a risk and asked for a hearing. His case is now being reviewed by a special panel headed by Gordon Gray, former Secretary of the Army.

Question of Past Ties

The Administration official said the big question was whether the Government should take the position that past association with Communists, even if foresworn, should forever after preclude Government service.

"I do not believe it should," he said. "I believe each case should be considered on its merits, particularly when dealing with an ideology which during the Nineteen Thirties had such an appeal among the intelligentsia and various other groups."

The official, who has been familiar with the Oppenheimer case since 1948 when the scientist was questioned by a Congressional committee, added that he had found Dr. Oppenheimer to be "cooperative, impressive and responsive" under questioning.

More recently, he said, he has had an opportunity to see the full file on the physicist and it presents "an extremely difficult problem."

"Dr. Oppenheimer, at least on the evidence I have seen, in my opinion is a loyal American," he asserted. "On the other hand the information in his file is voluminous and makes a prima facie case of security risk.

"But I am sure Dr. Oppenheimer will get a fair hearing."

The same official said that the disclosure of the security inquiry

Continued on Page 4, Column 2

U. S. PLEDGES TO KEEP FORCES IN EUROPE; WEIGHS FIGHTING IN INDO-CHINA IF NECESSARY

ASIAN PERIL CITED

High Aide Says Troops May Be Sent if the French Withdraw

By LUTHER A. HUSTON
Special to The New York Times.

WASHINGTON, April 16—A high Administration source said today that if France stopped fighting in Indo-China and the situation demanded it the United States would have to send troops to fight the Communists in that area.

He said he hoped this country would not have to send troops but if it could not avoid it the Administration would have to face up to it and would do it. As the leader of the free world, the United States cannot afford another retreat in Asia, he said.

The source of these statements does not hold press conferences and he is not the Administration spokesman on foreign policy. Those were the reasons he gave for refusing to permit his name to be used, his remarks to be attributed to him or the time or place where his statements were made to be disclosed.

He has, however, a voice in the formation of policy. He said that if the situation required it he would support sending troops to Indo-China.

Eisenhower Aide Silent

The statement on possible United States armed intervention in the fighting came in answer to a question after the highly placed official had expressed the opinion that there was no reason why the French could not win in Indo-China.

What prompted the question was his statement that while the Vietminh forces would continue fighting in event of a French withdrawal, Indo-China probably would be Communist-dominated within a month of that act.

James C. Hagerty, White House press secretary, now in Augusta with President Eisenhower, would not say whether the statements made by the Administration source reflected the views of the President.

"I have no knowledge of the story," said Mr. Hagerty. "I was not in Washington and I cannot comment on anything I did not hear."

Congressional reaction to the anonymous statement was scattered but to the point. Senators Bourke B. Hickenlooper, Repub-

Continued on Page 3, Column 2

President's Promise Heartens Europeans

Special to The New York Times.

PARIS, April 16—President Eisenhower's message guaranteeing the maintenance of United States forces in Europe was received today with greatest satisfaction in French official circles. The French said its terms were even stronger than those contained in the agreement with Britain.

Some of the most competent observers saw in the program in part one more step in the program that was arranged during the visits of Secretary of State Dulles this week to London and Paris. They hoped these visits would assist Foreign Minister Georges Bidault in getting action from the French National Assembly toward approval of the long-de-

Continued on Page 2, Column 5

FRENCH HOLD OFF DIENBIENPHU FOE

Prevent Reds From Widening Foothold at Fort—Enemy Clings to Airstrip Gains

By The Associated Press.

HANOI, Vietnam, April 16—French tanks, artillery and infantry kept the Vietminh rebels from widening their foothold, only 800 yards from the heart of Dienbienphu, today.

The French Union forces battled with the rebels at all points around the northwest Indo-China fortress.

Despite constant harassment of the Communist-led rebels clung to the trenches they carved out of the northern part of the main airstrip in their closest approach to the fortress headquarters of Brig. Gen. Christian de Castries, the French commander.

Under cover of darkness the rebels planted more explosives under the steel matting of the airstrip and blew up stretches to pave the way for additional trench digging. The digging went on during the day under covering mortar fire from the Vietminh side.

Mass Assault Awaited

By holding to the airstrip the Vietminh threatened communications between the east and west strong points of the fortress. A French Army spokesman said these strong points were being reinforced, however, by Union troops who managed to skirt the rebel trenches.

The French defenders still awaited a mass assault by the troops of the Vietminh commander, Gen. Vo Nguyen Giap. The rebel commander was reported to have around 40,000 fresh regulars to throw into the battle, in addition to 5,000 other young rebels just out of training camps.

[According to The United Press, the United States Navy carriers Boxer and Wasp, which had been reported maneuvering off Indo-China, were said by the area command officer at Sangley Point, in the Philippines, to have returned to Manila harbor Friday afternoon.]

Artillery battles continued during the day. French 155-mm. and 105-mm. artillery swept all around the dustbowl fortress, plastering rebel gun emplacements and shelling convoys on roads leading into rebel positions and anti-aircraft batteries. French war planes hammered at Vietminh troop concentrations and supply bases. The biggest strikes were centered in the northwestern, northeastern and eastern sections of the area around the fortress.

Foe at Barbed Wire Defenses

Special to The New York Times.

SAIGON, Vietnam, April 16—The Vietminh has brought its system of entrenchments up to the barbed wire of the French defense points in some places at Dienbienphu.

Yesterday the French struck back in the northwest sector. French vanguards were driven from the immediate vicinity and the defenses and trenches with

Continued on Page 3, Column 5

EISENHOWER ACTS

Assures France, Others in E. D. C. Troops Will Stay Till Threat Ends

Text of Eisenhower's message is printed on Page 2.

By JOSEPH A. LOFTUS

AUGUSTA, Ga., April 16—President Eisenhower assured France that United States armed forces will stay in Europe as long as a threat to the area exists.

This and other assurances have been conveyed to the Premiers of the six nations in the projected European Defense Community. Primarily, the President's statement was designed to give France certain guarantees that political leaders in that country felt were necessary to speed ratification of the European community treaty. The French Cabinet has set May 18 to discuss a date for Assembly debate of the treaty.

Italy, too, has delayed ratification. Belgium, West Germany, Luxembourg and the Netherlands have ratified the treaty, under which the six nations agree to integrate their forces into a European army for the common defense. The defense community would form an integral part of the North Atlantic Treaty Organization, to which the United States has committed armed forces.

Fears Delay French Action

French ratification of the defense community treaty has been delayed by special concerns. One is the old fear of German militarism. Another fear is that the United States might withdraw from the North Atlantic Treaty Organization and leave the defense community to itself, which might put France at the mercy of West Germany. A third is a fear that the new United States policy of "massive retaliation" might expose West Europe to land invasion at the start of any new war.

The President's declaration sought to allay these fears. He said he had discussed with the leaders of both political parties in Congress the essential elements of the United States' position between the European community and army on the one hand and the broader community of the North Atlantic Treaty Organization on the other.

In Washington some Senators, including Leverett Saltonstall, Republican of Massachusetts, protested that they had not been consulted on the latest statement on United States foreign and military policy.] President Eisenhower gave these assurances to the defense community nations:

¶The United States will continue to maintain in Europe, including Germany, such units of its armed forces as may be necessary and appropriate to contribute its fair share of the forces needed for the joint defense of the North Atlantic area while a threat to that area exists, and will continue to deploy such

Continued on Page 2, Column 2

$32,000 Payroll Lost In 'Wild West' Theft

Special to The New York Times.

ORANGEBURG, N. Y., April 16—A pair of bandits robbed two bank messengers of a $32,000 payroll here today in a bit of old-fashioned Wild West gunplay. No one was hurt, and the hold-up men made the classic "clean" getaway.

About 9:30 this morning, Clifford Summers, assistant vice president of the First National Bank of Spring Valley, N. Y., and John Johnson, a uniformed guard at the bank, arrived outside the main entrance to the Orangeburg Manufacturing Company here with two canvas bags containing the weekly wages for the company's employes.

As Mr. Johnson was lifting the money bags out of the automobile, another car carrying two men about 30 years old and wearing old trenchcoats pulled up alongside. One man jumped out and

Continued on Page 26, Column 2

Fog Cuts Holiday Air Travel but Sun Is Due to Shine for Easter Parade

The New York Times (by Ernest Sisto)
Prometheus and the lilies in the rain yesterday at Rockefeller Plaza. Partly shrouded R. C. A. Building is in background.

Fog, which thickened through a wet afternoon, brought air traffic to and from New York airports virtually to a standstill yesterday afternoon. With record holiday week-end bookings reported by most airlines.

Fog rolled down like a gray blind over the city and suburbs. It blurred the tops of buildings in Manhattan and slowed outbound automobile traffic to a crawl. The high-

The murky weather disrupted scores of carefully planned holidays. Eastern Air Lines chartered a Baltimore and Ohio train to take 160 of its Miami-bound passengers to Washington, where they were to board planes. Although the Weather Bureau expected the fog to lift this morning, and forecast clear, pleasant weather for tomorrow's Easter Parade, last night was certainly not promising.

Continued on Page 11, Column 2

"All the News
That's Fit to Print"

The New York Times.

LATE CITY EDITION
Fair, moderate temperatures to-day. Partly cloudy tomorrow.
Temperature Range Today—Max., 63 ; Min., 45
Temperatures Yesterday—Max., 59 ; Min., 47
Full U. S. Weather Bureau Report, Page 47

VOL. CIII.. No. 35,167.

Entered as Second-Class Matter,
Post Office, New York, N. Y.

Copyright, 1954, by The New York Times Company.

NEW YORK, FRIDAY, MAY 7, 1954.

Times Square, New York 36, N. Y.
Telephone LAckawanna 4-1000

FIVE CENTS

WESTERN BIG THREE AGREE ON INDO-CHINA COMPROMISE FOR 'PROTECTED ARMISTICE'

U.S. FOR PARIS PLAN

Allies Will Suggest Reds Retire in Vietnam, Quit Laos and Cambodia

By JAMES RESTON
Special to The New York Times.

WASHINGTON, May 6—The United States, Britain and France are now in substantial agreement on a compromise plan for a "protected armistice" in Indo-China.

It is understood that the Laniel Government in Paris has told Washington that it is prepared to fight on in Indo-China unless the Communists agree to evacuate Laos and Cambodia and withdraw to certain "fixed areas" in the third independent state of Vietnam.

The Eisenhower Administration, determined to block the Communist conquest of the whole peninsula, but unwilling to intervene at this time in the war with United States military power, is prepared to go along with France in its attempt to negotiate this compromise in Geneva.

The Secretary of State was reported tonight to have discussed this compromise arrangement with representatives of the Senate and the House of Representatives at the State Department last evening. He also outlined to them his own plans for the negotiation of an "extended" Southeast Asia security arrangement that would be designed to guarantee the terms of any honorable armistice that could be arranged.

Briefing by Dulles Reported

Washington tonight was full of gloomy reports that the Eisenhower Government had virtually abandoned hope of any "collective action" to save the major Indo-Chinese state of Vietnam, but as a matter of fact the Administration was actually a little more hopeful tonight that a "bearable compromise" could be negotiated.

President Eisenhower went over the Indo-China situation with the National Security Council today. John Foster Dulles, the Secretary of State, was represented by his associates in that body as having taken a solemn but not unhopeful view of the situation.

At the end of the meeting it was understood that the position of the United States was about as follows:

¶There was no question of direct United States intervention in the war in the foreseeable future, even though it was assumed that the French garrison of Dienbienphu would probably fall.

¶The United States should do what it could to negotiate a security pact for the defense of Southeast Asia, but there was no hope of doing so without a French promise of "unequivocal independence" to the three associated Indo-Chinese states of Vietnam, Laos, and Cambodia.

¶Meanwhile, the United States and Britain should go along with the French on trying to negotiate a "protected armistice" on the following terms: The Communists should withdraw from Southern Vietnam, Cambodia and Laos; there should be a "neutral zone" in

Continued on Page 2, Column 2

Democrats Launch Attack On Dulles' Foreign Policy

Truman and Johnson Lead Assault — Latter Fears U.S. 'Naked and Alone'

By WILLIAM S. WHITE
Special to The New York Times

WASHINGTON, May 6 — An all-out Democratic attack on the Eisenhower Administration's foreign policy, the first such attack since the President took office, was opened tonight.

The effect was to put the Administration on dual notice (1) that the bipartisanship of the last sixteen months was breaking up and (2) that the Congressional Democrats could not be counted upon for unquestioning general support in the field of world affairs.

Senator Lyndon B. Johnson of Texas, Democratic leader of the Senate, and former President Harry S. Truman both took the occasion to declare that the Administration was alienating allies of the United States.

Senator Johnson said that the

Senator Lyndon B. Johnson
Harris & Ewing

Administration had put the United States "in clear danger of being left naked and alone in a hostile world."

The results thus far of the

Continued on Page 14, Column 4

LANIEL IS UPHELD IN INDO-CHINA TEST

French Chamber, 311 to 262, Gives Him Confidence Vote —Deputies Avert Crisis

By LANSING WARREN
Special to The New York Times.

PARIS, May 6—Premier Joseph Laniel won a vote of confidence today on his refusal to hold a debate on the Indo-China war. The vote was 311 to 262.

By reason of abstentions the vote fell short by three of a majority of the Assembly members and it gave an indication of a serious uneasiness in France about the Government policies in the Indo-China conference at Geneva.

Premier Laniel, nevertheless, avoided the necessity of giving information that might hamper Foreign Minister Georges Bidault in the Geneva negotiations and gained time for him to get some limited achievement through that conference before the Assembly's restiveness returns.

Discussions by the Deputies gave an indication that this might be soon in case of adverse events, such as the fall of Dienbienphu or of rebuffs to France by the delegations of Ho Chi Minh of Vietminh or the Chinese Communists.

Most of the speeches made in the debate today gave the impression of the strong desire of the French to get a cease-fire in Indo-China war at once if only long enough to save the heroic garrison at Dienbienphu.

It was understood that one reason the Deputies avoided a crisis was the news that there was progress in the negotiations at Geneva and on the spot to get a truce at Dienbienphu for the evacuation of the wounded.

Continued on Page 3, Column 5

PEACE PRESSURES ON BIDAULT MOUNT

Geneva Observers Consider French Vote as Move for Indo-China Settlement

By TILLMAN DURDIN
Special to The New York Times.

GENEVA, May 6—Georges Bidault, French Foreign Minister, is believed in some quarters to be under increased pressure from Paris to agree to a settlement in Indo-China as a result of today's challenge to the French Government.

Although the Laniel Cabinet won today's Assembly confidence vote, informed French political sources here say that new moves against the Government can be expected shortly if M. Bidault does not achieve an early solution in Indo-China at the forthcoming Geneva negotiations.

Marc Jacquet, French Under-secretary of State for the Associated States of Indo-China, arrived here late today from Paris to report to M. Bidault on the result of the day's political activity in the French capital. It was reported that he brought new instructions on Indo-China for the Foreign Minister. He refused to give correspondents any indication of what they might be but the surmise in French quarters was that M. Bidault would be asked to reinforce his efforts to get an Indo-China settlement.

Start Remains Uncertain

However, the French Assembly vote at least gave M. Bidault assurance that he could look forward to continued participation in the Indo-China talks and plan accordingly. He dined tonight with M. Jacquet and representatives of the Associated States of Vietnam, Cambodia and Laos and there was a general discussion of prospects and policies for the talks.

Just when the Indo-China sessions will get under way remained uncertain tonight. Because a formal conference session on Korea has been arranged for tomorrow afternoon, and because the delegations for the Indo-China states are still incomplete, it was considered certain that there could be no Indo-China meeting tomorrow.

A French spokesman said it was possible that the Indo-China talks would start Saturday, but the Vietnamese representatives here doubt if the delegation will be ready by then. The chiefs for the Laotian and Cambodian delegations have not yet arrived in Geneva and these two delegations may also not be prepared to participate Saturday.

Nguyen Trung Vinh, chief of the Bao Dai delegation, arrived with a number of ranking delegation members this morning.

A Vietnamese spokesman said that Chief of State Bao Dai

Continued on Page 3, Column 2

SEAWAY IS VOTED BY HOUSE, 241-158; LONG BATTLE ENDS

Bill to Join Canada in Project Goes Back to the Senate for Approval of Minor Changes

By CLAYTON KNOWLES
Special to The New York Times.

WASHINGTON, May 6—The House of Representatives voted today, 241 to 158, to authorize the United States to join Canada in constructing the St. Lawrence Seaway.

The vote gave President Eisenhower his biggest legislative victory in his seventeen months in office. Since World War I every President has urged passage of legislation to accomplish the Seaway project.

Approved Jan. 20 by the Senate in slightly different form, the measure now must go back to the upper chamber for concurrence in minor changes voted by the House. The Senate passed the bill by 51 to 33.

As was the case in the Senate, Democratic help was needed in the House to pass the Administration bill. On final passage, 144 Republicans, ninety-six Democrats and the one independent voted with the President. Ninety-four Democrats and sixty-four Republicans voted in opposition.

Strong Administration pressure was exerted for passage of the bill without change. The vote was passed that the President "wanted the bill as it passed the Senate."

President Cites Satisfaction

Informed of the final vote, the President noted that it "marks the end of a long and fruitful effort." He said:

"It is a source of tremendous personal satisfaction to me that this Eighty-third Congress has made it possible for the United States to join hands with its close neighbor, Canada, in building this Seaway and by this means to contribute materially to the economic well-being and security of both our countries.

"The sponsors of the legislation are to be congratulated for developing a new approach to the St. Lawrence project which eliminated objectionable features responsible for the defeat of similar proposals in the past."

'Before final passage, Representative Charles A. Halleck of Indiana, the House Republican leader, led Administration forces in beating down a move that, it was contended, would "kill the bill."

The test came on an amend-

Continued on Page 18, Column 7

WIDER SALES TAX SEEMS INEVITABLE, MAYOR DECLARES

In Reply to Business Group's Protest, He Asks Its Help in Getting Action by State

Wagner and McGraw messages are printed on Page 34.

By PAUL CROWELL

Mayor Wagner declared yesterday that extension of the 3 per cent sales tax to commercial services was "seemingly" inevitable. Nothing else can be done, he said, unless a "practical" substitute source of revenue is made possible at a special session of the Legislature.

"We have an obligation to keep the government of the City of New York in first-class running order," the Mayor said. "To do this we need $30,000,000 more in funds than the state allows us to retain or collect except through the imposition of taxes like the 3 per cent service tax and others equally onerous. I regret to state that no practical substitute for that tax has yet appeared and that, barring an agreement on a special session and a program for that session, its imposition is seemingly our only present course of action."

Aid Asked for Special Session

The Mayor called upon business and financial interests opposing the extended sales tax to cooperate with the city in persuading Governor Dewey to call a special session.

The bill to impose the extended sales tax, estimated to yield an annual revenue of $30,000,000, is now in the hands of the Finance Committee of the City Council, which held a public hearing on the measure on April 20.

The Mayor's declaration of policy was made in a letter to Harold W. McGraw, chairman of the Joint Conference for Better Government, representing sixty-seven business, trade and taxpayer associations. The letter was in reply to a telegram sent to the Mayor by Mr. McGraw last Monday. The telegram urged the Mayor to drop the proposed extended sales tax and quit his "efforts to push responsibility for this vicious tax to Albany."

A spokesman for the Dewey Administration, commenting in Albany on the Mayor's letter, hinted broadly that the special session sought by the city with the aid of pressure from business and financial groups affected by

Continued on Page 34, Column 2

M'CARTHY DEMANDS A TEST OF EXECUTIVE RIGHT TO BAR SECRET DATA TO CONGRESS

McClellan Suggests 'Crime' By McCarthy on Security

Says Receiver of Secret May Be Just as Guilty as Person Who Passed It

By ELIE ABEL
Special to The New York Times

WASHINGTON, May 6—A suggestion that Senator Joseph R. McCarthy may have violated the law in accepting material officially classified as confidential was put up to the Department of Justice today.

Mr. McCarthy has testified under oath that he received an altered and abbreviated version of a confidential Federal Bureau of Investigation document from a young Army intelligence officer whom he refused to identify.

Senator John L. McClellan called on Herbert Brownell Jr., the Attorney General, to determine whether "a crime was committed" by the receiver of the paper, as well as the man who passed it to him.

He said it was for this purpose that he had proposed that the Attorney General examine the record

Continued on Page 13, Column 6

Senator John L. McClellan
The New York Times

of the Army-McCarthy dispute.

CHALLENGES RULE

Asks Colleagues to Join After Brownell Rules Against Publicity

Excerpts from transcript of the hearing, Pages 12 and 13.

By W. H. LAWRENCE
Special to The New York Times

WASHINGTON, May 6—Senator Joseph R. McCarthy threw down the gauntlet today to President Eisenhower and the entire Executive Branch of Government.

The Wisconsin Republican served notice that he would not be bound by any secrecy decisions by anyone in the Executive Department. He called on the Legislative Branch to join him in a clear-cut test of Presidential authority.

He demanded a closed session of the Senate Permanent Subcommittee on Investigations to decide "once and for all * * * this question of whether or not we are the lackeys to obey and afraid to overrule a decision made by someone in the Executive Department."

The oratory of Senator McCarthy highlighted a day in which there were these developments:

¶Herbert Brownell Jr., Attorney General, ruled that the Senator was not authorized to have possession of information from a confidential report of the Federal Bureau of Investigation. The Attorney General said it would not be in the public interest to make this information public. The Senator threatened to make it public anyway.

¶Senator McCarthy testified under oath yesterday that he had received an altered, condensed version of a classified F. B. I. report from a young Army Intelligence officer who realized he was violating a Presidential directive. He refused to name the informer, and was not required to do so.

¶Senator McCarthy, on his side, suggested possible perjury actions against Robert T. Stevens, Secretary of the Army, and Maj. Gen. Ralph W. Zwicker, Commanding General of Camp Kilmer, N. J., but was rebuked by the committee for improperly suggesting legal conclusions in the guise of questions.

¶The Army presented a legal opinion by the Attorney General supporting its contention, challenged by Senator McCarthy, that it is not required to honor subpoenas for members of loyalty-security boards when it is aware the questions deal with activities kept secret by Presidential directive.

¶There was a long but indecisive wrangle about "Mr. X," a former member of the Army's loyalty-security "screening board." It was alleged by Senator McCarthy and his associates that Mr. X had a record of Communist-front activities.

Secretary Stevens was succeeded on the stand by Mr. Adams, who developed testimony that the charges against Mr. X

Continued on Page 11, Column 1

NEW HAVEN DROPS COMMUTATION RISE

New President Wants Study of Railroad's Role—Dewey 'Discouraged' Over L.I.R.R.

The New York, New Haven and Hartford Railroad's new management withdrew yesterday a proposal its predecessor had made for a 24 to 30 per cent commutation fare increase.

Patrick B. McGinnis, newly elected president, said he first wished to study the various methods of travel used by commuters and to confer with governmental agencies on what part the railroad was to play in the future of mass transport.

Meanwhile, Governor Dewey in Albany termed "discouraging" the action by the Interstate Commerce Commission Wednesday, which he said in effect sought to force a 25 per cent increase in Long Island Rail Road commutation fares in sixty days by the State Public Service Commission.

Governor Dewey summoned members of the Long Island Transit Authority to meet with him "at their earliest"—probably late next week—to discuss that line's problems. If some kind of plan for private rehabilitation of the bankrupt Long Island can be worked out, Mr. Dewey plans to call a special session of the Legislature in June.

New Haven Filed Dec. 30

The New Haven's former management had filed a Dec. 30 petition with the Interstate Commerce Commission to raise commutation fares both interstate and within New York State. Plans were to ask the Connecticut, Rhode Island and Massachusetts Public Service Commissions for similar increases in their areas.

But Mr. McGinnis, who won control of the $500,000,000 New Haven in a management fight last April 16, asserted that "entirely new thinking must be introduced by railroad management to change the general trend from rails to rubber."

Asserting that rate increases are "attended by decreases in the number of commuters," Mr. McGinnis contended that the answer to problems of commutation trains rested in convincing more riders that it was as cheap and convenient to use trains as to use buses and automobiles.

The New Haven's new chief argued that the problem of mass transportation should be studied as a whole, rather than "merely as a railroad problem." He called for conferences with the Port of New York Authority, the Triborough Bridge and Tunnel Authority and officials of New York State, New York City and Westchester County.

"Thus far," he said, "the tendency has been for these other agencies to avoid even discussing the problem with the rail-

Continued on Page 17, Column 2

AUTHORITY SPURNS TRANSIT PLANT BID

Terms Edison Offer So Low as to Make Modernizing of Power Facility Feasible

By LEONARD INGALLS

The Transit Authority rejected yesterday an offer by the Consolidated Edison Company to buy one of the three city-owned subway power plants.

Acting on a recommendation by Sidney H. Bingham, executive director and general manager of the transit system, the authority decided that it would be cheaper in municipal agencies on what part the railroad was to play in the future of mass transport.

The authority's decision was basic. Up to yesterday the question of whether to sell the power plants and buy electricity or to retain and modernize them had been unresolved.

By rejecting the Consolidated Edison proposal, the authority placed itself on record as favoring the latter course which would cost an estimated $176,500,000 in city capital funds.

Consolidated Edison, the authority reported, submitted a bid of $8,000,000 on Feb. 5 for the plant at Kent and Division Avenues, Brooklyn, which supplies power for the B. M. T. division. The land, structure and equipment are valued by the city's real estate assessors at $18,000,000.

Two power plants serving the I. R. T. are operated by the Transit Authority in Manhattan —one at West Fifty-ninth Street and the Hudson River and the other at East Seventy-fourth Street and the East River. Power for the IND subway division is

Continued on Page 17, Column 1

Junta Reported Ruling Paraguay After Army Ousting of President

By The United Press

ASUNCION, Paraguay, May 6 —A junta took over the government today following an uprising by army cavalry forces that deposed President Federico Chaves yesterday.

In a statement signed by its leader, a civil engineer, Tomas Romero Pereira, the junta said the "present political situation in the country remains under the control of the Colorado party."

Dr. Chaves had been a leader of the Colorado party. There was no word on his fate.

The statement from the junta said order prevailed throughout the country.

The junta met here this afternoon to consider steps toward full restoration of political normalcy.

Gen. Alfredo Stroener, Commander in Chief of the Paraguayan Army, broadcasting over a nation-wide hook-up, assured the people that "order has been

re-established in units of the First Cavalry Division, all garrisons are still obeying the orders of the Commander in Chief and of the Government Junta, and calm reigns in the republic."

The First Cavalry Division was the main factor in the rise against the Chaves Government and earlier reports indicated Dr. Chaves was a virtual prisoner of the armed forces.

[Buenos Aires reported indications of a severe censorship in effect in Paraguay. Communications were generally open, but subject to delays.]

Lieut. Col. Mario B. Ortega, new police chief in Asuncion, also assured the country that order had been restored and that the Army supported the Junta.

Colonel Ortega succeeded Police Chief Robert L. Petit, who was killed yesterday when re-

Continued on Page 8, Columns 5

4-Minute Mile Is Achieved By Bannister of England

Associated Press Radiophoto
Roger Bannister hits the tape in 3 minutes 59.4 seconds

By DREW MIDDLETON
Special to The New York Times.

LONDON, May 6—Roger Gilbert Bannister ran a mile in 3 minutes 59.4 seconds tonight to reach one of man's hitherto unattainable goals.

The 4-minute time sought by every great miler for twenty years was beaten by the slim, sandy-haired medical student in a dual meet at Oxford University.

The 25-year-old miler ran under exceedingly unfavorable conditions. Running on the four-lap Iffley

Road track, Bannister swept through the first quarter in 57.5 seconds. The middle quarters of the race were run in 0:60.7 and 0:62.3. Then with a final explosive burst, Bannister raced to the record with 0:58.9 for the last quarter.

Continued on Page 29, Column 1

Crippled Airliner With 62 Aboard Jettisons 'Gas,' Lands Safely Here

In a superb show of airmanship, a Pan American World Airways pilot brought a Boeing Stratocruiser—the world's largest and heaviest commercial transport—in to a safe landing here yesterday in spite of a damaged nosewheel.

None of the fifty-three passengers or crew of nine was even jarred.

The plane, bound for London, had taken off from the New York International Airport, Idlewild, Queens, at 4:23 P. M. Shortly after the takeoff the pilot, Capt. Cameron Walker of 115 Fox Boulevard, Massapequa, L. I., learned that the nosewheel was twisted to a 65-degree angle and would not retract.

Deciding to return, the former Marine Corps combat pilot took his two-deck aircraft out over the Atlantic and dumped 2,500 gallons of the 4,000 gallons aboard. Normally Stratocruisers carry nearly 8,000

gallons, but because of bad weather in the North Atlantic the plane had been routed via Bermuda and the Azores, and could have been refueled there.

When Idlewild learned of the plane's plight and Captain Walker's decision to return for an emergency landing, all measures were taken to handle what might well turn out to be a disaster. Five police cars, four ambulances, four Port of New York Authority fire trucks, two buses, a small derrick and two jeeps were called out to the end of Runway 31—a 9,500-foot strip.

Meanwhile, the passengers had been informed that the plane was returning because of mechanical difficulties. In the control cabin Captain Walker and his co-pilot, John H. Brink of Westbury, L. I., were confronted with a number of decisions.

The Stratocruiser, which weighs

Continued on Page 33, Column 7

7

"All the News That's Fit to Print"

The New York Times.

LATE CITY EDITION
Cloudy, scattered showers today.
Partly cloudy, cool tomorrow.
Temperature Range Today—Max., 55; Min., 47
Temperature Yesterday—Max., 60; Min., 46
Full U. S. Weather Bureau Report, Page 27

Copyright, 1954, by The New York Times Company.

VOL. CIII..No. 35,168.
Entered as Second-Class Matter,
Post Office, New York, N. Y.

NEW YORK, SATURDAY, MAY 8, 1954.

Times Square, New York 36, N. Y.
Telephone LAckawanna 4-1000

FIVE CENTS

PLEAS FOR SCHINE LACED BY THREATS, STEVENS TESTIFIES

Phone Calls Mingled Them, He Tells Jenkins, Who Brings Army Case to Sharp Focus

OFFICIAL DENIES 'BANTER'

Mundt Asserts Subcommittee Hit a 'Security Roadblock' on Monitored Conversations

Excerpts from transcript of the hearing are on Page 8.

By W. H. LAWRENCE
Special to The New York Times.

WASHINGTON, May 7—The Secretary of the Army testified today that Senator Joseph R. McCarthy and his key aides had mixed, in the same conversations, repeated requests for favored treatment for Pvt. G. David Schine with "threats" of continued exposure of alleged Communists in the Army.

Ray H. Jenkins, special counsel for the Senate subcommittee, propounded the queries to Army Secretary Robert T. Stevens that brought into sharp focus the heart of the Army case.

This was that the Senator and his staff had used the investigating power of the Senate to back up their demands for special favors for Private Schine, who, until he was drafted, was an unpaid subcommittee consultant.

As Mr. Stevens, on his twelfth day on the stand, neared the end of his testimony, Mr. Jenkins propounded a series of climactic questions.

"I'll ask you, he said, 'whether or not * * * many telephone calls were either transmitted to you or Mr. Adams [John G. Adams, Army Counselor] with reference to Mr. Schine."

"Yes sir," the Secretary replied.

Subjects Intertwined

"I'll ask you," Mr. Jenkins continued, "whether or not in these telephone conversations there were discussions not only with reference to Schine but with reference to the McCarthy investigating committee's work at Fort Monmouth. Were those two subjects discussed in the same conversations, on numerous occasions or on a number of occasions, or on no occasions?"

"Yes, they were discussed on a number of occasions," Mr. Stevens declared.

"So that the conversations," Mr. Jenkins went on, "with reference to the investigation of Monmouth and with reference to Schine were intertwined, so to speak, in one telephone conversation. Is that right, Mr. Secretary?"

"Yes sir," the answer came.

"And did you not regard that," the counsel pursued, "as being a combination of a request for preferences for Schine, on the one hand, and correlated with a discussion or a threat of continued investigation of Fort Monmouth?"

"Yes, I couldn't separate the two," was Secretary Stevens' conclusion.

Mr. Stevens then coldly rejected suggestions by Senator Everett M. Dirksen, Illinois Republican, that the remarks-taken as threatening might have been good-natured "banter." The Army Secretary said he regarded the threats as a "very serious matter."

Other major developments in the
Continued on Page 8, Column 3

Seaway Bill Passed, Sent to Eisenhower

Special to The New York Times.

WASHINGTON, May 7—The Senate gave final Congressional approval today to the St. Lawrence Seaway bill.

It now goes to the White House where President Eisenhower has said he will sign the measure every President since Warren G. Harding has sought.

The Senate action was by voice vote. The Senate concurred in two minor changes made by the House of Representatives yesterday in giving approval of the bill by a vote of 241 to 158. The Senate had passed the measure, 51 to 33, on Jan. 20.

The bill, which authorizes the United States to join with Canada in constructing the project, calls for the establishment of a St. Lawrence Seaway Development Corporation to act for the United States subject to the supervision of the President. General Eisenhower has...
Continued on Page 18, Column 5

State to Get $113,000,000 Under New U.S. Road Law

Grants Will Be Allocated Over 2 Years— 4 Classes of Highways to Benefit— City Expected to Gain $5,000,000

Special to The New York Times.

ALBANY, May 7—The Public Works Department estimated today that New York would get $113,000,000 of the $1,932,000,000 in Federal highway grants authorized by President Eisenhower yesterday.

The figure in the new law represented an increase of $41,600,000 over New York's grants under the old Federal-aid highway measure. The new amounts will be spread over a period of two years, starting July 1, 1955.

The new Federal grants, as under the old law, will have to be matched by an equal amount of state funds. This represented no problem for the state since it already was planning a huge expansion in state highway construction funds.

At this year's legislative session alternative constitutional amendments to authorize state bond issues of either $500,000,000 or $750,000,000 for highway construction received initial approval. One of the two will be taken up for final legislative action.

proval and submission to the voters next year.

The Public Works Department analysis put the state's share of the new Federal funds at roughly $56,500,000 a year for the fiscal years 1956 and 1957. The first of these starts July 1, 1955, and the second July 1, 1956.

Four classes of roads will share in this amount: primary highways, secondary highways, urban arterial highways and interstate highway routes. More than $14,700,000 a year is provided for primary highways. This is $3,200,000 a year more than New York has been getting.

For secondary roads the new annual allocation is $5,900,000, an increase of $1,300,000. For urban arterial highways the new allowance is more than $22,900,000, an increase of almost $5,000,000. For interstate highways the new allocation is $12,700,000, an increase of $11,600,000.

Since New York City usually...
Continued on Page 36, Column 3

Steel Workers Set to Snub Union Anti-Raiding Accord

By A. H. RASKIN
Special to The New York Times.

PITTSBURGH, May 7—The 1,250,000-member United Steelworkers of America, C. I. O., intends to boycott the no-raiding pact between the American Federation of Labor and the Congress of Industrial Organizations.

The decision of David J. McDonald, president of the giant steel union, to withhold his signature from the peace plan represents as crippling a blow to the pact's effectiveness as the refusal of Dave Beck, an A. F. L. vice president, to bring his 1,300,000-member International Brotherhood of Teamsters under the agreement.

Word of the steel union's plan leaked out here just one week after Mr. McDonald had forged an informal alliance with Mr. Beck and John L. Lewis, president of the United Mine Workers, independent, at a luncheon conference in Washington.

Close associates of the steel union head said his decision had been formed well before the meeting. Mr. McDonald was a member of the joint A. F. L.-C. I. O. committee that drafted the no-raiding pact last summer. The agreement won unanimous approval from the 1953 conventions of both organizations.

However, Mr. McDonald was understood to feel his own union should not commit itself until specific questions relating to the union's jurisdiction had been settled to his satisfaction.

Mr. McDonald is eager to integrate into his organization dock workers employed at Great Lakes ports through which iron ore is shipped to steel mills from the Mesabi range in upper Minnesota. The steel union recently won control over the crews on most of the ore boats and it feels
Asked Business to Join Plea
Continued on Page 10, Column 4

BUSINESS TO OFFER 3% TAX SUBSTITUTE

'Top Committee' Representing 67 Groups Seeks a Meeting With Mayor Wednesday

By PAUL CROWELL

Mayor Wagner was asked yesterday to discuss with a "top committee" of outstanding business men next Wednesday a "sound nonpartisan" proposal for added city revenue. The adoption of it would make unnecessary the extension of the 3 per cent sales tax to commercial services, the civic group said.

It was expected that the Mayor, in line with his announced policy of discussing major city problems with all responsible organizations seeking endorsement, would grant the request, although the meeting might take place later in the week if the Mayor's office commitments prevented a Wednesday conference.

The request for the meeting was made in a telegram sent the Mayor by Harold W. McGraw and John T. Clancy, co-chairman of the Joint Conference for Better Government in New York City. This organization, claiming to represent sixty-seven business and taxpayers groups, is one of the leading opponents of the proposal to tax commercial services.

The telegram is in reply to the Mayor's letter of last Thursday in which he declared that extension of the sales tax to commercial services was "seemingly" inevitable unless a special session of the Legislature gave the city an acceptable substitute method of raising the $30,000,000 the broadened sales tax would yield in 1954-55.

In his letter the Mayor asked for the cooperation of the sixty-seven business and taxpayer groups in "a genuine non-partisan appeal to Albany." The McGraw-Clancy telegram assured the Mayor that the proposal to be presented for his consideration would represent the "high level non-partisan business thinking" of the "top committee," which would begin on Monday a series of executive meetings from which the plan would emerge.

The telegram expressed confidence that the plan would kill the "ruinous" sales tax proposal if the Mayor would "move sincerely" in cooperation with the business group.

The Mayor was informed that four members of the "top committee" had been chosen earlier in the day at a special meeting called to consider his letter.

They were Percy J. Ebbott, president of the Chase National Bank; Warren Lee Pierson, chairman of the board of Trans World Airlines, Inc.; Clinton W. Blume, president of the Real Es-
Continued on Page 23, Column 5

TAFT ACT CHANGES KILLED BY SENATE; DEMOCRATS SOLID

Party Prevails in 50-42 Vote to Return Bill — President Rebuffed on Program

Special to The New York Times.

WASHINGTON, May 7—The Senate today killed amendments to the Taft-Hartley Law for the 1954 session of Congress.

A vote of 50 to 42 sent the Administration bill to revise the labor act back to committee.

The Democrats engineered this with solidarity, something they had not achieved on a roll-call vote in the modern cycle of labor legislation going back to the Norris-LaGuardia Act of 1932. Three Republicans joined them, but their votes did not affect the result.

Forty-six of the Senate's forty-eight Democrats were for returning the bill and the two others were paired for recommittal.

Just before the tally, Senator William F. Knowland of California, the Republican leader, sternly told his colleagues what nearly everybody understood:

"A motion to recommit this bill is a motion to kill this bill as this session is concerned."

Nobody challenged this on or off the Senate floor.

Senator H. Alexander Smith, Republican of New Jersey, confirmed such a conclusion after the vote. As chairman of the Labor Committee, he was in charge of the bill on the floor, and though he lost he appeared happy that the fight was over.

Feels Sense of Relief

"I feel a sense of relief," he commented. "I'm just as cheerful as a dickey bird."

He said he did not think the issue of state's rights in labor matters would be opened again at this session by his committee, and he did not think the House of Representatives would produce a bill on the subject, either. The House Labor Committee has been writing a bill, but was deferring a final vote until the Senate acted.

The Republican Senators who voted to recommit were: William Langer and Milton R. Young of North Dakota and George W. Malone of Nevada. Senator Wayne Morse of Oregon, an Independent, also voted this way.

The stated reason for the Democrats' solid vote to recommit the bill was the fact that the Republicans' majority on the Labor Committee would not consider amendments outside the area of President Eisenhower's recommendations.

This was not considered the final reason, however, at least not the sole reason.

The Northern Democrats, most friendly to labor, had been persuaded that the Administration bill would make the Taft-Hartley Law more undesirable to them and that they might fare better by waiting until the next Congress was elected.

The Southern Democrats felt that some of the President's recommendations undeniably weakened some of the labor controls. Also, if the bill were not recommitted, they would face
Continued on Page 11, Column 2

Housing Unit Counsel Ordered To Answer Charges or Be Ousted

Acting Commissioner Directs Bovard, Now on Leave, to Act in 14 Days

By The United Press.

WASHINGTON, May 7—Norman P. Mason, acting Federal Housing Administrator, charged today that the agency's counsel, Burton C. Bovard, had failed to do his job "satisfactorily" and gave him fourteen days to answer the charges or be dismissed.

Mr. Mason, named to clean up alleged widespread housing scandals, said he had "no evidence of illegal activity" by Mr. Bovard. The charges involve his "failure to satisfactorily carry out the duties of general counsel of the F. H. A.," he explained.

While he gave Mr. Bovard fourteen days to show cause why he should not be removed, he said he might extend that time. If counsel fails to answer the charges, Mr. Mason added, he will be "removed from office" within thirty days.

Mr. Mason also offered to give Mr. Bovard a public hearing within twenty days if he agreed to testify under oath and be subject to cross-examination.

Associated Press
Burton C. Bovard

Meanwhile, Senator Harry F. Byrd, Democrat of Virginia, said he had sent to the Justice Department information that might be "helpful" in pinning down responsibility for Government housing...
Continued on Page 15, Column 7

DIENBIENPHU IS LOST AFTER 55 DAYS; NO WORD OF DE CASTRIES AND HIS MEN; DULLES SAYS UNITY CAN CHECK REDS

ASIA PACT PUSHED

Secretary Rules Out Armed Action Without Congress' Approval

Text of the Dulles address is printed on Page 4.

By WILLIAM S. WHITE
Special to The New York Times.

WASHINGTON, May 7—John Foster Dulles, Secretary of State, predicted tonight that the current efforts toward collective defense in Southeast Asia ultimately would halt Communist aggression short of its aims.

Reporting in a broadcast on the Geneva conference on the Far East, Mr. Dulles made two points plain:

1. That the possibility of ultimate United States military intervention in Indo-China, in association with other free nations, was real.

2. That there was no intention, in any event, of committing United States forces without the sanction of Congress.

The French Union fortress of Dienbienphu in Indo-China fell only at the cost of "staggering losses" to the Communists, Mr. Dulles noted.

"An epic battle has ended but great causes have, before now, been won out of lost battles," he added.

Steps Proposed for U. S.

He declared that the Eisenhower Administration regarded as important the following steps for a solution of the Indo-China crisis:

¶The French should give greater reality to their intention to grant full independence to Vietnam, Laos and Cambodia, the three Associated States of the country. This would take away from the Communists their false claim to be leading the fight for independence.

¶There should be greater reliance upon the national armies that would be fighting in their own homeland. He believed this could be done if the peoples felt that they had a good cause for which to fight and if better facilities for training and equipment were provided for them.

¶There should be greater free-world assistance. France is carrying on a struggle that is overburdening her economic resources. "Much progress" has been made toward all those goals, the Secretary asserted.

As to the current negotiations for creating a free-world alliance in Asia, Mr. Dulles reported that progress had been made and that "unity of purpose persists."

The fall of Dienbienphu will only "harden, not weaken, our purpose to stay united," he said.

Geneva Hopes Stand

While "present conditions" in Indo-China do not "provide a suitable basis" for armed intervention by the United States, the possibility under other circumstances of "serious commitments" by the United States nevertheless exists, Mr. Dulles said.

The Geneva conference, he went on, may yet find a settlement by which an honorable armistice can be arranged, but the United States "would be gravely concerned" if the outcome should "provide a road to a Communist takeover and further aggression."

"If this occurs, or if hostilities continue, then the need will be even more urgent to create the conditions for united action in defense of the area," he said.

"In making commitments which might involve the use of armed force, the Congress is a full partner," Mr. Dulles continued. "Only the Congress can declare war. President Eisenhower has repeatedly emphasized that he would not take military action in Indo-China without the support of Congress.

"Furthermore, he has made clear that he would not seek that unless, in his opinion, there would be an adequate collective effort based upon genuine mutuality of interest in defending vital interests."

This declaration took on added significance in light of the fact that earlier in the day Mr. Dulles had gone over with President Eisenhower for an hour and a
Continued on Page 4, Column 4

WEST STILL PLANS ARMISTICE TALKS

Negotiations on Indo-China Set to Open in Geneva, Subject to Paris Action

By THOMAS J. HAMILTON
Special to The New York Times.

GENEVA, May 7—The United States, Britain and France decided tonight to go ahead with the opening of the Indo-China negotiations here tomorrow despite the capture of Dienbienphu. Their decision, however, was made subject to the action of the French Cabinet.

The three Western powers had previously agreed to submit to the conference on Far Eastern affairs a proposal for an armistice under which the Vietminh would withdraw from southern Vietnam and the Red River delta in northern Vietnam.

This is the program that Foreign Minister Georges Bidault had been fighting for, and if the Cabinet backs him up the Indo-China phase of the Far Eastern conference will start at 3 P. M. tomorrow.

However, if the Cabinet overrules M. Bidault and orders him to propose a simple cease-fire, the new-found unity of the Western powers will be destroyed and it will be necessary to postpone the opening of the conference while a new formula is negotiated.
Continued on Page 4, Column 7

FRANCE IS SENDING MORE MEN TO WAR

No Protest Greets Laniel's Statement—Shock of Loss Seems to Unify Deputies

By LANSING WARREN
Special to The New York Times.

PARIS, May 7—The French Assembly heard Premier Joseph Laniel's statement on the fall of Dienbienphu in utter silence and adjourned for half an hour late this afternoon as a sign of mourning and respect for the valiant dead.

The three Western powers had previously agreed to submit to the conference on Far Eastern affairs a proposal for an armistice under which the Vietminh would withdraw from southern Vietnam and the Red River delta in northern Vietnam.

The shock was evidently great and most of the Deputies, as they discussed it, seemed to have been drawn together in a renewed determination that they would not now give up the fight. Even those members of the Assembly who had most strongly urged an end to the conflict were disposed today to show that France would not capitulate.

No one protested when the Premier made the announcement that more troops were on the way to Indo-China so that the expeditionary corps would not be weakened.

The Cabinet, in unison, decided upon military steps to aid the troops in the other parts of Vietnam to hold out.

The Vietminh tactics of overwhelming Dienbienphu on the eve of the opening of the Geneva conference on Indo-China seemed in a fair way to result in bolstering French resistance and in
Continued on Page 3, Column 2

ASSAULT SUCCEEDS

Fort Falls After 20-Hour Fight — Last Strong Point Is Silent

Special to The New York Times.

PARIS, May 7—The fall of Dienbienphu was announced today by Premier Joseph Laniel.

The news of the worst military defeat since the French have suffered since the Indo-China war began in December, 1946, came suddenly.

It was received with confused emotion. The heroic defense of Dienbienphu, besieged for fifty-five days, had been followed in screaming headlines since March 13, when the Vietminh launched its first attack—as if for the first time in more than seven years the public had fully realized that the country was fighting an enormously bloody and costly war.

M. Laniel told the Assembly that the heroic stronghold that had been taken after twenty hours of fighting and continuous alertness for the last two months. He could not say, any information as to the fate of the commander, Brig. Gen. Christian de Castries, or of the defenders or the wounded who have wasted underground for several weeks.

Final Concentration

All that he knew, the Premier said, was that the southern resistance point called Isabelle was still defended under the command of Col. André Lalande. French artillery with some tanks were concentrated at that center.

[Contact with the Isabelle outpost had been lost, according to an Associated Press dispatch from Saigon.]

"The Vietminh now are only a few meters away," were the last words heard from General de Castries over the radio-telephone, the French Cabinet was told. The last dispatch received from the battle was that the central strong point had been submerged.

For the defenders of Dienbienphu there was French pride in their heroism and sadness for their fate. There was also some grim anger against those who had engulfed them in defeat and, if not anger, at least unkindly feelings for those responsible for French political and military policy.

Before last March the name of Dienbienphu, now solidly entrenched in French military annals, was unknown here, but not in Indo-China, where it had some importance.

The Vietminh had taken Dienbienphu, a peaceful community of 9,000 persons, who grew rice and poppy for opium, in November, 1953, and used it to help launch operations against Laos in the following April.

French Seizure Nov. 21

Last November a Vietminh column was spotted heading northwest in the Thai country to the French base of Laichau, the French decided to evacuate Laichau and seize Dienbienphu, using parachutists from the Tonkin area.

A successful operation was launched Nov. 21 and after the Laichau garrison moved in the French began daily efforts to strengthen it by building underground fortifications, improving the airfield and setting up barbed wire.

The establishment of the Dienbienphu base had strategic and political reasons. Close to the Laotian border, it helped fend off Vietminh attacks southward into Laos and against the capital of Luang Prabang by threatening the Vietminh rear and blocking supply lines.

The fact that the Vietminh withdrew from Laos and did not attack Luang Prabang is attributed to French control of Dienbienphu. The French also wished to remain in the Thai tribal country to encourage and help the T'nai guerrillas hostile to the Vietminh.

Finally, Dienbienphu, because of its geographical position, was expected to require a large Vietminh force to attack it, thus relieving pressure on French defenses in the much more vital Tonkin delta area.

This is precisely what happened. The French garrison num-
Continued on Page 2, Column 4

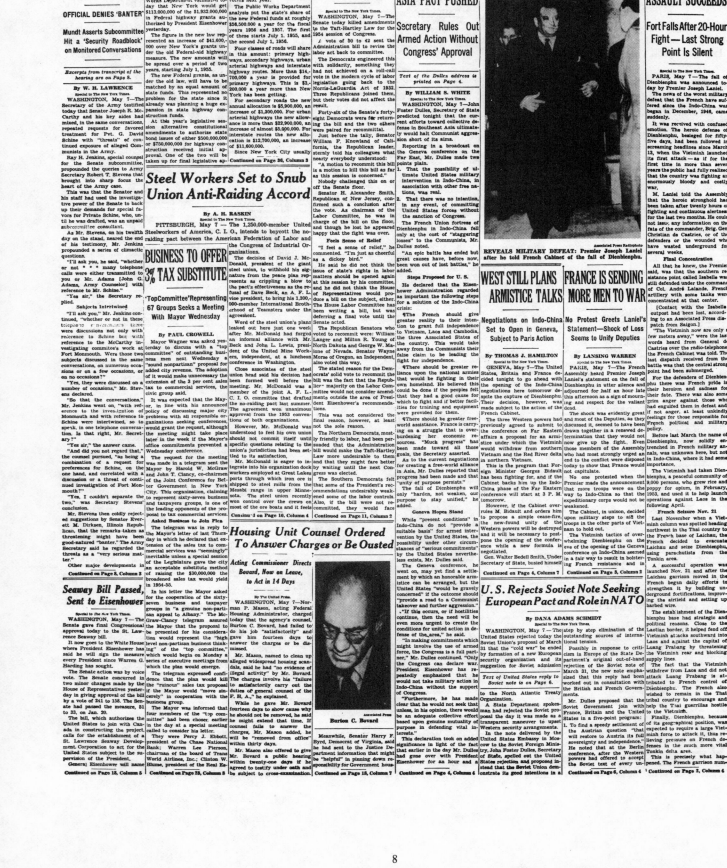

REVEALS MILITARY DEFEAT: Premier Joseph Laniel
after he told French Cabinet of the fall of Dienbienphu.
Associated Press Radiophoto

U. S. Rejects Soviet Note Seeking European Pact and Role in NATO

By DANA ADAMS SCHMIDT
Special to The New York Times.

WASHINGTON, May 7—The step by step elimination of the United States rejected today the Soviet Union's "cold war" ended outstanding sources of international tension.

Possibly in response to criticism in Europe of the State Department's original out-of-hand rejection of the Soviet note of March 31, the new note emphasized that this reply had been worked out in consultation with the British and French Governments.

Mr. Dulles proposed that the Soviet Government join with France, Britain and the United States in a five-point program:

1. To find a speedy settlement of the Austrian question. This will restore to Austria its full sovereignty and independence. He noted that at the Berlin conference, after the Western powers had offered to accept the Soviet text of every un-
Continued on Page 6, Column 4

Excerpts from the text of the Soviet note and United States reply

By the Soviet Union's "cold war" ended by formation of a new European security organization and suggestion for Soviet admission.

Text of United States reply to Soviet note is on Page 6.

to the North Atlantic Treaty Organization.

A State Department spokesman had rejected the Soviet proposal the day it was made as a transparent maneuver to upset Western security arrangements.

In the note delivered by the United States Embassy in Moscow to the Soviet Foreign Ministry, John Foster Dulles, Secretary of State, spelled out the United States rejection and proposed instead that the Soviet Union demonstrate its good intentions in a...
Continued on Page 6, Column 4

Soldiers of the former French-officered National Army of Vietnam and their families flee North Vietnam during a 300-day period of free movement between the two Vietnams provided for in the Geneva Agreements of 1954 after the fall of Dien Bien Phu.

Demonstrators march in front of the U.S. Information Service building in Saigon to mark "National Shame Day," July 19, 1964; the tenth anniversary of the partition of Vietnam by the Geneva Agreements.

Defeated French prisoners are led into captivity after the fall of Dien Bien Phu.

"All the News
That's Fit to Print"

The New York Times.

LATE CITY EDITION
Some cloudiness with a few
showers today. Fair tomorrow.
Temperature Range Today—Max., 86; Min., 70
Temperatures Yesterday—Max., 88.3; Min., 68.5
Full U. S. Weather Bureau Report, Page 47

Copyright, 1954, by The New York Times Company.

VOL. CIII No. 35,242.

Entered as Second-Class Matter,
Post Office, New York, N. Y.

NEW YORK, WEDNESDAY, JULY 21, 1954.

Times Square, New York 36, N. Y.
Telephone LAckawanna 4-1000

FIVE CENTS

M'CARTHY ACCEPTS COHN RESIGNATION, TRANSFERS SURINE

Puts the Assistant Counsel on Own Payroll—Panel Defers Any Action on La Venia

CONFIRMS REST OF STAFF

Carr Among 22 Approved— Senator Calls Loss of Cohn 'Great Victory' for Reds

Texts of Cohn letter, McCarthy statement are on Page 10.

By ANTHONY LEVIERO
Special to The New York Times
WASHINGTON, July 20—Senator Joseph R. McCarthy yielded today to the insistent demand for a staff housecleaning from a majority of the members of the Senate Permanent Subcommittee on Investigations.

The results, at the subcommittee met over a steak luncheon in the old Supreme Court chamber in the Capitol, were these:

¶Senator McCarthy reluctantly accepted the resignation of Roy M. Cohn, the subcommittee's chief counsel, denouncing those who had sought it and saying the result was a "great victory" for communism.

¶Mr. McCarthy transferred the controversial assistant counsel, Don Surine, from the subcommittee staff to his personal payroll, also with a vigorous defense of him.

Action on La Venia Deferred

Both these changes were personal actions of Senator McCarthy as chairman taken before the subcommittee met. In this way he headed off inevitable defeat on a staff housecleaning demanded by a majority of four of the seven members of the subcommittee led by Senator Charles E. Potter, Republican of Michigan.

The subcommittee itself then voted unanimously to withhold "without prejudice" confirmation of Thomas La Venia in his position as office manager and investigator until further consideration of his personal record.

The subcommittee then voted to confirm twenty-two other employes of the subcommittee in their present jobs. Among them were two others who had come under fire during the thirty-six days of the Army - McCarthy hearings that ended on June 17.

One was Francis P. Carr, staff director, who had been named as a principal in the controversy but was removed from that category before the hearings ended.

Juliana Approved

The other was James N. Juliana, a staff investigator, who assumed full responsibility during the hearings for cropping an Army colonel out of a photograph introduced in evidence. As produced by the McCarthy side, this photograph showed only Robert T. Stevens, Secretary of the Army, and Pvt. G. David Schine.

There was no discussion by the subcommittee on whether to oust Mr. Carr, who said he was staying "unless I am voted out." Senator McCarthy said that all votes today were unanimous.

On Capitol Hill the staff changes were regarded as one of the few reversals ever suffered by Mr. McCarthy in his Senatorial career which began in 1946.

The action today was a direct

Continued on Page 10, Column 5

Miss Connolly Breaks Leg, Out of U.S. Play

By The Associated Press.
SAN DIEGO, Calif., July 20—Maureen Connolly, the tennis queen, was so seriously injured when she was crushed against a big cement truck while riding her horse here today that she will be unable to defend her national title next month at Forest Hills, Queens.

Surgery and X-rays determined that the small bone in her lower right leg was broken and that muscle and tendons of the calf were damaged by a deep gash.

This definitely ends her hope of winning the United States championship for the fourth straight time.

She will hardly be able to get around, doctors said, by the start of the tournament on Aug. 28. "Little Mo," who will be 20 on Sept. 17, was wheeled into surgery within an hour after reaching the hospital.

She was conscious when the

Continued on Page 21, Column 2

House Inquiry Asked Into a House Inquiry

By C. P. TRUSSELL
Special to The New York Times
WASHINGTON, July 20—The House of Representatives was urged today to investigate one of its investigations.

At issue was the inquiry into tax-free educational and philanthropic foundations that began in May.

Early this month the investigators decided to hold no more public hearings. At that point the witnesses, including two committee researchers, had been eleven to one in criticism of foundations. The foundations were given permission to file sworn statements in rebuttal.

A resolution was introduced in the House this afternoon by Representative Jacob K. Javits, Republican of Manhattan. It called on the Rules Committee.

Continued on Page 30, Column 7

SHOWDOWN TODAY ON T.V.A. CURB SET

Democrats Decide to Permit Vote on President's Order for Power Contract

By WILLIAM M. BLAIR
Special to The New York Times
WASHINGTON, July 20—A band of Senate Democrats agreed tonight to a showdown vote tomorrow afternoon in their fight against President Eisenhower's order to the Atomic Energy Commission to carry out a private power contract.

They intimated, however, that if defeated they would renew what Senate Republican leaders have called a filibuster against the important atomic energy bill.

The President's order directed the commission to negotiate a contract with a private utilities group to supply the Tennessee Valley Authority with power.

The Senate recessed at 9:37 P. M. after Senator William F. Knowland, the Republican Floor Leader, had said he hoped for a vote in the power fight tomorrow and completion of the atomic energy bill by the start of the same time tomorrow night.

He announced that he had instructed the Sergeant at Arms to set up cots in the Senate wing of the Capitol in the event it was necessary to work through the night to complete the entire atomic energy bill.

The Democrats' decision at a strategy meeting ended temporarily seven days of unlimited talking in the Senate that stalled the Administration's program.

Continued on Page 8, Column 2

EISENHOWER LOSES ON PUBLIC HOUSING BY VOTE OF 234-156

House Rejects Plan to Build 140,000 Units in 4 Years —35,000 in One Voted

By CLAYTON KNOWLES
Special to The New York Times
WASHINGTON, July 20—The House of Representatives killed the last real hope today to enact President Eisenhower's public housing program at this session of Congress.

By a vote of 234 to 156, it rejected a proposal sponsored by Democrats to write the President's request for 140,000 housing units over a four-year period into the compromise housing bill that emerged last week from Senate-House conference.

Arrayed against the proposal were 155 Republicans and 79 Democrats. Supporting the President's position in the vote were 105 Democrats, 50 Republicans and one Independent.

Soon after this test, the House approved, 358 to 30, terms of the omnibus compromise on housing. It contained provision for only 35,000 units in a one-year extension of the public housing program. Many asserted that this authorization was meaningless because of restrictions in the provision. Some said only 10,000 units could be built under it.

Action Regarded as Final

The House action, which promises to create a major political issue for the Congressional campaign, was as good as final even though the Senate still has to ratify the conference report. The original Senate bill carried the President's "public housing program," but it was pared, almost beyond recognition, in conference.

Interruption Is Temporary

The general belief was that the Senate would not even attempt to restore the right of the free areas of the partitioned Indochina States to receive foreign military assistance would be interrupted only temporarily, so that no interference with their sovereignty would be entailed.

It was understood the temporary restriction on the receipt of military assistance from the United States and other free nations would end after a period of "disengagement" during which forces would be withdrawn from existing front-line areas.

Diplomatic officials conversant with, its terms held that the cease-fire generally came within the terms of the seven principles that President Eisenhower and Prime Minister Churchill laid down three weeks ago. These included division of the

Continued on Page 16, Column 4

Arrests Here Bare 'Sure Thing' Racing Fraud by Radio

AGREE ON TRUCE: Pierre Mendès-France, French Premier, as he appeared yesterday with Pham Van Dong, Vietminh Foreign Minister, left, at French headquarters in Geneva. Behind them are Guy de la Tournelle, wearing eyeglasses, and Georges Boris, aides to French leader.

Associated Press Radiophoto

CAPITAL CAUTIOUS

Accepts in Principle— Bars Any Guarantee Except by Alliance

Special to The New York Times
WASHINGTON, July 20—The United States Government will issue a unilateral statement tomorrow accepting in principle the terms of the Indochina cease-fire accord. It also will acknowledge its "ability to respect" such terms under the United Nations Charter, diplomatic officials disclosed tonight.

The decision to state the United States Government's position on the agreement—probably by President Eisenhower at his regular news conference tomorrow—was disclosed after diplomatic intelligence established the terms contained a clause permitting a free exchange of populations between northern and southern Vietnam.

For a period of one year, according to this understanding, no effort would be made to prevent movement between the two areas. Diplomatic officials attached the greatest importance to this clause, which they considered would avert the swallowing up of the anti-Communist and predominantly Catholic population of the Red regime.

SENATORS TO PUSH GERMAN REARMING

Leading Republicans Will Urge Action This Year in Addition to Granting Sovereignty

By WILLIAM S. WHITE
Special to The New York Times
WASHINGTON, July 20—Powerful Senate Republicans will advise the Eisenhower Administration that West German rearmament and sovereignty should be pushed this year.

They are prepared to suggest to the Administration that the United States-British plan to give sovereignty without the right to rearm, as an alternative to the faltering European Defense Community project, would not be realistic.

They will argue that implicit in the right of self-defense and that; the two concepts cannot be separated validly, as John Foster Dulles, Secretary of State, has proposed to do.

Senator Homer Ferguson of Michigan, chairman of the Senate Republican Policy Committee, who is one of the leaders in this movement, expects some sort of Congressional resolution backing both German sovereignty and German rearmament to be offered before Congress adjourns this month or early next month. Others, among them Senator William F. Knowland of California, Republican Senate floor leader, are taking a more reserved line pending a study by the State Department of the legal situation.

Mr. Dulles has adopted the position that the question of rearmament must be deferred un-

Continued on Page 5, Column 3

38 Jersey Forgeries Charged to Hoffman

Special to The New York Times
TRENTON, July 20—The preliminary report of a handwriting expert released here today said that former Gov. Harold G. Hoffman had apparently concealed his $300,000 defalcations by forging thirty-eight bank certifications in six years.

Attorney General Grover C. Richman made public the findings of Albert D. Osborne of Montclair, who for a month has been studying the signatures on the certifications from the South Amboy Trust Company.

The certifications of general state treasury funds deposited at the South Amboy bank cover a period from June 30, 1947, to Dec. 31, 1953. They all had the signature of George A. Kress, a vice president of the bank. No breakdown of the amount of

Continued on Page 48, Column 1

INDOCHINA ARMISTICE IS SIGNED; VIETNAM SPLIT AT 17TH PARALLEL; U. S. FINDS IT CAN 'RESPECT' PACT

LONG WAR ENDING

2 Accords Completed —One on Cambodia Due Later Today

By THOMAS J. HAMILTON
Special to The New York Times
GENEVA, Wednesday, July 21 —Armistice agreements bringing the fighting in Vietnam and Laos to a halt were signed this morning by representatives of the French and Communist Vietminh forces.

A French spokesman said the armistice would take effect forty-eight hours later.

The signing ceremony, witnessed by representatives of the nine delegations participating in the Far Eastern conference here, began at 3:42 A. M. (9:42 P. M. Tuesday, Eastern daylight time). It brought to a close the eight-year struggle for Indochina.

The armistice in Cambodia will not be signed until later this morning. The Far Eastern conference will hold its final session this afternoon to complete work on the final political settlement. Under it Laos and Cambodia will be neutralized and elections to create a unified government in Vietnam will be held within two years from the date of the armistice.

Pierre Mendès-France, French Premier, who had set July 20 as his deadline to obtain an armistice or resign, had missed it by a few hours. He canceled a radio speech to the French people and went to bed before the two agreements were signed at the Palais des Nations, former headquarters of the League of Nations, where conference sessions have been held since the Indochina negotiations began last May.

Rebels Get Northern Part

Under the Vietnamese agreement, Vietnam is to be divided into two parts, about equal in area and population, between the Communist-led Vietminh rebels who will hold northern Vietnam, north of a line along the seventeenth Parallel, and the French-sponsored Government of Bao Dai.

The partition line thus is far enough north to preserve Hue, the ancient capital of Annam; Tourane, an important port and naval and air base, and the only major highway leading to Laos from the coast.

The French will not give up Hanoi and Haiphong, in the Red River delta area, in the north, for approximately a year, which will give them time to evacuate personnel of the French expeditionary force in the territory remaining to them in the delta, plus civilians fearing persecution by the Communists.

Under the armistice agreements, the Communists recognize the Governments of Laos and Cambodia. However, regrouping areas for Communist troops were authorized in Laos. The forces of the Communist "resistance government" in Laos will be concentrated in two provinces near the frontier with Vietminh territory. [Some sources identified the two provinces as Samneua and Phongsaly.]

The Cambodian delegation held out against the provision, and prolonged sessions of the "drafting committee" of the Vietminh and Cambodian delegations were

Continued on Page 2, Column 5

French Call Pact No Victory But See Gains for Europe

By HAROLD CALLENDER
PARIS, July 20—The terms of agreement for the truce in Indochina were regarded here as probably a peace without victory. Some called it a peace that would confirm a defeat for the West in Asia and would mark the most notable loss in battle of French territories since Louis XV lost Canada in the eighteenth century.

But it was expected that this ill wind in Asia might blow some good for France and the Atlantic alliance in Europe.

The truce seemed likely to give great prestige to Premier Pierre Mendès-France, and to enable him to stay in office to seek a decision on the European army treaty and to press for a program to stimulate the French economy.

It appeared probable tonight that the Premier would submit the treaty to the National Assembly early in August with suggested modifications that would not require further action by the parliaments of the other signatories. The West German Chancellor, Dr. Konrad Adenauer, has indicated that he would consider changes that could be made without resort to parliaments.

New Unity a By-Product

Removal of the uncertainty that has surrounded the treaty for two years would clear up the question of West Germany's sovereignty and rearmament and permit in this sphere a unity among the United States, Britain and France that has not yet existed. Such a gain in Europe might be considered as offsetting to some extent the failure of Western policy in Indochina.

A severe blow to French prestige in Asia and probably in North Africa has foreseen in the truce. In North Africa that prestige is far more important than in Asia because France's African territories are more important to her. But M. Mendès-France's argument has been that France must cut her losses in Asia in order to conserve her strength in Europe; and if she revamps her economy, as he desires, the net result may be to increase her influence and even her prestige in Europe and Africa.

M. Mendès-France has urged that the failure to reconcile Vietnam with the French Union by a prompt grant of independence should not be repeated in North Africa, where nationalist movements now are menacing.

The truce in Indochina will mark the frustration of a prolonged Western effort to resist the conquest of Vietnam, Laos and Cambodia by a nationalist movement that was anti-West and Communist-led. Against it were employed unsuccessfully a French army, a native force and United States aid that was to amount to $800,000,000 this year.

The truce will mark an advance of communism in the sense that

Continued on Page 3, Column 4

HANOI PREPARING FOR TRUCE PERIOD

French Study Plans Designed to Preserve Calm in Delta and Effect Evacuation

By HENRY R. LIEBERMAN
Special to The New York Times
HANOI, Vietnam, July 20— Two kinds of preparations were being made here to cope with problems related to the surrender of North Vietnam to the Vietminh under a cease-fire agreement. North Vietnam will eventually be taken over by the Vietminh under a truce agreement.

French authorities were preparing security measures to "maintain calm" in this city of 340,000. Plans originally drawn up to evacuate French, foreign and a number of Vietnamese civilians under battle conditions were also being restudied in terms of a more leisurely evacuation.

It was being taken for granted today in this city, which is seven hours ahead of Geneva time, that the seven-and-a-half-year-old Indochinese war was drawing to a close.

Geneva reports aroused considerable interest in Hanoi but created no public excitement. In fact, despite a demonstration against partition yesterday by several thousand Vietnamese, there has been no major agitation

Continued on Page 2, Column 2

Reds Have Margin in Indochina Despite Even Split Under Truce

By TILLMAN DURDIN
Special to The New York Times
GENEVA, July 20—In statistical terms, a balanced settlement on Indochina seems to have been reached.

The Communist Vietminh has gained the northern half of Vietnam, inhabited by about 12,000,000 persons, while the Vietminh forces evacuate other areas according to the terms, the southern half of Vietnam and the states of Laos and Cambodia will remain in non-Communist hands. Approximately 10,000,000 Vietnamese, 4,000,000 Cambodians and 1,400,000 Laotians live in the territories to remain outside Communist control Northern Vietnam is somewhat smaller, both in population and area, than

Continued on Page 3, Column 3

Pocket transmitter at left sends race results to receiver near track, whence an agent phones data to an associate posted near a betting parlor. This man, using transmitter built into suitcase at right, relays result to a bettor, who gets electronic impulses through concealed dimes in left hand above. Agent then bets on horse that won.

The New York Times

The police cracked down yesterday on a gambling ring that has been using Dick Tracy techniques, complete with purse-size transmitters and shock radio receivers, to flash race results far in advance of official returns. Twenty-eight persons were rounded up in fast-hitting raids in Manhattan, Brooklyn and Queens. Fifty detectives and policemen, under the command of Supervising Assistant Chief Inspector James Nidds, fanned out through the three boroughs at 8 A. M. After the half-hour round-up, when the twenty-eight captives were paraded before Queens Assistant District Attorney Lawrence Peirez, a crime-comics story on the use of ingenious electronic devices was unfolded. Race-result plotters were pictured tapping

Continued on Page 28, Column 3

"All the News That's Fit to Print"

The New York Times.

LATE CITY EDITION
Warm, showers this morning; fair, cooler tonight. Fair tomorrow.
Temperature Range Today-Max., 83; Min., 68
Temperatures Yesterday—Max., 81; Min., 69
Full U. S. Weather Bureau Report, Page 41

VOL. CIII..No. 35,291. Entered as Second-Class Matter, Post Office, New York, N. Y.

NEW YORK, WEDNESDAY, SEPTEMBER 8, 1954. Times Square, New York 36, N. Y. Telephone LAckawanna 4-1000 FIVE CENTS

ASIAN AID TREATY SIGNED AT MANILA; DEFENSE LINE SET

COMPROMISE MADE

U. S. Drops Insistence Accord Aim Only at Red Aggression

By TILLMAN DURDIN
Special to The New York Times.

MANILA, Wednesday, Sept. 8—A defense treaty for Southeast Asia and the Southwest Pacific was signed here this afternoon.

The security arrangement was worked out in a three-day conference attended by representatives of the United States, Britain, France, Pakistan, Thailand, Australia, New Zealand and the Philippines.

The last important problem involved in completing the pact that binds the signers to resist aggression in the prescribed area was settled in a conference session this morning.

A compromise was reached with Britain, Australia and New Zealand over the question of including somewhere in the treaty a declaration on the right of peoples to independence and self-determination.

The morning session was not terminated until 1:15 P. M., more than four hours after it had begun. A round of clapping was heard from the closed conference hall before the delegates emerged smiling and remarked, "It's all over."

It is understood that purely technical details of drafting took a great deal of time after basic agreement had been reached on outstanding questions.

Issues Resolved Tuesday

All other major obstacles to the conclusion of the treaty were resolved at two intensive, three-hour closed sessions of the treaty conference delegates yesterday morning and afternoon. Difficulties were reported to have developed on a number of points.

But compromises were reached and most details were settled for a pact that will not differ greatly from the treaty proposals the United States submitted as a working draft to experts of the eight powers who assembled to produce a composite document here last week.

It was decided that the area of the treaty would be the general area of Southeast Asia, including the entire territories of the Asian members of the pact and the Southwest Pacific, not including the Pacific area north of Lat. 21 degrees 30 minutes N. This line excludes Hong Kong and Formosa.

Conference sources said one of the main treaty problems was solved yesterday when the United States compromised on its insistence that the pact be exclusively an anti-Communist one.

It was agreed that an American declaration, stating that as far as the United States was concerned the pact applied only to Communist aggression, would become a part of the treaty. In return, John Foster Dulles, United States Secretary of State, conceded the omission of the word Communist in the reference to aggression in the operative article of the treaty.

Pakistan, Britain, Australia,

Continued on Page 5, Column 3

U. S. Tactical Planes To Rotate to Europe

Special to The New York Times.

WASHINGTON, Sept. 7—The Air Force will start in the next few weeks to rotate fighter-bomber and troop-carrier squadrons from the United States to Europe.

One result of the plan will be a net increase in United States air power overseas. It also is designed to improve the mobility and flexibility of the Tactical Air Command.

The Strategic Air Command has been rotating long-range bomber wings to and from overseas bases for several years. Air Force headquarters said, in announcing the new program today, that it would mark the first time tactical units had been assigned to Europe on a temporary duty basis.

All the fighter-bomber squadrons involved are equipped with

Continued on Page 3, Column 5

FORMOSA STEPS UP ATTACKS ON COAST

Reports Air-Sea Raids on Red Ports and Gun Positions in Area Opposite Quemoy

Special to The New York Times.

TAIPEI, Formosa, Sept. 7—Nationalist China loosed today the biggest air and sea assault in five years against the Communist-held mainland.

The navy and air force pounded the "invasion coast" across from the Nationalist outpost of Quemoy Island. The all-day bombardment came amid new speculation about a Communist attempt to invade Quemoy, which is about five miles off the Fukien coast.

The Nationalist Defense Ministry reported the destruction of or damage to a Communist gunboat, more than 100 wooden junks and five motorized junks. Nationalist naval guns and aerial bombs also were aimed at Communist gun positions at Amoy, four other mainland forts and half a dozen islands surrounding Quemoy, according to Defense Ministry communiqués issued today.

The attack, paced by bombers, fighter-bombers and warships of the destroyer type, was launched early in the morning. By 11:30 A. M. the Nationalist bombers and fighter-bombers already had hit the mainland in more than 100 sorties, military sources said, while the Nationalist warships had entered Amoy Harbor to shell Communist gun positions and anchoring junks.

The Defense Ministry communiqués said at least five areas hit by the combined attacks were seen smoking. Attacking Nationalist planes encountered intense anti-aircraft fire over Amoy. After flak-suppression attacks, however, the Communist guns became silent, it was reported.

Meanwhile, other reliable

Continued on Page 5, Column 6

ADENAUER COOLS ON BRITISH PLANS FOR 9-POWER TALK

Uncertainty About Attendance of Dulles Is One Factor in New Bonn Attitude

By M. S. HANDLER
Special to The New York Times.

BONN, Germany, Sept. 7—Chancellor Konrad Adenauer put up obstacles today to a nine-power conference in London Sept. 14, as suggested by the British Government.

Last evening Government spokesmen were confident the Chancellor would accept the British invitation when it arrived. Something happened, however, to change the Chancellor's mind, although it is by no means certain he will refuse to go to London on the suggested date to discuss a new formula for the rearmament of West Germany.

The countries suggested as participants in the London conference are the United States, Canada, France, West Germany, Italy, Belgium, the Netherlands and Luxembourg, as well as Britain.

Dr. Adenauer outlined his doubts to Sir Frederick Hoyer-Millar, British High Commissioner. He also conferred with Dr. James B. Conant, United States High Commissioner.

The difficulties raised by the Chancellor were said to concern the agenda for the London meeting and the uncertainty that John Foster Dulles, United States Secretary of State, would be able to attend. Mr. Dulles is in Manila in charge of the United States delegation to the conference on a Southeast Asian alliance.

Dulles' Plans Are a Factor

The change in the Chancellor's attitude toward the projected conference was said to be related to the week-end trip of Prof. Walter Hallstein, Secretary of State for Foreign Affairs, and Dr. Herbert Blankenhorn, chief of the political department of the West German Foreign Office to Brussels and Paris.

Prof. Hallstein and Dr. Blankenhorn saw Paul-Henri Spaak, Belgian Foreign Minister, in Brussels. Prof. Hallstein also saw David K. E. Bruce, United States special representative on European Defense Community affairs, in Paris after the Brussels meeting.

It was not ascertained whether Dr. Blankenhorn accompanied Prof. Hallstein on the visit to Mr. Bruce. Government spokesman said Prof Hallstein had gone to Paris to see the German Ambassador.

It was regarded as symptomatic that the West German Government's enthusiasm for the proposed conference cooled between the time Prof. Hallstein returned to Bonn Monday and the meeting this morning be-

Continued on Page 3, Column 1

Cuban Ex-President Fined in Arms Plot

Carlos Prio Socarras, former President of Cuba, was fined $9,000 in Federal Court yesterday for conspiring to export arms from the United States to Cuba in violation of the Neutrality Act.

Segundo Curti Messina, former Minister of Interior in Dr. Prio's Cabinet, was fined $6,000 on the same charge.

Both men pleaded nolo contendere (no defense) before Judge Edmund L. Palmieri. Previously they had pleaded not guilty to the charge that they had purchased rifles, carbines, shells and other implements of war for shipment to Cuba. Arrangements to pay the fines were made through their attorneys.

Shortly after the fines had been levied Dr. Prio, who does not speak English, had an interpreter read a prepared statement, which said:

"I am glad that American justice has recognized the exceptional circumstances of this

Continued on Page 12, Column 3

U. S. IS SET TO SEND ARMS TO MID-EAST

Soviet 'Threat' Said to Force Action on Egypt and Iraq—No Peril to Israel Seen

By WALTER H. WAGGONER
Special to The New York Times.

WASHINGTON, Sept. 7—The United States was moving today to erect defenses against what the State Department has called the "threat posed by Soviet imperialism" in the Middle East.

The department indicated it was ready to approve Egyptian purchases of United States arms. These were barred during the several months of negotiations leading to the July 27 Suez Canal zone agreement between Egypt and Britain.

Preparations were under way also for the first shipment of arms aid to Iraq, with which the United States signed a military-assistance agreement last April. A Military Assistance Advisory Group is expected to go to Iraq in the near future to direct the use of the arms.

With the fact in mind that these United States actions will increase military aid to the Arab states, Israeli officials were pondering a new protest by the United States against Israeli border actions along the frontier with Jordan. The State Department has notified Reuven Shiloah, Israeli chargé d'affaires, that the Government "views with great concern" the reported activity by Israeli armed forces on Jordanian territory Sept. 2.

Summarizing the representa-

Continued on Page 14, Column 3

WINCHELL DENIES HE KNOWS SOURCE OF M'CARTHY DATA

Testifies He Is 'Pretty Sure' Senator or Staff Did Not Give Him F. B. I. Copy

Excerpts from transcript of the committee hearings, Page 16.

By ANTHONY LEVIERO
Special to The New York Times.

WASHINGTON, Sept. 7—Walter Winchell testified today that he had received a copy of the controversial Army Intelligence document that Senator Joseph R. McCarthy produced at the recent Army-McCarthy hearings.

The gray-haired syndicated newspaper columnist, questioned closely by the special committee considering the censure of the Wisconsin Republican, testified he was "pretty sure" it was not Senator McCarthy who had given him the document.

He also said he was pretty sure that no member of the McCarthy staff had given him the two-and-a-quarter-page document on alleged subversion at Fort Monmouth, N. J.

At other times during his testimony, however, Mr. Winchell said in positive terms that it was neither Senator McCarthy nor his aides. Moreover, he testified that even if he did recollect who it was, he would not disclose the person's identity. That was also the position taken by Senator McCarthy during the Army-McCarthy controversy.

Mr. McCarthy declared then that the paper had been given to him by a young Army officer, a contention that the Army, after investigation, disputed, referring the case to the Justice Department for action.

Mystery Is Intensified

Mr. Winchell's testimony today served only to intensify the mystery surrounding the "personal and confidential" abbreviated version of a fifteen-page report to the Army's former Chief of Intelligence, Maj. Gen. A. R. Bolling, by J. Edgar Hoover, Director of the Federal Bureau of Investigation.

Mr. Winchell was accused of violating the Espionage Act by possessing the document. This accusation was made today by Senator Ralph E. Flanders, Republican of Vermont, and sponsor of the censure resolution, in a memorandum he submitted to Senator Arthur V. Watkins, Republican of Utah, chairman of the special committee.

When in the Army-McCarthy hearings it was brought out that Senator McCarthy had obtained the document from an "officer" not entitled to give it, the document became "untouchable."

Robert T. Stevens, Secretary of the Army, refused in the cir-

Continued on Page 17, Column 1

DEWEY SAYS HE WON'T RUN BUT WILL AID IN CAMPAIGN; IVES LIKELY G. O. P. CHOICE

Associated Press
DECLINES TO RUN: Governor Dewey as he prepared speech yesterday in which he said he would not seek fourth term.

REFUSAL DEFINITE

Governor Reviews Main Achievements of His 12 Years in Albany

The text of the Dewey address is printed on Page 23.

By LEO EGAN

Governor Dewey eliminated himself last night as a possible candidate for a Republican renomination.

In a television address, carried over two state-wide networks, Mr. Dewey made his long-awaited announcement. He said:

"After the most thorough and even painful consideration, I have concluded that the time has come for me to return to private life. I shall not under any circumstances be a candidate for any public office this fall."

The emphasis on "this fall" in Mr. Dewey's statement was interpreted by some persons as leaving the door open to a third try for the Presidency in 1956 or 1960.

Mr. Dewey's self-elimination from the Republican ticket appeared to clear the way for the nomination of United States Senator Irving M. Ives of Norwich for Governor.

Mr. Dewey's statement appeared to preclude any possibility that he would accept an appointment to fill Mr. Ives' Senate seat if the latter were nominated and elected. Senator Ives' term runs for four more years.

Dewey Praises Dulles

The statement likewise ruled out the possibility that he might accept appointment as Secretary of State to replace John Foster Dulles. Answering a question dealing with this office Mr. Dewey said: "My statement speaks for itself. Besides we have an excellent Secretary of State."

Mr. Dewey's decision brought expressions of regret, and in some cases dismay, from national as well as local Republican leaders. Some of the latter, despite the finality of Mr. Dewey's statement, still hoped he could be persuaded to change his mind.

These planned a final appeal to him today at a meeting of the Republican State Executive Committee, which he is scheduled to attend along with Senator Ives.

President Eisenhower topped the list of Republicans to voice regret that New York's 52-year-old Governor had decided to retire. The President's statement made it clear, however, that he would not lend his prestige to a draft movement.

Richard H. Balch, Democratic state chairman, said Democrats would accept the Governor's statement at face value. But, he added, Mr. Dewey's record in office would be an issue in the campaign.

Balch Asks Air Time for Reply

The Democratic chairman announced that he had formally requested the television and radio networks for an equal amount of free air to reply to the Governor's claims of accomplishments.

Mr. Ives, as majority leader of the State Assembly during the first four years of Mr. Dewey's tenure in office, played a major role in translating many of the Dewey policies in New York into law.

The Senator was the legislative sponsor of New York's pioneering anti-discrimination law. This statute outlaws discrimination in employment because of race, color, religion or national origin.

This measure was cited last night by Governor Dewey as one of the major achievements of his twelve years in office.

Mr. Dewey's speech announcing his retirement from public life was delivered in the studios of the Columbia Broadcasting System at 111 East Fifty-eighth Street. It was carried simultaneously over the state-wide television networks of the Columbia Broadcasting System and the National Broadcasting Company, as well as over station WPIX in New York.

It was rebroadcast later over the state-wide radio facilities of both networks and the American Broadcasting Company and over a number of independent stations.

It had been awaited by poli-

Continued on Page 22, Column 3

EQUAL AIR RIGHTS IN ELECTIONS SET

F.C.C. Issues Rules to Insure All Candidates Are Treated Fairly on Time and Costs

Special to The New York Times.

WASHINGTON, Sept. 7—Equal rights for political candidates were the aim of new regulations covering radio and television broadcasting issued today by the Federal Communications Commission.

The rules are intended to insure that rival candidates get equal treatment, and that all are charged the same rate and receive the same discounts as ordinarily would be charged commercial advertisers under comparable circumstances.

The commission waived its own thirty-day waiting period and made the regulations effective immediately "because of the imminence of the November elections."

The regulations are designed to implement a 1952 Congressional amendment to the Communications Act. The amendment was intended, in general terms, to make certain that broadcasting companies did not raise their rates for political programs.

The new rules provide that charges by broadcasting companies shall be the same to all candidates for a given office without rebates either "direct or indirect." No station may make a contract or agreement that

Continued on Page 45, Column 2

BOTH CAMPS UPSET BY DEWEY'S ACTION

Republicans and Democrats See Withdrawal Affecting This Year and 1956

By W. H. LAWRENCE
Special to The New York Times.

WASHINGTON, Sept. 7—Republicans and Democrats agreed tonight that Thomas E. Dewey's refusal to seek a fourth term as New York's Governor might have major repercussions in both parties. Not only the election just ahead, but the one two years hence will be affected, they feel.

As the Republicans saw it, Mr. Dewey's unwillingness to run again transformed a "sure thing" into a "horse race" for the Governorship of the nation's most populous state. These Republicans also were concerned lest the loss of New York State in 1954 set in motion a trend that would help bring the Democrats back to national power when the Presidency is contested again in 1956.

Democrats wondered what effect Mr. Dewey's decision might have on their own fierce intra-party contest for the nomination. Representative Franklin D. Roosevelt Jr. was an early front-runner for the nomination, but he has not gained much in several weeks, as the leaders in the New York metropolitan area have refused to commit their large bloc of delegate votes.

Mr. Roosevelt's chief avowed rival is Averell Harriman, former

Continued on Page 24, Column 3

World's Loftiest Tower May Rise On Site of Grand Central Terminal

By DAMON STETSON

The New York Central System announced yesterday that it was considering plans to erect the largest privately owned office building in the world on the site of Grand Central Terminal.

The blueprints call for a structure that would tower over the 102 stories and the television tower of the Empire State Building, the tallest edifice ever built by man.

Meanwhile, the controlling interest in the Empire State was sold to Col. Henry Crown, chairman of the Empire State Building Corporation, by Roger L. Stevens of Ann Arbor, Mich., and New York, and Alfred Glancy Jr. of Detroit.

The sale price was not made public. The papers were signed here in the office of Thomas Halleran, a partner in the law firm of Cravath, Swaine & Moore. Mr. Halleran had represented the syndicate that bought the building in 1951 for more than $51,000,000 from the John J. Raskob estate. Colonel Crown, Mr. Stevens and Mr. Glancy were members of this syndicate.

Robert R. Young, chairman of the railroad's board, said the Central development was contemplated as a means by which the railroad could utilize to greater financial advantage its valuable property holdings in the area. His announcement was his most dramatic move since he won control of the New York Central last June.

Although plans for the office building are highly tentative at this stage, Mr. Young said that Webb & Knapp, Inc., real estate concern headed by William Zeckendorf, had estimated that a new building containing upward of

Continued on Page 26, Column 6

75 Crossing Guards Sworn In to Relieve Police

The New York Times
Mrs. Pearl Rabinowitz, left, and Mrs. Alice Maertz chat with Deputy Chief Inspector Michael Richter of the Bronx headquarters after being sworn in as school crossing guards. They will wear a white belt and a police cap with the insignia: School Crossing Guard, N. Y. P. D.

The first of the school crossing guards in the Bronx who will assume their duties when school opens Monday were sworn in yesterday at a ceremony at Police Headquarters.

In the group were sixty-six women and nine men. They will take a training course today through Friday on traffic regulations, first aid and subjects dealing with children at the Kingsbridge Armory, Kingsbridge Road and Jerome Avenue, the Bronx.

The guards will wear blue caps similar to the official Police Department cap, with the words, "School Crossing Guard, N. Y. P. D.," white gloves and white belts over civilian attire and they will carry white whistles. The women guards are mostly housewives, averaging more than 30 years in age and most are mothers with one or more children. They will work five hours a day at $1.50 an hour.

The remainder of the 117 guards scheduled for school-crossing duty will be selected by the end of the month.

Busy Peiping Impresses Attlee; Streets Swarming With Bicycles

Following is the second of a number of articles by Clement R. Attlee, former British Prime Minister, written in Hong Kong after his tour of Moscow and Communist China.

By CLEMENT R. ATTLEE
Distributed by United Feature Syndicate, Inc.

HONG KONG, Sept. 4—Leaving Russia at Altan Bulak, we flew for some hours over the Mongolian Desert. At first there was some scanty vegetation, but that gave way to stark barrenness. At a certain point we were told that we were now in China, but there was nothing to mark the change.

Later we came to a fantastic region cut up by hundreds of dry watercourses with deep gullies. Then the sides of these gullies began to be terraced and large villages appeared. These became increasingly numerous and the country was patterned into strips of cultivation. One began to appreciate the pressure of population, for every inch was cultivated.

Presently we came in sight of Peking [Peiping] and got a glimpse of the beauty of the Forbidden City from the air.

Just before 1 o'clock we landed at Peking amidst great heat. Six charming Chinese children came forward and presented us all with bouquets. We were then introduced to about thirty or forty notables with whom we shook hands. Among them were Lord and Lady Lindsay, who had come from Australia to help us with interpreting and by their knowledge of China, and Mr. Humphrey Trevelyan, the British chargé d'affaires.

We drove through fields and suburbs, then through a very nar-

Continued on Page 6, Column 2

"All the News That's Fit to Print"

The New York Times.

LATE CITY EDITION
Sunny and cold today. Fair and not so cold tomorrow.
Temperature Range Today—Max., 21; Min., 10
Temperatures Yesterday—Max., 23; Min., 14
Full U. S. Weather Bureau Report, Sec. 5, Page 9

NEWS SUMMARY AND INDEX, PAGE 95

Copyright, 1955, by The New York Times Company.

SECTION ONE

VOL. CIV..No. 35,449. Entered as Second-Class Matter, Post Office, New York, N. Y. NEW YORK, SUNDAY, FEBRUARY 13, 1955. Including Magazine and Book Review. TWENTY-FIVE CENTS

EISENHOWER DRAFT IS STARTED HERE AT LINCOLN FETE

Executive Body of National Republican Club Calls for Widespread Approval

'HIS FIRM HAND' PRAISED

Brownell Says President Has Built Up Mighty Military Force at Low Cost

By DOUGLAS DALES

The executive committee of the National Republican Club approved yesterday a resolution calling for a draft of President Eisenhower for a second term.

The action was announced last night by Daniel J. Riesner, president, at the club's Lincoln Day dinner in the Waldorf-Astoria Hotel.

The resolution called upon the club's members throughout the country "to express themselves freely and fully in favor of such a draft."

Referring to the "recent warlike tactics of Red China" and the "abdication" of Georgi M. Malenkov as Russian Premier, the resolution declared that "a firm, sure, determined hand in the White House, together with a far-reaching understanding of pressing international problems, military strategy and a knowledge of the Red Russian mind with its devious ramifications, are needed to safely guide the United States in its persistent efforts for world peace and prosperity at home."

Role Is Likened to Lincoln's

In announcing the resolution, Mr. Riesner compared President Eisenhower's services to the nation with those of Lincoln in the Civil War era.

Asserting that Lincoln's importance was such that his assassination delayed the reemergence of the South's economy and made for sustained confusion and lingering hatreds, he said, "the United States would unquestionably suffer another devastating loss in terms of world and national leadership if Dwight D. Eisenhower failed to be a candidate for re-election next year."

Another highlight of the dinner was the presentation to former Gov. Thomas E. Dewey of the club's first annual award for distinguished public service. The award, a bronze bust of Lincoln, was accepted by Mrs. Dewey. She read a letter from her husband, who was out of the state on business.

Mr. Dewey wrote that the award should have gone to all party members who "brought Republican direction to the nation at this time when every feeling of religious devotion, personal dignity and human freedom is under relentless attack."

Mr. Dewey went on to say:

"In Abraham Lincoln the Republican party gave to the nation the wise, strong but restrained leadership which carried us through our period of greatest internal peril. Once again it has fallen to the Republican party to give such leadership, this time to the entire free world, in the person of President Eisenhower."

Achievements Reviewed

Attorney General Herbert Brownell Jr. told the 1,000 guests at the dinner that President Eisenhower had combined his extraordinary military knowledge with a sensitive awareness of the taxpayers' burden to give the country a mightier military machine at lower cost.

In a review of the Eisenhower achievements, the Attorney General said:

"A surprise enemy attack would find us with increasing readiness to resist attack and retaliate with devastating effect." He added that "our offensive striking power is outstanding in the present world situation."

Mr. Brownell said that despite an increase in military power estimated defense costs for 1956 would be $9,500,000,000 less than actual 1953 expenditures.

The dinner was the second function sponsored yesterday by the club in observance of the

Continued on Page 67, Column 4

This section consists of 108 pages divided into three parts. The news summary and index will be found on Page 95. Society news begins on Page 88 and obituary articles will be found on Pages 86 and 87.

The New York Times

REPUBLICANS HONOR PARTY FIGURES: The National Republican Club last night gave its first annual public service award, a bust of Lincoln, to former Gov. Thomas E. Dewey. Here, with Attorney General Herbert Brownell Jr., center, and State Attorney General Jacob K. Javits, Mrs. Dewey admires award after accepting it in behalf of her husband. Mr. Brownell and Mr. Javits received merit citations at the Lincoln Day fete at the Waldorf.

Another Freezing Day Due; Drivers in Suburbs Warned

The cold wave that made a sudden and icy descent upon the metropolitan area Friday night is expected to last at least until tomorrow. The Weather Bureau said that the temperature today may go down to 10 degrees—it stood at 14 degrees at 1 A. M.—while the maximum probably would be no higher than 21.

As a result, there was little hope of much improvement in suburban driving conditions. Although roads were sanded, treacherous patches of ice remained from the rain, sleet and snow that preceded the sharp fall in temperature Friday night. Consequently the police in many areas warned against unnecessary travel.

Upstate, where as much as twelve inches of snow fell Friday night, driving conditions were far worse. Drifts made it necessary yesterday to close sections of several roads in the Malone area, near the Quebec line. Among them were U. S. Route 11 and New York Routes 10 and 37. Quebec Route 41 was also closed.

The cold here seemed the more intense because it followed two days of balmy, 55-degree weather and because it was accompanied by winds of twenty to thirty miles an hour, with higher gusts. The Weather Bureau said these would diminish today.

Manhattan temperatures yesterday were down to 14 degrees at 9 and 10 A. M.

At 7:30 A. M. yesterday, the wind blew out an 18-by-20-foot plate-glass window at the Chase National Bank branch, 575 Seventh Avenue, near Forty-first Street.

With drifts clogging highways in northern, central and western New York counties, local snow squalls continued yesterday, and wind gusts reached thirty-four miles an hour. Utica reported twelve inches of snow; Rome, eleven; Massena, ten, and Albany, five.

Near Nassau, in Rensselaer

Continued on Page 42, Column 4

PRESIDENT TARGET OF G. O. P. ATTACKS

Chicago Rally Cheers Censure —McCarthy Charges Drive Toward 'Defeat' in Asia

By RUSSELL BAKER
Special to The New York Times.

CHICAGO Feb. 12—The hard core of the Republican Old Guard convened here today to cheer verbal assaults on the United Nations, the State Department and the Eisenhower Administration.

Seventeen hundred persons representing twenty-six states listened to a day-long session of speechmaking. It ranged from attacks on the alleged evils of Washington to attacks on President Eisenhower's alleged captivity by "people of questionable Republicanism."

The speakers included Senators George W. Malone of Nevada, Everett M. Dirksen of Illinois, Joseph R. McCarthy of Wisconsin and Gov. J. Bracken Lee of Utah.

Senator McCarthy and his wife won one of the loudest and longest greetings. The Senator drew applause again with a denunciation of the Administration's Formosa policy. This he characterized as a "retreat" that would lead to "defeat" in Asia.

In another address, Governor Lee voiced an idea that had remained unexpressed among many of the participants—the possibility of a "third party."

The successful evacuation of

Continued on Page 54, Column 3

25 Derelicts Die in Hotel Fire; Chicago Blames 'Human Torch'

Special to The New York Times.

CHICAGO, Feb. 12—A fire early today swept a hotel on West Madison Street, killing at least twenty-five men. Fifteen others were injured.

Most of the victims were trapped in their cage-like "rooms" which they rented for 60 to 85 cents a night.

Because many were derelicts, without family connections, it is unlikely some of them ever will be identified.

It was estimated that 245 men were asleep in the Barton Hotel, which occupies the top four floors of the five-story building. The first floor was occupied by the Standard Store Fixture Company.

Their "rooms" were cubicles four feet wide, six feet long, and seven feet high. The bunks were separated from each other by corrugated iron sheets and each was covered at the top by meshed chicken wire. An aisle ran between each two rows of cubicles.

The fire started shortly before 2 A. M., supposedly when rubbing alcohol being used by one of the tenants on the second floor caught fire. This tenant, Joseph Armatyz, about 70 years old, ran screaming into an aisle, covered with flames. He was one of the men who died.

Within a few minutes, flames swept upward through the building. Smoke blinded and choked the tenants who ran screaming toward exits or cowered in their bunks. Many reached windows and a front fire escape and got out alive. The others died in their bunks or in aisles between their bunks.

Next to the La Salle Hotel fire on June 6, 1946, when sixty-one persons perished, the Barton Hotel fire took the highest death toll of any hotel fire in this city's history.

Firemen who responded to an

Continued on Page 56, Column 4

NEGRO NOMINATED FOR JOB IN CAPITAL

Hayes, Defender of Mrs. Moss in Security Hearing, Gets District Utilities Post

Special to The New York Times.

THOMASVILLE, Ga., Feb. 12—The Negro lawyer who successfully defended Annie Lee Moss against "security risk" charges won a District of Columbia job nomination today from President Eisenhower.

He is George E. C. Hayes of Washington, who was nominated to be a member of the District Public Utilities Commission. He will be the first of his race on this important regulatory body. The Senate must confirm him.

Mr. Hayes will replace Robert E. McLaughlin, who is being promoted to the three-man District of Columbia Government Commission. The three-year-term as Public Utilities Commissioner that goes to Mr. Hayes carries $11,000 a year salary.

Mr. Hayes stirred the wrath of Senator Joseph R. McCarthy, Republican of Wisconsin, when he insisted last spring that Mrs. Moss be allowed to deny charges of Communist affiliation without threat of perjury prosecution. Mr. Hayes represented her in subsequent hearings before Army security boards. His efforts won her continued employment with the Army.

A Virginian by Birth

Special to The New York Times.

WASHINGTON, Feb. 12—Mr. Hayes has lived and practiced law here most of his life.

He is a native of Richmond, Va., but came here as a youth and attended the public schools. He received his bachelor's degree at Brown University and his law degree from Howard University here.

He is 60 years old, has taught law at Howard for many years and is a former member of the city's Board of Education.

Mr. Hayes, who is highly respected among his colleagues, is a calm worker whose unassuming manner has for years kept him from wide public attention.

He recently became nationally known, however, because of two cases—the case against racial segregation in the public schools and the one involving Mrs. Moss.

Mr. Hayes was one of the lawyers who helped prepare the case against segregation in Washington's schools. The Supreme Court ruled last May 17 that segregation in the public schools was unconstitutional.

Mrs. Moss, a civilian employe of the Army Signal Corps, went to Mr. Hayes after Senator McCarthy had accused her of Communist affiliations. Mrs. Moss, appearing before the Senate Permanent Subcommittee on Investigations, then headed by Mr. McCarthy, repeatedly denied the charge.

Mr. Hayes at one point in these hearings clashed sharply with Mr. McCarthy. He chal-

Continued on Page 74, Column 3

U. S. HEAVY WATER SUPPLIED TO INDIA FOR ATOM REACTOR

A.E.C. Sells 10 Tons for Use in Research Plant as Joint Group Urges Action

By CHARLES E. EGAN
Special to The New York Times.

WASHINGTON, Feb. 12—The United States sold India ten tons of heavy water today for use in research on peaceful applications of atomic energy.

The sale, announced by the Atomic Energy Commission, coincided with the release of a report of a special Congressional subcommittee urging such action.

The subcommittee said that the atoms-for-peace plan outlined by President Eisenhower before the United Nations a year ago should be implemented at once by this country.

Under this plan the world's atomic resources would be pooled for peaceful uses.

Helping India meet her need for heavy water for peaceful atomic energy research was one of the specific recommendations advanced by the subcommittee of the Joint Congressional Atomic Energy Committee.

World prices for heavy water range from $80 to $100 a pound. It is one of the most efficient materials available for moderating atomic reactions under controlled conditions in an atomic reactor or furnace.

In heavy water, the hydrogen atom is twice as heavy as in ordinary water. This atom's nucleus has one proton and one neutron; an ordinary hydrogen nucleus consists of one proton.

Going to Bombay Plant

The quantity purchased by India today is to be delivered to an atomic furnace being built near Bombay. It will be used in the production of materials needed for research in medicine, agriculture and industry.

The Congressional subcommittee, headed by Senator John W. Bricker, Republican of Ohio, reported on a five-week visit it made to eleven nations in Europe and the Far East.

It said today that much of the goodwill won for the United States by General Eisenhower's dramatic appeal to the United Nations in December, 1953, would be lost unless this country came forward immediately with "some concrete and formal way of demonstrating its willingness to get on with atomic cooperation."

The United Nations has voted to set up a special international agency to further cooperation in peacetime atomic development, but Western and Russian-bloc nations have not been able to get together on details of how such an agency should be established or operate.

The subcommittee said in its report that it had learned in India that Russia's blatantly advertised offers to help Asian nations develop peaceful uses for atomic energy were hollow promises.

The subcommittee said that it found the response abroad to the United States offer to help in atomic development was "far

Continued on Page 24, Column 1

$12,000,000 Shop-Office Center To Rise on Old Armonk Airport

By JOHN STEVENS
Special to The New York Times.

ARMONK, N. Y., Feb. 12—The old Westchester Airport will be developed as a $12,000,000 shopping and executive-office center.

The airport was established here in 1920 as Westchester County's first commercial flying field. The larger Westchester County Airport at Purchase was opened in 1943 as a base for the air defense of New York City. It now handles commercial traffic, too.

Principals in the project said here today that the development would be another step in the rapid spread of business and industry to the suburbs. James R. Carosu, supervisor of the northern Westchester town of North Castle, whose residents have complained of the noise and danger of airplane traffic for thirty-five years, gave the proposal his blessing.

"We will be very happy to have the airport out of here," he said. He added that no zoning problems were involved, since the sixty-three-acre tract was already classified for shopping-center use, subject to certain restrictions.

A year ago the Town Council rejected a plan by a New York and White Plains syndicate to create a $7,000,000 shopping center on the airport site, principally because the plan involved an outdoor drive-in motion picture theatre, branded by opponents as a "passion pit."

Edward A. Lashins, White Plains builder and developer who on Feb. 7 executed an "unconditional" contract to purchase the property from J. David Finger, owner of the airport, said today no drive-in theatre was contemplated. He said he planned a "city of business," thirteen acres to be occupied by one-story buildings with shops and executive and professional offices, and the remaining fifty acres reserved for parking.

Mr. Lashins said construction of the shopping center, facing Route 22, would begin next fall and that already several large New York department stores were interested as potential tenants. The center will be close to small homes, the North Castle Town Hall and several old rural churches. It will serve northern Westchester and Putnam Counties in New York and Fairfield County, Conn.

Mr. Finger, who has operated

Continued on Page 49, Column 1

Normal Patrol of Formosa Resumed by Seventh Fleet

Jet Unit to Stay on Island—Nationalist Report of Junks Massing at Matsu Discounted by Admiral Briscoe

Special to The New York Times.

WASHINGTON, Feb. 12—The Navy and Air Force announced today that normal operations were being resumed now that the evacuation of the Tachen Islands had been completed.

The Formosa patrol of the Seventh Fleet will continue to guard Formosa and the Pescadores, but many of the units called in to reinforce it three weeks ago are returning to their permanent stations in Japan and the Philippines.

Vice Admiral Robert P. Briscoe, Deputy Chief of Naval Operations, said the evacuation had "turned out to be an entirely routine operation."

He discounted an announcement by the Nationalist Chinese Defense Ministry that the Communists were massing motorized junks near Matsu, one of the offshore islands Generalissimo Chiang Kai-shek has been urging the United States to defend.

He conceded that junks could be used to carry troops but said the Navy believed they were fishing boats on a peaceful mission.

The waters off Matsu are a popular fishing ground, Admiral Briscoe said, and it is not unusual to see 1,200 to 1,500 fishing boats there. He said the fishermen commonly were escorted by small patrol craft to protect them against China coast pirates.

Gen. Nathan F. Twining, Air Force Chief of Staff, announced at the same time that one squadron of Saberjets would be kept on Formosa. The two other squadrons of the Eighteenth Fighter-Bomber Wing, which provided high-altitude cover for the Tachens evacuation, will return to their bases on Okinawa and the Philippines.

A fighter-bomber wing nor-

Continued on Page 3, Column 1

Khrushchev Is Said to See Trade as Key to U. S. Ties

By HARRY SCHWARTZ

A visitor to the Kremlin said yesterday that Nikita S. Khrushchev was asking for normal relations with the United States based on freer trade. The visitor was Marshall MacDuffie, a New York lawyer.

He returned here Friday night. He interviewed Mr. Khrushchev, whom he has known for some time, Feb. 1, a week before Mr. Khrushchev, the First Secretary of the Communist party, apparently tightened his control of the Soviet Union.

"We want more normal relations with the United States, but the first prerequisite is more normal trade relations," Mr. Khrushchev was quoted as having said.

The Communist leader told Mr. MacDuffie that the Soviet Government was permitting more Americans to visit the Soviet Union and hoped more Soviet citizens could go to the United States. He disclosed that a visa had been granted to Supreme Court Justice William O. Douglas to visit the Soviet Union next summer.

"We hardly refuse any requests," Mr. Khrushchev was said to have commented.

Mr. Khrushchev expressed surprise when told that Americans wishing to visit the Soviet Union had to wait a long time for visas if they were fortunate enough to get them, Mr. MacDuffie asserted.

Mr. MacDuffie said that he was surprised that the interview was granted. He said he received only forty-five minutes' advance notice. The interview took place in the building in the center of the Kremlin area in which Stalin had his office and was probably in the same corridor as Stalin's old office, Mr. MacDuffie said.

The New York lawyer explained he became acquainted with Mr. Khrushchev almost a

Continued on Page 17, Column 1

O'DANIEL STARTS VIETNAM TRAINING

U. S. General Will Have Staff of 300—100,000 Army and 150,000 Reserve Planned

Special to The New York Times.

SAIGON, Vietnam, Feb. 12—Lieut. Gen. John W. O'Daniel, chief of the United States military mission here, assumed charge of the organization and training of the South Vietnamese army today.

In announcing this major step in the recasting of the non-Communist military forces, the South Vietnamese Premier, Ngo Dinh Diem, said General O'Daniel would act under the over-all authority of General Paul Ely, French Commander in Chief in Indochina.

It is learned that General O'Daniel will have an American staff of 300 officers and non-commissioned officers together with 1,000 French. Some of the American instructors are already here and will soon assume their functions in officers' schools and training camps.

During 1955 the United States will contribute $200,000,000 for the native military forces.

Details of Program

The program to be financed by these funds was drawn up after long discussions between the Vietnamese Government, the French High Command and the United States military mission. It includes the following points:

¶The army will be reduced from 220,000 to about 100,000 plus a mobile reserve of 150,000. Defense Minister Ho Thong Minh said the army would have an average of 140,000 in 1955. He added that demobilization had already begun.

¶Part of the private armies maintained by politico-religious sects will be disbanded while another part will be integrated into the national army.

¶The new army will be organized into divisions instead of the battalions that existed under the French regime.

¶Training methods will be based on those used to form the South Korean army, with emphasis on practice instead of the largely theoretical training given officers at the Dalat school, modeled after the French military academy of Saint-Cyr.

¶Army personnel will receive thorough political indoctrination to enable them to carry on propaganda in favor of the non-Communist regime among the people.

¶The army will be, above all, according to American ideas on the subject, a police force capable of spotting Communist guerrillas and Communist efforts at infiltration.

The Defense Minister said that

Continued on Page 5, Column 1

U. S. JOINS BRITAIN IN BARRING PARLEY EXCLUDING CHIANG

London Backed on Rebuffing Soviet Plan for Far East Talks Without Formosa

PROPAGANDA DEVICE SEEN

Moscow Broadcast on Offer Viewed as Effort to Play Up Advocacy of Asian Peace

Texts of the Soviet and British statements on Page 2.

By ELIE ABEL
Special to The New York Times.

WASHINGTON, Feb. 12—The United States and Britain agree that no useful purpose would be served by a conference on Formosa from which Nationalist China was excluded.

This became known today as Moscow broadcast its proposal, made earlier to Britain, for such a conference.

Washington is content to let the British continue their negotiations in Moscow looking toward a more acceptable framework outside the United Nations in which the tense Formosa issue can be discussed.

So far as today's broadcast of the Soviet proposal is concerned, Britain rejected it earlier this week. The fundamental objection of Sir Anthony Eden, British Foreign Secretary, was to the exclusion of Generalissimo Chiang Kai-shek's regime from the proposed ten-power conference.

The United States was in full accord with the British position. Sir William Hayter, British Ambassador to Moscow, delivered the rejection after extensive consultation between London and Washington.

The same view was said to have been taken by most of the British Commonwealth Prime Ministers, who talked over the Soviet proposal at their London conference that ended this week.

Divided on One Point

The two Governments remain divided, however, on the immediate future of the Nationalist-held coastal islands. The United States has made clear to the British, in recent diplomatic exchanges, that it will not consent to the surrender of the Quemoy or Matsu Island groups in the hope that this may persuade the Communists to stop fighting.

London, on the other hand, contends that all the coastal islands should go to the Communists and that only if the Nationalists are dislodged from these outposts will a cease-fire be possible.

The positions of both Governments are well known. United States policy-makers have not denied the ultimate possibility of letting the offshore islands go, but only as part of a long-range settlement in which Peiping would recognize the independent status of Formosa. For the present they see no evidence of Communist willingness to go along with such an arrangement.

Diplomats here were asking themselves why Moscow should have announced the proposal today, eight days after it was put to the British Ambassador by Foreign Minister Vyacheslav M. Molotov and when it had already been rejected. The answer, they

Continued on Page 3, Column 3

Pflimlin Due to List New Cabinet Today

By LANSING WARREN
Special to The New York Times.

PARIS, Feb. 12—Pierre Pflimlin, Popular Republican leader, who is trying to assemble a new French Government, began making Cabinet appointments today. The work was slow and the Premier-designate was not expected to announce his Ministers until tomorrow.

On the progress that he makes will depend the summoning of the National Assembly to approve or reject the Cabinet either Monday or Tuesday, in accordance with the present plans.

M. Pflimlin announced today that he had finished consultations on his program with the party groups. He said not all had yet agreed to join the Ministry, but that he found enough support to warrant the formation of a Government.

Unofficial lists of the new Cabinet were already circulating

Continued on Page 22, Column 3

"All the News That's Fit to Print"

The New York Times.

LATE CITY EDITION
Partly cloudy and warmer today.
Mostly fair, warmer tomorrow.
Temperature Range Today—Max., 68; Min., 49
Temperatures Yesterday—Max., 65; Min., 48
Full U. S. Weather Bureau Report, Page 35

Copyright, 1955, by The New York Times Company.

VOL. CIV. No. 35,525. Entered as Second-Class Matter, Post Office, New York, N. Y. NEW YORK, SATURDAY, APRIL 30, 1955. Times Square, New York 36, N. Y. Telephone LAckawanna 4-1000 FIVE CENTS

VIETNAMESE ARMY WINNING SAIGON FIGHT WITH REBELS; PREMIER REBUFFS BAO DAI

SENATE UNIT VOTES 5-YEAR ROAD PLAN; BARS A BOND ISSUE

Ignores President's Request on Financing—Asks Cent Rise in Gasoline Tax

VEHICLE WEIGHT LIMITED

$22 Billion Outlay by States and U. S. Passed—Ceiling on Federal Aid Is Lifted

By JOHN D. MORRIS
Special to The New York Times.

WASHINGTON, April 29—A Senate Public Works subcommittee approved today a five-year road building program calling for Federal and state outlays of $21,739,000,000. The measure differed sharply from the Administration's highway program.

The Senate bill recommended that part of the Federal share be financed by a 1 cent increase in the Federal tax of 2 cents a gallon on gasoline and other motor fuel instead of by special bonds as proposed by President Eisenhower.

But a separate tax bill, originating in the House of Representatives, would be required to put this into effect.

The President's program was for ten years and contemplated outlays of $101,000,000,000. About $29,000,000,000, however, was for streets and roads wholly financed by state and local governments not counted in the subcommittee's total.

The authorization bill, patterned on a measure sponsored by the subcommittee chairman, Senator Albert Gore, Democrat of Tennessee, was sent to the full committee by a vote of 6 to 3.

Passage Predicted

Mr. Gore predicted that the Public Works Committee would report it next Thursday and the Senate would pass it the following week.

The Federal Government's share of the program approved by the subcommittee would be $13,663,000,000 against $8,076,000,000 for the states.

The measure would authorize $7,750,000,000 of Federal appropriations for interstate highways in the five-year period starting a year from next July 1. The present matching formula of 60 per cent for the Federal Government and 40 per cent for the states would be changed by the bill to 75 and 25 per cent respectively.

The states consequently would pay $2,584,000,000 of the interstate system's cost of $10,334,000,000.

Authorized Federal contributions for interstate highways are limited by present law to $175,000,000 a year. The Gore bill, as revised, would allow an average of $1,550,000,000 annually over the five-year period. The authorized contributions would be graduated from $1,000,000,000 the first year to $2,000,000,000 in the fourth and fifth years.

For primary, secondary and urban roads the bill would authorize annual Federal appropriations of $1,100,000,000 against $675,000,000 under present law. The present 50-50 matching formula would be retained. The Federal Government and the states would consequently sup-

Continued on Page 7, Column 2

2 States Feud Over Truck Mud Flaps

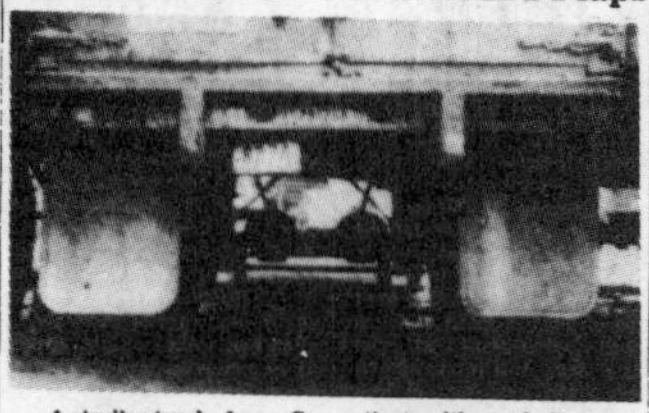

A trailer-truck from Connecticut with mud flaps

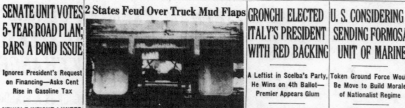

The New York Times
This is a New York trailer-truck, without flaps

By WAYNE PHILLIPS

The feud between New York and Connecticut over motor-vehicle regulations flared into the open again yesterday—this time over mud flaps. These gadgets dangle behind the rear tires of trucks. They are supposed to keep mud and stones from being thrown against the windshields of automobiles. Connecticut law requires them on all big trucks. New York law requires them only on those manufactured after 1953. And that's where the trouble started. Some Connecticut state policemen arrested a couple of unsuspecting New

Continued on Page 35, Column 8

GRONCHI ELECTED ITALY'S PRESIDENT WITH RED BACKING

A Leftist in Scelba's Party, He Wins on 4th Ballot—Premier Appears Glum

By ARNALDO CORTESI
Special to The New York Times.

ROME, April 29—Giovanni Gronchi, a member of the left wing of the Christian Democratic party, was elected today as the third President of the Italian Republic.

At a joint session of the Senate and Chamber of Deputies he was chosen by the votes of the Communists and their Left-Wing Socialist allies as well as by those of the Christian Democrats.

The three center parties apart from the Christian Democrats refused to go along with them in supporting the President of the Chamber, Signor Gronchi, and either turned in blank ballots or voted to re-elect President Luigi Einaudi.

Most of the extreme right voted blank ballots. In accordance with the Italian Constitution Premier Mario Scelba will hand in his and his Cabinet's resignation May 12 to the 67-year-old Signor Gronchi, who will take office the day before.

It is considered a foregone conclusion that Signor Gronchi will designate Signor Scelba to continue as Premier.

Out of 833 votes cast in today's balloting Signor Gronchi got 658 and Signor Einaudi 70. Ninety-two ballots were blank, eleven were in favor of several minor candidates and two were invalid.

Second Day's Balloting

In three ballots yesterday the Parliament failed to give the required two-thirds majority to any candidate and adjourned without having elected a president. On the fourth ballot today only a simple majority was needed.

The election of Signor Gronchi, especially with the help of the Communist votes, came as a jolt to many anti-Communist Italians. He is not suspected of Communist leanings but is identified in the minds of Italians as the man of the "opening to the left." In other words he is the man who would like the Socialist allies of the Communists and perhaps even the Communists themselves to be drawn into the Italian Government.

Many Italians think it dangerous to have a man with such ideas in the Presidency because it is he who designates new Premiers when there is a Cabinet crisis.

According to the Italian Constitution a new Premier takes over immediately on designation without waiting for confirmation from the Parliament.

Italy's President does not, as in the United States, fill the functions both of head of the State and head of the Government. He is head of the State only.

This means his powers are much narrower than those of the President of the United States. Nevertheless, he is not a figurehead.

He has the power of veto, he may call elections dissolving

Continued on Page 4, Column 4

U. S. CONSIDERING SENDING FORMOSA UNIT OF MARINES

Token Ground Force Would Be Move to Build Morale of Nationalist Regime

Special to The New York Times.

WASHINGTON, April 29—The United States is contemplating a token contribution of ground forces, probably Marines, to the defenses of Formosa.

Officials here said this move was one of several under consideration for strengthening the morale of the Chinese Nationalists while efforts to arrange a Formosa Strait cease-fire moved forward.

The proposal, these officials indicated, was discussed with Generalissimo Chiang Kai-shek at Taipei by Admiral Arthur W. Radford, chairman of the Joint Chiefs of Staff, and Walter S. Robertson, Assistant Secretary of State for Far Eastern Affairs.

Mr. Robertson and Admiral Radford are expected back in Washington this week-end. The decision whether to station United States Marines and additional jet planes on Formosa awaits their return. They are expected to see Secretary of State Dulles on Monday.

The contribution officials here have been discussing would be a symbol of United States support rather than a major reinforcement of the military power under General Chiang's command.

Spokesmen for the State and Defense Departments professed to know nothing about such a move. In other quarters, however, it was mentioned as a live possibility.

Defense Treaty Action

By assigning a small force of Marines to Formosa along with a fixed United States jet fighter base, Washington would reassure the Nationalists that the defense treaty concluded last December means what it says about joint resistance of aggression, officials remarked.

The effect of such a demonstration, the officials added, would be to offset Communist propaganda that the United States, in the end, would back away from a fight for Formosa, while at the same time making a cease-fire less distasteful to the Nationalists.

An effective cease-fire, according to widespread diplomatic opinion, would require a Nationalist evacuation of the Quemoy and Matsu Island groups. General Chiang has been doggedly resisting the idea that he should abandon these positions off the South China coast.

A single squadron of United States Sabre Jets has been based on Formosa since the Nationalists' evacuation of the Tachen Islands was completed last February. The United States Seventh Fleet and a wing (three squadrons) of the jet fighters screened the evacuation.

When it ended, the fleet steamed back to its main base in the Philippines and the fighter squadrons likewise returned to their permanent stations on Okinawa, Japan and the Philippines.

The Air Force announced, however, that as a safeguard

Continued on Page 3, Column 3

Faure Assails Saigon Chief; Holds Him Unequal to Task

French View Is Counter to U. S. Stand—Removal of Ngo Dinh Diem Held Unlikely While Fighting Persists

By HAROLD CALLENDER
Special to The New York Times.

PARIS, April 29—Premier Edgar Faure said today that the Government of Ngo Dinh Diem in South Vietnam was not equal to its task.

M. Faure's comment, made at a press conference, seemed in conflict with the official Washington attitude as reported in the press. But it is contended here that the conflict is not now nearly so sharp as it was and that Washington has revised its formerly favorable opinion of the Ngo Dinh Diem Government, in which the French have never placed any great confidence.

But a change of government while fighting continued was considered out of the question. Therefore, it was said here, Washington hesitated to emphasize at this moment its disappointed in Premier Ngo Dinh Diem.

It was predicted that Bao Dai's order transfering military power to Gen. Nguyen Van Vy, an opponent of the Premier, would tend to accentuate the split in the National Army and to increase the difficulty of finding a successful government. The latter would have been easier if Washington had changed its view before the fighting began.

Speaking of the Ngo Dinh Diem Government, M. Faure said that, as now constituted, it "is not adapted to the task it

Continued on Page 2, Column 6

500 DIE IN BATTLE

Ngo Dinh Diem Refuses to Go to France, Give Foe Army Power

By A. M. ROSENTHAL
Special to The New York Times.

SAIGON, Vietnam, Saturday, April 30—South Vietnam's army was winning the battle of Saigon yesterday against rebel forces. But its leader, Premier Ngo Dinh Diem, was fighting for his political life against the Chief of State, Bao Dai.

In polite defiance, the Premier refused Bao Dai's demand that, in effect, he step down and fly to the Riviera in France for conferences. The Premier also refused to follow an order to turn over the army command to one of his enemies.

The Premier and his backers believe the fate of his Government is largely in the hands of the United States. Right or wrong, they think that if Washington publicly and firmly supports the Premier, Bao Dai will back down. If not, they say, the Premier and his Government and the apparent victory of his army will be sacrificed.

The battle between the National Army and Binh Xuyen rebels tore this city apart for the second day. The Premier said he would fight to the finish against the Binh Xuyen, an army of mercenaries headed by Gen. Le Van Vien.

The National Army last night said it had swept the rebels from all posts north of their canal front headquarters except in the French protected security zone. An on-the-spot check by this reporter indicated the Binh Xuyen had been blasted out of all strongpoints except Le Grand Monde, a huge casino. The Premier's office said later during the night the casino also had been taken.

Rebels Still Hold Territory

But the rebel forces were not yet defeated. The Binh Xuyen still controls its canal bank headquarters, and many rebels were believed to have withdrawn to it. In addition the Binh Xuyen controls territory outside Saigon. And still in the city, within the French security zone, Binh Xuyen machine-gunners mounted guard over the old police headquarters.

In the first two days of the street fighting the army had scored important gains. The Boulevard Gallieni—Saigon's special street of death—had been cleared of rebel posts that had flanked army and police headquarters. The rebel headquarters on the south bank of the Chinese Arroyo had been hit hard by mortars. And the National Army was in control of the pile of rubble that was once the Rue de la Resistance, a street leading to the bridge to the rebel headquarters.

A reliable military source said early today that the Battle of Saigon already had taken 500 lives. The army's dead were put at 100 and its wounded at 300 or 400. The rebels were said to have lost 200 killed and 600 wounded. At least 200 civilians

Continued on Page 2, Column 4

EDEN DETERMINED ON SOVIET PARLEY

Pledges Effort to End Fear—Conservative Platform for Nuclear Aid in Industry

By DREW MIDDLETON
Special to The New York Times.

LONDON, April 29—The Government will make every effort to arrange a meeting with the Soviet Union, Sir Anthony Eden said today. He also pledged all efforts to reach solutions of international issues that will rid the world of fear.

There are "hopeful signs of better understanding with the Russians in Europe," the Prime Minister declared, and Britain is "ready for wider discussion."

Britain seeks talks that will deal with "all outstanding" issues between East and West, Sir Anthony said. "We wish them to lead to a reduction of tension and agreement about armaments which will banish the fear of the hydrogen bomb," he added.

These assurances by the leader of the Conservative party accompanied the release today of the party's election manifesto entitled, "United for Peace and Progress." The general parliamentary election will be held May 26.

The Conservative platform, with its emphasis on the use of nuclear energy in industry, the introduction of new industries and the expansion of production, struck some as a more revolutionary document than the man-

Continued on Page 6, Column 4

U. S. REITERATES VIETNAM BACKING

Renews Support for Premier After Paris Asks Removal—Mansfield Sees Plot

By ELIE ABEL
Special to The New York Times.

WASHINGTON, April 29—The United States is not prepared to abandon Premier Ngo Dinh Diem of South Vietnam, although it recognizes that his political life may be numbered in days.

An official expression of continued support for the Vietnamese leader was issued by the State Department today only a few hours after Premier Edgar Faure of France had pressed for his removal. London dispatches attributed a similar if unofficial view to the British Foreign Office.

On Capitol Hill, meanwhile, the Senate's leading authority on Vietnam proposed again that the United States cut off all but humanitarian aid to the anguished country if Premier Ngo Dinh Diem was overthrown.

Senator Mike Mansfield, Democrat of Montana, charged that the "decent and honest" Ngo Dinh Diem Government was the victim of a racketeers' conspiracy in Saigon abetted by the Chief of Government, Bao Dai, from his villa on the French Riviera.

The main developments here on Vietnam were these:

¶Gen. J. Lawton Collins, Pres-

Continued on Page 2, Column 8

300,000 Got Cutter Shots; City Tightens Rule on Sales

By MORRIS KAPLAN

Nearly 300,000 children in five states and Hawaii have been inoculated with the banned Cutter anti-polio vaccine. Dr. Hart Van Riper, medical director of the National Foundation for Infantile Paralysis, listed this figure yesterday in reporting on the foundation's nation-wide program.

The foundation now has donated the vaccine for 3,576,000 initial injections in twenty-eight states and the District of Columbia. The Cutter product has been withdrawn from use temporarily because of paralytic polio found in the areas where it has been administered.

In this city the Board of Health adopted temporary emergency regulations to tighten control of the distribution of the vaccine. It enacted a new section of the Sanitary Code making it unlawful to possess vaccine except on prescription unless the person was a physician, pharmacist or otherwise licensed.

The total of polio cases that have been discovered after inoculation with the vaccine stood at twenty-six last night, according to The Associated Press. In California there were fourteen, Idaho seven, Washington two, Illinois one, Colorado one and Georgia one.

Representatives of health agencies emphasized that nothing detrimental to health had been found so far in the Cutter vaccine. In Washington an inquiry was undertaken by a group of polio experts. Dr. Leonard Scheele, the Surgeon General, said they would go over every step of the Salk program to determine if any slip-ups could have contributed to outbreaks among inoculated children.

Dr. Jonas E. Salk, who devel-

Continued on Page 36, Column 4

SENATORS BATTLE TRADE BILL CURBS

Security Provision to Protect U. S. Industries Is Stressed in Committee Report

Special to The New York Times.

WASHINGTON, April 29—The Senate Finance Committee gave assurances today that domestic industries would be protected under the new national security clause of the reciprocal trade agreements bill.

In its report on the measure the committee thus sought to counter an expected drive on the Senate floor for specific protective amendments. The Senate will take up the measure Monday.

Managers of the bill meanwhile were prepared to spread the word privately during debate that President Eisenhower would use the proposed authority in curbing crude and residual fuel oil imports if they exceeded the 1954 proportion to domestic production.

The national security clause would give the President power to impose quotas on imports that threatened to impair the national security.

White House Report Cited

The committee wrote it into the bill as a substitute for proposed amendments for mandatory quotas on oil, fluorspar, lead and zinc.

The clause, the committee report said, "will provide a means for assistance to the various national defense industries which would have been affected by the individual amendments presented."

In this connection, it cited a report of the President's Advisory Committee on Energy Supplies and Resources Policy, issued by the White House on Feb. 26.

The advisory committee recommended "in the interest of national defense" that action be taken if crude and residual fuel oil imports rose significantly above the 1954 ratio to United States output.

The Finance Committee also noted that it had acted to tighten the escape clause provision of the Reciprocal Trade Agreements Act.

Under the escape clause procedure, the President must accept or reject Tariff Commission recommendations for higher duties where the commission finds that imports threaten serious injury to a domestic industry.

The bill, as reported to the

Continued on Page 6, Column 6

Bricker Flares Up At Treaty Witness

By The Associated Press.

WASHINGTON, April 29—Senator John W. Bricker clashed sharply today with a witness who opposed his constitutional amendment to limit the President's treaty-making powers.

The witness, Prof. Charles H. McLaughlin of the University of Minnesota, declared Mr. Bricker's "notion" of a conspiracy to surrender United States sovereignty to the United Nations was "laughable."

Flaring up, the Ohio Republican told Professor McLaughlin "you might as well wipe that laugh off your face."

He never had "intimated or suggested" there was such a conspiracy, the Senator added.

Professor McLaughlin, a political scientist testifying before the Senate's Judiciary subcommittee, acknowledged he might have misinterpreted a state-

Continued on Page 6, Column 7

Bonn Disavows Aim To Be Neutral State

By M. S. HANDLER
Special to The New York Times.

BONN, Germany, April 29—Government leaders acted today to dispel any opinion that neutralism had become rampant in West Germany since the Soviet-Austrian agreement on the terms of an Austrian treaty.

Repeated assurances were given to a group of United States and British reporters that the majority of the West Germans supported Chancellor Konrad Adenauer's policy of strict enforcement of the Paris agreements to arm West Germany.

The reporters also were assured that under no circumstances would the West German Government do the following:

¶Enter into bilateral negotiations with the Soviet Gov-

Continued on Page 6, Column 3

Associated Press Wirephoto (via Radio from Manila)
FLIGHT TO SAFETY IN SAIGON: Led by a man carrying a wounded child, refugees flee the fire and fighting in the South Vietnamese city. The blaze swept through thousands of grass huts and several of the public buildings.

Saigon Is 2 Cities, And One Is Dying

Special to The New York Times.

SAIGON, Vietnam, April 29—Saigon was two cities today, and one was dying.

Miles of this city—"fun-loving Saigon" it used to be called—were smoking rubble. Thousands of houses that had had people in them yesterday did not exist today.

To Saigon came the scene that has come to hundreds of other cities—listless survivors picking through ruins. One woman found a pair of scissors, picked it up, walked away a bit, came back, laid it down and then stared at it.

This was in the Vietnamese and Chinese sections of Saigon. People in these neighborhoods had Vietnamese Army posts and rebel Binh Xuyen strongpoints for neighbors. Their houses and shops were not particularly interesting militarily, but mortar shells often do not

Continued on Page 3, Column 6

"All the News That's Fit to Print"

The New York Times.

LATE CITY EDITION
Some cloudiness today; fair tonight and tomorrow.
Temperature Range Today—Max.: 66; Min.: 48
Temperature Yesterday—Max.: 45; Min.: 40
Full U. S. Weather Bureau Report, Page 41

*Copyright, 1955, by The New York Times Company.

VOL. CIV..No. 35,527.   Entered as Second-Class Matter, Post Office, New York, N. Y.   NEW YORK, MONDAY, MAY 2, 1955.   Times Square New York 36, N. Y. Telephone LAckawanna 4-1000   FIVE CENTS

ADAMS BIDS CITY STUDY GAMBLING AND YOUTH CRIME

Gravity of Problems Is Cited in '54 Report to Mayor— Overhaul of Force Urged

FELONIES SET A RECORD

Major Offenses Are Termed 'Province of the Young' by the Commissioner

By CHARLES GRUTZNER

Gambling and an "alarming" increase in juvenile crime are the most troublesome problems of New York's police. Commissioner Francis W. H. Adams said yesterday.

The Commissioner declared, in his annual report to Mayor Wagner, that the problem of enforcing gambling laws had "reached such magnitude that a serious study of the question in all its ramifications is urgently needed." He said he was offering the suggestion "without expressing any opinion as to the desirability of legal gambling."

On the question of juvenile crime, the Commissioner conceded that all efforts to deal adequately with youthful offenders and to prevent crime had not yielded results. He advised that "the effectiveness and value of the whole Juvenile Aid Bureau be restudied to determine if the bureau should be expanded or other means of dealing with the problem" be devised.

A structural overhaul of the plainclothes system was proposed by Commissioner Adams. Plainclothes patrolmen, who work out of uniform on gambling and vice assignments, have been exposed more over the years to the temptations of and opportunities for corruption than most other policemen. The plainclothes system has been raked periodically by charges of graft, such as were proved when the Harry Gross bookmaking empire fell apart.

Reorganization Proposed

Commissioner Adams suggested that the plainclothes force—now about 400 men—be reorganized into a separate division, somewhat like the Detective Division, with new controls and added pay.

He said this might keep out of plainclothes duty potentially crooked policemen who now seek such assignments. Also, he said, it might attract honest policemen who now accept such assignments unwillingly because of the bad name and "necessarily distasteful methods" that policemen use in gambling and vice investigations.

"Possibly service in the plainclothes division might be made a prerequisite for advancement to the Detective Division, far and away the most attractive assignment in the department," Mr. Adams said.

Commissioner Adams reported that major crimes in the city last year set a record high of 111,274 felonies, 2.3 per cent over 1953. There were also more misdemeanors than ever before—184,348, an increase over 1953 of 20.3 per cent.

Commissioner Adams expressed particular concern because offenses by youths had increased much more sharply than the over-all rise in crime. He repeated that the major crimes of robbery, burglary and

Continued on Page 15, Column 4

Hoodlum, 17, Seized As Slayer of Boy, 15

A 17-year-old hoodlum was charged yesterday with the unprovoked killing of a 15-year-old boy in the Bronx.

The dead youth, a sophomore at Mount St. Michael Academy, had been known as a well-mannered, good student. He had been on the football team.

The prisoner was one of twelve members of two teenage gangs arrested Saturday night and early yesterday morning after the shooting of William Blankenship Jr. of 3454 Fenton Avenue, the Bronx.

Young Blankenship's father has been active in civic affairs, including campaigns to curb juvenile delinquency. He is director of medical and chemical research for the International Latex Corporation and member of the Bronxwood Advisory Council.

Accused of homicide was Frank Santana of 696 Eagle

Continued on Page 12, Column 4

Harriman Vetoes Measures To 'Humanize' Income Tax

Terms G. O. P. Proposal 'Irresponsible'— Also Bans Supervision of Union Funds —Approves Delay on Car Inspection

By LEO EGAN
Special to The New York Times.

ALBANY, May 1—Governor Harriman announced today his veto of what the Republicans had called three "humanizing" amendments to the state personal income tax law.

In a veto message he said the measures were examples of an "irresponsible fiscal policy." Three of four new deductions

Text of Harriman's memorandum is printed on Page 15.

authorized in the bills would have provided the greatest benefits to persons of large incomes who least need relief, he explained.

The Governor said he was prepared to give sympathetic consideration in the future to proposals of this nature. However, he added, they must confer benefits on the lower income group

and they must be associated with measures that would provide the revenues clearly needed for essential services.

Mr. Harriman also disapproved Republican bills providing for the registration and supervision of labor union welfare funds by the State Insurance Department and for making it less costly for counties without large cities to substitute permanent personal registration for the present system of registering voters.

The veto of the union welfare fund bill was based on the statement that it was premature, in that the Insurance Department still was investigating the subject, and inadequate, in that it gave the department no power

Continued on Page 15, Column 1

Governor Approves 3 Bills For Belmont 'Dream Track'

Special to The New York Times.

ALBANY, May 1—Three bills authorizing the Jockey Club to go forward with its plans for a "dream track" at Belmont Park have been approved by Governor Harriman. Several obstacles remain to be overcome before the dream can take physical form.

These include the negotiation of agreements for the purchase of the outstanding stock of existing tracks and the development of an operating plan satisfactory to the State Racing Commission.

The measures whose approval was announced today would:

¶Authorize the creation of a single nonprofit racing association to acquire the outstanding stock of existing tracks and embark upon a $45,000,000 rehabilitation program financed by a bond issue.

¶Authorize the State Racing Commission to give the new nonprofit association a twenty-five-year franchise to conduct thoroughbred racing meets in New York State.

¶Permit the new association to retain the first $5,000,000 of pari-mutuel "take" at its tracks in any year, to make its bonds more salable, on condition that the full state and local share of the "take" be repaid subsequently in the same year.

¶Provide for the payment to the state, as an additional franchise tax, of any profits over and above those required to meet association obligations.

¶Give the State Racing Commission the right to pass on all directors of the new association and the right to require the dismissal of any association officers and employes of whom it disapproves.

The measures all had bipartisan sponsorship.

They were approved by the Legislature by narrow margins on the closing day. The vote in the Assembly was 77 to 63 and in the Senate 31 to 23. A con-

Continued on Page 15, Column 2

SALK VACCINE DUE IN CITY THIS WEEK

School Inoculations to Start a Few Days Later—Need for U. S. Controls Denied

By PETER KIHSS

Anti-poliomyelitis vaccine is expected to arrive late this week for the first phase of New York City's school inoculation program.

This would be free vaccine from the National Foundation for Infantile Paralysis. It would go to 281,000 pupils—all first and second graders, except for those third and fourth graders who were in six Salk vaccine test areas in 1954.

City and state efforts to buy vaccine to inoculate another 258,000 youngsters—those in kindergarten and the remaining third and fourth graders—appeared yesterday to be dependent once again on a move in Washington.

This is today's initial meeting on an eleven-member National Advisory Committee, set up to recommend a formula for distributing non-foundation vaccine state by state.

In Washington, Dr. Leonard A. Scheele, United States Surgeon General, discounted any immediate need for Federal control over the vaccine supply.

Arrival of foundation vaccine here has been delayed once more by the problem of re-shifting supplies to make up for 300,000

Continued on Page 14, Column 2

PRESIDENT FACES FIGHT IN CONGRESS ON HIS PROGRAMS

Reciprocal Trade Debate on Today in Senate—House to Act on Farm Support

By ALLEN DRURY
Special to The New York Times.

WASHINGTON, May 1—Both houses of Congress are squared away to do battle this week over major parts of the President's legislative program.

Tomorrow the Senate begins debate on the Reciprocal Trade Bill, H. R. 1.

On Tuesday, the House takes up a Democratic bill to replace the Administration's flexible farm price supports with the old fixed-supports system.

Under House debate rules the farm fight is expected to last three days. The Senate tussle over reciprocal trade may last three weeks. In both, the influence and prestige of the President are heavily committed.

As approved by the Senate Finance Committee, 13—2, H. R. 1 comes to the floor with substantial changes from the form in which it passed the House. It retains the President's request that his tariff-cutting powers be extended to June 30, 1958, with authority to reduce rates on foreign imports 5 per cent in each of the next three years.

Concession on Textiles

But it carries major concessions to two pressure groups to which the Administration yielded in the hope that these might avoid further amendments by the full Senate.

One concession, adopted at the request of Senator Walter F. George, Democrat of Georgia, would protect the textile industry against possible competition from Japan. It would do so by prohibiting the President from raising rates more than 50 per cent below the levels of last Jan. 1 on incoming Japanese products.

The amendment also would affect chemicals and some 300 other items now under negotiation between this country and Japan.

The other concession was made to a group of oil-state Senators who had demanded that the Administration impose a quota of 10 per cent of domestic production on incoming foreign oil.

To head off this group, the Administration agreed to accept a compromise amendment empowering the President to impose quotas on any import if, in his judgment, it injured a domestic industry vital to national security.

While this power is permissive rather than mandatory, the Administration promised backers of the oil quota that the President would use the powers if imports increased unduly.

It is on the basis of this promise that Administration supporters in the Senate are hoping they can avoid further amending of the bill in the debate. Because of the nature of the committee vote, most observers feel that chances for this were good. However, Senator Matthew M. Neely, Democrat of West Virginia

Continued on Page 15, Column 1

ZHUKOV STRESSES NEED FOR PARLEYS TO SETTLE DISCORD

Soviet Defense Chief Speaks at Moscow Rally — New Cannon Believed Atomic

By The United Press.

MOSCOW, May 1—The Soviet Army showed off today a huge new artillery piece that Western military attachés said might be an atomic cannon.

The cannon shared the center of attention at the annual May Day march with Marshal Georgi K. Zhukov, Soviet Defense Minister.

Marshal Zhukov said in a speech that Soviet policy was "aimed at solving controversial international questions by peaceful means." But he attacked West German armament and said it "hampers the lessening of international tension."

[It was Marshal Zhukov's first declaration since President Eisenhower disclosed last Wednesday that he had exchanged correspondence with the Soviet Defense Minister, whom he knew during World War II.]

In a march cut short by rain, the cannon was pulled on a rubber-tired platform past the reviewing stand on the roof of the Lenin-Stalin tomb in front of the Kremlin wall.

Taking the review were Premier Nikolai A. Bulganin, Nikita S. Khrushchev, the Communist party chief, Marshal Zhukov and members of the top Soviet leadership, including Vyacheslav M. Molotov, the Foreign Minister, and Georgi M. Malenkov, former Premier.

Radio Gives Account

The artillery pieces, including the new cannon, long-barreled anti-aircraft guns and Katyusha mortars, rolled past 20,000 spectators. The viewers included the foreign diplomatic and press corps.

A radio commentator giving an account said as the new cannon rolled by that "mighty tractors are now hauling guns so big that they are called installations."

"In the skilled hands of our artillerymen, guns of various types are capable of destroying the enemy on the ground, in the plains, the mountains and high up in the skies," the commentator continued.

"The conquests of Soviet science and technology, daring discoveries placed at the service of the armament of the Soviet Army—this is what we are reminded of by the guns that have now entered Red Square.

"They strike us not only by their size but also by their fantastic outline and unheard-of might, which are known only to the designers and the artillery-men themselves."

Also shown in the parade were the Soviet Army officers' new steel blue uniforms and the new dark blue of the Air Force officers. All were embroidered with gold braid.

The parade ended after forty-four minutes when the last military formation had marched past the reviewing stand. The civilian part of the parade was called off because of rain. Apparently for the same reason there were no

Continued on Page 3, Column 6

VIETNAM PREMIER CLINGS TO POWER AS RIVAL FLEES; GIVES BAO DAI NEW CHANCE

RETAINS MILITARY LEADERSHIP: Gen. Le Van Ty, Premier Ngo Dinh Diem's Army Chief of Staff in South Vietnam. After power struggle with Chief of State Bao Dai, the general and the Premier are still in control of Saigon.
Associated Press

COUP IS A FIASCO

Bao Dai Takes Milder Stand After His Man Fails to Win Army

By A. M. ROSENTHAL
Special to The New York Times.

SAIGON, Vietnam, Monday, May 2—Premier Ngo Dinh Diem is in control of South Vietnam's army after a struggle with Chief of State Bao Dai's backers.

It was a fifteen-hour struggle in which the weapons were not guns but personal loyalties and political strength.

The Premier's opponent in the fight for the army was Inspector General Nguyen Van Vy named by Bao Dai to take military command. At midnight Saturday the general was a prisoner in the Premier's palace. At 9 A. M. yesterday, he announced that the army was his and that there was no government in Saigon. At 3 P. M. he fled the city.

Last night the Premier cabled to Bao Dai, who lives on the French Riviera, that the army was loyal to the Government and that the general's coup had failed. The Premier warned Bao Dai that unless the Chief of State stopped his war-by-cablegram against the Government, the whole country would go up in revolution.

[The Chief of State Sunday told the Premier in a cablegram sent from Cannes that he was interested in avoiding a civil war. Bao Dai also said he sought a government with a broader base. The message was mild and was viewed as a backdown by Bao Dai.]

Premier 'Studying' Demands

Meanwhile, the Premier applied the brakes to a revolutionary committee of his backers. The committee on Saturday night had moved into the Government Palace and announced that Bao Dai was deposed. The Premier said he was "studying" the revolutionists' demands that the form a new government without allegiance to Bao Dai.

It was obvious the Premier was letting Bao Dai know that if the Chief of State tried to oust him he would not bow but would go along with the revolutionary committee.

"We are giving Bao Dai one more chance to come to his senses," said Ngo Dinh Nhu, the Premier's brother and adviser.

The French, who were backing Gen. Nguyen Van Vy against the Premier, were in a grim mood. French officials accused the Government of spreading anti-French propaganda among the people of Saigon and had the army accused the Government of endangering the security of the European population.

From Bien Hoa, about thirty-five miles north of Saigon, the French brought 10,000 Moroccan troops into the city to join 35,000 French soldiers already here. Instead of the usual night patrol of about ten men, the French put on a show of strength. A column of about forty tanks and armored vehicles rumbled

Continued on Page 6, Column 3

BIG 4 AIDES MEET IN AUSTRIA TODAY

Ambassadors to Pave Way for Foreign Ministers' Talks on Vienna State Treaty

By JOHN MacCORMAC
Special to The New York Times.

VIENNA, May 1—The Ambassadors of the United States, Britain, France and the Soviet Union will meet tomorrow to begin drafting a new state treaty for Austria.

Although the three Western Ambassadors have been working together for a week in an effort to achieve a common front, it is understood that final instructions from Washington arrived only today.

Austrian and other non-American diplomats attribute this delay in preparation to Secretary of State Dulles' insistence that no further Austrian treaty negotiations be conducted until the Paris agreements on arming West Germany were well on their way to ratification.

The Austrians had been discouraged from answering favorably a Soviet proposal last July for another state treaty conference. However, this did not prevent them from negotiating privately with the Russians. The upshot was the sudden Soviet invitation to Austria three weeks ago to send a delegation to Moscow.

This gave the Russians the initiative and it may be a hard task for the United States to re-

Continued on Page 9, Column 2

U.S. OFFICIALS HAIL TREND IN VIETNAM

Washington Reported Again Asking France to Support Premier in Showdown

By DANA ADAMS SCHMIDT
Special to The New York Times.

WASHINGTON, May 1—United States officials expressed deep satisfaction today that Premier Ngo Dinh Diem had won control of Saigon.

They were pleased, too, by indications that Chief of State Bao Dai had backed down from his previous demand that Ngo Dinh Diem report to him in Cannes and was adopting a more conciliatory attitude toward the South Vietnamese Premier.

The Chief of State changed his tune after Premier Diem won control of the army and the commanding general appointed by Bao Dai had fled. Reports reaching diplomats here suggested that relations between the Chief of State and the Premier might be patched up for the time being.

The exchange of telegrams between the two men led these diplomats to doubt reports that the Premier would press the United States for a decision on whether it would recognize a new provisional government formed without the Chief of State's consent.

Collins Due in Saigon

This would amount to recognition that Ngo Dinh Diem and the revolutionary committee had deposed Bao Dai. The Premier was said to be planning to put the question to the United States special representative, Gen. J. Lawton Collins, who is on his way back to Saigon.

The State Department declined meanwhile to discuss the issue, on the ground that it was hypothetical. "We haven't had to cross that legal bridge yet," one official remarked. Another State Department official observed that things were moving so rapidly in Saigon that the picture could be entirely changed again by the time General Collins arrived.

The officials were in doubt as to the importance and character of the revolutionary committee that yesterday announced the dismissal of Bao Dai as Chief of State—whether the Premier controlled the group, whether it controlled him, or whether it was playing an independent role.

Among the objectives of the revolutionary committee is to "drive out the French Expeditionary Army," and this is clearly embarrassing to the United States Government. The United States position is

Continued on Page 7, Column 4

Pope Declares May 1 Workers' Feast Day

By ARNALDO CORTESI
Special to The New York Times.

ROME, May 1—Pope Pius XII led the main observance of May Day today.

Last year the Communists were still able to assert with some truth that the May 1 celebration of Labor Day was theirs. This year the anti-Communist unions pushed them into the background in many places. In Rome they were pushed almost completely into the background.

The Pope seized the occasion to proclaim the liturgical feast of St. Joseph the Workman, assigning to it the first day of May. By this act today's rivalry between the Communists and Roman Catholics for the allegiance of the workers was made a permanent feature of May Day celebrations.

Justifying his choice of May

Continued on Page 4, Column 8

Chiang Urges Effort To Regain Mainland

By The Associated Press.

TAIPEI, Formosa, May 1—President Chiang Kai-shek today described the situation in the Formosa Strait as tense.

General Chiang in a message marking the establishment of the Chinese Association for Psychological Warfare apparently referred to reports of Communist Air Force and Army build-up opposite Formosa.

The President urged the association to do its utmost to help the Nationalist armed forces "hasten the downfall of the Communist puppets and recover the mainland."

A decree issued by the President today reduced the length of service of draftees to sixteen months from two years in the Army and three years in the Navy and Air Force.

Vice President Chen Cheng in a May Day speech inveighed against a cease-fire in Formosa

Continued on Page 3, Column 2

A SALUTE FOR ZHUKOV: Marshal Georgi K. Zhukov, Russia's new Defense Minister, as he rode through Mokhovaya Square yesterday en route to Red Square to attend May Day celebration. Zhukov made the principal address at festivities.
Associated Press Radiophoto

"All the News That's Fit to Print"

The New York Times.

LATE CITY EDITION
Fair and mild today and tonight. Some cloudiness, mild tomorrow.
Temperature Range Today-Max., 70; Min., 46
Temperatures Yesterday-Max., 68.3; Min., 43.4
Full U. S. Weather Bureau Report, Page 66

VOL. CV No. 35,705. Entered as Second-Class Matter, Post Office, New York, N. Y. NEW YORK, THURSDAY, OCTOBER 27, 1955. Times Square, New York 36, N. Y. Telephone LAckawanna 4-1000 FIVE CENTS

DEMOCRATS CHART LIBERAL PROGRAM IN NEW CONGRESS

Strategy Designed to Appeal to Left and Center Wings on Both Sides of Aisle

SCHISM TO BE FOUGHT

Chiefs Are Hoping to Avoid Major Conflicts by Barring Issues Like Civil Rights

By WILLIAM S. WHITE
Special to The New York Times.

WASHINGTON, Oct. 26—Powerful Senate Democrats have agreed in principle on the main program for the second session of the Eighty-fourth Congress.

This session will open in January in a Presidential election year.

They are ready to offer a complex of legislation somewhat more liberal in general tone than what was offered in the last session, but liberal mainly in such traditional areas as farm relief and flood control.

There is every intention to avoid, if possible, such issues as compulsory civil rights bills—for Federal sanctions against racial discrimination in hiring and so on—and repeal or basic alteration of the Taft-Hartley Labor Act.

Debate in these fields, if pursued to anything resembling ultimate tests, would split the party and reopen the old rupture between its Northern and Southern wings.

One of the great efforts of the session, in fact, will be an attempt by the Democratic hierarchy to restrain the party liberals from insisting on action in such matters as these.

Flood Control To Be Urged

Otherwise, the Democratic program will involve innovations, but innovations of a kind calculated to appeal to the left and center of the Republican as well as the Democratic party and to be unacceptable only to the right-wing of each.

For example, there will be an omnibus Democratic bill, involving possibly as much as $3,000,000,000 in Federal outlays, for a national flood control plan.

The Democrats reckon that this will appeal first of all to the Northeast, which has been hard hit by floods recently, but some assistance will be proposed for every area of the country.

There also will be a Democratic bill for Federal aid to public school construction. Such a measure remained inert in a Democratic-controlled Senate committee in the last session of Congress. This time the word will be passed that it is to be an absolute "must."

Apart from these items, the Democratic program may be thus described authoritatively:

¶A new approach to a Federal highway program, a matter on which the Democrats and the Eisenhower Administration fought inconclusively in the last session. The new approach will be intended immediately to provide perhaps $1,000,000,000, with much more to come later, in Federal assistance for road improvements.

¶Renewed attempts to cut individual income taxes. Many believe that the likely result of this effort will be an increase from

Continued on Page 16, Column 4

Gulick Predicts Kennedy Will Join City TV Project

Says Police Head Is Not Opposed to Plan if Special Problems Are Considered—Mayor Bars 'Unfair' Monopoly

By PAUL CROWELL

A prediction that Police Commissioner Stephen P. Kennedy would eventually participate in a properly safeguarded plan to dramatize the work of all city departments by means of commercial television shows was made yesterday by Dr. Luther Gulick, City Administrator.

Mr. Kennedy notified the Mayor last Saturday that he could not comply with Executive Order 27. This directed all city department heads to make their files, equipment and manpower available to a television production company headed by Theodore H. Granik, a personal friend of the Mayor's.

Dr. Gulick, whom the Mayor designated on Tuesday to head a special committee to study the entire problem of commercial telecasting of city activities, said that it would take "until after Jan. 1" to do the job.

"I am confident," Dr. Gulick declared at a City Hall press conference, "that we will produce a plan so sound and so reasonable that it will be impossible for any city department head to refuse cooperation."

"Does that apply to Police Commissioner Kennedy?" he was asked.

"Certainly it does," he replied. "He is the same as any other Commissioner. I have talked to him since my return to the city and he isn't opposed to television as a means of publicizing the work of his department, provided his special problems are considered. He is a Commissioner, the same as the others who

Continued on Page 67, Column 3

Profits of General Motors Driving Past Billion Mark

The General Motors Corporation, world's largest manufacturing enterprise, apparently will show record net income of well over $1,000,000,000 for 1955. The huge automotive producer yesterday reported record net income of $912,887,537 after taxes for the first nine months of this year, more than for any full year in its history.

The previous record for a full year was set in 1950, when net income totaled $834,000,000.

In their report, Harlow H. Curtice, president, and Alfred P. Sloan Jr., chairman, said the automobile industry was experiencing "the best year in its history." Confidence in the progress of the national economy is widespread and the public has the desire and ability to buy, they added.

General Motors sales for the first nine months were $9,543,778,894, only slightly below the $9,823,529,000 sales of all of last year. General Motors' record sales were made in 1953, at $10,027,985,000. This mark would seem about to topple.

For shareholders the net income figure for the first nine months represents $3.31 on each of an average number of 272,862,335 shares of common stock outstanding. This figure reflects the three-for-one stock split effective as of Sept. 30. In the first nine months last year net income amounted to $2.19 a share on each of 262,183,773 shares outstanding, adjusted to take into effect the stock split.

The report noted that sales of 7,300,000 cars and trucks by the United States and Canadian auto industries through September were greater than in any full year except 1950 and 1953. During the first nine months Gen-

Continued on Page 48, Column 6

MILK PEACE IS SET; NO PRICE RISE DUE

Industry Will Absorb Higher Costs in Settlement Here—Jersey Action in Doubt

By A. H. RASKIN

New Yorkers got simultaneous relief yesterday from the threat of a milk strike and a rise in milk prices.

Company and union negotiators agreed on a package settlement of $5 a week for wage increases, pensions and welfare benefits. The accord was reached at 5 A. M., after eighteen hours of almost continuous conferences at the Barbizon Plaza Hotel.

The industry promptly let it be known that there would be no increase in the cost to New Yorkers of the 4,000,000 quarts of milk they consume each day. Ordinarily, a $5 labor rise would be accompanied by an advance of half a cent a quart in milk prices. Such an increase would have added more than $7,000,000 a year to the city's milk bill.

The assurance of price stability did not extend to northern New Jersey. Distributors in that area avoided any commitment on whether the rise in labor costs would be absorbed or passed on to the consumer.

One factor in the decision of

Continued on Page 23, Column 3

BRITISH SALES TAX IS INCREASED 20%; HOUSING AID CUT

Supplementary Budget Also Raises Levy on Profits—Labor Bids Butler Resign

By THOMAS P. RONAN
Special to The New York Times.

LONDON, Oct. 26—R. A. Butler, Chancellor of the Exchequer, introduced today a supplementary budget cutting housing subsidies and other Government expenditures.

It also would increase the purchase tax and the tax on business profits. The purchase tax rise was set at 20 per cent.

Mr. Butler told the House of Commons also that the Post Office was raising charges for many of its services. Increases in postal rates for letters and parcels and in charges for telegrams and telephone services will bring the Government an extra $72,800,000 a year.

Mr. Butler said that Britain's economic situation had shown distinct improvement within the last month but that the steps he was taking were needed to carry on the fight against inflation.

The continuing high level of demand at home from both governmental and private sources, the persistent shortage of labor, the renewed pressure for higher wages and the strain to which the nation's gold and dollar reserves are still subjected, show that the economic restraints already applied have to be reinforced, he said.

Surplus Earnings Not Enough

Mr. Butler noted that Britain had earned a surplus of $106,400,000 in her business dealings with the rest of the world during the twelve months ended last June 30. But, he said, it was not nearly enough to meet her overseas commitments and responsibilities and to maintain confidence in the pound sterling.

Labor party members saw the supplementary budget, the first since 1947, as a confession of failure of the Government's economic policies. Throughout Mr. Butler's speech, they heckled him and at times they drowned out his words with jeers. When he sat down there were repeated cries of "resign."

The Laborites then took the unusual step of forcing a vote on the first resolution the Government introduced, one dealing with the purchase tax. Normally such a resolution is offered formally at this stage and a vote taken later.

The Government carried the resolution by 314 to 227, a majority of 87. But two Conservatives who opposed any rise in the purchase tax voted with the Laborites.

Mr. Butler, who spoke for more than an hour, ignored the interruptions and jeers. Some of his measures, especially those on subsidies and the purchase tax,

Continued on Page 4, Column 4

Associated Press Radiophoto

MOLOTOV REACHES GENEVA: An armed Swiss soldier stands guard at airport as Soviet Foreign Minister Vyacheslav M. Molotov, left, arrives for Big Four Conference.

ASSEMBLY BLOCKS FAURE IN 2 TESTS

After Procedural Defeats, French Premier Sets Vote of Confidence Tomorrow

By ROBERT C. DOTY
Special to The New York Times.

PARIS, Thursday, Oct. 27—Premier Edgar Faure, fighting to save his Government and its plan to call new Parliamentary elections, asked a predominantly hostile National Assembly for a vote of confidence early this morning.

M. Faure's defeat on two test votes led to his decision to invoke the Constitutional procedure. It foreshadowed the possibility of another French Government crisis that would leave France without a qualified spokesman at the Foreign Ministers Conference in Geneva opening today.

For the second time in two weeks, the Premier used the confidence vote procedure to rally his crumbling right-center majority in support of his explanations of Government financial prospects, the issue under debate. He won by 308 votes to 254 on the issue of Algerian policy on Oct. 18.

The Constitution requires a twenty-four-hour recess before the vote, which will take place at 10 A. M. tomorrow. A defeat would entail M. Faure's resignation. If the Premier were to lose by the Constitutional majority of 312 votes, it could lead to dissolution of the Assembly and bring M. Faure, in defeat, the new elections he sought.

The Assembly twice rebuffed

Continued on Page 6, Column 3

Acheson Criticizes Dulles And G.O.P. Foreign Policy

By JAMES RESTON
Special to The New York Times.

WASHINGTON, Oct. 26—Former Secretary of State Dean Acheson contended today that the Democrats had proved themselves superior to the Republicans in developing the unity and strength of the free world.

Breaking a long silence on controversial foreign policy questions and personalities, Mr. Acheson criticized the Republican party's foreign economic policy and characterized Secretary of State John Foster Dulles' threats of atomic retaliation as "a classic illustration of the way a leader among free nations should not proceed."

He also asserted that the difference between party attitudes on foreign affairs "may determine the success or failure" in the "cold war" and implied that the Republicans had not only followed wrong policies, but that they had shown little "hospitality to intelligence."

His observations on "The Parties and Foreign Policy" were published in the November Harper's Magazine and will be included in a book called "A Democrat Looks at His Party."

Cites 'Renaissance of Thought'

"In the conduct of our foreign relations in the years following the war," he wrote, "ideas were welcomed and respected. Men capable of having them were welcomed, respected, and both stimulated and supported.

"The result was a renaissance of thought and inventiveness which was unexcelled—and, it is not too much to say, unequaled—in any chancellery in the world."

Mr. Acheson did not say so, but he left to the reader to infer that the State Department had not been exactly a triumph of intellectual genius since Jan. 20, 1953, when Mr. Dulles took over.

Mr. Acheson's remarks were expected to revive the public dispute that divided him from many Republican and some Democratic leaders during his years in the State Department.

The Republicans are eager to debate the foreign policy issue in the coming Presidential campaign. They believe they can concede many disappointments in Indochina and Formosa, Ger-

Continued on Page 21, Column 3

EISENHOWER ASKS SOVIET GOODWILL

Issues a Statement Calling for 'Accommodation' at the Geneva Conference

Text of President's statement on Geneva is on Page 3.

By RUSSELL BAKER
Special to The New York Times.

DENVER, Oct. 26—President Eisenhower called upon the Soviet Union today to match the West's "genuine spirit of conciliation and accommodation" at the bargaining table in Geneva.

If the Soviet Union comes to the Big Four Foreign Ministers Conference, opening tomorrow, in this spirit, "much progress can be made" toward solving the major problems dividing East and West, the President said.

The proposals to be advanced by the Western powers will be designed "to promote a peace of justice, with increased security and well-being" for all peoples, the President added.

They will "reflect a genuine spirit of conciliation and accommodation" on the part of the West, he said. It is his "personal hope" that the Soviet Union will bargain in the same spirit to insure progress from the meeting, he added.

Message Sent From Hospital

The President's eve-of-conference statement was issued from his hospital room at Fitzsimons Army Hospital, where he is recovering from a heart attack.

In it, he again sounded the warning that the Foreign Ministers Conference would be "the acid test" of the "spirit of Geneva."

Developments in Geneva will "go far to demonstrate whether the spirit of Geneva marks a genuine change and will actually be productive of the peaceful progress for which the whole world longs," he said.

Again the President emphasized that he and Secretary of State Dulles were in complete harmony on United States policies to be enunciated at the conference. Mr. Dulles, who will head the United States delegation, has conferred twice with the President on strategy since General Eisenhower entered the hospital.

"Secretary Dulles and I think alike with respect to these matters," the President's statement said.

This was interpreted here as a further attempt to strengthen Mr. Dulles' hand at the bargaining table.

On Sunday, the White House published a letter, written by the President to Vice President Richard M. Nixon, stating in the strongest terms that Mr. Dulles was authorized to speak for him "with authority for our country" both "at the conference table and before the world."

The President's statement today was worked out jointly by

Continued on Page 3, Column 5

DULLES PROMISES CONCILIATORY AIM IN GENEVA TALKS

Says 'Necessary Steps Will Be Taken in Negotiating With Soviet at Parley

MOLOTOV IS OPTIMISTIC

West Is Prepared to Warn Moscow on Mideast at the Meeting Opening Today

By DREW MIDDLETON
Special to The New York Times.

GENEVA, Oct. 26—Secretary of State Dulles pledged the United States today to "necessary conciliation" in negotiating with the Soviet Union for Germany's unity, for disarmament and for improved contacts between the East and the West.

This statement by Mr. Dulles after he had stepped off a plane from Paris reflected the United States approach to the Foreign Ministers' Conference, which opens here tomorrow. It contrasted sharply with the strong warning the three Western delegations were prepared to issue on Soviet political and economic infiltration in the Middle East.

The Soviet Union's entry into this sensitive strategic area has altered the character of the conference. Mr. Dulles, Harold Macmillan, British Foreign Secretary, Antoine Pinay, French Foreign Minister, and Vyacheslav M. Molotov, Soviet Foreign Minister, were ordered here by the heads of their governments to discuss the great issues explored by the Big Four heads of government at their meeting here last July.

But it is apparent that informal contacts between Mr. Molotov and the Western ministers on the Middle East ultimately will be as important as formal discussion of items on the agenda.

First Agenda Item Stressed

Nevertheless, Mr. Dulles gave first priority to the first item on the agenda, "the closely linked subjects of the unification of Germany and European security."

Mr. Dulles declared the foreign ministers would meet "in the spirit of Geneva," that had become "identified with the hopes of the world."

The "spirit of Geneva" distilled by the four heads of government in July also was duly acknowledged by Mr. Molotov. The Soviet Foreign Minister, spruce and unusually voluble, arrived asserting that the spirit signified "a collaboration tending toward an improvement of international relations and a reinforcement of peace."

There was not the slightest hint in Mr. Molotov's statement or the subsequent comments of the Russian official spokesman of the Soviet Government's policy at the conference.

Mr. Molotov declared he expected from the participants in the conference "every effort toward finding agreeable solutions" that would end the "cold war" and improve relations.

"The Soviet delegation on its part will do all in its power to see that the conference achieves positive results corresponding to the aspirations of the peoples," Mr. Molotov added.

Mr. Molotov, in the view of diplomats, does not have to offer much. It is ruefully conceded by

Continued on Page 2, Column 3

60,000 Bright High School Pupils Vie for 400 College Scholarships

The New York Times (by Patrick A. Burns)

City pupils at the Bronx High School of Science taking part yesterday in first of a series of national scholarship tests

By BENJAMIN FINE

The nation's greatest talent hunt got under way yesterday. Sixty thousand boys and girls from 10,850 high schools in all the states spent two hours seeking the right answers for 115 brain-teasing questions.

The stakes were high—but so were the odds. Only 400 scholarships are to be awarded, making this a 1,500-to-1 contest. But the prizes will average $3,500 for a four-year college education. The awards may even go as high as $8,000 depending upon the needs of the individual student. Each winner may choose his college and will get free tuition, board, room, travel and maintenance. This was all part of the National Merit Scholarship Screening Test, the largest independent program of its kind in American education. The project was set up recently with a $20,500,000 grant from the Ford Foundation and the Carnegie Corporation. Funds

Continued on Page 26, Column 3

Arthur Dean Quits Fund for Republic

By PETER KIHSS

Arthur H. Dean, former United States peace negotiator in Korea, has resigned from the board of directors of the Fund for the Republic, reportedly "for policy reasons."

The often controversial fund says it seeks "to advance understanding of civil liberties." On Sept. 11, Seaborn P. Collins, then national commander of the American Legion, urged Legionnaires to boycott it for assertedly trying to depict communism as never a serious threat in this country.

At the law firm of Sullivan & Cromwell, of which Mr. Dean is a senior partner, it was said yesterday he had resigned Sept. 27. There was no explanation of the "policy reasons." Mr. Dean was unavailable for comment.

Paul G. Hoffman, chairman of the fund's board of directors,

Continued on Page 15, Column 4

British-Led Force Seizes Arab Oasis

By BENJAMIN WELLES
Special to The New York Times.

LONDON, Oct. 26—British-led Arab forces clashed today with a Saudi Arabian military unit occupying the Buraimi Oasis in southeastern Arabia.

Prime Minister Eden announced in the House of Commons that the Saudi Arabian force had been ousted from the oasis and areas to the west of it. According to Sir Anthony's cautiously worded statement, two Saudi Arabian soldiers were "slightly wounded" and were being cared for by the British-led troops.

The Buraimi Oasis has been a source of contention between Saudi Arabia on one hand and two pro-British native chiefs, the ruler of Abu Dhabi and the Sultan of Muscat, on the other. The borders in the area are not clearly defined.

Attempts to resolve the long-standing dispute through

Continued on Page 6, Column 4

South Vietnam Gets Status of Republic

By HENRY R. LIEBERMAN
Special to The New York Times.

SAIGON, Vietnam, Oct. 26—A new republic was born in South Vietnam at noon today. It was proclaimed by Premier Ngo Dinh Diem, who became its first President under a provisional constitutional act.

Thousands of Vietnamese congregated at the Palace of Independence to greet the birth of the new state. As church bells pealed and a twenty-three-gun salute sounded in the distance, they hailed their republic and their President.

Mr. Diem succeeded Bao Dai as Chief of State following an overwhelming victory in a referendum last Sunday. Mr. Diem received 98.2 per cent of the vote. Bao Dai, who was installed as Chief of State with French backing in 1949, has been in France for more than a year.

Recognition of the referendum

Continued on Page 3, Column 2

The New York Times.

LATE CITY EDITION
U. S. Weather Bureau Report (Page 36) forecasts:
Rain and cool today; drizzle, fog tonight. Some showers tomorrow.
Temp. range: 61–51; yesterday: 63–56.

VOL. CX..No. 37,729.   © 1961 by The New York Times Company. Times Square, New York 36, N. Y.   NEW YORK, FRIDAY, MAY 12, 1961.   10 cents beyond 50-mile zone from New York City except on Long Island. Higher in air delivery cities   FIVE CENTS

KENNEDY OFFERS PLAN TO COMBAT JUVENILE CRIMES

Urges a 5-Year Program to Curb Delinquency — Cost Is 10 Million First Year

CABINET GROUP SET UP

Attorney General Will Head Agency—A 'Total Attack' Proposed to Congress

Texts of Kennedy and Ribicoff letters are on Page 14.

By ALVIN SHUSTER
Special to The New York Times.

WASHINGTON, May 11 — President Kennedy urged Congress today to initiate a "total attack" on the growing menace of juvenile delinquency.

Expressing "serious concern," the President proposed a five-year program to prevent and control youth crime, treat offenders and train youth workers. The cost was put at $10,-000,000 for the first year, beginning July 1.

At the same time, the President issued an Executive Order creating a Committee on Juvenile Delinquency and Youth Crime to coordinate Federal efforts in a program to aid states and local communities in their fight against delinquency.

Committee Membership

The committee members will be Attorney General Robert F. Kennedy, the President's brother, who will serve as chairman, Abraham A. Ribicoff, the Secretary of Health, Education and Welfare, and Arthur J. Goldberg, the Secretary of Labor.

David L. Hackett, a 34-year-old special assistant to the Attorney General, will serve as the committee's executive director.

The Department of Health, Education and Welfare appointed Dr. Lloyd E. Ohlin, a 43-year-old professor of sociology at the New York School of Social Work, to be its special consultant on delinquency. The school is a graduate division of Columbia University.

A Citizens Advisory Council, composed of authorities on youth crime, will be selected by the Attorney General later to advise his Cabinet group.

Serious Problems Cited

In his letter to Speaker of the House Sam Rayburn asking Congressional action, the President said that expanding juvenile delinquency was evident in both urban and rural communities.

He said it affected particularly youths who dropped out of school, unemployed juveniles faced with limited opportunities and children from broken homes.

"I view the present trend with serious concern," he said. "Juvenile delinquency and youth offenses diminish the strength and vitality of our nation; they present serious problems to all the communities affected; and they leave indelible impressions upon the people involved, which often cause continuing problems."

To point up the need for the legislation, the President sent along figures compiled by Mr. Ribicoff showing the steady rise in youth crimes. Since 1948, the Secretary said in a letter to the President, court delinquency cases and juvenile arrests have more than doubled. If the pres-

Continued on Page 14, Column 4

Eisenhower Group Will Scrutinize Kennedy Policies

General Eisenhower with members of his group yesterday in Gettysburg, Pa. From left are Lewis L. Strauss, Charles E. Wilson, General Eisenhower and Frederick H. Mueller.
United Press International Telephoto

By FELIX BELAIR Jr.
Special to The New York Times.

GETTYSBURG, Pa., May 11—Dwight D. Eisenhower said today that he and his former Presidential aides would make a continuing review of the Kennedy Administration's domestic and foreign policies. The group will tell the public "the way we think the country should be going," he declared. After a five-hour meeting with a score of Cabinet officers and other high aides of his former Administration, the former President told newsmen that "there is no attempt here to dictate to our party." But it was clear from his remarks that he expected the group

Continued on Page 11, Column 1

Lefkowitz Gains as Choice Of Republicans for Mayor

By LEO EGAN

Attorney General Louis J. Lefkowitz was projected into the front ranks of possible Republican candidates for Mayor yesterday after Senator Jacob K. Javits had removed himself from consideration. A privately financed poll by an independent opinion-sampling concern was reported as crediting Mr. Lefkowitz with the power to make a "horse race" of a contest with Mayor Wagner.

The same poll gave Senator Javits a slight edge over Mr. Wagner. Its results were given to Governor Rockefeller and the city's five Republican county leaders several days ago.

Whether Mr. Lefkowitz has a good chance of getting Liberal party endorsement if he agrees to become the Republican candidate was still an open question last night.

Rose Not Antagonistic

Contrary to opinion in some quarters, a Liberal endorsement for Mr. Lefkowitz is not an impossibility, Alex Rose, the party's principal spokesman, indicated last night. Mr. Rose is a state vice chairman of the Liberal party and chairman of its policy committee.

Asked what the Liberal reaction would be to a Republican choice of Mr. Lefkowitz, he said:

"Attorney General Lefkowitz is a good public servant. We have a good opinion of him. If he were to be a candidate, the policy committee of the Liberal party would give his candidacy full consideration, together with other candidates. As of now the Liberal party is not committed to any individual."

A Liberal choice of candidates for this year's city election is not scheduled to be made until late this month or early next month. Most party leaders hope to know by that time whether Mayor Wagner will seek a third term, and, if so, who his running mates on the Democratic ticket will be.

Meanwhile Stuart Scheftel emphasized that he would chair-

Continued on Page 18, Column 4

WITNESSES SPLIT ON CITY CHARTER

Both Delay and Action Now Urged on Mayor's Unit at First Public Hearing

By PETER KIHSS

Mayor Wagner's Charter Revision Commission held its first public hearing yesterday. Some speakers warned against hasty Charter revision, but others called for the submission of a new Charter at this November's election.

Councilman Stanley Isaacs, a Republican-Liberal, said it would be "quite unfair to the people" to rush a new Charter through this year. The Women's City Club and the League of Women Voters likewise indicated willingness to delay action to get thoroughgoing revision.

However, witnesses from the New York Committee for Democratic Voters, representing forty insurgent Democratic clubs, the City Club of New York and the New York Americans for Democratic Action pressed for a Charter vote this fall.

Views Are Diverse

The consensus among fourteen witnesses appeared to favor strengthening the administrative power and accountability of the Mayor and introducing proportional representation or some other formula for insuring minority representation in the City Hall.

But the divergence of views on other aspects of the city's structure and administration was so great that John T. Cahill, the commission chairman, appealed to the city's civic groups to try to reconcile their views to help the commission. It will have to file a draft Charter by Aug. 9 if it is to be voted on this November.

Continued on Page 19, Column 2

JOB RISE IN APRIL HELD SIGNIFICANT

Gain of 384,000 Workers and Longer Factory Week Hailed by U. S. Aides

By PETER BRAESTRUP
Special to The New York Times.

WASHINGTON, May 11—The first "significant" upturn in employment since the start of the recession came last month, the Labor Department reported today.

The number of Americans on nonfarm payrolls rose by 384,-000 from mid-March to mid-April, to a total of 52,000,000. This increase was "substantially better" than usual for the season.

Helping this upturn, the department said, were an unseasonal steadiness in manufacturing employment and a 217,000 increase in construction jobs that was almost double the expected gain.

Some 'Good News'

Employed factory workers also enjoyed good news — a modest April increase in hours worked and wages earned. This continued what was termed another "significant" upward trend that began in January.

Arrayed against these "signs of strength," the Labor Department spokesman said, were the gloomy statistics of April's continued "serious" seasonally adjusted unemployment rate of 6.8 per cent, and a post-war high of 2,128,000 long-term jobless.

Seymour L. Wolfbein, Deputy Assistant Secretary of Labor, presented the department's elaboration of figures released last week. Those figures showed that from March to April employment—farm and non-farm—had risen by 218,000 to 65,-734,000, while unemployment fell by 533,000, to 4,962,000.

The modest improvements shown in April, Mr. Wolfbein said, are "not something you'd want to write home about, but in terms of what's been hap-

Continued on Page 16, Column 4

HOUSE COMMITTEE ASKS IF THE ICBM CAN WORK IN WAR

But McNamara Says Tests Have Proved That It Will —Two Experts Cited

By JACK RAYMOND
Special to The New York Times.

WASHINGTON, May 11—Doubts about the practicality and reliability of intercontinental ballistic missiles were raised today in a report to the House by its Armed Services Committee.

The committee, headed by Representative Carl Vinson, Democrat of Georgia, speculated that the use of nuclear weapons might be outlawed by international agreement.

This would give a strategic military advantage to countries with the greatest strength in conventional weapons, the committee said.

In addition, the committee report asked, "Who knows whether an intercontinental ballistic missile with a nuclear warhead will actually work?"

"Each of the constituent elements has been tested, it is true," the report said. "Each of them, however, has not been tested under circumstances which would be attendant upon the firing of such a missile in anger."

Total Placed at 27

The United States is believed to have a total of twenty-seven Atlas ICBM's as first deployment status at Vandenberg Air Force Base, Calif; Francis E. Warren Air Force Base, Cheyenne, Wyo., and Offutt Air Force Base, Omaha, Neb.

The committee cited no evidence that the warheads on ballistic missiles would fail. It emphasized the lack of evidence that they would succeed.

Secretary of Defense Robert S. McNamara dealt with the question in testimony before the Senate Armed Services Committee. A transcript of this committee's hearings was released yesterday.

Secretary McNamara said that the Defense Department had studied the problem. He confirmed that "while we have never actually tested a missile in the sense of firing one against an enemy target," the nuclear tests that have been carried out "all indicate beyond any reasonable doubt" that an ICBM would not lose its destructive power in space flight.

Refers to Dr. York

The Secretary cited the judgment of Dr. Herbert F. York, the Pentagon's outgoing director of Research and Development, and his successor, Dr. Harold Brown, as "international experts in this field."

Additional testimony by Secretary McNamara on this subject was deleted by security censors.

The House committee noted that an intercontinental ballistic missile would carry its nuclear warhead to great heights, subjecting it to great cold, then would arch downward and, upon re-entering the earth's atmos-

Continued on Page 8, Column 4

Johnson Assures Saigon Of Aid in Army Build-Up

Military and Other Backing Against Reds Pledged in Speech to South Vietnam Assembly—He Sees Ngo Dinh Diem

By The Associated Press

SAIGON, Vietnam, Friday, May 12—Vice President Johnson told South Vietnam's National Assembly today the United States was ready immediately to help South Vietnam increase its 150,000-man regular military forces by a substantial number.

In a speech to the Assembly, after talks with President Ngo Dinh Diem, Mr. Johnson said the United States would also assist in equipping and training the 50,000-man Civil Guard in the fight against the Communists. Also the United States would build up the Village Militia, which is known as the self-corps.

"I informed your President that the United States stands ready to assist in meeting the grave situation that confronts you," Mr. Johnson said.

"I've gone into details with your President," he added. "There are many things the United States is willing to do."

Among others, the Vice President added, were steps to improve Vietnam's capacity to resist the subversion and terrorism of the Communist guerrillas.

The address topped a warm and cheering welcome Vice President Johnson received from thousands of eager Vietnamese last night on his arrival here.

Setting out this morning on a day of activities, Mr. Johnson went first to Independence Palace. He was given full military honors, and President Ngo Dinh Diem extended a warm hand-

Continued on Page 2, Column 5

LAOS TALK FACES DELAY IN ABSENCE OF TRUCE REPORT

Rusk Will Not Join Geneva Parley, Scheduled Today, Till Cease-Fire Is Sure

GROMYKO IS INFORMED

3-Nation Panel in Battle Area Dispatches a Note for Britain and Soviet

By SEYMOUR TOPPING
Special to The New York Times.

GENEVA, May 11—The fourteen-nation conference on Laos scheduled to open here tomorrow may not itself participate pending verification of a cease-fire between the Government forces and the Communist-led rebels in the Indochinese kingdom.

Dean Rusk, Secretary of State, was understood to be standing by the United States position that political discussions could not begin here under any possible threat of a renewal of Communist military pressure in the Laotian civil war.

Andrei A. Gromyko, Soviet Foreign Minister, was informed of the United States attitude by the Earl of Home, British Foreign Secretary, at a private dinner at the lakeside villa of the British delegation.

It was expected that Lord Home, Foreign Minister Maurice Couve de Murville of France and Howard C. Green, Canadian Secretary of State for External Affairs, would endorse the United States position.

Opening Hinges on Report

Prospects for the opening of the conference on schedule hinge on the contents of a report en route from the International Control Commission in Laos. The commission, composed of delegates of India, Canada and Poland, has inspected the Laotian battlefronts to confirm the existence of an effective cease-fire.

The commission chairman, Samar Sen of India, dispatched the inspection report by courier to Bangkok. It will be handed to the Soviet and British Ambassadors there for transmission to their capitals.

Britain and the Soviet Union, as co-chairmen of the 1954 conference on Indochina, have responsibility for the preliminary arrangements on the talks here.

If the commission report is received in time and if it contains a satisfactory verification of a cease-fire, a brief procedural meeting of the foreign ministers may formally open the conference tomorrow.

Seeks Confirmation by U. S.

Mr. Rusk was understood to be insisting also on confirmation of a cease-fire from United States observers in Laos.

The Secretary of State believes the Western allies would be negotiating at a disadvantage if the Left-Wing forces of Capt. Kong Le and the pro-Communist Pathet Lao rebels were not bound by a clear definition of an effective cease-fire.

If, in the course of the conference, the Left-Wing forces break the truce, the United States will consider itself legally free to undertake political or military action, it was said.

There was little doubt that a conference would be convened

Continued on Page 2, Column 4

Security Inquiry in Britain Set in Wake of Spy Cases

By SETH S. KING
Special to The New York Times.

LONDON, May 11—A wide investigation of Britain's security system was ordered today by Prime Minister Macmillan. He announced in the House of Commons that, because of the public anxiety aroused by the case of George Blake, a Foreign Service employe convicted last week of spying for the Soviet Union, a top-level investigating committee would be appointed as soon as possible.

"This is really a very serious matter and I do not know what will be the outcome of this committee," Mr. Macmillan said.

"It might be that in all walks of life involving men who have anything to do with public services where secrecy is affected, a greater degree of responsibility and a greater curtailment of their liberty of thought and statements will have to be made," he declared.

Press Secrecy Requested

The Prime Minister also accepted responsibility for the request made to British newspapers last week that certain details of the Blake case not be published.

Even though this request was not complied with for as long as had been hoped, Mr. Macmillan said, the few days that it was heeded were "of value."

"There was some advantage in the time lag," he declared. "What happened subsequently confirms that it was an advantage." He refused to elaborate on these remarks.

The Blake case was the second major espionage case in two months. The Government has been deeply concerned over Blake's confession that he was a Soviet agent for nine and a half years. Blake pleaded guilty last Wednesday to charges of having violated the Official Secrets Act and was given a sentence of forty-two years in prison.

It is now believed that he

Continued on Page 3, Column 2

GHANAIANS SEIZED IN ANGOLA REVOLT

Portugal Reports 71 Taken in West African Fighting —Puts Dead at 1,000

By BENJAMIN WELLES

LISBON, Portugal, May 11—Portuguese authorities in Angola recently captured seventy-one Ghanaian nationals fighting alongside rebel bands in the strife-torn West African province.

Discussions of what to do with the Ghanaians are going on between Portuguese authorities here and in Luanda. Some Portuguese authorities favor bringing some or all of them here for a news conference to emphasize Portugal's assertion that "outside" instigation has played a role in the anti-Portuguese rebellion.

Nearly 1,000 persons are said to have been killed by the rebels in the fighting that is now in its seventh week. No figures are available here on the number of rebels killed by Portuguese forces.

Eventually, it is said here, the prisoners will be returned to the Ghanaian Government with a warning that any more captured fighting with the rebels may not receive lenient treatment.

The Portuguese have suspected for some time that the Gha-

Continued on Page 4, Column 3

Maglio Frees Girl In Raid-Drill Case

By ROBERT CONLEY

A city magistrate had second thoughts yesterday and freed a college girl he had sent to jail for thirty days for refusing to take cover in an air-raid drill.

The magistrate, Anthony E. Maglio, allowed the girl, Elizabeth Just, to withdraw her plea of guilty that had led to the sentence last Tuesday.

Setting aside the 20-year-old student's conviction and sentence, he ordered her released from the Women's House of Detention on parole to await a new trial May 22 in Adolescent Court.

Miss Just, a junior at New York University, was one of several persons who had joined in a protest against the Civil Defense test April 28 in City Hall Plaza.

The magistrate's turnabout,

Continued on Page 13, Column 4

U. S. and Japan at Odds on Use Of Army Base for '64 Olympics

By BERNARD KALB
Special to The New York Times.

TOKYO, May 11—The question whether the United States will relinquish a military base in the Tokyo environs for use in the 1964 Olympic Games threatened today to cause a new controversy between Japan and the United States.

The issue became front-page news here when United States military authorities, requested by the Japanese to yield Camp Drake to the Japanese Olympic Committee, offered the southern half of the base on two conditions: that it be returned immediately in the event of an emergency, and that, in any event, it be returned within sixty days after the games.

The Japanese have planned to convert the base, twelve miles north of Tokyo, into an Olympic village for housing foreign athletes.

The United States' answer "shocked" the Japanese Olympic Committee. At the committee's request, the Japanese Government has decided to take up the matter with the United States Government. If the matter is still unresolved, Premier Hayato Ikeda may be asked to discuss it with President Kennedy at their meeting in Washington next month, according to a committee official.

Meanwhile, a United States military spokesman said the United States was willing to consider any new proposals and was "desirous of extending the utmost cooperation" so that the Olympic Games could be staged successfully.

Ever since the Japanese began drafting blueprints for the 1964

Continued on Page 4, Column 5

COMMUNIST DELEGATIONS MEET IN GENEVA: Andrei A. Gromyko, right, Soviet Union's Foreign Minister, and Foreign Minister Chen Yi of Communist China applaud each other at airport in Swiss capital. The latter's delegation arrived yesterday from Moscow to join fourteen-nation conference, scheduled to open today, on situation in Laos.
United Press International Radiophoto

Senate Authorizes Red-Satellite Aid

By The Associated Press

WASHINGTON, May 11—The Senate voted, 43 to 36, today to grant President Kennedy wide authority to aid Eastern European satellites of the Soviet Union whenever he thought it would help wean them away from Moscow.

It did so over strong protests of a minority, who argued that any aid intended for the people would, in the end, be taken over by puppet Communist governments. This would tighten the Russians' dictatorial grip rather than loosen it, the opponents said.

Senator Strom Thurmond, Democrat of South Carolina, called it an example of "the naiveté of the self-styled humanitarians—whom I prefer to call misguided radicals." He said when the United States sent wheat to Poland a few years

Continued on Page 2, Column 6

General Maxwell D. Taylor, chairman of the U.S. Joint Chiefs of Staff, greets troops during a visit to South Vietnam in September 1962.

Female members of the South Vietnamese Civil Defense Guard drill with their male counterparts.

A U.S. Army aviator briefs a group of South Vietnamese troops as they prepare to board an H-21 Helicopter.

The New York Times.

LATE CITY EDITION
U. S. Weather Bureau Report (Page 69) forecast:
Mostly fair and cold today and tonight. Fair, not so cold tomorrow.
Temp. range: 46—32; yesterday: 46—35.

VOL. CXI...No. 37,911.   © 1961 by The New York Times Company. Times Square, New York 36, N. Y.   NEW YORK, FRIDAY, NOVEMBER 10, 1961.   10 cents beyond 50-mile zone from New York City except on Long Island. Higher in air delivery cities.   FIVE CENTS

SOVIET MODIFIES BERLIN PROPOSAL; U.S. UNIMPRESSED

THREE-POINT PLAN

Recognition of East Germany and Pact Said to Be Skirted

By SEYMOUR TOPPING
Special to The New York Times.

MOSCOW, Nov. 9—The Soviet Union has proposed informally to the Western powers a new compromise solution of the Berlin dispute.

The plan suggested by Moscow appears to involve a retreat from its previous stand, which has been rejected by the West.

It has been indicated to the Western powers that the Soviet Union is prepared to negotiate a Berlin settlement on the basis of the following points:

¶There shall be an agreement between the Soviet Union and the United States, France and Britain on a new statute for West Berlin that would guarantee the freedom of its inhabitants and the freedom of access to a free city of West Berlin.

¶An agreement shall be concluded between the Soviet Union and East Germany under which East Germany will undertake to respect the new statute for West Berlin and accept the guarantees agreed upon by the Soviet Union and the Western powers.

¶The Western powers shall conclude an agreement, with the participation of West Germany, to respect the sovereignty of East Germany.

Elaboration Sought

The Western powers were understood to be seeking an elaboration of the proposals communicated to them in general terms.

[Although Administration officials in Washington downgraded the report from Moscow, asserting that no new proposal had been received and that no significant retreat had been made by the Russians, all news agency dispatches, like that of The New York Times, reported an apparent change in the Soviet position.]

Moscow's plan seems to remove the chief obstacle to the opening of four-power negotiations for a settlement of Berlin and related German issues.

The Soviet Government previously insisted that any such formal talks be committed in advance to the conclusion of a German peace treaty that would recognize the division of Germany and terminate Allied occupation of West Germany.

The Western powers have stood by their pledge to seek German reunification through free elections and declined to make any such prior commitment.

Shift on Stand Seen

Moscow apparently is now prepared to leave the question of the signing of a peace treaty to a later date. It was understood, however, that the Soviet Government continued to insist that a peace treaty eventually should be signed to end the Allied occupation of West Berlin. The Soviet Union first gave ground on its peace treaty demand on Oct. 17, when Premier Khrushchev declared that he would not insist on the conclusion of a treaty this year if the Western powers displayed readiness to negotiate.

At a Kremlin reception on Tuesday Premier Khrushchev said Moscow would not wait indefinitely but that "it was not good for the time being to press one another."

By striking the peace treaty issue for the time being, the latest Soviet proposals seem to reduce the possibility of an East-West military collision on the approaches to West Berlin, 110 miles inside East Germany.

Earlier Premier Khrushchev threatened to sign a separate peace treaty with East Germany by the end of the year if the Western powers refused to join in a treaty on his terms. Under a separate treaty, Mr. Khrushchev said, control over Allied supply routes to West Berlin would be transferred to the East German.

Moscow had warned repeatedly

Continued on Page 10, Column 3

Albania Chief Airs Rifts With Moscow

By MAX FRANKEL
Special to The New York Times.

WASHINGTON, Nov. 9—Premier Khrushchev's repeated avoidance of a showdown in Berlin and his desire to pursue his objectives in Germany through negotiations with the West appear to be a major subject of debate within the world Communist movement.

This was suggested in a speech Tuesday by Gen. Enver Hoxha, leader of the Albanian Communists.

The nature of the program was defined—within the limits of "security"—by an official source today. The operation, he said, involves a movement of masses of United States equipment, planes and personnel. It does not include, the source added, the use of United States ground combat units.

The possibility of United States troop aid to South Vietnam against the Communist guerrillas has been debated for months, especially since the fact-finding mission by Gen. Maxwell D. Taylor, President Kennedy's special military adviser.

Whether the role of United States airmen already here on the way might be broadened to include tactical missions was not disclosed. The full extent of United States participation in the fighting in South Vietnam still awaits a decision by President Kennedy on the report of the Taylor mission, which included economic and political as well as military experts.

Aircraft Fly in Supplies

United States Globemaster transports have been flying into South Vietnam for the last week with equipment for bombing planes that are to be flown in later.

The transports have come from Clark Field in the Philippines with cars, trucks, radar equipment, generators, Quonset huts and other material needed to operate a number of medium bombers that will arrive soon.

A United States ground crew of about twenty men is already at Bienhoa, an airfield about twenty miles northeast of Saigon. Living in tents at the field, the ground crew is making preparations for the arrival of the bombers and their crews.

An informed source said that several hundred United States pilots and other personnel would come to South Vietnam in the "training mission" in the stepped-up aid program.

Helicopters in Program

In addition to the bombers, fighter planes and helicopters are included in the program. Some of these have arrived already and intensive training under United States supervision has begun.

This on-the-spot training of South Vietnamese pilots marks a sharp departure from previous practice. In the past all South Vietnamese military pilots were sent to the United States and the training took about eighteen months.

The helicopters will be employed to transport units quickly to beleaguered guard posts and also for attack missions, informed sources said.

The bombers and fighters will be used by the South Vietnamese to attack Communist guerrilla bases in the South Vietnam jungles and possibly the guerrillas' reported bases at the borders of Cambodia and Laos, according to military sources. The planes will also be available to support South Vietnamese ground forces.

The coming of United States

Continued on Page 14, Column 3

U.S. IS BOLSTERING VIETNAM'S AIR ARM TO COMBAT REBELS

Bombers, Armed Helicopters and 200 Instructors Are Included in Aid Plan

Special to The New York Times.

SAIGON, Vietnam, Nov. 9—The United States Air Force has begun a huge supply and training program here to strengthen South Vietnam's defenses against intensified Communist guerrilla operations.

NEHRU SAYS ENTRY TO BERLIN IS VITAL

Joins Kennedy in Terming Access Right 'Legitimate' —Neutral Laos Urged

Text of the joint communiqué is printed on Page 8.

By TOM WICKER
Special to The New York Times.

WASHINGTON, Nov. 9—President Kennedy and Prime Minister Jawaharlal Nehru issued a joint communiqué today asserting the West's "legitimate and necessary right of access to Berlin."

Mr. Kennedy, the communiqué said, "assured the Prime Minister that every effort would be made to seek a solution of the Berlin problem by peaceful means, and underlined the importance of the choices of the people directly concerned."

The communiqué was issued after a seventy-five-minute meeting between the President and the Indian leader, their fourth conversation since they met Monday at Newport, R. I.

Neutrality for Laos Urged

On another topic that occupied much of the discussions, Southeast Asian problems, the communiqué stated the "common objective" that Laos be "a genuinely neutral state, free of domination by any foreign power."

In an appearance at the National Press Club, Mr. Nehru spoke more specifically about his views on Southeast Asia and advocated a course that he reported to have urged on Mr. Kennedy during their conversation.

He recalled that after the 1954 Geneva conference that ended the 'Indochina war, the participating nations, including the Soviet Union and Communist China, had agreed "to leave those states [in Southeast Asia] to themselves."

This policy of neutralizing the

Continued on Page 9, Column 1

U.S. Army Company Will Drive To Berlin Over Autobahn Today

By DAVID BINDER
Special to The New York Times.

BERLIN, Nov. 9—The United States Army announced today that a motorized infantry company would drive up the autobahn from West Germany to West Berlin tomorrow in the first of a series of convoy exercises through Communist East Germany.

While the purpose of the move was said to be "routine training in convoy procedures," the exercise was seen here as a new demonstration of Western Allied rights of access to Berlin.

The United States mission in Berlin has informed Soviet authorities of the move, as is customary.

It was noted that the Army had markedly increased its traffic on the 110-mile autobahn stretch through East Germany since Soviet authorities held up American military police patrols on the highway eleven days ago. The Army has suspended the patrols.

Tonight a United States spokesman announced that American military policemen had begun checking the identity papers of all Soviet civilians, including diplomats, who cross into West Berlin at the Friedrichstrasse checkpoint in civilian cars.

For the last eight days the West Berlin police have carried

Continued on Page 11, Column 1

NKRUMAH GREETS ROYAL GUEST: President Kwame Nkrumah of Ghana with Queen Elizabeth at Accra airport.
Associated Press Radiophoto

QUEEN WELCOMED WARMLY IN GHANA

Reception in Accra Dispels Fears Foes of Nkrumah Will Repeat Violence

By HENRY TANNER
Special to The New York Times.

ACCRA, Ghana, Nov. 9—Queen Elizabeth II received an enthusiastic welcome from many thousands of Ghanaians here today at the start of her eleven-day state visit.

Fears of unrest that had overshadowed preparations for the visit were eased moments after the Queen's big four-engine jet touched down at Ghana Airport late in the afternoon. The Queen was accompanied by her husband, Prince Philip, Duke of Edinburgh.

Close to 10,000 men and women cheered and waved and praised the royal guest in rhythmic chants specially composed for the occasion.

Cancellation Weighed

"People said she should not come to Ghana, but Elizabeth has come, she has come" was the refrain of one of the chants repeated over and over by the gaily dressed, exuberant women.

The song was occasioned by the fact that as late as yesterday the British Government had considered the possibility of calling off the visit for fear that the internal political tension that has been building up here in recent weeks might threaten the Queen's personal safety.

Two bombs exploded in Accra, the capital, last Saturday, damaging the bronze statue of President Kwame Nkrumah and other Government property, and

Continued on Page 5, Column 3

AROSEMENA TAKES OATH IN ECUADOR

Armed Forces Support New President—Capital Calm —Death Toll Tops 35

By PAUL P. KENNEDY
Special to The New York Times.

QUITO, Ecuador, Nov. 9—Dr. Carlos Julio Arosemena Monroy became today President of Ecuador, as were his father and his grandfather before him.

Dr. Arosemena took over the office after mounting dissatisfaction over the regime of José Maria Velasco Ibarra had reached the point of violence and bloodshed more than a week ago.

At least thirty-five persons were killed in demonstrations throughout the country. Probably twice that many are in hospitals with gunshot wounds.

President Velasco Ibarra abandoned the palace early yesterday morning because he could no longer expect the support of the armed forces. In political asylum in the Mexican Embassy here, he maintains he is still the constitutional President.

The chiefs of staff, who informed him on Tuesday that they could no longer defend his Presidency, maintained that Señor Velasco Ibarra had promised he would resign. Señor Velasco Ibarra denied from the Mexican Embassy that he had done so.

The capital was going about its affairs calmly following the installation of Dr. Arosemena. There were no surface signs that Ecuador had only a relatively short time ago been on the verge of wide-scale revolutionary fighting.

The new President is being

Continued on Page 3, Column 1

X-15 Flies 4,070 Miles an Hour, Slightly Faster Than Its Goal

'Was Never in Any Danger,' Pilot Says Despite the Fact Windshield Shattered

By The Associated Press.

EDWARDS AIR FORCE BASE, Calif., Nov. 9—Air Force Maj. Robert M. White piloted the X-15 today to a speed of 4,070 miles an hour, exceeding the rocket plane's designed top speed of 4,000 miles an hour.

He achieved the mark in the first all-out test of the craft's maximum speed. He followed it with a perfect landing despite a shattered windshield. His comment was:

"I was never in danger at any time."

The speed reached by the X-15 today would take one from New York to Washington in three minutes and from New York to Los Angeles in thirty-six.

The 37-year-old major, who has maneuvered his way out of many tight spots in the edge-of-space craft, was asked if he had been afraid. He replied:

"The things you fear are the things you don't know about. As a result of intense planning

Continued on Page 21, Column 1

Maj. Robert M. White after he made flight yesterday.
Associated Press Wirephoto

ALBANY VOTES SHELTERS; APPROVES G. I. TAX RELIEF; REDISTRICTING IS ARGUED

G.O.P. WOULD GAIN

City Faces Loss of 3 Seats—Democrats Fight for Delay

By DOUGLAS DALES
Special to The New York Times.

ALBANY, Nov. 9—Republicans proposed legislation today designed to reduce drastically Democratic representation from New York in the next Congress.

Democratic legislators got their first glimpse of the bill revising the state's Congressional district lines as they arrived this morning for a two-day special session.

The measure, fixing the lines on which candidates for the House of Representatives will run for the next decade, was put on the calendar for tomorrow. Democrats this afternoon made an unsuccessful effort to have consideration of the bill put off until the regular session in January.

Attack Seems Doomed

The debate tomorrow is certain to see a revival of the recent campaign charges by Mayor Wagner that the new lines will "short change" New York City in its representation in Congress. Substantial G. O. P. majorities in both the Senate and Assembly, however, appeared to doom the minority attack to failure.

In New York Mayor the issued a statement appealing to Governor Rockefeller to recess the Legislature until Dec. 4, to permit a "deliberate" consideration of reapportionment.]

An analysis of the population figures for the districts indicated that, with the exception of the Bronx, the constituencies in Democratic districts in New York City were generally larger than those in Republican areas of the city and in the suburbs.

Carlino Optimistic

What appeared to be a slight hitch developed at a Republican Assembly conference this afternoon, when party leaders were able to produce only seventy-three votes for the bill. A majority of seventy-six is needed for passage. There were three absentees.

After the conference, however, Speaker Joseph F. Carlino said he was sure he would have sufficient votes to pass the measure.

The bill has the broadest changes in New York City, which will lose three of its present seats, and in Nassau and Suffolk Counties, which will gain two. The area north of the Bronx line will lose one district.

A redrawing of the state's Congressional lines is made necessary under the 1960 Federal Census, which showed that New York's relative population growth had lagged behind the rest of the country.

The state now has forty-three seats in the House. The Democratic party won a 22-21 edge in the House delegation elected last year. Under changes provided in the reapportionment bill, the Republicans hope to have a 25-16 majority after the next election.

The present Democratic majority

Continued on Page 28, Column 3

200 Professors Say Shelters Invite War

By FOSTER HAILEY

Almost 200 professors of five universities in the Boston area have declared that the money and effort spent on fall-out shelter programs could be better diverted toward "a positive program for peace."

"It appears to us," they declared in a public letter, "that the prodigious energy of our people is being channeled into wrong directions for wrong reasons, and that continuation of this trend may be extremely dangerous to the nation and to civilization itself."

The letter was signed by 183 members of the faculties of Boston University, Brandeis, Harvard, Massachusetts Institute of Technology and Tufts University, whose dental school is in Boston.

William Schreiber, Associ-

Continued on Page 15, Column 3

ROCKEFELLER SEES GAIN IN ELECTIONS

Results in State, Jersey and City Called a Good Omen for His Re-Election

Special to The New York Times.

ALBANY, Nov. 9—Governor Rockefeller pictured himself today as undismayed by Tuesday's election results.

He told a news conference he thought the outcome in New Jersey, New York City and elsewhere in New York State was a "good" omen for his re-election campaign next fall.

This was the way Mr. Rockefeller said the election returns looked to him.

¶Attorney General Louis J. Lefkowitz' losing campaign for Mayor in New York City showed "a very strong resurgence" of Republican strength because Mayor Wagner's plurality had been more than cut in half from four years before.

¶The New Jersey returns showed "a substantial drop in Democratic strength" because Governor - elect Richard J. Hughes won by 38,000 votes, compared with 270,000 for Gov. Robert B. Meyner, also a Democrat, in 1957.

¶The election of a Democratic County Executive in Nassau was "primarily a case of personalities"—a competition between "a popular, aggressive young Democratic candidate and a very experienced, less dramatic Republican candidate."

Referring to Rochester, which was taken over by the Democrats for the first time in twenty-four years, Mr. Rockefeller said the political situation was "confused" by a bus strike, which had "a very adverse affect on the administration in power."

The Governor pointed out that the Republicans had elected Mayors in Buffalo, Syracuse and Utica and that it was the first time a Republican candidate had ever been chosen for a second term in Utica, He also cited

Continued on Page 28, Column 6

Pro Golf Organization Ends Ban Against Nonwhites as Members

By LINCOLN A. WERDEN

The Professional Golfers Association eliminated the "Caucasian" clause from its constitution yesterday and thereby opened the way to membership for Negroes and Orientals. The action was taken unanimously at Hollywood, Fla., at the organization's forty-fifth annual convention.

The immediate result is a triumph only of principle. Because of the rigid qualifications that currently apply to Caucasians, no nonwhite can be expected to become a full-fledged member of any race. The candidate for membership can reach his goal either by serving a five-year apprenticeship in a golf shop or by adhering closely to the

business methods. One is given in Clearwater, Fla., and another in Los Angeles.

Merely by attending this one-week session, the young hopeful receives one year's credit toward his ambition in a five-year program. It is a concrete method introduced by P. G. A. officials who wish to streamline the entire process of becoming a professional.

The path to Class A (or full-fledged) membership in the P. G. A. is long for members of any race. The candidate for membership can reach his goal either by serving a five-year apprenticeship in a golf shop or by adhering closely to the

Continued on Page 44, Column 1

ACTION IS SPEEDY

Critics of 100 Million Fall-Out Plan Bow in Special Session

By WARREN WEAVER Jr.
Special to The New York Times.

ALBANY, Nov. 9—Governor Rockefeller won legislative approval today for a major fall-out shelter program.

An administration bill appropriating $100,000,000 for shelters at schools, colleges and state institutions passed both houses within six hours after the Legislature had convened in a special session called by the Governor.

In another, action before the two houses recessed until tomorrow, a package of five bills proposed by the Governor to provide benefits and protection for New York residents entering the armed forces during the present emergency was voted in the Senate and Assembly without opposition.

The most important of these bills exempts from the state income tax all military pay up to $100 a month received by New York residents for a twenty-one-month period, beginning last Oct. 1.

Votes Are Decisive

The votes on the fall-out program were decisive—44 to 13 in the Assembly and 93 to 51 in the Assembly. However, the tallies did not reflect the reluctance to support the plan that was evident in both parties.

In the two houses, only one Republican, other than the floor leaders, spoke in support of the shelter legislation. He was Assemblyman Verner M. Ingram of Potsdam. The others sat silently as Democrats, who finally voted for the measure, attacked the bill.

Two of the negative Assembly votes were cast by Republicans, Prescott B. Huntington of Suffolk and Kenneth R. Willard of Livingston. All other Republicans in both houses supported the Governor's proposal.

Score Late Receipt of Bill

The principal Democratic objection was that the text of the bill had not been made available until yesterday afternoon, and that many of the members had had no opportunity to finish reading its thirty-eight-page legal-sized mimeographed pages before the vote.

The Rockefeller bill provides state financial assistance for as much as half the cost of fall-out shelters to be built voluntarily by schools and colleges, public and private. It is estimated that this will use up $85,000,000 of the schools and colleges take advantage of the voluntary program.

In addition, $15,000,000 will be spent to build shelters at state institutions, particularly the units of the State University.

Road Funds Needed

If enough schools build shelters to exhaust the $100,000,000, legislatures in succeeding years presumably would add appropriations to keep the shelter construction plan moving.

It became known today that, to provide enough money for the shelter plan, the Legislature would have to "unfreeze" $100,000,000 that had been set aside at the regular session for possible future highway expenditure.

This money had been set aside earlier this year to match additional Federal highway funds. If Congress made them available, the Federal money was not forthcoming, so the state reserve is being transferred to the shelter program.

Actually, a relatively small amount of the $100,000,000 will probably be spent during the

Continued on Page 28, Column 2

The New York Times.

LATE CITY EDITION
U. S. Weather Bureau Report (Page 62) forecasts:
Partly cloudy and mild
today, tonight and tomorrow.
Temp. range: 68—51; yesterday: 62—42.

VOL. CXI..No. 37,914. © 1961 by The New York Times Company. Times Square, New York 36, N. Y.   NEW YORK, MONDAY, NOVEMBER 13, 1961.   10 cents beyond 50-mile zone from New York City except on Long Island. Higher in air delivery cities.   FIVE CENTS

U.N. SESSION TODAY WILL SEEK TO BAR CONGO CIVIL WAR

Council to Debate Steps to Prevent Widening of Strife Over Katanga Secession

USE OF FORCE OPPOSED

Major Powers Expected to Demur if Bomboko Urges New Military Moves

By SAM POPE BREWER
Special to The New York Times.

UNITED NATIONS, N. Y., Nov. 12—The Security Council will meet tomorrow to try to avert the threat of full-scale civil war in the Congo.

Heated debate is expected. Both Belgium and her former colony will be represented by top-ranking delegates. Belgium's Deputy Premier, Paul-Henri Spaak, arrived today to represent his country. Foreign Minister Justin A. Bomboko will represent the Congo.

Mr. Bomboko is expected to press for strong military action by the United Nations to force the secessionist province of Katanga into union with the rest of the Congo.

Spaak to Defend Belgium

M. Spaak's task presumably will be to defend Belgium against African charges that she has not taken decisive measures to end the presence of Belgian mercenary officers in Katanga's forces.

The major powers are said to be reluctant to enter into any action that might involve the United Nations in further military operations in the Congo. Yet the question of how else to end this crisis poses a major problem.

The strength of the United Nations force in the Congo is 15,490 men. A move by the United Nations command in mid-September to take control in Katanga failed, leaving United Nations units in a precarious and uneasy position in the area of Elisabethville, Katanga's capital.

Any effort to impose a settlement by force might require a considerable increase in the troops at the disposal of the

Continued on Page 3, Column 1

ADENAUER IS FIRM ON LINKS TO WEST

Asserts He Wants to Dispel Doubts on New Coalition

By GERD WILCKE
Special to The New York Times.

BONN, Germany, Nov. 12 — Chancellor Adenauer declared tonight that his new coalition Government would make no changes in West German foreign policy.

The Chancellor said he felt it necessary to reiterate his stand to stop "the talk that is starting up again here and there in foreign newspapers about the instability, the unreliability of the German people."

"That talk is completely false," he said in a television interview.

Dr. Adenauer did not go further than to cite the unspecified foreign reports as the basis for his strong reiteration of his Gov-

Continued on Page 13, Column 1

NEWS INDEX

Molotov Returns Quietly to Soviet to Face Accusers

Vyacheslav M. Molotov and daughter Svetlana at railroad station yesterday in Moscow
Associated Press Radiophoto

By THEODORE SHABAD
Special to The New York Times.

MOSCOW, Nov. 12—A discredited Vyacheslav M. Molotov, who is reported to have been ousted from the Communist party and a Soviet diplomatic post, returned to-day in quiet obscurity to the nation he once helped to rule.

The former Premier and Foreign Minister and his wife were met only by their daughter and son-in-law on their arrival by train from Vienna. No Soviet official was in sight. Answering newsmen's questions, the 71-year-old diplomat said he had had a "good trip" and was "going home." Asked for comment on his reported expulsion from the

Continued on Page 8, Column 5

American Jets Said to Fly Photo Missions in Vietnam

By The Associated Press.

SAIGON, Vietnam, Nov. 12—Reliable informants said today that United States Air Force jets were flying reconnaissance missions over South Vietnam to pin-point build-ups and movements of Communist rebel forces and their secret bases.

[In Washington, Government sources withheld comment Sunday night on the Saigon reports.]

The Saigon informants said highly detailed aerial photographs taken by the United States jets were being used to guide South Vietnamese fighter-bombers in strikes against well-guarded and almost inaccessible installations of the Viet Cong, as the Communist guerrillas are known.

Presumably the jets could also have provided what South Vietnamese authorities have termed conclusive photographic evidence that Communist rebels had extensive bases and large troop units in neighboring neutralist Cambodia. This charge in the past has been denied by the Cambodians.

Four Jets Involved

Four F-101 reconnaissance jets have been flying from Saigon's International Airport the last three weeks.

The United States Embassy's official explanation is that the jets arrived here Oct. 22 for an exhibition during the celebration of South Vietnam's National Day Oct. 26, which was canceled long in advance, and had remained to "log some flying time."

South Vietnamese press reports in the last few weeks have been telling of a continuing series of successful raids by Government warplanes, destroying hundreds of rebel thatch houses and other structures, sinking boats and killing troops.

Whether the United States jets in Saigon were providing only photographs was not known. However, it is an open secret

Continued on Page 19, Column 1

MOSLEM SENATOR SLAIN IN ALGERIA

Victim's Shift on Proposal to End Crisis Is Viewed as Possible Motive

By PAUL HOFMANN
Special to The New York Times.

ALGIERS, Nov. 12—A Moslem member of the French Senate was assassinated near here this afternoon in a machine-gun attack. The assailants escaped.

The victim, Salah Benacer, 62 years old, was elected to the Senate in 1959 on a "French Algeria" ticket. Lately, however, he had advocated negotiations between France and the rebel Provisional Government in Tunis.

Mr. Benacer was Mayor of Mekla, a Berber town of about 15,000 people, in the rugged mountains of the Grande Kaby-lie, seventy miles east of Algiers. At least two members of the Senator were killed by nationalist guerrillas during the first years of the rebellion.

Mr. Benacer was captured by guerrilla forces in 1958 after he had publicly declared support for President de Gaulle. He was a prisoner in a mountain field camp until a French Army unit freed him during a raid.

But well-informed sources here warned against any assumption that the Senator had been assassinated by the rebels. There is some evidence, it was authoritatively said, that he might have been murdered

Continued on Page 3, Column 4

PRESIDENT READY FOR EARLY MOVE ON FREER TRADE

Congress Is Expected to Get Tariff Proposals When It Reconvenes in January

By WALLACE CARROLL
Special to The New York Times.

WASHINGTON, Nov. 12 — The Kennedy Administration has taken all but the final decision to go to Congress in January with a revolutionary foreign trade program.

At a White House meeting last Thursday, President Kennedy apparently resolved most of the existing doubts that this was the time to risk an all-out political battle over tariff policy.

As he indicated at his news conference the previous day, however, his final decision may not come for two or three weeks. The Kennedy program is intended to meet what the Administration regards as the challenge and the opportunity of the Nineteen Sixties in the foreign economic field.

Aims of Kennedy Plan

It is aimed at forestalling the division of the non-Communist world into competing and mutually harmful trading blocs, at giving a big stimulus to the economic systems of the United States and its trading partners and at keeping the Soviet Union, with its latest twenty-year expansion program, well behind the West in production for decades to come.

Many of the refinements of the program remain to be worked out, but as it now stands it would broaden authorization for the President to reduce tariffs on industrial products in return for comparable reductions by other countries.

The President would be able to negotiate such items on an across-the-board basis, rather than item-by-item as at present. He would be able to make agreements not only with individual countries but also with such a unit as the European Common Market, now comprising France, West Germany, Italy, the Netherlands, Belgium and Luxembourg.

Powers of President

And he would be able to commit this country to automatic reductions on broad categories of products at fixed periods—say, 20 per cent every three years—until the tariffs had been eliminated.

The program also would include tax concessions and credits to help American industries threatened by foreign competition to modernize plants and equipment and funds to retrain workers in industries that cannot stand up to foreign competition and move them to new jobs.

Parallel programs would seek to keep foreign markets open to American farm products and to give the under-developed countries stable and profitable

Continued on Page 25, Column 1

U. S. ORBIT OF MAN SEEMS OFF TILL '62

Launching of Chimpanzee Is Delayed, Dimming Hopes for Astronaut This Year

By United Press International.

CAPE CANAVERAL, Fla., Nov. 12—United States hopes for sending a man into orbit this year apparently ended today when a flight with a chimpanzee was postponed at least a week.

The chimpanzee flight, set for Tuesday, was delayed because of troubles in the space capsule.

Scientists plan to send the chimpanzee three times around the earth as the last test before one of the seven United States astronauts gets a chance to follow the trails of Majs. Yuri A. Gagarin and Gherman S. Titov, Soviet astronauts.

But the chance of putting an astronaut into orbit this year depended on a successful launching and recovery of the chimpanzee no later than this week.

The manned flight is now off until early 1962, sources close to the Mercury program said. Most estimates are for February.

The postponement of the chimpanzee test came only hours after the body of a small monkey had been recovered off the north shore of Cape Canaveral.

Goliath, a one-and-a-half-

Continued on Page 20, Column 4

Rockefeller Sets Up Study Of Atomic Attack Survival

Phone Executive to Head Inquiry Into Problems of How to Rebuild

Special to The New York Times.

ALBANY, Nov. 12—Governor Rockefeller set in motion today a broad state study of how survivors of a nuclear attack could organize and rebuild.

He announced that he was appointing a special state committee on recovery from nuclear attack and named Benjamin H. Oliver Jr. of Albany, a vice president of the New York Telephone Company, as its chairman.

The Governor said this country had "two tremendous assets" for survival after a nuclear attack: a two-year stockpile of surplus food and "a reservoir of unused machinery and equipment constantly being replaced by new models, which, if stored rather than scrapped, would enable us to rapidly restore our industrial production."

The Russians, Mr. Rockefeller said, lack both these. Such a lack, he added, "raises serious questions as to the capacity for survival of their people and the habilitation of their industry in a post-attack period."

His committee's study will be financed by a part of the $100,-

Associated Press
Benjamin H. Oliver Jr.

000,000 appropriation in the fall-out shelter bill approved by a special session of the Legislature last week and signed by the Governor.

It is expected that the survival study will take only about $100,000 of this amount. The remainder is earmarked for shelters at state institutions and

Continued on Page 26, Column 3

600 Extra Policemen Put On Special Night Patrols

By EMANUEL PERLMUTTER

Police Commissioner Michael J. Murphy announced yesterday that he had assigned more than 600 additional members of his force to areas where crime incidence is high. The patrols, including detectives and policewomen, are on duty mainly from 4 P. M. to midnight, when street crime is at a peak.

Mr. Murphy said that the additional patrols had been on duty for the last week and that they had been instructed to concentrate on crimes of violence and on sex offenders.

He made the announcement in a talk before 900 members of the Police Department Shomrim Society at its annual breakfast in the Waldorf-Astoria Hotel.

Street-Crime Drive

In his talk and in a statement given out at Police Headquarters, Mr. Murphy said the new assignments would continue in the police drive against street crime.

The program also would include tax concessions and credits to help American industries. Many of the men sitting at coatless wearing skullcaps and side arms.

For the first time in many years, the police statement explained, detectives have been assigned to street patrol. They will tour the city around the clock in cars, wearing civilian clothes, on the lookout for muggers and street gangs. They will work out of the sev-

Continued on Page 21, Column 1

MAYOR SEEKS RISE OF 10C IN CAB FARE

Study Group Recommends Action—Drivers Would Get Medical Care Program

By PAUL CROWELL

Mayor Wagner will ask the City Council to consider increasing taxicab fares by 10 cents.

The present fare, set in 1952, is 25 cents for the first fifth of a mile and 5 cents for each succeeding fifth. The Mayor's proposal would fix the rate for the first fifth of a mile at 35 cents.

The Mayor's action would be based upon a report submitted by a special committee named by him on Sept. 2 to study the request of the taxicab industry for the 10-cent increase. The committee consists of Thomas J. Miley, chairman; James A. Parley and John A. Coleman.

Its recommendation of the fare rise was based upon conferences with representatives of the taxicab industry and the committee's analysis of fiscal data submitted by these representatives.

When he named the committee, the Mayor said he would not favor a rise in fares unless the lion's share of the additional revenue was used to give fleet drivers and other employes such benefits as medical care programs.

In the last few weeks the owners of about half of the 11,700 taxicabs in the city have

Continued on Page 35, Column 5

KENNEDY ORDERS AIR-SAFETY PLAN STARTED AT ONCE

Traffic-Control System Will Check Planes' Altitude by Skyborne Transmitters

500 MILLION IS NEEDED

Program Sets Up Restricted Areas for Use by Craft Under Ground Guidance

By RICHARD WITKIN

President Kennedy has ordered an immediate start on a radically revised program to modernize the nation's system of air-traffic control.

The new concept is keyed to the use of a special type of radio transmitter known as a beacon. Each plane under air-traffic control would carry a beacon that would radio the plane's altitude to traffic control centers.

The overhauling of the traffic control system is the major feature of a 146-page "Study of the State and Efficient Use of Airspace." The study, made public yesterday, was drawn up by an eight-man task force created last spring at the request of the President.

Suggestions Are Listed

Among the major recommendations of the study, known as Project Beacon, were these:

¶There should be a great expansion of the areas set aside exclusively for planes flying under strict guidance of the ground-control system. This would be done to minimize the dangerous mixing of controlled and uncontrolled flying.

¶All planes weighing 12,500 pounds or more should be required to carry the altitude-reporting beacons. These beacons would be usable not only in terminal areas but also between airports.

¶When a $500 short-range beacon is perfected, it should be required on all planes that land at designated controlled airports.

¶A new category of flight should be created to permit pilots who are not now qualified for controlled flights to take advantage of the control system when the weather is good. Today, only pilots qualified to fly in instrument weather—that is, in clouds—are permitted to make use of the ground-control network.

¶In busy terminal areas, planes should be segregated according to performance so that fast, medium-speed and relatively slow craft would approach and leave airports along different corridors.

¶A speed limit should be imposed on all planes flying below 8,000 feet.

Computers Are Used

Under the new program, the beacons would reply to pulses sent from radar equipment on the ground.

Each beacon, connected to an altimeter, would repeatedly transmit to the ground the altitude of the plane carrying it. It would also enhance, or strengthen, the radar blip, a small streak of light, indicating on the ground radarscope the plane's horizontal position.

The altitude information would be processed by a computer on the ground. It would be insert-

Continued on Page 16, Column 4

Nehru Spends 3 Hours on Smiling Tour of Disneyland

Prime Minister Jawaharlal Nehru tours park in an electric car with host, Walt Disney
Associated Press Wirephoto

Special to The New York Times.

LOS ANGELES, Nov. 12—Prime Minister Jawaharlal Nehru of India arrived at Los Angeles today and almost immediately began a three-hour tour of Disneyland. Mr. Nehru, who flew here from New York for a two-day visit was greeted by Mayor Samuel W. Yorty, who said with a smile, that he understood Mr. Nehru was making his first visit to Southern California so that he could see Disneyland. The Prime Minister, with a smile of his own, corrected the misapprehension. "I was invited here some time in the past and at that time the question of Disneyland did not arise," he said. "Of course, I

Continued on Page 7, Column 1

---

73 Polish Women, Nazi Victims, To Get Indemnities From Bonn

By ARTHUR J. OLSEN
Special to The New York Times.

WARSAW, Nov. 12 — The Polish Red Cross and West German Government will pay up to $10,000 in compensation to each of seventy-three Polish women victims of Nazi medical experiments during World War II.

An agreement announced by the Polish Red Cross today is the first instance of West German indemnification of persons living behind the Iron Curtain. In general Bonn rejects claims from Eastern Europe on the ground that it lacks assurance that the real victims would benefit.

The Bonn Government, which is represented in Polish propaganda as dominated by neo-Nazis, was mentioned only obscurely in the Polish Red Cross announcement.

The compensation agreement for the so-called Ravensbrueck guinea pigs was concluded be-tween the Polish Red Cross and the International Red Cross Committee, acting on behalf of the West German Government.

A key role in the negotiations was played by Norman Cousins, editor of The Saturday Review, who has taken an active interest in the women victims of the Hiroshima bombing and the Nazi medical experiments at the Ravensbrueck and Dachau concentration camps. Through his efforts groups of Japanese and Polish women have gone to the United States for treatment.

Benjamin Ferencz, a New York lawyer representing the Hiroshima Peace Center Association, which was set up by Mr. Cousins to help Japanese girls.

Continued on Page 12, Column 4

Charity Balls in City Increasing In Number, Size and Complexity

By NAN ROBERTSON

Among those who toil for charity there is an epigram that runs: "Name a disease and there's a ball for it."

This was never more true than today. About 120 charity balls of social importance have been scheduled in New York City for the 1961-62 social season, triple the number five years ago. This month and next the galas will be checking in and out of the hotels like traveling salesmen.

Most raise money for charities that try to prevent, cure or ease more physical and mental complaints than ever afflicted Job.

A few dances aid schools, churches, settlement houses, the poor of all ages and such causes as the officers of the former Imperial Russian Cavalry and Horse Artillery and Planned Parenthood for Pets, run this year by Mrs. Frothingham Wagstaff.

At the charity balls considered "social," good names attend in driblets or en masse. Almost all are held at five Manhattan hotels: Plaza, Pierre, St. Regis, Sheraton-East and Waldorf-Astoria.

The people who go come from a big range of backgrounds. Among those present at the latest April in Paris Ball were the Marquis de Montesquiou, Duc de Fezensac, flown from Paris, and Sal Mineo from Throgs Neck, the Bronx.

The roster of charity-ball faithfuls also includes society and fashion publicists, columnists, designers and manufacturers whose dresses are paraded at the party, merchants who underwrite some or all of the ball's expenses, stars of the stage, screen and television, and cafe society.

And this season, the guest

Continued on Page 39, Column 1

The Viet Cong's arms came from many diverse sources; among them were weapons captured in Korea and channeled through the Chinese. The guerrilla in the forefront carries a U.S.-made Browning Automatic.

The Vietnam Air Force's tactical fighters surprise a Viet Cong barracks area housing enemy soldiers, with a low-level fire bomb attack.

The New York Times.

LATE CITY EDITION
U. S. Weather Bureau Report (Page 66; forecast:
Cloudy today, tonight and tomorrow.
Cooler, possible rain tomorrow.
Temp. range: 46—34; yesterday: 40—34.

VOL. CXI..No. 38,020.   © 1962 by The New York Times Company.   NEW YORK, TUESDAY, FEBRUARY 27, 1962.   10 cents beyond 50-mile zone from New York City except on Long Island. Higher in air delivery cities.   FIVE CENTS

WAGNER SETS UP HOUSING AGENCY WITH WIDE GOALS

It Would Administer Rents, Municipal Lending and Tax-Relief Programs

AIM IS 'SLUMLESS' CITY

Mayor Says Local Law Will Treat Landlords Fairly but Penalize the 'Chiseler'

By CHARLES G. BENNETT

The creation of a city Rent and Rehabilitation Administration to carry out a broad new housing program was announced yesterday by Mayor Wagner.

At the heart of the new program will be the city's administration of rent control, a function it will take over from the state May 1. The Mayor described the new housing set-up as a massive effort to achieve a "slumless" city.

The Mayor proposes to assign to the new housing office, in addition to rent control, an expanded municipal lending program and the tax exemption and abatement program, both of which seek to spur housing rehabilitation and improvements.

The lending and tax abatement functions are now administered by the Housing and Redevelopment Board.

Mr. Wagner outlined his proposed new expanded housing program at a City Hall news conference yesterday and amplified his plans later in a 3,200-word statement.

Director Not Named

He declined to indicate whom he might select for the new top spot of commissioner or director of the projected rent administration. City Hall spec-ulation, however, included Mrs. Hortense W. Gabel, the Mayor's assistant for housing; Charles Abrams, former chair-man of the State Commission Against Discrimination, and Assemblyman Sam Spiegel.

As a new policy-making arm for housing, the Mayor designated the Housing Policy Board. He issued an executive order "confirming the existence" of this unit and establishing in it an executive committee. The Mayor noted he had created the board "informally" last year. James Felt, chairman of the city Planning Commission, was named to head the policy board executive committee.

"The executive committee and its parent body, the Housing Policy Board, will have responsibility for coordinating the entire range of the city's housing policy, subject, of course, to

Continued on Page 23, Column 2

GOVERNOR URGES CO-OP BUYING AID

Asks $200 Down Payment on Homes Up to $32,500

By LEO EGAN
Special to The New York Times

ALBANY, Feb. 26—Governor Rockefeller asked the Legislature tonight to approve a plan whereby any middle-income family with $200 in cash could buy a cooperative apartment worth up to $32,500.

In a special message, the Governor described his new plan as "a soundly practical, pioneering concept in home-financing assistance" for middle-income families.

"Thousands of financially reliable families have been barred from cooperative middle-income housing through inability to make the required down payments," Mr. Rockefeller's message said.

Under present law, down payments must represent at least 10 per cent of the purchase price of a cooperative middle-income apartment. In the case of a $32,500 apartment this would be $3,250.

Today's special message was the first of three dealing with housing and urban renewal that Governor Rockefeller expects to send to the Legisl'ure this week. The two others are expected to deal with income segregation of families in publicly assisted housing and with urban renewal.

The program for stimulating middle-income housing outlined

Continued on Page 23, Column 1

TRIUMPHANT WELCOME: Lieut. Col. John H. Glenn Jr. and his wife wave to cheering crowd on motorcade to the Capitol. Seated in the front are Vice President Johnson and Carolyn, the Glenns' 14-year-old daughter.
United Press International Telephoto

Supreme Court Reaffirms Ban on Travel Segregation

By E. W. KENWORTHY
Special to The New York Times

WASHINGTON, Feb. 26—The Supreme Court ordered a Federal court in Mississippi today to uphold quickly the right of Negroes to unsegregated transportation service.

The case came to the Supreme Court on appeal after a special three-judge Federal court in Jackson, Miss., refused to rule on the constitutionality of state and local laws requiring segregation in trains, buses, street cars, terminal waiting rooms and restaurants.

The special panel said that the meaning of these laws should first be determined by state courts that are now considering several Freedom Rider cases.

Today the Supreme Court, in a brief, unsigned opinion, said, in effect that the anti-segregation principle had been established in prior decisions.

Opinion by the Court

The Supreme Court said:

"We have settled beyond question that no state may require racial segregation of interstate or intrastate transportation facilities."

Since the question "is no longer open," the court said that there had been no need to convene the three-judge court. Under Federal law, such a tribunal is convened only when an injunction is sought to prevent enforcement of a state statute on the ground of its unconstitutionality.

"There is no such ground," the Supreme Court stated, "when the constitutional issue presented is essentially fictitious."

The court found this issue fictitious because "prior decisions" had made "frivolous any claim that a state statute on its face is not unconstitutional."

"Therefore, the court annulled the judgment of the three-judge court. It remanded the case to the district court to be heard by one judge with instructions "for expeditious disposition, in the light of this opinion, of the

Continued on Page 24, Column 2

MEANY DISPUTES GOLDBERG VIEWS

Says Government Must Not Go Beyond Mediation in Solving Labor Disputes

By STANLEY LEVEY

BAL HARBOUR, Fla., Feb. 26—George Meany served notice on Secretary of Labor Arthur J. Goldberg today to stay out of labor - management collective bargaining except in a peace-making capacity.

The President of the American Federation of Labor and Congress of Industrial Organizations made known his views in commenting on a speech last Friday by Mr. Goldberg.

His brusque rejection of what the Labor Secretary had called a "definitive" statement of the Kennedy Administration's labor - management philosophy brought clearly into focus the labor movement's increasing disenchantment with Mr. Goldberg.

View by Goldberg

In his talk before the Executives' Club in Chicago, Mr. Goldberg said that in the future, when the Government intervened in collective bargaining, it would define and assert the national interest. It would not just mediate the outstanding issues, he said.

Asked for his thoughts on the Goldberg policy, Mr. Meany said:

"I don't agree with it. The Government's role is mediation, conciliation or anything else it can do to help industrial peace.

"When he says the role of the Government is to assert the national interest, he is infringing on the rights of free people and free society, and I don't agree with him whatsoever.

"This is a step in the direction of saying the Federal Government should tell either or both sides [in an industrial dispute] what to do, and I don't agree with that."

Mr. Meany made clear that he was speaking his own mind in voicing these views. He said the Executive Council of the

Continued on Page 18, Column 1

RIGHTIST RAMPAGE KILLS 13 IN ALGIERS

Moslems Massacred in Busy City Streets—12 Others Wounded by Gunmen

By PAUL HOFMANN
Special to The New York Times

ALGIERS, Feb. 26—European terrorists went on a midday rampage in the heart of Algiers today, killing thirteen Moslems and wounding a dozen in an hour and a half.

The massacre took place in rush-hour traffic in the main streets of the European center.

The new wave of violence, following similar outbreaks in other parts of the city during the last few days, took the police and the army by surprise. Few troops were on patrol duty in the area when the attacks started at 11 A. M.

The forces were unable to prevent the killings and succeeded in arresting only one alleged terrorist, a young European brandishing a gun. His name was withheld.

More Troops Sought

An official said later that the civilian administration was exerting pressure on the army to deploy more troops in Algiers.

Military sources indicated that the army was resisting these civilian demands, preferring to keep at least half of its men in reserve in case major clashes broke out.

About 45,000 troops are understood to be concentrated in the Algiers area in view of the expected announcement of a cease-fire halting the Algerian war. Two beheaded bodies, be-

Continued on Page 8, Column 5

Democrats to Name McKeon State Chief

By CLAYTON KNOWLES

William H. McKeon, a 41-year-old Auburn lawyer, won unanimous backing last night from Mayor Wagner and key Democratic leaders in the state that assures him of election as Democratic state chairman.

The Democratic State Committee will meet under special call Thursday afternoon at the Biltmore Hotel to oust Michael H. Prendergast as chairman and to choose a successor.

The leaders who committed themselves to Mr. McKeon in a two-and-a-half-hour meeting at Gracie Mansion represented a dozen counties that cast 167 of the 300 votes on the state committee.

And leaders present, coming from points as remote as Erie and Nassau, Albany and Broome, could speak with reasonable authority for state

Continued on Page 20, Column 4

U. S.-French Strain Laid to Paris Plan For Nuclear Force

By ROBERT C. DOTY
Special to The New York Times

PARIS, Feb. 26—An authoritative French Government source said today that relations between France and the United States would remain unsettled as long as Washington opposed France's ambitions to become an independent nuclear power and a major European military force.

There was good evidence that the speaker was reflecting accurately the basic views of President de Gaulle, even if these were expressed in stronger language than the President might employ.

French discontent with the current balance of nuclear power and influence in the North Atlantic Treaty Organization is at the root of most of the frictions in the alliance.

France Refuses to Defer

These frictions include French resistance to further integration of French forces under international command, hostility to the idea of a nuclear test ban, refusal to envisage any negotiations with the Soviet Union on Berlin and criticism of United States policy in the African and Asian worlds and of the United States-backed action of the United Nations in the Congo.

French positions on all of these issues could be summarized as a refusal to defer to United States leadership and nowhere is this more apparent than in the domain of nuclear power.

France refuses, and is likely to continue to refuse, to rely for nuclear protection on the

Continued on Page 5, Column 1

GLENN IS CHEERED IN CAPITAL MARCH AND IN CONGRESS

Thousands Stand in the Rain to Welcome Astronaut— He Foresees New Era

Transcript of Glenn's speech to Congress, Page 16.

By RUSSELL BAKER
Special to The New York Times

WASHINGTON, Feb. 26—This normally blasé capital put up its umbrella and stood in a chilling downpour today to offer its unabashed admiration to the first American to orbit the earth.

Lieut. Col. John H. Glenn Jr. was cheered up Pennsylvania Avenue to the Capitol by thousands and thousands of drenched spectators in a demonstration of human and national emotion such as Washington rarely gives.

At the Capitol, his hair still damp from the bare-headed ride through the rain, Colonel Glenn spoke for seventeen minutes to a joint meeting of Congress and, through most of it controlled the politicians as nimbly as he handled his Mercury capsule last week.

One To Be Proud Of

Secretary of Defense Robert S. McNamara, spoke the consensus afterward when he called the Glenn appearance "magnificent."

"He showed poise and charm," the Secretary said. "He is an American that all of us can be proud of."

In his speech the 40-year-old marine did just about everything that befits the idolized American hero.

To the obvious delight of the Congressmen, who regard most joint meetings as trials of ritualistic solemnity, he smashed protocol by introducing his family, his friends and his colleagues in the galleries and on the floor.

Interpolating freely and with aplomb in his prepared text, he struck the patriotic chord.

"I know I still get a real hard-to-define feeling down inside when the flag goes by and I know all of you do, too," he said.

During today's outpouring of people along Pennsylvania Avenue, he said, "I got that same feeling. Let's hope that none of us ever lose it."

Advance in Knowledge Cited

Then the astronaut went on to talk about the advance of knowledge that would come from space exploration.

"Seriously, though," he said, "I feel we are on the threshold of an area of expansion of knowledge about ourselves and our surroundings that is beyond description or comprehension at this time."

"Knowledge begets knowledge," he said a little later. "The more I see, the more impressed I am not with how much we know but with how tremendous the areas are that as yet unexplored.

"Well, the real benefits we probably cannot even detail.

Continued on Page 16, Column 1

Voting Lead Taken By Krishna Menon

Special to The New York Times

BOMBAY, India, Tuesday, Feb. 27—Defense Minister V. K. Krishna Menon had gained a two-to-one lead in his North Bombay constituency by the time the counting of votes ended there last night.

Archarya J. B. Kripalani contested Mr. Krishna Menon's seat in the lower house of Parliament in one of the most bitterly fought campaigns of India's third general elections.

With less than one-fifth of an estimated total of 450,000 North Bombay ballots counted, Mr. Krishna Menon held 53,959 votes to 28,865 for Mr. Kripalani, who had been backed by all parties except the ruling Congress party and the Communists.

The final result will be

Continued on Page 6, Column 2

PRESIDENT URGES PEACE CORPS RISE

Proposes Doubling Strength to 6,700 by Mid-1963— Hails Achievements

By TOM WICKER
Special to The New York Times

WASHINGTON, Feb. 26—President Kennedy told Congress today that the Peace Corps had "successfully weathered its experimental period" and should be more than doubled in size.

He submitted legislation that would permit the corps to have 6,700 volunteer workers in the field by June 30, 1963. It now has an authorized strength of 2,480, he noted, and will reach that size by next June 30.

"Another 2,700 are scheduled to enter training in July or August of this year," Mr. Kennedy said in a letter accompanying the bill. The letter was sent to House Speaker John W. McCormack and Vice President Johnson.

To accomplish the proposed expansion, the Peace Corps budget would be more than doubled. Last year Congress authorized $40,000,000 for the corps in the 1962 budget, but appropriated only $30,000,000.

The President's bill would authorize $63,750,000 for the fiscal year ending June 30, 1963.

He said the measure was "clearly justified," as the corps' "early successes have fulfilled expectations."

The best proof, he said, is that "every one of the twelve countries in which volunteers are now at work has requested additional volunteers."

He said the volunteers had

Continued on Page 13, Column 1

TWO PLANES BOMB PALACE IN SAIGON; DIEM KEEPS RULE

LEADER IS UNHURT

Attack Believed Made by Dissident Pilots —Building Afire

By The Associated Press

SAIGON, Vietnam, Tuesday, Feb. 27—Two fighter-bombers bearing markings of the South Vietnam Air Force attacked President Ngo Dinh Diem's palace with bombs, rockets and machine guns today. The Saigon radio announced an hour later that the President and his family were safe.

One wing of the palace was left in flames. The attackers also strafed the Saigon Airport.

The 41-year-old bachelor President, his brother Ngo Dinh Nhu and Mme. Ngo Dinh Nhu were in the palace at the time.

The Government broadcast said one of the planes, identified by American sources as AD-6 Skyraiders, crashed near the capital. The AD-6 is an attack craft that was used by the United States Navy in World War II and later supplied by the United States to South Vietnam's Air Force.

Defense Line Set Up

It was not known who piloted the planes. The only military movements in Saigon were by Government troops, who were setting up a defense perimeter around the palace.

[In Tokyo, a report received from the South Vietnam press agency said the planes had been piloted by rebel members of the South Vietnam Air Force. The pilot of the plane that crashed was said to have been captured. In Washington, United States officials said President Ngo Dinh Diem was in control of the situation. They regarded the attack as an isolated incident and not as a widespread conspiracy.]

The planes made repeated passes over the Presidential Palace at low altitude, dropping napalm (jellied gasoline), firing rockets and strafing.

Attack Lasts 50 Minutes

The attack began at 4:50 A. M. Saigon time and lasted for fifty minutes. Light anti-aircraft guns and machine guns on the ground fired back at the planes as they circled over the heart of the city before each pass.

Six tanks and armored cars rolled up in front of the palace gate at the height of the attack and firemen rushed into the palace.

Small-arms fire was heard from the direction of the Saigon Airport, four miles from the palace.

In a broadcast after the attack the Vietnamese President said:

"Thanks to the Almighty's protection, I and all the people in the palace were unharmed. There was only some material damage.

"All defense and security measures have been taken. All

Continued on Page 5, Column 1

Irish Terrorists End Violence on Border

Special to The New York Times

DUBLIN, Feb. 26—The Irish Republican Army announced today the end of its campaign of violence against Northern Ireland.

In the last five years the outlawed army's hit-and-run attacks against Northern Ireland's police stations, custom posts and police patrols and blowing up of post office vans, telephone kiosks and bridges have caused damage estimated at the equivalent of $14,000,000. In that period six Northern Irish policemen and nine I. R. A. terrorists have been killed.

The announcement of the end of hostilities was made in a communication to all the daily newspaper offices in Dublin. It was signed by James McGarrity, who described himself as the secretary of the Irish Republican publicity bureau.

Mr. McGarrity has issued

Continued on Page 8, Column 5

PROTEST NUCLEAR TESTS which poison AIR, KIDNEYS, give cancer, race. Write Pres., Senator and Congressmen. See page 21.—Advt.

ALGIERS STREET SCENE: Pedestrian walks by body of Moslem shot by terrorists yesterday on Rue Michelet
United Press International Radiophoto

"All the News That's Fit to Print"

The New York Times.

LATE CITY EDITION

U. S. Weather Bureau Report (Page 66) forecasts: Warm, early and late showers today. Clearing tonight, fair tomorrow. Temp. range: 82—67; yesterday: 81—63. Temp.-Hum. Index: mid-70's; yesterday: 76.

VOL. CXII..No. 38,560. © 1963 by The New York Times Company. Times Square, New York 36, N. Y. NEW YORK, WEDNESDAY, AUGUST 21, 1963. TEN CENTS

CRISIS IN SOUTH VIETNAM DEEPENS AS DIEM'S FORCES RAID PAGODAS; U.S. SEES ITS TROOPS ENDANGERED

KENNEDY OPPOSES QUOTAS FOR JOBS ON BASIS OF RACE

Says Education Is Greatest Need of Negroes—Doubts U.S. Can 'Repair Past'

RIGHTS BILLS PRESSED

Congress Urged to Act This Session—Election Year Pressure in '64 Cited

Transcript of news conference and summary, Page 14.

By CABELL PHILLIPS
Special to The New York Times

WASHINGTON, Aug. 20 — President Kennedy said today that he disapproved of employment quotas based on race.

This device has been proposed as a means of correcting the effects of past discrimination against Negroes in hiring. The theory is that Negroes should be given jobs in rough proportion to their representation in the population.

The President told his news conference this afternoon, however, that he felt such a solution would lead to a "good deal of trouble." The American society, he said, is too complex and too mixed to make such a practice feasible. [Question 11, Page 14.]

Mr. Kennedy said that Negroes had suffered a long accumulation of injustices. But he doubted that the nation could repair the past through any scheme of special or preferential compensation.

Calls Education Vital

The greatest need of the Negro both in redressing his grievances of the past and improving his lot in the present, the President said, is education.

Negroes would like to see their children well educated, he said, "so that they could hold jobs" and become "accepted as equal members of the community."

"I don't think we can undo the past," Mr. Kennedy asserted. "I don't think quotas are a good idea. I think we'd get into a good deal of trouble."

The President was emphatic in saying that he saw no good reason that Congress should put over action on his civil rights bill until next year.

His comment came in response to a question suggesting that this probably would be the result of the crowding of the legislative calendar.

The Senate majority leader, Mike Mansfield of Montana, said yesterday that it might be Christmas before the civil rights bill was taken up.

Mr. Kennedy said that he could see no advantage in putting the bill over until next year.

He said there would be as many excuses by Congress "to

Continued on Page 23, Column 1

Khrushchev Is Welcomed by Tito

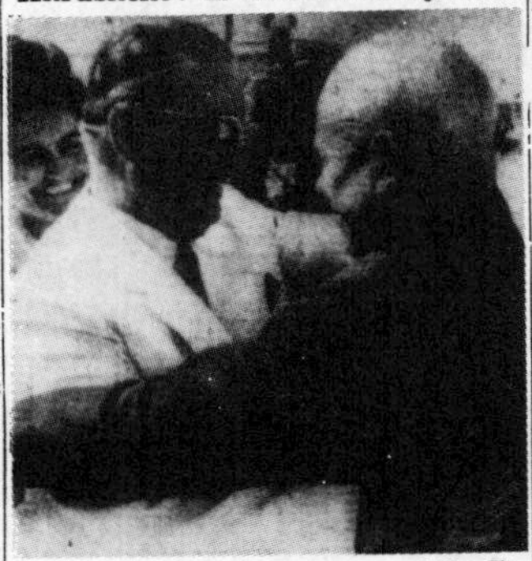

The Soviet Premier, right, with President and Mrs. Tito

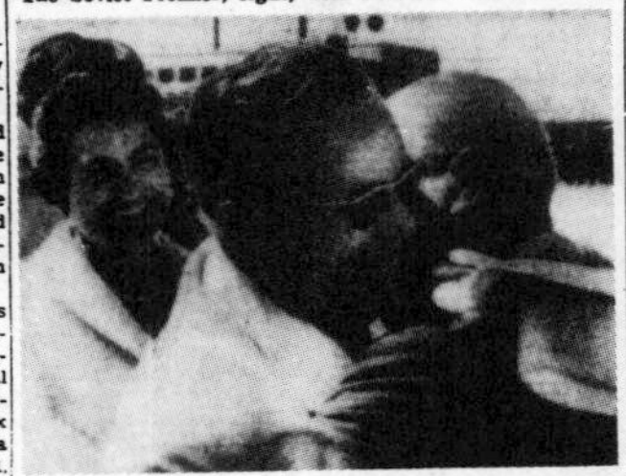

Associated Press

Soviet and Yugoslav leaders embrace at Belgrade Airport

MAYOR INDICATES TAX GAP IS LIKELY

In Annual Message, He Says City May Need New Levies —Pledges Economies

By CHARLES G. BENNETT

Mayor Wagner indicated yesterday that new or increased taxes would be required to meet the city's needs in the fiscal year beginning July 1, 1964.

In his annual message to the City Council, the Mayor said: "I cannot give assurance that our present tax resources will be sufficient to meet next year's needs."

Just before the Mayor spoke, his address was amended to include a promise to economize, to "maximize" available revenues and to avoid new taxes if possible.

Bill Is Before Council

The addition to the text apparently resulted from a feeling by the Mayor and his aides that the afternoon newspapers, TV and radio were unduly emphasizing the possibility of added taxes in 1964-65.

Speaking to an audience that included not only the City Councilmen, but also about 30 city commissioners, agency heads, deputies and aides, the Mayor asked the Council to establish a citizens' commission "to consider our entire fiscal picture in the light of our expanding budgetary needs."

Such a commission would review the city's sources of revenue and study "other possible sources." Bills calling for a commission of this nature are now pending before the City Council. If the group is to be

Continued on Page 21, Column 2

Khrushchev Begins Visit to Yugoslavia; Lauds Tito Regime

By DAVID BINDER
Special to The New York Times

BELGRADE, Yugoslavia, Aug. 20—Premier Khrushchev opened a 15-day visit to Yugoslavia today by declaring that the Soviet Union regarded the country as "Socialist" and "fraternal."

Although not a blanket endorsement of the type of socialism practiced by the independent Communist Government of President Tito, Mr. Khrushchev's remarks, made at the Belgrade Airport, appeared to be a direct rebuke to the Chinese Communist leadership.

The Peking regime, which was represented at the airport ceremony by a second secretary instead of its embassy's chargé d'affaires, has vehemently insisted for the last five years that Yugoslavia has been practicing heresy to Marxism-Leninism.

Premier Khrushchev, his face still pink from a holiday on the shores of the Black Sea, spoke with great warmth about Yugoslavia. He added that Moscow would continue to strive for closer relations with Belgrade as a matter of ideological principle.

"The Communst party of the Soviet Union and the Soviet Government," Mr. Khrushchev said, "are building relations with Socialist Yugoslavia, led by the Leninist principles of foreign policy, the principles of Socialist internationalism."

"There is no doubt," he added, "that the present visit will serve the cause of further strengthening friendship and cooperation between our countries and peoples." For his part,

Continued on Page 9, Column 1

COUNCIL APPROVES BET REFERENDUM

Voters to Be Asked to Back a Study Commission

By CHARLES GRUTZNER

The City Council ordered yesterday a referendum in the November election to let New York City voters indicate whether they favored off-track betting.

An emergency message of necessity from Mayor Wagner permitted the Council to vote the same day the measure was introduced, dispensing with a public hearing. The vote was 20 in favor, 3 against and 1 abstention.

The referendum, described privately by an aide of the Mayor as a "gimmick," can have no legal standing; off-track betting can be legalized only by the Legislature, whose Republican leadership has for the last 10 years turned a deaf ear on the city's plea for such action.

A strongly favorable vote, however, could bring pressure on Governor Rockefeller and the Republican legislative leaders to support permissive legislation.

The opposition in the Council made up for the scarcity of its numbers in the vehemence of its attack. The minority leader,

Continued on Page 20, Column 3

Court Backs Reform Democrats In Bid to List Slates in Primary

By RICHARD P. HUNT

A State Supreme Court justice ordered the Board of Elections yesterday to list candidates by slates on the primary election ballots, as a group of reform Democrats had urged.

Justice John J. Flynn said in a brief opinion that there was "ample" legal authority for putting slates on the ballot and that it would be "far less confusing for the average voter."

The Board of Elections immediately asked the Appellate Division of the Supreme Court to reverse Justice Flynn's decision. The Appellate justices will hear the case at 2 P.M. today, and the Court of Appeals will review it in Albany tomorrow.

This will enable the Court of Appeals, which is the state's highest court, to consider the ballot case on the same day it will review one to decide whether councilmen at large will be elected this year. The Appellate Division heard arguments in that case yesterday and reserved decision.

The Board of Elections had planned to use the form of the old paper ballot, which was used in the primary elections here until 1959, in listing candidates on the city's 2,750 new Shoup voting machines.

But four reform Democrats, acting with the support of the Committee for Democratic Voters, contended that the board's plan would make it difficult for the voters in the Sept. 5 primary to determine which candidates were running together as a team. Edward Greenfield, who

Continued on Page 20, Column 4

GET READY FOR BACK TO SCHOOL
Save time, money with ideas, advice on fall fitting-out. Page after page of valuable help in today's World-Telegram — *Advt.*

PRESIDENT VOWS U.S. WILL STEP UP ATOMIC READINESS

Disputes Teller on Danger to Security in Test Ban —Schriever Against Pact

By E. W. KENWORTHY
Special to The New York Times

WASHINGTON, Aug. 20—President Kennedy assured Congress and the country today that a program of safeguards would be vigorously carried out to insure that national security would not be jeopardized by any Soviet abrogation of the treaty to limit nuclear tests.

At his news conference, the President was asked to comment on fears expressed by some Senators during the hearings on the treaty that the safeguards proposed by the Joint Chiefs of Staff might not be diligently carried out.

"We are just as anxious," he said, "we appreciate the concern of the members of Congress, but this matter is of concern to us also and I can assure them we will do the job." [Question 1, Page 14.]

Commenting also in relation to the treaty, the President said that the United States was still "a good, long way" from formulating its final position on a possible agreement with the Soviet Union on safeguards against surprise attack. [Question 10.]

Rejects Teller View

He rejected the arguments of Dr. Edward Teller, the physicist, who continued his opposition to the treaty at a Senate hearing.

The President said "it would be very difficult, I think, to satisfy Dr. Teller in this field."

He said the physicist had "made it very clear that he is opposed" to the treaty, noting: "He opposed it all last week and this week." [Questions 3 and 16.]

There were these other developments on the treaty today:

¶In what appeared to be a gathering Air Force offensive, Gen. Bernard A. Schriever, chief of military space development, told the Senate Preparedness Subcommittee, that he could carry out his mission better without the treaty. Yesterday Gen. Thomas S. Power, head of the Strategic Air Command, opposed the treaty as inimical to the nation's interests in testimony before the same subcommittee.

¶Roswell L. Gilpatric, Deputy Secretary of Defense, told the Senate Appropriations Committee that the treaty "does not alter our assessment of the military threat confronting us now or likely to face us in the future." It was, he said, but "a small first step albeit a very important one."

¶Mike Mansfield of Montana, Senate Democratic leader, said that hearings were going well and floor debate should begin the first week in September.

Mr. Kennedy ticked off the

Continued on Page 15, Column 1

Red Force Overruns Hamlet in Vietnam

Special to The New York Times

SAIGON, Vietnam, Aug. 20 — A show-place strategic hamlet 30 miles north of here was overrun by Vietcong guerrillas yesterday morning and many of the homes were burned, military sources said today.

The hamlet, called Ben Tuong, is situated in a Communist-controlled region among rubber plantations. It was the first project of "Operation Sunrise," the plan for the organization of armed villages in the heart of the Vietcong area. The project was begun in March, 1962.

Critics of the operation say that the strategic hamlets are overextended and are neither

Continued on Page 3, Column 8

SOVIET TROOP CUT IN CUBA REPORTED

Kennedy Says Combat Units Are Departing—Others Train Castro Forces

By TAD SZULC
Special to The New York Times

WASHINGTON, Aug. 20—A decline in the number of Soviet troops in Cuba, possibly bringing the total down to about 10,000 men, was reported today by President Kennedy.

The Russians maintain a sizable program for training troops of the regime of Fidel Castro. The program concentrates on ground-to-air and coastal defense missiles, on operations of the Cuban Air Force, which is equipped with MIG jet fighters, and on other modern equipment.

The President said at his news conference that it was difficult to discuss the precise rate of the Soviet withdrawals, but his comments, combined with information from other Government quarters, seemed to indicate the Russians had removed most of their combat units from the island.

These units were estimated last June at between 4,000 and 5,000 out of a total of 12,500 men. The President said that in the opinion of the intelligence services the "primary emphasis" of the Soviet troops remaining in Cuba was "in training, and not in concentrated military units." [Questions 15 and 21, Page 14.]

Although this apparent dis-

Continued on Page 7, Column 3

State of Economy Called 'Good'; White House Presses for Tax Cut

Special to The New York Times

WASHINGTON, Aug. 20—The state of the economy was characterized today by President Kennedy as "good." But he indicated he would be worried about the future if Congress did not enact his tax reduction bill this year.

The President told his news conference that the upturn in business activity this year had been "slightly better, although not much better," than the Administration foresaw in January.

Favorable Congressional action on taxes this year, even though the actual reduction would not go into effect until January, 1964, could give a lift to economic activity in the final months of this year, he said. [Questions 6 and 14, Page 14.]

If hopes for a tax cut are disappointed and Congress takes until the middle of next year before voting tax reduction, "what would happen to the economy in the meanwhile?" the President asked.

"Right now," the President said, "I would say the state of the economy is good."

He noted in particular the rise in industrial production, which has increased from 119 per cent of its 1957-59 base in January to 127 per cent in July.

Statistics made public by the Commerce Department today bolstered the President's generally optimistic assessment. One key indicator of future business activity, the volume of new orders received by manufacturers of durable goods, rose in July. The rise followed a decline in June, which had caused some pessimism about the business outlook.

Personal income set a record in July, for the fifth straight month, although the wages received by factory workers failed to increase for the first time since January.

Housing starts were down, but this is a business indicator that has been notoriously erratic.

An increase in orders for industrial machinery was considered the most hopeful sign in the new orders statistics. Orders for this type of equipment, which fell in June, provide a clue to the future trend of business capital investment.

Government economists have

Continued on Page 16, Column 4

NEWS INDEX

BUDDHISTS SEIZED

Police Hurl Tear Gas and Grenades During Saigon Attacks

By United Press International

SAIGON, Vietnam, Wednesday, Aug. 21 — Hundreds of heavily armed policemen and soldiers, firing pistols and using tear-gas bombs and hand grenades, swarmed into the Xa Loi pagoda early today and arrested more than 100 Buddhist monks.

The big pagoda has been the scene of frequent clashes between Buddhists, demonstrating against what they call religious persecution by the Government, and Government troops.

Policemen and soldiers also stormed into three other pagodas in Saigon, but the Xa Loi pagoda is the main cathedral of the Buddhists, who have been embroiled in a religious and political crisis with the Government.

Grenade explosions were heard and tear-gas smoke could be seen rising from inside the walls of the main pagoda.

Outspoken Opponent

On Sunday more than 15,000 Buddhists held an all-day sitdown hunger strike in front of the pagoda to protest the policies of President Ngo Dinh Diem and of his sister-in-law, Mrs. Ngo Dinh Nhu, both Roman Catholics.

Mrs. Nhu, one of the most outspoken opponents of the Buddhists, has accused them of treason, murder and Communist tactics and has ridiculed the Buddhist suicides by fire.

Violence has also been reported in Hue and other Buddhist centers. Martial law was imposed yesterday in the coastal city of Danang after demonstrators clashed with soldiers during a Buddhist mass march.

Danang, about 380 miles northeast of Saigon, is headquarters for the Vietnamese First Army Corps and is a major military base on the northeast coast.

Regime Cites Protests

The Government press agency said officials imposed martial law after a Vietnamese soldier was wounded and a Government vehicle damaged during protests Sunday by about 1,000 demonstrators.

A Buddhist protest letter to President Ngo Dinh Diem said that 36 demonstrators were injured, 18 seriously, and that 200 Buddhists were arrested in Danang. It said eight priests and nuns were among those seriously injured.

Tinh Khiet, Vietnam's supreme Buddhist priest, charged that Government troops were too harsh in putting down the demonstrations.

Other sources in Saigon reported that the demonstrators in Danang numbered about 3,000. They said the trouble began when a Vietnamese Army captain and two soldiers riding in a jeep became entangled in a

Continued on Page 3, Column 6

The New York Times

RESORTING TO FORCE: President Ngo Dinh Diem of South Vietnam. His troops attacked pagodas in Saigon.

AID BILL IS 'VITAL', KENNEDY ASSERTS

In Plea to House Members for Passage, He Terms It Necessary to Security

By FELIX BELAIR Jr.
Special to The New York Times

WASHINGTON, Aug. 20—House members of both political parties were asked by President Kennedy today to support the $4,087,750,000 foreign aid authorization bill. He said it was "vital to the security and well-being of the United States and the free world."

"No party or group should call for a dynamic foreign policy and then seek to cripple this program," the President said in a statement opening his news conference.

As he was citing the fact that the legislation carries $850,000,000 less than his budget estimate of last January, Republican speakers were urging the House to cut deeper into the amount recommended by its Foreign Affairs Committee.

House Debate Limited

Debate in the House was limited to opening speeches for the record. It will be late tomorrow before the bill is read for amendment.

But an indication of the fireworks yet to come was supplied by Representative H. R. Gross, Republican of Iowa, who demanded that the Secretaries of State and Defense be prosecuted for the "lobbying" letter they sent to all House members yesterday. The letter urged support of the bill.

Nobody on either side of the aisle took Mr. Gross's proposal seriously. Wayne Hayes, Democrat of Ohio, called it "stupid."

The exchange served only as a demonstration that nothing so arouses members like the annual battle over foreign aid.

Even President Kennedy — although he read from a prepared statement — sounded impatient as he reached words anticipating efforts to "cripple"

Continued on Page 14, Column 6

Butts Gets 3-Million Libel Award For Saturday Evening Post Story

By JOHN SIBLEY
Special to The New York Times

ATLANTA, Aug. 20—A Federal jury awarded $3,060,000 today to Wally Butts, the former football coach and athletic director at the University of Georgia, in his libel suit against the publishers of The Saturday Evening Post.

The magazine, in an article March 23, had accused Mr. Butts of divulging the Georgia team's secret formations and plays to the University of Alabama coach before last season's Georgia-Alabama game in Birmingham.

The jury of 12 men announced its verdict after deliberating 7 hours 20 minutes. The jurors were closeted for slightly less than two hours this morning, after having been excused and sent to a hotel at 10:45 P.M., New York time, yesterday.

The Alabama coach, Paul (Bear) Bryant, has filed a separate libel suit against The Post in Federal Court at Birmingham. Mr. Bryant is demanding $10,000,000 damages, as did the 58-year-old Mr. Butts in this suit.

The award to Mr. Butts consisted of $60,000 in general damages to compensate him for loss of earnings and damage to his reputation, plus $3,000,000 in punitive damages. A jury may assess punitive damages only when it finds malice and "callous disregard" for the injured party.

This was the second-highest sum awarded in a libel action. In July, 1962, a New York Supreme Court jury awarded $3,500,000 to John Henry Faulk, a television entertainer who had been branded a Communist sym-

Continued on Page 41, Column 1

PHONE LINKS CUT

Threat of Martial Law Reported—U.S. Aide Protects Monks

By JAMES RESTON
Special to The New York Times

WASHINGTON, Wednesday, Aug. 21 — The United States is convinced that a major crisis is developing in South Vietnam.

Official reports reaching here indicated this morning that the conflict between the Government of President Ngo Dinh Diem and the Buddhists had created a situation that threatened the security of the Diem Government and of the United States forces in Vietnam.

Normal communications between Saigon, the South Vietnamese capital, and the United States were cut off yesterday afternoon. At that time, according to official reports reaching here, Vietnamese Government troops occupied the headquarters of the telephone and telegraph offices in Saigon.

Strict censorship was imposed on all outgoing cables and telephone calls after Government troops raided a Buddhist temple serving as the headquarters of the religious opposition to the Government.

Several Persons Hurt

It is understood that several persons were killed and several more injured in that raid.

William C. Trueheart, the United States chargé d'affaires in Saigon, is known to have reported to Washington that in the course of the Government's attack on Buddhist headquarters several monks fled into the headquarters of the United States mission. The mission has been supplying aid to the South Vietnamese Government.

Mr. Trueheart reported that Vietnamese soldiers demanded the right to enter the mission headquarters and take custody of the monks. On his own authority, Mr. Trueheart refused entry to the soldiers.

The South Vietnamese Defense Minister, Nguyen Dinh Thuan, thereupon informed Mr. Trueheart that the Diem Government would declare martial law in Saigon at 2 A.M. Saigon time (2 P.M. Tuesday, Eastern daylight time.)

But while this was reported to Washington, there was no subsequent message from Saigon to confirm that martial law had actually gone into effect.

The correspondent of The New York Times in Saigon, David Halberstam, could not be

Continued on Page 3, Column 2

ISRAEL ASKS U.N. TO MEET ON SYRIA

Appeals to Council to Curb 'Aggression' on Border

By W. GRANGER BLAIR
Special to The New York Times

JERUSALEM (Israeli Sector), Aug. 20—Israel accused Syria of aggression today and asked the United Nations Security Council to meet in urgent session.

Syrian and Israeli forces exchanged fire throughout the afternoon in the area of Ashmura, a border farm settlement in the demilitarized zone 10 miles north of the Sea of Galilee.

The army announced that two Israeli Mirage Jet fighters had attacked and damaged one of at least six Syrian MIG-17 jets that entered Israeli airspace over the demilitarized zone on the southeast shore of the Sea of Galilee. It was the first time the Mirages, recently acquired from France, had seen combat.

The Cabinet met to consider "a grave threat to peace" in the area. Haim Yahil, director general of the Foreign Ministry, said at a news conference tonight: "We feel there is a real danger to peace if the Syrian actions do not stop."

The Government acted after two Israelis were killed yesterday by Syrian armed forces

Continued on Page 2, Column 5

Airborne troops of the South Vietnamese Army trained by U.S. advisers, participate in a counterinsurgency program.

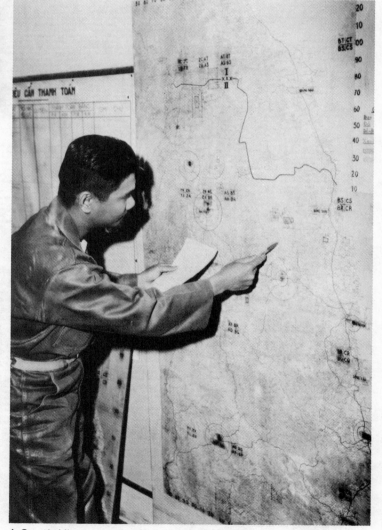

A South Vietnamese officer tries to locate a village under attack by the Viet Cong on a map. He will then direct air strikes against the guerrillas.

The New York Times.

LATE CITY EDITION
U.S. Weather Bureau Report (Page 80) forecasts:
Hazy, warm and humid today; clear and humid tonight. Fair tomorrow.
Temp. range: 86—70; yesterday: 84—69.
Temp.-Hum. Index: mid-70's; yesterday: 77.

VOL. CXII..No. 38,561. © 1963 by The New York Times Company. Times Square, New York 36, N. Y. — NEW YORK, THURSDAY, AUGUST 22, 1963. — TEN CENTS

AT-LARGE VOTING IN CITY UPHELD; NEW APPEAL DUE

Appellate Division Finds No Constitutional Violation in Council Election System

DAVIDSON RULING UPSET

Appeals Court to Hear Case Today in Albany—Decision Expected by Weekend

By LEONARD INGALLS

The city's right to hold an election for councilmen at large was upheld yesterday by the Appellate Division of the State Supreme Court.

The five-member court unanimously reversed the ruling by Justice Irwin D. Davidson on Aug. 8 that sections of the new City Charter providing for councilmen at large and their election by limited voting were unconstitutional.

In a firmly worded decision, the appellate court said that provisions for limited voting for councilmen at large in Section 22 of the Charter were "fully in accord" with the State Constitution.

It also declared that the city had the right under the home-rule powers granted by the state to determine the membership and mode of election of its local legislative body.

Action Brought by Candidate

Justice Davidson had ruled in an action brought by Robert B. Blaikie, an insurgent candidate for the Democratic nomination for councilman at large in Manhattan. Mr. Blaikie said yesterday through his lawyer, Harry H. Lipsig, that he would appeal the reversal.

The Court of Appeals, highest in the state, has agreed to hear the appeal at noon today in Albany. It has indicated it will give a decision by the end of the week.

This would leave time for the Board of Elections to prepare the ballot for the Sept. 5 primary election in which party nominations for councilman at large are being contested in Manhattan, the Bronx and Staten Island. The at-large posts are to be filled in the November election.

Council Membership Increased

The new City Charter, which became effective Jan. 1, increased the City Council from 25 to 35 members to provide greater minority representation. The Council now consists of 23 Democrats and two Republicans.

The Charter provided for election of two councilmen at large from each of the five boroughs, but limited each party to one candidate in each borough and each voter to one vote for the office.

Justice Davidson held that allowing a voter to cast only one ballot disfranchised him because he lost his vote for the second at-large post. He applied the same reasoning to the restricting of party nominations.

In its decision, the Appellate Division said:

"The provisions for limiting voting for councilmen at large contained in Section 22 of the New York City Charter, enacted as a local law of the city, are fully in accord, rather than in contravention to, constitutional provisions."

The court noted that the city

Continued on Page 31, Column 7

CONFER ON RAILROAD CRISIS: Facing camera, from left: J. E. Wolfe, chief management negotiator; Senator Warren G. Magnuson, Democrat of Washington; W. Willard Wirtz, Labor Secretary; H. E. Gilbert, head of firemen's union; Neil P. Speirs, head of switchmen's union. Foreground: John J. Gaherin, left, and E. H. Hallmann of railroads.

Associated Press

Rail Parleys Break Down On Arbitration Procedure

By HEDRICK SMITH
Special to The New York Times

WASHINGTON, Aug. 21—Efforts to devise a plan for a voluntary settlement of the nation's four-year rail dispute collapsed tonight. After virtual round-the-clock mediation, Secretary of Labor W. Willard Wirtz announced at 6:15 P.M. that there were irreconcilable differences between labor and management over the issues and procedures for voluntary arbitration.

He said he had adjourned his meetings with the two parties and was informing key Congressional leaders that there were no immediate prospects for breaking the stalemate.

This threw the problem into the lap of Congress with only seven days until a threatened national rail strike.

Senators Meet Today

The action was announced by Robert L. McManus, the Governor's press secretary, after Mr. Rockefeller and Mr. Stichman had conferred 20 minutes at the Governor's office, 22 West 55th Street.

"We're all ready to move," asserted the Washington Democrat. "We've been discussing this thing for weeks. There has to be expeditious action now."

The Senator said the committee had a number of amendments to the President's proposals to consider but that it was possible some legislation could be reported to the Senate in time for passage Friday.

He considered it more likely, however, that the Senate vote would come Monday, leaving the House three days to act before the scheduled strike.

"Of course," Mr. Magnuson added, "you always have a faint hope that something will happen to break the stalemate between labor and management."

Principle Accepted

Hopes had risen sharply five days ago when both the railroads and the five railway brotherhoods accepted voluntary arbitration in principle for two key issues—management's demands for reducing the size of train crews and eliminating 32,000 firemen's jobs.

Mr. Wirtz said that since then the two sides had exchanged proposals for the terms of an arbitration agreement that left significant differences as far as the issues to be arbitrated and the procedures to be followed.

Continued on Page 28, Column 5

WAGNER TO JOIN MARCH IN CAPITAL

Mayor Proclaims Aug. 28 as 'Jobs and Freedom Day'— Washington Maps Plans

By M. S. HANDLER

Mayor Wagner announced yesterday that he had accepted an invitation to participate in the march on Washington Aug. 28.

"I am clearing my desk so that I can get down there in time," he said.

The invitation was extended to the Mayor by Cleveland Robinson, administrative chairman of the march. Mr. Robinson said he thought Mr. Wagner might wish to be among the dignitaries who are going to the capital from all parts of the country to take part in the mass demonstration for civil rights and equal opportunities.

Mr. Wagner said that his role in Washington would be up to the persons who invited him. The leaders of the march are planning to seat all dignitaries on a platform at the Lincoln Memorial.

Mr. Wagner signed a proclamation at City Hall yesterday designating Aug. 28 as "Jobs and Freedom Day." In it, he urged all citizens to "lend their heartfelt support to the peaceful purposes" of the march on Washington.

"This demonstration of urgent protest is addressed not simply to the seat of government but to the heart and conscience of every American," the proclamation said.

The pledged participation of New York City officials and civil servants in the march was reinforced yesterday by a contingent of approximately 1,000 employes of the Welfare Department.

Commissioner James R. Dumpson, who will lead the con-

Continued on Page 18, Column 5

GOVERNOR ORDERS MARTINIS INQUIRY

Stichman Told to Examine Handling of Case Against Judge's Son in Car Deaths

Governor Rockefeller yesterday directed Herman T. Stichman, his special investigations commissioner, to "look into the handling" of the Gareth Martinis case.

The action was announced by Robert L. McManus, the Governor's press secretary, after Mr. Rockefeller and Mr. Stichman had conferred 20 minutes at the Governor's office, 22 West 55th Street.

Governor Rockefeller appointed Mr. Stichman as special investigations commissioner and special assistant attorney general on last Sept. 8. He has a staff of lawyers and investigators and the power of subpoena.

His general duties are to "investigate thoroughly and make appropriate recommendations concerning aspects of local law enforcement and the relationship between corruption or misconduct and government."

Mr. Martinis, 23-year-old son of Bronx Criminal Court Judge Joseph A. Martinis, was involved in a Bronx accident May 19 in which five persons were killed.

Wide criticism of the handling of the case followed his acquittal on July 1 of drunken driving and other charges stemming from the accident.

Subsequently, Mr. Martinis's driver's license was revoked

Continued on Page 28, Column 5

Teller's Midnight Ride Ended By Governors Wary of Speech

Opponent of Test Ban Treaty Believed Victim of Opposing Political Forces at Parley

By JOSEPH A. LOFTUS
Special to The New York Times

WHITE SULPHUR SPRINGS, W. Va., Aug. 21—Southern Governors almost heard an unscheduled speech today by Dr. Edward Teller, a foe of the treaty to limit nuclear testing.

However, when word of the invitation to the physicist got around last night, a backstage political uproar developed and a midnight ride by Dr. Teller to alert the Governors was called off quickly.

The physicist was presumably the innocent victim of opposing political forces here. His speech was scheduled and called off in a matter of hours, but there was a night of comic-opera confusion as his disappointed sponsors tried to find him and turn him back.

Dr. Teller was to take an overnight train from Washington, where he had testified against the treaty. He was to be flown back to Washington after an early morning speech so that he could address a National Press Club luncheon.

Somewhere during the night Dr. Teller left the train. Back

Continued on Page 34, Column 2

United Press International Telephoto
Dr. Edward Teller at National Press Club luncheon.

Court Reverses Ballot Ruling; Reform Plea for Slates Rejected

By RICHARD P. HUNT

The Appellate Division of the Supreme Court unanimously rejected yesterday a plea by reform Democrats to have candidates listed by slates on the primary election ballot.

The five-member court said that the Board of Elections had the legal right to rule out the old paper ballot for use on the city's voting machines.

The court thus reversed a decision handed down Tuesday by Justice John J. Flynn of the State Supreme Court, who held that listing candidates by slates would be "far less confusing to the average voter."

A lawyer for the four reform Democrats who brought the case will ask the Court of Appeals, the state's highest court, to remove the Appellate Division's ruling. The argument

Continued on Page 31, Column 1

NASSER'S FORCES ARE PUT ON ALERT AT ISRAEL BORDER

Iraq Places Her Units Under Syrians After Clashes at the Armistice Line

By Reuters

CAIRO, Aug. 21—The armed forces of the United Arab Republic were put on an emergency alert today to face "Israeli aggression against Syria," the Middle East News Agency reported tonight.

The Arab League was consulting on a "unified Arab plan" following receipt of a note from the Syrian Foreign Ministry on what Damascus called "Israeli aggression."

Meanwhile, Maj. Gen. Odd Bull, Norwegian chief of staff of the United Nations Truce Supervision Organization in Palestine, arrived in Damascus from Jordan to discuss the subject of the border situation with Syrian authorities. A United Nations spokesman said the border situation was quiet during the day.

In Amman, Jordan, Premier Sherif Hussein ben Nasser said his country always considered the eastern border between Arab countries and Israel an Arab defense line and any aggression would be considered a collective act against the Arab world.

During the day President Gamal Abdel Nasser welcomed to Cairo President Abdel Salam Arif of Iraq, who arrived for talks aimed at healing Egypt's rift with Syria and Iraq over Arab unity.

Syria Gets Iraqi Aid

DAMASCUS, Syria, Aug. 21 (AP)—Iraq placed her armed forces today under Syrian command to support Syria in the armed crisis with Israel.

Reports from Baghdad said that the Iraqi Government had placed territory adjoining Syria under military emergency.

Iraq's forces in this area, west of the Euphrates River, have been put on alert to answer any call for their service from Syria.

The Syrian Premier, Salah el-Bitar, called in the ambassadors of the United Nations Security Council members — including those of the United States, the Soviet Union, Britain and France—and gave them Syria's version of the air and land battles that flared along the armistice line yesterday.

A Foreign Ministry spokesman said that the Syrian Government also sent a telegram to the Arab League in Cairo demanding a unified Arab stand behind Syria to face "all possible eventualities" along the 70-mile demarcation line.

Syria and Iraq are parties to the Arab League Joint Defense and Economic Cooperation Treaty. The treaty says that armed aggression against one of its parties is to be considered as aggression against them all. Other members of the Arab League include the United Arab Republic, Lebanon and Yemen.

Syria called the border tensions

Continued on Page 10, Column 3

U.S. DENOUNCES VIETNAM FOR DRIVE ON BUDDHISTS; CHARGES BREACH OF VOW

Diem Orders Martial Law; More Pagodas Are Raided

All South Vietnam Placed Under Armed Forces' Control and More Buddhists Are Seized—Saigon Now Quiet

The following dispatch was transmitted from Saigon before censorship was imposed by the Vietnamese regime.

By DAVID HALBERSTAM
Special to The New York Times

SAIGON, South Vietnam, Aug. 21—President Ngo Dinh Diem ordered nationwide martial law today after Vietnamese troops and policemen had attacked Buddhist pagodas throughout the country.

Hundreds of Buddhist priests were arrested and many were beaten in the military and police action.

The situation was extremely unsettled tonight. A 9 P.M. curfew was ordered and Americans and Vietnamese both were

Continued on Page 2, Column 3

Text of martial law decree is printed on Page 2.

"bluntly warned that anyone trying to evade the police after that hour would be shot.

[Business and traffic were almost back to normal in Saigon Thursday morning, The Associated Press reported.]

High United States officials, caught by surprise by the lightning events, were reported to have been unable to see President Diem or other high South Vietnamese officials.

The tense day began shortly after midnight when heavily armed troops assaulted pagodas. Screams and gunfire were heard

---

KENNEDY CONFERS

C.I.A. Chief Is Among Aides Summoned to Discuss Strategy

By TAD SZULC
Special to The New York Times

WASHINGTON, Aug. 21 — The United States charged today that the Government of South Vietnam had violated its recent assurances that it was pursuing a policy of reconciliation with the Buddhists.

The State Department issued a strong statement within hours of being advised of the situation in South Vietnam by the United States Embassy in Saigon. It emphasized the Administration's concern and anger over violent attacks yesterday by Vietnamese forces on Buddhist pagodas in Saigon.

The statement said it appeared that the Government of South Vietnam had instituted serious repressive measures against Vietnamese Buddhist leaders.

The United States deplores repressive actions of this nature, the department said.

Kennedy Calls Meeting

At 10 A.M. President Kennedy held an emergency meeting on Vietnam. It was reported to have been attended by Under Secretary of State George W. Ball, who is acting as Secretary of State while Dean Rusk is on vacation; John A. McCone, director of the Central Intelligence Agency; Edward E. Rice, Deputy Assistant Secretary of State for Far Eastern Affairs, and other top officials.

The President canceled an appointment with A. S. J. Carnahan, the United States Ambassador to Sierra Leone, to hold the conference on Vietnam.

The vagueness of the situation in Saigon was said to have made it impossible for the President to recommend specific policy steps in what the Administration regards as a crisis of the utmost seriousness.

Mr. Kennedy ordered Henry Cabot Lodge, the new United States Ambassador to South Vietnam, to proceed at once to his post.

Lodge Gets Orders

Mr. Lodge, who had not been scheduled to fly to Saigon until next Monday, was reached by telephone in Tokyo and instructed to get to Saigon as soon as possible.

He left Tokyo for Saigon aboard a military aircraft.

[In Tokyo, Pan American World Airways reported Thursday morning that the Saigon airport had been reopened to all commercial air traffic, according to United Press International.]

Pending a clarification of the situation, officials here stressed that this morning's severe condemnation of the attacks on the Buddhists did not imply an immediate break with President Ngo Dinh Diem.

Plans here were to continue military and economic assistance to Saigon in its war

Continued on Page 2, Column 2

Tito's Worker Councils Win Khrushchev's Favor

By DAVID BINDER

RAKOVICA, Yugoslavia, Aug. 21—Premier Khrushchev said here today that the Soviet Union was ready for a "democratization" of its industrial management and workers' councils.

During a visit to an automotive and tractor factory, the Soviet leader praised the workers' councils, formerly denounced by the Soviet Union and other Communist-bloc countries as "revisionism" of Marxist-Leninist theory.

"I like the form of the workers' councils," Mr. Khrushchev said. "This is a progressive institution. Your workers' councils are not those that were formed ten years ago. They are better."

Workers' councils are management organs elected through trade-union and party units in a plant. They govern much of the administrative work and decide on wages and work quotas after consultation with the plant director.

Russians to Study System

"I am chairman of the commission that is preparing the new Soviet Constitution," Mr. Khrushchev continued.

"In this connection we are considering all sorts of new forms. We want to be more democratic and less bureaucratic.

"Our country is now ripe for a democratization of the management of enterprises. We are looking for forms that would not violate the Leninist principle of the unity of leadership. And this is why we are interested in the Yugoslav experience. In this connection we are planning to send a delegation of party workers, trade-union leaders and members of [regional] economic councils to study conditions here."

Mr. Khrushchev, who arrived in Yugoslavia yesterday on a 15-day tour, denounced the economic policies of the Chinese Communist regime. He said they preached go-it-alone Socialism while demanding Soviet credits to pay for it.

In what was regarded as an allusion to Rumania, the Soviet leader also spoke of "other countries that want to live on their own resources but only while utilizing our credits." The Rumanian Communist Government recently has pursued an economic development policy in

Continued on Page 5, Column 4

NATO BACKS BONN ON ATTACK ISSUE

Majority of Members State Opposition to Limiting of Observers to Germany

By HENRY GINIGER

PARIS, Aug. 21—A majority of the members of the North Atlantic Treaty Organization declared today their opposition to any treaty on surprise attacks that would confine observers to East and West Germany.

General support for the position of West Germany arose during discussion this morning in the Permanent Council of the organization. The effect, in the opinion of several allied diplomats here, is to make an agreement on this point with the Soviet Union extremely difficult.

The Council heard a report from Charles C. Stelle, United States delegate to the Geneva disarmament conference, that indicated that the Soviet Union was linking the question of safeguards against surprise attacks by either side to the problem of general security in Central Europe, which in practice means the two Germanys.

The two-and-a-half-hour session

Continued on Page 13, Column 1

House Rebuffs Kennedy on Aid; Passes Two Loan Restrictions

By FELIX BELAIR Jr.
Special to The New York Times

WASHINGTON, Aug. 21 — Administration forces were beaten decisively in the early voting today on the $4,087,750,000 foreign aid authorization bill. House Republicans fought determinedly against some of its provisions and many Southern Democrats avoided the battle.

The timely intervention of Speaker John W. McCormack saved the Administration from its third and most important defeat of the day. The Speaker made one of his uncommon appearances in the well of the House to remind the opposition that the revolving-fund principle in development lending, which they were about to scuttle, was a creation of the Eisenhower Administration.

With the hottest fighting over both policy and money amendments yet to come, the

Continued on Page 13, Column 1

Democratic leadership quickly adjourned the day's session so that the sectional whips could work overnight trying to regroup their forces. There had been three votes on amendments.

Even before the bill was read for amendment it was clear that reactions to other political issues were having an effect. Southern Democrats absented themselves in numbers in protest against civil rights legislation. Republicans were seizing every chance to persuade colleagues to ignore pleas for bipartisan support made yesterday by President Kennedy.

On the first real test the House voted, 142 to 126, to adopt a proposal by Representative E. Ross Adair, Republican of In-

Continued on Page 13, Column 1

U.S. ships at anchor in the bay off the Philippine Islands, preparing to set off for off-shore patrols in the Gulf of Tonkin.

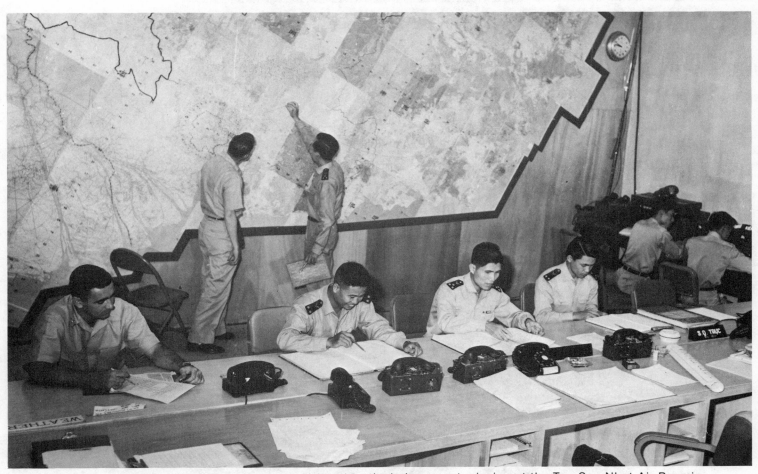

U.S. Air Force and Vietnamese Air Force personnel plan a tactical air support mission at the Tan Son Nhut Air Base in South Vietnam.

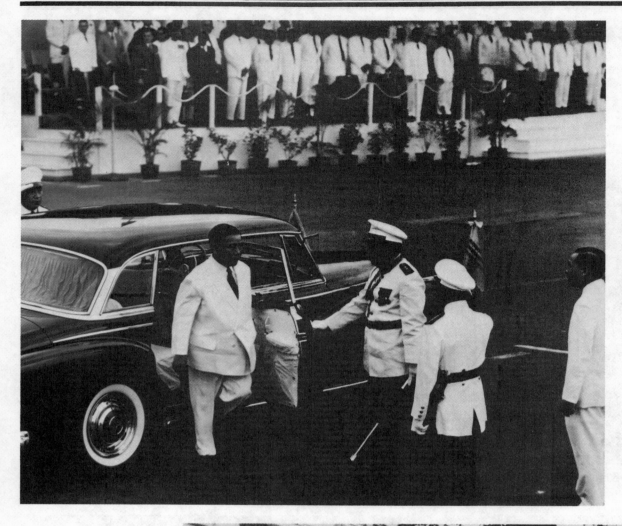

President Ngo Dinh Diem of South Vietnam arriving for the beginning of the National Day parade in Saigon in October 1962, just one year before his regime was overthrown by a coup.

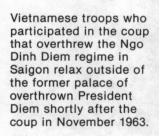

Vietnamese troops who participated in the coup that overthrew the Ngo Dinh Diem regime in Saigon relax outside of the former palace of overthrown President Diem shortly after the coup in November 1963.

"All the News That's Fit to Print"

The New York Times.

LATE CITY EDITION
U. S. Weather Bureau Report (Page 52) forecasts:
Cloudy, cool and windy today; fair and colder tonight. Fair tomorrow.
Temp. range: 52-42; yesterday: 53-48.

VOL. CXIII. No. 38,633.
© 1963 by The New York Times Company.
Times Square New York 36, N. Y.

NEW YORK, SATURDAY, NOVEMBER 2, 1963.

TEN CENTS

RUSSIANS REPORT LAUNCHING CRAFT THAT SHIFTS ORBIT

Major Advance Is Claimed for Rendezvous in Space —More Shots Predicted

KHRUSHCHEV JUBILANT

He Expresses Support for a U.S.-Soviet Lunar Trip if Tensions Are Eased

By THEODORE SHABAD
Special to The New York Times

MOSCOW, Nov. 1—The Soviet Union announced the launching today of a new type of maneuverable satellite in a major step toward perfecting rendezvous techniques in space. Shortly afterward Premier Khrushchev indicated support for a joint Soviet-American moon project.

The unmanned earth-controlled spaceship, called Polyot 1, or Flight 1, appeared to have the same capability as that sought in the United States Gemini project, which is still under development.

It reportedly performed extensive horizontal and vertical maneuvers that moved it from its initial nearly circular orbit with an apogee (maximum distance from earth) of 368 miles to a greatly elongated orbit with an apogee of 882 miles.

There was no indication whether the satellite was being guided by telemetry from the ground or had been programed before its launching.

Stresses Joint Flights

As the teletype machines of Tass, the Soviet press agency, clattered out the communiqué on the launching, Premier Khrushchev announced the news at a reception for Premier Prince Souvanna Phouma of Laos.

Smiling and triumphant, with his hands folded in a characteristic pose across his stomach, the Soviet leader said that the new vehicle offered "unlimited" possibilities in space exploration.

"Man is no longer a prisoner of his ship, but can make the ship obey his will," Mr. Khrushchev said.

Noting that the Soviet Union had studied "with attention" President Kennedy's proposal for a joint United States-Soviet manned moon flight, Mr. Khrushchev said:

"What could be better than to send a Russian and an American to the moon together, or better yet, a Russian man and an American woman?"

Anastas I. Mikoyan, a First Deputy Premier, who was standing behind Mr. Khrushchev during his first public appearance after a recent illness, joined in the general laughter that followed. Soviet propagandists have tried

Continued on Page 9, Column 1

WOODS REOPENED IN MOST OF STATE

Rain Permits Hunting Again —Water Still Short

Governor Rockefeller reopened virtually all the state's woodlands after intermittent rains had reduced the danger of forest fires. His order also meant, in most counties, the reinstatement of the hunting season, which had been halted Oct. 13.

However, the trace of rain that fell on New York City's watershed did little or nothing to replenish its reservoirs. Commissioner Armand D'Angelo of the Department of Water Supply, Gas and Electricity said that at 8 A.M. yesterday the city's water supply was at only 29.1 per cent of capacity.

Mr. D'Angelo pointed out that a year ago on this date, the city's six upstate reservoirs were at 42.7 per cent of capacity and that two years ago they contained 67.7 per cent of capacity.

Appealing for conservation of water, city officials said that care could save 100 million gallons of water by next June, or about one-fifth of the reservoirs' capacity.

More rain fell here in the first day of November than in the entire month of October. The weather bureau said it had recorded 0.59 inches of rain during the 24-hour period. The

Continued on Page 52, Column 2

14 Indicted on L. I. In Party Vandalism

Special to The New York Times

RIVERHEAD, L. I., Nov. 1—Thirteen young men and one young woman were indicted today for causing $3,202 worth of damage at a Southampton mansion after a debutante party on the night of Aug. 31. Several are members of prominent families in New York and Philadelphia.

A Suffolk County grand jury charged them with destruction of property, a misdemeanor carrying upon conviction a maximum penalty of six months in jail and a $250 fine.

District Attorney Bernard C. Smith said the 14 would be permitted to surrender voluntarily next Friday. But, he said, he will seek to extradite any of those living outside the state who do not

Continued on Page 12, Column 2

INSURRECTION LAW IN GEORGIA VOIDED

U.S. Court Prohibits, 2 to 1, Trial of 4 in Americus— Integrationists Bailed

By CLAUDE SITTON
Special to The New York Times

AMERICUS, Ga., Nov. 1 — A Federal court handed down an injunction today prohibiting the prosecution of four civil rights workers on state insurrection charges.

It declared, in a 2-to-1 decision, that the insurrection statute was unconstitutional.

The three-judge panel also directed local authorities to set reasonable bail on additional state and city charges against the four and two other persons. The six were freed immediately on bonds totaling $11,150. Officials of the state, Sumter County and Americus were given until next January by the court to prepare their defense against charges that they had engaged in a conspiracy to suppress the civil rights movement here.

Two Laws Affected

The injunction against these officials applies to prosecution of the insurrection charges, which carry a maximum penalty of death, and charges of unlawful assembly. Both statutes were held unconstitutional by the court.

Lawyers said the actions marked the first time that the Federal judiciary had halted a state court proceeding in a civil rights case at the request of a private party.

The court held that it had the power to do so under the Civil Rights Act of 1870 and an amendment to the Civil Rights Act of 1957.

The act of 1870 gives district courts jurisdiction over civil actions initiated by a person to end a denial of his constitutional rights by a state or its officials. It also entitles him to recover damages or obtain equitable relief under any Congressional act providing for the protection of civil rights.

The amendment of 1957 makes the statutory authority to enjoin a state court proceeding

Continued on Page 12, Column 5

SENATE REFUSES TO ASK DEEP CUT FOR FOREIGN AID

Turns Back, 46-29, Motion by Morse Urging Revision of Bill by Committee

By FELIX BELAIR Jr.
Special to The New York Times

WASHINGTON, Nov. 1—The Senate rallied behind its leaders today and blocked a move by dissident Democrats to return the $4.2 billion foreign aid authorization to the Foreign Relations Committee for possibly heavy pruning.

In a 46-29 vote it rejected a recommittal motion by Senator Wayne Morse and set the stage for a favorable vote next week on a proposal to cut the authorization by $385 million.

The proposal, designed to head off even deeper cuts on the floor, was sponsored by Mr. Morse, Democrat of Oregon, as the "powerhouse amendment."

The plan was put before the Senate late yesterday by Senators Mike Mansfield and Everett McKinley Dirksen, the Democratic and Republican leaders, respectively. It was cosponsored by the two top-ranking members of both parties on the Foreign Relations Committee.

Morse Is Ridiculed

Senator Dirksen mocked and ridiculed Senator Morse and his recommittal motion with mimicry and sarcasm. Although Mr. Dirksen left the Senators and gallery spectators rocking with laughter, Mr. Morse appeared more determined than ever to prolong consideration of the bill.

Assuming an attitude of high moral rectitude, and using the familiar gestures of the Oregon Senator, Mr. Dirksen recalled Mr. Morse's blanket objection to any agreement limiting debate and added that "he can just stew in his own juice."

Mr. Dirksen invoked a vision of Senators in red flannels, sitting around Christmas trees with their grandchildren, and then held his head in his hands as he enacted their frustration and despair at having to return to the Senate to resume consideration of the foreign assistance authorization.

Margin Nearly 2 to 1

He said, "The clock and the calendar are running out on this session of the Senate" and noted the important measures on which the Senate had yet to act. But he added:

"With a decent approach and with no Senator feeling that all the wisdom reposes in him alone, we can get out of here on schedule."

Winding up his performance, the Republican leader said the motion to return the bill to committee "comes with poor grace from the senior Senator from Oregon who, because of his personal frustration and because he doesn't like it, wants to take another whack at it."

In the voting that followed, 29 Democrats were joined by 17 Republicans to provide a margin of nearly 2 to 1 against the motion, while 21 Democrats and 8 Republicans were recorded in its support.

Normally, the unwritten rules of senatorial courtesy require that a member be notified when

Continued on Page 8, Column 2

Czechs, Malaysians To Split U.N. Term

By ALEXANDER BURNHAM
Special to The New York Times

UNITED NATIONS, N. Y., Nov. 1—The General Assembly gave its approval today to a gentlemen's agreement whereby Czechoslovakia and Malaysia would split a two-year term on the Security Council. It then elected Czechoslovakia for the first year.

The approval followed 11 ballots by the Assembly on Oct. 18 and Oct. 25 in an effort to choose between the two.

After two weeks of consultations with other countries, the Czechs and Malaysians agreed to share the term.

Before today's secret vote the Assembly president, Dr. Carlos Sosa Rodriguez, said that if the delegations agreed to the arrangement Czechoslovakia would be the sole candidate for election.

Czechoslovakia then received

Continued on Page 6, Column 6

MOROCCANS SAY TRUCE IS VIOLATED

Accuse Algeria of 2d Attack at the Border—Ben Bella Denies Earlier Charge

By Reuters

RABAT, Morocco, Saturday, Nov. 2—Moroccan military officials said early today that Algeria broke the cease-fire in border fighting a few minutes after it became effective at midnight.

The officials said Algerian forces launched a "violent attack" toward the Sahara town of Figuig.

The Moroccan announcement came shortly after the Algerian News Agency had reported that Algerian forces on the desert frontier ceased fire at midnight in accordance with the agreement reached Wednesday in Bamako, Mali, by President Ahmed Ben Bella of Algeria and King Hassan II of Morocco.

A local Moroccan Army command said firing was still heard from the heights above Figuig more than 45 minutes after the cease-fire time.

Yesterday King Hassan reported that Moroccan forces withdrew from Figuig earlier in the face of Algerian artillery.

[In Algiers, President Ben Bella said the accusation by King Hassan was a ruse. He countered with a charge that the Moroccans had shelled a village in Algerian territory.]

The Algerian agency said President Ben Bella's troops would remain on guard against provocations and the country would strictly observe the conditions of the agreement.

The truce agreement was

Continued on Page 5, Column 3

POLES TRY TO END SOVIET-CHINA RIFT

Tell Envoys to Use Every Chance for Mediation

By PAUL UNDERWOOD
Special to The New York Times

WARSAW, Nov. 1—Poland's Communist leadership was reported today to be trying to mediate the ideological quarrel between the Soviet Union and Communist China.

Many of the world's Communist parties, including the Polish, have made repeated calls for an end to the bitter polemics. Diplomatic sources report that the Polish Ambassadors in Moscow and Peking have been told by Warsaw to make themselves available if any opportunity for peace-making efforts arises. It is assumed that other Polish officials have received similar instructions.

The whole weight of Polish influence within the Communist world is being directed toward calming tempers on both sides.

The chances for a truce in the dispute seems to have improved as a result of Premier Khrushchev's call last Saturday for both sides to halt public denunciations.

This move was widely interpreted in the West as an effort by the Soviet leader to absolve himself of responsibility in advance of a gathering of world Communist figures in Moscow this month to celebrate the an-

Continued on Page 16, Column 5

OPTIMISM VOICED

American Complicity Denied but a Key Role Is Acknowledged

By MAX FRANKEL
Special to The New York Times

WASHINGTON, Saturday, Nov. 2—The Administration welcomes the coup d'état in South Vietnam, assumes that its policies helped to bring it about and is confident of greater progress now in the war against the Communist guerrillas.

There were, of course, no public statements to this effect even after the success of the coup appeared certain this morning. Officials denied any direct involvement in the military plot and are likely to explore the deaths of President Ngo Dinh Diem and his brother Ngo Dinh Nhu if reports of their deaths are confirmed.

It is conceded here, however, that the United States Government had created the atmosphere that made the coup possible. This had been done by President Kennedy's public denunciation of President Ngo Dinh Diem and by constant pressure from Washington for changes in his regime.

The belief here was that Washington's hostility and the political unrest in Saigon had virtually paralyzed the Ngo Dinh Diem regime and seriously impaired the conduct of the guerrilla war, to which the United States is deeply committed.

Useful if Not Essential

A change of government, therefore, was regarded as useful if not essential, and of benefit to both the people of South Vietnam and United States policy.

Administration leaders are confident that a new civilian government could quickly restore order in Saigon and turn its attentions back to the war effort. They believe the ouster of President Ngo Dinh Diem, his brother and principal political adviser, Ngo Dinh Nhu, and of only a few of their principal adherents will bring an end to internal repression and recurrent political turmoil. Because the Administration here so obviously welcomed the coup and had come close in recent weeks to inviting it, there was widespread discussion of the extent of Washington's involvement.

High officials insisted with

Continued on Page 3, Column 3

REBELS IN VIETNAM OUST DIEM, REPORT HIM AND NHU SUICIDES; SHARPER FIGHT ON REDS VOWED

Ngo Dinh Diem   Ngo Dinh Nhu
Associated Press

The New York Times   Nov. 2, 1963
Heavy fighting was reported at the Presidential Palace (1) in Saigon. Anti-Government forces seized the Defense Ministry (2) and police and navy headquarters (3 and 4).

U.S. Fleet Sent to Vietnam To Safeguard Americans

By JOHN W. FINNEY
Special to The New York Times

WASHINGTON, Nov. 1 — The Defense Department ordered ships of the Seventh Fleet to the vicinity of South Vietnam today to protect any Americans who might be endangered by disorders accompanying the overthrow of President Ngo Dinh Diem.

The Pentagon emphasized that the order was strictly a "precautionary measure" and did not signify any intention to intervene militarily in the Vietnamese crisis.

"This order has been given should it be necessary to protect American lives in South Vietnam," a brief Pentagon announcement said.

The order was issued by Secretary of Defense Robert S. McNamara shortly before 11 A.M. —about eight hours after Washington learned of the military revolt.

The first word of the outbreak of fighting in Saigon came shortly before 3 A.M., Eastern standard time, in a report from the United States Embassy in Vietnam teletyped to the White House situation room, a command center in the White House basement that receives diplomatic and military reports from around the world.

Kennedy Notified Quickly

The report set off a flurry of early-morning activity that turned on the lights in the White House, the State Department, the Pentagon and the Central Intelligence Agency.

Watch officers in the situation room called McGeorge Bundy, the President's special assistant for national security affairs, as soon as the embassy's report arrived. Mr. Bundy awakened President Kennedy with a 3 A.M. telephone call.

During the predawn hours, the President kept informed on developments by telephone. At 6 A.M. Mr. Bundy went to the President's bedroom to give him a briefing on the situation.

Mr. Kennedy did not go to his office until 9:20 A.M., shortly before he received the credentials of the new Ambassador from Norway. Until then he

Continued on Page 2, Column 2

MRS. NHU CHARGES U.S. INCITED COUP

Says Revolt Could Not Occur Without American Help— Won't Stay in Country

By JACK LANGGUTH
Special to The New York Times

BEVERLY HILLS, Calif., Nov. 1—Mrs. Ngo Dinh Nhu bitterly accused the United States Government today of inciting and backing the military revolt in South Vietnam. Uncertain whether her husband, the brother of South Vietnam's President, was alive or dead, Mrs. Ngo Dinh Nhu was angry and distracted during her first appearance since receiving news of the uprising in Saigon.

Later in the day she received reports that the Government of her family had been deposed. Secluded in her hotel room, with a policeman on guard at her door, she told aides that she would have no further comment until information was more definite.

Previous Attempts Alleged

She met reporters as she left her hotel for an All Saints Day noon mass at the nearby Church of the Good Shepherd. Mrs. Ngo Dinh Nhu began calmly by observing that "it was not the first time" that the American Government had tried to overthrow President Ngo Dinh Diem, her brother-in-law.

She became more agitated when asked whether the United States had played a role in the military coup. "Definitely," she replied. "No coup can erupt without American incitement and backing."

Asked whether she might seek political asylum in the United States, Mrs. Ngo Dinh Nhu replied, "Never!" She added, "I cannot stay in a country with people who have stabbed my Government."

"I believe that all the devils of the hell are against us," she said before being escorted to a limousine. "But we shall triumph."

She did not explain what she meant by triumph, but presumably she was alluding to the fight against the Communists. Accompanied by her 18-year-old daughter, Ngo Dinh Le

Continued on Page 8, Column 1

PALACE BESIEGED

Army, Air Force and Marines Combine to Oust President

Communiqués by coup leaders will be found on Page 4.

By HEDRICK SMITH
Special to The New York Times

WASHINGTON, Saturday, Nov. 2—The South Vietnamese Government of President Ngo Dinh Diem has fallen in a swift military coup d'état.

The insurgents reported over the Saigon radio this morning that Ngo Dinh Diem and his powerful brother Ngo Dinh Nhu had committed suicide.

High authorities here confirmed that President Ngo Dinh Diem surrendered to the rebels at 6:05 this morning, Saigon time (5:05 P.M. Friday, New York time), and that the brothers were arrested. There was no official confirmation of the suicide report, which was relayed by the United States Embassy in Saigon.

Anti-Red Drive Promised

All indications were that the military committee that staged the coup was firmly anti-Communist and pro-Western. It was viewed as eager to eliminate the repressive features of the Ngo Dinh Diem Government, which had so frustrated the United States recently.

The insurrectionists pledged to intensify the country's struggle against the Communist guerrillas—the cause that the United States feared might suffer from Ngo Dinh Diem's loss of popular support.

According to the Saigon radio, the brothers escaped the rebel forces after their surrender and sought asylum in a church. Then, the radio added, they were recaptured. The time of their suicide was given as 10:45 this morning (9:45 P.M., Friday, New York time).

Officials said that Vice President Nguyen Ngoc Tho, a Buddhist highly regarded in Washington, was expected to become Premier of a caretaker civilian government.

Discrimination Was Issue

Vu Van Mau, who resigned as South Vietnam's Foreign Minister last August, was also expected to play a prominent role. His resignation protested the Government's Aug. 21 destruction of Buddhist pagodas, which intensified the religious crisis that led to the coup.

Since last May South Vietnam's Buddhists had been charging the Government of the Roman Catholic Ngo family with religious discrimination.

The military leaders were reported to have assured Ambassador Henry Cabot Lodge that they intended to turn over control of the Government to responsible civilian officials.

This made it likely that the United States would extend diplomatic recognition to the

Continued on Page 2, Column 1

Dominicans Arrest Presidential 'Heir'

Special to The New York Times

SANTO DOMINGO, Dominican Republic, Nov. 1—Dr. Juan Casasnovas Garrido, a former president of the Senate who contends he is the rightful Provisional President of the Dominican Republic, was seized today by forces of the civilian junta.

Dr. Casasnovas was injured in the left arm as he attempted to escape arrest one block from the home in which he had been hiding for two days, according to Mrs. Digna D. Garrido, a relative of Dr. Casasnovas. He was hiding in her home in the Sanchez-Luperon district.

Another relative living in the house was also arrested.

At police headquarters this afternoon Dr. Casasnovas indicated that his arm had been injured by a tree branch, not a

Continued on Page 8, Column 5

NEWS INDEX

	Page		Page
Art	23	Music	15-17
Books	23	Obituaries	31
Bridge	22	Radio	63
Business	33	Real Estate	42
Churches	31	Screen	15-17
Crossword	23	Ships and Air	67
Editorial	24	Society	20
Fashions	22	Sports	19-23
Financial	33	Television	63
Food	14	Theaters	15-17
Letters	24	U. N. Proceedings	3
Man in the News	7	Weather	67

News Summary and Index, Page 27

Dwight D. Eisenhower's 'The White House Years' appears on Page 27.

FREED IN GEORGIA: Donald Harris, right, receives an enthusiastic welcome after he, Ralph Allen, left background, and Thomas McDaniel, center foreground, were released on bond following a precedent-setting decision by a three-man Federal court in Americus.
Associated Press Wirephoto

"All the News That's Fit to Print"

The New York Times.

LATE CITY EDITION

U. S. Weather Bureau Report (Page 95) forecasts: Partly cloudy and cold today; clear tonight. Fair and milder tomorrow. Temp. range: 50—36; yesterday: 48—40.

SECTION ONE

NEWS SUMMARY AND INDEX, PAGE 95

VOL. CXIII. No. 38,634. © 1963 by The New York Times Company. Times Square, New York 36, N. Y. NEW YORK, SUNDAY, NOVEMBER 3, 1963. 40c beyond 50-mile zone from New York City, except on Long Island. 50c beyond 200-mile zone from New York City, higher in air delivery cities. THIRTY CENTS

DIEM AND NHU ARE REPORTED SLAIN; ARMY RULING SAIGON AFTER COUP; KENNEDY REVIEWS VIETNAM POLICY

Associated Press

AFTER COUP: Crowd jeers as head of a demolished statue is carted through Saigon. The head was part of a monument that was destroyed by a mob because it was thought to bear a resemblance to Mrs. Ngo Dinh Nhu.

U.S. GIVES SOVIET COMPROMISE PLAN FOR WHEAT RATES

Suggests Providing Vessels for 20 to 30% of Grain at a Cost of $18 a Ton

RUSSIANS WEIGH OFFER

Approval Will End Deadlock—Bulgaria May Purchase 8 Million in Tobacco

By WILLIAM M. BLAIR

Special to The New York Times

WASHINGTON, Nov. 2—The United States has moved to break the impasse on its shipping rates that has held up sales of wheat to the Soviet Union.

A new proposal, which the Russians are understood to be considering over the weekend, would involve concessions by both sides. It includes a lowered United States cargo rate and a division of $250 million worth of wheat between American and foreign-flag vessels.

A spokesman for the Department of State denied tonight that the United States had suggested such a formula to the Russians.

The sale of up to four million tons of wheat has been blocked because United States cargo schedules have been $10 to $13 or more higher than foreign charter charges for shipments to Black Sea and Baltic ports.

Stipulation by Kennedy

President Kennedy stipulated that wheat sold to the Soviet Union and its satellites should be carried in American vessels, as available, supplemented by foreign ships.

It is understood that the United States is willing to provide a cargo rate of $18 a ton if 20 to 30 per cent of the wheat is carried in American vessels. Payment for this amount would be in dollars or gold.

The $18-a-ton rate compares with the $21 a ton recently offered by a group of tramp-ship owners to move wheat to the Soviet Union. The tramp-ship operators, whose unscheduled vessels ply between any ports where cargo is available, recently reduced their rate by $5 from $26 a ton.

Foreign Ships Would Be Used

Presumably, the remainder of the wheat purchase, 70 to 80 per cent, would be carried by foreign vessels at the world charter rate of about $12.50 a ton. This amount of wheat would be paid for through normal commercial credits of about 18 months.

The $18-a-ton figure was said to have been worked out with American tramp-ship owners, whose vessels are regarded as most suitable by wheat shippers, at an unannounced meeting earlier this week in New York. It was understood that ship representatives and officials of the Commerce Department had

Continued on Page 31, Column 1

Vatican Decides to Invite 5 Women to the Council

They Will Join Laymen's Panel Viewing Ecumenical Meeting for First Time—May Participate in This Session

By MILTON BRACKER

Special to The New York Times

ROME, Nov. 2—The Vatican has decided in principle to add five women to the list of delegates who are attending an ecumenical council for the first time.

Pope Paul VI announced Sept. 14 that qualified laymen would be permitted to attend the resumed session of Ecumenical Council Vatican II. The day after it opened, Sept. 29, the names of 10 laymen from six nations were listed.

Among them was James J. Norris of Rumson, N. J., assistant to the Most Rev. Edward E. Swanstrom, Auxiliary Bishop of New York and executive director of relief services of the National Catholic Welfare Conference. Mr. Norris has returned to the United States after having attended several Council meetings.

The precedent of adding women to the group may still be set during the present session, which is due to end Dec. 4.

Two references to the important part played by women in the organized Roman Catholic laity, and one specific demand that they be invited not only to listen but to be heard, have been made at the Council.

On Oct. 24 the Most Rev. Georges Hakim, Melchite Archbishop of Nazareth, criticized the chapter on the laity in the schema on the church for being "so silent as to the place of women in the church as to give the impression that they do not exist."

On Thursday the Right Rev. Giocondo Grotti, Prelate of Acre and Purus, Brazil, asserted that if laywomen were to be invited to the Council, they should be given an active role.

"They should be asked to talk

Continued on Page 4, Column 3

TRUCE IN SAHARA REMAINS IN DOUBT AFTER NEW CLASH

Moroccans and Algerians Exchange Accusations on Breach in Figuig Area

By PETER GROSE

Special to The New York Times

FIGUIG, Morocco, Nov. 2—An Algerian artillery barrage at this border town early today appeared to have erased the cease-fire agreement between Algeria and Morocco that was to have taken effect at midnight last night.

[On the Algerian side, the cease-fire breach was laid to Morocco. After having expressed the hope that the cease-fire would be successful, Algerian officials announced that all firing along the border area near Figuig had ceased.]

Algerian forces launched the attack on Figuig, an ancient Moroccan frontier fortress, at dawn. Heavy Moroccan artillery replied from hills around the town.

Attack and Counterattack

The bombardments followed a day of attack and counterattack yesterday, during which King Hassan II of Morocco announced at one point that his forces had withdrawn from the town of 8,000.

Diplomatic observers were flown to the scene from Rabat to confirm the attack described by the King yesterday. They listened in silence to this morning's battle reports, which revive the border crisis that flared into open fighting Oct. 8.

Included in the diplomatic party at Figuig was Ya Doumbouia, Ambassador of Mali, in whose capital, Bamako, King Hassan and President Ahmed Ben Bella of Algeria signed the truce. It was then heralded as a victory for African mediation and statesmanship under the aegis of King Haile Selassie of Ethiopia. The Ambassador declined to comment on the new situation.

Algerian Tells of Attack

An Algerian captured on the outskirts of Figuig last night told interrogators that his unit had been moved into position at 11 P.M. Thursday on the heights at the edge of Algerian territory overlooking the border fort. The first Algerian attack came early yesterday.

"We were told we would occupy Figuig," the prisoner said in the presence of newsmen.

He said no orders had been issued to cease fire at the time agreed upon.

Moroccan officers and men interviewed yesterday confirmed that they had received orders to stop firing at midnight. At 11 P.M. King Hassan sent personal instructions that the truce should be observed unless the front-line units had to defend themselves.

The first technical rupture of the cease-fire came only minutes after midnight. The artillery batteries of both sides had been

Continued on Page 18, Column 3

GOLDWATER WINS WIDE LEAD IN POLL

Backed in 85% of Replies by G.O.P. Leaders—Nixon and Rockefeller Far Behind

Senator Barry Goldwater of Arizona is the runaway choice in a nationwide poll of Republican Presidential preferences for 1964, taken by The Associated Press among Republican state and county leaders.

Of the 1,404 who answered a questionnaire, 1,194, or 85.1 per cent, voted Senator Goldwater the party's "strongest candidate" against President Kennedy as of today.

Fewer, however, believe that Mr. Goldwater will be nominated. Here his vote was 901, or 64.2 per cent of those who replied.

Governor Rockefeller received 56 votes as the "strongest candidate" and former Vice President Richard M. Nixon received 44.

See Nixon as Compromise

On the outlook for the nomination, Mr. Nixon had 72 votes to 65 for Mr. Rockefeller. Moreover, a sizable number of those who favor Mr. Goldwater for the nomination predicted that, if a deadlock should develop in the nominating convention, Mr. Nixon would emerge again as the candidate.

The convention, scheduled to open in San Francisco July 13, has a tentative apportionment of 1,308 delegate votes.

The survey was started early last month.

Correspondents in every state polled by mail and telephone 2,961 Republicans, including some city and town leaders. In Alaska, which has no counties, the national committeeman and committeewoman participated in the poll.

More than 47 per cent of those questioned replied. Republicans in New Jersey and Hawaii declined to participate.

The questionnaire asked opinions on two points:

"Who is the strongest potential G.O.P. candidate against

Continued on Page 46, Column 1

7 Feared Drowned As an Auto Plunges Into Harlem River

At least seven persons, including several children, were believed to have drowned early today when the car in which they were riding plunged into the Harlem River in the Bronx.

The police said there was a possibility that eight persons had died.

The only survivor was a man identified at Isias Martinez, of 366 South Second Street, Brooklyn. He apparently climbed out of the submerged car, scrambled up the pilings and walked two blocks to a tavern to telephone the police.

Mr. Martinez was taken to Lincoln Hospital and was treated for shock and submersion. The police said he was incoherent.

The accident occurred at the foot of Lincoln Avenue just south of East 132d Street in the Mott Haven section. There were no witnesses.

Grappling Is Begun

Police launches and a Coast Guard rescue craft rushed to the scene and began grappling operations.

A police helicopter hovered in the darkness over the scene. The area was lit by floodlights on shore and on the rescue vessels.

Mr. Martinez told the police that all the passengers had been returning from a wedding in the Bronx. He said the passengers had included his wife, Judith, 27 years old, and their two children, David, 9, and Dadala, 7.

He identified the other passengers as Robinson Aponte, whose address he did not know and who apparently owned the

Continued on Page 60, Column 1

MRS. NHU SAYS U.S. WILL BEAR STIGMA

Calls Americans Responsible for Fate of Her Family—Rules Out Suicide

Text of Mrs. Nhu's statement appears on Page 24.

By JACK LANGGUTH

Special to The New York Times

BEVERLY HILLS, Calif., Nov. 2—Mrs. Ngo Dinh Nhu, pausing to wipe away tears, said today that "no one can seriously believe in the disclaimer" that the United States Government had nothing to do with the military revolt in South Vietnam.

She said that "whatever happens to my family will be an indelible stigma against the United States."

Mrs. Ngo Dinh Nhu rejected the possibility that her husband and his brother, the deposed President of South Vietnam, had committed suicide. Her husband was the President's political adviser.

She Affirms Faith

In a brief news conference on her way to an All Souls' Day mass, Mrs. Ngo Dinh Nhu read a statement that did not accept as final the reports that Ngo Dinh Nhu and Ngo Dinh Diem were dead.

But she added: "If the news is true, if really my family has been treacherously killed with either the official or unofficial blessing of the American Government, I can predict to you all that the story in Vietnam is only at its beginning."

"Any crime against the Nhu family cannot be hidden under the label of suicide," she said, noting that suicide was incompatible with the family's religion. The Nhus are Roman Catholic.

Reliable military sources in

Continued on Page 24, Column 7

Washington Expects Ties With Saigon Within Week

By HEDRICK SMITH

Special to The New York Times

WASHINGTON, Nov. 2—President Kennedy met twice today with his top national-security advisers to formulate a United States policy on establishing relations with the Provisional Government of South Vietnam.

The President canceled plans to attend the Army-Air Force football game in Chicago so he could conduct a full policy review. Officials said the action did not indicate any new crisis in Saigon.

Washington was expected to extend recognition, probably early in the week, as soon as the revolutionary rulers of South Vietnam listed a cabinet and declared their policies.

The United States Ambassador, Henry Cabot Lodge, was reported to be in contact with the military leaders who overthrew President Ngo Dinh Diem this morning, but the White House and the State Department have not officially characterized Washington's reaction to the coup.

The Administration also made no official comment on reports of the deaths of Ngo Dinh Diem and his brother, Ngo Dinh Nhu. Although some members of Congress expressed regret at this news, the Administration maintained silence.

Officials accepted reports that the Ngo brothers had died in the wake of the coup, but Washington was unable to confirm reports that they had been assassinated. It was disclosed,

Continued on Page 25, Column 1

IZVESTIA DERIDES REVOLT LEADERS

Sees U.S. Behind Coup—Asserts New Chiefs Will Be Repressive as Diem

By THEODORE SHABAD

Special to The New York Times

MOSCOW, Nov. 2—The leaders of the South Vietnamese coup d'état were derided here today as puppets of the United States.

The Soviet press was evidently pleased with what Izvestia, the Government newspaper, called the "ignoble" end of President Ngo Dinh Diem. But it foresaw no fundamental changes in the struggle between the Communist guerrillas of the Vietcong and the Government forces backed by the United States.

"Judging from Saigon dispatches and from Washington's reaction, new American puppets have come to power," Izvestia's Washington correspondent wrote.

Anti-Red Stand Scored

"They came to power because the old ones compromised themselves to such an extent in the eyes of the Vietnamese people that they no longer suited their American masters. Leaders of the coup made clear their anti-popular program in their first appeal to the armed forces, calling for continued struggle against 'Communists,' meaning the patriotic forces seeking genuine progress for their country."

A commentator of Tass, the official Soviet press agency, said that Washington had undoubtedly engineered the coup and that the decision had probably been taken soon after the return of President Kennedy's fact finders, Secretary of Defense Robert S. McNamara and Gen. Maxwell D. Taylor, chairman of the Joint Chiefs of Staff.

"But the change of scenery," said the Tass commentator, Igor Orlov, "will not slow, let alone end, the dragging and deepening crisis in South Vietnam."

Echoing a point of view expressed repeatedly in the past by the Soviet Government, he added that only a withdrawal by the United States could

Continued on Page 27, Column 8

SUICIDES DOUBTED

Deposed Chiefs Fled, Then Were Seized—Throngs Exult

By DAVID HALBERSTAM

Special to The New York Times

SAIGON, South Vietnam, Nov. 2 — President Ngo Dinh Diem and his brother, Ngo Dinh Nhu, are dead in the wake of the military uprising that ended their regime.

While the Saigon radio announced that they had committed suicide, reliable private military sources said that they had been assassinated.

With Saigon under military rule, crowds of jubilant youths set fire to the homes of government security officials, offices of government-controlled newspapers and police stations.

[The military leaders set up a Buddhist-led provisional Government with Nguyen Ngoc Tho, former Vice President, as Premier, The Associated Press reported. The recently elected National Assembly was dissolved.]

Reports on Death Conflict

The military sources that reported that the brothers had been killed said they had escaped from the palace by a tunnel shortly before marines overran it.

Later, Ngo Dinh Diem was seen in a small Roman Catholic church in Cholon, a suburb of Saigon, it was reported. The military leaders sent troops and armored cars and both men were taken prisoner.

They were placed inside an armored personnel carrier and were guarded by several soldiers, according to this account. On the way to military headquarters, an informed source said, an order was given to kill both. When the armored car arrived at headquarters both men were dead.

Military men said that both men shot themselves while in transit.

Captured After Escape

The reports that the President and his brother, considered the most powerful man in his regime, had committed suicide were received skeptically in some quarters since both were Roman Catholics. The President was considered particularly devout.

The military, denouncing what it termed the Diem Government's despotism and corruption, suspended the Constitution and ended the presidential system. Imprisoned Buddhist monks were freed.

The military coup d'état ended nine years of Ngo Dinh Diem's rule shortly before 7 A.M. when the palace was stormed by marines. Moments before this, both Ngo Dinh Diem and Ngo Dinh Nhu had told the military they were surrendering.

Continued on Page 24, Column 1

Sports News

FOOTBALL

Army beat the Air Force yesterday before 76,660 fans at Soldier Field, Chicago.

Scores of major games:

Alabama	20	Miss St.	19
Army	14	Air Force	10
Auburn	19	Florida	0
Baylor	32	T. C. U.	13
Boston Coll.	19	Vanderbilt	6
Colgate	20	Lehigh	6
Cornell	18	Columbia	17
Georgia T.	30	Duke	6
Illinois	41	Purdue	21
Indiana	24	Minnesota	6
Miami (Fla)	20	Kentucky	14
Michigan	27	N'western	6
Mich. St.	30	Wisconsin	13
Mississippi	37	L. S. U.	3
Navy	35	N. Dame	14
Nebraska	13	Missouri	12
N. Carolina	28	Georgia	7
N. C. St.	15	Virginia	9
Ohio St.	7	Iowa	3
Oklahoma	35	Colorado	0
Oregon St.	10	Stanford	7
Penn	7	Harvard	2
Penn St.	17	Maryland	15
Pittsburgh	35	Syracuse	27
Princeton	34	Brown	13
Rutgers	21	Boston Univ.	6
Texas	17	S. M. U.	12
Villanova	22	Holy Cross	14
Washington	22	So. Calif.	7
West Va.	20	G. Wash.	16
Yale	10	Dartmouth	6

HORSE RACING

The Axe II won the $113,700 Man o' War Stakes at Aqueduct by five lengths.

Details in Section 5.

Last Hunting Curb Lifted by Governor

By RICHARD P. HUNT

Governor Rockefeller ended the state's forest-fire emergency yesterday by reopening the last of the woodlands and fields that had been closed because of a long autumn drought.

Sportsmen had been complaining about the ban on recreational use of open spaces in the hunting and fishing areas close to New York City. The drought was relieved by rain yesterday and Friday.

The Governor signed an order restoring the hunting season in seven Hudson Valley counties shortly after he had left a bridge-opening ceremony in Newburgh with the explanation that "a development has come up in the state."

Robert T. McManus, the Gov-

Continued on Page 55, Column 1

Kennan Says Congress Impeded His Work as Envoy in Belgrade

Asserts That U.S. Must Keep Foreign Policy Separated From Domestic Politics

By MAX FRANKEL

Special to The New York Times

WASHINGTON, Nov. 2 — George F. Kennan has told Congress that he would not have become Ambassador to Yugoslavia had he known how little value the legislators would assign to his judgment.

Reflecting, for a Senate subcommittee, upon his "recent ambassadorial experience," Mr. Kennan said Congressional actions had been the "main impediments" to his performance.

He also said that he had lacked access to information about Yugoslavia in the files in Washington, and he deplored what he called the general tendency to make foreign policy "a function of domestic political convenience."

The nation has a foreign service "second to no other," he said, "and better than it has a right to expect, given the lack of appreciation and respect exhibited by the public at large for its tasks, and its achievements."

Mr. Kennan, who has served the State Department and Foreign Service for more than 25 years, returned this autumn to Princeton, N. J., where he is a permanent professor in the School of Historical Studies at the Institute for Advanced Study.

A former director of the State Department's policy planning

Associated Press

George F. Kennan

Continued on Page 35, Column 1

Polish Army Drafts Priesthood Students

By PAUL UNDERWOOD

Special to The New York Times

WARSAW, Nov. 2—Poland's Communist regime has ordered students of four of the country's largest Roman Catholic seminaries to report for military service, church sources said today.

Seminarians have previously been exempt from army duty.

The action was the latest in a series of moves by the Government that have soured church-state relations and threatened the uneasy truce between these two powerful forces in Polish life.

The church sources said news of the order, which affected seminaries in Warsaw, Poznan,

Continued on Page 7, Column 1

Today's Sections

Index to Subjects

General Maxwell D. Taylor, chairman of the U.S. Joint Chiefs of Staff is greeted upon his arrival at the Montagnard Training Center in South Vietnam.

South Vietnamese soldiers move their 155mm Howitzer into a new position for firing on a band of Viet Cong that has been flushed out of hiding by a patrol. The Howitzer enables this outpost at An Hoa to control the entire Ven Tri Valley.

"All the News That's Fit to Print"

The New York Times.

LATE CITY EDITION

U. S. Weather Bureau Report (Page 70) forecasts: Sunny and mild today; fair tonight. Fair tomorrow. Temp. Range: 78—51; yesterday: 71—48.

VOL. CXIII..No. 38,835. NEW YORK, FRIDAY, MAY 22, 1964. TEN CENTS

© 1964 by The New York Times Company. Times Square, New York, N. Y. 10036

U.S. PUTS A JET WATCH OVER LAOS; INFORMS U.N. IT WILL BACK ASIANS SEEKING HELP AGAINST SUBVERSION

CONFER AT UNITED NATIONS: Adlai E. Stevenson, chief U.S. representative, with Secretary General Thant and Roger Seydoux, center, the Security Council president.

United Press International

AIR AID REQUESTED

Planes Scouting Reds Because Truce Unit Cannot Function

By HEDRICK SMITH
Special to The New York Times

WASHINGTON, May 21—The Government disclosed today that unarmed United States jet planes piloted by Americans had been flying reconnaissance missions over the Plaine des Jarres, in central Laos, to gather information on Communist forces.

A State Department spokesman said the missions had been undertaken at the request of the Government of Laos because of "the current inability of the International Control Commission to obtain adequate information" on recent attacks on neutralist and right-wing forces in Laos.

The commission, made up of representatives of India, Canada and Poland, is assigned to supervise the numerous truces in the fighting between pro-Communist Pathet Lao and anti-Communist forces in Laos.

U. S. Provides Bombs

Coupled with the disclosure of the reconnaissance flights was a report by qualified sources that the United States had provided bombs being used by the Laotian Air Force for raids against Pathet Lao and purported North Vietnamese forces.

These sources indicated that the bombs were supplied some time ago at the request of the Laotian Government under the July, 1962, Geneva agreements between East and West. Under these accords Laos was to be unified and neutralized, with a government to consist of neutralist, rightist and pro-Communist factions.

The current raids were the first in which the bombs were used.

The announcement of the reconnaissance flights was the first official acknowledgment since the signing of the Geneva accords that the United States was taking a military role in Laos.

Planes Fired On, Peking Says

The disclosure came in the wake of reports from Tokyo quoting the Peking radio to the effect that Pathet Lao troops had fired on American planes over Laos. Officials here could not confirm that any planes had been fired on.

[The United States jets were fired upon over Khang Kay and Phongsavan, the Peking radio said, according to United Press International.]

The State Department's acknowledgment of the flights was viewed by observers here as having more importance than the military value of the flights themselves.

It was interpreted as part of a carefully developed plan by the Johnson Administration to demonstrate that it was prepared to go beyond traditional diplomatic gestures of

Continued on Page 15, Column 4

Stevenson Rejects Appeal For New Geneva Meeting

By SAM POPE BREWER
Special to The New York Times

UNITED NATIONS, N.Y., May 21—Adlai E. Stevenson declared today that the United States would back the fight against Communist subversion in Southeast Asia as long as the people there "ask for our help" in preserving their independence.

Mr. Stevenson's remarks, in the Security Council, were directed especially at the Soviet Union. The Council was meeting officially on a complaint by Cambodia that the United States had directed raids into her territory from South Vietnam.

Text of Stevenson's speech, Fedorenko excerpts, Page 14.

However, Nikolai T. Fedorenko of the Soviet Union broadened the debate on Tuesday with a general attack on United States activities in Southeast Asia.

Meeting Proposal Rejected

Mr. Stevenson rejected suggestions for a new meeting of the 14-power Geneva conference that worked out agreements on neutrality for the Southeast Asian countries in 1954. He said respect for the agreements already signed was more important.

France has been favoring a new meeting of the Geneva conference. Washington has opposed it on the ground that it would give an opportunity for new Communist maneuvers.

First Western reaction here to Mr. Stevenson's statement was favorable. In British circles it was said that he had helped to clear up the situation and that his proposals on the Cambodian situation were interesting and welcome.

U. N. Watch Suggested

For the first time, Mr. Stevenson suggested that a solution of the problem might be a United Nations force to watch over the frontiers in question.

Mr. Fedorenko accused the United States of waging an aggressive war in the interests of capitalism. He said "ordinary Americans" were dying in defense of those interests.

Mr. Stevenson, the United States representative at the United Nations, was summoned home from Europe by Secretary of State Dean Rusk to present the United States stand. Mr. Stevenson's statement was known to have been worked out directly with President Johnson and Mr. Rusk.

It disappointed some observers because they found it less vigorous and sweeping than advance reports from Washington had led them to expect. There

Continued on Page 15, Column 1

LAOS NEUTRALIST REGROUPS FORCES

Kong Le Said to Have Four Battalions Left—Other Units Try to Join Him

By SEYMOUR TOPPING
Special to The New York Times

VIENTIANE, Laos, May 21—General Kong Le, the neutralist commander, regrouped his tired battalions southwest of the Plaine des Jarres today and turned to face advancing pro-Communist Pathet Lao troops.

The young general established his command post near Ba Na, a forested hill position about eight miles southwest of his fallen headquarters at Muong Phanh on the western fringes of the plain.

Only four battalions remained under his command of about 5,000 neutralist troops that held the Muong Phanh area when the Pathet Lao opened its offensive Saturday. The battalions are believed to have 400 to 600 men each.

Clustered about the Ba Na perimeter were thousands of refugees and members of the soldiers' families.

A neutralist communiqué broadcast by the Vientiane radio said isolated units were attempting to fight their way through the Pathet Lao lines to rejoin General Kong Le. It was said that a unit, presumably the lost Fourth Paratroop Battalion, which had held the southern anchor of the line at

Continued on Page 13, Column 1

CIVIL RIGHTS BLOC PREDICTS CLOSURE BY EARLY IN JUNE

Leaders Voice Confidence They Will Have Needed Votes After Holiday

NARROW MARGIN IS SEEN

6 Doubtful Republicans May Be Ready to Back Move to Halt the Filibuster

By E. W. KENWORTHY
Special to The New York Times

WASHINGTON, May 21—Leaders of the civil rights forces in the Senate confidently predicted today that they would have the votes to shut off the Southern filibuster in early June.

Senator Everett McKinley Dirksen of Illinois, the Republican leader, said that the votes would be in hand by the time a petition for closure of debate was filed. But Mr. Dirksen said:

"I must acknowledge the margin will be narrow."

Senator Hubert H. Humphrey of Minnesota, the Democratic floor manager of the civil rights bill, acknowledged it would be premature to say the leaders now had the necessary votes. But he said he was "confident we will have them."

Two-Thirds Vote Needed

Shutting off debate requires the votes of two-thirds of the Senators present and voting. If all 100 Senators are present, 67 votes are needed.

Senator Richard B. Russell, Democrat of Georgia, the Southern leader, who only two days ago said the civil rights leaders did not have votes for closure, apparently felt today the showdown was not long away.

"Pressure is increasing daily on Senators to support the bill," he said. "Pressure is also increasing for the gag rule. I therefore make no claim as to being able to beat the gag rule or the bill."

Mr. Humphrey said the Republican leaders felt certain that a package of amendments proposed by Mr. Dirksen and agreed to by the Justice Department "has produced some Republican votes" for closure.

Two May Stay Away

There was reason to believe that six Republican Senators, all of whom had been considered doubtful on closure, might be ready to vote for it after the three-day Memorial Day holiday. They are Senators Len B. Jordan of Idaho, Carl T. Curtis and Roman L. Hruska of Nebraska, Karl E. Mundt of South Dakota, Peter H. Dominick of Colorado and John J. Williams of Delaware.

Mr. Humphrey also said, "On our side, I think we've had some help." This could mean only two things.

The first was that Senator Frank J. Lausche of Ohio had been satisfied by the Dirksen amendments and was ready to vote for closure.

The second was that either Senator Howard W. Cannon or Senator Alan Bible of Nevada, or perhaps both of them, was willing to absent himself on the closure vote. When a Senator who opposes closure stays away during the vote, the number of votes necessary for a two-thirds majority is reduced.

Without elaboration, Mr. Humphrey said, "It's always

Continued on Page 22, Column 6

Head of Channel 13 Named State University President

Gould Expects to Mold the 58 Campuses Into a Unified Institution

By FRED M. HECHINGER

Associated Press

Dr. Samuel B. Gould

Dr. Samuel B. Gould, president of educational television station WNDT-TV (Channel 13), was appointed president of the State University of New York yesterday.

Dr. Gould said he expected to transform the university from "a loose federation" into an institution with a sense of unity.

He will be the fourth president of the university, which was created in 1948 through the fusion of a group of state-financed colleges. It has an enrollment of 76,500 full-time students on 58 campuses and an operating budget of $130 million.

The 53-year-old college administrator will take over on Sept. 1. The office has been vacant since the resignation in August, 1962, of Dr. Thomas H. Hamilton.

A successor to Dr. Gould will be named "in due course," said Howard C. Sheperd, chairman of the board of trustees of the Educational Broadcasting Corporation. Dr. Gould said he expected to remain with the station until the first week of August.

In Albany, the university trustees said that Dr. Gould would help the institution "attain the

Continued on Page 71, Column 3

PRESIDENT PLANS NEW SPENDING CUT OF $700 MILLION

Would Reduce the Deficit of Current and Next Fiscal Year by $300 Million

By EDWIN L. DALE Jr.
Special to The New York Times

WASHINGTON, May 21—The White House disclosed new budget estimates today showing a drop of $700 million in spending in the current and next fiscal years.

The announcement also showed a drop in estimated receipts of $400 million for the two years. The result is a drop in the deficit for the two years of $300 million.

The bulk of the drop in spending, $600 million, is to take place in the next fiscal year, beginning July 1. Today's statement said that for that year "estimated expenditures for agriculture have increased, but this rise is more than offset by reductions in the expenditure estimates for defense and a number of other programs."

Debt Ceiling Hearings

The new estimates were made public in advance of Congressional testimony by Administration financial officials next week on an increase in the ceiling on the national debt. Action on the debt limit is necessary before the current fiscal year ends on June 30.

Revised estimates of spending and receipts were also made at this time last year, although they were not published by the White House.

Today's statement noted that the passage of the tax reduction legislation in late February, instead of in January as assumed originally in the budget, had shifted the timing of tax receipts and refunds.

The new estimates put receipts in the current fiscal year $1.1 billion higher than the earlier estimate, and receipts in the next fiscal year $1.5 billion lower.

The new estimates show spending in the current fiscal year of $98.3 billion and receipts of $89.5 billion, with a deficit of $8.8 billion. This deficit estimate is $1.2 billion below the January estimate.

Over-All Reduction

For the next fiscal year, 1965, the new estimates show spending of $97.3 billion and receipts of $91.5 billion, for a deficit of $5.8 billion.

This deficit estimate is $900 million higher than the January estimate, caused entirely by the change in the receipts estimate.

The statement pointed out that spending in fiscal year 1965 is now put at about a billion less than in fiscal 1964, compared with an original estimate of $500 million.

For real economic purposes, as well as for political purposes, the significance of today's statement is not in the shifting estimates of the deficit for the two fiscal years but the over-all reduction in spending and in the two deficits put together.

Johnson's First 6 Months: Popularity and Problems

By TOM WICKER
Special to The New York Times

WASHINGTON, May 21—As President Johnson completed his sixth month in office today, he stood high in all the popularity polls, dominated the national political outlook, and was heavily favored to win the election next Nov. 3. He was firmly in command of the Administration.

Only half a year after the assassination of President Kennedy elevated Mr. Johnson from the Vice-Presidency to the White House, he has a substantial record of achievement at home, and has not been heavily challenged or set back in affairs abroad.

Both at home and abroad, however, the President is still confronted with the two major problems that disturbed the last year of Mr. Kennedy's life.

Rights Problems Persist

In the United States, evidence is mounting that the civil rights crisis threatens not only social but political stability, and that its effects have reached into almost every state and section. Both Negro and white moderates like Mr. Johnson—seem to have only a tenuous command of the situation, and in Congress there is no resolution of the bitter Senate debate on the Kennedy-Johnson civil rights bill.

In South Vietnam, most signs point to a deteriorating situation in the guerrilla warfare between the Vietcong, the Communist forces, and the Government troops with their United States advisers and support. The President asked this week for an increased United States commitment of military and economic assistance to South Vietnam, and there appears to be no immediate threat of a debacle such as the French suffered a decade ago at Dienbienphu.

Neither, however, does there appear to be hope of immediate or even reasonably quick success in ridding South Vietnam of the Communist threat. In neighboring Laos, Thailand and Cambodia, also, Communist influence is advancing by varying degrees, rounding out a picture of a hard-pressed United States position in Southeast Asia.

His Only Major Worries

These two problems—civil rights and South Vietnam—appear to many of Mr. Johnson's supporters and opponents to be the most likely—perhaps the only—areas in which he might suffer sizable setbacks between now and the Presidential election. Without such setbacks, few opponents and virtually no supporters believe that he can be defeated in November.

Among Republicans, however, a determined effort is being made to link President Johnson to the allegations of influence-peddling that have been made against Robert G. Baker, who as the former Secretary to the Senate Democrats was close to Mr. Johnson. Some Republicans hope at least to show that the President helped squelch a Senate investigation of Mr. Baker's activities. The Rules Committee has investigated Mr. Baker's dealings to see if he wrongly used his position for personal gain.

Most Democrats seem to think

Continued on Page 16, Column 1

LEVY SAYS HE GOT A BUCKLEY OFFER

Tells of Promise of Funds to Run and Split Reform Vote —Democrat Denies It

By RONALD SULLIVAN

David Levy said yesterday that a man from the Buckley camp had offered him unlimited funds to run as a Democratic insurgent candidate in an attempt to split the anti-Buckley Reform vote in the Bronx.

Mr. Levy, the Reform candidate who almost defeated Representative Charles A. Buckley in the 1962 primary, said in an interview that he was asked by the Buckley go-between to be a candidate this year in the 21st Congressional District.

Mr. Levy said he had rejected the offer.

The candidates in the 21st District are Representative James C. Healey, the chief political lieutenant of Mr. Buckley, the Democratic leader in the Bronx, and James H. Scheuer, his Reform opponent. There is also a third candidate, Isaac Ben Greenman, an independent insurgent.

The strategy behind the offer made to him, Mr. Levy said, was to split the Reform vote in the 21st District and insure a Healey victory.

Mr. Levy spoke of the offer after he had been bitterly attacked by Reform leaders, who accused him of having been approached by Buckley people to become a "spoiler" and run in Mr. Buckley's district, the 23d.

Mr. Levy snapped that his critics "got me in the wrong

Continued on Page 33, Column 1

ERHARD PLEDGES STABILITY MOVES

Chancellor Says He Will Act to Get West Germany Out of Inflationary Trend

By ARTHUR J. OLSEN
Special to The New York Times

BONN, May 21 — Chancellor Ludwig Erhard promised today new Government measures to maintain a stable economy in West Germany in the midst of its inflation-wracked European neighbors.

"We shall do everything necessary to get out of the inflationary trend," the Chancellor said in a speech at an international handicraft fair in Munich.

He offered no indication of what further stabilization measures he had in mind.

Last week the Government announced its intention to make substantial cuts on July 1 in West German tariffs on industrial goods. Parliament is considering a tax bill aimed at stemming the flow from abroad of "hot" money—that is, money seeking the highest possible interest rate.

Dr. Erhard has been sounding the alarm against the danger of "imported inflation" from neighboring countries where prices have been rising steeply. Flight capital has been entering West Germany and exports of relatively cheap German goods have soared.

In the first four months of

Continued on Page 2, Column 3

Chinese-Mongol Tension Rising; Ulan Bator Charges Subversion

Street Fights and Expulsion of Workers Followed by Tighter Border Watch

By HARRISON E. SALISBURY

The New York Times May 22, 1964

Area of tension (shaded)

A severe deterioration in relations between Mongolia and Communist China is reported in information received from Ulan Bator, capital of the remote Asian land.

Street clashes have erupted between Mongols and Chinese workers assigned by the Peking Government to construction projects in Mongolia.

Sharp protests have been sent to the Foreign Ministry in Peking against Chinese interference in domestic Mongolian affairs, distribution of "subversive propaganda" and other activities contrary to normal diplomatic practice.

The rising Mongol-Chinese tension, a by-product of the intensifying Moscow-Peking ideological struggle, has led the Mongolian authorities to carry out a series of far-reaching security measures.

There were suggestions that Ulan Bator feared the Chinese might attempt to carry out a coup d'état against the Government of Premier Yumzhagiin Tsendenbal, which firmly supports Moscow in the Communist dispute, and replace it with a regime inclined to the Peking side.

Security measures along the nearly 4,000-mile-long frontier between China and Mongolia were said to have been greatly tightened.

Adherents of the Chinese Communist viewpoint are known to exist within the top Communist party structure of Mongolia. It is also known that some Mongols of nationalistic inclination, hopeful of creating a "Greater Mongolia," saw in the Chinese-Soviet conflict an opportunity to advance their ambitions by playing politics with Peking. China has actually sought to win influence in Mongolia for at least eight years.

The most drastic step taken thus far by Mongol authorities since the deterioration of relations, it was reported, was a

Continued on Page 12, Column 1

Bronx Negro Minister to Head 3.2 Million U.S. Presbyterians

By GEORGE DUGAN
Special to The New York Times

OKLAHOMA CITY, May 21—A Negro minister from the Bronx was elected Moderator of the General Assembly of the United Presbyterian Church in the U.S.A. today. He is the first member of his race to head the 3.2 million-member, predominantly white Protestant denomination.

The new Moderator is the Rev. Dr. Edler G. Hawkins, the pastor of St. Augustine Church at Prospect Avenue and East 165th Street.

Dr. Hawkins, who will in effect serve as spiritual leader of the denomination for the coming year, defeated the Rev. Dr. A. Ray Cartlidge, a white minister from Erie, Pa., where he heads the Presbyterian Church of the Covenant. The vote was 465 to 368.

The election marked the opening of the church's 176th General Assembly at the Municipal Auditorium here. It undoubtedly set the tone for the days ahead, when the Presbyterians are expected to take a strong stand in support of civil rights demonstrations.

Dr. Hawkins was born in New York and educated in its public school system. He is a graduate of Bloomfield College, Bloomfield, N.J., and Union Theological Seminary.

The organization Dr. Hawkins will head is the largest of the Presbyterian bodies. Another, the Presbyterian Church in the United States, has about 930,-

Continued on Page 20, Column 1

WILL YOU OWE UNCLE SAM PLENTY? Experts say tax withholdings are too low. You'll owe plenty more. Let Charles Haskell help you. Today's World-Telegram.—Advt.

Cuba Said to Seek Spain's Aid For an 'Arrangement' With U.S.

By PAUL HOFMANN
Special to The New York Times

MADRID, May 21—Cuba is putting out feelers for an "arrangement" with the United States, a diplomatic source said today.

Representatives of Premier Fidel Castro's regime, the source disclosed, have lately hinted to Spanish diplomats in various capitals that a modus vivendi between Havana and Washington should be sought.

The implication was that Spanish diplomacy might be instrumental in bringing about contacts for such an improvement in Cuban-United States relations.

International observers here believe that Washington will not consider negotiations with Cuba before the Presidential elections next autumn.

Diplomats here suggest that the Administration emerging from the election may envisage an arrangement with Cuba if it obtains certain guarantees.

Specifically, Washington would not subscribe to a modus vivendi with the Cuban regime, it is believed, unless the latter formally renounced any idea of a military alliance with the Soviet Union and halted subversion in Latin America.

It is assumed that the Castro regime is turning to Spain for possible mediation because of the present good relations between Madrid and Washington. At the same time, Spain is showing goodwill toward Cuba and has recently increased commercial exchanges with her.

Spokesmen for the anti-Communist Spanish regime justify dealings with Premier Castro

Continued on Page 3, Column 3

NEWS INDEX

News Summary and Index, Page 37

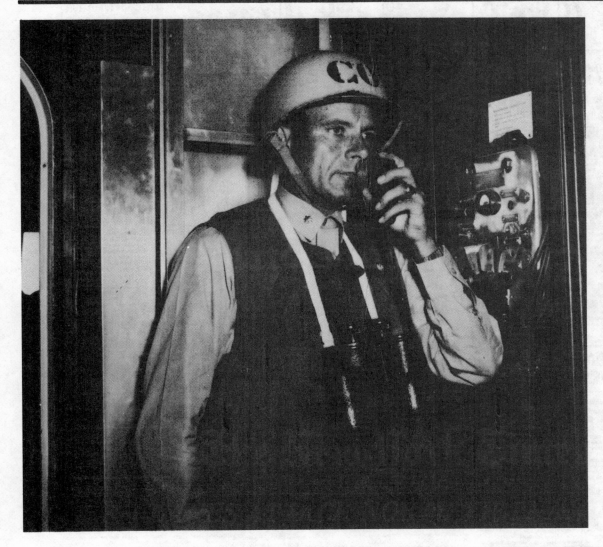

A member of the Pacific Fleet Mobile Photo Unit helps to compile information for reconstructing documentary coverage of the men, ships and planes involved in the Gulf of Tonkin incident.

The U.S.S. *Constellation* in 1963 prior to the Gulf of Tonkin attack.

The New York Times.

VOL. CXIII..No. 38,836.   © 1964 by The New York Times Company. Times Square, New York, N. Y. 10036.   NEW YORK, SATURDAY, MAY 23, 1964.   TEN CENTS

PRESIDENT URGES NEW FEDERALISM TO 'ENRICH' LIFE

In Talk to Michigan Class He Bids U.S., Localities Join in Rebuilding Country

CITES CITIES' PROBLEMS

Johnson Exhorts Students to Beautify Nation and to Raise School Standards

By TOM WICKER
Special to The New York Times

ANN ARBOR, Mich., May 22—President Johnson called today for a "creative federalism" of local and national authorities to rebuild American cities, preserve the American countryside and develop an educational system that "grows in excellence as it grows in size."

As a first step, he promised the 4,862-member graduating class of the University of Michigan, he will "establish working groups to prepare for a series of White House conferences and meetings—on the cities, on natural beauty, on the quality of education, and on other emerging challenges."

In an appeal directed primarily to the nation's youth, Mr. Johnson said that the "challenge of the next half-century" was to use American resources "to enrich and elevate our national life and to advance the quality of American civilization."

Challenge of the Cities

Nowhere is the challenge more pressing than in the cities, the President told about 85,000 persons sitting in the sun in the world's largest college-owned stadium.

"In the next 40 years," Mr. Johnson said, "we must rebuild the entire urban United States."

Outside the cities, he said, "we must act to prevent an ugly America"—turning back the threats of polluted air, water and food, disappearing fields and forests, and overcrowded recreational areas.

In the classroom, Mr. Johnson continued, "we must give every child a place to sit and a teacher to learn from."

"Poverty must not be a bar to learning and learning must offer an escape from poverty," he declared.

Interrupted by Applause

Even more important, the President said, is that the nation's educational system should "find new ways to stimulate the love of learning and the capacity for creation."

Mr. Johnson was interrupted frequently for applause, particularly when he urged better teacher salaries and spoke of civil rights.

At Detroit, where the President transferred from his jetliner to a helicopter for the flight to Ann Arbor, he was met by a crowd estimated by the police at 30,000 but which did not seem quite so large to other observers.

Gov. George Romney, a Republican who sometimes figures in Presidential speculation, met the President at the municipal airport at 9:09 A.M. So did Henry Ford 2d, the automobile magnate, who is also a Republican. Mayor Jerome Cavanaugh of Detroit, a Democrat, presented Mr. Johnson to the crowd.

Mr. Johnson delivered the

Continued on Page 10, Column 2

Barnes Scores Rule Of 'Mob' on Lights

Traffic Commissioner Henry A. Barnes criticized yesterday Mayor Wagner's order for the installation of a traffic light at a Harlem intersection after four days of demonstrations.

Mr. Barnes deplored "traffic improvements made on the basis of mob rule," and said it was unfair to give special priority to those using "pressure tactics."

Sit-ins and picketing, which led to 17 arrests, began Monday at the corner of 131st Street and Fifth Avenue, near Public School 133. They were halted Thursday, after the Mayor had promised the installation of a light.

Parents taking part in the protest had said that schoolchildren were endangered by the traffic. But in his written statement, Mr. Barnes said that there was no record of any traf-

Continued on Page 10, Column 6

Caplin Quits Post As U.S. Tax Chief

Mortimer M. Caplin

Special to The New York Times

WASHINGTON, May 22—Mortimer M. Caplin resigned today as Commissioner of Internal Revenue.

In his letter of resignation to President Johnson, Mr. Caplin said that "personal responsibilities are compelling me to return to private life."

While Mr. Caplin did not further define his reasons, associates indicated that a combination of financial and family reasons was behind the

Continued on Page 21, Column 2

RIGHTS BLOC NEAR AN ACCORD ON BILL

Humphrey-Dirksen Changes Almost Complete—Senate Action Due Next Week

By E. W. KENWORTHY
Special to The New York Times

WASHINGTON, May 22—Senator Hubert H. Humphrey said today that he and the Republicans' Senate leader, Everett McKinley Dirksen of Illinois, planned to introduce early next week their package of amendments to the civil rights bill.

Senate Republicans held their third meeting on the proposals this morning but did not complete their discussions. Mr. Dirksen said a final meeting would be held next Monday morning. He was hopeful of concluding then the consideration of several minor changes in language proposed by his colleagues.

When Mr. Dirksen went to the meeting today, he had with him three pages of changes suggested during the two earlier meetings. These had been gone over with Democratic staff members and representatives of the Justice Department.

Mr. Dirksen indicated that most of them had been accepted.

As an example of the changes made, Mr. Dirksen said it had been decided that any person who felt he had been defamed by a complainant in an execu-

Continued on Page 11, Column 2

CITY CONSIDERING SHIFTING CLASSES FOR INTEGRATION

Some 6th Grades Would Be Put in Junior High and 9th Grades in Senior High

By LEONARD BUDER

The school system may transfer some sixth grades to junior high schools and some ninth grades to senior highs to promote integration and improve education.

The contemplated changes were outlined at a private meeting yesterday by Dr. Calvin E. Gross, the Superintendent of Schools.

They would be the first step toward the possible reorganization of the school system along the lines recommended last week by a state advisory committee.

The transfer of sixth-graders would give the elementary schools additional space to expand their kindergarten programs and possibly add pre-kindergarten programs. These are considered especially important for children in underprivileged areas.

Full Sessions Possible

The additional space could also make it possible for these schools to operate full-day kindergartens, instead of the half-day sessions that are now provided.

The transfer of the ninth-grade classes would give the senior high schools a better racial balance. A recent study has shown that there are proportionately more Negro students in the ninth grade than in the upper grades.

The changes under consideration were disclosed by Dr. Gross at a meeting yesterday morning with assistant superintendents at Board of Education headquarters, 110 Livingston Street, Brooklyn.

No details were given as to which schools might be involved in the experiment. The assistant superintendents, who are in charge of local school districts throughout the city, were told to keep the matter confidential.

Board Approval Needed

The matter later came up at an informal meeting of the school board, which was attended by six of the nine members. Another informal meeting was scheduled for next Wednesday, and a source indicated that the board might take some action at that time. The changes could only be put into effect with the approval of the board.

The state committee, which was appointed by Dr. James E. Allen Jr., the State Education Commissioner, urged fundamental changes in the structure of the schools.

The committee called for an end of the present 6-3-3 arrangement—six years of elementary school, three of junior high and three of senior high school—and the establishment of a 4-4-4 pattern.

This would provide for neighborhood primary schools ex-

Continued on Page 10, Column 5

City Outlay Budget Of $3,354,501,789, A Record, Is Passed

By CHARLES G. BENNETT

A record expense budget of $3,354,501,789 for the fiscal year beginning July 1 was approved yesterday by the Board of Estimate and the City Council.

The figure was $3,048,000 higher than that in Mayor Wagner's proposed "austerity" budget, and $263,002,384 above appropriations in the present year.

All changes made in the Wagner budget by the two bodies were identical; they had been worked out Thursday by a joint subcommittee and submitted to full meetings of the Council and the board yesterday. Mayor Wagner, who was one of Thursday's conferees, is expected to accept the budget as revised.

In the City Council, the Republican minority assailed the new budget as laden with fat.

G.O.P. Seeks Staff

Minority Leader Angelo J. Arculeo, Brooklyn Republican, in a 1,500-word minority report, accused the Council's Democratic majority of deliberately "starving" the Republican group to keep it weak and ineffective. He called for an adequate staff to permit the minority to do its job.

Mr. Arculeo scored Mayor Wagner for having put through new and increased taxes—such as the rise in the retail sales tax from 3 to 4 per cent and the new professional occupancy tax—a year ago. As a result of these imposts, he charged, "in this year of general prosperity New York City's economy has been lagging behind that of the rest of the state."

Joseph Modugno, Queens Republican, said of the budget: "This budget is like a tremendous giant, with thin arms, emaciated legs, a bottomless stomach and no muscles at all."

The Board of Estimate dis-

Continued on Page 55, Column 2

Decision Due Soon On Kennedy Race

By WARREN WEAVER Jr.
Special to The New York Times

WASHINGTON, May 22 — Attorney General Robert F. Kennedy has told friends he will reach a decision on running for the Senate from New York State in a few weeks.

Earlier Mr. Kennedy had been described as unlikely to make a decision until after the Democratic National Convention, which opens in Atlantic City on Aug. 24.

His associates now report, however, that the Attorney General feels it would be unfair to New York Democratic leaders and the other potential candidates to delay his decision beyond mid-June or shortly thereafter.

Many New York Democrats want to choose a candidate to oppose Senator Kenneth B. Keating as early as possible

Continued on Page 28, Column 3

TAKES UP NEW POSITION: Gen. Kong Le, left, commander of Laotian neutralist forces, in Ba Na after retreat from the Plaine des Jarres. At right is Gen. Vang Phao, commander of Meo guerrillas, friendly to the neutralists.
Associated Press Radiophoto

SAIGON WELCOMES U.S. BORDER PLAN

Khanh Amenable to Idea of U.N. Inspection Team on Cambodian Frontier

By PETER GROSE
Special to The New York Times

SAIGON, South Vietnam, May 22 — Premier Nguyen Khanh welcomed today a United States suggestion that United Nations inspectors be stationed along the troubled frontier between South Vietnam and Cambodia.

He said the South Vietnamese Government would favor "any real international control" of the border, whether by the United Nations, the International Control Commission or any other international body that could be truly effective.

He said South Vietnam's Foreign Minister, Pham Huy Quat, would fly to New York to take part in the Security Council debate on Southeast Asian border tension.

It was in the Security Council yesterday that Adlai E. Stevenson suggested for the first time that a solution of the Cambodian border problem might be a United Nations force. He said contribute to the costs of maintaining a United Nations presence along South Vietnam's western border if this were voted by the Council.

Type Not Specified

The American delegate's suggestion left open the type of United Nations presence to be considered. American officials here believe the most practical force would be one composed of troops from South Vietnam and Cambodia working under the direction of a United Nations command.

The question of a United Nations presence along the frontier has been under careful study here in recent weeks. American officials have worked out tentative plans for a real border patrol, not just a token force. They believe the border patrol could be effective if other United Nations members would agree to the proposal.

General Khanh's willingness to accept border controls, possibly under the auspices of the International Control Commission, surprised some observers here. The commission, composed of India, Canada and Poland,

Continued on Page 6, Column 3

Laos to Ask Anti-Red Help Of U.S., Britain and France

By The Associated Press

VIENTIANE, Laos, May 22—Premier Souvanna Phouma announced today that "we are going to ask aid from France, the United States and Britain—both military and economic—for the defense of the country's unity."

The Laotian leader, whose neutralist army has been swept from the Plaine des Jarres by the pro-Communist Pathet Lao, said that "we are now in the process of establishing our needs."

Prince Souvanna Phouma spoke to newsmen after it became known that United States jets already were flying reconnaissance missions over territory held by the Pathet Lao, trying to pinpoint military concentrations and ascertain the intentions of the pro-Communist commanders.

Washington sources have said these unarmed craft started the flights yesterday at the Prince's request. He declined to comment on them.

[Moscow reported that the Soviet Government was informing Paris of its support for France's proposal that the 14-nation Geneva conference be re-convened to discuss the Laotian crisis.]

Defense Equipment Permitted

All foreign military forces were supposed to withdraw from Laos under the 14-nation Geneva agreements of 1962, which guaranteed the independence and neutrality of the Southeast Asian kingdom. But the accords permit the Government to bring in limited quantities of war matériel for defense.

The United States withdrew its contingents which had trained and advised Government troops in the civil war of 1959 to 1961.

But there never has been proof that foreign Communists—specifically combat and supply units of Communist North Vietnam—left the country.

The Pathet Lao broadcast today a bitter complaint about "provocative reconnaissance" by United States jets, saying there had been an American flight over the Pathet Lao area for the second consecutive day.

Pro-Reds Slow Attack

By SEYMOUR TOPPING
Special to The New York Times

VIENTIANE, May 22—The Pathet Lao forces slowed their advance today as low-level reconnaissance flights by United States planes appeared to warn of possible armed intervention if the offensive went forward.

Pathet Lao troops were reported to have probed the new position at Ba Na taken up by the neutralist forces of General Kong Le after his withdrawal from the Plaine des Jarres. The new portion is northwest of the plain in the forested hill country of the friendly Meo tribesmen.

The Pathet Lao was also active north of Borikane in an area 75 miles northeast of Vientiane. Some apprehension was felt that the Pathet Lao

Continued on Page 2, Column 3

Plane Maker's Wife Kidnapped in Paris

By The Associated Press

PARIS, Saturday, May 23—The wife of a multimillionaire airplane builder and publisher, Marcel Dassault, was kidnapped early today by two masked men who hit Mr. Dassault over the head with a pistol and knocked out his chauffeur.

Mrs. Madeleine Dassault, who is about 65 years old, fought back, striking one assailant in the stomach with her umbrella and losing her gold compact in the struggle.

The Dassaults had just driven up to their apartment house in their chauffeur-driven American limousine.

The chauffeur, Louis Dubois, 48, said that Mrs. Dassault was walking to the door when two men seized her. Mr. Dubois said they knocked him out when he tried to intervene.

One of the men also ran to

Continued on Page 8, Column 3

RUSK WARNS REDS WAR IN VIETNAM MAY BE WIDENED

He Says This Is Possibility if Communists Persist in 'Their Aggression'

U.S. JET HIT OVER LAOS

Navy Reconnaissance Craft Flies Back to Carrier— Pilot Reported Unhurt

Excerpts from Rusk's speech will be found on Page 4.

By HEDRICK SMITH
Special to The New York Times

WASHINGTON, May 22 — Secretary of State Dean Rusk raised the possibility tonight that the war in South Vietnam might be expanded "if the Communists persist in their course of aggression."

This was considered the most serious warning the United States has given during the deepening crisis in Southeast Asia touched off by leftist and Communist attacks in Laos.

Shortly before Mr. Rusk's speech, officials disclosed that one of the United States Navy reconnaissance jets flying over embattled central Laos had been hit by ground fire, but had made its way back to an American aircraft carrier at sea. Qualified sources said the plane's engine had been damaged, but not seriously, and that the pilot was unhurt. Despite the incident, these sources said, the reconnaissance flights are continuing.

Other Moves Envisioned

The reconnaissance missions were regarded as possibly only the first of a number of American military moves in Southeast Asia designed to underline the grave concern with which Washington views the latest attacks by pro-Communist Pathet Lao and North Vietnamese troops in Laos.

Secretary Rusk spoke before the American Law Institute. His speech was largely devoted to a history of the troubles and tensions that have gradually worn away the non-Communist position in Southeast Asia. The address was another element of Washington's carefully developed plans to bring a halt to Communist advances.

"We have made it clear that we are not going to abandon people who are trying to preserve their independence and freedom," Mr. Rusk said solemnly. "In this is the signal which must be read with the greatest of care in other capitals, and especially in Hanoi and Peiping.

"Both in Laos and in Vietnam there is a simple prescription for peace—leave your neighbors alone."

Mr. Rusk's firm tone and his reference to a "signal" that must be read clearly in Communist China and North Vietnam underlined the seriousness

Continued on Page 4, Column 3

U.S. CLERICS SCORE MOSCOW ON JEWS

Anti-Defamation League's Protest on Repressions Is Endorsed by 2,000

By GLADWIN HILL

BEVERLY HILLS, Calif., May 22—Two thousand Protestant and Roman Catholic clergymen and church officials in the United States joined Jewish leaders today in signing a protest against the treatment of Jews in the Soviet Union.

The endorsers included three Cardinals of the Roman Catholic Church, the heads of several major Protestant denominations and seven Bishops of the Protestant Episcopal Church. The Catholic leaders were Francis Cardinal Spellman, Richard Cardinal Cushing of Boston and Joseph Cardinal Ritter of St. Louis.

The communication was given to the State Department and to the United States delegation to the United Nations for transmission to Moscow. Three are estimated to be three million Jews in the Soviet Union.

The representation, termed a "letter of conscience," was drawn up by the Anti-Defamation League of B'nai B'rith, the international Jewish service organization, and was announced at the league's national executive committee meeting here.

The league charged that, in addition to systematic discouragement of Jewish religious traditions, the Soviet Union was engaging in a "campaign of vilification of the Jewish past and present in newspapers and other official publications."

"Jewish history is being falsified, anti-Semitic stereotypes exploited and the synagogue portrayed as a breeding ground for crime," it added.

The communication, referred to as a petition, set forth a

Continued on Page 7, Column 1

GUIANA DECLARES EMERGENCY RULE

Britain Adding to Troops as Race Strife Grows

Special to The New York Times

GEORGETOWN, British Guiana, May 22—A state of emergency was proclaimed in this British colony tonight as racial violence and terrorism rose to a new peak.

The proclamation was made by the Governor, Sir Richard Luyt, in a nationwide broadcast. He said more British troops would be coming to help preserve law and order.

All troops in the British garrison, which was reduced in January from two battalions to one, moved into positions tonight to prevent further disturbances. The heavily armed soldiers patrolled this capital and seven other trouble spots.

The police used tear gas on several occasions today on mobs looting the municipal markets and small business premises owned by East Indians.

Negro mobs attacked East Indians who were boarding a boat to leave the city.

Other Indians were badly beaten in the streets and had to be sent to a hospital. A man was severely injured when he

Continued on Page 8, Column 6

DELIVERS COMMENCEMENT ADDRESS: President Johnson speaking at University of Michigan. Others, from right: Gov. George Romney of Michigan, Prof. Marvin L. Niehuss, university vice president, and Joseph E. Maddy, of Interlochen music camp in Michigan.
Associated Press Wirephoto

A South Vietnamese fortified outpost goes up in flames after a surprise attack by Viet Cong guerrillas.

Three Viet Cong prisoners huddle in front of a bunker at the Soc Trang Airfield in South Vietnam.

"All the News That's Fit to Print"

The New York Times.

LATE CITY EDITION
U.S. Weather Bureau Report (Page 58) forecast: Sunny and hot today. Fair tonight. Chance of showers late tomorrow.
Temp. Range: 96—73; yesterday: 89—69.
Temp.-Hum. Index: about 80; yesterday: 80.

VOL. CXIII..No. 38,902. NEW YORK, TUESDAY, JULY 28, 1964. TEN CENTS

© 1964 by The New York Times Company. Times Square, New York, N.Y. 10036

COURT SAYS STATE MUST REDISTRICT BEFORE APRIL '65

U.S. Judges Set One-Year Terms for Legislators to Be Elected This Fall

SPECIAL SESSION LIKELY

December Meeting Expected—Plan for Connecticut Is Termed Unworkable

By R. W. APPLE Jr.

A Federal Court ordered the New York Legislature yesterday to pass a reapportionment measure by April 1, 1965.

The court directed that Assemblymen and Senators be elected Nov. 3 on the basis of the legislative districts now in effect. But it ruled that the legislators elected on that date could serve only one year instead of two.

By its actions, the three-judge court set the first definite timetable for the implementation of the United States Supreme Court's decision of June 15, which declared the state's formula for legislative apportionment unconstitutional.

The state must now hold three legislative elections in three years—the one in November; a special election in November, 1965, based on new districts, for one-year terms; and a regular election in November, 1966, also based on new districts, for two-year terms.

Democrats' Plea Denied

By ordering the short terms, the court advanced the effective date of the Supreme Court's reapportionment ruling by a full year — from November, 1966, to November, 1965.

The decision yesterday was a defeat for the Democrats, who had asked the court to order immediate redistricting. However, it was not an unqualified victory for the Republicans, who had hoped to delay the impact of reapportionment for two years.

In another development growing out of the Supreme Court's ruling, Gov. John N. Dempsey of Connecticut rejected a Federal Court's plan for redistricting in that state and asked permission to present a proposal of his own.

Mr. Dempsey described the court's plan as unworkable. It calls for a special session of the General Assembly by next week to begin preparations for a constitutional convention.

Sources in Albany reported that Governor Rockefeller was

Continued on Page 26, Column 4

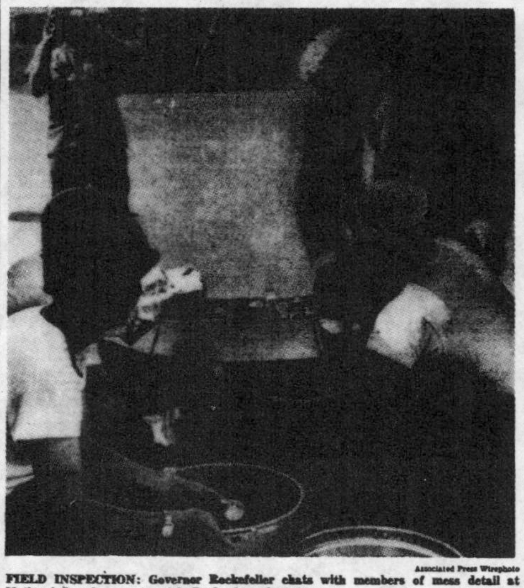

Associated Press Wirephoto

FIELD INSPECTION: Governor Rockefeller chats with members of mess detail at National Guard encampment in Rochester, where troops are on hand to prevent rioting.

Police Inspector Demoted In Gambling Graft Inquiry

By EDITH EVANS ASBURY

Police Commissioner Michael J. Murphy demoted a deputy police inspector to captain yesterday on a charge of permitting gambling operations "in an open and notorious manner" in Brooklyn. The officer, Deputy Inspector Anthony Obremsky, also came under fire from District Attorney Frank H. Hogan's office.

The Commissioner charged that the officer had failed to perform his duties properly as supervisor of plainclothes men in the Greenpoint - Williamsburg section of Brooklyn. He had been assigned to that post in the 14th Inspection Division last Jan. 29.

The Commissioner said charges would be brought against the officer, who is on vacation and whose whereabouts were not immediately known yesterday.

Two Charges Made

Mr. Hogan's office cited the manner in which the officer had answered grand jury questions about his activities while stationed in midtown Manhattan, and took note of his seeking retirement July 17 after a third appearance before the grand jury.

Two specific charges were made against Captain Obremsky.

The first alleged that he "failed and neglected to properly perform his duties between June 26 and July 14, 1964, between 7 and 10 P.M., and that within the area of his responsibility at Union Avenue and Withers Street, Brooklyn, during these times, a gambling operation took place in an open and notorious manner."

The second charge asserted that Captain Obremsky's alleged failure to perform his duties "did bring or tend to bring adverse criticism of this department and a loss of confidence and respect of the people."

12 Others Face Charges

The announcement, made by Deputy Commissioner Walter Arm, said that 12 other policemen stationed in the 14th Division would be served with similar charges.

Previously Captain Obremsky served as deputy inspector on plainclothes patrol duty in the Third Division of Manhattan, which handles vice and gambling cases in midtown.

The officer's appearance before the special New York County grand jury investigating allgeed links between the police and gamblers was disclosed yesterday when Assistant District Attorney Peter D. Andreoli applied to Supreme Court Justice Charles Marks for the release of testimony.

Mr. Andreoli stated, in an affidavit for the court, that the

Continued on Page 60, Column 1

GOVERNOR DENIES VOTING-LAW PLEA

Rejects Wagner Demand for Special Session to Revise Literacy Requirement

By DOUGLAS DALES
Special to The New York Times

ALBANY, July 27 — Governor Rockefeller rejected today Mayor Wagner's request for a special session of the Legislature to revise the state's literacy requirements for voting.

Mr. Wagner had said the state should act to make its literacy requirements conform with the Federal Civil Rights Act of 1964. However, Mr. Rockefeller said today that the Mayor's request had been based on a "misunderstanding" of the 1964 statute.

The New York law since 1923 has permitted literacy to be established by proof of an eighth-grade education.

Provisions of Law

The literacy provision in the new Federal law applies to suits in which the United States Attorney General alleges that discrimination exists in the voting process. It makes a sixth-grade education presumptive evidence of literacy. It does not intend to supersede state voting requirements, the Governor said.

[In New York, Mayor Wagner said he had not seen the Governor's statement and did not know what the basis for the Governor's decision was. But he added: "Of course, I disagree completely on the issue."]

In a letter to the Mayor, Mr. Rockefeller buttressed his position on the intent of the 1964 law with an opinion from the Department of Justice and by reference to statements by Senators Kenneth B. Keating, Republican of New York, and Hubert H. Humphrey, Democrat of Minnesota, during the debate on the 1964 law.

Confusion Feared

Mayor Wagner, in requesting the special session last July 8, expressed fear that the differences in the educational standards for literacy would create a chaotic situation, with some voters eligible to vote in national but not state elections.

Mr. Rockefeller said that there was no inconsistency between the Federal and state literacy requirements and that the state's requirements continue to apply to Federal and state elections alike.

"The Civil Rights Act of 1964," the Governor wrote, "is concerned with voter literacy

Continued on Page 26, Column 2

HARLEM KILLINGS REPORTED URGED

Police Testify That Leftist Called on Negroes There to Slay Patrolmen

By PETER KIHSS

A left-wing Harlem Negro was said yesterday to have urged Negroes to kill policemen and judges.

Testimony by police witnesses in Supreme Court ascribed the actions to William Epton, leader of the Harlem Defense Council and a top member of the Progressive Labor Movement. He was also said to have urged Negroes to lure policemen into side streets where they could be bombarded with bottles and other missiles.

Justice Gerald P. Culkin continued a restraining order against demonstrations in Harlem by Mr. Epton's group and by Jesse Gray's Community Council on Housing. The restraining orders have been sought by the city to avert further racial disorders.

5 Negroes Transferred

There were these other developments in the city's race problems:

¶Police Commissioner Michael J. Murphy transferred five Negro sergeants into the three Harlem precincts to replace five whites.

¶The Rev. Dr. Martin Luther King Jr., president of the Southern Christian Leadership Conference, flew here at the invitation of Mayor Wagner and met with the Mayor at Gracie Mansion late last night.

¶A Harlem unity committee held a press conference last night at which Dr. King's presence in the city was denounced. A spokesman said Harlem leaders were "mad as hell at Mayor Wagner for importing Dr. King from Atlanta to discuss problems of Harlem."

¶The City Council, in a move endorsed by Mayor Wagner, ar-

Continued on Page 15, Column 1

Teamsters Cut Off Liquor for Harlem

By EMANUEL PERLMUTTER

The teamsters' union placed a temporary embargo yesterday on liquor deliveries to Harlem and the Bedford-Stuyvesant section of Brooklyn.

Lester Connell, secretary-treasurer of Local 816 of the International Brotherhood of Teamsters, said the action had been taken primarily to protect the drivers and their helpers from assault and robbery.

He added that withholding liquor from the two areas might also reduce a cause of violence and disorder.

The embargo was imposed as the men returned from a two-week vacation during which wholesale liquor dealers observed their annual summer shutdown.

About 200 union members and several hundred bars and liquor

Continued on Page 14, Column 6

GOVERNOR TOURS ROCHESTER AREA, DENOUNCES RIOTS

He Finds 'Clear Evidence of Extremism'—Visits Troops and Meets Officials

By FRED POWLEDGE
Special to The New York Times

ROCHESTER, July 27—Governor Rockefeller flew here unannounced today and inspected the scene of three nights of racial rioting. He said he was saddened and shocked by what he saw.

The Governor toured the riot area in an automobile, and visited with the National Guardsmen he called out yesterday and congratulated them and the state policemen on their work.

He met with city, county and state officials for about an hour, and then returned to New York City.

Quiet prevailed throughout Rochester tonight. The police radio buzzed with routine traffic. In areas where violence had occurred earlier, the loudest noise came from television sets in houses and apartment buildings.

Governor Cites Extremism

The Governor was asked at a news conference late in the afternoon whether the racial violence here was the kind of extremism he had had in mind when he appealed to the Republican National Convention to adopt a platform plank condemning all forms of extremism.

Mr. Rockefeller replied: "Have you been downtown through the streets where these riots took place and seen the boarded-up stores? I think that's clear evidence of extremism, that anyone who had seen it would not hesitate to call it extremism.

"As Governor, and as a citizen, I deplore this kind of violence. Regardless of the objectives, it cannot be justified."

Question of Agitation

He said he saw no direct connection between the rioting here and the recent outbreaks in New York City. "There is no indication that I have from any source of outside agitators," he added.

Mr. Rockefeller said he had come here "because the state has committed some 450 police, and because I've called out the National Guard."

He said his reaction to the situation was "the same reaction that everyone has—a reaction of shock, a reaction of sadness."

Declaring that the state would take "all steps necessary" to preserve peace, he said he hoped it would not be

Continued on Page 14, Column 1

JOHNSON STRESSES ECONOMIC ISSUES AS CAMPAIGN KEY

He Counsels Party Leaders to 'Talk Jobs' in Dealing With 'White Backlash'

By EARL MAZO

President Johnson has sent word to Democratic leaders that "bread and butter" issues should be stressed in the coming political campaign to overshadow the possible adverse effect in some places of racial issues.

Mr. Johnson's message has been conveyed to top-rank party figures in New York and elsewhere by members of the Cabinet.

They revealed that the President lectured the Cabinet for more than an hour last week on campaign strategy and techniques. The President reportedly emphasized that the best way to deal with the "white backlash" vote was to "talk jobs, prosperity, opportunity . . . a good future."

Voter Trend Reported

One Cabinet member quoted Mr. Johnson as stating:

"When the people know how good things are and are going to be, they'll stop worrying about who is going to move next door."

His reference was to reports that some voters in overwhelmingly Democratic communities of the North and West believed that the Civil Rights Act might cause them to lose jobs to Negroes and accelerate the integration of their neighborhoods.

Mr. Johnson instructed his Democratic colleagues to talk "prosperity, people and peace" in the campaign.

Appearances Limited

The President also indicated that he was inclined to schedule relatively few barnstorming tours during the campaign. That chore would fall to his Vice-Presidential running mate, he implied. His own public appearances would be restricted to normal Presidential activities, such as news conferences, with major addresses to the nation on television.

Mr. Johnson reviewed in detail the campaign strategies of President Franklin D. Roosevelt in 1936 and 1940 and President Dwight D. Eisenhower in 1956. Mr. Johnson said he considered these campaigns models for an incumbent seeking reelection.

At one point, according to a Cabinet member, the President asked if anyone in the room realized that Mr. Roosevelt had

Continued on Page 9, Column 4

U. S. TO ENLARGE VIETNAM FORCE BY 5,000 ADVISERS

TOTAL TO BE 21,000

More Materiel Also Will Be Provided to Counter Reds

By EDWIN L. DALE Jr.
Special to The New York Times

WASHINGTON, July 27—The United States will add about 5,000 men to its 16,000-man military mission in South Vietnam, it was reliably reported tonight.

The Vietnamese Government announced in Saigon earlier today that the United States would increase its military assistance, but the magnitude was not disclosed. Officials in Washington said tonight that it would be "in the order" of 5,000 men.

It is understood that the additional troops will work mainly in the field, accompanying and advising Vietnamese units down to the battalion level. The Saigon announcement said that, in addition, the United States would send more military equipment to bolster the critical struggle against the Communist forces.

Evidence of Concern

The announcement of the step-up of about 30 per cent was viewed as further evidence of the deep concern in Washington about the trend of the war. However, there was still no sign of a United States decision to carry the war into North Vietnam or to throw American units into combat.

The 5,000 men will be sent to South Vietnam the next few months. The first contingent is expected to be a 600-man unit from Okinawa. Plans for the shipment of this unit had been announced before today's action.

The disclosure of a major increase in the United States mission illustrates a complete change from the more hopeful atmosphere of last year. In October, the White House announced that its goal was the withdrawal of all United States forces by the end of 1965.

Reduction Abandoned

This policy was changed before the year was out as the Vietcong guerrillas stepped up their military activity. The plan to reduce the United States forces was abandoned in December. Now, seven months later, comes the announcement of a major increase.

Already 158 American servicemen have lost their lives in the war even though they have not been serving as members of United States combat units.

The basic United States policy remains unchanged. This is to help the South Vietnamese fight the war on their own territory and gradually wear down the guerrilla forces.

There have been recent reports from Saigon that the Vietcong, now sometimes attacking in organized strength, may be preparing for a major military campaign in central Vietnam. One objective that has been mentioned is capture of the former capital city of

Continued on Page 5, Column 1

Makarios Proposes U.N. Assembly Step

By W. GRANGER BLAIR
Special to The New York Times

NICOSIA, Cyprus, July 27—Archbishop Makarios, President of Cyprus, said today that the Cyprus question should be taken "soon" to the United Nations General Assembly.

He prefaced the statement with the remark that he did not believe an "agreed solution" of the crisis was "possible."

The President expressed his views at the airport before leaving for Athens to consult with the Greek Government on the political and military situation relating to Cyprus.

Archbishop Makarios is expected back Wednesday after

Continued on Page 2, Column 6

GOLDWATER PLANS G.O.P. UNITY TALKS

Will Invite Party's Leaders and All Its Governors—Eisenhower Expected

By E. W. KENWORTHY
Special to The New York Times

WASHINGTON, July 27 — Senator Barry Goldwater announced today that he intended to call a meeting of all Republican Governors and other leading party figures in the interest of party unity.

The Republican Presidential nominee did not set a date for the meeting. He said it would come after two breakfast conferences to which he and Representative William E. Miller of upstate New York, the Vice-Presidential nominee, have invited Republican members of the House and Senate on Aug. 6 and 7.

At these breakfast sessions, Mr. Goldwater said, "we will discuss what we will have made by then for our campaign, and we will find out what is on their minds." Because of the number of Republicans in Congress—33 in the Senate and 178 in the House—it will be

Continued on Page 10, Column 2

Churchill Pays Last Visit to Commons

50-Minute Stay Ends 64-Year Service of Wartime Leader

By JAMES FERON
Special to The New York Times

LONDON, July 27 — Sir Winston Churchill, looking fit, spent what was probably his final hour in the House of Commons today.

Tomorrow the chamber he has served for 64 years will record, in an official tribute, its "unbounded admiration and gratitude for his services," but Sir Winston is not expected to be there.

The frail health of the 89-year-old former Prime Minister, his colleagues feel, would not permit the response he would feel obliged to give if he were present.

Instead, a written reply will be read to the House later in the week. Parliament will adjourn Friday and Sir Winston, who still represents the Woodford constituency, has said he intends to retire.

Today there was nothing to keep Sir Winston from a final visit to the House he has frequented for so long.

He entered the chamber shortly after 3 P.M. supported by two fellow Conservative members, Capt. Lawrence P. S. Orr and Sir Dudley Williams, and leaning on a cane.

Foreign Secretary R. A. Butler was answering questions as Sir Winston's colleagues guided him to his usual place on a front bench at the foot of the gangway. There were no cheers, no interruption, at his arrival.

He wore a dark bow tie

Continued on Page 7, Column 1

Associated Press Cablephoto

Sir Winston Churchill being escorted from London home for trip to Parliament. In foreground is one of his cats.

India Acts to Stop Grain Speculation

By JACQUES NEVARD
Special to The New York Times

NEW DELHI, July 27—India acted vigorously today to increase food supplies at prices her masses can afford to pay.

In a move aimed at forcing speculators to unload hoarded stocks, the Government announced the imposition of strict controls on the purchase, sale, storage and transportation of grains.

Prime Minister Lal Bahadur Shastri has called the shortage and high prices of food the "most formidable problem" facing India.

[The police in Bombay arrested about 700 persons during a demonstration over soaring prices, Reuters reported.]

The announcement of controls was made by Coimbatore

Continued on Page 5, Column 3

SENATE BARS PLAN TO LIST FINANCES

Then Clears Way to Set Up a Federal Ethics Panel

By CABELL PHILLIPS
Special to The New York Times

WASHINGTON, July 27—The Senate rejected all efforts tonight to require members to disclose details of their finances. It then paved the way for the creation of a special commission to study ethical practices in every branch of the Federal Government.

Final action will be taken tomorrow on a resolution sponsored by the minority leader, Everett McKinley Dirksen, that in effect sidetracks efforts by the Rules Committee to require Senators and Senate employes to make periodic disclosures of their outside financial holdings.

The Rules Committee disclosure plan, recommitted by a vote of 48 to 39, was the outgrowth of the committee's eight-month investigation of the outside business activities of Robert G. Baker, former secretary to the Democratic majority.

The proposal would have required all members of the Senate, and all Senate employes earning more than $10,000 annually, to identify periodically the sources of outside income exceeding 50 per cent of their Senate pay.

This proposal was vigorously opposed throughout a day of debate by Senator Dirksen and many other Senators of both parties.

Efforts to stiffen the Rules Committee's plan were defeated

Continued on Page 18, Column 1

NEWS INDEX

ONE OF THE GREAT PLAYS OF ALL TIME: "THE TROJAN WOMEN"—Advt.

A CHICKEN IN EVERY POT—or something more exotic if you choose from the many food suggestions on the women's page of The New York Times.—Advt.

A desolate woman walks with two South Vietnamese soldiers through the ruins of her village which was devastated by the Viet Cong.

One step ahead of the marauding Viet Cong guerrillas, South Vietnamese peasants evacuate their villages and homes by sampan.

South Vietnamese paratroopers drift earthward after jumping from C-123s on a mission near Saigon.

The U.S.S. *Ticonderoga* was one of several U.S. Navy ships attacked by the North Vietnamese in the Gulf of Tonkin incident, August, 1964.

North Vietnamese warships, similar to this patrol and attack craft, provoked and attacked the four U.S. Navy ships in the Gulf of Tonkin.

"All the News That's Fit to Print"

The New York Times.

LATE CITY EDITION
U. S. Weather Bureau Report (Page 44) forecasts:
Partly cloudy and cooler today, tonight and tomorrow.
Temp. Range: 78—65; yesterday 82—66
Temp.-Hum. Index: mid-70's; yesterday 76

VOL. CXIII . No. 38,908. NEW YORK, MONDAY, AUGUST 3, 1964. TEN CENTS
© 1964 by The New York Times Company. Times Square, New York, N. Y. 10036

MAYOR WILL SEEK MORE FEDERAL AID IN PARLEYS TODAY

He, Screvane and Dumpson to Hold Round of Talks on Antipoverty Drive

GROUP TO MEET WIRTZ

Wagner, in 'Social' Weekend With Johnson, Discusses the City's Program

By THOMAS P. RONAN

Mayor Wagner will explore with top Federal officials today the possibility of getting additional immediate and long-range aid in the city's antipoverty campaign.

The Mayor's office said yesterday that Mr. Wagner would spend the day in Washington in a round of talks with Congressional leaders and officials administering domestic aid programs.

City Council President Paul R. Screvane, Welfare Commissioner James R. Dumpson and Julius C. C. Edelstein will accompany the Mayor. Mr. Screvane is co-chairman of the Mayor's Poverty Council and Mr. Dumpson is its vice chairman, Mr. Edelstein is the Mayor's executive assistant.

Their first appointment, at 10 A.M., is with Secretary of Labor W. Willard Wirtz and Daniel P. Moynihan, Assistant Secretary of Labor for policy, planning and research.

Will Meet Celebrezze

At noon they are to confer with President Johnson's Task Force on Poverty and at 3 P.M. with Anthony J. Celebrezze, Secretary of Health, Education and Welfare.

They also plan to see Sargent Shriver, director of the Peace Corps, and officials of the Housing and Home Finance Agency.

The Mayor discussed the city's antipoverty program with President Johnson during his weekend visit to the White House with his sons, Robert Jr., 20 years old, and Duncan, 17.

The Mayor and his sons returned at 5 P.M. yesterday on an Air Force twin-engine jet. They went from Kennedy International Airport to their summer home at Islip, L. I. Mr. Wagner said at the airport that he also had talked to the President about the racial situation here, housing and the international situation.

Though he has often been mentioned as a possible nominee for Vice President, Mr. Wagner said this subject had not been

Continued on Page 28, Column 7

ANTIPOVERTY BILL FACES HOUSE TEST

Strong Opposition Planned by G. O. P. This Week

By MARJORIE HUNTER
Special to The New York Times

WASHINGTON, Aug. 2 — President Johnson's key foreign and domestic programs face crucial tests this week as Congress pushes toward adjournment.

Foreign aid will be debated in the Senate. The antipoverty bill is scheduled for House action. Both bills face strong opposition.

The fate of other Administration bills will be on the line this week. A decision is expected on whether to push for a program of medical care for the aged under Social Security. Clearance will be sought for the House to debate extending the area redevelopment program, which was once given up for dead.

The House debate over the Administration's $962.5 million antipoverty bill is expected to be one of the major legislative battles of the year.

The Senate passed an almost identical bill by nearly 2 to 1 last month after cutting out $15 million in funds and eliminating several farm programs.

In the House, however, the antipoverty bill has become caught up in far more partisan politics. Republicans, almost solidly opposed to the bill, have

Continued on Page 34, Column 3

NEW NUMBER FOR ORDERING WANT ADS in The New York Times. OXford 5-3311. Fast, direct-line service to want ad takers.—Advt.

Negroes and Police Clash in Jersey City; 30 Reported Injured

Special to The New York Times

JERSEY CITY, Monday, Aug. 3 — Scores of Negroes rioted here last night and early today, hurling debris, looting stores and shouting at the police.

At least 30 persons, including 10 policemen, were injured. Three of those hurt were white persons whose car was stopped by a mob.

All of the city's 150 available policemen were sent to the scene, in the predominantly Negro Lafayette section.

The police said that about 500 Negroes were concentrated in several spots in the area at the height of the rioting but that many of them were only onlookers. Observers said 200 people, most of them young toughs, made up the core of the rioters.

The trouble, which started shortly after 8 P. M., was generally under control at 1 o'clock this morning.

The trouble began when Miss Dolores Shannon, 26

Continued on Page 11, Column 4

U.S. PUSHING PLANS FOR '65 MOON TEST

Ranger 7 Experts Will Join Surveyor Project for an Unmanned Landing

By RICHARD WITKIN
Special to The New York Times

LOS ANGELES, Aug. 2—The success of Ranger 7 will lead to concentration on the Project Surveyor "soft" lunar landing, a space agency official said today.

The official said a number of top-grade engineers would be transferred from the Ranger to the Surveyor program to capitalize on their experience.

He indicated that other measures were also in the offing to assure that the late 1965 date for the first test flight would not have to be put off, as it has been several times already.

A landing is not a primary goal of the first launching. But the unmanned spacecraft will be fully equipped to try it if everything works in the initial stages of flight.

Vital Tests This Fall

Preparations are going ahead full tilt for vital tests early this fall in which the difficult soft lunar landing will be simulated in a 1,500-foot drop from a balloon over the White Sands, N. M., proving area.

The eventual landing on the moon will have to be as gentle as a parachute landing on earth.

But since the moon has no appreciable atmosphere, the landing cannot be made with parachutes. It will have to be done with reverse-thrust braking rockets automatically receiving precise instructions from sensitive radar on board.

Such a trick has never been performed on earth. It will be enormously more difficult 240,000 miles away.

In the Ranger program, the astonishing quality of the pictures received Friday has led to a diversity of suggestions about where the next landing should be made.

There are two more Ranger flights planned, virtual duplicates of the Ranger 7 mission.

Originally it had been thought

Continued on Page 3, Column 4

GOVERNOR ORDERS GUARD RECALLED FROM ROCHESTER

Move Is Made With Consent of Local Officials After 7 Days of Relative Calm

Special to The New York Times

ROCHESTER, Monday, Aug. 3—Governor Rockefeller last night ordered the withdrawal of all National Guard units from this city, and early this morning convoys of guardsmen slowly began winding their way home.

More than 1,200 officers and men had been on standby duty for a week to prevent new outbreaks of racial violence, which erupted here 10 days ago and resulted in four deaths.

The guardsmen learned of Governor Rockefeller's decision shortly after 9 o'clock last night, and immediately began dismantling pup tents and assembling their gear. Though the troops' morale was generally high, they cheered. Many headed for telephones to notify their families.

The Governor's statement, issued in Albany, noted that there had been seven consecutive days of law and order here. It said that the move had been made "with the consent of local and county authorities."

State Police to Stay

It added that the Governor had acted "after reviewing the steps being taken by local authorities to protect the citizens of Rochester after state forces are withdrawn."

Local officials said that the 300 state policemen on duty here would remain available. It was understood that state and local officials would meet today to discuss how long the troopers might be needed.

Beginning at 4 A.M. today, the city's police force resumes its regular eight-hour shifts and regular days off. However, leaves and furloughs remain canceled.

The guardsmen, who came here from eight neighboring communities, were never called into action. But their presence and their shows of force—touring the city with fixed bayonets—helped to bring relative quiet to the troubled city.

Among the guard units mobilized were three from Rochester. They will remain in the East Main Street Armory until later today.

Police Pelted

During the rioting, which broke out July 24, about 350 persons were injured and 973 were arrested. The violence started when the police attempted to arrest a Negro youth for disorderly conduct at a street dance.

Crowds of Negroes began pelting the police with bottles and stones and the police were hard-pressed, despite reinforcements, to cope with the rioters.

City Manager Porter W. Homer imposed a night curfew on this city of 325,000 on the next night and rescinded it last Monday. The sale of liquor was also banned during that time.

During the weekend of violence, stores were looted despite efforts by the police and firemen to stop the outbreaks with water hoses. The rioting broke out in two Negro districts, the Joseph Avenue section just east of the business district and an area across the Genesee River to the southwest.

The worst toll of the week-

Continued on Page 12, Column 3

CHINA COUNSELS SOVIET TO REMAIN GUARDIAN IN LAOS

Note Backs Call for Talks and Asks No Decision Until Then on Chairmanship

Special to The New York Times

HONG KONG, Aug. 2 — Communist China made it clear today that it did not want the Soviet Union to carry out its threat to withdraw as co-chairman of the 1962 conference on Laos.

In a note to Moscow, Peking expressed support for the Soviet Union's renewed call for another 14-nation meeting on Laos. Peking said that any Soviet decision on the 1962 co-chairmanship should await discussion at a new conference.

The Soviet Union shared the 1962 chairmanship with Britain. The two countries have maintained special responsibilities under the agreements reached in Geneva to neutralize and assure the Government of Laos.

The Chinese note, quoted by Hsinhua, the Chinese Communist press agency, was in reply to the Soviet proposal of July 25.

Warning With Proposal

In its proposal for a new meeting, the Soviet Union warned that it would have to re-examine its role as co-chairman if the United States and other Western powers continued to block the convening of the conference.

Last week, after a visit to Moscow by R. A. Butler, the British Foreign Secretary, the Soviet Union was reported to have agreed to defer a final decision on withdrawing as co-chairman.

The Peking statement said the Soviet Government had "rightly condemned the United States imperialists' violations of the Geneva agreements and their acts of interference in the internal affairs of Laos." The statement went on to say that Peking "expresses its approval of and support for" the Soviet bid for a new conference this month.

Peking recalled that a new conference was first proposed by Prince Norodom Sihanouk, the chief of state of Cambodia, and the French Government following a coup d'état April 19 in Vientiane.

Reds Support Call

Soon after the coup, directed by right-wing forces against Premier Souvanna Phouma, a neutralist, and his coalition regime, things returned to roughly their previous state except that the right-wing and neutralist military forces joined more closely. The French-Cambodian call for a new conference was backed by the Soviet Union, Communist China and North Vietnam.

The meeting failed to materialize, the Chinese note said, "owing to obstruction by the United States and its followers."

"The Chinese Government holds that the present grave situation in Laos is wholly created by United States imperialism," Peking said.

The Chinese note said it was "necessary that the Soviet Government should use its capacity and influence as co-chairman of the Geneva conference to persuade the United States to give up its unreasonable conditions and accept a proposal

Continued on Page 5, Column 5

U.S. Commander in Pacific Discusses Naval Clash

Associated Press Wirephoto

Adm. U. S. Grant Sharp Jr., center, talking with reporters yesterday in Honolulu. Admiral Sharp upheld the action of the U. S. destroyer and aircraft that responded to attack.

RED PT BOATS FIRE AT U.S. DESTROYER ON VIETNAM DUTY

Maddox and Four Aircraft Shoot Back After Assault 30 Miles Off Coast

ATTACKERS DRIVEN OFF

American Units Undamaged —Rusk Says 'Other Side Got a Sting Out of This'

By ARNOLD H. LUBASCH
Special to The New York Times

WASHINGTON, Aug. 2 — Three North Vietnamese PT boats fired torpedoes and 37-mm. shells at a United States destroyer in international waters about 30 miles off North Vietnam today.

The destroyer and four United States aircraft fired back, damaged them and drove them off.

The incident was announced here in an official statement by the Defense Department. It said that neither the destroyer nor the aircraft sustained casualties or damage.

The statement said that the destroyer, the 3,300-ton Maddox, was on a routine patrol when an unprovoked attack took place in the Gulf of Tonkin.

Cautious on Identification

At first Government officials were cautious in commenting that the attacking boats presumably came from North Vietnam, but Secretary of State Dean Rusk said in New York tonight that the attackers were North Vietnamese.

"The other side got a sting out of this," the Secretary said. "If they do it again, they'll get another sting."

Reports received here, apparently based on close air surveillance of the attacking boats, indicated there was no doubt that they were from North Vietnam.

President Johnson was informed immediately and received reports from top Government officials at a 45-minute White House meeting. He issued no statement.

Not Regarded as Crisis

Government officials said later that the attack was not regarded as a major crisis. They said the United States Seventh Fleet had been patrolling the area for some time would continue its patrols and had sufficient strength on hand.

Adm. U. S. Grant Sharp Jr., Commander in Chief in the Pacific, was advised of the incident by radio as he flew back to his Pearl Harbor headquarters from a visit to South Vietnam.

The Defense Department statement on the attack, issued also by the Pacific Command, said that the boats were damaged by gunfire from the Maddox and the four carrier-based jet aircraft. The statement said:

"While on routine patrol in international waters at 4:08 A.M., E.D.T., the United States destroyer Maddox underwent an unprovoked attack by three PT-type boats at latitude 19-40 north, longitude 106-34 east, in Tonkin Gulf. The attacking boats launched three torpedoes and used 37-mm. gunfire.

"The Maddox answered with

Continued on Page 6, Column 4

BELGIAN TO SPEAK FOR TSHOMBE HERE

Struelens, Once Information Chief of Katanga Regime, to Be Special Envoy

By J. ANTHONY LUKAS
Special to The New York Times

LEOPOLDVILLE, the Congo, Aug. 2—Michel Struelens, former director of the Katanga Information Service in New York, will serve as the personal representative for Premier Moise Tshombe of the Congo in his dealings with the United States Government.

Informed sources said today that Mr. Struelens, a Belgian who now lives in Canada, had been named as adviser to the Congolese Embassy in Washington and to the Congolese delegation to the United Nations.

However, he is expected to be more than an adviser. He will hold the title of Special Assistant on Foreign Affairs to Mr. Tshombe and observers here believe he will perform some of the functions normally performed by an ambassador.

Had Dispute With U.S.

In 1962, when Mr. Struelens was a spokesman and propagandist for Mr. Tshombe's secessionist government in Katanga Province, the United States moved to have him expelled from the country. Mr. Struelens, after a long battle, left the United States voluntarily a year ago for Canada.

Mr. Struelens, who has been here for the last five days, was scheduled to leave Leopoldville tonight on his way to the United States He is expected to confer with United States officials in Washington next week.

Mr. Struelens talked in Washington last month with McGeorge Bundy, President Johnson's Special Assistant on National Security Affairs, and W. Averell Harriman, Under Secretary of State for Political Affairs.

According to a source close to the Congolese Government, Mr. Harriman and Mr. Bundy indicated they would welcome the designation of an intermediary who had Mr. Tshombe's full confidence. They are reported to have said they would ac-

Continued on Page 4, Column 6

The New York Times Aug. 3, 1964

The U.S.S. Maddox was attacked in the Gulf of Tonkin (1). North Vietnam said U.S. planes raided a border area (2).

RAID FROM LAOS ALLEGED BY HANOI

Vietnam Communists Say 4 U.S. Planes Attacked Border Village and Post

By The Associated Press

TOKYO, Aug. 2 — Communist North Vietnam charged today that four United States fighter-bombers flew in from Laos and attacked a border post and village with bombs and rockets. Hanoi said the attack yesterday wounded a villager and destroyed homes and property.

A protest from the North Vitenamese Foreign Ministry accused the United States of a provocative act and said the Laotian Government "must bear heavy responsibility" for having allowed the United States to use its territory for the attack.

The United States has sent T-28 fighter-bombers to the Government of Prince Souvanna Phouma, the neutralist Premier of Laos, in its struggle against the pro-Communist Pathet Lao. The propeller-driven planes, piloted by Laotians, have been striking at Pathet Lao forces around the Plaine des Jarres in central Laos.

The Hanoi protest, broadcast by the North Vietnamese press agency, did not describe the attacking planes other than to say they were United States fighter-bombers.

United States Navy jets have been flying reconnaissance in

Continued on Page 5, Column 4

DIRKSEN PRESSES FOR POLICY STUDY

Asserts Destroyer Incident May Be Omen for U.S.—Democrats Cautious

By ROBERT B. SEMPLE Jr.
Special to The New York Times

WASHINGTON, Aug. 2 — Senator Everett McKinley Dirksen said today that the attack on the destroyer Maddox showed that "a hard look" at the Administration's policies in Vietnam was a matter of "the utmost urgency."

The Republican leader in the Senate, a frequent critic of United States policy in Southeast Asia, said that what most concerned him was that the attack appeared to be "one more item in the Communist bag of tricks," and that incidents of this sort, while seemingly isolated, might foreshadow "other attacks of a more serious nature."

A spot check of Congressional opinion here brought expressions of dismay over the attack from Republicans, while Democrats either withheld judgment altogther or took the position that such incidents were to be expected in view of the extent of the United States commitment in Southeast Asia.

The Senate majority leader, Mike Mansfield, speculated that the incident might cause considerable Congressional debate. The Montana Democrat asserted, however, that the episode did not appear to challenge in any way the United States policy in Vietnam.

"We have got to remember that we are rather heavily committed out there," he said, "and that in view of our involvement such occasions will arise from time to time. We hope they do not, but we should not be surprised if they do."

Most Congressmen seemed

Continued on Page 7, Column 2

Khrushchev's Year of Troubles: Policies Tested

By MAX FRANKEL
Special to The New York Times

WASHINGTON, Aug. 2—A year has passed since Premier Khrushchev turned his back on Communist China to sign the nuclear test ban treaty with the United States and Britain. It was a bitter choice, leading to a year of torment for Moscow. The anniversary finds Washington appreciative of both the choice and the torment.

The evidence of recent days alone demonstrates the pressure that Mr. Khrushchev must now face from all sides. He and his policies are in effect to be tested in two momentous elections at the same time—in the choice between Moscow and Peking that he is forcing upon the 90 Communist parties of the world and in the developing American campaign debate over East-West conciliation versus strife.

Analysts here believe that the Soviet leader has an enormous stake in both contests. Unless he can hold the allegiance of a great majority of the Communists against the Chinese, it is thought, Soviet influence in the world, Moscow's authority in the revolutionary movement and Mr. Khrushchev's standing in his country will be severly damaged.

But a comparable blow might be dealt him, officials note, by the United States electorate, over which he has no direct control.

Because Mr. Khrushchev's argument with Peking revolves around "coexistence" and the need to avoid nuclear war, his Communist enemies are expected to profit greatly if a sizable number of Americans can be shown to have rebelled against the recent efforts of Washington to negotiate and live more normally with the Soviet Union.

All this uncertainty, the analysts add, has hit Moscow at a time of great domestic strain as well. The long and apparently heated debate among the Soviet leaders about the allocation of limited capital continues with no sign of resolution. The champions of the military, of agriculture, heavy industry, chemistry, foreign aid and a dozen other activities are still vying for a share of the modest investment pie.

Under the circumstances, officials here say they know better than to seek consistency in Mr. Khrushchev's words and deeds. But, with some disagreement among themselves, they believe they can appreciate his major worries and problems at the moment and some of his reactions.

Their analysis begins with signs that Moscow has tried in many small ways to preserve the easier relations with the United States and the West as a whole that followed the Cuban missile crisis of 1962. They cite the restraint that Mr. Khrushchev has pressed on Cuba, his well-advertised deflation of the tension over Berlin and Moscow's correctness, and at times even courtesy, in scrapes and incidents that would have evoked storms in other years.

Since the test-ban treaty, Mr. Khrushchev has also cooperated with Presidents Kennedy and Johnson in some real and some largely contrived agreements to emphasize the value of negotiation—agreements on cultural exchanges, a consular convention, the banning of missiles in orbit and cutbacks in the production of fissionable materials.

The "peace issue" is thought to be important to Mr. Khrushchev not only in winning supporters against the Chinese but also to justify his administration to the Soviet people, whose ever greater desire for

Continued on Page 2, Column 3

NEWS INDEX

GOLDWATER AND THE SOUTH
Don't miss famed political pollster Samuel Lubell's first report on what the South thinks. Today's World-Telegram.—Advt

NEW NUMBER FOR ORDERING WANT ADS in The New York Times. OXford 5-3311. Fast, direct-line service to want ad takers.—Advt.

Orthodox Mission To Rome Expected

By ROBERT C. DOTY
Special to The New York Times

ROME, Aug. 2 — Prospects were reported good today that the Eastern Orthodox Church would soon establish a permanent mission in Rome to restore contacts broken nine centuries ago.

The Roman Catholic daily Il Quotidiano attributed to a monsignor who was recently in touch with Eastern Orthodox patriarchs the statement that the Orthodox Conference of Rhodes from Aug. 23 to Sept. 3 would "almost certainly" authorize the establishment of a liaison mission here.

The writer, Raniero la Valle, interviewed Msgr. Aristide Brunello, a member of the Italian Catholic Association for the Christian Orient, at an ecumenical meeting at La Mendola in

Continued on Page 2, Column 3

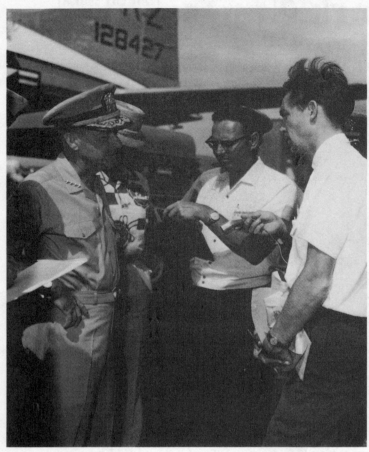

Admiral Grant Sharp, Commander-in-Chief of the Pacific Fleet, being interviewed by newsmen for his reactions to the provocative Gulf of Tonkin incident.

A photograph taken from aboard the U.S.S. *Maddox* during its attack by three North Vietnamese warships on August 2, 1964. One of the warships is shown approaching the *Maddox* at breakneck speed.

The U.S.S. *Turner Joy,* one of the four Navy ships attacked by the North Vietnamese.

The New York Times.

LATE CITY EDITION
U.S. Weather Bureau Report (Pg. 46) forecasts Variable cloudiness today; clear tonight. Fair and cool tomorrow.
Temp. Range: 86—65; yesterday: 81—57. Temp.-Hum. Index: low 70's; yesterday: 73.

VOL. CXIII—No. 38,910.   © 1964 by The New York Times Company. Times Square, New York, N. Y. 10036   NEW YORK, WEDNESDAY, AUGUST 5, 1964.   TEN CENTS

U.S. PLANES ATTACK NORTH VIETNAM BASES; PRESIDENT ORDERS 'LIMITED' RETALIATION AFTER COMMUNISTS' PT BOATS RENEW RAIDS

F. B. I. Finds 3 Bodies Believed to Be Rights Workers'

GRAVES AT A DAM

Discovery Is Made in New Earth Mound in Mississippi

By CLAUDE SITTON
Special to The New York Times

JACKSON, Miss., Aug. 4—Bodies believed to be those of three civil rights workers missing since June 21 were found early tonight near Philadelphia, Miss.

Federal Bureau of Investigation agents recovered the bodies from a newly erected earthen dam in a thickly wooded area about six miles southwest of Philadelphia, in east-central Mississippi.

The dam is several hundred yards off State Highway 21, near the Neshoba County fairgrounds.

Fulton Jackson, the county coroner, made a preliminary examination at the scene. The bodies were then sealed in plastic bags and brought by ambulance to the University of Mississippi Medical Center in Jackson, 70 miles to the southwest.

Pledge by Governor

Roy K. Moore, special agent in charge of the Jackson F.B.I. office, said physicians and forgerprint experts would seek to make positive identification and establish the cause of death.

[In Washington, authoritative sources said that President Johnson had telephoned Gov. Paul B. Johnson Jr. of Mississippi after having learned of the discovery of the bodies. However, this could not be confirmed immediately.]

Governor Johnson said in a statement:

"If these are the bodies of the three civil rights workers who have been missing several weeks, the investigative forces of the State of Mississippi will exert every effort to apprehend those who may have been responsible."

Area Searched Earlier

Mr. Jenaras said he understood F.B.I. agents had searched the area once before and had noticed the new dam. Later, when they saw that the dam had collected no water despite heavy showers, they returned for a further investigation.

Excavation uncovered the bodies in the fill of the dam, the Governor said.

Sheriff L. A. Rainey, who had just returned from a vacation, visited the scene a short while after the discovery.

The missing men were Michael H. Schwerner, 24 years old, and Andrew Goodman, 20, both white and both from New York City, and James E. Chaney, a Negro of Meridian, Miss.

All three had been taking part in the Mississippi Summer Project, a state-wide civil rights drive, which began on the week-

Continued on Page 27, Column 2

Scattered Violence Keeps Jersey City Tense 3d Night

400 Policemen Confine Most of Rioters to 2 Sections—Crowds Watch in Streets Despite Danger

By FRED POWLEDGE

JERSEY CITY, Aug. 4—Scattered violence broke out again here tonight as roving groups of Negroes hurled crude Molotov cocktails in the streets. There was some gunfire but no injuries were reported.

About 400 city policemen contained most of the young rioters to two predominantly Negro neighborhoods. There were at least six arrests.

Although it was dangerous to be on the streets on this third night of violence, many people watched from sidewalks and front porches as police cars, their red lights flashing, sped from one pocket of violence to another.

On Ocean Avenue the police trained spotlights on the roof of a three-story block of apartments. A man had been seen on the roof, and it was feared that he was armed with a rifle, fire bombs, or both. Yet on the sidewalk below, a woman walked her dog, apparently without concern, through throngs of helmeted policemen. From a front porch across the street, a baby cried.

Since the rioting started Sunday night, more than 30 persons have been injured, two of them with gunshot wounds. None of the wounds was critical. More than three dozen persons have been arrested.

Five hundred city and Jersey City policemen stood ready to

Continued on Page 26, Column 1

JOHNSON SEEKING EXTREMISM PLANK

Favors a Stand Against Far Left and Right Without Naming Any Groups

Special to The New York Times

WASHINGTON, Aug. 4—President Johnson wants the Democratic platform to take a stand against extremism of the right and the left, without naming any particular organization.

Mr. Johnson, at the moment, plans to attend the party's national convention in Atlantic City only on Thursday night, Aug. 27, when he is scheduled to make his acceptance speech. But his wish on the platform is likely to be enough to make his views effective.

As yet, however, he has had no detailed discussions with the platform drafters.

The President is also planning to follow a somewhat unusual procedure in having himself placed in nomination. This is to be done by "co-nominators" — Governors Edmund G. Brown of California and John B. Connally Jr. of Texas.

These and other fairly well-advanced plans of the President have been learned from high Democratic sources.

However, on the question of most current interest, Mr. Johnson's choice for a Vice-Presidential candidate, no decision has yet been made.

Senator Hubert H. Humphrey

Continued on Page 14, Column 6

Rockefeller to Join Goldwater's Parley On Campaign Unity

Special to The New York Times

ALBANY, Aug. 4—Governor Rockefeller has accepted the invitation of Senator Goldwater to attend a meeting of Republican Governors at Hershey, Pa., on Aug. 12.

The invitation was extended by the Republican Presidential nominee in telegrams last Saturday to the 16 Republican Governors.

Mr. Rockefeller, who was a candidate for the Presidential nomination until after his defeat in the California primary, June 2, was one of Senator Goldwater's severest critics through the Republican National Convention last month in San Francisco.

Mr. Goldwater has called the Hershey gathering in an effort to promote unity within the Republican party behind his candidacy.

The prospects for success of

Continued on Page 16, Column 1

Salinger Appointed to the Senate

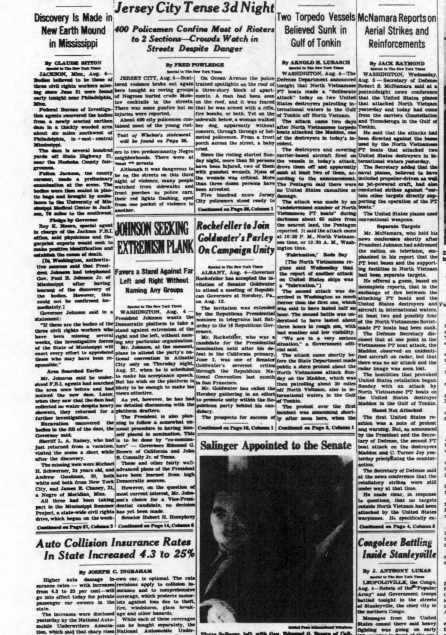

Pierre Salinger, left, with Gov. Edmund G. Brown of California after the announcement yesterday in Sacramento.

By WALLACE TURNER
Special to The New York Times

SAN FRANCISCO, Aug. 4—Pierre Salinger was appointed to the Senate today by Gov. Edmund G. Brown of California to fill the remaining five months of the term of the late Senator Clair Engle. Mr. Salinger is scheduled to be sworn in tomorrow noon. He will be escorted to the rostrum by Senator Thomas H.

REDS DRIVEN OFF

Two Torpedo Vessels Believed Sunk in Gulf of Tonkin

By ARNOLD H. LUBASCH
Special to The New York Times

WASHINGTON, Aug. 4—The Defense Department announced tonight that North Vietnamese PT boats made a "deliberate attack" today on two United States destroyers patrolling international waters in the Gulf of Tonkin off North Vietnam.

The attack came two days after North Vietnamese torpedo boats attacked the Maddox, one of the destroyers in today's incident.

The destroyers and covering carrier-based aircraft fired on the vessels in today's attack, drove them off and apparently sank at least two of them, according to the announcement. The Pentagon said there were no United States casualties or damage.

The attack was made by an "undetermined number of North Vietnamese PT boats" during darkness about 65 miles from the nearest land, the Pentagon reported. It said the attack came at 10:20 P. M. North Vietnam time, or 10:30 A. M., Washington time.

'Fabrication,' Reds Say

[The North Vietnamese regime said Wednesday that the report of another attack on United States ships was a "fabrication."]

The second attack was described in Washington as much fiercer than the first one, which was said to have lasted half an hour. The second battle was understood to have lasted about three hours in rough seas, with bad weather and low visibility.

"We are in a very serious situation," a Government official said.

The attack came shortly before the State Department made public a stern protest about the North Vietnamese attack Sunday on the Maddox, which was then patrolling about 30 miles off North Vietnam, also in international waters in the Gulf of Tonkin.

Hanoi Not Attacked

The first United States reaction was a note of protest and warning. But, as announced by the President and the Secretary of Defense, the second PT boat attack on the destroyers Maddox and C. Turner Joy yesterday precipitated the counteraction.

The Secretary of Defense said at the news conference that the retaliatory strikes were still under way at that time.

He made clear, in response to questions, that no targets outside North Vietnam had been attacked by the United States warpianes. He specifically ex-

Continued on Page 5, Column 1

2 CARRIERS USED

McNamara Reports on Aerial Strikes and Reinforcements

By JACK RAYMOND
Special to The New York Times

WASHINGTON, Wednesday, Aug. 5 — Secretary of Defense Robert S. McNamara said at a postmidnight news conference that the United States planes that attacked North Vietnam yesterday and today had come from the carriers Constellation and Ticonderoga in the Gulf of Tonkin.

He said that the attacks had been directed against the bases used by the North Vietnamese PT boats that attacked two United States destroyers in international waters yesterday.

The Secretary added that the naval planes, believed to have included propeller-driven as well as jet-powered craft, had also conducted strikes against "certain other targets directly supporting the operation of the PT boats."

The United States planes used conventional weapons.

Separate Targets

Mr. McNamara, who held his news conference shortly after President Johnson had addressed the nation on television, emphasized in his report that the PT boat bases and the supporting facilities in North Vietnam had been separate targets.

He offered a guess, based on incomplete reports, that in the exchange of fire between the attacking PT boats and the United States destroyers and aircraft in international waters, at least two and possibly four of the North Vietnamese Soviet-made PT boats had been sunk.

The Defense Secretary disclosed that at one point in the Vietnamese PT boat attack, the Maddox observed an unidentified aircraft on radar, but that there was no air attack and the radar image was soon lost.

The hostilities that provoked United States retaliation began Sunday with an attack by North Vietnamese PT boats on the United States destroyer Maddox in the Gulf of Tonkin.

Continued on Page 4, Column 3

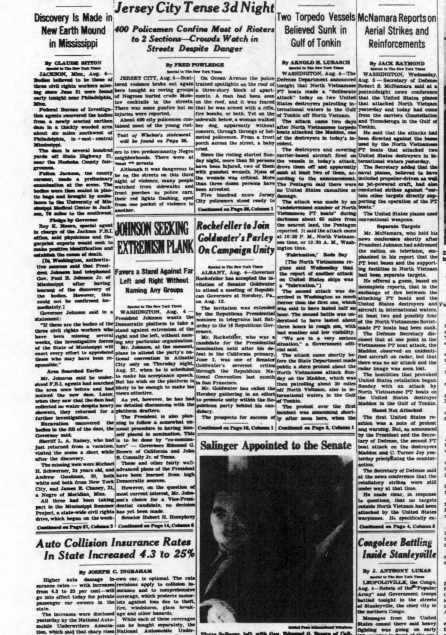

DECISION: President Johnson, in a nationwide broadcast, tells of action he ordered taken against North Vietnam.
Associated Press Wirephoto

The President's Address

Following is the text of the President's address on Vietnam last night, as recorded by The New York Times:

My fellow Americans:

As President and Commander in Chief, it is my duty to the American people to report that renewed hostile actions against United States ships on the high seas in the Gulf of Tonkin have today required me to order the military forces of the United States to take action in reply.

The initial attack on the destroyer Maddox on Aug. 2 was repeated today by a number of hostile vessels attacking two U.S. destroyers with torpedoes.

The destroyers and supporting aircraft acted at once on the orders I gave after the initial act of aggression.

We believe at least two of the attacking boats were sunk. There were no U.S. losses.

The performance of commanders and crews in this engagement is in the highest tradition of the United States Navy.

But repeated acts of violence against the armed forces of the United States must be met not only with alert defense but with positive reply.

Action 'Now in Execution'

That reply is being given, as I speak to you tonight. Air action is now in execution against gunboats and certain supporting facilities in North Vietnam which have been used in these hostile operations.

In the larger sense, this new act of aggression aimed directly at our own forces again brings home to all of us in the United States the importance of the struggle for peace and security in Southeast Asia.

Aggression by terror against the peaceful villages of South Vietnam has now been joined by open aggression on the high seas against the United States of America.

The determination of all Americans to carry out our full commitment to the people and to the Government of South Vietnam will be redoubled by this outrage. Yet our response for the present will be limited and fitting.

We Americans know—although others appear to forget—the risk of spreading conflict. We still seek no wider war.

I have instructed the Secretary of State to make this position totally clear to friends and to adversaries and, indeed, to all.

I have instructed Ambassador Stevenson to raise this matter immediately and urgently before the Security Council of the United Nations.

Congressional Resolution Asked

Finally, I have today met with the leaders of both parties in the Congress of the United States and I have informed them that I shall immediately request that our Government to pass a resolution making it clear that our Government is united in its determination to take all necessary measures in support of freedom and in defense of peace in Southeast Asia.

I have been given encouraging assurance by these leaders of both parties that such a resolution will be promptly introduced, freely and expeditiously debated, and passed with overwhelming support.

And just a few minutes ago I was able to reach Senator Goldwater and I am glad to say that he has expressed his support of the statement that I am making to you tonight.

It is a solemn responsibility to have to order even limited military action by forces whose over-all strength is as vast and as awesome as those of the United States of America.

But it is my considered conviction, shared throughout your Government, that firmness in the right is indispensable today for peace.

That firmness will always be measured. Its mission is

FORCES ENLARGED

Stevenson to Appeal for Action by U.N. on 'Open Aggression'

By TOM WICKER
Special to The New York Times

WASHINGTON, Aug. 4—President Johnson has ordered retaliatory action against gunboats and "certain supporting facilities in North Vietnam" after renewed attacks against American destroyers in the Gulf of Tonkin.

In a television address tonight, Mr. Johnson said air attacks on the North Vietnamese ships and facilities were taking place as he spoke, shortly after 11:30 P.M.

State Department sources said the attacks were being carried out with conventional weapons on a number of shore bases in North Vietnam, with the objective of destroying them and the 30 to 40 gunboats they served.

The aim, they explained, was to destroy North Vietnam's gunboat capability. They said more air strikes might come later, if needed. Carrier-based aircraft were used in tonight's strike.

2 Boats Believed Sunk

Administration officials also announced that substantial additional units, primarily air and sea forces, were being sent to Southeast Asia.

This "positive reply," as the President called it, followed a naval battle in which a number of North Vietnamese PT boats attacked two United States destroyers with torpedoes. Two of the boats were believed to have been sunk. The United States forces suffered no damage and no loss of lives.

Mr. Johnson termed the North Vietnamese attacks "open aggression on the high seas."

Washington's response is "limited and fitting," the President said, and his Administration seeks no general extension of the guerrilla war in South Vietnam.

Goldwater Approves

"We Americans know," he said, "although others may forget, the risks of spreading conflict."

Mr. Johnson said Secretary of State Dean Rusk had been instructed to make this American attitude clear to all nations. He added that Adlai E. Stevenson, chief United States delegate, would raise the matter immediately in the United Nations Security Council. [The Council was expected to meet at 10:20 A.M. Wednesday.]

The President said he had informed his Republican Presidential rival, Senator Barry Goldwater, of his action and

Continued on Page 2, Column 3

Khanh Is Fighting Threat of a Coup

By SEYMOUR TOPPING
Special to The New York Times

SAIGON, South Vietnam, Aug. 4—Premier Nguyen Khanh struggled today to strengthen the political stability of his Government as his aides privately warned of plots to drive him from office. United States officials were concerned about the political deterioration in Saigon.

The malaise in the capital was attributed more to a clash of rival political and military personalities than to pressure from the Vietcong insurgents.

United States sources said reports from provinces indicated that conditions there were generally better than in Saigon.

Once again rumors of a coup d'état were circulating in a sus-

Continued on Page 4, Column 7

Auto Collision Insurance Rates In State Increased 4.3 to 25%

By JOSEPH C. INGRAHAM

Higher auto damage insurance rates — with increases from 4.3 to 25 per cent—will go into effect today for private passenger car owners in the state.

The increases were disclosed yesterday by the National Automobile Underwriters Association, which said that sharp rises in auto thefts and in the cost of repairs had made them necessary.

The association said that although the statewide rise would be the lesser amount, the rates in most of the metropolitan areas had been increased as much as 25 per cent.

Physical damage insurance, which reimburses a car owner for loss of or damage to his

own car, is optional. The rate revisions apply to collision insurance and to comprehensive coverage, which protects motorists against loss due to theft, fire, windstorm, glass breakage and other hazards.

While each of these coverages can be bought separately, the National Automobile Underwriters Association, rating organization for more than 400 companies here, lumps the vari-

Continued on Page 67, Column 1

Congolese Battling Inside Stanleyville

By J. ANTHONY LUKAS
Special to The New York Times

LEOPOLDVILLE, the Congo, Aug. 4—Rebels of the "Popular Army" and Government troops battled tonight in the streets of Stanleyville, the chief city in the northern Congo.

Messages from the United States consul there said heavy fighting was going on early this evening in front of the consulate, about half a mile from the center of the city.

At 6:15 P. M. Stanleyville time, the consul, Michael P. E. Hoyt, telegraphed that the army was "advancing across front lawn of consulate" and seemed to be "pushing rebels back."

Eight minutes later he wired that the army troops were "advancing rapidly and in numbers beyond consulate on road to Wanie Rukula." He said that

Continued on Page 3, Column 6

News Summary and Index, Page 35

"All the News That's Fit to Print"

The New York Times.

LATE CITY EDITION

U.S. Weather Bureau Report (Page 56) forecasts: Mostly sunny and cool today; clear, cool tonight. Fair tomorrow. Temp. Range: 77—62; yesterday 81—62. Temp.-Hum. Index: 70—65; yesterday 73.

VOL. CXIII..No. 38,911. © 1964 by The New York Times Company. Times Square, New York, N. Y. 10036 NEW YORK, THURSDAY, AUGUST 6, 1964. TEN CENTS

U.S. PLANS NO NEW VIETNAM RAID AFTER HITTING 25 PATROL BOATS; TELLS U.N. OF HANOI AGGRESSION

EXPERTS IDENTIFY MISSISSIPPI BODIES AS RIGHTS AIDES'

Informer Reported to Have Been Paid $25,000 for Tip on the Graves

NEW EVIDENCE HUNTED

F.B.I. Declines to Say How 3 Were Slain—Coroner's Jury Visits the Site

By CLAUDE SITTON
Special to The New York Times

JACKSON, Miss., Aug. 5—Experts working from dental charts and other evidence identified today the three bodies found buried deep inside a cattle-pond dam as those of three missing civil rights workers.

Federal Bureau of Investigation agents declined to say how the two white men and one Negro were killed six weeks ago after their release from the Neshoba County jail at Philadelphia, Miss.

There were persistent reports that an informer who received $25,000 to $30,000 had led F.B.I. agents to the crude graves five miles southwest of Philadelphia in the rolling hills of east-central Mississippi.

These reports and other circumstances surrounding the finding of the bodies early last night indicated that investigators knew some details of the slaying and had some idea of who was involved. However, it was learned that no arrests were imminent.

[In Honolulu, Dick Gregory, the Negro entertainer, said tonight that three weeks ago he had turned over a letter to the F.B.I. naming five persons as responsible for the deaths and pinpointing the location of the bodies, according to United Press International.]

Said to Have Been Shot

County Coroner Fulton Jackson, Sheriff L.A. Rainey, Deputy Sheriff Cecil Price and a six-man coroner's jury visited the site last night and again this morning. No finding was announced immediately.

"We are not certain what was the cause of death," Mr. Jackson said.

He drove an ambulance bearing the bodies to Jackson last night. The bodies were encased in three black plastic bags, tagged X-1, X-2 and X-3.

A waiting team of pathologists and F.B.I. identification experts at the University of Mississippi Medical Center began examination of the bodies after the ambulance arrived at 12:30 A.M.

Mr. Jackson was asked today if it were true the autopsies had shown that the three men had been shot to death and that bullets had been removed from all the bodies. Such a report was published by The Jackson Daily News.

"I'm just not going to make any statement at this time," the coroner answered. "The matter is still pending."

J. Edgar Hoover, director of the F.B.I., announced this morning in Washington that the two white men had been definitely identified as Michael H. Schwerner, a 24-year-old field worker for the Congress of Racial Equality from New York, and Andrew Goodman, 20, a

Continued on Page 16, Column 5

Fall of Stanleyville To Rebels Reported

By J. ANTHONY LUKAS
Special to The New York Times

LEOPOLDVILLE, the Congo, Aug. 5 — The control-tower operator at the Stanleyville airport said this afternoon that the city had fallen to rebel forces.

There was no official confirmation, but it appeared that most of that city, the Congo's third largest, was in rebel hands.

Congolese Government troops, who pushed the rebels from the heart of the city last night, were reported late this afternoon to have fled.

If Stanleyville has fallen, the victory would be the most important yet scored by the rebels, who already control much of the eastern Congo. It

Continued on Page 2, Column 3

NEW NUMBER FOR ORDERING WANT ADS IN The New York Times: OXford 5-3311. Fast, direct-line service to want ad takers.—Advt.

Criminal Anarchy Charged to Epton In Indictment Here

By JACK ROTH

William Epton, the chairman of the Progressive Labor Movement in Harlem, an extreme left-wing organization, was arrested here yesterday on charges of advocating criminal anarchy.

This was the first such indictment voted in New York County since 1919, when three men associated with a Communist newspaper, Revolutionary Age, were convicted.

Mr. Epton, a Negro, is 32 years old. He describes himself as an electrical tester and lives at 1420 Amsterdam Avenue. He says he is a disciple of the Chinese Communists.

Mr. Epton was accused in the true bill of advocating overthrow of the organized government of the State of New York by force and violence and of calling for the killing of police officers and judges.

The defendant was arraigned before Supreme Court Justice Gerald P. Culkin, who

Continued on Page 18, Column 3

POLICE INTENSIFY NARCOTICS DRIVE

Squad Is Expanded, Review Panel Established and Training Extended

Police Commissioner Michael J. Murphy strengthened the department's program against narcotics yesterday.

The Commissioner ordered the formation of a departmental narcotics enforcement review board, the assignment of more men to the 200-member narcotics squad, and the extension of special training in narcotics enforcement to the 600 men and women in the Youth Division.

Deputy Commissioner Walter Arm, who announced the moves at Police Headquarters, said that the stepped-up drive against the illegal drug traffic would be concentrated in three areas—Harlem, East Harlem and the Bedford-Stuyvesant section of Brooklyn.

These are the areas, he said, where most narcotics addicts live. But, he added, the department's efforts would have their effect "all over the city."

Mr. Arm emphasized that the Commissioner's orders had not been prompted by the recent racial riots here or by the current Senate Government Operations subcommittee investigation into drug addiction.

Senator Jacob K. Javits had said Tuesday before the subcommittee that the removal of dope addicts from the streets of Harlem and Bedford-Stuyvesant would help to reduce tensions. He called the addicts an "incendiary element."

Mr. Arm said that the moves announced yesterday had been "studied and considered for a long time."

The new narcotics enforce-

Continued on Page 20, Column 1

DEMOCRATS YIELD TO STATES' RIGHTS IN POVERTY BILL

Administration, Courting the South in House Debate, Accepts Veto Principle

By MARJORIE HUNTER
Special to The New York Times

WASHINGTON, Aug. 5—The Administration, as a concession to the South, agreed today that Governors would be allowed to veto antipoverty projects in their states.

The move, designed to attract badly needed Southern votes, was announced as the House opened a partisan debate over President Johnson's antipoverty bill.

The states' rights amendment will be offered by supporters of the legislation tomorrow or Friday. The final vote on the bill is scheduled Friday.

Administration sponsorship of the veto proposal represents a reversal of the stand taken in the Senate just two weeks ago. There, Administration leaders fought off adoption of a similar proposal. Instead, the Senate adopted an amendment allowing Governors to veto only those projects originated by private organizations, such as the church groups or civic clubs.

Racial Overtones Voiced

The amendment to be offered in the House would allow Governors to veto city and county projects as well, possibly tying the hands of communities seeking Federal funds to wage local attacks on poverty.

Today's debate was marked by frequent clashes between Democrats and Republicans. The Republicans charged, as they had done previously, that they had been locked out from attempts to write a bipartisan bill.

There were strong racial overtones, too. Representative Howard W. Smith of Virginia, a leader of the conservative Southern bloc that has joined Republicans in opposing the bill, told the House:

"I want to say to any Southerners who plan to vote for this bill, you are implementing the civil rights bill that you opposed."

Calls Poverty a Disease

The Job Corps training camps that would be set up under the bill would be "integrated camps," Mr. Smith said pointedly. "They aren't going to be very popular south of the Potomac."

Mr. Smith also suggested that Federal funds could be channeled into the hands of the National Association for the Advancement of Colored People to wage local campaigns against poverty.

"And is there anything in this bill that would stop them from establishing a nudist colony in your community?" he asked.

Another Southerner, Representative Phil M. Landrum, Democrat of Georgia, is leading the floor fight for passage of bill.

Mr. Landrum spoke eloquently of the hopelessness that

Continued on Page 21, Column 1

PEACE CALLED AIM

Stevenson Says Goal Is to Keep Southeast Asia Independent

Text of remarks in Security Council debate, Page 9.

By THOMAS J. HAMILTON
Special to The New York Times

UNITED NATIONS, N. Y., Aug. 5—The United States told the Security Council today that despite "acts of deliberate aggression" by North Vietnam it was determined to maintain the "assured and guaranteed independence" of Southeast Asia.

"We are in Southeast Asia," Adlai E. Stevenson, the chief United States delegate, declared, "to help our friends preserve their own opportunity to be free of imported terror, or alien assassination managed by the North Vietnam Communists based in Hanoi and backed by the Chinese Communists from Peking."

Mr. Stevenson insisted that the United States bombing of North Vietnamese torpedo boats "and their facilities" was an act of self-defense against attacks on United States destroyers on the high seas and was authorized by international law and the United Nations Charter.

U.S. 'Cannot Be Diverted'

He said: "This is a single action designed to make unmistakably clear that the United States cannot be diverted by military attack from its obligations to help its friends establish and protect their independence."

R. W. Jackling, the British representative, supported the United States, holding that the bombing was authorized by Article 51 of the Charter, which recognizes the right of self-defense against an armed attack pending action by the Security Council to maintain international peace and security.

However, Platon D. Morozov, the Soviet representative, asserted that in the view of his Government the United States had committed an "act of aggression." He added that if such actions were repeated the United States "will have to bear a heavy responsibility."

The only other speaker on the merits of the question was Liu Chieh of Nationalist China, who said that the United States action was justified by international law and the Charter.

Official sources said that the primary aim of the United States was to report the North Vietnamese attacks to the Council and that it did not intend to introduce a resolution at this

Continued on Page 8, Column 8

The New York Times (by Patrick A. Burns)

EXPLAINS U.S. ACTION: Adlai E. Stevenson, U.S. delegate to U.N., addressing Security Council meeting on the Vietnamese crisis. At top is Platon D. Morozov, Deputy Soviet Representative. Center is R. W. Jackling, British Deputy Permanent Representative.

PEKING CONDEMNS U.S. 'AGGRESSION'

Chinese Won't 'Sit Idly By' While Americans Extend War, Statement Warns

Special to The New York Times

HONG KONG, Thursday, Aug. 6—Communist China accused the United States today of "deliberate armed aggression" against North Vietnam and said the Chinese people would not "sit idly by."

In an official statement distributed by the Hsinhua press agency, Peking Government said Washington had taken the first step toward extending the war in Indochina.

Referring to the American raids on North Vietnamese installations as a "surprise attack," the Peking statement said Washington had thus gone "over the brink of war."

This was Peking's first comment on the developments of the last few days. It gave no hint of what Peking intended to do, and analysts here speculated that the Chinese Communists might not yet have decided on any action.

As Peking's strongest statement on the situation so far, it appeared to commit China to some concrete move.

It spoke of "lending a helping hand" and added that "the debt of blood incurred by the

Continued on Page 6, Column 6

Johnson Tells Communists Not to Expand Hostilities

By JOSEPH A. LOFTUS
Special to The New York Times

SYRACUSE, Aug. 5—President Johnson warned the nations of the Communist world today not to support or widen aggression in Southeast Asia or to assume that in this election year the United States was divided.

In grave, measured tones, the President said:

"To any who may be tempted to support or to widen the present aggression, I say this: There is no threat to any peaceful power from the United States of America. But there can be no peace by aggression, and no immunity from reply. And that is what is meant by the actions that we took yesterday."

Text of President's speech will be found on Page 7.

The words rang out over the green, rolling campus of Syracuse University, where the President dedicated the first building of the Samuel I. Newhouse Communications Center.

Nation's Unity Stressed

A standing audience of many thousands replied with applause after nearly every sentence of the President's warning and his remarks about domestic politics.

To allies and adversaries alike the President addressed his closing words:

"Let no friend needlessly fear, and no foe vainly hope, that this is a nation divided in this election year. Our free elections—our full and free debate—are America's strength, not America's weakness."

This declaration of domestic unity was dramatized on the spot by Governor Rockefeller: When the President finished speaking, the Republican Governor stepped up and shook his hand.

Last night, as he prepared to

Continued on Page 7, Column 5

President Requests Support of Congress

Johnson message, proposed resolution are on Page 8.

By E. W. KENWORTHY
Special to The New York Times

WASHINGTON, Aug. 5—President Johnson asked Congress today to pass a joint resolution assuring him of full support "for all necessary action" he might have to take to protect the armed forces of the United States in Southeast Asia.

The President also asked that the resolution give prior sanction for any necessary steps, including the use of armed force, to assist nations covered by the Southeast Asia Treaty Organization that requested help in defense of their freedom.

As soon as the clerk had finished reading the special message from the White House,

Continued on Page 8, Column 1

MORE U.S. FORCES ARE SENT TO ASIA

Aircraft and Ships Rushed —Troops Alerted in Event Chinese Intervene

Special to The New York Times

WASHINGTON, Aug. 5—The United States rushed fighting men, planes and ships to Southeast Asia today. Secretary of Defense Robert S. McNamara, announcing the reinforcements at a news conference this morning, disclosed among these the assignment of an antisubmarine task force to the South China Sea.

This clearly was intended to thwart any possible intervention by the Chinese Communists. The North Vietnamese are not known to have any submarines.

In a television interview tonight, Mr. McNamara was asked to comment on the possibility of Soviet or Chinese Communist intervention.

"We are prepared for any action they may take," he replied.

Carrier Group Shifted

The Secretary announced at his news conference that an attack carrier group of the First Fleet had been transferred from the California coast to reinforce the Seventh Fleet in the Western Pacific.

It was subsequently made known that the aircraft carrier Ranger would lead the carrier group.

The Defense Secretary said that "selected" Army and Marine Corps units had been alerted and readied "for movement," but he did not identify them, tell how many or indicate from where or to where they might be moved.

In other reinforcements announced by the Defense Secretary, interceptor and fighter bomber planes were flown to South Vietnam and Thailand.

Unidentified interceptor and fighter bomber squadrons were transferred from the United

Continued on Page 7, Column 1

4 BASES BOMBED

Oil Depot Also Target of 5-Hour Attack —2 Planes Lost

Transcript of McNamara news conference is on Page 6.

By JACK RAYMOND
Special to The New York Times

WASHINGTON, Aug. 5—United States aircraft bombed North Vietnam bases, naval craft and an oil storage depot in a five-hour raid along 100 miles of coast early today.

Secretary of Defense Robert S. McNamara said that 25 North Vietnam patrol boats had been destroyed or damaged and that the oil installation had been 90 per cent destroyed.

He declared that unless the United States was further provoked, no new American attacks were planned.

The Defense Secretary also announced that strong reinforcements had been dispatched to the Southeast Asia crisis area. He said certain Army and Marine Corps units had been alerted.

Two of the attacking American planes were lost and two returned damaged from the raids, the Defense Secretary said. He attributed the casualties to antiaircraft fire in the vicinity of the bases.

Success Reported

In a second announcement, made before Columbia Broadcasting System television cameras tonight, the Defense Secretary reported that the air strikes had been "very successful."

Reconnaissance flights have confirmed initial reports of success, the Defense Secretary said.

The reconnaissance planes, unlike the attacking aircraft, did not encounter any antiaircraft fire, Mr. McNamara added. The planes took off from the same carrier from which the original attack was launched against the coastal bases.

Told of a North Vietnamese claim that one of the two lost Navy pilots had been captured, the Defense Secretary said that was "possible."

One Plane Lost at Sea

One of the lost planes may have been downed in North Vietnam although the other was believed to have been lost at sea, he said.

Mr. McNamara did not accept the entire claim of the North Vietnam Army High Command that five United States planes were downed and two returned damaged from the raids.

A United States spokesman said that the figures given by Mr. McNamara that two United States planes were lost "still hold."

The Defense Secretary reported on the hostilities at a news conference at the Pentagon this morning.

The atmosphere in the press conference room was reminiscent of the Cuba missile crisis of 1962. The Secretary, as in

Continued on Page 6, Column 1

North Vietnam Says It Downed 5 Planes

By SEYMOUR TOPPING
Special to The New York Times

SAIGON, South Vietnam, Aug. 5 — North Vietnam said tonight that antiaircraft batteries defending its coast had shot down five United States warplanes and damaged three others.

A communiqué from the military high command said that one of the pilots had been captured.

The armed forces were "overjoyed by their successes," the communiqué said, and were increasing their vigilance and combat readiness.

The announcement, broadcast by the Hanoi radio in Vietnamese and English, said that the report of losses inflicted on the United States planes during the four attacks was a preliminary one.

It gave no details about the

Continued on Page 6, Column 7

United Press International Telephoto

GRAVES OF RIGHTS WORKERS: Excavation at a dam near Philadelphia, Miss., is where bodies of Michael H. Schwerner, Andrew Goodman and James E. Chaney were discovered Tuesday by Federal Bureau of Investigation.

NEWS INDEX

The *Enterprise* replenished by the underway support ship, the U.S.S. *Sacramento,* while patrolling the hostile waters of the Gulf of Tonkin.

General William Westmoreland, Commander of the U.S. Military Assistance Command conferring with fellow officers at the Ton Son Nhut Airport, Saigon.

The New York Times.

LATE CITY EDITION

U. S. Weather Bureau Report (Page 64) forecast:
Mostly sunny with chance of showers late today; fair tonight, tomorrow.

Temp. Range: 85—67; yesterday: 84—61.
Temp.-Hum. Index: 75 to 70; yesterday: 75.

VOL. CXIII..No. 38,913.   © 1964 by The New York Times Company.
Times Square, New York, N. Y. 10036   NEW YORK, SATURDAY, AUGUST 8, 1964.   TEN CENTS

CONGRESS BACKS PRESIDENT ON SOUTHEAST ASIA MOVES; KHANH SETS STATE OF SIEGE

RESOLUTION WINS

Senate Vote Is 88 to 2 After House Adopts Measure, 416-0

By E. W. KENWORTHY
Special to The New York Times

WASHINGTON, Aug. 7.—The House of Representatives and the Senate approved today the resolution requested by President Johnson to strengthen his hand in dealing with Communist aggression in Southeast Asia.

After a 40-minute debate, the House passed the resolution, 416 to 0. Shortly afterward the Senate approved it, 88 to 2. Senate debate, which began yesterday afternoon, lasted nine hours.

The resolution gives prior Congressional approval of "all necessary measures" that the President may take "to repel any armed attack" against United States forces and "to prevent further aggression."

The resolution, the text of which was printed in The New York Times Thursday, also gives advance sanction for "all necessary steps" taken by the President to help any nation covered by the Southeast Asia collective defense treaty that requests assistance "in defense of its freedom."

Johnson Hails Action

President Johnson said the Congressional action was "a demonstration to all the world of the unity of all Americans."

"The votes prove our determination to defend our forces, to prevent aggression and to work firmly and steadily for peace and security in the area," he said.

"I am sure the American people join me in expressing the deepest appreciation to the leaders and members of both parties in both houses of Congress for their patriotic, resolute and rapid action."

The debates in both houses, but particularly in the Senate, made clear, however, that the near-unanimous vote did not reflect a unanimity of opinion on the necessity or advisability of the resolution.

Except for Senators Wayne L. Morse, Democrat of Oregon, and Ernest Gruening, Democrat

Continued on Page 2, Column 1

MOSCOW ASSURES HANOI OF BACKING

Gromyko Says U.S. Actions Risk Grave Consequences

By United Press International

MOSCOW, Aug. 7.—Foreign Minister Andrei A. Gromyko said tonight that the United States military action against North Vietnam could "entail dangerous consequences."

Mr. Gromyko, in a telegram to the North Vietnamese Foreign Minister, Suan Tui, accused the United States of "flagrant violation of international law" and an attempt to introduce "piratical arbitrariness" in foreign relations.

The text of the message was published by Tass, the Soviet press agency.

Mr. Gromyko gave North Vietnam assurances of Soviet diplomatic backing against the United States.

"Such actions, generating a threat to the security of the people of other countries, can entail dangerous consequences, the scope of which it is now hard to foresee," the message said.

"The Soviet Government has demanded that the United States should immediately stop military operations against the Democratic Republic of Vietnam [North Vietnam]."

Mr. Gromyko said the presence of United States ships in the Gulf of Tonkin was an "openly hostile challenge" to the nations whose shores are "washed by the waters" of the gulf—which would include Communist China.

"This armed demonstration, of course, cannot be justified by

Continued on Page 3, Column 4

TO TOUR ALLIED CAPITALS: Henry Cabot Lodge with President Johnson on White House steps yesterday.

SAIGON DECREES EMERGENCY RULE

Khanh Says Chinese Army Threatens Nation—Urges People of North to Rebel

By PETER GROSE
Special to The New York Times

SAIGON, South Vietnam, Aug. 7.—Premier Nguyen Khanh decreed a state of emergency throughout South Vietnam today and urged the people of North Vietnam to "stand up and overthrow the dictatorial party rule" of their Communist Government.

The Premier also ordered stringent measures to tighten his Government's control over the population and to safeguard the country against the threat of large-scale Communist attacks.

"The coming weeks will decide the destiny of our entire people," General Khanh said. "We will not accept becoming a minor province of Red China."

Quotes Intelligence Reports

According to intelligence reports, General Khanh said, Chinese Communist troops are massed along China's southern frontier and are "stationed—not infiltrated but stationed—in North Vietnam itself."

Emergency measures, to be put into effect immediately, include controls on travel and food distribution, regional curfews where dictated by security requirements, enlarged authority for detention and house arrest, unlimited search rights in private homes and a ban on strikes and meetings "considered harmful to public order."

The press and all public-information media are to be censored. [This apparently will not extend to foreign news dispatches and other communications leaving the country, The Associated Press said.]

For anyone taking part in

Continued on Page 2, Column 2

Lodge to See Allies Of U.S. to Explain Vietnam Situation

By TOM WICKER
Special to The New York Times

WASHINGTON, Aug. 7.—Henry Cabot Lodge, only a few months ago a leading Republican Presidential possibility, will tour allied capitals for President Johnson to explain the situation in South Vietnam.

Speaking in front of the White House today, Mr. Lodge said he and Gen. Dwight D. Eisenhower's approval for the mission. He will leave within a week.

Mr. Lodge was the United States Ambassador to South Vietnam for 10 months until he resigned in late June to return and work against the nomination of Senator Barry Goldwater by the Republicans.

He did not elaborate on what he would tell officials he would talk with during his trip, except to say that it would be "in support of our national policy." Presumably a large part of his mission will be to explain the reasons for and the intent of the retaliatory action taken this week against North Vietnam for attacks on American naval vessels.

Politics Not Discussed

While Mr. Lodge's announcement vibrated with domestic political overtones. However, he would not discuss politics, even whether he would support Senator Goldwater against Mr. Johnson in the fall campaign.

Asked if he would, he replied: "I do not think this is the time or the place to discuss partisan politics."

The domestic political significance of today's announcement was twofold:

One of the nation's leading Republicans, that party's Vice-Presidential nominee in 1960, agreed to a diplomatic assignment from the Democratic President, against whom Senator Goldwater is running.

By lending his support to the Administration's policy on South Vietnam, as he has con-

Continued on Page 2, Column 3

Hanoi Invited by U.N. Council To Testify on Clashes With U.S.

By SAM POPE BREWER

UNITED NATIONS, N. Y., Aug. 7.—The Security Council invited North Vietnam today to appear before it to testify on the recent armed clashes with United States naval forces in the Gulf of Tonkin.

The Council also asked South Vietnam to appear or to present pertinent information on the situation.

The Council adjourned without further action. It was agreed that the members would set the date for the next meeting, which presumably depends on the replies to the invitations.

Adlai E. Stevenson, the United States representative, rejected an assertion by Czechoslovakia's delegate, Jiri Hajek, that United States ships violated North Vietnamese territorial waters on July 30 before the first Vietnamese at-

on the U.S.S. Maddox, and Aug. 10—The Security Council had fired on Vietnamese territory.

Mr. Stevenson said there had been no attack on North Vietnam and no incursion into its territorial waters before the retaliatory attack of Aug. 5. United States ships were attacked on the high seas 65 miles from Vietnamese territory, he said.

It was not known here whether North Vietnam was interested in appearing. South Vietnam was invited because, although it was not directly involved in the clashes this week, the incidents grew out of the conflict with the North.

No vote was taken on today's action. This month's Council President, Sivert A. Nielsen of

Continued on Page 2, Column 7

TURKS SEND JETS TO WARN CYPRUS; STRAFING ALLEGED

But Ankara Denies Nicosia Accusation of an Attack— U.S. Aides Distressed

By The Associated Press

ANKARA, Turkey, Saturday, Aug. 8—Turkey reported early today that she was sending jet aircraft on warning and surveillance flights over Cyprus.

After an emergency Cabinet meeting, Deputy Premier Kemal Satir also warned that the island could be bombed if American conciliation efforts failed to ease the tension between Greek and Turkish Cypriotes.

Mr. Satir denied, however, a Greek Cypriote charge that four Turkish Air Force Sabrejets had already strafed the northwestern coastal town of Polis and had hit an Italian cargo vessel in the harbor.

[In Washington, high State Department officials described the Cyprus situation as "very serious." Other high officials said they had had some forewarning that the Turks "would probably try something like this."]

U.S. Envoy at Meeting

The Cabinet met under Premier Ismet Inonu. The session was attended by the United States Ambassador, Raymond A. Hare, and the chief of the Turkish general staff, Gen. Cevdet Sunay.

Mr. Satir said afterward that Ankara would "do everything in its power to ameliorate the tense situation in Cyprus."

In denying Cypriote charges of strafing and machine-gun fire by Turkish jets, Mr. Satir said, "They must have mistaken the planes' noise for machine-gun fire."

After the Cabinet meeting, Minister of Information Ali Hassan Gogush issued this statement:

"The Government is closely watching the latest developments in Cyprus. The Greek Cypriote Administration has increased its aggression against the Turkish Cypriote community. The Turkish Government is taking defensive precautions and making political contacts."

Nicosia Plans Protest

NICOSIA, Cyprus, Aug. 7 (AP)—The Cypriote Government said tonight that four Turkish Air Force jet fighters had strafed the northwestern coastal town of Polis and had hit an Italian cargo vessel in the harbor.

The Government said the planes, identified as United States-made Sabrejets, attacked a few minutes after 6 P.M. (11 A.M., Eastern daylight time). Witnesses said the four planes had made several low runs from

Continued on Page 5, Column 3

KENNEDY WEIGHS RACE FOR SENATE; HE SEES WAGNER

Attorney General's Backers Seeking Support Among Top State Democrats

By R. W. APPLE Jr.

Attorney General Robert F. Kennedy is once again seriously considering running for Senator from New York State this fall.

Authoritative sources disclosed yesterday that relatives and political allies of the Attorney General had begun tentative discussions with a number of important Democrats in the state, seeking a broad base of support for his candidacy.

Stephen Smith, Mr. Kennedy's brother-in-law, has told people eager to work for the Attorney General to expect a go-ahead signal by this weekend, barring unforeseen developments.

However, other intimates of Mr. Kennedy, while confirming that he has expressed a definite interest in a Senate campaign, said they expected no final decision for two weeks.

Talks to Wagner

Mr. Kennedy was in New York yesterday for a meeting with Mayor Wagner, the state's most powerful Democrat. They had breakfast together at Gracie Mansion and discussed the Senate situation as well as the recent racial riots in Harlem.

After studying the idea of making a race for the Senate for several weeks, Mr. Kennedy said on June 23 that he would not be a candidate. At that time he was hopeful that President Johnson would choose him as his running mate.

When Mr. Johnson eliminated the Attorney General and other Cabinet members from the list of potential Vice-Presidential candidates on July 30, Mr. Kennedy was immediately urged by influential New York Democrats to reconsider. He has now done so.

Strong Support in Sight

Mr. Kennedy is known to have the support of a powerful group of Democratic leaders, including Peter Crotty of Erie County (Buffalo), Stanley Steingut of Brooklyn, Charles A. Buckley of the Bronx and John F. English of Nassau County.

With the exception of Mr. English, each of these men is a political opponent of the Mayor. They will control close to 400 votes at the state Democratic convention on Sept. 1, with a total of 573 votes needed to win nomination.

While it is conceivable that Mr. Kennedy could win the nomination without the open endorsement of Mr. Wagner, it is not thought likely that he would attempt to do so. Mr. Wagner is considered re-

Continued on Page 8, Column 8

JOHNSON ANTIPOVERTY BILL APPROVED IN HOUSE, 228-190, BUT FOES BALK FINAL VOTE

Goldwater Sees a Victory If He Takes 5 Big States

Asserts California, Texas, Illinois, Ohio and Indiana and Smaller 'States Already for Me' Could Beat Johnson

By CHARLES MOHR
Special to The New York Times

WASHINGTON, Aug. 7.—Senator Barry Goldwater has told 200 Republican Congressmen that he could assure his election by carrying California, Texas, Illinois, Indiana and Ohio.

The Republican Presidential nominee was reported to have told the Congressmen that if he could win the 130 electoral votes of those major states and add them to the "states that are already for me" it would be possible to defeat President Johnson.

His reference to states already for him was understood to cover many smaller Western, Midwestern and Southern states support for the Senator.

C. Clifton White, a seasoned political professional who helped Mr. Goldwater win the

Continued on Page 8, Column 5

CRITICS REPULSED

Size of Victory Margin Surprises Backers— Action Due Today

By MARJORIE HUNTER
Special to The New York Times

WASHINGTON, Aug. 7 — President Johnson's antipoverty bill won an all-but-final victory in the House tonight by a surprisingly wide margin of 38 votes.

However, opponents succeeded in delaying final action until tomorrow.

Tentative approval came on adoption of the Administration-sponsored substitute bill, embodying all the changes made by both the Senate and the House. The vote was 228 to 190. Even sponsors of the bill were surprised at the wide margin of support. They had expected to get the votes of only six to ten Republicans.

Twenty Republicans joined 208 Democrats in voting for the measure. Voting against it were 153 Republicans and 37 Democrats, most of them conservative Southerners.

Thus, after a day of bitter wrangling and one close brush with defeat, the $947.5-million antipoverty program was on the verge of passage.

Engrossed Bill Demanded

But opponents delayed a final vote by demanding an engrossed bill—a printed copy of the measure and all its amendments. This demand automatically put off final action until the printers could prepare the document.

The delaying maneuver was viewed as a temporary setback for the Administration, which had pressed for quick passage while the votes were in hand. Many members usually go home for the weekend. It could prove difficult to keep the supporters, particularly those who reluctantly backed the Administration, in town for the final vote scheduled for tomorrow.

However, the tentative approval represented a major victory for President Johnson.

The antipoverty bill, one of

Continued on Page 6, Column 7

Rockefeller Denies That He Will Stump For National Ticket

By DOUGLAS DALES
Special to The New York Times

ALBANY, Aug. 7 — Governor Rockefeller's office said today that he had no intention of stumping for the Goldwater ticket either inside or outside New York State.

The Governor's press secretary, Robert McManus, made the statement as a result of a prediction yesterday by Fred A. Young, Republican State Chairman, that Mr. Rockefeller would stump for the national ticket.

[In New York, Representative Seymour Halpern of Queens was reported ready to disavow Mr. Goldwater and run as an independent Republican.]

While Governor Rockefeller was distressed at the action of the Republican National Convention in selecting Senator Barry Goldwater as the party standard-bearer, he had said before the convention that he would support any nominee.

He renewed his pledge of support at a meeting of Republican county chairmen and vice chairmen here yesterday.

However, as the Governor's

Continued on Page 8, Column 5

HARLEM LEFTISTS CURBED BY COURT

Three Barred From Staging Protests — Epton Freed on Bail Put Up by Texan

By FRED POWLEDGE

A state judge granted a temporary injunction yesterday against continued "illegal demonstrations" by three individuals and organizations in Harlem.

Supreme Court Justice Gerald P. Culkin said the "conduct" of Milton Rosen, William Epton Jr. and Jesse Gray "creates a clear and present danger of irreparable injury to life and property."

The three men and their organizations, the Progressive Labor Movement, the Harlem Defense Council and the Community Council on Housing, had been accused by the city and state of fomenting tensions during the recent period of racial violence in Harlem.

Mr. Rosen is chairman of the Progressive Labor Movement; Mr. Epton, head of the Harlem Defense Council, and Mr. Gray head of the Community Council on Housing.

The city obtained a restraining order on July 25 to prohibit a demonstration by the Harlem Defense Council, scheduled for that day. The order, and a show-cause order, were argued during the next week. Justice Culkin's injunction was the result of that hearing.

Mr. Epton, meantime, was freed on $10,000 bond yesterday in another action and told that he could not leave the city limits of New York. The son of a wealthy Texas oilman posted collateral for Mr. Epton, a professed Communist.

Mr. Epton was indicted

Continued on Page 7, Column 4

PHONE AIDE CITED IN POLICE INQUIRY

Investigator Implicated in Gambling Conspiracy

By JACK ROTH

A suspended chief investigator for the New York Telephone Company was identified yesterday as the man who allegedly sold information to two police officers about gamblers' telephone numbers. The gamblers were reportedly shaken down by the policemen.

The telephone employe, Harold A. McElroy, was named by Victor Herwitz, a lawyer, who represents one of the police officers—Capt. Anthony Obremski—in a departmental trial on conspiracy charges that began yesterday.

Captain Obremski is accused of conspiring to get information about the gamblers' telephones with Mr. McElroy, Lieut. James J. Sullivan, the other police officer, and Seymour Freedman, a plainclothesman who left the force five years ago.

Mr. McElroy was scheduled to be the first prosecution witness against Captain Obremski when Trial Commissioner Aloysius J. Melia adjourned the trial to Monday at 10 A.M. to permit Mr. Herwitz time to examine Mr. McElroy's recent testimony

Continued on Page 6, Column 6

U.S. and Belgium Plan Increased Aid to Bolster Congo

At meeting in Brussels, are, from left: Under Secretary of State W. Averell Harriman, Foreign Minister Paul-Henri Spaak of Belgium and Ambassador Douglas MacArthur 2d.

By EDWARD T. O'TOOLE

BRUSSELS, Aug. 7 — Belgium and the United States are ready to increase technical aid to shore up Premier Moise Tshombe's Government in the Congo, but neither country will provide military personnel for combat, informed sources indicated tonight.

W. Averell Harriman, United States Under Secretary of State for Political Affairs, arrived here from Washington today and conferred for five hours with Belgium's Foreign Minister, Paul-Henri Spaak. They refused to comment later on their discussions beyond saying that they had had a "useful exchange of views." A Belgian official said the visit of Mr. Harriman was initiated by the State Department after Premier Tshombe had requested more United

States aid to combat Communist-guided rebels in the Congo. Other sources disclosed that Mr. Harriman and Mr. Spaak had apparently reached a working agreement on a program under which the United States would provide matériel to the Tshombe Government and Belgium would supply experts to teach the Congolese troops how to

Continued on Page 4, Column 3

Nuclear Test Blast Set for Mississippi

Special to The New York Times

WASHINGTON, Aug. 7 — The Government announced today arrangements for evacuating residents in an area 28 miles southwest of Hattiesburg, Miss., next Sept. 22 when it touches off an underground nuclear detonation.

The blast will be the first of three in a series known as Project Dribble.

The project is part of the Department of Defense's Vela program, which is designed to develop techniques for detecting and locating underground nuclear explosions.

Earlier investigations in the Vela series contributed to the United States decision to press for the exclusion of underground tests in the treaty with the Soviet Union that prohibited nuclear explosions in the at-

Continued on Page 6, Column 6

The New York Times.

LATE CITY EDITION
U.S. Weather Bureau Report (Page 51) Forecast:
Cloudy, fog and drizzle today; cloudy tonight. Chance of rain tomorrow.
Temp. Range: 43—33; yesterday 37—30.

VOL. CXIV.No. 39,050. © 1964 by The New York Times Company
Times Square, New York, N. Y. 10036
NEW YORK, WEDNESDAY, DECEMBER 23, 1964. TEN CENTS

STEINGUT CHOSEN ASSEMBLY CHIEF; MAYOR REBUFFED

BUCKLEY IS KEY

Joins to Bar Zaretzki and Travia—Erway Gets Senate Post

By RONALD SULLIVAN
Special to The New York Times

ALBANY, Wednesday, Dec. 23—Assemblyman Stanley Steingut of Brooklyn and State Senator Julian B. Erway of Albany have been named by the Democrats to the top posts in the 1965 Legislature.

Mr. Steingut was selected Speaker of the Assembly at a conference of Democratic Assemblymen late last night. Mr. Erway was picked to be Senate majority leader at a conference early today of Democratic Senators and Senators-elect.

Their command of the Democratic leadership of the next legislative session had been assured late yesterday when they won the support of two of the state's most powerful county leaders, Representative Charles A. Buckley of the Bronx and Peter J. Crotty of Erie County.

Their victory was a setback for Mayor Wagner, who was backing Assembly Minority Leader Anthony J. Travia of Brooklyn and Senate Minority Leader Joseph Zaretzki of Manhattan.

Vote Made Unanimous

Mr. Steingut was chosen by 81 incumbent and newly-elected Assemblymen in a closed session that ended at 10 P.M. in the Crystal Room of the DeWitt Clinton Hotel, near the Capitol. There will be 86 Democrats in the next Assembly, but seven were absent.

The voting for Speaker began shortly after 9 o'clock. When Mr. Steingut's total reached 43, a majority, Assemblyman Moses Weinstein of Queens, an ally of the Mayor, moved that Mr. Steingut's designation be made unanimous.

Afterward, as a crowd converged around Mr. Steingut, the defeated Mr. Travia told reporters that the "expression of support for Stanley Steingut" was not official. But when asked whether Mr. Steingut had in fact been elected speaker, Mr. Travia replied, "yes."

Two and a half hours later the 33 Senators met in a smaller room upstairs and by a vote of 19 to 14 chose Mr. Erway. Anti-Wagner forces

Continued on Page 14, Column 1

MAYOR CONDEMNS BOSSES AT ALBANY

Indicates Surprise at Votes Defeating His Choices

Text of statement by Wagner is printed on Page 14.

Mayor Wagner, indicating surprise at the defeat of his candidates for the top posts in the coming Democratic-controlled Legislature, denounced his opponents last night for attempting "to install the institution of bossism at the state level."

The Mayor suggested that the elevation of Assemblyman Stanley Steingut of Brooklyn and State Senator Julian B. Erway of Albany to the posts of Speaker of the Assembly and Senate majority leader was a result of "the same old gang-up of the bosses."

Mr. Wagner had backed Assembly Minority Leader Anthony J. Travia and Senate Minority Leader Joseph Zaretzki. While conceding that the organization of the Legislature was, for the legislators themselves to decide, the Mayor said the selection of Mr. Travia and Mr. Zaretzki would have been logical.

"The bosses decided on the replacement of Assemblyman Travia and Senator Zaretzki and the votes were in accord with their will," Mr. Wagner said. "In the face of this, Tony

Continued on Page 14, Column 1

Politician Accused In L.I. Meter Bribes

By JACK ROTH

Philip B. Kohut, former Democratic leader and Public Safety Commissioner of Long Beach, L. I., was indicted here yesterday on charges of accepting parking-meter bribes.

He was accused of taking $23,500 between 1957 and 1960 to see to it that Long Beach bought more than $100,000 worth of parking meters from the Duncan Parking Meter Company of Chicago.

The former president of the company, Jerome J. Robinson of Chicago, has been convicted of perjury here for lying to a grand jury. He desired to the jury that he had told associates in 1961 that he had paid $25,000, with $25,000 still to pay, to sell parking meters to

Continued on Page 15, Column 4

PLAN 'A' IS VOTED

G.O.P. Said to Seek Actions Other Than on Redistricting

By R. W. APPLE Jr.
Special to The New York Times

ALBANY, Dec. 22—The Republicans pushed the first of their four reapportionment bills through the Legislature tonight, and Governor Rockefeller signed it minutes later.

The Senate and the Assembly also passed the second G.O.P. bill before recessing for the night. The vote in the Assembly was subsequently nullified because of a legal technicality, but the bill was assured of repassage tomorrow morning.

In both houses, every Republican legislator supported the proposals of the party leadership. The votes in the Senate were 31 to 24; those in the Assembly were 82 to 61.

The Legislature was expected to complete action on the reapportionment bills late tomorrow afternoon. But reliable sources said tonight that Governor Rockefeller was preparing for delivery tomorrow a message asking the special session to act on several other matters as well.

Details Not Available

Details of Mr. Rockefeller's plans were not available, and a spokesman for the Governor declined to comment.

The first bill acted upon by the Legislature tonight was Plan A, which includes neither of the features to which Democrats have most strenuously objected—fractional voting and the use of the 1962 vote for Governor as an apportionment base.

Next the Senate and the Assembly passed Plan B, which includes a voter-base provision but not fractional voting. When the Assembly passed it, it had been on the legislators' desks for only an hour and a half.

'Immoral Attempt'

Assembly Republicans, ignoring the protests of the Democrats, also established Sept. 14 as the date of the 1965 primary election. This was done in a measure modifying the election law to conform with the new apportionment plans.

Little Doubt of Result

The roll-call began only five hours after the Legislature reconvened following a five-day recess. Although many upstate Republicans had been dissatisfied with the districting bills, there had been no real doubt that they would be enacted.

Nevertheless, the Democrats in both houses made fiery speeches attacking the Republican strategy. They raised amendments that would have sidetracked the G.O.P. bills and set up a bipartisan reapportionment commission.

Senator Edward S. Lentol

Continued on Page 14, Column 2

GIVES CHRISTMAS MESSAGE: Pope Paul VI as he taped appeal for world peace yesterday at the Vatican.
Associated Press Cablephoto

EXPRESSWAY GETS 15-HOUR HEARING

Foes Bitter, but City Aides Laud Lower Manhattan Artery at Hearing

By CHARLES G. BENNETT

A public hearing in City Hall on the controversial Lower Manhattan Expressway plan ended at 12:53 A.M. today after nearly 15 hours of heated and, at times, angry debate.

The $100 million Expressway plan was praised during the hearing as "an essential key to business growth" and condemned as "an outrageous land grab."

The opponents, who provided most of the commotion inside and outside the hearing room during the hearing, went to City Hall by the hundreds—some in busloads—in an effort to defeat the project.

Nevertheless, it became evident as the session wore on that a heavy weight of official prestige had been brought to bear for approval of the road.

Top city officials — all appointees of Mayor Wagner—argued that, without the expressway, traffic in lower Manhattan would face complete stagnation, with millions of dollars in potential business and commerce losses.

Throughout the long session, City Hall swarmed with those who had come to testify. As he has done before, Assemblyman Louis F. DeSalvio, Manhattan Democrat, led the opposition.

His voice rising as he talked, Mr. DeSalvio rebuked the board for "this immoral attempt, at this time, three days before Christmas," to put through "this unneeded, unwanted, elevated monstrosity."

The amendments were shouted down in voice votes.

In the Senate, New York City Democrats complained in anguished voices about what one described as "this skulduggery foisted on the people of New York State" and another called "a plan that cuts the state up into Rorschach blots."

Continued on Page 14, Column 2

PONTIFF APPEALS FOR END OF RACISM

Christmas Message Calls on World Also to Halt Class Strife and to Disarm

Excerpts from the Pope's message appear on Page 8.

By ROBERT C. DOTY
Special to The New York Times

ROME, Dec. 22 — Pope Paul VI tonight made a fervent Christmas appeal to the world for brotherhood, disarmament and rejection of class, racial and national strife.

The spiritual leader of more than half a billion Roman Catholics addressed his message "to all men of all ages, of all countries, of all beliefs, toward whom we feel more than ever we feel we owe our esteem, our affection and our united efforts."

In this ecumenical spirit, he referred to his recent visit to predominantly non-Christian India as "something of inestimable human value" and "a moment of understanding and blending of many hearts."

Militarism Is Decried

In his most direct passage on current world affairs, the Pontiff expressed alarm over "militarism" and the stockpiling "of weapons ever more powerful and destructive."

This, he said, is "a process that consumes enormous quantities of money and manpower needed for humanitarian ends, "feeds the public mind on the thought of power and war and induces men to make mutual fear the treacherous and inhuman basis of world peace."

The Pope broadcast his 25-minute message from his pri-

Continued on Page 8, Column 2

U.S. WARNS VIETNAMESE MILITARY HELP IS BASED ON FREE CIVIL RULE; KHANH SPURNS 'FOREIGN' WAR AIMS

HE DEFIES TAYLOR

Aid Talks Suspended —9 Senior Officers Reported Retired

By PETER GROSE

SAIGON, South Vietnam, Dec. 22—Lieut. Gen. Nguyen Khanh supported today the resumption of supreme power by the armed forces despite United States opposition.

He declared that the Vietnamese military would not fight "to carry out the policy of any foreign country."

An order of the day signed by General Khanh as Commander in Chief appeared to be in direct defiance of the American stand against the purge of the civilian legislature, the High National Council, by a group of young officers last Sunday. The officers dissolved the Council and arrested a number of its members.

[Informed sources said that Phan Khac Suu, the chief of state, had signed orders at the insistence of the young officers compulsorily retiring nine senior generals, including Lieut. Gen. Duong Van Minh, Reuters reported. Page 4.]

Qualified United States officials considered General Khanh's declaration a "throwing down of the gauntlet" that could produce an entirely new situation in United States relations with South Vietnam.

Legal Regime Sought

Even before the general's statement was broadcast, officials let it be known that certain talks toward increasing United States aid to the South Vietnamese war effort had been suspended pending the restoration of a legal governmental structure.

Premier Tran Van Huong was reliably reported as willing to cooperate with the military commanders who dissolved the council. The United States Ambassador, Maxwell D. Taylor, urged him to defy them.

The scene appeared set for a showdown over American and South Vietnamese ideas of how best to fight the Communist insurgency.

In his critical assessment of the situation since Sunday, Mr. Taylor said that the military moves raised "serious questions" about the reliability of South Vietnam as an ally.

The suspension of aid talks, while not affecting any of the present American support to the South Vietnamese war effort, was intended as a warning to generals that the United States commitment here was predicated on the promise of a stable government.

In Mr. Taylor's view, accord-

Continued on Page 4, Column 3

U.S. Plans Military Plane That Can Carry 600 Men

Johnson Will Seek $157 Million to Start Developing Transport—Intends to Cut Defense Spending by $500 Million

By CHARLES MOHR

AUSTIN, Tex., Dec. 22—President Johnson ordered today the development of a gigantic new military transport plane that could carry 600 troops.

But he planned to cut overall defense spending by about $500 million in the next fiscal year.

Secretary of Defense Robert S. McNamara said after a budget conference with the President that Congress would be asked to appropriate $157 million next year to begin developing a new transport with three times the capacity of the largest existing cargo plane.

Mr. McNamara said that the new jet plane, which would be the largest in the world, would "greatly reduce our reaction time" in meeting brush-fire crises around the world by carrying both troops and heavy

divisional equipment to trouble spots.

Mr. McNamara also announced that the defense budget for the fiscal year 1966, which begins next July 1, would be "closer to $49 billion than $50 billion." Expenditures in the current year are estimated at $49.8 billion.

At a news conference here, the Secretary said that Mr. Johnson had decided to name Gen. John Paul McConnell to replace Gen. Curtis E. LeMay as Air Force Chief of Staff when General LeMay retires Jan. 31.

Mr. Johnson conferred at his LBJ Ranch, 65 miles west of here, with Mr. McNamara, Deputy Secretary of Defense Cyrus R. Vance and the Joint Chiefs of Staff.

Later he discussed budget

Continued on Page 11, Column 1

Three Castro Foes Arrested in Firing Of Bazooka at U.N.

By PETER KIHSS

Three Cubans, understood to be opponents of the regime of Premier Fidel Castro, were arrested last night in the Dec. 11 firing of a bazooka shell toward the United Nations Headquarters.

Chief of Detectives Philip J. Walsh asked each of the three was charged with endangering life maliciously by placing an explosive near a building, and with attempting to damage a building or a vessel, both of which are felonies. They were further charged with conspiracy, a misdemeanor.

Chief Walsh identified the three men as:

Julio Carlos Perez, 31 years old, of 247 Audubon Avenue, a teletype repairman who has been in the United States for three years. He was booked as 29.

Ignacio Nova, 26, of 535 West 50th Street, a shoe salesman who has been here for 12 years. He was booked, however, as "Ignacio Novo."

Guillermo Nova, 25, his brother, of 1414 91st Street, North Bergen, N. J., a doorman who has also been here for 12 years. Chief Walsh, Police Commissioner Michael J. Murphy and District Attorney Frank D. O'Connor of Queens said the ar-

Continued on Page 6, Column 4

CAPITAL WORRIED

Officials Unsure How to Solve Deepening Political Crisis

By JOHN W. FINNEY
Special to The New York Times

WASHINGTON, Dec. 22 — The United States warned military leaders in South Vietnam today that American support was based on maintenance of a government free of "improper interference" by military leaders in Saigon.

The warning was issued by the State Department in Washington, after a day in which Administration officials followed developments in Vietnam with some anxiety, uncertain how to change the course of the deteriorating political situation.

The Administration was surprised and disturbed by the move of military leaders, with the approval of Lieut. Gen. Nguyen Khanh, to undermine the authority of the new civilian Government.

Position of U.S. Unclear

It was apparent that the military move had provoked a political crisis in South Vietnam that could lead to a reappraisal of United States policy. For the moment the Administration was uncertain where the United States stood in the situation in Saigon and where it and South Vietnam were proceeding.

The Administration at first decided not to issue a statement on the ground that the situation was so unclear and so volatile that a statement might confuse the situation further.

Later, when word was received that General Khanh had criticized Ambassador Maxwell D. Taylor and the United States in an interview with a correspondent of The New York Herald Tribune, the Administration changed its mind.

[General Khanh was quoted in the interview that if Ambassador Taylor did not "act more intelligently, the United States will lose Southeast Asia and we will lose our freedom," he was said to have added that the Ambassador had acted "beyond imagination" in his reported efforts to obtain the release of politicians from jail and to restore the dissolved civilian legislature.]

A Rebuke to Khanh

In essence, the Administration's statement was a defense of Ambassador Taylor, a rebuke to the military leaders, and a restatement of American policy, which seeks a stable government.

Noting that the State Department had received inquiries about "allegations critical of our Ambassador as well as the U.S. Government," the department's press officer, Robert J. McCloskey, issued this statement on behalf of the Administration:

"Ambassador Taylor has been acting throughout with the full support of the United States Government.

"As we have repeatedly made clear, a duly constituted gov-

Continued on Page 5, Column 1

TSHOMBE PRESSED TO REVISE REGIME

U.S. and Belgium Advising Moves to Gain Support in African Capitals

By J. ANTHONY LUKAS
Special to The New York Times

LEOPOLDVILLE, the Congo, Dec. 22 — The United States and Belgium are putting heavy pressure on Premier Moise Tshombe of the Congo to take steps to improve his reputation in the rest of Africa.

Concerned by a rising chorus of criticism, Washington and Brussels have urged him to make his regime more palatable to the rest of the continent. Reliable sources here said today that a series of steps were strongly recommended to Mr. Tshombe during talks he had last week in Brussels with Belgium's Foreign Minister, Paul-Henri Spaak, and the United States Ambassador to Belgium, Douglas MacArthur 2d.

The sources here denied earlier reports that Mr. Tshombe was being urged to seek negotiations with rebel leaders to end the rebellion in the Congo. Instead, they said, the steps proposed include:

¶A broadening of Mr. Tshombe's Cabinet to include ministers more acceptable to other African countries.

¶An amnesty for all rebels not accused of acts punishable under the Congo's criminal code.

¶Guarantees that opposition parties will be free to participate in the campaign for the elections tentatively scheduled for February. This would also probably involve the release of certain opposition leaders now in prison.

¶An invitation to certain Af-

Continued on Page 5, Column 1

Soviet Wages Bitter Campaign Against NATO Nuclear Force

By HENRY TANNER
Special to The New York Times

MOSCOW, Dec. 22—The Soviet press, radio and television have waged one of their most extensive propaganda campaigns against the United States proposal for a mixed-manned nuclear force in the Atlantic alliance.

Soviet leaders, in the words of recent "authorized statement" by Tass, the press agency, are convinced that the nuclear fleet would have no practical

Continued on Page 10, Column 1

Even such frequent targets as American policy toward South Vietnam, Cuba and the Congo and international crises in the United Nations have not been treated with comparable heat and bitterness. They certainly have not received anything like the same amount of space.

The Soviet campaign is directed not so much against the fact that the Western powers are planning an integrated nu-

AT HEARING ON MANHATTAN EXPRESSWAY: Seated, from left, are Triborough Bridge and Tunnel Authority officials: Charles F. Preusse, John Thornton, Robert Moses and Peter J. Reidy, who are in favor of project. Standing at left is the Rev. Gerard LaMountain of Most Holy Crucifix Roman Catholic Church, who is opposed.
The New York Times (by Paul Bennett)

"All the News That's Fit to Print"

The New York Times.

LATE CITY EDITION
U.S. Weather Bureau Report (Page 60) forecasts:
Cloudy and mild today; light rain tonight. Chance of rain tomorrow.
Temp. Range: 51—40; yesterday: 42—32.

VOL. CXIV..No. 39,051.
© 1964 by The New York Times Company
Times Square, New York, N.Y. 10036

NEW YORK, THURSDAY, DECEMBER 24, 1964.

TEN CENTS

WAGNER BACKERS IN ALBANY MOVING TO BLOCK ERWAY

5 Senators From City Oppose Him as Majority Leader— 6th Is Urged to Join

HIS RECORD IS ATTACKED

Designee Is Assailed on Civil Rights — Ingalls Heads G.O.P. Assemblymen

By RONALD SULLIVAN
Special to The New York Times

ALBANY, Dec. 23—A handful of Democratic liberals from New York City sought today to upset the Senate leadership in the 1965 Legislature.

Anti-Wagner forces had picked Senator Julian B. Erway of Albany to be Senate majority leader at a Democratic caucus early today. But four Senators allied with the Mayor refused to make the designation unanimous and vowed to block Mr. Erway's election when the new Legislature convened Jan. 6.

By tonight, the fight had spread. A fifth Senator from the city said he would oppose Mr. Erway and a sixth was under enormous pressure to follow suit.

The Democratic liberals attacked Mr. Erway's record in the Senate, particularly his position on civil rights.

Would Lack Majority

If the six Senators joined in opposing Mr. Erway's election on Jan. 6, the Senate line-up would be 27 Democrats for Mr. Erway, 6 Democrats against him, and 25 Republicans who would have their own candidate. Mr. Erway would then be three votes short of a majority of 30 in the 58-member house. The Senate rules require a majority of those present and voting, provided that a quorum (at least 30 Senators) is present and voting, for the election of a leader. No Senator may abstain.

Sources close to the Republican leadership were confident that all 25 Republican Senators would be on hand, "so they can watch the Democrats tear each other to pieces."

In the Assembly, the designation last night of Assemblyman Stanley Steingut of Brooklyn as the next Speaker appeared secure.

Setback for the Mayor

Both Mr. Steingut, the Kings County leader, and Mr. Erway, a member of the old-line Democratic organization in Albany controlled by Daniel O'Connell, were selected after they had won the backing of two of the state's most powerful Democratic county leaders, Representative Charles A. Buckley of the Bronx and Peter J. Crotty of Buffalo.

Their victories were a setback for Mayor Wagner, who had supported Assembly Minority Leader Anthony J. Travia and Senate Minority Leader Joseph Zaretzki.

But the rebellion against Mr. Erway, if it is sustained when the Democrats organize the Legislature next month, would represent a remarkable recovery by the pro-Wagner forces here.

For the Mayor, it would be a personal victory over the Democratic leaders across the state who have lined up against him. Meanwhile, Republican As-

Continued on Page 6, Column 5

School Cabinet Post Is Urged by Powell

By CABELL PHILLIPS
Special to The New York Times

WASHINGTON, Dec. 23 — Representative Adam Clayton Powell Jr., chairman of the House Education and Labor Committee, will offer legislation in the new Congress to create a Cabinet-level Department of Education.

At a news conference here today, the Manhattan Democrat also said he would press for a $3 billion appropriation for the antipoverty drive — a billion above what President Johnson is said to contemplate. He further said he would seek legislation extending Federal aid to elementary and secondary schools.

Mr. Powell said he favored breaking up the "hydra-headed" Department of Health, Education and Welfare and making the field of education separate

Continued on Page 10, Column 1

Thousands Flee Floods in West; 11 Killed

The Eel River at Rio Dell, Calif., raging out of control, smashed a bridge and washed away part of Highway 101.
United Press International Telephoto

Slides in California, Oregon and Idaho Add to Havoc

By United Press International

SAN FRANCISCO, Dec. 23—The worst floods in years swamped the Far West today, leaving thousands homeless or stranded. Debris-filled flood waters receded in some places, but other areas braced for possible further disaster.

At least 11 persons have died in two days of wind and rain in Northern California, Oregon and Idaho. The storm, spawned by a rare, warm tropical air mass moving in from Hawaii, came on the heels of a blizzard that raced across the Northern prairies last week.

"In terms of totality and involvement of the entire state, this is the greatest disaster ever to hit Oregon," Gov. Mark O. Hatfield said.

New weather bulletins predicting less rain brought optimism to some areas, but elsewhere, especially in Oregon, rising rivers and streams caused increasing concern.

"At this time, it appears that the worst is over in California, but the picture could change at any time," said George Deatherage of the California Department of Water Resources. "If we get another heavy storm, we could be in more trouble."

In Oregon the Willamette River continued to rise over the flood level, threatening about 4,200 homes in the Salem suburb of Keizer, where evacuations began today. State officials warned that food was in short supply in some areas and asked residents to buy no more than was absolutely necessary.

Officers in Cassia County, Idaho, said the Dewey Dam had broken near Declo and was threatening the town

Continued on Page 20, Column 1

Governor Is Ready to Drop His 'Pay-as-You-Go' Policy

By R. W. APPLE Jr.
Special to The New York Times

ALBANY, Dec. 23—Governor Rockefeller made it clear today that he was ready to abandon his "pay-as-you-go" method of balancing the state's books. Although the Governor did not say so, Assemblymen and Senators of both parties agreed that this was clearly the meaning of two special messages he sent to the Legislature.

The messages asked for the passage of two bills to protect bond reserves against what one Republican called "the danger of political raids" by the Democrats, who are to take control of the Legislature on Jan. 6.

Both bills cleared the Assembly 119 to 19 and the Senate 32 to 25. They were then sent to Governor Rockefeller, who signed them in the Red Room of the Capitol.

After completing action on the fiscal measures and reapportionment, the Legislature recessed just before 7 P.M. It did not formally adjourn, but further sessions were considered extremely unlikely.

Thus it appeared that today was the last day of the long Republican reign in Albany as well as the end, at least for a while, of Walter J. Mahoney's tenure as Senate majority leader and of Joseph F. Carlino's term as Assembly

Continued on Page 6, Column 1

CITY HALL WEIGHS UPSET IN ALBANY

Mayor Stands on State Bent Charging Bosses Gave Victory to Steingut

By CLAYTON KNOWLES

The big question at City Hall yesterday was how deeply Mayor Wagner had been hurt by the coup that selected Stanley Steingut, a political enemy, to be Speaker of the 1965 Assembly.

Friend and foe asked how permanent the injury would be and whether there were offsetting factors that might indeed help Mr. Wagner.

The Mayor himself stood firm on his angry statement of late Tuesday night in which he charged that he was again under attack from "the same old gang-up of bosses."

He maintained that Assemblyman Anthony J. Travia and Senator Joseph Zaretzki, present minority leaders, were being denied majority leadership posts by an edict of the bosses "to strike back at me for the losses they [the bosses] had suffered in the past."

Questioned on O'Connell

He reread his statement before television batteries yesterday in the big reception room at City Hall. But despite the most insistent efforts of reporters who surrounded him, Mayor Wagner refused to spell out his case against "the bosses."

"How is it," he was asked, "that Dan O'Connell of Albany, who used to be your ally, is now characterized as a boss when he supports the change of leadership?"

The Mayor refused to answer the question for the record. An O'Connell man, Senator Julian Zaretzki as leader if he can pick up one more vote than he received in the conference Tuesday night.

The Mayor later strode out of the room, giving reporters

Continued on Page 6, Column 4

REPUBLICANS PASS DISTRICTING PLANS

Democrats Reduce Protests as Legislature in Albany Votes Last 2 of 4 Bills

By SYDNEY H. SCHANBERG
Special to The New York Times

ALBANY, Dec. 23—With almost no debate at all, the Republicans obtaining final approval of their four-part reapportionment plan tonight.

The last obstacle was moved at 6:53 P.M., when the Assembly passed the fourth and final part, known as Plan D, by a party-line vote of 80 to 52.

The Democrats had apparently talked themselves out yesterday, when their outcries were loud and bitter in both chambers as the first two bills, Plans A and B, were passed through.

Protest over Plans C and D was muted and surprisingly brief today. The only debate heard anywhere took place in the Senate on Plan C. Even that seemed perfunctory and lasted only a few minutes.

The plans were approved along strict party lines—by votes of 32 to 25 in the Senate and 80 to 52 in the Assembly.

Bills Are Signed

The Governor signed Plan A into law yesterday. By 8 o'clock tonight, he had signed all the rest.

These included not only Plans B, C and D, but also a "Serviceman's Bill" that amends sections of the election law and sets the rules for absentee voting to conform with the new redistricting system.

The Serviceman's Bill, passed yesterday by the Assembly and approved in the Senate's closing minutes today, also set Sept. 14 as the date for next year's primary elections.

The Democrats, who have traditionally favored a June primary date, were generally not too chagrined, because in 1965, for the first time in years, they will be in control of the Legislature. A late primary usually helps the "ins."

The effect of today's proceedings was to make Plan D—the Plan the Republicans like most and the Democrats least—the law of the state.

This is the plan that will be scrutinized first by the special three-man Federal Court in New York City set up last Dec. 1 for the specific purpose following the Supreme

Continued on Page 6, Column 6

President Planning Farm and Aid Cuts; Weighs Pay Rises

By CHARLES MOHR
Special to The New York Times

AUSTIN, Tex., Dec. 23 — President Johnson was reported today to be planning cuts in foreign aid and Agriculture Department expenditures but considering a new pay rise for Government employees.

It was also reported, after a third day of budget conferences at the President's ranch, that Mr. Johnson would offer legislation calling for modest increases in second- and third-class postal rates and a law requiring businesses to sort first-class mail by zip code number. Budget Director Kermit Gordon said that in the budgetary meetings this week the requests of Government departments, which had totaled $108.5 billion, had been "very, very substantially" cut by Mr. Johnson.

An Exchange of Views

His brief statement after the afternoon meeting said only that interested delegations had met and there had been an exchange of views.

Adlai E. Stevenson, the United States representative, said as he left the meeting that "there is an armistice but no peace treaty." Tewfik Bouattoura of Algeria, head of the Asian-African group, said the meeting registered "no progress but no despair."

Nikolai T. Fedorenko, the Soviet representative, informed the Secretary General, U Thant, of the new Soviet demands this morning. Later he said, "We are ready to proceed with the normal work of the Assembly at any time."

"Why wait?" the Soviet representative said. According to reliable sources, Moscow raised

Continued on Page 4, Column 3

Nasser, Angered by Criticism, Says U.S. Can 'Jump in Lake'

Asserts Cairo Would Refuse Aid Rather Than Accept Dictation of Policy

By HEDRICK SMITH
Special to The New York Times

CAIRO, Dec. 23—President Gamal Abdel Nasser lashed back tonight at American criticism and delays on economic aid. He told the United States in Egyptian slang to "jump in the lake" if Washington disapproved of Cairo's recent behavior.

He also declared that the Egyptian people were ready to "cut our rations" and do without $140 million in American aid rather than let the United States dictate Egyptian policy.

The President was replying to expressions of American irritation over the burning of the United States Embassy library in Cairo last month and the downing of an American oil company plane by Egyptian jets four days ago.

Gamal Abdel Nasser
Associated Press

have been sent to him by President Johnson through diplomatic channels, that Egypt stop sending arms to the Congolese rebels.

"Our policy is clear and we say it openly," Mr. Nasser told a cheering crowd at Victory Day celebrations at Port Said.

"We say that we sent arms to the Congolese people and we shall keep on sending arms to the Congo."

The Egyptian leader accused the United States and Belgium of aggression in the Congo and rejected an appeal, reported to

Continued on Page 6, Column 4

Burning of a Negro Arouses Louisiana

By JOHN HERBERS
Special to The New York Times

FERRIDAY, La., Dec. 23—At 2 A.M. on Dec. 10, the night attendant at the Billups service station here was startled by an explosion and fire in Frank's shoeshop.

An instant later the shop owner, Frank Morris, a 51-year-old Negro, ran from the building, his clothing afire. The attendant put out the flames.

Before he died in Concordia Parish Hospital from burns over 90 per cent of his body, Mr. Morris said that he had found two white men in the shop pouring gasoline about. When he tried to flee, he said, one of the men forced him back inside with a shotgun. The fire followed.

The Federal Bureau of Inves-

Continued on Page 17, Column 2

NEW CONDITIONS BY SOVIET IMPERIL U.N. FUND ACCORD

Moscow Insists on Resumed Voting—Assembly Meeting Put Off Until Tuesday

By THOMAS J. HAMILTON
Special to The New York Times

UNITED NATIONS, N. Y., Dec. 23 — New Soviet conditions jeopardized today a plan under which the United Nations would try to resolve its financial difficulties by soliciting donations from the entire membership.

Alex Quaison-Sackey, the president of the General Assembly, canceled the meeting at which he was scheduled to submit his plan to the General Assembly.

In essence, the Soviet Union demanded that the question of taking away its Assembly vote because it is $52.6 million in arrears be dropped in exchange for a Soviet promise to donate an unspecified sum to the organization.

United States sources had termed any such arrangement "buying a pig in a poke."

Moscow's Conditions

Under the conditions fixed by Moscow, the Assembly would resume normal voting procedure immediately after the adoption of Mr. Quaison-Sackey's proposal for raising funds.

This plan would shelve indefinitely the question of taking away the vote of the Soviet Union and other members that have refused to pay assessments for the United Nations Congo and Middle Eastern forces, as demanded by the United States.

Mr. Quaison-Sackey canceled the Assembly meeting scheduled for today and called one for tomorrow as soon as he had been informed of the new Soviet demands. But later, after he had met for two hours with representatives of the United States, the Soviet Union and other countries, he put off the meeting until Tuesday.

Continued on Page 16, Column 1

Helicopter rescuing flood victims near Molalla, Ore.
United Press International Telephoto

VIETNAM DEFIES U.S. INSISTENCE ON UNIFIED RULE

TAYLOR ADAMANT

Meets With Leaders to Emphasize Stand on Military Coup

By PETER GROSE
Special to The New York Times

SAIGON, South Vietnam, Dec. 23—United States efforts to restore a constitutional facade to South Vietnam's Government were stalled today as Ambassador Maxwell D. Taylor was accused of interference in the country's internal affairs.

Backed by a specific though firm statement of support from the State Department, Mr. Taylor met Premier Tran Van Huong and other Government leaders and again insisted that American aid to Vietnam was predicated on a promise of governmental stability and orderly political evolution.

He emphasized that a change of the power basis such as occurred Sunday, when the armed forces abruptly dissolved the civilian legislature and arrested opposition politicians, was not consistent with the United States purpose in aiding Saigon against the Communist insurgency.

U. S. More Determined

The American stand brought the most direct clash with Vietnamese leaders since the veiled threats leveled against the regime of Ngo Dinh Diem that was overthrown last year. Foreign observers believe that the United States is more prepared now to back up its warnings with a reduction of support commitment than it was last year.

Many Vietnamese believed, however, that the United States would back down when faced with an apparent fait accompli.

The most extreme expression of this view came yesterday from the armed forces Commander in Chief, Lieut. Gen. Nguyen Khanh, who issued a public declaration of independence from what he implied was foreign manipulation. In private, he was more specifically anti-American.

According to informed sources, General Khanh, a former Premier, proposed a positive anti-American campaign to the Armed Forces Council, a newly formed body of leading military commanders.

The sources said General Khanh had asserted that American aid was not necessary to the Vietnamese cause.

He urged that United States policy be criticized openly and to take pains not to worsen the

Continued on Page 3, Column 2

CRITICIZES DISUNITY: Secretary of State Rusk in Washington, where he urged end to feud within the Government in South Vietnam.
Associated Press Wirephoto

RUSK HINTS SAIGON FACES A CUT IN AID

Suggests That U.S. May Be Forced to Act if a Unified Regime Is Not Restored

Excerpts from Mr. Rusk's remarks appear on Page 2.

By JOHN W. FINNEY
Special to The New York Times

WASHINGTON, Dec. 23—Secretary of State Dean Rusk suggested today that the United States would be forced to curtail its aid to South Vietnam if a unified government were not re-established in Saigon.

Mr. Rusk appealed to the factions in the Southeast Asian nation to put aside "personal rivalries" for the sake of maintaining the strength and unity of the country.

"Unity," he declared, "would be worth many, many divisions." He called it a "primary requirement" for establishing the security and independence of South Vietnam against the Communist insurgents.

Comment Is Cautious

Mr. Rusk discussed the deteriorating political situation in South Vietnam in cautious, general terms during a news conference at the State Department.

The conference was arranged before the South Vietnamese military forces had provoked the crisis by challenging the authority of the civilian Government, and Mr. Rusk appeared to take pains not to worsen the crisis by saying anything too openly critical of the military.

He returned repeatedly to the theme of the need for unity between civilian and military authorities in South Vietnam. Only obliquely, and then in conciliatory tones, did he suggest that the initiative for restoring unity must come from the military and, in particular, Lieut. Gen. Nguyen Khanh, Commander in Chief of the South Vietnamese armed forces.

Military Initiative Recalled

Mr. Rusk observed that it was the military that took the initiative last summer, when General Khanh was Premier, in creating the civilian Government, with the understanding that the military would restrict its own activities to the war against the Vietcong.

The overriding need now, he said, is for "complete unity of action and loyal support to the arrangements which have been agreed upon."

Reflecting the difficult position of the United States in the internal political crisis in South Vietnam, Mr. Rusk emphasized that this country was

Continued on Page 2, Column 4

BONN CHALLENGES U.S. DEAL IN EAST

Bids Washington Give Data on Action of 2 Companies

By PHILIP SHABECOFF
Special to The New York Times

BONN, Dec. 23 — The West German Government called upon the United States today to provide full information about reported plans of two American companies to sell licenses and equipment to East Germany for the construction of a synthetic fiber plant.

The Government has been surprised by reports that the Standard Oil Company of Ohio has agreed to sell licenses covering the production of synthetic fibers to East Germany and that another American concern, the Litwin Engineering Company, of Wichita, Kan., will sell equipment to build the fiber plant.

These transactions were said to have been approved by the export control agency of the Department of Commerce. They were reported to involve about $25 million. This would equal the total of United States exports to East Germany for the last six years.

It would also be the first major transaction between United States companies and the Communist regime of East Germany.

Government sources noted to-

Continued on Page 34, Column 1

In retaliation for the unprovoked attacks by North Vietnamese patrol craft on U.S. destroyers in the Gulf of Tonkin, planes bombed North Vietnam facilities at Hongay (1), Loc Chau, Phuc Loi and Vinh (2). and at Quang Khe (3).

As hostilities escalated in Vietnam in early 1965, the entire area of Southeast Asia was a tinderbox about to catch fire. The United States bombed sites in North Vietnam (1) in retaliation for a Viet Cong raid in South Vietnam (2) Laos (3) had been the scene of fighting between pro-Communists and neutralists, and an attempt by a right-wing general to regain power in the army. Thailand (4) was concerned over pro-Communist moves in Laos and Cambodia (5), which had chronic border difficulties with South Vietnam.

A U.S. Air Force F-105 Thunderchief fighter bomber at a base in South Vietnam. These powerful planes were used to strengthen defense in the area against air attacks from North Vietnam.

"All the News
That's Fit to Print"

The New York Times.

LATE CITY EDITION
U.S. Weather Bureau Report (Page 58) forecasts:
Rain, then partly cloudy, mild today,
tonight. Showers likely tomorrow.
Temp. range: 60—50; yesterday: 52—57.

VOL. CXIV..No. 39,097.   © 1965 by The New York Times Company.
Times Square, New York, N. Y. 10036   NEW YORK, MONDAY, FEBRUARY 8, 1965.   TEN CENTS

ALBANY LEADERS PROMISE TO SLASH 'LULUS' AND JOBS

$1 Million Cut in Costs of Legislature Is Pledged by Zaretzki and Travia

AUDITS ARE SUGGESTED

Bronston to Seek Reforms —Fairness Assured on Top Committee Jobs

By PETER KIHSS

An overhaul of the Legislature's "lulu" system of trimming of the patronage plum tree were pledged yesterday by Democratic leaders.

Senator Joseph Zaretzki of Manhattan, the newly elected temporary president of the Senate, and Anthony J. Travia of Brooklyn, the new Speaker of the Assembly, promised a $1 million cut in the legislative budget.

The two, who were elected with Republican support, said they were "determined to cut out all superfluous and no-show jobs."

Senator Jack E. Bronston of Queens, a Democrat who was defeated by Mr. Zaretzki in last week's voting at Albany, announced he would fight for the "elimination of the lulu system," by which lump sum expense funds are given to legislators in lieu of detailed accounts.

Periodic Audits Favored

Mr. Bronston declared that he and Controller Arthur Levitt had agreed there should be complete periodic audits of the legislative budget by the Controller, including the "evaluation" of jobs. Last year the Legislature appropriated $12 million for its operation.

Mr. Levitt, the only elected Democratic state executive, said the Legislature had "some pretty big lulus, $16,000 in some cases," and he favored a careful study. But he said a lulu could "avoid red tape" and let proper when expenses could be reasonably and regularly anticipated.

Each of the 208 legislators gets a $1,000 lulu in addition to his $10,000 salary. Mayor Wagner precipitated an outcry last month when he charged that extra lulus for certain committee chairmanships had been offered in the leadership struggle, offers which he said were in effect attempted bribes.

Senator Zaretzki said yester-

Continued on Page 12, Column 3

A.M.A. MOBILIZES TO BEAT MEDICARE

Votes Own 'Eldercare' Plan and an Educational Drive

Special to The New York Times

CHICAGO, Feb. 7 — The American Medical Association's House of Delegates set the stage today for a campaign to defeat the Johnson Administration's medicare bill with its own "eldercare" plan.

The House passed a resolution endorsing and "enthusiastically" supporting the A. M. A. proposal, which will be promoted by a large-scale national "educational program."

The eldercare bill would expand the present Kerr-Mills state - administered plans by subsidizing private health insurance plans with Federal and state funds for the poor of age 65 and older.

The medicare bill would provide hospital and nursing home benefits under Social Security for persons 65 and older.

Adoption of the eldercare program today marked a change from the last House of Delegates meeting in Miami Beach in December. At that time—before eldercare had been proposed—the House reiterated its support of the Kerr-Mills Act. The Board of Trustees, which runs the A.M.A. between House sessions, announced the eldercare plan last Jan. 10.

Today's vote by the 234-member House came on the final day of a two-day special session in the Pick-Congress Hotel. The decision not only reaffirmed opposition to medicare and empowered the trustees to conduct a "vigorous" campaign for the A.M.A. plan.

Two standing committees and

Continued on Page 9, Column 3

5-Union Pact Ends Last Rail Dispute

By JOHN D. POMFRET

WASHINGTON, Feb. 7 — Five nonoperating rail unions and the nation's railroads reached final agreement tonight on a contract of major importance. The agreement protects most of the members of the unions against layoff and gives the carriers new flexibility to transfer workers.

For the first time in more than five years, the railroads now have no major national collective bargaining dispute pending with any union or group of unions. Tonight's was the 15th major labor settlement reached by the railroads since last spring.

The new agreement extends the attrition principle to about 290,000 railroad workers. This is the largest single group inside or outside of the rail industry to be covered by such

Continued on Page 11, Column 1

LEADING LAWYERS JOIN RIGHTS DRIVE

150 Will Be Recruited to Go to Mississippi in Summer —Jackson Office Planned

By FRED P. GRAHAM

Special to The New York Times

NEW ORLEANS, Feb. 7 — Plans were announced today to recruit 150 volunteers from the leading law firms of the nation to represent civil rights workers in Mississippi.

The plan has the approval of the Mississippi Bar Association.

Bernard G. Segal, a corporate lawyer of Philadelphia, Pa., who is co-chairman of the Lawyers Committee for Civil Rights Under Law, announced that the committee would establish a law office in Jackson, Miss., before the expected influx of civil rights workers occurs this summer. Efforts are under way to raise $200,000 to cover expenses for the first year of operation.

The office in Jackson is expected to consist of three full-time staff attorneys, secretarial help and a law library. A second office in another Mississippi city may be opened later, Mr. Segal said.

Training Course Planned

Leading law firms across the nation will make available the services of experienced lawyers for periods of at least one month. The committee will pay expenses, and will provide a training course in Philadelphia law and procedure. Lawyers will be available for duty in Mississippi on a year-round basis, although most of them will be used in the summer.

Last month the committee sent 18 volunteer lawyers to Mississippi to represent members of the National Council of Churches.

Mississippi law allows out-of-state lawyers to practice unless they are challenged by two members of the local bar. Pending a decision by the State Bar Association's Admissions Committee, the challenged lawyers cannot practice in the state courts.

Mr. Segal said he had been assured that the Mississippi Committee on Admissions

Continued on Page 17, Column 3

ACCORD REACHED ON DOCK CONTRACT IN PHILADELPHIA

Agreement Could Pave Way for Return to Work in All North Atlantic Ports

Striking longshoremen and shipping employers agreed to a new contract for the Port of Philadelphia last night in an action that could pave the way for the return to work of 40,000 dockworkers on the North Atlantic Coast.

Philadelphia had been the major holdout port in the strike that has halted work in ports from Maine to Texas since Jan. 11.

Thomas W. Gleason, the president of the International Longshoremen's Association, said here in a telephone interview that he would call a meeting of his executive council shortly to work out union policy.

He added that the 22-man council would give "special consideration" to the question of getting the men in the North Atlantic ports back on the job.

Other Pacts Pending

The convening of the meeting, Mr. Gleason said, hinges on negotiations in Philadelphia involving four craft locals representing such workers as coopers, carpenters and clerical employes. These locals are expected to follow the lead of the longshoremen and settle quickly.

Mr. Gleason said his council's meeting, to be held in New York, might come as early as tonight or tomorrow.

The longshoremen's union has traditionally refused to work until all ports under its jurisdiction have settled, but it now has a plan to send its men back to the piers from Searsport, Me., to Hampton Roads, Va. However, the executive council must approve each action.

Pressure for an end to the long tie-up on the Atlantic and Gulf Coasts has been mounting for days. President Johnson appealed more than a week ago through the Department of Labor for a return to work in ports that had reached contracts, and there have been fears among some union leaders that Congress may take action.

The strike has tied up 775 ships and cost nearly $1.7 billion to the nation's economy.

Similar to Pact Here

The announcement of the Philadelphia longshoremen's pact was made just before 11 P.M., after 33 hours of almost continuous negotiations. Assistant Secretary of Labor James J. Reynolds, needing a shave but otherwise looking fresh, emerged from the meeting and said "a complete and final settlement" had been achieved.

The agreement is similar to the one reached in New York on Jan. 21. It provides an 80-cent-an-hour wage and welfare increase spread over the four-year life of the contract.

The longshoremen had

Continued on Page 50, Column 4

REDS CLAIM TOLL

'Barbarous' Attackers Lost Four Planes, Hanoi Declares

Special to The New York Times

HONG KONG, Feb. 7 — Communist North Vietnam asserted today that four United States jets were shot down as they made retaliatory raids against North Vietnamese targets.

In a statement by the Defense Ministry, North Vietnam also declared that the attack "constituted a new and extremely serious act of aggression."

The North Vietnam press agency said in a report received here that United States jets "coming in several waves from the sea" strafed and bombed villages around Donghoi, the capital of Quangbinh Province, in two strikes.

[Communist China said the air strikes were an "extremely serious provocation." A Moscow radio broadcast called them a "large-scale provocation." Page 16.]

Time of Attack

The press agency said that the first strike began at 2 P.M. local time (1 A.M. Sunday, New York time) and lasted about 20 minutes.

It said that the "United States imperialists were so barbarous and brazen" as to strafe the Donghoi hospital and an area in front of the office of the International Control Commission.

This is the three-nation body established in 1954 to supervise the execution of the Geneva cease-fire agreement that ended the fight between French and Communist forces in Indochina. Its members are India, Canada and Poland.

The agency said that at 2:35 P.M. United States jets returned and strafed the same localities for 10 more minutes.

The Defense Ministry statement said the fact that the "brazen aggressive act" had taken place while McGeorge Bundy was in Saigon further exposed the "sinister designs of United States imperialists" to expand the war in South Vietnam.

U.S. 'Severely' Warned

It added: "The Ministry of National Defense of the Democratic Republic of Vietnam severely warns United States imperialists and their henchmen they must bear full responsibility for the extremely serious consequences of aggressive acts provoked by them."

Before today's air strikes, Premier Aleksei N. Kosygin of the Soviet Union, who is visiting Hanoi, renewed Moscow's pledge to help North Vietnam should it be attacked.

Speaking at a rally in the North Vietnamese capital this morning, he said: "We sternly

Continued on Page 16, Column 2

U.S. JETS ATTACK NORTH VIETNAM IN REPRISAL FOR VIETCONG RAIDS; JOHNSON ORDERS FAMILIES HOME

United Press International Telephoto

EXPLAINS TACTICAL PROBLEMS: Secretary of Defense Robert S. McNamara during news conference yesterday. He shows point in North Vietnam where attacks on the South (arrows) are believed to have started, as well as situation of carriers off the coast.

Associated Press Radiophoto

RESULT OF VIETCONG ATTACK: Wreckage of U.S. helicopter at Camp Holloway air base, which was shelled early yesterday by mortars in a surprise attack by guerrillas.

TAYLOR CONSULTS WITH SAIGON CHIEF

Bundy, Back From Saigon, Reports to Johnson— Vietcong in New Raid

By SEYMOUR TOPPING

Special to The New York Times

SAIGON, South Vietnam, Monday Feb. 8 — Ambassador Maxwell D. Taylor conferred twice yesterday with Acting Premier Nguyen Xuan Oanh.

The Ambassador has been in touch with President Johnson through the highspeed communications of the United States Military Assistance Command here since the Vietcong attacks on the air base at Pleiku.

Three hours before a joint statement was issued by South Vietnam and the United States, announcing that action had been taken against military installations in North Vietnam, Mc-George Bundy, special assistant to President Johnson on security affairs, left Saigon hurriedly to report to the White House.

[Mr. Bundy returned home Sunday night and promptly went to see the President, The Associated Press reported.]

Communist guerrillas made another hit-and-run attack on a United States installation last night. They staged a 15-minute assault on an American air base at Soctrang, 50 miles south of Saigon, with mortar and small-arms fire. There were no casualties or damage as the Communist fire fell north of the runway.

A United States spokesman said that about 30 aircraft at the base went aloft when the raid began. Except for two medical evacuation helicopters and four armed helicopters, all aircraft were diverted to a base at Cantho.

This is the first time since World War II that the army and navy have done such work. They have been called to dock duty now because Bermuda, a largely dependent upon imports for its food supplies.

The Soctrang attack came less than 24 hours after the Pleiku assault.

Mr. Bundy has been sched-

Continued on Page 14, Column 4

Vietnamese Guard Was Half Strength When Reds Struck

By United Press International

PLEIKU, South Vietnam, Feb. 7—Only 44 of the 100 available Vietnamese security guards were on duty when Communist guerrillas attacked the airfield and billet area here today. Eight Americans were killed and 108 wounded.

Col. Joseph Ulatoski, 37 years old, of Stamford, Conn., adviser to the II Vietnamese Corps, estimated the infiltrating Vietcong force at Camp Holloway at about two squads and one platoon. It is estimated that this would be about 300 men.

The colonel said there were 12 Vietnamese guards in a pillbox near the United States billets. "Apparently they did not see much of anything," the colonel added.

Lieut. Col. John C. Hughes, 42, of Herrin, Ill., commanding officer of the 52d United States Army Aviation Battalion, told President Johnson's special assistant, McGeorge Bundy, who toured the damaged area before leaving for the United States, that the Americans and the Vietnamese were

Continued on Page 14, Column 2

Strike in Bermuda Perils Food Supply

By MURRAY SCHUMACH

Special to The New York Times

HAMILTON, Bermuda, Feb. 7 —The armed forces of Bermuda will unload a grain ship tomorrow because dock workers, in sympathy with a strike by electric company employes, have refused to do it. The effects of the strike have spread steadily since the labor dispute began Jan. 19.

Soctrang is the main center for helicopter operations in the Mekong delta area.

Bermuda is the main center for its food supplies.

The use of troops to unload the grain is also an indication

Continued on Page 17, Column 1

U.S. VIEWED RAIDS AS A TEST OF WILL

Administration Retaliated in Belief That Inaction Would Be Seen as Defeatist

By MAX FRANKEL

Special to The New York Times

WASHINGTON, Feb. 7—The Administration ordered the airstrike against North Vietnam today in the belief that it faced the most serious test so far of its will to help resist aggression in South Vietnam.

Informed sources said the United States had acted on the assumption that North Vietnam's Communist Government organized that test without warning Soviet Premier Aleksei N. Kosygin, its guest in Hanoi at the moment.

Sensing that the Soviet leader might find himself in an awkward position there, the Administration sent a special message to Moscow to explain its raid as an act of retaliation rather than as a move to expand the war in Southeast Asia.

Sense of Challenge

President Johnson and his leading advisers were said to have had no doubt they were being tested. They were described as confident that a failure to respond would have been interpreted as a defeatist position in several Communist capitals.

Their sense of challenge as they met at the White House last night to plan the response was said to have been based on the following factors:

¶The severity of the Vietcong attack on a United States military compound in South Vietnam, in which eight Americans died. That attack, presumably coordinated with two other major Vietcong strikes, was interpreted here as an effort to demonstrate American vulnerability.

¶Secret but "clear" evidence that North Vietnam not only knew of this test but also participated in its planning. The

Continued on Page 14, Column 1

CAPITAL IS TENSE

But President Asserts Nation Still Opposes Widening of War

Text of the McNamara-Ball news conference, Page 15.

By TOM WICKER

Special to The New York Times

WASHINGTON, Feb. 7 — United States aircraft struck at North Vietnam early today in response to what President Johnson called "provocations ordered and directed by the Hanoi regime."

Mr. Johnson made it clear, however, that the air strike was a limited response rather than a signal for a general expansion of the guerrilla warfare in South Vietnam.

In what appeared to be the most threatening crisis in Southeast Asia since the Gulf of Tonkin clash last August, Washington replied to severe Vietcong attacks.

The guerrillas had struck without warning against major American installations at Pleiku in the central plateau of South Vietnam, at an airstrip in Tuyhoa and at villages near Nhatrang.

49 Aircraft in Action

At the President's order, 49 carrier - based fighter planes bombed and strafed areas of the Vietcong guerrillas in the vicinity of Donghoi, just north of the border between North and South Vietnam.

The raid occurred swiftly about 2 P.M. Sunday, Vietnamese time (1 A.M. Eastern standard time). Secretary of Defense Robert S. McNamara said one American plane had gone down in the South China Sea. The Hanoi radio in the North Vietnamese capital said four aircraft had been knocked out.

Today, amid tension, President Johnson ordered the evacuation of about 1,800 dependents of United States military and civilian personnel stationed in South Vietnam.

Missile Unit Dispatched

He also ordered into the Danang area of South Vietnam an air - defense battalion equipped with Hawk ground-to-air missiles.

In the Vietcong attack at Pleiku, 8 Americans were killed and 108 wounded, but first reports did not indicate American casualties in the two other attacks.

Tension in Washington was heightened, and the United States response appeared conditioned to some extent by the Hanoi visit of Premier Aleksei N. Kosygin of the Soviet Union. Mr. Kosygin said in a speech to a Hanoi group that Moscow would assist North Vietnam against any nation that encroached on its territory.

Johnson Repeats Pledge

Administration officials insisted that the air attack would not be considered a reply to Mr. Kosygin's visit to Hanoi and would have been staged even if he had not been there.

In a White House statement announcing the retaliatory attack, Mr. Johnson repeated the pledge, given at the time of the Tonkin incident, that "we seek no wider war."

But the President cautioned that "whether or not this course can be maintained lies with the North Vietnamese aggressors."

The response to the Vietcong attacks, he said, "was carefully limited to military areas which are supplying men and arms for attacks in South Vietnam." Thus, he said, "the response is appropriate and fitting."

Mr. McNamara, at a news conference with George Ball,

Continued on Page 14, Column 1

Visitors to Museum Hall See Man Slay Ex-Wife

Violin Maker, 72, Shoots His Former Mate After Talk

A 72-year-old master violin maker shot and killed his former wife in the main hall of the American Museum of Natural History yesterday afternoon.

About 30 people, including the couple's 12-year-old daughter, were in the cavernous, marble - pillared hall when the shooting occurred. The five shots, three of which struck the 43 - year - old woman, transformed the normally hushed lobby into a bedlam. Youngsters screamed and parents ran to protect their children as museum guards grappled with the slayer.

The embittered violin maker was identified by the police as Dmytro Didchenko, who had worked at his craft on two continents since leaving his native Russia after the 1917 Revolution. He and his wife, Gertrude, a German immigrant, had been battling in court for most of their marriage of 13 years. Last Thursday the marriage was annulled.

Associated Press

Dmytro Didchenko leaving 68th Street police station.

Lawyer in Marital Case Dies at Police Station House

lives at 101 West 85th Street, made an appointment with his former wife to discuss the visitation rights of their daughter, Susan. The dark-haired girl lived with her mother at 63-15 190th Street, Rego Park, Queens.

The couple were married in 1952. In 1956 a court case involving the two—by then separated—received some attention because Mrs. Didchenko said she was afraid her husband would kill her if she took her daughter for the visits stipulated by the judge.

Neighbors of Didchenko said yesterday that he had become an embittered and lonely man during the long round of court appearances. They said they had finally avoided him because he seemed obsessed with discussing his marital troubles and they had difficulty understanding him.

Before he died, Mr. Tompkins had said that the marriage was finally annulled on the ground that Didchenko had had an

Continued on Page 19, Column 2

A few hours after the 1:15 P.M. shooting, Mrs. Didchenko's lawyer, former State Senator Bernard Tompkins, collapsed and died on the steps inside the West 68th Street station house while being interviewed.

The day's events apparently began when Didchenko, who

Bombs explode on a naval facility in North Vietnam during an attack by U.S. Air Force fighter-bombers.

U.S. troops on a mop-up operation in the jungles of South Vietnam after saturation bombing by B-52 Stratofortresses.

Quarters at Pleiku Air Base, South Vietnam, damaged during a Viet Cong mortar attack.

"All the News That's Fit to Print"

The New York Times.

LATE CITY EDITION
U. S. Weather Bureau Report (Page 72) forecasts: Sunny, very mild today; increasing cloudiness tonight. Rain tomorrow. Temp. range: 56—37; yesterday: 38—36.

VOL. CXIV—No. 39,100. © 1965 by The New York Times Company. Times Square, New York, N. Y. 10036 NEW YORK, THURSDAY, FEBRUARY 11, 1965. TEN CENTS

JOHNSON URGES RESTRAINT IN U. S. INVESTING ABROAD TO CUT PAYMENTS DEFICIT

CURB ON TOURISTS

Would Cut Purchases for Travelers to $50 —Tax Widened

Text of President's message is printed on Page 56.

By EDWIN L. DALE Jr.
Special to The New York Times

WASHINGTON, Feb. 10—President Johnson called on American business and banking today for a broad new voluntary effort to cut down their lending and investing abroad to eliminate the deficit in the nation's international payments.

The President's specific measures in a special Balance of Payments Message to Congress were relatively few and relatively mild. But the potential savings from his appeal to private business and banking would be enormous, running into the billions of dollars, if he gets cooperation.

[Leading bankers and businessmen reacted cautiously, though generally favorably, to President Johnson's message. What seemed to impress them most was Mr. Johnson's request that they exercise voluntary restraint in lending money or making investments abroad. Page 57.]

Would Cut Outflow

Mr. Johnson asked Congress to reduce the duty-free exemption for purchases abroad by tourists from $100 to $50, with the $50 limit applying to the retail instead of the wholesale price. The exemption would be allowed only for goods actually carried by the traveler when he returned to the United States.

This set of changes, it is expected, would cut about $100 million from the nation's net tourist dollar outflow of $1.6 billion a year.

The President also announced, as a second specific measure, that he had extended the new interest-equalization tax to loans made abroad by banks. It now applies only to the purchase of foreign securities.

Congress was asked to extend the tax for two years beyond its scheduled expiration date of next Dec. 30, and to apply it, effective today, to loans by lenders other than banks.

The heart of the President's program was his appeal for a

Continued on Page 56, Column 1

Democrats Said to Reject Plan for State Sales Tax

Increase in Income and Other Levies Is Likely, Greenberg Asserts

By R. W. APPLE Jr.
Special to The New York Times

ALBANY, Feb. 10—A top Democratic spokesman on fiscal matters predicted today that the Legislature would enact a revenue and spending program without a state sales tax.

The spokesman, Senator Samuel L. Greenberg of Brooklyn, chairman of the Senate Finance Committee, also said that the Senate and Assembly should be able to trim at least $75 million from Governor Rockefeller's record $3.48 billion budget.

Mr. Greenberg indicated in an interview that the Democratic majorities in the two houses were considering increases in the pari-mutuel, corporation, liquor and gasoline taxes, as well as higher personal income taxes.

The 11-term Brooklyn legislator agreed with some other key Democrats here that the prospects of legislation to legalize off-track betting were slim. He said some members of his party and almost all Republicans would probably vote against it.

That view was challenged by a source close to the Senate

Continued on Page 33, Column 3

Fabian Bachrach
Samuel L. Greenberg

KENNEDY WARNS ALBANY LEADERS: AVOID PATRONAGE

Tells Travia and Zaretzki to Fill State Jobs on Merit or Party Will Suffer

Text of the Kennedy letter will be found on Page 35.

By RONALD SULLIVAN
Special to The New York Times

ALBANY, Feb. 10—United States Senator Robert F. Kennedy warned Assembly Speaker Anthony J. Travia and Senate Majority Leader Joseph Zaretzki today against handing out jobs on the basis of patronage.

He recommended instead that the State Democratic party begin a talent hunt—"like that which President Kennedy established in 1960"—to seek the best persons for the job without regard to whether they were Democrats or Republicans.

He suggested further that jobs "not in the public interest" be eliminated.

While acknowledging the "traditional right" of the leaders to choose the appointees, Senator Kennedy said:

"I had assumed that these positions would be filled on the basis of merit and, since this is a state matter, I had intended to remain uninvolved. However, it has come to my attention that telephone calls have been made to various political leaders around the state asking them to fill positions on the basis of patronage."

Further 'Injury' Feared

Such a move, if carried out, would only add to "the injury which we must agree has recently been sustained by the Democratic party as a result of the long leadership impasse," Mr. Kennedy said.

Mr. Travia, in his shirt sleeves behind his office desk, shook his head at the letter's bluntness and said, "No one has gotten any jobs yet."

He said that when he did make appointments, they would be based "on merit and ability alone."

Mr. Zaretzki declined at first to comment here, saying he had not read the letter thoroughly. But late tonight, after returning to his home in Manhattan, he said he was mailing a long reply to Mr. Kennedy.

Fears Held Unjustified

In it, he said that Senator Kennedy's fears were unjustified. He said there was a difference between staff positions in the legislative branch of government and administrative positions in the executive branch.

With a touch of sarcasm, Mr. Zaretzki asserted that he was "not aware" that Mr. Kennedy had followed his own recommended procedure "in filling the staff positions in your own office in the United States Senate."

Mr. Kennedy did not specify which jobs were being filled on a patronage basis. However, it was assumed that he was referring to the key legislative

Continued on Page 35, Column 4

165 Selma Negro Youths Taken on Forced March

By ROY REED
Special to The New York Times

SELMA, Ala., Feb. 10—Sheriff James G. Clark and a group of deputies with night sticks and electric cattle prods led 165 Negro demonstrators, all children and teen-agers, on a forced march into the Dallas County countryside today.

The youngsters were marched at a pace alternating between a run and a rapid walk while the sheriff and members of the Dallas County sheriff's posse rode in cars and spelled each other at the task of drill master.

Several youngsters told newsmen later that the sheriff's men had used night sticks and electric cattle prods on them. The sheriff said he had not seen anything like that.

"You've been wanting to march, now let's go," the possemen yelled as they trotted beside the Negroes. "Close up the ranks back there. Come on, close it up, close it up."

After 2.3 miles the exhausted youngsters rebelled and fled into a private yard beside the road. The sheriff and his men tried to herd them back on the road, but the Negroes refused to leave the yard. Many went into the house at the invitation of one of the Negro marchers who lived there.

The sheriff gave up after a few minutes and took his men

Continued on Page 19, Column 1

ABEL HOLDS LEAD IN STEEL ELECTION

A Narrow Margin Separates Him From McDonald in Contest for Presidency

By DAMON STETSON
Special to The New York Times

PITTSBURGH, Feb. 10 — I. W. Abel clung to a narrow lead over David J. McDonald today as the vote count continued in the election battle for the presidency of the United Steelworkers of America.

The margin was so small, however, that neither Mr. Abel nor Mr. McDonald, the incumbent president, would claim victory. Many of the big locals in basic steel, which have been tediously counting their votes, have been extremely slow in reporting their figures.

Unofficial returns compiled by United Press International from 2,779 of 3,203 locals in the union showed:

Abel	249,839
McDonald	238,267

Although Mr. Abel, now secretary-treasurer of the union, made no public comment on the outlook, he was reported to be confident that he would come out on top. Some of his aides were talking in terms of a winning margin of 40,000 votes, but accurate projections in a

Continued on Page 25, Column 2

PRESIDENT MOVES IN PIER DEADLOCK

Names Panel to Recommend Way Out by Tomorrow

By GEORGE HORNE

President Johnson took action yesterday in the month-long waterfront strike.

He named an informal committee of three men to make quick recommendations in the stalemate in South Atlantic and Gulf ports and set a deadline for noon tomorrow for the disputing parties to make up their minds on acceptance of the panel's settlement formula.

Sharply criticizing the International Longshoremen's Association for "unjustified" continuation of the strike in many ports where settlement has been reached, Mr. Johnson said the injury to the national economy had reached "staggering proportions."

The President named to his "informal" committee Secretary of Labor W. Willard Wirtz and Secretary of Commerce John T. Connor. He asked Senator Wayne Morse, Democrat of Oregon, to be the third member.

Senator Morse is familiar with the dispute because he was chairman of a panel named by President Kennedy to settle the last coastwide dock strike in the winter of 1962-63.

The President based his move

Continued on Page 73, Column 5

GET OUT OF THE AISLE, HERMAN. So Scrabble Crossword Cubes by Selchow & Righter are portable. So there's no board. So you can play anywhere. But Herman, an airplane aisle?—Advt.

City Brewers' Pact Bars Discrimination

By MORRIS KAPLAN

The city's breweries agreed yesterday to integrate Negroes and Puerto Ricans into the industry's permanent work force.

Representatives of five major beermakers—Schaefer, Liebmann (Rheingold), Schlitz, Ruppert and Piel's—and Locals 3 and 46 of the International Brotherhood of Teamsters and the Negro American Labor Council signed a pact to assure equal job opportunities.

The agreement was negotiated by the City Commission on Human Rights, which conducted a signing ceremony at its headquarters, 80 Lafayette

Continued on Page 25, Column 5

L. B. J. and THE BUSINESSMAN. A Special survey in February FORTUNE.—Advt.

SAIGON'S PLANES ATTACK NORTH; VIETCONG BLOW UP U.S. BARRACKS, G.I. KILLED, 24 HUNTED IN RUBBLE

JOHNSON IS SILENT

Confers With Security Aides Amid Secrecy Over Retaliation

By CHARLES MOHR
Special to The New York Times

WASHINGTON, Feb. 10—President Johnson summoned the National Security Council today to discuss new Communist military successes against American and South Vietnamese troops, but gave no hint whether the United States would respond.

On Sunday and Monday United States and South Vietnamese planes raided bases in North Vietnam in retaliation for an attack by Vietcong forces at Pleiku in South Vietnam. Eight Americans were killed and more than 100 wounded in the Pleiku attack.

Tight secrecy was imposed at the White House on the question whether Mr. Johnson would respond to the new Vietcong onslaughts with air strikes on North Vietnam.

Some usually informed sources said that they strongly doubted there would be any announcement of United States intentions until tomorrow at the earliest.

At the State Department, however, officials said that the new Vietcong attack was regarded here just as gravely as last weekend's.

Delay Is Expected

The President was informed this morning that a United States Army barracks at the seacoast town of Quinhon had been attacked by Vietcong terrorists. He was also told that South Vietnamese forces had been badly defeated in a clash in Binhdinh Province.

Mr. Johnson summoned his top military and diplomatic advisers to the National Security Council meeting in the Cabinet room at 2 P.M. The meeting lasted about an hour and 45 minutes.

A few minutes after it had ended Mr. Johnson unexpectedly walked through the lobby of the west wing of the White House and onto the driveway leading toward the northwest gate. He was accompanied by Marvin Watson, who reported to work Feb. 1 as a special assistant to the President.

Scores of newsmen and photographers tumbled excitedly after him, and pursued him to a point near the gate, where Mr. Johnson turned and followed the main drive toward the White House proper.

Asked by a reporter what he would do about Vietnam, the President said:

"I think I'll just walk up to

Continued on Page 12, Column 5

The New York Times Feb. 11, 1965

WIDESPREAD GUERRILLA ACTIONS: An American billet was blown up at Quinhon (1). Near the town of Phumy, just to the north, the Vietcong sprang a trap on five companies. Fighting was heavy near Danang (2) and paratroops were ambushed in Phuoc Tuy (3).

15 MEN WOUNDED

American Aides Hint at a New Air Strike Against North

By Reuters

DANANG, South Vietnam Thursday, Feb. 11—About 28 South Vietnam Air Force Skyraider fighter bombers took off from here today followed shortly by 20 U.S. jetfighters heading north and fully loaded with bombs.

The planes took off into a fair blue sky in the direction of North Vietnam. Danang is only 50 miles from the North Vietnam border. Hundreds of United States servicemen were at the edge of the runway.

By SEYMOUR TOPPING
Special to The New York Times

SAIGON, South Vietnam, Thursday, Feb. 11—Vietcong terrorists last night blew up a four-story building housing American enlisted men in the coastal city of Quinhon, 267 miles northeast of Saigon.

At 9 A.M. today, as drills and cranes picked through a mound of rubble a story tall, military spokesmen said one soldier was known dead, 15 were wounded and 24 were unaccounted for.

Shouts from six men were heard through the rubble.

Trap Sprung on Highway

Communist units were reported to have shattered five companies of Government troops—about 500 men—in a running battle that began shortly after the bombing of North Vietnam by United States and South Vietnamese planes on Sunday.

Military observers said that a trap sprung by the Vietcong along a coastal highway near Phumy in Bindinh Province, about 300 miles northeast of Saigon, had resulted in one of the most severe Government defeats of the war.

The attack on the Quinhon barracks, in which a demolition charge was used, "completely destroyed" the four-story building, a United States spokesman said.

A Vietcong assault force first rushed the barracks, opening up with small-arms fire. Sentries returned the fire, a United States spokesman said.

About 40 servicemen were believed to have been in the

Continued on Page 12, Column 1

Moscow Is Warned By the White House To Curb Its Mobs

Special to The New York Times

WASHINGTON, Feb. 10—The United States warned the Soviet Union today that continued failure to protect the American Embassy in Moscow against mob demonstrations could damage diplomatic relations between the two nations.

The warning was contained in an unusual White House statement sharply criticizing the Soviet Union for having failed to provide adequate police protection for the embassy in Moscow against a mob of demonstrators yesterday.

The statement, read this morning by the White House press secretary, George E. Reedy, said that President Johnson took "a most serious view" of the incident and that the United States "must insist" upon adequate protection for its diplomatic missions.

The strongly worded statement was not intended as a threat to break off diplomatic relations between the two countires. But it suggested that Soviet failure to provide the pro-

Continued on Page 12, Column 8

BONN WITHHOLDS ARMS FOR ISRAEL

Action Follows Demand by Nasser—Cairo Said to Give Pledge on East Germany

By ARTHUR J. OLSEN
Special to The New York Times

BONN, Feb. 10—Chancellor Ludwig Erhard has ordered a temporary halt in West German arms deliveries to Israel, qualified sources said tonight.

The decision is understood to have been taken yesterday and communicated to Cairo.

[Diplomatic sources in Cairo said that the United Arab Republic, in turn, had promised not to extend diplomatic recognition to East Germany. Page 2.]

The sources here said that a final decision on West Germany's $80 million military aid program to Israel would be made in the light of the United Arab Republic's reception of Walter Ulbricht, the East German chief of state. He is scheduled to arrive in Cairo on Feb. 26.

The West German Government was reported to be determined to insure, in any event, that Israel's security needs would be met.

The Government declined any comment on the reported decision. But Eugen Gerstenmaier, president of the Bundestag, the lower house of Parliament, confirmed that the Government had stopped arms deliveries to Israel.

It was disclosed in Cairo Monday that President Gamal Abdel Nasser had demanded that

Continued on Page 2, Column 5

PARIS AGAIN ASKS PEACE IN VIETNAM

De Gaulle Calls for Talks and End of Intervention

By DREW MIDDLETON
Special to The New York Times

PARIS, Feb. 10 — President de Gaulle appealed again today for the end of foreign intervention and a negotiated peace in South Vietnam.

France's objective is an international agreement barring outside interference and covering North and South Vietnam, Laos and Cambodia, according to a Government statement.

The statement was issued by Alain Peyrefitte, Minister of Information, after General de Gaulle and the Cabinet had discussed the United States' air strikes against North Vietnam and the Vietcong's attacks on United States installations in the south.

The United States was not mentioned in the statement. Allied diplomats said, however, that it was certainly directed

Continued on Page 13, Column 2

City Rejects Park Memorials to Slain Jews

Model of [illegible]

Art Board Member Calls One Too Big, One Too Tragic

By WILLIAM E. FARRELL

The city's Art Commission has rejected proposals for construction of two monuments in Riverside Park in memory of the six million Jews slain by the Nazis.

Eleanor Platt, a sculptor who is a member of the Art Commission, said that one of the monuments, a statue showing a Polish-Jewish leader engulfed by flames and about to pitch forward, showed so "tragic a posture" that it might distress children in the park.

The other memorial, consisting of two 26-foot-high scrolls mounted on a 40-foot-wide platform, was criticized by Miss Platt in a letter to other commission members as being "excessively and unnecessarily large."

Also, she wrote, construction of the monuments "would set a highly regrettable precedent" in that it might provide an opening for "other special groups" that wanted to erect memorials on public land.

Supporters of the project had hoped to have the monuments put in the park between 83d and 84th Streets, an area set aside in 1947 for a similar memorial that was never built.

The Art Commission rejected the designs at a Jan. 28 meeting at the home of Arnold Whitridge, a trustee of the Metropolitan Museum of Art, who is president of the commission.

The minutes of the meeting

Continued on Page 9, Column 1

The New York Times
Artur Zygelboim memorial is a tragic bronze figure.

Johnson Is Upheld On Food for Cairo

By FELIX BELAIR Jr.
Special to The New York Times

WASHINGTON, Feb. 10—Congress yielded today to President Johnson's appeal for a free hand to use surplus food shipments to the United Arab Republic as an instrument of United States foreign policy.

The grant of complete discretionary power was contained in a conference committee agreement on the $1.6 billion agricultural supplemental appropriation. The measure was quickly passed by the House and Senate and sent to the White House after the President bowed to Congressional

Continued on Page 2, Column 2

INTRIGUE IN THE DEN With Selchow & Righter's Tangle. It's just as much fun as their Scrabble® and Parcheesi® games.—Adv.

NEWS INDEX

[illegible] TEMPORARY OFFICE HELP!!! Special Office Staffs, [illegible]—Advt.

Children killed by the Viet Cong during a raid on a village 10 miles north of Saigon.

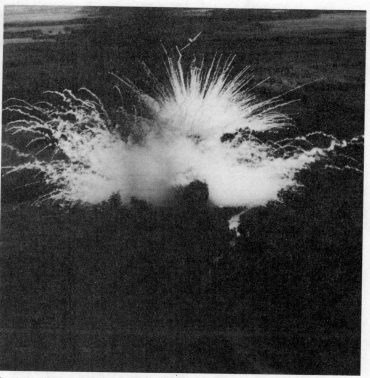

A phosphorous bomb explodes in a white hot spray over a cluster of Viet Cong military structures hidden in the Phong Dinh Province. The Vietnamese Air Force A-IE Skyraider which dropped the bomb, is visible banking away.

U.S. Air Force jet bombers including these F-100 Supersabres were used for the first time in the Vietnamese conflict in February, 1965.

The New York Times.

"All the News That's Fit to Print"

LATE CITY EDITION
U. S. Weather Bureau Report (Page 37) forecast:
Rain today; clearing tonight. Fair and seasonable tomorrow.
Temp. range: 46-38; yesterday: 49-37.

VOL. CXIV. No. 39,101.   © 1965 by The New York Times Company.   NEW YORK, FRIDAY, FEBRUARY 12, 1965.   TEN CENTS

U.S. COURT ORDERS I.L.A. HERE TO END WALKOUT AT ONCE

Top Union Officials, Who Must Be Served, Are at Washington Inquiry

HIRING CENTERS TO OPEN

But Writ Is Not Yet Binding — 2 Other Ports Get Similar Injunctions

By GEORGE HORNE
Special to The New York Times

WASHINGTON, Feb. 11 — Striking longshoremen in the Port of New York were ordered back to work by a Federal judge in New York this afternoon as President Johnson's special panel opened an inquiry here.

Federal Judge Sidney Sugarman signed a five-day temporary order enjoining the 24,000 New York dockers on a petition filed by the National Labor Relations Board regional office in New York.

The New York Shipping Association had asked for the injunction on Tuesday, charging unfair labor practice. The 145-member employer group said that New York had a contract with the International Longshoremen's Association and that the union was continuing to strike in support of the ports that have not yet reached agreement.

[Similar restraining orders were issued in Baltimore Thursday and in New Orleans Friday morning. An injunction was issued in Mobile, Ala., last week.]

Officials at Inquiry

All of the top New York union officials are here attending the inquiry that was set in motion yesterday when President Johnson intervened in the month-old walkout that has brought huge losses to the national economy.

Judge Sugarman used the word "forthwith" in ordering a stop to the walkout.

The court's order cannot be legally binding until it has been served on union officials and there was some question here as to how this could be quickly accomplished. Thomas W. Gleason, president of the I.L.A., said when informed of the order:

"I haven't been served."

Union men here, however, were informed tonight that Local 1814 in Brooklyn had already sent out orders for its men to return to the docks tomorrow. Anthony J. Scotto, an international vice president and the head of Local 1814, said

Continued on Page 57, Column 3

ROCKET ACHIEVES 3 ORBITS IN TEST

Air Force Fires Titan 3-A for Space Station Trial

By United Press International

CAPE KENNEDY, Feb. 11 — A Titan-3A rocket was put into three different orbits today in a test of maneuverability needed for possible use on trips to space stations.

After executing a four-and-a-half-hour series of space acrobatics, the Titan's third stage swung out into space to launch a 69-pound experimental communications satellite.

The satellite apparently separated from the third stage as planned but failed to shoot itself into the 11,500-mile orbit expected. Even so, a spokesman reported late tonight that the satellite was working well.

The primary goal of the mission, however, was the versatile third stage's three starts and stops. Its first firing sent the 7,000-pound rocket-payload up

Continued on Page 6, Column 3

Final Seconds of DC-7B: Pilots Differ on Near-Miss

Radio Log Recounts Airliner's Plunge Into Ocean—Wreckage Is Located by Divers From Fishing Boat

By FREDRIC C. APPEL

The two Pan American World Airways pilots who witnessed Monday night's fatal plunge of Eastern Air Lines Flight 663 off Jones Beach, L. I., apparently differed on whether the two planes were in a "close miss."

While one pilot had reported, "We had a close miss here."

However, two F.A.A. officials expressed doubt that the aircraft had really come very close together. Both officials estimated the separation of the planes at 1,200 to 1,700 feet vertically and three to four miles laterally, well within legal limits.

Civil Aeronautics Board officials, on the other hand, declined to comment on this reconstruction, indicating they thought it was too early to try to draw any conclusions. The C.A.B. is officially charged with investigating the accident in which all 84 persons on the DC-7B, a piston propeller craft, were killed.

At the crash scene, wreckage of the doomed aircraft was located by six amateur divers

Continued on Page 34, Column 1

Excerpts from transcript of air messages, Page 34.

the second, in the same cockpit, said: "He was well over the top of us. And it looked like he went into an absolute vertical turn and kept rolling."

This dramatic description of Flight 663's final seconds emerged from recorded tapes of the pilots' radio transmissions, released yesterday by the Federal Aviation Agency.

In separate news conferences,

Judgment Against Powell Is Increased to $210,000

By WILL LISSNER

A judgment of $46,500 for defamation of character that Representative Adam Clayton Powell has avoided paying was increased in State Supreme Court yesterday to $210,000.

A jury awarded Mrs. Esther James, 68-year-old former domestic worker, $100,000 compensatory damages against Representative Powell and his wife and $250,000 punitive damages against the Representative alone for transferring a Puerto Rican beach house to his wife's relatives to avoid its attachment.

Justice Frederick Backer held that $350,000 in lieu of the $46,500 was "totally excessive" and reduced compensatory damages to $60,000 and punitive damages to $150,000.

Powell Not in Court

Mr. Powell was convicted on April 3, 1963, of having publicly defamed the Harlem widow by calling her a "bag woman" who collects money from gamblers for payments to the police. The judgment of $211,500 was reduced to $46,500 by the Appellate Division of the State Supreme Court on Feb. 6, 1964.

The action concluded yesterday was brought by Mrs. James on the basis of the transfer of the beach house. Representative Powell did not participate in the proceeding, though his counsel, George D. Covington, appeared when the jury brought in its verdict. Mr. Covington said he had sought to intervene on Wednesday, but the judge had denied his request without prejudice.

Because Mr. Powell did not accept service of a summons and complaint, and participate in the proceeding, it was a jury inquest, not a trial of a suit for

Continued on Page 30, Column 6

RACE ISSUES FAN BERMUDA UNREST

Strikes Seen as Outgrowth of Negroes' Discontent— Whites Voice Concern

By MURRAY SCHUMACH
Special to The New York Times

HAMILTON, Bermuda, Feb. 11—Beneath the surface of Bermuda's wave of labor disputes, racial currents are sweeping the oldest of the British Crown colonies from Victorian serenity toward the anxieties of the present.

The tourist does not notice this. He speaks longingly of this land without income tax. He relaxes in a horse-drawn barouche, rejoices in the sea air in a secluded cove or on green golf courses. He finds solace in the coveys of attendants at hotels and restaurants and in the friendliness of pubs.

To him this is still just a land of sunshine and of bargains in cashmere sweaters, liquor and crockery. And he is encouraged in this by the residents, who do not like to think about racial problems themselves, much less discuss them with tourists.

Racial differences seemed to be a public secret and a private obsession in Bermuda.

They are one reason that the

Continued on Page 4, Column 3

MAYOR AND G.O.P. DISPUTE KENNEDY ON ALBANY JOBS

Defend Zaretzki and Travia Against Patronage Charge —Rockefeller Caustic

Text of Zaretzki's letter is printed on Page 14.

By DOUGLAS DALES

Mayor Wagner took issue yesterday with intimations by United States Senator Robert F. Kennedy that the Democratic legislative leaders might seek to fill jobs on a patronage basis.

"I don't think it should disqualify any individual," the Mayor said, "if the recommendation for his appointment came through someone in political life."

The Mayor's observation was in response to questions dealing with a letter by Mr. Kennedy to the legislative leaders warning against handing out jobs on a patronage basis.

Mr. Wagner was high in his praise for the two principal selections made at Albany so far — John McKennan, former Utica Mayor, for Assembly Clerk, and George Van Lengen of Syracuse for Secretary of the Senate.

Kennedy's Goal at Issue

Mr. Kennedy's letter, addressed to Senate Majority Leader Joseph Zaretzki and Assembly Speaker Anthony J. Travia, was widely interpreted as projecting Mr. Kennedy in the middle of the bitter intra-party fight that held up organization of the Legislature for five weeks.

But in Washington Senator Kennedy denied that he was taking sides in the Albany leadership battle. He said that his warning on patronage would have been sent to anti-Wagner men if they had been elected and if they had ignored merit in making appointments.

Senator Zaretzki and Assemblyman Travia, elected as leaders with the aid of Republican votes, had the support of leaders who had been the early advocates of the nomination of Mr. Kennedy for the Senate.

Rockefeller Comments

Governor Rockefeller, touring in the Southern Tier counties yesterday, charged that Mr. Kennedy's letter had been "something brought because he was "sore" over the issue of the leadership fight by "his boss-controlled candidates."

"I think what he is doing is carrying on the fight," the Governor said during a brief news conference at the Chemung County Airport.

"His boss-controlled candidates lost. He obviously is sore and is carrying on his fight by writing this letter."

The Governor asserted that Mr. Kennedy was "assuming a holier-than-thou attitude" toward Mr. Zaretzki and Mr. Tra-

Continued on Page 14, Column 1

PONTIFF APPEALS FOR PEACE EFFORT

Implies Support for a U.N. Role in Vietnam Solution

By ROBERT C. DOTY
Special to The New York Times

ROME, Feb. 11—Pope Paul VI made an appeal for peace today that was interpreted by informed sources as indirect support for a negotiated settlement in Vietnam sponsored and guaranteed by the United Nations.

The Pontiff made no specific reference to the increasing hostilities in North and South Vietnam. But, in an address to pilgrims at a general audience, he expressed concern over growing dangers of war and appealed to statesmen "of whatever side" for wise action to avert a new world holocaust.

"May international institutions capable of preventing the attacks of force be reinforced," he said in an allusion to the United Nations. "May these be adapted, surrounded with general respect, to assure the honest execution, the honest observance of treaties."

According to qualified observers, this appeared to lend papal support to the theory, advanced principally by President de Gaulle, that only negotiations can end the hostilities in Vietnam. The French President has also proposed a review by the big powers of the functioning of the United Nations Charter.

Pope Paul said it was almost incredible that there could be

Continued on Page 13, Column 5

160 U. S. AND VIETNAMESE PLANES ATTACK MILITARY BASES IN NORTH; WASHINGTON SEEKS TO LIMIT WAR

U.S. BARRACKS DESTROYED: Hotel at Quinhon, South Vietnam, used as an enlisted men's barracks, lies in ruins after Vietcong attackers blew it up in a raid on Wednesday.
Associated Press Radiophoto

Mao Is Said to Bar War Unless China Is Attacked by U.S.

Special to The New York Times

BONN, Feb. 11—An article prepared for a West German pictorial magazine quotes Mao Tse-tung as having said that the crisis in Vietnam will not lead to war between the United States and Communist China so long as China itself is not attacked.

Mr. Mao, chairman of the Chinese Communist party, made the remark during an interview that Stern, a leading Hamburg weekly, is to publish Monday.

[Premier Kosygin of the Soviet Union, feted in North Korea after visits to Hanoi and Peking, appealed for unity among the world's Communist parties. Page 12.]

A summary of the Mao interview, given to Edgar Snow, an American journalist, was made public today. The interview took place several weeks ago.

Mr. Mao said that Communist China did not maintain any troops abroad, nor did it intend to fight as long as its own territory was not attacked.

This precludes war over Viet-

Continued on Page 12, Column 5

LIMIT ON CONFLICT STRESSED BY U.S.

Officials Point to Distinction Between Retaliatory Raids and Outright Hostilities

Text of U.S. announcement appears on Page 13.

By CHARLES MOHR
Special to The New York Times

WASHINGTON, Feb. 11 — Administration officials insisted today that there remained in their own minds a distinction between outright war against North Vietnam and retaliatory air strikes of the kind they ordered three times in five days this week.

The latest attacks this morning, the White House said in a formal statement, were ordered "in response to further provocations by the Hanoi regime." It invoked a number of new guerrilla actions against Americans and South Vietnamese.

Administration sources added, however, that they still hoped to prevent the "spreading" of the war. There was said to be considerable pressure from military leaders for permission to continue raids against North Vietnam, with or even without the pretext of retaliation.

President Johnson was said to have resisted that advice.

[Stock prices plunged sharply as concern over the situation in Vietnam grew. The Dow-Jones industrials fell 11.04 points, the biggest loss since Nov. 22, 1963, the day President Kennedy was assassinated. Page 37.]

Officials acknowledged that their unwillingness to say precisely the circumstances under which they would retaliate in the future might have blurred definitions and given the impression that virtually

Continued on Page 13, Column 1

Rubble of Barracks In Quinhon Sifted; G.I. Dead Put at 21

By JACK LANGGUTH
Special to The New York Times

QUINHON, South Vietnam, Friday, Feb. 12 — The last American known to be alive in the wreckage of the bombed United States barracks here was dragged free this morning after almost 36 hours in the rubble.

Army and Marine Corps engineers were preparing to sift through the ruins for the bodies of 20 American soldiers still missing.

The survivor was brought out grinning and joking with his rescuers. "Don't tell me I need a shave," he said.

Barring the discovery, considered unlikely, that some of the buried men are still alive, the explosion will have taken 21 American lives—the largest number lost in a single incident in Vietnam.

25 Are Extricated

By late yesterday, a day after Vietcong terrorists blew up the building, the body of an American and 25 wounded servicemen had been pulled from the wreckage. A foot of one man was amputated so he could be freed.

At least eight Vietnamese civilians were killed by three explosions of TNT, now believed to have been carried in suitcases by Communist guerrillas who entered the building. The bodies of two women and five children were taken from a small house next door.

As exhausted rescue teams dug by hand through beams and plaster, they spoke most often of retaliation against North Vietnam.

"I hope we blast the hell out of them," a sergeant said. Drawn by the large number of Americans at the rescue scene, Vietcong troops tried to strafed and bombed the area of

Continued on Page 12, Column 2

THREE CRAFT LOST

Hanoi Claims 4 More and Says It Holds American Pilot

By SEYMOUR TOPPING
Special to The New York Times

SAIGON, South Vietnam, Feb. 11—In the biggest air attack of the Vietnamese war, more than 160 United States and South Vietnamese fighter planes struck today at military installations in North Vietnam.

The action was a swift reprisal for Vietcong thrusts, including the terrorist attack last night on a United States Army barracks in Quinhon, a coastal city 200 miles northeast of Saigon. Casualties were heavy in the barracks explosion.

In a communiqué, the United States and South Vietnam asserted that air strikes had been carried out in response to "continued acts of aggression by Communist Vietcong under the direction and with the support of the Hanoi regime."

More than 100 Navy planes from three aircraft carriers and a joint strike force of United States Air Force and South Vietnamese fighter-bombers hit military barracks and supply depots in two coastal areas in the southern part of North Vietnam.

2 Planes Down in Sea

A United States military spokesman said at a news conference that three Navy aircraft had been lost. Two fell into the sea, presumably after being hit by ground fire. One pilot was rescued, and a search was begun for the other.

[North Vietnam asserted that its armed forces had shot down seven United States planes and had captured an American named Robert H. Shumaker. Page 12.]

Less than an hour before the air strikes were announced, two explosions ripped a Saigon hall in which students were meeting. Terrorists had attached charges to bicycles standing against a wall of the meeting place in the center of the city. Three Vietnamese women students were wounded.

Hanoi Link Still Charged

United States officials, asked about a connection between the Vietcong terrorism and Hanoi's role in the war, said they were certain that the general pattern of attacks on Americans had been agreed to or ordered by the North Vietnamese capital.

There was certainty about Hanoi's responsibility for raids such as the one against Quinhon.

The new assault on North Vietnam lasted three and a half hours. It was larger than those of Sunday and Monday in retaliation for the Vietcong attacks on two camps in the Pleiku area, in which 8 Americans were killed and 126 wounded.

For 18 minutes, Navy planes from the aircraft carriers Ranger, Hancock and Coral Sea

Continued on Page 12, Column 1

Orderly Students Picket the Soviet Embassy in U.S.

Students march in the neighborhood of the Soviet Embassy in Washington, protesting, they said, the demonstration that took place at the U.S. Embassy in Moscow last Tuesday.
Associated Press Wirephoto

By CABELL PHILLIPS
Special to The New York Times

WASHINGTON, Feb. 11 — Four hundred American students picketed the Soviet Embassy here today—a distance of a block and a half. The demonstration was an orderly retaliation for a rock-throwing, ink-splatter-

ing attack on the United States Embassy in Moscow by 2,000 students two days ago. The marchers here, most of them from Georgetown University, obeyed a local ordinance prohibiting demonstrations within 500 feet of an embassy. They marched up and down the

street, across from the Statler Hotel, more than a block from the embassy. A police detail of about 100 patrolmen and motorcycle officers had more trouble getting homeward-bound spectators to clear the sidewalks than they

Continued on Page 13, Column 1

The U.S. in Vietnam: Why It Is There

By MAX FRANKEL
Special to The New York Times

WASHINGTON, Feb. 11— The deepening involvement of the United States in the war in Vietnam has revived, even in parts of this capital, the insistent question: What are we doing out there anyway?

There is no easy answer, because the involvement embraces not only Vietnam but also all of Southeast Asia and because it cannot be traced to any specific decision or time. It is the result of a gradual, often uncharted, evolution of American policy throughout Asia, dating at least to World War II.

Fundamentally, the American efforts represent a continuing search for a postwar settlement there, and an adjustment to the collapse of British, French and Dutch colonial empires and to the emergence of an ambitious Communist Government on the Chinese mainland.

With varying degrees of enthusiasm, the United States has tried since 1945 to promote the independence and the national

veloped in response to similarly shifting policies and tactics by competing as well as cooperating Communist nations.

At times, these two objectives threatened to become contradictory; anti-Communism produced policies that looked to some like antinationalism, even antineutralism. At other times, Washington's policies were undermined by rivalries among the nations of Southeast Asia and by the instabilities and idiosyncrasies of their politics.

Since containment of China came to be the primary objective, the temptations invariably increased to apply American power wherever the local governments seemed too weak for the job. And though Washington has all along disclaimed colonial ambitions in the region, it has found itself in the indirect contest with China for political and economic influence and

Continued on Page 13, Column 2

News Analysis

Lincoln's Birthday

Today is Lincoln's Birthday, and following is a list of services and facilities that are or are not affected:

Public and parochial schools, banks, New York Coffee and Sugar Exchange, Cocoa Exchange and New York Commodity Exchange —Closed.

Department stores and retail businesses, general and some bank branches (for deposits only)—Open.

All major securities exchanges —Open.

Post Office—Normal service.

Parking—Alternate-side parking rules suspended.

U.S. soldiers keep under cover while watching out for the enemy.

Always alert troopers move cautiously through the jungle 8 miles from Bien Hoa.

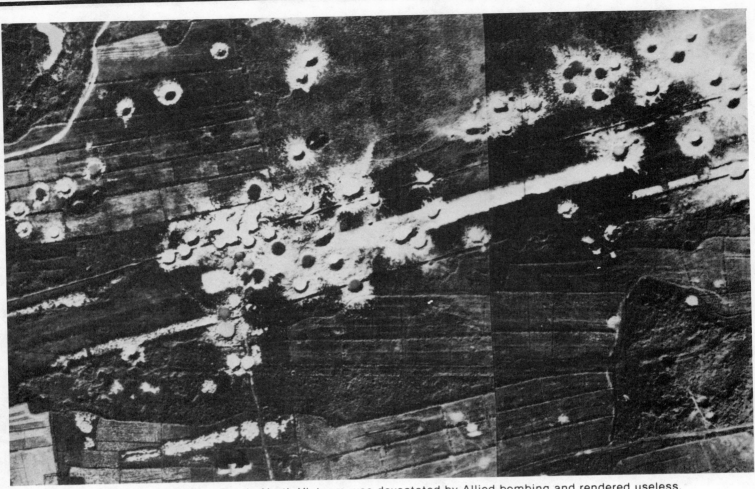

This once-vital airstrip at Dien Bien Phu in North Vietnam was devastated by Allied bombing and rendered useless.

A Vietnamese Air Force A-1 Skyraider begins a bombing pass on a Viet Cong concentration along a canal in the Mekong Delta.

The New York Times.

LATE CITY EDITION
U. S. Weather Bureau Report (Page 8) forecast:
Fair, windy and cold today; clear and very cold tonight. Sunny tomorrow.
Temp. range: 38—24; yesterday: 40—28.

VOL. CXIV..No. 39,111. © 1965 by The New York Times Company. Times Square, New York, N. Y. 10036

NEW YORK, MONDAY, FEBRUARY 22, 1965.

TEN CENTS

SCHOOL AID DELAY BRINGS A DEMAND FOR HOUSE ACTION

Administration Is Seeking to Get a Decision This Week From Powell Group

SHOWDOWN IS VOWED

Supporter Pledges Move if Measure Is Not Called Up at Thursday Session

By MARJORIE HUNTER
Special to The New York Times

WASHINGTON, Feb. 21 — The Administration is determined to get House committee action this week on the $1.25 billion school aid bill, a virtual legislative truant in the last few weeks.

This was to have been the week that the bill was to have come up for floor action in the House. Instead, the measure has not even been brought up before the full House Education and Labor Committee.

President Johnson and House leaders are "deeply concerned" over the failure of Representative Adam Clayton Powell, Democrat of Manhattan, to move the bill out of his committee, sources close to the President said today.

The bill, which has top priority on the President's legislative list, got off to a fast start early in the new Congress.

Met on Saturdays

Working day and night, House subcommittee held 10 days of public hearings. The subcommittee even met on Saturdays, almost unheard of so early in a new session, in order to speed the bill.

The measure was approved Feb. 5 by the six subcommittee Democrats. The three Republicans boycotted the voting session in protest against failure to hold longer hearings.

"We were in good shape to move the bill right along," Representative Frank Thompson Jr., Democrat of New Jersey, a member of the subcommittee, said today. "But nothing happened."

Representative Powell failed to call the full committee into session the following week. And he did not call a meeting after the long Lincoln birthday holiday recess.

The committee is required under its own rules to meet next Thursday.

"If the chairman doesn't bring up the bill then, we'll have a showdown," Representative Thompson promised.

Linked to Travel Funds

Representative Powell could not be reached today to comment on whether he intended to call up the bill at the Thursday meeting.

Administration sources said that the delay over the education bill appeared to be tied in with Representative Powell's effort to win favorable House action on a resolution determining how much money will be authorized for his committee's travel and investigation this year.

The House is expected to vote this week on a number of such authorization measures, including one for the Powell committee.

Meanwhile, Republicans have used the more than two-week breather to draft proposed

Continued on Page 18, Column 1

Malcolm X Shot to Death at Rally Here

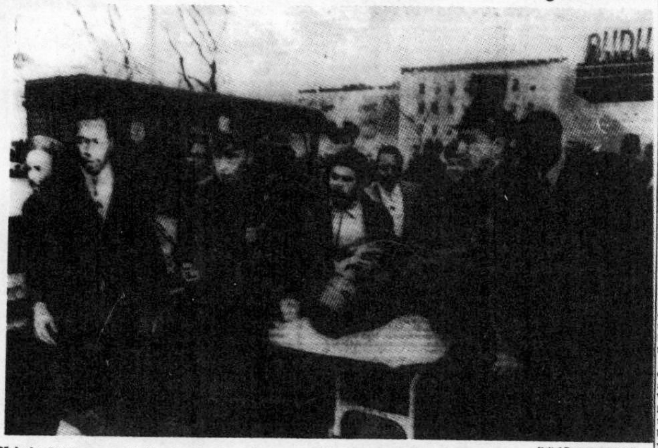

Malcolm X being taken to hospital from Audubon Ballroom yesterday after he was shot while addressing a meeting
United Press International

Three Other Negroes Wounded—One Is Held in Killing

By PETER KIHSS

Malcolm X, the 39-year-old leader of a militant black nationalist movement, was shot to death yesterday afternoon at a rally of his followers in a ballroom in Washington Heights.

Shortly before midnight, a 22-year-old Negro, Thomas Hagan, was charged with the killing. The police rescued him from the ballroom crowd after he had been shot and beaten.

Malcolm, a bearded extremist, had said only a few words of greeting when a fusillade rang out. The bullets knocked him over backward.

Pandemonium broke out among the 400 Negroes in the Audubon Ballroom at 166th Street and Broadway. As men, women and children ducked under tables and flattened themselves on the floor, more shots were fired. Some witnesses said 30 shots had been fired.

3 Weapons Fired

The police said seven bullets had struck Malcolm. Three other Negroes were shot.

About two hours later the police said the shooting had apparently been a result of a feud between followers of Malcolm and members of the extremist group he broke with last year, the Black Muslims. However, the police declined to say whether Hagan is a Muslim.

The Medical Examiner's office said early this morning that a preliminary autopsy showed Malcolm had died of "multiple gunshot wounds." The office said that bullets of two different calibers as well as shotgun pellets had been removed from his body.

One police theory was that as many as five conspirators might have been involved, two creating a diversionary disturbance.

Hagan was shot in the left thigh and his left leg was broken, apparently by kicks. He was under treatment in the Bellevue Hospital prison ward last night; perhaps a dozen policemen were guarding him, according to the hospital's night superintendent. The police said

Continued on Page 10, Column 1

Malcolm Knew He Was a 'Marked Man'

By THEODORE JONES

"I live like a man who's already dead," Malcolm X said last Thursday in a two-hour interview in the Harlem office of his Organization for Afro-American Unity.

"I'm a marked man," he said slowly as he fingered the horn-rimmed glasses he wore and leaned forward to give emphasis to his words. "It doesn't frighten me for myself as long as I felt they would not hurt my family."

Asked about "they," Malcolm smiled, shook his head, and said, "those folks down at 116th Street and that man in Chicago."

The references, Malcolm quickly confirmed, were to his former associates in the Black Muslim movement and to Elijah Muhammad, the organizer and head of the movement. Before Malcolm X left the movement 18 months ago, he was the minister of the Black Muslims' Harlem mosque at 116th Street and Lenox Avenue.

"No one can get out without trouble." Malcolm continued, "and this thing with me will be resolved by death and violence."

Why were they after him? "Because I'm me," he replied. But realizing that was not enough to say, he pushed into an almost endless flow of sentences.

"I was the spokesman for the Black Muslims," he said. "I believed in Elijah Muhammad more strongly than Christians do in Jesus. I believed in him so strongly that my mind, my body, my voice functioned 100 per cent for him and the movement. My belief led others to believe.

"Now I'm out. And there's the fear if my image isn't shattered, the Muslims in the movement will leave. Then, they know I know a lot. As long as I was in the movement, anything he [Elijah Muhammad] did was to me by divine guidance."

Malcolm said that he knew many things that made him a

Continued on Page 11, Column 2

POWELL OPPOSING NEW MOTLEY POST

Says Senator Can Be More Effective in Albany Than in Borough Presidency

By MARTIN GANSBERG

Representative Adam Clayton Powell asserted yesterday that the elected leaders of Harlem were opposed to the selection of State Senator Constance Baker Motley as Manhattan Borough President.

In a sharply worded telegram to Mayor Wagner, Mr. Powell, who heads the 12th District South, said that he also was speaking for Hulan Jack, Mark T. Southall and Percy Sutton in insisting that Mrs. Motley would "be much more effective in Albany than as Borough President."

"Not one of the elected leaders representing the Harlem community has sponsored her," Mr. Powell asserted. "Unfortunately, and once again, the selection of a Negro is apparently being made by the white man."

Mr. Jack is leader of the 14th District North, Mr. Southall of the 12th District North and Mr. Sutton is a State Assemblyman from the 11th District. The other Harlem leaders are George Miller of the 11th District and J. Raymond Jones of the 13th District.

Mr. Powell's statement, released here by a spokesman for him, was issued at 1:30 yesterday morning after he had completed telephone conversations from Puerto Rico.

Continued on Page 17, Column 1

Rise of 24 Million In U.S. Labor Force Is Forecast by 1980

By JOHN D. POMFRET
Special to The New York Times

WASHINGTON, Feb. 21 — The Labor Department issued new projections today indicating that the nation's labor force would grow to 86 million in 1970 and 101.4 million in 1980.

It was 77 million in 1964 and 73 million in 1960.

Although the projected increase between 1970 and 1980 — 15.4 million — is 2.4 million higher than the projected increase between 1960 and 1970, the rate of gain would be about the same — 17.7 per cent from 1960 to 1970 and 17.9 per cent from 1970 to 1980.

An increase of 24 million workers between 1964 and 1980 would mean that 1.5 million new jobs would have to be created each year, on the average, merely to absorb growth in the labor force. Still more jobs would be needed to offset gains in output per manhour and to reduce the level of unemployment.

The projections were compiled by Miss Sophia Cooper and Denis F. Johnston of the Bureau of Labor Statistics.

According to their study, the rest of this decade will show

Continued on Page 19, Column 1

AGE IS A PROBLEM IN LABOR COUNCIL

Some in A.F.L.-C.I.O. Feel Older Chiefs Should Quit —Most Are Over 65

By DAMON STETSON
Special to The New York Times

BAL HARBOUR, Fla., Feb. 21—Some leaders of the American Federation of Labor and Congress of Industrial Organizations are beginning to worry about the superannuated character of the organization's executive council.

The 29-member council, which opens its winter meeting here tomorrow in the plush surroundings of an alabaster-white beachfront hotel, is getting along in years. Fifteen members—more than half—of the labor organization's top policy-making body are 65 years old or over, nine are 70 or over, and one is 82.

One of these elder statesmen of the labor movement, who is still playing an energetic role as leader of his own union, said that he did not feel age alone was any criterion of a labor leader's effectiveness. But he said that he was disturbed that some former union presidents were continuing as members of the council long after having given up active direction of their unions and going into retirement.

If the labor movement isn't careful, he said, the council will become little more than a fraternal organization of old men who like to come to Florida in the winter to play gin rummy.

Although some labor leaders here are willing to talk privately about the need for an infusion of new blood in the council, no one is saying much publicly about it at this time.

Among some of the younger council members, there is a feeling that the council and the merged labor organization ought to become more dynamic and aggressive. But there is a reluctance, at the same time, to push out old war horses of an earlier era.

George Meany, president of the A.F.L.-C.I.O., who is 70, is one member who has shown no

Continued on Page 22, Column 7

Democrats in Legislature to End Duplicate Bill-Filing as Waste

By SYDNEY H. SCHANBERG
Special to The New York Times

ALBANY, Feb. 21—Democratic leaders disclosed today that they had decided to abolish the wasteful practice of duplicate bill-filing in the Legislature.

Senate Majority Leader Joseph Zaretzki said he and Assembly Speaker Anthony J. Travia reached the decision at a meeting last week.

Under present practice, sanctioned by existing rules, hundreds of times every year several different legislators sometimes dozens file the same bill.

The bills are printed separately, but the wording is identical. It costs the state $12.32 a page to print legislative bills, and the cost of the duplication runs into tens of thousands of dollars.

Senator Zaretzki said that from now on, if more than one legislator wanted to introduce the same bill they would have to sponsor it cooperatively. That is, instead of many bills on one subject there would be only one, with the names of the sponsors affixed, whether Republican or Democratic.

Mr. Zaretzki said that although the change was based so far solely on a leadership decision, a formal change of rules might be proposed this week in the Legislature's rules. The Senate leader said he was assured of enough votes in both houses to carry the proposal.

The Manhattan Democrat said he had already asked Earl W. Brydges, the Republican minority leader in the Senate, not to introduce any bills on Governor Rockefeller's program without

Senator Zaretzki said that *Continued on Page 17, Column 5*

Washington's Birthday

Today is Washington's Birthday, a Federal and state holiday, and following is a list of services and facilities that are or are not affected:

Public and parochial schools, banks, stock and commodity exchange—Closed.

Department stores and retail business in the city and suburban areas—Some open, some closed.

Post offices—Special delivery only, no business transacted.

Parking—Alternate-side rules suspended, all others, including parking meter rules, in effect.

Sanitation—No refuse collection.

Congo Seeks Return Of Ousted Teachers

By JOSEPH LELYVELD

LEOPOLDVILLE, the Congo, Feb. 21—The Congolese Government sent an urgent message to Athens today inviting the UNESCO teachers it expelled yesterday as subversives to return to their classes here as soon as possible.

Among some of the teachers was taken last night before their plane departed from Leopoldville for Athens. But something went wrong with official communications and the security police at the airport insisted that the teachers and their dependents, a total of 35 persons, board the plane.

The snag in communications was eventually straightened out to the satisfaction of the security police, but not before the plane was airborne. Leopoldville

Continued on Page 6, Column 1

PANEL OF 7 NAMED TO TRY TO IMPROVE TRANSIT FINANCES

Governor and Mayor Join In Attempt to Avert a Rise in the 15-Cent Fare

By EMANUEL PERLMUTTER

The appointment of a seven-man citizens' committee to try to solve the financial problems of the city's transit system was announced yesterday by Governor Rockefeller and Mayor Wagner.

The naming of the committee followed a recent announcement by Joseph E. O'Grady, chairman of the Transit Authority, that the 15-cent fare might have to be increased in view of the system's growing deficit.

With the election of a Mayor coming up this fall, and that of a Governor next year, both Mr. Wagner and Mr. Rockefeller have been reported to be trying to avoid a fare rise. One has been avoided in the last few years by increases in financial assistance from the city, with the acquiescence of the Legislature.

Purpose of the Panel

The chairman of the citizens' study committee, named by Mr. Rockefeller and Mr. Wagner, will be J. Victor Herd, board chairman of the Continental Insurance Company.

Other members of the committee are John A. Coleman, former president of the New York Stock Exchange; J. Clarence Davies, former chairman of the city Housing and Redevelopment Board; Charles Garrahan, vice president of the Amalgamated Clothing Workers of America; George S. Moore, president of the First National City Bank of New York; Clifton W. Phalen, president of the New York Telephone Company, and Walter N. Rothschild Jr., president of Abraham & Straus.

The announcement said the committee had been appointed "to make recommendations for the immediate and long-term solution of the substantial financial problem presented by the city subway and surface lines."

Review Is Planned

It "will review the administration and economics of public mass transit in the city and its relationship with other forms of transportation serving New York City," the statement continued.

"The committee will report to the Governor and the Mayor as quickly as their recommendations can be developed."

Although no time limit was set within which the committee is to make its recommendations, it is virtually under obligation to make them before the end of the year. The authority would have to know where it could get additional revenues before it could make a contract offer to its union employes late this fall.

The committee was envisaged almost 14 months ago in the contract settlement between the Transit Authority and the Transport Workers Union.

The committee made its appearance yesterday at the right moment, too.

On Feb. 2, Mr. O'Grady said the authority expected a deficit of more than $33 million in the fiscal year starting July 1. He said this prospect made it doubtful that the 15-cent fare

Continued on Page 3, Column 7

U.S. FINDS BACKING IN WORLD'S PRESS

Extent of Support for Action in Asia Surprises Capital, U.S.I.A. Director Says

By JOHN W. FINNEY
Special to The New York Times

WASHINGTON, Feb. 21 — Foreign editorial reaction to the United States air strikes in North Vietnam has been generally favorable—more so than some Administration officials expected, according to Carl T. Rowan, director of the United States Information Agency.

An analysis by the agency this month drew almost universal support in the South American press, strong support in Southeast Asia and guarded endorsement in some countries of the Middle East and South Asia.

The only strong opposition, except from the Communist press, came from Africa and some sections of the Middle East and South Asia.

World Reaction 'Good'

Summarizing the reaction, Mr. Rowan said in an interview: "The general world reaction to our actions in Vietnam has been good, and considerably better than I had expected."

Among newspapers supporting the United States air strikes, they were viewed as a legitimate and necessary response to the Communist attacks on American installations in South Vietnam and as a demonstration of American firmness.

There was a nearly unanimous feeling that the United States should not widen the war in South Vietnam. But a majority of the newspapers accepted the repeated policy statements of the Johnson Administration that it was seeking only to press the Communists into ceasing aggressive activities in South Vietnam.

A majority of the editorial

Continued on Page 3, Column 1

MILITARY COUNCIL DISMISSES KHANH; HE BOWS TO EDICT

French Official Asks Talks to Stop War

By JACK RAYMOND
Special to The New York Times

WASHINGTON, Feb. 21 — Maurice Couve de Murville, the French Foreign Minister, urged before a nationwide American television audience today that negotiations for a settlement in Vietnam be attempted "as soon as possible."

His public advocacy of negotiations followed three days of private talks with President Johnson, Secretary of State Dean Rusk and other officials during which he was unable to win them over to the idea.

In reply to a question, Mr. Couve de Murville said: "We think that the negotiations [to end the fighting in Vietnam] should be engaged as soon as possible.

"A long time, in our

Continued on Page 3, Column 6

VOTE UNANIMOUS

Tran Van Minh Named Acting Commander of Armed Forces

By JACK LANGGUTH
Special to The New York Times

SAIGON, South Vietnam, Monday, Feb. 22 — Lieut. Gen. Nguyen Khanh bowed today to a unanimous decision of the Armed Forces Council to replace him with Maj. Gen. Tran Van Minh as commander in chief.

After the council voted late yesterday to oust him, General Khanh spent the night telephoning military commanders throughout the country to rally support. Unsuccessful, he called the council's headquarters in Saigon early this morning from the resort of Dalat, northeast of the capital, to admit defeat.

Council members said they hoped to bring General Khanh into the capital later in the day for a news conference.

Earlier, Brig. Gen. Nguyen Chanh Thi, commander of the army's I Corps, said the South Vietnamese Air Force would bomb any troops or tanks that moved toward Saigon.

Saigon Wary About Firing

General Thi, who helped to keep General Khanh in power in the past, had become a leader in the movement to drop him.

Unusual troop movements and some mortar fire on the outskirts of the capital kept Saigon wary after the broadcast announcement of General Khanh's removal. But the mortar fire and flares dropped around Tansonnhut Airport were apparently connected with operations against the Vietcong.

The ouster came a day after General Khanh, aided by loyal paratroops and air units, defeated a brief and bloodless attempt at a military coup d'état. Some of the officers who backed him were among those who now voted for his dismissal.

Suu Agrees to Action

General Khanh did not attend the council meeting.

The council's announcement did not specify whether General Minh, who was named acting commander in chief, would also inherit General Khanh's second post, the chairmanship of the Armed Forces Council. The new Premier, Dr. Phan Khac Suu, to tell him about the vote. The new Premier, Dr. Phan Huy Quat, was present.

Dr. Suu readily agreed to sign an order to dismiss General Khanh and appoint General Minh.

In his order, Dr. Suu said General Khanh would be reassigned. The general's ambitions and his courting of Buddhist political support have long made him suspect among his colleagues.

Second Meeting Held

Council members met again near midnight to map a strategy that would keep General Khanh from regaining power. Air Vice Marshal Nguyen Cao Ky first insisted that General Khanh be required to leave the country.

But General Khanh was not yet ready to give up. From his command post at the southeastern beach resort of Cap Saint-Jacques, he telephoned offers to junior officers, not on the council, who he thought might support him.

Brig. Gen. Nguyen Van Chuan, General Thi's deputy, was offered command of the I Corps if he would send troops to support General Khanh. General Thi countered the call with a message of his own, cautioning the deputy that General

Continued on Page 3, Column 1

Moscow Announces a Relaxation Of Attitude Toward Intellectuals

By THEODORE SHABAD
Special to The New York Times

MOSCOW, Feb. 21 — The Soviet Communist party proclaimed today a relaxed attitude toward the Soviet Union's intellectuals.

An article that appeared in Pravda, the principal party newspaper, assailed what was described as a trend toward anti-intellectualism under the Khrushchev era and asserted that "genuine creativeness" was possible only through search.

The Pravda editor, a leading ideological spokesman of the administration, said party "genuine creativeness" is criticism of literature would be guided by a policy statement made in 1925, long before Stalin imposed rigid controls over the arts.

The 40-year-old pronouncement, which he quoted, said: "Communist criticism must rid itself of the tone of literary command. The party must in every way eradicate attempts at homebred and incompetent administrative interference in literary affairs." Mr. Rumyan-

Continued on Page 7, Column 1

"All the News That's Fit to Print"

The New York Times.

LATE CITY EDITION

U.S. Weather Bureau Report (Page 42) forecasts: Snow, then rain today; clearing tonight. Fair tomorrow. Temp. range: 38—30; yesterday: 38—32.

VOL. CXIV..No. 39,114.

NEW YORK, THURSDAY, FEBRUARY 25, 1965.

TEN CENTS

HUNT FOR KILLERS IN MALCOLM CASE 'ON RIGHT TRACK'

Police Express Confidence as They Query Witnesses —3 to 5 Men Sought

THOUSANDS VIEW COFFIN

Funeral for Negro Leader Set for Saturday—More Bomb Threats Spiked

By PETER KIHSS

The police asserted yesterday that they were "on the right track" in the hunt for the Negro killers of Malcolm X, militant black nationalist leader.

Assistant Chief Inspector Joseph L. Coyle, in charge of Manhattan North detectives, said witnesses were being shown photographs, which he would not otherwise identify.

One man, Thomas Hagan, also known as Hayer, was arrested immediately after the murder Sunday, but three to five men are believed to have been involved.

While the police effort went on, 5,000 persons, overwhelmingly Negroes, visited the Harlem funeral home where Malcolm's body was on public display. Two thousand visitors filed past the open coffin during the first four hours Tuesday night.

Saturday Funeral Set

A funeral service for the 39-year-old founder of his own Muslim sect was announced for 9:30 A.M. Saturday. It will be held at Faith Temple, Church of God in Christ, 1763 Amsterdam Avenue at West 147th Street, whose two floors can hold nearly 2,000 persons.

Both the church and the funeral home were targets of unfounded bomb threats during the day. In Chicago, Saturn Airlines announced it had canceled a charter flight that was to have brought 150 Black Muslims, members of the movement from which Malcolm had split, to their national convention tomorrow because of what Ronald Grillman, regional manager, said was fear of bombing.

Meanwhile a survey of various investigators indicated that Malcolm's own Organization of Afro-American Unity had remained small and had apparently been fading even more than the segregationist parent group.

Hate Drive Feared

But there was concern that his assassination might build him up as a symbol. Chinese Communist propagandists were already seeking to invoke him for a hate campaign, such as followed the murder of Congo Premier Patrice Lumumba.

While his own group withheld data, responsible outside quarters estimated Malcolm's movement had perhaps only 40 "hard core" or "full-fledged" members and 200 more "hangers-on." This was a decline from an estimated total of 400 members at its start in March, 1964, when Malcolm's first public black nationalist meeting drew 1,000 spectators for his call for Negro "ballots — or bullets."

The Black Muslims — Elijah Muhammad's Nation of Islam — have fallen off to 7,000 members in the country, according

Continued on Page 18, Column 1

Associated Press Cablephoto

EAST GERMAN PRESIDENT IN CAIRO: Walter Ulbricht, left, the East German Communist leader, waving from open car with President Gamal Abdel Nasser of the United Arab Republic. Mr. Ulbricht is on a week's visit.

FAIR EXECUTIVES DIVIDED ON MOSES

He Gets Vote of Confidence, but 6 Abstain, Including the Mayor's 3 Men

By ROBERT ALDEN

Robert Moses received a vote of confidence at a meeting of the executive committee of the World's Fair yesterday.

Mr. Moses did not participate, and six others of the 15 at the meeting refrained from putting support for him on record.

Significantly, three of the abstainers represented Mayor Wagner at the meeting—Paul Screvane, president of the City Council; Edward F. Cavanagh Jr., Deputy Mayor, and Richard C. Patterson Jr., Commissioner of the Department of Public Events.

Just before the meeting, Mr. Moses, president of the fair, sent an angry telegram to George V. McLaughlin, vice chairman of the Triborough Bridge and Tunnel Authority, who had resigned as a director of the fair because Mr. Moses had tentatively suggested that $6.4 million of the authority's funds be used to restore Flushing Meadow Park at the close of the fair.

Called Within the Law

A colleague said that Mr. Moses was "deeply hurt" by the resignation of a friend of 30 years' standing.

Mr. Moses told Mr. McLaughlin that "the law clearly permits park and other improvements related to the Triborough program," but the subject "has not come up for decision at any Triborough meeting."

"If and when the matter does come to the decision stage," Mr. Moses said, "you will be fully informed, if you are still interested, and will have every opportunity . . . to present your point of view and cast your vote. . . .

"You have rendered a distinct and completely gratuitous disservice to Triborough by your

Continued on Page 19, Column 4

Abolition of Death Penalty Gains Among Legislators

Zaretzki Pledges Vote

By R. W. APPLE Jr.

Special to The New York Times

ALBANY, Feb. 24 — The chairman of an influential bipartisan commission said today that it would probably propose that capital punishment be abolished in New York State.

Assemblyman Richard J. Bartlett, who heads the Temporary Commission on Revision of the Penal Law, emphasized that no final decision had been reached. He also said that the 12-member group might not make a unanimous recommendation.

"We can't afford to dally on this," the 39-year-old Glens Falls Republican declared in an interview. "I expect some decision within about 10 days."

Joseph Zaretzki of Manhattan, the Senate majority leader, said he thought there was a "pretty good chance" that the upper house would vote this year to do away with the death penalty. He said he personally would support such a measure.

But the majority leader in the Assembly, Moses M. Weinstein of Queens, indicated that he had reservations about the outright abolition of execu-

Continued on Page 20, Column 1

Last Execution in '63

By McCANDLISH PHILLIPS

Special to The New York Times

OSSINING, N. Y., Feb. 24—Opponents of capital punishment are making their strongest bid in years to put the death penalty to a legislative death in New York State. They are doing so at a time when executions have been almost halted by legal maneuvers and new court rulings.

The electric chair at Sing Sing Prison here, which has taken 614 lives since 1891, has been remarkably vacant lately. It has executed just four men in the last four years.

This is by far the lowest number of executions in any four-year period since the first of four men was strapped into the electric chair here on a July morning 74 years ago.

That first man was Harris A. Smiler, who had shot Maggie Drainey to death at 284 Seventh Avenue two years earlier.

There are now 21 men awaiting execution at Sing Sing. Recent court rulings regarding confessions used in criminal trials have given hope to thousands of convicted felons, whose cases may be reopened. These

Continued on Page 20, Column 5

FREE TUITION IDEA MIRED IN ALBANY

Democrats Pessimistic on Ending State U. Fees Now

By DOUGLAS ROBINSON

Special to The New York Times

ALBANY, Feb. 24—Democratic leaders have almost abandoned their plan for ending tuition fees at the State University at this session of the Legislature.

Although some 20 free-tuition bills have been introduced this year, the leaders said today that the terms of the outstanding bonds for school construction were a great obstacle to passage.

These leaders, however, are still pressing for legislation that would remove the power to impose tuition from the New York City Board of Higher Education. So far, the board has not exercised this power.

Senate Majority Leader Joseph Zaretzki pointed out that $290 million in construction bonds had been issued by the state and that the security for them was the $30 million a year the schools collect in tuition.

Some units of the State University, such as Harpur College and the so-called contract colleges at Cornell and Alfred Universities, have always charged tuition. The tuition schedule adopted by the Board of Trustees two years ago applied to the University's four-year colleges (former teachers' colleges), the two-year agricultural and technical institutes, and graduate and professional programs. The tuition for undergraduate schools is $400 a year.

A Senate bill that would guarantee free tuition at the City University of New York

Continued on Page 21, Column 6

JENKINS DENIES USING PRESSURE

Former Johnson Aide Gives Replies in Baker Inquiry

By BEN A. FRANKLIN

Special to The New York Times

WASHINGTON, Feb. 24 — Walter W. Jenkins denied for a second time today that he had ever used coercion or pressure on Don B. Reynolds, an insurance salesman, to buy advertising time on a Texas television station owned by President Johnson's family.

Mr. Jenkins, former special assistant to the President, also denied other assertions by Mr. Reynolds, who sold two $100,000 policies on Mr. Johnson's life before he became President. Mr. Reynolds was once a business associate of Robert G. Baker, former secretary to the Senate's Democratic majority.

Mr. Jenkins's denials were made in answers to 40 written questions submitted to him Feb. 10 by the Senate Rules Committee, which is investigating Mr. Baker's private business affairs. A transcript of the questions and answers was made public by the committee today.

Mr. Jenkins was excused from appearing personally before the committee earlier this month. He has been under intensive psychiatric treatment for "severe depression" since resigning from the White House staff last October after his two arrests on morals charges were disclosed. His statement today said two psychiatrists had informed him his appearance would be "injurious to my health."

Mr. Reynolds, a key witness in the Baker investigation, testified before the committee in

Continued on Page 11, Column 8

ULBRICHT HAILED BY CAIRO CROWDS

Nasser Gives East German Leader All-Out Reception —Bonn Cuts Off Aid

By HEDRICK SMITH

Special to The New York Times

CAIRO, Feb. 24—The United Arab Republic rolled out the red carpet today for Walter Ulbricht, the East German President, at the start of his first official visit to a non-Communist country.

His presence here was a personal political triumph for the 72-year-old President and a severe setback for West Germany and its claim to be considered the only legitimate representative of divided Germany.

Chancellor Ludwig Erhard of West Germany warned last week that Bonn would retaliate against Cairo for Mr. Ulbricht's visit by stopping economic aid and possibly by taking political countermeasures.

Defiance and Conciliation

President Gamal Abdel Nasser went the limit in defying warnings from West Germany. The Egyptian leader provided Mr. Ulbricht with as ardent a welcome as possible for a visiting chief of state from a country that Cairo does not formally recognize.

Then, a few hours later, after Bonn announced that it had now halted economic aid to the United Arab Republic, Mr. Nasser struck a surprisingly conciliatory note toward West Germany.

At a state banquet in Mr. Ulbricht's honor, Mr. Nasser declared that Egypt was "still exerting our maximum and most sincere efforts so that matters do not deteriorate any further" in Cairo-Bonn relations.

"We have always been careful to maintain good relations with Federal [West] Germany," he asserted, blaming the current crisis on a "stab in the back," his term for West Ger-

Continued on Page 4, Column 3

Thant Asks Vietnam Talks Leading to a U.S. Pullout

U.N. Chief Reports He Has Offered Some Proposals—Says That if Americans Had Facts They Would Back Him

By THOMAS J. HAMILTON

Special to The New York Times

UNITED NATIONS, N. Y., Feb. 24—The Secretary General, U Thant, advocated today informal negotiations for the establishment of a stable government in South Vietnam and the withdrawal of United States forces "from that part of the world."

The Secretary General said at a news conference that he had presented "concrete ideas and proposals" to "some of the principal parties directly involved in the question of Vietnam," including the United States. He declined to disclose their responses.

Mr. Thant reiterated his belief that the prospects for a peaceful settlement would become more and more remote "with the passage of time" but that it was not too late to make an attempt at "diplomatic and political methods." He did not directly criticize the Johnson Administration's refusal to agree to negotiations on Vietnam.

[Premier Phan Huy Quat of South Vietnam said Thursday his country was "suffering too much" and "we want to end the war with honor," Reuters reported. But he told a Saigon audience, the agency added, that the Vietcong wanted to sell Vietnam to Communism. Page 2.]

Decries More Bloodshed

Mr. Thant said he had "the greatest respect for the great American leader, President Johnson, whose wisdom, moderation and sensitivity to world public opinion are well known."

At the same time, Mr. Thant declared:

"I am sure that the great American people, if only they know the true facts and the background to the developments in South Vietnam, will agree with me that further bloodshed is unnecessary.

"The political and diplomatic method of discussions and negotiations alone can create conditions which will enable the United States to withdraw gracefully from that part of the world. As you know, in times of war and of hostilities the first casualty is truth."

A United States spokesman declined to comment on Mr. Thant's statement.

Plan Deals With Technique

The Secretary General was informed after his news conference that the Soviet Union and France had decided to take preliminary action toward a conference on Vietnam. He commented that this was "not unexpected."

Reliable sources said that Mr. Thant's proposals dealt with the technique of negotiating rather than the substance of a settlement. According to these sources, Mr. Thant has suggested a series of informal talks, with himself or some other third party as an intermediary. The talks would involve the principal parties, the United States, Communist China, North and South Vietnam, France, the Soviet Union and Britain.

The Secretary General, it was understood, envisions a series of interlinked "dialogues" as a preliminary to a formal conference.

The Secretary General did not explain what "facts" regarding Vietnam were not known by the American people.

A United Nations source said Mr. Thant felt that Americans were not adequately informed about two "facts" he considers important: that military action will not resolve the situation

Continued on Page 2, Column 3

U.S. JET BOMBERS ATTACK VIETCONG; FIRST SUCH STRIKE

Crews Are Solely American, Another Change in Policy in War in the South

SAIGON REQUESTED STEP

Massing of Guerrilla Units, a Shift in Tactics, Called Reason for the Flights

By JACK LANGGUTH

Special to The New York Times

SAIGON, South Vietnam, Feb. 24—The United States Embassy disclosed today that American jet aircraft were sent on air strikes against the Vietcong in South Vietnam during the last week.

The bombing raids, including one today in Binhdinh Province, where there is a heavy guerrilla concentration, mark the first use of jet bombers in the war in the south.

An announcement by the United States mission said the strike today had been made by F-100's and B-57's from Bienhoa and Danang air bases. [A Pentagon spokesman said he had no information on the number of planes involved.]

An embassy spokesman said information on the strikes was not made public earlier because an element of surprise had still been possible during the "several" raids made since the first use of the jets last Thursday.

Government Unit Trapped

The target today was a large concentration of Vietcong troops in a mountain pass between Ankhe and Pleiku, where a strong attack by the Communist insurgents had trapped a Government unit.

The United States statement began by observing that the strikes had been made "at the request of the Government of Vietnam." A spokesman declined to say when authorization for the use of jet bombers had been given by Washington.

In the past the bombing raids on which American pilots have flown, in propeller-driven A-1H Skyraider fighter-bombers, have been officially described as "training flights."

To conform with the United States' position that its troops here are military advisers and not combatants, the American mission had maintained that a Vietnamese trainee accompanied the United States pilot on all flights in the two-seat Skyraiders. No such statement was

Continued on Page 3, Column 2

U.S. ADMITS SHIFT IN VIETNAM STAND

'Advising and Assisting' Role for Americans Omitted in Report on Air Raid

By MAX FRANKEL

Special to The New York Times

WASHINGTON, Feb. 24—The Administration tacitly acknowledged today that it had changed the rules of United States involvement in the war in South Vietnam. It cited Congressional authority for the move.

The use of American planes and crews on combat missions against the Vietcong guerrillas supplants an earlier policy of having Americans "advise and assist" the South Vietnamese, and fight only in self-defense. The acknowledgment of the change had the effect of stiffening Washington's position in the face of continuing appeals abroad for negotiations.

The White House summarized official responses to these appeals by stating that it had received "no meaningful proposals" for negotiation. By implication, the statement made little of the mediation efforts of U Thant, Secretary General of the United Nations, and of British and French diplomats who have been sounding out the Soviet Union.

Nothing Is 'Authorized'

"There are no authorized negotiations under way with Mr. Thant or any other government," George E. Reedy, the White House press secretary, said.

"I am not going into any diplomatic chitchat that may be going forth, or way-out feelers," he added. "But authorized or meaningful negotiations—no."

His statement also implied that no encouraging offer of a settlement developed at the regularly scheduled meeting in Warsaw today between the Ambassadors of the United States and Communist China.

Officials here have repeatedly said that they cannot envision negotiations until Communist China and North Vietnam indicate a willingness to "leave South Vietnam alone." They say they have seen no such indication and doubt that Moscow can speak for its Communist allies.

Administration Backed

This view is also being endorsed more vigorously on Capitol Hill. A growing number of members of both houses of Congress are speaking out in defense of the Administration's reluctance to define the limits of possible military action in both North and South Vietnam and its refusal to consider negotiations now.

The "advise and assist" definition of the role of American troops in Vietnam was abandoned by the State Department today in its assessment of the disclosure that B-57 bombers and F-100 fighter-bombers with American crews were now being used to attack Vietcong troops in support of ground action.

The jets were sent into action at the request of the Gov-

Continued on Page 2, Column 5

POLICE IN MADRID BATTLE STUDENTS

Many of 5,000 in Protest and 4 Teachers Arrested

Dispatch of The Times, London

MADRID, Feb. 24 — Five thousand students led by four professors clashed today with hundreds of policemen in University City.

Many students were arrested, some of them bleeding from head wounds. The professors, Garcia Calvo, José Luis Aranguran, Montero Dias and Garcia Vercher, also roughed up, were detained, too.

At student-faculty meetings in the last few days, a list of goals was drawn up and approved. One was the right to democratically organized student unions as opposed to the Government-controlled syndicate to which all students in Spain have been compelled to belong since the civil war.

It has become increasingly clear that a majority of students are now supporting this movement in Madrid University against the Government syndicate.

A demonstration to present the program to the rector of the university was set for today.

A procession of students, mostly from the faculties of philosophy and letters, sciences, law and medicine, formed. Headed by the four professors, they marched in silence until they met a barrier of policemen. They all sat down on the pavement.

Dozens of jeeps of policemen

Continued on Page 7, Column 1

Virginia Parties Woo the Negro; G.O.P. Names One to High Post

By JOSEPH A. LOFTUS

Special to The New York Times

RICHMOND, Feb. 24—Both major parties for the first time are openly courting the Negro vote in Virginia.

For the Democrats this is a dramatic departure from the cries of "massive resistance" to integration heard in recent years throughout the Old Dominion. Some of the once-loudest white-supremacy voices are now the softest in wooing the Negro. Apparently the Negro is responding.

Two developments illustrate the competition for votes that may be crucial as early as the fall of this year, when Virginia elects a Governor.

Today, Clarence L. Townes Jr., a Negro, was appointed assistant to the state chairman of the Republican party. Mr. Townes, 37 years old, is a Richmond insurance executive. Robert J. Corber, the state chairman, announced the appointment.

On Saturday night, between 12 and 15 Negroes were welcomed at a Democratic function —the annual fund-raising Jefferson-Jackson Day dinner. They not only dined without discrimination but also made the rounds of the after-dinner parties. A year ago one Negro attended this dinner. He ate at a table for two—alone.

The Richmond dinner guests included Senator Harry Flood Byrd, State Senator Harry Byrd Jr., Representative William M. Tuck, a former Governor; Representative Watkins M. Abbott and Lieut. Gov. Mills E. Godwin Jr., all identified with "massive resistance" of recent years.

The personification of this turnaround is Mr. Godwin, who

Continued on Page 17, Column 1

West German Cabinet Supports Extension of Nazi Crimes Law

By PHILIP SHABECOFF

Special to The New York Times

BONN, Feb. 24 The West German Cabinet voted unanimously today to support the proposed extension of the statute of limitations for the prosecution of Nazi war criminals beyond the May 8 deadline.

A Government statement said that the decision was based on the fact that new evidence indicated that criminal acts committed during World War II would go unpunished if the 20-year statute were allowed to expire as scheduled.

Today's vote in effect reverses the decision last Nov. 5 when the Cabinet declared that legal obstacles prevented extension of the statute.

Chancellor Ludwig Erhard said at the time that he disagreed with that decision but would go along with his Cabinet.

However, the Government took pains in today's gingerly worded statement to note that it had not specifically reversed its previous decision.

"The Federal Government," the statement said, "will support the German Bundestag [lower house of Parliament] in its efforts to create the possibility of satisfying justice while maintaining the principles of legality."

In other words, the Federal Government will not itself make any suggestions to extend the statute of limitations, but will support legislation introduced in Parliament that is designed to do just that.

A Bundestag debate on extension of the statute is scheduled for March 10.

The cautious tone of the Cabinet statement was a case of

Continued on Page 5, Column 1

NEWS INDEX

"All the News That's Fit to Print"

The New York Times.

LATE CITY EDITION

U.S. Weather Bureau Report (Page 50) forecasts: Mostly sunny and cold today; partly cloudy tonight. Fair tomorrow. Temp. range: 31—21; yesterday: 35—24.

VOL. CXIV ... No. 39,116.

NEW YORK, SATURDAY, FEBRUARY 27, 1965.

TEN CENTS

U.S. JUDGE ORDERS CONSPIRACY TRIAL IN RIGHTS DEATHS

Allows One Count Against 17 in Mississippi but Drops Other Charges for 14

SHERIFF FACES 2D TRIAL

Cox Says 3 Law Aides Must Be Tried for Misdemeanor Beyond the Plotting

By JOHN HERBERS
Special to The New York Times

JACKSON, Miss., Feb. 26 — Judge W. Harold Cox of the United States District Court ruled today that Sheriff Lawrence A. Rainey of Neshoba County and 16 other men must stand trial under a misdemeanor charge in the deaths of three civil rights workers last summer.

He did this by upholding one count of an indictment charging all 17 with conspiring to violate a "color of law" statute of 1870.

Judge Cox also dismissed three other counts of the indictment, charging actual violation of the law, for 14 of the accused. He left these additional counts standing against three law-enforcement officers named in the indictment — Sheriff Rainey, Deputy Cecil Price and Richard A. Willis, a policeman in Philadelphia, Miss.

Judge Cox said that all the defendants would be tried first for conspiracy and that the trials of the three officers on charges of direct violation would be held later.

Felony Charge Barred

Yesterday, Judge Cox dismissed a felony indictment brought against all 17 on the ground that the Federal Government had no jurisdiction.

In Washington a spokesman for the Justice Department said:

"While aspects of the decision today and yesterday raise certain legal questions which the department may decide to appeal, the trial can now be scheduled on issues unaffected by the decisions. Consequently, the department is now preparing for trial."

Judge Cox will decide a date and place for the trial. Normally, persons accused of Federal crimes in Neshoba County are brought to trial in Meridian, where today's order was filed.

Maximum penalty under the indictment is one year imprisonment and a $1,000 fine. The indictment that was dismissed yesterday could have brought 10 years' imprisonment and a $5,000 fine.

Government attorneys were reported to believe there was

Continued on Page 10, Column 1

Black Muslim Guard Held In Murder of Malcolm X

Stores Defy Demand to Close—Police Prepared for Funeral Today

By HOMER BIGART

A member of the Black Muslim guard was arrested early yesterday and charged with the slaying of Malcolm X, the black nationalist leader.

Norman Butler, also known as Norman 3X, a husky, round-faced expert in karate, was seized at his apartment in the Soundview housing project in the Bronx, and was questioned for three hours before Assistant District Attorney Herbert Stein ordered him booked on a homicide charge.

The arrest marked the first direct police linkup of the Black Muslims to the assassination of Malcolm X. The police had worked on the theory that Malcolm's defection from Elijah Muhammad's Black Muslims last spring lay behind the slaying.

Since the shooting last Sunday of the 39-year-old Malcolm at a black supremacist rally at Broadway and 166th Street, some Negroes have voiced the suspicion that although the slayers were black, the orders to kill had come from whites.

Fearing that racial tensions might explode on the eve of today's funeral for Malcolm X, the police yesterday blanketed Harlem. Stores on 125th Street, most of them owned by whites, had been threatened with

Continued on Page 10, Column 2

Associated Press

Norman 3X Butler after his arrest in the city yesterday.

Muhammad Says Muslims Must 'Protect' Themselves

By AUSTIN C. WEHRWEIN
Special to The New York Times

CHICAGO, Feb. 26—Elijah Muhammad, leader of the Black Muslims, warned followers of Malcolm X today that "we will fight" if necessary to combat assassination attempts and attacks on mosques, and to "protect ourselves."

With a sharp denunciation of his murdered rival, Muhammad roused several thousand Negroes to a chanting shout of "All praise to Muhammad!"

He addressed an annual meeting of his cult after his son Wallace Delaney Muhammad recanted his defection from the Black Muslims and begged forgiveness for saying last July that his father had betrayed Allah's teachings.

At the same meeting two brothers of Malcolm vowed their faith in Muhammad and assailed their slain brother.

Tension Is High

Their denunciation of Malcolm was the most dramatic moment during an afternoon when the tension in the gloomy arched arena could almost be tasted.

One of them, Philbert X of Lansing, Mich., warned, "Do not let the white man come between us."

He said he had vainly tried to convince Malcolm to change his "dangerous course." In explaining why he would stand by Muhammad tomorrow rather than be at Malcolm's funeral, he said, "Now that he is dead there is nothing I can do—or anybody else."

The other brother, Wilfred X, of Detroit Temple No. 1, where the movement began, said he had recruited Malcolm when Malcolm was in prison. He said the teachings of Muhammad had reformed him

Continued on Page 10, Column 4

WOUNDED NEGRO DIES IN ALABAMA

He Said Trooper Shot Him—Statement by Assailant Reported by Prosecutor

By ROY REED
Special to The New York Times

SELMA, Ala., Feb. 26—Jimmie Lee Jackson, a 26-year-old Negro who said he was shot by a state trooper as policemen broke up a civil rights march the night of Feb. 18 at Marion, Ala., died today in a hospital here.

The immediate cause of death was listed as infection and respiratory difficulty.

Mr. Jackson had suffered a bullet wound in the stomach and a lacerated scalp the night of the march. His doctor was quoted today as saying that he had been badly beaten and that his back had been bruised.

Blanchard McLeod, circuit solicitor (prosecutor) for the district that includes Perry County, said today that he had a signed statement from the man who shot Mr. Jackson.

Mr. McLeod said he would turn over the results of the investigation to the Perry County grand jury about March 10 and let the grand jury use its own judgment about returning an indictment. The prosecutor said

Continued on Page 10, Column 5

PRICE INDEX RISES 5TH MONTH IN ROW

Rate in New York Drops—U. S. Increase Moderate

By The Associated Press

WASHINGTON, Feb. 26—The Consumer Price Index rose one-tenth of 1 per cent in January but can be expected to remain relatively stable throughout 1965, the Labor Department reported today.

The increase, bringing the index to 108.9 per cent of the 1957-59 average, was the fifth consecutive monthly advance. It was attributed mainly to higher costs of housing, gasoline and automobile insurance.

It brought a wage increase of a cent an hour to 950,000 automobile, farm machinery and aerospace employes whose contracts tie their wages to consumer prices.

[In the New York metropolitan area, the index dropped two-tenths of 1 per cent. Page 23.]

The new index level is 1.1 per cent higher than a year ago. The department's Bureau of Labor Statistics said that the index was expected to rise in 1965 at about the same annual rate as in recent years, from 1 to 1.5 per cent.

This relative price stability, the department said, is not expected to be threatened by the 4.5 per cent rise in national output forecast for this year. "A significant gap will continue between output and the economy's over-all capacity to produce," the department ex-

Continued on Page 23, Column 1

Associated Press Wirephoto

ELIJAH MUHAMMAD UNDER GUARD: The Black Muslim leader is surrounded by guards as he addresses opening of convention of followers in Chicago. He remained seated.

LEADERS SUPPORT ROCKEFELLER PLAN TO BUY THE L.I.R.R.

New York Central Plans to Increase Fares 4.4% on Its Hudson and Harlem Lines

By RICHARD WITKIN

Governor Rockefeller's proposal that the state buy the financially distressed Long Island Rail Road if a "reasonable price" could be agreed on drew considerable support yesterday.

But some officials balked at important aspects of the plan.

Among the issues that generated debate were what might be a "reasonable price," the method of payment and provisions for significant annual contributions by Nassau and Suffolk Counties.

Commuters using another line, the New York Central Railroad, were informed yesterday that the management had asked the Public Service Commission to approve fare increases that would average 4.4 per cent of monthly tickets.

The increases would be applied from New York to Poughkeepsie on the Hudson Division and to Pawling on the Harlem Division. They would go into effect on tickets put on sale April 21 for May commutations, unless blocked by the Public Service Commission.

Zaretzki Backs Plan

The railroad said that recent wage increases were the cause of the petition to raise fares. The Central estimates the new fares would add $1.596 million to its income.

Senator Joseph Zaretzki, majority leader of the Democratic-controlled State Senate, strongly approved the broad outlines of the Governor's plans for the Long Island. He questioned, however, the need to pay for the commuter line from tax dollars, suggesting instead that it be financed from operating revenues.

Senator Earl W. Brydges, minority leader of the State Senate, said:

"We've got to do almost anything within reason to keep the Long Island operating. And it begins to look as though this is the only thing we can do."

Nickerson Opposes Increase

Mr. Zaretzki, who is from Manhattan, seemed to be more worried about the willingness of upstate taxpayers to help pay for Long Island commuting than the Republican leader, who is from Niagara Falls.

The Democratic County Executive of Nassau, Eugene N. Nickerson, strongly opposed the provision that his county increase its contribution to maintain rail stations.

His counterpart in Suffolk County, H. Lee Dennison, also a Democrat, said he was against any subsidies from either county because he did not think they would be necessary.

New York City also would be asked to increase its annual contribution to the Long Island. Reaction from city officials was not immediately available.

The blueprint for taking over the Long Island, the largest commuter railroad in the country, was worked out by a special five-man committee named by the Governor last fall. Its chairman was William J. Ro-

Continued on Page 21, Column 4

INDONESIA SEIZES RUBBER ESTATES OF U.S. CONCERNS

Holdings Put at $80 Million—More American Property Take-Overs Expected

By United Press International

JAKARTA, Indonesia, Feb. 26—Indonesia announced today that she was taking over American-owned rubber plantations in North Sumatra. The value of the seized property was estimated at $80 million.

The seizure was the latest move in a series of developments in Indonesia that included the closing of American libraries, withdrawal from the United Nations and the strengthening of economic ties with Communist China.

The Minister of Estates, Frans Seda, read a decree signed by Foreign Minister Subandrio that announced the seizure of plantations owned by the United States Rubber Company of New York and the Goodyear Tire and Rubber Company of Akron, Ohio.

The decree marked the first time that Indonesia had directly seized American property. It is believed that moves will soon be made against other American holdings in Indonesia.

The decree said that the estates would be managed by the Indonesian Government but that American ownership rights were "recognized."

Labor Teams Installed

Informed sources said Indonesian labor teams had been installed on the plantations. Dr. Subandrio and Dr. Seda returned today from a three-day visit to Medan, the capital of North Sumatra, to settle the take-over.

Previously, Indonesia nationalized Dutch and British businesses but prevented the outright take-over of American investments, which are worth $180 million. These investments include holdings by the Standard Vacuum Oil Company and Caltex and lesser holdings by the Union Carbide Corporation, the General Electric Company, the Westinghouse Electric Corporation and the Singer Company.

Earlier this week, President Sukarno informed the United States Ambassador, Howard P. Jones, that Indonesia had "no intention" of taking over the plantations.

The Indonesian Herald, an English-language paper unofficially published by the Foreign Office, said foreign correspondents in Jakarta were "salesmen of hate" who could use mental examinations.

"They would do us a great service if they would just pack up and leave," the paper said.

President Sukarno denounced

Continued on Page 2, Column 7

GOVERNOR ORDERS BUFFALO INQUIRY

State Investigator to Study City's Garage Purchase

By R. W. APPLE Jr.
Special to The New York Times

ALBANY, Feb. 26—Governor Rockefeller announced today that the state planned to investigate a transaction in which the City of Buffalo bought a garage for $800,000 from a company that had purchased it two minutes earlier for $657,000.

The Governor said he would name a special prosecutor to conduct an inquiry and "appropriate criminal proceedings" in connection with "alleged crimes" growing out of the city's purchase of the garage in 1963.

Mr. Rockefeller disclosed in a statement that the prosecutor would supersede the Democratic District Attorney of Erie County, Michael F. Dillon, who had been investigating the situation himself. Buffalo is the seat of Erie County.

A member of the Governor's staff said Mr. Dillon would retain jurisdiction over matters not related to the garage.

The District Attorney wrote to Mr. Rockefeller on Wednesday urging him not to send in an outsider to investigate. But the Governor called him to New York City for a conference this afternoon and then issued his statement in Albany.

Mr. Rockefeller said he was acting "in the public interest." He explained that Mr. Dillon had a close personal relation-

Continued on Page 21, Column 7

U.S. WHITE PAPER BRANDS HANOI AS AN 'AGGRESSOR' AND HINTS AT AIR ATTACKS

Associated Press Wirephoto

ENLISTED AS CONSULTANT: Henry Cabot Lodge, former Ambassador to South Vietnam, with President Johnson yesterday. He will study Vietnamese situation.

POLICY IS ALTERED

Washington Now Feels Military Effort Must Go Beyond South

By MAX FRANKEL
Special to The New York Times

WASHINGTON, Feb. 26—The Administration is about to issue a long indictment of North Vietnamese "aggression" against South Vietnam to justify air attacks against the North.

The white paper, portraying an "intensified" Communist campaign to conquer South Vietnam, concludes that military efforts aimed solely at the Vietcong guerrillas in the south are no longer sufficient to meet the threat.

It stops just short of predicting further air strikes against North Vietnam, but it invites Hanoi, the North Vietnamese capital, to choose between peace and an "increasingly destructive" conflict.

Publication of the document is scheduled for this weekend as part of a mounting Administration campaign to hold North Vietnam accountable for the guerrilla war in the South.

Shift in U. S. Position

In policy terms, it represents a clear departure from the United States' position that despite Hanoi's support of the guerrillas, the "main problem" lies inside South Vietnam.

State Department and intelligence officials were still making last-minute changes in the paper today, but its essential policy statements and compilations of evidence against Hanoi had been approved for distribution.

In advance of its distribution, Administration sources gave the following account of the paper:

It is a sequel to a similar indictment published in December, 1961, to justify the assignment of large contingents of United States military advisers to South Vietnam.

The paper estimates the increase in the flow of men and arms from North to South Vietnam since then, and it describes political, economic and communication links between the Vietcong rebels and the Hanoi Government.

'64 Was Peak Year

On the basis of incomplete and previously published estimates, the paper concludes that 1964 was probably the year of the greatest infiltration of men, a majority native Northerners, into South Vietnam.

It also reports an increase in the southward flow of "more sophisticated" weapons; the most conclusive proof was obtained 10 days ago after the sinking of a 100-ton cargo ship in a cove on Vungro Bay, 235 miles northeast of Saigon.

The vessel was said to have carried three North Vietnamese nautical charts, the health records of two North Vietnamese soldiers and other personal effects.

Its cargo was said to have included 2,000 rifles of a 7.95-mm. Mauser type, 1,000 submachine guns, 500 other rifles, more than a hundred 7.62-mm. carbines, more than 1,000 stick

Continued on Page 2, Column 2

Lodge Will Aid on Vietnam; U.S. to Send More Troops

By CHARLES MOHR
Special to The New York Times

WASHINGTON, Feb. 26—President Johnson enlisted Henry Cabot Lodge today as a special consultant on the Vietnam crisis. Meantime, Secretary of Defense Robert S. McNamara said that a "few hundred" more American military men would be sent to South Vietnam and indicated that long-delayed plans to expand the South Vietnamese Army by 100,000 men would be carried out.

[In Saigon it was reported that the United States was increasing its force in Vietnam by more than 1,000 men.]

Mr. Lodge, a Republican and Maxwell D. Taylor's predecessor as Ambassador to South Vietnam, met with the President at the White House and then said he would serve as a consultant, "for a few days," probably three or four.

Mr. Lodge said he would be briefed on the situation in Vietnam, would study it and then would report to Mr. Johnson. He said Mr. Johnson wanted to be "sure that we're not overlooking anything we could do."

Military and Political Study

He indicated he would study and make recommendations on military as well as political and civic action programs. His assignment would not involve a return to Vietnam.

Mr. Lodge had asked for the appointment with the President. But Mr. Johnson was believed to be taking advantage of the meeting to associate a leading Republican with Administration policy.

The former Ambassador, who was Republican Vice-Presidential candidate against Mr. Johnson in 1960, endorsed the recent air raids on North Vietnam and said of Mr. Johnson, "What he's done has been very, very good."

He added that Mr. Johnson's silence since the raids was wise. "He ought to have the opportunity to play his hand," said Mr. Lodge.

"I don't think he ought to be pressured into saying what he would do" if provocations by North Vietnam continue, Mr. Lodge said. "That puts your adversary in the position of controlling what you do."

Mr. Lodge said he was "neither associating or disassociating" himself from former Vice President Richard M. Nixon, who yesterday suggested con-

Continued on Page 2, Column 4

KOSYGIN SAYS U.S. RISKS WAR SPREAD

Warns It to End 'Aggression' in Vietnam or Conflict Will Cross 'Original' Borders

By HENRY TANNER
Special to The New York Times

MOSCOW, Feb. 26—Premier Aleksei N. Kosygin declared today that unless the United States halted its "aggressive actions," the war in Vietnam would "inevitably transcend its original boundaries."

His declaration was interpreted by diplomatic observers here as an implied warning that the Soviet Union as well as Communist China would be drawn into the conflict if the United States carried the war into North Vietnam.

The Premier reviewed previous Soviet calls for a withdrawal of American forces from South Vietnam and South Korea.

He indicated that the Soviet Government felt that a resumption of American air attacks on North Vietnam would destroy whatever chances existed for negotiation of a peaceful settlement.

"First and foremost," he said, American "aggressive actions" have to cease in order to "create conditions for the exploration of avenues leading to the normalization of the situation in Indochina." This appeared to bear

Continued on Page 2, Column 6

Nasser, in Apparent Bid to West, Restates Differences With Reds

By HEDRICK SMITH
Special to The New York Times

CAIRO, Feb. 26—President Gamal Abdel Nasser has reasserted his differences with world Communism, apparently to quiet Western fears that the United Arab Republic is veering dangerously toward the Eastern bloc.

"We differ on many points with Communism," Mr. Nasser was reported to have told members of the National Assembly last night a few hours after he had held formal talks with Walter Ulbricht, the East German chief of state.

"Our differences with Communism are radical," the Cairo press quoted President Nasser as having said. "We believe in religion and we reject the dictatorship of any class. We look forward to national unity. We do not liquidate any class by use of violence. But we do liquidate privileges enjoyed by any class."

Mr. Nasser's reference to Arab national unity was seen as a reaffirmation of his stand in the discussion last May with Nikita S. Khrushchev, then Soviet Premier, who tried to persuade him to accept international solidarity of the working class rather than emphasize Arab unity.

A number of foreign observers considered it significant that President Nasser would

Continued on Page 3, Column 3

NEWS INDEX

Closeup of the A-4E aircraft that was widely used by the U.S. military forces in Vietnam against the Viet Cong.

The U.S. embassy in Saigon, following a terrorist bombardment in 1965.

"All the News That's Fit to Print"

The New York Times.

LATE CITY EDITION
U. S. Weather Bureau Report (Page 93) forecast:
Fair, cool today; clear, cold tonight. Fair tomorrow.
Temp. range: 46—30; yesterday: 40—35.

VOL. CXIV—No. 39,147. © 1965 by The New York Times Company. Times Square, New York, N.Y. 10036

NEW YORK, TUESDAY, MARCH 30, 1965.

TEN CENTS

BOMB IN VIETNAM RIPS U.S. EMBASSY; AT LEAST 6 DEAD

MANY ARE INJURED

Deputy Envoy Johnson Cut—Blast Set Off in Front of Building

By The Associated Press

SAIGON, South Vietnam, Tuesday, March 30—A huge bomb exploded at the United States Embassy today, causing scores of casualties.

One American woman secretary was killed and an unidentified man, believed to have been an American military policeman, also was killed.

Four Vietnamese were known to be dead. It was believed many more dead Vietnamese were in hospitals scattered throughout the city.

Scores of Vietnamese pedestrians were in the vicinity of the embassy at the time of the explosion.

The weight of the bomb was estimated at 250 pounds. It was apparently planted in a vehicle outside the embassy.

An American medical officer said that about 30 Americans had been wounded, 10 gravely.

Envoy Last to Leave

Deputy Ambassador U. Alexis Johnson, the ranking American in the building, was cut on the face by flying glass. He said he was not hurt badly and added: "We have been hit. We will need some medical assistance."

Mr. Johnson supervised the removal of the injured by ambulance to a United States Navy hospital 10 blocks away. He was the last of the injured to leave the scene.

The blast heavily damaged the office of Ambassador Maxwell D. Taylor, who is in Washington for talks on the war against the Communist guerrillas and on the United States air strikes against North Vietnam.

An American official in Saigon said that 150 persons were in the embassy at the time of the blast. Most of the injuries were from flying glass and bricks.

Hole Torn in Building

Deputy Ambassador Johnson was at his desk when the explosion ripped through the building. The blast overturned furniture and smashed windows.

A hole was ripped in the facade of the five-story concrete building.

Sgt. Lyle Goodwin of Pekin, Ill., who came upon the scene just before the blast, said he had seen a large French automobile make a halt near the embassy and two men leap out. The two ran, he said, and the police may have fired at them.

[The police killed one terrorist and seized a 37-year-old Vietnamese identified as Nguyen Van Hai, Reuters reported.]

The injured included Robert H. Miller, first secretary of the embassy's political section. His condition was not immediately known.

The blast occurred at 10:55 A.M. (9:55 P.M. Monday, New York time).

Continued on Page 14, Column 4

France Bars Parley On European Unity

By ROBERT C. DOTY
Special to The New York Times

ROME, March 29—France in effect vetoed today an Italian proposal for a meeting of Common Market foreign ministers this spring to discuss European political unity.

Maurice Couve de Murville, France's Foreign Minister, was reported at the end of a three-day visit here to have agreed in principle to the proposal of Italy's Foreign Minister, Amintore Fanfani.

But the French minister declined to be pinned down on a date. He was reported to have said that there was not enough evidence of sufficient agreement among the six nations to give a spring conference much

Continued on Page 2, Column 3

U.S. Bombers Hit Radar Post Again

By JACK LANGGUTH
Special to The New York Times

SAIGON, South Vietnam, March 29—Forty-two United States Navy aircraft today carried out a second raid over the Bachlong radar station, 60 miles off North Vietnam.

Jets and propeller-driven planes bombed the island, about 120 miles southeast of Hanoi. A smaller Navy force, also from carriers of the Seventh Fleet, attacked the island last Friday.

At least one plane, an A-4 Skyhawk, was downed by ground fire after the raid. The pilot was recovered at sea.

The naval commander who led the flight said in Saigon afterward that the mission had been more successful than the previous strike against the radar installation and other military targets.

Comdr. Henry P. Glindeman of Coeur d'Alene, Idaho, was permitted today to disclose the kind of information on the raid that had been withheld after other recent air strikes.

He said that 12 Navy planes had flown on a support mission, principally to suppress Communist antiaircraft fire, and that 45 tons of bombs had been dropped. These included

Continued on Page 19, Column 2

POPE ASKS RULING ON BIRTH CONTROL

Exhorts Study Panel to Act Soon on Issue Causing 'Anguish' to Many

Special to The New York Times

ROME, March 29—Pope Paul VI has urged his commission of priests, scientists and laymen to recommend soon a Roman Catholic policy on birth control in response to "the anguish of so many souls" on the issue.

The Pontiff met with the members of the commission "for the study of problems of birth" on Saturday at the end of their fourth secret study session. His speech to the 55 members who attended was published today by the Vatican newspaper L'Osservatore Romano.

"The people of the United States," he said, "are proud of the achievements of these two young men and I am sure that New York, rain or no rain, will give them a welcome the likes of which they have never had."

Commission Year Old

The commission was set up last year in response to demands by Catholic clerics and laymen for review, in the light of modern scientific, social and demographic conditions, of the church's traditional ban on any chemical or mechanical means of birth control.

The position of the church has been that the only permissible form of birth control is the limitation of marital sexual relations to the nonfertile period of the female menstrual cycle.

The participants in the meetings have scrupulously observed the secrecy rule. Pope Paul has reserved to himself the right to resolve the thorny conflict between the church's stand and the consciences of many Catholic married people.

This difference was emphasized by Maximos IV Cardinal Saigh, Melchite Patriarch of Antioch, at the last session of the Ecumenical Council Vatican II. He said the church rule on contraception was not observed "in the immense majority" of Catholic marriages.

Pope Paul, in his speech, gave

Continued on Page 6, Column 4

Spacemen Receive A Rousing Welcome Despite Chilly Rain

By GAY TALESE

New Yorkers littered the sky yesterday with tons of swirling ticker tape, confetti and old newspaper headlines — and at the bottom of it all, moving slowly up lower Broadway, surrounded by marching bands, were two quiet Americans: Virgil I. Grissom and John W. Young.

It was no day for a parade. It rained hard and the wind was raw. And yet at noon several thousand people waited along Broadway to cheer the astronauts who last week rocketed into space — and yesterday rode past at 7 miles an hour in a Lincoln convertible.

Sitting between them, poised and gregarious—so different from the astronauts—was Vice President Hubert H. Humphrey, who had flown to New York an hour before. At La Guardia Airport he greeted the spacemen, their families and dignitaries.

Pride Is Expressed

Then the motorcade, consisting of 25 autos and 40 police motorcycles, formed and the ride began from La Guardia to the starting point of the parade —Bowling Green Park in downtown Manhattan.

This is New York's oldest park. In 1776 there was a riotous scene there with patriots knocking off the British crowns that capped the park's fence. But at 12:05 P.M. yesterday, as the parade began to move, the fence and the park's trees were streaming with ticker tape tossed from a dozen skyscrapers by hundreds of people

Continued on Page 8, Column 3

Washington Is Cool To Alabama Boycott

Special to The New York Times

WASHINGTON, March 29—Important Johnson Administration sources responded coolly today to a proposal by the Rev. Dr. Martin Luther King Jr. for an economic boycott of Alabama and a withdrawal of Federal funds and support from the state.

The sources said Dr. King had not discussed the plan with the Administration before proposing it on a national television program yesterday. They made it obvious that his proposal would not have Administration support.

George E. Reedy, White House press secretary, would not comment at a news conference on Dr. King's proposals that labor unions refuse to

Continued on Page 28, Column 3

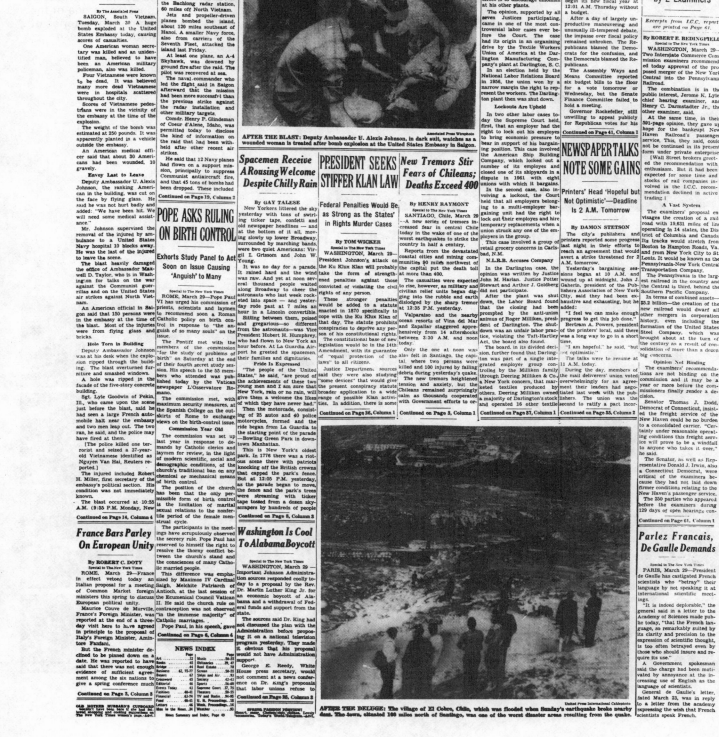

AFTER THE BLAST: Deputy Ambassador U. Alexis Johnson, in dark suit, watches as a wounded woman is treated after bomb explosion at the United States Embassy in Saigon.

Associated Press Wirephoto

PRESIDENT SEEKS STIFFER KLAN LAW

Federal Penalties Would Be as Strong as the States' in Rights Murder Cases

By TOM WICKER
Special to The New York Times

WASHINGTON, March 29—President Johnson's attack on the Ku Klux Klan will probably take the form of strengthened penalties against those convicted of violating the civil rights of any person.

These stronger penalties would be added to a statute enacted in 1870 specifically to cope with the Ku Klux Klan of that day. The statute prohibits conspiracies to deprive any person of his constitutional rights.

The constitutional base of new legislation would be in the 14th Amendment, with its guarantee of "equal protection of the laws" to all citizens.

Justice Department sources said they were also studying "some devices" that would give broader application to a wide range of possible Klan activities. In addition, there is some

Continued on Page 26, Column 1

New Tremors Stir Fears of Chileans; Deaths Exceed 400

By HENRY RAYMONT
Special to The New York Times

SANTIAGO, Chile, March 29 —A new series of tremors increased fear in central Chile today in the wake of one of the worst earthquakes to strike the country in half a century.

Reports from the devastated coastal cities and mining communities 90 miles northwest of the capital put the death toll at more than 400.

The casualties were expected to rise, however, as military and civilian relief units began digging into the rubble and earth dislodged by the sharp tremor at 12:35 P.M. yesterday.

After the plant was shut down, the Labor Board found that the closing had been prompted by the anti-union animus of Roger Milliken, president of Darlington. The shutdown was an unfair labor practice, violating the Taft-Hartley Act, the board also found.

Valparaiso and the nearby ocean resorts of Vina del Mar and Zapallar staggered apprehensively from 14 aftershocks between 3:30 A.M. and noon today.

Only the one at noon was also felt in Santiago, the capital, where two persons were killed and 100 injured by falling debris during yesterday's quake.

The new tremors heightened tension and anxiety, but the Chileans remained surprisingly calm as thousands cooperated with Government efforts to or-

Continued on Page 3, Column 1

HIGH COURT HOLDS CONCERN MAY SHUT TO BALK UNIONISM

But Finds It Illegal to Close Only Part of a Company to Keep Out Labor

By JOHN D. POMFRET
Special to The New York Times

WASHINGTON, March 29—The Supreme Court held today that an employer could close down his business entirely to avoid dealing with a union, but not partly that the intent and effect is to discourage unionism at his other plants.

The opinion, supported by all seven Justices participating, came in one of the most controversial labor cases ever before the Court. The case had its origin in an organizing drive by the Textile Workers Union of America at the Darlington plant at Darlington, S. C.

In an election held by the National Labor Relations Board in 1956, the union won by a narrow margin the right to represent the workers. The Darlington plant then was shut down.

Lockouts Are Upheld

In two other labor cases today the Supreme Court held, first, that an employer had the right to lock out his employes to bear in support of his bargaining position. This case involved the American Ship Building Company, which locked out a number of its employes and closed one of its shipyards in a dispute in 1961 with eight unions with which it bargains.

In the second case, involving a lockout, the Court held that all employers belonging to a multi-employer bargaining unit had the right to lock out their employes and hire temporary replacements when a union struck any one of the employers in the group.

N.L.R.B. Accuses Company

In the Darlington case, the opinion was written by Justice John M. Harlan. Justice Potter Stewart and Arthur J. Goldberg did not participate.

The board, in its divided decision, further found that Darlington was part of a single integrated employer group controlled by the Milliken family through Deering Milliken & Co., a New York concern, that marketed textiles produced by others. Deering Milliken owned a majority of Darlington's stock and operated 16 other textile

Continued on Page 37, Column 1

NEWSPAPER TALKS NOTE SOME GAINS

Printers' Head 'Hopeful but Not Optimistic'—Deadline Is 2 A.M. Tomorrow

By DAMON STETSON

The city's publishers and printers reported some progress last night in their efforts to reach an agreement that would avert a strike threatened for 2 A.M. tomorrow.

In the Darlington case, the opinion was written by Justice John M. Harlan. Justice Potter Stewart and Arthur J. Goldberg did not participate.

The union's bargaining sessions began at 10 A.M. and wound up at midnight. John J. Gaherin, president of the Publishers Association of New York City, said they had been exhaustive and exhausting, but he added:

"I feel we can make enough progress to get this job done."

Bertram A. Powers, president of the printers' local, said there was a long way to go in a short time.

"I am hopeful," he said, "but not optimistic."

The talks were to resume at 11 A.M. today.

During the day, members of the mail deliverers' union voted overwhelmingly for an agreement their leaders had negotiated last week with the publishers. The union was the second to ratify a pact incor-

Continued on Page 35, Column 2

I.C.C. AIDES BACK CENTRAL MERGER WITH THE PENNSY

NEW HAVEN LOSES

Passenger Service Is Excluded From Plan by 2 Examiners

Excerpts from I.C.C. report are printed on Page 61.

By ROBERT E. BEDINGFIELD
Special to The New York Times

WASHINGTON, March 29—Two Interstate Commerce Commission examiners recommended today approval of the proposed merger of the New York Central into the Pennsylvania Railroad.

The combination is in the public interest, Jerome K. Lyle, chief hearing examiner, and Henry C. Darmstadt Jr., the other examiner, said.

At the same time, in their 591-page opinion, they gave up hope for the bankrupt New Haven Railroad's passenger service. This, they said, could not be continued in its present form under private enterprise.

[Wall Street brokers greeted the recommendation with enthusiasm. But it had been expected for some time and stocks of rail companies involved in the I.C.C. recommendation declined in active trading.]

A Vast System

The examiners' proposal envisages the creation of a railroad with 19,631 miles of line operating in 14 states, the District of Columbia and Canada. Its tracks would stretch from Boston to Hampton Roads, Va., and from New York City to St. Louis. It would be known as the Pennsylvania-New York Central Transportation Company.

The Pennsylvania is the largest railroad in the country and the Central is third, behind the Southern Pacific Company.

In terms of combined assets— $5.2 billion—the creation of the new railroad would dwarf all other mergers in corporation history, even including the formation of the United States Steel Company, which was brought about as a result of consolidation of more than a dozen big concerns.

Opinion Not Binding

The examiners' recommendations are not binding on the commission and it may be a year or more before the commissioners finally render a decision.

Senator Thomas J. Dodd, Democrat of Connecticut, insisted the freight service of the New Haven could be no burden to a consolidated carrier. "Certainly under reasonable operating conditions this freight service will prove to be a windfall to anyone who takes it over," he said.

The Senator, as well as Representative Donald J. Irwin, also a Connecticut Democrat, were critical of the examiners because they had not laid down firmer conditions relating to the New Haven's passenger service.

The 250 parties who appeared before the examiners during 129 days of open hearings in-

Continued on Page 61, Column 1

Budget by April 1 Doubted in Albany

By R. W. APPLE Jr.
Special to The New York Times

ALBANY, March 29—It appeared all but certain tonight that the state would begin its new fiscal year at 12:01 A.M. Thursday without a budget.

After a day of largely unproductive maneuvering and unusually ill-tempered debate, the impasse over fiscal policy remained unbroken. The Republicans blamed the Democrats for the confusion, and the Democrats blamed the Republicans.

The Assembly Ways and Means Committee reported six budget bills to the floor for a vote tomorrow or Wednesday, but the Senate Finance Committee failed to hold a meeting.

Governor Rockefeller, still unwilling to appeal publicly for Republican votes for his

Continued on Page 41, Column 1

Parlez Francais, De Gaulle Demands

Special to The New York Times

PARIS, March 29—President de Gaulle has castigated French scientists who "betray" their language by not speaking it at international scientific meetings.

"It is indeed deplorable," the general said in a letter to the Academy of Sciences made public today, "that the French language, so remarkably suited by its clarity and precision to the expression of scientific thought, is too often betrayed even by those who should insure and require its use."

A Government spokesman said the charge had been motivated by annoyance at the increasing use of English as the language of scientists.

General de Gaulle's letter, dated March 23, was in reply to a letter from the Academy expressing the wish that French scientists speak French.

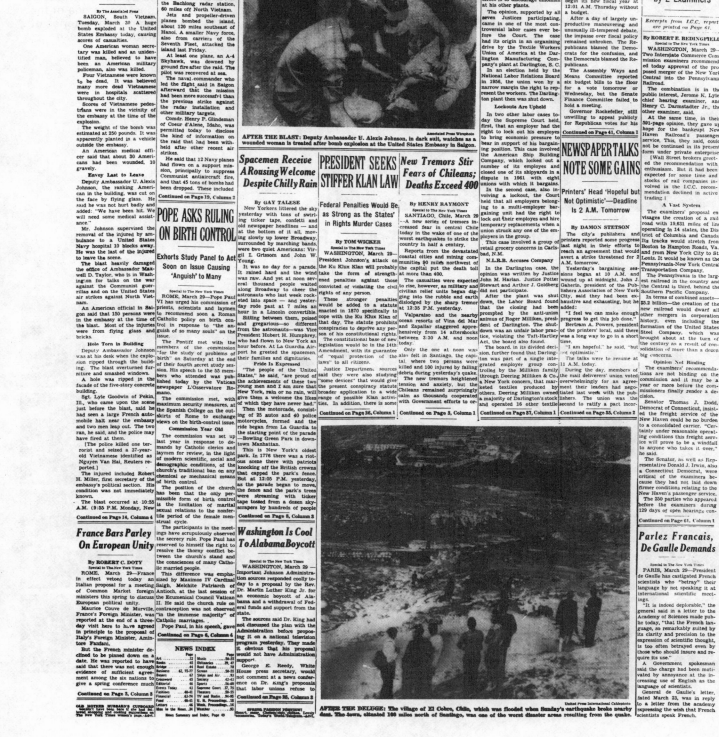

AFTER THE DELUGE: The village of El Cobre, Chile, which was flooded when Sunday's earthquake broke nearby dam. The town, situated 100 miles north of Santiago, was one of the worst disaster areas resulting from the quake.

United Press International Cablephoto

POST-STRIKE DONG PHONG THUONG RR BR

DESTROYED SPAN

4 APRIL 1965

The Dong Phong Thuong Railroad and Highway Bridge was struck on April 3, 1965 by Allied forces, thus destroying one of the most important arteries of the North Vietnamese.

DONG HOI BRIDGE AND FERRY

VIEW NORTHEAST

BUILT UP LANDING

NO BRIDGE REPAIRS

NO FERRY LANDING

4 APRIL

FERRY LANDING UNDER CONSTRUCTION
BOMB CRATERS FILLED IN

9 APRIL

LANDINGS UNDER CONSTRUCTION

14 APRIL

LANDINGS NEAR COMPLETION

23 APRIL

The Dong Hoi Bridge and Ferry Landing in North Vietnam was destroyed by Allied forces in early April 1965—and promptly rebuilt by the Viet Cong by the end of the same month.

"All the News That's Fit to Print"

The New York Times.

LATE CITY EDITION
U. S. Weather Bureau Report (Page 61) forecasts
Sunny and mild today; fair tonight.
Increasing cloudiness tomorrow.
Temp. range: 58—38; yesterday: 57—34.

VOL. CXIV..No. 39,153. © 1965 by The New York Times Company. Times Square, New York, N. Y. 10036 NEW YORK, MONDAY, APRIL 5, 1965. TEN CENTS

CONGRESS NEARS TEST ON MEDICARE AND SCHOOL BILL

Senate Is Expected to Begin Floor Debate Wednesday on Aid to Education

JOHNSON PUSHES PLANS

House Committee Is Likely to Clear Medical Proposal for Action Same Day

By MARJORIE HUNTER
Special to The New York Times

WASHINGTON, April 4 — Congress moves tomorrow into what could be the single most important week of the session, with action scheduled on medical care for the aged and aid to the nation's schools.

Seldom have two such major bills come up for floor action in a single week. Both are being pushed vigorously by President Johnson.

The $1.3 billion school-aid bill, already passed by the House, is expected to reach the Senate floor on Wednesday and could become law before the end of the week.

The House is expected to begin debate Wednesday on a bill to provide medical care for the aged and increases in Social Security benefits.

Waiting in the wings, once the Senate completes action on the school bill, will be the Administration's voting-rights legislation.

A Friday Deadline

The Senate Judiciary Committee faces a Friday deadline for reporting the voting-rights bill to the floor. It is possible, but not likely, that Senate action on the school legislation will be completed in time for floor debate to begin Friday on voting rights.

Mike Mansfield of Montana, the Senate majority leader, said today that he thought the school bill "will take us at least through Friday, maybe even Saturday."

Senator Mansfield and other Democratic leaders hope to steer the school-aid bill through the Senate without change. This would avoid having to send the bill to conference to work out differences with the House.

The school bill cleared a Senate Education subcommittee Thursday in exactly the same form in which it passed the House. The full Senate Labor and Public Welfare Committee is scheduled to act Tuesday, in time for floor action Wednesday.

Long-Standing Battle

Its passage would mark the end of a series of Congressional battles, dating back many years, over providing Federal aid to the nation's elementary and secondary schools.

The money would go only to public schools, but there would be aid to parochial-school students in the form of library materials, textbooks and such special services as shared-time classes.

The bill would focus on largely impoverished neighborhoods. Supplementary educational centers, open to both adults and youths, also would be established.

While the Senate debates school aid, the House will be involved with another Congres-

Continued on Page 20, Column 4

The Car and Smog: A Growing Controversy

Auto Industry Says Evidence Does Not Warrant Controls

By DAVID R. JONES
Special to The New York Times

DETROIT, April 4—A little-noticed controversy involving the family car, which seems destined to have significant influence on the welfare and pocketbooks of millions of Americans in the years ahead, is raging throughout the nation.

The controversy centers on the question of how much the automobile contributes to the nation's air-pollution problem, in which the major metropolitan areas, such as Los Angeles, face the prospect of eventually choking on their own exhaust.

What should be done to control the gases vehicles spew into the air? The question is pitting the automobile industry against Federal, state and local authorities.

This debate over automotive air pollution will be in the spotlight this week as the Senate Public Works Committee's subcommittee on air and water pollution begins three days of hearings Tuesday in Washington. Senator Edmund S. Muskie,

Continued on Page 27, Column 1

Smog enveloping a section of downtown Los Angeles. Motor vehicle exhaust is said to be a major contributing factor to the condition, but industry sources question this theory.

BRANDT IS HALTED BY EAST GERMANS ON ROAD TO BERLIN

Mayor Forced to Fly to City as Harassment Continues —Reds to Bar Deputies

By PHILIP SHABECOFF
Special to The New York Times

BONN, April 4—Mayor Willy Brandt of West Berlin was barred by the East German police from traveling on the autobahn to his own city today.

The Mayor's car was turned back at a control point near the town of Lauenburg, 174 miles from Berlin, as the Communist regime stepped up its harassing tactics in reprisal for a scheduled meeting of the Bundestag in West Berlin Wednesday. The Bundestag is the lower house of the West German Parliament.

Tonight the East German Government announced that Bundestag Deputies and "other persons" who planned to take part in the meeting would be barred from the land corridors to West Berlin.

The announcement, made by the East German press agency A.D.N., made no mention of barring air traffic.

Mayor Assails 'Impudence'

Mayor Brandt said the East German officials had acted with "boundless impudence" in turning him back at the border. It was the first time a governing Mayor of West Berlin had been prevented from passing through East Germany to the city.

The Mayor had been returning from the northern city of Lübeck in West Germany, where he visited his mother, who is ill. Later in the day he arrived in Berlin from Hamburg by plane.

[The Allied commandants in Berlin formally protested Monday on the action against Mr. Brandt, Reuters said.]

Mayor Brandt was not the only motorist left fuming by the East German tactics. At the Helmstedt-Marienborn control point farther south, hundreds of autos were kept waiting in a line stretching back two miles.

The Communist authorities saw to it that only 10 cars an hour passed into East German territory for the trip to Berlin.

Baggage Is Inspected

Waiting time to get through the Helmstedt check point exceeded three hours. The East German guards forced motorists to get out of their cars and open their baggage for inspection. At one point last night the waiting time was about seven hours.

The East German Government has acknowledged that its harassment techniques on the Berlin autobahns are a direct reprisal for the scheduled Bundestag meeting. East Germany contends that West Berlin is not a part of West Germany and that the Bundestag has no right to assemble there.

The East German authorities had indicated before the weekend that they would not permit members of the West German Parliament to drive through their territory. Last Thursday the wife and secretary of a Deputy were denied passage on the autobahn.

The West German Parliament last held an official assembly in Berlin in 1958. This year, after repeated urging by West German officials, the Western

Continued on Page 4, Column 4

HANOI MIG'S DOWN 2 AMERICAN JETS IN FIRST AIR CLASH

U.S. RAIDS 4 SITES

Red Planes Appear During a Bombing Attack on Bridge

By JACK LANGGUTH
Special to The New York Times

SAIGON, South Vietnam, Monday, April 5—North Vietnamese MIG fighter planes shot down two United States Air Force jets that were taking part in a bombing attack on a bridge yesterday.

The MIG's appeared during one of four attacks by planes of the United States Air Force and Navy and the South Vietnamese Air Force on bridges and roads in North Vietnam.

The assault by the MIG's marked the first clash between Communist and American planes in Vietnam.

The drowned body of one American pilot was later found at sea. Search operations were continuing for the second American flier, military sources said.

One Vietnamese A-1H Skyraider, piloted by an American, was downed by fire from a Communist vessel. The pilot has been given up as dead. Other aircraft were also known to have been destroyed by ground fire, but details were withheld while the search continued.

F-105's Are Faster

The supersonic jet interceptor aircraft that accompanied the American bombers did not appear in time to head off the four MIG-15 and MIG-17 jets that downed the two American F-105 fighter-bombers. The F-105 is about twice as fast as the old MIG's.

Maj. Gen. Joseph H. Moore, commander of the Second Air Division, said United States planes had returned the fire of the MIG's, which he said bore North Vietnamese markings. But he added, "We didn't knock down any."

The general said the attacks by the MIG's were "not unexpected." He added, "We have felt that at some point they would feel bold enough to try out their aim."

An American mission spokesman said, however: "We have obviously entered a new phase."

Asked why the American jet bombers, with their greater

Continued on Page 15, Column 1

The New York Times April 5, 1965

MIG jets downed two U.S. planes near Thanhhoa (1) during a raid on bridges. Another target was a span just south of Donghoi (2).

Wagner Urges New Talks To Avert Strike on Papers

By DAMON STETSON

Mayor Wagner urged the printers and publishers last night to continue to make "every conceivable effort" to settle their dispute and avoid a strike that might affect seven of the city's daily newspapers.

The Mayor made his plea after receiving a report from Theodore W. Kheel, his labor adviser who has been attempting to mediate the controversy.

The possibility of a strike, starting as early as today, arose when negotiations collapsed at 3 A.M. yesterday after more than 12 hours of bargaining on economic issues. These issues have been the major block to a settlement.

Mayor Is Notified

After the talks broke up, Bertram A. Powers, president of New York Typographical Union No. 6, said he had notified the Mayor through Mr. Kheel that he had been unable to reach agreement with the publishers. This notification, he said, fulfilled the union's promise to give at least 24 hour's notice before calling a strike and left the printers free to strike after 3 A.M. today.

Mr. Powers emphasized last night that the union was reserving the right to strike any time after that hour.

"It could be tomorrow [Monday], Tuesday or Wednesday," he said. "A time and a day will be set. We may or may not give advance notice."

Mr. Powers said he saw no purpose in further meetings with the publishers.

"We've now met 30 times and we have not been able to resolve the situation," he said. "We are prepared to strike at

Continued on Page 24, Column 3

HUGHES PROPOSES JERSEY RAIL PLAN

$5.8 Million, 16-Month Trial Seeks More Revenue and Riders for the Lines

By WALTER H. WAGGONER
Special to The New York Times

TRENTON, April 4 — Gov. Richard J. Hughes made public today a plan for preserving and improving commuter service of the Erie-Lackawanna Railroad and other rail lines in the state.

The plan would first establish a $5.8 million, 16-month Demonstration Project for putting in effect recommended schedule and service changes designed to ttract passengers and increase revenues for the Erie-Lackawanna.

Beyond that, it would utilize a $50 million fund, half state and half Federal, for a two-year capital improvement program to reduce the operating costs of both the Erie-Lackawanna and other passenger lines in the state.

The plan is set forth in a comprehensive 75-page study of the state's railroad problems by State Highway Commissioner Dwight R. G. Palmer, whose department has a Division of Railroad Transportation.

The objectives of the plan, Mr. Palmer said, are two-fold:

1. "Preserve and improve essential rail passenger service" while ending the present year-to-year subsidy program.

2. "Preserve the railroads themselves, and strengthen their ability to operate in a competitive atmosphere, so that

Continued on Page 26, Column 3

U.S. AND INDONESIA BACK AMITY MOVE

Sukarno and Bunker Agree to Try to Ease Irritants —No Real Gain Seen

By NEIL SHEEHAN
Special to The New York Times

JAKARTA, Indonesia, April 4—President Sukarno and Ellsworth Bunker agreed today that the United States and Indonesia should try to minimize some of the irritants that have resulted in a grave deterioration in their relations.

Mr. Bunker, a former ambassador who is here as a special envoy of President Johnson, met with the Indonesian President and Dr. Subandrio, the Foreign Minister, for two hours and 45 minutes at the Merdeka (Freedom) Presidential Palace.

It was Mr. Bunker's second meeting with Mr. Sukarno since his arrival last Wednesday.

Sides Agree 'to Disagree'

Dr. Subandrio said after the meeting that the talks had brought "an agreement to disagree" on specific issues, but that this "should not mar the relationship between both sides."

"Even if we cannot reach an agreement on all specific issues," he said, "then at least we should minimize irritations on both sides."

Despite the optimistic tone of these statements, diplomats did not believe the Bunker-Sukarno talks would lead to any real improvement in relations.

It was felt that differences between the two countries were so great that they could not be

Continued on Page 11, Column 1

Guantanamo Plant Helping Base End Reliance on Cuba

By HANSON W. BALDWIN
Special to The New York Times

UNITED STATES NAVAL BASE, Guantánamo Bay, Cuba, April 4—The largest plant in the world that both produces electric power and removes the salt from sea water will be formally turned over to the United States Navy in a few days.

The ceremony will mark a definitive milestone in making the United States naval base here completely independent of Fidel Castro's Cuba.

The base now generates all its own electricity and processes all its fresh water from the sea. The Cuban "commuters" working on the base, who once numbered thousands, have been reduced to 561.

Jamaican laborers under 120-day contracts have been imported to replace the Cubans. All food and other supplies—much of them once bought in Cuba—now come to the base by ship or plane.

Likened to a U.S. City

Rear Adm. John D. Bulkeley, the base commander, has likened the base to a small American city of 8,300 people. But unlike most American cities, the 45-square-mile enclave is virtually self-contained.

The $10 million desalting and generating plant was constructed in record time by the Westinghouse Electric Corporation and the Burns & Roe Construction Corporation.

The base was formerly supplied with water by pipelines from the Yateras River, five miles outside the naval reservation. The United States Government paid Cuba about $14,000 a month for about two million gallons a day used at the base.

The Yateras River lines were closed and then cut by the removal of a section of pipe on Feb. 17, 1964. This action by Mr. Castro caused the construction of the desalting plant and the other measures that have

Continued on Page 8, Column 3

U.S. SAYS BOMBING CUT VITAL ROUTES

Stresses Effect of Attacks on Bridges Linking North Vietnam With South

By TAD SZULC
Special to The New York Times

WASHINGTON, April 4—The Defense Department announced today that United States air strikes in the last two days had made "impassable" three bridges that were "vital links in the North Vietnamese transportation system supporting Communist guerilla operations in South Vietnam and Laos."

A department statement said that "the vital importance of these bridges to the North Vietnamese was indicated by the heavy antiaircraft defense and the fact that the MIG interceptor aircraft were employed for the first time."

The statement, which acknowledged that six United States aircraft were lost in the attacks between Friday and last night, said two Air Force fighter planes "were shot down in a hit-and-run attack by Communist MIG aircraft."

The MIG's, which first appeared during the early Saturday strikes, came back to attack the United States planes in the second attack on the Thamhhoa railroad-and-highway bridge over the Ma River.

The 540 foot-long, two-span, steel and concrete bridge is 76 miles south of Hanoi, the North Vietnamese capital, and is one of the farthest points of penetration in the North by United States aircraft in the now daily raids.

Officials observed that the MIG's appeared only in this area, close to Hanoi, though the weekend strikes ranged along the North Vietnam coast from the Ma River, about 65 miles south of Hanoi, to as far south as a bridge on a coastal highway near Donghoi, just above the 17th Parallel, the dividing

Continued on Page 14, Column 4

PANEL TO STUDY TRADE WITH REDS

Johnson Picks 12-Man Unit on Expansion Possibilities

Special to The New York Times

WASHINGTON, April 4—President Johnson named today a 12-man special Presidential committee to study the possibilities and implications of expanding United States trade with Eastern Europe and the Soviet Union.

The panel, composed of outstanding business and industrial leaders, educators and foreign policy specialists, is headed by J. Irwin Miller, board chairman of the Cummins Engine Company, Inc., of Columbus, Ind., and a member of the executive committee of the World Council of Churches.

It includes a representative of organized labor, which on occasion has expressed doubts about expanding trade with Communist nations. He is Nathaniel Goldfinger, director of research for the American Federation of Labor and Congress of Industrial Organizations.

The White House announcement said that "on completion of its investigations, the committee will report its findings and recommendations to the President."

In his State of the Union

Continued on Page 18, Column 4

Integration of Harlem by 1975 Is Aim of Area Planning Group

A neighborhood planning group is drawing up guidelines to transform Harlem into a quality, integrated community in 10 years.

District Planning Board No. 10, an advisory body on Central Harlem to the Borough President's office, which is in charge of the project, is gathering information on the problems and needs of the area and possible solutions.

The study covers all of Harlem and small parts of adjoining communities—from 110th to 165th Street and from the Hudson to the East and Harlem Rivers. Most of the area's 500,000 residents are Negroes and Puerto Ricans.

Among the proposals already suggested are the transformation of 125th Street into a new commercial area, the establishment of a community college, new transportation facilities to bring commercial and commuter traffic into Harlem, and the construction of a television center.

To further integration, the shifting of large blocs of Negroes and Puerto Ricans both within the area under study and to outside communities has been suggested.

Undertaken with the cooperation of Columbia University, the study is intended to provide for "a substantially integrated Harlem based on excellence by 1975," according to George Gregory Jr., chairman of the planning board.

Mr. Gregory, a tall, lanky Negro who is a City Civil Service Commissioner, explained in a recent interview that his group hoped to avoid the pit-

Continued on Page 22, Column 4

SOCIAL DYNAMITE. Read "What Hit the Teenagers," April FORTUNE.—Adv.

A Prince Can't Drop In at a Pub, Philip Notes With Some Regret

By The Associated Press

LONDON, April 4—Prince Philip said today his role as husband of Queen Elizabeth II prevented him from indulging in small pleasures like visiting a pub or catching a movie.

"These are things that I miss, but on the other hand I've got a lot of advantages which compensate for it," Philip told a British radio audience.

The Prince was on an unrehearsed question-and-answer radio show with a panel of four young people. The British Broadcasting Corporation taped the program a few days ago and put it on the air today.

Philip was asked what he would like to do but could not because of his position.

"There are a lot of things," Philip replied: "Just being able to walk into a cinema or go out to a nightclub or go to a pub, or something like that.

"I can do it, but it isn't always particularly enjoyable because if you're recognized, the atmosphere changes and people nudge each other and conversation stops and somebody asks you for your autograph or something."

"Do you ever wish you could go off to a desert island, or do you feel that you're better when you're under tremendous pressure?" Susan Bucknell, a student at Oxford University, asked.

"No, I think the essence of the exercise is to vary it, you know, if you can," Philip replied.

He said his travels abroad brought Britain to the minds of other peoples. "It makes them realize that we're both living in the same world," he said.

A 16-year-old student, Christopher Hall, asked:

"Is there anywhere left you'd particularly like to visit?"

"I'd like to go to a lot of places," Philip replied. "I'd like to go to China, I'd like to go to Russia. I haven't been to Japan."

Vivienne Barton, 18, who is training to be a reporter on a Brighton newspaper, asked: "Does the decision lie solely with you? If you want to go to China next week, can you do so?"

"No, not really," Philip replied, "because as you can imagine people would say it would — it would attract a certain amount of political attention

Continued on Page 4, Column 5

Associated Press Cablephoto

HIGHWAY INCIDENT: Mayor Willy Brandt of West Berlin with West German customs officers at Lauenburg. Later, East Germans forbade him to continue to Berlin on autobahn.

NEWS INDEX

"All the News That's Fit to Print"

The New York Times.

LATE CITY EDITION
U.S. Weather Bureau Report (Page 78) Forecast:
Fair and mild today and tonight;
becoming cloudy tomorrow.
Temp. range: 59–39; yesterday: 47–41.

VOL. CXIV..No. 39,156
© 1965 by The New York Times Company
Times Square, New York, N. Y. 10036

NEW YORK, THURSDAY, APRIL 8, 1965.

TEN CENTS

G.O.P. BLOCKS VOTE ON STATE BUDGET; FIGHTS SALES TAX

Governor's Program Cut in Senate, but Not Enough to Satisfy Republicans

WEEK'S DELAY IS LIKELY

Exemptions From 2% Levy Sought—City Housing Bill Sent to Rockefeller

By SYDNEY H. SCHANBERG
Special to The New York Times

ALBANY, April 7—The minority Republicans, maneuvering to water down Governor Rockefeller's sales-tax proposal, scuttled Democratic hopes of passing a state budget in the Senate today.

Approval of a sales tax is the key to passing the budget. Democratic amendments to exempt haircuts, laundry and other personal services from the sales tax were approved in the Senate today. The vote was 37 to 18, with 15 Republicans joining 22 Democrats in voting for the exemptions.

However, Republicans said they wanted even more exemptions. The Republican leader in the Senate, Earl W. Brydges, said that his side was not satisfied with the amended bill and would not vote for it.

When the day's political skirmishing was over, it appeared that before a sales tax is approved its scope will be reduced even further by the Republicans.

G.O.P. Help Needed

Though the Democrats have a majority in the Senate, the leadership cannot round up enough votes to approve a sales tax without Republican help.

In another development, the Legislature gave final approval to a bill that would help New York City recover the hundreds of thousands of dollars it spends to repair tenements.

The Senate Republicans are apparently delaying action on a budget for two reasons: to get their own amendments incorporated into the sales tax and to await a resolution of the situation in the Assembly, where the minority leader, George L. Ingalls, has been unable to line up much Republican support for the tax bill.

During a recess, Senator Brydges told reporters that the Republicans were considering "a lot" of additional amendments to ease the impact of Governor Rockefeller's proposed 2 per cent tax.

Among items the Republicans were thinking of exempting, Mr. Brydges said, were farm machinery and equipment, fuel used by manufacturers and the

Continued on Page 22, Column 1

ENGRAVERS' UNION AGREES TO A PACT

Accepts Same $12 Taken By Newspaper Printers

By DAMON STETSON

The publishers of seven of the city's daily newspapers reached an agreement with the photoengravers last night. The publishers' dispute with the printers was settled early yesterday morning.

The announcement of the engravers' accord was made after negotiations in the afternoon and evening.

The agreement expresses a money increase in terms of a wage percentage, which the union had asked for, rather than in absolute number of dollars. But John J. Gaherin, president of the publishers' association, and Frank A. McGowan, president of the photoengravers, agreed that the settlement was on the basis of a package increase valued at $12 a week over two years.

Mr. Gaherin and Mr. McGowan did not disclose the details of the agreement but said they would do so today. Mr. McGowan said he would recommend its acceptance to his members.

Negotiators for the publishers and the photoengravers met through the afternoon and early evening in an effort to conclude another agreement among the 10 unions that represent 17,000 employes on the

Continued on Page 42, Column 1

JETS HARASS BUNDESTAG MEETING: Soviet MIG fighter planes swoop over Congress Hall in West Berlin to protest first session of Parliament there in seven years.
United Press International Cablephoto

POWELL RETURNS TO FIGHT WARRANT

Ends Weekday Absences—Paroled in Fund Transfer Linked to Slander Case

By JACK ROTH

Representative Adam Clayton Powell came to New York yesterday. It was the first time in five months that he had been known to have set foot here on a weekday.

If the Harlem Democrat had come to New York on any day but a Sunday he would have been arrested. No legal process is served on Sunday.

Yesterday, Mr. Powell surrendered to answer a Criminal Court warrant that had been issued for his arrest on the charge of violating a section of the Penal Law by fraudulently transferring funds to his wife's name.

The warrant was issued on the basis of a complaint made against Mr. Powell by Mrs. Esther James, who had won a judgment against him for slander. He had called her a "bag woman," or graft collector, for the police. Mrs. James charged that Bertha Klausner, a literary agent, had sent to Mrs. Yvette Powell a $900 check that should have been sent to the Representative.

Mr. Powell appeared before Judge Arthur Braun. He was flanked by two of his lawyers.

Continued on Page 26, Column 3

Soviet Jets Harass Berlin As Bundestag Meets There

By ARTHUR J. OLSEN

BERLIN, April 7—Soviet jet fighters zoomed low over West Berlin's Congress Hall today in angry protest against the presence there of the West German Parliament. Communist authorities again blocked land access to the city for part of the day.

Throughout the four-hour session of Parliament, Communist aircraft—apparently executing a well-planned operation above the sleekly modern structure—crisscrossed at low altitude where the 100 West German Deputies were meeting. It was their first plenary session here of the Bonn Parliament in seven years.

Some of the politicians left the chamber to watch the show overhead.

The planes cracked windows throughout the city with sonic booms and shattered virtually every air safety regulation governing the skies above West Berlin.

[In Washington, the State Department assailed the Soviet flights as "dangerous and provocative." It also called in the Soviet Ambassador, Anatoly F. Dobrynin, to protest "in the strongest terms" Russian harassment of Berlin access routes and the flights over the city. Page 6.]

Continued on Page 6, Column 3

CORE TO OPPOSE WAGNER IN FALL

Re-election of Mayor to Be Fought With Bigger Rallies Than in '64, Group Says

By RICHARD WITKIN

City chapters of the Congress of Racial Equality announced yesterday they were unalterably opposed to the re-election of Mayor Robert F. Wagner. To dramatize their position, they plan a series of demonstrations, including an opening-day action at the World's Fair.

The CORE leaders said they were "declaring war" on the Mayor because of his "complete apathy," his "disregard for the Negro and Puerto Rican communities and the major problems" of the city.

The decision marked the first time a major civil-rights group had moved to defeat the Mayor for re-election. Such organizations have for the most part maintained a nonpartisan position in election campaigns.

The local CORE officials said they were not ready to support any alternative candidate. They were waiting to see who might indicate a readiness to go along with their program for better job opportunities, schools and houses and for measures to end alleged police brutality.

They also said no decision had been made on the kind of demonstration that would be conducted when the fair is opened April 21. It was probable, they said, that that and other demonstrations would be bigger than those conducted last year.

A request for comment from Mayor Wagner on CORE's de-

Continued on Page 24, Column 3

Strike Halts School Buses Here; Impact on Attendance Is Slight

By LEONARD BUDER

A wildcat strike by 1,000 drivers and mechanics left 81,350 public and parochial school pupils without bus service yesterday.

Leaders of the walkout said that the strike would continue until the men received guarantees that their jobs and accumulated benefits would be protected. The strikers are employes of the Children's Bus Service, which plans to go out of business at the end of June. The walkout had only a small impact on school attendance, according to Board of Education officials. No attendance checks were made, but a board spokesman said:

"Based on past experience, probably no more than 10 per cent of the pupils affected were absent because of the strike."

This would indicate that the number who missed classes was

Most of the children walked to school in the morning, despite the rain—or were transported in car pools or public conveyances. About two-thirds of the pupils carried by buses live "within a mile or slightly more of school and can walk to school in an emergency," the board spokesman said.

But thousands of handicapped pupils could not get to school. Some of these require buses that can accommodate wheel chairs.

"I realize that these drivers are going to lose their jobs but I think it is highly unfair of them to take it out on the children, particularly handicapped children who depend on the school buses," said the mother of a high school student confined to a wheel chair because of infantile paralysis.

Continued on Page 32, Column 4

PRESIDENT MAKES OFFER TO START VIETNAM TALKS UNCONDITIONALLY; PROPOSES $1 BILLION AID FOR ASIA

HANOI GETS ARMS

Chinese Now Reported Allowing Russians to Transship Materiel

By HENRY TANNER
Special to The New York Times

MOSCOW, April 7 — The Chinese Communists were reported tonight to have ceased putting obstacles in the way of Soviet arms shipments to North Vietnam.

Reliable diplomatic sources quoted high-ranking Soviet officials to the effect that negotiations with the Chinese on the subject of the transit of Soviet arms through China had been concluded satisfactorily and that weapons and missiles were flowing smoothly to the North Vietnamese.

The report came 10 days after Communist sources here had reported that the Chinese refused to grant permission for Soviet arms to be sent to Hanoi by air via Peking.

The same sources had quoted Soviet officials as having said that the Chinese were using obstructionist tactics to drag out negotiations on the transshipment of arms by rail. The Chinese negotiators insisted on the right to inspect the shipments, which are believed to include antiaircraft missiles, statements attributed to the Soviet officials said.

No Official Confirmation

The Soviet complaints were given wide distribution by circles close to the leadership here, but they were never repeated officially. Similarly, no official confirmation could be obtained for the reports that the difficulties had been overcome.

Discussing another phase of the Vietnam problem, President Anastas A. Mikoyan told Pakistani journalists tonight that the first requirement was for "the Americans to withdraw their forces and to stop killing innocent people."

He spoke to the correspondents at a reception given for Soviet officials by President Mohammad Ayub Khan of Pakistan, who has been here on a state visit since Saturday. The Pakistani Foreign Minister, Zulfikar Ali Bhutto, signed a trade agreement with the Soviet Union under which Soviet trade with Pakistan will double during the next three years. The agreement also calls for the shipment of farm machinery and industrial equipment to Pakistan.

Kosygin Denounces U.S.

By DAVID HALBERSTAM
Special to The New York Times

WROCLAW, Poland, April 7 — Premier Aleksei N. Kosygin of the Soviet Union condemned United States activities in Vietnam today and said "peace-loving nations will never forgive the United States imperialists' barbarism" there.

At the same time, Leonid I. Brezhnev, First Secretary of the Soviet Communist party, con-

Continued on Page 18, Column 3

Johnson's Speech Viewed As Bid to World Opinion

Washington Is Reported Shifting Stand in Effort to Tempt North Vietnamese Away From Aggressive Course

By MAX FRANKEL
Special to The New York Times

WASHINGTON, April 7 — Two discussion" and a "billion dollar major considerations were understood here to have prompted President Johnson's offer tonight to talk with anyone at any time about Vietnam.

One was a personal desire to yield to and appeal to opinion at home and abroad, to convey sincere hope for peace in Asia and to its appearance before the world. The pressures upon the President and his country were heartless, stubborn and unreasonable where peace was at stake.

The other was a wish within the Administration to venture another step forward in the complicated and subtle effort to bring North Vietnam to terms to suggest that Hanoi would profit from a settlement while emphasizing how Hanoi would suffer, largely alone, in further combat.

The offers of "unconditional

Continued on Page 17, Column 1

major considerations were understood here to have prompted Southeast Asia were chosen to drama-tize both these purposes. It was not just propaganda that led the Administration to take a position that it had long resisted, at considerable cost to its appearance before the world.

The pressures upon the President to say what he said tonight—that the United States would discuss the war in Vietnam so long as no conditions were set by any party have been immense.

Especially since the start of American air attacks upon North Vietnam two months ago, he has faced public and private demands for negotiations from leading Democrats and, largely alone, in further attacks from intellectuals.

STUDENT DEMAND GRANTED BY SPAIN

Regime, After 6 Weeks of Unrest, Decrees Reform of Academic Organization

Special to The New York Times

MADRID, April 7 — A reorganization of the university student's organization on a more representative basis was decreed today by the Spanish Government.

The decree followed a six-week drive by students at Spain's 13 university centers for a relaxation of Government controls over student affairs. It was approved last Friday by the Generalissimo Francisco Franco and his Cabinet.

The decree will allow students to elect all representatives to the governing councils of the Student Union, the principal demand of the students' agitation. Previously the national head of the organization and his immediate subordinates were appointed by the Government. With student-elected delegates limited to lower posts.

Continued on Page 10, Column 4

FIGHT WILL GO ON

President Says Saigon Must Be Enabled to Shape Own Future

Text of the speech by Johnson is printed on Page 16.

By CHARLES MOHR
Special to The New York Times

BALTIMORE, April 7 — President Johnson said tonight that the United States was ready to begin, without prior conditions, diplomatic discussions to end the war in Vietnam.

In a speech at Johns Hopkins University that was carried on television and radio, Mr. Johnson also said he would ask Congress to approve a $1 billion American investment in a vast Southeast Asian regional development program that eventually could include North Vietnam.

The President made it clear that while he would begin "unconditional discussions" for peace, any settlement in Vietnam demanded "an independent South Vietnam—securely guaranteed and able to shape its own relationship to all others."

He said, however, that South Vietnam could be a neutral state, "tied to no alliance, a military base for no country."

Two Months of Air Attacks

The speech, which came two months after the start of intensive American air strikes against North Vietnam, was the first statement of willingness by the United States to enter negotiations on Vietnam without prior conditions. Heretofore the Administration has said that negotiations could begin only after some "signal" from North Vietnam that it was willing to end aggression against its southern neighbor.

Government officials indicated that they had had no indication that either Hanoi or Peking would accept an invitation to unconditional talks.

High officials said that Mr. Johnson's use of the word "unconditional" meant "exactly what it says," and that the United States would be willing to enter into any kind of diplomatic contact with such Communist powers as North Vietnam and China even while the Vietcong continued to fight in South Vietnam.

The officials hinted that the United States might insist on

Continued on Page 16, Column 1

U.S.-JORDAN PACT ON ARMS AID NEAR

Talks With Israelis Advance Also as Washington Tries to Keep Mideast Stability

By JOHN W. FINNEY
Special to The New York Times

WASHINGTON, April 7 — The United States is nearing agreement with Jordan to supply additional arms, including tanks, to help modernize her army.

At the same time, after some initial negotiating difficulties, progress has been reported in talks between the United States and Israel over the purchase of American arms. It is expected that the two nations will reach agreement soon.

The pending arms agreements with two ostensibly hostile nations underline the dilemma facing the Johnson Administration in the Middle East arms race.

U.S. Being Pushed to Act

At the policy-making levels of the Administration there is a desire to curb the race, or at least not contribute to its acceleration by becoming a major supplier of arms to the Middle East.

But political and diplomatic factors are pushing the Administration into a more active role of supplying arms on a selective basis in an attempt to maintain a military balance and political stability in the Middle East.

The commissioner will also provide liaison between the students and the state.

The decree stipulates that political activity outside the student organization will be con-

Continued on Page 9, Column 3

Since 1957 the United States has provided Jordan with about $36 million in arms, and Jordan

Continued on Page 9, Column 3

800 POLICE BEGIN SUBWAY PATROL

Every Train and Station Is Guarded in Night Hours

By EMANUEL PERLMUTTER

A small army of policemen patrolled New York's crime-plagued subways last night and early today as a campaign opened to make them safer.

By 8 P.M. there was an armed patrolman on every train and station along the 237 miles of the subway system. They remained on duty until 4 o'clock this morning, working through the high hours of highest crime incidence.

The approximately 800 men in blue were a welcome sight to many of the nighttime riders of the subways, where there has been an increase of 106 per cent in muggings, assaults and other serious crimes since 1963.

Some passengers, immersed in newspapers or dozing fitfully, paid the police scant attention. But as many seemed openly pleased by their presence.

"People smiled and said they were glad to see me and that it was about time," Patrolman Fred Waldman reported as his IRT Lexington Avenue express pulled into South Ferry after a trip down from 180th Street.

Mrs. Robert Kane, a linotype operator at The New York Times, reported as she left an IND Eighth Avenue train at 175th

Continued on Page 43, Column 1

Head of Buddhist Sect Dies in a Tenement Here

Scholar and Former Ruler of 900 Lamas Was 82

By WILL LISSNER

In the living room of a tiny ground-floor rear flat in a shabby tenement at 204 East 32d Street, the Dilowa Hutukhtu—Living Buddha of the Yellow Sect of Mahayana Buddhism—died at 7:15 A.M. yesterday.

Once he was the spiritual and temporal ruler of 900 lamas, or monks, and the head of three lamaseries. For nine years he was also the governor of one of Outer Mongolia's four provinces. Then, after the Communists drove him into exile, he was able to spend three years in Lhasa, Tibet, as tutor to the present Dalai Lama, who is the head of the Yellow Sect.

At his death the distinguished Orientalist and Buddhist scholar was just an old man of 82 suffering from cancer, in exile among strangers. He was

Shabby Rooms Were a Home to Outer Mongolia Exile

The New York Times, 1955
The Dilowa Hutukhtu

died were the Most Rev. Da Lama, head of all Mongolian lamas at the court of the Dalai Lama in exile in Mussoorie, northern India; the Rev. Dornpa Jampal Dorje and the Rev. Napsang Chanjo from Outer Mongolia; and the Revs. Rabjampa Sandjejye, Yarphla Lharanpa and Basang Badmaev. Kalmuk lamas from the Soviet Union, who now live near Farmingdale, N. J.

These were joined by the Rev. Salting and the Rev. Baksha Menkov, who are also Kalmuk lamas.

All were clad in their robes, which consist of brown cassocks, surmounted by maroon tunics with a saffron blouse on top, and are partly covered by a maroon toga-like garment

Continued on Page 3, Column 1

U.S. planes bombarding Viet Cong hideouts 40 miles west of Hanoi.

A column of smoke rises from a burning Vietnamese Air Force helicopter, forced down by the Viet Cong.

"All the News That's Fit to Print"

The New York Times.

LATE CITY EDITION

VOL. CXIV .. No. 39,227. © 1965 by The New York Times Company. Times Square, New York, N. Y. 10036 NEW YORK, FRIDAY, JUNE 18, 1965. TEN CENTS

JOHNSON REPORTS DEFICIT REDUCED TO $3.8 BILLION

Figure Is $2.5 Billion Less Than January Estimate—Tax Cut Impact Cited

JOBLESS AREAS FEWER

President, at News Parley, Discloses Reclassification of 16 Manpower Centers

Transcript of news conference is on Pages 14 and 15.

By JOHN D. POMFRET
Special to The New York Times

WASHINGTON, June 17—President Johnson said today that the Federal budget deficit for the year ending June 30 would be about $3.8 billion, or $2.5 billion less than his estimate of last January.

The announcement was the third since April of a drop in the estimated deficit. It came at a rapid-fire 80-minute news conference in the President's White House office. [Opening statement, Page 14.]

Mr. Johnson commented on a wide variety of foreign and domestic issues, told some favorite stories and jokingly accused reporters crowded around his desk of stirring up trouble for him by writing that no one was opposing him.

Employment Gain

He also announced these further developments on the economic front:

¶The Labor Department has reclassified 16 major manpower centers to categories denoting lower unemployment. This reduced the number of major areas classified as having substantial unemployment to 22, the lowest figure since May of 1957 and 17 below the number thus classified a year ago.

¶A new report from the Budget Bureau shows that the Administration's program to cut the dollar drain of Government programs abroad has reduced the net balance-of-payments costs of these programs by 23 per cent, or $635 million, in the two years ending this June 30.

The President also congratulated Congress on passing the measure reducing excise taxes. He indicated that he would sign it soon.

Mr. Johnson said that the excise reductions would release about $1.75 billion in extra purchasing power into the economy during the rest of 1965 and another $1.75 billion next January.

The excise tax reduction, Mr. Johnson said, "will help maintain the steady growth of jobs

Continued on Page 15, Column 5

Goldwater Forms Group For Political Education

Asserts New Unit Will Not Be a 3d Party but Will Try to Guide Conservative Voters Away From Extremism

By TOM WICKER
Special to The New York Times

WASHINGTON, June 17—Barry M. Goldwater formally announced today a new "crusade of political education" designed to give the millions who supported him for President last year a "focus" for their political activities.

Mr. Goldwater insisted at a news conference here that the Free Society Association, of which he will be honorary chairman, was not the nucleus of a new political party and that he would not participate in any such movement.

Sources close to him said that a major purpose of the new "educational organization" would be to channel conservative voters and political action into a more moderate and acceptable force than the John Birch Society or other right-wing groups.

"I wish to make it crystal clear," Mr. Goldwater said in a prepared statement, "that the Free Society Association will perform no organizational tasks—no precinct, district, or other political subdivision task. It will back no candidates nor raise any money other than that needed for its research and educational efforts."

Nevertheless, there were reports of some dismay at the Republican National Committee's headquarters and in some organizations such as the American Conservative Union. Their officials were said to regard the Free Society Association as a

Continued on Page 20, Column 1

LAWN SPRINKLING IS BARRED IN CITY; SUMMONSES DUE

350 Inspectors to Enforce Rules on Saving Water—The Problem Worsens

By WILLIAM E. FARRELL

The watering of lawns, gardens, tennis courts, sidewalks and other surfaces was banned entirely yesterday by the Department of Water Supply, Gas and Electricity as part of an intensified campaign to conserve the city's dwindling water supply.

In a directive superseding one issued on April 19, Commissioner Armand D'Angelo prohibited the use of city water in sprinklers and other lawn devices and barred the use of hoses for any purpose other than fighting fires, unless special permission is obtained from him.

The earlier directive permitted the watering of lawns and gardens on Saturdays from 6 to 9 A.M. and 8 to 11 P.M.

Ban Is Immediate

The new order takes effect at once. The department said studies had shown that 200 million gallons of water were used every Saturday on lawns and gardens.

Mr. D'Angelo declared that it was "absolutely necessary to impose this restriction" because "the storage in our reservoirs is dropping daily and the water supply is growing progressively worse."

The latest figures from the department show that the city's reservoirs contain 256.4 billion gallons, or 53.8 per cent of capacity. Last year at this time there were 412.9 billion gallons in storage, or 86.7 per cent of capacity.

The Commissioner also announced that beginning Monday 350 inspectors would no longer give warnings to those who "willfully waste water."

Summonses to Be Given

Instead, summonses will be issued calling for a fine of up to $50 or 30 days in jail or both. A spokesman for the department said that it was expected that the police would aid the inspectors in issuing the summonses.

Mr. D'Angelo was interviewed as he ate lunch at his desk in his office in the Municipal Building. He said many owners of the 50,000 private swimming pools in the city "have indicated their displeasure" at his order barring the filling of noncommercial pools when the water now in the pools dropped below the reach of recirculating equipment.

"We're talking about hundreds of millions of gallons of water here," he said, explaining his reason for the order.

Continued on Page 36, Column 2

27 HEAVY BOMBERS FROM GUAM HIT VIETCONG FORCE IN SOUTH VIETNAM; WILSON WILL LEAD PEACE MISSION

United Press International Radiophoto

DESCRIBES CLASH: Comdr. Louis C. Page, right, relates details of duel over North Vietnam. With him are, from left: Lieut. Comdr. Robert C. Doremus; Lieut. Jack E. Batson Jr., his radar operator, and Lieut. John C. Smith Jr., radarman for Commander Page.

2 B-52'S ARE LOST

Missiles of Navy Jets Down 2 MIG-17's Close to Hanoi

By JOHN W. FINNEY
Special to The New York Times

WASHINGTON, June 17—Twenty-seven B-52's based on Guam carried out today—early Friday in Vietnam—the first attack by these heavy bombers in the war in Vietnam, the Defense Department announced tonight.

Thirty planes started out on the raid against a Vietcong concentration north of Bencat in Binhduong province, 30 miles north of Saigon. One B-52 went down about 100 miles northwest of Luzon Island in the Philippines after a collision with another B-52.

There was radio silence during the flight, and the fall of the second plane was not observed, so its fate was not known. But it was missing and was believed to have fallen into the sea.

One survivor from the first plane was rescued and others were sighted, the Pentagon said. The B-52's usually have crews of six men.

A third plane reached the target area but because of mechanical difficulties was unable to release its bomb load.

First Combat Use

The attack by the big, jet-powered bombers was the first mass bombing raid in Vietnam on World War II tactics. The action also marked the first use of the planes in combat.

[The Pentagon reported early Friday that the two B-52's that had collided on the way to Vietnam crashed; 27 of the bombers returned to the Guam base, and the plane that had mechanical trouble was diverted to Clark Air Base in the Philippines, The Associated Press said.

[Over North Vietnam, United States Navy jet fighters, using air-to-air missiles, downed two Communist MIG-17 fighters 40 miles south of Hanoi. Page 2.]

There was no immediate information on the effectiveness of the B-52 attack, which was carried out at the request of the Vietnamese Government.

In the bombing raids in Vietnam up to now, the United States has used tactical

Continued on Page 2, Column 5

Lindsay Urges Computers To Raise Police Efficiency

By RICHARD L. MADDEN

Representative John V. Lindsay proposed yesterday that the Police Department be "computerized" to increase its efficiency by as much as 20 per cent. "It is time we realized that the two-way radio is no longer the hottest innovation in law-enforcement circles," the Republican candidate for Mayor said.

To combat what he called "the crisis in crime," Mr. Lindsay said that the Police Department should employ, "on a top priority basis, the resources offered by planning and modern technology in communications and electronic data-processing systems."

Excerpts from Lindsay speech will be found on Page 21.

Second Police Proposal

Mr. Lindsay's proposal, called a major policy statement, was made in a luncheon speech to about 100 persons at a meeting of the Idlewild Lions Club in the International Arrivals Building at Kennedy International Airport.

It was the second of a series of Lindsay statements on law enforcement. On May 20 he proposed the addition of four civilians to the Police Department's board of three deputy commissioners for reviewing complaints of police brutality.

A spokesman for Police Commissioner Vincent L. Broderick said there would be no comment on Mr. Lindsay's latest proposals.

Talking with reporters after

Continued on Page 21, Column 6

MEDICARE REVISED TO HELP THE POOR

Senate Committee Rewrites Measure in Major Upset for the Administration

By JOHN D. MORRIS
Special to The New York Times

WASHINGTON, June 17—The Administration program of medical care for the aged was radically revamped by the Senate Finance Committee today to shift a greater share of the benefits to persons with low income.

The surprise action was a major upset for the Administration. If sustained by the Senate and House, it would have the effect of converting the program's basic concept from one of limited benefits for everyone over 65 years old to one of unrestricted benefits mainly to those in low-income brackets.

Patient Would Pay More

The committee adopted two fundamental amendments to the hospitalization and nursing-care provisions of the House-approved medicare bill. Both were sponsored by Russell B. Long of Louisiana, the Democratic whip, or assistant leader, of the Senate.

The first would remove all restrictions on the length of time a beneficiary could stay in a hospital or nursing home and on the number of home-nursing visits to which he would be entitled after discharge.

To offset the added cost to the Social Security insurance system, the second amendment would require the patient to pay a larger part of his hospital bill. The higher his income, the more he would have to pay.

The vote was 8 to 6 on the first amendment and 10 to 3

Continued on Page 18, Column 5

JOHNSON ACCUSES DOMINICAN REBELS

Charges Them With Seeking to Block Political Accord—Plan Expected Today

By RICHARD EDER
Special to The New York Times

WASHINGTON, June 17—President Johnson today accused the rebel side in the Dominican conflict of "flagrant violation" of the cease-fire that had been established in Santo Domingo.

Displaying considerable emotion, the President said at a news conference that elements on the rebel side had engaged in what appeared to be "premeditated" attacks on the inter-American peace-keeping force for the purpose of obstructing efforts toward a political settlement.

[In Santo Domingo it was expected that an inter-American peace plan calling for elections this year would be presented to both factions Friday. Page 10.]

As Mr. Johnson made his statement, the State Department moved to quell a report that had gathered considerable momentum among diplomatic circles here.

This report attributes to the

Continued on Page 10, Column 3

5 Commonwealth Nations To Seek Peace in Vietnam

By CLYDE H. FARNSWORTH
Special to The New York Times

LONDON, June 17—Leaders of the British Commonwealth decided today to take an initiative toward bringing the war in Vietnam to an end. Prime Minister Wilson of Britain and leaders of four other Commonwealth countries will visit the Governments principally concerned to try to lay the groundwork for a peace conference.

The mission will try to go to Peking and Hanoi as well as to Moscow, Washington and Saigon. There was no indication whether it would be received in Peking or Hanoi.

The Chinese Communists have rebuffed earlier initiatives toward a peace conference. In addition, Peking and Hanoi refused to give visas to former Foreign Secretary Patrick Gordon Walker, who undertook a peace mission on behalf of Britain earlier this year.

21 Nations at Conference

The decision to send the new mission was taken at the first day of the Commonwealth Prime Ministers' Conference in London, at which 21 countries, mostly in Asia and Africa, are represented. It was announced before President Johnson held a news conference at which the Vietnam issue was discussed.

The Prime Minister, as chairman of the Commonwealth conference, would head the mission. Those invited to participate are: President Kwame Nkrumah of Ghana, Prime Minister Sir Abubakar Tafawa Balewa of Nigeria, Prime Minister Eric E. Williams of Trinidad and Tobago, and Prime Minister Dudley Senanayake of Ceylon.

It was not yet clear whether all four would be able to accept. Mr. Senanayake is not at the conference, his country being represented by Minister of Justice A. F. Wijemanne.

The suggestion to send the mission came from Mr. Wilson, who opened the afternoon ses-

Continued on Page 3, Column 2

PRESIDENT SAYS HANOI BARS TALKS

Calls Reds Unresponsive—Reiterates Stand Against Dealing With Vietcong

By MAX FRANKEL
Special to The New York Times

WASHINGTON, June 17—President Johnson said today that North Vietnam had shown itself opposed to any kind of negotiations now and reiterated his stand against diplomatic dealings with the Vietcong in the south.

Expressing a strong wish to settle the war through discussions, the President said his Administration had found the Communist side wholly unresponsive. He predicted that its next move would be to try to force the United States to deal directly with the rebels.

He said that idea had been carefully studied here and rejected on the ground that negotiations were proper only with a recognized government. The Administration has condemned the hard core of the Vietcong as intruders from North Vietnam and therefore as mere agents of that country.

If the Vietcong have anything to offer or to negotiate, Mr. Johnson said at a news conference in his office, they would have no difficulty in finding a government with which to discuss it.

Mr. Johnson warmly endorsed

Continued on Page 2, Column 2

CONGRESS PASSES EXCISE TAX CUTS

Johnson Indicates He'll Sign $4.6 Billion Bill Quickly

Special to The New York Times

WASHINGTON, June 17—Congress approved today the final text of legislation for $4.6 billion in reductions on excise taxes on a wide variety of consumer goods.

Both the House and Senate acted by voice vote after brief discussions, sending the Administration-backed bill to the White House. President Johnson thus could sign it in time for shoppers to benefit this weekend.

The first big batch of cuts will take effect the day after the President signs the bill. He indicated at his news conference this afternoon that he would sign it quickly. [Opening statement, Page 14.]

If he signs tomorrow, about $1.75 billion annually in taxes on sales that occur after midnight tomorrow would be eliminated.

The bill, a compromise between versions passed June 2 by the House and two days ago by the Senate, provides for additional cuts of about $1.6 billion next Jan. 1, with other reductions scheduled for Jan. 1 in 1967, 1968 and 1969.

Under the bill, the reduction of the tax on passenger automobiles, which will fall from 10 per cent to 7 per cent, and the repeal of the 10 per cent levy on air-conditioners are

Continued on Page 22, Column 1

New Yorkers Face Record Realty Tax

By LAWRENCE O'KANE

The city's property owners can expect to pay a record basic tax of $4.54 for each $100 of assessed valuation next year.

The new basic tax, an increase of 13 cents above the current rate of $4.41, was indicated yesterday when figures for the taxable value of city property were released. In addition, property owners also will pay varying borough taxes.

William E. Boyland, president of the City Tax Commission, reported to Mayor Wagner that the total assessed value of taxable city property, beginning on July 1, would be $30,901,763,159.

This total is an increase of $1,149,023,050 above the 1964-65 figure. As usual the total was less than the tentative estimate released in February, which was $31,377,694,465 this

Continued on Page 21, Column 7

Astronauts Leave Today for Goodwill Trip Abroad

Associated Press Wirephoto

President Johnson receives flag carried on Gemini 4 flight from Maj. James A. McDivitt, left, and Maj. Edward H. White 2d. Vice President Humphrey is at center. President Johnson cited astronauts and Charles W. Mathews, right, manager of Gemini program office.

By ROBERT B. SEMPLE Jr.
Special to The New York Times

WASHINGTON, June 17—President Johnson said tonight that he was sending the Gemini 4 astronauts on another trip at 4 A.M. tomorrow, starting with the Paris Air Show. The President's announcement, made in the presence of the pair, was a climax to their 12-hour triumphal orbit of Washington today. This began with ceremonies in the White House Rose Garden this morning and ended—after a sudden change in flight plans—in the guest rooms three flights up. Along the way, Maj. James A. McDivitt and Maj. Edward H. White 2d received medals from the President, applause from a crowd lining Pennsylvania Avenue and the unabashed praise of Congressmen and diplomats. Charles W. Mathews, the manager of

Continued on Page 18, Column 1

Colleges Face U.S. Aid Cutoff If They Permit Fraternity Bias

By WALLACE TURNER
Special to The New York Times

DENVER, June 17—The terms of the Civil Rights Act of 1964 require individual colleges to make certain that fraternities do not discriminate on racial grounds, Francis Keppel, Commissioner of Education, declared today.

Under the legislation, Mr. Keppel could cut off all Federal funds to the colleges if they allowed the fraternities to continue discriminating.

His statement was in a letter to Senator Lee Metcalf, Democrat of Montana, who had asked about the situation involved in the suspension last April of the Sigma Chi chapter at Stanford University.

The suspension came in a letter from the national fraternity dated four days after a Negro student had accepted a bid to pledge the Stanford chapter.

The issue touches on the entire system of Federal grants to colleges and universities.

If Mr. Keppel found that a fraternity was practicing racial discrimination, he would then question the "assurances of compliance" filed by the schools under Title VI of the Civil Rights Act, which empowers Federal agencies to withhold funds from any recipients practicing discrimination. The

Continued on Page 24, Column 1

AILES RESIGNING AS HEAD OF ARMY

President Names Resor as Secretary's Successor

By MARJORIE HUNTER
Special to The New York Times

WASHINGTON, June 17—President Johnson announced today the resignation of Secretary of the Army Stephen Ailes and the choice of Stanley R. Resor as his successor.

Mr. Resor, a New York lawyer, has been Under Secretary of the Army since April 5 of this year. He is 47 years old.

Mr. Ailes is scheduled to testify tomorrow before a House Banking subcommittee that is investigating his connection with a concern that makes loans to servicemen.

The shift in the Army's top civilian post, effective July 1, was one of several personnel changes at the Pentagon and the White House announced today by the President at his news conference. [Opening statement, Page 14.]

Mr. Johnson disclosed the resignation of Kenneth E. BeLieu as Under Secretary of the Navy, effective July 1, and the choice of Robert H. B. Baldwin of New Jersey as his successor.

The President said that David E. McGiffert, now assistant to the Secretary of Defense for legislative matters, would replace Mr. Resor as Under Secretary of the Army.

The President also announced that two of his personal White House assistants, Horace Busby

Continued on Page 15, Column 2

NEWS INDEX

The B-52s that struck targets in Southeast Asia from bases in Guam needed 12 hours for flying time and refueling in the air. From the base at U-Tapao, Thailand, shown here, targets could be reached in two to five hours.

Loading bombs on a B-52's underwing pylons.

A bomb-laden B-52D takes off from the switchback runway at Guam. The B-52Ds carried up to 70,000 pounds of bombs.

U.S. Air Force B-52 bomber en route to an enemy target in South Vietnam.

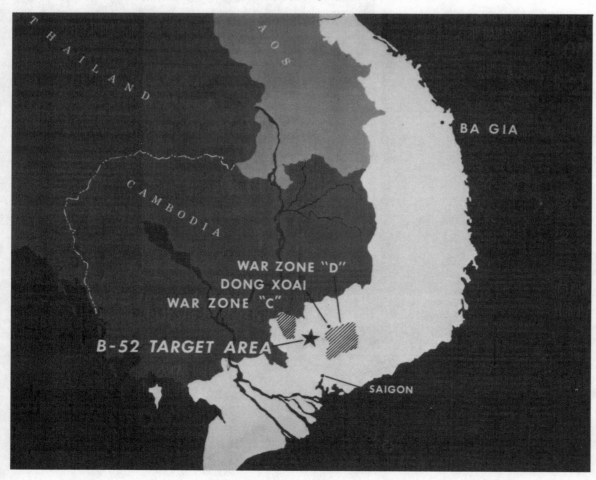

A map of South Vietnam indicating B-52 target areas aimed at flushing out enemy concentrations.

"All the News That's Fit to Print"

The New York Times.

LATE CITY EDITION

VOL. CXIV. No. 39,248. © 1965 by The New York Times Company Times Square, New York, N. Y. 10036 NEW YORK, FRIDAY, JULY 9, 1965. TEN CENTS

LODGE TO RETURN AS SAIGON ENVOY; TAYLOR RESIGNS

Associated Press
Henry Cabot Lodge

The New York Times
Maxwell D. Taylor

YEAR'S TERM ENDS

Shift Linked to Prior Agreement—Policy Held Unchanged

Johnson-Taylor exchange of letters is on Page 2

By MAX FRANKEL
Special to The New York Times

WASHINGTON, July 8 — President Johnson nominated Henry Cabot Lodge today to resume the position of Ambassador to South Vietnam, in place of Maxwell D. Taylor.

Mr. Taylor, who replaced Mr. Lodge in Saigon a year ago, pleaded personal obligations in asking the President to accept his resignation. He reminded Mr. Johnson of his commitment to serve only a year.

In a warm and grateful response, Mr. Johnson said he had acquiesced "only" because he felt bound to honor the one-year limit upon which they had agreed.

Defense Secretary Robert S. McNamara and Mr. Lodge will fly to Saigon Wednesday to confer with Mr. Taylor and to bring their own impressions up to date. The Ambassador-designate will then return to Washington for a round of briefings before assuming his post in mid-August.

Letters' Contents Stressed

Administration sources said the exchange of letters between Mr. Taylor and the President gave the real reasons for the shift. No fundamental policy changes are envisioned or implied by the move, officials said.

Although Mr. Taylor has given military advice on the Vietnamese war far beyond that which would customarily come from an ambassador and although he was among the early advocates of a greater American involvement, all decisions, even on relatively minute matters of tactics, have been made by President Johnson and four or five of his principal advisers here.

These men, above all Secretary of State Dean Rusk, Secretary of Defense McNamara and McGeorge Bundy, special Presidental assistant for national security affairs, will continue to be the main policy counselors.

At the same time, officials acknowledged that the return of Mr. Lodge, a prominent liberal Republican, could have an important bearing on the conduct of United States diplomacy in Saigon and might have considerable political significance. While loyally supporting the Administration's military

Continued on Page 2, Column 3

WHITE MAN IS SHOT BY NEGRO IN CLASH IN BOGALUSA, LA.

Police Jail Rights Marcher in an Unidentified Town—Victim in Critical State

TENSION RISES IN AREA

Assailant Said to Belong to Deacons for Defense—2d Negro Is Arrested

By ROY REED
Special to The New York Times

BOGALUSA, La., July 8—A Negro shot and seriously wounded a white man who attacked him today during a civil rights march on a downtown street.

Police Chief Claxton Knight said the Negro was believed to be a member of the Deacons for Defense and Justice, an armed Negro organization formed last spring to defend Negroes against white terrorists.

The white man, Alton D. Crowe Jr., 25 years old, of Pearl River, La., 35 miles south of here, was rushed to a hospital with two bullet wounds, one in the chest and one in the neck. His condition was listed as critical.

He was transferred to New Orleans Charity Hospital for possible emergency surgery.

His wife, Evelyn, accompanied him. They have five children, ranging in age from 5 years to 10 months. Mr. Crowe is employed in a Kaiser Aluminum plant in nearby Chalmette.

Tensions Are Increased

The man who fired the shot and a second Negro were arrested at the scene and taken to an unidentified town to protect them from angry whites.

A small crowd of whites shouted threats while policemen held the Negroes. Some whites attacked news photographers.

The shooting tightened tensions in this racially unsettled papermill town. A small group of white men talked grimly among themselves outside the City Hall and police station. Others stood silently on the downtown streets, their eyes watchful and their lips set hard.

Two rallies were held here tonight, one by the Bogalusa Civic and Voters League, which is leading the Negro movement, and the other by the National States Rights party, a white supremacist, anti-Semitic organization with headquarters in Birmingham.

Gov. John J. McKeithen dispatched 150 additional state troopers to the city at the re-

Continued on Page 13, Column 2

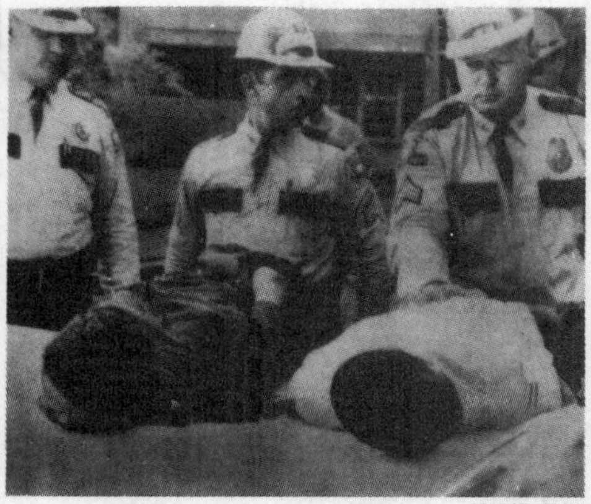

Associated Press Wirephoto

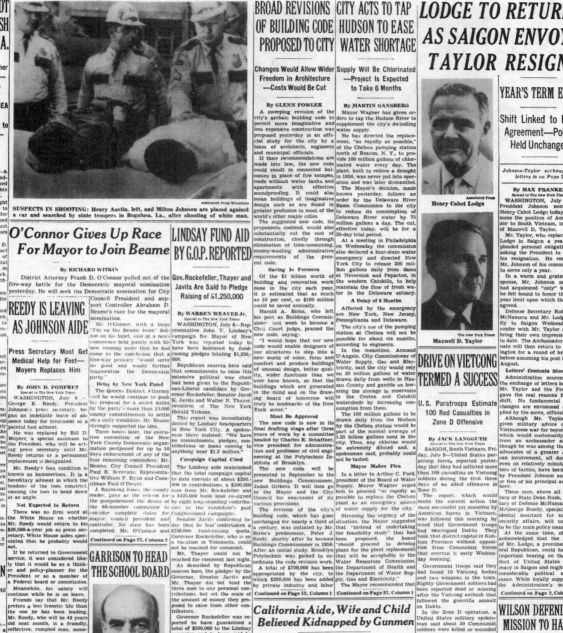

SUSPECTS IN SHOOTING: Henry Austin, left, and Milton Johnson are placed against a car and searched by state troopers in Bogalusa, La., after shooting of white man.

O'Connor Gives Up Race For Mayor to Join Beame

By RICHARD WITKIN

District Attorney Frank D. O'Connor pulled out of the five-way battle for the Democratic mayoral nomination yesterday. He will seek the Democratic nomination for City Council President and support Controller Abraham D. Beame's race for the mayoral nomination.

Mr. O'Connor, with a large "I'm on the Beame team" button on his lapel, said at a news conference held jointly with his new running mate that he had come to the conclusion that a five-way primary "would serve no good and would further fragmentize the Democratic party."

Delay by New York Panel

The Queens District Attorney said he would continue to push his proposal for a secret ballot by the party's more than 15,000 county committeemen to settle on a unity candidate. Mr. Beame strongly supported the idea.

Three hours later, the executive committee of the New York County Democratic organization postponed for up to 10 days endorsement of any of the four remaining contenders: Mr. Beame, City Council President Paul R. Screvane, Representative William F. Ryan and Councilman Paul O'Dwyer.

J. Raymond Jones, the county leader, gave as the reason for the postponement the desire of the 66-member committee to consider complete slates for mayor, council president and controller. No slate has been completed. Mr. O'Connor and

Continued on Page 27, Column 2

REEDY IS LEAVING AS JOHNSON AIDE

Press Secretary Must Get Medical Help for Feet—Moyers Replaces Him

By JOHN D. POMFRET
Special to The New York Times

WASHINGTON, July 8 — George E. Reedy, President Johnson's press secretary, began an indefinite leave of absence today for treatment of a painful foot ailment.

He was replaced by Bill D. Moyers, a special assistant to the President, who will be acting press secretary until Mr. Reedy returns or a permanent replacement is designated.

Mr. Reedy's foot condition is known as hammertoes. It is a hereditary ailment in which the tendons of the toes constrict, causing the toes to bend down at an angle.

Not Expected to Return

There was no firm word at the White House on whether Mr. Reedy would return to his $28,500-a-year job as press secretary. White House aides speculated that he probably would not.

If he returned to Government service, it was considered likely that it would be as a thinker and policy-planner for the President or as a member of a Federal board or commission.

Meanwhile, his salary will continue while he is on leave.

Friends say that Mr. Reedy prefers a less frenetic life than the one he has been leading. Mr. Reedy, who will be 48 years old next month, is a friendly, reflective, rumpled man, somewhat in the professorial tradition. His friends say he sometimes thinks he would like to make the resemblance a reality.

The new acting press secretary is an ordained Baptist minister who, at 31 years of

Continued on Page 11, Column 3

LINDSAY FUND AID BY G.O.P. REPORTED

Gov. Rockefeller, Thayer and Javits Are Said to Pledge Raising of $1,250,000

By WARREN WEAVER Jr.
Special to The New York Times

WASHINGTON, July 8—Representative John V. Lindsay's campaign for Mayor of New York was reported today to have been bolstered by fund-raising pledges totaling $1,250,000.

Republican sources here said that commitments to raise this extensive political war chest had been given to the Republican-Liberal candidate by Governor Rockefeller, Senator Jacob K. Javits and Walter N. Thayer, president of The New York Herald Tribune.

This report was immediately denied by Lindsay headquarters in New York City. A spokesman there insisted: "We have no commitments, pledges, contributions or loans coming to anything near $1.2 million."

Campaign Capital Cited

The Lindsay aide maintained that the total campaign capital to date consists of about $200,000 in contributions, a $100,000 loan from Mr. Rockefeller and a $425,000 bank loan co-signed by eight long-standing contributors to the candidate's past Congressional campaigns.

Senator Javits confirmed today that he had undertaken a $250,000 fund-raising quota. Governor Rockefeller, who is on a vacation in Venezuela, could not be reached for comment.

Mr. Thayer could not be reached for comment last night.

As described by Republican sources here, the pledges by the Governor, Senator Javits and Mr. Thayer did not bind the three men to any personal contributions, but set the scale of the amount of money they proposed to raise from other contributors.

Governor Rockefeller was reported to have guaranteed a total of $500,000 to the Lindsay campaign and to have said he would advance $100,000 as a ready cash fund while he is soliciting the $500,000.

Mr. Thayer's quota is also understood to be $500,000. This total was scaled down from an original figure of $650,000 after

Continued on Page 27, Column 5

BROAD REVISIONS OF BUILDING CODE PROPOSED TO CITY

Changes Would Allow Wider Freedom in Architecture—Costs Would Be Cut

By GLENN FOWLER

A sweeping revision of the city's archaic building code to permit more imaginative and less expensive construction was proposed yesterday in an official study for the city by a team of architects, engineers and municipal officials.

If their recommendations are made into law, the new code could result in connected balconies in place of fire escapes, roofs without water tanks and apartments with effective soundproofing. It could also mean buildings of imaginative design such as are found in greater profusion in most of the world's other major cities.

The suggested new code, its proponents contend, would also substantially cut the cost of construction, chiefly through elimination of time-consuming, money-wasting administrative requirements of the present code.

Saving Is Foreseen

Of the $1 billion worth of building and renovation work done in the city each year, it is estimated that as much as 10 per cent, or $100 million could be saved annually.

Harold A. Birns, who left his post as Buildings Commissioner last week to become a Civil Court judge, praised the new code, saying:

"I would hope that our new code would enable designers of our structures to step into a new world of color, form and comfort and produce buildings of unusual design, better quality, wider functions than we ever have known, so that the buildings which are generated in the mind and on the drawing board of tomorrow will truly be landmarks of the New York scene."

Must Be Approved

The new code is now in its final drafting stage after three years of work by a committee headed by Charles E. Schaffner, vice president for administration and professor of civil engineering at the Polytechnic Institute of Brooklyn.

The new code will be presented in September to the new Buildings Commissioner, Judah Gribetz. It will then go to the Mayor and the City Council for enactment of its various provisions.

The revision of the city's building code, which has gone unchanged for nearly a third of a century, was initiated by Mr. Birns's predecessor, Peter J. Reidy, shortly after he became Buildings Commissioner in 1958. After an initial study, Brooklyn Polytechnic was picked to coordinate the code revision work.

A total of $700,000 has been appropriated by the city, to which $200,000 has been added by private industry and labor

Continued on Page 12, Column 1

CITY ACTS TO TAP HUDSON TO EASE WATER SHORTAGE

Supply Will Be Chlorinated—Project Is Expected to Take 6 Months

By MARTIN GANSBERG

Mayor Wagner has given orders to tap the Hudson River to supplement the city's dwindling water supply.

He has directed the replacement, "as rapidly as possible," of the Chelsea pumping station north of Beacon, N. Y., to provide 100 million gallons of chlorinated water every day. The plant, built to relieve a drought in 1950, was never put into operation and was later dismantled.

The Mayor's decision, made known yesterday, follows an order by the Delaware River Basin Commission to the city to reduce its consumption of Delaware River water by 75 million gallons a day. The cut, effective today, will be for a 30-day trial period.

At a meeting in Philadelphia on Wednesday the commission also declared a four-state water emergency and directed New York City to release 200 million gallons daily from dams at Neversink and Pepacton, in the western Catskills, to help maintain the flow of fresh water in the Delaware estuary.

A Delay of 6 Months

Affected by the emergency are New York, New Jersey, Pennsylvania and Delaware.

The city's use of the pumping station at Chelsea will not be possible for about six months, according to engineers.

In the meantime, Armand D'Angelo, City Commissioner of Water Supply, Gas and Electricity, said the city would rely on 30 million gallons of water drawn daily from wells in Nassau County and gamble on lowering the storage in reservoirs in the Croton and Catskill watersheds by increasing consumption from them.

The 100 million gallons to be drawn daily from the Hudson by the Chelsea station would be part of the normal average of 1.25 billion gallons used in the city. Thus, any chlorine would be extremely diluted and, a spokesman said, probably could not be tasted.

Mayor Makes Plea

In a letter to Arthur C. Ford, president of the Board of Water Supply, Mayor Wagner urged him to proceed "as rapidly as possible to replace the Chelsea plant as an emergency source of water supply for the city."

Stressing the urgency of the situation, the Mayor suggested that "instead of undertaking the feasibility study" that had been proposed, the board "should proceed to develop plans for the plant replacement that will be acceptable to the Water Resources Commission, the Department of Health and the Department of Water Supply, Gas and Electricity."

The Mayor recommended that

Continued on Page 32, Column 1

DRIVE ON VIETCONG TERMED A SUCCESS

U.S. Paratroops Estimate 100 Red Casualties in Zone D Offensive

By JACK LANGGUTH
Special to The New York Times

SAIGON, South Vietnam, Friday, July 9—United States paratroop forces reported yesterday that they had inflicted more than 100 casualties on Vietcong soldiers during the first three days of an allied offensive in Zone D.

The report, which would make the current action the most successful yet mounted by American forces in Vietnam, was followed this morning by word that Government troops had reoccupied Dakto. They took that district capital in Kontum Province without opposition from Communist forces that overran it early Wednesday morning.

Government troops said they had found 10 Vietcong bodies and two weapons in the town. Eighty Government soldiers had been reported dead or missing after the Vietcong ambush that followed the guerrilla assault on Dakto.

In the Zone D operation, a United States military spokesman said about 50 Communist soldiers were killed or wounded Wednesday and their bodies carried off by their colleagues through an intricate system of tunnels. Another group of about 50 Vietcong guerrillas were killed later in the day, he added.

The spokesman said the cost

Continued on Page 3, Column 6

JOHNSON WARNS OF LONG SESSION

Would Hold Congress Until November for Program

By DAVID S. BRODER
Special to The New York Times

WASHINGTON, July 8—President Johnson warned a group of lawmakers today that he might hold Congress in session until November to pass his entire legislative program for the session.

He was quoted as telling members of the Washington State delegation who visited the White House today that there were a hundred bills he wanted enacted before adjournment.

"If I have my way," the President was reported to have said, "you're going to be here until November."

The President's remarks came as a surprise. Democratic Congressional leaders had held out the hope of adjournment by Labor Day.

The meeting was an off-the-record social and briefing session, and members of the delegation refused to confirm publicly the President's remarks.

However, word of his views began to spread after the delegation returned to Capitol Hill. A reliable source said the President's plans had been confirmed by the House Democratic leadership.

The last official word of adjournment plans came last Thursday from the Senate Democratic leader, Mike Mansfield of Montana. He told his colleagues they should be "prepared to continue to operate with the deliberate speed and effectiveness" of the last six months

Continued on Page 10, Column 5

Baruch Left Bulk Of Estate to School

By ROBERT E. TOMASSON

The bulk of Bernard M. Baruch's multimillion-dollar estate will be given in grants and loans to students attending City College's Baruch School of Business and Public Administration, it was disclosed yesterday.

Lawyers representing the estate declined to estimate its value after filing Mr. Baruch's will for probate in Surrogate's Court in Manhattan. Following standard procedure with large estates, its value was characterized as being "in excess of $1 million."

A final accounting was expected to take a year or longer.

The 23-page will was dated May 20, one month before Mr. Baruch died here at the age of 94.

Five trust funds totaling $1.75

Continued on Page 60, Column 1

GARRISON TO HEAD THE SCHOOL BOARD

The New York Times
Lloyd K. Garrison

By GENE CURRIVAN

The Board of Education, which has been without a president for more than a week, announced yesterday the election of Lloyd K. Garrison to fill the post.

At the same time the board named its newest member, Alfred A. Giardino, to succeed Mr. Garrison as vice president.

The action was taken at an informal session Wednesday night and will be ratified formally at the next regular meeting on July 21.

Although the election of Mr. Garrison was considered virtually certain in view of the stature he has attained on the board, it carries with it a new significance because of his re-

Continued on Page 16, Column 1

Dean Gildersleeve Of Barnard Dead

By The Associated Press

CENTERVILLE, Mass., July 8 — Virginia C. Gildersleeve, dean emeritus of Barnard College, the women's branch of Columbia University, died last night at the age of 87. She had been in a nursing home here for the last year.

There are no known immediate survivors.

An Academic Leader

Miss Gildersleeve, who was dean of Barnard College for more than 36 years until 1947, was regarded as one of the country's foremost educators. But she was much more besides.

Intensely interested in foreign affairs, she played a leading role in several international organizations. Her role was later recognized when she became the only woman delegate from the United States to the

Continued on Page 29, Column 2

California Aide, Wife and Child Believed Kidnapped by Gunmen

By The Associated Press

SACRAMENTO, Calif., July 8—California's top appointive official, his wife and their baby daughter vanished early today. Gov. Edmund G. Brown said he believed they were kidnapped by two armed Oregon ex-convicts fleeing from murder, bank robbery and kidnapping charges.

A search was under way throughout the Far West for State Finance Director Hale Champion, 42 years old, his wife, Marie, 39, and their 19-month-old daughter, Katherine Marie. Governor Brown said:

"I'm sure that these felons, acting irrationally, are using them as hostages. I believe and police believe, too, that they have been kidnapped."

The Governor referred to Mr. Champion as "my closest friend."

The Federal Bureau of Investigation said there was "an obvious presumption" that the Champions had been seized by the ex-convicts at the Champions' home and forced to flee with them at gunpoint. To avoid harm to the Champions, the California Highway Patrol warned the police not to stop the 1962 Green Ford Galaxie.

Capt. L. G. Williams of the Highway Patrol said the Champions disappeared from their Sacramento home between midnight and 6 A.M. Their absence was not discovered until Mr. Champion failed to keep a 9 A.M. appointment with Governor Brown in the State Capitol.

The Champions' 10-year-old son, Tommy, was found asleep at home, with no knowledge of what had happened. The home is about four miles from where the fugitives were last seen.

Mr. Champion, a former Sacramento Bee and San Francisco Chronicle reporter, became Governor Brown's press secretary in 1959 and State Finance Director in 1961.

The gunmen, both released from Oregon State Prison last week, are Wilfred Marion Gray, 30 years old, and Carl Cletes Bowles, 24. They are accused of robbing a Portland bank of $14,000 on Tuesday and murdering Deputy Sheriff Carlton E. Smith that night. The deputy had stopped their car near Springfield, Ore.

Shortly after Deputy Smith was gunned down with a shot-

Continued on Page 15, Column 1

F.C.C. Will Tell TV To Tune Down Ads

By JACK GOULD

Loud commercials that jolt the television viewer out of his electronic euphoria will be officially frowned upon by the Federal Communications Commission in a statement of policy to be issued either today or next week.

In the first direct governmental assault on excessively noisy pitches and selling blabs, the regulatory agency will declare that the public interest demands a decline in jarring loudness over the airwaves.

A spokesman for the F.C.C. confirmed that the policy statement was now being circulated among the commissioners for their individual signatures and that its formal release would then follow.

The chief purpose of the F.C.C. policy statement is to

Continued on Page 59, Column 2

WILSON DEFENDS MISSION TO HANOI

Commons in Heated Debate Over Dispatch of Davies

By ANTHONY LEWIS
Special to The New York Times

LONDON, July 8—A political and diplomatic storm blew up today over Prime Minister Wilson's dispatch of a left-wing Labor Member of Parliament to North Vietnam.

The news leaked early this morning that Harold Davies, parliamentary secretary at the Ministry of Pensions, was on his way to North Vietnam. He was said to be going to try to persuade Hanoi to admit a four-man Commonwealth mission that seeks to mediate the Vietnam war.

Confusion and conflict over the trip mounted during the day.

Government sources said Mr. Davies had been invited by the Government in Hanoi and was going officially. Two North Vietnamese journalists who arranged the trip for him insisted that there had been no invitation and that it was a private visit.

Conservative leaders pressed Mr. Wilson in the House of Commons to clarify the issue. When they warned against any move toward "appeasement," they set off a bitter partisan

Continued on Page 2, Column 1

NEWS INDEX

The New York Times.

LATE CITY EDITION
U.S. Weather Bureau Report (Page 70) forecasts:
Fair today; becoming cloudy tonight; cloudy tomorrow.
Temp. Range: 84—69; yesterday: 78—69.
Temp.-Hum. Index: around 75; yesterday: 73.

VOL. CXIV...No. 39,267. © 1965 by The New York Times Company, Times Square, New York, N. Y. 10036   NEW YORK, WEDNESDAY, JULY 28, 1965.   TEN CENTS

CELEBREZZE QUITS; EDUCATOR TO GET HIS CABINET POST

John W. Gardner, Carnegie Corporation President, to Head Welfare Agency

CHOICE WINS APPROVAL

Johnson Hails the Retiring Secretary, Who Will Be Appointed U.S. Judge

By ROBERT B. SEMPLE Jr.
Special to The New York Times

WASHINGTON, July 27 — President Johnson announced today the resignation of Anthony J. Celebrezze as Secretary of Health, Education and Welfare and named John W. Gardner to replace him.

Mr. Celebrezze resigned to accept a Federal judgeship.

Mr. Gardner has been president of the Carnegie Corporation for the last 10 years and is regarded as one of the most influential figures in American education.

The President announced the Cabinet change at a brief ceremony this morning in the Rose Garden outside his office. As Mr. Celebrezze and Mr. Gardner looked on, Mr. Johnson praised the outgoing Secretary as a man who had "widened the dimensions of his adopted land" and his successor as a man who had been, "for all of his adult life, an explorer in the search for excellence."

Vacancy in 6th Circuit

Mr. Johnson said that within a few days he would nominate Mr. Celebrezze to fill an impending vacancy in the United States Court of Appeals for the Sixth Circuit, which has its headquarters in Cincinnati. If approved by Senate, Mr. Celebrezze will replace Judge Lester L. Cecil of Dayton, Ohio, who is resigning Aug. 1.

Mr. Celebrezze was serving his fifth consecutive term as Mayor of Cleveland when named by President Kennedy in 1962 to head the Department of Health, Education and Welfare. He confided to friends in recent weeks that if an opening occurred he would like to return to Ohio and accept a judgeship.

Mr. Gardner, who is a Republican, served as chairman of the White House Conference on Education last week. He also served on a special education study group established by President Kennedy in late 1960 and headed the study group on education established last July by Mr. Johnson to make policy recommendations.

The selection of Mr. Gardner as Mr. Celebrezze's successor was widely applauded here today, although his willingness to accept the post came as a surprise to some of his friends.

In his capacity as a private citizen, he has played such a

Continued on Page 18, Column 4

GOVERNORS BACK A SCHOOL COMPACT

Endorse Interstate Panel to Improve Education

By DAVID S. BRODER
Special to The New York Times

MINNEAPOLIS, July 27 — The nation's Governors pledged their support today to a cooperative effort to improve the quality of American education.

They endorsed a report urging a formal national compact for education. Twenty-six of the Governors signed individual statements promising to send representatives to a meeting in September to create a clearinghouse for innovations in education from the grade school level through the university.

The Governors also asked President Johnson to renew his study of the possibility of turning back a share of Federal tax collections to the states.

The closely related problems of education and finance dominated the day's agenda of the 57th annual National Governors' Conference.

In a speech at a conference banquet tonight, Vice President Humphrey warned the Governors that the step-up in the Vietnam war would "touch the lives of thousands of American families.

Continued on Page 32, Column 5

NEW CABINET MEMBER: John W. Gardner, left, with President Johnson, who named him Secretary of Health, Education and Welfare, and Anthony J. Celebrezze, whom he is to succeed. They are shown at White House, Mr. Celebrezze is to become a Federal judge.

United Press International Telephoto

U.S. Is Suing for Damages In Glass Fiber Trust Case

By FRANKLIN WHITEHOUSE

The Government filed suit in Federal Court here yesterday to recover damages from six textile companies accused of trying to fix prices and rig bids in sales of glass fiber fabrics used in the aerospace and missile programs.

The amount of the alleged damages was not specified in the civil suits, but a Government lawyer said it might run into millions of dollars.

The defendants had pleaded no contest in January and March to a criminal information charging a similar conspiracy in the field. The companies, and several of their officers, were fined a total of $106,000.

Defendants Listed

The defendants are Burlington Industries, Inc., J. P. Stevens & Company, Inc., United Merchants & Manufacturers, Inc., and Clark-Schwebel Fiber Glass Corporation, all of New York City; Exeter Manufacturing Company, Inc., Exeter, N. H., and the Coast Manufacturing and Supply Company, Livermore, Calif. No individuals were named in the complaint.

In two actions on Friday and Monday, 10 steel companies that had been allowed to change their pleas from not guilty to nolo contendere (no contest) were fined by Federal judges.

"We are in the process of trying to reconsider policy as to when a nolo plea will be accepted and when it won't," said Donald F. Turner, chief of the Justice Department's antitrust section said.

"There has been a feeling in the last few years in the Justice Department not to accept nolos when there are a large number of private parties who have been damaged by alleged conspiracies," he said in a telephone conversation.

Mr. Turner said there were about 80 to 100 antitrust cases in all industries still pending across the country.

The Justice Department contended that yesterday's defendants held secret meetings in various New York hotels and restaurants in which they agreed to fix prices and rig bids in sales of fabric to such governmental organizations as the National Aeronautics and Space Administration, the Philadelphia

Continued on Page 47, Column 2

EARNINGS OF G.M. HIGHEST IN WORLD

If '65 Sales Pace Continues, 12-Month Net Will Exceed Record Set by A.T.&T.

By RICHARD RUTTER

Dramatic evidence of the strength of the national economy and particularly of the boom in the automotive industry came yesterday in the latest profit statement of the General Motors Corporation.

General Motors in both the second quarter and first half of 1965 showed the largest earnings of any corporation in history.

If the present trend of record new-car sales continues, G.M. will easily top the existing 12-month record in profits of any company. The record now is held by the American Telephone and Telegraph Company, which earned $1.76 billion in the year ended on May 31.

Donner-Roche Statement

In a separate development, the United States Steel Corporation reported yesterday its best second-quarter and first-half earnings in five years. U. S. Steel in the second quarter registered a profit of $81 million. For the first half of this year, earnings totaled $154.8 million.

G.M., the biggest manufacturing enterprise in the world, reported that its operations in the second quarter and first half of 1965 set records for unit sales, dollar sales, earnings, dividends, employment and payrolls.

Frederic G. Donner, chairman, and James M. Roche, president, in a joint statement said net income in the second quarter rose to $639 million, or $2.23 a share, from $602 million, or $2.11 a share, in the 1964 period. Sales in the latest period

Continued on Page 47, Column 4

State Democrats Replace McKeon With Burns, Binghamton Mayor

By RICHARD L. MADDEN

Mayor John J. Burns of Binghamton was elected by acclamation yesterday as Democratic State Chairman to succeed William H. McKeon.

The election was unopposed at a meeting of the 300-member Democratic State Committee at the National Democratic Club here. After he was chosen, Mr. Burns said "the biggest task is to unite the party."

A measure of that task came a few minutes after Mr. Burns was elected when State Controller Arthur Levitt attacked the record of the Democratic-controlled Legislature.

Mr. Levitt echoed the appeal for unity, but he told the state committee that the Legislature had displayed "a sorry, inconsistent record" on state finances. He said that there was a lack of "courage" to reduce Governor Rockefeller's budget

effectively and that most of the budget cuts were later restored.

The Democratic Controller was applauded when he called for repeal of the "obnoxious" 2 per cent statewide sales tax enacted by the Legislature.

Mr. Levitt also criticized the Legislature for not taking "a truly bipartisan approach" to reapportionment of legislative districts.

"The majority of the Legislature was inadequate here [the softened the word "defaulted," which had been in his prepared text] in a high responsibility and the punishment is correspondingly severe," he declared. It was an apparent reference to the special legislative session ordered this fall by a Federal District Court under a Republican

Continued on Page 39, Column 2

BRITAIN TO SLASH RATE OF SPENDING TO PROTECT POUND

Austerity Move in Defense, Building and Credit Aimed at Speeding Deflation

By CLYDE H. FARNSWORTH
Special to The New York Times

LONDON, July 27 — Tough austerity measures were introduced today to speed deflation and to convince foreign creditors of the nation's determination not to devalue the pound.

The Government is risking unpopularity at home, since the measures could tighten the financial squeeze on the public.

The most important action was to slow the increase in public spending. Other measures tightened installment-buying controls and affected exchange controls, imports and exports.

The public-spending measure will hit particularly hard at local government bodies, which have been taking vast sums from the Treasury and borrowing heavily in financial markets to build everything from new roads to schools to swimming pools. Only the most essential spending projects will now be permitted.

In addition, home mortgages granted by local authorities are to be cut back. This will affect many prospective homeowners.

Defense Cutback Set

The national Government and nationalized industries, meanwhile, are to defer capital spending projects, and defense spending next year will be cut by £100 million ($280 million).

The effect of these measures will be to hold public spending within an annual increase of 4¼ per cent.

This year it was headed much higher. Last year total public spending reached £11.5 billion.

Observers of the British economic scene have long contended that failure to curb public expenditures was the weak link in the Government's earlier efforts, including budgets last April and November, to defend sterling.

The public will also feel the effects of the tighter controls on installment buying. The maximum repayment period is to be reduced from three years to 30 months, which means monthly payments will be increased.

Callaghan Announces Steps

The Labor Government actions on exchange controls, imports and exports are aimed at a direct and immediate improvement in the balance of payments.

The Chancellor of the Exchequer, James Callaghan, announced the measures in the House of Commons in a 14-minute statement punctuated occasionally by "ah's" and "oh's" from the Conservative benches.

The general feeling of the Opposition was that the measures had to come, and probably should have come sooner. Some of the Labor benches were restive, and Parliamentary experts said the Government might have trouble selling the measures to its supporters.

Left-wing Laborites pointed-

Continued on Page 3, Column 2

HEATH IS ASSURED OF TOP TORY POST

Gets Majority on First Vote for Leader—Maudling and Powell Withdraw

By ANTHONY LEWIS
Special to The New York Times

LONDON, July 27 — Edward Heath, a tough professional politician with reformist ideas about Britain's future, appears certain to be the new leader of the Conservative party.

He took a commanding lead today on the first ballot for the Tory leadership. There must be a second ballot, but his is likely to be the only candidacy when nominations close tomorrow.

Mr. Heath polled 150 votes among the 298 Conservative members of the House of Commons who cast ballots. Reginald Maudling had 133 and Enoch Powell 15. Five members were absent.

Under the new Conservative party rules, Mr. Heath had to have a margin of 15 per cent of the ballot over the runner-up. On the second ballot a simple majority wins.

Opposition Disappears

Mr. Maudling cut through the elaborate procedure by dropping out of the race and all but assuring Mr. Heath's election. Mr. Powell withdrew also.

"We are in the process of" possibilities said they would not enter on the second ballot.

Mr. Maudling heard the news at his bank, Kleinwort, Benson Ltd., where he was lunching with his fellow directors. He immediately telephoned Mr. Heath and promised his support.

It was a dramatic end to the first elective leadership race in the Tories' history. They formerly were said to have let a leader "emerge" from private meetings — a process much criticized when it produced Sir Alec Douglas-Home as leader in 1963.

After Sir Alec's resignation last Thursday, Mr. Heath had at first been rated the front-runner to succeed him. But Mr.

Continued on Page 3, Column 3

U.S. RAIDS 2 MISSILE SITES IN VIETNAM, WRECKING ONE; JOHNSON TO SPEAK TODAY

COUNTERTHRUST: The Pentagon issued this map on missile sites in North Vietnam. Newly revealed ones, designated 6 and 7, were attacked by U.S. planes. Others, numbered 1 through 5, surround Hanoi. The map does not denote five more reported at the port of Haiphong. The arrow marks where a plane was downed last Saturday.

SIX PLANES LOST

Strike 40 Miles West of Hanoi Follows Downing of Jet

By HANSON W. BALDWIN
Special to The New York Times

WASHINGTON, July 27 — United States Air Force jet fighter-bombers, attacking at low level, destroyed one antiaircraft missile site 40 miles west of Hanoi and damaged another early today, the Pentagon said.

It was the first attack on such sites in North Vietnam.

The attack followed the loss of an F-4C Phantom jet fighter last Saturday and damage to three other Phantoms. The Pentagon confirmed that the Phantom had been downed by a missile launched from the ground.

The attacked sites were described by the Pentagon as "recently constructed" and "semimobile." Arthur Sylvester, Assistant Secretary of Defense for Public Affairs, interpreted this to mean that the missiles could be set up and made operational within 24 to 48 hours.

The attack, covered by an unspecified number of fighters flying at high altitudes, was made by 46 F-105 fighter-bombers. The Defense Department announced the loss of three F-105's through "intense conventional ground fire," and Hanoi claimed the downing of six planes and the capture of three pilots.

Two Planes Collide

The Pentagon said pilots had seen two parachutes. Congressional sources insisted that six planes had been lost and that one pilot had been rescued. They said that three of the aircraft were shot down and that at least one other was severely damaged.

On its way back to base, according to these sources, the damaged plane collided with another F-105 and both were lost. The sources added that a sixth plane, on a reconnaissance mission over the missile sites, was shot down.

On Saturday a formation of four F-4C's were flying at an altitude between 20,000 and 30,000 feet in an area west of Hanoi that was well beyond the range of the five missile sites known to be emplaced around North Vietnam proper.

A salvo of two SAM-2 surface-to-air missiles of Soviet design was fired at them. One of the missiles destroyed an aircraft and caused minor damage to three others.

Intensive photographic and communication reconnaissance

Continued on Page 2, Column 2

President, on TV, to Give Results of Policy Review

By JOHN D. POMFRET
Special to The New York Times

WASHINGTON, July 27 — President Johnson will report to the nation tomorrow on the results of the Administration's intensive review of United States policy in Vietnam. The White House would not say whether the President would announce any major decisions.

Mr. Johnson will deal with Vietnam in his opening statement on a nationally televised news conference at 12:30 P.M.

[A Georgia newspaper said that a 15,000-man Army division at Fort Benning has been packing its gear to move to South Vietnam, United Press International reported. Page 2.]

Legislators Called

For the first time in a week of discussions with top military and foreign policy advisers on Vietnam, Mr. Johnson brought Congressional leaders into the recess, with the United States consultations tonight. He met with House and Senate leaders of both parties at the White House.

Senator Mike Mansfield, the majority leader, said later: "The President will make his decision and he will do his very best on behalf of the country and leave no stone unturned to seek an honorable settlement that will safeguard Southeast Asia and allow it to go its own independent way."

The President planned to meet tomorrow morning with Democratic and Republican leaders of the House and Senate appropriations, armed services and foreign relations committees.

These committees would be involved in reviewing any Presidential request to Congress for authority to summon reservists to active military duty.

They would also have to pass

Continued on Page 4, Column 3

17-NATION PARLEY ON ARMS RESUMES

U.S. and Soviet Agree Time Is Running Out for Accord but Clash on Solutions

By M. S. HANDLER
Special to The New York Times

GENEVA, July 27 — The disarmament conference reconvened today at the Palais des Nations after a 10-month recess, with the United States and Soviet delegations agreeing that time was running out for curbing the nuclear danger to world peace. But they strongly disagreed on how this danger should be restrained or averted.

In a message to the conference, President Johnson described nuclear control and disarmament "as the most important task on earth." He also told the delegates that "if we man, nothing is more important than the effort to diminish the weapons of war under increasing control."

The President's message was read by William C. Foster, head of the United States delegation to the 17-nation conference.

"No difference among any of our nations, on any other issue, can be allowed to bar agreement in this critical area," the President continued. "This is not in any single nation's interest, nor is it in the interest of the multitude of nations and peoples whose future is so tied to the good sense of those at this conference table."

Mr. Johnson spoke of the four

Continued on Page 4, Column 3

POMPIDOU REJECTS ROLE OF E.E.C. UNIT

Stand Indicates Continued Common Market Crisis

By HENRY TANNER

PARIS, July 27 — France is determined to retain full control of her economy and will not accept dictation from the international civil servants working for the European Economic Community, Premier Georges Pompidou declared tonight.

His remarks, in a rehearsed television interview, marked the first detailed, official French statement on the Common Market crisis.

The Premier gave the impression that France would not permit a solution of the crisis on any terms but her own.

It was obvious from his statement that he did not expect an early solution. This was in keeping with earlier semiofficial

Continued on Page 6, Column 4

Policeman Cleared In Negro's Slaying

By DAVID ANDERSON

A Brooklyn grand jury found yesterday that a young white policeman who shot and killed a Negro ex-convict in Brooklyn July 15 had "acted in a lawful and justifiable manner in defense of himself."

District Attorney Aaron E. Koota presented the case to the jurors—4 women and 18 men, all white—10 days ago, when it became apparent that witnesses were giving several conflicting versions of the shooting.

The prosecutor's prompt action was praised in many quarters because Bedford-Stuyvesant, where the shooting took place, has been the scene of racial violence in the past.

The ex-convict was slain as he grappled with the patrolman

Continued on Page 39, Column 4

APPEARS CERTAIN OF TORY LEADERSHIP: Edward Heath leaving his London apartment yesterday for House of Commons, where Conservative party is choosing leader.
Associated Press Radiophoto

U.S. troops on a mop-up operation in the jungles of South Vietnam following a massive bombing by U.S. B-52s to flush out Viet Cong guerrilla bases.

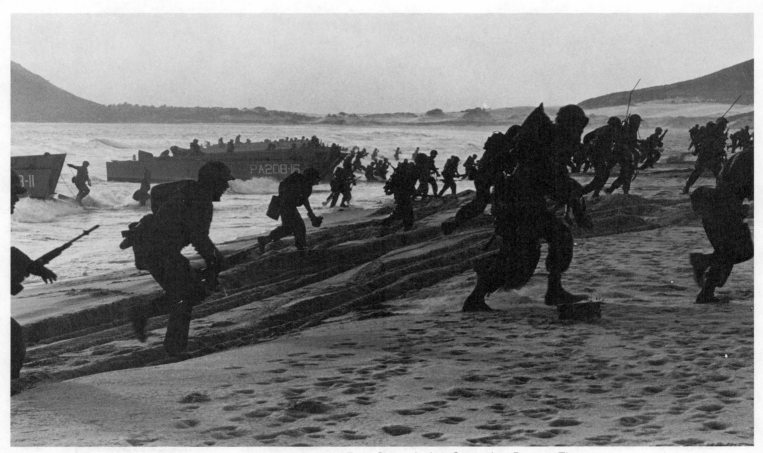

A wave of U.S. infantry men come ashore at the beach at Tam Quan during Operation Dagger Thrust.

**QUI VINH RR BR
9 APRIL 1965**

DESTROYED SPAN

Destroying North Vietnamese bridges and roads was a major goal of the U.S. and South Vietnam. Here, a photograph of the Qui Vinh Railroad Bridge after its destruction by South Vietnamese forces.

U.S. Marines wade ashore at Da Nang. These were the first land combat troops committed by the U.S. to South Vietnam.

"All the News That's Fit to Print"

The New York Times.

LATE CITY EDITION
U.S. Weather Bureau Report (Page 56) forecasts.
Cloudy with showers today, tonight; sunny tomorrow.
Temp. Range: 78—67; yesterday: 83—62.
Temp.-Hum. Index: 72—61; yesterday: 74.

VOL. CXIV..No. 39,268.   © 1965 by The New York Times Company. Times Square, New York, N. Y. 10036   NEW YORK, THURSDAY, JULY 29, 1965.   TEN CENTS

FORTAS TAKING GOLDBERG SEAT ON HIGH COURT

LIBERAL IS NAMED

Lawyer First Refused Post, Then Acceded to President's Plea

By ROBERT B. SEMPLE Jr.
Special to The New York Times

WASHINGTON, July 28—President Johnson today named his long-time friend Abe Fortas, the Washington lawyer, to succeed Arthur J. Goldberg on the Supreme Court.

Mr. Fortas's appointment, in the view of students of the Court, means that there probably will be no appreciable change in the liberal course charted by the Court since 1962, when Mr. Goldberg replaced Justice Felix Frankfurter.

It also keeps alive the tradition of a Jewish seat on the Court. Justice Louis D. Brandeis was appointed in 1916, and Justice Benjamin Cardozo was appointed in 1932. Justice Cardozo was succeeded by Justice Frankfurter, who was Mr. Goldberg's predecessor.

Mr. Goldberg resigned from the Court last week to become, at Mr. Johnson's request, the United States representative at the United Nations. There was immediate and widespread speculation that Mr. Fortas would be named to replace him, particularly in view of his close relationship with the President and his immense prestige in the legal profession.

First Choice for Post

However, officials here, including at least one Cabinet member and the President's press secretary, Bill D. Moyers, tried hard to dampen this speculation. Thus, until yesterday it was generally assumed that, despite the earlier rumors, Mr. Fortas had either withdrawn himself from consideration or had not been considered at all.

Today informed sources said that Mr. Fortas was not only the President's first choice, as Mr. Johnson disclosed at his news conference, but was also the only man to whom he had offered the job.

The President, in announcing his first appointment to the Supreme Court, said, "In this instance, the job has sought the man." [Opening statement, Page 12.]

Mr. Johnson made his first overture to Mr. Fortas Monday evening, July 19, the same night that he asked Mr. Goldberg to take the United Nations assignment. At that time the offer was conditional on Mr. Goldberg's taking his new post.

When Mr. Goldberg agreed to the President's request to

Continued on Page 13, Column 1

U.S. RULE DEFIED BY JERSEY COURT

Weintraub Is Supported on Admitting Confessions

By SIDNEY E. ZION

The New Jersey Supreme Court, in a unanimous decision, has supported its Chief Justice's defiance of a Federal court ruling on confessions.

The decision upheld the murder convictions of two youths who had confessed without having been advised of their constitutional rights.

The ruling, which was handed down July 12 but which has not yet been published in official court reports, creates a Federal-state judicial conflict that will be appealed to the United States Supreme Court—the only court that can finally resolve the dispute.

The conflict arose May 20 when the United States Court of Appeals for the Third Circuit, covering New Jersey, Pennsylvania and Delaware, reversed two New Jersey murder convictions because the police had not advised the defendants, before taking their confessions, of their right to counsel and their right to remain silent.

Two weeks later, Chief Justice Joseph Weintraub of the New Jersey Supreme Court sent

Continued on Page 17, Column 1

U.S. AIRLINES TOLD TO PUT PROSPERITY INTO LOWER FARES

C.A.B. Also Tells Carriers to Add Coach Seats and Allow Free Stopovers

By FREDRIC C. APPEL

The Civil Aeronautics Board told the nation's airlines yesterday that they were making too much money and should start passing some of it on to the consumer in the form of lower fares and better service.

The board said it thought the following improvements could be made:

¶Lower fares on short trips. The board noted that the new short-range jets now coming into use had lower operating costs that could make possible lower fares over routes such as that between New York and Washington.

¶More coach seats. The board suggested a higher ratio of coach seats to first-class seats to reflect the public's desire. Last year 76 per cent of domestic air passengers flew coach, according to the Air Transport Association. The board also called for more coach service into more communities.

¶More service to smaller cities. This suggestion was apparently a reaction to a hearing, ended two weeks ago, by the Senate Aviation subcommittee, in which the airlines were severely criticized for neglecting the less profitable service to smaller cities.

¶Additional economy services on highly traveled routes.

¶Free stopover privileges. With such privileges, a man flying from New York to Los Angeles might stop in Chicago for a few days at no extra cost. The board, which abolished these privileges in 1958 when the airlines were having financial problems, said that now that the airlines' finances had improved, they should be revived as a method of stimulating vacation travel in the United States and from abroad.

No Reaction Yet

There has been no official reaction from the airlines yet, but one industry source privately predicted "a very strong" one.

Addressing itself to air fares, the board virtually told the airlines to forget about any increases and concentrate on reductions.

After first noting that the rate of return of the 11 domestic trunk carriers had risen to 10.6 per cent in the 12 months ended March 31, 1965, the board said:

"In this setting, the board believes it is difficult to find justification for fare increases. Rather, the C.A.B. feels, the present favorable earnings position of the airlines offers an excellent opportunity for carriers themselves to consider reductions in fares or improvements in service without fare

Continued on Page 56, Column 5

HOUSE VOTES END OF UNION SHOP BAN

Acts, 221 to 203, to Repeal Part of Taft-Hartley Law —Labor Is Jubilant

By MARJORIE HUNTER
Special to The New York Times

WASHINGTON, July 28—The House handed organized labor its biggest victory in years by voting today to outlaw state "right to work" laws. The vote was 221 to 203.

The bill now goes to the Senate, where passage is expected.

The measure seeks repeal of Section 14(b) of the Taft-Hartley Act of 1947. Under this 44-word section, states are permitted to pass laws that forbid labor contracts making union membership a condition for keeping a job.

Nineteen states, most of them in the South and Midwest, now have such "right to work" laws.

The House action marked another in a long string of Administration victories. President Johnson had pledged he would seek repeal of 14(b) this year.

Forecast Off by One Vote

The final vote closely tallied with an informal count made months ago by union lobbyists. They said then that they could count on 222 votes for repeal—just one more than today's tally.

Voting for repeal were 209 Democrats and 21 Republicans. Voting against were 117 Republicans and 86 Democrats.

Labor leaders were jubilant at the outcome, for it was the first pro-labor legislation involving the internal affairs of unions since the House since World War II.

During that period, two major labor laws have been enacted over bitter protests of organized labor. The Taft-Hartley Act of 1947 created categories of unfair labor practices by unions for the first time. The Landrum-Griffin Act of 1959 imposed internal controls on union operations.

Amendments Rejected

Administration forces held firm against a barrage of amendments offered by Republicans and a lone Democrat, Representative Edith Green of Oregon.

The amendments were held as "not germane" by the presiding officer, Representative Leo W. O'Brien, Democrat of upstate New York.

Discovering that avenue closed, the House minority leader, Gerald R. Ford of Michigan, asked that the bill be sent back to the House Education and Labor Committee.

"This body today is precluded from working its will," he protested. "The people are not having their day in court."

The Ford motion for recommittal was defeated, 223 to 200.

"We're being paralyzed," rep.

Continued on Page 6, Column 4

LETTER TO THANT

Goldberg Delivers It— U.S. Would Discuss Hanoi's 4 Points

Johnson's letter to U Thant is printed on Page 10.

By TOM WICKER
Special to The New York Times

WASHINGTON, July 28—The United States has asked the United Nations to employ its "resources, energy and immense prestige" in finding ways "to halt aggression and to bring peace in Vietnam," President Johnson said today.

The President conveyed this request to U Thant, the Secretary General of the United Nations, in a letter delivered by Arthur Goldberg, the new United States representative.

The letter contained Mr. Johnson's "hope that the members of the United Nations, individually and collectively, will use their influence to bring to the negotiating table all governments involved in an attempt to halt all aggression and evolve a peaceful solution."

The President described the action in a statement at his news conference. [Opening statement, Page 12.]

Opportunity Is Seized

High Government sources expressed no great confidence that the United Nations, acting as a body, could find a way to bring the Vietnamese question to the conference table.

They said, however, that the President wished to seize the opportunity of Mr. Goldberg's arrival at the United Nations to emphasize that the United States would welcome any possible initiatives and to give him a chance to work on the matter with strong backing from the White House.

In addition, the sources said the possibility was not discounted that new emphasis on the United Nations might lead to "corridor talk" or informal meetings between delegates that would be useful in working toward negotiations.

For months Mr. Thant has been trying behind the scenes to initiate negotiations but has met with rebuffs from Hanoi and Peking.

Mr. Johnson emphasized again that the United States' objective in Vietnam still was a negotiated settlement, not the military defeat of North Vietnam. That settlement, he again made plain, could be based on

Continued on Page 10, Column 1

John Chancellor of N.B.C. Named Director of the Voice of America

Johnson Selects White House Reporter as First Working Newsman in the Post

By LLOYD GARRISON
Special to The New York Times

WASHINGTON, July 28—John W. Chancellor, White House correspondent for the National Broadcasting Company, was named by President Johnson today to head the Voice of America.

The 38-year-old reporter and broadcaster succeeds Henry Loomis, the long-time director of the Government's overseas radio, who resigned last March with a charge that the Voice was losing credibility because of an overdose of propaganda.

This controversy was discussed in connection with Mr. Chancellor's appointment. Reliable sources said that he and President Johnson had talked at length on the role of the Voice and that Mr. Chancellor would be free to emphasize the bad as well as the good in the treatment of United States affairs.

In a farewell address to Voice employees, Mr. Loomis contended that the Voice's reputation for objectivity was being undermined because the United States Information Agency, which has over-all responsibility for overseas broadcasts, was insisting

John W. Chancellor after his appointment yesterday.

that news commentaries reflect and reinforce Administration policies and de-emphasize dissenting opinion.

Carl T. Rowan, the head of U.S.I.A., countered that news reports of the Voice had the same "judicial balance" of the favorable and unfavorable "that a responsible newspaper gives."

Mr. Rowan later resigned as U.S.I.A. director and on July 13 Mr. Johnson named Leonard H. Marks, a Washington communications lawyer, to succeed him.

In announcing Mr. Chancel-

Continued on Page 15, Column 4

JOHNSON ORDERS 50,000 MORE MEN TO VIETNAM AND DOUBLES DRAFT; AGAIN URGES U. N. TO SEEK PEACE

PRESENTS CREDENTIALS AT U.N.: Arthur J. Goldberg, right, the new United States representative at the United Nations, with U Thant, the Secretary General.

Associated Press

ECONOMIC IMPACT IS CALLED SLIGHT

Prosperity Cited by Johnson in Rejecting Declaration of National Emergency

By EDWIN L. DALE Jr.
Special to The New York Times

WASHINGTON, July 28—The moderate increase in the war effort in Vietnam announced today by President Johnson will impose no noticeable strain on the national economy, high economic officials said today.

In answer to a question on this point at his news conference, Mr. Johnson said he was certain the American people would face "whatever it is necessary to face." [Question 4, Page 12.] But he cited the current prosperity and added:

"I see no reason for declaring a national emergency and I rejected that course of action earlier today when I made my decision."

War Days Recalled

Mr. Johnson had been asked whether he believed the nation would face the choice of "guns or butter." The exchange brought to mind the days of World War II when rationing was in effect and some materials, such as butter, gasoline, food and clothing, were in short supply.

The economic impact of the Vietnam war so far has been minimal. Today's decision will increase in defense spending and military manpower will leave it minimal, officials believe, though a few defense industries will be affected.

The extra effort is not expected to put any notable strain on the nation's supply of labor, its plant capacity for production or its budgetary resources, top officials said after the President's announcement.

Several measures of the relatively small impact of the expanded war effort were cited.

Revenues Are Growing

The increase of 17,000 in monthly draft calls compares with an expected growth of the labor force this year of 1,250,000. It also compares with a regular monthly turnover of about 115,000 workers in the nation's manufacturing industries alone, and at least five times that for the economy as a whole. And it compares with a currently unemployed total of 3.5 million.

The prospective increase in defense spending is generally put in the range of $2 billion to $3 billion during the fiscal year that has just begun, and almost certainly no more than $5 billion. The Government's revenues, with no change in tax rates, now grow by $7 billion a year with an expanding economy, or more than enough to accommodate the defense increases.

The moderate rise in defense outlays will probably enlarge somewhat the prospective small

Continued on Page 15, Column 6

Most in Congress Relieved By the President's Course

By E. W. KENWORTHY
Special to The New York Times

WASHINGTON, July 28—Most members of Congress received President Johnson's statement on the Vietnam crisis today with a sense of relief. First, there was general satisfaction that the President had decided to increase the draft and postpone a decision on calling up reserve units. Second, there was approval of his avowal to seek an honorable resolution of the conflict through the United Nations.

These feelings were especially keen in those members who have circumspectly voiced doubts and reservations about the course of Administration policy since last February, when the President made the decision to bomb selected military installations in North Vietnam.

'Honorable Settlement'

Mike Mansfield of Montana, the Senate Democratic leader, spoke the sentiments of many of these members when he said the President had spoken in a "calm and deliberately measured manner" and was plainly desirous of "seeking an honorable settlement."

Even before Secretary of Defense Robert S. McNamara went to Saigon two weeks ago, there had been an expectation that the President would call up some Army and Marine Corps reserve units. This belief became firmer during the first days of intense review of military needs following the Secretary's return.

Consequently, it was widely believed on Capitol Hill today that the President had "backed off" this decision in the last few days.

Some of the leaders who attended one or both of the meetings with the President last night and this morning thought there were three reasons for

Continued on Page 11, Column 2

City Faces 'Order' To Meter Water

By HOMER BIGART
Special to The New York Times

PHILADELPHIA, July 28—New York City may be forced to adopt universal metering as a condition of its further use of Delaware River water.

The Delaware River Basin Commission accepted today a report by its advisory council recommending that universal metering be "ordered" by the commission throughout the basin and its service area.

That report, according to one committee member, was designed to prod Mayor Wagner into an early decision to impose metering on New Yorkers regardless of political consequences.

The Mayor has been reluctant to sponsor universal metering. At present New York compels water meters only for business, which accounts for

Continued on Page 57, Column 1

NO RESERVE CALL

Additional Troops Will Be Sent as Needed, President Says

Transcript of news conference and summary, Page 12.

By JOHN D. POMFRET
Special to The New York Times

WASHINGTON, July 28—President Johnson announced today that United States military strength in South Vietnam would be increased from the present 75,000 men to 125,000 "almost immediately."

Draft calls, Mr. Johnson said, will be gradually raised to 35,000 men a month from the current rate of 17,000 and the campaign for voluntary enlistments will be stepped up.

However, the President said at a nationally televised news conference at the White House that it was not necessary now to order reserve units into active duty. [Opening statement, Page 12.]

The purpose of Mr. Johnson's announcement was twofold: to disclose the military measures being taken in the Vietnam war and to emphasize the desire of the United States for negotiations on ending the conflict.

The President opened his statement by quoting a letter he had received recently from "a woman in the Midwest." She wrote that she had a son in Vietnam and that her husband had served in World War II, and she concluded: "Our country was at war, but now, this time, it is just something that I don't understand that."

He Tries to Meet Question

The President said he had tried to answer that question dozens of times. "Let me again now discuss it," he said, and continued with his statement.

Mr. Johnson announced that the United States was asking the United Nations to make a major effort to bring peace to South Vietnam. He also said that the United States was prepared to discuss the peace proposals put forward by the Government of North Vietnam.

The 50,000-man increase in United States forces in Vietnam is considerably smaller than some Congressional and military sources had expected. It apparently does not involve military units beyond those already alerted for service in South Vietnam.

The President said that additional forces would be needed later and would be sent as requested. He did not specify how many more troops would be needed. Qualified sources said it was impossible to estimate the number because it would depend on the extent of the fighting.

The President said that he ordered the First Cavalry Division (Airmobile) to Vietnam today, as well as other forces. The Airmobile Division, which had been tentatively marked for Vietnam service, began

Continued on Page 11, Column 1

HANOI PREPARES PEOPLE FOR WAR

Defense Minister Says U.S. May Invade North—Soviet Scores Johnson Speech

By SEYMOUR TOPPING
Special to The New York Times

SAIGON, South Vietnam, July 28—North Vietnam has begun to prepare its people for possible involvement in a full-scale war with the United States.

The Hanoi leadership, in its statements and in domestic propaganda, is demonstrating growing concern about the build-up of United States troop strength in South Vietnam. Gen. Vo Nguyen Giap, the Defense Minister, has warned that these troops might be used in an invasion of North Vietnam.

These North Vietnamese developments preceded President Johnson's announcement today that United States forces in Vietnam would be enlarged.

[The Moscow radio said President Johnson was taking a "colossal risk" in increasing American armed strength in Vietnam, The Associated Press reported. Page 9.]

No Big Expansion Noted

Apart from a decision taken by Hanoi in April to extend the tour of duty of conscripts indefinitely, no reports have been received here by United States officials of any rapid expansion of the North Vietnamese Army to meet a United States invasion. North Vietnamese men are normally drafted into the 250,000-man army for three-year terms and subsequently enrolled in the militia of 1.5 million.

A Youth Volunteer Brigade made up of men between 17 and 30 years old was founded on July 7 for defense duty. Detachments have been identified in connection with work on such projects as road-building, repair of bridges and other emergency tasks.

Since the systematic United States bombings of North Vietnam began on Feb. 19, Hanoi has been gradually mobilizing the population. Women have been organized to do the work of men called away for defense duty.

General Giap, writing in the current issue of Hoc Tap, the theoretical journal of the Lao Dong, or Communist, party, declared: "We need to make every preparation to defeat the United States aggressors in South Vietnam.

Continued on Page 11, Column 1

White Youth Is Shot Near Georgia Rally

By GENE ROBERTS

AMERICUS, Ga., Thursday, July 29—A white teen-ager was shot in the head from a car early today three blocks from a night-long civil rights protest rally in the rain.

Police officers and witnesses said that a Negro was the assailant.

The shooting took place near a street corner where only an hour before a group of about 20 white youths had been yelling "nigger, nigger," and hurling stones and bottles at passing Negroes.

Wounded in the shooting was Andy Whatley, 19 years old, a projectionist at an Americus drive-in theater.

Dr. R. A. Collins, an Americus surgeon, called his condition "critical—very bad," and transferred him to an Albany hospital, 40 miles away. Dr. Collins

Continued on Page 15, Column 1

69

"All the News That's Fit to Print"

The New York Times.

LATE CITY EDITION
U.S. Weather Bureau Report (Page 59) forecasts:
Warm, humid, showers later today; warm, humid tonight and tomorrow.
Temp. Range: 86—73; yesterday: 86—72.
Temp.-Hum. Index: near 80; yesterday: 79.

VOL. CXIV—No. 39,289. NEW YORK, THURSDAY, AUGUST 19, 1965. TEN CENTS

ACCORD REACHED BY HANOVER BANK IN ANTITRUST SUIT

Compromise on Merger Set With Justice Department —Court to Study Plan

WALL ST. IS SURPRISED

Agreement Is Announced by Katzenbach — Up to 40 Branches Would Close

By ROBERT FROST

Attorney General Nicholas deB. Katzenbach disclosed yesterday that the Manufacturers Hanover Trust Company had reached agreement with the Government on a plan to settle the antitrust suit pending against the bank.

The compromise is reported to involve the giving up of as many as 40 of the bank's branches.

In a statement that took a large part of the financial community by surprise, Mr. Katzenbach told the House Banking Committee the settlement was "entirely satisfactory to the Government."

When asked by Representative Wright Patman, Democrat of Texas, chairman of the committee, what the plan covered, Mr. Katzenbach said the bank had requested that he not disclose the details. Mr. Patman then agreed not to press for further data.

Branches at Stake

However, neither the bank nor the Department of Justice would confirm the reports of the divestiture plan.

The suggestion that the divestiture might involve as many as 40 branches was offered by a Justice Department spokesman. Banking sources here felt that the total was more likely to be about "two dozen."

Manufacturers Hanover has 135 branches, the same number that it had at the end of 1961, the year that the Manufacturers Trust Company and the Hanover Bank were merged.

As a result of the merger, Manufacturers Hanover became the fourth largest bank in the nation, ranking behind the Bank of America, the First National City Bank and the Chase Manhattan Bank.

If the bank is forced to divest itself of some branches, it may do so either by selling them to other banks or by using them as a nucleus in the formation of a new bank.

More Logical Plan

Bank industry representatives suggested that the sale of the branches was the more logical plan.

The bank's only statement on the settlement noted that "since the case is still pending in the court, we cannot comment on it. Any resolution between the bank and the Justice Department is subject to court approval."

An assistant to Mr. Katzenbach said in a telephone interview that before the details of the plan could be disclosed, the settlement would have to be presented to Judge Lloyd F. MacMahon in the United States District Court here.

It was Judge MacMahon who ruled last March that the 1961 bank merger was in violation or antitrust sections of the Sherman and Clayton Acts. His

Continued on Page 41, Column 3

U.S. Declares 4-State Drought Disaster; City Allowed to End Delaware Diversion

200 Million Gallons a Day to Be Put in 'Bank' for Use in an Emergency

By WARREN WEAVER, Jr.
Special to The New York Times

WASHINGTON, Aug. 18—New York City was relieved today of its obligation to pour 200 million gallons of water into the Delaware River system every day.

In an agreement to give the city that relief, President Johnson declared the Delaware Valley watershed and the communities it serves in four states a disaster area.

The agreement goes into effect Sept. 10, when the present drought emergency declared by the Delaware River Basin Commission will expire. But the commission has the right to authorize New York to start storing the water before then.

The 200 million gallons of water will not automatically go into the city's supply. It will be stored in a "bank" in the city's Catskills reservoir system and be made available to New York or Philadelphia in time of need.

This arrangement, a major victory for Mayor Wagner, was agreed upon by representatives of New York, New Jersey, Pennsylvania and Delaware at a White House conference today. Mr. Wagner called it "real progress for New York."

By providing specific Federal drought assistance for New Jersey and Pennsylvania, President Johnson and Secretary of the Interior Stewart L. Udall were able to get those two states to agree to eliminate the re-

Continued on Page 28, Column 6

The New York Times Aug. 19, 1965

City no longer must release water into Delaware River from Pepacton and Neversink Reservoirs (1). Pumps near Chelsea (2) will be rebuilt. New Jersey may draw water from Greenwood Lake (3), Lake Hopatcong (4), underground lake near Passaic (5). Philadelphia will draw water from improved intake to be built at Torresdale (6).

City Believed Safe From Water Crisis Till Spring Runoff

By McCANDLISH PHILLIPS

The threat that New York City would run out of water next winter was ended yesterday, barring unforeseen difficulties, a spokesman for the Department of Water Supply said last night.

The agreements reached in Washington, he said, mean that the city will have a "one-month reprieve from real water famine," which had been threatened by mid-February.

The reprieve means enough water, but with none to spare, to carry the city through March. That is when spring thaws start the runoff season that usually adds billions of gallons of water to the reservoirs in three months.

In March, too, the Hudson River pumping station at Chelsea may be in operation to draw 100 million gallons of water a day from the river. The City Planning Commission approved $7 million yesterday for that purpose, but its action does not constitute final approval of the project.

The agreement reached in Washington yesterday among members of the Delaware River Basin Commission allows New York to stop releasing up to 200 million gallons of fresh water a day into the Delaware.

Instead, the city will store that amount in a kind of savings bank, on which drafts may be made by the commission in the interest of Philadelphia or

Continued on Page 28, Column 5

SCREVANE TO GET BEST BALLOT LINE

Assigned First Democratic Column on Basis of Most Candidates on Ticket

By WILLIAM E. FARRELL

City Council President Paul R. Screvane was given the preferred position on the voting machines yesterday among Democrats running for the mayoral nomination in the Sept. 14 primary.

The four commissioners of the Board of Elections voted unanimously to place Mr. Screvane's slate in the third vertical column on the left side of the voting machines on the ground that he was the Democratic candidate with the longest ticket.

The spot is the first Democratic designation on the ballot. The first and second columns are reserved for the Republican party because the election law provides that the party with the largest vote in the last gubernatorial election be given first place.

Candidates covet the left side of the ballot because people read from left to right.

The Board of Elections decided to allocate the spots on the eight-column voting machines on the basis of the number of candidates throughout the city running on each of the Democratic mayoral candidates' tickets. This method was favored by Mr. Screvane, Controller Abraham D. Beame and Councilman at Large Paul O'Dwyer.

94 on Beame Ticket

Commissioner Maurice J. O'Rourke said that a check of papers filed by candidates listing their slate preference disclosed a total of 126 persons seeking to run on the Screvane ticket.

Mr. Beame had 94 candidates on his ticket and was assigned the fourth column. Representative William F. Ryan had a total of 33 candidates and was given the fifth column on the voting machine. Mr. O'Dwyer had a total of 16 candidates and his slate will appear in the sixth column. This leaves the seventh column for Jesse Gray, whose petitions are being challenged.

The number of candidates in each column will vary throughout the city, depending on how many offices are being contested in each district.

The commissioners anticipate some difficulty because of the large number of citywide slates. Each is entitled to one column on the voting machine, as are independent candidates for various offices.

If there are too many inde-

Continued on Page 18, Column 8

Astronauts Ready For Flight Today; Record Is Sought

By EVERT CLARK
Special to The New York Times

CAPE KENNEDY, Fla., Thursday, Aug. 19—The United States will seek an official world record for the longest manned space flight when the Gemini 5 begins its eight-day journey here today.

The final countdown for the flight began at 1:30 A.M. today and space agency officials said the rocket, spacecraft and crew were ready for the launching, which is set for 10 A.M. Eastern daylight time. The astronauts retired early and slept in seclusion at this sprawling missile base.

There are two primary goals for the flight. One is to test a spacecraft radar, vital for joining later spaceships in orbit, by chasing an electronic Rendezvous Evaluation Pod. The other is to see if eight days in space adversely affects the human body.

It was learned yesterday that the International Federation of Aeronautics, official aviation and space record-keeping body, had been asked to monitor the flight.

Lieut. Col. Valery F. Bykovsky of the Soviet Union now holds the record for the longest space flight with 119 hours and six minutes, almost five days, in space. He set the

Continued on Page 15, Column 1

WHITE HOUSE SAYS MOST EXCISE CUTS GO TO CONSUMERS

But Survey Reports Some Manufacturers Have Failed to Pass On the Reductions

By EDWIN L. DALE Jr.
Special to The New York Times

WASHINGTON, Aug. 18—The White House reported today that consumers had received the benefit of about three-fourths of the $1.75 billion excise tax reduction enacted two months ago.

The report was sharply critical, however, of manufacturers of phonograph records, pens and pencils, matches and some golfing equipment for raising wholesale prices by the full amount of the tax cut.

Consumers, according to the report, benefited from a complete or almost complete pass-through of the tax cut on such major items as new automobiles, women's handbags, men's wrist watches, typewriters and home permanent kits.

Some of these items were taxed at the manufacturers' level and some at retail, but in either case the price to the consumer was reduced by the amount of the tax cut at nearly all retail dealers, the report said.

Based on Survey

The report was based on a detailed survey made last month by several Government agencies on some, but not all, of the items affected by the tax reduction. The survey covered what the report called a "representative sample" of items in each of the broad categories of goods affected.

Thus there were details on home permanent kits but not on perfume or face powder, on television sets but not on radios, on matches but not on cigarette lighters.

Bill D. Moyers, the White House press secretary, told reporters:

"Secretary of the Treasury [Henry M.] Fowler informed the President that the over-all results are encouraging, but that the failure of some manufacturers to pass on the reduction bears closer examination.

"The President urged the Secretary to request these manufacturers to keep faith with the hope of the Administration and Congress in passing this legislation and to pass on the benefits."

Exceptions Listed

The report, submitted to the President by the Council of Economic Advisers, showed that "major manufacturers" of phonograph records, pens and mechanical pencils, and matches had passed on none of the cut, and that only 30 per cent of the manufacturers of golfing equipment had passed it along.

On these items, the report said, "future surveys will show whether the manufacturers will succeed in retaining the benefits or whether competition will be sufficient to assure that the benefits will be passed on."

Manufacturers of all other items in the sample passed the reduction along fully to the re-

Continued on Page 21, Column 1

COAST RIOT AREA GETS $1.7 MILLION FOR CLEANUP JOB

U.S. Antipoverty Funds Will Finance Project—Troops Begin Withdrawing

By GLADWIN HILL
Special to The New York Times

LOS ANGELES, Aug. 18—Gov. Edmund G. Brown announced tonight the allocation of $1,770,000 in Federal funds to aid the 45-square-mile site of Negro rioting here, as National Guard troops began leaving the area.

Under a "work experience training" project of the Government's antipoverty program previously approved for Los Angeles County, up to 1,600 men and women will be hired for cleanup activities, the Governor said.

Damage from five days of violence that began last Wednesday night, following the arrest of a Negro for drunken driving, has been estimated as high as $200 million.

Officers of the California National Guard, which was brought in Friday night to help quell the rioting of thousands of Negroes, began a large-scale withdrawal by order of the Governor.

10,000 Leaving

A military spokesman said 10,000 men of the 40th Armored Division were on their way to regular summer duty at Camp Roberts at Paso Robles, 200 miles north of Los Angeles.

Some 5,000 troops of the 49th Infantry Division are scheduled to start leaving tomorrow. Some of these men will still be in the city over the weekend.

The Guard last night began reducing patrols in the Negro area in southwestern Los Angeles centering on the Watts district.

The start of the withdrawal followed the first night without a curfew in the riot area since Saturday.

Only one major clash occurred following the lifting of restrictions on night-time movement on the streets.

An early-morning battle between 50 policemen and a number of Black Muslims at their mosque led to the arrest of 59 persons and the hospitalization of four others.

Arms Movement Reported

The police said they had been met by gunfire when they went to investigate a report of arms being trucked to the headquarters of the militant Negro racist movement.

The death toll in the rioting rose to 34 today with the death of a Negro woman shot by a guardsman over the weekend. The total of persons arrested reached more than 3,800.

Late today the Governor conferred with the Rev. Dr. Martin Luther King Jr. The civil rights leader, who arrived here yesterday to explore ways of easing interracial tensions resulting from the disorders, said after the meeting that it had been "very fruitful and amicable."

The Atlanta clergyman said he had asked Mr. Brown to urge appointment of a civilian board to review Los Angeles

Continued on Page 16, Column 2

Associated Press Wirephoto

ANSWER QUESTIONS ON RIOTS: Governor Edmund G. Brown of California and the Rev. Dr. Martin Luther King Jr. at news conference in Los Angeles last night.

U.S. Steel and 2 Others Fined For Fixing Prices of Steel Parts

By ROBERT A. WRIGHT

Three steel companies were fined a total of $100,000 yesterday on price-fixing charges after they changed their pleas from not guilty to no contest.

Federal District Judge Sylvester J. Ryan fined the United States Steel Corporation $40,000, and the Armco Steel Corporation $35,000 on a 1963 indictment obtained by the Federal Government charging price fixing of railroad wheels.

The Erie Forge and Steel Corporation, indicted for price fixing of steel castings, was fined $25,000. Judge Ryan first imposed a fine of $35,000 on Erie, but reduced it after Arnold Bauman, its lawyer, told the court that Erie was in a "precarious financial situation" because it had lost about $4 million in the last several years.

The wheels involved in the one indictment are the kind used by the New York subway system. A spokesman for the Transit Authority, described in the indictment as one of the principal purchasers of the product during the cited period, said yesterday that the authority was considering a damage suit against the companies.

The use of no contest pleas, at first strongly opposed by the Government, permits a defendant to accept punishment without admitting guilt.

A plea of guilty or conviction after trial provides companies wishing to press private damage suits in antitrust cases with a ready-made brief.

In cases where defendants have pleaded no contest, purchasers suing for damages would have to prove the de-

Continued on Page 44, Column 1

U.S. MARINES TRAP 2,000 OF VIETCONG, KILL 'HUNDREDS'

U.S. Tells Advisers To Avoid Ambushes

Special to The New York Times

SAIGON, South Vietnam, Aug. 18—United States military advisers to South Vietnamese troop units have been ordered to refuse to accompany them on operations likely to lead to ambushes and to refuse the use of United States-controlled resources such as helicopters in such operations.

The instructions, issued recently by the United States military commander in Vietnam, Gen. William C. Westmoreland, came after a number of American advisers lost their lives in ambushes by the Vietcong this spring and summer.

The instructions became known today. There have been cases in which advisers refused to endorse or participate in actions that appeared

Continued on Page 2, Column 7

FIGHTING INTENSE

Ships and Planes Aid Drive—Reds Strike at Mountain Camp

By CHARLES MOHR
Special to The New York Times

SAIGON, South Vietnam, Thursday, Aug. 19 — United States marines have trapped about 2,000 Vietcong guerrillas with their backs to the sea and killed "hundreds" of them in the first major battle involving American troops in Vietnam, a military spokesman reported yesterday.

But as the successful attack near Chulai continued this morning, other Vietcong troops were attacking and threatening to overrun a Special Forces camp at Daksut, manned by 12 United States defenders and mountain tribesmen they have armed and trained.

Daksut is an isolated mountain post 300 miles north of Saigon and about 90 miles southwest of the scene of the Marine battle.

Marine casualties were described officially as "light," but it appeared they were the highest ever suffered by an American unit in one battle in Vietnam. Communist mortar fire did most of the damage, Marine sources indicated.

Landing by Air and Sea

The marines landed yesterday morning and throughout the day by helicopter and from the sea by landing craft in the area of Vantuong, a village 315 miles northeast of Saigon.

By late last night they reported that they had surrounded the guerrillas and "continued to grind" them toward the South China Sea. The enemy had been reported as being "heavily entrenched" and armed with such weapons as recoilless rifles.

[A Marine Corps spokesman said the bodies of 552 Vietcong had been counted at the end of the first day's fighting on Vantuong peninsula, The Associated Press reported.]

The area of the fighting, which is 16 miles south of the United States air base at Chulai, has been controlled and held by the Vietcong for two years, the spokesman said.

500 to 600 in Force

The force that attacked at Daksut was estimated at a battalion, or 500 to 600 men.

By early this morning, the Vietcong guerrillas were reported to have occupied about half of the 400-man Vietnamese sector of the camp and to have penetrated the American Special Forces compound.

Communications with the camp were cut off about dawn. A radio report shortly before midnight said that the camp was afire in several places and that ammunition bunkers were exploding.

The operation by the marines near Chulai was given the code name Starlight. It began with elements of the Third and Fourth Marine Regiments landing in helicopters near Van-

Continued on Page 3, Column 1

JOHNSON DENIES EISENHOWER RIFT

Unity of Goals on Vietnam Cited by White House After Statement by General

By JOHN W. FINNEY
Special to The New York Times

WASHINGTON, Aug. 18 — The White House, seeking to prevent any partisan breach on Vietnam policies, insisted today that there was no difference between President Johnson and former President Dwight D. Eisenhower over the historical basis of the American military commitment in Vietnam.

The Presidential press secretary, Bill D. Moyers, said President Johnson saw no difference between himself and the former President and believed the objectives of the Johnson Administration in Vietnam were the same as the Eisenhower Administration's.

General Eisenhower seemed to demur yesterday at President Johnson's oft-repeated suggestion that America's military commitment in Vietnam springs from a letter from General Eisenhower to Premier Ngo Dinh Diem in 1954.

In a four-minute reply to a question, Mr. Moyers blended Presidential praise of General Eisenhower with variously phrased assertions of unity of purpose between the Eisenhower and Johnson Administrations.

Appropriation Approved

On Capitol Hill, meanwhile, with no partisan differences, the Senate Appropriations Committee approved a $1.7 billion emergency fund to help pay the costs of the increasing American military oommitment in the South Vietnamese war. The additional appropriation, sure to be approved by Congress, will increase the special funds for the Vietnam war to $2.4 billion in the current fiscal year.

Senator John C. Stennis of Mississippi, chairman of the defense appropriations subcommittee, emphasized that the new emergency fund was "only a small down payment upon the ever-increasing cost of our operations in Vietnam." He predicted that at least $7 billion to $10 billion in additional funds would be required to support combat operations and to replace equipment diverted there.

In the letter to the late South Vietnamese leader, President Eisenhower offered to "assist the Government of Vietnam in developing and maintaining a strong, viable state, capable of resisting attempted subversion or aggression through military means."

President Johnson, who has

Continued on Page 2, Column 2

NEWS INDEX

Talk With Pakistan Is Canceled by India

By J. ANTHONY LUKAS
Special to The New York Times

NEW DELHI, Aug. 18 — A scheduled conference of the Indian and Pakistani Foreign Ministers has been canceled because of what the Indian Government described as "a sharp and serious deterioration" of relations between their countries.

In a note to Karachi last night, Foreign Minister Swaran Singh of India suggested that Zulfikar Ali Bhutto of Pakistan call off his trip here this week.

The Indian said that, because of the deterioration of relations, there was little prospect of reaching agreement on the disputed border in the Rann of Cutch at talks the two ministers had been scheduled to hold here on Friday. The Rann is a desolate wasteland on India's western border.

Reports from Karachi tonight

Continued on Page 4, Column 5

U.S. Air Force F-100 Supersabres hit enemy targets 15 miles south of Hanoi.

In 1965 multi-national forces joined the U.S. operation in Vietnam. Here, Austrailian troops engage the enemy.

The New York Times.

LATE CITY EDITION
U. S. Weather Bureau Report (Page 82) forecasts:
Fair, then becoming cloudy today;
cloudy tonight. Fair tomorrow.
Temp. Range: 50—32; yesterday: 43—30.

VOL. CXV...No. 39,394.   © 1965 by The New York Times Company. Times Square, New York, N.Y. 10036   NEW YORK, THURSDAY, DECEMBER 2, 1965.   TEN CENTS

---

3 U.S. AIDES MOVE TO OFFSET WORRY OVER INFLATION

Meeting Called by Johnson With Economic Advisers Termed Merely Routine

PUBLIC CONCERN NOTED

Wirtz and Connor Speeches Urge Expansion—Peril in 'Braking' Is Stressed

By EDWIN L. DALE Jr.
Special to The New York Times

WASHINGTON, Dec. 1—The Johnson Administration struck back on three fronts today to counter what appeared to be growing public concern over the threat of inflation.

In Austin, Tex., Joseph Laitin, the assistant White House press secretary, in contrast with reports from the Texas White House yesterday, said the President was not showing "undue concern" over inflation and that this was not the reason for a meeting a the next few days between Mr. Johns in and his four top economic advisers.

"We don't consider inflation a major threat at this time, but the President's advisers always are watching the situation and studying it very carefully," Mr. Laitin said.

This was an apparent reversal of the word given to some reporters in Austin yesterday about the President's attitude of concern following the announcement of another increase in the Consumer Price Index. This attitude was reported in The New York Times and some other newspapers this morning.

Administration's Position

Mr. Laitin's picture of the President's attitude was backed up in speeches by two Cabinet officers and was in line with the Administration's position that has obtained for some time. Officials have been saying, in public and private, that serious inflation is no immediate threat, though they concede the danger is greater than for some years past.

The Administration again today sought to calm public fears on the point. One aim is to avert any outbreak of inflationary psychology.

In San Francisco, Secretary of Labor W. Willard Wirtz spoke in even stronger terms than Mr. Laitin. In a speech to the Building and Construction Trades Department of the A.F.L.-C.I.O., the text of which was made available here, he repeatedly stressed that unemployment remained high at 4.3 per cent of the labor force.

"The worst mistake today would be to get the idea that we've got it made, that we are where we started to go, that it is time to put on some brakes," he said. The economy

Continued on Page 28, Column 1

U.S. JUDGES ENJOIN KLAN IN BOGALUSA

Panel Orders Halt to Acts of 'Terror and Intimidation'

By The Associated Press

NEW ORLEANS, Dec. 1—A Federal court ordered Ku Klux Klansmen today to halt "acts of terror and intimidation" aimed at preserving white supremacy in Bogalusa, La.

In a strongly worded injunction requested by the Justice Department, the court said that further interference with the civil rights of Bogalusa Negroes would not be tolerated.

The three-judge court listed as defendants the Original Knights of the Ku Klux Klan, "its dummy front, the Anti-Communist Christian Association," and 38 individuals, including the top Klan officials in Bogalusa.

The injunction is the second issued by Federal courts in recent months in an effort to aid civil rights demonstrators in Bogalusa, a papermill town of 25,000 persons 70 miles north of New Orleans. The earlier order directed police officials to provide adequate protection to peaceful Negro demonstrators.

Bogalusa erupted in racial turmoil last spring when Negroes began a drive to desegregate public facilities and obtain better job opportunities. In the months that followed,

Continued on Page 36, Column 4

5-Alarm Fire Destroys W. 84th St. Church

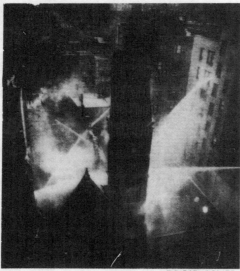

Episcopal Church of St. Matthew and St. Timothy after fire destroyed the interior
The New York Times (by Robert Walker)

120 Pupils Evacuated as Nearby Tenants Are Led to Street

By MARTIN GANSBERG

A five-alarm fire destroyed the Episcopal Church of St. Matthew and St. Timothy at 26 West 84th Street yesterday afternoon as 240 firemen fought to prevent it from spreading to adjacent apartment houses.

However, the flames ate through an airshaft on the second floor of a nine-story apartment house at 20 West 84th Street, which abuts the church. Tenants were forced to evacuate the building through smoke-filled corridors.

The fire, which was reported at 3:09 P.M., was one of three in Manhattan that drew heavily on men and equipment in the afternoon. The department ordered the transfer of 120 men and 22 pieces of equipment from Queens to cover vacated stations in Manhattan.

The other fires were in a five-story vacant tenement building on 111th Street between Park and Lexington Avenues and a three-story vacant tenement in Harlem, at 2324 Third Avenue near 126th Street. Because larger fire companies had been

Continued on Page 51, Column 6

Jury Finds Robles Guilty In Wylie-Hoffert Killings

By THEODORE JONES

A Supreme Court jury last night found Richard Robles guilty of first-degree murder in the 1963 slayings of Janice Wylie and Emily Hoffert. After the jury deliberated almost five hours, the five women and seven men returned to the dimly lit court room at 6:50 P.M. to announce the verdict against the 22-year-old defendant.

The jury foreman, Thomas McDade, an electrician with the Long Island Rail Road, said that Robles had been found "guilty."

CONFESSIONS HELD CRUCIAL BY HOGAN

He Contradicts View That Admissions Are Unneeded in Solving of Crimes

By STEVEN V. ROBERTS

District Attorney Frank S. Hogan sharply contradicted yesterday the recent contention of State Supreme Court Justice Nathan R. Sobel that confessions do not play a crucial role in the solution of major crimes.

In countless incidents, Mr. Hogan said, "it is the defendant, and only the defendant, who gives the evidence that results in his conviction.

Mr. Hogan also criticized Brooklyn District Attorney Aaron E. Koota and others who had advocated the broadening of a suspect's right to counsel early in a criminal investigation. The presence of counsel virtually eliminates the possibility of a confession, Mr. Hogan said.

"Obviously the whole purpose of a police investigation is frustrated," Mr. Hogan said, "if a suspect is entitled to have a lawyer during preliminary questioning, for any lawyer worth his fee will tell him to keep his mouth shut."

Police Heads Honored

Mr. Hogan made his remarks at a luncheon sponsored by the Grand Jury Association of New York County to honor former Police Commissioner Michael J. Murphy and the present Commissioner, Vincent L. Broderick.

He thus entered a heated controversy over the nature and use of confessions that began in June 1964, when the United States Supreme Court first voided a voluntary confession because the police had prevented a suspect from seeing his lawyer.

Mr. Hogan sided with those who maintain that law enforcement would be seriously impaired if the police were prevented from taking confessions by the presence of counsel.

The opposing viewpoint con-

Continued on Page 52, Column 1

The jury began its deliberations at 1 P.M., moments after it had received a two-hour charge from Justice Davidson.

It returned to the courtroom twice to hear testimony taken during the trial and parts of two public tape recordings on which Robles was alleged to have discussed details of the slayings with two friends who testified against him at the trial. It also had taken into the

Continued on Page 45, Column 1

Conviction on a charge of first-degree felony murder, which involves killing a person during commission of a felony, carries a life sentence. The death penalty no longer exists in New York except in cases involving the killing of a law officer or prison personnel during an escape attempt.

The jury deliberated almost five hours, the five women and seven men returned to the dimly lit court room for their "dedicated service." He then announced that Robles would be sentenced Jan. 11.

Life Sentence

The defendant had been found guilty of a felony murder in the first degree on each charge of the two-count indictment.

Robles received the verdict standing and showed no emotion. Then he sat down and folded his hands on his lap.

Justice Davidson dismissed the jury after he had thanked them

---

QUILL CALLS HALT TO TRANSIT TALKS

Denounces Lindsay's Stand in City Contract Dispute as 'Height of Stupidity'

By EMANUEL PERLMUTTER

The Transport Workers Union yesterday broke off contract negotiations with the Transit Authority.

Michael J. Quill, the union's international president, said he had halted the talks because of a telegram from John V. Lindsay in which the Mayor-elect said he would not enter the situation personally until he had evidence that both sides were bargaining in "good faith."

The union leader charged that Mr. Lindsay had "shot to hell" any hope of an agreement before the union's strike deadline of 5 A.M. Jan. 1.

"It's all in the lap of Mr. Lindsay," he said angrily. "We won't move an inch. His telegram is the height of stupidity."

Mr. Lindsay's telegram to Mayor-elect said "Mr. Lindsay stands on his telegram."

"It's all in the lap of Mr. Lindsay," he said angrily. "We won't move an inch. His telegram is the height of stupidity."

Mayor Wagner was questioned about the negotiation stalemate when he left City Hall last night. He was asked whether he would intervene in the impasse should prove prolonged.

"We've still got a responsi-

Continued on Page 53, Column 1

City's High Schools Doctoring Records That Go to Colleges

By MARTIN TOLCHIN

A dozen city high schools systematically upgrade, or conceal, student failures on transcripts sent to colleges.

These practices, long known to college admissions officers, were documented yesterday by the University Application Processing Center at Brooklyn College, which is preparing computerized transcripts for students at 40 of the city's 60 academic high schools.

The concealments were confirmed, moreover, by city school officials. Harold Zuckerman, the Board of Education's co-ordinator of college guidance and scholarships, said that the problem was "a matter of policy that has to be clarified."

'Of Course It's Dishonest'

Specifically, some schools simply do not record failures on transcripts sent to colleges. In two-term courses, students who fail the first term and pass the second term are given passing marks for the first term's work. Some schools do not record summer-session failures.

"Of course it's dishonest," said Prof. Louis M. Heil, director of the center, which processes all applications to the City University. "It means the difference between kids getting into the City University" and being rejected, he said.

The practices were reminiscent of the upgrading of marks by New Haven's Hillhouse School. In hearings last September, the school's clerks testified that when a student received

Continued on Page 44, Column 3

State Will Raise Aid To City $101 Million

By HOMER BIGART
Special to The New York Times

ALBANY, Dec. 1—Governor Rockefeller has informed Mayor-elect John V. Lindsay that New York City will receive $903.8 million in total state aid next year—an increase of $101.2 million over the amount in this year's state budget.

This mandated increase is higher than was estimated by the Temporary Commission on City Finances in forecasting a budget gap of at least $500 million for New York City in the fiscal year ahead.

Lacking the estimates of the Rockefeller administration on the state tax yield for 1966-67, the commission calculated that mandatory state assistance would come to $77 million. Thus the Governor's estimate would apparently shave roughly

Continued on Page 53, Column 4

BRITISH WOULD PUT FORCE IN RHODESIA IF DAM IS PERILED

Wilson Adds Sanctions and Says Regime Is Willing to Send Troops to Zambia

By ANTHONY LEWIS
Special to The New York Times

LONDON, Dec. 1—Britain, moving sharply toward a tougher policy, said today that she was prepared to send troops to Rhodesia if necessary to protect the power supply from the Kariba Dam.

Prime Minister Wilson made the statement in announcing his Government's willingness to send a token military force to Zambia, just across the Rhodesian border. It would be a Royal Air Force squadron with ground protection.

Mr. Wilson also imposed stringent new economic measures. Virtually all imports from Rhodesia are now banned. No pensions or dividends or interest may be paid from Britain to anyone in Rhodesia. Bank loans are forbidden.

[A dispatch from Salisbury said that Rhodesia was starting to shift her trade from Britain to South Africa. Page 6.]

Basis of British Action

Britain has opposed Rhodesia's seizure of independence because the Rhodesian regime has made no provision for the eventual political rights of the black majority. Now Britain is attempting to bring down the Rhodesian regime so she can reassert her authority and move the blacks toward political authority.

The strong moves by Mr. Wilson today brought protests from the Conservative side in the House of Commons. The greatest concern was expressed at the dispatch of troops and their possible use at Kariba, on the Rhodesia-Zambia border.

At the same time, Zambia was resisting Mr. Wilson's troop proposal as too limited. Mr. Wilson told the House that President Kenneth D. Kaunda of Zambia wanted ground forces and frankly wanted them to move into Rhodesia.

Bottomley in Lusaka

The Commonwealth Secretary, Arthur Bottomley, is in Lusaka, the Zambian capital, trying to reach an agreement on the troops. Mr. Wilson said communications from Lusaka were "in a shocking state" because of atmospheric conditions; he did not know how the discussions were going.

In any event, the decisions now taken by the Wilson Government are a significant step toward the black African view. Mr. Wilson is committed to bringing the rebel regime of Prime Minister Ian D. Smith down quickly. He is prepared to do so even at the cost of losing Conservative support on the Rhodesian issue — which for the last few weeks he has been eagerly courting.

Continued on Page 6, Column 1

RED CHINA SPURNS WORLD ARMS TALK

Bars Ties With U.N. Before the Restoration to Peking of 'Legitimate Rights'

By SEYMOUR TOPPING
Special to The New York Times

HONG KONG, Dec. 1—The Chinese Communist Foreign Ministry said today that Peking "will certainly not take part" in the world disarmament conference proposed by the United Nations.

A resolution, approved by the General Assembly Monday by a vote of 112 to 0, with France abstaining and Nationalist China not participating, called for the convening not later than 1967 of a world conference to which all countries would be invited.

[At the United Nations voted Wednesday to bar nuclear weapons from Africa. The vote was 105 to 0. Page 2.]

The Statement by Peking

Observers in Hong Kong mentioned the refusal of Communist China, one of the nuclear powers, to participate in the projected disarmament conference would deprive it of much of its significance. There are several forums for discussion open to the other major powers and the world conference was intended to bring Communist China into disarmament negotiations.

The Foreign Ministry statement, made by a spokesman in Peking, said:

"Under United States control, the United Nations has all along

Continued on Page 4, Column 3

THANT REBUFFED BY HANOI REGIME ON PEACE TALKS

Peace Conferees Submit 300 Ideas

By JOHN W. FINNEY
Special to The New York Times

WASHINGTON, Dec. 1—The White House Conference on International Cooperation ended today by submitting some 300 recommendations to the Administration on steps that could be taken to further cooperation and peace in the world.

In the opinion of both Government officials and conference leaders, the four-day meeting of 5,000 citizens had achieved its principal objective of establishing a productive dialogue between the Government and the citizenry in staking out possible new avenues of international cooperation.

Probably never before had so many citizens gathered at one time to discuss the problems and possibilities of international cooperation. And cer-

Continued on Page 2, Column 3

U.S. BACKS HIS BID

Go-Betweens Used— Rusk Says Reds Get 'Weekly' Appeals

By DREW MIDDLETON
Special to The New York Times

UNITED NATIONS, N. Y., Dec. 1—North Vietnam has shown no interest in recent indirect soundings by Secretary General Thant on the possibility of negotiations to settle the war in Vietnam, reliable sources said today.

The Secretary General has had no direct contact with the Hanoi Government this autumn. His inquiries, like those of the United States, have been channeled through intermediaries.

Washington has reacted favorably to the suggestions of negotiations, the sources here said.

[In Washington, Secretary of State Dean Rusk said Hanoi had received and ignored inquiries "every week" on the prospect that a halt in American bombings would lead to negotiations. Page 3.]

Hanoi Called Tougher

Informants at the United Nations described North Vietnam's silence as an indication that the Government of President Ho Chi Minh had embraced Communist China's intransigence on a settlement.

They added that what was possible in 1964, when Hanoi still exercised independent judgment on peace talks, was impossible in 1965, with Hanoi dutifully following Peking's policy.

Last year, diplomats suggested, Hanoi oscillated between the moderation advised by the Soviet Union and the intransigence of the Chinese. It was then that Secretary General Thant was informed by the North Vietnamese Government that it was prepared to send a representative to Rangoon, Burma, to discuss negotiations with the United States.

Goldberg Describes Bids

Today, the diplomats added, Hanoi is increasingly a captive of Peking's policy. The North Vietnamese now demand, as conditions for talks, the withdrawal of all United States forces from South Vietnam and American acceptance of independence, sovereignty and unity for all of Vietnam.

Arthur J. Goldberg, chief United States representative at the United Nations, disclosed today that he had probed Hanoi's attitude toward a cease-fire that would involve a progressive reduction of military activity, including the United States bombing of North Vietnam.

Mr. Goldberg said the United States mission had asked Communist delegations "whether there is willingness to enter into an equitable arrangement for a cease-fire that would call for a diminution of military activity on both sides."

Again, Mr. Goldberg said, there was no response from Hanoi.

A prevailing opinion among

Continued on Page 3, Column 1

Cuba Air Exodus On As 75 Exiles Arrive

By MARTIN WALDRON
Special to The New York Times

MIAMI, Dec. 1—Seventy-five Cuban refugees, who said they had been stripped of most of their belongings by Premier Fidel Castro's Government, were flown here this afternoon by the United States. It was the first flight in what may become one of history's great exoduses.

Two and a half hours after the plane landed, immigration officials began releasing some of the refugees in care of relatives in this country.

The United States expects to fly in from 3,000 to 4,000 refugees a month until the last of those who wish to leave Cuba under an airlift agreement between Washington and Havana have arrived.

Premier Castro announced nearly two months ago that Cubans who wanted to leave

Continued on Page 20, Column 3

Lindsay, in Alfresco Setting, Names New Commissioner of City Parks

By TERENCE SMITH

Mayor-elect John V. Lindsay announced yesterday that Thomas P. F. Hoving would be the city's next Parks Commissioner.

Mr. Hoving, who is 34 years old, is the curator of the Cloisters, the medieval branch of the Metropolitan Museum of Art in Fort Tryon Park.

He will succeed Newbold Morris, who has been Commissioner of Parks for the last five and a half years, at a salary of $25,000 a year.

Mr. Lindsay, in making the announcement, at an alfresco news conference at the boathouse in Central Park, took a page from President Johnson in his selection of a site for introducing the new commissioner. In recent months Mr. Johnson has held news conferences at a variety of spots, ranging from a Texas country post office to the base of the Statue of Liberty.

Shivering in the 40-degree cold, the Mayor-elect and Mr. Hoving answered questions on the boarding ramp behind the boathouse. A few feet beyond them, sunlight glittered off the partly frozen Central Park lake.

After Mr. Lindsay described

Continued on Page 57, Column 3

Thomas P. F. Hoving on Central Park lake with Mrs. Hoving and daughter, Petra Bell
The New York Times

Austrailian troops first engaged the Viet Cong near Bien Hoa in 1965. Here, a 105mm howitzer of the Australian 1st Field Regiment in action.

Reconnaissance photographs of the My Hoa bridge 25 miles south of Dong Hoi in North Vietnam revealed that the bridge was still serviceable after several bombardments. The bridge was finally put out of commission shortly thereafter.

"All the News That's Fit to Print"

The New York Times.

LATE CITY EDITION
U. S. Weather Bureau Report (Page 71) forecast:
Snow flurries, very windy today;
fair, very cold tonight, tomorrow.
Temp. range: 34—21; yesterday: 59—52.

NEWS SUMMARY AND INDEX, PAGE 71

SECTION ONE

VOL. CXV..No. 39,418.   © 1965 by The New York Times Company
Times Square, New York, N. Y. 10036   NEW YORK, SUNDAY, DECEMBER 26, 1965.   50c beyond 50-mile zone from New York City, except
on Long Island, higher in air delivery cities   THIRTY CENTS

MEDIATORS SEEK HELP OF LINDSAY IN TRANSIT TALKS

Meeting With Both Parties in Contract Dispute May Come in a Day or Two

PARLEYS ARE STALLED

T.W.U. Members Vote Today on Authorizing a Walkout at 5 A.M. on Saturday

By EMANUEL PERLMUTTER

The mediation panel in the transit contract dispute has asked Mayor-elect John V. Lindsay to speak to the Transit Authority and its unions to try to avert a strike.

This became known yesterday as the Transport Workers Union prepared for a mass meeting at 2 P.M. today in Manhattan Center, where the officers will ask the members to authorize a strike for 5 A.M. next Saturday.

It is expected that Mr. Lindsay will meet tomorrow or Tuesday with the three mediators in their suite at the Americana Hotel. The panel will then ask him to address representatives of the Transit Authority and of its two unions, who have been negotiating in the same hotel.

Plea by Mayor Earlier

Last week, Mayor Wagner talked to officers of the authority, the T.W.U. and the Amalgamated Transit Union at their bargaining session. He urged them to speed up their talks to avoid a New Year's Day strike.

Until now, Mr. Lindsay has confined his involvement in the talks to conferences with Dr. Nathan P. Feinsinger, the chairman, and Theodore W. Kheel and Sylvester Garrett, the other two members of the mediation panel.

The pressure for intervention by the Mayor-elect has resulted from the fact that those close to the negotiations see little genuine progress.

Mediator Returning

Dr. Feinsinger said yesterday by telephone from his home in Aspen, Colo., that the mediators had asked Mr. Lindsay on Friday to meet with them tomorrow afternoon at the Americana.

The mediator said he was cutting his Christmas vacation short and coming here today by plane so that he could participate in the resumption of negotiations at 10 A.M. tomorrow after their weekend recess.

"We have been urging both sides to speed up their negotiations," he said. "I think everyone concerned should set them an example by talking to them as soon as possible."

Joseph E. O'Grady, the Transit Authority chairman, said yesterday at his home that he had been informed that Mr. Lindsay would meet with both sides tomorrow afternoon.

A spokesman for Mr. Lindsay said yesterday that the Mayor-

Continued on Page 32, Column 1

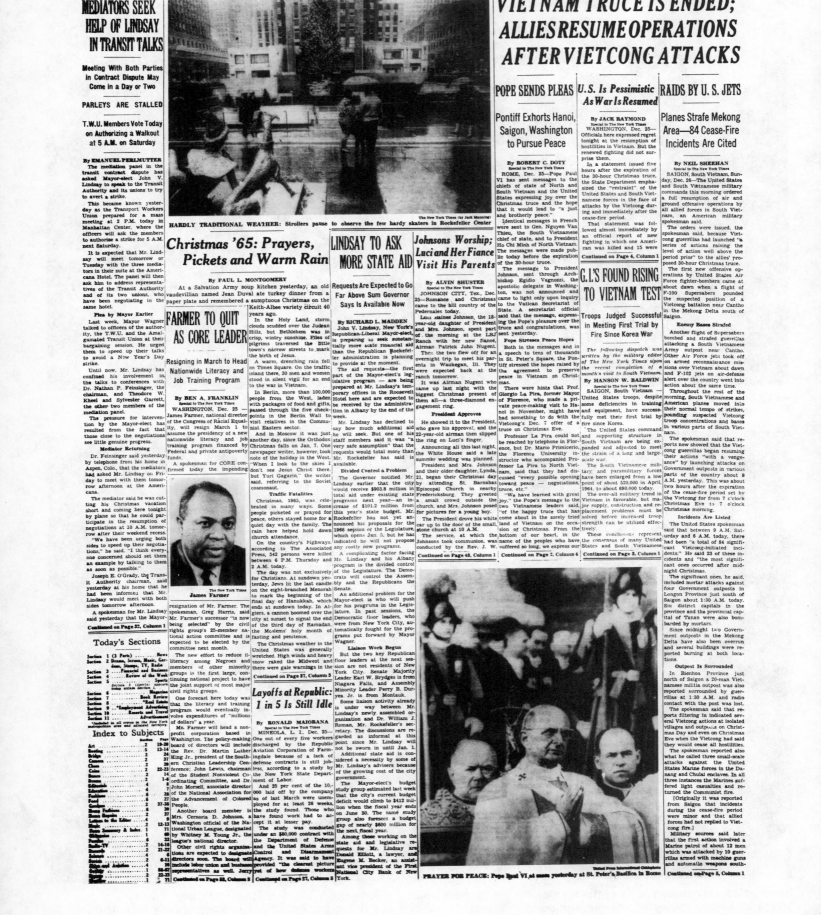

THE NEW YORK TIMES (by Jack Manning)
HARDLY TRADITIONAL WEATHER: Strollers pause to observe the few hardy skaters in Rockefeller Center

Christmas '65: Prayers, Pickets and Warm Rain

By PAUL L. MONTGOMERY

At a Salvation Army soup kitchen yesterday, an old vaudevillian named Jean Duval ate turkey dinner from a paper plate and remembered a sumptuous Christmas on the Keith-Albee variety circuit 40 years ago.

In the Holy Land, storm clouds scudded over the Judean Hills, but Bethlehem was in crisp, wintry sunshine. Files of pilgrims traversed the little town's narrow streets to mark the birth of Jesus.

A warm, drenching rain fell on Times Square. On the traffic island there, 30 men and women stood in silent vigil for an end to the war in Vietnam.

In Berlin, more than 100,000 people from the West, laden with packages of food and gifts, passed through the five checkpoints in the Berlin Wall to visit relatives in the Communist Eastern sector.

And in Moscow it was just another day, since the Orthodox Christmas falls on Jan. 7. One newspaper writer, however, took note of the holiday in the West. "When I look to the skies I don't see Jesus Christ there, but Yuri Gagarin," the writer said, referring to the Soviet cosmonaut.

Christmas, 1965, was celebrated in many ways. Some people picketed or prayed for peace, others stayed home for a quiet day with the family. The rain here helped hold down church attendance.

On the country's highways, according to The Associated Press, 542 persons were killed between 6 P.M. Thursday and 2 A.M. today.

The day was not exclusively for Christians. At sundown yesterday, Jews lit the last candle on the eight-branched Menorah to mark the beginning of the final day of Hanukkah, which ends at sundown today. In Algiers, a cannon boomed over the city at sunset to signal the end of the third day of Ramadan, the Moslems' holy month of fasting and penitence.

The Christmas weather in the United States was generally wretched. High winds and heavy snow raked the Midwest and there were gale warnings in the

Continued on Page 37, Column 3

FARMER TO QUIT AS CORE LEADER

Resigning in March to Head Nationwide Literacy and Job Training Program

By BEN A. FRANKLIN
Special to The New York Times

WASHINGTON, Dec. 25 — James Farmer, national director of the Congress of Racial Equality, will resign March 1 to assume the presidency of a new nationwide literacy and job training program financed by Federal and private antipoverty funds.

A spokesman for CORE confirmed today the impending

The New York Times
James Farmer

resignation of Mr. Farmer. The spokesman, Greg Harris, said Mr. Farmer's successor "is now being selected" by the civil rights group's 25-member national action committee and is expected to be elected by the committee next month.

The new effort to reduce illiteracy among Negroes and members of other minority groups is the first large, continuing national project to have the joint support of most major civil rights groups.

One forecast here today was that the literacy and training program would eventually involve expenditures of "millions of dollars" a year.

Mr. Farmer will head a nonprofit corporation based in Washington. The policy-making board of directors will include the Rev. Dr. Martin Luther King Jr., president of the Southern Christian Leadership Conference; John Lewis, chairman of the Student Nonviolent Coordinating Committee, and Dr. John Morsell, associate director of the National Association for the Advancement of Colored People.

Another board member is Mrs. Cernoria D. Johnson, a Washington official of the National Urban League, designated by Whitney M. Young Jr., the league's national director.

Other civil rights organizations are expected to designate directors soon. The board will include labor union and business representatives as well. Jerry

Continued on Page 52, Column 3

Layoffs at Republic: 1 in 5 Is Still Idle

By RONALD MAIORANA
Special to The New York Times

MINEOLA, L. I., Dec. 25 — One out of every five workers discharged by the Republic Aviation Corporation of Farmingdale because of a lack of defense contracts is still jobless, according to a study by the New York State Department of Labor.

And 25 per cent of the 10,000 laid off by the company as of last March were unemployed for at least 26 weeks, the study found. Those who have found work had to accept it at lesser pay.

The study was conducted under an $80,000 contract with the Department of Defense and the United States Arms Control and Disarmament Agency. It was said to have provided "the clearest picture yet of how defense workers

Continued on Page 27, Column 5

LINDSAY TO ASK MORE STATE AID

Requests Are Expected to Go Far Above Sum Governor Says Is Available Now

By RICHARD L. MADDEN

John V. Lindsay, New York's Republican-Liberal Mayor-elect, is preparing to seek substantially more state financial aid than the Republican Rockefeller administration is planning to provide at the moment.

The aid requests—the first part of the Mayor-elect's legislative program — are being prepared at Mr. Lindsay's temporary offices in the Roosevelt Hotel here and are expected to be received by the administration in Albany by the end of the week.

Mr. Lindsay has declined to say how much additional aid he will seek. But one of his staff members said it was "a very safe assumption" that the requests would total more than Mr. Rockefeller has said is available.

Divided Control a Problem

The Governor notified Mr. Lindsay earlier that the city would receive $903.8 million in total aid under existing state programs next year—an increase of $101.2 million from this year's state budget. Mr. Rockefeller has not yet announced his proposals for the 1966 session of the Legislature, which opens Jan. 5, but he has indicated he will not propose any costly new programs.

A complicating factor facing Mr. Lindsay and his Albany program is the divided control of the Legislature. The Democrats will control the Assembly and the Republicans the Senate.

An additional problem for the Mayor-elect is who will push for his programs in the Legislature. In past sessions, the Democratic floor leaders, who were from New York City, automatically fought for the programs put forward by Mayor Wagner.

Liaison Work Begun

But the two key Republican floor leaders at the next session are not residents of New York City. Senate Majority Leader Earl W. Brydges is from Niagara Falls, and Assembly Minority Leader Perry B. Duryea Jr. is from Montauk.

Some liaison activity already is under way between Mr. Lindsay's newly assembled organization and Dr. William J. Roman, Mr. Rockefeller's secretary. The discussions are regarded as informal at this point since Mr. Lindsay will not be sworn in until Jan. 1.

Additional state aid is considered a necessity by some of Mr. Lindsay's advisers because of the growing cost of the city government.

The Mayor-elect's budget study group estimated last week that the city's current budget deficit would climb to $412 million when the fiscal year ends on June 30. The same study group also foresees a budget gap of nearly $600 million for the next fiscal year.

Among those working on the state aid and legislative requests for Mr. Lindsay are Donald Elliott, a lawyer, and Eugene M. Becker, an assistant vice president of the First National City Bank of New York.

Johnsons Worship; Luci and Her Fiance Visit His Parents

By ALVIN SHUSTER
Special to The New York Times

JOHNSON CITY, Tex., Dec. 25—Romance and Christmas came to the hill country of the Pedernales today.

Luci Baines Johnson, the 18-year-old daughter of President and Mrs. Johnson, spent part of the morning at the LBJ Ranch with her new fiancé, Airman Patrick John Nugent. Then the two flew off for an overnight trip to meet his parents in Waukegan, Ill. They were expected back at the ranch tomorrow.

It was Airman Nugent who came up last night with the biggest Christmas present of them all—a three-diamond engagement ring.

President Approves

He showed it to the President, who gave his approval, and the 22-year-old airman then slipped the ring on Luci's finger.

Announcing all this last night, the White House said a late summer wedding was planned.

President and Mrs. Johnson and their older daughter, Lynda, 21, began their Christmas day by attending St. Barnabas Episcopal Church in nearby Fredericksburg. They greeted a small crowd outside the church, and Mrs. Johnson posed for pictures for a young boy.

The President drove his white car up to the door of the small stone church at 10 A.M.

The service, at which the Johnsons took communion, was conducted by the Rev. J. W.

Continued on Page 48, Column 1

VIETNAM TRUCE IS ENDED; ALLIES RESUME OPERATIONS AFTER VIETCONG ATTACKS

POPE SENDS PLEAS

Pontiff Exhorts Hanoi, Saigon, Washington to Pursue Peace

By ROBERT C. DOTY
Special to The New York Times

ROME, Dec. 25—Pope Paul VI has sent messages to the chiefs of state of North and South Vietnam and the United States expressing joy over the Christmas truce and the hope that it would lead to "a just and brotherly peace."

Identical messages in French were sent to Gen. Nguyen Van Thieu, the South Vietnamese chief of state, and to President Ho Chi Minh of North Vietnam. The messages were made public today before the expiration of the 30-hour truce.

The message to President Johnson, sent through Archbishop Egidio Vagnozzi, the apostolic delegate in Washington, was not announced and came to light only upon inquiry to the Vatican Secretariat of State. A secretariat official said that the message, expressing the Pope's pleasure over the truce and congratulations, was sent yesterday.

Pope Stresses Peace Hopes

Both in the messages and in a speech to tens of thousands in St. Peter's Square, the Pontiff stressed the hopes raised by the agreement to preserve peace in Vietnam on Christmas.

There were hints that Prof. Giorgio La Pira, former Mayor of Florence, who made a private peace-making visit to Hanoi in November, might have had something to do with the Vietcong's Dec. 7 offer of a truce on Christmas Eve.

Professor La Pira could not be reached by telephone in Florence, but Dr. Mario Primicerio, the Florence University instructor who accompanied Professor La Pira to North Vietnam, said that they had discussed "every possible opening toward peace — negotiations, truce, etc."

"We have learned with great joy," the Pope's message to the two Vietnamese leaders said, "of the happy truce that has come about in the sorely tried land of Vietnam on the occasion of Christmas. From the bottom of our heart, in the name of the peoples who have suffered so long, we express our

Continued on Page 2, Column 4

U.S. Is Pessimistic As War Is Resumed

By JACK RAYMOND
Special to The New York Times

WASHINGTON, Dec. 25—Officials here expressed regret tonight at the resumption of hostilities in Vietnam. But the renewed fighting did not surprise them.

In a statement issued five hours after the expiration of the 30-hour Christmas truce, the State Department emphasized the "restraint" of the United States and South Vietnamese forces in the face of attacks by the Vietcong during and immediately after the cease-fire period.

That statement was followed almost immediately by an official report of new fighting in which one American was killed and 15 were

Continued on Page 4, Column 1

G.I.'S FOUND RISING TO VIETNAM TEST

Troops Judged Successful in Meeting First Trial by Fire Since Korea War

The following dispatch was written by the military editor of The New York Times upon the recent completion of a month's visit to South Vietnam.

By HANSON W. BALDWIN
Special to The New York Times

SAIGON, South Vietnam — United States troops, despite some deficiencies in training and equipment, have successfully passed their first trial by fire since Korea.

The United States command and supporting structure in South Vietnam are being expanded and adjusted to meet the strain of a long and large-scale war.

The South Vietnamese military and paramilitary forces have been enlarged from a low point of about 520,000 in April, 1964, to about 690,000 today.

The over-all military trend in Vietnam is favorable, but major supply, construction and replacement problems must be solved before increased troop strength can be utilized effectively.

These conclusions represent the consensus of many United States and South Vietnamese

Continued on Page 3, Column 1

RAIDS BY U. S. JETS

Planes Strafe Mekong Area—84 Cease-Fire Incidents Are Cited

By NEIL SHEEHAN
Special to The New York Times

SAIGON, South Vietnam, Sunday, Dec. 26—The United States and South Vietnamese military commands this morning ordered a full resumption of air and ground offensive operations by allied forces in South Vietnam, an American military spokesman said.

The orders were issued, the spokesman said, because Vietcong guerrillas had launched "a series of actions raising the level of action well above the period prior" to the allies' proposed 30-hour Christmas truce.

The first new offensive operations by United States Air Force fighter-bombers came at about dawn when a flight of F-100 Supersabers pounded the suspected position of a Vietcong battalion near Cantho in the Mekong Delta south of Saigon.

Enemy Bases Strafed

Another flight of Supersabers bombed and strafed guerrillas attacking a South Vietnamese Army outpost near Cantho. Other Air Force jets took off on armed reconnaissance missions over Vietnam about dawn and F-102 jets on air-defense alert over the country went into action about the same time.

Throughout the rest of the morning, South Vietnamese and American planes moved into their normal tempo of strikes, pounding suspected Vietcong troop concentrations and bases in various parts of South Vietnam.

The spokesman said that reports now showed that the Vietcong guerrillas began resuming their actions "with a vengeance" by launching attacks on Government outposts in various parts of the country about 9 A.M. yesterday. This was about two hours after the expiration of the cease-fire period set by the Vietcong for from 7 o'clock Christmas Eve to 7 o'clock Christmas morning.

Incidents Are Listed

The United States spokesman said that between 9 A.M. Saturday and 6 A.M. today, there had been "a total of 84 significant Vietcong-initiated incidents." He said 23 of these incidents "were the most significant ones that occurred after midnight Christmas.

The significant ones, he said, included mortar attacks against four Government outposts in Longan Province just south of Saigon about 1:30 A.M. today. Six district capitals in the province and the provincial capital of Tanan were also bombed by mortars.

Since midnight two Government outposts in the Mekong Delta have also been overrun and several buildings were reported burning at both locations.

Outpost Is Surrounded

In Bienhoa Province just north of Saigon a 20-man Vietnamese militia outpost was also reported surrounded by guerrillas at 1:30 A.M. and radio contact with the post was lost.

The spokesman said that reports filtering in indicated several Vietcong actions at isolated villages and outposts on Christmas Day and even on Christmas Eve when the Vietcong had said they would cease all hostilities.

The spokesman reported also what he called three small-scale attacks against the United States Marine forces in the Danang and Chulai enclaves. In all three instances the Marines suffered light casualties and returned the Communist fire.

[Originally it was reported from Saigon that incidents during the cease-fire period were minor and that allied forces had not replied to Vietcong fire.]

Military sources said later that the first action involved a Marine patrol of about 12 men which was attacked by 10 guerrillas armed with machine guns and automatic weapons south-

Continued on Page 5, Column 1

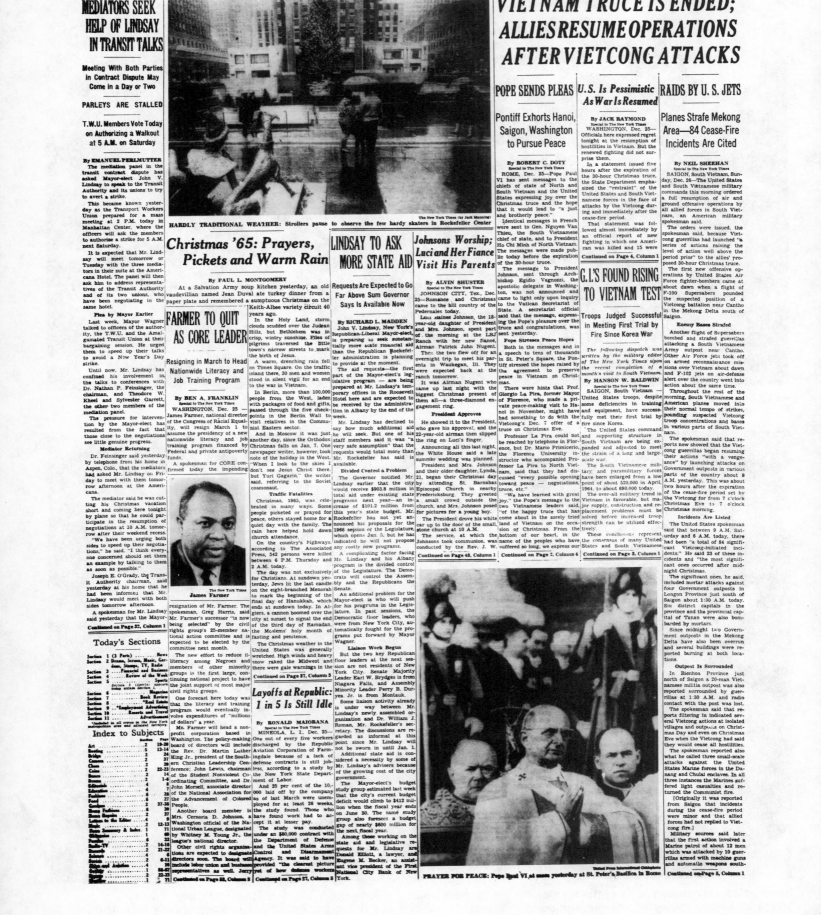

United Press International Radiophoto
PRAYER FOR PEACE: Pope Paul VI at mass yesterday at St. Peter's Basilica in Rome

As evidenced by these varied Viet Cong uniforms captured by the Allied forces, the guerrillas move in many disguises and can easily infiltrate the most secure areas.

Buddhist monks who were already displeased by President Thieu's domestic policies, demonstrated against the war.

"All the News That's Fit to Print"

The New York Times.

NEWS SUMMARY AND INDEX, PAGE 59

LATE CITY EDITION
U. S. Weather Bureau Report (Page 59) forecasts:
Windy and sunny today; fair tonight. Cloudy and cold tomorrow.
Temp. range: 10—25; yesterday: 44—16.

SECTION ONE

VOL. CXV.... No. 39,432. © 1966 by The New York Times Company, Times Square, New York, N. Y. 10036 NEW YORK, SUNDAY, JANUARY 9, 1966. 50c beyond 50-mile zone from New York City, except on Long Island, higher in air delivery cities THIRTY CENTS

STRIKE TALKS SHOW GAIN; LINDSAY STRIVES FOR END OF TIE-UP BY TOMORROW

8,000 G.I.'S OPEN BIGGEST ATTACK OF VIETNAM WAR

Australians Join in a Drive on Vietcong 20 Miles Northwest of Saigon

HEAVY GUNS IN ACTION

Start of Operation Withheld From South Vietnamese to Bar a Leak to Foe

By United Press International

SAIGON, Sunday, Jan. 9—United States forces have launched their largest offensive operation of the Vietnam war to sweep clean the Communists' Hobo Forest stronghold 20 miles north-northwest of Saigon, military officials said today.

About 8,000 American troops, aided by Australians and New Zealanders, converged on the Vietcong's Iron Triangle yesterday morning in the wake of a strike by B-52 strategic bombers and an artillery barrage unprecedented in this war.

Military sources said the operation was kept secret from the South Vietnamese Army command and the Government for fear of an intelligence leak.

Headquarters of the South Vietnamese Army's III Corps here is known to be riddled with Vietcong agents. For that reason word of the operation was confined to the allies involved. It was believed to have been the first such operation kept secret from the South Vietnamese command.

Copters Take in Troops

American military authorities at the forward command post at Trunglay, in Haunghia Province, 24 miles northwest of Saigon, said at least five United States Army helicopters were riddled with machinegun fire as elements of the First Infantry Division and the 173d Airborne Brigade were lifted into landing zones both north and south of the forest.

Artillerymen said that never in the history of the Vietnamese war had so much artillery been used to soften up suspected Vietcong positions.

Howitzers and cannons of all sizes, ranging up to 8-inch guns, began pounding the landing zones 90 minutes before the 100 troop-carrying helicopters appeared from the directions of Bienhoa and Laikhe, the bases of the 173d Airborne Brigade and the First Infantry Division's Third Brigade.

After a brief but furious skir-

Continued on Page 3, Column 6

Hanoi Praises Soviet Military Aid

Associated Press Radiophoto

Aleksandr N. Shelepin and President Ho Chi Minh in Hanoi

By The Associated Press

TOKYO, Jan. 8—Premier Pham Van Dong of North Vietnam praised the Soviet Union tonight for its aid to the Vietcong war effort. In greeting a Soviet delegation led by Aleksandr N. Shelepin, who also met with President Ho Chi Minh, the Premier seemed to be rebutting Chinese Communist criticism of Moscow. Mr. Dong assailed United States peace gestures as tricks and said peace could come only when the United States halted bombing of North Vietnam "unconditionally and for good." He spoke

Continued on Page 2, Column 4

Lynd Says Hanoi Denies Getting a Direct U.S. Bid

By PETER GROSE

Special to The New York Times

MOSCOW, Jan. 8—Prof. Staughton Lynd of Yale came here from a private "fact-finding" tour of North Vietnam tonight and criticized the Johnson Administration for "the apparent failure to make direct contact" with the Vietnamese Communists in its offer of peace talks.

The 36-year-old history teacher disclosed that he had sent a cablegram to Senator J. W. Fulbright from Hanoi with an offer to present "significant information" to the Senate Foreign Relations Committee. The Arkansas Democrat is its chairman.

Mr. Lynd spoke with newsmen at Moscow's Sheremetyevo Airport along with his traveling companions, Herbert Aptheker and Thomas Hayden. The three men spent 10 days in Hanoi on a privately financed trip to seek clarification of Communist terms for ending the war in South Vietnam.

90-Minute Talk With Premier

In a prepared joint statement, they said that they had spoken for 90 minutes with the North Vietnamese Premier Pham Van Dong, as well as with representatives of the South Vietnamese National Liberation Front, the political organization of which the Vietcong are the fighting forces.

"Our conversations convince us that many of the ingredients of an honorable solution exist," their statement said. They promised further elaboration after their scheduled arrival in New York tomorrow evening.

During their overnight stop in Moscow, their first formal encounter with Western newsmen since their conversations in Hanoi, they offered only one conclusion, which was as follows:

"We asked Premier Pham Van Dong whether the United States had made direct contact with the Government of the Democratic Republic of Viet-

Continued on Page 6, Column 1

POPE EMPHASIZES NONALIGNED ROLE

Sees Church as Independent of World's Vying Blocs—Vows New Peace Steps

By ROBERT C. DOTY

Special to The New York Times

ROME, Jan. 8 — Pope Paul VI declared today that his peace efforts and those of the Roman Catholic Church were totally independent of "the competitions of this world."

This does not mean, the Pontiff said, that the church is "indifferent" to errors or ignorant of the "ambiguities of worldly values." But it concentrates its attention, he said, on positive aspects of those values—presumably from all of the world's ideologies—"on what they contain that is valuable for the construction of a better, more just society."

Pope Paul made these statements at a reception for diplomats accredited to the Holy See. His words appeared aimed at dissolving any suspicion that the Vatican was acting as the agent of any national or ideological interest in its public and private efforts to achieve peace in Vietnam.

"God is our witness," he said, "that we are ready, for our part, to attempt all steps—even outside the generally accepted protocol forms—every time we believe that the Church can usefully bring to world leaders the weight of its moral authority

Continued on Page 2, Column 7

U.S. RAIDS IN LAOS CALLED EFFECTIVE

Pilots Say Heavy Strikes Smash Vietcong Convoys

By The Associated Press

SAIGON, Jan. 8 — United States jet pilots are reporting excellent results from massive raids on the Ho Chi Minh Trail through eastern Laos during the lengthening pause in the bombing of North Vietnam, informed sources said today.

Squadrons totaling up to 300 planes, carrying nearly 1,000 tons of bombs and rockets, are hitting daily at strategic junctions and southbound Communist convoys on the maze of roads and waterways making up the trail, the sources said.

"To do any less would be madness," one source said. "We simply cannot let the Communists arrive in South Vietnam with all that stuff intact."

Pilots told of numerous secondary explosions from ammunition-laden sampans and trucks that North Vietnam dispatched to take advantage of the pause ordered by President Johnson Christmas eve in air attacks on North Vietnam.

The informants, who reported today on results of the raids in Laos, are reliable, but they preferred not to be identified. Nor was there a pinpointing of the bases that the jets used. No official United States or Vietnamese spokesman would comment.

At one time or another in the last year pilots based in Thailand, in South Vietnam and aboard Seventh Fleet carriers in the South China Sea have made runs over Laos. Announced combat activity of the latter

Continued on Page 3, Column 3

Mansfield Report Seen as Urging U.S. to Get Peace Pact Quickly

By E. W. KENWORTHY

Special to The New York Times

WASHINGTON, Jan. 8 — A bleak report on the situation in Vietnam by Mike Mansfield and four other Senators appears to suggest that the United States should take the best peace settlement it can get that is consistent with honor.

The report to the Senate Foreign Relations Committee, which was made public last night, does not actually make such a recommendation.

Yet the inference can be drawn from the way the report describes the situation in Vietnam and poses the alternatives facing the United States. Almost certainly such an inference will be drawn by some Senators opposed to further widening of the war.

A longer, more detailed, franker and tougher version of this public report was given to President Johnson by Senator Mansfield, the Majority Leader, on Dec. 19, the day after his return.

So grim, in fact, was the secret report to the President that officials agree it was a strongly contributing factor in Mr. Johnson's decision to order the pause in the bombing of North Vietnam.

The report of the Mansfield group, which made a world-circling tour at the request of President Johnson before Christmas, said the alternatives in

Continued on Page 2, Column 4

WAR COST ISSUE IN CONGRESS PUTS JOHNSON TO TEST

Domestic Program Will Feel Vietnam Impact in Session That Opens Tomorrow

By JOHN D. MORRIS

Special to The New York Times

WASHINGTON, Jan. 8 — Rising costs of the war in Vietnam promise to bring about severe tests of President Johnson's leadership in the 1966 session of Congress, which opens Monday.

The President apparently faces no serious difficulty in obtaining whatever appropriations he may request for carrying out the broadened commitment of United States combat forces to that conflict.

However, he is already beset by strong cross-pressures in dealing with the war's impact at home.

On one side, many Republicans and some Democrats are demanding sharp cutbacks in expenditures for social welfare and other nondefense purposes. On the other, leading spokesmen for liberal causes are urging full steam ahead in achieving Great Society goals.

Curtailment Is Expected

President Johnson's immediate problem is to chart a middle course in his State of the Union and Budget Messages, one that will satisfy the most pressing demands for economy on the domestic front without inviting a revolt by a sizable group of liberals in his own party.

Mr. Johnson has given notice of his intention to restrict the expansion of Great Society programs in seeking to cope with the fiscal and economic effects of the war. The word from the White House is that nondefense domestic spending will be greatly curtailed, but that does not necessarily mean that major cutbacks are in prospect.

Secretary of Labor W. Willard Wirtz said today that budgeted expenditures for the campaign against poverty were likely to be substantially increased.

Noted Rise in Programs

In a speech in Little Rock, Ark., the text of which was made public here, the Secretary estimated that about $17.7-billion in Federal funds would be spent in the current fiscal year for "programs directed entirely to helping the poor of this country or for those parts of broader programs which are properly allocable to benefitting this disadvantaged group."

He said such outlays had risen by an average of about $1.7-billion annually in the last three years and added:

"There is every reason to expect that the increase in next year's budget, now under consideration, will include further increases on an even larger scale."

Administration sources reported Monday that the President had trimmed his spending budget for the fiscal year 1967, starting July 1, to slightly less than $115-billion. Expenditures in the present fiscal year are now es-

Continued on Page 31, Column 4

WYSZYNSKI'S TRIP BARRED BY POLES

United Press International

Stefan Cardinal Wyszynski

By The Associated Press

WARSAW, Sunday, Jan. 9—The Polish Government accused Stefan Cardinal Wyszynski early today of having harmed Polish national interests while in Rome recently and barred the Roman Catholic Primate from further travel abroad.

A statement from Janusz Wieczorek, head of the office of the Polish Council of Ministers, said the Cardinal had been "refused a passport to go abroad. It

Continued on Page 13, Column 1

The New York Times (by Robert Walker)

LISTENING TO THE PEOPLE: Mayor Lindsay pausing at a frankfurter stand on De Kalb Avenue, Brooklyn, as he made quick tour to get views on effect of transit strike.

Mayor Chats With Victims of Strike

By TERENCE SMITH

Mayor Lindsay made a hurried tour yesterday of three of the city's areas hurt most by the transit strike.

He talked to shopkeepers and residents of the Bedford-Stuyvesant section of Brooklyn, the South Bronx and Harlem in the course of his three-hour visit to the depressed areas.

Huge crowds pressed against the Mayor as he moved along the sidewalks of the predominantly Negro and Puerto Rican neighborhoods.

"Are you O.K.? Are you getting to work all right?" Mr. Lindsay asked the people who pushed through to shake his hand.

"I haven't been able to get to work all week," one woman in Bedford-Stuyvesant told him.

"Are you being paid?" the Mayor asked.

"No," the woman said.

"Well, that's why we're trying to settle this thing—quick," Mr. Lindsay said.

The depressed, or low-income, areas such as those he visited yesterday have suffered most from the strike, in the opinion of the city's labor specialists. The residents, many of whom are paid on an hourly or daily basis, in most cases cannot afford to ride by taxi to their jobs.

Their rate of absenteeism, according to the Emergency Control Board, has been markedly higher than that for residents of more prosperous neighborhoods.

The Mayor decided on the spur of the moment to make the tour in the early afternoon. Frank D. O'Connor, the City Council President, and Mario A. Procaccino, City Controller, were invited to

Continued on Page 42, Column 8

JOHNSON RETAINS BUSINESS BACKING

But Survey Shows His Stand on Price Increases Has Aroused Apprehension

By EILEEN SHANAHAN

Special to The New York Times

WASHINGTON, Jan. 8—Business support for President Johnson has been "cracked but not shattered" by the President's recent successful attempts to control prices by threats and persuasion.

This was the consensus that emerged from a series of telephone interviews this week with business leaders in all sections of the country.

Businessmen who supported Mr. Johnson for re-election in 1964 stated, without exception, that they did not regret that decision even though their enthusiasm for the President had diminished.

But these supporters of 1964 expressed considerable anxiety over the President's use of the vast economic powers of the Federal Government to induce producers of aluminum, copper and steel to hold prices down.

Inflation Fear

The fears over what the President might next try to do to force business to do things his way were tempered, however, by a very substantial agreement among businessmen that the President was right in fearing inflation.

"Each time we read that pressure has been applied, that causes apprehension," said John Watlington, president of the Wachovia National Bank of Winston-Salem, N. C. "But there is also substantial apprehension about what will happen if prices rise," he added.

A Midwestern manufacturer put it another way.

"Business is disturbed at the meat-ax tactics," he said, "but also relieved that prices are being held down."

Last week's confrontation with the steel industry, which resulted in a compromise, added only a little to business appre-

Continued on Page 31, Column 3

New Yorkers Relax And Traffic Eases After Hectic Week

By THOMAS BUCKLEY

Battered by a week of pavement-pounding and traffic jams, New Yorkers decided to rest their weary feet yesterday.

The decision was made easier by blasts of cold air that engulfed the city. Temperatures were in the 20's during the sunny afternoon, with readings as low as 10 forecast overnight.

Traffic was lighter than usual for a Saturday, according to the Traffic Department. There was congestion in the garment center but no jams. The trucks were moving finished garments while the streets were relatively clear on the weekends.

Later in the day, traffic picked up and the police described it as generally very heavy in midtown Manhattan from 5 to 7 P.M., but no serious tie-ups were reported. Traffic was reported to be generally moderate last night.

The 27,000 members of the Police Department enjoyed a respite. After seven days of 12-hour tours of duty, they were

Continued on Page 42, Column 4

Physicians Urged To Tell the Dying

By NATALIE JAFFE

The taboo against talking of death to the dying may produce feelings of helplessness and isolation far more difficult to bear than the threat of death itself, according to a panel of psychologists and psychiatrists.

In a report published today by the Group for the Advancement of Psychiatry, several doctors who have worked extensively with the aged and the seriously ill agreed that fatally ill patients knew, somehow, that they were dying.

How they handle that knowledge—with acceptance, denial, severe depression, thoughts of immortality, attention to practical details or involvement with the treatment of their disease

Continued on Page 27, Column 1

'65 TRANSIT PAY EXCEEDED FARES

Riders Paid $280-Million, $5-Million Less Than Total Payroll Costs

By RICHARD PHALON

About $280-million in nickels, dimes and tokens clinked into Transit Authority fare boxes last year, but for the first time the fares failed to provide enough cash to meet the payroll.

An official of the authority said yesterday that the city's buses and subways took in $283.3-million from all operations, which included fares, advertising space rentals and concessions, in the year that ended June 30.

Wage costs, including checks, pension payments, Social Security and health insurance, came to $285-million.

Besides its income from fares, advertising space and concessions, the authority received aid from the city. This included $5.5-million to help pay off bonds, $13.7-million for the transit police force and $20-million for electrical power costs, among other items.

Deficit Put at $14-Million

However, the authority still operated at a deficit estimated at about $14.3-million.

The authority has budgeted a payroll of $301.4-million for the year ending June 30, 1966, but that figure does not include whatever the Transport Workers Union will win in the current bargaining. Since fare collections are running about the same as last year, the authority expects another deficit.

The law that set up the authority says that it must pay its operating costs out of its operating revenues or raise its fare. It has been able to avoid raising the fare because of the City aid it has received.

It has been estimated that a fare increase to 25 cents would bring in an additional $126.9-million. An increase to 20 cents would bring in about $63.5-million. When the authority ran in the red in the past, it got some

Continued on Page 42, Column 5

HARD WORK AHEAD

But Agreement Today Is Termed 'Possible' by Chief Mediator

By EMANUEL PERLMUTTER

Mayor Lindsay and the three mediators in the transit strike were pressing early today for a contract agreement in time to get the subway trains and buses rolling again by tomorrow morning.

Negotiations involving the Transit Authority and the two striking unions went on continuously yesterday and early this morning. Mr. Lindsay's aides said he would stay indefinitely at City Hall and keep in touch by telephone with the mediators at the Americana hotel, where the contract negotiations are taking place.

At 3 A.M. the Mayor was still at City Hall.

Both sides were reported to have modified their positions in separate private talks with the mediators and to have come close to agreement on some minor contract proposals.

However, many unsolved issues still remained on the ninth day of the strike, which has created monumental transportation difficulties.

'Meaningful Progress' Seen

A source close to the talks said there was still a "wide gap" between the authority and the two unions, the Transport Workers Union and the Amalgamated Transit Union.

The two sides did not meet face to face in the bargaining sessions.

Nathan P. Feinsinger, chairman of the mediation panel, had said yesterday morning that "meaningful progress has been made."

The Mayor said soon afterward that although the two sides were "still apart," he was urging them to "stay at the negotiating table steadily without letup."

Wages the Main Problem

"We are trying to get the subways and buses moving by Monday morning," Mr. Feinsinger said at his news conference in the Americana.

Asked if he thought that a settlement could be reached by today, he replied: "It is possible. I don't think the positions of the parties are so far apart as to preclude this."

Mr. Feinsinger said that the main problem still to be resolved was the wage settlement.

"If we get over the wage problem, the other issues will fall into place," he explained.

Mayor Lindsay said at a news conference in City Hall that "it is critical and essential that this dispute be brought to a fair,

Continued on Page 42, Column 1

Today's Sections

Index to Subjects

U.S. and Vietnamese forces headed for their destination in the Mekong Delta as a series of heavy U.S. raids on North Vietnam began.

U.S. Air Force volunteers help extinguish a burning gas tank which caught fire during a Viet Cong mortar attack at Tan Son Nhut Air Base.

"All the News That's Fit to Print"

The New York Times.

LATE CITY EDITION

U. S. Weather Bureau Report (Page 3): Forecast:
Cloudy, windy and cold today; fair,
cold tonight and tomorrow.
Temp. Range: 17—14; yesterday: 38—19.

VOL. CXV..No. 39,454.

© 1966 by The New York Times Company,
Times Square, New York, N. Y. 10036

NEW YORK, MONDAY, JANUARY 31, 1966.

TEN CENTS

BLIZZARD BRINGS 7-INCH SNOW HERE, SNARLING TRAVEL

Bitter Cold and High Winds Likely to Continue Today —Emergency Declared

EAST COAST IS BATTERED

Pennsylvania Turnpike Shut —Albany Cancels Session —9 Deaths Laid to Storm

By PETER KIHSS

A Sunday blizzard whistled through the city and the East Coast states yesterday, dumping seven inches of snow here and causing the second declaration of a snow emergency in eight days.

The bitter cold weather, with west winds gusting to 40 and 50 miles an hour, was expected to continue into today.

At least nine deaths in the metropolitan area were attributed to the storm. Among the deaths was that of an 18-month-old baby in Harlem who was the 11th child killed by fire in the city since last Thursday.

Road travel was hazardous and the New York Thruway was ordered closed at 5 P. M. from Albany to Buffalo. The entire Pennsylvania Turnpike was closed and Governor Mills Godwin of Virginia declared that in his state "no one can be assured of safe travel to any given destination."

Legislative Session Postponed

For the first time in many years, the New York State Legislature called off its session in Albany for today because snow tie-ups would have prevented many members from getting back to the capital. This week's meetings were rescheduled for tomorrow and Wednesday.

John F. Kennedy International Airport was closed from 2 P. M. to 6:18 P. M. Most airports from Charleston, S. C., north were reported closed earlier in the day. Newark Airport kept operating.

La Guardia Airport was closed to passenger traffic at 2 P. M. and remained closed through the night. The airport was open to freight traffic.

The Pennsylvania Railroad said it was unable to run trains between Baltimore and Washington because of snow trouble, and for 11 hours southbound trains were halted at Baltimore.

The New York Central's 20th Century Limited from Chicago encountered so much storm trouble that it reached Grand Central Terminal at 2:00 P.M. —four hours and 30 minutes late.

5,218 Complain

Buildings Commissioner Charles Moerdler reported 5,218 telephone calls to his central complaint bureau at WOrth 4-3000—most of them dealing with lack of heat—during the 24 hours ended at 4 P.M.

More than 100 volunteers, including Republican and Democratic political figures, responded to appeals to man telephones for incoming calls and 10 for outgoing calls at the complaint bureau, 53 Chambers Street.

Commissioner Moerdler said a number of buildings had been ordered vacated during the weekend, and armory and hotel space remained available for

Continued on Page 29, Column 1

The Plow's the Thing, So to Speak

Plow dumping snow into a Sanitation Department truck on Fifth Avenue yesterday north of St. Patrick's Cathedral.

In the suburbs it was often worse. This man uses small snow blower at Fairfield Street in Valley Stream, L. I.

The New York Times (by Allyn Baum and Ernest Sisto)

500 City Tenants Will Get New Homes With U.S. Aid

By SAMUEL KAPLAN

Five hundred low-income families here will receive Federal subsidies so they can move into privately owned middle-income apartments under a new public housing program.

The program will be carried out by the City Housing Authority, which announced yesterday that it planned to lease about 500 middle-income apartments in private buildings and then sublease them at lower rents to families eligible for public housing.

The leasing agreement will be known only to the landlord, the authority and the tenant to avoid any possible social ostracism of the tenant by other residents of the building.

The authority explained that it would charge the low-income family the same rent it would pay if it moved into a comparable apartment in a public housing project.

Program Explained

For example, a four-bedroom apartment in a Federally aided low-income project rents for about $76 a month. If a four-bedroom apartment is found in a middle-income development renting for $190 a month, the authority would pay the landlord $114 a month. The tenant would pay $76.

The cost of the program, which was not disclosed, will be borne by the Federal Department of Housing and Urban Development under the rent-subsidy section of the 1965 Housing Act.

The experimental program was developed to provide needed

Continued on Page 17, Column 3

COURT APPORTIONS SHUBERT ESTATES

Partnership's Value Is Put at $33.5-Million, Divided in 2 Parts by State Justice

By MILTON ESTEROW

A State Supreme Court justice has ruled that the estate of Lee Shubert is entitled to receive about $28-million from the estate of his brother, J. J. Shubert.

Justice John L. Flynn said that the partnership of the brothers who built Broadway's most powerful theatrical dynasty was worth $33.5-million when Lee Shubert died in 1953. J. J. Shubert died in 1963.

Justice Flynn, in a decision handed down Friday, held that the Lee Shubert estate was entitled to half of the value of the partnership, or $16.7-million, plus 6 per cent interest for every year since 1953—more than $11-million.

The ruling supported every recommendation made several months ago by Edwin L. Weisl Sr., who has been serving as a court referee in the dispute, which began in 1954.

The decision by Justice Flynn may be appealed by both sides as well as by the Federal Government. The Government intervened in the case to protect tax claims of $15.7 million made in 1963 against the Lee Shubert estate. There are no tax claims against the J. J. Shubert estate.

Theatrical sources said yesterday that the case could ultimately force a reorganization of the Shubert enterprises.

No agreement has been

Continued on Page 22, Column 1

Fund Goal Passed By Lincoln Center

By RICHARD F. SHEPARD

The fund drive to build and launch Lincoln Center for the Performing Arts has reached its goal — one of the largest ever set for this purpose — and brought in several millions extra.

The campaign has reaped $165.4-million, well above the $160.7-million set in 1963 as its objective. However, unforeseen expenses incurred since 1963 have absorbed the difference, and an additional $1.4-million not included in the fund drive target must now be raised to complete the Juilliard School. The total cost of the center is now $166.5-million.

Four of the six buildings on the 14 West Side acres are in

Continued on Page 22, Column 4

BRODERICK URGES $50 PARKING FINES IN MIDTOWN AREA

Barnes Backs Idea, but Notes Scofflaw Problem—Mayor Says Cleanup Is Needed

By ROBERT E. DALLOS

Police Commissioner Vincent L. Broderick urged yesterday that fines for illegal parking in midtown Manhattan be raised to $50. Traffic Commissioner Henry A. Barnes immediately supported the idea.

The increase from the present $15 fine, Mr. Broderick said, "would be a deterrent" to illegal parking and would be "more realistic."

The Commissioner, who was interviewed on "Direct Line" over WNBC, said that the plan must be worked out with the traffic commissioner and with the courts.

In a telephone interview after Mr. Broderick's radio and television appearance, Commissioner Barnes said: "I think the idea is good. The $15 fine hasn't in any way been a deterrent to parking in midtown Manhattan."

Scofflaw Problem Cited

But Mr. Barnes added: "Even a $50 fine or a $100 fine isn't going to deter anyone unless means can be developed to apprehend scofflaws.

"I can put in all the signals, all the systems, all the signs and all the regulations but if people don't pay attention to them, we can save the money."

He suggested that the registration and driver license files of scofflaws be flagged at the Department of Motor Vehicles and that renewal of such documents be denied to such persons.

A spokesman for Mayor Lindsay said that Mr. Lindsay agreed that traffic in Manhattan "must be cleaned up." But the spokesman added that Mr. Lindsay could not comment on whether or by how much fines should be raised since he had not talked with either of his commissioners.

Mayor Has Started Drive

On Friday Mr. Lindsay had announced a drive on illegal parkers. He said cars double parked would be ticketed and towed from congested midtown areas.

The Automobile Club of New York said it would be difficult to oppose higher fines for people who "flout the law" but it decried the sweeping nature of Commissioner Broderick's proposal. Gilbert B. Phillips, the club's president, said the city "should stop dragging its feet on providing of off-street parking space."

Final authority for higher parking fines must come from the First and Second Departments of the Appellate Division of the State Supreme Court.

Presiding Justice Bernard Botein of the First Department said in a telephone interview last night that it would be "unrealistic" to think that such action would be taken unless the police and traffic commissioners requested it.

Although he refused to speculate on any action the court might take, he said a request to raise parking fines "would engage our serious consideration."

These courts used their jurisdiction during the transit strike by temporarily raising $15 parking fines to $25 at the request

Continued on Page 30, Column 5

RAIDS ON NORTH VIETNAM RESUMED BY U.S. PLANES AS 37-DAY PAUSE IS ENDED

A MISSION OF MERCY: Although he had been hit in eye by enemy fire, Pfc. Thomas Cole, medical corpsman from Richmond, administers first aid to First Cavalry Division (Airmobile) comrade in trench in landing zone near Anthai during bitter fighting there.

Associated Press Radiophoto

JOHNSON TO TALK

Saigon Reports Strike by Navy and Air Force Bombers

By CHARLES MOHR
Special to The New York Times

SAIGON, Monday, Jan. 31—United States war planes resumed bombing attacks on North Vietnam today.

The bombing raids on that Communist country had been suspended for 37 days from 6 P.M. on Christmas Eve, Dec. 24, until today as one step to encourage Hanoi to negotiate a peaceful settlement of the Vietnam war.

[The White House said that President Johnson would make a statement at 10 A.M. on the renewed bombing of North Vietnam.]

Today's action apparently signaled the end of the so-called Washington peace offensive and marked a return to a hard military line toward the North Vietnamese.

Embassy Announcement

Barry Zorthian, Minister Counselor of Information for the United States Embassy here, summoned reporters to a press briefing at 3 P.M. (2 A.M., Monday, New York time) and read the following announcement:

"The Prime Minister of the Republic of Vietnam (South Vietnam) and the American Ambassador to Vietnam announce that United States aircraft today attacked targets in designated areas of North Vietnam."

Mr. Zorthian added that the raids today had already been completed and that full details would be made available later at the regular daily military briefing.

He turned aside other questions.

It was not stated whether the planes that struck North Vietnam today followed the same rules of engagement which had governed airstrikes before the long pause. These prohibited pilots from striking the population centers of Hanoi or Haiphong.

Efforts at Negotiation

The United States has twice ordered cessation of bombing in the North to encourage negotiations. The first pause was for a period of five days last May.

Air raids against North Vietnam began almost a year ago, on Feb. 7, 1965 after Vietcong guerrillas raided an American compound at Pleiku and caused a number of American deaths.

It was noted that the resumption of bombing came at a time when military activity in general was being elevated by the United States. A series of large-scale military operations, involving United States Army and Marine Corps troops along the Central Vietnam coast, amounted to a general offensive in that area.

Other large scale operations

Continued on Page 8, Column 3

BRITAIN TIGHTENS CURB ON RHODESIA

Blocks Remainder of Imports —Treasury Warns Against Loans to Smith Regime

By W. GRANGER BLAIR
Special to The New York Times

LONDON, Jan. 30—The Government announced today that it would charge the relatively small amount of Rhodesian imports that had still been permitted to enter Britain.

Effective next Wednesday, the 5 per cent of imports that had not been covered by earlier British economic sanctions against the rebellious regime in Rhodesia will be barred from Britain.

The Board of Trade, making public the new measures, said licenses for British exports to Rhodesia would "in general" be refused from Wednesday on, thus virtually halting all trade between the two countries.

The Treasury issued a warning that anyone who extended credit to Rhodesia risked losing his money when constitutional government was restored. The Rhodesian regime, which is controlled by the territory's

Continued on Page 6, Column 5

Troops From North Fight First Cavalry In Binhdinh Province

Special to The New York Times

SAIGON, Jan. 30. Military developments this weekend added to rest a feeling that the war in South Vietnam might be gradually "fading away."

Troops of the 18th North Vietnamese Army Regiment have been identified as among those in battle against the United States First Cavalry Division in Binhdinh Province 303 miles northeast of Saigon, an American military spokesman said today.

Four major United States spokesman said the South Vietnamese were conducting 42 military operations that each involved a battalion or more of troops.

This represents about 40 per cent of Saigon's combat battalions.

The enemy forces also were active. In addition to doggedly fighting the First Cavalry troops near Bongon in Binhdinh Province, they harassed a

Continued on Page 8, Column 1

GOLDBERG STATES PEACE BID STANDS

Says Ho Chi Minh, in Letter 'Plainly' Spurning Talks, Is Now on Defensive

By IRVING SPIEGEL

Arthur J. Goldberg declared last night that despite the "intransigent" position taken by President Ho Chi Minh of North Vietnam, the United States would continue to press for peace in Vietnam.

In a speech delivered here, the chief United States delegate to the United Nations directly rebutted remarks by the North Vietnamese leader.

Last week, writing to the leaders of Communist and some other countries, President Ho Chi Minh sharply denounced United States offers of unconditional peace talks as an "effort to fool public opinion."

Peace Wish Unaltered

Mr. Goldberg asserted that the letters "plainly" spurned the peace offer. Voicing regret over this, he added: "In no way, however, does it change or diminish our desire for peace. In no way does it change or diminish our effort to seek an honorable settlement. It will continue."

Mr. Goldberg was the principal guest at a dinner session of the 53d annual meeting of the Anti-Defamation League of B'nai B'rith, at the New York Hilton Hotel. He accepted the league's America's Democratic Legacy Award for "distinguished contributions to the enrichment of our democratic heritage."

Dore Schary, national chairman of the league, made the presentation and cited Mr. Goldberg for "lifelong dedication and commitment to assuring constitutional principles of freedom and dignity to all Americans."

President Johnson sent a message describing Mr. Goldberg as "a man who epitomizes the highest qualities of public life."

In his address Mr. Goldberg noted the requests addressed to the United States "by individuals and nations of many ideologies" for a pause in bombing attacks on North Vietnam "for a reasonable period of time" so that

Continued on Page 10, Column 3

'Arty' Therapy Is Criticized by Scholar

By RAYMOND H. ANDERSON

A growing abuse of the term "creativity" in occupational therapy, entertainment and business is vulgarizing original thought in modern society, according to Dr. Michael Wyschogrod, an assistant professor of philosophy at City College.

Creativity must be served for its own sake, not for psychological needs, he said yesterday at a meeting of the American Association of Existential Psychology and Psychiatry.

"We cannot pretend that dabbling with creativity is the solution to the problem of the housewife and the salesman who find their lives empty," the professor added. "The only result we will achieve is to cheapen creativity

Prof. Michael Wyschogrod

Fred Stein

solely "to improve his story or his picture, his poem or his song." If this is not done, he added, the result is "a form of occupational therapy that is destructive of the dignity of labor, particularly creative labor."

"The person who attempts to create in order to find a meaning in his life, to convert a pointless existence into one that is no longer pointless is using creativity to his own end and that cannot be done," he declared.

The theme of the association's two-day meeting was "Imagination and Existence." Among the participants were Ben Shahn, the artist; Saul Bellow, the writer; Dr.

out solving their problems."

The true artist, Professor Wyschogrod said, must work

Continued on Page 14, Column 3

Wyszynski Defies Regime in Poland

By HENRY KAMM
Special to The New York Times

CZESTOCHOWA, Poland, Jan. 30 - Stefan Cardinal Wyszynski defiantly declared today that the Roman Catholic Church of Poland could not be vanquished by any temporal power.

His stern sermon, delivered at an occasion of special significance in Poland's holiest shrine, was a clear reply to the Government's present campaign against the church.

It was the Cardinal's strongest statement of the dispute since he was refused a passport to visit the Vatican early this month.

It was well understood as such by a densely packed crowd of worshipers at the Basilica of

Continued on Page 5, Column 4

NEWS INDEX

	Page		Page
Books	37	Music	29-33
Bridge	36	Obituaries	29
Business	39-39	Real Estate	40
Buyers	34	Screen	29-33
Chess	36	Sermons	29
Crossword	37	Ships and Air	20
Editorials	38	Society	29
Fashions	34	Sports	30-35
Financial	39-33	Theaters	29-33
Food	34	TV and Radio	79
Letters	38	U. N. Proceedings	5
Man in the News	9	Weather	35

The News Summary and Index will be found on Page 2 today.

"All the News That's Fit to Print"

The New York Times.

LATE CITY EDITION
U.S. Weather Bureau Report (Page 54) forecasts
Clearing today after early snow;
fair, cold tonight and tomorrow.
Temp. Range: 32–25; yesterday: 34–10

VOL. CXV..No. 39,456.   © 1966 by The New York Times Company, Times Square, New York, N. Y. 10036   NEW YORK, WEDNESDAY, FEBRUARY 2, 1966.   TEN CENTS

CATHOLIC CHURCH BIDS LEGISLATURE DELAY ON DIVORCE

Senator Who Led Drafting Panel Views Action as 'Declaration of War'

REFORM FEARED DEAD

Wilson Attack on Letter to All Members Brings Hot Reply From Leaders

By SYDNEY H. SCHANBERG
Special to The New York Times

ALBANY, Feb. 1.—The Roman Catholic Church has sent a letter to all state legislators calling on them not to take any immediate "affirmative action" on the bill to reform the state's divorce law.

Senator Jerome L. Wilson, head of the joint legislative committee that drafted the bill, viewed the letter as "seemingly a declaration of war ... in opposition to meaningful divorce reform." It puts the bill "in deep trouble," the Manhattan Democrat declared.

The leaders of the Legislature took a less alarmist view and told Mr. Wilson there was no need for him to get excited. Nevertheless, almost everyone in the Capitol agreed that the move by the Catholics had not helped the bill.

Letter From State Group

The letter, dated yesterday, came from Charles J. Tobin Jr., secretary of the New York State Catholic Welfare Committee, the spokesman for the church in the state.

The Catholic Church does not recognize divorce and in the past has successfully opposed any liberalization of the state's 178-year-old divorce law, which provides only one ground for divorce—adultery.

The letter was actually a missive to the chairmen of the committees handling the bill in both houses—Senator John H. Hughes, head of the Senate Judiciary Committee, and Speaker Anthony J. Travia, who runs the Assembly Rules Committee. However, copies were sent to all the other lawmakers.

While the letter did not register outright opposition to the Wilson bill, it asked the Legislature to "postpone" any action until more "supporting data and explanations" were available.

"We are confident that there are many groups in our state who will be seriously disappointed in and critical of the

Continued on Page 38, Column 3

MOLLEN TESTIFIES IN STATE INQUIRY

Tells of Meeting With 2 Who Figured in Housing Case

By EDITH EVANS ASBURY

The State Investigation Commission heard testimony yesterday that a Brooklyn insurance salesman received $75,000 and insurance contracts after arranging a meeting between the applicant for a housing project and Milton Mollen at Mr. Mollen's home.

Mr. Mollen, chairman of the Housing and Redevelopment Board at the time of the meeting, denied that the meeting had figured in approval of the state-aided project.

Mr. Mollen said he had known the insurance salesman only as a rabbi and did not know he had any personal interest in the project.

The meeting at Mr. Mollen's home at 4619 Avenue H in Brooklyn took place on an evening in January or February of 1963, according to the testimony of Mr. Mollen and the other two participants. They were Reuben Glick, the builder, and Philip Gruberger, the insurance salesman.

It had been arranged, according to all three witnesses, to discuss a charitable event, "Music Under the Stars," to be held in Madison Square Garden in June, at which Mr. Mollen was scheduled to be a guest of honor.

During the discussion, "inadvertently it turned to the subject of housing," according to Mr. Gruberger.

The specific housing was Brightwater Towers, a proposed $16-million, 735-family develop-

Continued on Page 42, Column 2

EJECTED FROM AIR BASE: Impoverished Negroes and civil rights workers are carried from a deactivated Air Force base at Greenville, Miss. Group has occupied barracks to dramatize appeal for food, housing and jobs.
Associated Press Wirephoto

NEW RIGHTS CHIEF CRITICIZES UNIONS

Booth, Sworn In Here, Vows Fight on Discrimination in Building Trades

By TERENCE SMITH

William H. Booth was sworn in as the new chairman of the city's Commission on Human Rights yesterday and promptly declared that he regarded the building-trades unions as "particularly guilty" of job discrimination.

Within minutes after being sworn in by Mayor Lindsay at City Hall, Mr. Booth said he intended to "get after the construction unions — not with brickbats, but with the law."

He promised to hit the unions "in their economic breadbaskets," but he did not specify what economic pressures he had in mind.

Mr. Booth, who is resigning as state chairman of the National Association for the Advancement of Colored People, replaces Earl Brown as chairman of the commission. The post pays $25,000 a year.

100 at Ceremony

Mr. Brown was among the 100 guests who attended the swearing-in ceremony in the Board of Estimate chamber. He said he had known for some time that he would be replaced, but that he felt the move was "just a change-over, not an expression of disappointment in me."

In introducing Mr. Booth, the Mayor praised Mr. Brown, thanking him in the name of the city "for his stewardship of the civil rights movement."

The 15-member Human Rights Commission currently meets in closed session once a month and its chairman is the only salaried member. In order for Mr. Booth to replace Mr. Brown it was

Continued on Page 38, Column 2

Air Force Ejects Negroes Occupying A Mississippi Base

By GENE ROBERTS
Special to The New York Times

GREENVILLE, Miss., Feb. 1.—Air Force troops weathered a flurry of kicks, bites and curses today while ejecting 110 civil rights workers and impoverished Negroes from a deactivated Air Force base.

A major general — flanked by three colonels, two lieutenant colonels and two majors —gave the ejection order to 140 air policemen after the demonstrators refused to leave a barracks they occupied yesterday.

They were occupying the barracks at Greenville Air Force Base, the demonstrators said today, to dramatize an appeal for free food, housing and job training programs.

3 Bite Policemen

"Kick 'em!" shouted one woman as the air police began carrying the demonstrators bodily from the building. "Kick hell out of 'em!"

At least three persons bit air policemen on the hands and legs. And one white civil rights worker leaped on the back of an airman, then kicked, struggled and cursed as he was carried away.

Although the idea for the "live-in" was developed in subfreezing temperatures over the weekend as a way of protesting delays in a food distribu-

Continued on Page 15, Column 4

Buster Keaton, 70, Dies on Coast; Poker-Faced Comedian of Films

By The Associated Press

HOLLYWOOD, Feb. 1.—Buster Keaton, the poker-faced comic whose studies in exquisite frustration amused two generations of movie audiences, died of lung cancer today at his home in suburban Woodland Hills. His age was 70.

Someone once remarked of Buster Keaton that he looked like the kind of man that dogs kick.

A mournful little fellow, sadfaced as a basset, usually wearing a saucer-brimmed porkpie hat, oversized suit and floppy bow tie, Joseph Francis Keaton stood with Charlie Chaplin and Harold Lloyd as one of the three great clowns of the silent screen.

In 20 or more films, mostly two-reelers filled with windfalls and custard pie slapstick, Buster Keaton established a screen character—the sad and silent loner who persevered stoically against a mechanized world.

Unlike Mr. Chaplin, he was never sentimental and he never resorted to maudlin pathos. He turned a granite face to the widely comic and nightmarish cries that befell him—and he always prevailed over impending doom.

Buster Keaton

His strength was his ability to survive. He displayed that perseverance not only in his comic characterizations but also in his private activities. For his life was marked by periods of triumph and frustration—wealth, a descent into

Continued on Page 28, Column 3

New Midwest Storm Moves Into the East

By BERNARD WEINRAUB

A new storm piled up snow and ice across the Midwest yesterday and moved into the East last night, dusting New York with a new layer of snow.

Snow flurries began at 11:20 P.M. and the Weather Bureau predicted "moderate amounts"— two to four inches—of snow by this morning. At 2:30 A.M. the snow measured less than an inch.

"It won't be anything like it was Sunday," said one forecaster, taking note of the storm that froze crops in the South, stranded motorists in the Midwest and buried parts of the Atlantic Coast under drifts of up to 30 feet.

Commissioner of Traffic Henry A. Barnes, who had lifted the

Continued on Page 28, Column 2

PRESIDENT URGES WORLD AID DRIVE, BUT TRIMS FUNDS

Request for Foreign Help Is $3.4-Billion—Self-Help Is Key to Poverty Attack

Excerpts from aid message appear on Page 4.

By FELIX BELAIR Jr.
Special to The New York Times

WASHINGTON, Feb. 1.—President Johnson told Congress today that the appalling conditions of the underdeveloped half of the world "challenge our own security and threaten the future of the world." He then requested the smallest appropriation for improving them in the 18-year history of foreign aid programs.

In a special message, the President asked for $3.38-billion in the fiscal year 1967, which begins July 1 — $2.46-billion of the amount to go for loans and grants to developing countries "in new attacks upon the root causes of world poverty."

Despite increases in some economic aid categories, his total asking figure for funds to improve economic and social conditions in the developing world remained well under the current fiscal year's comparable figure of $2.7-billion, and the combined economic and military aid total of $4.17-billion for the period.

First Sought $3.3-Billion

A year ago the President's initial request was for $2.2-billion in economic aid and $2.17-billion in military assistance.

These were later increased by supplemental requests for an additional $494-million in economic grants, primarily for South Vietnam, and $300-million more for military assistance. In requesting the supplemental amounts, aid officials acknowledged that they had underestimated actual requirements at the outset.

A total of $917-million was asked today for military aid "to keep our commitments to our allies and friendly armed forces." This would not include such aid for South Vietnam, for which a separate, classified request was included in the Defense Department budget.

'Absolute Minimum'

Mr. Johnson labeled his asking figure for economic aid as "the absolute minimum to meet presently foreseeable needs." He said it was submitted "with the understanding that I will not hesitate to request a supplemental appropriation if a clear need develops."

At the same time, the President placed such emphasis on self-help criteria through economic, fiscal and social reforms, including population controls measures, as to raise the question of how many developing countries might qualify for aid.

Officials responsible for carrying out the aid program said the guidelines laid down by the President called for "a severe and exacting" application of the principle of self-help.

The guiding principle of fu-

Continued on Page 4, Column 2

GOLDBERG SPEAKS ON VIETNAM AGENDA ISSUE: Arthur J. Goldberg, U.S. representative, addressing the Security Council. At lower left is Nikolai T. Fedorenko, the Soviet delegate. Lord Caradon, the British delegate, is seated next to Mr. Goldberg.
The New York Times (by Patrick A. Burns)

SECURITY COUNCIL WEIGHS VIETNAM; DEFERS VOTE ON U.S. AGENDA ITEM; HANOI BARS ANY U.N. INTERVENTION

JORDAN HOLDS KEY

Russians and French Opposing Move — Ballot Due Today

Excerpts from statements in Security Council, Page 14.

By DREW MIDDLETON
Special to The New York Times

UNITED NATIONS, N.Y., Feb. 1.—Jordan held the key tonight to whether the Security Council could debate a draft United States resolution seeking peace in Vietnam.

Jordan's delegate, Waleed M. Sadi, obtained a postponement of the voting until 3 P.M. tomorrow while he seeks instructions from his Government in Amman.

The decision to delay the vote followed a series of sharp exchanges in the Council between Arthur J. Goldberg, the United States representative, and Nikolai T. Fedorenko of the Soviet Union, who bitterly denounced the United States. The Soviet Union and France opposed action on the resolution.

Seven other members of the newly enlarged 15-member Council support the United States proposal to place on the agenda a resolution calling on the Council to arrange a conference that would achieve a durable settlement of the war in Vietnam. The resolution also looks to the restoration of stability in neighboring Laos and Thailand.

Nine Votes Needed

A ninth vote, Jordan's, is necessary for a majority in support of placing the item on the agenda. Since the question is procedural, the veto power of the permanent members cannot be exercised. If the issue is placed on the agenda, any action on it will then be subject to veto by the Soviet Union or France.

Supporting the United States are Britain, New Zealand, Argentina, the Netherlands, Nationalist China, Japan and Uruguay. Bulgaria, like the Soviet Union and France, is opposed to the agenda move, and Mali, Nigeria and Uganda are expected to abstain.

Mr. Goldberg, who spoke twice during the long, increasingly sharp debate, said he expected that the United States proposal would win the necessary votes.

The virulence of the Soviet and Bulgarian opposition, the cool rejection by France and the wavering of the African delegations foreshadowed hard passage for the resolution if it gets to the stage of debate in the Council.

The resolution, some diplo-

Continued on Page 15, Column 1

20,000 Troops in Vietnam Hunt 4 Enemy Regiments

Offensive Is Joint Action

By NEIL SHEEHAN
Special to The New York Times

SAIGON, Feb. 1.—The United States and South Vietnamese high commands have launched a major offensive in the rice deltas of central Vietnam in an ambitious effort to trap and destroy four enemy regiments.

The offensive involves more than 20,000 American, South Vietnamese and South Korean troops, including helicopter, air force, artillery and armor-support elements.

It has actually been in progress for seven days, but a United States military spokesman here has reported it as two large but separate operations, one in Binhdinh Province and the other in the adjacent northern province of Quangngai. But today it was reliably reported that the forces are part of a coordinated military effort.

Biggest Since French Drive

The targets of the offensive are the 18th and 98th North Vietnamese Regiments of regulars, which infiltrated into South Vietnam last winter, and the First and Second Vietcong Regiments.

The four regiments are estimated at a total strength of about 8,000 men.

Nothing on the scale of the current allied offensive has taken place in Central Vietnam since 1953 during the French Indochina war, when the French high command staged a vast offensive north of Hue in a vain attempt to annihilate an enemy regiment.

The first stage of the current offensive, known as Operation Masher, began last Tuesday

Continued on Page 15, Column 5

Port in North Bombed

Special to The New York Times

SAIGON, Feb. 1.—American planes bombed North Vietnamese port facilities and communications lines for the second day today, following the end of Washington's pause to allow a response to its peace offensive.

A United States military spokesman said three American fighter-bombers were lost during the first day of the resumption of bombing after the 37-day pause, which began Christmas Eve.

One pilot is missing and presumed dead or captured. The three crewmen of the two other planes were plucked safely from the South China Sea by helicopters.

The spokesman gave only sketchy details of the new raids. He said full reports were still being processed by command centers and were not yet available for news media.

The spokesman said that as far as he knew the raids were on the southern portion of North Vietnam and that there were no strikes near Hanoi or the major port of Haiphong.

One target was the port of Benthuy, about five miles southeast of Vinh, a coastal

Continued on Page 15, Column 8

'54 PACT IS CITED BY NORTH VIETNAM

Statement Says That Only Parties to Geneva Parley Can Join Negotiations

By SEYMOUR TOPPING
Special to The New York Times

HONG KONG, Feb. 1.—North Vietnam declared today that the United Nations Security Council had no right to deal with the Vietnam question.

A terse statement from the Foreign Ministry, issued several hours before the Security Council met in New York, warned that any resolution it might adopt "intervening in the Vietnam question would be null and void."

This eliminated any immediate possibility that the Security Council could become a forum for direct negotiations to end the war.

"The Government of the Democratic Republic of Vietnam reaffirms that, on the international plane, consideration of the United States war acts in Vietnam falls within the competence of the 1954 Geneva Conference on Indochina, and not of the United Nations Security Council," the Foreign Ministry said.

Invitation Would Be Needed

The 1954 Geneva Conference, which ended the French Indochina war, was initially attended by representatives of the United States, Britain, France, the Soviet Union, Laos, Cambodia, the French-sponsored "Associated States of Vietnam," and of the "Democratic Republic of Vietnam," who spoke for the Communist-led Vietminh insurgents.

Any peace talks in the Security Council would not include the representatives of either side in Vietnam, unless they, as nonmembers, were specifically invited to participate.

The North Vietnamese statement denounced the United States initiative in calling a Security Council meeting. It declared:

"As on previous occasions, this time the United States is seeking again to use the United Nations to cover up its aggression in the war of aggression and to force on the Vietnamese people a settlement of the Vietnam question, accord-

Continued on Page 15, Column 5

VIETNAM PROTEST SNARLS TIMES SQ.

32 Demonstrators Arrested in Sitdown at Rush Hour

By DOUGLAS ROBINSON

A sitdown demonstration against the resumption of bombing and the continuing war in Vietnam snarled traffic in Times Square last night at the rush hour.

Thirty-two demonstrators, who made themselves limp and had to be carried to police vans, were arrested on charges of disorderly conduct after sitting and lying on the slush-covered streets.

The protest was carried out by at least 1,000 persons who marched into Times Square from the United Nations Plaza, where many had participated in a silent 24-hour vigil against President Johnson's decision to resume bombing North Vietnam.

The demonstrators, shouting and chanting, arrived in Times Square at 6:20 P.M. and were herded behind police barricades. They ringed the Allied Chemical Building and the armed forces recruiting station at 43d Street.

Others marched in a long line in front of the bookstores

Continued on Page 15, Column 2

G.O.P. Sees Issue In Expanded War

By TOM WICKER
Special to The New York Times

WASHINGTON, Feb. 1.—Republican Congressional strategists believe divisions within the Democratic party and the prospect of an expanding land war in Vietnam may be giving them a winning political issue against President Johnson.

They believe the country may eventually turn against a President whose party does not fully support him and whose war policy may produce long casualty lists without military victory or a negotiable settlement.

To take political advantage of this, the Republican leaders are pulling back from direct criticism of the Johnson policy and are de-emphasizing their former

Continued on Page 11, Column 1

FAILURE FOR U.S. SEEN BY GEN. GIAP

Hanoi's Defense Chief Says Size of Force Is Irrelevant

Excerpts from Giap article will be found on Page 16.

By MAX FRANKEL
Special to The New York Times

WASHINGTON, Feb. 1.—North Vietnam's Defense Minister, Gen. Vo Nguyen Giap, has issued an analysis of American war aims that predicts inevitable failure for the United States regardless of the size of its commitment.

Granting American military superiority, General Giap does not forecast a battlefield victory of the kind scored over the French at Dienbienphu in the Indochina War. He expects a long and hard war, but insists that the United States can never triumph because it cannot, win over the people of South Vietnam, occupy enough of its territory or create a viable army and government there.

The top analysis by the general, who is also a Deputy Premier of North Vietnam, aug-

Continued on Page 16, Column 1

"All the News That's Fit to Print"

The New York Times.

LATE CITY EDITION
U. S. Weather Bureau Report (Page 77) forecast:
Mostly cloudy today and tonight.
Rain developing late tomorrow.
Temp. Range: 40—28; yesterday: 34—19.

VOL. CXV..No. 39,462.

© 1966 by The New York Times Company, New York, N. Y.

NEW YORK, TUESDAY, FEBRUARY 8, 1966.

TEN CENTS

MAYOR PREPARING A BILL TO CONTROL TRANSIT AGENCIES

It Would Allow Him to Name Heads of Triborough and Transit Authorities

SEEKS TO UNIFY SYSTEM

Lindsay Would Also Assume Direction of Both Expense and Capital Budgets

By SYDNEY H. SCHANBERG
Special to The New York Times

ALBANY, Feb. 7—Mayor Lindsay is preparing to put a bill before the Legislature that would remove the heads of the Transit Authority and the Triborough Bridge and Tunnel Authority and give the Mayor virtually full control over the naming of their successors.

The legislation to unify and strengthen the city's transportation system would also give the Mayor virtually full control over the capital and expense budgets of both the Transit and Triborough Authorities. At present, his control is limited to the Transit Authority's capital budget.

The bill, however, does not call for the merger of the two authorities.

It is also understood to be Mr. Lindsay's plan to create an over-all city transportation agency into which the separate city departments that deal with transportation—such as traffic, highways and marine and aviation—could be shifted by local law or executive order.

Since such a merger can be carried out without state legislation, it is not known whether this part of the Mayor's plan is either mentioned or incorporated in his transit bill.

Still Conferring on Bill

Mr. Lindsay's bill has reportedly been drafted, but is not scheduled for introduction in the Legislature until next week at the earliest. It will be the Mayor's first major legislation to be introduced.

Richard M. Rosen, the Mayor's legislative representative, refused comment tonight on the specifics of the bill. Mr. Rosen said that he was still holding numerous discussions over the bill with legislative leaders and that as a result the legislation was in a state of flux and could undergo some changes before its formal introduction.

One source reported tonight that most of Mr. Rosen's discussions have been with the Governor's office and with Earl W. Brydges, the Republican majority leader of the Senate.

These talks, it was reported,

Continued on Page 22, Column 3

O'CONNOR OPPOSES PROSECUTOR PLAN

Disputes Lindsay on Merger of 5 District Attorneys

By TERENCE SMITH

City Council President Frank D. O'Connor vehemently objected yesterday to a proposal to consolidate the five district attorneys' offices in the city.

Mr. O'Connor, who was the Queens District Attorney until his election last fall, described the plan, put forward by Mayor Lindsay's task force on law enforcement, as "illegal, impractical and not feasible."

He also objected to the group's proposal Sunday to appoint a special assistant to the Mayor to coordinate the work of all law-enforcement agencies. He described this as unwarranted "interference" with the affairs of the Police Department.

Mr. O'Connor, who is the highest-ranking Democrat in the city government, made his comments on the report in a hastily called news conference in his City Hall office.

At about the same time, in Utica, N. Y., Mayor Lindsay was telling a pre-luncheon press conference that the proposals of the task force, which include the establishment of a civilian-dominated police review board, must be put into practice "as soon as possible."

The Mayor refused to say whether he would retain Police Commissioner Vincent L. Broderick.

Continued on Page 28, Column 3

Close Vote Seen Today in the 17th

The New York Times (by John Orris)
Orin Lehman, left, and Theodore Kupferman at WCBS studio

By PAUL L. MONTGOMERY

An extremely close contest is expected today in the special election in the 17th Congressional District for Mayor Lindsay's former seat.

City Councilman Theodore R. Kupferman, the Republican candidate, and Orin Lehman, the Democrat, predicted victory yesterday in their last day of campaigning, but both acknowledged that the vote would probably be near 50-50. Jeffrey St. John is the Conservative party candidate.

The 311 polling places in the district will be open from 6 A.M. to 9 P.M.

Mr. Lehman, an unsuccessful candidate for Controller in last September's mayoral primary, urged his workers to last-minute canvassing by recalling the 1954 contest in the 17th District. Mr. Lehman worked in that campaign, in which Frederic R. Coudert, the Republican, defeated An-

Continued on Page 27, Column 1

F.H.A. Mortgage Interest Raised From 5¼ to 5½%

By EILEEN SHANAHAN
Special to The New York Times

WASHINGTON, Feb. 7—The Government increased today from 5¼ to 5½ per cent the maximum interest rate on home mortgages insured by the Federal Housing Administration. The rate increase was ordered, according to Robert C. Weaver, Secretary of Housing and Urban Development, only after it became clear that the recent rising trend of interest rates would not reverse itself soon.

He said the action "was required to assure a flow of funds for F.H.A.-insured loans," which have been increasingly hard to get because many lenders have preferred to put their money into other types of loans on which interest rates are higher and the return larger.

Others Earn More

Mortgages without Government backing earn more than F.H.A.-insured mortgages and so do many types of business and personal loans, especially in recent months.

Interest rates began to rise as early as last fall and took a sharp upward turn in December following the Federal Reserve Board's increase in the discount rate, its basic lending rate to banks.

The increase in the F.H.A. maximum rate on home mortgages is expected to facilitate, in particular, the sales of older houses, which are more frequently sold with F.H.A. insurance than new homes are.

Lenders tend to work less F.H.A.

Continued on Page 21, Column 4

LOTTERY IS VOTED IN STATE SENATE

Bill Passed 39 to 22 After Debate About Morality— Assembly Acts Today

By JOHN SIBLEY

ALBANY, Feb. 7—The Senate voted today to establish a state lottery, with the proceeds to be spent exclusively for education. The Assembly is expected to follow suit tomorrow.

The proposal was approved by a vote of 39 to 22 after nearly three hours of debate on the morality of using the proceeds of gambling to help pay for government.

Authorizing a public lottery requires an amendment to the State Constitution, so the measure—if approved by the Assembly—will be put to the voters in a referendum in November.

The bill was approved by the Legislature last year, but constitutional amendments require passage by two successive Legislatures and then the electorate.

Although details would be left to the 1967 Legislature, proponents of the lottery envision one similar to that now operated by New Hampshire.

Estimates of revenue range from $65-million a year, forecast by T. Norman Hurd, the State Budget Director, to $500-million a year, forecast by the lottery's more enthusiastic advocates.

Continued on Page 25, Column 1

Divorce Law Called 'Unfair' by Kennedy

By HOMER BIGART
Special to The New York Times

UTICA, N. Y., Feb. 7—Senator Robert F. Kennedy said here today that he favored liberalization of New York State's "archaic" divorce laws. He did not say how he wanted the laws to be changed, but he said that he was concerned over the fact that the only ground for divorce in the state was adultery.

The support of Mr. Kennedy, a prominent Roman Catholic, for revisions in the divorce laws came only four days after bills that have been introduced by other leading Roman Catholic laymen urged the Legislature to adopt "significant revisions" in the state's divorce laws.

Earlier, however, a spokes-

Continued on Page 24, Column 4

ALBANY LEADERS REACH AN IMPASSE ON REDISTRICTING

Rival Bills Are Introduced As Compromise Plan Fails —Courts May Take Over

By RICHARD L. MADDEN
Special to The New York Times

ALBANY, Feb. 7—Efforts to reach a bipartisan compromise on reapportionment of the Legislature stalled today, and Republican and Democratic leaders began pushing their conflicting plans for new Senate and Assembly districts.

With a Court of Appeals deadline for enacting a reapportionment plan only eight days away, both sides said that they would continue negotiations, but agreed that an impasse had been reached.

"I'm not as optimistic as I was earlier on the outcome," said Senate Majority Leader Earl W. Brydges, Republican of Niagara Falls, said at a news conference.

Unless the stalemate is broken soon, it appeared likely that the courts might have to resolve the dispute. Many Democrats and Republicans said it was doubtful that either plan for new district lines could pass both houses of the divided Legislature.

Travia Is Optimistic

"I'm doing what I can as fast as I can," Assembly Speaker Anthony J. Travia, Democrat of Brooklyn, said with a shrug. "If the court takes over, the court takes over."

The Court of Appeals, the state's highest court, has given the Legislature until Feb. 15 to adopt a new plan for allocating Senate and Assembly seats. If it is no done by then, the judiciary has said that it will undertake the job and redraw the districts.

The decision for each party to go its separate way with its own reapportionment plans came after a closed meeting here this morning between Senator Brydges and Speaker Travia.

Democrats Offer Plan

Last week, when the legislative leaders said they were moving closer together on a compromise, each side agreed to hold up the introduction of its competing plans to allow the compromise talks to proceed.

But after today's meeting, Mr. Travia announced that he had introduced in both the Assembly and Senate his so-called "professors' plan" for legislative districts. The plan was drafted by a group of political scientists appointed by the Democratic leaders.

Mr. Travia said he doubted that the Assembly could act on the plan this week. Asked if he had the votes to pass it in the Democratic-controlled Assembly, Mr. Travia said: "I don't know. I'm going to try."

A few hours later, Senator Brydges announced details of a revised Republican plan and the bill was introduced immediate-

Continued on Page 35, Column 1

Sir Isaiah Berlin, Philosopher, To Join City University in Fall

By LEONARD BUDER

Sir Isaiah Berlin of Oxford University, who is regarded as one of the world's foremost scholars, will join the faculty of the City University of New York next fall, serving for at least a year.

The 56-year-old philosopher, whose erudition is almost legendary in academic circles, will become a professor of humanities at the university's Graduate Center. Although his schedule has not been completed, it is expected that he will teach doctorate-level courses in social and political theory, conduct seminars and direct research. He will also give at least one lecture on each of the four senior campuses to afford a maximum exposure to students.

Sir Isaiah is now Chichele Professor of Social and Political Theory and a Fellow of All Souls College at Oxford. He has lectured at several American universities and is the author of books on philosophy, political theory, intellectual history and biography.

At the City University he will receive a salary of $20,150 a year—the top salary paid to a full professor on regular appointment.

Sir Isaiah's appointment, which will be for the 1966-67 academic year, is expected to

Continued on Page 25, Column 1

give impetus to the city's fledgling doctorate program. The university started the program in 1961, a year after it was raised from college to university status, and last June awarded its first two Doctor of Philosophy degrees.

The City University is also in the midst of discussions with Arthur M. Schlesinger Jr., the noted historian and former adviser to the late President Kennedy, to take a special state-financed professorship. An agreement is expected soon.

This professorship, the Albert Schweitzer Chair in the Humanities, has been endowed by the state with a stipend of $100,000 a year. Part of this would be used to pay Mr. Schlesinger's salary and the rest would be used to cover research and related expenses.

The discussions that led to Sir Isaiah's decision to join the City University were started last fall while he was a visiting lecturer at Princeton University and were continued during his visits to this city.

The negotiations for the city institution were conducted by Dr. Mina S. Rees, the dean of graduate studies, and Dr. Albert H. Bowker, the chancellor of the university.

Dr. Rees, who is credited

Continued on Page 25, Column 1

NEW G.I. BILL WINS IN HOUSE BY 381-0; PRESIDENT LOSES

Johnson Sought to Limit Aid in Housing and Education to 'Hot Spot' Veterans

By MARJORIE HUNTER
Special to The New York Times

WASHINGTON, Feb. 7—A new G. I. Bill of Rights for veterans sailed through the House today after years of active blocking from three Administrations. The vote was 381 to 0.

The Senate has passed a more costly bill last year, but it is expected to accept the House version and send it along to the White House.

President Johnson had sought to head off the broad program of educational and housing benefits by offering a modest proposal covering only veterans of such "hot spots" as Vietnam, Berlin, the Dominican Republic and the Formosa Straits.

However, sources close to the President said that he was not expected to veto the bill.

$327-Million First Year

The House bill sets up a permanent program of educational and housing benefits for veterans with more than 180 days of active military service since Jan. 31, 1955. That was the date the Korean War G.I. Bill expired.

The first-year cost has been estimated at $327-million, with a gradual rise to $494-million when the program became fully effective in 1970.

The Senate version called for outlays of $360-million the first year, rising to $589-million by 1970. The Administration proposed benefits of about $150-million a year.

With Congressional sentiment running strongly toward even more liberal benefits than those in either the Senate or House bills, the Administration quietly arranged through White House aides and legislative leaders for the bill to be brought to the House floor under a procedure barring amendments.

Advocates of far larger benefits angrily denounced the move. They argued that the benefits fall far short of those given veterans of both World War II and Korea.

"It's a disgrace," Representative John P. Saylor, Republican of Pennsylvania, told the House.

The Government owes its fighting men "much more than we are giving them here," Representative Paul A. Fino, Republican of the Bronx, insisted.

Senate Bill Higher

"I'm sorry it took this feeling over Vietnam to get this bill to the floor," he said. "This should not have had to depend on the Administration's slow surrender to public opinion."

Under the House bill, veterans enrolled in approved colleges or vocational schools would receive monthly payments to partially cover their living and educational expenses. Single persons would receive $100 a month; those with one dependent, $125, and those with two or more dependents, $150.

Both the Korean G.I. bill and the Senate bill passed last year provided $110 a month for a single person, $135 a month for one dependent and $160 for each of these categories.

Veterans of World War II received $50 a month in living allowances, plus $25 for each dependent. This was later raised to $75 for single persons, $105 for those with one dependent

Continued on Page 16, Column 5

Publisher's Heir, 25, Held in Girl's Death

By PAUL HOFMANN

A 25-year-old member of a prominent family was charged with homicide yesterday after the police found the body of a 19-year-old girl in the trunk of his rented car.

The police said he had caused the victim's death about two weeks ago by giving her a narcotics shot in his East Side apartment.

The suspect is Robert Friede, a grandson of the late Moses L. Annenberg, former publisher of The Philadelphia Inquirer and owner of a communications empire.

Friede told the police he was living on the $27,000-a-year income from a trust fund set up by his grandfather. The police

Continued on Page 78, Column 1

Associated Press Wirephoto
AS THE VIETNAM CONFERENCE OPENED IN HAWAII: President Johnson and Secretary of State Rusk face Air Vice Marshal Nguyen Cao Ky, left, South Vietnamese Premier, and Lieut. Gen. Nguyen Van Thieu, chief of state, at Pacific command headquarters.

JOHNSON-KY TALKS BEGIN WITH ACCORD ON REFORMS AS A KEY TO WINNING WAR

Fulbright Fears Conflict With China Over Vietnam

By E. W. KENWORTHY
Special to The New York Times

WASHINGTON, Feb. 7—Senator J. W. Fulbright expressed fear today that the war in Vietnam might lead to a conflict with Communist China. The chairman of the Senate Foreign Relations Committee told reporters that the committee's inquiry into the Administration's policies in Southeast Asia was "a very serious matter" involving "policies beyond Vietnam, very major policies."

"Communist China overshadows the whole thing," he said. "There are rumors of very drastic action."

Asked later to clarify this statement, Mr. Fulbright said:

"I am fearful that if the war in Vietnam is not handled extremely well, the Chinese Communists will come in."

Suggestions on Action

By "rumors of very drastic action," he said, he was referring to suggestions made publicly by some members of Congress and privately by some military officials on the course to be followed if the Chinese Communists entered the war in response to an extension of the bombing of North Vietnam.

There are those who have advocated use of nuclear weapons to wipe out Communist China's nuclear capacity and her warmaking potential.

For example, on Jan. 27 Senator John Stennis, Democrat of Mississippi, in a speech to the Mississippi Legislature advocated "all-out air attacks on North Vietnam." He agreed that this raised the "very serious question" of provoking "Red China to full intervention in the war." He recommended that this risk be accepted and, if "our boys" were put in "mortal conflict against the hordes of Red Chinese coolies," the United States should use "every weapon we have."

The purpose of the Foreign

Continued on Page 15, Column 1

5 Texans Accused In Latin Arms Plot

By The Associated Press

EL PASO, Tex., Feb. 7—Federal charges were filed today against five El Paso men in connection with what United States Customs officials called an arms conspiracy involving persons in the United States, Mexico, Panama and other Latin-American countries.

Customs agents investigating the case said the conspiracy involved transactions of planes, tanks, guns, submarines, destroyers and other items on a national and international basis.

The investigation is continuing in the United States, Mexico and other Latin-American countries," said Joe F. Ray, customs agent in charge.

Arraigned before United States

Continued on Page 21, Column 7

BRITAIN RESTRICTS TIME BUYING AGAIN

Bigger Down Payments on Household Items Required in Anti-Inflation Move

By CLYDE H. FARNSWORTH
Special to The New York Times

LONDON, Feb. 7—The Government clamped down further today on the use of installment credit. The move is part of the effort to restore Britain's balance of payments equilibrium by the end of the year.

The new restrictions raise the minimum down payment on appliances and most other household goods to 25 per cent from 15 per cent. Down payments on furniture and mattresses go to 15 per cent, from 10 per cent. For new cars there is no change in initial payments, but the maximum repayment periods are reduced to 27 months, where formerly 30 months were allowed.

The restrictions were termed "moderate" by the Government, but manufacturers and traders said that they would have an upsetting effect.

The measures, which supplement an extended freeze on bank lending imposed last week, come amid growing concern that rapidly rising wages and prices will jeopardize financial recovery.

Jay Makes Announcement

They were announced in the House of Commons this afternoon by Douglas Jay, President of the Board of Trade.

And at a banquet for overseas bankers, Prime Minister Wilson and the Earl of Cromer, Governor of the Bank of England, stressed a need for continued tough action. This will probably be reflected in the budget in two months.

Mr. Wilson said there was still "some way to go" to put the balance of payments on a sound footing and once again pledged that he would take "whatever measures are needed" to keep the pound sterling strong.

He described the improvement in Britain's reserve position since last September as mainly "a reflux of short-term funds." During the period, published re-

Continued on Page 3, Column 5

PEACE BID PRESSED

But Saigon's Premier Bars Negotiations From Weakness

By TOM WICKER
Special to The New York Times

HONOLULU, Feb. 7—President Johnson and the leaders of the Saigon Government agreed today that social and economic reform in South Vietnam was a key element in winning the war against Communist aggression and infiltration.

They pledged to continue that war, in President Johnson's words, as "brothers in arms." But they agreed also that the search for a "just and honorable peace" would continue.

The leaders held talks throughout the day. They are to conclude the conference tomorrow.

Premier Nguyen Cao Ky, who led the Saigon delegation to the bilateral talks opened here this morning, stressed his Government's belief that there must be no negotiations with Communist forces from a position of weakness.

Determination Emphasized

Strength, he said, is the only language the Communists understand.

Mr. Johnson, emphasizing "our resolution and our determination to see this thing through," nevertheless welcomed Air Vice Marshal Ky's acknowledgment that the search for peace had to be continued.

"In our hearts," the President said, "we know that is so."

Marshal Ky also pledged his country's "determination not to surrender or to compromise with the Communists whether in the North or South."

While on its face this seemed to be a guarantee that South Vietnam would not seek a peace or compromise settlement of its own, observers familiar with South Vietnamese attitudes considered it also a veiled warning to Mr. Johnson that the Saigon Government would never deal with the Vietcong.

Thant Position Recalled

In the worldwide debate on the question of arranging a negotiated settlement, one of the most frequently advocated courses is for the United States to recognize the National Liberation Front, the parent political organization of the Vietcong, as a direct party in any negotiations. Secretary General Thant of the United Nations, among others, has taken that position.

So far, the United States has been willing to say only that the Vietcong would have no difficulty in having their views represented at any conference, possibly by attending as an independent political party.

Statements by Mr. Johnson, Marshal Ky and Lieut. Gen.

Continued on Page 16, Column 1

U.S. Army troops during a search for tunnels and bunkers used by the Viet Cong, as part of Operation Attleboro when more than 22,000 troops were deployed, with massive air support, in the largest operation of the war to date in North Vietnam.

A camouflaged U.S.A.F. F-105 armed with the lethal "Shrike" missiles, en route to its target near Hanoi.

General William Westmoreland (r) commander of all U.S. forces in Vietnam, inspects the damage inflicted on the Tan Son Nhut Air Base by a Viet Cong mortar attack on April 14, 1966.

A U.S. Air Force F-100 Supersabre drops two 500-pound bombs on a Viet Cong target in the lower Mekong Delta.

"All the News
That's Fit to Print"

The New York Times.

LATE CITY EDITION
U.S. Weather Bureau Report (Page 73) Forecast:
Mostly sunny today; mostly cloudy
tonight. Showers likely tomorrow.
Temp. Range: 75—50; yesterday 74—49.

VOL. CXV..No. 39,559.   © 1966 by The New York Times Company.
Times Square, New York, N. Y. 10036   NEW YORK, MONDAY, MAY 16, 1966.   TEN CENTS

BIG BUSINESS SEES A PROFIT SQUEEZE; OPPOSES TAX RISE

Council of Major Executives Fears New Federal Curbs but Still Likes Johnson

HIGHER COSTS EXPECTED

Drop in Employe Efficiency in Tighter Labor Market Also Causes Concern

Special to The New York Times

HOT SPRINGS, Va., May 15—The nation's big-business executives overwhelmingly oppose a tax increase and fear that profit margins will go down after midyear. They also see a fresh drive toward greater government regulation of business, which disturbs them. And they still like Lyndon Johnson.

This was the consensus over the weekend after a three-day meeting at the Homestead Hotel of the Business Council, a private organization that periodically advises the Government on policy issues affecting business. The council's 100-odd members are nearly all presidents or board chairmen of large corporations.

The big businessmen think there is a good chance the Administration will decide a tax increase is not needed this year. However, they heard nothing from Cabinet-level officials who attended their meeting to change the assessment made several months ago by Secretary of the Treasury Henry H. Fowler that a tax increase this year was a 50-50 bet.

Ackley and Connor Attend

Mr. Fowler was here along with two other officials who will play key roles in the tax decision — Gardner Ackley, chairman of the President's Council of Economic Advisers, and Secretary of Commerce John T. Connor.

The businessmen think that chances are better than even for avoidance of a tax increase because they see signs that the pace of the business boom is slowing.

They intensely hope that the Administration will not be forced to recommend a tax increase to control the boom and inflation, largely because they are fearful of the form the tax increase might take.

Although they know the Administration has never given serious thought to recommending the kind of tax increase business hates worst—an excess profits tax—they fear that Congress might pass one anyhow if it is requested to raise taxes at all.

They also fear that Congress might, over Administration objections, repeal the 7 per cent credit given for business expenditures.

Continued on Page 14, Column 4

SCHOOLS BECOME TAX WHIPPING BOY

Suburban Budget Defeats Laid to General Protest

By FRED M. HECHINGER

Suburban school budgets are turned down in alarming number, not so much because the voters resent school spending, but more because they rarely have a chance of voting against any other spending.

This is the conclusion reached after a survey by New York Times reporters, following increasingly unfavorable balloting on school budgets on Long Island and in Westchester County.

With state and Federal taxes appearing to most voters as inevitable as death, they exercise their right to say "no" to school expenditures, less in protest over what the schools are doing than in anger against those levies on which they have no direct voice.

"The privilege of voting in suburban school districts is the last refuge for people who want to register a protest against something with immediate results," said Bowen Sterling, a New York building contractor who is president of the Lakeland Board of Education, a district covering six towns in northern Westchester and southern Putnam Counties. The district's $7,613,058 school budget was defeated recently.

"They may be disturbed about food prices or the war," he

Continued on Page 41, Column 8

Mayor Warns Both Sides to Settle the Taxi Dispute

The New York Times (by Allyn Baum)
Michael Mann, left, the regional director of A.F.L.-C.I.O., reporting on negotiations to striking taxi drivers and their families gathered outside City Hall yesterday.

By EMANUEL PERLMUTTER

Mayor Lindsay told negotiators in the five-day-old taxi strike yesterday to continue meeting without break until they reached an agreement to get the cabs back on the street. The Mayor was grim as he spoke to the union and management representatives. He said that the public was being seriously inconvenienced and that the city's convention business had already been endangered by cancellations caused by the shortage of taxis. About 9,000 cabs have been idled by the strike. Mr. Lindsay made his remarks during day and night conferences that he held starting at noon in City Hall with the Taxi Drivers Organizing Committee and negotiators for 80 fleet garages. The talks were still under way at 3 A.M. The union's bargainers were led

S.E.C. Report Will Urge Reforms in Mutual Funds

The following is the first in a series of three articles on the problems that are facing the mutual-fund business.

By EILEEN SHANAHAN

Special to The New York Times

WASHINGTON, May 15—New laws and regulations designed to make sure that people get their money's worth when they buy mutual funds are about to be proposed by the Government. The reforms will be recommended in a long-awaited report by the Securities and Exchange Commission.

Based on studies done by and for the commission over the last eight years, the report will call for fundamental changes in the way the $35-billion fund industry does business, both for its 3.5 million present shareholders and for those who will buy mutual fund shares in the future.

While revisions are still being made in the final wording of the report, which is scheduled for completion by June, the commission has decided to seek, among other things:

¶Restrictions, and possibly an outright ban, on the sale of one of the most rapidly growing types of mutual funds—the "contractual" or "front-end load" plan. Under the front-end load plan, the investor agrees to buy stated amounts of a fund regularly over a period of years, usually 10 or 12, and half of his first year's payments are deducted for the salesman's commission and other selling charges.

¶A reduction in management fees charged by the funds, which bear no relationship to the actual cost of running a fund and which can, annually, take up as much as 50 per cent of a mutual fund shareholder's dividend income.

¶Rules aimed at reducing commissions—the sales charges imposed on purchasers of all but a handful of funds. These commissions are often more than four times as large as the commissions charged on regu-

Continued on Page 55, Column 2

MEDICARE 'CRISIS' CITED BY KENNEDY

Senator Calls for $2-Billion Expansion of Aged Care to Meet Future Demand

By MICHAEL STERN

Senator Robert F. Kennedy proposed last night a $2-billion Federal program of building, training and research to meet what he called "a national crisis in medical facilities" on the eve of the start of Medicare.

Without such a program, he said, "the bright hopes of Medicare can be dashed."

In a speech at the Americana at the Judy Holliday Memorial Dinner of the American Medical Center, the Senator said:

"What is the value of offering medical treatment to our aged if there are no doctors available to administer it? What is the value of offering nursing-home care to our old people if there are no nursing homes where they can go? What is the value of offering hospital treatment to those aged who are seriously ill if there are no hospital beds waiting for them?"

10-Year Fund Urged

To meet the needs of the 15 million Americans over 65 who will become eligible for Medicare benefits on July 1, Senator Kennedy said he was preparing a bill that he would submit to the Congress soon. It would commit the Federal Government to spending $2-billion over a 10-year period.

Aides to the Senator later outlined the provisions of the bill. It would provide $1.8-billion as grants to voluntary, nonprofit organizations, so they could build quarters for 200,000 long-care beds for the aged. First call on the money would be given to existing hospitals and nursing homes that were willing to expand or replace their facilities for long-term care.

Voluntary, nonprofit health organizations established by unions and by farm and fraternal groups also would be eligible for the building grants.

The bill also would provide $200-million to train the professional

Continued on Page 28, Column 2

HOSPITALS DELAY CLINIC SHUTDOWN IN NURSING CRISIS

But Will Consider Alternate Proposals as Fact-Finding Conferences Continue

By PETER KIHSS

The Department of Hospitals said yesterday that it was deferring the closing of out-patient clinics in the municipal hospitals, earlier announced to begin today. But this morning it will go over a series of alternate plans to cope with a threatened wholesale loss of nurses.

Of the department's 3,260 registered nurses, 1,470 have filed resignations effective a week from today as a result of a deadlock over pay and working conditions.

George Moskowitz, who has been accepted by both sides as a fact-finder with power to make recommendations for settling the dispute, spent more than seven hours yesterday hearing seven witnesses presented by the directors of nursing at four municipal hospitals.

The fact-finding sessions recessed at 10 P. M. until 11:30 A. M. today. Mr. Moskowitz said he hoped to complete this phase today. His goal then, he said, will be to make a report to both sides within 48 hours.

Help for 12,000 Daily

Dr. Harvey Gollance, Deputy Commissioner of Hospitals, said the closing of outpatient clinics was among plans whose timing and sequence would be re-examined this morning in the light of continuing negotiations. The clinics provide medical help for 12,000 persons a day who are able to go back and forth from their own homes.

The alternative would be checked with administrators of the 21 municipal hospitals. Some persons involved in the negotiations contended that an immediate closing of outpatient clinics today would be premature while all the nurses remained on duty, and while other moves in the meantime could be reducing the total number of bed patients.

"It depends on what happens in the negotiations," Dr. Gollance said. "If they haven't come to a definite conclusion, then it would seem the first thing we would have to do would be to limit admissions to emergencies. Even if we had a nursing staff in some hospitals, it would have to take up the slack from others."

There are 17,500 beds and 15,000 patients in the municipal hospitals. Medical, surgical and pediatric beds are usually crowded at this time of year, Dr. Gollance said.

8,000 Jobs Provided

There are 8,000 positions for registered nurses in the department's books. But more than half are already occupied by practical nurses or nurses' aides, because of an inability to hire more highly qualified nurses.

The actual peak number of registered nurses was reduced yesterday to have been about 5,400 in 1940, just before World War II, with the number in the last eight years running at about 3,500. The New York State Nurses Association contends that 300 of the resigning nurses have already agreed to take jobs elsewhere.

In yesterday's fact - finding session at Mr. Moskowitz's law

Continued on Page 27, Column 2

HOSPITALS SHORT OF ANESTHETISTS

Resulting Practice Is Being Investigated—Many Jobs Go to Independent Teams

By MARTIN TOLCHIN

An acute shortage of anesthesiologists in hospitals here has led to practices that are now being investigated by medical authorities.

Hospital directors, confronted with a growing difficulty in staffing their anesthesia sections, have increasingly turned the job over to groups of anesthesiologists who provide complete service. The groups often hire their own resident physicians and nurses to administer anesthetics, and their own clerical help. Patients are billed directly by the groups, some of which serve five and six hospitals each.

By and large, this widespread group practice is regarded by medical authorities as a practical solution to the shortage of anesthesiologists. The overwhelming majority of groups are believed to provide excellent medical care.

However, United Medical Service and the New York State Society of Anesthesiologists are investigating whether some groups have overextended themselves beyond their ability to provide competent medical care.

Specifically, they are studying whether hospitals retain sufficient control over the groups. They are also studying the quality of supervision exercised by physicians who are the chief anesthesiologists at several hospitals. Finally, they are studying billing procedures to determine whether patients have always received the services for which they are billed.

The State Health Department is considering a Health Code provision that was first recom-

Continued on Page 28, Column 3

KY FORCES HOLD DANANG; BUDDHISTS FEAR CIVIL WAR; U.S. APPEALS FOR ACCORD

Washington Is Concerned And Surprised by Ky Step

Instructs Americans in Saigon to Attempt to Bring Sides Together—Johnson Sees Rusk, McNamara and Lodge

By RICHARD EDER

WASHINGTON, May 15—The Administration, surprised and deeply concerned over the South Vietnamese junta's move against dissidents in Danang, began an immediate effort today to prevent the action from leading to civil war.

A State Department spokesman announced, after clearance by the White House, that United States representatives in Vietnam had been instructed "to make every effort to bring the South Vietnamese leaders together to resolve their differences."

President Johnson met this afternoon with Secretary of State Dean Rusk, Defense Secretary Robert S. McNamara, Walt W. Rostow, special Presidential assistant, and Ambassador Henry Cabot Lodge. Later the President went to his country retreat at Camp David, Md.

A State Department spokesman, W. Marshall Wright, stressed that the United States had been caught unawares by Premier Nguyen Cao Ky's seizure of Danang. He refused to characterize the Administration's attitude toward the move.

It was clear, however, that Administration officials were gravely distressed by the move.

In the context of Premier Ky's military initiative, there was little doubt that the instruction to the United States Embassy to press for a settlement—besides being an unusually frank

Continued on Page 2, Column 4

What Premier Ky Did

Hope for Quiet Shift to Civilian Rule Appears Ended by Events in Danang

By CHARLES MOHR

Special to The New York Times

SAIGON, May 15—The whine of bullets and the clank of tank treads today probably erased the possibility of harmonious transition from military to civilian government in South Vietnam. Those in South Vietnam and elsewhere who did not want a civilian government will applaud Air Vice Marshal Nguyen Cao Ky's sudden armed occupation of Danang. But even they realize that Premier Ky has now apparently taken an irreversible step that forecloses the possibility of a new agreement between the Premier and his enemies to work peacefully toward a popular government. Those in power, some observers say, Premier Ky will have to continue to do what he did today—use force.

As usual, the latest development in South Vietnamese politics is complex, and its explanation requires a look at the recent past.

On March 10 Premier Ky pre-

News Analysis

cipitated a political crisis by purging his chief military and political rival, Lieut. Gen. Nguyen Chanh Thi, commander of the I Corps, which embraces South Vietnam's five northernmost provinces, and the cities of Danang and Hue.

General Thi's protégés—most of the public officials in the Ky campaign. They were joined then by the leaders of the Unified Buddhist Church, who demanded a quick end of military rule and an elected government. Although Premier Ky was pledged to the installation of an elected government by late 1967, he at first resisted such pressures. At one point early in April he threatened to "liberate" Danang, a center of agitation against him, then backed down.

But the pressure spread to Saigon. It became apparent that Premier Ky could end the Buddhist demonstrations by compromise or harsh use of re-

Continued on Page 2, Column 5

SEAMEN'S STRIKE STARTS IN BRITAIN

Long Walkout Could Cripple Economy of the Nation

By JOSEPH LELYVELD

Special to The New York Times

LONDON, Monday, May 16—The first strike by British merchant seamen in 55 years started at 12:01 A.M. today.

Its immediate effects were comparatively slight, but it could eventually cripple major sectors of the British economy.

Less than 15 per cent of the country's merchant fleet was in British ports when the strike started. Under maritime law the 62,500 members of the National Union of Seamen are entitled to join the walkout only when their ships have berthed in Britain.

Thus it would be more than a month before even half the union's members could join the stoppage. Ships are expected to be immobilized at the rate of 300 a week; eventually 2,500 could be affected.

Prime Minister Wilson had appealed in vain to union leaders to call off the strike to avoid damage to the economy. He spent yesterday at 10 Downing Street going over contingency plans after hearing from the Minister of Labor, Ray Gunter, that the seamen seemed determined to strike.

Mr. Wilson will address the nation on television tonight, and is expected to warn against panic buying. About half of

Continued on Page 10, Column 5

FIGHT LASTS A DAY

10 Are Reported Dead in Wild Shooting— Rebels Hole Up

By NEIL SHEEHAN

Special to The New York Times

DANANG, South Vietnam, May 15 — The ruling junta appeared tonight to have seized control of most of this city after a day of wild shooting between troops loyal to the Government and rebel military units allied with Buddhist insurgents.

In a surprise move, Premier Nguyen Cao Ky and the other junta leaders flew 1,000 Vietnamese marines to the air base on the outskirts of this port and garrison city in the hours before dawn.

At dawn the marines, supported by tanks and Vietnamese Air Force planes, buzzed the town, moved into the city and began systematically seizing vital points.

Marines Are Reinforced

The marines were later reinforced by some 500 paratroopers and Rangers. They met disorganized resistance from a force estimated to number 300 to 500 soldiers, but succeeded in occupying the I Army Corps headquarters, the civilian and military police stations, the radio station and other major installations.

There was a great deal of shooting today in Danang, including one strafing attack by

The New York Times   May 16, 1966
Danang (cross) is under the control of the Ky regime.

air force planes on rebels in the central market.

Most of the shooting was apparently wild and inaccurate and casualties were reported to be light. Although estimates varied, it appeared that about 10 people on both sides, including civilians, had been killed and at least a dozen wounded.

[In Saigon, Buddhist monks denounced the Government move on Danang as an "act of treachery" that would "surely lead to civil war." Page 3.]

Danang settled into an uneasy quiet at night, with only an occasional stray shot breaking the silence. Vietnamese Air Force C-47's kept the city illuminated with flares and observation planes circled overhead. Premier Ky, who has designated himself Air Vice Marshal, is head of the air force as well as Premier.

Rebels Retreat to Pagodas

The streets were deserted except for patrols of Vietnamese marines and paratroopers. The thousands of United States marines stationed here were confined to camps on the outskirts of the city.

The remaining rebel soldiers, estimated at 150, were holed up in and around two Buddhist pagodas that have served as headquarters for opposition to the Government junta. Several Buddhist laymen, as well as Buddhist priests, have taken shelter in the pagodas. Rebel soldiers said they intended to defend the pagodas to the death.

Danang had been in the hands of Buddhists and rebel military units since mid-March, when Buddhist leaders began agitation to displace the military-dominated junta with a civilian government.

In Hue, 50 miles north of here, the Buddhist movement and rebel military units that hold the

Continued on Page 3, Column 1

8,000 IN CAPITAL PICKET FOR PEACE

Demonstrators Circle White House for Two Hours

By JOHN HERBERS

WASHINGTON, May 15—The moderate wing of the American peace movement staged a large demonstration here today in an effort to increase Congressional opposition to President Johnson's policies in Vietnam.

A crowd variously estimated at from 8,000 to 11,000 adults, youths and children strolled around the White House for almost two hours, then gathered on a hillside beneath the Washington Monument for speeches deploring American military involvement in Southeast Asia.

It was a perfect day for an outing. A warm breeze kept the American flags around the monument fluttering, and the grass and foliage, green from spring rains, glistened in the sunlight.

Except for their signs, it was hard to distinguish the peace marchers from the sightseers, who also were out in numbers. Most were neatly dressed adults, and the form of their protest, although embittered and impatient with the Administration, was politically conventional.

Sanford Gottlieb, coordinator of the march, announced that the demonstrators had brought with them more than 73,000 pledges signed by voters saying they would work for a candidate in this year's elections who ad-

Continued on Page 5, Column 3

Arts for All: A Rising Tide in America

By HOWARD TAUBMAN

The nineteen-sixties seem certain to become the decade in which the arts in this country achieved the broad, democratic base that the prophets had long talked about.

For the first time in American history there is a determined drive to make them available to people everywhere, regardless of income level, remoteness from metropolitan centers, their ages and previous exposure. For the first time huge amounts of Government money are being spent to bring children into the schools in direct contact with music, drama, dance and the visual arts.

To this observer, who has visited large and small communities in the Northeast, the South, the Midwest and the Southwest in recent weeks, the artistic tide is rising and there is no telling how far and deep it will spread.

The forces that are bringing about this cultural revolution are many: civic pride, economics, affluence, greater educational opportunities, new leisure, higher aspirations for the life of the mind and the spirit and the discovery by countless Americans of the exaltations and consolations to be found in a play or a poem, a symphony or a painting.

Consider the element of civic pride. A good many large cities and some small ones are eager to be in the swim and to have their own cultural institutions like New York's Lincoln Center and Los Angeles's Music Center. But some, like Atlanta, which is about to start building one, have a really urgent need for such facilities to provide proper accommodation for their music and drama.

In Atlanta the most important business leaders, men like Robert Woodruff of Coca-Cola and Richard C. Rich of Rich's Department Store, are in the vanguard of those pushing for a new arts center.

In Kansas City, where a plan to build a new theater and establish a repertory company has been hanging fire for months, a decisive meeting called by Mayor Ilus W. Davis took place last week. A businessman, William Deramus, president of the Kansas City Southern Railway, made the first substantial offer of funds with a pledge of $75,000.

His friends describe Mr. Deramus as anything but "a culture type." Like other local businessmen, he wants the new theater to be downtown rather than on the campus of the University of Missouri in Kansas City. Merchants and bankers are eager

Continued on Page 41, Column 1

"All the News That's Fit to Print"

The New York Times.

LATE CITY EDITION

U. S. Weather Bureau Report (Page 95) forecasts: Morning showers then fair today, tonight and tomorrow. Temp. Range: 77—60; yesterday: 85—64.

NEWS SUMMARY AND INDEX, PAGE 95

SECTION ONE

VOL. CXV..No. 39,565. © 1966 by The New York Times Company. Times Square, New York, N.Y. 10036 NEW YORK, SUNDAY, MAY 22, 1966. 50c beyond 50-mile zone from New York City, except on Long Island, higher in air delivery cities THIRTY CENTS

PRESIDENT FINDS ECONOMY IS FIRM DESPITE PRICE RISE

Calls News Conference to Report Good Signs—Says Nation Can Be Thankful

SILENT ON TAX ISSUE

But His Remarks Are Taken As a Hint That Prospects for Increase Are Lower

By JOHN D. MORRIS
Special to The New York Times

WASHINGTON, May 21—President Johnson viewed the problem of inflation as one of mixed blessings today and observed that "we have much to be thankful for" in present economic conditions.

His remarks on inflation and related fiscal matters at a surprise news conference encouraged speculation that prospects of a tax increase had lessened. He specifically declined to say, however, whether this speculation was justified.

He said he did not want to "create any false impressions" until a decision had been reached on whether a tax rise would be recommended to Congress.

Cites Prices Abroad

The President exhibited a graph to show that consumer prices in Japan, Italy, France, Britain and Germany had increased more since 1960 than they had in the United States.

He noted with pride that the rise in this country had averaged less than 1½ per cent while the other countries experienced increases at least twice as great.

While the present economic problem is recognized and is receiving a good deal of attention by the Administration, he said, "it is one that we prefer to have than ones we have had."

"I would rather face the problems I face now for this reason: Increases in wages have come faster than the prices," he said.

'People Have Work'

"The fact that people have work," he said, "and the fact that we have income coming into our Treasury to permit us to increase our educational efforts, our health efforts, our beautification efforts, our conservation efforts—I would rather have these problems than problems that come when unemployment is high and incomes low."

The President also reported that higher-than-expected revenues would enable the Government to end the present fiscal year June 30 with a deficit of about $4-billion, perhaps less, compared with the $6.4-billion deficit that he had forecast in his Budget Message last January.

The improved outlook is expected to influence the Administration in making a decision on whether to seek a tax increase. This is because the smaller deficit now in prospect is likely to contribute less to

Continued on Page 44, Column 8

Hoving Discloses Plans for Coney Island Renaissance as Beach Opens

The New York Times (by John Orris)

At Coney Island, the water temperature was 55 degrees—not very warm, but tempting enough for the hardy souls

By BERNARD WEINRAUB

Parks Commissioner Thomas P. F. Hoving announced at Coney Island yesterday that a committee of architects, showmen and community officials would be formed to bring about "a renaissance" on the three-mile-long amusement park.

"We want to make Coney Island magnetic," the Commissioner said at the opening of the swimming season at Coney Island and other municipally operated beaches. "We want to make it a beach and entertainment area that you have to come to, not just during the day but at night."

As the Commissioner spoke, waves rolled in five feet away, but only a handful of the 75,000 to 100,000 persons who showed up actually stepped into the 55-degree waters. On a summer weekend day, 800,000 to a million persons crowd the beach. With the temperature hitting 85 at 2:35 P.M.—the warmest day of the year—about 30,000 persons visited the Rockaways and about 75,000 went to Jones Beach, which also opened yesterday.

For most, it was a day of sunbathing. But for Mr. Hoving it was a day of disclosing plans for the renaissance at Coney Island and discussing the plans with a group of Brooklyn Congressmen at a luncheon of antipasto, cheesecake and espresso in a restaurant just off the boardwalk. "Everyone's very enthusiastic," said the Parks Commissioner.

He said that the next step, which was discussed Friday at City Hall with Brooklyn Borough President Abe Stark, would be discussions on and

Continued on Page 47, Column 3

FINNISH COALITION TO INCLUDE REDS, KEPT OUT SINCE '48

4 Parties Reach Agreement to Form Government After Month's Negotiations

By United Press International

HELSINKI, Finland, May 21—Political leaders agreed today to form a four-party coalition that would include Communists in the Government for the first time since 1948.

The agreement was reached after a month of negotiations and two months after the general elections of March 20-21.

The coalition would be headed by Rafael Paasio, chairman of the Social Democratic party, largest of the four in the coalition.

The new Government is scheduled to be formed next week after the leaders of the four parties meet separately to approve today's agreement.

In addition to the Social Democrats, the coalition would also include the predominantly Communist People's Democratic League, the agrarian Center party of President Urho Kekkonen and the Left-wing Socialist party, a Social Democratic splinter group.

6 Seats for Social Democrats

The agreement provides that the Social Democrats, winners in the election, are to hold six seats in the 15-member Cabinet. The Center party, which heads the caretaker non-Socialist coalition, would receive five, the Communists three and the Left-Wing Socialists one.

The coalition would command 152 of the 200 seats in Parliament, with the Social Democrats holding 55, the Centrists 49, the Communists 41 and the Left-Wing Socialists 7. In opposition would be the Conservatives, with 26; the Swedish People's party, with 12; the Liberal People's party, with 9, and the Smallholders, with 1.

The negotiations leading up to the agreement have been complicated by divergent economic demands. The Social Democrats and the Center have been at odds over the agrarians' request for rural social legislation and a farm-income subsidy law. The Communists have objected to a Social Democratic proposal for an increased sales tax.

Finns See No Red Peril

By WERNER WISKARI

The agreement to include Communists in the Government underscores a growing feeling in Finland that neither the Soviet Union nor the domestic Communist party now poses a threat to the nation's security.

In 1948, Communists were ousted from the Government amid suspicion that they were planning to seize power by force. There was talk of giving them government responsibility again during a Soviet-Finnish crisis in 1959, but this idea was quashed by the agrarians, who then formed a minority regime.

The agrarian Center party has

Continued on Page 25, Column 1

JOHNSON APPEALS FOR UNITY IN WAR; KY'S FORCES GAIN

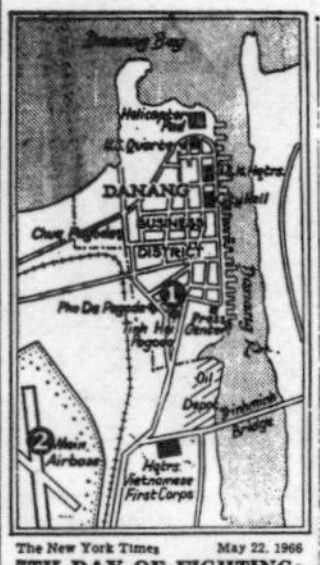

The New York Times May 22, 1966

7TH DAY OF FIGHTING: Dissident forces in Danang are falling back on the main pagoda (1). U.S. jet planes were evacuated from the big strategic air base (2).

UNREST DEPLORED

President Also Urges U.S. to Be Patient in Midst of Strife

Transcript of news conference will be found on Page 44.

By MAX FRANKEL
Special to The New York Times

WASHINGTON, May 21 — President Johnson deplored the political strife in South Vietnam today as a diversion from the war against the Vietcong and from efforts to establish a constitutional government there.

Mr. Johnson, described by aides as deeply troubled by the turmoil and the effect it is having on American opinion, pleaded for patience and understanding in both Vietnam and the United States.

He called on the rival factions in Vietnam to hold together until elections are held —they are scheduled for later this year — and asked Americans to bear with the frustrations of building a nation in the midst of war.

Administration officials, reflecting the same concerns, urged Americans to see the crisis in perspective and not to imagine from the headlines that the entire war effort was falling apart.

Annoyance Conceded

They said they found it natural for Americans to feel fed up with the internal struggles in South Vietnam. They acknowledged growing annoyance in the Administration and said the Vietnamese were being warned not to try Washington's patience too long.

President Johnson called a small group of reporters into his office at noon for a news conference and began by reading a brief and carefully worded statement, his first since Premier Nguyen Cao Ky provoked the latest in the long series of South Vietnamese political crises by moving troops into the dissident city of Danang a week ago.

The President said the United States had no desire to dictate South Vietnam's form of government and wanted to see the South Vietnamese grow in the ability to manage their own affairs, with the participation of an ever-broader segment of the population.

'Regret Any Diversion'

"We regret any diversion from that task and from efforts to defeat the Communists' attempt to take over South Vietnam," he said.

Mr. Johnson refused, however, to distribute blame for the conflict between Premier Ky and the Buddhist leaders based in Hue and Danang. He declined specifically to describe his attitude toward Marshal Ky, saying that it would not contribute to a solution.

Asked about American opinion polls showing a drop in support for his handling of the war, Mr. Johnson said that as the nation made more sacrifices, there was bound to be

Continued on Page 4, Column 1

DISSIDENTS' AREA IN DANANG SHRINKS

Cease-Fire in Effect at Some Points After Clash—U.S. Moves Planes to Safety

By NEIL SHEEHAN
Special to The New York Times

DANANG, South Vietnam, Sunday, May 22 — Dissident troops fought a half-hour gun battle with Government units in front of the Tinh Hoi pagoda this morning. By noon the firing had dwindled almost to nothing.

An informal cease-fire was in effect at several of the points where pro-Government and anti-Government troops face each other across barricades. There were reports that formal negotiations might take place later today, but these were denied by a spokesman for the dissidents.

More than 40 bodies, draped with Buddhist flags, lay in an anteroom off the sanctuary of the pagoda. One of the bodies was that of an infant about 2 years old.

The dissident troops, forced back in heavy fighting yesterday and in this morning's brief action, were compressed into an area about four blocks wide and six blocks long.

The Government commander, Brig. Gen. Du Quoc Dong, appeared to be setting the stage for a climactic assault.

As a result of a brief mortar attack on the big American and Vietnamese air base yesterday, the United States moved many of the Air Force and Marine fighter-bombers to more secure locations elsewhere in South Vietnam. A military source estimated that 40 to 100 planes were involved.

About 15 American service-

Continued on Page 3, Column 2

Clay Halts Cooper in 6th; Kauai Wins the Preakness

Associated Press Cablephoto

THE WINNER: Cassius Clay after bout last night.

Cassius Clay retained the world heavyweight boxing championship last night by stopping Henry Cooper in the sixth round of a scheduled 15-round title bout at London.

For five rounds, Clay, a 24-year-old native of Louisville, toyed with Cooper, a 32-year-old Englishman, and seemed almost disinterested. In the sixth, Clay opened a bad cut over Cooper's left eye, and the cut bled so freely that the referee halted the bout after 1 minute 38 seconds of the round.

José Torres retained the world light-heavyweight title by scoring a unanimous decision over Wayne Thornton in a 15-round bout at Shea Stadium. Torres, in his first title defense, twice floored Thornton in the opening round. The first professional bout held outdoors in New York in six years was witnessed by a disappointingly small crowd of about 12,000.

HORSE RACING

Kauai King, the even-money favorite, won the 91st running of the Preakness Stakes at the Pimlico track in Baltimore.

Kauai King passed Stupendous in the stretch and beat him by 1¾ lengths. Amberoid ran third in the field of nine.

The Preakness is the second jewel in the Triple Crown series for 3-year-olds. The first of the three races was the Kentucky Derby, won by Kauai King two weeks ago. The final race is the Belmont Stakes June 4 at Aqueduct in Queens.

Kauai King is owned by Michael J. Ford and was ridden by Don Brumfield. He ran the 1-3/16 miles in 1 minute 55 2/5 seconds, and he earned $129,000.

At Aqueduct, Summer Scandal scored a five-length victory in the $55,300 Top Flight Handicap for fillies and mares. She ran 1⅛ miles in 1:49 2/5. Malhoa finished second.

BASEBALL

The New York Yankees defeated the Minnesota Twins, 4-2, at Yankee Stadium by scoring four unearned runs in the seventh inning.

The Giants won from the New York Mets, 4-3, at San Francisco. In a night game at Los Angeles, the Dodgers beat the Pittsburgh Pirates, 5-4, in 12 innings.

Details in Section 5.

CITY NURSES SPURN 2 NEW PAY OFFERS

Talks With Public Health Aides Collapse—300 Due to Resign Tomorrow

Public health nurses working for the city rejected two new wage offers yesterday as a mediator tried to avert the resignation of three-fourths of them, scheduled for tomorrow.

"It looks very serious," said Morris Tarshis, the labor mediator, who has been acting on Mayor Lindsay's behalf in the dispute. He said that no new talks were scheduled.

Three hundred of the 415 nurses plan to resign from their jobs of caring for patients of all ages at health centers and special clinics throughout the city if their demand for more money is not met. In their jobs they get patients ready for doctors, conduct interviews, prepare vaccines and work up medical charts. They also visit families at home.

After yesterday's session ended in failure, J. Jerome Olitt, an attorney representing the nurses, said: "We have reached an impasse. The city has seen fit to play politics with the public's health and the need for nursing."

Mr. Tarshis reported that he was ready to meet with the nurses' group at any time, "through the night or around the clock." But he added that he knew of no plans for further discussions.

The mediator explained that at yesterday's meeting, held in the office of Budget Director Eugene Becker, he had first of-

Continued on Page 34, Column 1

5th Ave. Sitdown Holds Up Parade Of Armed Forces

By DOUGLAS ROBINSON

Thousands of servicemen marching in the 17th Annual Armed Forces Day Parade were forced to mark time for five minutes yesterday when antiwar demonstrators sat down in their path on Fifth Avenue.

The demonstrators broke through police barricades just after a five-man color guard, the vanguard of a 10,000-man parade force, passed.

Uniformed policemen and detectives in plainclothes quickly surrounded the sitters, but not before several spectators had dashed from the sidelines to tear up signs protesting the war in Vietnam and drop the pieces on the heads of the protesters.

Fifty demonstrators, of whom 18 were women carrying bouquets of flowers, were taken away in a police van and a Department of Corrections bus. Some of the men had to be dragged from the street, and a few women were carried away on stretchers.

One man, a spectator who threw a rolled newspaper at the demonstrators but hit a detective instead, was charged with

Continued on Page 82, Column 3

The New York Times (by Carl T. Gossett Jr.)

STAGING A PROTEST AT PARADE: Demonstrators sitting in roadway on Fifth Avenue yesterday as the Armed Forces Day paraders approached. Police cleared them away.

Berkeley Rated Over Harvard in Graduate Study

By FRED M. HECHINGER

The University of California at Berkeley has emerged over Harvard as the nation's "best balanced distinguished university" in graduate education, according to an assessment by the powerful American Council on Education.

But it was only because Berkeley ranked high in engineering, in addition to all the other major academic areas, that it took the prize for overall excellence away from Harvard.

In fact, Harvard was ranked slightly higher than Berkeley in all other categories, but its engineering division failed to achieve "distinguished" rank.

Stanford University was ranked third, after Harvard, in all-around excellence of graduate education. Like Harvard, Stanford was rated distinguished in four of the five categories.

The five categories, analyzed by thousands of academic experts, were the humanities, social sciences, biological sciences, physical sciences and engineering.

Rated after Stanford for all-around distinction were Columbia University, the University of Illinois, Yale, Princeton, the University of Michigan and the California Institute of Technology. These institutions were ranked as distinguished in three of the categories.

Next in line, rating distinguished in two of the areas, were the Massachusetts Institute of Technology and the Universities of Chicago and Wisconsin.

Regionally, the Eastern Seaboard maintained its strong academic lead, followed by the Middle West and the Far West.

While no Southern university has yet achieved top place in the study's judgment, the report predicted that the South might make "the greatest advance in institutional quality in the next decade or two."

It considered Duke University, the Universities of Texas and North Carolina, Rice University, Tulane and Vanderbilt as poised near the point of "achieving major national status in the years ahead."

In addition, seven other public universities in the South may be close to these top leaders in the race toward

Continued on Page 35, Column 1

4 Good Samaritans: 3 Succeed, 1 Killed

By ALFRED E. CLARK

A man in his 50's who went to the aid of three teen-age girls being pestered by two strangers was stabbed to death in the Jamaica Bus Terminal in Queens early yesterday.

A short time later, on a bustling Greenwich Village street, three Philadelphia visitors leaped from their convertible automobile to rescue a taxicab driver whose passenger was holding a pistol to the driver's head. A shot was fired during the fight in the cab's back seat but the bullet struck harmlessly in the seat.

The body of the man killed while helping the girls lay unidentified yesterday in the Medical Examiner's morgue at 520 First Avenue. He was described

Continued on Page 81, Column 2

Today's Sections

Index to Subjects

Members of U.S. Army Company A fire from the shelter of an abandoned Viet Cong trench as they push the Viet Cong back from Tou Morong, Kontum Province.

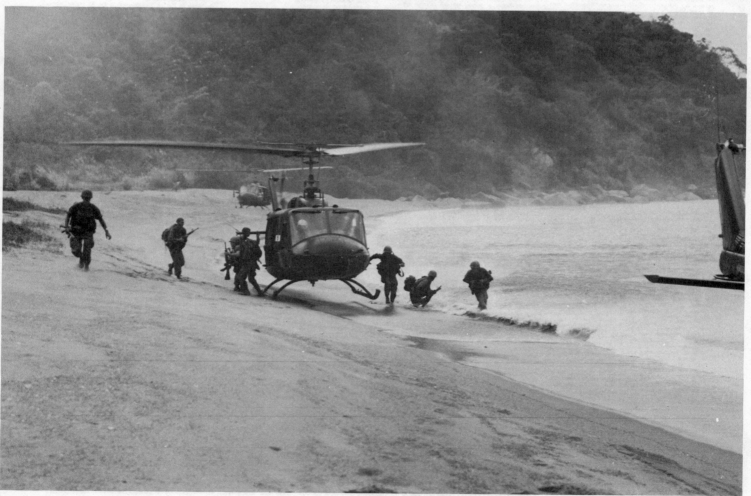

U.S. troops dismount from a helicopter at Vung Ro Bay during phase I of Operation John Paul Jones aimed at sweeping the area clean of Communist guerrillas.

"All the News That's Fit to Print"

The New York Times.

LATE CITY EDITION
U.S. Weather Bureau Report (Page 81) forecasts: Mostly sunny today; fair tonight and tomorrow.
Temp. Range: 77—57; yesterday: 75—60.

VOL. CXV..No. 39,566. | © 1966 by The New York Times Company. Times Square, New York, N.Y. 10036 | NEW YORK, MONDAY, MAY 23, 1966. | TEN CENTS

LINDSAY WILLING TO HALVE HIS TAX ON COMMUTERS

Reverses Stand on Income Impost in Face of Strong Legislative Opposition

PAYROLL LEVY SCORED

Mayor Calls 'Tax on Jobs' Unfair to Poor—Charges 'Cowardice' in Albany

By SYDNEY H. SCHANBERG

Mayor Lindsay, facing tough opposition to his tax package in the Legislature, did a turnabout yesterday and said he would agree to let commuters pay a smaller income tax than city residents.

The Mayor, who had heretofore said — at least publicly — that he would not accept any compromise on his proposed city income tax, said in a radio interview:

"We realize there ought to be an adjustment for commuters. The commuters ought to pay less."

When asked what compromise he might accept, Mr. Lindsay said that "a reasonable suggestion" might be to have the commuter pay only half of what residents would pay.

Mr. Lindsay's proposed income tax, as presently drafted, would fall on commuter and resident without distinction. It would be half of what the current state income tax is and would raise an estimated total of $385-million.

Acceptance Uncertain

It was far from certain late yesterday that the compromise offered by the Mayor would satisfy the powerful bloc of state legislators from suburban counties, who have vehemently opposed any income levy at all on commuters.

Republican legislative leaders in Albany have suggested that Mr. Lindsay exempt the commuters from the income tax and impose on them instead a payroll tax that the city already has the power to impose.

This tax is only one-half of 1 per cent of payrolls—half to be paid by the employer and half by the employe—and would mean, in effect, that the nonresident commuters would have to pay only one-ninth of what residents would be paying under the income tax.

Payroll Tax Opposed

The Republican Mayor and Democratic leaders, both in the Legislature and the City Council, have rejected this idea.

Mayor Lindsay repeated his opposition to using the payroll tax during his radio interview on "The WINS News Conference," which was taped on Friday afternoon and broadcast last night.

The payroll tax, the Mayor said, is "too much" of a concession to the quarter of a million suburbanites who commute to work in New York City and would induce the city's middle-income and high-income residents to move to the suburbs and become commuters themselves.

He added that the City Council had never implemented the tax because "it's a tax against expanded payrolls."

Burden on Poor Decried

"Therefore," he said, "it's a tax on jobs. And also it's a tax in which the poor person pays the same amount, same rate, as does the rich man, and that violates traditional American notions about what fair taxation is all about."

Mr. Lindsay addressed himself in particular to a proposal made by the Republican minority leader of the Assembly, Perry B. Duryea Jr., under which city residents would pay the income tax, commuting wage-earners would pay the payroll tax and commuting professional people would pay a self-employment tax.

The Mayor said the reason why Mr. Duryea—who is from Montauk, L. I.—and other suburban legislators were suggest-

Continued on Page 31, Column 3

NEWS INDEX

	Page		Page
Books	39	Man in the News	44
Bridge	38	Music	48-50
Business	56, 63	Obituaries	41
Buyers	63	Real Estate	63
Chess	38	Screen	48-50
Congress Vote	19	Ships and Air	78-81
Crossword	39	Society	46
Editorials	40	Sports	51-56
Events Today	45	Theaters	48-50
Fashions	47	TV and Radio	82-83
Financial	56-63	U. N. Proceedings	2
Food	47	Weather	81

News Summary and Index, Page 43

125 Leaders Are Chosen To Shape 2d Regional Plan

Association Focuses on Jobs, Education, Stores, Transportation and Housing in 31 Counties by the Year 2000

By PETER KIHSS

A blue-ribbon advisory committee of 125 leaders was announced yesterday to help draw a plan running through the year 2000 on how the New York metropolitan region can become a better place to live and work.

Morris D. Crawford Jr., 50-year-old lawyer and president of the Bowery Savings Bank, was designated chairman of the new group by the Regional Plan Association. The association has been working since 1929 to promote the original regional plan developed at that time for the 22-county region in New York, New Jersey and Connecticut extending 50 miles from Manhattan.

The new efforts will be twofold. One part is to offer recommendations for location of major activities — jobs, stores, education and other services—and the transportation to link them. The other would seek new designs and techniques to improve housing, neighborhoods and older cities.

Of the 1929 proposals projected for 1965 targets, association officials contend that major elements — highways, water crossings, airports, parks, superblock housing, even the Lincoln Center concept — have been carried out.

Population Up 7 Million

The major difference has been that population grew only from 10 million to 17 million, scattered over 2,000 square miles, instead of the predicted 20 million residents over only 1,000 square miles. The planners ascribe this to failure to carry out recommended railroad improvements, while stress went to highways.

Seventy members of the new 125-member Committee on the Second Regional Plan are to meet in closed-door sessions Wednesday, Thursday and Friday at the Princeton Inn in Princeton, N. J.

The committee includes civic, education, business, labor and religious leaders. Members were named by James S. Schoff, chairman of Bloomingdale's, before he retired as the association's chairman last week.

'Sounding Board'

Key associates in forming the committee — which Mr. Crawford yesterday called a "sounding board" — included Andrew Heiskell, board chairman of Time, Inc.; Gustave L. Levy, partner in Goldman, Sachs & Co., investment bankers; Dean Courtney C. Brown of the Columbia University Graduate School of Business, and Roger Hull, president of the Mutual Life Insurance Company of New York.

Preliminary studies have raised the question whether the metropolitan area by the end of the century may extend beyond the present 22 counties. Research has covered 31 counties, from New Haven to Trenton, westward to the Pennsylvania border.

The location patterns on

Continued on Page 44, Column 3

350 NURSES READY TO LEAVE CITY JOBS

Accuse Lindsay Regime of 'Double-Crossing' Them in Pay Negotiations

By WILL LISSNER

Three-quarters of the city's public health nurses are scheduled to withdraw en masse today from service in health centers and clinics.

A spokesman for the nurses charged the Lindsay administration with "duping" and "double-crossing" them in negotiations in which the nurses sought a $1,000-a-year raise to keep their pay equal to that of head nurses in city hospitals.

J. Jerome Olitt, counsel for the Professional Public Health Nurses Association, said that 350 out of 482 public health nurses in the city's employ would not report for work this morning and would allow resignations, handed in to the city Personnel Department last Friday, to take effect.

No attempt was made to resume negotiations yesterday. Acting Health Commissioner Arthur S. Bushel waited in vain for a call from Morris Tarshis, the city's mediator. Mr. Tarshis waited for a call from Mr. Olitt. Mr. Olitt said that when negotiations were resumed he would not take part unless Mayor Lindsay was present.

The public health nurses supervise 900 other public health workers and 485 public health assistants in 28 health centers, 46 child health stations, 12 consultation services and 105 clinics. They care for patients of all ages, get patients ready to see doctors, conduct interviews, prepare vaccines, work up medical charts and visit patients in their homes to give prescribed treatments.

A spokesman for the Depart-

Continued on Page 33, Column 1

Governor Sees Big Saving Under State Medical Plan

By PAUL HOFMANN

Governor Rockefeller rebutted widespread criticism of the state's new medical aid program yesterday, asserting that it would both expand the state's help to the needy and save money for New York City and other local communities.

"This program will lift the burden of fear from people who have worried that they would not be able to meet the needs of their loved ones for medical care," the Governor said. "It will not bankrupt the government."

He appeared on television here and in eight other viewing areas across the state to defend the three-week-old state law intended to help New Yorkers with low or moderate incomes to pay for physicians, dentists, hospital treatment and drugs.

Will Consider Changes

However, speaking to reporters after taping his remarks here Saturday, the Governor said he was willing to consider "amendments to correct any defects" in the new legislation. He expressed hope that the law's substance — help for about 40 per cent of the state's citizens who are not necessarily poor but who cannot afford medical treatment—would remain intact.

Opposition to the program, particularly from upstate, is expected to be voiced at a legislative hearing in Albany tomorrow. The bill passed the legislature with only one Senator and 15 Assemblymen voting against it, but since Governor Rockefeller signed it on April 30, public criticism of it has been rising.

Critics generally charge the program is overly generous in its eligibility specifications, under which a family of four with one wage earner would not have to pay any medical bills if its annual net income did not exceed $6,000. Professional groups have attacked the law as a step toward socialized medicine.

Enacted in 1929

In the television appearance, Governor Rockefeller took pains to recall that the state has had medical assistance legislation for needy persons since 1929, and that since 1963 any family of four with a net income of less than $5,200 yearly income was covered by it.

The Governor also contended that Federal funds for medical aid in the state would go up by about 300 per cent under the new program, while state and local contributions this year would be "the same or less than they were last year."

The Federal contributions are to be granted under the recently enacted Title 19 of the Federal Social Security Act that was passed at the same time as Title 18, which established the Federal Medical program for the aged.

New York City, in particular,

Continued on Page 32, Column 3

United Press International Radiophoto

THEN HE WAS KILLED: A Danang dissident keeps his arms high after his capture Saturday by South Vietnamese marines loyal to Saigon junta. Troops said he had been throwing grenades at them. He was questioned by marine officer, who then shot him.

Heart Patient Aided By Pump Implanted In Chest 5 Days Ago

By HAROLD M. SCHMECK Jr.

The successful use of an artificial auxiliary heart chamber was reported yesterday by a team of surgeons, physicians and other specialists at Maimonides Hospital of Brooklyn.

The device was implanted in the chest of a 63-year-old woman, severely ill with heart disease and its complications, during a six-hour operation Wednesday by the team, headed by Dr Adrian Kantrowitz. The purpose was to help the heart pump blood through the body.

Because the natural heart's main pumping chamber is called the left ventricle, the artificial device is described as an auxiliary left ventricle.

It has been in use on a roughly two-hours-on, two-hours-off basis since the operation and will be left in place permanently. Its external power and control mechanisms can be disconnected and later reconnected if necessary by means of a five-sixteenths of an inch tube through the patient's chest wall.

A statement released yesterday by the hospital said:

"At present her condition is good, and she appears to have the best chance of surviving such an implantation. However, she has undergone major surgery and in any new procedure unforeseen problems can arise."

Dr. Kantrowitz, who is director of surgery at the hospital, said it was too early to describe the implantation as a complete success.

"We can say with certainty that the equipment has worked magnificently, that it has helped her heart enormously but that she is a very sick woman," he said during a news conference at the hospital.

The patient, Mrs. Louise

Continued on Page 45, Column 1

PROCEDURE EASED ON MINOR ARRESTS

Police Will Have Option of Releasing Many Suspects With Only a Summons

By ERIC PACE

Many suspects arrested for minor crimes will be allowed to go home instead of being locked up to await arraignment, under a new police procedure to go into effect throughout Manhattan this fall.

The program, disclosed by Police Commissioner Howard R. Leary in an interview, will put the arrested person back on the street in about an hour. Otherwise he would be held in a cell in a station house and later in a detention pen at court while waiting an average of eight hours to be arraigned.

The suspects so released will be carefully selected and will be given a summons — like those served on speeders — directing them to appear in court later for arraignment.

Extension Is Planned

In the interview in his paneled office at Police Headquarters last weekend, Mr. Leary said this innovation, to be employed on a scale not tried in other American cities, would save the time of policemen and "eliminate embarrassment and inconvenience suffered by persons arrested for minor offenses."

If the measure is successful in Manhattan it may be extended to all boroughs. Persons arrested for crimes such as disorderly conduct, malicious mischief, simple assault and petit larceny would be eligible.

The procedure has been tried out in three central Manhattan precincts (the 13th, 14th and

Continued on Page 27, Column 1

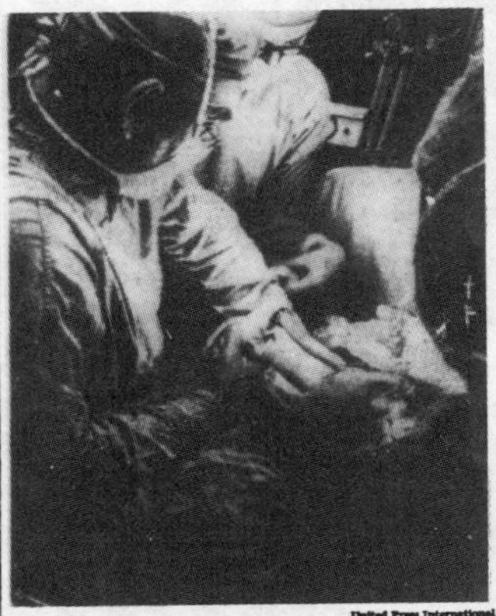

United Press International

AUXILIARY LEFT VENTRICLE is implanted by Dr. Adrian Kantrowitz, left, into chest of a 63-year-old woman during operation at the Maimonides Hospital of Brooklyn.

Mrs. Gandhi Chides Critics Who Charge 'Non-Nehru' Policy

By J. ANTHONY LUKAS
Special to The New York Times

BOMBAY, India, May 22 — Prime Minister Indira Gandhi delivered today her most stinging reply to party colleagues who accuse her of abandoning the policies of her father, the late Prime Minister Jawaharlal Nehru.

In an emotional speech to the governing body of the Congress party, Mrs. Gandhi snapped, "Don't tell me I don't know Nehru's ideology."

"Apart from being my father, he was a coworker and a comrade," she said, standing before a huge painting of Mr. Nehru. "We worked together. I was intimately connected with all his thinking. I knew about his policies before they came about."

But she said she also knew that her father had been flexible.

"New situations arise and new problems come along for which it is necessary to find new solutions," she declared, and added:

"If you disapprove of my approach, then change your leadership, remove me."

Mrs. Gandhi's half-hour declaration of conscience ended a day of lively debate during which several of the 500 delegates di-

Continued on Page 5, Column 5

East-West Trade Grows; U.S. Lags Behind Europe

By RICHARD E. MOONEY
Special to The New York Times

PARIS, May 22—Piero Savoretti looks into the Soviet market for his Italian employers—Fiat, Olivetti and others—from a small suite in Moscow's Sovietskaya Hotel. Britain's giant Imperial Chemical Industries, which sells almost 10 per cent of its exports to the Soviet Union, has a staff of Russian-speaking specialists.

And last winter Berthold Beitz, manager an dsupersalesman of the mighty house of Krupp, spent a long weekend stalking deer in the Carpathian Mountains with Premier Ion Gheorghe Maurer of Rumania.

Rewarding But Limited

This is East-West trade: tantalizing, often rewarding, but still limited. Twenty years after the world divided into East and West, commerce between the two spheres has yet to become substantial.

For Western businessmen, dreams of millions of clamoring Communist customers are becoming more realistic. For Western politicians, there remains a quandary: the inherent complexity of making friends with enemies, at the same time satisfying their own business community pressures.

This summary article of the current situation and the prospects is drawn from special reports by correspondents of The New York Times in London, Rome, Bonn, Paris, Tokyo, New York, Washington and Moscow.

Eleven days ago, President Johnson proposed a modified version of the "bridge-building" legislation that he had been talking about for more than a year, a bill to give imports from Communist countries the same most-favored-nation tariff treatment enjoyed by non-Communist goods. In it, the Administration sought to demonstrate to the Communist world that United States foreign policy is flexible, despite its rigidity on Vietnam.

Eligible for Same Right

The most-favored-nation principle provides that the nations subscribing to a treaty will grant to each other any tariff concession they may give to any other nation.

For some time now, Washington has tried to capitalize on the natural tendencies of the Soviet Union and Communist China to separate, and of the smaller Eastern European countries to pull away from Moscow. For example, in contrast to the normally strict United States definition of strategic goods that may not be sold to Communist countries, Washington has tried to push through the sale of an atomic reactor—a peaceful one—to Rumania.

But, if the executive branch is flexible, the legislative branch is not. Anti-Communism runs

Continued on Page 14, Column 3

DISSIDENTS YIELD TO KY IN DANANG, SURRENDER ARMS

ATTACK IN SAIGON

Buddhist Mob Burns U.S. Vehicles After Slaying of Soldier

By R. W. APPLE Jr.
Special to The New York Times

SAIGON, Monday, May 23—South Vietnamese marines and paratroopers moved in around Buddhist headquarters today after one Vietnamese was killed in front of the headquarters and two American vehicles were burned by an angry mob.

Some Buddhists and some Vietnamese passersby who said they had been eyewitnesses reported that the man who was killed was shot by an American soldier riding in a truck convoy.

There was no confirmation of this from American sources, but United States officials said they were checking.

The first report made to embassy officials by United States military operations officers was that a Vietnamese driver of an American fuel truck had fired the fatal shot.

The victim was Nguyen Van Ngoc, a sergeant in the Regional Forces. He had been bicycling to work past the compound of the Unified Buddhist Church's Institute of Secular Affairs, the Vien Hoa Dao.

Soldiers Reported Attacked

After he had died from a shot through the stomach, a mob overturned and burned one United States Army jeep and a yellow pickup truck reported to belong to Vietnam Builders, a United States construction company consortium.

The United States soldiers in the jeep were reported to have escaped into a nearby military installation after having been pummeled by the crowd.

There was no immediate word as to what happened to the occupants of the construction company pickup or whether they were Vietnamese or American employes of the company.

The killing, which set off the burning, was apparently a senseless act. Sergeant Ngoc had stopped his bicycle near the gate of Buddhist headquarters and was resting on one foot, possibly to peer into the busy compound.

Some Vietnamese witnesses asserted that a shot came from the last tank truck of an American convoy, which was passing on the street.

The soldier's body was car-

Continued on Page 3, Column 1

400 TROOPS GIVE UP

Soldiers and Civilians Leave Main Pagoda Without a Fight

By The Associated Press

DANANG, South Vietnam, Monday, May 23—The main rebel force of about 400 troops in Danang's Tinh Hoi pagoda surrendered without a fight today to troops loyal to Premier Nguyen Cao Ky.

The troops and Buddhist civilians, who had resisted the rule of South Vietnam's military Government since last March, walked out of the pagoda and gave up hundreds of weapons, which they stacked along a roadside.

South Vietnamese marines, flown by Premier Ky to Danang a week ago to put down the dissidence, stood outside the pagoda as the rebels gave up.

A crowd of curious civilians also watched the surrender.

Government troops had surrounded the pagoda last night with 13 armored personnel carriers. Previously, Government headquarters had asserted that 600 dissidents had been taken prisoner or had surrendered during the fighting of the last week.

Ky Men Bar Negotiation

By NEIL SHEEHAN
Special to The New York Times

DANANG, South Vietnam, May 22—Leaders of the Buddhist and military opposition to the Ky regime, whose position is rapidly deteriorating, offered today to negotiate peace with Government commanders here if the United States would sponsor and mediate the talks.

Representatives of the Government junta declined to negotiate and pressed their call to the dissident soldiers and officers to surrender by 6 P.M. tomorrow or be considered deserters. The refusal to negotiate was reported to have been made on instructions from Premier Nguyen Cao Ky and the rest of the junta in Saigon.

The call for surrender, made by Government loudspeaker planes and trucks, promised the rebels that they would not be punished if they gave up before the deadline.

Punishment Is Hinted

Informed Vietnamese sources said, however, that Premier Ky intended to treat severely any who surrendered or were captured. So far no leader has given himself up. Those who have surrendered have been ordinary soldiers or noncommissioned officers.

[In the war against the Vietcong, South Vietnamese and American forces reported having killed 228 of the enemy in two actions, one south of Danang and one in the Mekong Delta. Page 4.]

Thich Minh Chieu, senior Buddhist leader in Danang, said he and other leaders of the opposition to the regime would be willing to attempt to reach a compromise with the junta if Lieut. Gen. Lewis W. Walt, commander of the United States Third Amphibious Force, which is based here, sponsored and mediated the negotiations.

Pagoda Virtually Surrounded

Thich Minh Chieu made the offer at the Tinh Hoi pagoda the Buddhist and rebel headquarters, which was virtually surrounded by Government tanks and armored personnel carriers.

The monk, who seemed nervous, specified that General Walt would have to guarantee the personal safety of the rebel leaders. He said the junta would have to agree not to encroach further on the rebel positions while the talks were in progress. The offer was transmitted to General Walt by marine officers.

Informed sources said the United States Embassy in Saigon had told General Walt that the United States would not mediate any peace talks. The embassy was reported to have said that the United States was willing to sponsor the talks to the extent of attempting to arrange them and guaranteeing the safety of dissident leaders.

Brig. Gen. Du Quoc Dong,

Continued on Page 2, Column 2

U.S. Air Force F-102 revetment area at Da Nang, South Vietnam.

U.S. aircraft from the aircraft carrier U.S.S. *Oriskany* attacked petroleum-oil-lubricant barges and PT boats east of Haiphong. The smoke is rising from a burning barge.

"All the News That's Fit to Print"

The New York Times.

LATE CITY EDITION

U. S. Weather Bureau Report (Page 77) forecasts: Fair, hot, less humid today; cooler tonight. Fair, seasonable tomorrow.
Temp. Range: 90—73; yesterday: 92—73.
Temp.-Hum. Index: about 70; yesterday: 80.

VOL. CXV..No. 39,604. NEW YORK, THURSDAY, JUNE 30, 1966. TEN CENTS

U.S., EXTENDING BOMBING, RAIDS HANOI AND HAIPHONG OUTSKIRTS; CITES REDS' DISPERSAL OF FUEL

PRIME LOAN RATE IS RAISED TO 5¾% BY MAJOR BANKS

Chemical Initiates Increase on Business Borrowings —Others Due to Join

AIDES AT RESERVE WARY

Action Sets Off Speculation That Upturn in Discount Charge May Follow

By H. ERICH HEINEMANN

The cost of business borrowing at the nation's banks started to move up another notch yesterday.

Late in the afternoon, the Chemical Bank New York Trust Company, the fourth largest commercial bank in New York City and the fifth largest in the United States, announced that, effective immediately, its prime or minimum rate on loans to businesses would be raised to 5¾ per cent from 5½ per cent.

Almost at once, the First National Bank of Chicago announced a similar increase in the prime rate, the interest charged by banks on short-term loans to large depositors with the highest credit rating.

In Los Angeles, the Union Bank, which specializes in corporate banking, also increased its prime rate to 5¾ per cent.

[In Washington, Federal Reserve Board officials reacted cautiously to the Chemical Bank's increase in the prime rate, noting that it was "not out of line" with the general pressures on banks and money-market conditions.]

Reaction at Other Banks

The move to a higher business-lending rate came against the background of mounting demands for bank credit, selective rate increases by banks on some types of loans, and an increasingly restrictive credit policy by the Federal Reserve.

Some bankers speculate that the Federal Reserve might follow by increasing its discount rate.

The action came too late in the day for other major banks in New York City and elsewhere to react formally. However, there were strong indications from several of the country's largest banks—in New York, Chicago, San Francisco, and Boston—that they would join in today.

If the increase does become general, it will be the third time since last December that

Continued on Page 61, Column 1

HOUSE UNIT EASES HOUSING BIAS BAN

Exempts Individual Sales— Bill Cleared for Floor

By JOHN HERBERS
Special to The New York Times

WASHINGTON, June 29—The House Judiciary Committee approved President Johnson's civil rights bill today after accepting a compromise amendment to the open housing section that would exempt the vast majority of individual home sales.

By a vote of 21 to 13, the committee adopted the amendment sponsored by Representative Charles McC. Mathias Jr., Republican of Maryland.

This broke a two-day deadlock over the controversial section that would ban discrimination in the sale or rental of all types of housing.

The committee then approved the entire bill by a vote of 24 to 9 and asked that it be brought to a vote by the full House as soon as possible.

However, the committee also accepted an amendment sponsored by civil rights groups and offered by Representative John Conyers Jr., Democrat of Michigan, to establish an enforcement agency for open housing with power to issue cease-and-desist orders.

The vote on this amendment was 13 to 4, and there were indications that some members were not aware of how strong it was, although Mr. Conyers announced that it would give the agency powers beyond conciliation, similar to those of the National Labor Relations Board.

It was the Mathias amendment that made the housing

Continued on Page 23, Column 4

City Tax Program Mired as Senators Fail to Rally Votes

By RICHARD L. MADDEN
Special to The New York Times

ALBANY, June 29—Senate leaders struggled again today to round up enough votes to pass New York City's tax program, and again they failed.

After a day of huddles and whispered conversations in the red-carpeted Senate chamber, the members recessed until tomorrow without having acted on the tax package, which the city is counting on for the fiscal year starting at 12:01 A.M. Friday.

The Democratic-controlled Assembly is not scheduled to act on the city tax bills until the Senate moves. The Assembly spent much of today wrangling over Republican efforts to soften the impact of the state's controversial new medical assistance program.

The Senate leaders appeared to be in about the same position they were in last week when they first postponed action on the tax

Continued on Page 17, Column 1

A.M.A. FOR POLICY OF DIRECT BILLING

Urges All Members to Act Under Medicare Provision —Choice Is Retained

By AUSTIN C. WEHRWEIN
Special to The New York Times

CHICAGO, June 29 — The House of Delegates of the American Medical Association adopted today a resolution that recommended direct billing of patients by every member under Medicare.

Under direct billing, doctors would be enabled to ignore the machinery of Medicare, which goes into effect Friday. But in its zeal to encourage use of the method, the 238-member policy-making house went beyond the wishes of its leadership.

But later the delegates, by reinterpreting the resolution, apparently accepted the leadership view of how doctors should act under the new plan.

The leadership also favors direct billing, but in a carefully worded form to avoid any possible antitrust action. In their short-lived revolt, the delegates were seeking doubly to emphasize that they favored "individual responsibility" on the part of the patients and their conviction that they were protecting the doctor-patient relationship.

Picked by Acclamation

The development was seen as indicative of the dominant conservative sentiment in the House of Delegates, most of whose members are unreconciled to the whole Medicare law and intend to employ direct billing as one means of demonstrating this to patients, the public, Congress and the Johnson Administration.

Although the dispute over how hard to push doctors toward direct billing was smoothed over, it left the A.M.A. sharply split. There was no immediate explanation from the leaders on exactly what the policy was after the revolt.

Also, the A.M.A. was split over the question of discrimination against Negro doctors, especially in the South, although a debate on the floor on this issue was avoided.

By acclamation, the delegates

Continued on Page 19, Column 3

G.O.P. RELUCTANT ON OPEN SUPPORT FOR KLEIN IN FALL

Javits 'Not Enthusiastic' and Price Cool to Backing Democrat for Surrogate

By RICHARD WITKIN

Republican Senator Jacob K. Javits said yesterday that he deplored "very much" the fact that "we now have a candidate for Surrogate who has been rejected by his own party."

In an interview here in which he commented on the results of Tuesday's Democratic primary, Mr. Javits said it was "now essential for me to maintain a much closer eye on my own party and the details of its internal operations."

In the Surrogate primary, State Supreme Court Justice Arthur G. Klein, an old-line Democrat, was roundly defeated by Justice Samuel J. Silverman, who was backed by a coalition led by Senator Robert F. Kennedy.

But because Justice Klein also had been designated, unopposed, by the Republican regulars, he will be the Republican candidate in November against Justice Silverman.

Support in Doubt

Mr. Javits, asked if he would support Justice Klein in the fall, said:

"I am not very enthusiastic about the prospect, but I'll consider it."

Mr. Javits's comments reflected the wide Republican embarrassment over seeing the party maneuvered into being the only backer of an Old Guard Democrat.

"The general odor of a deal seems to have been pervasive enough," the Senator said, "to move a majority of the Democratic voters to reject Justice Klein in favor of Justice Silverman. I don't know what the deal was or even if there was one. I propose to keep a much closer eye on my own party than heretofore because of what has happened."

Governor Rockefeller, whose chances of winning re-election could suffer from having Justice Klein on his ticket, refused comment on the situation.

So did Mayor Lindsay, who said after the Republicans had picked Justice Klein that he had tried to stop it and was not happy.

Focus on Governorship

Sources close to Deputy Mayor Robert Price indicated that he would vote for Justice Klein but that he would campaign actively only for Governor Rockefeller and for Representative Theodore R. Kupferman, his former law partner.

Mr. Javits was interviewed at the offices of the First National City Bank, 399 Park Avenue, near 54th Street, just before addressing a group of business executives seeking to have the Federal Government add a huge new accelerator to the Brookhaven National Laboratory in Suffolk County.

Politicians everywhere yesterday were turning their attention again to the scramble for the Democratic nomination for Governor.

It was almost universally agreed that Mr. Kennedy could have a dominant voice in picking the candidate, if he wanted to. The guessing game over whom he might prefer picked up momentum.

There was some feeling that, among the active candidates, Franklin D. Roosevelt Jr. and Nassau County Executive Eugene H. Nickerson had been

Continued on Page 24, Column 1

Reading Standards Are Raised For Promotion in City Schools

By LEONARD BUDER

Higher standards for promotion have been put into effect in the city school system in an effort to improve academic performance.

The new policy emphasizes higher requirements in reading as a condition for promotion of pupils to the next grade.

Its impact will be felt for the first time today when the city's school year ends and pupils receive their report cards, which will tell them whether they have been promoted or "left back."

For the first time in nearly two decades, pupils will be retained in the first grade if they fail to meet minimum requirements in reading. Until now the policy has been to promote all first-graders, regardless of academic performance, so that they would not be discouraged by failure.

In most of the upper grades, two months have been added to the reading scores required for promotion.

This means that youngsters who previously could have lagged two years behind in reading and still be promoted, will now be retained in the same grade if they are more than a year and eight months behind in reading. (There are 10 months in the school year.)

An even more dramatic change will take effect in June, 1968, when students will be re-

Continued on Page 42, Column 3

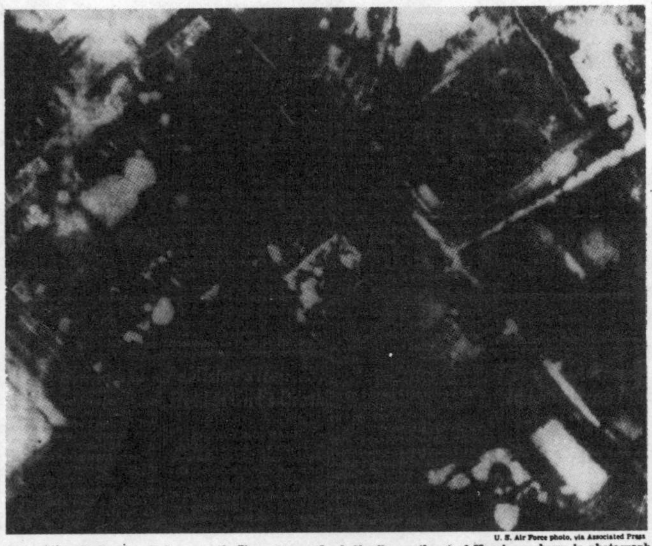

U. S. Air Force photo, via Associated Press

U.S. TARGET: Burning fuel storage facilities three-and-a-half miles northeast of Hanoi are shown in photograph taken from American plane after raid yesterday. Flames rose 12,000 feet. Bomb craters are visible at upper left.

United Press International Telephoto

DESCRIBING THE TARGETS: Defense Secretary Robert S. McNamara uses maps of Haiphong and Hanoi as he tells reporters about U.S. strikes against oil facilities. Arrows, which have been added to photograph, show raided areas.

HEAVY LOSS SEEN

Oil-Storage Capacity Is Reduced by 50%, Pilots Indicate

By CHARLES MOHR
Special to The New York Times

SAIGON, South Vietnam, June 29—United States bombers struck close to the heart of Hanoi and Haiphong today in raids that military informants said had damaged the gasoline and oil supplies of North Vietnam severely.

The raids marked a change from restrictions that had kept American planes well away from the two major cities since they began hitting the North in February, 1965. It also marked an important escalation of the United States effort against the North Vietnamese-backed guerrillas in South Vietnam.

Whether the restrictions will now be further altered to allow raids on manufacturing plants, military airfields and other targets around Hanoi and Haiphong was unclear, but some informed sources believed that such targets would soon be hit. The decision, like that to carry out today's raids, must be made in Washington.

Air Force Joins Attack

Navy A-4 and A-6 jet fighter-bombers attacked a large tank farm for petroleum products at the very edge of Haiphong, two miles northwest of the center of the city.

The complex, which represents 40 per cent of the fuel-storage capacity of North Vietnam and 95 per cent of the facilities for unloading tanker ships, was 80 per cent destroyed, according to preliminary damage reports by returning pilots.

Air Force F-105 jet fighter-bombers struck another large tank farm 3½ miles from the center of Hanoi that contained 20 per cent of the nation's storage facilities. The pilots estimated that they had destroyed 90 per cent of the target area.

Haiphong, the port for Hanoi, is about 60 miles from the capital.

In a Single Stroke

If the assessments are correct, the raids, in a single stroke, destroyed 50 per cent of North Vietnam's fuel-storage capacity as well as most of its ability to unload petroleum products from ships efficiently and expeditiously.

Another petroleum facility at Doson, 12 miles southeast of Haiphong, was also bombed, but there was no damage assessment.

The United States command made it clear that it had staged the raids because previously restricted air action had failed to deal with the major problem of North Vietnamese infiltration of troops and supplies to the Vietcong.

The Hanoi radio claimed seven United States planes shot down, three near Haiphong and four near Hanoi. Such reports have been exaggerated and there was no reason to doubt the accuracy of an American statement that only one plane, an F-105, had been lost.

The nearest previous strike in relation to Haiphong was a

Continued on Page 14, Column 1

WILSON DEPLORES LATEST ATTACKS

Backs General U.S. Policy —Thant Scores Raids on 'Populated Areas'

Text of Wilson's statement is printed on Page 14.

By DANA ADAMS SCHMIDT
Special to The New York Times

LONDON, June 29 — Prime Minister Wilson reaffirmed general British support of the United States policy in Vietnam today but declared that "we must dissociate ourselves" from the American bombing of oil storage installations at Hanoi and Haiphong.

The Conservative leader, Edward Heath, expressed full understanding and support of the American action.

Before a gravely silent House of Commons, Mr. Wilson expressed guarded disapproval for the first time of a major United States move in the war.

[At the United Nations, Secretary General Thant voiced "deep regret" over the bombings of what he termed "the heavily populated areas." In Moscow, there was no hint of an intensified Soviet commitment in Vietnam, although the raids were sharply criticized.]

Mr. Wilson explained that Britain had "made it clear on many occasions that we could not support an extension of the bombing to such areas, even though we were confident that

Continued on Page 14, Column 6

Bombing Evokes Criticism And Praise in Both Parties

By E. W. KENWORTHY
Special to The New York Times

WASHINGTON, June 29—On Capitol Hill today, President Johnson's decision to bomb oil depots at Hanoi and Haiphong was regretted, praised, denounced and accepted with resignation.

Those who have been urging expansion of the bombings endorsed the decision, as might be expected, and those who have counseled against stepping up the war were deeply angered or despondent.

The reactions cut across party lines, with influential Senators lined up on opposite sides.

Mike Mansfield of Montana, the Senate Democratic leader, who has steadily urged the President not to extend the bombing, was described as angry by those close to him.

In his customary exchange with reporters just before the Senate session, Mr. Mansfield was reluctant to comment. When pressed, he said, "I think it indicates a new stage in the war. I think it will also bring about a greater amount of aid from the Soviet Union and Peking.

"The destruction of petrol facilities won't deter infiltration. It may slow it down for the time being, but the end result may be increased infiltration that will make the road to the negotiating table that much more difficult."

Senator Richard B. Russell, Democrat of Georgia, chairman of the Armed Services Committee, said of the bombing:

"I approve of it. It seems to me we have exhausted every effort to arrive at negotiations. Any further delay in drying up the sources of supply for the Vietcong and the North Vietnamese troops in the South could only increase the casualty lists of American dead and wounded."

Senator Leverett Saltonstall

Continued on Page 14, Column 4

M'NAMARA GIVES REASON FOR RAIDS

Rise in Infiltration and Move by North to Camouflage Depots Are Mentioned

Transcript of news conference appears on Page 15.

By BENJAMIN WELLES
Special to The New York Times

WASHINGTON, June 29 — Defense Secretary Robert S. McNamara today attributed the timing of the United States bombing attacks near Hanoi and Haiphong to increasing infiltration into South Vietnam and recent moves to camouflage the North Vietnamese oil storage and distribution system.

The "perishable" nature of the vital petroleum targets, he said at a news conference, made an attack now "much more desirable" than it might have been earlier in the year.

Crisp and alert, despite his all-night vigil waiting in the Pentagon for reports on the raid, Secretary McNamara looked as if a weight had been lifted from his shoulders. Mounting speculation that the United States would strike at North Vietnam's remaining oil supplies had reached fever pitch.

Policy Aims Underlined

While he declined to speculate on future United States air attacks or on reactions by Communist China, he emphasized the following points:

¶The United States will continue a policy of military "restraint," hitting only "military" and not civilian targets.

¶American objectives in Vietnam remain "limited." These objectives are not to destroy the Communist Government in the North; not to destroy or damage the North Vietnamese people; not to make South Vietnam a military ally nor even to develop permanent military bases in the South.

¶The United States aims are

Continued on Page 15, Column 1

British Ship Strike Called Off One Year for Study of Industry

By W. GRANGER BLAIR
Special to The New York Times

LONDON, June 29—The leaders of Britain's National Union of Seamen decided today to end the 45-day-old maritime strike.

By a vote of 29 to 16, the union's executive council, which Prime Minister Wilson said yesterday had a "lack of guts," ordered the seamen back to work as of midnight Friday.

After a four-hour meeting at its headquarters in south London, the council voted to "adjourn strike action" for a year to permit the special committee of inquiry headed by Lord Pearson to conclude its scheduled study of seagoing employment and the shipping industry.

When a spokesman for the union came out to announce the decision, a group of placard-carrying seamen broke into boos and catcalls. The placards read, "Don't Let Us Down."

One seaman shouted, "You will have to get somebody else to sail your ships." Another, referring to the union leaders, cried, "None of you lads will be here in 12 months' time."

While some of the seamen were smashing their placards on the entrance steps to the headquarters, another wrote "Judas Hogarth" in red chalk on the steps, a reference to William Hogarth, head of the union.

There were also reports of

Continued on Page 6, Column 4

U.S. Sounds Latins On Argentine Ties

By RICHARD EDER
Special to The New York Times

WASHINGTON, June 29—The United States has begun, with a deliberate lack of haste, to consult other nations in the Western hemisphere about the question of resuming relations with Argentina's new military government.

Although ultimate United States policy toward the regime of Lieut. Gen. Juan Carlos Ongania, the new President, is still undetermined, it was evident that no quick move would be made to reverse Washington's initial coldness towards the coup d'état.

The consultations, which are being conducted in the Latin-American capitals, are expected to take three or four weeks. It

Continued on Page 5, Column 3

NEWS INDEX

	Page		Page
Art	36	Music	27-29
Books	36-37	Obituaries	39
Bridge	36	Real Estate	63
Business	50-51, 53	Screen	27-29
Buyers	51	Ships and Air	77-78
Chess	36	Society	32-33
Crossword	37	Sports	43-48
Editorials	38	Theaters	27-29
Fashions	30-31	TV and Radio	79
Financial	48-63	U. N. Proceedings	6
Food	30	Wash. Proceedings	23
Man in the News	19	Weather	77

News Summary and Index, Page 41

"All the News That's Fit to Print"

The New York Times.

LATE CITY EDITION

Mostly sunny, pleasant today; cool tonight. Fair tomorrow.

Temp. Range: 66-...; yesterday: 62-5...

VOL. CXVI..No. 39,722.

© 1966 by The New York Times Company.
Times Square, New York, N.Y. 10036

NEW YORK, WEDNESDAY, OCTOBER 26, 1966.

10 CENTS

FOOD-PRICE RISES LAID TO RETAILERS AND PROCESSORS

Federal Trade Unit Blames 2 Groups for Most Higher Bread and Milk Costs

END OF SPIRAL FORECAST

Agency Reports Increase by Farms Is Small Factor—O'Connor Starts Drive

By ROBERT E. BEDINGFIELD
Special to The New York Times

WASHINGTON, Oct. 25.—The Federal Trade Commission said today that retailers and processors were responsible for most of the recent increase in bread prices and nearly half of the increase in milk prices.

The commission forecast, however, that bread prices, at least, might come down soon.

It found that only a portion of the price increases on bread and milk was traceable to dwindling of supplies that had caused the farmers to raise prices.

The report was made at the specific request of Secretary of Agriculture Orville L. Freeman in a letter to Paul Rand Dixon, chairman of the commission. The trade agency started the study on Aug. 4.

[In New York, City Council President Frank O'Connor began an effort to drive down the price of milk by at least 2 to 3 cents a quart. Page 31.]

In the case of bread, the commission said, the increase in prices was three times the increase in the prices of farm products that go into bread. In the case of milk, the increase was double the amount of the increase in the prices received by farmers.

Margins Found Expanded

"Retailers not only passed on the increases but added to them by expanding their own gross margins, both absolutely and proportionately," the commission said.

The report found that in July, August and September retail prices for bread and milk were up 7.5 per cent and 7.8 per cent respectively above the January, 1966, level.

The commission predicted that the upward price spiral "will not be extended." It said that, although the usual seasonal advances in milk prices in the winter months might be expected, it is likely that some of the recent advances in bread prices "will not stick."

According to the agency, the gross profit margins of retailers of bread and milk have become

Continued on Page 31, Column 3

City Plans Containership Terminal

STATEN ISLAND

The New York Times Oct. 26, 1966

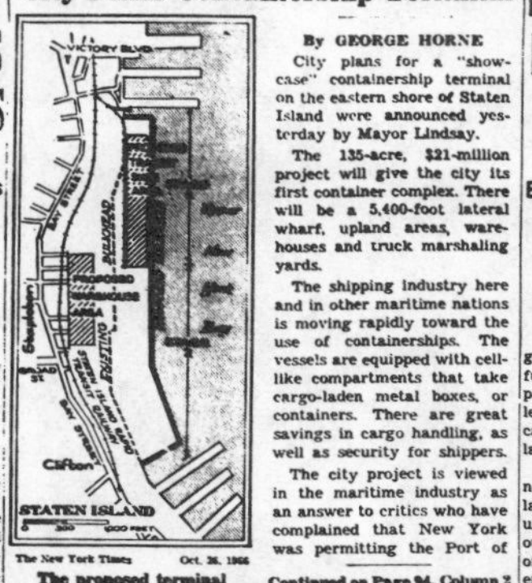

The proposed terminal

By GEORGE HORNE

City plans for a "showcase" containership terminal on the eastern shore of Staten Island were announced yesterday by Mayor Lindsay.

The 135-acre, $21-million project will give the city its first container complex. There will be a 5,400-foot lateral wharf, upland areas, warehouses and truck marshaling yards.

The shipping industry here and in other maritime nations is moving rapidly toward the era of containerships. The vessels are equipped with cell-like compartments that take cargo-laden metal boxes, or containers. There are great savings in cargo handling, as well as security for shippers.

The city project is viewed in the maritime industry as an answer to critics who have complained that New York was permitting the Port of

Continued on Page 94, Column 2

U.S. STEEL AND G.M. SHOW PROFIT DROP

Former Surprises Wall St. by Raising Its Dividend 10c a Share to 60c

By VARTANIG G. VARTAN

The United States Steel Corporation raised its quarterly dividend yesterday in a move that caught Wall Street by surprise, while the General Motors Corporation issued a report of disappointingly lower earnings for the third quarter.

The twin actions by industrial giants—one bullish and the other bearish—served to dramatize the paradoxes developing within the nation's economic machine, which is still racing at near-breakneck pace.

Directors of U.S. Steel voted the dividend increase—to 60 cents a share on the common stock, from 50 cents—in a move "to do something for stockholders," despite a drop in the company's third-quarter profits.

Big Steel's net income in the July-to-September period fell to $61.1-million, or $1.13 a share, from the year-earlier figure of $71.7-million, or $1.31 a share.

G.M.'s net income for the three-month period fell to $99.5-million, or 34 cents a share, from $263.8-million, or 91 cents a share, a year earlier. It marked the poorest third-quarter profits since 1961 for the largest manufacturing concern in the world.

The action by both U.S. Steel and General Motors took place shortly after the close of the New York Stock Exchange at 3:30 P.M. On the Big Board.

Continued on Page 57, Column 1

Mayor May Debate Cassese on Merits Of Review Board

By BERNARD WEINRAUB

Mayor Lindsay said yesterday that he would be "delighted" to debate John J. Cassese, the president of the Patrolmen's Benevolent Association, on the merits of the Police Department's Civilian Complaint Review Board. Mr. Cassese promptly accepted.

"John Cassese has been willing to debate John Lindsay from the outset, any time, any place," said Norman Frank, the P.B.A.'s community relations counsel.

The Mayor made his comment in reply to a question at a City Hall news conference. The conference followed a sidewalk campaign for the board in the Bronx where both the Mayor and Franklin D. Roosevelt Jr. were heckled by opponents of the board, which investigates complaints of police brutality and discourtesy.

At the news conference, Mr. Lindsay said:

"I'd be delighted with a confrontation if it were offered to me. If the great networks extend an invitation to us, I will accept."

By last night, offers to carry the debate had come in from WCBS-TV, WNBC-TV, WNEW-TV, WABC-TV and the radio stations WNEW and WABC.

"We have not accepted any one specifically yet, but we will," said David L. Garth, the campaign manager of the Federated Associations for Impartial Review, which supports the

Continued on Page 52, Column 1

LABOR IS FEARFUL BACKLASH VOTING WILL HURT UNIONS

Believes Reaction to Negro Pressure Will Cut Into Support for Liberals

By DAVID R. JONES
Special to The New York Times

WASHINGTON, Oct. 25.—Organized labor has become fearful that white backlash to Negro pressure for civil rights may lead to votes against liberal candidates, who support pro-labor legislation.

Such a development could negate much of the value of labor's efforts to get out the union vote this year and seriously undercut the effectiveness of labor's massive 1966 political effort.

The leaders of the American Federation of Labor and Congress of Industrial Organizations, from George Meany, its president, down to those at the local level, are expressing such fears and groping for ways to prevent such a white reaction, particularly in major cities.

"If it weren't for the race issue, I'd feel a lot more confident," says Alexander E. Barkan, executive director for labor's Committee on Political Education. "Who can tell what this madness is going to do? This is our biggest problem."

Worry Plagues Leaders

The labor leaders are plagued by this worry in the final stages of what they believe has otherwise been their most successful political drive so far. The political committee has begun some potentially significant experiments with computers. And officials say most local unions are working hard politically, despite disappointment over the defeat of most labor legislation in the 89th Congress.

These leaders also report that there is no significant shift within labor toward endorsing Republican candidates, even though strained relations between President Johnson and organized labor in February led Mr. Meany to hint that this might occur. The problem, union men say, is that there are few Republicans worth endorsing.

Top labor political strategists forecast early this year that the Democrats would lose no more than 20 to 30 House seats in the 1966 elections. But now that white backlash has shown up in various primary elections and polls, observes one leader, "all bets are off."

"There's clear evidence that by exploitation of race prejudice, the opposition has moved to split our vote," says W. Don Ellinger, political director for the International Association of Machinists. A top official of

Continued on Page 53, Column 1

U.S. AND ALLIES PLEDGE TO LEAVE SOUTH VIETNAM WITHIN 6 MONTHS AFTER HANOI ABANDONS THE WAR

Associated Press Cablephoto

ENDING MANILA CONFERENCE: President Johnson and South Vietnamese Premier Nguyen Cao Ky, right, as they signed a joint communiqué yesterday at the Malacanan Palace in Manila. Between them are Secretary of State Rusk and the South Vietnamese chief of state, Nguyen Van Thieu. Signing came last on conference agenda.

INDONESIAN COURT DOOMS SUBANDRIO

Ex-Foreign Minister, Found Guilty of Aiding Revolt, May Appeal to Sukarno

By ALFRED FRIENDLY Jr.
Special to The New York Times

JAKARTA, Indonesia, Oct. 25—Dr. Subandrio, Foreign Minister of Indonesia for nearly nine years until his arrest last March, was sentenced to death tonight by the Extraordinary Military Tribunal here. The one-time intimate of President Sukarno stood quietly and calmly in the crowded courtroom while Lieut. Col. Ali Said read the decision of the five military judges.

The former Foreign Minister, who is 52 years old, was convicted of having aided and conspired in the unsuccessful Communist-led attempt to seize power in Indonesia a year ago.

Second Such Decision

Dr. Subandrio, who is the second former high Cabinet Minister to be sentenced to death since President Sukarno delegated most of his authority to General Suharto in March, is expected to ask the President for clemency.

President Sukarno has not yet acted on a similar appeal made by Jusuf Muda Dalam, one-time Minister for Central Banking, who was sentenced to death last month.

Colonel Said announced the court's verdict three and a half hours after the session began and the judges had alternated in reading excerpts from testimony taken during the 17 earlier sessions. The tribunal chairman said that Dr. Subandrio had been found guilty of having given "information or opportunity to other persons with the intention of confusing

Continued on Page 33, Column 1

Cost of City Bonds Soars to 4.759%

By ROBERT ALDEN

New York City had to pay an interest rate of 4.759 per cent yesterday to borrow $123,530,000—the highest rate it has been charged in 34 years.

The single noncompetitive bid by a joint syndicate caused consternation in the financial community and among some city officials.

In recent weeks the municipal bond market has been getting firmer. The expectation was that the city would have to pay less for its money than it did in July, when the rate was 4.65 per cent for borrowing $112,925,000.

But at 11 A.M., when Comptroller Mario A. Procaccino opened the little metal box in his office used to receive bids on the city's borrowings, there was only one. It had been dropped in the box by a representative of a syndicate headed

Continued on Page 94, Column 1

Soviet Bloc Said to Favor A Softer Stand by Hanoi

By HENRY KAMM
Special to The New York Times

WARSAW, Oct. 25 — Informed Polish sources reported today that nine Communist nations at their conference in Moscow last week were in general agreement on the need to soften North Vietnam's stand on peace terms.

No agreement was reported on how to attain this goal, nor was optimism expressed that it could be attained.

The desirability of persuading Hanoi to agree to reasonable terms for a peace conference was said by the sources to have been at the center of discussion.

No confirmation was available from official sources. However, ranking diplomats found the reports in keeping with a mood they sensed here, a feeling that a move for peace in Vietnam might be in the offing.

Two steps that together might clear the way for a peace conference were said to have been discussed by the Soviet Union, its East European allies, Mongolia and Cuba.

The first would be to try to convince Hanoi that its insistence that the National Liberation Front, the political arm of the Vietcong, be the sole representative of South Vietnam at the conference table was unrealistic. This would open the way for participation by the Saigon Government, as the United States has insisted.

Second, the nine nations might suggest to President Ho Chi Minh to halt the dispatch of North Vietnamese troops to the South. Such a move could lead the United States to suspend bombing raids on the North.

The Communist nations were described as eager to receive a firm United States assurance on this point. They were reported to have been encouraged by recent conciliatory statements by the United States.

According to the Polish sources, the tone of the discussions, which were said to have evoked no controversy despite the presence of the Rumanians, who follow their own line on

Continued on Page 20, Column 6

YEMEN EXECUTES 7 FORMER AIDES

Pro-Cairo Regime Convicts al-Salal Foes of Treason

By HEDRICK SMITH
Special to The New York Times

CAIRO, Oct. 25 — Seven former officials of Yemen, including a Minister ousted last week, were convicted of high treason in a brief trial today and immediately executed by President Abdullah al-Salal's pro-Egyptian regime in Sana.

The executions, reported by the official Egyptian news agency, followed the sweeping purge in Yemen carried out by President al-Salal after the wholesale ouster of the government of former Premier Hassan al-Amri last month.

According to well-informed sources, more than 300 persons have been arrested and 140 are to go before state security courts in the coming days.

In the last month, the al-Salal regime has dismissed or retired nearly 100 military officers, shifted others to civilian jobs and replaced scores of civilian officials sympathetic to General al-Amri's "Yemen first" line and opposed to President al-Salal.

According to the Egyptian News Agency, today's executions were carried out against seven key defendants charged with trying to overthrow President al-Salal recently. They were shot by a firing squad in one of Sana's public squares.

The leader of the executed defendants was identified as Brig. Mohammed al-Ruaini, who until last week was Minis-

Continued on Page 7, Column 4

MANILA TALKS END

Proposal of Timetable Is Seen as Response to Russian Hints

Text of Manila communiqué appears on Page 20.

By MAX FRANKEL
Special to The New York Times

MANILA, Oct. 25 — The United States and five other nations said today that their troops would be out of South Vietnam within six months after North Vietnam had disengaged itself from the war.

Repeating the call for a gradual withdrawal of all foreign forces from South Vietnam, President Johnson attached a time factor to the offer to try to persuade the Communist nations of his sincerity.

According to responsible sources, the President was responding specifically to Soviet intimations that a timetable of withdrawal would make the American peace proposals more credible.

Several foreign diplomats, and especially Foreign Minister Andrei A. Gromyko of the Soviet Union, who on a recent visit to the United States are said to have urged announcement of a timetable to offset doubts that the United States would ever dismantle its costly military machine in South Vietnam.

Logistical Estimate

A six-month period was chosen, officials said, on the basis of purely logistical estimates of the time needed to evacuate all foreign forces, including more than 320,000 Americans, 44,000 South Koreans, 4,500 Australians, 2,000 Filipinos and several hundred Thais and New Zealanders.

The offer of total withdrawal was carefully wrapped in condition.

The offer was given dramatic emphasis, however, by inclusion in the communiqué signed here in the two-day meeting by the leaders of seven nations fighting in South Vietnam. The leaders of South Vietnam agreed to request withdrawal by the six others as the conditions are met.

Of the allied forces it said: "They shall be withdrawn, after close consultation, as the other side withdraws its forces to the North, ceases infiltration, and the level of violence thus subsides. Those forces will be withdrawn as soon as possible and not later than six months after

Continued on Page 21, Column 1

LEADERS UNWIND AT MANILA FIESTA

Most Wear Colorful Garb to the Going-Away Party

By ROBERT TRUMBULL
Special to The New York Times

MANILA, Oct. 25 — Old hands in the lively social life of Manila averred that there had never been such a "barrio" fiesta.

They were talking about the gigantic party given tonight by President Ferdinand E. Marcos and his wife, Imelda, for the visiting leaders at the conference of anti-Communist allies in South Vietnam.

For most of the leaders at the two-day meeting, which ended tonight, the glittering spectacle at Malacanan Palace, the Philippine White House, was the last social event of their stay. President Johnson is staying for another day of sightseeing in this former American colony but the others, except for President Marcos, will leave tomorrow.

The others are President Chung Hee Park of South Korea, Prime Ministers Keith J. Holyoake of New Zealand and Harold Holt of Australia, Premiers Thanom Kittikachorn of Thailand and Nguyen Cao Ky of South Vietnam, and Nguyen Van Thieu, the South Vietnamese chief of state.

More than 3,000 guests, most of them in the colorful native dress of the Philippines, wandered under palms and banyan trees illuminated with bright paper lanterns of traditional Malay design and watched island dances that suggested the

Continued on Page 21, Column 5

Bishops Assail Pike but Oppose a Trial for Heresy

The Right Rev. James A. Pike speaking yesterday before the Episcopal House of Bishops at meeting in Wheeling

Associated Press Wirephoto

By EDWARD B. FISKE
Special to The New York Times

WHEELING, W. Va., Oct. 25—The Episcopal House of Bishops overwhelmingly approved tonight a report recommending that threatened heresy charges against the Right Rev. James A. Pike be dropped but charging him with "irresponsibility" and "vulgarization of great expressions of faith."

Bishop Pike immediately retaliated by charging that he had not been given a fair hearing and invoking a little-used canon to demand an investigation of the charges against him.

The House of Bishops, which is holding its annual meeting at Oglebay Park here, voted 103 to 36 to accept the report of a special six-member committee that had investigated possible heresy charges against the retired Bishop of California.

Nineteen bishops later asked that their names be dissociated from the censure move. After the tabulation of the vote, Bishop Pike walked to the podium and said that he was invoking Section 56:4 of the church's canon.

This section states that "whenever a bishop shall have reason to believe that there are in circulation rumors, reports, or allegations affecting his personal or official character" he may demand an investigation of such allegations.

"I may be leading myself into formal charges," he said.

But Bishop Pike said later that he would insist that the investigation cover "everything that is said about me in the censure document as well as all charges that some of my views are heretical."

The Right Rev. John A. Hines, Presiding Bishop, said after the stormy session that the step asked by Bishop Pike "is not the same as a heresy procedure; it's merely an investigation."

Continued on Page 28, Column 5

The New York Times.

VOL. CXVI..No. 39,723.   © 1966 by The New York Times Company. Times Square, New York, N. Y. 10036   NEW YORK, THURSDAY, OCTOBER 27, 1966.   10 CENTS

COURT LIMITS VOTE ON POLICE BOARD TO P.B.A. PROPOSAL

Appeals Panel Upsets Ruling That Barred Conservatives From Dropping Petition

CITY'S MOVE DEFEATED

Police Group Will Have Only Plan on the Ballot to Kill Civilian Review

Special to The New York Times
ALBANY, Oct. 26—The Court of Appeals ruled today that one question on the New York Police Department's Civilian Complaint Review Board—not two—would face the voters on the Nov. 8 referendum.

In a unanimous decision, the seven-man court reversed a ruling by the Appellate Division that the city could place two questions on the ballot.

The court decision today said: "Order of the Appellate Division reversed. . . . All concur." There was no written opinion.

The court ruled, in effect, that the proposal of the Patrolmen's Benevolent Association to kill the board would appear on the ballot and that the proposal of the Conservative party to do so would not.

Who Drew Support

The board itself drew new support, meanwhile, from a Bronx Protestant group, the United Federation of Teachers and nine groups representing 1.5 million Jews. One of the Jewish organizations contended that the John Birch Society "was playing a major role" in the drive to defeat the board.

Last month, in a surprise move, the city fought the efforts of the Conservative party to drop its petition. The party said it wanted to do so to prevent confusion among voters because the P.B.A. had obtained a place on the ballot for a question that also sought to kill the complaint board.

In arguing to retain the Conservative petition, the city's Corporation Counsel said, "We have a duty to the citizens who signed this petition."

The patrolmen's association, however, said that the city was seeking to keep the two questions "to confuse the voters." Mayor Lindsay, who is leading the campaign to keep the board, denied this.

Association Pleased

The association was jubilant today. "Mayor Lindsay's concerted effort to create confusion among the voters has been finally and firmly frustrated by the courts," said Norman Frank, its community relations counsel.

Even supporters of the board did not appear gloomy about the decision.

"Now the emphasis can be placed where it belongs — on the P.B.A.'s attempt to pass a referendum which, while ostensibly dealing only with the review board, gives the police virtual immunity from all scrutiny and surveillance by all agencies of local government," said David L. Garth, the campaign director of the Federated Associations for Impartial Review, which supports the board.

In a statement, Mr. Garth added: "If it passes, this referendum would not only kill the civilian review board, it would, under a 'sleeper clause,' also

Continued on Page 52, Column 7

Ackley, in Shift, Ties Job Gain to Training

By EILEEN SHANAHAN
Special to The New York Times
WASHINGTON, Oct. 26—The President's chief economic adviser said today that the Government should not attempt to reduce unemployment below its current level by its tax and spending policies.

The cost in inflation of such an effort would be too high, Gardner Ackley, chairman of the President's Council of Economic Advisers, said.

With his statement, Mr. Ackley, in effect, moved over to the enemy camp.

Mr. Ackley's shift means that there is no one left in the high economic policy councils of Government who advocates Government action to increase total demand as the solution to remaining unemployment problems.

Labor groups and possibly

Continued on Page 21, Column 2

10-YEAR PLAN AIMS AT POVERTY'S END

Rights, Religious and Labor Leaders Ask $185-Billion U.S. 'Freedom Budget'

By THOMAS A. JOHNSON
A $185-billion "freedom budget for all Americans" designed to end poverty in the United States in the next 10 years was proposed yesterday by a coalition of civil rights, religious and labor leaders.

Conceived by A. Philip Randolph, Negro rights and labor official, the budget would be requested from the Federal Government to extend greatly the operations of social, educational and antipoverty programs.

Such a grant would require an act of Congress.

The plan, as outlined at a two-hour conference at the Salem Methodist Church, Seventh Avenue and 129th Street, attacks the causes of poverty on several fronts. It seeks a guaranteed annual income, increased welfare and Social Security payments, full employment, a rise in farm income and health, housing and educational opportunities for all persons.

New Taxes Barred

The proposal's monetary concepts were worked out by a team of economists, headed by Dr. Leon Keyserling, who said the program would neither require new taxes nor cut into expenditures for the war in Vietnam.

Dr. Keyserling, chairman of a former President Harry S Truman's Council of Economic Advisers, maintained that the money could come from projected "economic growth dividends" of the nation's gross national product for the next 10 years.

The sponsors estimate that the "economic growth dividend" from our gross national product [the sum of the nation's goods and services] would total $2,442-billion from 1966 through 1975 from which the needs of the freedom budget could be met.

This dividend was explained as the still uncommitted taxes the Federal Government would collect during this 10-year period, known as Federal surplus income.

The conference, attended by close to 100 persons, stressed

Continued on Page 26, Column 3

The President Salutes American Fighting Men in Person on Secret Trip to Vietnam

President Johnson leans from here to shake hands with servicemen at Camranh Bay. At his side is Gen. William C. Westmoreland, U.S. commander.
Associated Press Cablephoto

He pins the Distinguished Service Cross on Sgt. Charles B. Morris of Galax, Va. The sergeant is a paratrooper.

He dines with the troops in the base mess hall. Next to him is Lieut. Martin J. Hammer of Saint Marys, Pa. Earlier, the army officer was awarded Distinguished Service Cross.
Associated Press Cablephoto

PRESIDENT VISITS G.I.'S IN VIETNAM IN SURPRISE TRIP

Spends 2½ Hours at Base at Camranh Bay, Greeting Men and Praising Them

PRESENTS DECORATIONS

He Jests and Shakes Hands —After Return to Manila, He Flies On to Thailand

Text of the Johnson talk appears on Page 14.

By MAX FRANKEL
Special to The New York Times
CAMRANH BAY, South Vietnam, Oct. 26—President Johnson flew to South Vietnam today to salute his troops, to thank them, to decorate them, to eat with them, to joke with them, to be photographed with them.

And after 2 hours and 24 minutes of solemn ceremony, happy banter and urgent pep talk, he flew off again—speed and surprise serving, as intended, as his best protection.

Before many people could miss him in Manila, the jumping-off point, the President had crossed the South China Sea and landed amid the dunes of this enormous natural harbor, the newest and most secure of American bases in an insecure and embattled land.

The President's plane flew the 735 miles from the Philippines to South Vietnam in an hour and 40 minutes, arriving at 4:30 P.M.

Under 6 Hours in All

The entire trip took only 5 hours and 53 minutes out of his schedule, which calls for him to fly on to Thailand, Malaysia and South Korea before returning to Washington next Tuesday.

[President Johnson landed at Sattahip Air Base, 75 miles southeast of Bangkok, at 1:07 P.M., Thursday (2:07 A.M., Eastern daylight time), after a flight of about three hours from Manila, The Associated Press reported.]

Before an official word was spoken about the journey to South Vietnam, the Commander in Chief had reviewed some troops, met some wounded, eaten some chow, pressed many hands.

Wearing a ranch suit with the seal of his office on his breast, the tall Texan President loped through the sand or rode the back of a jeep, nodding, winking, yielding both hands to the crowds, a figure in tan in a milling throng of green combat fatigues.

"Thank you, thank you," he kept saying informally. "Y'all come back safe and sound now."

"I came here today for one good reason," he said formally, "simply because I could not come to this part of the world and not come to see you."

Pride and Sentiment

He spoke many more words before the sun disappeared behind the contested hills across the bay from this peninsula. They were words of pride and sentiment and patriotism and lavish praise for the two men who daily are concerned with the war on his behalf, Secretary of State Dean Rusk and Gen. William C. Westmoreland.

But above all they were words aimed simultaneously at a hobbled private in an air-conditioned quonset hospital and at a contentious world beyond.

"I give you my pledge," the President declared. "We shall never let you down, nor your fighting comrades, nor the 15-million people of South Vietnam, nor the hundreds of millions of Asians who are counting on us to show here in Vietnam that aggression does not pay, and that aggression cannot succeed."

It was the best prepared army, the most skilled army, the most compassionate army, the best-led army that he had come to see, Mr. Johnson kept saying. Despite some criticism of the

Continued on Page 14, Column 1

Laboratory Tests Improve Duplication Of Photosynthesis

By STUART H. LOORY
Working with the juice of fresh-cut spinach, two California scientists are believed to have taken mankind a big step closer to the use of sunlight for the production of nourishing foods out of such waste plants as jungle leaves and grass.

They have been able to duplicate the photosynthesis process outside a living cell to a degree that is regarded as insignificantly different from that taking place naturally inside a living cell.

Photosynthesis is the process in which the sun's energy is used by green plants to manufacture proteins, fats, sugars and starches, while at the same time giving off free oxygen to the atmosphere.

The process is one of nature's fundamental activities, taking light energy from the sun and converting it into chemical energy that plays a major role in helping plants to grow.

The scientists who succeeded in the new experiment are Dr. James A. Bassham, a chemist on the staff of the University

Continued on Page 26, Column 3

NEW DODD INQUIRY SLATED IN SENATE

Hearings Set on Finances —Democrat Declares, 'I Will Be Vindicated'

By E. W. KENWORTHY
Special to The New York Times
WASHINGTON, Oct. 26—The Senate ethics committee announced today that it would conduct hearings on "certain financial affairs and other activities" of Senator Thomas J. Dodd, including his use of campaign funds raised on his behalf between 1961 and 1965.

In a joint announcement the committee chairman, John Stennis, Democrat of Mississippi, and the vice chairman, Wallace F. Bennett, Republican of Utah, said that preliminary investigation of the Connecticut Democrat's financial affairs was now sufficiently complete to "provide a basis for hearings."

Mr. Dodd, who has contended that the committee lacks authority to look into his campaign finances, said in a statement:

"I stand ready to defend myself against all the allegations that have been made against me."

Travel Payments Cited

Mr. Stennis and Mr. Bennett said the hearings would also deal with payments by the Senate Disbursing Office for travel expenses of Senator Dodd.

Documents available to the ethics committee have indicated that on several occasions Senator Dodd submitted two bills for travel expenses — one to an organization that had invited him to speak, in his capacity as chairman of the Subcommittee on Juvenile Delinquency or as vice chairman of the Subcommittee on Internal Security, and a second to the Senate.

In his statement today, which he issued immediately after the committee's announcement, Senator Dodd declared:

"I am completely certain, as I was when I asked the ethics committee to investigate the allegations against me, that I will be vindicated when all the facts are in."

The allegations to which Mr.

Continued on Page 26, Column 1

43 Die in Fire on Carrier Off Vietnam; Accident Is U.S. Navy's Worst of War

Special to The New York Times
SAIGON, South Vietnam, Oct. 26—Flames swept through the blunt gray nose of the United States aircraft carrier Oriskany today in the worst naval accident of the war in Vietnam.

At least 43 men were reported to have died and 16 to have been injured in the fire.

The Oriskany, along with the carriers Constellation and Franklin D. Roosevelt, was cruising in the Gulf of Tonkin where for the last several weeks she has been sending attack planes into North Vietnam daily.

Flare in Hangar Ignited

A United States Navy spokesman said the fire was apparently touched off at 7:28 A.M. by a flare that ignited in Hangar Bay 1, a compartment in the forward third of the ship where planes are stored, refueled, armed with bombs, rockets and 20-mm. cannon shells and given minor maintenance.

A locker filled with flares then burst into flames and within minutes the forward section of five decks of the carrier was engulfed, the spokesman said.

Both sides of the hangar bay

are lined with officers' quarters and a number of the dead were believed to have been officers trapped in their staterooms by the flames.

An elevator used for lifting planes to the flight deck opens at the forward end of the hangar bay, which is approximately 100 feet long and 80 feet wide. Beyond the elevator are the quarters of enlisted men. It was not clear whether the flames had extended to them.

Two Helicopters Destroyed

In an initial damage report, officers aboard the ship said two helicopters were destroyed and four A-4E Skyhawk jet bombers damaged.

In addition, the officers said, extensive damage was done to the bulkheads and low ceiling of the hangar bay and to the forward officers' quarters, the catapult areas, forward elevators and electrical circuits.

It appeared likely that the ship would be pulled off Yankee Station, as the carrier positions off North Vietnam are known, and taken to a nearby port, possibly Subic Bay in the Philippines, for repairs.

Teams of firefighters spraying

streams of sea water and flame-smothering foam struggled three hours to bring the blaze under control, the spokesman said. Flash fires continued to break out as late as noon and it was not until 3:23 P.M. that the last embers were extinguished.

"The firefighters were extremely brave in charging into the dense smoke and flames to quell the blaze," said Comdr. F. T. Brown, the carrier's executive officer. "Their prompt and courageous actions were directly responsible for reducing the damage and casualties."

Help Flown Aboard

As the flames crackled through the ship, seamen in blue jerseys pushed planes to safety while red-shirted ordnance specialists wrestled with bombs, rockets and fuses in danger of exploding.

Navy doctors, hospital corpsmen and chaplains aboard the Constellation and the Roosevelt were flown to the Oriskany. Some of the injured were transferred to the other two ships for medical treatment while

Continued on Page 15, Column 2

Pope Names Sheen Bishop of Rochester Diocese

By GEORGE DUGAN
The Most Rev. Fulton J. Sheen, Auxiliary Bishop of New York and national director of the Society for the Propagation of the Faith, was named Bishop of the Rochester, N. Y., Diocese yesterday by Pope Paul VI.

Announcement of the appointment was made in Washington by Archbishop Egidio Vagnozzi, Apostolic Delegate to the United States. But the drama was here.

For half an hour, Cardinal Spellman and Bishop Sheen, the lean, youthful-looking 71-year-old prelate, held a news conference in the Cardinal's residence at 452 Madison Avenue.

Bishop Sheen, one of the church's few bishops without diocesan responsibilities, and Cardinal Spellman, whose spiritual leadership goes far beyond

Continued on Page 95, Column 2

Bishop Sheen with Cardinal Spellman after announcement.
The New York Times

Paris Resists Plan for European Atom Control

Stance Spurs U.S. Effort for Polish-Czech Proposal — Bonn Agrees to Study It

By JOHN W. FINNEY
Special to The New York Times
WASHINGTON, Oct. 26 — Diplomatic sources reported today that France was resisting a move begun by Communist countries to extend international nuclear controls into Western and Eastern Europe.

The French position has set off intensive diplomatic maneuvering in the Atlantic community over what is viewed in American circles as a potentially far-reaching offer from Poland and Czechoslovakia. The two nations recently offered to put their atomic facilities under the control of the International Atomic Energy Agency, a United Nations affiliate, if West Germany did the same.

Bonn issued a statement today that did not close the door on the offer.

The statement was at least a temporary victory from the United States in the maneuvering now going on with France

over how to respond to the offer.

Within the Atlantic community, but particularly among the six members of the European Atomic Energy Community [Euratom], the United States has been urging favorable consideration of the proposal.

It is accepted that the Communist offer may have some ulterior political motives aimed at weakening the Atlantic Alliance. But American officials believe acceptance could set an important East-West precedent. It could establish international controls to prevent military use of the fissionable byproducts of atomic power plants.

France at first advocated a favorable response but now is

urging the West German Government to reject the proposal. In recent weeks Paris was said to have threatened to veto any intrusion by the international agency into the inspection and control responsibilities now exercised by Euratom over atomic facilities in its six members—West Germany, France, Italy, the Netherlands, Belgium and Luxembourg.

Legally, there is some question whether France could veto a German decision to accept controls by the international agency as well as by Euratom. But France can cause considerable political difficulty for the European community and West Germany in particular.

In the process, France can also upset American hopes that the Polish-Czech offer can be used as one stepping stone to the improved East-West relations in such areas as trade and disarmament that are being

Continued on Page 3, Column 1

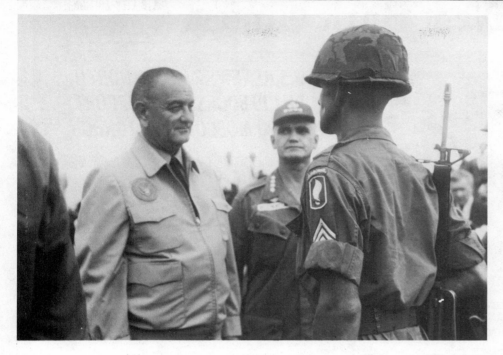

President Lyndon B. Johnson and General Westmoreland during Johnson's surprise visit to Vietnam in October, 1966.

General William C. Westmoreland, greets the U.S. 3rd Brigade upon its arrival in Vietnam in 1966.

Vice President Hubert Humphrey visiting a field hospital in Saigon in 1966.

"All the News That's Fit to Print"

The New York Times.

LATE CITY EDITION
U. S. Weather Bureau Report (Page 83) Forecast:
Partly cloudy, milder today; fair
tonight, partly cloudy tomorrow.
Temp. Range: 42—23; yesterday: 23—4.

VOL. CXVI...No. 39,833. © 1967 by The New York Times Company.
Times Square, New York, N. Y. 10036.   NEW YORK, TUESDAY, FEBRUARY 14, 1967.   10 CENTS

A STUDENT GROUP CONCEDES IT TOOK FUNDS FROM C.I.A.

National Association Says It Received Aid From Early 1950's Until Last Year

ROLE IN SPYING DENIED

Leader Asserts All Money Was Used to Help Pay for Overt Activities Abroad

By NEIL SHEEHAN
Special to The New York Times

WASHINGTON, Feb. 13—The National Student Association, the largest college student organization in the country, conceded today that it received funds from the Central Intelligence Agency from the early nineteen-fifties until last year.

Eugene Groves, president of the association, said the C.I.A. funds had been used to finance the association's international activities, including sending representatives to student congresses abroad and funding student exchange programs.

The intelligence agency refused tonight to comment on the matter.

The association has chapters on more than 300 American colleges and university campuses, where about 1.5 million students are studying. The local student government organizations rather than the individual students themselves form the membership.

Article in Ramparts

Mr. Groves's statement was in response to inquiries about a forthcoming article in the March issue of Ramparts magazine. According to a Ramparts spokesman, the article discusses in detail the relationship between the student association and the C.I.A.

Mr. Groves said the money was received through foundations that acted as go-betweens for the agency. He declined to name the foundations.

A Ramparts spokesman, Marc Stone, a New York public relations executive, said that the magazine would list the Sidney and Esther Rabb Charitable Foundation of Boston and the Independence Foundation of Boston.

Mr. Rabb was on a fishing trip in Florida and could not be reached for comment. Representatives of the Independence Foundation were also unavailable.

Uncertain of Amount

Mr. Groves, who has been president of the student association since last September, said Rockefeller today and called for an increase in state aid to public schools.

"I am firmly convinced there must and can be a record increase in 1967," Mr. Duryea said at a news conference.

Mr. Rockefeller, in submitting his proposed record budget of nearly $4.7-billion to the Legislature on Feb. 1, did not recommend any increase in the formula under which the state pays financial aid to local schools. This aid is scheduled to rise automatically by $117-million in the next fiscal year under the existing aid formula.

Mr. Duryea proposed an additional increase of $32-million for the fiscal year starting April 1.

Estimates Called 'Solid'

He said he thought the extra money could be provided because the Governor's proposed budget had "slightly underestimated" the anticipated income from existing tax revenues. He added: "I feel there can be a realignment of certain items in the budget."

Mr. Duryea said he had not discussed his proposal with the Governor. Reaction from Mr. Rockefeller and the legislative leaders was guarded.

"This is a very tight budget," the Governor said through his press spokesman, Leslie Slote. "Any proposed increase in state expenditures will have to be accompanied by proposed revenue-producing measures."

Asked about Assemblyman Duryea's suggestion that the Rockefeller budget had underestimated certain tax yields, Mr. Slote said: "The budget estimates are solid estimates based on previous experience and will surely hold up."

The Senate majority leader, Earl W. Brydges, Niagara Falls Republican, said: "I haven't closed the door on the possibility of an increase, but my feeling is that it might be difficult in the light of the tight fiscal situation."

"It's up to him. Rockefeller can be a stronger candidate than he was in 1964."

Only last Saturday, Mr. Rockefeller repeated that he was not a candidate and was "determined not to be used as an in-

Continued on Page 34, Column 2

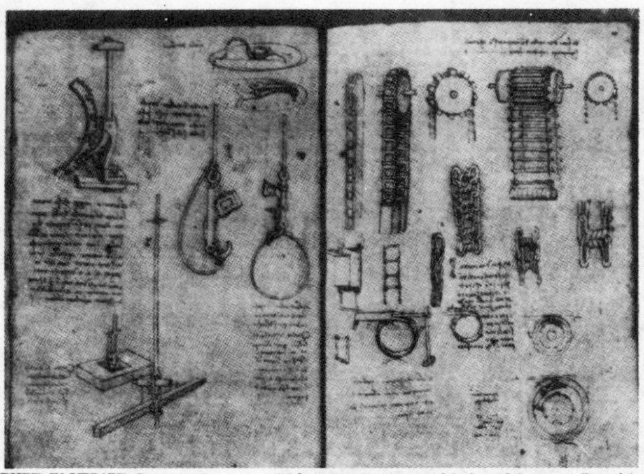

DURYEA ASKS RISE IN AID TO SCHOOLS

G.O.P. Leader in Assembly, in a Split With Governor, Urges $32-Million More

By RICHARD L. MADDEN
Special to The New York Times

ALBANY, Feb. 13—The Republican minority leader in the Assembly, Perry B. Duryea Jr. of Montauk, split with Governor Rockefeller today and called for an increase in state aid to public schools.

"I am firmly convinced there must and can be a record increase in 1967," Mr. Duryea said at a news conference.

Mr. Rockefeller, in submitting his proposed record budget of nearly $4.7-billion to the Legislature on Feb. 1, did not recommend any increase in the formula under which the state pays financial aid to local schools. This aid is scheduled to rise automatically by $117-million in the next fiscal year under the existing aid formula.

Continued on Page 68, Column 6

Scarcity of Recruits Worrying the Police

By MARTIN ARNOLD

The manpower pool from which the city's police recruits traditionally are drawn is shrinking so fast that police officials say the department's future effectiveness is jeopardized.

"We used to get 20,000 men taking a single written exam for the department," a police recruiter said yesterday. "Now we're lucky to get 4,000. It's getting harder and harder to come up with 1,000 new men a year."

The problem was crystallized on Sunday by John J. Cassese, president of the Patrolmen's Benevolent Association. He said radio cars were standing idle outside some station houses because there were not enough men to man them. The statement

Continued on Page 86, Column 4

FOUND IN LIBRARY: Two pages from manuscript by Leonardo da Vinci show variety of his inventions. At right are links and chain drives, much like those on bicycles.

Escapement, upper left, is used to convert linear into rotary motion as plunger is pushed down. At left center are two simple release mechanisms, like those in cranes.

700 Pages of Leonardo MSS. Found in Madrid

By WALTER SULLIVAN
Special to The New York Times

BOSTON, Feb. 13 — Some 700 pages of manuscript and drawings by Leonardo da Vinci, lost for almost two centuries, have been found in the National Library in Madrid.

The drawings, most of them done near the end of the 15th century, are said to establish Leonardo as the inventor of several devices, including the chain drive familiar to all bicycle riders.

They increase by a substantial amount the surviving fruits of Leonardo's genius. About 5,000 pages of his manuscript material were hitherto available. The added 700 pages contain some of his most elaborate and careful drawings.

They are arranged in two extended manuscripts more systematically organized than was the wont of the "great doodler," whose output during the period when he wrote his famous fresco, "The Last Supper," in a monastery in Milan.

The finding was announced today jointly by two scholars, Dr. Jules Piccus, who made the discovery accidentally two years ago, and Dr. Ladislao Reti, a leading authority on Leonardo drawings, who authenticated the documents two weeks ago.

Dr. Piccus is a professor of Romance languages at the University of Massachusetts in Amherst. He was searching the library at Madrid for popular ballads of the medieval period when he noticed a gap in the numerical sequence of catalogue cards.

Suspecting that the missing

Continued on Page 49, Column 1

Confirmation Age Raised By Sheen to Late Teens

Special to The New York Times

ROCHESTER, Feb. 13 — Bishop Fulton J. Sheen announced yesterday that Roman Catholic children in his diocese would be confirmed at about the time they graduate from high school instead of at the traditional church confirmation age of 9 to 12.

The Bishop's announcement runs counter to a 20-year-old trend, officially encouraged by the Vatican, to lower the age of confirmation. However, the question of lowering the age has come under debate by a study commission since the last Vatican Council.

Priests from the United States Catholic Conference and the Archdiocese of New York said yesterday that they believed the Diocese of Rochester would have the oldest Roman Catholic confirmation age in the world.

The 71-year-old prelate, who became Bishop of Rochester last December after serving as Auxiliary Bishop of New York, said the change would be effected over the next five years to allow young people to receive the Sacrament of Confirmation at a more mature age.

"Bishops are now being asked to confirm 11-year-olds who haven't yet reached the age of puberty," Bishop Sheen told 1,300 parochial schoolteachers this morning at an annual conference in the Columbus Civic Center.

"The Army would never induct at that age," he said later during an interview. "We say to these young people that they are now in the army of Christ—go out and fight for the church."

"Confirmation must become a

Continued on Page 25, Column 1

NIXON FORESEES OPEN CONVENTION

Says Rockefeller Remains a Presidential Possibility

By WARREN WEAVER Jr.
Special to The New York Times

WASHINGTON, Feb. 13 — Richard M. Nixon is looking forward to a "wide open" Republican National Convention in 1968, with three or more candidates and several ballots.

He made this prediction in an interview published in The Saturday Evening Post today. What the former Vice President did not say was that, in the opinion of most observers, a wide open convention would probably provide the most likely forum for his nomination.

Mr. Nixon particularly emphasized his belief that Governor Rockefeller remained a real and local governments.

If the Administration continues to oppose proposals for general tax sharing, Republican leaders say they are prepared to push for tax sharing on a piecemeal basis. This would amount to having any new grants-in-aid money bypass the Federal bureaucracy and go directly to the states.

As grant-in-aid appropriation bills come up on the floor, the Republican leaders would attempt to have them sent back to committee with instructions to substitute part or all of the money in block grants to the states.

Thus, if the appropriation were for education, the money

Continued on Page 20, Column 6

HOUSE G.O.P. PLANS TAX SHARING STEP

Will Attack Federal Reins on Domestic Aid Funds

By JOHN HERBERS
Special to The New York Times

WASHINGTON, Feb. 13 — Republican leaders in the House of Representatives have developed a four-point plan of policy and strategy for dealing with Administration proposals and for developing a party record in the 90th Congress.

The first point and cornerstone of the plan is an effort to reduce Federal controls in President Johnson's Great Society programs. The Republicans have become increasingly interested in the concept of the Federal Government's sharing a portion of its revenue with state and local governments.

Continued on Page 20, Column 2

U.S. RENEWS RAIDS IN NORTH, BUT PLEDGES PEACE EFFORT, AS DO MOSCOW AND LONDON

SOVIET SHIFT SEEN

Kosygin Ends British Visit With Pledge to Seek Halt in War

Text of London communiqué is printed on Page 10.

By ANTHONY LEWIS
Special to The New York Times

LONDON, Feb. 13—The Soviet Union and Britain pledged today to "make every possible effort" for peace in Vietnam and agreed to "maintain contact to this end."

This modest language was regarded by the British as signifying a shift in Soviet policy—toward a willingness to speak out and work for an end to the fighting in Vietnam. The British feeling is that the Russians urgently want the conflict to stop.

In a communiqué issued at the end of Premier Aleksei N. Kosygin's seven-day visit here, the British and Soviet Governments also announced that they would install a hot line similar to the one between Moscow and Washington. It will connect teleprinters in the Kremlin and 10 Downing Street.

New Treaty Planned

Britain accepted Mr. Kosygin's proposal for a treaty of "friendship and peaceful cooperation" between the two countries. Mr. Wilson said negotiations would begin "right away."

These were the high points of the communiqué. Mr. Wilson called it a "landmark in Anglo-Soviet history" and spoke of "the evident desire of the Soviet Government for the best possible relations between our two countries."

There was an atmosphere of euphoria about the whole visit as the Soviet Premier departed. Mr. Wilson told Mr. Kosygin at Gatwick Airport that he had "almost become part of the British way of life."

On Vietnam, the resumption of American bombing today marked the failure of hopes that immediate steps to peace could be arranged through Mr. Kosygin. But the British nevertheless saw hopeful signs.

Wilson Voices Optimism

The Prime Minister told the House of Commons this afternoon:

"I believe that despite the deeply held differences in the attitudes of the major participants, the gap is not unbridgeable, given a realistic appreciation of the political and military factors involved and above all given a belief on each side that the other desires a negotiated settlement."

At a news conference, Mr. Wilson said: "We believe the road to a solution is open. Even if we are disappointed on this occasion, there is no reason why—at an appropriate moment—the road should not be opened up again."

He spoke those words about half hour before the bombing was resumed. Mr. Wilson's phrasing indicated that he knew certain to cause "dissension, division and controversy" within the party.

One of the proposals would make it "prima-facie evidence of discrimination" for any state with a population of more than 20 per cent Negroes to select a convention delegation that has less than 10 per cent Negro representation.

This proposal, if adopted by the convention credentials committee, would apply to all of the Deep South states and to some border states. The states with 20 per cent Negro population, according to the 1960 census, are Virginia, North Carolina, South Carolina, Georgia, Alabama, Mississippi, Arkansas and Louisiana. The District of Columbia would also be affected.

This proposal is expected to draw especially heavy fire from supporters of Gov. Lester G. Maddox of Georgia and of former Gov. George C. Wallace of Alabama, who has indicated he is seeking the Presidency.

Mr. Maddox once closed a fried chicken restaurant in Atlanta rather than desegre-

Continued on Page 21, Column 1

Ho Chi Minh Asks Pope to Press U.S.

The text of message to Pope will be found on Page 8.

Special to The New York Times

HONG KONG, Feb. 13 — President Ho Chi Minh of North Vietnam called on Pope Paul VI today to urge the United States to "respect the national rights of the Vietnamese people."

The message, which was broadcast by the Hanoi radio, was in reply to the Pope's plea of Feb. 8 for action to transform the lunar new year cease-fire into negotiations for "a just and stable peace."

The reply was made public before the United States resumed raids on the North.

Observers here said that while President Ho Chi Minh placed on the United States the responsibility of bringing about conditions for a settlement, his message was a more encouraging response than any previous reaction by

Continued on Page 8, Column 1

JUSTICES REJECT DRAFT TEST CASE

High Court Bars a Hearing in Conviction for Burning Card at '65 Rally Here

By FRED P. GRAHAM
Special to The New York Times

WASHINGTON, Feb. 13—The Supreme Court refused today to review the first test case challenging the constitutionality of the 1965 law that forbids the burning of draft cards.

The refusal to review the appeal does not necessarily mean that the Justices consider the law to be constitutional. It gives, however, a strong indication that they have decided to steer clear of the issue, and it also virtually removes any doubt that persons burning their draft cards can be legally punished.

In today's action the Supreme Court declined to review the petition for certiorari (review) of David J. Miller, 24 years old, a Roman Catholic lay social worker who burned his draft card at an antiwar rally in Manhattan on Oct. 15, 1965.

Sentence Suspended

Miller, the first of 16 persons who have been prosecuted under the law, was given a three-year suspended sentence and placed on probation for two years.

Although he has married since his conviction and has a 2-month-old daughter, Miller said today he would go to jail rather than violate his beliefs by carrying a draft card. One condition of his probation is that he carry a draft card and obey all other Selective Service regulations.

Mr. Miller is a native of Syracuse and a graduate of Le Moyne College, a Jesuit institution there. He burned his draft card during a speech near Whitehall Street in Manhattan.

Four days later he was arrested and charged with violating the law that had been passed by Congress the previous August in reaction to a wave of draft card burning protests against the Vietnam war.

Attorneys for the New York Civil Liberties Union, which is handling a number of draft card burning cases, argued that the law violated the First Amendment's free speech guarantee because it was deliberately enacted to suppress dissent.

They contended that Miller's act was "symbolic speech,"

Continued on Page 12, Column 3

JOHNSON EXPLAINS

Says Foe Used Pause to Send Supplies to Troops in South

By JOHN W. FINNEY
Special to The New York Times

WASHINGTON, Feb. 13—The United States resumed the bombing of North Vietnam today after a pause of nearly six days.

In explaining its decision to resume the attacks, President Johnson said he had "no alternative but to resume full-scale hostilities" in view of the use of the truce by the North Vietnamese for "major resupply efforts of their troops in South Vietnam" rather than to seek a peaceful settlement of the war.

The President emphasized, however, that "the door is open and will remain open" to a negotiated settlement.

The President's statement was issued about four hours after the bombing was resumed at 12:07 P.M. Eastern standard time (1:07 A.M. Tuesday, Saigon time) with strikes against targets in the southern section of North Vietnam.

The United States suspended the bombing at 6 P.M. Eastern standard time last Tuesday for the four-day Tet truce marking the lunar new year. On Presidential orders, the pause was extended until today.

White House Statement

Through the White House press secretary, George Christian, Mr. Johnson issued the following statement:

"It had been our hope that the truce periods connected with Christmas, New Year's and Tet might lead to some abatement of hostilities and to moves toward peace. Unfortunately, the only response we have had from the Hanoi Government was to use the periods of truce to improve their troops in South Vietnam.

"Despite our efforts and those of third parties, no other response has yet come from Hanoi. Under these circumstances, unless to our own troops and those of our allies, we had no alternative but to resume full-scale hostilities after the ceasefire period. But the door is open and will remain open, and we are prepared at any time to go more than halfway to meet

Continued on Page 10, Column 6

TRIAL OF SUKARNO IS ASKED BY COURT

Indonesian Congress Urged to Act on Treason Charge

By United Press International

JAKARTA, Indonesia, Feb. 13 —The Indonesian Supreme Court demanded today that President Sukarno be tried for treason on charges of having stolen large amounts of money for his personal bank accounts and having given his blessing to an attempted Communist coup 16 months ago.

In a 120-page decision, the court demanded that Indonesia's Congress act against Mr. Sukarno when it meets next month. The court's report was based on documents presented by the military strongman, General Suharto, who assumed most of Mr. Sukarno's powers last March.

The court concluded that President Sukarno had had prior knowledge of the plot, knew that its purpose was seizure of the Government and approved of the final execution of the plan. It said he had an "obligation to account for everything he knew, for the action he took in regard to the coup."

In its statement, the court said Mr. Sukarno had stolen funds estimated at the equivalent of $7-mill on and charged that some of the money was deposited in banks in Tokyo and Amsterdam. The court also

Continued on Page 17, Column 1

DEMOCRATS WEIGH '68 RIGHTS PLEDGE

Plan Would Bar Delegations From South if Negroes Were Not Included

By GENE ROBERTS

ATLANTA, Feb. 13—A move is developing among some Democratic national committeemen to close the doors of the 1968 convention to any delegation from the Deep South that does not have Negro members and does not promise to uphold Federal civil rights laws.

The plan is outlined in a seven-page set of proposals that is awaiting action in March by the special equal rights committee of the Democratic National Committee.

The proposals are still regarded as confidential by their authors — members of an equal rights subcommittee headed by Mrs. Mildred Jeffrey, Democratic committeewoman from Michigan. But they are being quietly circulated in the South and are delighting white liberals and Negroes.

'Obnoxious' to Carolinian

State Senator Edgar A. Brown, a member of the equal rights committee from South Carolina, called the proposals "obnoxious" and said they were certain to cause "dissension, division and controversy" within the party.

'What's My Line?' Leaving TV in Fall

By ROBERT E. DALLOS

"What's My Line?" the second oldest program on television, and one of the last remaining network shows produced live, will be dropped from the schedule of the Columbia Broadcasting System next fall. It will probably be replaced by a Western.

The panel show, which has been on the air since February, 1950, is not listed on the network's program schedule for next season. Only the Ed Sullivan Show, which went on the air 17 months earlier, has been televised longer.

Network executives are now pondering schedules for the 1967-68 season. The cancellation of "What's My Line?" is the most significant of a number of casualties that can be ex-

Continued on Page 86, Column 3

"All the News That's Fit to Print"

The New York Times

LATE CITY EDITION

Weather: Snow ending this afternoon; partly cloudy through tomorrow. Temp. range: today 36-30; Mon. 38-33. Full U.S. report on Page 82.

VOL. CXVI..No. 39,854

NEW YORK, TUESDAY, MARCH 7, 1967

10 CENTS

JOHNSON PLANS DRAFT BY LOTTERY, WITH 19-YEAR-OLDS CALLED FIRST; WOULD CUT DEFERMENTS SHARPLY

1969 DEADLINE SET

Message to Congress Calls for Debate on Students' Status

Text of Johnson's message is printed on Page 32.

By MAX FRANKEL
Special to The New York Times

SAN ANTONIO, Tex., March 6—President Johnson announced today in a special message to Congress that he intended to establish by Jan. 1, 1969, a kind of lottery that would determine which young men were drafted for military service.

By the same date, the White House said, and possibly sooner—unless Congress inhibits his present freedom of action—the President also plans to decree by Executive order:

¶That 19-year-old men be the first exposed to the random call-up each year, along with older men whose deferments had expired.

¶That deferments for all graduate students, except those preparing to be physicians, dentists or ministers, be abolished.

¶That all deferments for fathers and men in so-called essential occupations be abolished, and that rules governing deferments in other categories be tightened and made uniform.

Undergraduate Deferments

Mr. Johnson left undecided for the time being the question whether undergraduates should be deferred until they obtain a bachelor's degree.

He invited the nation to debate the issue of college deferments, noting that his expert advisers could not agree. Officials expect him to make up his mind before the end of the year.

In no event, however, will he permit college students "to pile deferment on deferment" to evade the risk of call-up, the President said.

Even if student deferments are continued under stricter rules, he indicated, each year's eligible graduates will be entered in the next lottery pool.

Disruption Doubted

Mr. Johnson's principal request of Congress was for a four-year extension of the draft law, which expires next June 30. If Congress agrees and adds no inhibiting amendments, the President will be able to make the changes he wants by Executive order, without further legislative action.

Mr. Johnson was aware that the idea of a lottery and other changes would meet strong resistance in Congress, especially among Southern delegations. By revealing his intentions many months before he would be ready to act, he apparently hoped to stimulate public support for his plans.

The problems posed by transition to the new system have not yet been thought through, officials said, but the chances are that the new rules will not be used to disrupt the plans of

Continued on Page 33, Column 1

CRITICISM VOICED

Some Democrats Seek a Change in Laws to Bar Random Choice

By NEIL SHEEHAN
Special to The New York Times

WASHINGTON, March 6 — Democratic leaders of the House Armed Services Committee said today they would attempt to block President Johnson's decision to create a lottery system for drafting young men.

In his special message on the draft sent to Congress today, Mr. Johnson announced that he was ordering the creation of a system of random selection, or lottery, for eligible 19-year-olds. It would be put into operation by Jan. 1, 1969.

The President has the discretionary power under the Selective Service Act to set up such a lottery on his own authority. Crucial portions of the act are due to expire June 30, but Mr. Johnson asked Congress today to renew the act for four more years.

In a telephone interview today, Representative L. Mendel Rivers, Democrat of South Carolina, who is chairman of the House committee, said: "I do not favor a lottery."

Change in Law Predicted

Mr. Rivers indicated he would work for legislation to prevent the President from setting up a lottery.

"I suspect we'll change the law, as far as I'm concerned," he said.

Representative F. Edward Hébert, Democrat of Louisiana, who is senior Democratic member of the committee, said he also "will certainly work toward the end of preventing a national lottery."

"While I appreciate the President's interest and desire to extend the law," Mr. Hébert said, "the Congress has a responsibility under the Constitution to raise and maintain the Army and Navy, and certainly the Congress should discharge this responsibility to the fullest."

The attitude of Representatives Rivers and Hébert toward the President's draft message was considered by observers as the most significant Congres-

Continued on Page 33, Column 5

KOSYGIN DECLARES U.S. STEP-UP SPURS MORE AID TO HANOI

Soviet Leader Also Assails Rejection of North's Peace Offer Based on Bomb Halt

IT IS CALLED VITAL MOVE

Americans Are Accused of Hiding Aggressive Intention Behind New Ultimatums

By RAYMOND H. ANDERSON
Special to The New York Times

MOSCOW, March 6—Premier Aleksei N. Kosygin declared today that United States escalation of the Vietnamese war would bring retaliatory increases in Communist aid to North Vietnam.

The Soviet leader denounced Washington's rejection of Hanoi's offer of peace talks in exchange for an unconditional halt in the United States bombing raids.

Hanoi's gesture, made Jan. 28 by Foreign Minister Nguyen Duy Trinh, was described by Premier Kosygin as "an extremely important peace initiative."

The United States refused to respond to the proposal unless Hanoi indicated that it would reciprocate for a bombing halt by a curtailment of military operations against South Vietnam.

Opportunity Called Genuine

Mr. Kosygin, speaking at a rally for candidates in the election Sunday of members of the Supreme Soviet (parliament) of the Russian Republic, reiterated Moscow's insistence that Foreign Minister Trinh's proposal had opened a genuine opportunity for settling the conflict.

"The American Government, however, did not avail itself of this opportunity," he said. "On the contrary, trying to camouflage its aggressive intentions, it hastened to set forth ultimatums that were absolutely unacceptable to the Vietnamese people."

Instead of responding to the peace overtures, Mr. Kosygin declared, the United States violated the lunar new year truce last month by redeploying troops and preparing to step up the war.

The escalation followed, he continued, with the resumption of bombing raids on North Vietnam, artillery attacks on the demilitarized zone between North Vietnam and South Vietnam, naval bombardment of the North Vietnamese coastline and the mining of rivers in North

Continued on Page 16, Column 1

The, via United Press International Cablephoto

CONDEMNS U.S. AT RALLY: Premier Aleksei N. Kosygin speaking at an election rally yesterday in Moscow. He said that U.S. escalation of the war in Vietnam would bring increased Communist aid to the Hanoi regime.

CHOU SAID TO TAKE THE HELM IN CHINA; SOFTER LINE SEEN

East Europeans in Peking Say He and 4 Top Aides Run Nation's Affairs

By Agence France-Presse

PEKING, March 6—Informed East European sources said today that Premier Chou En-lai, assisted by a small "working group," had assumed control of China's governmental, Communist party and military affairs, as well as the guidance of the Cultural Revolution.

It is not yet clear whether the present pre-eminence of Mr. Chou signifies a permanent shift in the direction of the Cultural Revolution, or merely masks a "tactical withdrawal" by Mao Tse-tung, the party chairman, and his followers, the sources said.

They said that Mr. Mao and his group remained as militant and intransigent as ever. The chief members of the group are Mr. Mao's apparent successor, Defense Minister Lin Piao; a Politburo member, Kang Sheng; the Cultural Revolution leader, Chen Po-ta, and Chairman Mao's wife, Chiang Ching.

Soviet Break Favored

The "toughest" members of this group, including Mr. Kang, favor a break with the Soviet Union and more active Chinese intervention in Vietnam, the sources said.

Other members, including Mr. Lin, are more cautious concerning Vietnam. However, they envisage a long period of isolation for China, which in their view must become a fortress prepared to fight on two fronts—against "imperialism" in the east and south, and against Soviet "revisionism" in the west.

The working group assisting Premier Chou includes Li Fu-chun, chairman of the Planning Commission; Hsieh Fu-chih, Minister of Public Security; Liu Po-chang, a deputy chairman of the Defense Commission, and Foreign Minister Chen Yi.

Concerned With Theory

While this group handles the practical running of the country, Mr. Mao and Mr. Lin are devoting themselves mainly to theoretical and ideological aspects of the Cultural Revolution, the sources said.

Mr. Lin, whose activities have not been mentioned officially since last November, rarely leaves his Peking residence except to confer with Mr. Mao or to attend meetings of the Central Committee's Military Commission, of which he is chairman.

The East European sources were pessimistic about the durability of the new softer line of the Cultural Revolution, the inauguration of which was heralded in a speech by Premier Chou.

The new line was marked by the halting last Feb. 11 of demonstrations outside the Soviet Embassy here, the dissolution of the Red Guards and other Maoist organizations, and a call

Continued on Page 7, Column 1

Lodge Reported Seeking To Leave Post in Vietnam

By R. W. APPLE Jr.
Special to The New York Times

SAIGON, South Vietnam, March 6—Ambassador Henry Cabot Lodge has asked to be relieved of his duties in Saigon late in the spring or early in the summer, according to friends. Mr. Lodge has declined to discuss his plans publicly.

Informed sources said that the White House was conducting an intensive search for a successor. The search has proved more difficult than expected, the sources indicated, so the Ambassador's departure date has not yet been set.

In any case, observers believe that Mr. Lodge would not want to leave until after the promulgation of the new South Vietnamese constitution, which he considers a major step forward not only for South Vietnam but also for American policy here.

Charter by March 27

The Constituent Assembly is scheduled to complete a draft of the document by March 27, after which the governing military junta will have 30 days to evaluate it and to propose any changes before making the text public.

It is unlikely, then, that Mr. Lodge would depart before May. His departure could be delayed—possibly until after the scheduled Vietnamese elections in July, August or September—if a replacement cannot be found.

A tall, elegant New England Brahmin, Mr. Lodge is 65 years old. He has served two terms as Ambassador in Saigon, the first from August, 1963, to June, 1964, the second beginning on Aug. 19, 1965.

If he leaves when he hopes to, his departure will coincide roughly with those of two advisers.

Philip C. Habib, the embassy's chief political officer, is to depart next Tuesday. Barry Zorthian, who had headed public information and propaganda operations for three years, is

Continued on Page 16, Column 3

U.S. GUNS SHELLED; 5 MARINES KILLED

Attacks on Artillery Position Near Border Wound 11—Weapons Undamaged

By The Associated Press

SAIGON, South Vietnam, March 7 — North Vietnamese forces staged two mortar attacks early today against long-range United States artillery that fires across the demilitarized zone into North Vietnam, the United States command reported.

Five United States marines were killed and 11 were wounded in the two shellings, headquarters said. The bombardments were directed against the United States Army's 175-mm. guns on the artillery plateau at Camp Carroll, about eight-and-a-half miles south of the demilitarized zone.

These guns, the biggest in Vietnam with a 20-mile range, only recently began a campaign of bombardments into the demilitarized zone and beyond the zone into North Vietnam.

The United States headquarters said 150 rounds of enemy mortar fire struck the camp perimeter shortly after last midnight and 35 more rounds hit the camp just before daybreak. Spokesmen said there was no damage to the big guns or to other equipment.

Only a few miles south of the demilitarized zone, outnumbered United States marines clashed

Continued on Page 15, Column 1

Election for Powell's Seat Set by State for April 11

Harlem Leader Expected to Run Again and Win Even Without a Campaign—Liberals Will Not Enter Contest

By SYDNEY H. SCHANBERG
Special to The New York Times

ALBANY, March 6—Governor Rockefeller today called a special election for Tuesday, April 11, to fill the Congressional seat of Adam Clayton Powell.

The Harlem Democrat, excluded from his place in the House by a 307-to-116 vote of its members last Wednesday, is considered a sure winner if he runs for the seat again.

Mr. Powell, who is still at his vacation retreat on the island of Bimini in the Bahamas, has said that if necessary he will run for the seat again, "and win."

The necessity may arise, since most observers believe that two lawsuits being prepared by Mr. Powell's lawyers in an attempt to overturn the exclusion vote will probably not be decided before the April 11 election date.

Both suits will be filed in Federal courts—one in Washington against the House Speaker, John W. McCormack, charging that the House exceeded its authority, and the other in New York against Governor Rockefeller, seeking to enjoin him from calling a special election.

Some of the Governor's advisers are concerned that, by acknowledging that the Powell seat is vacant and calling such an election, he may antagonize many Harlem voters.

The Governor is said to be-

Continued on Page 35, Column 1

Hoffa Goes to Jail Today After Losing New Appeal

By DAVID R. JONES
Special to The New York Times

WASHINGTON, March 6—James R. Hoffa today lost a crucial court appeal in his long battle to stay out of prison and was due to begin an eight-year sentence for jury tampering tomorrow. Imprisonment was assured for the president of the International Brotherhood of Teamsters after the Federal Court of Appeals here rejected his plea.

Hoffa can carry his case to Chief Justice Earl Warren, and there were indications that he would do so. But the Supreme Court head is traveling in South America, and Hoffa's lawyers apparently decided not to appeal to him until he returns here later this week.

Hoffa is to appear at the United States marshal's office in the Federal Courthouse here at 9 A.M. tomorrow to be put under arrest. He is then to be taken to the Federal penitentiary at Lewisburg, Pa.

10-Year Struggle

The 54-year-old head of the nation's largest labor union—1.7 million members — approached the end of the legal road 10 years to the month after the Justice Department began to pursue him on what turned out to be a variety of charges. The conviction under which he will be jailed came in 1964.

Hoffa still has two motions for a new trial pending in the Court of Appeals for the Sixth Circuit, in Cincinnati. He also has filed with the Federal District Court in Chattanooga what he contends is new evidence that the Government illegally eavesdropped on him and the jurors in his trial there for jury tampering in 1964.

The teamster leader's lawyers apparently hoped that Chief Justice Warren would take their appeal and perhaps free Hoffa while his motions were pending, because he was the only Justice

Continued on Page 28, Column 4

CAR SAFETY RULE TERMED ILLEGAL

Companies Tell U.S. They Can't Meet Standard on 'Interior Impact' by '68

By United Press International

DETROIT, March 6—The nation's leading auto makers told the Federal Government today that its safety rule governing passenger protection from crash injury was impossible to meet in time to include on 1968 models.

Two of them, the General Motors Corporation and the Chrysler Corporation, said that the so-called "interior impact" rule was illegal. Chrysler warned that it would take the issue to court unless the rule was changed.

The complaints came in separate replies to 20 Federal car safety standards proposed by Dr. William Haddon Jr., administrator of the new National Traffic Safety Agency.

The Ford Motor Company had a few minor complaints about other rules.

The American Motors Corporation said only that it did not have time to finish the engineering and test work needed, and doubted that it could meet the deadline even if all the testing was finished.

But the industry threw up a united front against the rule that would outlaw protruding knobs

Continued on Page 28, Column 3

BONN IS OPTIMISTIC ON U.S. TROOP PLAN

Says Talks Cleared Way to Solve Problem of Costs

Special to The New York Times

BONN, March 6 — A West German spokesman said today that the way had been cleared for a solution of problems related to meeting the foreign exchange costs of the 225,000 American troops in Germany.

Conrad Ahlers, deputy spokesman for the Government, said that talks held by John J. McCloy, President Johnson's special envoy, with Chancellor Kurt Georg Kiesinger in Stuttgart Saturday and Foreign Minister Willy Brandt here yesterday had proceeded "smoothly." They produced "a clarification and strengthening of German-American relations," according to Mr. Ahlers.

These talks, following the announcement Friday by the State Department that the United States would no longer insist on West Germany's buying exclusively military equipment in the United States to offset the local costs of maintaining

Continued on Page 3, Column 3

U.S. to Arm Observer Craft in Vietnam

Twin-engine Cessna Super Skymaster. With minor modifications, this commercial craft is being turned into a plane, with machine guns and rockets, for air patrol in Vietnam.

By WILLIAM BEECHER
Special to The New York Times

WASHINGTON, March 6—The Pentagon has decided to provide new planes armed with machine guns and rockets for the few hundred Air Force pilots in Vietnam who now fly reconnaissance missions over guerrilla positions in unarmed, single-engine Cessnas.

These forward air controllers are assigned to American and South Vietnamese combat units. They spend hours each day winging low over jungles, marshes and mountains looking for signs of enemy activity.

Black-shirted figures suddenly diving into the underbrush on hearing the plane's approach, a hut appearing overnight in a "deserted" hamlet, a herd of water buffalo grazing where they have not appeared before, fires at dusk in a strange place—any of these signs can alert the air controller to new guerrilla activity. He then calls in a jet strike or a ground patrol to check the sighting.

Often the first inkling of untoward activity is the sight of small red-yellow flashes and wisps of smoke as enemy sharp-shooters fire at a controller.

For the most part, the only armament on the Cessna observer plane today is a rifle

Continued on Page 14, Column 4

U.S. RANKED LOW IN MATH TEACHING

12-Nation Study Says Japan Does Best Job in Subject

By FRED M. HECHINGER

American public schools have been found to rank low in an international comparison of pupils' achievements in mathematics, and Japan's schools to be doing "the best over-all job" in that field.

But although American schools were found to be doing poorly in cultivating mathematical talent among young teenagers, they recouped some of the losses by enrolling relatively large numbers of students in mathematics courses in the upper years of high school.

These findings are the result of a 12-nation educational endeavor, sponsored by the International Project for the Evaluation of Educational Achievement, which had the support of the participating countries' top-level education authorities.

Of the Japanese 13-year-olds tested, 76 per cent scored in the upper half, 31 per cent in the upper tenth, and 5 per cent in the upper 1 per cent on the internationally devised test scale.

By contrast, of the American 13-year-olds, only 43 per cent were in the upper half, 4 per cent in the upper tenth and only one-third of 1 per cent in the upper 1 per cent.

However, they lagged only slightly behind Scottish, English and French youngsters.

A comparison of accomplish-

Continued on Page 18, Column 4

Doctors Upheld in Barring an Abortion

By RONALD SULLIVAN
Special to The New York Times

TRENTON, March 6—The State Supreme Court held today that a defective child's right to life was greater than the wish of his parents to employ an abortion to keep him from being born.

In a 4-to-3 decision, marked by a vigorous dissent by Chief Justice Joseph Weintraub, the court dismissed the suit of Mr. and Mrs. Irwin Gleitman of North Arlington, who charged that two physicians were guilty of malpractice for allowing the birth of their 7-year-old son, Jeffrey, who is blind, deaf, dumb and mentally retarded.

Jeffrey was born at Margaret Hague Hospital in Jersey City after Mrs. Gleitman, who is now 27 years old, had contracted German measles during the early months of her pregnancy.

The parents alleged in their suit that two obstetricians, Dr. Robert Cosgrove Jr. and Dr. Jerome Dolan of Jersey City, were negligent in failing to warn Mrs. Gleitman that German measles could result in a defective child.

"Though we sympathize with the unfortunate situation in which these parents find themselves, we firmly believe the right of the child to live is greater than and precludes their right not to endure emotional and financial injury," Justice Haydn Proctor wrote for the majority.

In a 15-page dissent, Chief Justice Weintraub warned of the effects of today's ruling so far as it affected abortion.

"When the highest court of the state even intimates the practice may be criminal, I would doubt that a reputable doctor or reputable institution would take the risk [of permitting an abortion]. Rather the question will likely be presented by some back-alley abortionist with all the diversion from the merits that a character of that kind can induce.

"Meanwhile, we can be sure, the pregnant woman who up until now has had the services of the highest run of medical men and the safety of a hospital will deliver herself to dirty hands, if she can afford it, for a woman unwilling to

Continued on Page 35, Column 2

NEWS INDEX

"All the News That's Fit to Print"

The New York Times

LATE CITY EDITION

Weather: Variable cloudiness today; fair tonight and tomorrow. Temp. range: today 34-26; Wed. 45-29. Full U.S. report on Page 93.

VOL. CXVI . No. 39,863 | © 1967 The New York Times Company. | NEW YORK, THURSDAY, MARCH 16, 1967 | 10 CENTS

JOHNSON DEFENDS BOMBING BUT INVITES PEACE TALKS; BUNKER TO REPLACE LODGE

NEW ENVOY NAMED

Pacification Plans and Growth of Economy to Be Emphasized

By HEDRICK SMITH
Special to The New York Times

WASHINGTON, March 15—President Johnson announced today that he would appoint Ellsworth Bunker, a 72-year-old diplomat with a reputation as a skillful trouble shooter, to replace Henry Cabot Lodge as United States Ambassador to South Vietnam.

The President, who said last Thursday that he was not looking for a successor to Mr. Lodge, inserted his announcement into a speech on Vietnam before the Tennessee Legislature in Nashville. He did not say when Mr. Bunker would take over.

Mr. Lodge was reported to have spoken privately of his desire to complete his tour as Ambassador in Saigon this summer.

Officials here said Mr. Bunker would attend the President's Vietnam strategy meeting at Guam next weekend. But they added that Mr. Lodge would continue to serve as Ambassador in Saigon after the Guam conference, probably for several weeks, and the Mr. Bunker would probably come to Washington for more briefings on Vietnam.

Locke Is Appointed Deputy

The President also announced that Eugene M. Locke, the United States Ambassador to Pakistan since last August, would replace William J. Porter, who has served as Deputy United States Ambassador in Saigon since Sept. 13, 1965. Mr. Locke, a former Texas attorney, is a close associate of Mr. Johnson.

Another change made known by the President was that Robert Komer, White House special assistant for the civilian pacification effort in Vietnam, would expand his operations in Saigon and spend more time there than in Washington.

Administration officials and allied diplomats said they expected these changes to bring a renewed emphasis on economic development and civilian pacification—"the other war" in Vietnam, as it is often called.

Officials said they expected the Guam meeting, disclosed by the President at his news conference March 9, to be largely concerned with working out the changes in the American command.

There has been speculation

Continued on Page 9, Column 4

That Note to Hanoi: Returned to Sender

By TOM WICKER
Special to The New York Times

WASHINGTON, March 15—President Johnson offered today an inside glimpse of the difficulties of diplomatic dealings with North Vietnam.

He did so in referring to an incident involving a United States letter handed to a doorman at the North Vietnamese Embassy in Moscow, returned in a plain envelope to the American Embassy, but probably not before it was steamed open, read and resealed.

There are some indications that the North Vietnamese returned the note somewhat surreptitiously, rather than dignify it with any kind of official notice.

Mr. Johnson, who made his disclosure in a speech to the Tennessee Legislature at Nashville, said only:

"We stopped [bombing North Vietnam] for five days and 20

Continued on Page 8, Column 5

POLICY AFFIRMED

President, in Nashville Talk, Says U.S. Will 'Stay the Course'

Text of Johnson's speech appears on Page 8.

By ROY REED
Special to The New York Times

NASHVILLE, Tenn., March 15 — President Johnson chose this Upper South capital, with its long tradition of patriotism and military pride, for a strong defense and reassertion of his Vietnam policy today.

"America is committed to the defense of South Vietnam until an honorable peace can be negotiated," he said with emphasis, adding that if this point got through to the other side, peace talks could start at once.

He made a lengthy justification of the bombing of North Vietnam, repeated his willingness to end the war if the other side would show the same willingness and expressed his firm determination to "stay the course."

Guam Parley Broadened

Mr. Johnson used his address to the Tennessee Legislature for a surprise announcement of the replacement of Henry Cabot Lodge by Ellsworth Bunker as Ambassador to South Vietnam.

He also declared:

The leaders of South Vietnam will join him and his advisers for the discussion of the war scheduled this weekend on Guam. Premier Nguyen Cao Ky of South Vietnam had announced this earlier in the day.

Representatives of all the nations fighting with the United States in Vietnam will meet in Washington April 20-21 for "a general appraisal of the situation."

"Additional top-flight military personnel," none of them specified, will be sent to help Gen. William C. Westmoreland, the American commander, "in the intense operations that he will be conconducting in the months ahead."

Mr. Johnson departed from his advance text to make these statements as the capstone to one of his strongest affirmations of his position on Vietnam.

Mr. Johnson got his warmest response of the day when he told the legislators of his determination to stay the course. Their applause was one of the few really warm demonstrations of support during his day of speaking, touring and visiting

Continued on Page 8, Column 1

ASSEMBLY PASSES 3 PRIMARY BILLS FOR STATE VOTING

Travia Proposal, One Other Are Voted Unanimously and Third by 125-20

A CONVENTION OPPOSED

Governor Gets a Plan Now, May Receive Two Others After Senate Action

By THOMAS P. RONAN
Special to The New York Times

ALBANY, March 15 — The Democrats and the Republicans joined in the Democratic-controlled Assembly tonight in approving with surprising speed three bills, each containing a different proposal for nominating candidates for state offices.

Two of the bills were passed unanimously and without debate. The third was approved by a vote of 125 to 20 after a brief discussion. Most of the dissenters were Democrats but there was also a scattering of Republican opposition.

One of the three has already passed the Republican-dominated Senate and will now be sent to Governor Rockefeller. If the Senate ratifies the two others, it will be up to the Governor to decide which version of a statewide primary he prefers for choosing statewide candidates.

Governor's Intent Unclear

The Governor said during his campaign for re-election last year that he would sign a bill for a simple direct primary, but he did not define precisely what he meant. Some of his advisers have questioned whether the measure already approved by both houses will satisfy his requirements.

At present, statewide candidates are chosen by state conventions. For years this method has led to charges of boss-control. All three of the bills passed tonight would make it easier for insurgents to bid for the nominations.

The version on its way to the Governor provides that a party state committee would designate a candidate. Anyone receiving at least 25 per cent of the committee vote could challenge the party designee in the primary election.

Aspirants for the nomination could also get on the primary ballot by collecting 10,000 petition signatures of members of their party. At least 50 of the signatures would have to come from each of three-quarters of the state's 62 counties.

Travia Bill Approved

The Assembly approved the measure unanimously, and without debate, a few minutes after acting similarly on a bill sponsored by Speaker Anthony J. Travia, Brooklyn Democrat.

The Travia version, which is the one preferred by the Democratic State Committee, also would do away with the system of nominating candidates at conventions. It would permit any candidate getting 7,500 signatures on his petitions to get a listing on the primary ballot.

The candidate would have to obtain at least 50 signatures, or 5 per cent of his party's enrollment, whichever is smaller, from each of any 47 counties.

The third version, and the only one to encounter opposition, would permit any candidate who received 15 per cent of the vote at a state nominating convention to challenge the con-

Continued on Page 57, Column 1

Defense Department via Associated Press Wirephoto

AS GRAVE WAS CONSECRATED: With President Johnson, members of John F. Kennedy's family view ceremonies at new Kennedy gravesite at Arlington National Cemetery. [redacted] Edward M. Kennedy, Senator Robert F. [redacted] Serviceman behind Mr. Johnson, Mrs. [redacted], Senator Edward M. Kennedy.

Johnson at Grave With the Kennedys

By ROBERT B. SEMPLE Jr.
Special to The New York Times

WASHINGTON, March 15—Members of the Kennedy family and President Johnson stood together shortly after dawn today for a brief private ceremony to consecrate the new and permanent grave of John Fitzgerald Kennedy.

The service, unannounced and carried out in secrecy, took place at 7 A.M. in a cold, driving rain on the same graceful Virginia hillside in Arlington National Cemetery where Mr. Kennedy was buried Nov. 25, 1963.

Ten hours before today's service, workmen had moved the coffins of the 35th President and of two infant Kennedy children 20 feet downhill from their temporary sites to a permanent monument of granite and marble. The transfer was witnessed by the late President's brothers, Senators Robert F. Kennedy and Edward M. Kennedy, and by Richard Cardinal Cushing of Boston.

Early this morning, an hour before the cemetery opened to the public, Mr. Johnson and 10 members of the Kennedy family — including the two Senators and President Kennedy's widow—huddled under umbrellas around the new site as Cardinal Cushing said a short prayer and blessed the grave.

President Johnson had been

Continued on Page 25, Column 1

ALBANY ADOPTS REDUCED BUDGET

Rejects Pleas for Changes —Clears Way for Drive to End Session Soon

By RICHARD L. MADDEN
Special to The New York Times

ALBANY, March 15 — The politically divided Legislature voted grudging but overwhelming approval tonight for a slightly marked-down version of Governor Rockefeller's proposed $4.6-billion budget.

The Republican-controlled Senate passed the stack of 25 budget bills unanimously shortly before 9 P.M., a few hours after the Democratic-controlled Assembly had approved them with only token opposition.

Passage of the record budget for the state's fiscal year starting April 1 opens the way for a major drive to complete the Legislature's work and adjourn the session by the end of this month.

Legislative leaders have expressed determination to wind up the session before the opening of the state Constitutional Convention here April 4, and tonight's activity had much of the numbing aura of an adjournment rush.

The Assembly worked until 11:10 P.M. in its chamber, littered with coffee containers and discarded bills, to wind up its work for the week. The Senate adjourned after passing the budget but wil come back for a rare late-week meeting by itself tomorrow.

Both Senators and Assemblymen found things to complain about in the budget, but most of them voted for it anyway.

Senate Minority Leader Jo-

Continued on Page 57, Column 2

CATHOLICS SEEK NEW JEWISH TIES

Bishops' Guidelines Suggest Official and Lay Contacts and Prayer in Common

Text of the Catholic-Jewish guidelines is on Page 32.

By EDWARD B. FISKE

An agency of the National Conference of Catholic Bishops issued yesterday a set of guidelines for Jewish-Catholic relations that urges Roman Catholics to initiate contacts between the two faiths at both official and "grassroots" levels.

The guidelines call for prayer in common with Jews and for acknowledgment by Catholics of the "living and complex reality of Judaism after Christ."

They urge a "frank and honest" treatment of historic Christian anti-Semitism and state that the Crucifixion story should be presented "in such a way as not to implicate all Jews of Jesus' time or of today in a collective guilt for the crime."

2,000-Word Document

The guidelines are contained in a 2,000-word document issued by the Bishops' Committee for Ecumenical and Interreligious Affairs, which was created last November at the founding meeting of the National Conference of Catholic Bishops.

The conference was established in accordance with Ecumenical Council instructions for the formation of a conference of Bishops in each country.

The chairman of the committee is the Most Rev. John J. Carberry, Bishop of Columbus, Ohio. The Most Rev. Francis P. Leipzig, Bishop of Baker, Ore., is chairman of the Subcommission for Catholic-Jewish Relations, which drafted the guidelines.

Msgr. William W. Baum, executive director of the committee, described the document yesterday as "a sign that the

Continued on Page 32, Column 4

Senate Panel Hears How Dodd Dinners Paid Personal Bills

By E. W. KENWORTHY
Special to The New York Times

WASHINGTON, March 15—The Senate ethics committee heard detailed testimony today that Senator Thomas J. Dodd had used campaign funds and the proceeds of testimonial dinners to pay thousands of dollars' worth of personal bills.

Michael V. O'Hare, former office manager for the Connecticut Democrat, told the committee that he had paid some bills himself and sent others to Hartford to be paid by Edward F. Sullivan, head of Mr. Dodd's office there.

With the exception of two purchases of Army-Navy game tickets to be given by the Senator to prominent constituents, Mr. O'Hare said, he paid the bills on orders from Mr. Dodd.

The facts on which Mr. O'Hare's testimony were based were not in dispute because they had been stipulated to by Benjamin R. Fern, committee counsel, and John F. Sonnett, chief counsel for Mr. Dodd. Mr. Fern's questioning was ad-

Continued on Page 35, Column 1

Rent Control Called A Cause of Slums

By STEVEN V. ROBERTS

A major landlord group predicted yesterday that "New York's housing will become a massive and growing slum" if rent control is continued.

Many landlords echoed this contention at a turbulent City Council meeting through the day and late last night on Mayor Lindsay's proposals to extend and to slightly modify the rent control law. Controls were first imposed by the Federal Government in 1943 as a wartime measure to protect tenants from exploitation.

The day was set aside for opponents of rent control, traditionally an emotional issue here. Extra police were stationed all

Continued on Page 58, Column 4

CONSULAR TREATY CLEARED FOR VOTE

Senate Blocks All Moves by Republicans to Alter It—Approval Today Likely

By JOHN W. FINNEY
Special to The New York Times

WASHINGTON, March 15—The Senate cleared the way today for approval of the United States-Soviet consular treaty by rejecting a series of Republican-sponsored reservations.

A final vote on the three-year-old pact was put off until tomorrow. It appeared that the convention—the first bilateral treaty between the two nations—would be approved by substantially more than the required two-thirds vote.

The treaty, signed in 1964 but not brought up for Senate action until this year, has become symbolically important in the Administration's current "bridge-building" policy toward the Soviet Union.

Senate approval of the treaty would mark the first legislative endorsement of that policy.

Two Features

The treaty lays down the guidelines for resumption of consular relations between the two nations, broken off in 1948. Basically it follows the pattern of other consular conventions, but it has two distinctive features.

One provision, incorporated for the first time in any consular agreement signed by the United States, extends immunity from criminal charges to officials and employes of consulates. Much of the controversy over the treaty has focused on this provision, which opponents say would provide protection for Soviet spies.

The other distinctive provision establishes strict rules of consular notification and access for Americans arrested in the Soviet Union. This measure has been emphasized by the Administration as necessary for the protection of the growing num-

Continued on Page 3, Column 1

G.O.P. Chooses a Grandmother To Run Against Powell April 11

By HOMER BIGART

Republicans yesterday chose a 50-year-old grandmother, Mrs. Lucille Pickett Williams, to run against Adam Clayton Powell.

Simultaneously followers of the controversial Harlem Democrat pushed plans to welcome him when he returns from the Bahamas on Sunday.

Mrs. Williams, a former beautician, was the unanimous choice of Republican leaders of the 18th Congressional District who met at county headquarters in the Roosevelt Hotel. She replaces James H. Meredith, the civil rights hero who suddenly quit the race early Monday morning, six days after receiving the nomination. Both Mrs. Williams and Mr. Meredith are Negroes.

Her nomination was a matter of scant interest in much of Harlem, where Negro organizations ranging from the ultranationalist Mau Mau Society to the National Association for the Advancement of Colored People were planning demonstrations of support for Mr. Powell.

Mr. Powell risks arrest on his return to New York. Sheriff John J. McCloskey is under court orders giving him discretion to seize Mr. Powell, even on a Sunday, for civil and criminal contempt of court. Yet most civil rights leaders were of the

Continued on Page 45, Column 1

BUSINESS TAX AID WIDENED IN HOUSE

Committee Adds Retroactive Provision as It Clears Bill

By JOHN D. MORRIS
Special to The New York Times

WASHINGTON, March 15—The House Ways and Means Committee approved today a liberalized version of an Administration bill to restore tax incentives for business investment in equipment and buildings.

The bill, as amended and sent to the House floor for debate tomorrow, would save business and industry about $1.8-billion in income taxes, according to unofficial estimates.

The prospective saving is about $500-million above what the Administration contemplated in recommending that the tax benefits, suspended last Oct. 10, be restored as of March 9.

The suspension was intended to dampen what the Administration regarded as an unhealthy boom, which has now abated, in the capital goods market. It applied to a 7 per cent tax credit on outlays for machinery and other equipment and to liberal tax allowances

Continued on Page 36, Column 1

PRO-MAO TROOPS CONTROL CANTON

Residents of Chinese City Celebrate With Drums and Firecrackers

By Reuters

CANTON, China, March 15—Army trucks roared through the streets of this South Chinese city today announcing over loudspeakers that pro-Mao Tse-tung troops had taken over Canton and the province of Kwangtung, of which it is the capital.

In large demonstrations following the announcement, streets in the center of Canton were choked with marchers and vehicles. Drums and cymbals, blaring loudspeakers, firecracker explosions and singing turned the area into a riot of noise.

Army trucks with large red stars on their radiators and colored portraits of Mr. Mao and red banners on their roofs were hung with red bulbs, casting an eerie glow on the marching thousands.

Traffic at Standstill

Thousands of Red Guards and other Maoist supporters marched through the streets under forests of red flags and portraits of the party chairman.

Traffic was at a standstill in the city center and the marching thousands were held up for varying periods of time by the crush and confusion.

Earlier this month the Canton radio said the army had issued a warning that "class enemies" were active in the city. Informed sources said today the Mayor had come under criticism in wall newspapers.

The army takeover was preceded this morning by an editorial in the Canton daily newspaper, which said that "a handful of people in authority, seeking the capitalist road, are not yet reconciled to their failure" and would look for a chance to counterattack.

The Opposition, reputedly led by President Liu Shao-chi and the party's general secretary, Teng Hsiao-ping, has been the target of the Cultural Revolution. This is the name given to Chairman Mao's campaign to impose a more austere form of Communism in China.

Army Control Elsewhere

PEKING, March 15 (Reuters)—Newspapers reaching Peking today from Sinkiang and Inner Mongolia reported that army

Continued on Page 4, Column 4

CUBA SAID TO PLAN NEW REBEL HELP

Castro Talk Called Indication of More Militant Policy

By JUAN de ONIS
Special to The New York Times

UNITED NATIONS, N. Y., March 15 — Political observers said today that the slashing attack on Venezuela's "rightist" Communist party by Premier Fidel Castro of Cuba indicated a new, militant line of Cuban support for Latin-American guerrilla movements.

Mr. Castro's broadcast speech yesterday condemned "revolutionaries who don't fight." It coincided with a recently published Cuban article indicating that Maj. Ernesto Che Guevara, a Cuban leader missing since last May, was engaged in "insurrectional work on the international plane," presumably in Latin America.

"When Che Guevara reappears, it is likely that it will be at the head of a guerrilla movement as its undisputed political and military chief," said the article, entitled "Revolution in the Revolution?" It was written by Regis Debray, a French Marxist, and appeared in the first issue of Cuadernos de la Casa de las Americas, a

Continued on Page 20, Column 1

NEWS INDEX

A U.S. Air Force control team directs the aerial delivery of equipment during Operation Junction City in 1967. As a direct result of the operation, the Communist headquarters of South Vietnam was forced into Cambodia and its activities were seriously disrupted.

The heavy cruiser U.S.S. *Newport News* fires its guns in support for the allied forces fighting the ground war south of the Demilitarized Zone during Operation Sea Dragon in 1967.

"All the News That's Fit to Print"

The New York Times

LATE CITY EDITION

Weather: Snow, then rain today; ending tonight. Partly cloudy Wed. Temp. range: today 40-30; Monday 40-23. Full U.S. report on Page 86.

VOL. CXVI..No. 39,868 — © 1967 The New York Times Company. — NEW YORK, TUESDAY, MARCH 21, 1967 — 10 CENTS

FIREMEN REJECT NEW WAGE OFFER; STRIKE VOTE SET

Proposal by a Fact-Finding Panel Is Shouted Down by 5,000 at Meeting Here

POLICE MAY DO SAME

Suspension of All Services Except Emergencies and Alarms Is Authorized

By EDWARD C. BURKS

Five thousand city firemen shouted down the wage proposal of a fact-finding panel last night and called for an immediate mail ballot on whether to strike.

While their meeting hall reverberated with shouts, whistles and applause, the firemen also voted to authorize suspension of all services except responding to fire alarms and emergencies.

Under that authorization, the executive board of the Uniformed Firemen's Association will decide when and how to suspend nonemergency services, which include building inspections, training and clerical work.

This would be an interim move pending the outcome of the strike ballot. Then, should a strike be voted, all services would terminate, association officials announced.

The association is Local 94 of the International Association of Fire Fighters, American Federation of Labor - Congress of Industrial Organizations.

Represent 10,500 Firemen

Leaders of the association, which represents the city's 10,500 firemen below the rank of fire officer, said that a strike, if called, would be the first in the department's history.

The firemen took their vote at a meeting of the association at Manhattan Center, on 34th Street near Eighth Avenue, after a months-long contract dispute with the city.

The association's 10-man executive board, which conducted the meeting, recommended rejection of the fact-finding panel's proposals and approval of the strike vote. These recommendations and others made by the board won immediate unanimous approval.

Since the firemen and the Patrolmen's Benevolent Association, representing 24,000 policemen, negotiate together, a rejection by one group is a rejection by both, fire association leaders stated.

The fact-finding panel had been agreed on by the city, the patrolmen's association and the firemen's association, with the understanding that its recommendations would not be binding.

The panel had proposed a two-

Continued on Page 34, Column 3

L.I.U. Students, Protesting Provost's Resignation, Mob Chancellor

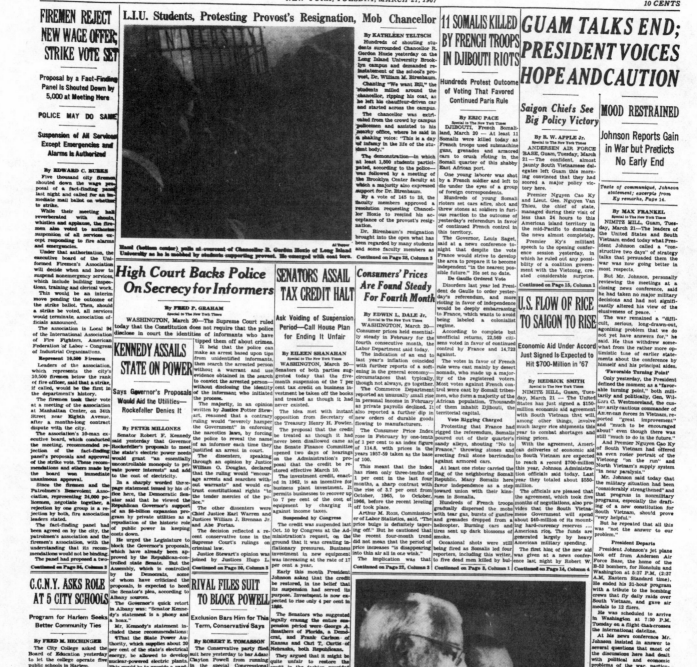

Al Tepper

[illegible] (bottom center) pulls at overcoat of Chancellor R. Gordon Hoxie of Long Island University as he is mobbed by students supporting provost. He emerged with coat torn.

By KATHLEEN TELTSCH

Hundreds of shouting students surrounded Chancellor R. Gordon Hoxie yesterday on the Long Island University Brooklyn campus and demanded reinstatement of the school's provost, Dr. William M. Birenbaum.

Chanting "We want Bill," the students milled around the chancellor, ripping his coat, as he left his chauffeur-driven car and started across the campus.

The chancellor was extricated from the crowd by campus policemen and assisted to his nearby office, where he said in a shaking voice: "This is a day of infamy in the life of the student body."

The demonstration—in which at least 1,500 students participated, according to the police—was followed by a meeting of the Brooklyn Center faculty at which a majority also expressed support for Dr. Birenbaum.

By a vote of 145 to 38, the faculty members approved a resolution requesting Chancellor Hoxie to rescind his acceptance of the provost's resignation.

Dr. Birenbaum's resignation brought into the open what has been regarded by many students and some faculty members as

Continued on Page 28, Column 3

11 SOMALIS KILLED BY FRENCH TROOPS IN DJIBOUTI RIOTS

Hundreds Protest Outcome of Voting That Favored Continued Paris Rule

By ERIC PACE
Special to The New York Times

DJIBOUTI, French Somaliland, March 20 — At least 11 Somalis were killed today as French troops used submachine guns, grenades and armored cars to crush rioting in the Somali quarter of this shabby East African port.

One young laborer was shot by a French soldier and left to die under the eyes of a group of foreign correspondents.

Hundreds of young Somali rioters set cars afire, shot and threw stones at soldiers in furious reaction to the outcome of yesterday's referendum in favor of continued French control in this territory.

The Governor, Louis Saget, said at a news conference tonight that despite the vote France would strive to develop the area to prepare it to become independent "in the nearest possible future." He set no date.

De Gaulle Ordered Vote

Disorders last year led President de Gaulle to order yesterday's referendum, and more rioting in favor of independence would be deeply embarrassing to France, which wants to avoid being labeled a colonialist regime.

According to complete but unofficial returns, 22,569 citizens voted in favor of continued control by France and 14,723 against.

The votes in favor of French rule were cast mainly by desert nomads, who made up a majority of the registered voters. Most votes against French control were cast by Somali tribesmen, who form a majority of the African population. Thousands of them inhabit Djibouti, the territorial capital.

Vote Rigging Charged

Protesting that France had rigged the referendum, Somalis poured out of their quarter's sandy alleys, shouting "No to France," throwing stones and erecting frail stone barricades against armored cars.

At least one rioter carried the flag of the neighboring Somali Republic. Many Somalis here favor independence as a step toward union with their kinsmen in Somalia.

Hundreds of French troops gradually dispersed the mobs with tear gas, bursts of gunfire and grenades dropped from a helicopter. Burning cars and tires sent up dark blossoms of smoke.

Occasional shots were still being fired as Somalis led four reporters, including this writer, to five dead men killed by bul-

Continued on Page 8, Column 1

GUAM TALKS END; PRESIDENT VOICES HOPE AND CAUTION

Saigon Chiefs See Big Policy Victory

By R. W. APPLE Jr.
Special to The New York Times

ANDERSEN AIR FORCE BASE, Guam, Tuesday, March 21 — The confident, almost jaunty South Vietnamese delegates left Guam this morning convinced that they had scored a major policy victory here.

Premier Nguyen Cao Ky and Lieut. Gen. Nguyen Van Thieu, the chief of state, managed during their visit of less than 24 hours to this American island territory in the mid-Pacific to dominate the news almost completely.

Premier Ky's militant speech to the opening conference session yesterday, in which he ruled out any possibility of a coalition government with the Vietcong, created considerable surprise.

Continued on Page 15, Column 1

MOOD RESTRAINED

Johnson Reports Gain in War but Predicts No Early End

Texts of communiqué, Johnson statement; excerpts from Ky remarks, Page 14.

By MAX FRANKEL
Special to The New York Times

NIMITZ HILL, Guam, Tuesday, March 21—The leaders of the United States and South Vietnam ended today what President Johnson called a "constructive two days" of strategy talks that persuaded them the war was now going better in most respects.

But Mr. Johnson, personally reviewing the meetings at a closing news conference, said he had taken no major military decisions and had not significantly altered his view of the elusiveness of peace.

The war remained a "difficult, serious, long-drawn-out, agonizing problem that we do not yet have answers for," he said. He thus withdrew somewhat from the rather more optimistic tone of earlier statements about the conference by himself and his principal aides.

'Favorable Turning Point'

Only yesterday, the President defined the moment as a "favorable turning point," both militarily and politically. Gen. William C. Westmoreland, the customarily cautious commander of American forces in Vietnam, reported "great improvement" and "much to be encouraged about" even though there was still "much to do in the future."

And Premier Nguyen Cao Ky of South Vietnam had offered an even rosier portrait of the Vietcong "on the run" and North Vietnam's supply system "in near paralysis."

Mr. Johnson said today that the military situation had been "considerably strengthened" and that progress in nonmilitary programs, especially the drafting of a new constitution for South Vietnam, should prove "very helpful."

But he repeated that all this was "not the answer to our problem."

President Departs

President Johnson's jet plane took off from Andersen Air Force Base, the home of the B-52 bombers, for Honolulu and Washington at 5:37 P.M. (2:37 A.M. Eastern Standard time). He ended his 31-hour program with a tribute to the bombing crews that fly daily raids over South Vietnam, and gave air medals to 12 fliers.

He was scheduled to arrive in Washington at 7:30 P.M. Tuesday on a flight that crosses the international dateline.

At his news conference Mr. Johnson insisted in answer to several questions that most of the discussions here had dealt with political and economic problems of the war, particularly the Saigon leaders' plans

Continued on Page 14, Column 1

High Court Backs Police On Secrecy for Informers

By FRED P. GRAHAM
Special to The New York Times

WASHINGTON, March 20—The Supreme Court ruled today that the Constitution does not require that the police disclose in court the identities of informants who have tipped them off about crimes.

It held that the police can make an arrest based upon tips from unidentified informants, then search the arrested person without a warrant and use evidence obtained in the search to convict the arrested person—without disclosing the identity of the informant who initiated the process.

The majority, in an opinion written by Justice Potter Stewart, reasoned that a contrary ruling would "severely hamper the Government" in enforcing the narcotics laws, by forcing the police to reveal the name of an informer each time they justified an arrest in court.

The dissenters, speaking through an opinion by Justice William O. Douglas, declared that the ruling would "encourage arrests and searches without warrants" and would entrust constitutional rights "to the tender mercies of the police."

The other dissenters were Chief Justice Earl Warren and Justices William J. Brennan Jr. and Abe Fortas.

The decision reflected a recent conservative tone in the Supreme Court's rulings on criminal law.

Justice Stewart's opinion was joined by Justices Hugo L.

Continued on Page 20, Column 3

KENNEDY ASSAILS STATE ON POWER

Says Governor's Proposals Would Aid the Utilities—Rockefeller Denies It

By PETER MILLONES

Senator Robert F. Kennedy said yesterday that Governor Rockefeller's proposals to meet the state's electric power needs would grant "an essentially uncontrollable monopoly to private power interests" and add to the cost of electricity.

In a sharply worded three-page statement issued by his office here, the Democratic Senator said that he viewed the Republican Governor's support of an $8-billion expansion program by private utilities as a repudiation of the historic role of public power in keeping costs down.

He urged the Legislature to block the Governor's proposals, which have already been approved by the Republican-controlled state Senate. But the Assembly, which is controlled by the Democrats, some of whom have criticized the proposals, is expected to heed the Senator's plea, according to Albany sources.

The Governor's quick retort in Albany was: "Senator Kennedy's statement is a phony and a hoax."

Mr. Kennedy's statement included these recommendations:

¶That the State Power Authority, which supplies about 20 per cent of the state's electrical energy, be allowed to develop nuclear-powered electric plants. This would be to provide a yard-

Continued on Page 53, Column 2

SENATORS ASSAIL TAX CREDIT HALT

Ask Voiding of Suspension Period—Call House Plan for Ending It Unfair

By EILEEN SHANAHAN
Special to The New York Times

WASHINGTON, March 20—Senators of both parties suggested today that the five-month suspension of the 7 per cent tax credit on business investment be taken off the books and treated as though it had never existed.

The idea met with instant opposition from Secretary of the Treasury Henry H. Fowler.

The proposal that the credit be treated as though it had never been disallowed came as the Senate Finance Committee opened two days of hearings on the Administration's proposal that the credit be restored effective March 10.

The investment credit, enacted in 1962, is an incentive for business plant investment. It permits businesses to recover up to 7 per cent of the cost of equipment by charging it against income taxes.

Suspended by Congress

The credit was suspended last Oct. 10 by Congress at the Administration's request, on the ground that it was creating inflationary pressures. Business investment in new equipment was increasing at the rate of 17 per cent a year.

Early this month President Johnson asked that the credit be restored, in the belief that its suspension had served its purpose. Investment is now expected to rise only 4 per cent in 1968.

The Senators who suggested legally erasing the entire suspension period were George A. Smathers of Florida, a Democrat, and Frank Carlson of Kansas and Carl T. Curtis of Nebraska, both Republicans.

They argued that it might be quite unfair to restore the credit in the fashion provided

Continued on Page 21, Column 4

Consumers' Prices Are Found Steady For Fourth Month

By EDWIN L. DALE Jr.
Special to The New York Times

WASHINGTON, March 20—Consumer prices held essentially steady in February for the fourth consecutive month, the Labor Department said today.

The indication of an end to last year's inflation coincided with further reports of a softening in the general economy—circumstances that typically, though not always, go together.

The Commerce Department reported an unusually small rise in personal income in February as private payrolls declined. It also reported a further dip in new orders of durable goods flowing to manufacturers.

The Consumer Price Index rose in February by one-tenth of 1 per cent to an index figure of 114.8, with prices in the years 1957-59 taken as the base of 100.

This meant that the index has risen only three-tenths of 1 per cent in the last four months, a sharp contrast with the rise of 3.7 per cent from October, 1965, to October, 1966, before the recent leveling off took place.

Arthur M. Ross, Commissioner of Labor Statistics, said, "The price bulge is definitely tapering off." But he cautioned that the recent four-month trend did not mean that the period of price increases "is disappearing into thin air all in one wink."

The implication was that

Continued on Page 22, Column 3

U.S. FLOW OF RICE TO SAIGON TO RISE

Economic Aid Under Accord Just Signed Is Expected to Hit $700-Million in '67

By HEDRICK SMITH
Special to The New York Times

NIMITZ HILL, Guam, Tuesday, March 21 — The United States has just signed a $150-million economic aid agreement with South Vietnam that will, among other things, involve much larger rice shipments this year to combat shortages and rising prices.

With the agreement, American deliveries of economic aid to South Vietnam are expected to reach a record $700-million this year, Johnson Administration officials said today. Last year they totaled about $550-million.

The officials are pleased that the agreement, which took five months of negotiations, also provides that the South Vietnamese Government will spend about $40-million of its mounting hard-currency reserves for American rice. The funds are generated largely by heavy American military spending.

The first hint of the new aid was given at a news conference last night by Robert W.

Continued on Page 14, Column 4

C.C.N.Y. ASKS ROLE AT 5 CITY SCHOOLS

Program for Harlem Seeks Better Community Ties

By FRED M. HECHINGER

The City College asked the Board of Education yesterday to let the college operate five public schools in Harlem.

The plan's aim is to demonstrate how community and university participation, new teacher-training methods and a revised curriculum may solve the city's school problems. The college - supervised schools would eventually range from nursery school to high school.

"What this amounts to is our invitation to the board, the United Federation of Teachers and the parents to join in a genuine effort to do a job for the urban schools," Dr. Buell G. Gallagher, president of the college, said.

Dr. Bernard E. Donovan, the Superintendent of Schools, and Albert Shanker, president of the United Federation of Teachers,

Continued on Page 32, Column 3

L.I. Judge on Trial; 'Gross' Acts Charged

By F. DAVID ANDERSON

Suffolk County Judge Floyd Sarisohn went on trial yesterday charged with helping a prostitute to flout the law, locking up an innocent elderly woman, tampering with court records, fixing a friend's ticket for speeding and other "highly improper" and "grossly illegal" actions.

The nine counts of asserted misconduct were made public for the first time when the slender, curly-haired district judge from Commack, L.I., went before a five-judge panel of the Appellate Division of State Supreme Court in Brooklyn.

The 38-year-old judge, the first member of the bench to face such disciplinary proceedings in that department since

Continued on Page 31, Column 2

RIVAL FILES SUIT TO BLOCK POWELL

Exclusion Bars Him for This Term, Conservative Says

By ROBERT E. TOMASSON

The Conservative party filed suit here yesterday to bar Adam Clayton Powell from running in the special Congressional election April 11 to regain the House seat he had held for 22 years.

The suit was based on one essential contention: that the 307-116 vote by the House of Representatives on March 1 that excluded Mr. Powell from the 90th Congress precluded him from running for re-election to the current session.

An hour after the suit was filed in State Supreme Court, Justice Irving L. Levey ordered a hearing for Monday morning to decide whether the Board of Elections should be compelled to strike out the name of Mr. Powell as a certified candidate in the special election.

The suit was brought by the Rev. Ervin F. Yearling, a 35-year-old Conservative who is making his first bid for political office against Mr. Powell in what is viewed as at best an uphill fight.

Like Mr. Powell, Mr. Yearling is a Negro and an ordained Baptist minister.

Mr. Yearling is represented

Continued on Page 30, Column 3

Sanchez Bars Race In San Juan in '68

By PETER KIHSS

Governor Roberto Sánchez Vilella of Puerto Rico announced last night that he and his wife had separated and that he would refrain from seeking re-election to keep his personal life out of politics.

The 54-year-old Governor, target of rumors about the break-up of his 30-year-old marriage for the last several months, said in a statement in San Juan that he would fill out the remainder of his $25,000-a-year, four-year term, which expires in January, 1969.

Governor Sánchez was believed to desire a divorce, a wish that was meeting with a refusal from his wife, the former Conchita Dapena Quiñones. Even a public separation is po-

Continued on Page 18, Column 3

Associated Press Wirephoto

SUMMING UP THE TALKS: President Johnson is flanked by Henry Cabot Lodge, right, retiring Ambassador to South Vietnam, and Ellsworth Bunker, his successor, as he talks to reporters on Guam after conclusion of conference with the leaders of South Vietnam.

U.S. Marines Land Near Buffer Zone

By The Associated Press

SAIGON, Tuesday, March 21—United States marines landed just south of Vietnam's demilitarized zone yesterday in a new drive, and enemy forces rained heavy mortar and rocket fire on allied forward bases close to the landing area.

United States military headquarters announced that a landing force of marines from Seventh Fleet ships moved ashore by helicopter and assault landing craft just a mile south of the demilitarized zone separating North and South Vietnam.

An estimated total of 1,500 to 2,000 marines made the assault, a search-and-destroy sweep called Operation Beacon Hill.

Some of the landing forces

Continued on Page 15, Column 2

NEWS INDEX

"All the News That's Fit to Print"

The New York Times

LATE CITY EDITION

Weather: Mostly sunny and mild today; fair tonight and tomorrow. Temp. range: today 69-40; Saturday 56-41. Full U.S. report on Page 91.

SECTION ONE

VOL. CXVI..No. 39,894

NEW YORK, SUNDAY, APRIL 16, 1967

30c beyond 50-mile zone from New York City, except Long Island. Higher in air delivery cities. 35 CENTS

F.B.I. IS WATCHING 'ANTIWAR' EFFORT, PRESIDENT SAYS

Press Aide Refuses to Tell if Hoover Is Checking on the Vietnam Protests

LODGE SENDS WAR DATA

Copter Plant in Connecticut Struck—Johnson Moves to Prevent Long Tie-Up

By MAX FRANKEL

Special to The New York Times

SAN ANTONIO, Tex., April 15—President Johnson's attention was turned again to the war in Vietnam today only a few hours after he returned to his Texas ranch from the conference with Latin American leaders in Uruguay.

His preoccupation was evident as he received reports from J. Edgar Hoover on "antiwar activity" and from Ambassador Henry Cabot Lodge on progress in the war and as he moved to prevent a long tie-up at a helicopter plant in Connecticut that produces engines for Vietnam.

[A strike began at the plant, the Lycoming Division of the Avco Corporation in Stratford, Conn., early Sunday after expiration of the contract at midnight. A spokesman at the plant said the strike's major effect would not be felt until Monday.]

F.B.I. Work Disclosed

The President reached the ranch shortly after midnight this morning, after a 14-hour flight from Punta del Este, Uruguay, with a refueling stop in Surinam (Dutch Guiana).

Mrs. Johnson had come here earlier this week from Washington, and the President apparently planned to spend a few days here to catch up on accumulated paper work.

With major demonstrations being held against the Vietnam war today, Mr. Johnson let it be known that the Federal Bureau of Investigation was keeping an eye on "antiwar activity." The President's spokesman refused, however, to make any connection between this disclosure and the demonstrations.

The disclosure was made by George Christian, White House press secretary, in listing a series of reports that were awaiting the President when he awoke at 6:30 A.M.

Mr. Christian was asked if the "antiwar activity" referred

Continued on Page 8, Column 1

100,000 Rally at U.N. Against Vietnam War

The Rev. Dr. Martin Luther King Jr. addresses antiwar rally outside United Nations. He praised march and rally. The New York Times

Many Draft Cards Burned — Eggs Tossed at Parade

By DOUGLAS ROBINSON

Thousands of antiwar demonstrators marched through the streets of Manhattan yesterday and then massed in front of the United Nations building to hear United States policy in Vietnam denounced.

The Police Department's Office of Community Relations said that police officers at the scene estimated the number of demonstrators outside the United Nations at "between 100,000 and 125,000."

It was difficult to make any precise count because people were continually leaving and entering the rally area. It was also almost impossible to distinguish the demonstrators from passersby and spectators.

On Friday the police had announced that they were preparing for a crowd of 100,000 to 400,000.

Leaders of Parade

It was the largest peace demonstration staged in New York since the Vietnam war began. It took four hours for all the marchers to leave Central Park for the United Nations Plaza.

The parade was led by the Rev. Dr. Martin Luther King Jr., Dr. Benjamin Spock, the pediatrician, and Harry Belafonte, the singer, as well as several other civil rights and religious figures, all of whom linked arms as they moved out of the park at the head of the line.

The marchers — who had poured into New York on chartered buses, trains and cars from cities as far away as Pittsburgh, Cleveland and Chicago—included housewives from Westchester, students and poets from the Lower East Side, priests and nuns, doctors, businessmen and teachers.

Chant From Youths

As they began trooping out of Central Park toward Fifth Avenue, some of the younger demonstrators chanted: "Hell no, we won't go," and "Hey, Hey, L. B. J., How Many Kids Did You Kill Today."

Most of the demonstrators, however, marched silently as they passed equally silent crowds of onlookers. At several points—notably Central Park South from the Avenue of the Americas to Fifth Avenue—the sidewalks were swarming with onlookers. Other blocks were almost deserted.

Some of the marchers were hit with eggs and red paint. At 47th Street and Park Avenue, several demonstrators were struck by steel rods from a building under construction. Some plastic cups filled with

Continued on Page 2, Column 3

NAVY'S NEW PLANE UNDERGOES A TEST

Flown in Rain to Determine if Jet Engine Will Stall in Vietnam-Like Squalls

By HANSON W. BALDWIN

The Navy's newest aircraft, the A-7A Corsair 2, is hunting thunderstorms in Florida to find out whether or not its jet engine will lose power or stall in rain squalls.

The basic engine in the A-7A is the same as that in the swept-wing General Dynamics F-111, a fighter-bomber that has also experienced engine problems, though of a different nature.

The Florida tests for the Ling-Temco-Vought A-7A are part of a "quick-fix" program that the Navy and Pratt & Whitney Aircraft Division of the United Aircraft Corporation, makers of the engine, are pushing to insure deployment of the new plane in Vietnam by November.

The Navy attack plane, meant to supplement and ultimately replace the Navy's Douglas A-4 Skyhawk, has been ordered in quantity, and the Navy has been counting on the aircraft to help replace Vietnam combat losses and losses from accidents.

Sees Quick Resolution

Production models of the plane are now being delivered to the Navy and two development squadrons have flown hundreds of hours.

High Navy spokesmen insist that the plane will meet its November deployment date unless the Florida tests show a more serious deficiency than is expected.

One naval aviator admiral said last week that in his experience he had never seen "an airplane program that has gone as fast or as well as the A-7", and he predicted that the engine problems would be resolved quickly. He added that the Navy was planning to fly one of the planes nonstop—and without air refueling—to the Paris air show in late May.

But the same admiral, as well as other Defense Department and naval sources, said that the A-7A had encountered a number of technical and other problems.

At the least, the officials said, the problems might delay for a considerable period the capability of the plane to meet its design specifications. At the worst, they might result in an

Continued on Page 60, Column 1

DR. FAGER VICTOR IN GOTHAM STAKES

Damascus Finishes Second in Feature at Aqueduct

Dr. Fager, making his first start of the season, became a strong pre-Kentucky Derby favorite yesterday by capturing the $57,800 Gotham at Aqueduct

The crowd of 50,522 saw Manuel Ycaza ride the 3-year-old, who outran Damascus, with Willie Shoemaker riding, in the stretch to win the mile race and return $4.60 for $2.

At Pimlico in Baltimore, Dawn Glory broke the track record for 1⅛ miles, winning the $31,150 Survivor Stakes. Ridden by Gilberto Vasquez, Dawn Glory was timed in 1:49 4 5 and paid $10.

BASEBALL

Mel Stottlemyre pitched his second consecutive shutout, defeating the Boston Red Sox, 1-0, at the Stadium. Horace Clarke drove in the Yankee run.

The Mets became the victims of Tony Gonzalez's first major league home run with the bases filled and dropped a 6-2 decision to the Phillies at Philadelphia.

ROWING

Princeton's varsity crew, starting at a fast 44 strokes a minute, went on to defeat Navy by almost two lengths in a 1¾-mile race on Lake Carnegie. The Tigers were timed in 9 minutes 19.3 seconds.

HOCKEY

The Toronto Maple Leafs took a 3-2 lead in their four-of-seven-game semi-final Stanley Cup series with the Black Hawks by scoring a 4-2 victory at Chicago.

Details in Section 5.

OPTIMISM VOICED ON BIRTH CONTROL

World Population Assembly Ends With Plea to All Lands to Promote Programs

By JUAN de ONIS

Special to The New York Times

SANTIAGO, Chile, April 15—The World Planned Parenthood assembly adjourned today with a call on all governments to adopt national programs that would help their people utilize birth control.

Sir Colville Deverell of Britain, Secretary General of the International Planned Parenthood Federation, said family planning of the number and spacing of children was "a contemporary human right" that governments and international bodies such as the United Nations must support.

The eighth international conference of the federation, which attracted official and private delegates from 87 countries and international organizations, closed at the municipal theater with a basically optimistic assessment by delegates of the possibilities of controlling the world "population explosion" in this century.

But, summing up the general

Continued on Page 38, Column 4

LINDSAY PROMISES AID FOR PROGRAMS OF PUERTO RICANS

Key Officials Told to Work With Representatives of All Levels of Community

By PETER KIHSS

Mayor Lindsay yesterday ordered every key city agency to designate a top-level representative to work with Puerto Ricans on proposals to better their life here.

The proposals will come out of the city's first conference with representatives of all segments of the Puerto Rican community, which started yesterday.

The Mayor declared, for example, that there was a need for a fundamental review of the teaching methods and curriculum for the more than 200,000 Puerto Ricans among the one-million youngsters in public schools. This 20 per cent proportion, he said, "calls for a greater voice of the Puerto Rican community on all levels of the educational structure."

About 1,000 persons started the two-day conference, called by the Mayor, at the High School of Art and Design, Second Avenue at East 57th Street.

Wide Range of Leaders

The conference, in preparation for four months, brought together the whole wide range of leaders of the 700,000 Puerto Ricans here.

At least 15 commissioners and deputies were on hand to attend a dozen panels. A panel headed by Nick Ortiz, manager of the Banco Popular, said the city had 10,000 Hispanic-owned businesses, but said they were marginal and in ghetto areas, victimized in many ways.

On the social side, Dr Efrén Ramirez, the city's Narcotics Coordinator, said addiction was growing faster among Puerto Ricans than any other ethnic group here. He estimated that they made up 24.2 per cent of the city's addicts in 1964 while at the same time totaling only 3 per cent of the over-all population.

Progress Is Cited

Nevertheless, Borough President Herman Badillo of the Bronx noted that "when all of us came here from Puerto Rico, we were all living below the poverty level" — as was he on his arrival at the age of 12. Now, he said, half had climbed above that median despite society's demands for more and more education — as against only 3 per cent of New Yorkers having had high school training in 1860.

Under the administrations of former Mayors Vincent R. Impellitteri and Robert F. Wagner, the city had held three conferences in San Juan and one here on migration problems—but on an intergovermental level. When another such San Juan session was set for last December, objections from New York Puerto Ricans led to its replacement by yesterday's self-help effort here instead.

Mayor Lindsay had assigned

Continued on Page 45, Column 1

School Board Gets Mayor's Assurance Of Budget Freedom

By THOMAS P. RONAN

The Lindsay administration told the Board of Education yesterday that it intended to exercise only limited control over how the board spent its funds.

For the last five years the city has given the board a lump-sum appropriation and complete freedom to shift funds within its budget without getting approval from City Hall. But on Friday an aide to Mr. Lindsay said the Mayor felt this freedom should be ended. The board quickly complained that this would hamper the flexibility of its operations.

Yesterday, one of the Mayor's budget experts said that the board would have the power to transfer certain funds, but not all. He said that the board would be given appropriations for broadly stated programs, and that it could switch funds within each of these programs. However, it will not be allowed to

Continued on Page 79, Column 6

SPECK IS GUILTY AND FACES DEATH

But the Judge Can Soften Jury's Recommendation With Prison Sentence

By EDWARD C. BURKS

Special to The New York Times

PEORIA, Ill., April 15—Richard Speck was found guilty here this afternoon of the murder of eight young nurses in Chicago last July.

The jury of seven men and five women recommended that his punishment be death in the electric chair. Under Illinois law the jury alone can fix the death penalty. But the judge in imposing sentence can give the convicted man a prison term. This term cannot be less than 14 years.

Judge Herbert C. Paschen, in leaving the courtroom today, said that it would be "better than 30 days probably" before sentencing.

The jurors deliberated only 49 minutes.

As the verdicts were read out, the 25-year-old pockmarked native of Monmouth, Ill., appeared to be chewing on a piece of gum. He stopped and turned his furrowed brow aside, closed his eyes for a second, but showed no emotion. There was no sound in the courtroom.

Seems Resigned

As George Weiman, a steel and wire company foreman, continued reading the verdicts, Speck seemed resigned to his fate. But he did not flinch or lower his head. When the public defender, Gerald Getty, asked for a polling of the jury, Speck turned his somewhat lopsided gaze on them, then for a moment he looked at the 100 spectators packed into the small courtroom.

Opposing attorneys will meet with Judge Paschen here Monday morning to discuss defense motions.

Parents of four of the slain nurses, whose ages ranged from 20 to 24, were in the courtroom this afternoon. The evidence showed that five of the girls were strangled and three stabbed to death. Altogether there were 32 stab wounds.

Family Not in Court

Speck's mother and six brothers and sisters had testified during the trial, giving a picture of a ninth-grade dropout who was borrowing money from a sister just a few days before the crime. None of them appeared in court today.

During the final summations by the two sides this morning, Speck was flushed and attentive. As the jury filed out at 2 P.M. to begin its deliberations he turned to smile broadly at others at the defense table.

The prosecutor, William Martin, had presented his case, buttressed by 42 witnesses, in an even-toned methodical way. But today his voice alternated between a whisper and a shout as he reminded the jury of the way in which the girls were killed.

He used repetition to drive home his argument. Speaking of one of the girls, the prosecu-

Continued on Page 56, Column 3

12% RISE PROPOSED IN CITY SPENDING, WITHOUT NEW TAX

Lindsay Asks $5.18-Billion, With Biggest Shares for Schools and Welfare

GAP IN REVENUE CLOSED

$803-Million Allotted Health Services — $502-Million Goes to Fight on Crime

Digest of the budget message will be found on Page 78.

By SETH S. KING

New York City will provide for the governmental needs of its eight million people in the coming fiscal year by spending more money than ever before without asking for new taxes.

This was shown yesterday in the executive budget Mayor Lindsay gave to the Board of Estimate and City Council calling for expenditures of $5,183,508,877. This was an increase of $584.8-million, or 12.7 per cent, over the current year's budget, making it the largest budget in the city's more than 300-year history.

The money for the increased expenditures will come in part from the normal growth of revenue in the city's existing taxes, from the new educational lotteries and from increased state and Federal aid.

The budget covers the expenditure of all funds for the day-to-day operating expenses of the city for the year beginning July 1. A capital budget of $1.059-billion was approved Tuesday by the board and the Council to pay for permanent improvements. It is financed by borrowing, with the debt service on the loans provided for in yesterday's executive budget.

Schools Head List

Again, education leads the list of expenditures in the executive budget, with a total appropriation of $1.093-billion. Among other large allocations are these for welfare and community development, which will total $1.015-billion. Health and hospital programs will take $803.2-million.

Police, court and prison costs total $502.2-million. Collection of garbage and air and water pollution control are given $216.1-million.

Appropriations for transportation (not including direct subway operating costs) total $177.3-million. Parks and recreation get $114.8-million. Finally, the payment of interest and principal on the city's debts will cost $648.3-million.

There has been virtually no change in the city's population in the last year. But in the coming year the cost for each man, woman, and child will reach $650, compared with $591 in the current year. Ten years ago it was $237.

In presenting his budget, Mayor Lindsay said that it had been formulated in a time of

Continued on Page 79, Column 1

O'Brien Prices Modern Postal Service at $5-Billion

Special to The New York Times

WASHINGTON, April 15 — Postmaster General Lawrence F. O'Brien believes that it will take annual expenditures of a billion dollars for five years to equip the postal service to handle efficiently the increasing volume of mail.

This is the first time that the Postmaster General has publicly put a price tag on his department's over-all need for modernizing post offices, for new post offices, and for new equipment, including computers and mail-sorting machinery.

In addition, the Postmaster General remains convinced that his own Cabinet-level post must be abolished and the functions of his department turned over to a non-profit corporation.

Mr. O'Brien believes that both the commission named by President Johnson to investigate the postal system and Congress should review the present postal rate structure, which gives a wide variety of preferential rates to certain senders of mail.

He says, however, that the postal system must continue to subsidize some categories of mail for "public service" reasons.

These and other views—in-

Continued on Page 66, Column 3

The New York Times (by George Tames)

Postmaster General Lawrence F. O'Brien as he discussed the problems and plans of his department at an interview in his office. He favors nonprofit corporation to handle mail.

Today's Sections

Index to Subjects

"All the News That's Fit to Print"

The New York Times

LATE CITY EDITION

Weather: Sunny today, cloudy tonight; chance of showers tomorrow. Temp. range: today 63-44; Thurs. 65-43. Full U. S. report on Page 76.

VOL. CXVI..No. 39,899

NEW YORK, FRIDAY, APRIL 21, 1967

10 CENTS

SENATE STALLED ON TAX INCENTIVE AND CAMPAIGN AID

Mansfield Moves to Strip Bill on Investment Credit of Unrelated Riders

FILIBUSTER IS PROMISED

Long Objects to Proposal to Repeal Contribution Plan, Restored by 46-42 Vote

By EILEEN SHANAHAN
Special to The New York Times

WASHINGTON, April 20 — The Senate worked itself into an angry stalemate today over legislation that would restore the 7 per cent tax bonus for business investment and also modify the new law permitting taxpayers to contribute $1 to finance Presidential campaigns.

The controversial campaign financing proposal, which the Senate voted to repeal only a week ago, was reinstated in the bill early this afternoon by a vote of 46 to 42.

Immediately after the vote on the campaign funds issue, Senator Mike Mansfield of Montana, the Democratic leader, moved that the bill be returned to the Senate Finance Committee, there to be stripped of the campaign financing proposal and other amendments unrelated to the restoration of the investment tax credit.

Seeks Quick Action

Mr. Mansfield's motion also provided that the new stripped-down measure, to be reported "forthwith" by the Finance Committee, contain a provision repealing the campaign financing law next July 31.

In the House, meanwhile, Representative Wilbur D. Mills, chairman of the Ways and Means Committee, rejected the view of the Administration's chief economist that frequent tax changes were necessary to keep the economy prosperous and growing.

Mr. Mansfield, explaining his motion on the tax bill in the Senate, said that he did not wish the campaign financing law to be permanently repealed. He said, however, that he thought every member of the Senate agreed that the law needed amendment.

He proposed the July 31 date for expiration of the present law, he said, so that the Senate Finance Committee and the Senate as a whole would face a deadline in rewriting the meas-

Continued on Page 20, Column 3

Associated Press Wirephoto

PROTEST TEACHER'S DISMISSAL: Students of Catholic University of America, in Washington, demonstrating for reinstatement of the Rev. Charles E. Curran, who was dismissed as instructor effective Aug. 31. In background is Immaculate Conception shrine.

ARMY IS REPORTED RULING IN GREECE ON KING'S ORDER

Military Radio Asserts Step Was Taken to Keep Peace —Curbs Announced

By The Associated Press

LONDON, Friday, April 21—An army radio station in Athens said today that the military had taken control of Greece under a royal proclamation signed by King Constantine, Premier Panayotis Kanellopoulos and his Cabinet.

The broadcast, monitored in London, said the army took over at midnight last night to preserve public order.

Vehicles were ordered off city streets and the public was warned against hoarding food.

Monitors said the broadcast was made by the Athens army radio.

Telephone service to Athens was not obtainable. Early yesterday, Greek telecommunications personnel went on a 24-hour strike for higher pay.

First word of the army takeover did not make it clear which side in Greece's political crisis the army had taken. There was immediate speculation in London, however, that the army action was a move to strengthen 26-year-old King Constantine in his long struggle with the 80-year-old former Premier, George Papandreou, leader of the powerful Center Union party. Observers believed that if the army had taken over, it had done so to strengthen the King's position by disbanding political parties.

Origins of Crisis

The speculation seemed to be borne out by the army broadcast.

There was no immediate word on what had happened to the country's political leaders.

Mr. Papandreou and his son Andreas have been outspoken critics of the monarchy, accusing it of meddling in politics, while many of the top army officers are known partisans of the throne.

Greece's latest political crisis began last month when the interim Government of Premier Ioannis Paraskevopoulos resigned after three months in office.

King Constantine summoned a meeting of all parliamentary leaders to try to form a coalition Government, but the meeting was boycotted by the elder Papandreou, whose Center Union held 122 of the 300 seats in Parliament.

New Government Falls

King Constantine then asked the National Radical Union leader, Panayotis Kanellopoulos, to form a Government pending new elections. Premier Kanellopoulos took over on April 3, but his Government was unable to function. Last Friday he dissolved Parliament and ordered elections for May 28.

His Government was to stay in power during the campaign

Continued on Page 17, Column 3

U.S. JETS BOMB HAIPHONG; FIRST ATTACK INSIDE CITY KNOCKS OUT POWER PLANT

2D UNIT ALSO HIT

Port Area Is Spared —One Residential Section Damaged

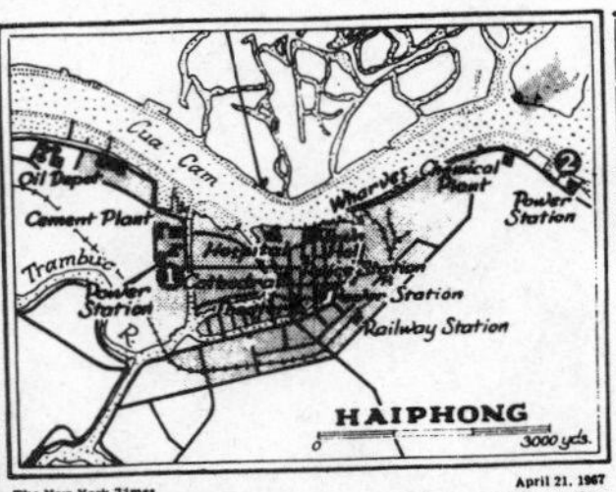

The New York Times — April 21, 1967

PORT CITY RAIDED: A power plant (1) in the city and another (2) northeast of downtown section were hit. The built-up areas of Haiphong are indicated by shading.

By R. W. APPLE Jr.
Special to The New York Times

SAIGON, South Vietnam, April 20—United States planes struck targets in Haiphong today for the first time.

Dozens of fighter bombers from the aircraft carrier Kitty Hawk pounded a power plant a mile from the center of the port city's business district. At the same time, planes from the carrier Ticonderoga hit a second power plant on the northeastern fringe of the city, two miles from downtown.

Rear Adm. David C. Richardson of Meridian, Miss., commander of the carrier task force operating in the Gulf of Tonkin, conceded that some damage had been inflicted on a residential district in the attack on the plant a mile from the center of the city.

On board the Kitty Hawk, the admiral said: "Between the power plant and a small canal to the east of it, there is a little street. There was some destruction in there but very few places. We saw no evidence of damage to any significant number of houses in our photographs."

Admiral Richardson emphasized that all possible precautions against extensive civilian casualties had been taken.

No U. S. Plane Losses

Despite heavy antiaircraft fire, no United States planes were reported lost.

Both targets were well removed from the docks, where ships of the Soviet Union and, occasionally, non-Communist nations are moored. The presence of these ships has often been cited as a reason for avoiding attacks on Haiphong.

One senior American official, who was unwilling to permit the use of his name, described the strike on Haiphong as a "tremendously important intensification — escalation, if you will—of the air war."

He said it was part of a series of steps ordered by the White House to penalize North Vietnam for refusing to agree to negotiations.

Other power plants have been struck in the past, including a number substantially larger than either of those hit today. But the symbolic significance of bombing Haiphong itself for the first time outweighed this fact, diplomats here said.

A pilot who took part in the

Continued on Page 6, Column 1

7 Vietnam Allies Confer; Troop Needs Are Studied

By HEDRICK SMITH
Special to The New York Times

WASHINGTON, April 20—The United States and its six allies in the Vietnam war held their first high-level strategy conference in six months today amid private talk of the need for more troops for the war effort.

An authorized conference source said that American and Asian spokesmen mentioned the increasing Communist "aggressiveness" in the northern provinces of South Vietnam, but said they did not deal directly with the question of new troop commitments in their formal discussions.

Excerpts from communiqué are printed on Page 6.

Some participants indicated privately, however, that rising tensions near the demilitarized zone dividing north and south had increased the need for sizable new American forces in Vietnam.

Reds' Propaganda Noted

Two themes dominated today's session, conference sources reported. One was the allies' concern that a worldwide Communist propaganda campaign had put them on the defensive. The other was the caution expressed by some delegations over the dangers of being lured into false cease-fires or sham peace talks by the Communists.

The seven allies, who held their first strategy meeting last October in Manila, met behind closed doors this afternoon after the conclusion of a three-day ministerial meeting of the Southeast Asia Treaty Organization.

In a final communiqué, the SEATO group indirectly endorsed continued American bombing of North Vietnam until Hanoi agreed to scale down its own military activities. "It is agreed that reciprocity is an essential element of any acceptable proposal for reduction in the fighting" the declaration by the treaty group's council declared.

The treaty organization and the seven-nation Manila group largely overlap. Australia, New Zealand, the Phillippines, Thailand and the United States are members of both groups. Britain and Pakistan are members

Continued on Page 7, Column 1

TOLL OF CIVILIANS RISING IN VIETNAM

First Official U.S. Figures on Wounded in the South Show a 3-Year Climb

By JONATHAN RANDAL
Special to The New York Times

SAIGON, South Vietnam, April 20—United States officials have disclosed that the number of civilian casualties in South Vietnam is rising as the tempo of the war increases.

About 50,000 civilians may be treated for war-related injuries in Government hospitals this year, according to an estimate by Maj. Gen. James W. Humphreys, director of the United States aid mission's Office of Public Health.

In an interview, the Air Force general disclosed the first major American statistical effort to keep track of civilian casualties in South Vietnam.

Critics' Role Cited

Before the survey, no reliable statistics were kept by either South Vietnamese or United States authorities. Civilian casualties were not distinguished from other hospital cases. The change is generally attributed to criticism from opponents of the Johnson Administration's position in Vietnam.

General Humphreys disclosed his estimate at a time when American military and civilian officials were voicing concern over such criticism. In particular, there is bitter resentment of an article in the January issue of Ramparts magazine, which asserted that allied weapons had caused "at least a million child casualties since 1961."

Barry Zorthian, director of the United States public-affairs office here, has called the article "a fantasia of numbers"

Continued on Page 8, Column 1

PARENTS WILL GET CITY SCHOOL VOICE

East Harlem and West Side to Choose Administrators in Experimental Plan

By GENE CURRIVAN

For the first time the Board of Education is planning to give parents and community representatives an authoritative role in administering schools.

The experiment will be conducted in East Harlem and the upper West Side where each of two communities will elect its own board and choose an administrator who will share "the full administration of the schools." If successful, the plan would be extended to other schools.

The plan, announced yesterday at a news conference at the board's headquarters, 110 Livingston Street, Brooklyn, is part of a decentralization program providing for greater community involvement and the delegation of authority to school districts.

Under the plan, which will not be put into effect until parents, local boards and community representatives help work out details, there will be two groups of schools, each with its own elected board and administrator. No deadline was set for implementation.

One of the groups will include Intermediate School 201, in East Harlem, where the parents conducted boycotts and demonstrations last September demanding "control" of the school and the right to select the principal. The dispute was never resolved inasmuch as the board refused to abdicate its rights.

I.S. 201 is in District 4, which includes its feeders,

Continued on Page 26, Column 2

Catholic U. Classes Stopped as Protest Spreads in Faculty

By JOHN D. MORRIS
Special to The New York Times

WASHINGTON, April 20—Nearly all classes were suspended today in a spreading strike of students and teachers at the Catholic University of America.

Protests against the threatened dismissal of the Rev. Charles E. Curran, 33-year-old assistant professor of moral theology, took on aspects of a full-scale revolt against the Cardinals and Bishops who govern the institution.

Father Curran, who is known for his liberal views on birth control and other doctrinal issues, was notified Monday that his two-year contract would not be renewed after it expired Aug. 31. No reason was given.

It is generally assumed on the campus that the action was prompted by Father Curran's written and spoken theological views, particularly those in favor of relaxing the church's stand against the use of contraceptives by Catholics.

Faculty Votes

The decision against renewing Father Curran's contract was taken at a recent secret meeting of the university's board of trustees, which consists of 33 Cardinals, Archbishops and Bishops and 11 laymen. The board, which governs the university on behalf of the Pope, is headed by Cardinal Spellman of New York.

With almost all of the 6,600 students boycotting classes since the start of the day, faculty members from the university's 11 schools voted at a mass meeting this afternoon to go on strike.

"We cannot and will not function as members of our respec-

Continued on Page 50, Column 2

RIGHTS PROGRESS URGED BY ROMNEY

Legislation on All Levels Is Sought in Speech Here at A.J.C. Banquet

Gov. George Romney said yesterday that "more is needed" in Federal civil rights legislation. It was the second major message of his undeclared campaign for the Republican nomination for President.

In his address he did not spell out precisely what legislation he had in mind.

Addressing a banquet of the American Jewish Committee in the Americana hotel, Mr. Romney declared: "The elimination of social injustice depends not only on Federal action, but on state action, local action and private, personal action. All four are needed."

With a grin, the Michigan Governor began his 15-minute speech by alluding to the public fund-raising effort at the dinner. It produced $1-million in pledges. "As my contribution," he said, "I've discarded my script."

He then skipped in and out of his five-page text, interpolating a long reference to his Mormon sect, which he had mentioned only briefly in his prepared remarks.

The Mormons, he said, con-

Continued on Page 26, Column 2

CITY IS CHECKING ON COST OF BOOKS

Rankin Charges Conspiracy on Works for Children

By HENRY RAYMONT

An investigation has been started by the Lindsay administration to determine whether New York City's schools and public libraries have been paying artificially high prices for children's books for years.

Corporation Counsel J. Lee Rankin said yesterday that although the data from the inquiry were not complete, he was convinced that the city had been overcharged by major book publishers.

Mr. Rankin disclosed in an interview that he was planning to file an antitrust suit against publishing houses, possibly as an adjunct to litigation already initiated in Philadelphia and by several other cities, including Rochester, Los Angeles and Madison, Wis. A Federal suit against children's book publishers has also been filed.

"There's no question in my mind that conspiracy is involved in the sale of library editions of children's books," the Corporation Counsel declared. "We are now trying to assess to what extent this has damaged New York City schools and public libraries."

He added that he expected the city's claim to be "very substantial."

In the lawsuit that was started last June by the public libraries of Philadelphia, 14 publishers and three wholesale distributors were charged with conspiracy to fix prices of library editions. The plaintiffs asked the Eastern District Court of Pennsylvania to award

Continued on Page 36, Column 4

40,000 Rubber Workers Strike Three Big Tire Manufacturers

By BEN A. FRANKLIN
Special to The New York Times

AKRON, Ohio, Friday, April 21—The United Rubber Workers union struck three of the Big Four tire manufacturers early today.

The union struck all plants of the Firestone Tire and Rubber Company, the B. F. Goodrich Company and UniRoyal, Inc., in a deadlocked dispute mainly over a proposal for a guaranteed annual wage.

It was the biggest strike in the union's 32-year history.

The strike was not the first simultaneous walkout against three of the Big Four tire companies. In 1959, the union pulled workers out of plants of the same three companies for a brief time and continued the strike against two of them—Firestone and Goodrich — for eight weeks.

The issues this time were regarded as far more complex.

The strike called early today affects more than 40,000 workers at 39 plants in Ohio and 15 other states. The struck companies were expected to resume meetings with union negotiators later today.

The talks had been under way for a month, against a strike deadline of midnight last night. The Firestone sessions, which were broken off by the union late last night, were held in Cleveland. Bargaining with Goodrich was in Columbus and with UniRoyal in Cincinnati.

The union said it would continue negotiations on a "day-to-day basis" with the Goodyear Tire and Rubber Company. But midnight shift workers at the

Continued on Page 50, Column 5

Word 'Idiot' in Paris Assembly Raises Passions to Dueling Point

By HENRY TANNER
Special to The New York Times

PARIS, April 20—Premier Georges Pompidou was shouted down for several minutes in the National Assembly today as he refused to yield the floor while defending his Government against Opposition criticism.

Feelings became so heated and the language so strong that Gaston Defferre, Mayor of Marseilles and one of the four leading figures of the non-Communist left, was challenged to a duel by a Gaullist deputy.

The Gaullist, René Ribière, asserted that Mr. Defferre had called him an "idiot." Afterward, when Mr. Defferre confirmed that this was so, Mr. Ribière sent him his two seconds.

The duel, which is not likely to draw much blood, is scheduled for tomorrow morning. Since dueling is against the law, the place must be kept secret or the police will be there.

"I want to get this over quickly, I have to be back in Marseilles tomorrow afternoon," Mr. Defferre said. He, too, named two seconds, and the four seconds conferred after the close of the session. Nobody, so far as could be found out, was slapped with a glove.

The angry scene came toward the end of a three-day debate in which the Assembly demonstrated its new unruly spirit. The unruliness results from last month's legislative election in which the Gaullists lost more than 40 seats to the parties of the left.

The Gaullists retain a narrow working majority in the Assembly, but the debate showed that the Opposition is determined to keep Mr. Pompidou under strong and constant pressure.

Mr. Pompidou, early during his rebuttal speech, had yielded the floor to François Mitterrand, the leader of the non-Communist Federation of the Left. Mr. Mitterrand, his voice nearly drowned out by Gaullist voices and banging of desk covers, repeated earlier charges of large-scale election frauds in overseas territories.

Later Mr. Pompidou refused to yield to Guy Mollet, the Socialist leader and former Premier.

Mr. Mollet felt insulted by Mr. Pompidou's assertion that the Mollet Government, which was in power shortly before General de Gaulle's return, had brought the country to the brink of bankruptcy.

The Assembly President, Jacques Chaban-Delmas, a Gaullist, told the Assembly that he

Continued on Page 4, Column 4

U.S. Guarantees Aid to Thais; Plans to Let China Get Drugs

Spur to Private Capital

By FELIX BELAIR Jr.
Special to The New York Times

WASHINGTON, April 20 — The United States began blazing a new trail today to induce private capital to help increase agricultural production in developing countries.

In a radical departure from its usual government-to-government loans and technical assistance grants, the Agency for International Development issued an "extended risk" guarantee of a $3-million bank loan by the Chemical Bank New York Trust Company to modernize agriculture in Thailand.

The bank loan goes to the Thailand subsidiary of Calabrian Company of New York. The effect of the arrangement is that the New York trading concern is guaranteed against

Continued on Page 18, Column 4

New Gesture to Peking

By B. DRUMMOND AYRES Jr.
Special to The New York Times

WASHINGTON, April 20—The United States is prepared to relax its strict trade embargo of Communist China so that American drugs may be sold or donated to thousands of Chinese suffering from cholera, meningitis and infectious hepatitis, Government officials said tonight.

The relaxation of the embargo was described by the officials as a humanitarian gesture motivated by reports that parts of China are being swept by various epidemics that the Chinese Government is having difficulty controlling because of drug shortages.

But the move also was seen as another step by Washington to improve relations with

Continued on Page 18, Column 2

U.S. GETS GO-AHEAD ON NUCLEAR PACT

NATO Backs Reopening of Talks With Soviet on Text

By RICHARD E. MOONEY
Special to The New York Times

PARIS, April 20 — United States officials said today that they had received "a green light" from the Atlantic allies to resume negotiations with Moscow for a treaty to prevent the spread of nuclear weapons. They declared that the talks would be reopened soon.

A West German official, reflecting the fact that his Government and others still objected to some fundamental aspects of the proposed treaty, said: "It looks more like a yellow light to us."

These comments followed a two-hour meeting of the permanent council of the North Atlantic Treaty Organization. For

Continued on Page 3, Column 1

NEWS INDEX

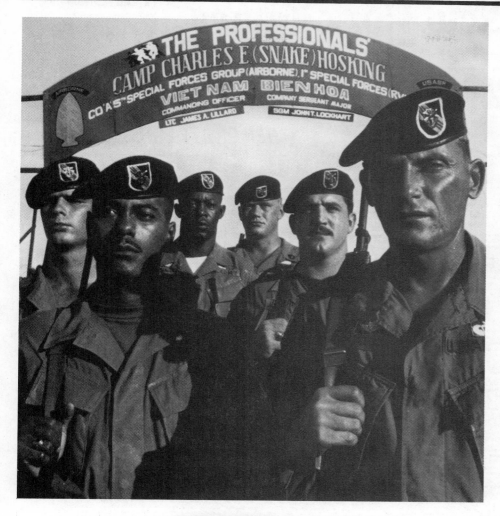

A squad of the elite Green Beret commandos at their home base, Bien Hoa, Vietnam.

The bloody battles along the Mekong Delta left countless dead and wounded. Here, Viet Cong guerrillas lie dead following a skirmish.

"All the News That's Fit to Print"

The New York Times

LATE CITY EDITION

Weather: Sunny today; fair tonight. Cloudy, cool tomorrow. Temp. range: today 52-35; Monday 45-35. Full U.S. report on Page 85.

VOL. CXVI..No. 39,903 | © 1967 The New York Times Company. | NEW YORK, TUESDAY, APRIL 25, 1967 | 10 CENTS

U.S. PLANES RAID HANOI RAIL YARD AND 2 MIG FIELDS

NEW STAGE IN WAR

Bombing Is 2¼ Miles From Center of the North's Capital

By JONATHAN RANDAL

Special to The New York Times

SAIGON, South Vietnam, Tuesday, April 25—American warplanes struck today at Hanoi's railroad repair yards and its electricity transformer site only hours after they had bombed two MIG airfields near the North Vietnamese capital.

The raids marked the end of what had been two privileged sanctuaries in the air war over North Vietnam. They were seen as part of an intensifying American effort to force the Hanoi regime to the bargaining table.

The raids had been widely expected since the bombing on Thursday of a power plant within the city limits of Haiphong, which had also previously been exempt from air strikes.

Closest to Capital

The attack today was the closest reported raid to the center of Hanoi since the air war against North Vietnam began 32 months ago.

Air Force F-105 Thunderchiefs carried out the raids this morning. It was the first time in more than four months that American warplanes had bombed within 15 miles of the center of the capital.

The railroad repair yards are situated 2¼ miles northeast of the city's center, across the Red River. The transformer site is seven miles to the northeast.

Pilots on the raids reported encountering the Soviet-built MIG's, surface-to-air-missiles and antiaircraft fire over the target areas. No bomb damage assessment or figures on American or enemy losses were available.

The transformer station is a major element in the electric power grid system that channels electricity to other parts of North Vietnam.

'Limited Response'

American F-4-C Phantom jets shot down two MIG's late yesterday in raids against two airfields near Hanoi where enemy jet interceptors are based. The two MIG's brought to 42 the number of Communist planes shot down in North Vietnam. MIG's have shot down 11 United States planes.

The bombing in the vicinity of Hanoi called into question official American military statements that the three raids yesterday against the airfields did not constitute another step in the escalation of the air war.

Unlike the Haiphong raid, which was clearly if reluctantly labeled an escalation in the war by American officials here, the bombing of the airfields was described yesterday by military spokesmen as a "limited response to increased MIG activity in the last few days—a very limited response."

The closest point to Hanoi bombed previously by American

Continued on Page 8, Column 4

The New York Times

HARDER WAR AHEAD: Gen. William C. Westmoreland tells publishers he foresees bitter fighting.

WESTMORELAND DECRIES PROTESTS

In A.P. Talk Here, He Says Support in U.S. and Abroad Is Giving Enemy Hope

Text of Westmoreland talk, question period, Page 14.

By PETER KIHSS

Gen. William C. Westmoreland declared yesterday that the enemy in Vietnam had "gained support" in the United States and abroad that "gives him hope that he can win politically that which he cannot accomplish militarily."

The commander of United States forces in Vietnam somberly told 1,500 newspaper executives and others at the annual luncheon of The Associated Press at the Waldorf-Astoria Hotel that he foresaw, "in the months ahead, some of the bitterest fighting of the war."

But he asserted that "the military picture is favorable," even though, he said, "I do not see any end of the war in sight." And he appealed for the unified support of the American people for his forces.

Truce Moves a Worry

General Westmoreland said he was delighted over the first bombing of MIG airfields in North Vietnam yesterday. He added that he was "concerned about cease-fire proposals" because experience had shown that the enemy had used the cease-fire periods to strengthen his forces both militarily and politically.

Earlier, at the news agency's annual membership meeting, Senator Charles H. Percy, Republican of Illinois, deplored the airfield bombing. He said the State Department had told his office last Friday that "if we began bombing North Vietnam airfields, the planes would seek sanctuary in Red China and this would expand China's role in the war."

The Defense Department, he said, told his office the same day that "in two years of bombing, only 11 United States aircraft had been lost to the North Vietnamese aircraft, and their aircraft does not pose a serious threat to our bombers."

Byrd Opposes Restraints

At the same meeting, Senator Harry F. Byrd Jr., Democrat of Virginia, called for the removal of restrictions on North Vietnamese military targets.

He opposed further "pauses" in military operations unless there was assurance against enemy reinforcement. He urged the United States to get more combat troops from other nations in a fight to "keep Asia free from Communism."

A million Americans were drafted or enlisted last year, and this total will be duplicated this year, the Senator asserted. American casualties totaled 35,000 last year, but may reach 65,000 this year based on the rate so far, he added.

Senator Percy suggested that "the best avenue to peace" might be an all-Asian conference, including North Vietnam and Communist China. This, he

Continued on Page 15, Column 1

KING SAID TO TELL U.S. AIDE IN ATHENS HE OPPOSES JUNTA

Monarch's Goal Is Reported to Be Re-establishment of Constitutional Rule

By JOHN W. FINNEY

Special to The New York Times

WASHINGTON, April 24—King Constantine was reported by diplomatic sources today to have made clear to American officials that he disapproved of the military seizure of power in Greece on Friday.

In two conversations with Ambassador Phillips Talbot in Athens, the King was reported to have explained that he was resisting the military dictatorship that a junta of relatively junior military officers was seeking to impose upon Greece and that he was seeking to use his influence to restore constitutional government.

Just how much influence the 26-year-old monarch can exert at present was unclear to State Department and diplomatic officials.

Ambiguous Position

While apparently distressed over the political consequences of the military coup d'état, the King was believed to be in a somewhat ambiguous position in opposing the military junta.

In conversations with foreign envoys, he was said to have emphasized that he felt a duty to the Greek people to resist a military dictatorship. At the same time, diplomatic observers feel, if he resists the military junta too forcefully or openly, he could lose his throne or cause a civil war.

At this point, the King appears to diplomatic observers here to be assuming a role of passive opposition, refusing to sign decrees suspending constitutional guarantees and declining to speak out in endorsement of the new military regime.

Dispatches Discounted

This view was not altered by dispatches from Athens today reporting that the junta had announced the King would preside over a Cabinet meeting "in the course of a week." The dispatches pointed out that the King had made no statement of support for the new Government and that the junta had not produced the decrees it said the King had signed suspending parts of the Constitution.

Eventually, diplomats here believe, the King can become a rallying point for public opposition in forcing the military junta to back down and accept a restoration of constitutional government.

If this public opposition is to be rallied, however, it is believed essential that the Greek people be informed that the King is not supporting the junta—a point not being made by the military-controlled radio stations and censored newspapers in Greece.

It was a point being made,

Continued on Page 5, Column 1

Miniskirts Banned By Junta in Greece

By HENRY KAMM

Special to The New York Times

ATHENS, April 24—The new Government of Greece proscribed miniskirts for girls and long hair for boys today and called for regular church attendance by all youths.

The emphasis on austere morality, in a country where moral laxity is not evident, in combination with the general right-wing trend of the military junta that seized power last Friday, reminded Greeks of the Fascist-style dictatorship of Gen. John Metaxas, who governed Greece from 1936 to 1940.

The Interior Minister, Brig. Stylianos Patakos, called on the Education Ministry to instruct school principals to tell their pupils to go to confession and communion next Sunday, the Eastern Orthodox Easter, and to attend

Continued on Page 5, Column 1

TEAMSTERS' VOTE MAY BAR ACCORD

Early Tally Indicates Locals Rejected National Pact—Strike Still Uncertain

By DAVID R. JONES

Special to The New York Times

WASHINGTON, April 24—Members of the International Brotherhood of Teamsters appeared tonight to have voted down a tentative national trucking contract reached 12 days ago.

An Associated Press tabulation of partial early returns showed that the union's 450,000 freight truckers voted nearly two-to-one against the pact. A United Press International survey of early returns showed about 58 per cent voting against the agreement.

The teamsters' headquarters here said it would not give out any results of the weekend vote until the tabulation from 360 locals across the nation was completed tomorrow. Some informed sources hinted, however, that the vote was closer than the incomplete tabulations indicated.

The union's constitution provides that a "final offer" from management goes into effect if the majority of those voting accept the contract. The members may strike if two-thirds turn down the "final offer." The union leadership may determine what course to follow if the vote falls between those extremes.

The uncertainty tonight about the vote margin left it unclear what practical effect a turndown would have. But most sources speculated that the rejection would not be large enough to precipitate a strike. This would permit the continuation of talks without immediate strife.

A contract rejection would be

Continued on Page 25, Column 6

NEW YORK BACKS 5-STATE COMPACT ON AIR POLLUTION

Governor Signs Bill Paving Way for Commission to Enforce Regional Rules

By THOMAS A. JOHNSON

Governor Rockefeller signed a bill into law yesterday providing for New York's membership in a proposed Mid-Atlantic States Air Pollution Control Compact with four other states and the Federal Government.

The compact would empower the agency to set standards, conduct research and enforce pollution abatement measures within the states.

New York is the first state to approve the compact. The New Jersey Legislature was expected to pass a similar measure yesterday but it was held up because of a controversy over other legislation. The compact will be considered on Thursday.

Other states invited to join the compact are Connecticut, Pennsylvania and Delaware.

2 States Need to Approve

After at least two states approve the compact, the Federal Government will be asked to ratify the agreement and thus give final approval for setting up the regional agency.

The compact will not affect existing state and local laws that "are consistent with the commission's authority . . . nor would the compact prevent member states and local governments from administering stronger or more restrictive air-pollution controls," a memorandum issued by the Governor's office said.

In a related matter, Austin N. Heller, the New York City Air Pollution Control Commissioner, said that incinerators that failed to meet the May 20 deadline for the installation of upgrading equipment would "be sealed within five days."

Fines Now Provided

New York State laws now provide fines up to $1,000 for persons violating Public Health Laws concerning air pollution with a $200 fine for each day the violation continues.

A spokesman for the Department of Health, Education and Welfare said yesterday that the Federal position was to "try our best to encourage local governments to develop ways to deal with pollution on a regional basis."

At a brief signing ceremony at his mid-Manhattan offices, Governor Rockefeller called the compact "a major step forward" and "the most effective vehicle in the nation for fighting air pollution on a regional basis."

The compact would be the first in the nation, he said.

Later in the day, Mr. Rockefeller told a meeting of the American Medical Association's National Congress on Environmental Health that New York

Continued on Page 33, Column 1

SOVIET ASTRONAUT KILLED AS HIS SPACESHIP CRASHES WHEN CHUTE LINES SNARL

U.S. ASSAYS EFFECT

Expects Russians Will Slow Space Drive but Not Halt It

By EVERT CLARK

Special to The New York Times

WASHINGTON, April 24—The death today of a Russian astronaut will slow but not halt the Soviet Union's space program, officials here believe.

One source disclosed that the Soviet Union had three times secretly put into earth orbit weights that would have been great enough to send men on a looping flight around the moon.

This was cited as a clear indication that plans were laid, resources committed and training begun long ago for far more ambitious flights than the fatal flight of Col. Vladimir M. Komarov in Soyuz 1.

Meanwhile, James E. Webb, head of the National Aeronautics and Space Administration, voiced sorrow at the Soviet spaceman's death and said that closer cooperation between the United States and the Soviet Union might reduce the chances of subsequent space accidents.

In Bonn, President Johnson wired his sympathy to the Soviet people and the family of the astronaut, who, Mr. Johnson said, "died in the cause of science and in the eternal spirit of human adventure."

Weight Limit Suggested

Official sources here believe that Colonel Komarov was testing a wholly new spacecraft, no heavier than 15,000 pounds, that may have been intended as the passenger cabin for later flights of several men to the moon, or as a ferry vehicle to lift astronauts to a moon ship as it orbited the earth.

That means that the Soyuz was only a little larger than the 12,500-pound Voskhod 2, which made the last Russian manned flight in March, 1965. Voskhod 1 weighed 11,700 pounds, not far above the 10,400 pounds of the first manned Vostok capsules, and probably was an adaptation of the Vostok, officials said.

They believe that Colonel Komarov's mission was to go into orbit and await the launching, apparently planned for last night, of a second and similar vehicle that would join his and permit at least one astronaut to transfer from the second ship into the Soyuz 1.

This would have given the Soviet Union its first practice at the rendezvous and docking needed to join vehicles in space,

Continued on Page 20, Column 6

Associated Press

KILLED IN CRASH: Col. Vladimir M. Komarov, Soviet astronaut, died in crash at the end of his mission.

DIES IN RE-ENTRY

Komarov First Known Fatality During Any of Manned Flights

By RAYMOND H. ANDERSON

Special to The New York Times

MOSCOW, April 24—Col. Vladimir M. Komarov, pilot of the Soviet Union's first manned space flight in more than two years, was killed today when his craft's main re-entry parachute snarled and the ship plummeted 4.3 miles to earth.

He had been in orbit around the earth a little more than 24 hours before attempting to land. No details were given on where or exactly when the spacecraft crashed or on how many orbits had been completed.

The Soviet astronaut is the first man known to have died on a space flight.

Colonel Komarov, the only man aboard, was testing the Soyuz 1, a heavy new craft intended for a series of manned Soviet space flights this summer.

An Account From Tass

Tass, the Soviet press agency, said the ship had performed normally in orbit and had been successfully braked with retro-rockets for re-entry into the earth's atmosphere.

"However, when the main parachute was opened at an altitude of seven kilometers [about 23,000 feet], the lines of the parachute, according to preliminary information, got snarled and the spaceship descended at great speed, which resulted in Komarov's death," the press agency stated.

Tass did not report whether Colonel Komarov had a personal parachute with him to attempt an escape from the spaceship in such an emergency.

[American officials were unable to confirm reports of a Russian radio broadcast indicating that the astronaut had fought to control his spacecraft for the last three orbits. But they noted that the troubles described in the reported broadcast were similar to what American experts believed actually occurred.]

Many Russians in Tears

In earlier Soviet manned flights, some of the astronauts bailed out of their spaceships after they had re-entered the atmosphere.

Many Russians broke into tears when the death of the astronaut was broadcast shortly before 5:30 P.M., Moscow time (9:30 A.M. Eastern standard time).

The Presidium of the Supreme Soviet decorated posthumously Colonel Komarov, who was a Hero of the Soviet Union, with a second Gold Star medal for heroism, courage and valor displayed during the Soyuz 1 flight.

Groups of men and women clustered on Red Square around small transistor radios, listening solemnly to reports of the accident and quietly exchanging

Continued on Page 20, Column 2

TEACHER REGAINS CATHOLIC U. POST

Students Cheer as Trustees Reverse Earlier Decision—Boycott Is Ended

By JOHN D. MORRIS

Special to The New York Times

WASHINGTON, April 24—Striking teachers and students at the Catholic University of America won the reinstatement and promotion today of a liberal young theology professor.

Classes, suspended since last Wednesday, will be resumed tomorrow.

The settlement was a complete victory for the strikers, who had accused the governing Roman Catholic hierarchy of violating the principle of academic freedom by dismissing the Rev. Charles E. Curran, 33-year-old assistant professor of moral theology.

The Most Rev. Patrick A. O'Boyle, Archbishop of Washington and chancellor of the university, drew wild applause and cheers from several thousand students when he announced from the steps of Mullen Memorial Library that the board of trustees had rescinded its order against Father Curran's reappointment.

Students Cheer Promotion

The students applauded and cheered with equal fervor when the Most Rev. William J. McDonald, rector of the university, announced the promotion of the young priest to associate professor.

The board of trustees, consisting of 33 Cardinals, Archbishops and Bishops and 11 laymen, had decided at a closed meeting April 10 that Father Curran's employment was to be ended when his contract expired Aug. 31. No reason was given for the decision.

When the decision became known on the campus last week, virtually the entire faculty and student body decided to stay away from class until it had been rescinded.

In response to a formal appeal for reinstatement from the faculty of the theology school, meanwhile, Archbishop O'Boyle polled the trustees to determine if they wanted to reverse themselves.

In view of the faculty's appeal "and further information surrounding the nonrenewal of the appointment of Father Curran," the Archbishop said, "the board of trustees has voted to abrogate its action."

"Since in this case no charges have been preferred by the board of trustees," he added, "I would emphasize that their present action must not be interpreted as in any way affecting the theological issues injected by the news media."

"In particular," he said, "this

Continued on Page 35, Column 1

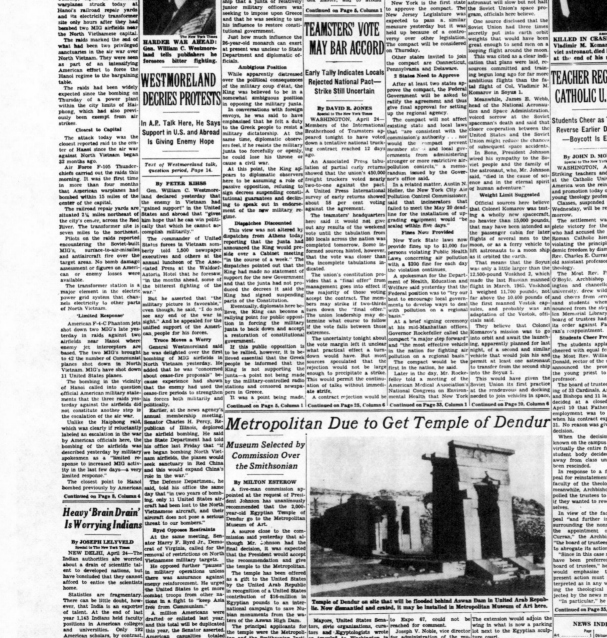

Metropolitan Due to Get Temple of Dendur

Museum Selected by Commission Over the Smithsonian

By MILTON ESTEROW

A five-man commission appointed at the request of President Johnson has unanimously recommended that the 2,000-year-old Egyptian Temple of Dendur go to the Metropolitan Museum of Art.

A source close to the commission said yesterday that although Mr. Johnson had the final decision, it was expected that the President would accept the recommendation and give the temple to the Metropolitan.

The temple has been offered as a gift to the United States by the United Arab Republic in recognition of a United States contribution of $16-million in Egyptian pounds to an international campaign to save Nubian monuments from the waters of the Aswan High Dam.

The principal applicants for the temple were the Metropolitan and the Smithsonian Institution in Washington. A private group in Cairo, Ill., and the Brooks Memorial Art Gallery in Memphis had also shown interest. Requests also came to the State Department from 20 other cities, among them Phoenix, Ariz.; Philadelphia and Miami.

Temple of Dendur on site that will be flooded behind Aswan Dam in United Arab Republic. Now dismantled and crated, it may be installed in Metropolitan Museum of Art here.

Mayors, United States Senators, civic organizations, curators and Egyptologists wrote or traveled to Washington in the last 16 months to lobby for the temple.

Thomas P. F. Hoving, the Metropolitan's director, appeared at a meeting of the commission in Washington two weeks ago to present the museum's case. Mr. Hoving, who was in Montreal yesterday on a visit to Expo 67, could not be reached for comment.

Joseph V. Noble, vice director for administration of the museum, said by telephone yesterday that the museum had received no word about the temple.

"If we get it, we plan to place it in a new extension of our north wing," he said. The wing is on Fifth Avenue between 82d and 83d Streets. The extension would adjoin the wing in what is now a parking lot next to the Egyptian sculpture court.

Neither the size nor the cost of the extension has been determined, Mr. Noble said. But "we would hope to have it ready in time for our centennial in 1970," he said.

The temple is one of five,

Continued on Page 40, Column 1

Heavy 'Brain Drain' Is Worrying Indians

By JOSEPH LELYVELD

Special to The New York Times

NEW DELHI, April 24—The Indian authorities are worried about a drain of scientific talent to developed nations, but have concluded that they cannot afford to entice the scientists home.

Statistics are fragmentary. There can be little doubt, however, that India is an exporter of talent. At the end of last year 1,143 Indians held faculty positions in American colleges and universities. Only 192 American scholars, by contrast, were teaching in Indian institutions.

Nearly 10 per cent of all Indians holding medical degrees are believed to be working in the United States and Britain, despite the critical shortage of medical skills here. According

Continued on Page 24, Column 3

Convent Sheltered Stalin's Daughter

Special to The New York Times

GENEVA, April 24—Svetlana Alliluyeva spent nearly three of her six weeks in Switzerland in a Roman Catholic convent, the Swiss Government disclosed today.

Sister Marguerite Marie, one of 52 members of the Order of the Visitation community near Fribourg, in western Switzerland, said Stalin's daughter lived there until she left Friday for the United States.

Sister Marguerite said Mrs. Alliluyeva did not participate in the religious life of the community and showed no interest in any special form of religion. She was reported, however, to have attended mass at the Catholic St. Nicholas Cathedral in Fribourg.

In a statement issued Friday when she arrived in the United

Continued on Page 30, Column 3

NEWS INDEX

"All the News That's Fit to Print"

The New York Times

LATE CITY EDITION

Weather: Mostly sunny today; fair, seasonable tonight and Sun. Temp. range: today 72-55; Friday 81-59. Full U.S. report on Page 70.

VOL. CXVI...No. 39,928

NEW YORK, SATURDAY, MAY 20, 1967

10 CENTS

SENATE'S DEBATE ON DODD CENSURE IS OFF TO JUNE 13

Mansfield and Dirksen Drop Monday Start After Plea by Connecticut Democrat

LONG'S TACTICS DECRIED

His Efforts to Gain a Delay Violated Usual Courtesies, Majority Chief Indicates

By E. W. KENWORTHY
Special to The New York Times

WASHINGTON, May 19—Senate leaders agreed today to postpone for three weeks the debate on a resolution of censure against Senator Thomas J. Dodd, Democrat of Connecticut.

The majority leader, Senator Mike Mansfield of Montana, and the minority leader, Senator Everett McKinley Dirksen of Illinois, announced on May 9 that the censure resolution would be called up May 22. There had been no objection to that date by Mr. Dodd, who was consulted by the leaders beforehand.

Yesterday, Senator Russell B. Long of Louisiana, the assistant Democratic leader, unexpectedly announced on the Senate floor that he had volunteered to be counsel to Mr. Dodd and requested a six-week postponement to prepare "a proper defense."

Thereupon Mr. Dodd rose and said he welcomed Mr. Long's help and appealed for extra time.

"I don't think I'm asking for very much," he said.

Plea Is Supported

His plea was supported by Senator John O. Pastore, Democrat of Rhode Island, and Senator Albert Gore, Democrat of Tennessee.

In announcing the extension today, Mr. Mansfield emphasized that he and Mr. Dirksen were responding to the plea of Senator Dodd and not to that of Senator Long.

At first Mr. Mansfield said that the resolution would be called up Monday, June 12. Mr. Pastore objected. Yesterday he rejected Mr. Mansfield's argument that a postponement would be an inconvenience to Senators who had canceled engagements, saying that it "doesn't carry much weight."

But today he said:

"On June 12 my son graduates from medical school. Can't you make it June 13? I've waited 25 years for this."

Mr. Mansfield hesitated a moment and then replied, "June 13."

Senator Mansfield, without openly rebuking Senator Long, made plain that he believed the assistant leader had been inconsiderate and had transgressed the accepted courtesies due a Senate leader.

Mr. Mansfield told the Senate that the first indication he had that Mr. Long would seek a six-week postponement came Wednesday afternoon when a news ticker quoted a Senate ad-

Continued on Page 16, Column 6

A Tax on Profits Of Churches Urged By Episcopal Group

By EDWARD B. FISKE

An organization of Episcopal lawyers and clergymen here has urged that an income tax be imposed on real estate and other untaxed commercial interests owned by churches, but not used for religious purposes.

About half of the group, the Guild of St. Ives, recommended that churches also be taxed on income from stocks, savings accounts and other "passive" investments that are now tax-free.

In addition, the guild urged that churches be required to issue the same kind of periodic financial statements now required of other nonprofit organizations.

The recommendations are contained in "A Report on Churches and Taxation," which follows a 15-month study of the question by guild lawyers.

The guild was founded in 1965 to study church-related legal matters. Its 19 mem-

Continued on Page 20, Column 2

WELFARE CLIENTS TO GET INCENTIVES

City to Let Them Keep More of Their Earnings if They Work While on Relief

By CHARLES G. BENNETT

A plan to offer welfare recipients a financial incentive to work was announced yesterday by Mayor Lindsay.

The idea has been approved by the Federal Government. New York will be the first city to try it and officials here expect that if it succeeds it will be copied elsewhere.

At present, except for the first $40 a month of earned income for working mothers and the first $20 a month for other welfare clients, the welfare payment to a person on relief is reduced exactly by the amount he earns.

Under the new arrangement, effective at once, for the first $85 a month a client earns there will be no reduction in assistance allowance. From the amount in excess of the first $85 a month in earnings, the public assistance will be reduced by 70 per cent.

The Welfare Department estimates that for an average family of four persons all public assistance will stop when the wage-earner's pay reaches about $4,900 a year. The average aid now for such a family, supported entirely by public assistance, is $2,850 a year.

The cost of the new incentive plan will be wholly administrative, and is estimated at $43,000 a year. Of this, the Federal Government will pay 75 per cent and the state and city each 12.5 per cent.

Mayor Lindsay announced the plan at a crowded news conference in the Blue Room of his City Hall suite. Seated behind the large mahogany table, the Mayor was flanked by sev-

Continued on Page 19, Column 3

U.N. TROOPS END 10-YEAR MISSION IN MIDDLE EAST

Begin Withdrawal as Thant Meets Cairo's Demands—U.S. Joins Urgent Talks

By SAM POPE BREWER
Special to The New York Times

UNITED NATIONS, N.Y., May 19—The United Nations Emergency Force ended today its 10-year-old mission to keep peace between Israel and the United Arab Republic.

At the request of the Egyptian Government, it halted its patrols in the Sinai Peninsula and the Gaza Strip on the Egyptian side of the armistice line between the two countries. Israel has never permitted United Nations patrols on her side.

The Emergency Force, consisting of troops from India, Canada, Yugoslavia, Sweden, Brazil, Norway and Denmark, began drawing back to its base camps on the Mediterranean coast of the Gaza Strip.

Secretary General Thant expressed "serious misgivings" about this development.

'Grave Implications' Seen

He said in a report to the General Assembly that the force "has been an important factor in maintaining relative quiet in the area of its deployment during the past 10 years." Its removal, he declared, "may have grave implications for peace."

Private talks were begun here on possible Security Council action to fill the gap in peace measures for the area in view of tensions caused by recent Israeli warnings and by Egyptian troop movements. Israel said yesterday that she was taking "appropriate measures" following an Egyptian build-up in the Sinai Peninsula.

Arthur J. Goldberg, the United States representative, issued a statement today indicating American willingness to join in some energetic move to maintain the peace.

He said the United States fully shared Mr. Thant's misgivings.

Background of the Crisis

"In the light of today's developments," Mr. Goldberg added, "we are giving urgent consideration, in consultation with others, to the further steps that might be required in support of peace and the role of the United Nations in preserving it in the Middle East."

No specific suggestions were put forward today for new action as the Emergency Force moved out.

The current crisis grew out of demands by officers of the United Arab Republic for removal of observers from areas where Cairo foresaw possible conflict with Israel. It was said Cairo feared an Israeli attack on Syria and wanted to be able to go to Syria's aid without overrunning the United Nations force.

Mr. Thant emphasized that although the troops of the Emergency Force were on Egyptian territory by consent of the Egyptian Government, they took orders only from the

Continued on Page 6, Column 3

American Men and Materiel Move Into Demilitarized Zone in Vietnam

Associated Press Radiophoto

Tanks and landing craft carrying marines push along the Benhai River in first U.S. offensive within the buffer zone

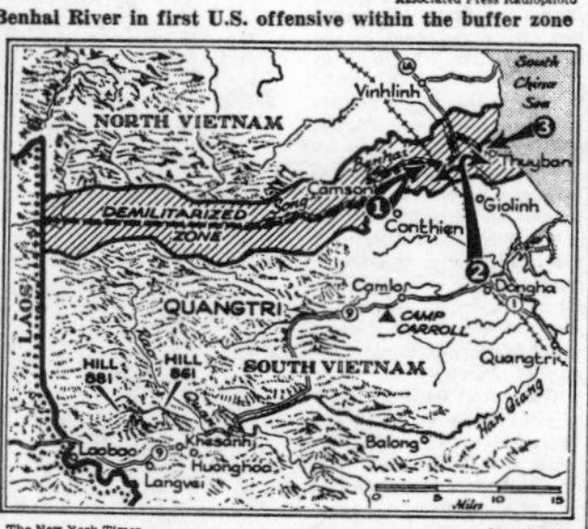

The New York Times May 20, 1967

Drive into the neutral zone involved marines at Camson and Conthien (1), who were to meet South Vietnamese troops moving north of Dongha (2). U.S. landing force at mouth of Benhai River (3) met stiff enemy resistance.

Soviet Ratifies Pact to Bar Nuclear Weapons in Space

By United Press International

MOSCOW, May 19—The Soviet Union, after waiting four months, ratified today the treaty banning nuclear weapons in outer space. The treaty was signed here Jan. 27 by the United States, the Soviet Union and Britain. Dozens of other nations signed later, and the United States ratified it.

The treaty, negotiated under United Nations auspices, established the peaceful use of outer space. It was the first major East-West agreement since the treaty of 1963 imposing a limited ban on nuclear tests. That treaty also was signed here.

The new pact bans nuclear weapons in orbit or in space. It also bars the use of the moon, planets or other celestial bodies for military bases.

Delay Spurred Fears

The treaty signing, coming as it did during the Vietnam war, had raised hopes that the Southeast Asian crisis would not block East-West progress on unrelated issues.

But the four-month delay between signing and Soviet ratification had led to fears that the Kremlin was holding up ratification out of irritation at United States escalation in Vietnam.

Those fears ended with the announcement today by Tass, the official Soviet press agency, that the Presidium (executive body) of the Supreme Soviet (parliament) had ratified the pact. The Presidium acts for the Supreme Soviet when the full parliament is not in session.

Consular Treaty Pending

The action paved the way for Supreme Soviet ratification of another outstanding Soviet-American treaty—the consular convention.

That accord was ratified by the United States earlier this year. It would establish Soviet and American consulates in each other's country and provide protection for Americans arrested here or Russians arrested in the United States.

The Supreme Soviet has yet to act on the consular convention. Western observers here have said the delay is not necessarily significant, and ratification is expected in due time.

Another recent Soviet-American agreement provides for di-

Continued on Page 5, Column 3

'CLEAN' WARHEADS SOUGHT FOR NATO

Major Effort Being Made to Develop Small, Precise Weapons for Defense

By WILLIAM BEECHER
Special to The New York Times

LONDON, May 19—A major effort is under way to perfect small, precise tactical nuclear warheads, including some that are practically free of fallout.

"We're increasing our efforts to perform those technological tricks that could make nuclear weapons more usable in Europe," according to a top American military planner.

He stressed the importance of this work in addressing the question how the North Atlantic Treaty Organization is going to plan for the defense of Western Europe in the face of diminishing forces and the loss of room to maneuver.

Most military strategists interviewed in the course of a visit to six alliance nations are convinced that the announced reductions of American and British ground and air elements, combined with the loss to them of French territory and forces, increase the likelihood that if war starts nuclear weapons will be used, and used sooner than would normally be the case.

Weapons Need Foreseen

"A thrust through northern Germany," said one British planner, "could only be held for two or three days with conventional weapons. After that, we'd either have to go nuclear or give up."

But the potential destructiveness of nuclear weapons in heavily populated regions of Western Europe, such as fallout on civilians and blast damage in towns and cities, has caused serious second thoughts, particularly among West German officials, about whether the cure might not be as bad as or worse than the disease.

Thus the major program to develop what one general called "cooky-cutter nuclear weapons."

"We're fast developing smaller warheads offering very precise, predictable effects," he said. "One family of warheads, if detonated up in the air over the target, produces little or no fallout, but very heavy blast and heat effects."

"Another development," he said, "enhances short-term radiation as its principal element, allowing you to go after troops ensconced in an evacuated town without destroying the

Continued on Page 11, Column 3

NEWS INDEX

Thieu Will Oppose Ky for Presidency

By JONATHAN RANDAL
Special to The New York Times

SAIGON, South Vietnam, May 19—Lieut. Gen. Nguyen Van Thieu, South Vietnam's chief of state, said today that he had decided to oppose Premier Nguyen Cao Ky for the presidency.

The 43-year-old general's statement, made to visitors, came a week after the Premier declared his candidacy. General Thieu said, "There is no need for Premier Ky to withdraw his candidacy," a reference to the Premier's offer to stand down if the chief of state chose to run.

Behind this mask of polite formality, with General Thieu playing Alphonse to Premier Ky's Gaston, lies an increasing animosity between them.

General Thieu said that although his decision to seek the

Continued on Page 2, Column 4

Allies Pushing Into Zone; Action Called 'Defensive'

Enemy Resistance Stiff

By TOM BUCKLEY
Special to The New York Times

THUYBAN, Demilitarized Zone, South Vietnam, May 19—American marines and South Vietnamese infantrymen fanned out today along the Benhai River, the border of the two Vietnams, in their first offensive within the demilitarized zone.

Stiffening enemy resistance against the three-pronged assault, which began yesterday, inflicted a rising toll of casualties on the 5,500-man allied force.

By midafternoon, military spokesmen reported, 30 men had been killed and 307 wounded. The bodies of 136 enemy troops were counted, with 56 listed as probably killed.

In the easternmost assault, a battalion landing team of 1,000 marines drove against stubborn defenders north of this hamlet on the headland south of the mouth of the Benhai.

Navy Bombards Foe

While the marines pushed through sand under a blazing sun against heavy mortar and machine-gun fire from deeply burrowed bunkers, a naval task force led by the heavy cruisers St. Paul and Boston and five destroyers bombarded North Vietnamese artillery emplacements on the north bank of the river.

Five battalions of the South Vietnamese First Division that sped up Route 1 in trucks and armored personnel carriers yesterday to the "peace bridge" across the Benhai fanned out to the east and west and then swung back south.

To the west, the Marine battalion that was lifted by helicopter to a landing zone on the south bank near the hamlet of Camson, about 12 miles inland from the South China Sea, began moving southeast.

It is to link with two Marine battalions moving northward from the hard-pressed outpost at Conthien, a mile south of the demilitarized zone. These units will then sweep eastward on a broad front to meet the South Vietnamese.

Maj. Gen. Bruno Hochmuth, commander of the Third Marine Division, said at his headquarters at Dongha that the purpose of the offensive was to deny a sanctuary to the North Vietnamese and the Vietcong.

He said the troops were scheduled to withdraw from the

Continued on Page 3, Column 1

Northern Build-up Cited

By HEDRICK SMITH
Special to The New York Times

WASHINGTON, May 19—The United States Government said today that the American-South Vietnam military thrust into the southern half of Vietnam's demilitarized zone was a "purely defensive measure" against a "considerable build-up" of North Vietnamese forces.

In Paris, a North Vietnamese officer, Col. Ha Van Lau, said at a news conference that the allied attack had been a violation of the 1954 Geneva agreement that prohibited troops from entering the buffer zone but that it was not an invasion.

The State Department, through its spokesman, said the action "is not in any sense an invasion of North Vietnam."

Well-placed Administration sources said that there were no plans for an attack by allied ground forces into the northern half of the demilitarized zone, which lies in North Vietnam, or regions farther north. But they would not totally exclude the possibility of such an attack at a later time.

Well-placed sources indicated that President Johnson approved the thrust into the demilitarized zone several days ago. Giving no hint of it at an impromptu

Continued on Page 2, Column 6

DOWNTOWN HANOI RAIDED FIRST TIME BY U.S. BOMBERS

North's Major Power Plant, Mile From City's Center, Is Target of Navy Jets

FOUR MIG-17'S DOWNED

American Plane Toll Is Put at 5 by U.S. Spokesman, 10 by North Vietnamese

By R. W. APPLE Jr.
Special to The New York Times

SAIGON, South Vietnam, Saturday, May 20—United States pilots bombed downtown Hanoi yesterday for the first time. Five planes were lost, an American military spokesman said.

[The North Vietnamese press agency said 10 American planes had been downed and five pilots captured, United Press International reported. It said two of the pilots had been displayed at a news conference within hours of their capture. Page 2.]

Navy fighter-bombers, using air-to-air missiles, shot down four enemy MIG-17 jets during battles high above the capital, the military spokesman said. A fifth was reported damaged.

Hoalac Airfield Bombed

Jets from the carrier Bon Homme Richard in the Gulf of Tonkin struck early in the afternoon at a 32,000-kilowatt power plant, the largest in North Vietnam.

In another raid, Air Force Thunderchief jet from the 355th Tactical Fighter Wing in Thailand dropped 750-pound bombs on the MIG airfield at Hoalac, 20 miles west of Hanoi.

The Hoalac strip was reported to have been put out of operation last week after repeated strikes. The new raid, the spokesman explained, was intended "to keep the air field unusable."

Other planes of the 355th struck an area just south of the field, where aerial photographs had shown three MIG-17 jets hidden under camouflage. Two nearby structures were said to have been destroyed, but there was no word on whether the planes had been hit.

The spokesman added that all the downed planes had been carrier-based Navy craft.

3 Bases Still Untouched

For more than two months, American planes have been blasting objectives that were previously ruled off limits by the White House—MIG bases, targets within Haiphong and targets on the outskirts of Hanoi.

[illegible] major targets remaining untouched are the Haiphong docks and three large fighter-bomber bases.

In the past, the closest strike to the North Vietnamese capital was a raid on the railroad repair shops two miles northeast of the city, on April 28.

According to the spokesman, the power plant, which supplies about 20 per cent of North Vietnam's electricity, is 1.1 miles from the center of the city, as measured from the Cuanam market. It is within the city limits and the built-up area of Hanoi.

The old French Governor General's house, in which President Ho Chi Minh has some-

Continued on Page 2, Column 4

'Terrible Barrage' of Hanoi Fire Downed U.S. Jets, Witness Says

The following dispatch is by Jacques Moalic, correspondent of Agence France-Presse in North Vietnam.

HANOI, North Vietnam, May 19—Three or perhaps four United States fighter-bombers were shot down in Hanoi today by the most terrible barrage of antiaircraft fire I have ever seen.

The planes were downed during the day's second American attack against the suburbs of Hanoi. A third raid occurred later, but a storm rolling into Hanoi prevented me from seeing the attackers and the effects of the antiaircraft fire.

The day's total air losses promised to be very heavy. The Hanoi radio said four planes had been brought down in the morning raid. According to available information, about an equal number were shot down in the afternoon.

The day's first action in the capital was a violent raid over the southern suburbs, after a four-day pause in the bombing here.

At least two waves of planes swept over shortly after 10 A.M., dropping their bombs for a quarter of an hour through a barrage of antiaircraft fire and Soviet-made missiles. One plane was apparently shot down and its pilot captured in this raid.

Several groups of North Vietnam's MIG-17 jets flew overhead, but it was impossible to see whether they were actually engaged in combat.

An American rocket—apparently the Bullpup type, guided by heat—struck the city's diplomatic section during this first raid, at about 10:15. It exploded on the curb of the sidewalk,

Continued on Page 2, Column 3

United Press International Telephoto

AFTER SENATE GRANTED DELAY: Senator Thomas J. Dodd, left, Connecticut Democrat, with his lawyer, John F. Sonnett, after censure proceeding was set for June 13.

"All the News That's Fit to Print"

The New York Times

LATE CITY EDITION

Weather: Cloudy, warm, humid, chance of showers today, tonight. Temp. range: today 83-71. Thurs. 81-69. Temp.-Hum. Index 78. Thurs. 77. Full U.S. report on Page 58.

VOL. CXVI..No. 40,004

NEW YORK, FRIDAY, AUGUST 4, 1967

10 CENTS

JOHNSON ASKS FOR 10% SURCHARGE ON PERSONAL AND BUSINESS TAXES; 45,000 MORE MEN TO GO TO VIETNAM

GOAL NOW 525,000

Troop Action Reflects Compromise—Rise in Spending Seen

By WILLIAM BEECHER
Special to The New York Times

WASHINGTON, Aug. 3 — President Johnson announced plans today to dispatch 45,000 to 50,000 more American troops to Vietnam, beyond the number already committed. This will bring the total to 525,000 by June 30, he said.

The decision, disclosed in Mr. Johnson's budget and tax message to Congress, represents a compromise between the 70,000 men sought by Gen. William C. Westmoreland and the 15,000 to 30,000 men suggested by Secretary of Defense Robert S. McNamara.

[South Korea's President, Chung Hee Park, proposed to send 3,000 military reservists to Vietnam to free Korean and American support troops for combat duty. Page 2.]

President Johnson also declared that military spending for the fiscal year ending next June might rise as much as $4-billion over the $73.1-billion that was foreseen in January, when he presented his budget request. But he asked Mr. McNamara to defer as many nonessential military expenditures as possible to absorb some of this increase, he said.

Plane Purchases Deferred

It is understood that Secretary McNamara has already pressed the services to eliminate or postpone at least $3-billion in spending. Pentagon sources say, for example, that because aircraft losses in Vietnam have been lower than expected, purchases of replacements will probably be slowed.

Mr. Johnson's action countered any suggestion that he was seriously thinking of reverting to a holding position while seeking a quick solution that would allow him to liquidate the burdensome war effort.

His intentions were indicated by the size of the troop increase, by the reports that he had assured the military that he was not foreclosing further reinforcements and by the language used in justifying the increase in troops.

Mr. Johnson repeated a passage from his State of the Union address conceding that the end of the war was not in

Continued on Page 2, Column 3

Congress Likely to Delay Effective Date of Tax Rise

By JOHN D. MORRIS
Special to The New York Times

WASHINGTON, Aug. 3—Congress scrutinized President Johnson's tax-increase program today with a mixture of resignation, pain and hostility.

Despite the unfavorable tone of many public statements, especially by Republicans, few members of either party expressed outright opposition.

This, coupled with private assessments of the outlook by key legislators, indicated that a bill patterned on the President's recommendations would be reluctantly enacted.

It was highly doubtful, however, whether action would be completed in time to put the 10 per cent surcharge on individual income taxes into effect on Oct. 1 as proposed.

It was also uncertain whether the full 10 per cent asked by the President for corporations as well as individuals would be approved.

The House Ways and Means Committee scheduled public hearings starting Aug. 14 with Henry H. Fowler, Secretary of the Treasury, as the opening witness.

The chairman, Representative Wilbur D. Mills, Democrat of Arkansas, declined to estimate how long the hearings would continue. But other members expressed doubt that a bill would reach the House floor before Labor Day, at the earliest.

With the Senate following the usual practice of waiting for the House to act before starting work on a tax bill, it

Continued on Page 10, Column 1

INFLATION FEARED

Message to Congress Seeks Withholding Increase Oct. 1

Text of Johnson's message is printed on Page 10.

By EDWIN L. DALE Jr.
Special to The New York Times

WASHINGTON, Aug. 3—President Johnson asked Congress today for a 10 per cent surcharge on personal and corporate income taxes, excepting only those individuals with the lowest incomes.

Mr. Johnson said the increase was needed to head off "an unsafe and unmanageable deficit" in the Federal budget, which he said might exceed $28-billion without the tax increase. Such a deficit, he continued, could bring these results:

¶"A ruinous spiral of inflation."

¶"Brutally higher interest rates."

¶"An unequal and unjust distribution of the cost of supporting our men in Vietnam."

¶"A deterioration in our balance of payments by increasing imports and decreasing exports."

[Stock prices fell sharply in an initial reaction to the President's tax proposals, but a strong afternoon rally trimmed many of the earlier losses. Volume of 13.44 million shares was the third highest of the year.]

Affects Withholding

If enacted as proposed, the 10 per cent surcharge would take effect for individuals Oct. 1 and be reflected at once in withholding from paychecks. The present amount withheld each week or month will rise 10 per cent.

Next April, the individual taxpayer will calculate his tax as usual on income for the year as a whole and then add 2.5 per cent, because the surcharge would be in effect for only one quarter of 1967. Some or all of this extra payment due will already have been covered by withholding in the case of most wage earners.

A similar 10 per cent surcharge would be applied to corporate profits taxes, but retroactive to July 1. Thus in the case of taxes on 1967 incomes, corporations would be hit a little harder than individuals, though the burden would be equal in later years.

The President asked that the tax remain on the books until mid-1969 "or continue for so long as the unusual expenditures associated with our efforts in Vietnam require higher revenues."

There would be no surcharge on the tax of a family of four with an income up to $5,000, on a married couple with income up to $3,600 or on a

Continued on Page 11, Column 1

U.S. Combat Loss In Vietnam Drops To Six-Month Low

Special to The New York Times

SAIGON, South Vietnam, Aug. 3—American combat casualties dropped last week to their lowest level in six months, a United States command spokesman said today.

During the week, 114 soldiers were killed and 893 wounded, the spokesman said. The week before, United States losses were 164 killed and 1,442 wounded.

Enemy casualties dropped to 1,399 killed, from 1,780 the previous week, but with the low allied losses this week the announced ratio of allied to enemy deaths was 6.8 to 1, the largest of the year.

Vietnamese Losses at 61

South Vietnamese losses were listed by the United States command at 61 dead for the week, which equaled the figure for the first week in May. A South Vietnamese military spokesman said Government losses were 76 killed and 368 wounded, with 14 missing, equaling the losses of the last week in April.

Other allies suffered 30 killed during the week. The United States command does not break down the losses by country, but South Korean and Australian troops have seen the most recent action.

The spokesman said military activity for the period ranged

Continued on Page 2, Column 7

2 IN VIETNAM RACE URGE PEACE TALKS

Presidential Campaign On —'We Must De-escalate,' One Candidate Says

By R. W. APPLE Jr.
Special to The New York Times

SAIGON, South Vietnam, Aug. 3—The South Vietnamese presidential campaign opened today with pledges from two civilian tickets that they would try to open immediate negotiations with North Vietnam if they were elected.

Dr. Phan Quang Dan, a Harvard-educated physician seeking the vice-presidency on a slate headed by Phan Khac Suu, Speaker of the Constituent Assembly, issued a ringing call for radical change in Government policy.

"It is impossible to fight the Communists the way we are now," he said at a news conference in a smoke-filled restaurant this morning. "It would be better to have a shouting war rather than a shooting war. We must de-escalate."

Speaking in English, he said he favored negotiations "at all levels, including the Vietcong." But his running mate, Mr. Suu, replied to the question in Vietnamese and said he would "deal with Hanoi," not with the Vietcong guerrillas of the South.

The Suu-Dan slate is one of

Continued on Page 3, Column 1

United Press International Radiophoto

ACCIDENT IN SOUTH VIETNAM: A U.S. transport, shot down by American gunners, plummeting to earth in Haphan, about 15 miles west of Quangngai, yesterday. Plane, loaded with ammunition, was about to land at a Special Forces camp when a single round of artillery from the ground cut it in half. All three crewmen died in the mishap.

Levitt Finds Taxes Trail State Estimate

By RICHARD L. MADDEN
Special to The New York Times

ALBANY, Aug. 3—Tax collections in the first one-third of the state's fiscal year lagged behind Governor Rockefeller's budget estimates, State Controller Arthur Levitt indicated today.

The Controller reported that tax collections for the first four months of the current fiscal year increased less than 1 per cent over the comparable period last year.

Mr. Levitt, a Democrat and frequent critic of the Republican Governor's budget policies, noted in his brief statement that the current state budget of nearly $4.7-billion is based on the forecast of an 8 per cent increase in revenue during the full fiscal year to stay in balance.

The Controller's report did

Continued on Page 32, Column 3

LINDSAY FORMING GROUP TO ASSIST SLUM BUSINESSES

Leaders of Corporations and Unions Are Recruited as Members of a Coalition

LOAN NEEDS STRESSED

Mayor Says Banks Are Not Sufficiently Involved in Negro Sections Here

By RICHARD REEVES

Mayor Lindsay is recruiting civic leaders to become members of a new organization—the New York Coalition—designed to unite corporations, unions, churches and other private organizations in an attack on the problems of the city's slums.

The city group, which is similar to the national Urban Coalition formed in Washington last Monday, would attempt to handle such problems as persuading city banks to grant more loans to Negro and Puerto Rican small-business men.

The Mayor, who hopes to announce the formation of the local coalition within two weeks, said yesterday that large banks were not sufficiently involved in helping solve the problems of New York's slums.

Banks 'Better Equipped'

"The banks know the problem—each day they have a greater awareness of the need for ghetto investment," Mr. Lindsay said at a press conference, "But I would like to remind the banks that there is great gain for themselves in vigorous investment in ghetto areas [with] valuable land that isn't being used and great talent that isn't being tapped."

Large banks and insurance companies "are better equipped than the city" to finance small-business men in slum areas, the Mayor continued. He then added that his goal was to help the residents of Harlem and Bedford-Stuyvesant become "their own butchers, bakers and candlestick makers—help them own the haberdasheries and delicatessens."

In an interview after the press conference, Mr. Lindsay said a local organization parallel to the Urban Coalition could help persuade bankers to invest in slum businesses. Other city officials later revealed that a parallel organization, the New York Coalition, was already being recruited by the Mayor and Andrew Heiskell, chairman of Time, Inc.

The mayor and Mr. Heiskell were among 22 leaders in government, business, labor, civil rights and religion who formed the Urban Coalition in Washington earlier this week.

A statement issued by the na-

Continued on Page 13, Column 1

Halo Stolen From Statue of Mary in Jerusalem Shrine

The Rev. Kevin Mooney points to the statue of the Virgin Mary in the Church of the Holy Sepulcher, Jerusalem, from which a golden halo was stolen. Earrings were also removed.

By JAMES FERON
Special to The New York Times

JERUSALEM, Aug. 3—A golden halo studded with precious stones was stolen last night from a statue of the Virgin Mary in the Church of the Holy Sepulcher, one of Christendom's holiest sites.

The church is in the former Jordanian sector of Jerusalem, which was seized by the Israelis during the war in June.

Platinum earrings, similarly studded, and a row of ornamental hearts also were removed from the three-foot-high statue inside the church's Franciscan Chapel.

Neither church officials nor the Israeli police could estimate the value of the missing items, which are among many thousands of precious and historic offerings in the ancient church.

The carved wooden statue, a gift of Queen Maria of Portugal in 1624, was in a glass case before the altar on a balcony in the southwest side of the church.

The balcony, just inside the main entrance, is revered

Continued on Page 8, Column 7

Associated Press Cablephotos

Statue, a gift from Queen Maria of Portugal, before theft

U.S.-AIDED SCHOOL HELD ANTIWHITE

Police Official Says Negroes in Nashville Teach Hatred in Name of Liberation

By JOHN HERBERS
Special to The New York Times

WASHINGTON Aug. 3 — A Nashville police captain testified today that the Federal Government was subsidizing a "liberation school" in his city that taught "unadulterated hatred" of whites and was run by an official of the Student Nonviolent Coordinating Committee.

The captain, John A. Sorace, told the Senate Judiciary Committee that the school director was Fred Brooks, whom he identified as the Nashville chairman of the student committee and who he said was receiving funds from the Office of Economic Opportunity.

Captain Sorace charged that national leaders of the student committee had fomented riots in Nashville last April and that Mr. Brooks was at the scene of the violence.

Later in the day, Senator James O. Eastland of Mississippi read a memorandum from the poverty agency denying that Mr. Brooks was on the Federal payroll. Whereupon, Mr. Sorace whipped out a "list" showing Mr. Brooks to be on the payroll for $300 a month.

Edward M. Kennedy, Democrat of Massachusetts, demanded that Mr. Sorace disclose the source of his "list." The police captain refused to do so publicly.

Senator Eastland, the committee chairman, who had charged that Communist influences were at work in the Negro movement in Nashville, broke off this exchange by saying he would demand that a poverty agency official appear before the panel for questioning.

So ended the second day of

Continued on Page 12, Column 1

Saudis Are Believed Receptive to Offer By Cairo on Yemen

By ERIC PACE
Special to The New York Times

KHARTOUM, the Sudan, Aug. 3—Authoritative sources reported that Saudi Arabia reacted favorably to an Egyptian offer made formally today, to end the struggle for power between the two countries in Yemen.

The sources, who declined to be identified for publication, said the Saudis' reaction made it probable that an Arab summit meeting would be held, most likely later this month, here in Khartoum.

It would be the first gathering of Arab leaders since the 1965 meeting in Casablanca and its purpose would be to close ranks in the wake of the Israeli military victory in June.

Ten of the 13 nations represented at the Arab foreign ministers' conference here have made it known that they favor holding a summit meeting. The exceptions were Saudi Arabia, Algeria and Syria, but these three countries are now expected to agree if the Yemen issue is resolved.

At today's session, the sources reported, the Saudi delegate, Omar Saqqaf, gave a warm initial response to the Egyptian offer, saying all differences between the two countries should be resolved. The Saudis de-

Continued on Page 7, Column 2

DUVALIER FAMILY IN HAITI DIVIDED

Dictator's Struggle to Keep Control Has Caused Open Conflict With His Kin

By HENRY GINIGER
Special to The New York Times

PORT-AU-PRINCE, Haiti, Aug. 2 — President François Duvalier's struggle to maintain his 10-year dictatorship has caused open conflict within his own family.

The family quarrel adds to a growing picture of desperation in the regime.

The latest target of the President's ceaseless hunt for "traitors" among Haiti's mostly black population of 4,660,000 was his son-in-law, Lieut. Col. Max Dominique, now abroad. Last Saturday he was dismissed from the army "for the good of the service" and has been ordered to return within 30 days to face trial on a charge of conspiracy against the President.

Colonel Dominique, the husband of the eldest of the three Duvalier daughters, Marie-Denise, left for Europe late in June, taking his wife and the youngest of the sisters, Simone, with him.

As soon as they left, Colonel

Continued on Page 6, Column 6

New York Air Pollution Worst Of Nation's Major Urban Areas

By HAROLD M. SCHMECK Jr.
Special to The New York Times

WASHINGTON, Aug. 3—New York has the most severe air pollution problem of any major metropolitan area in the nation, the Public Health Service reported today.

Chicago was ranked second, Philadelphia third, the Los Angeles-Long Beach area fourth and Cleveland fifth. The report named 65 areas and cautioned against complacency by those that appeared low on the list.

"In all the large urban areas covered in our report the public health and welfare are threatened by air pollution," said Dr. John T. Middleton, director of the Public Health Service's National Center for Air Pollution Control.

The center ranked each of the 65 urban centers on the basis of air pollution measurement and on information on fuel use supplied by the Bureau of Census.

The ratings were based on the following factors:

The average total of air pollution particles in the atmosphere; the average number of particles defined as benzene-soluble particles, mostly associated with man-made pollution; the frequency and severity of excessive air pollution episodes; the area's total gasoline consumption; the population density of automobiles in the area; the average concentration of sulphur dioxide in the atmosphere; the area's total emissions of sulphur dioxide; the density of sulphur

Continued on Page 34, Column 1

NEWARK COLLEGE TO HELP NEGROES

Willing to Set Aside Site for a Slum Area Complex

By RONALD SULLIVAN
Special to The New York Times

TRENTON, Aug. 3—The Newark College of Medicine and Dentistry has agreed in principle to use a major part of its proposed Newark campus for an urban welfare center in the Negro slums.

The complex that is envisioned would contain low-income housing, child care and health centers and facilities for employment and welfare.

After a three-hour meeting here between Gov. Richard J. Hughes and his aides and leaders of the college, John V. Spinale, special assistant to the Governor, reported that everyone had agreed that there "must be full participation of the Negro community" in the development of a 66-acre tract that the college has set aside for future development.

The tract is near the heart of the area that was torn by

Continued on Page 12, Column 6

NEWS INDEX

Smoke, dust and mud boil skyward as a Navy A-4 Skyhawk from the carrier U.S.S. *Oriskany* attacks the Phuong Dinh railroad bridge, vital to the North Vietnamese.

A Supersabre pilot swoops low over the jungle to bomb an enemy concentration in Dak To, South Vietnam.

"All the News That's Fit to Print"

The New York Times

LATE CITY EDITION

Weather: Fair and pleasant today, tonight and tomorrow. Temperature range: today 81-57. Sunday 80-52. Temp.-Hum. Index 73; Sunday 72. Complete U.S. report on Page 42.

VOL. CXVI..No. 40,035 | NEW YORK, MONDAY, SEPTEMBER 4, 1967 | 10 CENTS

THIEU AND KY ARE VICTORS IN SOUTH VIETNAM BALLOT; 83% OF ELECTORATE VOTES

Associated Press Radiophoto

BABY SITTERS ARE SCARCE: A South Vietnamese woman balloting near Saigon.

TWO GENERALS WIN

Their Goal Was 40% but They Get Only 27% of Total

By R. W. APPLE Jr.
Special to The New York Times

SAIGON, South Vietnam, Monday, Sept. 4—Lieut. Gen. Nguyen Van Thieu, the candidate of the armed forces, won a four-year term as President of South Vietnam yesterday in the country's momentous national election.

General Thieu, the incumbent chief of state, and his vice-presidential running mate, Premier Nguyen Cao Ky, built their victory on two strongpoints — the 700,000-man army and the minority groups whose support they had sought: hill tribes, Roman Catholic refugees, ethnic Cambodians and Chinese, and religious splinter sects.

But the military candidates, in a field of 11 slates, fell far short of the 40 per cent of the vote that their supporters had hoped for. With the count nearing completion, the generals had only 27 per cent of the vote, even though they outpolled their closest rival by better than two to one.

Lawyer Finishes Second

In a major surprise, Truong Dinh Dzu, a wealthy Saigon lawyer, finished in second place, running well ahead of both Tran Van Huong, a former Premier, and Phan Khac Suu, the Speaker of the Constituent Assembly. Mr. Suu, although his campaign had appeared to gain momentum in the last week, was a badly beaten fourth.

At 2:30 P.M. today (2:30 A.M. New York time), with 90 per cent of the vote counted, a New York Times tabulation showed:

Nguyen Van Thieu	1,398,581
Truong Dinh Dzu	651,745
Tran Van Huong	428,680
Phan Khac Suu	425,341

A total of 4,868,266 persons —51 per cent of the 8.5 million persons of voting age and 83 per cent of the 5,853,384 registered voters—marched to the polls on a brilliant, cloudless Sunday.

About 2,650,000 persons of voting age were not registered, most of them because they live in Vietcong-controlled or contested areas. Parts of nearly every province, including some places within 15 miles of Saigon, were on the list of non-voting localities.

The turnout exceeded the expectations of the Government. It was slightly larger

Continued on Page 2, Column 1

Consensus of U.S. Team Is That Voting Was Fair

By TOM BUCKLEY
Special to The New York Times

SAIGON, South Vietnam, Sept. 3—The consensus today among the 22 American observers of the South Vietnamese election was that, as far as they could see, it had been conducted fairly. Several of those active in politics at home shared a view expressed by Gov. William L. Guy of North Dakota, a Democrat.

He said that, while instances of fraud might come to light, the election "as far as I can see has been carried out with greater detail and checks and balances than many of our own."

[Officials in Washington were surprised and encouraged by the size of the turnout in the election and by the Vietcong's inability to destroy the election machinery through terrorism. Page 3.]

John S. Knight publisher of the Knight Newspapers and the only member of the team who has expressed sharp public criticism of the Johnson Administration's Vietnam policy, implied reservations.

Field Trips Included

"I could see no evidence of wrongdoing," he said, "but we're observers, not inspectors of elections. If I were an inspector, I'd have brought Dick Daley and Ray Bliss along."

Richard J. Daley, Mayor of Chicago and chairman of the Cook County Democratic organization, and Mr. Bliss, chairman of the Republican National Committee, are regarded as among the most astute political organizers of their parties.

The Americans did their observing in Saigon and on field

Continued on Page 2, Column 4

TERRORISTS KILL 26 DURING VOTING

Vietcong Incidents Reported in 21 of 43 Provinces—Polling Places Blasted

Special to The New York Times

SAIGON, South Vietnam, Sept. 3—The Vietcong staged a series of election day terrorist attacks and shellings today in which at least 26 South Vietnamese were killed and 82 wounded.

A South Vietnamese military spokesman said 54 incidents were reported today and 80 in the 24 hours preceding the opening of the polls at 7 A.M. It will be two or three days before all the incidents are reported.

The spokesman said there were incidents or shellings in 21 of South Vietnam's 43 provinces.

Despite the widespread attacks, a United States Embassy spokesman said the Vietcong had prevented voting in only three villages, all in Quangtri Province, the northernmost in South Vietnam. The spokesman said balloting was held at 8,821 polling places in the country.

The most serious incidents were reported in or near Sai-

Continued on Page 4, Column 1

EDUCATION'S COST IN SUBURBS STIRS GROWING CONCERN

Taxpayers Are Scrutinizing Budgets as Area Spending Increases 11 Per Cent

13 COUNTIES SURVEYED

Free-Busing Law in Jersey Poses Obstacles—Broader Curriculums Scheduled

By LEONARD BUDER

Taxpayers' revolts against rising school costs have cast a shadow over many suburban school systems as they prepare to reopen this week.

"There's a fiscal crisis at our heels," said Dr. Carroll F. Johnson, Superintendent of Schools in White Plains, where taxpayers approved an increase in school spending powers last spring after twice voting it down.

"We're in for rougher times ahead," added a Nassau County school board member. On Long Island, 43 school budgets for 1967-68 were initially voted down last spring, compared with 18 the year before.

"The voters are carefully scrutinizing the budgets," the board member continued. "We'll salvage the basic programs, but the extras will suffer. This will probably mean cutbacks in recreation, adult education and special programs."

Free Busing in Jersey

Adding to the concern of school officials in New Jersey is the effect of a new state law requiring districts to provide free bus transportation to children attending private and parochial schools if they generally do so for public-school pupils.

The state will reimburse the districts for 75 per cent of the cost, but the remaining 25 per cent has many officials worried.

"We adopted our budget before we knew how many kids would apply under this law," one superintendent said. "What are we going to do for our share of the cost?"

Implementation of the law is also causing a logistical headache. Districts in some counties, such as Bergen, have joined under what they consider to be a feasible arrangement. But other districts, working on their own, admit

Continued on Page 22, Column 1

Labor Day

Today is Labor Day. Following are services affected:

Parking—Sunday regulations in effect.

Post Offices—Closed except for special delivery.

Stores—Department and most retail stores closed.

Banks and Stock Exchanges—Closed.

Sanitation—No regular refuse collection.

Central Park Drives—Closed to autos, 6 A.M. to 6 P.M.

All Goes Right as Sweden Shifts Her Traffic Pattern

Associated Press Cablephoto

Swedish motorists on King Street in Stockholm turned out at 5 A.M. to participate in change to right-hand driving. There had been a ban on traffic since midnight Saturday.

By The Associated Press

STOCKHOLM, Sept. 3—Swedes took to the highways by the tens of thousands today to test their country's new right-hand driving regulations. The resulting traffic jams had a holiday flavor. Despite the switch from driving on the left, the first hours of the traffic revolution were almost bloodless. No serious accidents were reported. Most city drivers seemed to enjoy the early chaos on the streets. Smaller cities and towns changed over at 6 A.M. after a five-hour prohibition on all traffic. Bystanders cheered as cars moved into right-hand traffic lanes. Townspeople on foot, bicycles and horseback joined the throngs in the roadways. Policemen and soldiers assigned to traffic duty were presented with bunches of flowers. In Stock-

Continued on Page 26, Column 1

REUTHER BLAMES FORD FOR IMPASSE IN NEGOTIATIONS

U.A.W. Chief Says Failure of Company to Supply Data Could Force Walkout

By JERRY M. FLINT
Special to The New York Times

DETROIT, Sept. 3—Walter P. Reuther, president of the United Automobile Workers, said today that unless the Ford Motor Company changes its bargaining approach, "there will be a strike, but they will have called it."

The union president demanded that Ford produce figures on company productivity for use in the bargaining on wages. He said that Ford refused this request today. Mr. Reuther said that he also was rebuffed when he sought to discuss higher wages in terms of company profits.

"If the company isn't prepared to talk about economic facts," Mr. Reuther told newsmen after a bargaining session, then the union has "no recourse but to strike."

In another development, Mr. Reuther announced tonight that William E. Simkin, Director of the Federal Mediation and Conciliation Service, would sit in on tomorrow's talks. Mr. Reuther emphasized that the invitation was extended because the union wanted a Government official to see firsthand what some of the problems are.

Calls Data Essential

The union leader made it clear that he believed Ford's productivity increase was at least 6 per cent a year and that he wanted wages and benefits to equal the productivity gains. This translates into 90 cents an hour over a three-year contract. Ford has offered a three-year contract with wage and fringe benefit increases of close to 4 per cent a year, or 55 to 60 cents an hour over three years.

Mr. Reuther called the company's refusal to talk in terms of productivity and profits the equivalent of saying: "Let's lay the facts aside." Without this information, he said, the only way to decide the size of the wage and benefit increases in a new contract is a strike.

Malcolm L. Denise, Ford's chief negotiator, who is a company vice president, said wages did not change as plant productivity "jiggles up or down."

"They haven't in the past," he said.

Mr. Denise said the amount of wage and benefit increases was determined by collective bargaining.

Federal Mediator Arrives

"If you want to call that a jungle battle, you can call it that," he said, but added, "we've reasoned together in the past."

Mr. Reuther always asks the car manufacturers to produce their productivity figures. The companies always refuse and even decline to say if such figures exist.

Although the strike deadline was only three days away, Ford and union negotiators appeared to be marking time.

Today's bargaining sessions at Ford's headquarters building in Dearborn, west of Detroit, began at 11:25 A.M., adjourned for lunch at 1:30 P.M., and resumed at 4:05 P.M.

Both sides made it clear that

Continued on Page 14, Column 1

A 'BILL OF RIGHTS' DUE FOR TENANTS

City Will Order It Printed on New Leases in Both English and Spanish

By EARL CALDWELL

The City Rent Administrator said yesterday that landlords would be required to print a "tenants' bill of rights" on the back of every lease as a means of reducing abuses of the rent control law.

The Administrator, Frederic S. Berman, said the document would "advise tenants of what their rights are under the rent control law," and would be printed in both Spanish and English.

Mr. Berman said that a number of other major forms used by his department would also be printed in Spanish and English.

The first of these, one used by tenants in applying for rent reductions, is to become available in both languages this week.

The changes, Mr. Berman said, are designed to cope with the "small handful" of landlords who take advantage of their tenants by overcharging, harassment and illegal eviction.

He said the city had found that "a good deal of this" took place in areas where there was a language problem, "where the tenants are not as aware of their rights."

The Administrator also an-

Continued on Page 15, Column 4

New-Politics Group Gives Equal Votes To Negro Minority

By WARREN WEAVER Jr.
Special to The New York Times

CHICAGO, Sept. 3—The National New Politics Convention agreed tonight to demands from its Negro minority for equal voting power.

Supporters of the move called it a gesture of reparation and an earnest of good faith. Opponents said it was a violation of democratic principle and "a farce."

The convention of American radicals, in which white delegates outnumbered Negroes by about 1,500 to 600, thus met in full the second major demand submitted in two days by the convention's Black Caucus as the price of continued racial unity.

In practical terms, the move increased the number of votes that can be cast by the militant all-Negro group from 5,341 to 28,498. All other delegates combined, some representing white groups and some integrated, will retain their collective voting power of 28,498.

Originally, the votes represented the membership of the anti-Vietnam war, civil rights and other local groups that sent delegates to the six-day convention called by the National Conference on New Politics. With tonight's action, this relationship ceased.

Yesterday the convention accepted a controversial 13-point policy statement dictated by the Black Caucus. If the white

Continued on Page 15, Column 2

PARTY IS ACCUSED BY CZECH WRITERS

300 Intellectuals Reported to Implore West to Rescue Their 'Spiritual Freedom'

Special to The New York Times

LONDON, Sept. 3—More than 300 Czechoslovak intellectuals have accused the Communist party in their country of conducting "a witchhunt of a pronounced fascist character" against "the entire Czechoslovak writers' community."

The accusation was made, The Sunday Times of London reported today, by Czechoslovak writers, artists, scientists, publicists and other intellectuals in a "writers' manifesto."

The 1,000-word statement appealed to writers in the West, particularly those of "leftist" sympathies, to join in a protest campaign against restrictions on the freedom of expression of Czechoslovak writers, The Sunday Times said.

The newspaper said it had obtained a copy of the document but was withholding the names of the signers "to reduce the risk of instant reprisals by the regime."

Positions Said to Be Denied

As published by The Sunday Times, the manifesto accused party representatives of having "expressly ordered the crossing-off at first of 12 and later of 4 of the names of the most courageous colleagues from the list of candidates" for the Writers Union's Governing Committee.

The party representatives "threatened to silence" the candidates, the statement said. It contended that the candidates had been "put under police surveillance and prohibited from publishing their works" and were "being subjected to persecution that is endangering their livelihood and personal freedom."

The manifesto said the events occurred during and after the Fourth Congress of Czechoslovak Writers held in Prague June 27 to 29.

Czechoslovakia's acting chargé d'affaires in London, Jan Pátek, said: "I very much doubt whether this document is true. It has all the appearances of being fabricated."

The manifesto said that participants in the congress and

Continued on Page 12, Column 7

Foreclosed Homes Sought for Poor

By MAURICE CARROLL

Some of the people living in city slums should be moved into houses already standing in the suburbs, the chairman of President Johnson's Commission on Urban Problems suggested yesterday.

The chairman, former Senator Paul H. Douglas, said Federal Housing Administration mortgages on 43,000 single-family houses, many of them in the suburbs, were foreclosed each year.

"Why not use some of them, discreetly, for public-housing clients?" he asked.

Mr. Douglas, a former Democratic Senator from Illinois, emphasized that he spoke for himself, not for the commission, which will open hearings here on Wednesday.

The commission was set up to make "a penetrating review of zoning, housing and building codes, taxation and development standards" and to report to the President and the Congress on "ways in which the efforts of

Associated Press

Paul H. Douglas

the Federal Government, private industry and local communities can be marshaled to increase the supply of low-cost decent housing."

On Friday, Robert Moses is scheduled to appear before the group at a hearing at the Community Church of New York, 40 East 35th Street.

Mr. Douglas said the erection of 500,000 public-housing units a year—"we've been building 31,000," he said—seemed a reasonable goal to ease the pressures of the nation's slums.

He suggested four sources of public-housing sites or dwellings: urban vacant lots, dilapidated urban buildings, pockets of Federally owned land and the houses on which the F.H.A. has foreclosed mortgages.

When the mortgage is foreclosed, the Senator said, the house could be turned over to a public-housing agency rather than put on the market.

Mr. Douglas indicated there would not be legal obstacles to this sort of transfer. "My staff is working on it," he said.

Mr. Douglas said that in the committee hearings so far, the clear belief had emerged that "units of local govern-

Continued on Page 15, Column 7

NEWS INDEX

	Page		Page
Art	19	Man in the News	2
Bills in Washington	13	Music	24-26
Books	19	Obituaries	21
Bridge	18	Real Estate	34
Business	32	Screen	24-26
Chess	18	Ships and Air	42
Crossword	19	Society	18
Editorials	20	Sports	28-31
Fashions	17	Theaters	24-26
Financial	32-34	TV and Radio	43
Food	17	Weather	42

News Summary and Index, Page 23

In Leningrad, Three Rubles for a Job

By HENRY KAMM
Special to The New York Times

MOSCOW, Sept. 3—A tale of graft and corruption reminiscent of the most damning Soviet recitals of the evils of capitalism was unfolded this weekend in Leningrad, the birthplace of the Bolshevik Revolution.

Leningradskaya Pravda, the newspaper of the city's government and Communist party organization, told of a chauffeur's vain efforts to make an honest living in a business whose wheels appeared to turn only on bribery and cheating.

The article was viewed here with considerable interest because of muffled reports of dissatisfaction with the party leadership in Leningrad and of an article published last July 21 in Pravda, the Communist party paper. In the Pravda article, party leaders in Leningrad were warned against brushing aside "justified criticism voiced by workers."

The Leningrad paper described Nikolai Nikolayevich Ipatov as a first-class driver with an unblemished record and as a former paratrooper to whom all the highest socialist virtues were attributed.

Presumably, his criticisms are therefore to be taken as justified and not to be brushed aside.

Nikolai Nikolayevich's passport contains stamps indicating that he has been accepted for work 20 times and 11 stamps showing his resignation. The editors of Leningradskaya Pravda said he had dropped in on them on his day off, prompted by righteous indignation. They said he was thinking of going to work in a factory, far from garages and those who run them.

He told them that whenever he quit a job in despair over the prevalence of graft, no one would ever look at his immaculate working papers when he went to apply elsewhere. He got action only when he put on the table three rubles, about $3.30, for a half-liter of vodka.

Then, he said, they would

Continued on Page 12, Column 5

"All the News That's Fit to Print"

The New York Times

LATE CITY EDITION

Weather: Sunny and pleasant today; sunny and milder tomorrow. Temp. range: today 64-43; Saturday 66-48. Full U.S. report on Page 95.

SECTION ONE

VOL. CXVII....No. 40,083 NEW YORK, SUNDAY, OCTOBER 22, 1967 · 60¢ beyond 50-mile zone from New York City, except Long Island. Higher in air delivery cities. · 40 CENTS

HOUSE PANEL HITS U.S. HEALTH UNITS FOR BUDGET ROLE

Public Health Service and National Institutes Scored on Administering Grants

EXTRAVAGANCE CHARGED

But Operations Committee Study Finds No Fault With the Quality of Research

By HAROLD M. SCHMECK Jr.

Special to The New York Times

WASHINGTON, Oct. 21 — The House Committee on Government Operations issued a report today criticizing severely the performance of the United States Public Health Service and the National Institutes of Health in administering the large research budgets they control.

The report used such terms as "inadequate" and "inept" in describing some of the specifics of the research administration.

"Our nation is presently facing a financial crisis," said Representative L. H. Fountain in a statement that was issued with the report.

"Strong inflationary pressures have developed and will continue to mount as we head toward one of the largest Federal budget deficits in history. In view of the budget situation and the heavy costs of our Vietnam commitment, we can ill afford to subsidize waste and extravagance in any Federal program."

Drafted By Subcommittee

Mr. Fountain, Democrat of North Carolina, is chairman of the Inter-Governmental Relations Subcommittee which drafted the report.

Representative William L. Dawson, Democrat of Illinois, is chairman of the full Committee on Government Operations.

The subcommittee estimates that the Federal Government's contribution to health research amounts to two-thirds of all the money spent for this purpose in the nation. In 1966, the Federal share was $1.6-billion, of which the Public Health Service accounted for $900-million. The National Institutes of Health, the chief research arm of the Public Health Service, spent $808-million of this.

Generally, the committee re-

Continued on Page 28, Column 1

Talks at Ford Push Conclusion of Pact

By JERRY M. FLINT

Special to The New York Times

DETROIT, Oct. 21—Negotiators for the Ford Motor Company and the striking United Automobile Workers went back to the bargaining table this morning in hopes of putting the finishing touches on a new contract agreement.

The major provisions of the proposed pact have been agreed upon, but already there were signs of dissatisfaction among some union men.

The dissatisfaction centered on these areas:

¶A special pay increase of 30 cents an hour a year for

Continued on Page 37, Column 1

HOSPITAL REPORT LISTS NEW CURBS

Progress Study by Terenzio Finds Better Supervision of Voluntary Institutions

By EMANUEL PERLMUTTER

The city reported yesterday that it had tightened its controls over voluntary hospitals and medical schools affiliated with municipal hospitals.

They must now submit monthly expense reports to the city, and physicians they assign to municipal hospitals are strictly limited in the amount of time they spend in outside teaching.

These changes in the hospital affiliation program are among the highlights of a 28-point progress report that has been submitted by Hospitals Commissioner Joseph V. Terenzio to the State Investigation Commission.

Its contents were disclosed yesterday by Mr. Terenzio, one day after City Controller Mario A. Procaccino asked six voluntary hospitals to return $1.5-million to the city that he said had been spent improperly.

Public Hearings Planned

Under the affiliation program, the city pays the private, nonprofit voluntary hospitals and medical schools to provide equipment and personnel and to perform medical, surgical and other professional services at 19 municipal hospitals.

In general, yesterday's report cites in detail improved supervision and control of financial, personnel and professional programing in the affiliation contracts that were signed in July. Many of the improvements were made public previously. These contracts replace agreements drawn up in 1962, which had caused much criticism.

Myles J. Lane, chairman of the Investigation Commission, said yesterday, "We want to study this report before we can comment on its achievements."

"But we intend to continue the investigation of the affiliation program that we started a year ago," he added. "Our accountants have checked the books of the hospitals and we plan to hold public hearings on the whole subject in the next several weeks."

Mr. Procaccine had charged that some hospital directors had improperly certified that physicians were working in

Continued on Page 30, Column 3

Scuffles at the Pentagon Follow Rally and March by Opponents of Policy on Vietnam

U.S. marshals clubbing antiwar demonstrators who tried to storm the Pentagon yesterday

Associated Press Wirephotos

Demonstrators shouting at a military policeman at barrier

GUARDS REPULSE WAR PROTESTERS AT THE PENTAGON

6 Break Through Line Into Building — Mailer and Dellinger Are Arrested

THOUSANDS HEAR TALK

Spock Tells Demonstrators at Lincoln Memorial That Johnson Is Real 'Enemy'

By JOSEPH A. LOFTUS

Special to The New York Times

WASHINGTON, Oct. 21—Thousands of demonstrators stormed the Pentagon today after a calm rally and march by some 50,000 persons opposed to the war in Vietnam.

The protesters twice breached the lines of deputy Federal marshals backed by soldiers armed with bayonet-tipped rifles. But they were quickly driven back by the rifle butts of the soldiers and the marshals' nightsticks.

Six demonstrators succeeded in entering a side door at the main Mall entrance of the building but were pushed out immediately by marshals.

There were no reports of serious injuries but the Pentagon steps were spattered with blood.

128 Held at Pentagon

Soldiers and marshals arrested at least 128 persons at the Pentagon, including David Dellinger, Chairman of the National Mobilization Committee to End the War in Vietnam, which organized the rally and march.

Also arrestted were Norman Mailer, the novelist, who was seized for technical violation of a police line, and the Rev. John Boyles, the Episcopal chaplain at Yale University.

The surging disorderly crowd that milled about the vast Pentagon shouted obscenities and taunted the forces on guard there. Some threw eggs and bottles as darkness fell, built bonfires and waved what they said were burning draft cards.

They clashed with the guards several times.

Use of Tear Gas Denied

Several tear gas canisters exploded outside the building at various times. The Defense Department announced that the Army had not used tear gas at any time and charged that the demonstrators had.

Two soldiers were reported to have been injured, one by tear gas and one by a missile that struck him in the eye.

At the Lincoln Memorial and elsewhere, the police reported ten persons arrested, most of them for demonstrations against the demonstrators.

A police and military consensus put the size of the crowd at the Lincoln Memorial, where the demonstrators first

Continued on Page 58, Column 1

112 Major Concerns Would Build in Slum If Decay Is Halted

By STEVEN V. ROBERTS

More than 100 of 700 major corporations questioned by a leading consulting company have indicated a willingness to build new plants in or near slum areas. But not one of them said it would make such a move under current conditions.

The 112 corporations responding favorably to the survey listed a set of stiff conditions, ranging from the elimination of surrounding decay to the presence of "responsible" leadership, that would have to be met before they would consider relocating in rundown neighborhoods.

The survey was made by the Fantus Company, a subsidiary of Dun and Bradstreet, which specializes in finding new locations for industry.

Response Called 'Amazing'

Leonard C. Yaseen, Fantus's chairman, acknowledged that the conditions laid down by the companies do not exist in any city today. But he insisted they might be met "five years from now" if municipal governments went to work immediately.

The response to the survey was "amazing in view of what's been going on in the cities these days," Mr. Yaseen said. The business executive declined to say whether he thought the conditions set by the company were realistic.

"I want to concentrate on the positive side," he said.

Mayor Lindsay, Senator Robert F. Kennedy and other political figures have stressed the importance of attracting industry to poor neighborhoods, both to provide jobs and bolster the city's tax base.

However, such critics as

Continued on Page 46, Column 3

THANT SUGGESTS STAFF RESHUFFLE

Urges Reduction in Number of Top Secretariat Posts to Increase Efficiency

By JOHN M. TAYLOR

Special to The New York Times

UNITED NATIONS, N. Y., Oct. 21 — Secretary General Thant proposed today that the United Nations Secretariat be reorganized. It is expected that the General Assembly's Committee on Budget and Administration will accept the proposals without serious objection.

In his report to the committee, Mr. Thant urged that the top echelon of the Secretariat be divided into two levels, "with proper geographcal distribution at both levels."

"While the placement of serving officers at either of the two levels will not prove an easy task," Mr. Thant said, "I believe that in the long-term interests of the organization this has to be undertaken."

Growth of U.N. Is Cited

He explained that the continuous growth of the United Nations and the expansion of its activities made reorganization necessary.

At present, there are 14 Under Secretaries in secretariat headquarters and five at regional offices abroad. Altogether the senior staff numbers 36, all of whom report directly to the Secretary General.

In the interests of efficiency, Mr. Thant wishes to reduce this number to 11, with the rank of Under Secretary General. The lower level of the topmost echelon would hold the rank of Assistant Secretary General.

This is the first time the

Continued on Page 10, Column 1

Israeli Destroyer Is Sunk By Missiles of Egyptians

By JAMES FERON

Special to The New York Times

JERUSALEM, Sunday, Oct. 22 —An Israeli destroyer, the 2,500-ton Elath, was sunk by Egyptian missiles last night off the northern coast of Sinai.

An Israeli announcement said the ship had been on routine patrol 14 miles outside Egyptian territorial waters when she was apparently attacked by an Egyptian missile boat.

According to the Cairo radio, the Elath entered Egyptian territorial waters north of Port Said, a coastal town at the northern end of the Suez Canal. "Our naval units engaged and sank it," the Cairo announcement said.

The Israelis said the attack occurred at 5:30 P.M. opposite the village of El Rumana. They conceded that the missiles might have been launched from Port Said.

The vessel was abandoned about 8 P. M. when it became apparent that she would sink, the Israelis said.

There were no immediate reports of casualties, but Israeli Air Force and Navy units were sent to the scene to assist in rescue work, the Israelis said. The 362-foot ship would have carried between 180 and 220 men, according to estimates here. The Central Negev Hospital in Beersheba was alerted to handle any casualties.

Later reports of the incident came from the Cairo radio, which announced the ship's sinking. At first the Israelis confirmed that a destroyer had been hit but declined to say much more.

They did say, however, that

Continued on Page 4, Column 2

1,000 AT VIGIL HERE TO SUPPORT G.I.'S

Battery Park Rally Will Last 31 Hours—Motorists Turn Lights on During Daylight

By PAUL HOFMANN

Almost 1,000 persons attended a vigil in Battery Park yesterday in support of American fighting men in Vietnam.

The 31-hour rally, in which war veterans and youths of draft age are participating, began at noon with speeches and ceremonies.

The vigil, scheduled to end at sundown today, is part of a nationwide series of demonstrations organized by the National Committee for Responsible Patriotism, which comprises organizations of former servicemen and other patriotic groups.

Bus and Taxi Lights On

The events sponsored by the committee for this weekend are also designed to stress respect for law and order. The organizers have said that the demonstrations were planned before yesterday's antiwar march in Washington was announced.

The committee had urged motorists to keep their headlights burning while driving in the daytime during the weekend, and had called on householders to leave a light burning in their homes all night from yesterday to today. Both actions were aimed at displaying backing for the soldiers in Vietnam.

Thousands of autos in the metropolitan area yesterday had their headlights or parking lights on. Conspicuous was the participation of bus drivers and tax drivers in the silent demonstration.

Signatures Collected

Yesterday morning many police patrol cars also had their headlights burning. Later, the more than 1,000 patrol cars on duty were ordered by the chief inspector's office to turn their lights off during the daytime.

"All units will operate on the normal daylight procedures," the directive said.

The order was prompted by complaints from citizens about what they termed a display of the policemen's feelings by driving around neighborhoods with headlights burning. Later yesterday, the police vehicles circulated again with turned-off lights.

In the metropolitan area, five parades in support of the armed forces in Vietnam are scheduled for today—in the Bronx, Brooklyn, Hempstead, L. I., Newark and Waterbury, Conn. The demonstrations, called Opera-

Continued on Page 59, Column 1

PURDUE, ALABAMA AND NAVY UPSET

Oregon St., Tennessee and William and Mary Victors

Purdue, Alabama and Navy were defeated in major college football upsets yesterday. Oregon State dumped the second-ranked Boilermakers, 22-14. Tennessee trounced the Crimson Tide, 24-13. William & Mary rallied to sink the Middies, 27-16.

Scores of other leading games:

Army	14	Rutgers	3
Auburn	28	Ga. Tech.	10
Bucknell	28	Penn	27
Clemson	13	Duke	7
Colorado	21	Nebraska	16
Dartmouth	41	Brown	6
Georgia	56	V. M. I.	6
Harvard	14	Cornell	12
Houston	43	Miss. St.	6
Indiana	27	Michigan	20
Miami (Fla.)	58	Pitt	0
Minnesota	21	Mich. St.	0
N. Dame	47	Illinois	7
Penn St.	21	West Va.	14
Princeton	28	Colgate	0
Syracuse	20	Calif.	14
Texas	21	Arkansas	12
U. S. C.	23	Washington	6
U. C. L. A.	21	Stanford	16
Wyoming	30	Wichita St.	7
Yale	21	Columbia	7

THOROUGHBRED RACING

Tartan Stable's Ruffled Feathers, ridden by Dave Hidalgo, scored a dramatic upset in the $116,100 Man o' War Stakes at Aqueduct. The long shot scored by a head over Fort Marcy and paid $82.40, $31.60 and $19.80 for $2 across the board.

Dr. Fager, the odds-on favorite, won the $121,360 Hawthorne Gold Cup in Chicago and returned $2.60 for $2 to win.

Details in Section 5

Beauty Is Now in Fashion in Soviet

By HENRY KAMM

Special to The New York Times

MOSCOW, Oct. 21—An article in the current issue of the influential weekly Literaturnaya Gazeta demands that the Soviet Union break the Western monopoly on beauty contests.

The author, Dr. S. P. Letunov, a specialist in the medical aspects of sports, said Soviet beauty competitions should not imitate the advertising and commercial features that mar Western contests but should be held in the spirit of Socialist competitions.

Russians should acquire beauty by working for it, with physical exercises 30 minutes a day, Dr. Letunov urged. The exercises should be designed to develop grace and reduce weight rather than add muscle.

Beauty would thus be created by man's own hand and not by "God," Dr. Letunov declared. The quotation marks are his. The beauty-through-work theme appeared to make the idea of beauty contests ideologically acceptable.

This ideological approach to beauty was also reflected in the doctor's affirmation of the perfectibility of man by man. We cannot control the physical beauty of a face now, Dr. Letunov said, although cosmetic surgeons have done much to correct the grossest defects. But he added that it would probably be possible to do much more about creating personal beauty through science in the future.

The article was marked by a spirited defense of beauty for beauty's sake, a new idea in a country where social utility remains the ultimate criterion of value. While inner beauty is of principal importance, the doctor said, people have never despised mere outward beauty.

"Everything must be beautiful in a human being—face, clothes, soul and thought," Dr. Letunov said, quoting Chekhov. "We must cultivate, from childhood on, a taste for beauty and must not be ashamed to speak of it."

The kind of athletic training practiced in the Soviet Union today results in great, but unharmoniously devel-

Continued on Page 13, Column 1

School Board Ends Racial Attitude Test After Protest Here

By MALCOLM W. BROWNE

A Board of Education test designed to measure the racial attitudes of pupils toward each other has brought on a controversy between parents and school officials on Manhattan's West Side.

As a result, the test has been canceled and "another wedge has been driven between the community and the teaching professionals," according to Dr. Nathan Jacobson, assistant superintendent for District 5, in which the test was administered.

The test consisted of 18 stories, with each one containing a hero or villain. The pupils were supposed to mark an answer sheet indicating whether they thought the hero or villain was "Negro, white or 'Spanish-speaking.'" They also indicated their own races or linguistic backgrounds. A typical test question was:

"One day the teacher said, 'I have to go out of the room for a few minutes. If everyone is very good while I am gone, we will have a surprise when I come back.'

"When the teacher came back, everyone was working very quietly and good. Everyone except one child. That child was running around the room and shouting. The teacher said: 'Well, I'm very sorry. Now we cannot have our surprise.'

"Put an X on the child (Negro, white or 'Spanish-speaking') who spoiled the surprise

Continued on Page 44, Column 3

WAR COMPROMISE RULED OUT BY GIAP

Hanoi General Says U.S. Bombs Won't Force Talks

By RAYMOND H. ANDERSON

Special to The New York Times

MOSCOW, Oct. 21 — Any form of compromise with the United States in the Vietnam war was ruled out today by Gen. Vo Nguyen Giap, Defense Minister of North Vietnam.

The general asserted that United States bombing attacks on North Vietnam would never break the will of its people to help the Vietcong in South Vietnam achieve victory. The Vietnamese, he added, are ready to pay "any price" for victory.

[Two United States planes bombed six North Vietnamese torpedo boats in the Gulf of Tonkin and reported that four had been sunk. Page 3.]

General Giap outlined Hanoi's stand in an article in Krasnaya Zvezda, newspaper of the Soviet Ministry of Defense.

His assertion that bombing would never force Hanoi to submit to negotiations came amid reports from Washington that President Johnson was believed to be weighing the pros and cons of a bombing halt in response to widening demands for such a step.

The North Vietnamese military leader praised Moscow's expanding assistance, but he carefully balanced the praise of the Russians with appropriate acknowledgments of help from the Chinese Communists.

General Giap reiterated Hanoi's insistence that the only

Continued on Page 3, Column 5

Today's Sections

Index to Subjects

Two exhausted U.S. Naval officers stand in front of their aircraft aboard the U.S.S. *Constellation* minutes after downing an enemy Mig-21 over North Vietnam.

A U.S. Air Force pararescueman rides a jungle penetrator as he is hoisted up to a helicopter during a practice rescue exercise held at Pleiku Air Base.

"All the News That's Fit to Print"

The New York Times

LATE CITY EDITION

Weather: Cloudy and windy today; fair tonight. Fair, cold tomorrow. Temp. range: today 38–29; Thurs. 36–31. Full U.S. report on Page 51.

VOL. CXVII...No. 40,151   © 1967 The New York Times Company   NEW YORK, FRIDAY, DECEMBER 29, 1967   10 CENTS

TROWBRIDGE SEES A $50-BILLION GAIN IN GROSS PRODUCT

Commerce Secretary Puts 1968 Increase at 6½% —Asks Higher Taxes

ECONOMISTS OPTIMISTIC

417 in Survey Expect Growth but Support Eases a Bit for Rise in Levies

By EILEEN SHANAHAN
Special to The New York Times

WASHINGTON, Dec. 28 — The Johnson Administration made its first official forecast today of business conditions in 1968 and concluded that "we like what we see."

The nation's total output of goods and services — the gross national product — should rise next year by "a minimum" of $50-billion, or about 6½ per cent from the estimated 1967 total of $785-billion, Secretary of Commerce Alexander B. Trowbridge said. He presented his forecast to a meeting of the Allied Social Sciences Association at the Washington Hilton Hotel.

The Government's official predictions for 1968 will be contained in the major Presidential messages delivered to Congress after the turn of the year — the State of the Union address, the budget and the economic report. It was considered unlikely, however, that Secretary Trowbridge's predictions would be significantly different from those contained in these documents.

One Warning Note

Mr. Trowbridge sounded only one note of warning. He emphasized the need that the Administration still sees for enactment of a tax increase next year and cautioned both labor and management against excessive price and wage increases.

The Commerce Department's optimistic forecast of 1968 business conditions received independent backing today from 417 academic, private-industry and Government economists, who took part in a survey on the economic outlook in connection with the social scientists' meeting.

The median forecast of the economists involved in the survey of next year's G.N.P. was $835-billion, the same figure

Continued on Page 37, Column 1

MAYOR CRITICIZES 'VILLAGE' DECISION

Lindsay Says Court Lacked Facts on Cleanup Order

By SETH S. KING

Mayor Lindsay responded yesterday to a court order to clean up "the madness and unhealthy situation" in Greenwich Village by blaming judicial laxity for some of the problems and by declaring that the justice who issued the order lacked knowledge of the facts.

Referring to what he called "the extraordinary decision" by Justice Charles A. Tierney, on Tuesday, Mr. Lindsay said there had been a marked improvement in the Macdougal Street area since special police and licensing actions had been undertaken at his direction.

"The tactical patrol force was in there long before Judge Tierney took his look," Mr. Lindsay asserted.

The Mayor said the real problem was that the courts were not severe enough on offenders taken before them.

In a decision sustaining dozens of complaints by residents of disorderly conduct and ordinance violations, Justice Tierney ordered the Mayor and other city officials to take "effective" action to correct the conditions immediately.

At a news conference in the Board of Estimate chamber yesterday, the Mayor ticked off a list of actions the city had taken in the Macdougal Street area.

"This is a congregating area for youngsters, and we're involved in a sensitive problem

Continued on Page 34, Column 5

LEAVING COURT: James L. Marcus, right, former City Commissioner of Water Supply, Gas and Electricity, outside Federal Courthouse with attorney, Edward Bennett Williams.

The New York Times (by Meyer Liebowitz)

Lindsay to See Both Sides In Tangled Transit Talks

By DAMON STETSON

Mayor Lindsay is scheduled to take a personal role in the transit negotiations today. He has been keeping in close touch with bargaining developments through his panel of mediators, but is planning to go to the Americana Hotel to meet directly with negotiators for the two unions and the Transit Authority.

Earlier in the negotiations, the Mayor had conferred with officials of both the authority and the unions. But his office said he had decided to step into the talks again today after receiving reports yesterday from the panel. He is due at the Americana at 11:30 A.M.

With only three days left before the New Year's Day deadline for a citywide strike of bus and subway workers, the mediators sought yesterday to pave the way for a money proposal by the authority. They are also expected to seek a revised statement of union demands that would provide a more realistic basis for direct negotiation. The Mayor may attempt to give a push to both sides.

Theodore W. Kheel, one of the mediators, said late in the afternoon that the panel was trying to determine whether the authority would submit a statement of position on money issues to the mediators for transmission to the unions—

Continued on Page 23, Column 1

LABOR COSTS RISE 5% IN 12 MONTHS

Increase Reflects Lagging Productivity Growth Rate and Sizable Wage Gains

By EDWIN L. DALE Jr.
Special to The New York Times

WASHINGTON, Dec. 28 — The labor cost of each unit of output in manufacturing rose again in November after a temporary decline in October and is now about 5 per cent higher than a year ago.

This large rise in labor costs, reported by the Commerce Department today, reflects a combination of sizable wage gains over the last year and a much lower growth than normal in productivity, or output per manhour.

For the whole of the decade up to early 1966, unit labor costs in manufacturing were essentially stable. This was a major factor in the general price stability of that period.

Began to Rise in '66

But the cost index, which uses the years 1957 to 1959 as a base of 100, after fluctuating near or below 100 for years, began to rise in the spring of 1966. Last month it reached a record peak of 108.3, after dipping slightly to 107.7 in October from 108.1 in September.

The figure for November of last year was 103.1. Thus the rise in the last 12 months has been 5.04 per cent.

Today's report was in Business Cycle Developments, a monthly publication.

Higher unit labor costs in manufacturing mean one of two things, or a combination of the two—higher prices and lower profits. There is abundant evidence this year that both have been happening in the manufacturing sector.

Productivity the Key

The key to the steep rise in unit labor costs this year appears to be the weak performance of productivity. This, in turn, is associated with what until only recently has been the sluggish nature of manufacturing output for most of this year.

Although the figures are not final, it appears that productivity growth in manufacturing this year may be as low as 1 per cent, the smallest in many years.

From 1960 to 1964, when the economy was expanding, productivity in manufacturing grew an average of 4 per cent a year, helping to keep unit labor costs down even though wages were rising.

Productivity growth in manufacturing was 3.4 per cent in 1965 and 3.1 per cent in 1966.

WORLD'S FAIR LOSS PUT AT $21,159,660

Bondholders Cover Major Share of Deficit, With City Writing Off the Rest

By RICHARD E. MOONEY

The New York World's Fair of 1964-65 lost exactly $21,159,660.30, according to an official city audit.

The report, from the office of City Controller Mario A. Procaccino, said that the final deficit stood "in sharp contrast" to the fair management's original predictions of a $50-million surplus.

The deficit was covered by a court settlement with the fair's bondholders — under which they received $18.4-million less than they were owed — and by the city's agreement to write off $2.7-million of the fair's commitment to restore the grounds when the fair ended.

At the end of 1966, the report said, the fair had $4.1-million remaining in assets, and liabilities of the same amount.

"Barring any unfavorable court decision on the numerous legal actions against it," the report said, the fair had "barely sufficient funds available to meet its outstanding obligations."

There were $14-million of lawsuits pending against the

Continued on Page 14, Column 4

MARCUS, 5 OTHERS PLEAD NOT GUILTY IN KICKBACK CASE

Further Hearing to Be Held Next Month on Charges Involving City Contract

By RICHARD REEVES

James L. Marcus and five other defendants stood among their 14 lawyers in Federal court here yesterday and pleaded not guilty to charges involving an alleged $40,000 kickback on a contract for cleaning a city reservoir.

When his name was called by a court clerk, Mr. Marcus and his lawyer, Edward Bennett Williams, pushed their way through the small crowd of men in front of Judge Constance Baker Motley.

Mr. Williams said: "The defendant James L. Marcus waives the reading of the charges and enters a plea of not guilty."

Mr. Marcus nodded and murmured "Yes."

A Federal grand jury charged two weeks ago that Mr. Marcus, when he was Commissioner of Water Supply, Gas and Electricity, shared in a $40,000 kickback on an $835,000 contract he awarded for cleaning of the Jerome Park Reservoir in the Bronx.

Conspiracy Is Charged

The contract was awarded to S. T. Grand, Inc., whose president, Henry Fried, was indicted on conspiracy charges along with Mr. Marcus; Antonio (Tony Ducks) Corallo, a reputed Mafia leader; Daniel Motto, a union leader, and two lawyers, Herbert Itkin and Charles J. Rappoport.

The six defendants all made the same plea during the 20-minute hearing in Judge Motley's gloomy courtroom. After listening to the pleas, the judge scheduled a hearing for motions on Jan. 30.

Lawyers and defendants milled into a shifting mass as the case was called at 10:50 A.M. Corallo and Mr. Fried, who are both short men, changed positions several times when their view of the judge and clerk was blocked by the 6-foot-1 Mr. Williams.

Corallo was represented by Jacob Kossman, who has represented James R. Hoffa, former president of the International Brotherhood of Teamsters.

Mr. Williams has also represented Hoffa, who is now in prison, and a long list of prominent clients, including the late Senator Joseph R. McCarthy, Representative Adam Clayton Powell and Robert G. Baker, a onetime secretary to the

Continued on Page 14, Column 1

DIRKSEN DOUBTS JOHNSON POLICY POINTS TO PEACE

Cites Rising War Costs and Casualties — Aggressive Line for 1968 Is Seen

By E. W. KENWORTHY
Special to The New York Times

WASHINGTON, Dec. 28 — Everett McKinley Dirksen, the Senate Republican leader, says "there is no prospect of peace, no promise of stability, no hope for the better" in the policies of the Johnson Administration.

He issued the indictment in an "extension of remarks" dated Dec. 15, the last day of the Congressional session, that appeared today in the session's final issue of The Congressional Record.

The Senator, in his most severe attack on President Johnson's conduct of the Vietnamese war and diplomacy, said that "as our casualties mount daily, the skyrocketing costs of combat soar beyond sight, the unpopularity of the war among our people intensifies hourly and there is little evident reason to hope for victory in the foreseeable future."

"For there is no prospect of peace, no promise of stability, no hope for the better in the policies of this Administration," he said.

Moreover, he went on, the Administration has given little evidence of looking beyond Vietnam and considering "where we shall stand and with whom we shall sit when this conflict ceases."

Little Genuine Effort

"The Congress and the people have seen all too little evidence of genuine effort to explore and exploit the diplomatic opportunities available to us in this regard," he said. "Channels of diplomacy—economic and otherwise—still remain open for our use."

Traditionally the final issue of The Congressional Record is given over to back-dated speeches and extensions of remarks composed after the close of the session. Party leaders often use it for a partisan summation and defense of the party record and, prior to election years, for attacks on the opposition.

Mr. Dirksen has hitherto given almost unqualified support to the Vietnam policies of President Johnson, with whom he has a cordial and confiding relationship.

Consequently his sharp attack was interpreted here as an indication of the line that he will probably take in the

Continued on Page 2, Column 4

SIHANOUK EASES STAND OPPOSING INCURSION BY U.S.

Foe Counterattacks On Vietnam's Coast

Special to The New York Times

SAIGON, South Vietnam, Friday, Dec. 29 — Vietcong guerrillas counterattacked a force of several battalions of South Vietnamese rangers, infantrymen and militia early today in a fierce battle near Hoian, on the South Vietnamese coast, 380 miles northeast of Saigon.

Government forces said the counterattack was made after the Vietcong had lost 52 men in a series of bitter actions yesterday in which the South Vietnamese called in reinforcements. The South Vietnamese were supported by American artillery fire and helicopter gun ships.

Last night, after continuous fighting through the day, the Vietcong launched a heavy counterattack that lasted until 3:30 this morning. South Vietnamese casualties were officially described as light.

Heavy fighting was also

Continued on Page 4, Column 3

CITES HOT PURSUIT

Says Units of Vietcong Entered Cambodia but Were Ousted

By Agence France-Presse

PNOMPENH, Cambodia, Dec. 28—Prince Norodom Sihanouk, the Cambodian chief of state, said today that under certain conditions Cambodian troops would not try to stop United States troops from entering the country in hot pursuit of Vietcong or North Vietnamese forces.

The Prince added that he would take such a position only if he was convinced that Vietcong or North Vietnamese troops had entered Cambodia illegally and were in an "uninhabited outlying region difficult to control."

Prince Sihanouk took that position in reply to questions submitted to him by The Washington Post. The main points of his reply were made public by Cambodian Information Services.

[In Washington, State Department officials said they would have no comment on the Prince's statements until they could study a complete text. The United States is widening its diplomatic efforts to keep the enemy from using Cambodian territory as a sanctuary. Washington has tried repeatedly to convince Prince Sihanouk that the enemy is doing so.]

Prince Adds a Warning

The Prince coupled his statement with a sharp warning that if there were "serious raids or bombings" against frontier areas inhabited by Cambodians or Vietnamese who had been living there a long time, Cambodian troops would strike back as strongly as possible.

He also warned the United States against sending South Vietnamese troops onto Cambodian soil, maintaining that

Continued on Page 2, Column 3

FRENCH PARTNERS CRITICAL OF VETO

Even Pompidou Seems to Be Fearful Common Market May Have Been Impaired

Special to The New York Times

PARIS, Dec. 28 — Premiers and foreign ministers of five European countries expressed or implied various degrees of fear today that the French veto on British membership might have seriously weakened the European Economic Community.

The views of the Premiers of France, Belgium and Luxembourg and the Foreign Ministers of Italy and the Netherlands were quoted in separate interviews by Le Figaro, a pro-Government French newspaper. Chancellor Kurt Georg Kiesinger of West Germany as well as Foreign Minister Willy Brandt refused to answer its questions, Le Figaro said.

The newspaper quoted the four partners of France as being severely and sometimes bitterly critical of the French position.

Premier Georges Pompidou, though staunchly defending French opposition to British entry, appeared to betray apprehension that in retaliation against France the other member countries might send the Common Market into limbo.

1968 Termed Crucial

The coming year, he said, will be crucial because "it will show, depending on the attitudes of the member nations, whether the Europe of the Six is resigned to a sort of progressive dissolution or whether on the contrary it is determined to be economically and politically united."

He expressed the hope that France's partners would "respect the commitments already entered . . . that the agricultural Common Market will be completed" and "that the customs union will be realized by the first of July of 1968."

France, being the foremost agriculture country in the community, has long been manifesting a greater interest in agricultural unification than her partners.

Premier Paul Vanden Boeynants of Belgium charged that

Continued on Page 8, Column 3

PROTESTERS WIN SIDEWALK RIGHTS

State Court Voids City Ban on Obstructions as Vague

By SIDNEY E. ZION
Special to The New York Times

ALBANY, Dec. 28 — The Court of Appeals declared unconstitutional today a New York City law that has often been used by the police to break up peaceful sidewalk protests against the Vietnam war.

In a 5-to-2 decision, the state's highest court reversed the conviction of Elliot Katz, a 20-year-old college student, who had set up a card table in Queens with a sign that said: "Stop the War in Vietnam."

The court also handed down a number of significant criminal law rulings.

The city statute it threw out was Section 692H-1.0 of the Administrative Code. It provided: "It shall be unlawful for any person . . . to encumber or obstruct any street . . . with any article or thing whatsoever."

In a four-page opinion that cited a number of libertarian rulings of the United States Supreme Court, Judge Kenneth B. Keating concluded: "Where a statute is couched in such broad language that it is subject to discriminatory application, the resulting infringement on the exercise of freedom of speech far outweighs the public benefit sought to be achieved."

Aryeh Neier, executive director of the New York Civil Liberties Union, which handled the case for Mr. Katz, praised the

Continued on Page 3, Column 2

Unionists Gather at Jail in Rain to Protest Holding of Shanker

Demonstrators gathering in front of the jail on West 37th Street, right, where Albert Shanker, president of the United Federation of Teachers, is serving a 15-day sentence. The bad weather held their number to several hundred.

The New York Times

By M. A. FARBER

Several hundred labor union members, buffeted by the wind and drenched by rain and sleet, demonstrated for an hour in front of Civil Jail yesterday to protest the imprisonment of Albert Shanker, president of the United Federation of Teachers. The unionists, circling within wooden police barricades under a blanket of umbrellas, chanted, "Lindsay In, Shanker Out" and "One-Two-Three-Four—Open Up the Stinking Door." They carried placards saying, "Labor Can't Be Put Behind Bars" and "The Right to Strike Is Basic to Freedom." Mr. Shanker is serving a 15-day sentence in the jail at 434 West 37th Street for leading the city teachers' stoppage in September. He entered the jail Dec. 20. The tall, 39-year-old leader of the teachers' union could not see the spirited demonstration because prisoners, who live in dormitories instead of cells, were kept in the rear of the jail. Highlighting the demonstration—which began about 4:15 P.M. and was expected to draw more than 10,000 people before the bad weather set in—were at

Continued on Page 23, Column 2

NEWS INDEX

	Page		Page
Books	25	Music	12-27
Bridge	25	Obituaries	33
Business	44	Real Estate	32
Crossword	25	Screen	25
Editorials	26	Ships and Air	70
Fashions	22	Society	
Financial	35-43	Sports	
Food	22	Theaters	25
Letters	26	TV and Radio	52
Man in the News	25	Weather	

News Summary and Index, Page 29

"All the News That's Fit to Print"

The New York Times

LATE CITY EDITION

Weather: Showers today; periods of rain tonight and tomorrow. Temp. range: today 45-36; Monday 39-36. Full U.S. report on Page 81.

VOL. CXVII . . No. 40,183 NEW YORK, TUESDAY, JANUARY 30, 1968 10 CENTS

RECORD 186-BILLION BUDGET IS PRESENTED BY JOHNSON; TAX RISE REQUIRED, HE SAYS

20-BILLION DEFICIT

This Would Be Cut to 8-Billion by Passage of 10% Surcharge

Text of the Budget Message and related articles are on Pages 16 through 21.

By EDWIN L. DALE Jr.
Special to The New York Times

WASHINGTON, Jan. 29—President Johnson presented to Congress today a budget of $186.1-billion—the biggest ever and one that he said required a tax increase to reduce the deficit and the Government's need to borrow.

The rise in total spending in the fiscal year 1969, beginning July 1, is $10.4-billion, but a third of that is for defense and most of the rest for increases in such areas as Social Security payments that are fixed by law, interest on the debt and Federal pay.

"We have had to set priorities," the President said. "We cannot do everything we would wish to do."

'User' Charges Included

The growth in spending is much less than in the last three budgets, partly because the cost of the war in Vietnam is leveling off. Still, there would be a second consecutive deficit of more than $20-billion without the requested tax increase, mainly the 10 per cent surcharge, which is stalled in Congress.

With the tax increase, the deficit would drop to $8-billion in the new fiscal year. Receipts would be $178.1-billion, of which $12.9-billion depends on the tax bill. The receipts total also includes $280-million of unspecified new "user" charges on trucks, barges and airlines.

Apart from defense and "built-in" increases, the budget has nearly offsetting ups and downs in expenditures. The reductions, many of which are controversial, will require Congressional approval.

Altogether, 50 specific reductions are proposed from the levels in laws and appropria-

Continued on Page 16, Column 1

Associated Press

SIGNS FEDERAL BUDGET: President Johnson puts his signature to document. At rear are Charles L. Schultze, left, the outgoing Director of the Bureau of the Budget, and Charles J. Zwick, who was sworn in as his successor.

Congress Cool to Budget; Mahon Backs a Tax Rise

By MARJORIE HUNTER
Special to The New York Times

WASHINGTON, Jan. 29—The chairman of the House Appropriations Committee threw his support behind a tax increase today, but he said that Congress must first trim President Johnson's budget.

Representative George H. Mahon, Democrat of Texas, had refused to support the Administration's proposed 10 per cent surtax last year.

His switch in positions could be influential in prying the long-stalled bill from the House Ways and Means Committee.

The Appropriations Committee generally sets spending patterns in Congress. The Ways and Means Committee handles revenue measures.

The budget received a chilly reception on Capitol Hill, with key Democrats and Republicans calling for substantial reductions in domestic spending.

In supporting a tax increase, and promising to trim the budget, Mr. Mahon, in effect, was saying to Wilbur D. Mills, chairman of the Ways and Means Committee: We'll cut spending if you will increase revenues.

Mr. Mills, an Arkansas Democrat, was not present today to answer the Mahon challenge. He is spending a week in his home state and was not available for comment.

However, just last week, Mr. Mills told high Administration officials that they had "not yet established" to his satisfaction that they had "done the best

Continued on Page 21, Column 6

DEFENSE FIGURE 3-BILLION HIGHER

But Johnson Indicates That the Proposed 79.8-Billion May Be Insufficient

By WILLIAM BEECHER
Special to The New York Times

WASHINGTON, Jan. 29—President Johnson's $79.8-billion defense budget that went to Congress today represents an increase of about $3-billion over expected spending for the current fiscal year.

In remarks at the White House, however, Mr. Johnson hinted that even this level of expenditure might prove insufficient.

Top military leaders had sought more than $100-billion, he said. While this total was "cut back to $80-billion we may have to put some of it back," he said.

The President did not mention the Korean crisis in his remarks, made at the swearing in of his new Budget Bureau Director, Charles J. Zwick.

But other officials conceded that defense spending could go substantially higher should North Korea's seizure of the United States intelligence vessel Pueblo lead to new hostilities.

They ascribed the $3-billion

Continued on Page 16, Column 5

A NEW U.S. OFFER OF PEACE TERMS IS SENT TO HANOI

Halt in Air Raids on North and 'Normal' Infiltration by Enemy Are Related

SOME SEE STAND EASED

But Officials Insist Proposal Is Consistent With Johnson Stand in San Antonio

By HEDRICK SMITH
Special to The New York Times

WASHINGTON, Jan. 29—The United States has directly informed North Vietnam that it would be willing to stop bombing North Vietnamese territory and talk peace if Hanoi did not take advantage of this move to raise the infiltration of men and supplies to South Vietnam beyond "normal" levels.

Administration officials said today that there had been no response to this offer, which was transmitted privately to Hanoi through diplomatic channels during the last two weeks.

Though some diplomatic observers viewed the offer as a softening of United States requirements, the State Department insisted that its terms were consistent with the view expressed by President Johnson at San Antonio, Tex., last Sept. 29.

Hanoi Allegation Denied

The Administration officials said that diplomatic probings of Hanoi, which began after the North Vietnamese offered on Dec. 29 to hold talks in return for an "unconditional" cessation of the bombing and "other acts of war," were continuing.

The State Department forcefully denied a North Vietnamese allegation that Washington was ignoring Hanoi's overture. "That is not true and North Vietnam knows it," Robert J. McCloskey, the State Department spokesman, asserted.

Administration officials declined to elaborate on the terms of the latest offer to North Vietnam or to define the level of infiltration that President Johnson would find acceptable.

But they emphasized that Washington would not tolerate either an intensified resupply effort from North to South Vietnam or a halt in the bombing in the face of a major build-up of North Vietnamese forces in the South, such as that said to be going on around Khesanh.

American military officers

Continued on Page 2, Column 5

Vietcong Attack 7 Cities; Allies Call Off Tet Truce

Rockets Destroy 6 U.S. Planes at Danang—Prisoners Freed

By TOM BUCKLEY
Special to The New York Times

SAIGON, South Vietnam, Tuesday, Jan. 30—Vietcong raiders drove into the center of seven major Vietnamese cities early today, burning Government buildings, freeing prisoners from provincial jails and blasting military installations and airfields with rockets and mortars.

The surprise thrusts, which were accompanied by scores of attacks on smaller centers, came only hours after the allied forces canceled their 36-hour cease-fire for the lunar new year in the five northern provinces because of the massive South Vietnamese build-up there. Today was the first day of the new year.

As word of the attacks flooded into American headquarters this morning, the high command abruptly called off the cease-fire for the rest of South Vietnam as well in the name of President Thieu, who was reported not immediately available to sign the proclamation.

[American sources in Saigon said the bombing pause over the heart of North Vietnam was not affected, Reuters reported.]

The heaviest attack took place at Danang, the second largest city in the country and the base area for military operations along the demilitarized zone.

The guerrillas smashed the giant airbase at the southern edge of the city with rockets and mortars, destroying four F-4 Phantoms and two A-6 Intruders on the ground.

Other units fought their way

Continued on Page 3, Column 1

The New York Times Jan. 30, 1968

Truce in South Vietnam was canceled after attacks on major centers (underlined).

U.S. SEES A DELAY IN MOVES TO FREE CREW OF PUEBLO

Reconciled to a 2-to-3-Week Wait for Their Release—Ship May Take Longer

By PETER GROSE
Special to The New York Times

WASHINGTON, Jan. 29—The United States appeared reconciled today to the likelihood that diplomatic efforts to free the 83-man crew of the intelligence ship Pueblo, held by North Korea, would take at least two or three weeks.

American officials indicated that demands for the release of the ship had far lower priority than the freeing of the men.

[At the United Nations, the United States was prepared to discuss all aspects of the Korean issue with North Korea provided the men aboard the Pueblo were not held as hostages during talks. Page 7.]

Military contingency planning continued in a series of announced conferences at the White House and the State Department. But the early impatience voiced in some official quarters for prompt military moves to obtain satisfaction has faded.

Support in Congress

Even on Capitol Hill, where a number of Senators warned that the incident must not be left dangling, there was general support for the Administration's insistence that diplomacy be exhausted before any use of force.

George Christian, the White House press secretary said the United States is making a "prudent and orderly and limited deployment" of American military force in the Korean area. At the same time, a large number of diplomatic channels are "active," he said.

The United States has asked foreign governments to make formal approaches to North Korea and the Soviet Union, building the widest possible diplomatic pressure toward obtaining release of the crew. Since most of the United States allies have no diplomatic relations with Pyongyang, they have been asked to work through Moscow.

One Channel Promised

At least one nonaligned government has promised to convey the United States demands directly to Pyongyang. Administration spokesmen declined to identify the countries that have been asked to intercede.

The International Committee of the Red Cross has been asked to arrange prompt release of the four members of the Pueblo crew who were reported wounded when the ship was seized last Tuesday.

Of immediate concern is the threat by the North Koreans to put the crewmen on trial as "criminals." This threat, made first in a North Korean newspaper last week, was repeated by a spokesman today.

After the first threat, the

Continued on Page 6, Column 1

SANITATION UNION, IN SUDDEN ACTION, MAY STRIKE TODAY

Negotiators Go Into Night Session—Talks Moved to Gracie Mansion

By DAMON STETSON

The city's 10,000 sanitationmen threatened yesterday to go on strike today, causing a flurry of mediation activity aimed at bringing about a quick agreement.

Negotiators for the city and the Uniformed Sanitationmen's Association sought during the night to work out terms of a settlement that would avert a stoppage of refuse collections with consequent fire and health hazards.

Herbert L. Haber, director of the city's Office of Labor Relations, said shortly after 1 A.M. today that the negotiations were being moved from the union's headquarters to Gracie Mansion, where Mayor Lindsay would participate.

"We have been negotiating steadily," Mr. Haber reported, "and we have been unable to resolve some major problems separating us."

Mr. Haber said he had called Mayor Lindsay to recommend that the Mayor talk with the union president, the mediators and himself.

"He agreed," Mr. Haber said, "and we are going to Gracie Mansion to continue negotiations."

Shift Due at 7 A.M.

Mr. Haber declined to answer questions about whether a strike was in progress. He said the next shift was scheduled to start at 7 A.M.

The union's negotiating committee was remaining at union headquarters while the principals conducted the talks at Gracie Mansion, Mr. Haber added.

By 3 A.M. there was no statement from the participants at the Gracie Mansion talks.

The sanitationmen's union, which had not set any deadline previously for achieving an agreement, suddenly announced yesterday that its members would strike today if there was no settlement.

The state's Taylor Law prohibits strikes by public employes, but some unions have threatened strikes in an effort to speed up the collective bargaining process. The sanitationmen have been negotiating since last summer.

Mediators Assist

City officials did not announce immediately any emergency measures of instructions for coping with the problem of uncollected household garbage and refuse if the walkout were to occur. But a press spokesman at the Department of Sanitation said that administrators there were "following the situation very carefully."

John J. DeLury, president of the Uniformed Sanitationmen, and Mr. Haber said in a joint statement yesterday afternoon that two mediators had been

Continued on Page 29, Column 2

HIGH COURT VOIDS 2 GAMBLER CURBS

Says Excise Tax and Yearly Stamp Endanger Right to Avoid Self-Incrimination

By FRED P. GRAHAM
Special to The New York Times

WASHINGTON, Jan. 29—The Supreme Court declared unconstitutional today key provisions of the Federal law that required gamblers to buy a $50 gambling stamp each year and to pay a 10 per cent excise tax on their gross wagers.

In a related decision the Court struck down a section of the National Firearms Act that made it a crime to possess an unregistered sawed-off shotgun, machine gun, or other weapon subject to Federal regulation.

The Court ruled in both cases that the laws violated the Fifth Amendment's privilege against self-incrimination because they required persons to file information with the Government that amounted to confessions of guilt.

Both decisions were by votes of 7 to 1, with Chief Justice Earl Warren dissenting.

He objected that the gambling decision put gamblers in a privileged class by making it impossible for the Government to collect taxes similar to those that legitimate businessmen must pay.

Chief Justice Warren also said that the theory in to-

Continued on Page 25, Column 3

Steel Union Calls Big Rise in Wages Key Goal in Talks

By DAVID R. JONES
Special to The New York Times

WASHINGTON, Jan. 29—The United Steelworkers of America placed major emphasis today on winning "a substantial wage increase" in forthcoming labor negotiations with big aluminum and steel producers.

The union's 163-member wage policy committee gave "priority status" to wage needs in a broad policy statement. The panel set forth a long list of demands, including improved pensions and an expansion of layoff benefits "so that we may reach our goal of a guaranteed annual income."

As justification for its wage and related demands, the committee cited "greatly increased living costs" since the aluminum and steel contracts of 1965 were achieved, sustained economic growth, the profitability of the companies and recent labor agreements in other major industries.

The union's policy statement is traditionally kept vague to give the union leadership maximum flexibility in dealing with the aluminum and steel companies. The specific demands to be made on those two industries will be refined from the broad document at two conferences due to be held around March 21.

I. W. Abel, the union president, declined after to-

Continued on Page 28, Column 2

SKELETONS FOUND AT PRISON FARM

3 Dug Up in Arkansas and Linked to 'Escapees'

By United Press International

CUMMINS PRISON FARM, Ark., Jan. 29—Three human skeletons were found buried in crude wooden coffins today on the Cummins State Prison Farm, where scores of convicts have disappeared, classed as "escapees," over the last 60 years.

State officials said that the coffins had been found by convicts digging to build a pigpen in an outlying area of the 15,000-acre farm, about 75 miles southeast of Little Rock.

One of the skeletons was headless and the legs of another had been crushed, apparently to get the bodies into the coffins, the officials said.

The discovery was announced by a spokesman for the state prison superintendent, Thomas O. Murton, a former criminology professor brought in by Gov. Winthrop Rockefeller to investigate conditions at the prison.

Mr. Murton expressed little concern earlier today over reports that convicts were buried on the grounds of the prison farm, but three hours later his secretary announced the discovery of the skeletons.

Cummins, headquarters of the state prison system in Arkansas, and the Tucker Prison Farm, its companion institution,

Continued on Page 30, Column 2

Spock, Coffin and Three Others Arraigned on Charge of Conspiring to Aid Draft Evaders

By JOHN H. FENTON
Special to The New York Times

BOSTON, Jan. 29—Dr. Benjamin Spock, the author and pediatrician, and the Rev. William Sloane Coffin Jr., chaplain of Yale University, were arraigned today in Federal District Court with three other defendants on a charge of conspiring to help young men evade the draft laws.

Judge Francis J. W. Ford released the five in $1,000 bond each without surety—the equivalent of personal recognizance—and granted the Government and the defendants a total of 50 days in which to file special motions. A trial date will be scheduled sometime after that.

Specifically, the five defendants were charged with conspiring to counsel, aid and abet those who wish to refuse to serve in the armed forces and comply with other duties required by the draft law. The maximum penalty on conviction is five years in prison and

Continued on Page 4, Column 3

United Press International

Four of the five defendants who appeared before the Federal District Court yesterday in Boston, singing at a teach-in held later in Arlington Street Church. From the left they are Mitchell Goodman, of New York; Michael Ferber, of Buffalo; the Rev. William Sloane Coffin Jr., of Yale, and Dr. Benjamin Spock, accompanied by his wife.

Two on IRT Seized Terrorizing Riders

By MARTIN GANSBERG

Two unshaven youths wearing leather jackets boarded a crowded Lexington Avenue IRT car at 14th Street yesterday morning and swinging heavy bicycle chains and brandishing knives, threatened to "take over."

Rush-hour passengers cowered and tried to escape to other cars, but within a minute the two youths were seized by Transit Authority detectives who had followed them.

Pushing their way through frightened standees, the detectives cornered the youths and captured them at gunpoint.

The detectives, part of a special squad assigned to the mid-

Continued on Page 51, Column 1

LINDSAY ATTACKS MARSHAL SYSTEM

Attorneys Told Ending Jobs Would Save City $750,000

By RICHARD REEVES

Mayor Lindsay called last night for the abolition of the 312-year-old city marshal system and said the city would make an annual profit of $750,000 if the marshals' duties were transferred to the city Sheriff's office.

"Almost every form of avarice and bullying can be found someplace in the history of marshals," Mr. Lindsay told 200 members of the Association of the Bar of the City of New York. "Let's abolish this embarrassment to our court structure."

The Mayor said he would have bills introduced in the Legislature today to abolish the jobs of the 79 marshals and transfer the responsibility for service and execution of Civil Court papers to Sheriff John J. McCloskey.

In his speech, Mr. Lindsay cited Department of Investigation records showing that six

Continued on Page 82, Column 3

NEWS INDEX

"All the News That's Fit to Print"

The New York Times

LATE CITY EDITION

Weather: Fair, mild today and tonight; becoming cloudy tomorrow. Temp. range: today 50-39; Tuesday 42-36. Full U.S. report on Page 82.

VOL. CXVII..No. 40,184 NEW YORK, WEDNESDAY, JANUARY 31, 1968 10 CENTS

FOE INVADES U.S. SAIGON EMBASSY; RAIDERS WIPED OUT AFTER 6 HOURS; VIETCONG WIDEN ATTACK ON CITIES

United Press International

Helicopter carrying blood to a military aid station lands in downtown Saigon in the midst of a sniper attack

NATION IS WARNED UNREST IN CITIES IMPERILS SYSTEM

Advisory Unit Calls Failure to Solve Issue Greatest Threat Since Civil War

AUTHORS 'PESSIMISTIC'

Report Says Abdication at Lower Levels Challenges Federal Political Setup

Excerpts from commission report are on Page 18.

By BEN A. FRANKLIN
Special to The New York Times

WASHINGTON, Jan. 30—The failure of government to prevent rioting, despair and "threatened anarchy" in the nation's large cities has brought the Federal system to the brink of its greatest crisis since the Civil War, a Government study commission declared today.

In a report its authors characterized as "pessimistic," the Advisory Commission on Intergovernmental Relations said the historic American system of plural government—local, state and national—was in danger.

The abdication or inability of the states, of city government, and of the Federal Government, singly or jointly, to hold back the deterioration of urban life, the commission said, raises the prospect of pervasive Federal dominance in the name of security.

14-Page Preamble

In a strongly worded 14-page preamble to its ninth annual report to the President and Congress, the commission warned that Federal authority over governmental responsibilities that had traditionally been those of states, counties and cities might be—might have to be—greatly expanded to maintain law and order. It said many cities were "seething" with racial and class revolt and that many were near public bankruptcy.

"The manner of meeting these challenges," the commission declared, "will largely determine the fate of the American political system; it will determine if we can maintain a form of government marked by partnership and wholesome competition among national, state and local levels, or if instead—in the face of threatened anarchy—we must sacrifice political diversity as the price of the authoritative action required for the nation's survival."

The commission is not confident the sacrifice can be avoided. Its report virtually acknowledged that some cities

Continued on Page 18, Column 7

State Senate Votes to End Ban on Church-School Aid

Repeal Backed 35 to 17

By THOMAS P. RONAN
Special to The New York Times

ALBANY, Jan. 30—After a two-and-a-half-hour debate, the State Senate voted 35 to 17 today to repeal the state's constitutional ban on state aid to church-related schools.

Twenty-six Republicans and nine Democrats voted for repeal. Fifteen Democrats and two Republicans voted against it. Four members were absent and the 57th seat in the Senate is vacant.

Before the repeal can become effective, it must be approved by the Assembly at this session, by both houses at the next legislative session and by the voters in a statewide referendum, which could not be held before November, 1969.

There is some doubt whether the bill calling for repeal will be approved by the Assembly this year. The Assembly Speaker, Anthony J. Travia, said recently that while he still favored repeal he opposed taking action on it during the present session.

Mr. Travia said he thought that the issue "should be studied a little better" and considered for action at a future session.

This morning he told news-

Continued on Page 44, Column 1

Aid to All Colleges Urged

By M. A. FARBER

A special committee appointed by Governor Rockefeller has recommended that private colleges and universities, including many with religious affiliations, be given direct state financial support for general use.

The panel, headed by McGeorge Bundy, president of the

Excerpts from Bundy report are printed on Page 44.

Ford Foundation, proposed an annual program of assistance providing the state's 143 independent institutions of higher learning with about $33-million in 1970.

"We see the need as critical," the committee said. For many institutions, it added, the funds "would represent the margin of difference between gradual decline and continuing improvement."

"It is small price to pay for the continued vigorous health of private higher education in New York State," the panel said.

Although the committee opposed public assistance to institutions "whose central purpose is the teaching of religious

Continued on Page 44, Column 5

PRESIDENT URGES WIDER PROGRAM TO AID VETERANS

Congress Asked to Provide Incentive Pay for Those Joining Public Service

By MAX FRANKEL
Special to The New York Times

WASHINGTON, Jan. 30—President Johnson advised Congress today that he had earmarked $50-million in his new budget for incentive payments to veterans who agree to take special public service jobs.

This was one of several benefits he suggested adding to the nation's veterans programs.

The money would be used to supplement the salaries or Government training grants of veterans who volunteer to help teach the children of the poor, to man understrength police forces and fire brigades, to join the staffs of undermanned hospitals or to be enrolled in various new job-training and antipoverty programs.

Mr. Johnson proposed the new program in a special message to Congress urging legislative action and announcing administrative steps for veterans. Most of his other recommendations are relatively low-cost improvements of services rather than payments to veterans.

Pattern of Benefits

The pattern of benefits in the public service program would vary, the President said, depending on the individual and the occupation he pursues.

A veteran might get $50 extra a month for schooling, Mr. Johnson explained, for every month he agrees to teach, and once on the job, he might be given a gradually declining series of training allowances. Or, he added, he might be given extra benefits under the G. I. bill for graduate school.

The President said he expected the veteran population of 26 million to grow by more than 70,000 new veterans each month in the coming year. He asked for expenditures of $7.1-billion for all veterans benefits and services in the fiscal year starting July 1, an increase of $300-million over estimated spending in the current year.

Besides passage of the Veterans in the Public Service Act, Mr. Johnson asked Congress for several other adjustments.

Request Revived

He revived his year-old request for higher group life insurance policies, from a current maximum of $10,000 to some as high as $30,000, and for regulations to keep veterans from losing certain pension benefits if their private income should increase.

The President proposed raising the Government's maximum guarantee on G.I. home loans from $7,500 to $10,000 and proposed training allowances for disabled veterans in part-time as well as full-time rehabilitation programs.

By administrative action, Mr. Johnson announced the following new services to veterans:

¶The hiring of veterans on a priority basis and without examination for the first five levels of the Civil Service, which pay a maximum of about $5,000 a year, provided the

Continued on Page 10, Column 5

Precinct Mergers to Free Policemen for Street Duty

By RICHARD E. MOONEY

The city's 79 police precincts will be merged into 55 in the next four years, freeing "hundreds" of deskbound policemen for street duty, Mayor Lindsay announced yesterday.

The consolidation is part of what the Mayor called "the largest police construction program ever undertaken anywhere in the nation"—a program that demonstrates "our full commitment to the war on crime."

The city will spend $97-million during the coming four years on the construction of 31 new precinct houses, renovation of five old ones, building the new 15-story police headquarters in the civic center north of City Hall, and completing the department's computerized communications network.

Program Accelerated

These are not new projects, but all are being accelerated to get the whole job done three years sooner than had been planned.

Mr. Lindsay's announcement was an official sneak preview of his annual capital budget message, due tomorrow. The preview served to highlight the "crime in the streets" issue, and the Mayor's attention to it.

Police Commissioner Howard R. Leary, in a companion statement to the Mayor's, said that the present precinct arrangement, unchanged in more than 65 years, "is extremely outdated."

Viewing the precinct structure in terms of fighting crime, he said that with modern communications, patrol cars and scooters "the distance from a precinct house no longer influences the effectiveness of protection on the street."

Chicago and Washington have

Continued on Page 45, Column 1

STATE UNIVERSITY SETS DRUG CURBS

Gould Issues New Controls in Reaction to Raid on Stony Brook Campus

By SYDNEY H. SCHANBERG
Special to The New York Times

ALBANY, Jan. 30—The chancellor of the State University announced stringent new regulations tonight for all campuses of the university, forbidding the illegal use of drugs and barring any "sanctuary for those who violate state and Federal narcotics laws."

The chancellor, Dr. Samuel B. Gould, issued the new rules for the 60-unit university in reaction to the "deeply disturbing" situation at the Stony Brook campus on Long Island.

Two weeks ago, the Suffolk County police, in a 5 A.M. raid, arrested 33 persons—eight of them nonstudents—in the Stony Brook dormitories and houses in the area. The police charged that university officials had refused to cooperate with them.

One of the new regulations issued by Dr. Gould, who just returned from an Arizona vacation, called for university and police action against outsiders and loiterers who have no "legitimate reason" for be-

Continued on Page 45, Column 4

4TH SUPERAGENCY VOTED BY COUNCIL

Reorganization Advanced by Approval of Finance Unit

By RICHARD REEVES

Leaders of the City Council, which had previously approved three of Mayor Lindsay's 10 proposed superagencies in 14 months, said yesterday that they could complete final approval of the Mayor's reorganization program in the next two months.

The proposed revamping of 51 agencies into 10 administrations advanced yesterday when the Council unanimously approved another of the superagencies—the Finance Administration.

At the same time the Democratic leadership introduced legislation modifying the reorganization by creating a new Department of Consumer Affairs combining the Departments of Licenses and Markets.

The new department, which Mr. Lindsay is not expected to oppose, would represent the most important modification of the program made by the Council. Under the original Lindsay plan, the Markets and Licenses

Continued on Page 45, Column 2

Lawyer Sues Over Wedding Photos

By RONALD SULLIVAN
Special to The New York Times

TRENTON, Jan. 30—A lawyer is suing the photographer at his wedding, saying that pictures of his bride were "so grotesque and repulsive" that they got him in trouble with in-laws and hurt his practice.

The lawyer, William L. Boyan, assistant Mercer County prosecutor, said that the pictures taken by the Pro-Photo Service Company were so bad that "neither they nor a story about the wedding could be submitted to any newspaper."

Mr. Boyan said in his suit in Superior Court that the lack of publicity "had diminished his income" and that the career of his wife, Tia, a model, had also suffered.

He emphasized that he was prevented from normal advertising by the canons of professional ethics.

In addition, Mr. Boyan said that he had to pay to take the entire wedding party—the best man, the matron of honor and the soloist who sang at the ceremony two years ago in Toms River—on a $2,000 trip to the Netherlands "for the purpose of assuaging the bride's family."

He said his in-laws in the Netherlands were upset and disappointed because they did not receive the wedding pictures he had promised them, making the trip necessary.

"Because there were no acceptable photographs," he said "the relationships between the plaintiff and the bride on one hand and the bride's family on the other became somewhat strained."

In his breach-of-contract complaint, Mr. Boyan, a former deputy state attorney general, also said that the photographer had failed to take candid shots of attending dignitaries.

These included: Superior Court Judge David A. Furman; Brig. Gen. Chester Charles of the New Jersey National Guard; Miss June Strelecki, director of the division of motor vehicles in the State Department of Law and Safety; Floyd Hoffman, who was then director of the Office of Milk Industry in the State Department of Agriculture, and William Druz, assistant chief examiner of state civil service.

Mr. Boyan said that he filed the suit early this month after hearing that he was going to be sued for the $150 photography bill.

EGYPT AND ISRAEL IN CLASH AT CANAL

2 Hours of Shelling Follow Cairo Effort to Send Boat North on Clearance Job

By JAMES FERON
Special to The New York Times

JERUSALEM, Jan. 30—Israeli and Egyptian forces exchanged artillery fire across the Suez Canal today in a dispute over the clearance project that began Saturday for the release of 15 vessels trapped in the waterway since June.

The shooting started in the Ismailia area, at the center of the 105-mile-long canal, and later spread northward to Qantara and southward to Great Bitter Lake.

United Nations observers who patrol both banks of the canal restored the much-broken cease-fire about two hours after the shooting started. Sporadic fire was heard during the afternoon, but all was quiet by nightfall.

[A spokesman for the Suez Canal Authority said in Ismailia that the effort to free the vessels would be suspended indefinitely. Page 16.]

The Israelis said that five of their soldiers were wounded in the exchange but that they had

Continued on Page 16, Column 1

Rockefeller's Aides Plan Write-in Drive In Oregon Primary

By WARREN WEAVER Jr.
Special to The New York Times

LOS ANGELES, Jan. 30 — Governor Rockefeller's Presidential supporters, working with his knowledge, are planning an intensive write-in campaign for the Oregon primary next May designed to move him into contention for the Republican nomination.

These backers are also preparing a position from which the New York Governor could follow up this bid in the California primary in June if circumstances then seemed to warrant a bold challenge to Gov. Ronald Reagan in his home state.

This strategy is designed to resolve the current Rockefeller dilemma by permitting the Governor to remain publicly loyal to Gov. George Romney through two or three early primary tests without excluding himself from competing personally in a fourth and conceivably a fifth.

These plans assume that Mr. Romney will [illegible] the nation's earliest primary in New Hamp

Continued on Page 22, Column 7

U.S. Aide in Embassy Villa Kills Guerrilla With Pistol

By CHARLES MOHR
Special to The New York Times

SAIGON, South Vietnam, Wednesday, Jan. 31—The Vietcong terrorist attack on the United States Embassy ended this morning with a gun battle between an embassy official and a guerrilla on a staircase.

Col. George Jacobson, retired, who holds the title of United States Mission Coordinator, had been trapped in his white stucco villa in a corner of the spacious embassy grounds throughout the fierce fighting, which raged in the compound from about 3 A.M. until 9 A.M. today.

Using a .45-caliber automatic pistol that had been tossed to his second-story window by an American military policeman, Colonel Jacobson turned and killed a wounded Vietcong rifleman stumbling up the stairs to get away from tear gas fumes filling the ground floor.

"I was very lucky," said Colonel Jacobson. "He got in the first shots and shot three times but missed. I didn't do much because the military police and Marine guards had already crippled him and he couldn't shoot straight."

7 Americans Killed

At least five American military policemen and two United States Marine guards were killed in a wild night that saw the Vietcong terror squad overrun and then hold a section of the embassy grounds against initial attempts by rescue forces to fight their way in.

Bodies of Vietcong littered the grass and graveled terrace around the modernistic eight-story chancery building.

An initial count by military policemen said that there were 17 bodies of Vietcong after the fight ended.

In one of the strangest scenes of the Vietnam war, helmeted American troops ran crouching across broad Thong Nhut Boulevard to assault the gate of their own embassy at dawn today.

Seven American helicopters landed on the roof to discharge a platoon of American paratroops who raced down the stairways to come to the aid of Marine guards fighting to keep the enemy out of the main chancery building.

Meanwhile, the rattle of gunfire and explosions could be heard from the area of the nearby Independence Palace and numerous other parts of Saigon

Continued on Page 2, Column 5

NEWS INDEX

JOHNSON RECEIVES FLOW OF REPORTS

He Meets With Advisers on Saigon Raid, Viewed as New Step-Up in War

Special to The New York Times

WASHINGTON, Jan. 30—The bold Vietcong commando raid on the United States Embassy in Saigon, viewed here as part of a well-planned intensification of the war by enemy forces, took the Administration by surprise.

But officials asserted that despite reports to the contrary from Saigon, the Vietcong had not seized the embassy building proper, and expressed relief that it had been held.

Some officials termed the embassy raid and the attacks on seven South Vietnamese provincial capitals, American air fields and scores of other Vietcong's single biggest coordinated terrorist offensive in the war, apparently designed for shock effect. They said they expected more of the same.

25 Reports Go to President

Tonight more than 25 reports were sent to President Johnson in a steady stream to keep him continuously informed on the progress of the battle in the embassy compound in Saigon.

The first word of the attack reached Washington about 4 P.M., minutes after the attack began at 3 A.M. Wednesday, Saigon time. The all-clear report came by telephone from the embassy from Gen. William C. Westmoreland, the United States commander in South Vietnam.

During the attack, the President met for about an hour with his principal national security advisers—Secretary of State Dean Rusk, Secretary of Defense Robert S. McNamara, Secretary of Defense-designate Clark M. Clifford, Gen. Earle G. Wheeler, who is chairman of the Joint Chiefs of Staff, and Walt W. Rostow, special assistant for National Security Affairs.

The President also had briefings for the Republican leaders, Senator Everett McKinley Dirksen and Representative Gerald R. Ford, on the situation at the embassy and on efforts to get North Korea to release the

Continued on Page 2, Column 4

AMBASSADOR SAFE

Guerrillas Also Strike Presidential Palace and Many Bases

By TOM BUCKLEY
Special to The New York Times

SAIGON, South Vietnam, Wednesday, Jan. 31—A 17-man Vietcong squad seized parts of the United States Embassy in the center of Saigon and held them for six hours early today.

The Vietcong, wearing South Vietnamese Army uniforms, held off American military policemen firing machine guns and rocket launchers. Finally the invaders were routed by squads of American paratroopers who landed by helicopter on the roof of the building.

[Ambassador Ellsworth Bunker was taken from his residence about five blocks from the embassy to what was described as a secure area, The Associated Press reported. He returned to the embassy at 11 A.M., about two hours after the last enemy resistance was wiped out. Others of the embassy staff were also said to be safe. The American flag was raised in front of the embassy at 11:45 A.M., almost five hours later than normal.]

The daring raid was the most dramatic of scores of attacks launched by enemy commando units that carried the Vietcong's Lunar New Year offensive to the capital.

Fighting was continuing in Saigon at 2 P.M. local time (1 A.M., New York time.) A Vietcong squad, armed with a captured American machine gun and rocket launchers, was firing from among the concrete

Continued on Page 3, Column 1

A Pueblo Crewman Is Dead, U.S. Is Told

By HEDRICK SMITH
Special to The New York Times

WASHINGTON, Jan. 30—The Defense Department said tonight that it had received word that one crew member of the intelligence ship Pueblo, captured eight days ago by North Korea, had died.

The statement was issued by the Pentagon a few hours after the White House said that the United States had been informed that the 83-man crew of the Pueblo was being "properly treated" and given necessary medical aid.

At the United Nations, the Hungarian delegation, apparently in touch with North Korea, reported to other members of the Security Council that one crew member had died and the

Continued on Page 5, Column 3

"All the News That's Fit to Print"

The New York Times

LATE CITY EDITION

Weather: Rain, mild temperatures today, tonight. Showers tomorrow. Temp. range: today 42-35. Thurs. 36-32. Full U. S. report on Page 70.

VOL. CXVII . . . No. 40,186 © 1968 The New York Times Company. NEW YORK, FRIDAY, FEBRUARY 2, 1968 — 10 CENTS

PRESIDENT ASKS PAY-PRICE CURBS AND RISE IN TAX

INFLATION FEARED

Economic Report Says Failure to Act Risks a 'Feverish Boom'

Text of Johnson's Economic Report, Pages 20 and 21.

By EDWIN L. DALE Jr.
Special to The New York Times

WASHINGTON, Feb. 1—The Johnson Administration asserted today that there would be "no prospect" of slowing the pace of inflation this year unless negotiated union wage settlements were "appreciably lower" than the average 5.5 per cent increase last year.

The warning came in the Annual Report of the Council of Economic Advisers, which accompanied the Economic Report of the President, transmitted to Congress today. President Johnson, in his report, said:

"I must again urge—in the strongest terms I know—that unions and business firms exercise the most rigorous restraint in their wage and price determinations in 1968."

Speedy Action Urged

Apart from the appeal for restraint, and the 5.5 per cent bench mark for wage increases, the main thrust of both reports was an urgent further request for the Administration's proposed 10 per cent surcharge on income taxes.

Asking action on the bill "in the next few weeks," the President said:

"We must choose whether we will conduct our fiscal affairs sensibly; or whether we will allow a clearly excessive budgetary deficit to go uncorrected by failing to raise taxes, and thereby risk a feverish boom that could generate an unacceptable acceleration of price increases, a possible financial crisis, and perhaps ultimately a recession."

In discussing the outlook for

Continued on Page 19, Column 2

Associated Press
Richard M. Nixon in official campaign photograph.

NIXON ANNOUNCES FOR PRESIDENCY

Discloses Plans in a Letter to New Hampshire Voters —Opens Drive Today

By ROBERT B. SEMPLE Jr.

Richard M. Nixon formally announced yesterday, as expected, that he was a candidate for the Republican Presidential nomination.

The announcement, which Mr. Nixon had presaged by his energetic preliminary campaigning in the last few months, was in the form of a letter to the voters of New Hampshire.

Copies of the letter were handed to newsmen at Nixon campaign headquarters at 521 Fifth Avenue at about the same time that others were reaching the mailboxes of 150,000 New Hampshire homes—85 per cent of the state's households, Nixon aides said.

The New Hampshire primary, the first of a series of Presidential trial heats, will be held March 12. The former Vice President will begin his campaign with a news conference in Manchester today.

'Special Responsibility'

The letter, composed by Mr Nixon himself, told New Hampshire voters of their "special responsibility" as participants in the first Presidential primary in the nation.

Explaining why he had decided to become a candidate, Mr. Nixon suggested that his 14 years as a member of Congress and as Vice President and his eight years as a private citizen since then had given him the experience and the perspective necessary to provide the "new leadership" he said the nation required.

Mr. Nixon—who lost the Presidency to John F. Kennedy by a narrow margin in 1960—declared:

"Peace and freedom in the world, and peace and progress

Continued on Page 9, Column 1

HOUSE, 382-4, VOTES HELP TO CONSUMER

'Truth-in-Lending' Measure Now Goes to Conferees

By JOHN D. MORRIS
Special to The New York Times

WASHINGTON, Feb. 1—The House passed today a comprehensive "truth-in-lending" bill designed to give consumers full and clear information on how much they pay in interest and other finance charges on loans and credit purchases.

The bill, which its supporters call an unusually strong consumer protection measure, was approved on a roll-call vote of 382 to 4.

The Senate unanimously passed a less comprehensive bill last year. A Senate-House conference committee will try to work out a compromise version.

President Johnson issued a statement praising the House for bringing "every American consumer another step closer to knowing the cost of the money he borrows."

"I urge the House and Senate to resolve their differences promptly and to give the American consumer a strong truth-in-lending bill," he added. "I hope this will be the first of many measures that will mark this Congress as the consumers' Congress."

The four votes against the bill today were cast by Representatives Thomas G. Abernethy and G. V. Montgomery, Democrats of Mississippi; Robert G. Stephens Jr., Democrat

Continued on Page 19, Column 1

I LOVE YOU SANDY—Sl.
—Advt.

Bond Issue Sought To Clean State Air

By PETER KIHSS

New York City's Air Pollution Control Commissioner called yesterday for a $1-billion state bond issue to pay for new clean-air facilities, including incinerators to burn refuse for heat and power.

The Commissioner, Austin N. Heller, said this would follow the precedent set by the state's $1-billion clean-water program. The water bond issue was approved by the Legislature and Governor Rockefeller and then by the voters in 1965 to pay for construction of sewage treatment and other water purification systems throughout the state.

Mr. Heiler's proposal was

Continued on Page 18, Column 3

LINDSAY REDUCES OUTLAY OF FUNDS FOR NEW SCHOOLS

Cites Unused Backlog as He Submits a 'Tight' Capital Budget of $996-Million

Excerpts from capital budget appear on Page 22.

By RICHARD E. MOONEY

Mayor Lindsay submitted a $996-million capital budget yesterday for the coming fiscal year—slightly reduced from the current year's record total, but sharply reduced in the sensitive area of schools.

"This is a tight budget," the Mayor said, adding that he had decided to keep it well under the legal limit for city borrowing. It is also "a realistic budget," he said, because it does not include funds for projects that are not moving fast enough to need money next year, such as school construction.

The cut in school funds brought an immediate charge from Alfred A. Giardino, president of the Board of Education, that the Mayor was recommending "retrogressive education."

Counteroffer by Mayor

The Mayor countered with an offer to set up a school construction task force to expedite school construction, and a pledge that there will be funds for every school project that is ready for them.

The new budget covers city spending for construction and other capital projects—new subway cars and buses, hospital renovation, and the like—in the fiscal year 1968-69, starting next July 1. The city's current operating expenses, which will run close to six times as large, will be covered in a separate message two months from now.

The Board of Estimate and the City Council, both controlled by Democrats, have until mid-March to act on the capital budget. They usually add a little to it.

Few New Programs

Thereafter the Mayor has two weeks to veto changes he does not like, and the Board and the Council then have two more weeks to override him if they can muster a two-thirds majority in each body.

One striking feature of yesterday's message was the almost total absence of new programs. There was only one, to subsidize vest-pocket industrial sites for factories that threaten to leave the city.

In the major categories, there was an eight-fold increase to

Continued on Page 22, Column 1

M'NAMARA SAYS SOVIET DOUBLED ITS ICBM'S IN '67

But Secretary, in Farewell Report, Tells Congress U.S. Force Is Bigger

Excerpts from the McNamara report are on Page 16.

By WILLIAM BEECHER
Special to The New York Times

WASHINGTON, Feb. 1—The Soviet Union took a giant step toward closing the nuclear missile gap last year by more than doubling its force of intercontinental ballistic missiles, Defense Secretary Robert S. McNamara disclosed today.

But the outgoing defense chief indicated he did not regard the development as particularly ominous. Each nation, he said, now possesses strategic forces capable of withstanding a surprise attack and retaliating overwhelmingly against the other.

Making it clear that he believed a nuclear stalemate had been achieved between the two superpowers, he declared:

"It is precisely this mutual capability to destroy one another, and conversely, our respective inability to prevent such destruction, that provides us both with the strongest possible motive to avoid a strategic nuclear war."

A Valedictory Message

In a voluminous farewell report to a joint session of the Senate Armed Services Committee and the Defense Appropriations subcommittee, a 220-page unclassified version of which was made public, Mr. McNamara delivered what amounted to a valedictory message covering his seven years as Defense Secretary.

Clark M. Clifford, whose nomination to succeed Mr. McNamara was approved by the Senate earlier this week, is expected to take over by the end of this month.

Senator John Stennis, Democrat of Mississippi, expressed concern as he emerged from the hearing at the scope of the Soviet strategic buildup and the American response. "I am not nearly as optimistic as the Secretary that the [defense] budget is adequate to meet all our needs," he said.

Noting a growing sense of disillusionment and war-weariness on the part of the American public, Mr. McNamara warned against the temptation to renounce growing burdens around the world in favor of a neo-isolationist "fortress America."

Such a move, he insisted,

Continued on Page 16, Column 4

CITY U. WILL BUILD IN BROOKLYN SLUM

Community College to Rise in Bedford-Stuyvesant

By M. A. FARBER

The City University will build its next community college in Bedford-Stuyvesant, a predominantly Negro and Puerto Rican section of Brooklyn.

It will be the first of the university's seven two-year institutions to be placed in a slum neighborhood and will be particularly designed for "equalizing educational opportunities" for minority-group youths.

In announcing the decision yesterday, the Board of Higher Education said the college would experiment with liberalized admissions policies and increased community service programs.

Dr. Albert H. Bowker, the university's chancellor, also disclosed that he would recommend a Southeast Bronx site for an eighth two-year institution in the municipal system.

The Bronx site, Dr. Bowker said, is in the neighborhood of the new Lincoln Hospital, which is to be bounded by Park and Morris Avenues and 144th and 149th Streets. This college would be modeled after the one planned for Bedford-Stuyvesant.

Like the central Brooklyn in-

Continued on Page 32, Column 1

WESTERNER GETS CITY HEALTH POST

Dr. Bucove of Washington Will Succeed Dr. Brown

By MARTIN TOLCHIN

A public health physician who advocates decentralization of the city's health services was named yesterday to head the Health Service Administration.

Mayor Lindsay announced the appointment of Dr. Bernard Bucove, director of health for the State of Washington, to the $37,500-a-year post. The 55-year-old physician will receive $2,500 a year more than Dr. Howard J. Brown, who resigned last December after 17 stormy months as the city's chief health officer.

In an interview from his Olympia, Wash., office, Dr. Bucove asked:

"Are you amazed that somebody finally took the job?"

The physician said he agreed with a recommendation to create a public corporation to operate the city's health facilities, thereby freeing the facilities from municipal red-tape. The recommendation was made by a committee led by Gerard Piel, publisher of Scientific American magazine.

"I would hope to be able to implement the major part of

Continued on Page 32, Column 4

STREET CLASHES GO ON IN VIETNAM, FOE STILL HOLDS PARTS OF CITIES; JOHNSON PLEDGES NEVER TO YIELD

GUERRILLA DIES: Brig. Gen. Nguyen Ngoc Loan, national police chief, executes man identified as a Vietcong terrorist in Saigon. Man wore civilian dress and had a pistol. A picture sequence of the execution is on Page 12.

Associated Press
HIS FAMILY SLAIN BY VIETCONG: A South Vietnamese officer carries the body of one of his children from his home. Terrorists overran the base of his unit in Saigon, beheaded an officer and killed women and children.

A RESOLUTE STAND

President Won't Halt Bombing—Predicts Khesanh Victory

By MAX FRANKEL
Special to The New York Times

WASHINGTON, Feb. 1—President Johnson responded today to the new enemy challenges in South Vietnam with a vow that "the enemy will fail again and again" because "we Americans will never yield."

The enemy in South Vietnam has been met and matched, he said, and will be thrown back in the hills around Khesanh.

The enemy in North Vietnam will continue to be bombed "with a very precise restraint," he said, until there are "some better signs than what these last few days have provided" that he will not step up his terrorism or accelerate his aggression.

Mr. Johnson seized upon a previously scheduled ceremony of honor for an Air Force officer to give a reaction to the assaults on dozens of American installations in South Vietnam this week and to the major enemy build-up around Khesanh.

"Let those who would stop the bombing," he said, "answer this question: What would the North Vietnamese be doing if we stopped the bombing and let them alone?

"The answer, I think, is clear. The enemy force in the South would be larger. It would be better equipped. The war would

Continued on Page 13, Column 1

A.C.L.U. Bars Help To Draft Resisters

By JOHN LEO

The American Civil Liberties Union said yesterday it would not defend individuals who refuse to register for military service as a protest against war or the draft.

In a formal statement on civil disobedience, the union said: "We have assumed that the [draft] laws are constitutional, regardless of how unwise or unjust they may be from the viewpoint of the individual who violates them."

The A.C.L.U. thus opposes four of its own largest affiliates. The Civil Liberties Unions of New York, Southern California, Massachusetts and New Jersey do not consider the

Continued on Page 3, Column 6

Hanoi Says Aim of Raids Is to Oust Saigon Regime

Special to The New York Times

HONG KONG, Friday, Feb. 2—The Hanoi radio declared today that the latest attacks by the Vietcong were part of a general offensive aimed at overthrowing the Saigon Government.

The radio, monitored here, broadcast an appeal by the Vietcong to the people of South Vietnam to aid "in attacking and tracking down the U.S. and puppet forces and in capturing all their agents."

"Compatriots," the broadcast said, "the long-awaited general offensive against the Thieu-Ky puppet administration has come. The revolutionary armed forces, representing the will of the entire people, have opened fire at our archenemy.

"We would like to tell our compatriots that we are determined to overthrow the Thieu-Ky puppet administration."

The radio said the aim of the Vietcong struggle was to "win independence for the nation, peace for our country and democracy and happiness for the people" and to build a political power "entirely for the fatherland and the people."

The appeal was issued in the name of the South Vietnam Revolutionary Armed Forces Command.

A representative of the Vietcong's political arm, the National Liberation Front, said in Hanoi yesterday that the Vietcong had staged the "most all-out and widespread attacks ever known."

The representative, Nguyen Phu Xoai, said at a news conference reported by the Hanoi radio that in some places, such

Continued on Page 12, Column 8

ENEMY TOLL SOARS

Offensive Is Running 'Out of Steam,' Says Westmoreland

By CHARLES MOHR
Special to The New York Times

SAIGON, South Vietnam, Friday, Feb. 2—Vicious street fighting continued today in many South Vietnamese towns and cities, and the Vietcong attacked three more province capitals.

The United States military commander, Gen. William C. Westmoreland, said yesterday that there was some evidence that the enemy's general offensive ...s "about to run out of steam," but he also conceded that the enemy had the capability to continue "this phase of their campaign for several more days."

[The United States command announced that 10,593 enemy soldiers had been killed since 6 P.M. Monday—by far the heaviest losses ever inflicted by the allies in Vietnam, United Press International reported. American losses were put at 281 killed and 1,195 wounded and South Vietnamese losses at 632 killed and 1,588 wounded.]

Some Question Totals

The assertion today that more than 10,000 of the enemy had died in the outbreaks was viewed with reserve by some observers. One, a press release, said that in a fight near Pleiku in the central highlands, 208 of the enemy were killed and one Vietnamese militiaman wounded.

Since Monday, the Vietcong have attacked 26 of the country's 44 province capitals, penetrating some of them deeply.

New attacks were reported yesterday and today on the towns of Baria, Muchoa and Phucuong, all province capitals. Other important cities, such as Danang, have also been attacked in the Vietcong drive.

Five battalions of Vietcong and North Vietnamese troops were still fighting heavily within the walls of the ancient

Continued on Page 12, Column 1

Vietcong's Attacks Shock Washington

By TOM WICKER
Special to The New York Times

WASHINGTON, Feb. 1 — Widespread Vietcong attacks on cities throughout South Vietnam dealt this city a hard blow, too.

From the State Department to Capitol Hill and the Pentagon, the well-coordinated and tenacious attacks were under discussion. They were recognized as costly but also as what Senator John Stennis, Democrat of Mississippi, called them—"embarrassing" and "humiliating" to the Johnson Administration and the South Vietnamese Government.

Doves tended to believe that their criticism of the war was

Continued on Page 12, Column 7

NEWS INDEX

Heavy fighting continued in Saigon and its suburbs despite the monsoon season with its drenching rains and strong winds.
United Press International

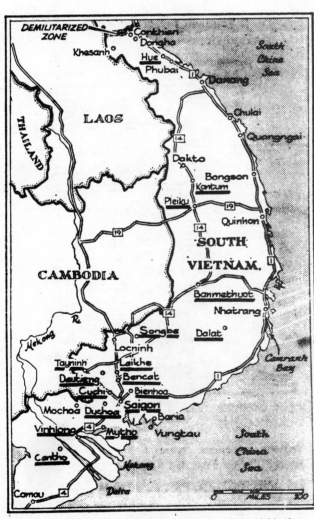

While the controversies raged in the United Nations as to who was right or wrong in the Vietnam conflict, the Tet Offensive raged on and both sides paid no attention to diplomatic efforts to ease the hostilities. This map documents North Vietnam's continued drive. Underlining marks battle areas.

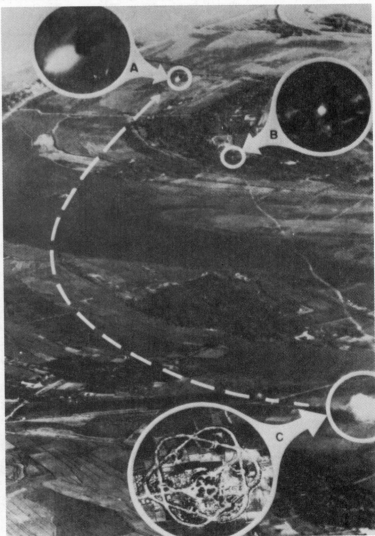

Deadly surface-to-air-missiles (SAM) were used by the Communists in the late Sixties in Vietnam. This U.S. Air Force reconnaissance photo shows two SAMs fired at an Air Force plane. Insert A shows one of the missiles in normal flight and its path from its launch pad (Insert C). The second missile had developed trouble as shown by its erratic flight path marked with smoke. Insert B shows an enlargement of the missile's exhaust seconds before it exploded near Hanoi.

"All the News That's Fit to Print"

The New York Times

LATE CITY EDITION

Weather: Sunny and windy today. Clear and seasonable tomorrow. Temp. range: today 45-34: Friday 48-35. Full U.S. report on Page 58.

VOL. CXVII..No. 40,187 NEW YORK, SATURDAY, FEBRUARY 3, 1968 — 10 CENTS

JOHNSON SAYS FOE'S RAIDS ARE A FAILURE MILITARILY; SAIGON, HUE BATTLES GO ON

SANITATION STRIKE BEGUN BY 10,000; CITY OBTAINS WRIT

Stoppage Follows a Rally at Which Angry Unionists Pummel Their Leader

WAGE DEMAND IS RAISED

New Figure of $600 Rejected by Mayor — Neither Side Sees an Early Accord

By DAMON STETSON

The city's 10,000 uniformed sanitationmen went on strike yesterday after a tumultuous demonstration at City Hall Park, where they rejected proposals for a settlement and hooted down their president's plea for a strike vote by mail.

The 7,000 rebellious sanitationmen who milled about in the park for five hours subsequently cheered and applauded their leader, John J. DeLury, when he stood atop a truck and shouted, "I accept the motion for go-go-go!"

At the beginning of the demonstration, which started at 7 A.M., the men had booed Mr. DeLury and roughed him up. An egg was thrown at him, but missed.

Shortly after noon, however, the fiery union leader returned from a meeting with Mayor Lindsay and told the crowd that he had submitted new demands, including a proposal for a $600 pay increase. The original figure has not been made public.

Rejected by City

Mr. DeLury's new proposals were rejected by the city. In his report to members in the park, he declared, "No contract, no work." The crowd responded with cheers and shouts of approval.

With residential collection of trash and garbage at a standstill throughout the five boroughs, the city's Corporation Counsel went into State Supreme Court and got a temporary restraining order under provisions of the Taylor Law, enjoining the union from any strike, slowdown or stoppage. The law prohibits strikes by public employes.

There was no immediate indication the strikers would go back to work before the contract dispute was settled. A top union official late in the afternoon declined to comment

Continued on Page 15, Column 1

AFTER THE DECISION—'NO CONTRACT, NO WORK': John J. DeLury, center, gesturing with hands before his face, trying to get through a crowd of sanitation men yesterday outside City Hall. Union members wanted to congratulate the leader on the decision.

The New York Times (by Neal Boenzi)

ATTEMPTED BRIBE LAID TO JUDGE ROE

L.I. Jury Says He Tried to Get Traffic Ticket Dropped

By FRANCIS X. CLINES

Special to The New York Times

RIVERHEAD, L. I., Feb. 2—State Supreme Court Justice James A. Roe Jr. was indicted today on charges of trying to bribe two policemen who gave him a speeding ticket last summer on Shelter Island.

Justice Roe, who sits in Queens, allegedly offered $10 bribes to the policemen if they would forget the matter. The policemen stopped him Aug. 24 while he was driving near his summer home on the resort island in eastern Suffolk County.

Justice Roe and his father, the late James A Roe Sr., a former Democratic leader of Queens, have maintained a large family compound, Westmoreland Farm, on the southwest shore of Shelter Island for several decades.

A plea of not guilty was entered by the 45-year justice, who was notified of the charges by the office of the

Continued on Page 13, Column 1

NEWS INDEX

Lindsay Proposes a Shift To Public Works for Poor

By RICHARD REEVES

Mayor Lindsay said yesterday that city antipoverty programs must shift their emphasis from community organization to public works projects employing poor people to improve their own neighborhoods.

The Mayor said he was pressing the Council on Poverty, the citywide agency that approves antipoverty programs, to give public works projects higher priority than such programs as organizing the poor to demand better schools or more police protection.

"Community action work in the past has tended to be in the field of community organization," Mr. Lindsay said at a news conference. "But this must give way to the higher priority of public works-type activities, particularly in the area of rehabilitation of physical structures."

Mr. Lindsay gave one example of what he believes poverty agencies should be doing.

Cites Maintenance Need

"In the cold snap that we had this winter I think that it would have been useful if community action programs had been so geared that maintenance men could have been supplied through the poverty program to work in the buildings in the neighborhoods that were in trouble.

"I think this is the direction in which the Council Against Poverty should move, and I hope that I will be able to bring sufficient influence to bear to interest the council in doing so."

The council is composed of 28 members appointed by the Mayor. Half of them represent the city's 26 antipoverty community corporations and half represent social service organizations, labor, business and religious institutions. The members must approve the $37-million worth of programs operated by the community cor-

Continued on Page 35, Column 6

CITY PROPERTY TAX MAY RISE 5C TO 8C

Fiscal Chief Sees Increase Over '67's $5.07 Per $100 —Valuations Climb 4%

By THOMAS W. ENNIS

Property owners here can expect an increase in the basic tax rate of 5 to 8 cents for each $100 of assessed valuation in the 1968-1969 fiscal year, the president of the city's Tax Commission estimated yesterday.

The current basic realty tax is $5.07 for each $100 of assessed value.

The new tax rate was indicated when the head of the commission, Michael Freyberg, made public the tentative assessments of the city's taxable real estate in his offices in the Municipal Building. The commission is in charge of assessing property; the final tax rate will be set this spring by the City Council.

Assessed Value $33-Billion

The Citizens Budget Commission, a private civic group, recently estimated that the tax would be increased to $5.16. Last year, Mr. Freyberg correctly estimated a tax increase of 11 cents for the current fiscal year, which ends June 30, but he said he regarded this as purely accidental.

The tentative total assessed value of the city's taxable real estate, affecting 860,000 parcels in the five boroughs, is $33,849,357,210, an increase of

Continued on Page 24, Column 1

Hundreds of Pupils Rampage In Protest at Brooklyn School

Disorder at J.H.S. 258

Hundreds of eighth grade pupils—surging through corridors, trading blows, barging into classes, shouting, jeering and turning in a false fire alarm—created havoc yesterday in a Bedford-Stuyvesant junior high school after demonstrating to win better food, more freedom and more dances.

Only when half a dozen policemen were rushed to the school was order restored and the children herded back to their classrooms, where there was no further instruction for the day.

Assistant Superintendent Henrietta B. Purcell, who was summoned to Junior High School 258, at Marcy Avenue and Macon Street, said a complete investigation of the disorder would be made by the Board of Education.

She said there were indica-

Continued on Page 30, Column 4

Teacher Quits at I.S. 201

By LEONARD BUDER

A new teacher turned down his assignment to Intermediate School 201 as the result of an allegedly antiwhite play presented in the school auditorium Thursday by LeRoi Jones, the militant Negro writer.

Three other teachers reportedly "walked out in disgust" during the performance but did not quit and were at work yesterday.

The new teacher, after working one day—Thursday—at the East Harlem school, went to district headquarters and said: "Please take me out of there." The teacher was reassigned.

Martin W. Frey, the district superintendent, said yesterday that he had learned about the play after it had taken place and was looking into the situation? "I heard to-

Continued on Page 30, Column 1

ACCORD REACHED IN GARAGE STRIKE

Employers and Employes to Submit Pact to Vote— Union Ballots Tomorrow

Negotiators for both sides in the parking garage strike agreed last night to submit to their members this weekend mediators' recommendations for settlement.

The six-day strike against 650 parking garages in Manhattan and the Bronx could end tomorrow night if the recommendations are approved by members of the striking union and the Metropolitan Garage Board of Trade.

A spokesman for the board, representing the owners, said it would accept the recommended settlement because the owners had given their negotiators complete authority to agree to terms.

The union leadership, mindful that the members had rejected a proposal for a three-year contract last Saturday that they had recommended, refrained from formally recommending approval this time.

A union spokesman said, however, that "we certainly hope the strike will be over as soon as possible."

The acceptance by the negotiators was announced last night by Vincent D. McDonnell, the chairman of the State Mediation Board.

Local 272 of the Teamster Garage Employes Union informed Mr. McDonnell that it would present his recommendations to the union membership

Continued on Page 26, Column 7

U.S. IS REBUFFED AGAIN ON PUEBLO BY NORTH KOREA

President Says 2d Meeting at Panmunjom Produced No Satisfactory Result

By PETER GROSE

Special to The New York Times

WASHINGTON, Feb. 2—North Korea has rebuffed a second United States demand for the release of the intelligence ship Pueblo and her crew, seized 10 days ago.

President Johnson announced today that a meeting between American and North Korean representatives at Panmunjom had "not produced any satisfactory results as far as the United States is concerned."

But he indicated that diplomatic efforts would continue, even though he conceded that he had no confidence that the United States could expect to have the ship and her crew back in the near future.

"I don't want to hold out any hopes, on information that I have," the President said at a hastily summoned news conference at the White House. "All I can say is that things take time." [Question 3, Page 8.]

The tone of the President's remarks indicated that the Administration had, for the time being, laid aside military plans drawn up on a contingency basis to free the ship and the American prisoners by force. Eighty-three crewmen were seized, but there have been reports that one of them has died.

More Talks Urged

"We hope there will be additional meetings," the President said. But he declined to elaborate on the meetings that have already taken place with the North Koreans or on what approaches were planned for the future.

[In Seoul, Government sources said South Korea had formally asked the United States for additional American troops to help guard against any invasion by North Koreans, The Associated Press reported. In Washington early Saturday, the Pentagon declined to comment on the report.]

The second direct discussion between American and North Korean officials apparently took place within the last 24 hours. It is understood that the meeting was an informal one between the officers representing the two countries at the Military Armistice Commission at Panmunjom.

On Jan. 24, the day after the Pueblo was seized, these officers met formally. The transcript of the statements made at that time showed such a gulf between the two sides that the United States temporarily aban-

Continued on Page 4, Column 3

ENEMY HOLDS OUT

Street Fighting Rages Within Mile of the Capital's Center

By TOM BUCKLEY

Special to The New York Times

SAIGON, South Vietnam, Saturday, Feb. 3—Deadly fighting broke out again this morning in narrow streets and alleys within a mile of the center of Saigon and in the suburbs.

The Vietcong, who attacked the city early Wednesday, clung to strongpoints in Cholon, the Chinese section of the city, near the Anquang pagoda, headquarters of the anti-Government wing of Buddhism, and around the Children's Hospital.

Heavy fighting continued in Giadinh Province, three to six miles north of the center of the city. In the delta and the Central Highlands, South Vietnamese and American troops, supported by tanks and helicopter gunships, were trying to corner guerrilla units that appeared to be leaving Saigon.

12,704 Enemy Dead Reported

The United States command announced that by last midnight 12,704 enemy troops had been killed and 3,576 suspects detained.

A total of 1,814 hand weapons and 545 crew-served weapons, such as machine guns, were said to have been captured. The casualty count, compiled mainly by South Vietnamese sources, was believed to be considerably inflated.

Allied casualties throughout the country for the four days of fighting were put at 983 killed—a far higher figure than for any previous full week—and 3,483 wounded. Of these, 318 of the dead and 1,639 of the wounded were Americans.

This was the situation elsewhere in the country, according to official American and South Vietnamese sources:

In the I Corps area, embracing the five northernmost provinces, most of the city of Hue was still in the hands of the enemy. But about five battalions of enemy troops who had occupied the Citadel and royal palace grounds, the symbol of Vietnamese imperial authority, were said to have been driven into its northern corner by midnight.

Air strikes were called in against the moated fortress,

Continued on Page 9, Column 7

6 U.S. Missionaries Killed by Vietcong

Six American missionaries, three of whom were women, were killed this week in a Vietcong assault on the town of Banmethuot in the highlands of South Vietnam, the Christian and Missionary Alliance announced yesterday.

A seventh missionary was wounded and another was said to have escaped into the woods that surround the town, 170 miles northeast of Saigon. Another missionary was reported captured by the Vietcong.

The slayings occurred at a leprosarium operated by the alliance. Bodies of the missionaries were left in the area and were wired with booby traps, the alliance reported.

The missionary buildings, including the leprosarium

Continued on Page 10, Column 4

ENEMY MAINTAINS TIGHT GRIP ON HUE

Force Put at 5 Battalions— U.S. Marines Hold Two Square Blocks of City

By GENE ROBERTS

Special to The New York Times

HUE, South Vietnam, Feb. 2—Enemy battalions weathered repeated attacks by Marine tanks and South Vietnamese aircraft today to maintain a tight grip on the ancient city of Hue.

At nightfall, the Marines held only two square blocks of the smoking city. And seven South Vietnamese Army battalions struggled unsuccessfully to push North Vietnamese and Vietcong troops from the Citadel—a 19th-century fortress built to shield the nation's historic imperial palace.

The strength of the enemy resistance caught the South Vietnamese by surprise. As late as yesterday, Vietnamese commanders in the area were saying that the enemy troops in Hue were weak and ill supplied and would fall with the first major allied push.

But today the assessment has changed. "Enemy forces in the ancient Citadel are believed to number five battalions," the

Continued on Page 9, Column 2

WARNING IS GIVEN

President Terms U.S. Ready for a Push by Enemy at Khesanh

Transcript of news conference will be found on Page 8.

By MAX FRANKEL

Special to The New York Times

WASHINGTON, Feb. 2—President Johnson said today that the Vietcong suffered "a complete failure" militarily throughout South Vietnam this week and he expressed confidence that as the facts became known the enemy would gain nothing psychologically either.

Measuring his comments at a news conference with extreme care, Mr. Johnson said the second stage of a long-planned enemy winter-spring offensive was imminent around Khesanh.

He has tried to provide his commanders with everything they think they need to repulse that expected assault, he said, and is "reasonably sure" and "confident" about their readiness. [Opening statement. Page 8.]

Only when the engagement is over, the President said, will he be able to give an over-all appraisal of the position of anti-Communist forces in South Vietnam. So far, he added, no basic changes in strategy seem necessary.

Cites Riots in Detroit

Mr. Johnson acknowledged that the Vietcong's simultaneous attacks on cities throughout South Vietnam had disrupted life in many communities and inflicted casualties on civilians. But "a few bandits can do that in any city," he remarked, pointing to the disruptions caused by riots in Detroit and other American communities.

The important thing, the President said, was that their plan and ability to do this was "anticipated, prepared for and met" and that the enemy took more than 10,000 battle deaths against a loss of 249 American and 553 South Vietnamese soldiers. Later casualty figures were higher.

"I can count," Mr. Johnson asserted. "It looks like somebody has paid a very dear price for the temporary encouragement that some of our enemies had." Mr. Johnson said the Administration had known for several months that the Vietcong and North Vietnamese were planning an offensive whose purpose, in part, was to set the stage for a "general uprising" that would destroy the Saigon Government and force the United States to accept a "Communist-dominated" coali-

Continued on Page 9, Column 1

Thieu Asks Action To Penalize North

By Agence France-Presse

SAIGON, South Vietnam, Feb. 2—President Nguyen Van Thieu today urged an extension of the bombing of North Vietnam to cover all military objectives as a "punishment" for the present enemy offensive in the South.

Speaking in a television broadcast, the President said that "to save time" in clearing the Vietcong out of occupied urban sectors, the armed forces would have to "act ruthlessly."

He expressed once again his opposition to the idea of any coalition government with the National Liberation Front, political arm of the Vietcong.

He emphasized that South Vietnam's allies were agreed on what he termed "this essential point."

Mr. Thieu predicted that the present Vietcong offensive against the country's main towns was only the prelude to

Continued on Page 9, Column 2

Associated Press

RESCUE UNDER FIRE: Members of the U.S. Marine Corps dragging a wounded comrade back across a bridge at Hue after an unsuccessful attempt to dislodge North Vietnamese and Vietcong troops from positions in the city.

U.S. and South Vietnamese aircraft retaliated to
Communist attacks by striking Chanh Hoa (1) and
Chap Le (2) in reprisal for the terrorist attacks at
Quinhon (3). A powerful American naval force was
concentrated in the China Sea (4).

As the Viet Cong continued undeterred by American
reprisals, the reprisals were escalated. American jets from
Da Nang (1) and Bien Hoa (2) attacked rebels in South
Vietnam. One raid was carried out near Pleiku (3). The Viet
Cong were endeavoring to cut the country in two at the
southern border of the Binhdinh Province.

Elite troops of the Viet Cong carrying Soviet AK 47 assault
rifles.

"All the News That's Fit to Print"

The New York Times

LATE CITY EDITION

Weather: Occasional snow flurries today. Sunny and cold tomorrow. Temp. range: today 32-18; Friday 41-24. Full U. S. report on Page 66.

VOL. CXVII . No. 40,194

NEW YORK, SATURDAY, FEBRUARY 10, 1968

10 CENTS

G.I.'S ENTER SAIGON TO HELP ELIMINATE ENEMY HOLDOUTS

Move Seen as Sign of U.S. Dissatisfaction at Pace of Government Effort

AIR RAID NEAR HAIPHONG

Bombing Appears to Signal End of Month-Long Curb on Attacks in North

By CHARLES MOHR
Special to The New York Times

SAIGON, South Vietnam, Saturday, Feb. 10—American infantry troops were brought to Saigon yesterday to help clear the city of guerrillas who have held out here for 12 days.

Ten helicopters carrying about 60 United States soldiers landed in the infield of the Phuto race track in the troubled Cholon section in the southern part of the city.

There was no fighting in the immediate area at the time, and the troops, part of the 199th Light Infantry Brigade, fanned out slowly over the weedy race track and began to open cans of rations.

The riflemen were later reinforced by road with what was called a "battalion minus" of other men from the 199th Brigade. An Army battalion is about 750 men.

Most G.I.'s on Outskirts

The arrival of combat troops—there were already many American support troops and security and military policemen in the city — was graphic evidence of American dissatisfaction, previously expressed by informed sources, at the slow pace taken by South Vietnamese forces in driving guerrilla forces out of town.

[American military headquarters in Saigon said that carrier-based United States Navy planes had bombed an airfield four miles southeast of Haiphong, The Associated Press reported. The attack appeared to end a month-long restraint on the bombing of targets around Haiphong and Hanoi. Page 10.]

With American agreement, the South Vietnamese took sole responsibility for the fight in Saigon six days ago, and United States combat forces took up screening positions around the city limits.

People Moving Freely

The South Vietnamese had first said they expected that it would take seven to 20 days to clean up Saigon. American officials suggested that they try to complete the job in 10.

The estimate of the number of Vietcong still operating within the city is vague. In recent days official spokesmen have put it at 500 to 1,000 men.

On the surface, the situation in Saigon seemed to be much better than it had been for many days. A three-hour tour of its streets showed that people were moving freely almost everywhere and returning to normal activities.

In South Vietnam's northwestern corner, at the Marine stronghold of Khesanh, no significant fighting was reported, military spokesmen here said.

On Thursday, however, Amer-

Continued on Page 10, Column 1

Associated Press

AMERICANS GO TO CHOLON: Members of the 199th Light Infantry Brigade at the race track in southern Saigon, after arrival in copters to aid South Vietnamese troops.

U.S. Girding at Khesanh To Avoid a 'Dienbienphu'

Washington Mood Tense

By HEDRICK SMITH
Special to The New York Times

WASHINGTON, Feb. 9—As never before in the bewildering warfare of Vietnam, the forces of the United States and North Vietnam are gathered for battle, and world attention is focused on one point—Khesanh.

For weeks the enemy has made intensive preparations for combat there. Yet no United States military officer can predict with certainty that the North Vietnamese will make a sustained assault against the American Marine stronghold at Khesanh, in the northwest corner of South Vietnam.

There is an air of expectancy here, a sense that a titanic test of strength and will is about to take place.

Five North Vietnamese divisions—40,000 to 50,000 regulars—are poised along or just south of the demilitarized zone, which separates North and South Vietnam, two of the divisions closely menacing Khesanh.

Some Attacks Begun

The allied garrison at Khesanh is manned by the United States' 26th Marine Regiment, some Army Special Forces troops and a few hundred South Vietnamese rangers—5,000 to 6,000 men in all.

Probing attacks against some of Khesanh's outlying positions have taken place. The nearby army Special Forces outpost at Langvei on the western approach to Khesanh fell two days ago.

American forces already confront the enemy along all parts of the demilitarized zone, and sizable reserves have been made ready to reinforce Khesanh and other outposts, as necessary. About 55,000 allied troops are now on station in South Vietnam's northernmost province.

The military and political stakes have become so great that President Johnson ordered the Joint Chiefs of Staff last month to review plans to de-

Continued on Page 10, Column 5

Johnson Holds Reins

BY MAX FRANKEL
Special to The New York Times

WASHINGTON, Feb. 9—The ultimate command post for the developing battle at Khesanh is really a mansion on Pennsylvania Avenue here — the office and residence of the Commander in Chief, Lyndon B. Johnson.

Is this battle really necessary?

What do we do if we lose that heliport?

Who guards those roads, especially if the weather grounds our planes?

Are you sure you can hold that bridge?

Almost daily, these and other tense and urgent questions flow from the pen of the President, probing policy, tactics, preparations, morale.

Jammed Into Packet

The response they evoke adds up to the largest volume of messages and reports ever gathered by the White House for a tactical engagement in the war. They are jammed into Mr. Johnson's "night reading" packet and fed into the basement Situation Room, in the west wing of the White House, where maps and charts are ready for the President's survey of battle at any moment.

As he waits for the Vietcong and North Vietnamese forces to "drop the other shoe" by moving on Khesanh — if indeed they mean to drop it — Mr. Johnson embodies the concern

Continued on Page 10, Column 2

PRESIDENT URGED TO CLARIFY DRAFT

House Panel Wants Him to Explain Deferment Policy for Graduate Students

By NEIL SHEEHAN
Special to The New York Times

WASHINGTON, Feb. 9—The Special House Subcommittee on Education voted today to ask President Johnson for immediate action to end the uncertainty over draft policy toward graduate school students.

The vote came after Dr. Nathan M. Pusey, the president of Harvard University, testified that the abolition of blanket graduate school draft deferments would have a disastrous effect on the production of college teachers unless the current draft selection process was changed.

He also called upon President Johnson to solve the problem.

"It is a terribly urgent matter," he said.

Pusey Supported

Dr. Pusey was supported in his testimony before the subcommittee of the House Committee on Education and Labor by three other prominent education specialists.

They were John Morse, director of the Commission on Federal Relations of the American Council on Education; Dr. Merriam H. Trytten, special consultant to the president of the National Academy of Sciences, and Dr. William G. Shannon, associate executive

Continued on Page 6, Column 3

TRIBOROUGH PACT ENDS LAST BLOCK TO TRANSIT UNITY

Superagency Will Control Authority, but Is Curbed on Transfer of Funds

By ROBERT E. TOMASSON

An attempt by the Metropolitan Commuter Transportation Authority to take over the Triborough Bridge and Tunnel Authority and its surpluses was resolved yesterday in an out-of-court settlement.

The agreement removes the last major block to Governor Rockefeller's plan to consolidate all major transit agencies in the state into a new superagency to be called the Metropolitan Transportation Authority.

Under the terms of a court-approved stipulation, commissioners of the Metropolitan Authority will become officers of the Triborough Authority. However, they will not be allowed to transfer any of Triborough's surplus funds unless the bonds are paid off or amended.

Weeks of Negotation

The agreement was reached after weeks of intensive negotiations, with the decisive meeting being held shortly after 9 A.M. yesterday in the Manhattan office of Governor Rockefeller at 22 West 55th Street, near Fifth Avenue.

Those present at the meeting, according to the Governor's office, were Mr. Rockefeller, his brother David, president of the Chase Manhattan Bank; former Gov. Thomas E. Dewey, special counsel for the bank, and Dr. William J. Ronan, chairman of the Metropolitan Transportation Authority.

The court action was instituted more than seven months ago by the Chase Manhattan Bank, acting as trustee to protect the rights of the holders of $362.7-million of Triborough bonds.

Under the transit unification plan, approved by the Legislature last year, the Metropolitan Transportation Authority is to become what has been termed a "giant umbrella agency."

Policy and Planning

It is to take over the policy and planning control of the city's Transit Authority, the Triborough Authority, the Long Island Rail Road (which the Metropolitan Commuter Transportation Authority now owns) and, eventually, the Staten Island Rapid Transit Service and the commuter service of the New Haven Railroad.

The urgency of the complex negotiations between the two large authorities resulted from the fact that the Governor's unification plan is scheduled to go into effect March 1. If a settlement had not been reached with Chase Manhattan by then, the implementation of the program was in danger.

Following the 50-minute meeting in the Governor's office yesterday, a three-page stipulation was drawn up and submitted, late in the day, to State Supreme Court Justice William C. Hecht Jr.

The stipulation was also agreed to by Corporation Counsel J. Lee Rankin, on behalf of the city, and by Attorney General Louis J. Lefkowitz, repre-

Continued on Page 19, Column 6

GOVERNOR PRESSES TALKS TO END GARBAGE WALKOUT AND RESISTS USING GUARD

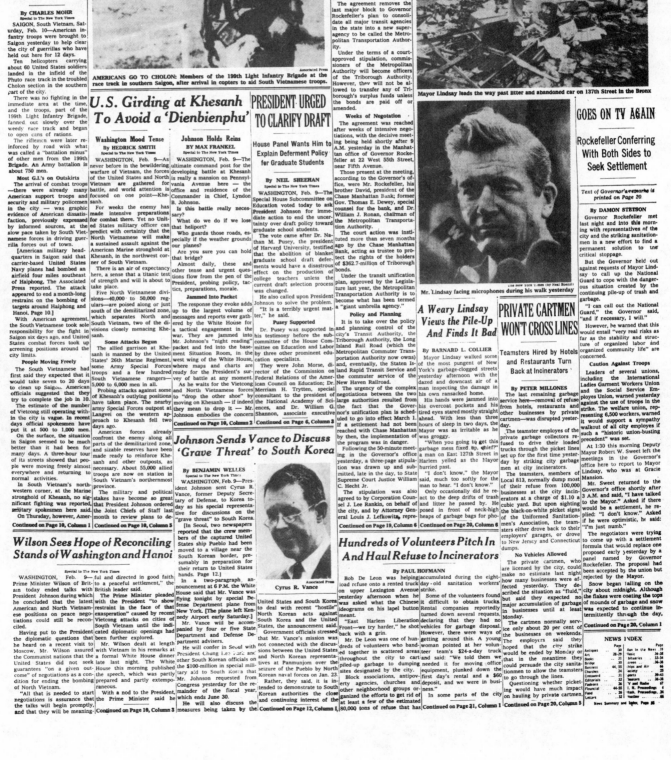

Mayor Lindsay leads the way past litter and abandoned car on 137th Street in the Bronx

The New York Times (by Neal Boenzi)

Mr. Lindsay facing microphones during his walk yesterday

GOES ON TV AGAIN

Rockefeller Conferring With Both Sides to Seek Settlement

Text of Governor's remarks is printed on Page 20.

By DAMON STETSON

Governor Rockefeller met last night and into this morning with representatives of the city and the striking sanitationmen in a new effort to find a permanent solution to the critical stoppage.

But the Governor held out against requests of Mayor Lindsay to call up the National Guard to cope with the dangerous situation created by the continuing pile-up of trash and garbage.

"I can call out the National Guard," the Governor said, "and if necessary, I will."

However, he warned that this would entail "very real risks as far as the stability and structure of organized labor and organized community life" are concerned.

Caution Against Troops

Leaders of several unions, including the International Ladies Garment Workers Union and the Social Service Employes Union, warned yesterday against the use of troops in the strike. The welfare union, representing 6,500 workers, warned it would support a sympathy walkout of all city employes if such a "historic union-busting precedent" was set.

At 1:30 this morning Deputy Mayor Robert W. Sweet left the meetings in the Governor's office here to report to Mayor Lindsay, who was at Gracie Mansion.

Mr. Sweet returned to the Governor's office shortly after 3 A.M. and said, "I have talked to the Mayor." Asked if there would be a settlement, he replied: "I don't know." Asked if he were optimistic, he said: "I'm just numb."

The negotiators were trying to come up with a settlement formula that would replace one proposed early yesterday by a panel named by Governor Rockefeller. The proposal had been accepted by the union but rejected by the Mayor.

Snow began falling on the city about midnight. Although the flakes were coating the tops of mounds of garbage and snow was expected to continue intermittently through the day,

Continued on Page 20, Column 1

A Weary Lindsay Views the Pile-Up And Finds It Bad

By BARNARD L. COLLIER

Mayor Lindsay walked some of the most pungent of New York's garbage-clogged streets yesterday afternoon with the dazed and downcast air of a man inspecting the damage in his own ransacked home.

His hands were jammed into his overcoat pockets and his tired eyes stared mostly straight ahead. With less than three hours of sleep in two days, the Mayor was as irritable as he was groggy.

"When you going to get this garbage mess fixed up, chief?" a man on East 127th Street in Harlem yelled as the Mayor hurried past.

"I don't know," the Mayor said, much too softly for the man to hear. "I don't know."

Only occasionally did he react to the deep drifts of trash and litter he passed by. He posed in front of neck-high heaps of garbage bags for pho-

Continued on Page 20, Column 6

PRIVATE CARTMEN WON'T CROSS LINES

Teamsters Hired by Hotels and Restaurants Turn Back at Incinerators

By PETER MILLONES

The last remaining garbage service here—removal of refuse from hotels, restaurants and other businesses by private cartmen—was disrupted yesterday.

The teamster employes of the private garbage collectors refused to drive their loaded trucks through the picket lines set up for the first time yesterday by striking city garbage men at city incinerators.

The teamsters, members of Local 813, normally dump most of their refuse from 100,000 businesses at the city incinerators at a charge of $1.10 a cubic yard. But upon sighting the black-on-white picket signs of the Uniformed Sanitationmen's Association, the teamsters either drove back to their employers' garages, or drove to New Jersey and Connecticut dumps.

No Vehicles Allowed

The private cartmen, who are licensed by the city, could make no estimate last night how many businesses were affected yesterday. They described the situation as "fluid," but said they expected no major accumulation of garbage in businesses until at least Monday.

The cartmen normally service only about 20 per cent of the businesses on weekends. The employers said they hoped that the city strike would be ended by Monday or that in the meantime they could persuade the city sanitationmen to allow the teamsters to go through the lines.

Questioning whether picketing would have much impact on hauling by private cartmen,

Continued on Page 20, Column 5

Wilson Sees Hope of Reconciling Stands of Washington and Hanoi

Special to The New York Times

WASHINGTON, Feb. 9—Prime Minister Wilson of Britain today ended talks with President Johnson during which he concluded that the latest American and North Vietnamese positions on peace negotiations could still be reconciled.

Having put to the President the diplomatic questions that he heard on a recent visit to Moscow, Mr. Wilson assured the Communist nations that the United States did not seek guarantees "on a given outcome" of negotiations as a condition for ending the bombing of North Vietnam.

"All that is needed to start negotiations is assurance that the talks will begin promptly, and that they will be meaningful and directed in good faith to a peaceful settlement," the British leader said.

The Prime Minister pleaded with the President "to show restraint in the face of that exasperation" caused by recent Vietcong attacks on cities of South Vietnam until the indicated diplomatic openings had been further explored.

Mr. Wilson dealt at length with Vietnam in his remarks at a formal White House dinner late last night. The White House this morning published the speech, which was partly prepared and partly extemporaneous.

With a nod to the President, the Prime Minister said he

Continued on Page 10, Column 3

Johnson Sends Vance to Discuss 'Grave Threat' to South Korea

By BENJAMIN WELLES
Special to The New York Times

WASHINGTON, Feb. 9—President Johnson sent Cyrus R. Vance, former Deputy Secretary of Defense, to Korea today as his special representative for discussions on the "grave threat" to South Korea.

[In Seoul, two newspapers reported that the crew members of the captured United States ship Pueblo had been moved to a village near the South Korean border, presumably in preparation for their return to United States hands. Page 12.]

In a two-paragraph announcement at 6 P.M. the White House said that Mr. Vance was flying tonight by special Defense Department plane from New York. [The plane left Kennedy Airport early Saturday.]

Mr. Vance will be accompanied by four or five State Department and Defense Department advisers.

He will confer in Seoul with President Chung Hee Park and other South Korean officials on the $100-million in special military aid to South Korea that Mr. Johnson requested from Congress yesterday for the remainder of the fiscal year, which ends June 30.

He will also discuss the measures being taken by the

Associated Press

Cyrus R. Vance

United States and South Korea to deal with recent "hostile" North Korean acts against South Korea and the United States, the announcement said.

Government officials stressed that Mr. Vance's mission was not connected with the discussions between the United States and North Korean representatives at Panmunjom over the seizure of the Pueblo by North Korean naval forces on Jan. 23.

Rather, they said, it is intended to demonstrate to South Korean authorities the close and continuing interest of the

Continued on Page 12, Column 1

Hundreds of Volunteers Pitch In And Haul Refuse to Incinerators

By PAUL HOFMANN

Bob De Leon was helping load refuse onto a rented truck on upper Lexington Avenue yesterday afternoon when he was asked what the Chinese ideograms on his lapel button meant.

"East Harlem Liberation Front—we try harder," he shot back with a grin.

Mr. De Leon was one of hundreds of volunteers who banded together in scattered areas throughout the city to cart piled-up garbage to dumping sites designated by the city.

Block associations, antipoverty agencies, churches and other neighborhood groups organized the efforts to get rid of at least a few of the estimated 80,000 tons of refuse that has accumulated during the eight-day-old sanitation workers' strike.

Some of the volunteers found it difficult to obtain trucks. Rental companies reportedly turned down several requests, declaring that they had no vehicles for garbage disposal. However, there were ways of getting around this. A young woman pointed at her volunteer team's $24-a-day truck and said: "We told them we needed it for moving office equipment, plunked down the first day's rental and a $60 deposit, and we were in business."

In some parts of the city

Continued on Page 21, Column 1

NEWS INDEX

"All the News That's Fit to Print"

The New York Times

LATE CITY EDITION

Weather: Partly sunny, windy and cold today. Fair, cold tomorrow. Temp. range: today 32-19; Friday 36-20. Full U. S. report on Page 57.

VOL. CXVII...No. 40,201 NEW YORK, SATURDAY, FEBRUARY 17, 1968 10 CENTS

MOST DEFERMENTS TO END FOR GRADUATE STUDENTS; JOB EXEMPTIONS LIMITED

EXCEPTIONS MADE

Medical, Dental and Allied Fields Listed —Educators Upset

Texts of statements on draft are printed on Page 10.

By NEIL SHEEHAN

Special to The New York Times

WASHINGTON, Feb. 16—The Johnson Administration abolished today most graduate deferments from the draft. Exceptions were granted for medical and dental students, students in allied fields and those who will have completed two or more years of their studies by June.

The National Security Council also suspended indefinitely the list of critical occupations and essential activities that has formed the basis for about half the 339,474 occupational deferments now held by draft registrants.

Administration officials said they expected about 150,000 men to be drafted during the fiscal year beginning July 1 as a result of the decision on graduate deferments.

This group will include eligible youths who will graduate from four-year colleges in June, men who will complete their first year of graduate school at that time and individuals receiving their master's degree in June.

Expected to Volunteer

Officials said they expected about 75,000 other men now faced with the draft to volunteer for service during the next fiscal year.

Other graduate students who had completed a year of graduate study by last Oct. 1 toward a doctoral or equivalent professional degree, or a combination of master's and doctoral degrees, will continue to be deferred for five years, including any years of graduate school before Oct. 1, 1967.

The Administration left unchanged the current system of draft selection, under which the oldest men are taken first in the chronological order of their birth dates.

The effect on the nation's graduate schools was expected to be severe under these circumstances and educators re-

Continued on Page 10, Column 1

President Declares Hanoi Doesn't Want to Negotiate

By MAX FRANKEL

Special to The New York Times

WASHINGTON, Feb. 16—President Johnson said today that North Vietnam was no more ready to negotiate now than it was one, two or three years ago and that "I don't think it has been at any time during any of that period."

Despite some semantic adjustments in their statements about negotiations, the President said, he has never found any sign that the leaders of North Vietnam have changed, modified or moderated their position.

On the contrary, he asserted, their answer to recent explorations and offers that went "as far as honorable men could go" was given in attacks on innocent civilians during what was to have been a truce on a sacred holiday. And that, Mr. Johnson added, "ought to be an answer that any elementary schoolboy and girl could understand." [Question 12, Page 8.]

The President gave his assessment of all recent diplomatic activity at an unplanned news conference at which he also vigorously reasserted his confidence in Gen. William C. Westmoreland, the American commander in Vietnam. He expressed the hope that his statement would put an end to damaging discussion about the general.

Mr. Johnson sidestepped a question about whether more troops than the scheduled total of 525,000 would be needed in South Vietnam. The subject was under constant review, he said, and he would provide whatever manpower was needed. [Question 16.]

And he brushed aside a question about comments on the war by Gov. George Romney of

Continued on Page 5, Column 1

AIRLINE EXECUTIVE IS CHOSEN TO TAKE TROWBRIDGE POST

Johnson Selects C. R. Smith as the Successor to Ailing Commerce Secretary

C.A.B. TO GET NEW HEAD

Lawyer to Take Over Job of Murphy, Who Will Help Out at White House

Transcript of news conference will be found on Page 8.

By EILEEN SHANAHAN

Special to The New York Times

WASHINGTON, Feb. 16 — President Johnson announced at a news conference today that Secretary of Commerce Alexander B. Trowbridge had resigned and that C. R. Smith, chairman of the board of American Airlines, would be nominated to replace him. [Opening statement, Page 8.]

Mr. Trowbridge's resignation, which the President ascribed solely to reasons of health, is the third by a Cabinet member in the last three months. [Question 3.]

Mr. Smith, if confirmed by the Senate, as expected, would take over the Commerce job on March 1, when Mr. Trowbridge's resignation is effective. That is the same date on which Clark M. Clifford, the Washington lawyer, is scheduled to replace Robert S. McNamara as Secretary of Defense.

The President indicated, however, that he had no immediate plans to fill the top job at the Department of Health, Education and Welfare. The resignation of John W. Gardner, announced last month, is also scheduled to become effective March 1. [Question 7.]

Praise for Cohen

Mr. Johnson, under questioning at his news conference, said that this department had "a very outstanding man" as Under Secretary — Wilbur J. Cohen, a career man—and that he expected Mr. Cohen to continue as Acting Secretary "at least a few weeks."

Mr. Johnson also formally announced the long-expected resignation of Charles S. Murphy as chairman of the Civil Aeronautics Board, which regulates commercial airline rates and routes. Mr. Murphy will become a counsel at the White House on a part-time basis. [Opening statement.]

While Mr. Murphy is generally considered, along with Mr. Clifford, to have been one of the main architects of Pres-

Continued on Page 8, Column 1

Associated Press

AT THE WHITE HOUSE: President Johnson during the news conference at which he announced the resignation of Secretary of Commerce Alexander B. Trowbridge. Standing next to Mr. Johnson is George Christian, his press secretary. The conference was held in the Fish Room. Painting hanging on wall is "The Cowboy," an oil by Frederic Remington.

A POLICE SHAKE-UP SHIFTS 3 TOP AIDES IN NARCOTICS UNIT

Renaghan Replaces Bluth as Chief in Midst of Four Inquiries Into Bureau

By DAVID BURNHAM

The top three commanders of the Police Department's Narcotics Bureau, which is under investigation by four different agencies, were relieved of their posts yesterday and assigned to less important duties.

The sudden removal of Chief Inspector Ira Bluth and his two top assistants surprised many police officials. Officers at headquarters said it was the most dramatic shake-up they could remember in the bureau, which is the largest narcotics enforcement agency in the world.

Jacques Nevard, Deputy Police Commissioner for Press Relations, said the reassignments had been made for the "good of the service," and that the department's investigation of the bureau was continuing.

In addition to the department's investigation, the City Controller, the Commissioner of Investigations and the United States Attorney for the Southern District are all looking into reports of irregularities in the bureau.

Transfers Announced

"The investigators are tripping over each other," said one top police official who asked not to be identified.

Yesterday's announcement by Commissioner Howard R. Leary said that Chief Bluth, who had headed the bureau since 1964, had been transferred to the office of the Detective Division in Queens.

Chief Bluth was replaced by Assistant Chief Inspector Thomas C. Renaghan, who has a reputation in the department as a disciplinarian. In his last post, Chief Renaghan had commanded the uniformed forces in the Bronx.

Also transferred out of the Narcotics Bureau were Deputy Inspectors Francis J. Wolfe and Cyril Regan. Inspector Wolfe, who had served in the bureau for the last 10 years, was transferred to a detective division in Brooklyn, and Inspector Regan was sent to a detective division in Manhattan.

During the last few months, a number of serious charges have been raised about the men and operational procedures of the Narcotics Bureau.

Last Dec. 13, three detectives of the bureau's special investigating unit were indicted by a Federal grand jury on charges of selling narcotics to peddlers. A trial date has not yet been set. Last week, the Police De-

Continued on Page 58, Column 6

Good Progress Reported By Sanitation Conferees

By DAMON STETSON

Negotiators for the city and the sanitation union reported "considerable progress" last night in their bargaining talks and said they would continue their discussions today.

The joint announcement at the end of an afternoon negotiating session eased concern caused by an earlier warning by the union.

That warning was the statement that it would not continue the talks beyond yesterday without getting new instructions from the executive board and shop stewards.

Jack Bigel, one of the negotiators for the union, the Uniformed Sanitationmen's Association, had issued the warning, but last night he said the day's bargaining session had brought progress.

Both Deputy Mayor Robert W. Sweet and Herbert L. Haber, director of the city's Office of Labor Relations, agreed with the assessment.

Details Withheld

None of the negotiators would disclose any details of the day's discussions or the areas in which the talks had moved forward.

The two sides are attempting to work out an agreement that would satisfy both the city and union members, who were promised by Governor Rockefeller that they would be paid at a higher annual rate if they would end the strike and return to work.

The period covered by the Governor's promise was only for the duration of the health emergency and was premised on a state take-over of Sani-

Continued on Page 34, Column 1

52 REFUSE TO QUIT HOMES IN ARMORY

Harlem Families Relocated Last Month Resist Orders to Move to New Quarters

By EDWARD C. BURKS

Fifty-two persons, including 40 children, who moved from unheated homes to a Harlem armory during last month's severe cold wave, were resisting eviction orders yesterday.

The Community Council on Housing, a tenants' group of 300 West 121st Street, advised them to stay put until all were assured of "decent housing."

Originally the city housed more than 100 people under emergency conditions at the armory, 2366 Fifth Avenue at 142d Street, but some had agreed to leave.

Both city and state agencies have been trying to remove the remaining families on the grounds that more suitable substitute housing is available.

Families Resist Move

The city's Relocation Department reported that it had found other quarters for the families, either in hotels or in "standard housing." But the remaining families refused to budge last night.

The Social Services Department, hoping to dislodge the families after days of futile argument, attempted to institute child-neglect proceedings in Family Court yesterday.

The argument was that the camp-out conditions in the armory—the families in two large make-shift dormitories—constituted neglect of the children's welfare by their parents, who had been offered better facilities. But the department reported that the court threw out the case, saying it lacked jurisdiction.

A spokesman for the Mayor's office, said last night: "The people are still there. We have better housing for them. The city is going to have to vacate the armory. We can't let the kids stay there because it's not a fit place for them."

Women and children are in one dormitory, the men in the other.

Mrs. Beraneece Sims, assistant director of the Community

Continued on Page 58, Column 8

CITY MAY WIDEN TOWAWAY AREA

Order Expected in March Covering 72d to 96th St. —Parking Fines Up $10

By JOSEPH C. INGRAHAM

Fines for illegal parking will rise $10 in the area from 72d to 96th Street, starting the first week in March, and violators' cars will probably be towed away.

The decision to impose the stiffer fines in the new area was ordered by Mayor Lindsay, according to Traffic Commissioner Henry A. Barnes.

"If the Police Department gives the word that they have the manpower and equipment, there will be a tough crackdown on towing away cars," he said yesterday.

Mr. Barnes added that a major towaway drive was essential "in view of the fantastic amount of illegal parking north of 72d Street."

Fines for illegal parking were increased to $25 and those for overtime parking at meters to $15 in all of Man-

Continued on Page 58, Column 3

DR. PARRAN DEAD; EX-HEALTH CHIEF

Surgeon General, 1936-48, Leader in Medical Advance

Special to The New York Times

PITTSBURGH, Feb. 16—Dr. Thomas Parran, Surgeon General of the United States Public Health Service from 1936 to 1948 and a founder of the World Health Organization, died last night in Presbyterian-University Hospital. He was 75 years old.

Dr. Parran was also a former Health Commissioner of New York State. He established the Graduate School of Public Health at the University of Pittsburgh and was its first dean.

A Dynamic Fighter

By ALDEN WHITMAN

A tenacious, dynamic fighter against such scourges as tuberculosis, venereal disease, diphtheria, malaria, hookworm and high maternal and infant mortality, Dr. Thomas Parran lifted public health in the United States from its role as an ill-regarded stepchild of medicine to a front rank in the medical family.

Serving as Surgeon General of the United States Public Health Service from 1936 to

Continued on Page 29, Column 1

De Gaulle and Kiesinger Agree British Market Entry Is Distant

By HENRY TANNER

Special to The New York Times

PARIS, Feb. 16—President de Gaulle and Chancellor Kurt Georg Kiesinger of West Germany, in a joint declaration here today, supported the principle of enlarging the European Common Market, but added that Britain was still far from eligible.

The two leaders noted that Britain had made a worthwhile start toward qualifying for membership, but they left no doubt that the day of British entry was still far off. They said their governments would be willing to consider interim arrangements to develop commercial exchanges between the Common Market and the nonmember countries that had expressed the wish to join.

They added that in the meantime "all the efforts" of the two governments should be devoted to the task of strengthening the existing community of six members. The four [illegible] lands, Belgium and Luxembourg.

The issue of British membership dominated the two days of top-level French-German talks as well as the final declaration.

German diplomats noted with satisfaction that President de Gaulle had refrained from merely repeating his opposition to British entry and had gone on record for the first time in favor of the idea of eventually including new members—notably Britain.

Günther Diehl, the West German spokesman, said that "the perspective of a free trade zone" including Common Market members and candidates for membership was behind the decision to consider interim arrangements for reducing trade barriers.

But French observers stressed that throughout their talks the two leaders had made it clear the interim arrangements for Britain as well as the issue of British membership would have to be decided by the six Common Market members together.

France, it was felt, thus retains all her leverage for keeping the British out until President de Gaulle judges them eligible.

"A German wrapping for a French policy" was the way one diplomatic observer summed up the result, for Britain, of the two-day conference.

The next test will come Feb. 29 in Brussels when the Foreign

Continued on Page 8, Column 6

Two Soviet Bombers Spotted Off Canada

By BENJAMIN WELLES

Special to The New York Times

WASHINGTON, Feb. 16—The Department of Defense disclosed today that two Soviet bombers were intercepted by United States jet fighters while approaching the Newfoundland coast last Friday.

It also disclosed that last Monday and Tuesday three Soviet bombers flew along the coast of Alaska about 80 miles offshore, at an altitude of about 30,000 feet. After flying the full length of the northern coast, Pentagon sources said, the planes left in the direction of the Soviet Union.

Both incidents, they said, appeared to involve Soviet training flights. Only in the flight off Newfoundland were United States fighter-interceptors reported to have gone up to iden-

Continued on Page 10, Column 7

Johnson Denies Atom Use In Vietnam Is Considered

By JOHN W. FINNEY

Special to The New York Times

WASHINGTON, Feb. 16—President Johnson said today that no recommendation had been made to him for the possible use of nuclear weapons in the Vietnam war and indicated that no such step was being considered by the Administration.

In emphatic, almost emotional terms, the President sought at a White House news conference to end the growing speculation in Congressional circles that nuclear weapons were being considered in Vietnam, particularly for the defense of the Marine outpost at Khesanh. [Question 11, Page 8.]

Such speculation, he said, is "against the national interest" and has no foundation in fact.

"It is reasonably apparent and known to all that it is very much against the national interest to carry on discussions about the deployment of nuclear weapons," he said.

Strongest Denial Yet

"So far as I am aware, they [the Secretaries of State and Defense and the Joint Chiefs of Staff have at no time even considered or made a recommendation in any respect to the employment of nuclear weapons.

"They are on our planes on training missions from time to time."

The President's statements represented the strongest denial yet on the matter.

Secretary of State Dean Rusk and Gen. Earle G. Wheeler, chairman of the Joint Chiefs of Staff, sought in the last week to dismiss the idea that

Continued on Page 2, Column 3

Refugees Find Hue Provides No Haven

By THOMAS A. JOHNSON

Special to The New York Times

HUE, South Vietnam, Feb. 16—When the Vietcong's Lunar New Year offensive started here 17 days ago, thousands of South Vietnamese refugees fled to Hue University on the south side of the Huong River for safety.

Today, there are more than 16,000 people cramped in the three main university buildings, about half of this city's new refugee population, and safety is nowhere in sight.

"Several refugees have been killed and many wounded during artillery, rocket, and mortar duels between the enemy forces, along the southern end of the city's historic Citadel, and American forces directly across the river.

"Several South Vietnamese

Continued on Page 3, Column 2

FOE STILL CLINGS TO HUE POSITIONS

Again Defies Bombardment and Tear Gas—Enemy's Tanks Seen at Conthien

By GENE ROBERTS

Special to The New York Times

SAIGON, South Vietnam, Saturday, Feb. 17—Enemy forces withstood the third successive day of heavy bombing and a thick fog of tear gas yesterday to continue their tight hold on large sections of the walls of Hue's historic Citadel.

United States Marines took advantage of the bombardment to bring another block and a half of territory under the control near the Citadel, which was built as the capital of the Annamese empire in the 19th century. But at nightfall they were still two blocks from a major enemy strongpoint at the southeastern corner of the wall.

Foe's Tanks Sighted

This morning, marines near the demilitarized zone reported that enemy tanks had been sighted near Conthien, a fortress that the North Vietnamese shelled repeatedly last fall.

This was the third time tanks had been sighted near the border of North Vietnam. "Marine tank and artillery crews fired at long range on the enemy tanks," the United States military command said. "The North Vietnamese tanks did not return the fire and immediately disappeared."

A Marine observer first reported having sighted the tanks at 2:30 P.M. north of the Benhai River, on the enemy side of the border. Airborne observers later reported the tanks four miles from Conthien in the demilitarized zone.

In the Hue battle at one

Continued on Page 3, Column 5

HANOI RELEASES THREE U.S. FLIERS

They Arrive in Thailand—Are Due Home Today

By HEDRICK SMITH

Special to The New York Times

WASHINGTON, Feb. 16—North Vietnam released three captured American pilots today, the first United States prisoners to be freed by Hanoi.

The men were downed last fall in air raids in North Vietnam. They arrived safely at an American air base in Thailand this afternoon and were quickly put on an Air Force plane for a flight to the United States. They are expected to arrive in this country tomorrow evening, officials said.

[The North Vietnamese Premier, Pham Van Dong, was quoted by an American pacifist who helped arrange the fliers' release as having said that Hanoi would "talk peace seriously" once the United States stopped its bombing of North Vietnam unconditionally.]

The release welcomed officially by the State Department, had been expected. North Vietnam announced on Jan. 27 that it would free three airmen as a humanitarian gesture for Tet, the lunar New Year,

Continued on Page 7, Column 3

NEWS INDEX

	Page		Page
Antiques	26	Music	32-34
Art	24-26	Obituaries	26, 29
Books	27	Screen	32-34
Bridge	26	Ships and Air	57
Churches	23	Society	37
Crossword	27	Sports	19-22
Editorials	28	Theaters	32-34
Fashions	16	TV and Radio	58-59
Financial	38-46	U. N. Proceedings	3
Letters	28	Wash. Proceedings	13
Man in the News	58	Weather	57

News Summary and Index, Page 31

"All the News That's Fit to Print"

The New York Times

LATE CITY EDITION

Weather: Sunny, cold today. Fair, continued cold tonight, tomorrow. Temp. range: today 28-15; Sat. 34-17. Full U. S. report on Page 79.

SECTION ONE

VOL. CXVII . No. 40,209

NEW YORK, SUNDAY, FEBRUARY 25, 1968

60¢ beyond 50-mile zone from New York City, except Long Island. 75¢ beyond 200-mile radius. Higher in air delivery cities.

40 CENTS

TOP BUSINESSMEN JOIN U.S. EFFORT TO FIND MORE JOBS

President, at Ranch, Gives Names of 60 Leaders—Meets With Henry Ford

AID FOR SLUMS MAPPED

But Auto Executive Doubts That Employment Alone Would Avert Rioting

By ROY REED

Special to The New York Times

AUSTIN, Tex., Feb. 24 — President Johnson announced today that 60 leading businessmen had agreed to join a private-public effort to find jobs for the hard-core unemployed in the nation's slums.

He made public the names of the businessmen as Henry Ford 2d and two other business leaders flew from Washington to the LBJ Ranch, where Mr. Johnson is resting and working, to report on the progress of the job-finding effort.

Mr. Ford, chairman of the board of the Ford Motor Company, is the chairman of the National Alliance of Businessmen, a group that is working with the Federal Government in one part of an attempt to head off further racial rioting.

Rein on Optimism

Mr. Ford, meeting reporters here after his session with the President, was not hopeful that the employing of slum people would be enough to stop rioting. He confirmed that a study had shown that most of the rioters last year in his home city, Detroit, had been employed.

But employing those who have traditionally been considered unemployable will go far toward giving those people a feeling of belonging to the larger society, he said.

Mr. Ford said he was not pretending that his job program would solve the nation's racial problems. But he repeated a warning that he said he had been giving to his fellow businessmen.

"It is no longer merely a matter of social justice and the principles of democracy," he said. "Our very national unity and domestic peace are at stake."

"And it is also plain that bringing these disadvantaged people out of the ghettos and into the mainstream of the American economy is a goal

Continued on Page 32, Column 1

Nixon Catches Up To Johnson in Poll

Special to The New York Times

PRINCETON, N. J., Feb. 24 —Richard M. Nixon has drawn even with President Johnson in the latest test of election strength, according to the Gallup Poll.

The former Vice President trailed the President by a sizable margin in a survey conducted before the recent Vietcong attacks in the cities of South Vietnam.

Mr. Nixon, as reported this week, holds a commanding lead—his widest to date—as the top choice of Republicans and independents for the 1968 Presidential nomination. Governor Rockefeller of New York is the runner-up with both groups.

Although Mr. Nixon has registered impressive gains on President Johnson since last month, his support falls

Continued on Page 36, Column 1

ROCKEFELLER SAYS HE'D ACCEPT DRAFT

Says in Detroit He Would Agree to Will of Convention —Still Backs Romney

Special to The New York Times

DETROIT, Feb. 24—Governor Rockefeller said today that he would run for President if he was drafted by the Republican National Convention.

The Governor, at a news conference here, asked by a newsman if he would accept the will of the convention, replied, "I would accept."

A top aide of the New Yorker said that was the first time he had said that he would run if drafted.

Mr. Rockefeller came here today to attend a fund-raising luncheon for Gov. George Romney of Michigan. Mr. Rockefeller repeated at the news conference that he had no desire to be President and expressed confidence that Mr. Romney would be the convention choice.

He also said, in answer to queries, that he would support former Vice President Richard M. Nixon if Mr. Nixon were nominated. Asked if he would support Mayor Lindsay, if he were nominated, the Governor grinned and said:

"The question has not come up."

Earlier in the news conference, Governor Rockefeller was asked if he would enter the race as a moderate candidate

Continued on Page 31, Column 1

M'NAMARA SAYS DESTROYERS IN '64 WARNED OF ENEMY

Tells Senators That 2 Ships Remained on Patrol Despite Threat of Hostile Action

Excerpts from the McNamara testimony are on Page 28.

By JOHN W. FINNEY

Special to The New York Times

WASHINGTON, Feb. 24—Some 15 hours before they came under attack in the Gulf of Tonkin in August, 1964, two American destroyers warned higher command that North Vietnam regarded them as enemy craft.

Despite the warning, Congressional testimony disclosed today, the destroyers were not instructed to break off their intelligence-gathering patrol off the coast of North Vietnam.

About 15 hours later—on the night of Aug. 4, 1964—they became involved in a naval encounter with North Vietnamese patrol boats that was to mark a turning point in the American involvement in the Vietnam war.

This new facet of the controversial Gulf of Tonkin incident was disclosed with the release of testimony by Secretary of Defense Robert S. McNamara before the Senate Foreign Relations Committee.

Reason for Retaliation

The testimony was given by Mr. McNamara on Tuesday in defense of the Administration's decision to retaliate by ordering the first air strikes against North Vietnam and by seeking Congressional approval of a resolution endorsing "all necessary measures to be taken by the Administration to prevent further aggression" by North Vietnam.

Throughout the 110 pages of testimony ran two principal themes:

First, was there an element of provocation on the part of the destroyers that induced the North Vietnamese to attack? And, second, did the Administration have sufficient proof of the attack at the time to warrant a decision that was later to be described by the State Department as "a functional equivalent" of a declaration of war against North Vietnam?

In the course of the all-day closed hearing, Mr. McNamara emphatically denied that there was any element of provocation. He was equally emphatic in insisting that the Adminis-

Continued on Page 29, Column 1

Associated Press

PLAN REBUILDING IN SAIGON: Nguyen Van Loc, at center in dark tunic, Premier of South Vietnam, confers with aides amid devastation of Cholon. Bulldozers have cleared Chinese section, which was a stronghold of the Vietcong.

SOUTH VIETNAMESE SEIZE HUE PALACE; ENEMY RETREATS

Troops, After 21-Day Siege, Find Most of Foe Gone—Fight Seems Near End

U.S. BOMBS HANOI PIERS

They Are Struck First Time —Two Americans Killed in Tansonnhut Clash

By CHARLES MOHR

Special to The New York Times

HUE, South Vietnam, Feb. 24 — South Vietnamese troops, throwing hand grenades and shouting an exultant war cry, captured the Imperial Palace here today.

They met no resistance. The North Vietnamese troops who had occupied the palace for 24 days had retreated, probably last night.

[In the air war, American bombers struck for the first time at Red River piers and warehouses in Hanoi, 1.8 miles from the center of the city. In Saigon, new fighting broke out along the northern boundary of Tansonnhut Airfield, with 2 Americans and 10 enemy soldiers reported killed. Page 24.]

The capture of Hue's 700-yard-square walled palace area seemed to signal the collapse of heavy enemy resistance, and the battle for the city appeared to be nearing its end.

Some fighting continued, however, in the Chinese quarter of the city and in the western sections of Hue, both inside and outside the wall that surrounds the major part of the city north of the Huong River.

Hue, which had a population estimated at 120,000, is bisected by the broad Huong.

Wall Surrounds Palace

The older, northern sector is enclosed by a high red-brick wall and is known as the Citadel.

The Imperial Palace compound, surrounded by its own 20-foot wall, lies in the south-central area of the Citadel.

Perhaps 1,000 North Vietnamese Army troops have occupied most of the Citadel as well as the palace since the early morning of Jan. 31, when they attacked Hue as part of a Lunar New Year offensive throughout South Vietnam.

Although the enemy had gradually been driven back into the southern part of the Citadel, heavy resistance was expected when the palace was attacked. But the main enemy forces evidently escaped through the southwestern section of the Citadel area, which enemy troops still controlled until late this afternoon.

The Citadel walls and the palace area they enclose were built by the Nguyen Dynasty of Annamese, or central Viet-

Continued on Page 25, Column 3

Mayor Urges Board To Avoid Showdown On Rally at I.S. 201

By RICHARD REEVES

Special to The New York Times

BEND, Ore., Feb. 24—Mayor Lindsay said today that New York City officials should avoid a confrontation with black militants over last Wednesday's angry antiwhite meeting at an East Harlem school because such a showdown could force the majority of Negroes to support a small minority preaching violence.

"The Board of Education must find a middle ground that prevents an impossible confrontation over I.S. 201," Mr. Lindsay said in interviews on the impact of growing Negro militancy on the city government.

Siding With Militants

"It pays to avoid showdowns over questions that force the majority of the black community on to the side of a few militants."

At the Wednesday meeting, which was organized as a memorial to Malcolm X, Negro militants urged 600 Harlem residents, including some students, to arm themselves for self-protection against white men and to practice using the weapons so they would be ready for the "hunting season."

The Board of Education later expressed "shock" over the program. It directed the Superintendent of Schools to "establish clear control" over the

Continued on Page 64, Column 1

NEW DRAFT RULES ANGER GRADUATES

Confusion and Resignation Also Found—Minority Is Seeking to Defy Law

By FRED M. HECHINGER

College seniors and first-year graduate students across the nation have responded to the new draft regulations with a mixture of anger, confusion and resignation, but without panic. An outspoken minority is debating means of defying the draft—even at the cost of going to jail—or evading it by moving to Canada, taking teaching jobs without first completing their studies, or finding legal loopholes.

From 160,000 to 200,000 undergraduate students and first-year graduate students are now eligible for the draft.

The Reserve Officers Training Corps on many campuses reports being flooded with as much as a 100 per cent increase in applications.

Few units are able to accommodate the influx and in many instances the applicants are not admitted until the following term.

Estimates of Administrators

Inventiveness in devising ways of avoiding the call-up ranges from simulating homosexuality to entering agriculture as a critical occupation. But the overwhelming majority of students appear to be girding for the draft, without enthusiasm. A few applaud the new regulations as an equitable measure to prevent middle-class intellectuals from becoming a privileged group.

This picture emerged from a check of leading graduate schools by correspondents of The New York Times across the country.

The interviews followed the announcement by the National Security Council that draft boards would be instructed to halt all deferments of graduate students in any field other than medicine, dentistry and related health professions, except of those who will have completed two or more years of graduate study by next

Continued on Page 61, Column 1

Thant Urges U.S. Assume Hanoi Good Faith in Talks

By DREW MIDDLETON

Special to The New York Times

UNITED NATIONS, N. Y., Feb. 24—Secretary General Thant declared today that if the United States unconditionally ended the bombing in Vietnam, it could reasonably assume that North Vietnam would deal in "good faith" with the issue of ground fighting.

This assessment by Mr. Thant, in a report on his inquiry into Hanoi's views on peace-making and his talks with Soviet leaders, appeared to diplomats here to be an attempt to bridge the gap between President Johnson's San Antonio formula and North Vietnam's position.

Text of Thant's statement will be found on Page 24.

The President said in a speech at San Antonio on Sept. 29, 1967, that he would halt the bombing if this action would bring prompt, productive discussions, and that he would "of course assume" that Hanoi would not take advantage of the cessation during the talks.

U. S. Issues Statement

The United States, in a statement issued tonight by its mission to the United Nations, took a less positive view of the prospect of talks than did the Secretary General.

Noting that Mr. Thant believed that the discussions would start in a matter of days after an end to the bombing, the statement said that the United States "would welcome confirmation from Hanoi that talks would start promptly in circumstances where we could reasonably assume that North Vietnam would not take military advantage of the bombing cessation."

The wording of the statement indicated that the Administration remained unconvinced by Mr. Thant's references to a reasonable assumption that North Vietnam would not take military advantage of a cessation of bombing. The words "would welcome" indicated that the United States wanted assurances more concrete than those offered by Mr. Thant on this point.

The statement had been ap-

Continued on Page 24, Column 4

U.S. ADMITS BLOW TO PACIFICATION

High Official in Saigon Says Foe's Attacks Resulted in a Rural 'Vacuum'

By BERNARD WEINRAUB

Special to The New York Times

SAIGON, South Vietnam, Feb. 24—The United States mission conceded today for the first time that the allied effort to pacify the countryside had suffered a "considerable setback" as a result of the Vietcong offensive.

"There has been a loss of momentum, there has been some withdrawal [of security troops] from the countryside, there has been a significant psychological setback both on the part of pacification people themselves and the local population," said a high official of the mission.

The pacification effort, which seeks to win the allegiance of South Vietnam's peasants, has been regarded here as having the same importance as the military drive.

Teams Termed Shaken

The comments today, unusually blunt for a high-level official, were made at a formal news conference. The official asked that he not be identified.

While the impact of the enemy offensive has varied from province to province, the official said that there was "little doubt" that local security forces as well as Government pacification teams had been shaken by the attacks, which began in earnest three and a half weeks ago during the Lunar New Year celebrations.

"Unquestionably there's been a considerable setback," the official said. "The real question

Continued on Page 20, Column 1

Johnson Unit Assails Whites in Negro Riots

Will Urge Drive on Prejudice, Neglect and Ignorance

Special to The New York Times

WASHINGTON, Feb. 24—The President's National Advisory Commission on Civil Disorders plans to recommend drastic changes in the operation of city governments, police departments and other institutions to help stem rising militancy and estrangement between whites and Negroes in urban areas.

The commission, appointed by President Johnson last July 27, has found that the primary cause of last summer's riots was a massive failure of the white majority, through prejudice and neglect, to deal justly with the Negro minority.

It found no evidence of organized direction or control, on either a national or local level, of the violence that broke out in American slums during the summer.

Militant black organizations and leaders, by their rhetoric, contributed to an atmosphere conducive to rioting, the commission concluded. But the thrust of its forthcoming report is to put the burden of responsibility chiefly on the white society.

Consequently, the commission is expected to say, the white society must assume the burden of initiating reforms that will attack the injustices, neglect and ignorance of Negro

The New York Times (by George Tames)

Gov. Otto Kerner of Illinois, right, is chairman of President Johnson's Commission on Civil Disorders. Mayor Lindsay, beside him, talking with aide, is group's vice chairman.

problems that are the root causes of disorder.

The commission, headed by Gov. Otto Kerner of Illinois, has prepared a broad set of recommendations that will touch various aspects of the society, with the Federal Government in the leadership role. The 11-member commission will meet next week to complete its voluminous report, scheduled for publication March 3.

The following recommendations, though far from inclusive and still tentative, are planned:

¶City governments should drastically decentralize their operations to make them more

Continued on Page 63, Column 1

Impact of Vietnam on Europe Grows

By HENRY TANNER

Special to The New York Times

PARIS, Feb. 24—The Vietcong's offensive in the cities of South Vietnam and the signs of American military vulnerability have made the war in Vietnam burst upon the European consciousness as never before.

Reports by correspondents of The New York Times from all the countries of Western Europe show a far greater sense of involvement and far stronger feelings than existed when the ground fighting took place in remote rice paddies and Europeans thought of the war primarily in terms of bombs falling on Hanoi.

There seems to be an almost universal feeling of revulsion over the horror of a war that most Europeans regard as unnecessary, unjustified, stupid and impossible to win.

The United States Administration's decision to continue bombing of the North appears to be regarded by the overwhelming majority of Europeans as the only important obstacle to negotiation and hence to ultimate peace.

Many editorialists do not believe that the Administration sincerely desires negotiation. Many see a link between the war and the Presidential election and are convinced that President Johnson is cynically making decisions that he thinks will help him at home.

Europeans view the setback to the pacification program in the countryside as meaning the collapse of the last possible pretense that the United States war effort might be in the interest of the South Vietnamese.

Maurice Couve de Murville, the French Foreign Minister, told the foreign policy commission of the National Assembly a few days ago that the South Vietnamese as well as the North Vietnamese Army were now "at war with the United States." The Foreign Ministry later said this was not an official statement.

But to judge from correspondents' reports, it is fairly close to the way most Europeans see it. In neutral Sweden a Cabinet Minister and the famous economist Gunnar Myrdal both took part

Continued on Page 27, Column 1

Today's Sections

Index to Subjects

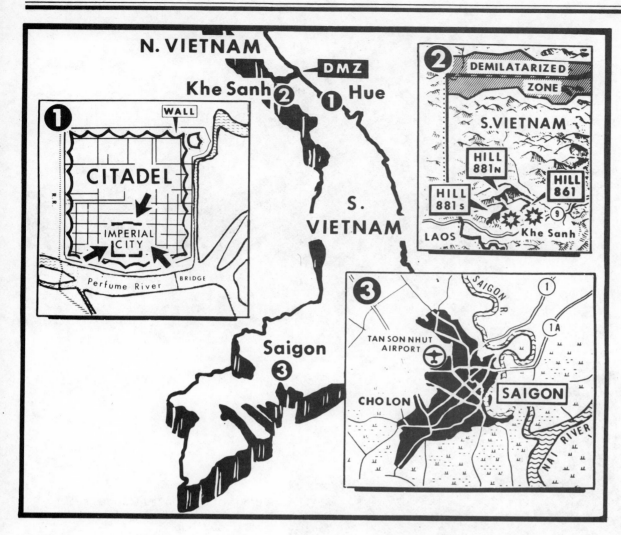

The numbered insets show the three main battlegrounds during the vicious Tet Offensive of early 1968: Hue, Khe Sanh and Saigon.

United Press International

His guitar and M-16 rifle slung from his shoulder, a Marine waits to be evacuated from the beleaguered fortress of Khe Sanh at the height of the Tet Offensive.

United Press International

A Marine observation plane makes a low level pass over Hue, the besieged Imperial City, during the Tet Offensive of 1968.

A group of surrounded Marines seek cover behind a wall in the Citadel during the Battle of Hue.

Fleeing refugees stream pass approaching tanks while the Battle of Hue rages.

"All the News That's Fit to Print"

The New York Times

LATE CITY EDITION

Weather: Snow today, clearing and windy tonight; fair, cold tomorrow. Temp. range: today 38-26; Tuesday 48-34. Full U.S. report on Page 93.

VOL. CXVII..No. 40,219

NEW YORK, WEDNESDAY, MARCH 6, 1968

10 CENTS

VIETCONG ATTACK CITY IN THE DELTA; FIGHTING IS HEAVY

Allied Units Retake Hospital After Hours of Battling—Report 250 of Foe Dead

1,000 HOMES DESTROYED

North Vietnamese Continue Shelling Khesanh Base—Shipyard Near Hanoi Hit

By JOSEPH B. TREASTER

Special to The New York Times

SAIGON, South Vietnam, Wednesday, March 6 — Vietcong guerrillas stormed into the capital of South Vietnam's southernmost province yesterday and occupied a hospital for several hours.

In fighting that raged most of the day, the hospital, the American military compound and some public buildings were extensively damaged. More than 1,000 homes were destroyed.

Through the night snipers' shots echoed in the streets of Quanlong, the usually quiet capital of Anxuyen province in the Mekong Delta. The city, formerly known as Camau, has a population of 6,000 to 8,000.

Mortar Raid Repeated

At 2 o'clock this morning, the guerrillas struck again with mortar rounds, setting fire to a dispensary. The extent of damage and casualties in the latest attack was not immediately known. There was apparently no follow-up ground assault.

Initial reports on the fighting yesterday indicated that at least 20 civilians had been killed and 50 wounded.

Allied military officials placed the number of Vietcong dead at 250 to 275. Losses among the Government troops who were called in to rout the enemy were said to be 10 dead and 41 wounded. Two American advisers were also wounded.

According to a Government spokesman, the Vietcong advanced into the city yesterday at 2:25 A.M. under cover of mortar fire and recoilless-rifle shells.

"They hit us from all sides," a military man said.

Attacks Widespread

Other enemy units struck American and South Vietnamese positions throughout the country with mortar fire and rockets. Generally, the damage was light.

Near the demilitarized zone, North Vietnamese troops continued to shell the United States Marine outpost at Khesanh despite steady pounding from American artillery and bombers.

American pilots flew 71 combat missions over North Vietnam. In one of them, Air Force bomber pilots struck for the first time at the Hadong shipyard six miles southwest of Hanoi. There was no report of damage.

Quanlong, the scene of the fighting in the delta, is a city of airy stucco buildings and macadam streets, surrounded on four sides by rivers and streams. The banks are crowded with thatched peasant huts. The city is 153 miles south-

Continued on Page 3, Column 1

United Press International

AT KHESANH: An American jet fires rockets into North Vietnamese positions that surround the Marine outpost

Nixon Vows to End War With a 'New Leadership'

By ROBERT B. SEMPLE Jr.

Special to The New York Times

NASHUA, N. H., March 5—Richard M. Nixon pledged today that "new leadership" in Washington—by which he presumably meant a new Republican Administration headed by himself—would "end the war" in Vietnam.

Mr. Nixon has said several times during the last seven days of his campaign for the Republican Presidential nomination that the American people would be justified in electing a new President if the present Administration failed to bring the war to a satisfactory conclusion by November.

The former Vice President appeared to take that position one step further with the following statement to a largely Republican crowd gathered at the American Legion Hall in Hampton, N. H., this morning:

"If in November this war is not over, after all of this power has been at their disposal, then I say that the American people will be justified to elect new leadership. And I pledge to you the new leadership will end the war and win the peace in the Pacific—and that is what America wants."

Cautions on Promise

Mr. Nixon went on to say that he could promise "no push-button technique" to end the war. He said he was not suggesting "withdrawal from Vietnam."

However, he went on, "I am saying to you" that the war "can be ended" if "we mobilize our economic and political and diplomatic leadership."

The American Legion Hall in Hampton was the first of six stops on an all-day tour that swept Mr. Nixon through six snow-covered towns in Rockingham County.

Apart from his statement on Vietnam, the most notable characteristic of today's tour was Mr. Nixon's apparent effort to breathe new life into the New Hampshire primary by turning it into a contest between himself and President Johnson and

Continued on Page 32, Column 7

PRAGUE DISMISSES IDEOLOGICAL CHIEF

Hendrych, Intellectuals' Foe, Out—Party to Publish Details on Shake-Up

By JONATHAN RANDAL

Special to The New York Times

PRAGUE, March 5—The new Communist leadership of Czechoslovakia announced tonight the dismissal of Jiri Hendrych from his influential post as secretary for ideological matters.

The 15-member party presidium, which met yesterday under Alexander Dubcek, the First Secretary, decided to publish a "full account" of the Central Committee sessions that culminated Jan. 5 in the ouster of Mr. Dubcek's predecessor as party leader, Antonin Novotny.

The decision to publish such an account was seen by observers as strengthening the position of those who are demanding that Mr. Novotny be stripped also of his remaining job as President of Czechoslovakia.

Mr Hendrych's replacement by Josef Spacek, one of the four new presidium members elected when Mr. Dubcek took power in January, reflected deep-seated opposition by Czechoslovak intellectuals.

Mr. Hendrych incurred their wrath by attacking rebellious writers and students last summer and autumn during the final months of Mr. Novotny's leadership.

He retained his job as Central Committee secretary by

Continued on Page 6, Column 4

JOHNSON BARS BID IN MASSACHUSETTS

Refusal to Go on the Ballot Leaves Field to McCarthy —Write-in Drive Hinted

Special to The New York Times

BOSTON, March 5—The chairman of the Democratic State Committee of Massachusetts announced today that President Johnson had decided against having his name on the ballot for the state's Presidential preference primary on April 30.

The chairman, Lester S. Hyman, said he had also been told that the President did not wish to be represented by a stand-in candidate.

Although Mr. Hyman held out the possibility of a write-in campaign for the President, one prominent Massachusetts Democrat said that he planned to resign as a delegate to the Democratic National Convention this summer rather than cast a ballot for Senator Eugene J. McCarthy of Minnesota.

The delegate, Edward J. McCormack, a former state Attorney General, said he was speaking for himself, but understood that other prominent members of the party also would resign as delegates. In this he included his uncle, John W. McCormack, the Speaker of the House, and Postmaster General Lawrence F. O'Brien.

Close to the Deadline

"Since we are all strong supporters of President Johnson," Edward McCormack said, "we find that as a matter of conscience we could not be delegates to a national convention required by law to vote against the President."

President Johnson's decision not to be represented on the ballot, announced just before a 5 P.M. filing deadline, meant that only the name of Senator McCarthy would be on the ballot for the Massachusetts Presidential preferential vote. Under the new Massachusetts primary law, effective in the April voting, the winner of the primary must get all the state's 72 votes on the first ballot at the convention.

In a prepared statement, distributed minutes after Mr. Hyman had made his announcement, Paul Counihan, Massachusetts campaign manager for the McCarthy for President Committee, said that the President's action "allows an easy victory by default for the Senator."

Mr. Hyman made a point of noting, however, that there was space on the ballot for

Continued on Page 32, Column 3

2 Medical Groups Urge Big Increase In Doctor Training

By HAROLD M. SCHMECK Jr.

Special to The New York Times

WASHINGTON, March 5—Two of the nation's key medical organizations joined today in a call for large increases in the number of doctors trained in the United States.

In a joint policy statement, the American Medical Association and the Association of American Medical Colleges said that the opportunity to go to medical school must be made available for all qualified men and women who want to do so.

Existing medical schools must be expanded and new ones built to make this possible, the presidents of the two organizations said at a news conference here at the Mayflower Hotel.

No Student-Aid Plan

They offered no specifics, however, on how much this might cost or who would pay for it. Nor were there any new proposals for helping would-be medical students pay the high cost of medical education.

The joint statement, read by Dr. Milford O. Rouse, president of the American Medical Association, said that the necessary financial support for expanded medical school facilities must be provided by the public, foundations, industry and government.

At present, the nation's 94 medical schools accept fewer than half of the applicants. Some of the rejected applicants are not properly qualified, but Dr. John Parks, president of the Association of American Medical Colleges, said that some qualified men and women who would like to be doctors do not apply.

He estimated there should be an increase of about 20 per cent in the number of new medical students during the next five years.

Dr. Rouse said that the capacity of medical schools must be increased 40 per cent during the next 25 years.

During the 1967-68 year the

Continued on Page 30, Column 6

L.I.R.R. SEEKS RISE OF 7 TO 10C A RIDE, TO BEGIN MARCH 22

Commutation Tickets Would Go Up by $3.10 to $4.60 —State Plans Hearings

By RICHARD WITKIN

The Long Island Rail Road, citing a "critical financial problem," has requested fare increases ranging from 7 to 10 cents a ride, effective March 22.

The request was announced yesterday by the Metropolitan Transportation Authority, the state agency that owns the railroad and is empowered to set fares. The authority said it would hold a public hearing here on the request on March 18.

Under the proposed rate schedule, the five-day-a-week monthly commutation ticket would be increased $4.60 for riders traveling to and from stations this side of Suffolk County. Suffolk commuters would pay only a $3.10 increase.

For trips this side of Suffolk, the March 22 fare increase would mean: 10 cents more for a one-way ride; 20 cents for a round-trip; $4.60 for a restricted monthly ticket; $6.00 for an unrestricted monthly ticket; and $1.20 for a unrestricted weekly ticket.

Suffolk Fares Lower

For Suffolk commuters, the increases would be: 7 cents one way; 14 cents round trip; $3.10 restricted monthly; $4.00 unrestricted monthly; and 80 cents weekly.

On the 27-mile run between Penn Station and Hicksville, in Nassau County, the one-way fare would go up from $1.55 to $1.65; the restricted monthly from $37.75 to $42.35; the unrestricted monthly from $43.55 to $40.55; and the unrestricted weekly from $10.40 to $11.60.

On the 39-mile run between Penn Station and Babylon in Suffolk County, the one-way fare would increase from $2.15 to $2.22; the restricted monthly from $43.50 to $46.60; the unrestricted monthly from $50.30 to $54.30; and the unrestricted weekly from $11.95 to $12.75.

The cost of school commutation tickets would increase $4.60 a month for non-Suffolk runs and $3.10 for Suffolk runs. Ten-trip tickets would cost $1 more for non-Suffolk runs and 70 cents more for Suffolk runs.

Counties Refuse to Help

The difference was not a matter of discrimination. It merely relieved Suffolk riders of a three-cents-a-ride penalty they started paying in 1963 when the county ceased making voluntary contributions to the cost of maintaining stations. The county is now making payments for the stations.

The issue of station costs throughout the system apparently had much to do with the request for a fare increase at this time.

The Metropolitan Transportation Authority is empowered under state law to charge such costs to local governments through whose areas the railroad runs. But the amounts of the bills sent out have been

Continued on Page 94, Column 1

Legislature Widens Shoot-to-Kill Power Of Police in Arrests

By SYDNEY H. SCHANBERG

Special to The New York Times

ALBANY, March 5 — The Legislature, in one of the most emotional debates of the session, voted tonight to broaden the powers of policemen and householders to shoot at suspected criminals and intruders.

The controversial shoot-to-kill bill, which is expected to be signed shortly by Governor Rockefeller, also includes a "no-sock" provision. This would make it a felony for a person to physically resist arrest by a policeman even if the arrest were illegal.

The Senate, after a debate that lasted more than two hours, passed the measure by 51 to 6. The Assembly, which debated the bill even longer, voted 126 to 17 to approve it.

Of the 17 negative votes in the Assembly, all but two were cast by Democrats. All six opposition votes in the Senate came from the Demo-

Continued on Page 43, Column 1

FRENCH AIRLINER CRASHES WITH 62

Hits a Guadeloupe Mountain and Bursts Into Flames —No Survivors Found

By United Press International

POINTE - A - PITRE, Guadeloupe, Wednesday, March 6—An Air France jetliner with 62 persons aboard crashed into the side of a mountain near the village of Saint Claude last night and burst into flames.

An Air France spokesman in Paris said that the first rescue teams to reach the crash site on Basse-Terre, one of the three main islands of Guadeloupe, reported no signs of survivors.

The plane, a Boeing 707 carrying 51 passengers and 11 crew members, crashed into the mountain, called Soufrière, at an altitude of about 3,900 feet. A French Air Force helicopter first spotted the wreckage on a part of the peak known as the Camp des Anglais.

Similar Crash in 1962

The crash was the second air disaster in the small overseas department of France in recent years. On June 22, 1962, an Air France Boeing 707 crashed in a storm over Guadeloupe, killing 113 people.

The circumstances surrounding the 1962 crash and the one last night were similar. In 1962, the plane was also on a regular scheduled run from Santiago, Chile, to Paris. It also crashed into a mountainside on Basse-Terre.

The plane last night was coming in for a landing at Pointe-a-Pitre, Guadeloupe's chief port and commercial center. It was running about a half hour late from its stop in Caracas, Venezuela.

Flames from the crash were visible in neighboring villages on Basse-Terre. The authorities from several surrounding villages rushed to the crash site

Continued on Page 16, Column 3

RIOT CURB ADDED TO BILL ON RIGHTS BY SENATE, 82-13

Amendment Would Make It U.S. Crime to Cross State Lines to Incite Disorder

LIBERALS ARE DEFEATED

Chamber Later Turns Down Plan to Weaken Provisions Calling for Open Housing

By MARJORIE HUNTER

Special to The New York Times

WASHINGTON, March 5 — The Senate expanded a controversial civil rights bill today to make it a Federal crime to cross state lines with intent to incite a riot.

The vote was 82 to 13, with opposition coming only from the stanchest liberals.

Later, the Senate rejected, 48 to 43, a move that would have drastically weakened the open housing provisions of the bill. The amendment by Senator Howard W. Baker, Republican of Tennessee, would have removed from the discrimination ban some 29 million single - family, owner - occupied homes — about 44 per cent of the nation's housing market.

The two roll-call votes highlighted a day of parliamentary tangles, sharp debate and increasing signs of frayed tempers as the Senate slowly waded through some of the dozens of pending amendments in an effort to move the rights bill closer to a final vote.

Provisions of Measure

As it now stands, the bill would do the following:

¶Provide a major step in breaking down housing barriers for Negroes and other minorities by banning discrimination in the sale and rental of about 45 million of the estimated 65 million housing units in the nation.

¶Provide stiff Federal penalties for persons convicted of intimidating or injuring civil rights workers or Negroes in such fields as schooling, housing, voting, registering to vote, jury duty and using public facilities.

¶Make it a Federal crime to travel from one state to another — or to use radio, television or other interstate facilities —with intent to incite a riot.

Continued on Page 31, Column 3

CITY OPENS DRIVE ON BUILDERS' BIAS

Says Contractor for School Shuns Minority Workers

By EDITH EVANS ASBURY

The City Human Rights Commission has begun a crackdown on contractors doing business with the city who refuse to employ Negroes and Puerto Ricans.

The commission issued a complaint yesterday against a contractor who is building an annex to a school in the Bedford-Stuyvesant section of Brooklyn, and also against eight union organizations involved.

The complaint was issued after an investigation disclosed that the company and the unions "have failed to recruit, accept and refer Negro and Puerto Rican journeymen and apprentices as members or employes on the same basis as whites," the commission said.

If, after a hearing, the contracting concern and the unions are found guilty of refusal to eliminate discrimination, their officers could be fined or jailed, the contract could be canceled, and the contractor could be banned from future city contracts for a period of time, according to the commission.

The annex to Primary School 21 is going up at 180 Chauncey Street and is in a predominantly Negro area.

"This is what the President's riot study report is all about," William H. Booth, chairman of the commission, said yesterday.

"These people in Bedford-

Continued on Page 28, Column 5

Soviet Pollution Foes Suffer a Defeat

By RAYMOND H. ANDERSON

Special to The New York Times

MOSCOW, March 5—A mood of defeat and despair appears to be emerging among Soviet scientists and conservationists in their bitter, decade-long struggle to prevent Lake Baikal, in Siberia, the world's largest body of fresh water by volume, from becoming a cesspool.

Despite pleas by conservationists and assuring promises of purification measures by industrial officials, a flow of yellow and odoriferous waste water is already being dumped into the lake by a huge wood-pulp plant at the mouth of the Solzan River on the lake's southern shore.

Conservationists are alarmed that the polluted water will ultimately destroy Lake Baikal's unique plant and animal life, which adapted

The New York Times March 6, 1968

over millions of years to the peculiarly cold and mineral-free environment.

Many species of water plants, mollusks and fish are found in no habitat other than Lake Baikal. They include the nerpa, a seal, and the golomyanka, a fish that produces living young instead of eggs.

The controversy over Lake Baikal was touched off nearly a decade ago when industrial planners unveiled a project for a vast pulp and paper-making complex to exploit the region's timber reserves.

The outcry from conservationists, including some of the country's most prominent scientists and writers, compelled the government to allocate millions of rubles to build the world's largest purification facilities for the complex.

The conservationists have insisted, nonetheless, that the industrial project was a mistake and demanded that

Continued on Page 11, Column 1

NEWS INDEX

Johnson and the Riot Panel's Report

By MAX FRANKEL

Special to The New York Times

WASHINGTON, March 5—No day passes at the White House now without someone asking for President Johnson's reaction to the grave warnings and far-reaching recommendations of his National Advisory Commission on Civil Disorders. But Mr. Johnson sits silent and his official spokesmen keep weaving, ducking and dodging.

The reason—though no one at the White House thinks it politic to say so in public at the moment—is that Mr. Johnson thinks the pleas for action and reaction are being wrongly addressed to the President.

Anyone can figure out how to spend more money, he believes, but his problem—even at present levels of commitment to help the cities and the poor—is to squeeze the money out of a reluctant Congress and a stingy public.

Plainly, Mr. Johnson does not want to quarrel openly with the commission over its failure to praise his programs and its low estimate of the progress he thinks has been made. But he is obviously displeased that the report offers so little aid and comfort in his immediate political battles on the same front.

Yes, the President has reviewed the report, his press secretary, George Christian, keeps saying.

Mr. Johnson expects it to be "carefully evaluated" by the Administration, Mr. Christian reiterated today. The President wants the executive branch to "check every phase" of the report. He "appreciates" the commission's work. He "certainly wants to examine any suggestions."

Did the report—in advocating massive new spending for the slums and bold efforts to integrate Negroes and whites —really tell Mr. Johnson anything he did not already know?

Well, of course, Mr. Christian replied, there has already been "substantial progress in the attacks on poverty" and some of the commission's proposals are already being tested or even applied in Administration programs. He is sure, he added, "the subject will be of continuing interest."

Doesn't it seem strange, with all this attention focused on a report by the President's own commission, that Mr. Johnson himself has made no comment? "Well," said Mr. Christian, "it'll just have to strike you as strange."

The subject arose at the

Continued on Page 23, Column 1

"All the News That's Fit to Print"

The New York Times

LATE CITY EDITION

Weather: Partly cloudy, warm today, some showers; colder tomorrow. Temp. range: today 73-43; Friday 48-43. Full U.S. report on Page 62.

VOL. CXVII . No. 40,236 — NEW YORK, SATURDAY, MARCH 23, 1968 — 10 CENTS

WESTMORELAND TO LEAVE VIETNAM, HEAD THE ARMY; U.S. MAY ADD 30,000 TROOPS

565,000 Total Is in View; Strategy Change Weighed

By WILLIAM BEECHER

Special to The New York Times

WASHINGTON, March 22—The Administration is moving toward adoption of a plan to send 30,000 more fighting men to Vietnam over the balance of the year.

The troop increase, well-placed Administration sources said, is likely to include an Army division or its equivalent, four to six Air Force squadrons and a few thousand Navy men.

The increase would be beyond the 525,000 men already approved for Vietnam and 10,500 paratroopers and marines rushed in as reinforcements last month. It would bring the new force level to about 565,000 men.

If the troop increase is limited to 30,000 men, the added budgetary costs above the estimates made in January would be only $1-billion or slightly more, according to both Administration estimates and outside calculations. Charles J. Zwick, the Director of the Budget, has testified that the cost of each additional man would be $20,000 to $40,000.

The budget estimated total defense spending at $77.2-billion, of which $26-billion was attributed to Vietnam. House and Senate members have placed the cost of the war at $30-billion a year.

It was still uncertain tonight whether a mobilization of reservists also would be ordered. The expectation was that roughly 40,000 men in the Army Reserve and National Guard might well be called to

Continued on Page 13, Column 1

SHIFT DUE BY JULY

President Announces Change for General Recently Criticized

News conference transcript appears on Page 12.

By MAX FRANKEL

Special to The New York Times

WASHINGTON, March 22—President Johnson announced today at a news conference his intention to appoint Gen. William C. Westmoreland as Army Chief of Staff, replacing him as commander of American forces in Vietnam sometime before July 2. [Opening statement, Page 12.]

No successor for the Vietnam command was announced.

If approved by the Senate, General Westmoreland would succeed Gen. Harold K. Johnson, who plans to retire.

The shift of General Westmoreland, whose tactics in the war have been heatedly debated here in recent weeks, was recommended to the President, he said, by both Robert S. McNamara, the former Secretary of Defense, and his successor, Clark Clifford.

The first suggestion from Mr. McNamara, the President said at the news conference in his office, came on Jan. 19 — eight days before the start of the enemy's Lunar New Year offensive against the South Vietnamese cities. [Opening statement.] The offensive seriously set back General Westmoreland's campaign.

Shows McNamara Note

Mr. Johnson held up a handwritten note from Mr. McNamara and went on to praise General Westmoreland as a "very talented and very able officer."

Mr. Johnson said no changes in strategy or tactics were implied by the change of personnel as such. But he left open the possibility that the new commander might make some new strategic or tactical recommendations.

General Westmoreland has been criticized particularly for his "search and destroy" concept of chasing enemy forces even into uninhabited terrain so as to inflict high casualties and wear them down by attrition.

Questions have also been raised concerning his willingness to stand in static defense

Continued on Page 12, Column 1

O'CONNOR TO LEAD STATEWIDE GROUP BACKING JOHNSON

Council President Concedes Electing Delegates Will Be a Difficult Task

WON'T ATTACK KENNEDY

Senator, Accused by Weisl of 'Lust for Power,' Says He Was 'Forced' to Run

By THOMAS P. RONAN

City Council President Frank D. O'Connor announced yesterday that he had agreed to serve as chairman of a statewide committee of Democrats supporting President Johnson for renomination.

He said the committee would establish headquarters here and elsewhere in the state to win support for the President and to elect pro-Johnson delegates to the Democratic national convention in August.

Mr. O'Connor conceded that it would be difficult in Senator Robert F. Kennedy's "quote home unquote state" to elect pro-Johnson delegates, but said he believed many of them would be chosen. Massachusetts was the Senator's home state until he ran in New York for the Senate.

Mr. O'Connor spoke at a news conference at the National Democratic Club, 233 Madison Avenue.

Shuns Personal Attacks

He said he thought Mr. Kennedy would be "in difficulty" in his effort to get the Democratic nomination for President if he did not obtain at least 100 of the state's 190 delegates to the national convention. He predicted Mr. Kennedy would not get that many.

Mr. O'Connor insisted that his committee was not designed "to stop Senator Kennedy or anyone else," but to bring home to the people of this state "the tremendous record of President Johnson."

He said he would not at any time personally attack Mr. Kennedy, whom he supported for United States Senator, or question the Senator's "motives, intentions or patriotism."

Edwin L. Weisl, Democratic national committeeman from the state and a long-time friend of Mr. Johnson, held the news

Continued on Page 17, Column 3

Powell Back, Granted Parole Pending Appeal in Contempt

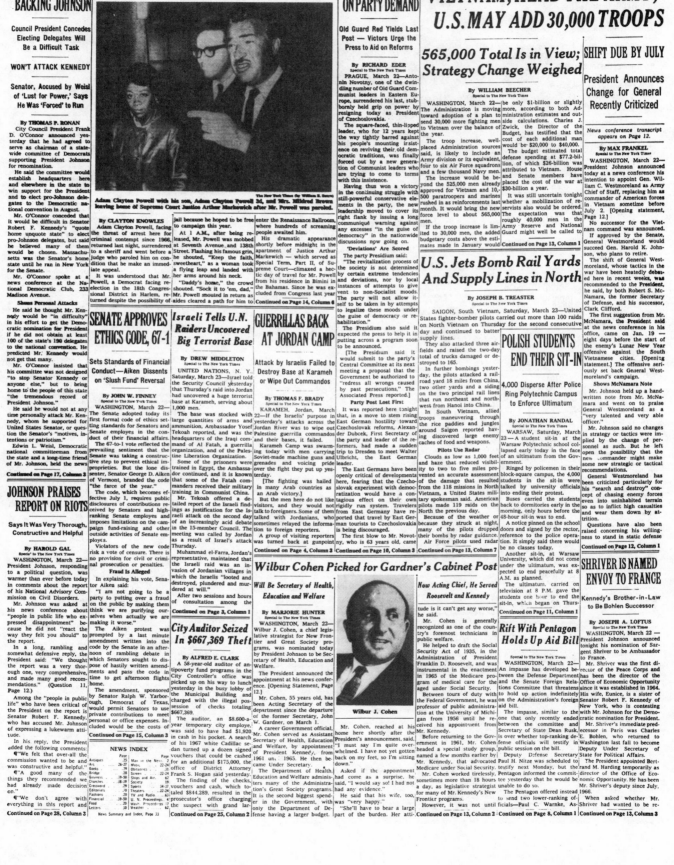

The New York Times (by William E. Sauro)

Adam Clayton Powell with his son, Adam Clayton Powell 3d, and Mrs. Mildred Brown leaving home of Supreme Court Justice Arthur Markewich after Mr. Powell was paroled.

By CLAYTON KNOWLES

Adam Clayton Powell, facing the threat of arrest here for criminal contempt since 1966, returned last night, surrendered to a sheriff and went before a judge who paroled him on condition that he make an immediate appeal.

It was understood that Mr. Powell, a Democrat facing re-election in the 18th Congressional District in Harlem, returned despite the possibility of jail because he hoped to be free to campaign this year.

At 1 A.M., after being released, Mr. Powell was mobbed at Seventh Avenue and 138th Street. Flashing his famous grin, he shouted, "Keep the faith, sweetheart," as a woman took a flying leap and landed with her arms around his neck.

"Daddy's home," the crowd shouted. "Sock it to 'em, dad," Mr. Powell shouted in return as aides cleared a path for him to enter the Renaissance Ballroom, where hundreds of screaming people awaited him.

His dramatic appearance shortly before midnight in the apartment of Justice Arthur Markewich — which served as Special Term, Part II, of Supreme Court—climaxed a hectic day of travel for Mr. Powell from his residence in Bimini in the Bahamas. Since he was excluded from Congress last year

Continued on Page 14, Column 6

NOVOTNY RESIGNS CZECH PRESIDENCY ON PARTY DEMAND

Old Guard Red Yields Last Post — Victors Urge the Press to Aid on Reforms

By RICHARD EDER

Special to The New York Times

PRAGUE, March 22—Antonin Novotny, one of the dwindling number of Old Guard Communist leaders in Eastern Europe, surrendered his last, stubbornly held grip on power by resigning today as President of Czechoslovakia.

The square-faced, thin-lipped leader, who for 12 years kept the way tightly barred against his people's mounting insistence on reviving their old democratic traditions, was finally forced out by a new generation of Communist leaders who are trying to come to terms with this insistence.

Having thus won a victory in the continuing struggle with still-powerful conservative elements in the party, the new leadership moved to cover its right flank by issuing a long communiqué warning against any excesses "in the guise of democracy" in the nationwide discussions now going on.

'Deviations' Are Scored

The party Presidium said:

"The revitalization process of the society is not determined by certain extreme tendencies and deviations, nor by local instances of attempts to give vent to non-Socialist moods. The party will not allow itself to be taken in by attempts to legalize these moods under the guise of democracy or rehabilitation."

The Presidium also said it expected the press to help it in putting across a program soon to be announced.

[The Presidium said it would submit to the party's Central Committee at its next meeting a proposal that the Government be authorized to "redress all wrongs caused by past persecutions," The Associated Press reported.]

Party Post Lost First

It was reported here tonight that, in a move to stem rising East German hostility toward Czechoslovak reforms, Alexander Dubcek, First Secretary of the party and leader of the reformers, had made a sudden trip to Dresden to meet Walter Ulbricht, the East German leader.

The East Germans have been openly critical of developments here, fearing that the Czechoslovak experiment with democratization would have a contagious effect on their own rigidly run system. Travelers from East Germany have reported that travel by East German tourists to Czechoslovakia is being discouraged.

The first blow to Mr. Novotny, who is 63 years old, came

Continued on Page 10, Column 3

U.S. Jets Bomb Rail Yards And Supply Lines in North

By JOSEPH B. TREASTER

Special to The New York Times

SAIGON, South Vietnam, Saturday, March 23—United States fighter-bomber pilots carried out more than 100 raids on North Vietnam on Thursday for the second consecutive day and continued to batter supply lines.

They also attacked three airfields and raised the two-day total of trucks damaged or destroyed to 165.

In further bombings yesterday, the pilots attacked a railroad yard 18 miles from China, two other yards and a siding on the two principal rail lines that run northeast and northwest from Hanoi into China.

In South Vietnam, allied troops maneuvering through the rice paddies and jungles around Saigon reported having discovered large enemy caches of food and weapons.

Pilots Use Radar

Clouds as low as 1,000 feet and haze that reduced visibility to two to five miles prevented an accurate assessment of the damage that resulted from the 118 missions in North Vietnam, a United States military spokesman said. American pilots made 119 raids on the North the previous day.

Because of the weather or because they struck at night, many of the pilots dropped their bombs by radar guidance.

Air Force pilots used radar

Continued on Page 13, Column 7

POLISH STUDENTS END THEIR SIT-IN

4,000 Disperse After Police Ring Polytechnic Campus to Enforce Ultimatum

By JONATHAN RANDAL

Special to The New York Times

WARSAW, Saturday, March 23 — A student sit-in at the Warsaw Polytechnic school collapsed early today in the face of an ultimatum from the Government.

Ringed by policemen in their block-square campus, the 4,000 students in the sit-in were talked by university officials into ending their protest.

Buses carried the students back to dormitories early in the morning, only hours before the 48-hour sit-in was to end.

A notice pinned on the school doors and signed by the rector, reference to the police operation. It simply said there would be no classes today.

Another sit-in, at Warsaw University, which did not come under the ultimatum, was expected to end peacefully at 8 A.M. as planned.

The ultimatum, carried on television at 8 P.M. gave the students one hour to end the sit-in, which began on Thurs-

Continued on Page 11, Column 1

SENATE APPROVES ETHICS CODE, 67-1

Sets Standards of Financial Conduct—Aiken Dissents on 'Slush Fund' Reversal

By JOHN W. FINNEY

Special to The New York Times

WASHINGTON, March 22—The Senate adopted today its first formal code of ethics setting standards for Senators and Senate employes in the conduct of their financial affairs.

The 67-to-1 vote reflected the prevailing sentiment that the Senate was taking a constructive step to prevent ethical improprieties. But the lone dissenter, Senator George D. Aiken of Vermont, branded the code "the farce of the year."

The code, which becomes effective July 1, requires public disclosures of contributions received by Senators and high-ranking Senate employes and imposes limitations on the campaign fund-raising and other outside activities of Senate employes.

Violators of the new code risk a vote of censure. There is no provision for civil or criminal prosecution or penalties.

Fraud Is Alleged

In explaining his vote, Senator Aiken said:

"I am not going to be a party to putting over a fraud on the public by making them think we are purifying ourselves when actually we are making it worse."

The Aiken protest was prompted by a last minute amendment written into the code by the Senate in an afternoon of rambling debate in which Senators sought to dispose of hastily written amendments and pass the code in time to get afternoon flights home.

The amendment, sponsored by Senator Ralph W. Yarborough, Democrat of Texas, would permit Senators to use private contributions to meet personal or office expenses. Included would be the costs of

Continued on Page 15, Column 3

Israeli Tells U.N. Raiders Uncovered Big Terrorist Base

By DREW MIDDLETON

Special to The New York Times

UNITED NATIONS, N. Y., Saturday, March 23—Israel told the Security Council yesterday that Thursday's raid into Jordan had uncovered a huge terrorist base at Karameh, serving about 1,000 men.

The base was stocked with large quantities of arms and ammunition, Ambassador Yosef Tekoah reported, and was the headquarters of the Iraqi command of Al Fatah, a guerrilla organization, and of the Palestine Liberation Organization.

Some of the prisoners were trained in Egypt, the Ambassador continued, and it is known that some of the Fatah commanders received their military training in Communist China.

Mr. Tekoah offered a detailed report of the Israeli findings as justification for the Israeli attack on the second day of an increasingly acid debate in the 15-member Council. The meeting was called by Jordan as a result of Israel's attack Thursday.

Muhammad el-Farra, Jordan's representative, maintained that the Israeli raid was an invasion of Jordanian villages in which the Israelis "looted and destroyed, plundered and murdered at will."

After two sessions and hours of consultation among the

Continued on Page 3, Column 1

GUERRILLAS BACK AT JORDAN CAMP

Attack by Israelis Failed to Destroy Base at Karameh or Wipe Out Commandos

By THOMAS F. BRADY

Special to The New York Times

KARAMEH, Jordan, March 22—If the Israelis' purpose in yesterday's attacks across the Jordan River was to wipe out Palestine guerrilla commandos and their bases, it failed.

Karameh Camp was swarming today with men carrying Soviet-made machine guns and grenades and voicing pride over the fight they put up yesterday.

[The fighting was hailed in many Arab countries as an Arab victory.]

But the men here do not like visitors, and they would not talk to foreigners. Some of them talked with Jordanians, who sometimes relayed the information to foreign reporters.

A group of visiting reporters was turned back at gunpoint

Continued on Page 4, Column 3

JOHNSON PRAISES REPORT ON RIOTS

Says It Was Very Thorough, Constructive and Helpful

By HAROLD GAL

Special to The New York Times

WASHINGTON, March 22—President Johnson, responding to a political question, was warmer than ever before today in comments about the report of his National Advisory Commission on Civil Disorders.

Mr. Johnson was asked at his news conference about "people in public life who expressed disappointment" because he did not "react the way they felt you should" to the report.

In a long, rambling and somewhat defensive reply, the President said: "We thought the report was a very thorough one, very comprehensive, and made many good recommendations." (Question 11, Page 12.)

Among the "people in public life" who have been critical of the President on the report is Senator Robert F. Kennedy, who has accused Mr. Johnson of expressing a lukewarm attitude.

In his reply, the President added the following comments:

¶"We felt that over-all the commission wanted to be and was constructive and helpful."

¶"A good many of the things they recommended we had already made decision on."

¶"We don't agree with everything in this report and

Continued on Page 28, Column 3

City Auditor Seized In $667,369 Theft

By ALFRED E. CLARK

A 58-year-old auditor of antipoverty fund programs in the City Controller's office was picked up on his way to lunch yesterday in the busy lobby of the Municipal Building and charged with the illegal possession of checks totaling $667,369.

The auditor, an $8,600-a-year temporary city employe, was said to have had $1,920 in cash in his pocket. A search of his 1967 white Cadillac sedan turned up a dozen signed vouchers that could be cashed for an additional $175,000, the office of District Attorney Frank S. Hogan said yesterday.

The finding of the checks, vouchers and cash, which totaled $844,289, resulted in the prosecutor's office charging the suspect with grand lar-

Continued on Page 25, Column 2

NEWS INDEX

Wilbur Cohen Picked for Gardner's Cabinet Post

Will Be Secretary of Health, Education and Welfare

Now Acting Chief, He Served Roosevelt and Kennedy

By MARJORIE HUNTER

Special to The New York Times

WASHINGTON, March 22—Wilbur J. Cohen, a chief legislative strategist for New Frontier and Great Society programs, was nominated today by President Johnson to be Secretary of Health, Education and Welfare.

The President announced the appointment at his news conference. [Opening Statement, Page 12.]

Mr. Cohen, 55 years old, has been Acting Secretary of the department since the departure of the former Secretary, John W. Gardner, on March 1.

A career Government official, Mr. Cohen served as Assistant Secretary of Health, Education and Welfare, by appointment of President Kennedy, from 1961 until 1965. He then became Under Secretary.

The Department of Health, Education and Welfare administers many of the Administration's Great Society programs. It is the second biggest spender in the Government, with only the Department of Defense having a larger budget.

Wilbur J. Cohen

Mr. Cohen, reached at his home here shortly after the President's announcement, said, "I must say I'm quite overwhelmed. I have not yet gotten back on my feet, so I'm sitting down."

Asked if the appointment had come as a surprise, he said, "I would say so! I had not had any evidence."

He said that his wife, too, was "very happy."

"She'll have to bear a large part of the burden. Her attitude is it can't get any worse," he said.

Mr. Cohen is generally recognized as one of the country's foremost technicians in public welfare.

He helped to draft the Social Security Act of 1935, in the Administration of President Franklin D. Roosevelt, and was instrumental in the enactment in 1965 of the Medicare program of medical care for the aged under Social Security.

Between tours of duty with the Federal Government, he was professor of public administration at the University of Michigan from 1956 until he received his appointment from Mr. Kennedy.

Before returning to the Government in 1961, Mr. Cohen headed a special study group, named a few months earlier by Mr. Kennedy, that advocated Medicare under Social Security.

Mr. Cohen worked tirelessly, sometimes more than 18 hours a day, as legislative strategist for many of Mr. Kennedy's New Frontier programs.

However, it was not until

Continued on Page 13, Column 2

Rift With Pentagon Holds Up Aid Bill

Special to The New York Times

WASHINGTON, March 22—An impasse has developed between the Defense Department and the Senate Foreign Relations Committee that threatens to hold up action indefinitely on the Administration's foreign aid bill.

The impasse, similar to the one that only recently ended between the committee and Secretary of State Dean Rusk, is over whether top-ranking defense officials will testify in public session on the bill.

Deputy Defense Secretary Paul H. Nitze was scheduled to testify next Monday, but the Pentagon informed the committee yesterday that he would be unable to do so.

The Pentagon offered instead to send two lower-ranking officials—Paul C. Warnke, As-

Continued on Page 8, Column 1

SHRIVER IS NAMED ENVOY TO FRANCE

Kennedy's Brother-in-Law to Be Bohlen Successor

By JOSEPH A. LOFTUS

Special to The New York Times

WASHINGTON, March 22 — President Johnson announced tonight his nomination of Sargent Shriver to be Ambassador to France.

Mr. Shriver was the first director of the Peace Corps and has been the director of the Office of Economic Opportunity since it was established in 1964. His wife, Eunice, is a sister of Senator Robert F. Kennedy of New York, who is contesting with Mr. Johnson for the Democratic nomination for President.

Mr. Shriver's immediate predecessor in Paris was Charles E. Bohlen, who returned to Washington last fall to become Deputy Under Secretary of State for Political Affairs.

The President appointed Bertrand M. Harding temporarily as director of the Office of Economic Opportunity. He has been Mr. Shriver's deputy since July, 1966.

When asked whether Mr. Shriver had wanted to be re-

Continued on Page 13, Column 3

Smoke rises from a fuel dump at Khe Sanh in the northern Quang Tri Province after a Communist mortar barrage.

Leathernecks of the Second Battalion, Fourth Marines, wait for gas to clear before assaulting a North Vietnamese stronghold in the Quang Tri Province.

Marines and South Vietnamese forces open fire on a sniper while on a patrol outside of Quang Tri City.

"All the News That's Fit to Print"

The New York Times

LATE CITY EDITION

Weather: Partial clearing today; fair, cool tonight and tomorrow. Temp. range: today 62-53; Sunday 68-48. Full U.S. report on Page 90.

VOL. CXVII..No. 40,245

NEW YORK, MONDAY, APRIL 1, 1968

10 CENTS

JOHNSON SAYS HE WON'T RUN; HALTS NORTH VIETNAM RAIDS; BIDS HANOI JOIN PEACE MOVES

ROCKEFELLER URGES ALBANY LEADERS TO SPEED BUDGET

Ready to Work With Them to Provide Funds as Fiscal Year Opens Today

By PETER KIHSS

Governor Rockefeller urged Republican and Democratic legislative leaders yesterday to agree quickly on a new budget as the state moved into the 1968-69 fiscal year today without a budget.

The Republican - controlled Senate has passed one version of the budget, but the Democratic-controlled Assembly is pondering a counter-version. The Governor said in a statement he was "ready to work with the leadership in both houses" for "a budget that meets the needs of the people of our state and provides the revenues necessary to finance it."

After the Legislature does act, the Governor will presumably seek a supplemental appropriation to restore some of the spending cuts that both parties' legislative fiscal committees make in his proposed school, urban, crime and construction programs. This is a traditional technique.

Assembly May Act Today

Fiscal aides to Assembly Speaker Anthony J. Travia analyzed the Senate proposals through the night. Mr. Travia himself said he was considering two interim moves. One would have the Assembly approve the budget appropriations and cuts already agreed on; the other would seek a temporary authorization for state spending at the rate for the last quarter of the fiscal year just ended.

Joseph Zaretzki, Senate Democratic minority leader, charged here yesterday that the budget bills rammed through the Senate early Saturday by the Republican leader, Earl Brydges, and his party followers aimed only "to get by next November's election."

Senator Zaretzki asserted that two of its key elements—

Continued on Page 38, Column 3

Liberals Designate Javits; Nickerson Race Confused

Baron May Enter Race

By CLAYTON KNOWLES

The Liberal party State Committee designated Senator Jacob K. Javits for re-election late yesterday, but under conditions that confronted him with the prospect of waging a primary fight to gain the extra line on the voting machines.

A bloc of unionists in the party, contending that an endorsement of Mr. Javits would aid Richard M. Nixon in his Presidential bid, put up Murray Baron, a long-time Liberal leader. Although Mr. Baron lost, he rolled up enough votes to qualify to run in the June 18 primary.

The Liberals acted several hours before President Johnson's withdrawal. Mr. Baron came under heavy attack in the prevote debate as "more

Continued on Page 50, Column 1

Johnson Causes Upset

The contest for the Democratic Senate nomination in New York was thrown into confusion last night by President Johnson's announcement that he would not seek the party's nomination for re-election.

Eugene H. Nickerson, the organization's candidate for the nomination and a supporter of Senator Robert F. Kennedy, said of the Johnson announcement: "I was very surprised. It just comes as such a complete surprise to me that I think we have to sleep on it."

Representative Joseph Y. Resnick of Ellenville, a Senate candidate who supports President Johnson, sent a telegram to the President urging the President to reconsider his decision.

"Mr. President," the Resnick

Continued on Page 50, Column 5

3 Beachfront Hotels Destroyed by Fire In Rockaway Park

By LAWRENCE VAN GELDER

Flames spurred by howling ocean winds raged through the Rockaway Park section of Queens yesterday, destroying three beachfront hotels, damaging small stores and bungalows, charring police and fire equipment and forcing the evacuation of hundreds of residents.

As the number of alarms climbed swiftly to eight, more than 400 firemen and 60 pieces of equipment were pitted against the intense blaze, which sent up a column of gray smoke visible for more than a dozen miles in the afternoon sky.

Despite the fury of the fire and the menacing wind-whipped embers that flew through the neighborhood around Beach 116th Street and Ocean Promenade, no serious injuries were reported from the blaze, which was attributed by officials to three small children. Four firemen, however, were reported

Continued on Page 36, Column 4

HOUSE PLAN SPURS INVESTING ABROAD

Committee Asks Creation of Quasi-Public Corporation to Attract Private Capital

By FELIX BELAIR Jr.

By The Associated Press

WASHINGTON, March 31—The House Foreign Affairs Committee urged in a report today that the Federal Government consider creating a quasi-public corporation to promote private American investments in underdeveloped countries.

The report, originated by Representative Leonard Farbstein, Democrat of Manhattan, won the unanimous approval of the committee.

The gist of the report was that the investment guarantee program of the Agency for International Development was no longer able to attract sufficient private capital to spur economic growth in the poor countries of Latin America,

Continued on Page 8, Column 1

TAX RISE PUSHED

Increase in War Costs Cited—No Specific Cuts Suggested

By EILEEN SHANAHAN

Special to The New York Times

WASHINGTON, March 31—President Johnson called on Congress tonight to "move from debate to action, from talking to voting" on a tax increase.

He pledged himself to accept any appropriate reductions in Federal spending that Congress voted, but he proposed nothing specific in the way of economy moves.

He announced, in fact, that there would be an increase in Government outlays because of the war. These, he said, would amount to $2.5-billion in the current fiscal year, which ends June 30, and $2.6-billion in the next fiscal year.

What effect the President's decision not to run for re-election might have on the long fight over the tax increase and Government spending was not immediately clear. A lame duck President is usually considered to have greatly diminished power to influence Congress, but the President's removal of himself from the campaign could also remove some of the partisanship from the tax and spending issue.

Deficit to Increase

The increases the President announced in defense spending would raise the deficit for the current year to $22.3-billion and for next year to $20.5-billion, if the 10 per cent tax surcharge is not enacted, and assuming that there are no other changes in spending from the official January estimates.

If the tax increase is enacted, with April 1 the effective date for individuals and Jan. 1 for corporations, as the President has asked, this year's deficit would be $20.4-billion and next year's, $10.6-billion.

"Enactment of a tax increase now, together with expenditure control, is necessary to protect our security, continue our prosperity and meet the needs of our people," Mr. Johnson said.

He said he believed there

Continued on Page 30, Column 3

DMZ IS EXEMPTED

Johnson Sets No Time Limit on Halting of Air and Sea Blows

By MAX FRANKEL

Special to The New York Times

WASHINGTON, March 31—President Johnson announced tonight that he had ordered a halt in the air and naval bombardment of most of North Vietnam and invited the Hanoi Government to join him in a "series of mutual moves toward peace."

The President said:

"Tonight, in the hope that this action will lead to early talks, I am taking the first step to de-escalate the conflict. We are reducing—substantially reducing—the present level of hostilities. And we are doing so unilaterally and at once."

The President said that attacks would continue only in the area just north of the demilitarized zone, which separates North Vietnam from South Vietnam, and where, he said, the "continuing enemy build-up directly threatens allied forward positions and where movements of troops and supplies are clearly related to that threat."

Hanoi's Stand Recalled

The President set no time limit for his restraint order. Until now, North Vietnam has demanded an "unconditional" —apparently meaning permanent—halt in the bombing of all its territory and all other acts of war against it.

North Vietnam's restraint and other unspecified events, the President indicated, can make possible an early end of "even this limited bombing."

The areas to be spared, he said, include almost 90 per cent of North Vietnam's population and "most of its territory."

The White House refused to give a more specific geographical delineation.

[In Saigon, the United States command said that the order went into effect at 9 P.M. Sunday, New York time, when President Johnson began his address, The Associated Press reported. Page 15.]

At the same time, Mr. Johnson used a televised address to the nation to urge the Soviet Union and Britain to do everything possible to move from his "unilateral act of de-escalation" toward a genuine peace.

He designated Ambassador at Large W. Averell Harriman and the American Ambassador to Moscow, Llewellyn Thomp-

Continued on Page 28, Column 1

Associated Press

ADDRESSES THE NATION: President Johnson last night

SURPRISE DECISION

President Steps Aside in Unity Bid—Says 'House' Is Divided

Text of Johnson's address will be found on Page 26.

By TOM WICKER

Special to The New York Times

WASHINGTON, March 31—Lyndon Baines Johnson announced tonight: "I shall not seek and I will not accept the nomination of my party as your President."

Later, at a White House news conference, he said his decision was "completely irrevocable."

The President told his nationwide television audience:

"What we have won when all our people were united must not be lost in partisanship. I have concluded that I should not permit the Presidency to become involved in partisan decisions."

Mr. Johnson, acknowledging that there was "division in the American house," withdrew in the name of national unity, which he said was "the ultimate strength of our country."

"With American sons in the field far away," he said, "with the American future under challenge right here at home, with our hopes and the world's hopes for peace in the balance every day, I do not believe that I should devote an hour or a day of my time to any personal partisan causes or to any duties other than the awesome duties of this office, the Presidency of your country."

Humphrey Race Possible

Mr. Johnson left Senator Robert F. Kennedy of New York and Senator Eugene J. McCarthy of Minnesota as the only two declared candidates for the Democratic Presidential nomination.

Vice President Humphrey, however, will be widely expected to seek the nomination now that his friend and political benefactor, Mr. Johnson, is out of the field. Mr. Humphrey indicated that he would have a statement on his plans tomorrow.

The President informed Mr. Humphrey of his decision during a conference at the latter's apartment in southwest Washington today before the Vice President flew to Mexico City. There, he will represent the United States at the signing of a treaty for a Latin-American nuclear-free zone.

Surprise to Aides

If Mr. Humphrey should become a candidate, he would find most of the primaries foreclosed to him. Only those in the District of Columbia, New Jersey and South Dakota remain open.

Therefore, he would have to rely on collecting delegates in states without primaries and on White House support if he were to head off Mr. Kennedy and Mr. McCarthy.

Former Vice President Richard M. Nixon is the only announced major candidate for the Republican nomination, although Governor Rockefeller has said that he would accept the nomination if drafted.

Mr. Johnson's announcement tonight came as a stunning surprise even to close associates. His main political strategists, James H. Rowe of Washington, White House Special Assistant Marvin W. Watson, and Postmaster General Lawrence F. O'Brien, spent much of today conferring on campaign plans.

They were informed of what was coming just before Mr.

Continued on Page 27, Column 1

Political Chiefs Stunned; Kennedy Sets News Parley

By SYLVAN FOX

Political leaders across the country reacted with shock, surprise and—in some cases—admiration to President Johnson's announcement last night that he would not seek re-election in November. Some political leaders immediately focused attention on Vice President Humphrey as a possible contender for the Democratic Presidential nomination.

Others suggested that Mr. Johnson's withdrawal could alter the position of Governor Rockefeller, who pulled out of contention for the Republican Presidential nomination on March 21.

Neither Mr. Humphrey nor Mr. Rockefeller was commenting immediately on his political plans in the light of Mr. Johnson's withdrawal.

Senator Robert F. Kennedy, like many others, was left almost speechless by the President's announcement.

"I don't know quite what to say," Senator Kennedy commented when he got the word of the President's decision. The Senator, a leading contender for the Democratic Presidential nomination, scheduled a news conference for 10 A.M. today.

Continued on Page 27, Column 4

WISCONSIN WEIGHS IMPACT ON VOTING

Primary Excitement Turns to Surprise—McCarthy and Nixon Wind Up Campaign

By DONALD JANSON

Special to The New York Times

MILWAUKEE, March 31—Excitement over a spirited contest between Senator Eugene J. McCarthy and President Johnson in the Wisconsin Democratic Presidential primary turned to surprise tonight with the President's announcement that he was not a candidate for re-election.

Thousands of Wisconsin voters, who had expected to choose between the two on Tuesday, saw and heard the President on television take himself out of the contest.

The announcement ended speculation that the Wisconsin primary, the first in the nation to have the President's name on the ballot, would produce a record vote.

It left only Senator McCarthy as an active candidate on the Democratic ballot and only former Vice President Richard M. Nixon as a major candidate on the Republican side. It eliminated the urgency that thousands of Republicans had felt to cross over to the Democratic contest to vote against the

Continued on Page 48, Column 1

Top Saigon Officials Confused By Refusal of Johnson to Run

By GENE ROBERTS

Special to The New York Times

SAIGON, South Vietnam, Monday, April 1—President Johnson's refusal to seek re-election plunged the top level of the South Vietnamese Government into confusion today and touched off a meeting of key American officials.

It was apparent, according to Americans who were at the presidential palace at the time, that President Johnson's announcement caught the South Vietnamese by surprise.

"Top advisers and officeholders began rushing toward the Vice President's office in obvious states of agitation," said one American who was waiting for a conference with Vice President Nguyen Cao Ky. "A few minutes later, Ky's military aide appeared and said all appointments had been canceled."

There was similar excitement at the United States Embassy. A receptionist said that no high officials were available for comment and explained that they were all in a top-level meeting.

There was also a rash of meetings at the headquarters of the military command here.

While many military officers and virtually all South Vietnamese officials are op-

Continued on Page 28, Column 5

The New York Times (by William E. Sauro)

AT ROCKAWAY PARK BLAZE: More than 400 firemen were called out to fight eight-alarm fire that raged on Beach 116th Street in the Rockaway Park section of Queens. Jamaica Bay is in rear. Four firemen were slightly hurt.

NEWS INDEX

News Summary and Index, Page 47

Marines of the 11th Engineer Battalion quickly put up a new bridge en route to Khe Sanh.

U.S. colors as seen from the Command Bunker on top of beleaguered Hill 881.

This chopper was one of eight used in a giant resupply effort in the Khe Sanh area in February 1968. Here, the helicopter is shown carrying a 3,000-pound load of ammunition on its cargo hook.

"All the News That's Fit to Print"

The New York Times

LATE CITY EDITION

Weather: mostly fair today; chance of showers tonight and tomorrow. Temp. range: today 60-42; Tuesday 61-36. Full U.S. report on Page 94.

VOL. CXVII . No. 40,247 | © 1968 The New York Times Company. | NEW YORK, WEDNESDAY, APRIL 3, 1968 | 10 CENTS

M'CARTHY WINS WISCONSIN; POLLS 57% TO JOHNSON'S 35; G.O.P. GIVES 80% TO NIXON

REAGAN GETS 10%

Kennedy Write-in 6% —Turnout Heavy in Primary Contests

By E. W. KENWORTHY
Special to The New York Times

MILWAUKEE, Wednesday, April 3—Senator Eugene J. McCarthy won a decisive victory yesterday over President Johnson in the Wisconsin Presidential primary.

With 90 per cent of the precincts reported, Senator McCarthy had 57 per cent of the Democratic vote, against 35 per cent for the President.

This fell slightly short of what some analysts had predicted prior to the President's announcement three days ago that he would not seek or accept renomination.

However, the margin was substantial enough, coming after Mr. McCarthy's showing in New Hampshire, to make him now a serious contender for the nomination and to give him the needed impetus for the crucial test against Senator Robert F. Kennedy in Indiana on May 7.

In the Republican primary, former Vice President Richard M. Nixon captured 80 per cent of the vote against 10 per cent for Gov. Ronald Reagan of California and 6 per cent for Harold E. Stassen.

With 2,880 of the state's 3,291 precincts reported, these were the totals in the two primaries:

DEMOCRATIC	
McCarthy	371,664
Johnson	231,441
Kennedy	38,401
Wallace	3,076
Humphrey	2,083
REPUBLICAN	
Nixon	357,320
Reagan	47,043
Stassen	26,425
Rockefeller	6,720
Wallace	1,255

Mr. McCarthy captured 52 of the 60 delegates by winning in eight of the 10 Congressional districts, which gave him 32 delegates. And by winning the statewide preferential vote he captured the prize of 20 delegates-at-large.

President Johnson got eight delegates by winning the pref-

Continued on Page 28, Column 5

Associated Press

THE WINNER: Senator Eugene J. McCarthy, Democrat of Minnesota, giving the victory sign in Milwaukee last night.

M'CARTHY URGES LEADERS TO WAIT

Bids Daley and Others Bar Rush to Kennedy—Cites 'Significant Victory'

By STEVEN V. ROBERTS
Special to The New York Times

MILWAUKEE, April 2—Senator Eugene J. McCarthy has asked many of the country's Democratic leaders to "stand firm" and not make any hasty commitments in the party's contest for the Presidential nomination.

With President Johnson out of the competition, Senator McCarthy hopes to forestall any rush to Senator Robert F. Kennedy and give himself time to increase the political strength he has been slowly gaining since he entered the race last November.

Senator McCarthy appeared before a tumultuous group of several thousand screaming supporters at about 11 P.M. and declared:

"We have demonstrated our ability here in Wisconsin to win the election in November."

"I am sorry my principal opponent didn't last out the home stretch," he added, "but by any interpretation this is a most significant victory."

The Senator spoke at a news conference earlier today at Eppley Field in Omaha. He flew to Nebraska for a noontime rally before returning here to await the outcome of the voting in Wisconsin.

Senator McCarthy said that Mayor Richard J. Daley of Chicago and Gov. Warren Hearnes of Missouri were two

Continued on Page 28, Column 6

Humphrey Is Silent On Entering Race, But Support Grows

By ROY REED
Special to The New York Times

WASHINGTON, April 2—Vice President Humphrey remained silent today on whether he would enter the race for the Democratic Presidential nomination, but support for him continued to build up in various parts of the nation.

However, there was a prediction that President Johnson, the man who could probably do more than any other to help a Humphrey candidacy, would not take sides in the race.

The prediction came from Mike Mansfield, Senate majority leader, who said after a breakfast meeting with Mr. Johnson, Mr. Humphrey and Democratic Congressional leaders:

"I think he [the President] will keep hands off and let the Democratic convention decide."

[Mr. Humphrey arrived in New York Tuesday night and refused to take himself out of the race. Page 28. Meanwhile, a meeting of Democratic Governors was called April 15 to discuss the Presi-

Continued on Page 28, Column 2

SENATE APPROVES SLASH IN SPENDING AND A 10% SURTAX

Votes, 53-35, to Cut Outlay $6-Billion and Curb Hiring of Federal Employes

By EILEEN SHANAHAN
Special to The New York Times

WASHINGTON, April 2—The 10 per cent tax surcharge, coupled with a mandatory cut of $6-billion in Government spending and strict controls on hiring Government employes, passed the Senate today by a vote of 53 to 35.

The size of the margin surprised even those who had predicted an improvement in relations between Congress and the White House as a result of President Johnson's decision not to run for re-election and his steps toward de-escalation of the war in Vietnam.

How the House of Representatives would react to the Senate's decision remained uncertain, however.

It was considered out of the question for the House simply to accept the Senate's bill, if only because many extraneous amendments had been added before today's key vote on the tax and spending issue.

Compromise Is Needed

The task of developing a compromise bill acceptable to both the House and the Senate is therefore likely to be put in the hands of a joint House-Senate conference committee. This would be made up of the senior members of the House Ways and Means Committee and the Senate Finance Committee.

It was considered unlikely, but not impossible, that the House members of the conference committee would agree to the Senate action that added the tax surcharge and expenditure control to a fairly simple and noncontroversial bill continuing automobile and telephone excise taxes. The House has passed its own bill.

The Senate bill also carries another major provision of the House bill—the acceleration of corporate tax collections. The House members of the joint conference committee will be led by Wilbur D. Mills of Arkansas, chairman of the Ways and Means Committee.

Mr. Mills has opposed the tax surcharge throughout the eight months since it was first proposed by President Johnson. He has argued that Government spending should be sharply reduced first, and has repeatedly indicated recently that he considered a reduction of $6-billion in Federal outlays inadequate.

In addition, House members

Continued on Page 34, Column 3

ACCORD REACHED ON STATE BUDGET; GOVERNOR BALKS

He Calls Plan Irresponsible —It Proposes to Scrap Most of His Tax Rises

By SYDNEY H. SCHANBERG
Special to The New York Times

ALBANY, Wednesday, April 3—The Republican and Democratic blocs defied Governor Rockefeller this morning to press for passage in the Assembly of their unorthodox plan to balance the state's budget.

The fiscal plan was announced late yesterday afternoon. It would balance the record $5.5-billion state budget for fiscal 1968-69—now three days overdue—largely by delaying state aid payments to localities to avoid enacting most of the $494-million in tax increases sought by the Governor.

Within hours of the announcement of the bipartisan compromise agreement, the Governor declared the plan irresponsible and hinted strongly that he might veto at least parts of it—in particular, the delay in state-aid payments.

At 3 A.M., the Assembly was in recess, waiting for certain amended bills to return from the printer so it could finish enacting the entire compromise budget package at one sitting.

Night Session Held

The Democratic-controlled Assembly passed several of the many bills in the bipartisan budget yesterday afternoon, before the Governor issued his veto warning. The legislators then went on to hold a raucous session, which continued well past midnight, to pass the rest of the measures.

Because some of the bills required last-minute amendments, Assembly Speaker Anthony J. Travia had to recess the Assembly several times to await the return of the revised measures from the printer.

The Assemblymen spent the recesses at restaurants and bars near the Capitol. Some appeared extremely convivial when they returned to their seats, throwing wads of paper at each other, laughing and cheering at the speeches.

Mr. Travia's Republican counterpart, Earl W. Brydges, the leader of the G.O.P.-controlled Senate, said that although he was not completely satisified with the compromise plan, "it represents a position acceptable to me."

Conference Set

Mr. Brydges said that if the Assembly passed the package he would bring it up at a conference of Senate Republicans scheduled for 10 o'clock this morning, along with the Governor's complaint.

The indications were that the Senate would follow the Assembly's example.

The plan would close an estimated $488.5-million gap in the budget of approximately $5.5-billion for fiscal 1968-69, largely by postponing until 1969-70 nearly $200-million in state-aid payments to localities and by paying back the state for $95-million in loans simply by selling $95-million in state bonds.

Mr. Rockefeller, who can-

Continued on Page 22, Column 4

U.S. DEFINES BOMBING LIMIT AS 225 MILES ABOVE DMZ IN REPLY TO WIDE OUTCRY

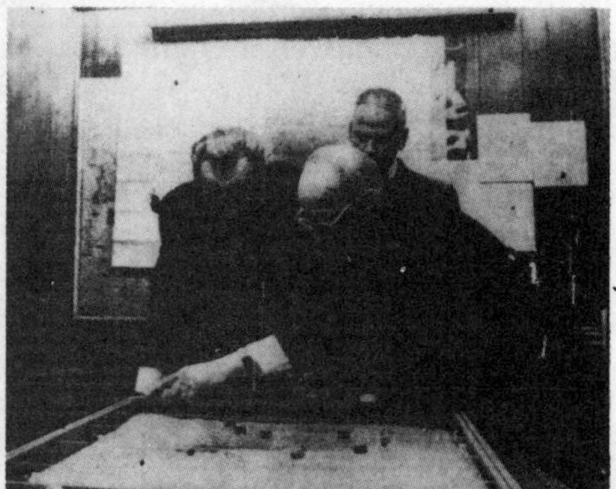

STRATEGY: President Johnson studying a model of Vietnam with Walt Rostow, an adviser, in situation room of White House on Feb. 15. Brig. Gen. Robert Ginsburgh, representing Joint Chiefs of Staff, is at rear in this photograph just released by White House.

AT 20TH PARALLEL

Charge That Johnson Misled the Country Upsets Officials

By MAX FRANKEL
Special to The New York Times

WASHINGTON, April 2—Reacting to a wide wave of criticism of its peace moves, the Johnson Administration identified the 20th Parallel in North Vietnam today as the line north of which it had halted all air and naval bombardment.

The 20th Parallel crosses North Vietnam approximately midway between its northern and southern frontiers, about 225 miles north of the demilitarized zone, which straddles the border with South Vietnam.

But because North Vietnam is funnel-shaped, almost 90 per cent of the population and 76 per cent of the territory are in the area now being spared from attack.

Officials at the White House and a formal statement by the Defense Department said the parallel was the line that President Johnson had in mind when he announced the bombing restraint Sunday night. The officials said that the line was explicitly cited in the military orders to the field and was identified to Congressional leaders in briefings before the President's speech.

Reference Is Deleted

The Administration was deeply chagrined by charges in Congress and elsewhere that Mr. Johnson had misled the country about the degree of restraint. The news of the bombing today of targets near the river, road and rail center of Thanhhoa, more than 200 miles north of the demilitarized zone, set off a new debate in the Senate.

Preliminary drafts of the President's speech are said to have contained a reference to the 20th Parallel. This was dropped, apparently because Mr. Johnson was persuaded not to commit himself publicly to the fixed border of a "sanctuary" for military activity.

In delivery, Mr. Johnson used the following words in defining the new bombing policy:

"Tonight I have ordered our

Continued on Page 12, Column 1

Fulbright, in Debate, Calls Curb on Raids Misleading

By JOHN W. FINNEY
Special to The New York Times

WASHINGTON, April 2—Senator J. W. Fulbright reopened Senate criticism of United States policy in Vietnam today by complaining that President Johnson had taken only a limited and misleading step in curtailing the bombing of the north.

In the face of a Fulbright assertion that the curtailment would not lead to peace talks,

Excerpts from Senate debate will be found on Page 14.

the Senate majority leader, Mike Mansfield, Senator John Sherman Cooper, Republican of Kentucky, and senior Democrats on the Senate Armed Services Committee came to the defense of the Administration.

They contended, in an outburst of spontaneous debate on the Senate floor, that the Administration was following a prudent military course in continuing to bomb North Vietnamese supply lines.

Mood Abruptly Changes

Despite such public defense, however, it was apparent from private comments that the mood of the Senate had abruptly changed from initial enthusiasm over the President's announcement to confusion, skepticism and misgivings as a result of the disclosure that the bombing halt did not preclude strikes at targets far north of the demilitarized zone.

Standing as a lonely critic on the Senate floor, Senator Fulbright, the Foreign Relations Committee chairman, gave voice to these misgivings. Initially, the Arkansas Democrat sought only clarification of what the Administration meant by the cessation, announced

Continued on Page 14, Column 4

HANOI PRESS CALLS PEACE BID A FRAUD

Army Paper Says Johnson Tries to Deceive Public With Bombing Curb

By The Associated Press

TOKYO, April 2 — North Vietnam's official newspaper said the United States was planning a new plot in Vietnam and described an American peace offer as a fraud, a Japanese report from Hanoi said today.

The newspaper Nhan Dan apparently was alluding to President Johnson's order Sunday halting the bombing of "most" of North Vietnam and calling for peace talks. But it made no mention of Mr. Johnson's offer.

The North Vietnamese army newspaper, Quan Doi Nhan Dan quoted by the Soviet press agency, Tass, said Mr. Johnson was trying to mislead public opinion and had not called for an unconditional halt to bombing. This was considered the first North Vietnamese reaction to Mr. Johnson's offer.

Quoted by Japanese

The Japanese press agency Nihon Dempa quoted Nhan Dan as having declared:

"The United States is planning a new plot to maintain its new colonialism and increasing its troops to reconstruct the South Vietnamese puppet regime and troops.

"The United States is attempting to increase bombing of North Vietnam, and the so-called fraudulent proposal for peace talks is aimed at getting rid of isolation from the people of the world."

The army newspaper, as quoted by Tass, said Mr. Johnson had not agreed to halt bombings and other military action against North Vietnam, the condition set by it before peace talks can begin.

Hanoi Broadcasts News

HANOI, North Vietnam, April 2 (Agence France-Presse) — The North Vietnamese radio reported today the American decision to call a halt in the bombing of much of North Vietnam by quoting an editorial comment by the Soviet press agency Tass.

A news program in French

Continued on Page 13, Column 1

U.S. Pilots Attack Near 20th Parallel

By DOUGLAS ROBINSON
Special to The New York Times

SAIGON, South Vietnam, Wednesday, April 3—Navy warplanes, on the second day after President Johnson's order curtailing air action over North Vietnam, have made bombing attacks on a railroad siding about 220 miles north of the demilitarized zone.

The strikes, carried out yesterday by A-6 Intruder jets, were among more than 105 missions flown against North Vietnamese targets. The number was about normal for the existing weather conditions.

The spokesmen said the attack on the railroad siding—12 miles north-northeast of Thanhhoa — fell within the President's definition of the area where air attacks could be expected to continue.

In Washington yesterday,

Continued on Page 12, Column 5

ANTIRIOT POWERS ASKED BY LINDSAY

He Seeks Ability to Ban Sale of Firearms and Liquor

By CHARLES G. BENNETT

Mayor Lindsay asked the City Council yesterday to give him emergency powers to ban the sale of firearms and alcoholic beverages and to impose a curfew in outbreaks of civil disorder.

The legislation sent to the Council by the Mayor would empower him to declare a state of emergency, either citywide or in a specified area, upon written certification by the city's Emergency Control Board. The board is made up of high city officials, including the Police and Fire Commissioners and is headed by the Mayor.

The bill would also empower the Mayor to close theaters and other places normally used for public entertainment and prohibit vehicular and pedestrian traffic in the emergency area, except for emergency services.

The emergency would be in force for 15 days, a period that the Mayor could reduce or extend. Violators of emergency measures would be subject to fines up to $500, one-year jail sentences, or both.

It was indicated that the

Continued on Page 19, Column 1

PRAY FOR ROSEMARY'S BABY. —Advt.

Lev Landau Dead; Soviet Physicist, 60

Special to The New York Times

MOSCOW, April 2—Dr. Lev D. Landau, one of the world's foremost theoretical physicists and a Nobel Prize winner, died here yesterday of injuries received in an automobile accident six years ago. He was 60 years old.

Dr. Landau never recovered his full powers after the accident, but he was able to give guidance to students and colleagues.

A Brilliant Scientist

By ALDEN WHITMAN

Dr. Landau was only 32 years of age when he explained in rigorous mathematical terms the superfluidity and the superconductivity of helium cooled to a liquid at near absolute zero. It opened the way for a new understanding of the prop-

Continued on Page 47, Column 1

Soviet Believed Testing Rocket Able to Guide Bomb From Orbit

By EVERT CLARK
Special to The New York Times

WASHINGTON, April 2 — The Soviet Union is apparently flight-testing in secret a maneuverable rocket stage that could be used to guide bombs down from orbit or to send instruments to the moon.

Three Russian space payloads launched in recent months have performed maneuvers not seen before. They were the Cosmos 185 on Oct. 27 and Cosmos 198 on Dec. 27, 1967, and the Cosmos 209, flown on March 22 this year.

All were launched from Tyuratam into orbits inclined at 65 degrees from the Equator. American tracking networks observed that all three went first into low orbits, then climbed to near-circular orbits about 500 miles above the earth.

Observers here are paying close attention to the three flights. The memory is fresh here of Moscow's clandestine development in 1966 and 1967 of a so-called fractional orbital bombardment system.

The system uses a missile to put a warhead into a very low earth orbit from which it can be ordered down onto enemy territory before it completes one circuit of the earth.

Intercontinental missile warheads usually are lobbed high into space, like a mortar shell, and defensive radars can spot them as much as 15 minutes before they are due to strike a target.

On the other hand, the warhead on the bombardment system comes in so low that the warning time is only about one-third that long.

Some observers here fear that the recent Russian shots may represent a step upward from this FOBS system to the so-called MOBS — multiple-orbit bombardment system —that Soviet officials have discussed publicly since 1961.

A multiple-orbit system would station the warhead in orbit for a time, rather than have it travel only part-way around the earth. The weapon could be left in space for many months — or sent up during a time of crisis, for psychological purposes or for use. It could be recalled safely to earth later if not used during the crisis.

It is understood that there is no strong evidence now to link the recent launchings to the development of the fractional orbit system. On the other hand, Government analysts argued among themselves for some months before they accepted the system for what it was. Former Secretary of Defense Robert S. McNamara

Continued on Page 4, Column 4

City Seeks to Raise Tax on Commuters

By RICHARD E. MOONEY

The City Council voted unanimously yesterday in favor of taxing the income of commuters at the same rates as city residents. But the chances of accomplishing it seemed slim.

The Council acted on a home-rule resolution, asking the State Legislature to approve a bill that has been submitted by Assemblyman Alexander Chananau, Bronx Democrat.

Most commuters pay a flat rate of one-quarter of one per cent. The rate for residents ranges from four-tenths of one per cent to 2 per cent.

The Lindsay administration has always wanted commuters taxed at a rate closer to that paid by residents, but its original proposal to this effect—two years ago when the city

Continued on Page 25, Column 2

If you live South of 14th St., you'll dig "LOOT" —now Biltmore Thea.—Advt.

NEWS INDEX

	Page		Page
Art	44	Music	36-42
Books	45	Obituaries	47, 51-52
Bridge	44	Screen	36-42
Business	62-63, 74	Ships and Air	94
Buyers	62	Society	53
Crossword	45	Sports	54-62
Editorials	46	Theaters	36-42
Fashions	50	TV and Radio	95
Financial	65-75	U. N. Proceedings	9
Food	50	Wash. Proceedings	30
Man in the News	3	Weather	94

News Summary and Index, Page 49

PRAY FOR ROSEMARY'S BABY. —Advt.

"All the News That's Fit to Print"

The New York Times

LATE CITY EDITION

Weather: Cloudy with showers today, tonight. Clearing tomorrow. Temp. range: today 59-48. Wed. 66-45. Full U.S. report on Page 94.

VOL. CXVII ... No. 40,248 NEW YORK, THURSDAY, APRIL 4, 1968 10 CENTS

NORTH VIETNAM AND U.S. AGREE TO CONTACT; JOHNSON CONSULTS SAIGON; TO GO TO HAWAII

President Sees Kennedy, Then Talks to Humphrey

Senator at White House for an Hour—Parley Reported as Cordial

By JOHN HERBERS
Special to The New York Times

WASHINGTON, April 3—President Johnson and Senator Robert F. Kennedy met at the White House for almost an hour today.

The White House press secretary, George Christian, said that they had discussed international developments and the "implications" of President Johnson's decision not to seek or accept renomination.

Mr. Kennedy, who had sought the meeting with the President, had no comment, and his office said that none would be made, in deference to the President. It was understood, however, that Mr. Kennedy considered the meeting to be "cordial."

The meeting, which began at 10 A.M., took place shortly after Mr. Johnson received word that North Vietnam was willing to discuss the possibility of peace negotiations.

Late today, Mr. Kennedy issued through his Presidential campaign office this statement

Continued on Page 22, Column 7

Vice President Is Later Endorsed by Labor and Farm Groups

By ROY REED
Special to The New York Times

WASHINGTON, April 3 — Vice President Humphrey conferred with President Johnson, picked up two more important endorsements and moved perceptibly closer today to a race for the Democratic Presidential nomination.

The details of the meeting were not disclosed. But Mr. Humphrey told reporters a few hours later:

"You know our relations have always been warm and friendly. They have not changed at all, and I don't expect that they will."

The President is expected to stay aloof from the Presidential contest, at least for a time.

Mr. Humphrey told a farm group later in the day, "I'm perfectly willing to stick around this town a long time."

A Humphrey associate who is also a friend of the President said that members of the White House staff were quietly helping Mr. Humphrey. The asso-

Continued on Page 22, Column 4

NEW ALLIED DRIVE

Push Toward Khesanh Aims at Lifting Siege at the Marine Base

By DOUGLAS ROBINSON
Special to The New York Times

SAIGON, South Vietnam, April 3—A major offensive aimed at relieving the isolated Marine fortress at Khesanh has been opened by American and South Vietnamese troops, the military command said tonight.

A force of 20,000 to 30,000 troops was reported moving along Route 9, which passes near the beleaguered outpost.

The operation, called Pegasus by the military, began Monday at Calu, a hamlet 15 miles east of Khesanh. First reports said the force had covered seven miles and had met light resistance.

[Advance elements pushed to within three miles of their goal Thursday, The Associated Press reported.]

Gen. Cao Van Vien, chairman of South Vietnam's Joint General Staff, has resigned. There were also reports here that a Governmental shake-up was imminent. [Page 19.]

No Evacuation Planned

In the push toward Khesanh, advance elements of the allied force were shelled by enemy artillery today.

Military spokesmen said there were no plans to evacuate the Khesanh outpost, which has been under almost continuous rocket, mortar and artillery attack since Jan. 21.

Although the military command in Saigon has estimated in recent weeks that more than 20,000 North Vietnamese regulars were ringing the garrison, intelligence officers at the scene believe that some of the enemy troops have withdrawn into Laos, leaving 10,000 to 12,000 near the outpost.

The force moving toward Khesanh includes elements of the First Cavalry Division (Airmobile), United States marines and an airborne unit of the South Vietnamese army.

For the last several months, the 6,000 marines and 1,000 South Vietnamese rangers at Khesanh have been encircled by enemy forces.

Bombardment Intense

Recently, the bombardment of the outpost has been so intense that supplies have had to be dropped by parachute.

The successful opening of Route 9, in the opinion of most military men here, would almost completely nullify any chance that enemy troops might overrun Khesanh.

They also said that if the enemy resisted the offensive, it could mean a conventional type of battle that might cause heavy allied casualties, but even heavier losses to the enemy.

In the past, enemy troops

Continued on Page 19, Column 1

United Press International

EN ROUTE TO KHESANH: Support forces of the U.S. First Cavalry Division (Airmobile) moving along Route 9 in an operation to clear a land route to the Marine post. It has been dependent on aircraft for troops and supplies.

FOE'S BID LIMITED

Direct Talks Proposed by Hanoi to Arrange End of All Raids

Text of the North Vietnamese statement is on Page 16.

By MAX FRANKEL
Special to The New York Times

WASHINGTON, April 3—North Vietnam and the United States exchanged public statements today in which they agreed to establish contact between their representatives.

Officials here said they were looking toward a face-to-face meeting. There was no indication from either side, however, about the time and place of possible talks or who would participate.

President Johnson, announcing American readiness to meet, also disclosed that he would fly to Honolulu tomorrow night for a weekend of consultations with his military and diplomatic aides stationed in South Vietnam.

Response Is Direct

North Vietnam's offer to make contact came in direct response to President Johnson's speech Sunday night announcing a halt in the bombing of much of Vietnam and appealing for discussions.

But Hanoi's offer was conditional. The initial contacts, Hanoi stipulated, should be arranged to bring about an "unconditional" end to all American bombing of North Vietnam and "all other acts of war" against it "so that talks may start."

Hanoi's offer came at the end of a long declaration denouncing American aggression, reiterating North Vietnam's past formulas for peace and suggesting that Mr. Johnson's moves were a "perfidious trick" forced on him by battlefield defeat and great domestic difficulties.

U.S. Proposal Reiterated

President Johnson intentionally ignored these statements and focused instead on North Vietnam's readiness to appoint representatives to make contact with Americans. He reiterated his own offer to send representatives to a meeting and declared:

"We will establish contact with the representatives of North Vietnam. Consultations with the Government of South Vietnam and our other allies are now taking place."

The President made his statement shortly after 5 P.M. The contacts were presumably begun even before that by Secretary of State Dean Rusk at the meeting of the Southeast Asia Treaty Organization in New Zealand and by American representatives in other capitals.

Understanding and cooperation from the South Vietnamese Government is seen here as crucial. Saigon, fearing that its in-

Continued on Page 16, Column 1

Governor Forces Leaders To Restudy Budget Plan

By SYDNEY H. SCHANBERG
Special to The New York Times

ALBANY, April 3—Governor Rockefeller, promising to use his veto on "fiscally irresponsible" parts of a bipartisan budget package worked out by the legislative leaders yesterday, forced the leaders today to halt the unorthodox package in midpassage and consider changing it.

Under the unusual pressure from the Republican Governor, the leaders of both the Republican-controlled Senate, which was on the brink of voting final passage for the budget plan, and the Democratic-controlled Assembly, which had already passed it, adjourned their houses for the week to try to work out a new plan acceptable to Mr. Rockefeller.

"We're looking for a way out of a little bit of an impasse in the light of the Governor's threatened veto," Senate Majority Leader Earl W. Brydges told newsmen grimly, after a 15-minute meeting with Mr. Rockefeller in Mr. Brydges's office.

The effect of the Governor's move was to force the leaders to reconsider the idea of balancing his $5.5-billion state budget for 1968-69 with taxes they had rejected as politically unpalatable. Among these were Mr. Rockefeller's requests for increases in the state income, gasoline and liquor taxes and the Senate Republican proposal

Continued on Page 32, Column 4

ABORTION REFORM DIES IN ASSEMBLY

Expected Support Fails to Materialize—Blumenthal to Try Again in 1969

By JOHN KIFNER
Special to The New York Times

ALBANY, April 3—The Assembly rejected today, after five hours of emotional debate, an attempt to reform the state's 85-year-old abortion law.

It was the second straight year that an attempt to liberalize the controversial abortion law had failed. Last year's bill was killed in committee.

The bill was sent back to the Assembly Codes Committee, effectively killing it for this year, when it became apparent that it had no chance of passage.

The Senate, meanwhile, voted to authorize eavesdropping by law-enforcement officials in carefully specified situations.

Supporters of the abortion bill had been saying privately in the last few days that they had three or four votes more than the 76 needed for passage.

But when Speaker Anthony J. Travia asked for a show of hands of those opposed to the bill, there was a gasp in the chamber as a forest of hands shot up on both sides of the aisle.

Several co-sponsors of the bill rose to request a roll-call vote, forcing the members to be recorded as for or against the bill.

Only about a dozen names had been called when the bill's

Continued on Page 31, Column 2

Gambling at Capitol Disclosed as House Adopts Ethics Code

By MARJORIE HUNTER
Special to The New York Times

WASHINGTON, April 3—The House adopted its first code of ethics today amid charges that a gambling ring was quietly flourishing on Capitol Hill.

The code, approved 405 to 1, would require all members and chief employes of the House to disclose publicly their principal sources of income.

But even as framers of the code sought to assure members that critics of the House might now be silenced, Representative John Kyl, Republican of Iowa, disclosed for the first time that a gambling ring was operating "in every building on Capitol Hill."

Mr. Kyl said he was "personally satisfied" that no member of Congress nor any Senate or

Continued on Page 13, Column 1

STOCKS SPURRED TO SALES RECORD

19 Million Shares Traded —Big Board's Tape Runs Up to 47 Minutes Late

By VARTANIG G. VARTAN

Volume on the New York Stock Exchange soared to a record of 19.29 million shares yesterday as investors bid up prices amid renewed prospects for peace in Vietnam.

From the opening bell, the market was spurred by news reports that the Hanoi Government stood ready to meet with United States representatives to discuss a total halt in bombing raids.

The Dow-Jones industrial average, up more than 13 points in frenzied late-morning trading, finished the day with a gain of 5.15 points, at 869.11. The stock-market tape, which lagged as much as an unprecedented 47 minutes behind floor transactions at mid-session, did not catch up until less than an hour before the close.

On Monday, trading set the previous record of 17.73 million shares amid sharply rising prices as stocks rallied in response to President Johnson's move to de-escalate the war in Vietnam. Until then the volume record had been the 16.41 million shares traded on Oct. 29, 1929, the "Black Tuesday" of the market crash.

Around the world, markets reflected the strength of the dollar as gold-mining shares

Continued on Page 19, Column 7

The President's Statement

Special to The New York Times

WASHINGTON, April 3—Following is a transcript of a statement made by President Johnson today before news correspondents in the west lobby of the White House:

Today the Government of North Vietnam made a statement which included the following paragraph, and I quote:

"However, for its part, the Government of the Democratic Republic of Vietnam declares its readiness to appoint its representative to contact the United States representative with a view to determining with the American side the unconditional cessation of the United States bombing raids and all other acts of war against the Democratic Republic of Vietnam, so that talks may start."

Last Sunday night I expressed the position of the United States with respect to peace in Vietnam and Southeast Asia, as follows: "Now, as in the past, the United States is ready to send its representatives to any forum at any time to discuss the means of bringing this war to an end."

Accordingly, we will establish contact with the representatives of North Vietnam. Consultations with the Government of South Vietnam and our other allies are now taking place.

So that you may have as much notice as I'm able to give you on another matter, I will be leaving tomorrow evening late for Honolulu. I will meet with certain of our representatives, American representatives from South Vietnam, for a series of meetings over the weekend in Hawaii.

Administration Wary

U.S. Eager for Talks, but Feels Hanoi Merely Wants to End War on Its Terms

By JAMES RESTON
Special to The New York Times

WASHINGTON, April 3—The Administration is eager to talk to North Vietnam about Hanoi's latest peace proposals, but it is frankly suspicious that it is merely being invited to talk about ending the war on the enemy's terms.

News Analysis

The fear in official quarters here is that the Hanoi Government has misjudged the recent political convulsion in the United States, and may be acting on the illusion that the departure of former Secretary of Defense Robert S. McNamara, the replacement of Gen. William C. Westmoreland and the forthcoming retirement of President Johnson mean that the Administration is prepared to accept Hanoi's four-point peace plan.

This, of course, the Johnson Administration is not prepared to do. It still regards the Hanoi proposals as an invitation to surrender, and is standing on President Johnson's statement of last Sunday that "the United States will never accept a fake solution to this long and arduous struggle and call it peace."

Nevertheless, the main thing about this new development out of Hanoi is that it breaks the pattern of the past. As in the American domestic political scene of the past few weeks, the frustrating stalemate of old contentions has been broken. Nobody knows where the negotiations on the war will go—and the outlook is not very hopeful—but the imponderable is important in the minds of officials here. Hanoi took Washington by surprise, but it produced something new and anything new in the diplomacy of the war is a relief.

The main difference between Hanoi's latest proposals and its previous suggestions is that the North Vietnamese Government has dropped its demand that all bombing and other acts of war against North Vietnam be stopped before it would talk. Now it has offered to talk first, but only about acceptance of precisely the same terms.

Nevertheless, the Administration is following up the latest proposal in the hope that the preliminary talks will lead to a wider agenda, and, hopefully, to some kind of arrangement to limit military activity on both sides while the talks proceed.

The purpose of President Johnson's trip to Hawaii tomorrow night is apparently to review the strategic and diplomatic situation in the light of the recent enemy offensive against the cities and Hanoi's quick but limited response to the President's Sunday night appeal for peace.

It is also important to de-

Continued on Page 17, Column 2

Doubling of Police In Housing Sought

By CHARLES G. BENNETT

Fear of criminals has made residents of City Housing Authority projects virtual prisoners in their own apartments, a City Council committee was told yesterday.

The accounts of terror in authority projects led Councilman Saul S. Sharison, chairman of the committee, to pledge that he and other Councilmen would seek to compel the Lindsay administration to double the size of the housing police force.

In a five-hour public hearing, the Council's Committee on Housing heard 42 witnesses demand more police protection for the 500,000 residents of low-cost housing projects.

At one point, Councilman Carlos Rios, Manhattan Demo-

Continued on Page 30, Column 2

NEWS INDEX

Brooklyn Teacher Is Beaten in Class

By LEONARD BUDER

A 23-year-old teacher was beaten by a teen-ager in a Brooklyn junior high school yesterday while, the teacher said, pupils kept him trapped behind his desk and encouraged his assailant.

During the attack, which took place in a second-floor classroom, a policeman on permanent duty at the school was patrolling the lobby and seven school aides recently hired for security purposes were watching school doors to prevent illegal intrusions.

The teacher did not know if his assailant was a member of the class or even a pupil at the school.

The incident occurred at Junior High School 258, at Marcy Avenue and Macon Street, in the Bedford-Stuy-

Continued on Page 29, Column 1

CZECHS WILL OPEN MASARYK INQUIRY

'48 Death to Be Investigated —Defense Chief Quits

By United Press International

PRAGUE, April 3 — The Czechoslovak State Prosecutor's Office announced today that it would reinvestigate the controversial death of Foreign Minister Jan Masaryk 20 years ago.

The body of Dr. Masaryk, son of the founder of Czechoslovakia, Thomas G. Masaryk, was found in the courtyard of the Foreign Ministry on March 10, 1948.

The Communist regime, which had just seized power, said he had committed suicide by jumping from a bathroom window. For two decades belief has circulated both here and abroad that he was murdered.

[In another development of the continuing democratization in Czechoslovakia, the Defense Minister, Gen. Bohumir Lomsky, offered his resignation at a session of the Central Committee of the Communist party.]

Plans for a new inquiry into the Masaryk case were announced by Frantisek Zabransky, a deputy prosecutor, apparently in response to a demand for such an investigation published yesterday in Student, a weekly of the Czechoslovak student organization.

Student listed these facts to back its charge that Dr. Masaryk had met with foul play:

¶Frantisek Borkovec, deputy security chief of the Min-

Continued on Page 7, Column 1

De Gaulle Praises Action by Johnson

By JOHN L. HESS
Special to The New York Times

PARIS, April 3—President de Gaulle saluted President Johnson today for "an act of reason and political courage" in limiting the bombing of North Vietnam.

A Government spokesman said that at a Cabinet meeting the general had stated his view of the Johnson declarations Sunday in the following sentence:

"Regarding the President of the United States, the fact that he publicly prescribes the halt of the bombings of North Vietnam, even though this halt is not yet either general or unconditional, seems to be a first step in the direction of peace and, consequently, an act of reason and political courage."

The statement, which was

Continued on Page 17, Column 7

Congress Cheered By Hanoi Response

By JOHN W. FINNEY
Special to The New York Times

WASHINGTON, April 3 — With a nearly unanimous voice, Republicans and Democrats and hawks and doves in Congress gave support today to acceptance of Hanoi's call for discussion of a cessation of the bombing.

Congressional doves foresaw that the North Vietnamese reply to President Johnson's de-escalation move would open the door to peace in Vietnam. The hawks were less vocal and more cautious about the reaction from North Vietnam.

Senator J. W. Fulbright, who accused the Administration yesterday of not having gone far enough with its bombing pause, described Hanoi's reply as a favorable development and ex-

Continued on Page 17, Column 1

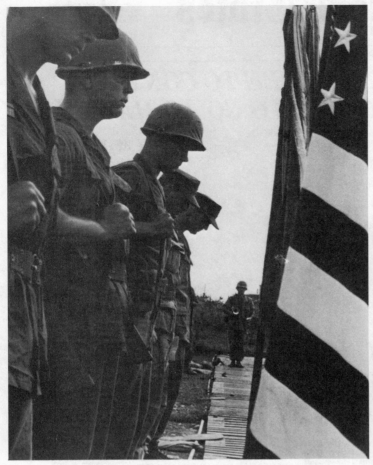

A memorial service for Marines killed at Dong Ha, Vietnam.

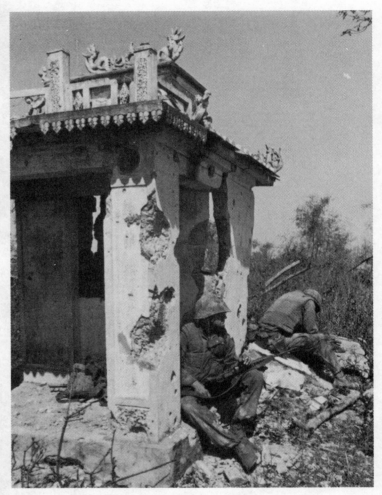

A battle-scarred Buddhist shrine is used by Marines as protection during a short pause in the Tet Offensive.

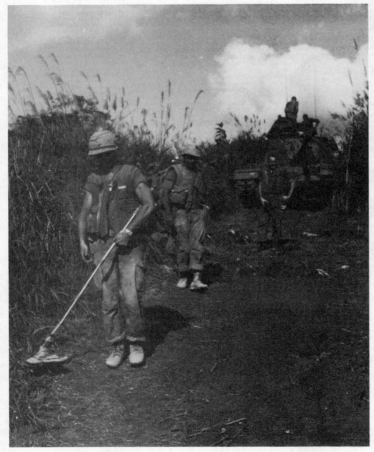

A mine sweep team checks a road ahead of an advancing tank. The tanks supported the Marines in an operation just south of the DMZ.

"All the News
That's Fit to Print"

The New York Times

LATE CITY EDITION

Weather: Fair and mild today and tonight. Continued fair tomorrow. Temp. range: today 64-42; Thurs. 65-42. Full U. S. report on Page 70.

VOL. CXVII..No. 40,256

NEW YORK, FRIDAY, APRIL 12, 1968

10 CENTS

PRESIDENT SIGNS CIVIL RIGHTS BILL; PLEADS FOR CALM

Acts a Day After Final Vote on Measure That Stresses Open Housing in Nation

FINDS MUCH TO BE DONE

In White House Ceremony, He Calls for Enactment of Rest of His Program

Text of Jonnson's statement is printed on Page 18.

Special to The New York Times

WASHINGTON, April 11—With another plea against violence and for the legal redress of injustice, President Johnson signed today the Civil Rights Act of 1968.

Its major provision is intended to end racial discrimination in the sale and rental of 80 per cent of the nation's homes and apartments.

Mr. Johnson read swiftly but with feeling through a brief speech that invoked the memories of the slaying of the Rev. Dr. Martin Luther King Jr. a week ago and the rioting that ensued in many cities.

But the President also displayed the pride that comes, he said, with the signing of the "promises of a century." Few thought when he proposed it at a White House meeting two years ago that fair housing would "in our time" become the law of the land, he said, "and now at long last this afternoon its day has come."

'Roots of Injustice'

"We all know that the roots of injustice run deep," the President asserted, "but violence cannot redress a solitary wrong or remedy a single unfairness.

"Of course all America is outraged at the assassination of an outstanding Negro leader who was at that meeting that afternoon in the White House in 1966.

"And America is also outraged at the looting and the burning that defiles our democracy. And we just must put our shoulders together and put a stop to both. The time is here. Action must be now."

The action he wants, the President said to leaders of Congress who received a pen symbolizing attendance at the signing, is the enactment of all his domestic programs and appropriations.

These include programs for the accelerated construction of low-cost housing, improved vo-

Continued on Page 18, Column 2

Associated Press

RIGHTS BILL BECOMES LAW: Around President Johnson are, from the left: Senator Hugh Scott, Representative William M. McCulloch, Senators Edward W. Brooke and Jacob K. Javits; House Speaker John W. McCormack; Representative Emanuel Celler; Senator Walter F. Mondale and Supreme Court Justice Thurgood Marshall.

ALABAMIAN NAMED IN DR. KING INQUIRY

F.B.I. Seeking to Question 36-Year-Old White Man —Car Found in Atlanta

By MARTIN WALDRON
Special to The New York Times

MEMPHIS, Tenn., April 11—The Federal Bureau of Investigation was seeking a 36-year-old Alabama man tonight for questioning in connection with the slaying of the Rev. Dr. Martin Luther King Jr., who was killed by a sniper's bullet here a week ago tonight.

The man was identified as Eric Starvo Galt, a 5-foot 11-inch white man weighing 175 pounds.

An F.B.I. bulletin said that Mr. Galt was last seen driving a white Mustang automobile. The car, bearing Alabama license plate 1-38993, was found abandoned tonight near a housing project in Atlanta.

A resident of the project said that the automobile was abandoned at 8:30 A.M. last Friday by a white man who was about 5-feet 9-inches tall, who weighed about 165 pounds and who had sandy colored hair.

Inadvertently Released

The bulletin describing Mr. Galt was apparently released inadvertently by the F.B.I., which has been conducting its investigation in the case under the strictest secrecy. The bulletin was withdrawn two hours after its release in an attempt to avoid publicity.

The F.B.I.'s headquarters in Washington refused to comment, but a source said that agents wanted to talk with Mr. Galt in connection with the slaying of Dr. King.

The source stressed that seeking Mr. Galt for questioning did not necessarily mean he would be charged with complicity in the slaying of Dr. King.

Mr. Galt was said to have blue eyes and brown hair and his birth date was listed as July 20, 1931.

The F.B.I. bulletin said that his last known address was

Continued on Page 19, Column 5

2-Block U.N. Expansion Is Planned for East Side

By CHARLES G. BENNETT

A proposal to develop a two-block area across First Avenue from the United Nations Headquarters, with new buildings to serve visitors and expanding United Nations organizations, was disclosed here yesterday.

The new development, for which cost estimates and specific plans are still to be produced, is provided for under bills filed yesterday with the Legislature in Albany.

Governor Rockefeller and Mayor Lindsay jointly announced the proposal, which they said was drawn up "as part of the state and city's responsibility as hosts to the United Nations."

New construction would include a center for 6,000 daily visitors to the United Nations, an underground bus terminal and parking facilities, offices for U.N. missions and related organizations, housing for United Nations personnel and some commercial and industrial facilities.

Concourse Proposed

The proposed legislation would set aside most of the area from 43d to 45th Street between First and Second Avenues, together with a walkway to connect the area with Hammarskjold Plaza at 47th Street.

The formal announcement described the walkway, as well as many other features of the proposed complex, only in general terms. But Ralph G. Schwarz, president of the Fund for Area Planning and Development, said last night that there would be a concourse running through the area from 41st to 47th Street, enabling pedestrians to walk that distance without crossing any streets.

Preliminary sketches indicate

Continued on Page 51, Column 2

TRUMAN TO ASSIST HUMPHREY DRIVE

Becomes Honorary Head of a Committee in Capital—Vice President in South

By ROY REED
Special to The New York Times

BATON ROUGE, La., April 11—A Humphrey for President campaign committee office was formally opened today in Washington. The announcement of the opening of the office came as Vice President Humphrey began a speaking tour in the South.

The committee's official formation was announced by Mr. Humphrey's fellow Minnesotan, Senator Walter F. Mondale. Former President Harry S. Truman is honorary chairman.

The Vice President acknowledged the committee's formation with gratitude but still delayed an announcement of his candidacy for the Democratic nomination.

Meeting Party Leaders

Mr. Humphrey was beginning a two-state Southern tour to speak to students and labor representatives and to meet with the party leaders who control delegate votes at the nominating convention.

He had interrupted his speaking schedule after the assassination of the Rev. Dr. Martin Luther King Jr. Today he bore down once again on the need for law and order and national unity in a time of discontent.

In his first talk following Dr. King's funeral, he urged: "Let us now join arms and hands—black and white, brown and yellow, adult and child—in the single cause of America." The talk was at Wake Forest University, Winston-Salem, N. C.

Mr. Humphrey was in politically friendly territory today in North Carolina and Louisiana. He is a friend of both Governors, Dan K. Moore of North Carolina and John T. McKeithen of Louisiana.

In addition, he received a

Continued on Page 22, Column 1

ISRAEL REPORTED BACKING U.N. PLAN

Jarring Formula Is Said in Cairo to Have Approval of Jordanians Also

By ERIC PACE
Special to The New York Times

CAIRO, April 11 — Highly placed Egyptian sources reported today that Israel had approved a formula worked out by Dr. Gunnar V. Jarring for acceptance of the United Nations resolution on the Middle East.

The Jordanian Government was also said to have expressed approval of the formula, a short statement of acceptance that stipulates vaguely that the parties involved are to deliberate about implementing the Security Council resolution.

No Reply from U.A.R.

The resolution, adopted Nov. 22, established the Jarring mission and called for withdrawal of Israeli forces from Arab territories occupied during the war last June, and for the establishment of "secure and recognized boundaries free from threats or acts of force."

The United Arab Republic had been insisting that Israel agree to implement the resolution in its entirety as a next step toward a settlement.

The Egyptian informants said that the Cairo authorities had not yet responded officially to Israel's acceptance of the formula since they had not yet been informed of it by Dr. Jarring. Word of the Israeli

Continued on Page 12, Column 3

U.S. CALLS 24,500 RESERVES; SETS G.I. CEILING AT 549,500, GIVING SAIGON MAJOR ROLE

POLICY TRANSFER

Clifford Asserts Main Job Will Be Handed Over Gradually

By WILLIAM BEECHER
Special to The New York Times

WASHINGTON, April 11—Defense Secretary Clark M. Clifford announced today a ceiling of 549,500 on the American troop strength in Vietnam and declared that the Johnson Administration had adopted a policy aimed at the gradual transfer to South Vietnam of the major responsibility for the war effort.

He linked the transfer policy to a decision by President Johnson to treat the level of 549,500 men, which was previously announced, as a ceiling beyond which the Administration does not intend to go at this time.

But Mr. Clifford was careful not to make his remarks sound like an ultimatum to Saigon. He did not fix any specific timetable for the assumption of principal responsibility by South Vietnam and he did not say when American forces would draw back from front-line positions.

The implications of his remarks, however, were that the United States was telling Saigon for the first time that it could not look forward to an unending flow of American reinforcements. If more troops are needed, Mr. Clifford was saying in effect, Saigon must supply them.

First News Conference

In his first news conference since he took over at the Pentagon from Robert S. McNamara six weeks ago, Mr. Clifford slipped the following statement into a discussion about plans to provide the South Vietnamese army with more modern rifles, mortars and communications equipment:

"Now that the policy decision has been made to turn over gradually the major effort to the South Vietnamese, we are now starting to give them a degree of preference in our most modern weapons."

Asked for elaboration, the Defense Secretary said that "for some months" such consultations had been under way with Saigon. "I don't know that it occurred on any one date."

He referred approvingly to comments by South Vietnam's President, Nguyen Van Thieu, last week "in which he stated that his hope was that some time in the foreseeable future their forces could be developed

Continued on Page 4, Column 4

120 of Foe, 14 G.I.'s Die in Vietnam Fight

By The Associated Press

SAIGON, South Vietnam, Friday, April 12—The Vietcong mounted a heavy assault early today against a unit of the United States 25th Infantry Division about 50 miles northwest of Saigon, but were thrown back by a ground, air and artillery counterattack.

The United States spokesman said that 14 Americans were killed and that a sweep of the battlefield turned up 120 enemy dead. It was the first major action reported in Operation Complete Victory, a sweep by 100,000 men in 11 provinces near Saigon, since it opened Monday.

Military spokesmen said the

Continued on Page 3, Column 1

U.S. REBUFFS HANOI ON WARSAW TALKS

Foe's Use of Soviet Press Agency to Send Suggestion Also Irritates Capital

By MAX FRANKEL
Special to The New York Times

WASHINGTON, April 11—North Vietnam proposed Warsaw today as the site for ambassadorial contacts with the United States, but the White House objected immediately and held out for a "neutral" setting.

The public exchange between Hanoi and Washington included a questioning by each of the good faith of the other. It left officials here with a new appreciation of the difficulty they face in any negotiations toward peace talks.

However, private exchanges to select a meeting place were said to be continuing.

Annoyed by Dispatch

In an official statement, the Administration betrayed annoyance with Hanoi's suggestion of Warsaw and with publication of the suggestion by Tass, the Soviet press agency, before it was placed in diplomatic channels.

The statement deplored the use of "propaganda" during the efforts to arrange contacts. It complained that North Vietnam had failed to respond to American proposals of "neutral countries"—India and Burma and perhaps others.

Warsaw was not actually rejected in the statement, read by President Johnson's press secretary, George Christian. But the Polish capital did not qualify as the "neutral" setting that the Administration wants, largely to assure free access for officials and newsmen of its allies. There is particular

Continued on Page 2, Column 4

88 UNITS INVOLVED

10,000 Men Slated for War Duty—Rest Will Join Strategic Force

List of units ordered to duty will be found on Page 5.

By NEIL SHEEHAN
Special to The New York Times

WASHINGTON, April 11 — President Johnson has ordered 24,500 military reservists called to active duty to meet the needs of the Vietnam war and strengthen the depleted Active Strategic Reserve.

Secretary of Defense Clark M. Clifford, announcing the call-up today, said that 10,000 of the reservists would be sent to Vietnam as entire units. The remaining 14,500, he said, will be used to replenish the Strategic Reserve, a force of Army, Marine and Air Force units that is kept in the United States for contingencies elsewhere.

Those placed in the Strategic Reserve, however, will then become eligible for assignment to Vietnam as individual replacements as the need arises, Mr. Clifford said.

Of the activated reservists, 13,633 will be drawn from the Army National Guard and 6,401 from the Army Reserve. There will be 2,201 called from the Air National Guard and 1,287 from the Air Force Reserve. The remaining 1,028 will be Navy reservists.

To Serve Two Years

Mr. Clifford said that the men were being summoned for two years of service less any time they might have already spent on active duty.

A total of 88 units from 34 states, with a total of about 20,900 men, are involved, including seven units from New York City and the state. The 3,600 other reservists will be individuals summoned from the Reserve manpower pool to bring the activated units up to full strength or to provide specialists for the Strategic Reserve divisions.

Mr. Clifford said that the 10,000 men to be sent to Vietnam in units would be support elements for the 11,000 combat troops rushed to Gen. William C. Westmoreland in February as emergency reinforcements after the enemy's Lunar New Year offensive.

Mr. Clifford said that General Westmoreland, the American commander in Vietnam, had been permitted to keep those emergency reinforcements and to get support elements for them under the new Vietnam troop ceiling of 549,500 men that has been set by President Johnson.

Mr. Clifford declined to specify at a Pentagon news conference, his first as Defense Secretary, which Reserve units

Continued on Page 5, Column 3

ROCKEFELLER HINTS HE'LL ENTER RACE

Says He Might Make Move Before the Convention

By RICHARD WITKIN

Governor Rockefeller said yesterday that he might formally enter the Presidential race before the Republican convention in August. He expressed confidence that he could win the election if he received the party's nomination.

"If I didn't think so, I wouldn't be here," Mr. Rockefeller declared at a news conference before a luncheon appearance at the New York Hilton Hotel.

Toward the start of the conference, the Governor said there had been no change in the position he enunciated March 21: that he would enter no primaries but was available for a draft.

The impression Rockefeller aides believe the public got from the statement—not precisely what the Governor intended—was that he was reluctant to run.

Politicians have viewed his more recent statements as intended to correct that impression, particularly yesterday's statements that he might formally declare before convention time and was confident he could win in November.

The consensus in the political

Continued on Page 22, Column 2

Religious Holidays

Today is Good Friday and the start of Passover, and although these are not legal holidays, many business offices will be closed. Following is a list of services and facilities that are or are not affected:

Public and parochial schools Closed.

Banks, department stores and retail businesses—Generally open.

Stock markets and major commodities exchanges—Closed.

Sanitation—Normal service.

Postal service—Normal.

Libraries—Open.

Parking — Alternate-side-of street parking regulations suspended.

NEWS INDEX

News Summary and Index, Page 37

The New York Times (by Barton Silverman)

EXPANSION SITE is bound by 43d and 45th Streets between First and Second Avenues. The U.S. Mission (1) and Tudor City buildings (2) are not included in the plan. In photo, Second Avenue runs diagonally at left, intersecting 43d Street at the bottom.

West Berlin Gunman Wounds Leader of Left-Wing Students

Special to The New York Times

BERLIN, April 11—A gunman fired three shots at Rudi Dutschke on Kurfürstendamm, Berlin's main shopping street, today, critically injuring the 27-year-old left-wing student leader.

It was the first attempt at political assassination in Germany in the postwar period. Mr. Dutschke was rushed to a hospital with two shots in his head and a breast wound.

An hour later, the West Berlin police captured the assailant after a gun battle in a nearby basement where the man had barricaded himself. He was hit by two police bullets and was seriously injured, officials said. The man carried no papers and his identity was not known.

Kurt Neubauer, Deputy Mayor of West Berlin, said he was "shocked at the crime," and called on Berliners to remain calm and come to the aid of the police in the investigation. Mr. Neubauer and other officials made it clear they feared the murder attempt could intensify unrest among radical students and other left-wing groups.

Late tonight, as doctors fought to save Mr. Dutschke's life in a four-hour operation, clashes broke out in various parts of the city.

The police used water cannon in an attempt to disperse some 2,000 students who marched to the newspaper publishing house of Axel Springer to protest the shooting. Police officials said demonstrators hurled rocks and flaming torches at the multi-

Continued on Page 7, Column 1

The New York Times

VOL. CXVII...No. 40,288   © 1968 The New York Times Company.   NEW YORK, TUESDAY, MAY 14, 1968   10 CENTS

COLUMBIA SPURS MASSIVE RENEWAL NORTH OF 125TH ST.

Negro Labor Committee and City Join in Planning the $150-Million Project

JOBS FOR 15,000 SEEN

Complex to Include Housing, Industries, Marina and Recreational Facilities

By PETER KIHSS

Columbia University, the Negro Labor Committee and the city's Housing and Development Administration are working on a renewal project aimed at producing 15,000 to 20,000 jobs, 3,000 housing units and recreational and cultural facilities.

The over-all cost of the renewal for the area between 125th and 135th Streets from Broadway west to the Hudson River has been talked of in terms of $150-million to $200-million.

The city agency would assemble the properties, now largely factories and warehouses, under a plan it has submitted to Columbia for study. The university and the Negro Labor Committee already have architects developing plans that Mayor Lindsay had been expected to announce shortly.

Courtney C. Brown, dean of the Columbia School of Business, reluctantly disclosed the project in outline last night after The New Republic magazine had made public an article in its May 18 issue on Columbia's real-estate ventures.

Uris Pledges Cooperation

The magazine suggested that "a major renewal project affecting thousands of people in New York City is being undertaken by a small group of university trustees operating behind closed doors."

Percy Uris, chairman of the board of the Uris Buildings Corporation and a Columbia trustee, said, "As an individual I have told Courtney Brown that I would devote myself to this project without compensation or reward." It will not be an enterprise of his company, he said.

Dean Brown said Prof. Percival Goodman of the Columbia School of Architecture "originally conceived this to be an area of great potential." The dean said the proposal "would not involve a large amount of relocation either of businesses or families."

Dean Brown credited Jason R. Nathan, head of the Housing

Continued on Page 34, Column 4

SHANKER BACKS OUSTED TEACHERS

Hints at Strike in 5 Schools Unless 13 Are Accepted

By LEONARD BUDER

The president of the teachers' union said last night that no union members would serve in five Brooklyn schools until the local governing board allowed 13 "dismissed" teachers to return to the schools.

"No teachers will work in these schools until all teachers are admitted," Albert Shanker told a meeting of 175 union chapter chairmen. He said that the teachers would assemble at points near their schools this morning to await developments.

Asked whether the union might call a citywide strike if the 13 were not restored to their posts, Mr. Shanker said: "We are not ruling out more drastic action."

A spokesman for the United Federation of Teachers said that about 90 per cent of the teachers in the affected schools were members of the union. The schools are in the Ocean Hill-Brownsville section.

Yesterday afternoon two of the schools were shut down for the rest of the day, as a safety measure after Superintendent

Continued on Page 44, Column 2

Strikers Walk Out As Inquiry Starts On Columbia Crisis

By SYLVAN FOX

Leaders of the Columbia University student protest stalked out of a fact-finding commission hearing yesterday after denouncing it as an attempt "to divert attention" from the real issues in the three-week-long dispute.

The walkouts came as the five-member commission, headed by Prof. Archibald Cox of the Harvard Law School, began what is expected to be a lengthy series of hearings on the underlying causes of the disturbances that have crippled Columbia since April 23.

In another development, Dr. Grayson Kirk, the president of Columbia, expressed opposition to proposals made recently in Congress and the Albany Legislature that Federal aid and state aid be withdrawn from students who participate in university uprisings like Columbia's.

"Any attempt by governmental authorities to deprive these offending students of financial aid which they are now receiving under Federal or state programs," Dr. Kirk said "would be difficult to administer equitably and would pave the way for the adoption of tests of political orthodoxy that would endanger the freedom of

Continued on Page 34, Column 1

AUTO UNION GETS A MEANY THREAT

He Says A.F.L.-C.I.O. Will Drop U.A.W. on Thursday Unless It Pays Levy

By JOSEPH A. LOFTUS

WASHINGTON, May 13 — George Meany announced today that the United Auto Workers would be automatically suspended from the A.F.L.-C.I.O. on Thursday unless it paid one month's affiliation tax before then.

This would mean that the American Federation of Labor and Congress of Industrial Organizations would loose its largest affiliate and one of its course of a global nuclear strategy some 20 years ago, founders and more provocative leaders, Walter P. Reuther.

No one expects the payment to be made. In Detroit, top auto union officers said today the union would not change the position established last week when Mr. Reuther made it clear that the money would not be paid unless a special convention was called to air U.A.W. complaints.

Council Statement

"This doesn't change anything," Emil Mazey, the union's second in command, declared. "I thought they would be a little more conciliatory, but nothing they do surprises me."

Mr. Meany pointed out, however, that the federation's Executive Council had agreed to give Mr. Reuther the special convention provided the U.A.W. agreed to attend and abide by its results. Mr. Reuther rejected those conditions.

The auto workers had been holding up payment of its per capita tax on about 1.3 million members. At 7 per cent per member, the tax amounted to more than $90,000 a month. The union will be three months in arrears on May 15.

The break would be the first major one since the federation expelled the 1.7 million-member International Brotherhood of Teamsters in 1957 for being under corrupt influences.

Mr. Meany said the separation—which he called "a withdrawal"—would be unfortu-

Continued on Page 59, Column 3

U.S. and North Vietnam Open Paris Talks With No Illusions of Easy Road to Peace

W. Averell Harriman, chief U.S. delegate, second from left, across from Xuan Thuy, his North Vietnamese counterpart, at conference table yesterday

Defense Budget and Policy Face Broad Senate Attack

By JOHN W. FINNEY
Special to The New York Times

WASHINGTON, May 13 — For the first time in recent years a concerted attack is being mounted in the Senate on the multibillion-dollar defense budget. Somewhat to the surprise of senior members of the Senate Armed Services and Appropriations Committees, the normally sacrosanct defense budget is being challenged in influential quarters in the Senate both as to its size and its strategic assumptions.

To a degree this Senate move is being stimulated by the economy mood in Congress. If Congress is to cut $10-billion in appropriations from the Administration budget—as proposed in the spending and tax package being prepared for Congressional approval—it is apparent that some of the reductions are going to have to be made in the $79.1-billion defense budget proposed for the fiscal year that starts July 1.

Move Goes Deeper

But the Senate move goes deeper than the normal economizing desires in Congress. Probably for the first time since the nation set off on a course of a global nuclear strategy some 20 years ago, some of the basic strategic assumptions in the defense budget are being critically challenged in the Senate.

Some influential Senators, for example, are questioning the need to keep six Army divisions stationed in Western Europe. Others are challenging the plan to start deploying a ballistic missile defense system.

Perhaps in reaction to the Vietnam war, protests are also being raised against construction of a new type of fast deployment logistic ship on the ground that such vessels could lead to greater military commitments for the United States.

Significantly, senior Senators believe the attack on the defense budget no longer is being directed by back-row liberals

Continued on Page 14, Column 3

Assembly Kills Gun-Control Bill With a Massive Show of Hands

By JOHN KIFNER
Special to The New York Times

ALBANY, May 13—The State Assembly killed Governor Rockefeller's gun-control bill today.

The bill, which would have required the statewide licensing of rifles and shotguns, was sent back to the Committee on Rules by an overwhelming show of hands after a 45-minute debate that flared briefly into animosity.

The action came as the legislators—and a noticeably large number of lobbyists—returned to the Capitol to attempt to dispose of the backlog of this year's bills by the end of the week.

But the general outlook here was that, because of the volume of remaining business, adjournment might not be possible until Tuesday or Wednesday of next week.

The Assembly moved at its

'CITY' OF THE POOR BEGUN IN CAPITAL

Abernathy Vows to 'Plague Pharaohs of Nation' for Help Against Poverty

By BEN A. FRANKLIN
Special to The New York Times

WASHINGTON, May 13—The Rev. Ralph David Abernathy today dedicated "Resurrection City, U.S.A.," with a vow "to plague the Pharaohs of this nation with plague after plague until they agree to give us meaningful jobs and a guaranteed annual income."

Construction of the "city" of plywood shelters near the Lincoln Memorial began at once. They will house 3,000 participants in the Poor People's Campaign who are coming here from various parts of the nation.

Mr. Abernathy pledged again to conduct a nonviolent protest "to arouse the conscience of the nation." But he said that "we cannot give you any other further guarantee" that the city will not be disrupted by massive acts of civil disobedience.

"Unlike the previous marches which have been held in Washington," he said, "this march will not last a day, or two days, or even a week. We will be here until the Congress of the United States decide that they are going to do something about the plight of the poor people by doing away with poverty, unemployment and underemployment in this country."

If necessary, Mr. Abernathy

Continued on Page 26, Column 4

Before conference started, Mr. Harriman, right, and Mr. Thuy shook hands in a salon of the conference building.

Two Die in Violence After Panama Vote; Arias Victory Seen

By HENRY GINIGER
Special to The New York Times

PANAMA, May 13—Two persons died and more than a dozen were injured here today as violence flared in the wake of yesterday's presidential election.

Black fumes from burning cars and buildings hung over the city of Panama as the battle for political power was fought in the streets and in voting places.

Contending factions continued to claim victory, but the evidence appeared to point to the election of Dr. Arnulfo Arias, the Opposition candidate. The elections tribunal, which is believed to be heavily weighted toward the Government of President Marco A. Robles and his candidate, David Samudio, said that it would issue no official returns in view of the disorders.

Some Stations Attacked

In generally quiet voting yesterday, there were several instances of attacks on polling stations, and in most cases the attackers were reliably reported to have been Government supporters.

Before dawn today there was a new attack on one of the city's biggest polling stations, on the Via Espana near the Minimax supermarket. One of the leaders was said to have been Rigoberto Paredes, a prominent Government deputy who was seeking re-election in the Panama city area.

Later in the morning, Mr. Paredes and his brother Rogelio were identified as part of a group that had attacked a radio station that had been particularly virulent in its opposition. The station, the Soberana radio, was attacked with machine guns, and one person was killed and four were seriously injured in the street.

The Paredes brothers took

Continued on Page 3, Column 1

FRENCH WORKERS JOIN HUGE PROTEST

Student Ranks Swelled to Hundreds of Thousands in Marches in Many Cities

By JOHN L. HESS
Special to The New York Times

PARIS, May 13—Hundreds of thousands of French students and workers joined today in an extraordinary protest against "police repression" and the de Gaulle regime.

It was the most massive outpouring in the recent international wave of student-led demonstrations. Students here, latecomers to the movement, chanted "Berlin, Warsaw, Rome—Paris!"

A majority of organized labor held a one-day strike in sympathy with the students, who had battled the police for 10 nights in the Latin Quarter.

In cities across the country, students occupied universities, and unions joined demonstrations as large as scores of thousands.

Size of Crowd Disputed

In Paris, the actual size of the demonstration was disputed. The police estimated the crowd at 200,000 people, while leaders of the protest put it at 500,000 to a million. The French state television network said the figure was "somewhere between."

In any case for four hours, marchers, 40 abreast, chanting "De Gaulle assassin!" filled the three-mile route from the Place de la République on the Right Bank, across the Seine and up the Boulevard St-Michel to Place Denfert-Rochereau.

The police were invisible, and order was maintained by thousands of volunteers. Else-where, heavy police forces kept activists from approach-

Continued on Page 17, Column 1

PARIS TALKS OPEN WITH REPETITION OF OLD CHARGES

U.S. Accused of 'Monstrous Crimes' — Aggression Is Laid to Regime in Hanoi

BROADER ISSUES RAISED

On Bombing, Neither Party Gives Sign of Shift During Session of Three Hours

Texts of North Vietnam and U.S. statements, Page 18.

By ANTHONY LEWIS
Special to The New York Times

PARIS, May 13—The United States and North Vietnam threw the whole range of familiar charges at each other today as they began substantive talks on the war.

W. Averell Harriman, chief American delegate, spoke of long-continued North Vietnamese "aggression." Xuan Thuy of North Vietnam, in a statement more strident in tone, accused the United States of "monstrous crimes."

On the first vital issue, United States bombing of the North, there was no shift from established positions. Mr. Harriman called for restraint by Hanoi in return for a total halt in the bombing. Mr. Thuy scorned the principle of "so-called reciprocity."

Small Formal Flourishes

The opening session in the French Foreign Ministry's International Conference Center on the Avenue Kléber lasted three hours. French protocol officers brought the two sides together with such formal flourishes as morning coats and white gloves for the attendants, and then the accusations began.

Afterward the American delegation's spokesman, William J. Jorden, told reporters in a United States Embassy auditorium that he had heard nothing that he had not heard before. A mile away, in the French press center, the North Vietnamese spokesman, Nguyen Thanh Le, saw "no new elements" in the Harriman speech.

Neither delegation had had any illusion that there would be an easy road to peace in Vietnam through these "official conversations," and, despite all the hard words, both made clear their intention to keep talking—and for a long time.

Discussions Enlarged

It was also interesting that both sides dealt at large with the issues facing Vietnam and Southeast Asia generally. Despite Hanoi's position that it is here to talk only about bombing, and Washington's that the political future of South Vietnam cannot be discussed without Saigon's representatives, it seemed that a broad negotiating process had begun.

The next meeting will take place Wednesday, again in the same building. Each side said it would go over the other's statements — "with a microscope," Mr. Harriman told the meeting — and make points to discuss.

Continued on Page 19, Column 1

VICTORY IN SAIGON CLAIMED BY ALLIES

Foe's Offensive Is Crushed, Generals Say — Outpost in Quangtin Abandoned

By CHARLES MOHR
Special to The New York Times

SAIGON, South Vietnam, May 13—Allied generals said today that the main thrust of Vietcong attacks on Saigon had been crushed.

Vietcong and North Vietnamese soldiers who had tenaciously held a neighborhood south of the Y-shaped bridge just outside the city limits finally withdrew overnight.

In northern South Vietnam, meanwhile, a camp of antiguerrilla Special Forces at Khamduc in Quangtin Province, led by Americans, was evacuated by air to avoid encirclement of North Vietnamese troops. The evacuation apparently reflected a belief that the camp could not be held against the gathering enemy force.

In Saigon, almost 3,000 American infantrymen occupied and searched the area of the Y bridge after seven days of sharp street fighting to the south and southwest of it.

Generals Issue Statement

The assertion that the enemy offensive that began May 5 had been crushed was made in a joint statement issued by Lieut. Gen. Fred C. Weyand and Lieut. Gen. Le Nguyen Khang. General Weyand is commander of American forces in the 11 provinces around Saigon and General Khang is the commander of South Vietnamese forces in the same area.

"Although isolated small attacks, terrorism and harassment by fire, including rockets, are still possible, a large number of the enemy have been attempting to withdraw from the battlefield for the past 48 hours, many being intercepted in the process," the statement said.

In the only enemy offensive near the capital today, about

Continued on Page 19, Column 2

Czechs Score Critics in Bloc; Populace Polled on Democracy

Three Papers Assailed

By DAVID BINDER
Special to The New York Times

PRAGUE, May 13 — The Prague radio today accused three newspapers of Soviet-bloc countries of slandering Czechoslovakia with "evil intent."

At the same time, the new party leadership of Alexander Dubcek got encouragement for its democratization from the visiting Yugoslav Foreign Minister, Marko Nikezic, who conferred at length with his counterpart, Jiri Hajek.

A late Prague broadcast also indicated that Janos Kadar, the Hungarian party leader, whom it described as a "friend of Czechoslovakia," would be visiting here soon.

The broadcast suggested that Czechoslovakia should renew

Continued on Page 3, Column 3

Questionnaire Printed

By TAD SZULC
Special to The New York Times

PRAGUE, May 13—Czechoslovakia's Communist leadership is asking the people to tell it, in effect, whether they think Communism is compatible with democracy.

That question and 22 others—all of them relating to fundamental issues concerning the validity of the Communist system in Czechoslovakia—are contained in a questionnaire published today in Rude Pravo, the party newspaper.

The questionnaire has been prepared by the Institute of Political Sciences of the Central Committee and the editors of Rude Pravo.

Since the start of liberaliza-

Continued on Page 4, Column 3

The New York Times

LATE CITY EDITION

Weather: Sunny, mild today; fair and milder tonight and tomorrow. Temp. range: today 77-56; Wed. 75-57. Temp.-Hum. Index yesterday 69. Complete U.S. report on Page 70.

VOL. CXVII..No. 40,395   © 1968 The New York Times Company.   NEW YORK, THURSDAY, AUGUST 29, 1968   10 CENTS

HUMPHREY NOMINATED ON THE FIRST BALLOT AFTER HIS PLANK ON VIETNAM IS APPROVED; POLICE BATTLE DEMONSTRATORS IN STREETS

SOVIET TO LEAVE 2 BLOC DIVISIONS ON CZECHS' SOIL

Svoboda Tells the Cabinet Other Forces Will Depart in 'Several Months'

By TAD SZULC
Special to The New York Times

PRAGUE, Aug. 28—President Ludvik Svoboda told his Cabinet today that the withdrawal of the Soviet-led occupation troops from Czechoslovakia would take "several months and stages" and that at least two divisions would remain permanently stationed on the West German border.

Authoritative sources that provided the account of the Cabinet meeting at Hradcany Castle quoted the President as having informed the ministers that no exact date had been set to begin the withdrawal of the forces of the Soviet Union and the four other Warsaw Pact countries that invaded Czechoslovakia a week ago.

The National Assembly adopted an eight-point resolution asking that a firm date be set forthwith for removal of the occupying forces and declaring that the Czechoslovak Army of 200,000 men was capable of guarding its own frontiers.

Prague Back at Work

Meanwhile, Prague was back at work, but a curfew was maintained and Soviet armored scout cars and motorized infantry trucks with machine guns mounted on their cabs continued to cruise through the city's crowded streets.

In a speech to the nation tonight, Premier Oldrich Cernik announced that today's Cabinet session had drafted a proposal to the Soviet Union, Poland, Hungary, Bulgaria and East Germany to begin "soon" the actual negotiations for the departure of their armies.

He said that within two weeks economic talks with the Soviet Union were to begin "during which compensation for damages" caused by the invasion would be discussed among other topics.

Czechoslovakia has long been

Continued on Page 3, Column 1

PRAGUE'S LEADERS WARNED BY SOVIET

It Says It Will Be Vigilant— Hints Doubt on Outcome

By RAYMOND H. ANDERSON
Special to The New York Times

MOSCOW, Aug. 28—The Soviet Union warned today that the reform leaders of Czechoslovakia, although allowed to return to Prague and to retain their positions after the negotiations here, were on a short leash and under the vigilant eyes of the Kremlin.

Soviet commentators asserted that a counterrevolutionary threat continued to exist in Czechoslovakia, and they indicated that Moscow had doubts that the Prague leadership could or would cope with the dangers adequately.

[In Bonn, the West German Government called for a complete restoration of Czechoslovakia's sovereignty and a pullback of all Soviet invasion forces. Page 6.]

Pravda, the Communist party organ, expressed indignation that underground radio stations in Czechoslovakia had broadcast criticism of the agreement worked out in Moscow between the Soviet leadership and a Czechoslovak delegation headed by President Ludvik Svoboda.

Yuri Zhukov, the political

Continued on Page 4, Column 3

John Gordon Mein
Associated Press

U.S. ENVOY SLAIN IN GUATEMALA

Terrorists Shoot Mein After Ambushing Car—Johnson and Rusk Ask Inquiry

By Reuters

GUATEMALA, Aug. 28—The United States Ambassador, John Gordon Mein, was slain here this afternoon by unidentified youths who had ambushed his limousine.

The 54-year-old career Foreign Service officer tried to put up a fight, but fell under a hail of pistol and machine-gun fire, dying instantly. At least nine bullets struck his body.

As the Ambassador was driving along Avenida Reforma to the embassy, several youths leaped out of two small Japanese-made cars and opened the limousine's rear door to force him out. He resisted and they opened fire.

[In Washington, President Johnson and Secretary of State Dean Rusk expressed shock and grief and called on Guatemala to investigate the assassination.]

Campaign of Terror

Mr. Mein is believed to be the first United States Ambassador assassinated at his post.

The kidnapping of prominent people has been an element of the terror campaign that has been waged by extremist political elements in this uneasy Central American country, which has a population of more than 4.6 million.

The shooting occurred three blocks from the Biltmore Hotel, where Mr. Mein had attended a luncheon given by the Foreign Minister, Emilio Arenales Catalán. The scene was about 10 blocks from the embassy.

The Ambassador's chauffeur,

Continued on Page 16, Column 3

Dubcek Was Put in Handcuffs: An Account of Confrontation

The following chronological account of the confrontation of Soviet and Czechoslovak leaders after the invasion of Czechoslovakia was written by Vincent Buist of Reuters.

PRAGUE, Aug. 28—Alexander Dubcek, the Czechoslovak Communist leader, was hauled out of his party headquarters last Wednesday, handcuffed and flown to a secret destination in Slovakia in a Soviet military aircraft.

All the way he sat on the plane's metal deck.

This was disclosed in an account of the Moscow negotiations given to me today by an official of the Czechoslovak Communist party's Central Committee.

The official said Mr. Dubcek was in his private room speaking on the telephone when the Central Committee building was surrounded by Soviet paratroopers with light tracked vehicles last Wednesday morning.

The party leader was trying to find out details of the extent of the invasion as a Soviet security officer and two soldiers armed with light machine guns burst into the room.

They tore the telephone out of Mr. Dubcek's hands and ripped the wire out of the wall, the official said.

The party leader was taken away and locked in a room in

Continued on Page 2, Column 5

HUNDRED INJURED

178 Are Arrested as Guardsmen Join in Using Tear Gas

By J. ANTHONY LUKAS
Special to The New York Times

CHICAGO, Thursday, Aug. 29—The police and National Guardsmen battled young protesters in downtown Chicago last night as the week-long demonstrations against the Democratic National Convention reached a violent and tumultuous climax.

About 100 persons, including 25 policemen, were injured and at least 178 were arrested as the security forces chased down the demonstrators. The protesting young people had broken out of Grant Park on the shore of Lake Michigan in an attempt to reach the International Amphitheatre where the Democrats were meeting, four miles away.

The police and Guardsmen used clubs, rifle butts, tear gas and Chemical Mace on virtually anything moving along Michigan Avenue and the narrow streets of the Loop area.

Uneasy Calm

Shortly after midnight, an uneasy calm ruled the city. However, 1,000 National Guardsmen were moved back in front of the Conrad Hilton Hotel to guard it against more than 5,000 demonstrators who had drifted back into Grant Park.

The crowd in front of the hotel was growing, booing vociferously every time new votes for Vice President Humphrey were broadcast from the convention hall.

The events in the streets stirred anger among some delegates at the convention. In a nominating speech Senator Abraham A. Ribicoff of Connecticut told the delegates that if Senator George S. McGovern were President, "we would not have these Gestapo tactics in the streets of Chicago."

When Mayor Richard J. Daley of Chicago and other Illinois delegates rose shouting angrily, Mr. Ribicoff said, "How hard it is to accept the truth."

Crushed Against Windows

Even elderly bystanders were caught in the police onslaught. At one point, the police turned on several dozen persons standing quietly behind police barriers in front of the Conrad Hilton Hotel watching the demonstrators across the street.

For no reason that could be immediately determined, the blue-helmeted policemen charged the barriers, crushing the spectators against the windows of the Haymarket Inn, a restaurant in the hotel. Finally the window gave way, sending screaming middle-aged women and children backward through the broken shards of glass.

The police then ran into the restaurant and beat some of the

Continued on Page 23, Column 1

FIGHTING INTENSE IN SAIGON REGION

G.I.'s Battle Through Night With Foe on Infiltration Routes Near Capital

Special to The New York Times

SAIGON, South Vietnam, Thursday, Aug. 29—Sharp fighting flared around Saigon last night and this morning as United States infantrymen battled a sizable enemy force on flatland infiltration routes northwest of the capital.

For no reason that could be immediately determined, the blue-helmeted policemen charged the barriers, crushing the spectators against the windows of the Haymarket Inn, a restaurant in the hotel. Finally the window gave way, sending screaming middle-aged women and children backward through the broken shards of glass.

So far, a total of 86 enemy soldiers have been killed in the fighting. American spokesmen said. Reports from the scene were sketchy, but United States spokesmen termed American casualties light.

101st Division Involved

According to the spokesman, the fighting began Tuesday after soldiers of the 101st Air Cavalry Division set up a cordon around an area and began moving in.

Fighting tapered in the evening, but by noon yesterday units of the division, trudging through muddy fields, came under sharp fire. Fighting continued into the morning.

Farther north, near another key infiltration route into Saigon, soldiers of the United States 25th Infantry Division fought two enemy companies seven miles southeast of Tayninh. During the four-hour battle

Continued on Page 10, Column 1

AT CONVENTION: Cheering in the amphitheatre after Vice President Humphrey's name was placed in nomination
The New York Times (by Neal Boenzi)

IN STREETS: Police attempting to clear demonstrators on Michigan Avenue outside Conrad Hilton Hotel last night
United Press International

Defeat for Doves Reflects Deep Division in the Party

By JOHN W. FINNEY

CHICAGO, Aug. 28—A deeply divided Democratic National Convention, after a climactic floor clash between the Administration's supporters and its critics, adopted today a White House-dictated plank supporting President Johnson's policy in Vietnam. The whole platform was then approved.

By a vote of 1,567¾ to 1,041¼, the convention rejected a plank advanced by Democratic doves calling for an unconditional halt in the bombing of North Vietnam. Instead, it adopted a plank that called for a bombing halt but only on conditional terms.

The vote reflected the deep, emotional division within the party over the Vietnam issue. The division manifested itself in nearly three hours of increasingly acrimonious debate, conducted against a backdrop of sporadic chants of "Stop the war!" from the galleries and the New York and California delegations.

It was a division that Vice President Humphrey, in his bid for the Presidential nomination, had hoped to avoid. But he could not avoid it when Mr. Johnson intervened behind the scenes to toughen the language of the plank so that it would correspond to Administration policy.

In the wake of the policy confrontation, the major question was whether Mr. Hum-

Continued on Page 25, Column 1

Excerpts from the debate on platform, Page 22.

The Party and the Police

By JAMES RESTON
Special to The New York Times

CHICAGO, Aug. 28 — The Democratic party was deeply hurt politically here tonight by the vicious clashes between demonstrators and the police in the streets of Chicago. Though the party itself had no direct responsibility for the incidents, it held its convention here knowing of the dangers of violence and counted on Mayor Daley and his police to handle the situation without embarrassment to the party. This gamble failed, despite all the barbed wire barricades, the police, secret agents and National Guardsmen. It was not only that Mayor Daley was condemned from the rostrum and

stood in the aisles mocking Senator Abraham Ribicoff, who had condemned the police action, but tens of millions watched the incidents on television to the obvious detriment of the Democratic party.

By the end of the night, Daley had become a symbol in the convention of the opposition within the party to the turbulent conditions of American life. So strong was the feeling against Mayor Daley and his police that even the name of Illinois was loudly booed when the roll of the states was called for nominations for the Presidency.

Thus the convention pre-

Continued on Page 20, Column 3

News Analysis

VICTOR GETS 1,761

Vote Taken Amid Boos For Chicago Police Tactics in Street

Excerpts from the nominating speeches are on Page 22.

By TOM WICKER
Special to The New York Times

CHICAGO, Thursday Aug. 29 — While a pitched battle between the police and thousands of young antiwar demonstrators raged in the streets of Chicago, the Democratic National Convention nominated Hubert H. Humphrey for President last night, on a platform reflecting his and President Johnson's views on the war in Vietnam.

Mr. Humphrey, after a day of bandwagon shifts to his candidacy, and a night of turmoil in the convention hall, won nomination on the first ballot over challenges by Senator Eugene J. McCarthy of Minnesota and George S. McGovern of South Dakota.

The count at the end of the first ballot was:

Humphrey	1,761¾
McCarthy	601
McGovern	146½
Phillips	67½
Others	32½

There was never a moment's suspense in the balloting, and throughout a turbulent evening, the delegates and spectators paid less attention to the proceedings than to television and radio reports of widespread violence in the streets of Chicago, and to stringent security measures within the International Amphitheatre.

Repeated denunciations of Mayor Richard J. Daley from convention speakers and repeated efforts to get an adjournment or recess were ignored by convention officials and Mr. Daley.

He sat through it all, usually grinning and always guarded by plainclothes security men, until just before the roll call. Then he left the hall. A few miles away, the young demonstrators were being clubbed, kicked and gassed by the Chicago police, who turned back a march on the convention hall.

Watched From Hotels

Most of the violence took place across Michigan Avenue from the convention headquarters, the Conrad Hilton, in full view of delegates' wives and other watching from its windows.

From the convention rostrum, Senator Abraham A. Ribicoff of Connecticut, denounced "Gestapo tactics in the streets of Chicago."

Julian Bond, the Negro insurgent leader from Georgia, in announcing his delegation's

Continued on Page 20, Column 1

HUMPHREY AIDES LIST 4 FOR TICKET

Say Muskie, Harris, Alioto and Shriver Are Leading for the No. 2 Spot

By STEVEN V. ROBERTS
Special to The New York Times

CHICAGO, Aug. 28—Aides of Vice President Humphrey advanced four names today as leading candidates for the Vice-Presidential nomination: Senators Edmund S. Muskie of Maine and Fred R. Harris of Oklahoma, Mayor Joseph L. Alioto of San Francisco and Sargent Shriver, the Ambassador to France.

The list contained no surprises. All four men have figured in recent speculation.

However, Mr. Humphrey met in his hotel suite today with key political figures, including Mayor Richard J. Daley of Chicago, and aides said the Vice-Presidency was one topic of discussion. It was generally believed that the final decision would not be made until tomorrow.

It was considered a remote possibility that Mr. Humphrey would try to heal the deep breach in the party over the Vietnam war by choosing a prominent war critic. Senators Eugene J. McCarthy of Minnesota, George S. McGovern of South Dakota and Edward M.

Continued on Page 22, Column 2

Gruening Defeated In Alaska Primary

By LAWRENCE E. DAVIES
Special to The New York Times

ANCHORAGE, Alaska, Aug. 28 — A dramatic, unexpected victory by a dark, good-looking, 38-year-old challenger has terminated the long political career of Senator Ernest Gruening, an 81-year-old warhorse known to his admirers as "Mr. Alaska."

Mike Gravel, a real estate developer from Anchorage and former Speaker of the state's House of Representatives, won the Democratic nomination for the Senate in yesterday's primary election in Alaska.

Unofficial returns to Secretary of State Keith Miller in

Continued on Page 26, Column 5

Vietnamese naval forces disembark from a U.S. Navy patrol boat to begin an assault against Viet Cong holdings on Tan Dinh Island.

U.S. marines aboard a C-117 en route to a jump zone near Phu Bai.

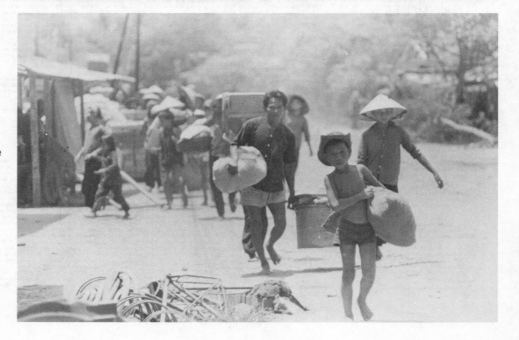

Vietnamese families evacuate their village of Hoa Vang as enemy mortars and rockets shell indiscriminately.

"All the News That's Fit to Print"

The New York Times

LATE CITY EDITION

Weather: Sunny, mild today; fair, cool tonight. Fair, mild tomorrow. Temp. range: today 60-39; Thurs. 55-36. Full U.S. report on Page 93.

VOL. CXVIII . No. 40,459 © 1968 The New York Times Company. NEW YORK, FRIDAY, NOVEMBER 1, 1968 10 CENTS

ATTACKS ON NORTH VIETNAM HALT TODAY; JOHNSON SAYS WIDER TALKS BEGIN NOV. 6

LINDSAY, SHANKER COOL TO HOLDING A SPECIAL SESSION

But Teachers' Union Leader Agrees to Public Hearing as Proposed by McCoy

By LEONARD BUDER

Mayor Lindsay and the president of the teachers' union both reacted coolly yesterday to a suggestion that Governor Rockefeller convene a special session of the State Legislature to deal with the city school crisis.

Informed of their reactions, Governor Rockefeller said:

"Wonderful. All they have to do is settle it. I certainly don't want to call a special session but I am deeply concerned about the children and the parents."

Mr. Rockefeller has been under increasing public pressure to summon a special session because of the school crisis, which has led to three citywide teachers' strikes this fall. City pupils have had only 12 days of regular schooling since the term began on Sept. 9.

Albert Shanker, the president of the teachers' union said last night he would be willing to take part in a public hearing as proposed by Rhody A. McCoy, the administrator of the Ocean Hill-Brownsville school district.

McCoy for Public Hearing

Mr. McCoy had suggested earlier in the day that a public hearing be held before "some responsible and high-ranking public official" that would go into union charges that its members have been harassed and threatened in the district.

At issue in the dispute is the reinstatement of a group of union teachers in the predominantly Negro and Puerto Rican Ocean Hill-Brownsville district in Brooklyn.

The district's governing board originally defied the city Board of Education and refused to reinstate the teachers, asserting that they were a detriment to the district. It has now agreed to permit the teachers to return, but the union has questioned the local board's sincerity.

Dr. James E. Allen Jr., the State Education Commissioner, said last night that he was con-

Continued on Page 32, Column 2

COST FOR WELFARE NOW TOP CITY BILL

Exceeds Outlay for Schools by Using 26% of Budget

By RICHARD PHALON

Welfare has supplanted education as the city's biggest expense item.

Controller Mario A. Procaccino's annual report, released yesterday, shows that welfare costs in the fiscal year ended last June 30 rose to 26.6 per cent of the city's $5.29-billion expense budget, while education declined to 21.4 per cent of the total.

A year earlier, when the total budget was $800-million less, education was the big expense item. It amounted to 22.7 per cent all funds, compared with 20.7 per cent for welfare.

In all, the city last year spent $1.4-billion on such welfare programs as aid to dependent children and stipends to the aged and handicapped. This compared with $931.8-million the year before.

The outlay for education was $1.1-billion, an increase of $200-million over fiscal 1967.

The cost curves on welfare have continued to rise in this fiscal year. The Human Resources Administration, which administers the city's welfare and antipoverty programs, is budgeted at about $348-million over last year. That outlay rep-

Continued on Page 32, Column 2

Nixon Hopes Johnson Step Will Aid the Talks in Paris

By ROBERT B. SEMPLE Jr.

Richard M. Nixon expressed last night his hope that the halt in the bombing of North Vietnam would "bring some progress" in the Paris talks on the war.

But Mr. Nixon, who addressed a colorful and enthusiastic crowd of some 19,000 partisans gathered in lusty communion in Madison Square Garden, did not offer any further opinion on President Johnson's announcement of the bombing halt.

Pointing to Gov. Spiro T. Agnew of Maryland, his Vice-Presidential running mate, sitting on the stage behind him, the Republican Presidential nominee suggested that it would be unwise for either of them to say anything more because it might upset the delicate talks in Paris.

"Neither he nor I will destroy the chance of peace. We want peace," he said.

According to Nixon aides, the President telephoned Mr. Nixon at his New York apartment about 6 P.M., roughly four hours before the candidate spoke, to inform him of the substance of his address.

Mr. Nixon made his comments at what some observers called "the rally of all Nixon rallies." A man who has often been exposed to well-orchestrated gatherings, Mr. Nixon has not in this campaign seen a noisier and more demonstrative crowd.

One hour of the proceedings, including the candidate's speech, was televised over 247 stations of the American Broadcasting Company at a cost of roughly $200,000.

The show included appear-

Continued on Page 51, Column 1

Israeli Commando Units Attack Two Nile Bridges

By JAMES FERON

Special to The New York Times

JERUSALEM, Friday, Nov. 1—Israeli commandos struck deep into the United Arab Republic early today in retaliation for Egyptian incursions Saturday on the eastern bank of the Suez Canal.

A Government announcement said that Israeli commandos had attacked a transformer station and two bridges on the Nile between Aswan and Cairo and had returned safely.

Accompanying the announcement was a statement by Premier Levi Eshkol characterizing the Israeli incursion as a warning intended to underline the dangers of violating the cease-fire agreement between Israel and the United Arab Republic.

Egyptian commandos, he said, have been crossing the Suez Canal cease-fire line with the full knowledge and cooperation of the Egyptian Army.

By striking well within Egyption territory, Mr. Eshkol said, Israel intended to demonstrate the capability of the Israeli Army in this type of warfare.

Result Not Described

The announcement of the Israeli foray did not describe the result of the raid. Read to correspondents at 2:30 A.M., it said:

"Israeli commando units attacked three objectives in southern Egypt tonight on the road between Cairo and Aswan about 230 kilometers [140 miles] north of Aswan.

"The objectives were a transformer station and two bridges on the Nile. Our forces returned safely."

This meant that the Israeli troops would have had to travel more than 200 miles from the southern region of the Sinai Peninsula, their closest base.

It also indicated that the

Continued on Page 17, Column 1

STATE WILL BUILD 4 HOSPITALS HERE

City to Run Them—8 Health Centers and 2 Housing Projects Also Planned

A state corporation created by the 1968 Legislature will build and outfit four new hospitals, eight neighborhood health-care centers and two housing projects for hospital staffs in this city at a cost of $276.4-million dollars, Mayor Lindsay announced yesterday.

The city will eventually pay off the construction costs, either in rents or by long-term purchase of the buildings, but the new plan can have them ready for use within five years, as against 10 to 15 years if the city were to build them, the Mayor said.

Mr. Lindsay said state and city health officials had resolved some legal and other problems and reached agreement that the new corporation, called the State Health and Mental Facilities Improvement Corporation, would finance the construction out of the $700-million bond issue authorized by the Legislature.

State and city officials will meet here Monday to work out remaining details, including de-

Continued on Page 32, Column 6

Ramon Novarro Slain on Coast; Starred in Silent Film 'Ben-Hur'

Special to The New York Times

LOS ANGELES, Oct. 31—Ramon Novarro, the Mexican-born star of scores of Hollywood movies made in the nineteen-twenties and thirties, was found bludgeoned to death in his $125,000 Hollywood Hills home early this morning. He was 69 years old.

The actor's nude body was discovered on the king-sized bed in the master bedroom at 8:30 A.M. by Edward Weber, 42, Mr. Novarro's private secretary and long-time friend.

According to detectives of the North Hollywood division of the Los Angeles police department, there was evidence that Mr. Novarro, a slightly built man, had put up a strong fight for his life. Furniture was overturned and vases and other small articles were broken in the den, living room and bedroom.

Several hours after the body was discovered, and while two dozen reporters and photographers were milling around outside the house, a young sightseer, Ted Grezlok, found a pile of bloody clothing in an ivy bed on the far side of the

Continued on Page 43, Column 3

Bob Martin

Ramon Novarro in 1964

CAUTION IS VOICED

U.S. Officials Expect the Sessions to Be Long and Difficult

By BERNARD GWERTZMAN

Special to The New York Times

WASHINGTON, Oct. 31—Administration officials cautioned tonight against expecting an early end of the war in Vietnam as a result of the agreement to stop the bombing of North Vietnam announced by President Johnson.

There was no mood of exultation in Washington as Administration officials met with newsmen at the White House, State Department and the Pentagon. Instead, officials were warning that the road ahead looked extremely difficult.

One high official, in fact, said that the next round of talks in Paris might turn out to be one of the most complicated diplomatic exercises in history, with the opposing sides spending much time attacking each other publicly and haggling over protocol details of seating, recognition, and prestige.

Details Are Secondary

The American view, however, is that these details are secondary to the major question, which was posed colloquially by one official: "Can the powers with guns in their hands sit around a table and make peace?"

No agenda has been arranged with North Vietnam on the forthcoming talks, to which the Government in Saigon and the National Liberation Front have been invited to participate.

There is some question whether South Vietnam will be able to assemble a delegation in time for the first session next Wednesday. But American officials said that if Saigon was not present, then the Front would not be allowed to take part.

Officials said that they expected the two sides to spend the first weeks, and perhaps months, on the issues of how the talks should proceed and what kind of agenda to follow.

Neither Saigon nor the Front recognizes the other as a competent spokesman for the South Vietnamese people. And the United States and North Vietnam have publicly shared the view of their allies.

Thus President Johnson said

Continued on Page 10, Column 6

LOST A-SUBMARINE FOUND OFF AZORES

Parts of the Scorpion's Hull Sighted at 10,000 Feet

By MARJORIE HUNTER

Special to The New York Times

WASHINGTON, Oct. 31—The Navy announced today that part of the hull of the nuclear submarine Scorpion had been located more than 10,000 feet below the surface of the Atlantic, 400 miles southwest of the Azores.

The discovery ended a five-month search for the atomic-powered submarine and her crew of 99 officers and men.

The Scorpion was last heard from May 21. When she failed to arrive on schedule May 27 in Norfolk, Va., a vast air and sea search was begun.

In announcing the photographic sightings today, Adm. Thomas H. Moorer, Chief of Naval Operations, said that a seven-man Navy court of inquiry would be reconvened in Norfolk. He set no date.

Findings by an inquiry last June have not yet been released.

Admiral Moorer said that reports of the photographic sightings came last night from a United States Navy oceanographic research ship, the Mizar.

"Mizar reports that the submarine's location has been con-

Continued on Page 6, Column 1

John Soto for The New York Times

ANNOUNCING HALT: President Johnson as he was seen on television yesterday

HUMPHREY HAILS DECISION AS WISE

Asserts 'Vast Majority' Will Support It—Aides Look for Campaign Upturn

By R. W. APPLE Jr.

Special to The New York Times

BATTLE CREEK, Mich., Oct. 31—Vice President Humphrey reacted cautiously but with scarcely concealed exuberance tonight to the news that President Johnson had ordered a halt in the bombing of North Vietnam.

"I've been hoping for months that it would happen," he said, "for months."

Standing on the ramp of his campaign plane at Newark Airport, Mr. Humphrey said that he fully supported Mr. Johnson's "very wise and prudent" decision and was sure "the vast majority of the American people will also support it."

Displays Good Spirits

Asked whether he thought the breakthrough would help his Presidential campaign, the Vice President replied:

"This is going to help people. I don't think it has much to do with the candidates as such. I suggest that you just look at the President's message and then study it."

But Mr. Humphrey then walked back to the press plane, past the spotlights that had been set up on the runway, and demonstrated that he was in the best spirits imaginable.

He hectored his press secretary, Norman Sherman, for not producing quickly enough a transcript of his remarks, joked with reporters, and made a "my-lips-are-sealed" gesture when asked about the possible political implications of Mr. Johnson's statement.

Will Refer to Vietnam

The plane's cabin was festooned with orange and black crepe paper, and the stewardesses were wearing black sweaters and miniskirts in anticipation of a Halloween party.

"Happy Halloween," the Vice President exclaimed when he spotted the stewardesses. "We've had tricks—and look at the treats."

Chatting informally with the newsmen, he said that he planned to refer "in guarded phrases" to the Vietnam developments during the rest of his campaign.

He also insisted that he had received no word earlier this

Continued on Page 51, Column 7

22 Days of Tension Led To Turning Point in Talks

By PETER GROSE

Special to The New York Times

WASHINGTON, Oct. 31—On Oct. 9, 1968, North Vietnam began asking the United States some serious questions. These questions and the American replies dominated 22 days of tense and tangled diplomacy, involving a dozen capitals, and led today to an order to cease all bombing of North Vietnam.

As the President announced his long-awaited decision, high Administration officials lifted the tight cover on the dossier of secret diplomatic exchanges, revealing a large part of the substance behind the public speculation around the world for weeks past.

A basic proposition of fewer than 100 words was the core of the diplomatic maneuvering. The formula was drafted by the Johnson Administration early in September, accepted by Hanoi last weekend and approved by the Government of South Vietnam this afternoon.

A Meeting at 2:30 A.M.

It was the basis of a White House meeting at 2:30 A.M. on Tuesday, when President Johnson called in his top Cabinet advisers to talk with the American military commander in Vietnam, Gen. Creighton W. Abrams, within minutes of the general's unannounced arrival.

The essence of the formula was to cut through the deadlock set up by Hanoi's insistance on a bombing halt without conditions and Washington's equal insistence that there could be no further cessation of bombing without reciprocity.

Here is how Administration officials say the diplomatic efforts unfolded:

For many months after the

Continued on Page 11, Column 5

President Is Offered Million for Memoirs

Special to The New York Times

WASHINGTON, Oct. 31—President Johnson has received at least one, and possibly more, conditional offers of an advance in excess of $1-million for his memoirs.

One condition is understood to be that the first volume deal with the major events of his Administration, such as his decisions to begin the bombing of North Vietnam, to send American combat troops into the war, to announce that he would not seek another term and, now, to halt the bombing of North Vietnam.

Although the President has not firmly decided what he will do, he is said to have tentatively agreed to write such a volume in advance of a multi-volume series of memoirs. He also plans to write some magazine articles.

The President is understood to have indicated to prospec-

Continued on Page 22, Column 4

ROCKET ATTACKS ON SAIGON KILL 21

Most Victims at Early Mass —Hue Is Also Shelled, With 9 Feared Dead

By GENE ROBERTS

Special to The New York Times

SAIGON, South Vietnam, Friday, Nov. 1—A series of the war's most damaging rocket attacks in terms of human life rocked Saigon last night and this morning as President Johnson was instructing the military to halt the bombing of North Vietnam.

South Vietnamese police officials said that more than 20 rockets had been fired, killing at least 21 Vietnamese civilians and wounding 40 others.

About 15 rockets also fell on Hue, the former imperial capital, killing 9 civilians and wounded 13, according to United States military spokesmen.

They also said that Mytho, the largest city in the Mekong Delta, had been shelled heavily with mortar rounds, but that there had been few casualties there.

U.S. Official Surprised

A high American official, who apparently knew that the bombing halt was being ordered, seemed incredulous when he received his first word of the Saigon attack from a newsman.

"You can't be serious," he said. Seconds later, he recovered his composure and said, "I'm sure there won't be any comment on this—at least for a while."

Ton That Thien, the South Vietnamese Minister of Information, denied that these had been rocket attacks when he was awakened after midnight by newsmen calling for comment.

Then, after becoming convinced that the reports were true, he said, "Hanoi has ruined Vice President Humphrey's chances now."

Most of the casualties in Saigon occurred at 6:30 A.M. today when a rocket struck the Xom Moi Roman Catholic Church just before mass.

"Beaucoup deaths—women, children, men," said the Rev. Nguyen Van Tri in a mixture of French and English as he twisted a key ring over and over in his palm and paced back and forth near the debris.

The church and its yard

Continued on Page 13, Column 1

PEACE CALLED AIM

Saigon and N.L.F. Can Join in the Enlarged Paris Discussions

Text of the Johnson speech is printed on Page 10.

By NEIL SHEEHAN

Special to The New York Times

WASHINGTON, Oct. 31—President Johnson announced tonight that he was ordering a complete halt to all American air, naval and artillery bombardment of North Vietnam as of 8 A.M. Friday, Eastern standard time (9 P.M., Vietnam time).

"I have reached this decision on the basis of the developments in the Paris talks," the President said, "and I have reached it in the belief that this action can lead to progress toward a peaceful settlement of the Vietnamese war."

"What we now expect—what we have a right to expect," the President said in a television broadcast, "are prompt, productive, serious and intensive negotiations in an atmosphere that is conducive to progress."

Face Shows Fatigue

His face showed fatigue as he made the announcement culminating weeks of secret negotiations.

Mr. Johnson did not announce any reciprocal military commitments from North Vietnam, which he has often said he must have in order to halt the air and naval bombardment that began on Feb. 7, 1965.

[Word of the President's action reached Paris about 2 A.M. Friday, and North Vietnamese negotiators said they might have a statement later in the day. Page 11.]

Washington officials said the bombing of infiltration trails in Laos would continue and that there was no prohibition against reconnaissance flights over North Vietnam.

'Reason to Believe' Foe

Senior Administration sources said the United States had "reason to believe" North Vietnam would not escalate the war in South Vietnam as a result of the bombing cessation.

They said Hanoi "clearly understood" that Mr. Johnson would resume the bombing if it attacked South Vietnamese population centers or took military advantage of the demilitarized zone.

On its side, North Vietnam had apparently not obtained the unconditional bombing halt it has consistently demanded.

Mr. Johnson said that in exchange for the bombing halt Hanoi had agreed to accept participation of the South Vietnamese Government at the Paris talks and the United States had in turn accepted the

Continued on Page 11, Column 1

Channel 13 Ahead 20 Minutes on Talk

By MICHAEL T. KAUFMAN

Channel 13 broke an embargo and televised the President's speech 20 minutes before it was officially released last night.

The violation — which the educational station ascribed to honest error—resulted in angry and indignant protests by the White House and the commercial networks.

"No one told us that the film was embargoed," said Lee Hays, producer of Channel 13's nightly news show. He acknowledged that the unauthorized early showing of the film of Mr. Johnson's speech was put on the air at 7:40 P.M.

Neither he nor station officials were able to say whether the premature broadcast was picked up by any of the 16 other outlets of the Eastern Educational Network, which serves an area from Maine to Washington.

Within minutes after the em-

Continued on Page 10, Column 5

"All the News
That's Fit to Print"

The New York Times

LATE CITY EDITION

Weather: Chance of showers today; partly cloudy tonight and tomorrow. Temp. range: today 70-47; Friday 64-42. Full U.S. report on Page 73.

VOL. CXVIII . . No. 40,460 | NEW YORK, SATURDAY, NOVEMBER 2, 1968 | 10 CENTS

THIEU SAYS SAIGON CANNOT JOIN PARIS TALKS UNDER PRESENT PLAN; U.S. TO STEP UP BOMBING IN LAOS

TEACHERS REJECT A PLEA BY MAYOR FOR ARBITRATION

Shanker Calls Lindsay Plan to Get the Schools Open a 'Warmed Over' Proposal

YOUNG QUITS CITY PANEL

Urban League Leader and Union Head Trade Charges —Pupil Attendance Dips

By LEONARD BUDER

Mayor Lindsay called on the city's striking teachers yesterday to return to work and to submit the issues in the school dispute to binding arbitration.

However, Albert Shanker, the president of the teachers' union, rejected the proposal, which was the same as one made by the Mayor and Vincent D. McDonnell, the chairman of the State Mediation Board, earlier in the week.

Rhody A. McCoy, the administrator of the Ocean Hill-Brownsville school district in Brooklyn, also reacted coolly to the Mayor's proposal. "I hardly think there is anything to submit to arbitration," he said.

There was no comment from the Board of Education. But it was learned that earlier in this week, John M. Doar, the city board's president, told a representative of the Mayor that he was opposed to submitting to arbitration a key issue in the dispute—the union's demand for the removal of the district's seven principals.

Brydges Gives View

In Hartford, a teachers' strike—called despite a court injunction—forced that city to virtually shut down its school system yesterday. Twenty-four thousand pupils were sent home when their teachers failed to go to work. The remaining 4,000 pupils stayed for curtailed classes.

State Senator Earl W. Brydges, the Majority Leader of the Senate, predicted yesterday that no strong school decentralization plan for New York City could get through the 1969 Legislature. Governor Rockefeller, in comments to newsmen, did not go this far but he asserted that the delay in resolving the city school dispute was "threatening the future of decentralization."

Referring to the Mayor's plan for arbitration, Mr. Shanker

Continued on Page 24, Column 3

U.S. COURT WIDENS VOTE IN VILLAGES

Rules It Cannot Be Limited to Owners of Property

By EDWARD RANZAL

A Federal Court ruled unconstitutional yesterday a section of state law that requires voters on village propositions to be property owners.

The effect of the court's ruling, which was made in a case brought by seven Ossining residents [illegible] statewide. The legislation that is involved, Section 4-402 (b) of the Village Law of New York, applies generally to all village elections concerning propositions.

The court granted a preliminary injunction to the Ossining residents, all registered voters, who, under the law, would not have been able to cast a ballot on a local proposition to replace the mayor with a business manager because they were not property owners on the last village assessment roll.

The court—composed of a United States Court of Appeals Judge, Wilfred Feinberg, and District Judges John F. X. McGohey and Inzer B. Wyatt—said exclusion from the vote on changing the form of village government would be "an invidious discrimination," disqualifying about 55 per cent of the 9,840 registered voters in the coming elections.

The seven plaintiffs either

Continued on Page 20, Column 3

O'Dwyer Backs Humphrey As Result of Bombing Halt

Democratic Candidate for Senator Ends Holdout and Will Campaign Here Today With Vice President

By EDWARD C. BURKS

Paul O'Dwyer, the Democratic candidate for the United States Senate, ended a long political holdout yesterday and endorsed Vice President Humphrey for President.

The two will campaign together today in Nassau and Suffolk Counties and in Harlem, Brooklyn and Queens.

Mr. O'Dwyer, who has based much of his campaign on attacking the Johnson Administration's Vietnam war policies, cited President Johnson's announcement of a bombing halt as the reason for his decision to support Mr. Humphrey.

Speaking at a news conference at the Commodore Hotel, Mr. O'Dwyer called the President's decision "a victory for the forces of peace, here in America and abroad."

In particular, he said, it was a victory for the movement within the Democratic party that has been led by Senator Eugene J. McCarthy of Minnesota and the late Senator Robert F. Kennedy.

"I believe the President's announcement last night indicates the Administration has finally chosen to alter its discredited policies in Vietnam and to seek instead a genuine political settlement of the war," Mr. O'Dwyer said.

"That change in policy, for which my supporters and I have all worked so hard, now enables me to indicate my preference for our nation's highest offices. I, therefore, endorse the candidacies of Hubert Humphrey for President and Edmund Muskie for Vice Presi-

Continued on Page 17, Column 3

NIXON LINKS RIVAL TO 'SECURITY GAP'

Terms Humphrey a 'Fuzzy Thinker' Who Would Risk War Through Weakness

By E. W. KENWORTHY
Special to The New York Times

SAN ANTONIO, Tex., Nov. 1—Richard M. Nixon chose the home state of Lyndon B. Johnson to restate tonight in harsher language his charge of a week ago that the President had permitted "a security gap" to develop in the nation's military strength relative to that of the Soviet Union.

When the Republican nominee for President first made this charge on Oct. 24, he aroused President Johnson—who, until then, had taken no open part in the campaign—to enter the lists with the accusation that Mr. Nixon was making "ugly and unfair" charges.

Secretary of Defense Clark M. Clifford had countered Mr. Nixon's charges with statistics to back his contention that the United States still had a considerable lead over the Soviet Union in intercontinental ballistic missiles, long-range bombing planes and nuclear-powered submarines with nuclear weapons.

Vice President Humphrey, the Democratic nominee, had seized upon Mr. Nixon's speech to charge that his opponent was insensitive to the imperative need of arms control.

Return to Attack

Apparently convinced that in this confrontation he had widespread popular support, Mr. Nixon returned to the attack before a cheering crowd of 5,600 at the San Antonio Municipal Auditorium.

Mr. Humphrey, he said, is one of those "fuzzy thinkers" and "false prophets" who "profess to believe that keeping America strong is somehow being against peace."

"They will, if they have their way, get America into war, not because they want war but because they don't understand how to keep the peace," Mr. Nixon said.

Mr. Nixon said that it was necessary to "deal with the world as it is, not as we wish it were."

"We cannot wishful think our way to peace with a Soviet Union that is rapidly escalating its arms," Mr. Nixon declared.

"Until we have in fact displaced the dangerous confrontations that transfix all humanity with horror and fear, until we have in fact developed

Continued on Page 21, Column 7

Humphrey Greeted By Daley but Hails Party's Dissenters

By R. W. APPLE Jr.
Special to The New York Times

CHICAGO, Nov. 1—Vice President Humphrey came back to Chicago tonight.

When he left here on Aug. 30 to begin his Presidential campaign, his mind and those of his countrymen were full of images of turmoil—the battles between the police and the demonstrators, the ugly schisms on the Democratic National Convention floor and the seemingly limitless divisiveness of the Vietnam war.

It appeared likely that he could make no more than a perfunctory race for the White House in the nine weeks remaining to him.

But as Mr. Humphrey returned, his party had achieved a measure of unity, his standing in the polls was steadily rising, a Vietnamese peace initiative was under way—and if victory still seemed improbable, it no longer seemed impossible.

Welcomed by Daley

Mayor Richard J. Daley provided a big red and green movie marquee, reading "Welcome Mr. Vice President—On to Victory," at Midway Airport. Mr. Daley himself was there to welcome the nominee, clapping his hands and doffing his gray fedora when he saw Mrs. Humphrey come down the ramp of the chartered campaign jet.

The Vice President had a warm greeting for Mr. Daley, who symbolized for many people the old politics of the Democratic convention of 1968, but he also tried to make clear his debt to the dissenters and critics who fought for the new politics.

His message was change—"peaceful and constructive change" in the social and economic organization of the nation, in the structure of the Democratic party, and in international relations. "Tonight,"

Continued on Page 20, Column 3

A WIDER U.N. ROLE ON MIDEAST PEACE PROPOSED BY U.S.

At Urgent Session, Wiggins Bids Council Act to Halt Cease-Fire Violations

By DREW MIDDLETON
Special to The New York Times

UNITED NATIONS, N.Y., Nov. 1—The United States called upon the Security Council tonight to strengthen United Nations machinery for maintaining the cease-fire in the Middle East and thus prevent further fighting between Israel and the Arab nations.

J. R. Wiggins, in his first appearance before the Council, said that Washington believed that it was incumbent upon the Council to determine promptly what could be done to "increase the effectiveness of the United Nations cease-fire machinery and prevent further violations of the cease-fire by either party."

The Council met, under the presidency of Otto R. Borch of Denmark, to hear accusations of aggression voiced by the United Arab Republic and Israel, whose delegations had asked for an "urgent" meeting of the Council.

Seriousness Stressed

Mr. Wiggins said that the recent fighting had more serious political implications than any since October, 1967, when the Israeli ship Elath was sunk in the Mediterranean off the Egyptian coast.

Mr. Wiggins's view reflected a diplomatic consensus that the recent fighting and the bitter exchanges in the Council tonight had stiffened positions on both sides and had drastically reduced the prospects for substantive negotiations between the United Arab Republic and Israel in the talks conducted here by Dr. Gunnar V. Jarring of Sweden, Secretary General Thant's mediator.

The new United States representative briskly rejected the United Arab Republic's justification of its attacks across the Suez Canal as "preventive or protective defense" and "the Israeli defense of 'reprisal' or 'retaliation.'"

Accounts Differ Sharply

The immediate issue between Mohamed Awad el-Kony of the United Arab Republic and Yosef Tekoah of Israel was the raid last night by Israel on two bridges across the Nile between Aswan and Cairo and on a transformer station. But the two envoys sounded as if they were talking about two different events.

Mr. el-Kony spoke of a raid by aircraft. Mr. Tekoah spoke of an attack by "an Israel commando unit."

The Egyptian's implication was that troops had not been employed. Western diplomats said that the Nasser Government wished to avoid public admission that the Israelis could penetrate to the Nile within 150 miles of the Aswan High Dam, which patriotic Egyptians describe as "our future."

Denouncing the Israeli attack as "illegal, immoral and inhuman," Mr. el-Kony asked

Continued on Page 3, Column 1

LeMay Loses His $50,000 Job Because He Runs With Wallace

By GLADWIN HILL
Special to The New York Times

LOS ANGELES, Nov. 1—Gen. Curtis E. LeMay has been dropped as board chairman of an electronics company because of his Vice-Presidential candidacy with the American Independent party, the company's president said today. The job paid $50,000 a year.

Mihai D. Patrichi, president and principal stockholder of the Networks Electronic Company of suburban Chatsworth, took the action. He said he had felt impelled because the company's stock dropped sharply after the retired Air Force Chief of Staff became the running mate of former Gov. George C. Wallace of Alabama.

Mr. Patrichi, a one-time Rumanian air force officer, said in a telephone interview that numerous Wall Street securities firms had "told me I had to do something." The company's stock slipped from $13 to $8 a share "because of the unfavorable reaction to the Wallace business," he said.

The company has issued more than a million shares to some 5,000 stockholders, so the market drop represented a paper loss of $5-million, Mr. Patrichi noted.

General LeMay took a "leave of absence" from the company Oct. 1 after deciding to join the Wallace ticket. The leave was supposed to be up Nov. 11.

At the time, Mr. Patrichi, a former Democrat now supporting Richard M. Nixon, the Republican nominee for President,

Continued on Page 23, Column 5

NEWS INDEX

United Press International

IN SAIGON: President Nguyen Van Thieu of South Vietnam after addressing the Assembly

N.L.F. IS TOP ISSUE

South Vietnam Bars Any Separate Seat for the Vietcong

By GENE ROBERTS
Special to The New York Times

SAIGON, South Vietnam, Saturday, Nov. 2—President Nguyen Van Thieu said this morning that his Government would not attend peace talks in Paris until the North Vietnamese agreed to negotiate without the participation of the National Liberation Front as a separate delegation.

President Thieu said that because three key conditions had not yet been met by Hanoi, "The Government of South Vietnam deeply regrets not to be able to participate in the present exploratory talks." The talks are scheduled to begin next Wednesday.

[The White House declined to comment on reports of Mr. Thieu's speech. Other Washington sources said there would be no United States reaction until officials had thoroughly studied the remarks.]

Assembly Enthusiastic

Speaking to a wildly enthusiastic joint session of the National Assembly, President Thieu outlined the three conditions that he said Hanoi must meet.

Specifically, Mr. Thieu called on the North Vietnamese Government to pledge publicly that it advocated serious peace talks and that such discussions would be an "entirely new phase of talks, not just a continuation of the present exploratory talks between the United States and North Vietnam."

The most important point raised by Mr. Thieu, however, was one demanding that North Vietnam appear alone at the bargaining table and not "bring along representatives of the National Liberation Front as a separate delegation."

Coalition Regime Opposed

"This would just be another trick toward a coalition government with the Communists in South Vietnam," the President said.

Mr. Thieu's speech was interrupted 15 times by applause and cheers. After his speech, more than 50 senators and representatives poured into the street, raised the red and yellow flag of South Vietnam and began singing the national anthem.

A few minutes later the group, now grown to more than 100 members of the Assembly, began to march across town to the Presidential Palace. The members walked quietly behind five Senators carrying flags. They were allowed to enter the palace, where President Thieu later joined them.

In imposing his three condi-

Continued on Page 14, Column 4

RUSK NOW URGES HANOI BE PRESSED

He Says That Governments and Leaders Should Insist on Steps Toward Peace

By BERNARD GWERTZMAN
Special to The New York Times

WASHINGTON, Nov. 1—Secretary of State Dean Rusk called on governments and leaders today to put pressure on Hanoi to take steps toward peace now that the United States had stopped bombing North Vietnam.

At a late-afternoon news conference, Mr. Rusk said that "we have our own reasons" to believe that the cessation would open the way to serious talks and would not endanger allied lives in South Vietnam.

"But we shall also be interested in what others may do to insist upon actions by Hanoi that will move us toward peace," he added.

Asked by newsmen whether the reasons he cited included anything specific or were merely assumptions, Mr. Rusk replied: "We're acting on more than assumptions."

Johnson Was Vague

President Johnson, in announcing the bombing halt last night, was vague on any commitments that he might have received from Hanoi to insure that the Saigon Government could take part in enlarged Paris talks, that the demilitarized zone would not be abused or that South Vietnam cities would not be shelled.

On the military aspects of the agreement, senior officials have said that there is no agreement that Hanoi will not take military advantage of the cessation. But Mr. Rusk said:

"North Vietnam clearly understands what is expected of them in this situation. They know what we expect with respect to talks, and they know what we expect with regard to the circumstances in which serious talks can proceed. They know that we shall take care of the security of our own and allied forces in the field.

'Situation Is Clear'

"So there's no misunderstanding on that point. The situation is very clear—to them and in our own minds."

Mr. Rusk refused to go into the details of the understanding. But under newsmen's questions, he said that last weekend "things began to clarify," giving the Administration "good reasons to believe" that the Paris talks would be expanded and that military advantage would not be taken on the field.

"We could be disappointed," he said, "but there's no doubt about not only our expectations, but also the understanding of the other side with respect to those expectations." A news-

Continued on Page 15, Column 6

Laos Route to Be Pounded To Cut Enemy Arms Flow

By WILLIAM BEECHER
Special to The New York Times

WASHINGTON, Nov. 1—The United States intends to triple the level of bombing along the Ho Chi Minh Trail in Laos in an effort to compensate for the effects of the cessation of air strikes against North Vietnam, high Administration officials disclosed today.

This is understood to be a principal reason behind the willingness of top American military commanders to endorse President Johnson's decision to cease all raids against the North.

[Prince Souvanna Phouma, Premier of Laos, said in Vientiane Friday that a halt in American bombing of the Ho Chi Minh trail in Laotian territory would depend on events, and added: "We certainly wish it would happen."]

Other factors that are said to have influenced the views of the military commanders concerning the bombing halt include these:

¶Granting of authority by the President to his field commander, Gen. Creighton W. Abrams, to bomb North Vietnamese forces and facilities within the demilitarized zone, and even just north of it, if General Abrams feels that enemy activities in that area threaten his or allied forces. The general would not have to check back with Washington to order such raids. This authority does not empower General Abrams himself to reinstitute general bombing of North Vietnam.

¶The decision to maintain active reconnaissance over all North Vietnam despite Hanoi's strong public opposition to such flights.

¶Evidence of substantial dis-

Continued on Page 14, Column 2

PLAN IS ACCEPTED BY HANOI ON TALKS

Thuy, in a Paris Statement, Doesn't Mention Demand for 'Unconditional' Halt

By HEDRICK SMITH
Special to The New York Times

PARIS, Nov. 1—The North Vietnamese issued a statement here this afternoon indicating their agreement to broadened Vietnam talks including the South Vietnamese Government as a participant.

The first official reaction from Hanoi to President Johnson's announcement of an end to bombardments against North Vietnam came about two and a half hours after the American bombing ended.

It came in the form of a three-paragraph press communiqué issued by a spokesman for Xuan Thuy, the chief North Vietnamese negotiator. North Vietnamese officials refused to make any immediate further comment or to elaborate on the statement.

The statement confirmed that the United States had not offered an "unconditional" halt in bombing, as Hanoi has long demanded.

Hint on Reconnaissance

It also seemed to confirm that Hanoi had been advised in advance that although the bombardments were ending, American aerial reconnaissance over the North would continue.

[A broadcast by the Hanoi radio said the United States had been forced to end the bombing because it was facing "great defeats in Vietnam and increasing condemnation and pressure from peoples throughout the world." Page 15.]

The [illegible] press statement, couched in diplomatic language without propaganda, said that W. Averell Harriman and Cyrus R. Vance, the American negotiators, had communicated to Mr. Thuy that the President was stopping "bombardments and all other acts involving the use of force" against North Vietnam.

This was a variation on Hanoi's standard demand for an end to bombing and "all other acts of war"—terminology that presumably covered reconnaissance flights.

Diplomatic sources said the shift to "acts involving the use of force" appeared to exclude

Continued on Page 14, Column 1

Citizens of Prague, On TV, Rebut Soviet

By TAD SZULC
Special to The New York Times

PRAGUE, Nov. 1—"Not true," said the young editor. "Not true," said the Prague factory worker. "Not true," said the economist. "Not true," said the army lieutenant colonel.

They were among the "witnesses for the defense" in a starkly dramatic hour-long program on Czecholovak television tonight in rebuttal of the Soviet charges last summer that a counterrevolution was in progress in this nation that justified the August invasion.

It was a part of the mounting Czechoslovak propaganda counteroffensive against the Soviet accusations circulated in a "white paper" produced by a "Group of Soviet Journalists."

The counteroffensive involves not only all the mass

Continued on Page 12, Column 3

Chinese Reds Expel Liu From the Party

By TILLMAN DURDIN
Special to The New York Times

HONG KONG, Nov. 1—At an unheralded plenary session in Peking, the Central Committee of the Chinese Communist party formally expelled Liu Shao-chi, the country's disgraced head of state, from the party and from all party and other posts, Communist China announced today.

The committee denounced Mr. Liu by name as a "traitor, renegade and scab" and a "lackey of imperialism, modern revisionism and the Kuomintang," or Chinese Nationalist party. There was no indication what punishment, if any, he would receive.

A surprise Peking report that the Central Committee had met was received here tonight from Hsinhua, the Chinese Com-

Continued on Page 5, Column 2

U.S. Air Force personnel move out to secure the perimeter of Tan Son Nhut Air Base in South Vietnam as the base is attacked by Viet Cong guerrillas.

The 71st Evacuation Hospital at Pleiku Air Base, South Vietnam, showing the damage sustained during a Viet Cong rocket attack.

"All the News That's Fit to Print"

The New York Times

LATE CITY EDITION

Weather: Becoming cloudy today, tonight. Partial clearing tomorrow. Temp. range: today 60-50; Saturday 77-55. Full U.S. report on Page 95.

SECTION ONE

VOL. CXVIII..No. 40,461 | NEW YORK, SUNDAY, NOVEMBER 3, 1968 | 60¢ beyond 50-mile zone from New York City, except Long Island. 75¢ beyond 200-mile radius. Higher in air delivery cities. | 50 CENTS

Associated Press

TEXAS LOOKS MIGHTY SMALL: President Johnson holds photo of his home state taken by astronauts. Region where Mr. Johnson's ranch is situated is blocked by booster section of the Saturn rocket, which covers most of the view. Astronauts are, from left, Capt. Walter M. Schirra Jr., Lieut. Col. Donn F. Eisele, Walter Cunningham.

HANOI INSISTING VIETCONG HAVE FULL ROLE IN TALKS; U.S. URGES SAIGON TO JOIN

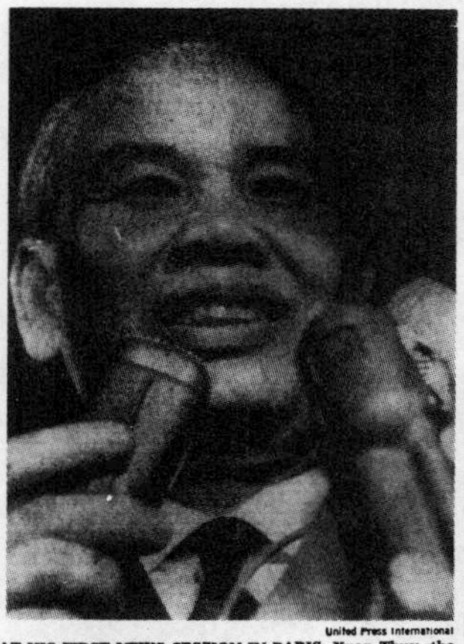

United Press International

AT HIS FIRST NEWS SESSION IN PARIS: Xuan Thuy, the chief negotiator for North Vietnam, at the microphones.

THUY GIVES VIEW

4 Groups With Right to Speak Must Be Seated, He Says

Excerpts from the Xuan Thuy news conference, Page 3.

By HEDRICK SMITH
Special to The New York Times

PARIS, Nov. 2—North Vietnam asserted today that the United States had agreed to admit the National Liberation Front to the next phase of the talks on Vietnam as an independent delegation with the full right to speak.

Xuan Thuy, the North Vietnamese chief negotiator, said at a packed news conference that the secret agreement with the Americans provided that the next phase of talks would involve "four delegations—independent delegations with the right to speak."

He indicated clearly for the first time that Hanoi was prepared to treat Saigon as an equal negotiating partner—without formal recognition as a political entity—provided that Saigon would do the same for the National Liberation Front, or Vietcong.

[In Hanoi, President Ho Chi Minh issued an appeal urging the people to increase their determination to "fight and to win." He called on them to "resolve to liberate the South, defend the North and proceed toward the peaceful reunification of the fatherland." Page 2.]

Statement by Thieu

President Nguyen Van Thieu of South Vietnam said emphatically earlier today that Saigon would not attend the talks if the Front were a separate delegation.

Mr. Thuy contended that if Saigon persisted in refusing to talk, "that will mean that they do not desire peace, and the American side will have to bear the full responsibility."

But his contention that the new talks would be four-sided conflicted with the American interpretation that the next phase would involve just two sides—the United States and South Vietnam on one, and Hanoi and the National Liberation Front on the other.

Washington is prepared to overlook such differences as a

Continued on Page 2, Column 3

DEMOCRATS FEAR SAIGON'S BOYCOTT MAY COST VOTES

Find Possibility of Damage Instead of Profit From Halt in the Bombing

By WARREN WEAVER Jr.
Special to The New York Times

WASHINGTON, Nov. 2—Democrats who had been hoping to realize a modest political profit from the bombing halt in North Vietnam began wondering today whether the ensuing international controversy might not instead cost them votes next Tuesday.

The refusal of South Vietnam to participate in the Paris talks on the war announced by President Johnson two days ago raised the possibility among politicians of both parties that the apparent breakthrough toward peace might backfire and hurt, rather than help, Vice President Humphrey's closing drive for the Presidency.

Thinly veiled Republican suggestions that the President's announcement on Thursday had been motivated by a desire to influence the election moved a step closer to open charges today as Richard M. Nixon, the party's Presidential nominee, campaigned through Texas.

Assurances Reported

In Austin, a Nixon aide told United Press International that the President assured the candidate two days ago that all parties to the expanded Paris talks were in agreement before the public announcement of the bombing halt was made.

As a result of the new developments, the Republican adviser said, Mr. Nixon fears that the military and diplomatic situation in Vietnam would be jeopardized and, further, would cast doubt on President Johnson's "credibility in stopping the bombing.

Mr. Nixon had confined his original reaction to the President's announcement to an expression of hope that the move would bring some progress in the Paris talks. He said that he and his running mate, Gov. Spiro T. Agnew of Maryland, would not say anything more lest they endanger improved prospects for peace.

In New York City, the Nixon headquarters made public the results of a telephone survey of 300 persons selected at random in nine major industrial states. It demonstrated, the Republicans said, "no appreciable shift in voting preference as a result of the bombing halt."

The telephone survey was

Continued on Page 75, Column 1

APOLLO SHAPES UP FOR MOON FLIGHT

Head of Space Center Finds December Lunar Orbit Not 'Precluded' by Last Trip

By NEIL SHEEHAN
Special to The New York Times

JOHNSON CITY, Tex., Nov. 2—Robert R. Gilruth, director of the Manned Spacecraft Center at Houston, implied today that nothing had happened during the recently completed Apollo 7 space mission to "preclude" orbiting the moon on the next American space flight in December.

He cautioned, however, in a news conference at President Johnson's ranch near here at noon, that the results of the Apollo 7 flight were not the "only determinant" of whether the United States would attempt a lunar orbit by Christmas on the Apollo 8 flight.

Timetable May Move Up

If a successful lunar orbit is made in December, it could accelerate the timetable for a landing attempt on the moon from September of 1969 to July of that year.

Dr. Gilruth mentioned the vibration problem with an engine in the Saturn 5 booster rocket during the Apollo 6 mission last April as one of a number of problems that still had to be solved completely before a lunar orbit could be attempted.

He said that "a number of engineering changes" had been made in the Saturn 5 booster to overcome the vibration difficulty, but that the National Aeronautics and Space Administration had not yet made the final decision to try the lunar orbit.

This decision would not be

Continued on Page 34, Column 1

Humphrey Here, Bids Faithful Return; Nixon, in Texas, Sharpens His Attack

Humphrey Tours the City

By MAX FRANKEL

Hubert H. Humphrey blasted on his bugle from seven sides of the New York metropolitan area yesterday, exuding a fervent faith that Richard M. Nixon's campaign was on the verge of collapse.

Dashing exuberantly among excellent crowds from the white suburbs of Suffolk, Nassau and Queens Counties to the centers of Negro, Puerto Rican and Jewish life in Harlem and Brooklyn, Mr. Humphrey summoned errant Democrats of the left and right to repent and return to the fold.

With an expansive show of generosity, he bade special welcome to the last two big-name converts—Paul O'Dwyer, the antiwar Democratic candidate for the Senate, and Allard K. Lowenstein, the dump-Johnson leader who is now the party's nominee for the House in Nassau.

Glad to See O'Dwyer

"Hello, Paul, glad to see you here," said Mr. Humphrey to Mr. O'Dwyer at their first encounter at Suffolk's MacArthur Field in Islip.

Democrats want the right to be different, the Vice President told the crowd of 2,500, and having made room for difference they are now determined to beat back the common foe.

So, too, did Mr. Humphrey readmit Mr. Lowenstein to the faith in what was the final

Continued on Page 80, Column 2

Nixon Scores 'Indulgence'

By E. W. KENWORTHY
Special to The New York Times

EL PASO, Tex., Nov. 2—Richard M. Nixon, who has said at every stop this week that he would not indulge in "personal charges" against his opponents, wound up his formal speechmaking today with a harsh attack on both Hubert H. Humphrey and Edmund S. Muskie.

In the last of a series of nationwide radio speeches, Mr. Nixon accused the Vice President of having "a personal attitude of indulgence and permissiveness toward the lawless."

1952 Speeches Recalled

And he charged Mr. Muskie with "giving aid and comfort to those who are tearing down respect for law across this country" when he said he had no quarrel with those who burn draft cards in his presence provided they were willing to pay the penalty for their illegal act.

Mr. Nixon has steadily criticized Mr. Humphrey on the issue of "law and order" and he has also criticized Mr. Muskie for the statement cited above. But he has rarely attacked them in such personal terms or in language that recalled the tone of his controversial speeches in 1952 and 1954.

Mr. Nixon attributed Mr. Humphrey's "attitude of indulgence and permissiveness" to what he called the Vice President's "near-exclusive em-

Continued on Page 79, Column 3

Wallace Denies He's Slipping

By United Press International

ATLANTA, Nov. 2—George C. Wallace wound up his political roadtrips today with a blast at the Federal Government and a denial that his popularity was slipping.

Forced by weather to cancel an appearance at Joplin, Mo., the third party Presidential candidate flew from St. Louis to Atlanta, where he will make a television appearance tomorrow and then end his campaign with a final rally at the Georgia capitol on Monday.

Mr. Wallace, who addressed a rally in Chicago last night, landed in St. Louis after the Weather Bureau warned of thunderstorms and possible tornadoes in the Joplin area.

On Narcotics Problem

He spoke to the Joplin audience by a telephone-loudspeaker hookup, which linked a lounge at the St. Louis airport with an auditorium in Joplin.

In his 30-minute talk, he charged that the Federal Government was more interested in busing children from one neighborhood to another than in cracking down on the use of narcotics, which he said "have destroyed so many young people in the United States."

He also told the audience not to worry about polls that indicated his support was slipping.

"We are receiving great receptions, but they're trying to play it down," he said re-

Continued on Page 77, Column 4

Thieu's Position on Paris Stirs Concern in Capital

By BERNARD GWERTZMAN
Special to The New York Times

WASHINGTON, Nov. 2—United States officials said today they were concerned over President Nguyen Van Thieu's decision to boycott the Paris talks but were under strict orders to refrain from official comment.

"We expected trouble from Saigon, but not this much," one reliable source said privately.

Mr. Thieu told the National Assembly this morning that South Vietnam would not attend the talks unless North Vietnam negotiated without the participation of the National Liberation Front, or Vietcong, as a separate delegation.

A reliable source here said that the Administration was maintaining absolute silence on the matter in order not to worsen the already strained relations between Washington and Saigon. The Texas White House also remained silent.

Change Needed Quickly

Mr. Thieu's speech has put the Johnson Administration in an embarrassing position, officials here said.

The Communist side will appear to the world to be more interested in serious talks than the allied side unless Mr. Thieu changes his mind soon, the officials felt.

Efforts are believed to be under way in Saigon to put diplomatic pressure on the Thieu Government to reconsider its decision, but this may take some time to accomplish, officials asserted.

Mr. Thieu is said here to be under heavy pressure from his "warhawks" in Saigon. They are unhappy with the bombing halt announced by President

Continued on Page 4, Column 1

U.S.-SAIGON RIFT ON TALKS WIDENS

Relations Are 'Strained'—Anti-Americanism Among Politicians Increases

By GENE ROBERTS
Special to The New York Times

SAIGON, South Vietnam, Nov. 2—The relationship between the South Vietnamese Government and the United States mission continued to deteriorate today after President Nguyen Van Thieu declared that his government would not participate in the Paris talks next week.

The mission was known to be taking the position that South Vietnam could stay away from the talks for a couple of weeks to get its delegation organized—providing President Thieu promised to send a delegation reasonably soon.

However, President Thieu, according to high-ranking diplomats, was refusing to give the mission the assurances it was seeking. They said he was still insisting that the National Liberation Front could not act as a "separate entity" at the Paris talks.

One diplomat, who said last

Continued on Page 3, Column 1

Basque Resentment at Franco Regime Intensifies

By RICHARD EDER
Special to The New York Times

SAN SEBASTIAN, Spain—The fishing port of Bermeo curves around an inlet on the Bay of Biscay, with the white, red-roofed houses climbing steeply up the deep green hills that mark the coastline of the Spanish Basque country.

An ancient stone watchtower, still serving as a beacon for the town's 135 tuna boats, stands on the quay beside the two-story shed that is the warehouse, auction hall and meeting place of the fishing cooperative.

Late one afternoon, the owner of a fishing-boat was showing a visitor around the dock, where young women pushed baby carriages and old women loaded nets into donkey carts.

The fisherman pointed to the reports of tides, weather and fishing conditions that are chalked on slates and hung outside the cooperative. He spoke with anger:

"There are 18,000 people in this town, and virtually all of us speak Basque. Yet those signs are required to be written in Spanish."

It is perhaps in the towns and villages of Vizcaya and Guipúzcoa—two of the four Basque provinces of Spain—that resentment of the regime of Generalissimo Francisco Franco is at its bitterest. It is in these towns and rural areas that the repressive acts of the authorities, usually the local detachment of the Civil Guard, are most severe. And it is in these areas that resistance, which has increased sharply this year, is the most frequent.

Bermeo, 15 miles north of Bilbao, lives almost completely estranged from the authorities. The Civil Guard detachment, housed in the former residence of an official of the pre-Civil war republic, is virtually an occupation garrison. Its troopers exercise and play soccer alone. The troopers—few of whom are Basque—were taken there from other parts of the Spain, as is the cus-

Continued on Page 24, Column 3

Lara for The New York Times

Fishermen at Bermeo, one of the areas where Basques struggle to preserve ethnic identity

Colleges Offer Admission Help To City's Strikebound Seniors

By FRED M. HECHINGER

College admissions officers across the country have promised "the widest possible latitude" to high school seniors here to assure that they will not be penalized as a result of the teachers' strikes that have kept students out of school for all but 12 days since Sept. 9.

The Board of Education's director of college guidance said yesterday that the college officials were prepared to help the students "with respect to deadlines, application forms and other requirements" to meet the emergency.

Many colleges are even prepared to offer the city's public high school seniors some of the advisory services they would normally get from their own guidance counselors.

Harold Zuckerman, the Board of Education's expert on college admissions, called on public high school seniors and their parents to avoid hysteria and misinformation and to take full advantage of a variety of options to protect their chances of college admission.

The assurance was offered as Dr. James E. Allen Jr., the State Education Commissioner, conducted secret negotiations here yesterday in an effort to narrow the gap between disputants in the citywide teachers' strike.

He was trying to win support for some variation of a plan he suggested last Tuesday, but which was rejected by the United Federation of Teachers.

This was the proposal that the state name a trustee for the controversial Ocean Hill-

Continued on Page 54, Column 3

Sports News

COLLEGE FOOTBALL

Top-ranked Southern California, Ohio State, Penn State, Harvard and Yale scored their sixth consecutive victories of the season yesterday, Notre Dame walloped Navy and Columbia scored its first triumph, beating Cornell.

Scores of leading games:

Amherst	42	Tufts	6
California	7	Washington	7
Colgate	27	Lehigh	11
Columbia	34	Cornell	25
Georgia	10	Houston	10
Harvard	28	Penn	6
Michigan	35	N'western	0
Notre Dame	45	Navy	14
Ohio State	25	Mich. St.	20
Penn State	27	Army	24
Princeton	50	Brown	7
Purdue	35	Illinois	17
Rutgers	23	Delaware	14
So. Calif.	20	Oregon	13
Syracuse	47	Holy Cross	0
Tennessee	42	U.C.L.A.	18
Union	17	Williams	7
Wake For'st	38	Maryland	14
Yale	47	Dartmouth	27

HORSE RACING

Dr. Fager, with Braulio Baeza aboard, won the $57,000 Vosburgh Handicap at Aqueduct by six lengths in the track record time of 1:20 1/5 for seven furlongs. The Tartan Stable horse paid $2.60 and earned $37,050 for the victory.

Details in Section 5.

Today's Sections

Index to Subjects

"All the News That's Fit to Print"

The New York Times

LATE CITY EDITION

Weather: Sunny today; clear tonight. Fair, seasonable tomorrow. Temp. range: today 43-28. Tuesday 45-30. Full U.S. report on Page 93.

VOL. CXVIII..No. 40,583 — NEW YORK, WEDNESDAY, MARCH 5, 1969 — 10 CENTS

© 1969 The New York Times Company.

NIXON WARNS FOE TO STOP RAIDING VIETNAM CITIES; ASKS SOVIET AID ON CRISES

TELLS OF HIS TRIP

President Says U.S. Weighs 'Response' if Assaults Go On

Transcript of news conference is on Pages 8 and 9.

By ROBERT B. SEMPLE Jr.
Special to The New York Times

WASHINGTON, March 4 — President Nixon declared tonight that the United States "will not tolerate" continued attacks on South Vietnamese cities. He warned that an "appropriate response will be made to these attacks if they continue."

Mr. Nixon emphasized that the recent wave of enemy attacks was still under review and that no decision had been made on what would constitute an "appropriate response." [Question 5, Page 8.]

At the same time, he said the Paris peace talks were now moving into a new phase of "hard bargaining," adding that he was encouraged by South Vietnam's desire to explore new approaches "rather than simply resign ourselves to a military decision."

The President's warning—his first public statement on the attacks in Vietnam—came during a 55-minute news conference televised nationwide from the East Room of the White House.

Topics Range Widely

Briefly describing his eight-day European trip, which ended Sunday night, Mr. Nixon went on to entertain a wide range of foreign-policy questions and covered these points:

¶Issued a broad invitation to the Soviet Union to share with the United States the burden of resolving a wide range of problems, including those of the Middle East, Vietnam and the arms race [Question 19.]

¶Warned that "harassment" in West Berlin by the Communist regimes would jeopardize projected negotiations with the Soviet Union. But he predicted hopefully that the Soviet Union would do its best to prevent disturbances there. [Question 3.]

¶Disclosed his hope that one major result of forthcoming four-power talks on the Middle East would be an agreement among the four to "guarantee" a middle East settlement. [Question 18.]

¶Declared that he would make and announce a decision early next week on whether the United States should proceed with an antiballistic missile system. [Question 6.]

¶Said that the Israeli Foreign Minister, Abba Eban, would soon visit the United States for discussions in Washington.

Mr. Nixon spoke without notes behind a free-standing

Continued on Page 9, Column 1

The New York Times (by Mike Lien)

AT NEWS CONFERENCE: President Nixon answering newsmen during televised session at White House last night.

Nixon Is Hopeful Moscow Will Help in Peacemaking

By MAX FRANKEL
Special to The New York Times

WASHINGTON, March 4—President Nixon tonight held out a vision—and to some extent an expectation—of Soviet-American collaboration to snuff out the world's most dangerous crises.

Cautiously disclosing at his news conference the impressions he and his advisers have drawn from talks with Soviet officials, Mr. Nixon said he was encouraged in the hope that Moscow "will play possibly a peacemaking role in the Mideast and even possibly in Vietnam."

Moreover, the President gave the Russians the benefit of the doubt in the current tension over Berlin. There, too, he said, he expects them to use their influence to reduce tensions that would otherwise propel the great powers toward confrontation. [Question 3, Page 8.]

Soviet Interests Noted

Mr. Nixon held the Soviet Union accountable for its military aid to North Vietnam and to Israel's Arab neighbors. Without that aid, he said, Hanoi could not sustain the war against the United States, and the Middle East would have no crisis of great concern.

But the President showed himself solicitous of special Soviet interests. Trying to explain the apparent ambivalence in Soviet policy of both belligerence and negotiations, he said the Russians could not readily abandon North Vietnam and other commitments without jeopardizing their leadership of the Communist world. [Question 12.]

But the "overwhelming fact" about the crises on Vietnam,

Continued on Page 9, Column 6

GOVERNOR SCOLDS LINDSAY FOR TALK OF STATE-AID 'CUT'

Asserts 'in Reality' City Will Get $238-Million More, in Spite of Budget Slash

MAYOR STANDING FAST

Democrats in Albany Favor Closing Tax 'Loopholes' to Bar Sales-Levy Rise

By WILLIAM E. FARRELL
Special to The New York Times

ALBANY, March 4—Governor Rockefeller said today that while he was "absolutely sympathetic" with Mayor Lindsay's fiscal problems, the Mayor's estimates of proposed state aid to the city for 1969-70 were inaccurate.

"Mayor Lindsay has said that the proposed state budget now before the Legislature will reduce the state's assistance to New York City," Mr Rockefeller said at a news conference in the State Capitol.

"In reality, the state budget that I have recommended to the Legislature provides for an increase of $238-million in state aid to New York City over the present year."

Mr. Rockefeller also said that the city "will have an increase in its next year's revenues of about $700-million over this current year—not a cut of $600-million as was implied by the Mayor."

'Draw Your Own Conclusions'

After reading his statement, the Governor was asked if Mr. Lindsay was "misrepresenting" the facts.

Mr. Rockefeller replied: "Well, I would suggest that you take the statement that I have just read and compare it to the statement that he made and draw your own conclusions."

On Saturday Mr. Lindsay released details of cuts anticipated in city services if Mr. Rockefeller's proposed reductions in projected state aid were passed by the Legislature. Mr. Lindsay said that with the Governor's reduction, there could be a municipal budget gap of $600-million in the next fiscal year.

[Mayor Lindsay, answering questions at a City Hall press conference, insisted his figures were "entirely accurate and correct."]

Mr. Rockefeller said that his proposed budget included $1,769,000,000 in state aid to New York City.

'Doesn't Grow on Trees'

"I am absolutely sympathetic with Mayor Lindsay's concern for more money for New York City," the Governor said. "I would like to recommend even more, but money doesn't grow on trees and the state can't print it."

Mr. Rockefeller's proposed budget for the 1969-70 fiscal year beginning April 1 calls for a 5 per cent across-the-board cut in projected spending, which would trim a proposed $6.7-billion budget to $6.4-billion.

This would still result in a

Continued on Page 33, Column 1

Associated Press

DEMONSTRATION IN PEKING: Chinese carrying portraits of Mao Tse-tung and a banner saying, "Soviet revisionists invade our country's territory," allusion to border clash.

Procaccino's Office Cited In 2 Investment Inquiries

By RICHARD REEVES

Investigators from two agencies have reported indications of mismanagement and possible fraud in the investment of city employe pension funds in mortgages by the office of Controller Mario A. Procaccino.

Investigations into a five-year-old city program to invest pension funds in mortgages for apartment and office buildings and shopping centers have been under way for almost a year by the city's Department of Investigation and District Attorney Frank S. Hogan.

The inquiries have resulted in the cancellation of at least one mortgage that involved many irregularities.

Fund Totals $5-Billion

One Department of Investigation report on the 19 mortgages totaling $147-million that Mr. Procaccino has approved in the last three years stated:

"Preliminary study revealed a number of questionable practices in the appraisal of property, the approval of loans rejected by the Controller's Mortgage Advisory Committee and the appointment of less than qualified 'experts' who represent this city

Continued on Page 32, Column 1

APOLLO 9 PROVES ITS LINKUP IS FIRM

Combined Craft and Lunar Module Taken on a Rough Ride on 2d Day in Orbit

By JOHN NOBLE WILFORD
Special to The New York Times

HOUSTON, March 4—Whipping through a series of orbital gyrations, the Apollo 9 astronauts shook, rattled and rolled their linked spacecraft and lunar module today to prove them a solid, flyable combination for future trips to the moon.

Col. James A. McDivitt and Col. David R. Scott of the Air Force and Russell L. Schweickart, a civilian, tried twice deliberately to give the 60-foot-long combined vehicle a rough ride by swiveling the nozzle of Apollo's main rocket engine as it fired.

The two ships remained securely linked nose to nose, not bending or twisting. An autopilot system was able to stop the induced rolling, as was Colonel Scott when he took over manual control.

Eugene Kranz, the flight director, said that the rocket firings "were accomplished as planned and as far as we can

Continued on Page 20, Column 6

RED CHINA LIKENS KREMLIN TO CZARS

Says Present Leaders Are 'More Gluttonous' and Seek Bigger Empire

By TILLMAN DURDIN
Special to The New York Times

HONG KONG, March 4—Communist China today called the rulers of the Soviet Union imperialists "more gluttonous than the Czars" as new mass demonstrations swept cities of mainland China in protest over the border clash between Chinese and Soviet frontier guards last Sunday.

Today's denunciation came in a violent editorial in two official Peking dailies, Jenmin Jih Pao and Chiehfang Chun Pao. The editorial, relayed here by Hsinhua, the Chinese Communist press agency, accused the Soviet regime of seeking to occupy Chinese territory as part of a scheme to recreate and expand the old Czarist colonial empire.

The editorial and the continuing demonstrations brought anti-Soviet feeling to a new height.

But political observers here

Continued on Page 6, Column 3

COMMUNISTS SHUT AUTOBAHN AGAIN, BUT RENEW OFFER

Closures Persist on Eve and Day of West German Vote —Red Bid Rebuffed

By DAVID BINDER
Special to The New York Times

BERLIN, March 4 — East German border troops closed the main autobahn out of Berlin this afternoon for two hours at both ends — a somewhat stiffer measure than the two previous blockades at the western end Saturday and Sunday.

[The eastbound lane was shut again Wednesday morning, Reuters reported.]

But, at the same time, the regime of Walter Ulbricht, in an 11th-hour bid to get Bonn's Presidential election tomorrow shifted away from West Berlin, renewed the offer of a concession to West Germany.

Under the offer, more than a million West Berliners would be permitted to visit relatives in East Berlin for the first time since 1966, in exchange for transfer of the election. The electoral college meeting is to be held in East Prussia Hall starting at 10 A.M.

West Berlin's Mayor, Klaus Schütz, said that the offer was "nothing new," and a West German spokesman called it "now as before, no basis for negotiations."

Maneuvers Discussed

This afternoon, while the negotiators of East Berlin and West Berlin, Michael Kohl and Horst Grabert, were still meeting, A.D.N., the official Communist press agency, announced that East German and Soviet troops holding maneuvers around the main autobahn were "preparing for a further complicated highpoint of the exercise."

The offer made by Mr. Kohl, according to a late-evening dispatch by A.D.N., included willingness to talk about "further passes" for West Berliners to visit East Berlin later this year —what Bonn wants in exchange for shifting the election.

Despite the initial rejections, it was understood that the West German side kept open its options almost until midnight, when A.D.N. published an announcement that the negotiations had again collapsed.

Calm Is Indicated

However, virtually all political signs pointed to relative calm in and around Berlin.

The West German Parliament, almost fully assembled here along with delegates of the 11 state parliaments, went ahead with preparations for the electoral process tomorrow.

Neues Deutschland, the East German Communist party organ, assumed a pacific stance toward West Germany for the first time in many months.

The editorial said that the Government was "preoccupied with problems of peaceful international cooperation," with a "peaceful political concept" and a "peaceful socialist construction."

Noting that Mr. Ulbricht was visiting the spring fair in Leipzig, 123 miles south of Berlin, for the third day, the editorial

Continued on Page 3, Column 1

HANOI WELCOMES A VIETCONG GROUP

High Delegation From Front Honored by Ho Chi Minh at a Formal Reception

By JOSEPH B. TREASTER
Special to The New York Times

SAIGON, South Vietnam, March 4 — North Vietnamese officials have enthusiastically welcomed a high-ranking delegation of the National Liberation Front to Hanoi this week, according to broadcasts from the North monitored in Saigon.

The Vietcong delegation was honored at a formal reception by President Ho Chi Minh, and its activities have received unusual coverage from North Vietnamese news agencies.

The delegation, led by Dr. Phung Van Cung, the senior vice chairman of the Liberation Front, is the first group of high officials of the Front to make a formal and publicly announced visit to Hanoi in six years.

Three Clerics in Group

The full composition of the delegation is not known, but it includes at least three clerics—a Buddhist monk, a Roman Catholic priest and a priest of the small South Vietnamese Cao Dai sect. All are members of the Central Committee of the Liberation Front.

The primary purpose of the visit, according to American analysts, is to enhance the status of the Front in the eyes of the world and of the Vietnamese. A secondary objective, they believe, is to bolster support for the war in the South among the North Vietnamese people.

"When the bombing stopped, a lot of North Vietnamese people seemed to think the war was over," one well-informed American official said. "This visit is a kind of re-

Continued on Page 6, Column 3

Columbia Appoints Dr. Kusch, Physicist, as Its Vice President

By LAWRENCE VAN GELDER

Two major posts at Columbia University were filled yesterday when Dr. Andrew W. Cordier, the acting president, announced the appointment of Dr. Polykarp Kusch as vice president and of Paul D. Carter as provost.

In addition, Dr. Kusch, a 59-year-old Nobel Prize-winning physicist who has been a member of the Columbia faculty since 1937, was named dean of faculties.

As vice president and provost, Dr. Kusch and Mr. Carter succeed Dr. David B. Truman, who announced his resignment from both posts last January.

Dr. Cordier said that Dr. Kusch and Mr. Carter would assume their new duties in mid-month, when Dr. Truman, who has held the posts since 1967, leaves to become president of Mount Holyoke College in Massachusetts. The appointments were confirmed at a meeting of the university's board of trustees on Monday night.

As vice president, Dr. Kusch will hold the university's second highest post. As dean of faculties, the university announced, he will be charged with maintaining the excellence of the academic program, and will be responsible for staffing and coordination among Columbia's schools and departments.

The post of dean of faculties has been vacant since it was relinquished in 1967 by Dr. Jacques Barzun, who now holds the title of university professor,

Continued on Page 16, Column 2

KARROO. Look THAT up in your Funk & Wagnall's Standard College Dictionary.—Advt.

Ex-Bookie Held Contract Agent Of Mafia-Controlled Companies

By CHARLES GRUTZNER

A former bookmaker, whom subpoena servers have been unable to locate, was described to the State Investigation Commission yesterday as a man of mystery who was able to obtain nightclub supply contracts for Mafia-controlled meat, liquor, linen, labor relations and fuel oil companies.

The missing witness, Joseph Gulmi, was named by other witnesses at a public hearing as having induced a doll manufacturer to pay him $40,000 to stop pilferage at his plant. He also was accused of having influenced a union to transfer $350,000 of its welfare funds into a bank where a friend was employed.

Gulmi, it was said, apparently had connections in the Internal Revenue Service that enabled him to get advance information about a tax claim against a businessman.

Convicted in 1937 and 1948 of gambling, Gulmi is not listed in law enforcement files as a member of any of the Mafia families that control much of organized crime here but was characterized by the S.I.C. as an "associate" of several members of the Carlo Gambino family.

Benjamin Maksik, who expanded a frankfurter stand on Brooklyn's Flatbush Avenue into the Town & Country Club, which he called the world's biggest nightclub, testified that Gulmi, who also used the name Joe Miller, virtually became a daily visitor in 1955 after the latest addition to the club was built.

He said Gulmi said he was a union delegate (which it developed later he was not) and "had business with the waiters and boys."

Mr. Maksik, who closed the club last fall, testified that in 1955 and 1956 he was "having trouble with the union." He said that Gulmi, who told him employes "were stealing from me," suggested he hire S.G.S. Associates, a concern of labor consultants, "and all my labor problems would be solved."

The witness said he met with Carlo Gambino, the "G" in the firm, and one of his partners and engaged them at $2,500 a month after the manager of the Concord Hotel at Lake Kiamesha, N. Y., another S. G. S. client, told him they had solved his labor problems and could Mr. Maksik's. Federal investigators have identified Gambino

Continued on Page 32, Column 1

ATTEND A THEATRE PARTY in London. yet. 8 shows. 15 days. From $300 including air fare. Japan Air Lines—Advt.

Scientists Halt Work for a Day, Troubled Over Role in Research

By ROBERT REINHOLD
Special to The New York Times

CAMBRIDGE, Mass., March 4—Scientists here and throughout the country put down their slide rules and test tubes, turned off their centrifuges and gathered today to ponder what they had wrought.

Here at the Massachusetts Institute of Technology, where a national movement to suspend scientific research temporarily as a symbolic gesture began about two months ago in the physics department, many scientists gathered for a full day's discussion on the uses and misuses of scientific knowledge.

Similar programs were held on as many as 30 campuses across the country. At one school, the University of Pennsylvania in Philadelphia, all undergraduate classes were canceled for the day.

The movement, which was not an official function of M.I.T., reflected a growing concern among scientists over the consequences of their work.

Few were willing to guess how many M.I.T. scientists had closed down their laboratories for the day. However, a shifting audience of professors and students often filled the 1,200-seat Kresge Auditorium on the campus to hear speeches on reconversion to nonmilitary research, the relationship of the university to the Government, disarmament and the responsibilities of intellectuals.

Other scientists, however, have dissented from the stop-

Continued on Page 13, Column 1

INSTANT MAIL. We'll electronically deliver your letter or contract in L. A. today. CALL INSTA-FAX (212) 866-6000.—ADVT.

Pentagon Bares Cost Of Germ War Study

By JOHN W. FINNEY
Special to The New York Times

WASHINGTON, March 4 — Because a Congressman's wife was upset after watching a television program, the Army disclosed today that the Pentagon was spending $350-million annually to develop and produce chemical and biological warfare weapons.

At a private briefing for a group of Senators and Representatives, the Army said that the United States effort in this field was outmatched by that of the Soviet Union. According to Army estimates, the Russians have seven to eight times the capability of the entire non-Communist world for waging chemical and biological warfare.

The briefing also brought out that the Army was regularly

Continued on Page 12, Column 1

NEWS INDEX

"All the News That's Fit to Print"

The New York Times

LATE CITY EDITION

Weather: Fair today. Cloudy and seasonable tonight and tomorrow. Temp. range: today 40-19. Wed. 36-22. Full U.S. report on Page 84.

VOL. CXVIII ... No. 40,584

NEW YORK, THURSDAY, MARCH 6, 1969

10 CENTS

M'CRACKEN URGES RESTRAINT TO CUT WAGE-PRICE RISES

Chairman of Nixon Council of Advisers Issues Call for Voluntary Curbs

CITES 'NEW BALL GAME'

Warns Environment Will Be 'Less Inflationary' for Business and Unions

By H. ERICH HEINEMANN

The Nixon Administration called on business and labor yesterday to use restraint in raising prices and wages.

In a speech to the Economic Club of New York, Paul W. McCracken, chairman of the President's Council of Economic Advisers, said that price and wage decisions in 1969 "must be consistent with the economic environment of the future, which will be less inflationary."

Business and unions, Mr. McCracken said, "face a new ball game," in which the growth of demand for goods and services will be rising "at a slower rate more nearly consistent with the growth in our productive capacity."

Mr. McCracken warned his audience of businessmen at the Waldorf-Astoria Hotel here that if they ignored the Administration's determination to halt inflation, they would face "uncomfortably soft markets in this new environment."

Guidelines Rejected

He added: "Wage bargains which assume continued inflation at recent rates will court the risk of less employment."

Mr. McCracken, who was a professor of economics at the University of Michigan before his appointment, specifically rejected—as did President Nixon during the campaign — the use of numerical guidelines for acceptable price and wage increases.

Later, Mr. McCracken said in an interview that he would be "glad" if the nation's banks could avoid another increase in their basic charge on business loans.

This "prime rate" is now at a record 7 per cent, following three rapid-fire increases in December and January.

"We've already got some problems in the housing area," Mr. McCracken said, "that an-

Continued on Page 78, Column 1

G.O.P. to Join Rivals In Convention Study

By WARREN WEAVER Jr.
Special to The New York Times

WASHINGTON, March 5—Representative Rogers C. B. Morton, the incoming Republican National Chairman, plans to join the Democrats in a bipartisan study of reform of the national convention system.

Although he will not formally assume the party leadership for six weeks, Mr. Morton has already discussed with his political associates a joint study on how to modernize procedures under which Presidential candidates are chosen. The Democratic National Committee is cosponsor of the project.

The implications of such a project for the American political system are far-reaching. It would tend to create pressure for uniform structure and procedures in both

Continued on Page 22, Column 1

BERLIN VOTE HELD BY WEST GERMANS IN SPITE OF REDS

Gustav Heinemann Elected President—Harassment Rises, Then Is Eased

By DAVID BINDER
Special to The New York Times

BERLIN, March 5—Dr. Gustav Heinemann, Justice Minister of West Germany, was elected President of the Federal Republic today on the third ballot of voting by the electoral assembly of state and federal parliaments.

Dr. Heinemann edged out Defense Minister Gerhard Schröder by a six-vote margin—512 to 506 with 3 abstentions.

During the voting the blockade of roads to West Germany was intensified by East German border troops. The East Germans, who termed the election in Berlin illegal, lifted their blockade measures at 6 P.M., a half hour before the election result was announced in East Prussia Hall of the West Berlin fairgrounds.

At 2 P.M. heavily armed East German guards moved to close all of the roads leading out of Berlin, including the highway to Hamburg. Blockades in the three preceding days affected only the main western autobahn to Helmstedt.

Military Traffic Delayed

United States and British military traffic was also delayed by the blockades today, but less so than civilian traffic.

Though the blockades were annoying to travelers, Western officials were much more disturbed by an East German move in the morning, when a truck carrying commercial goods was turned back for the first time. The East Germans said that it was carrying "illegal" military products.

Noting that the truck bore a load of "shoulder straps, hooks, 500 belts and 2,250 brass rivets," a spokesman for the unidentified West Berlin manufacturer said that the allegation that these constituted military goods was ridiculous.

To the Western Allies the barring of the truck from transit across East Germany represented the first application of a threat by the Soviet and East German Governments to cripple West Berlin's industry by curbing its exports. The threat was made in notes sent on Friday.

An Insistent Threat

East Germany and the Soviet Union have been threatening insistently in recent days to apply restrictions on West Berlin's purported "arms production."

About 70 per cent of West Berlin's annual industrial shipments of 12 million tons move by truck on the vulnerable land routes through East Germany to West Germany and beyond.

Less than 1 per cent of West Berlin's industrial products can be profitably flown out of the city through the three Allied air corridors to the West. For this reason the Communist threat to the land routes is viewed as a distinct menace to the economy of the city.

The federal election, held un-

Continued on Page 2, Column 4

South Vietnamese Rangers Flush Enemy From Stronghold in Bienhoa

South Vietnamese troops rushing a building during fighting last week in Bienhoa, 18 miles northeast of Saigon

United Press International

Three North Vietnamese who surrendered are marched from the bullet-riddled building following the all-out attack

22 DIE IN SAIGON IN ROCKET ATTACK; SCORES WOUNDED

Slum Neighborhood Heavily Shelled—Vietcong Radio Says Tempo Will Rise

CAPITAL HIT 4TH TIME

At Least 7 Missiles Fired—Shooting at Premier Laid to Guerrilla Agent

Special to The New York Times

SAIGON, South Vietnam, Thursday, March 6—The heaviest and most damaging rocket attack of the year hit Saigon early this morning, killing at least 22 civilians and wounding scores.

Military sources said that the number of deaths might reach 35 when final police and hospital reports were received.

The enemy fired at least seven rockets into the capital. Most of them landed in a densely populated slum neighborhood on the city's fringes.

The bombardment came less than 24 hours after President Nixon said that the United States "will not tolerate a continuation of this kind of attack without some response that will be appropriate."

[The Vietcong radio said in a broadcast heard in Hong Kong that the offensive would not stop and that the tempo of ground fighting would increase. Guerrilla forces must keep up their fighting spirit for weeks to come, the broadcast added, according to Agence France-Presse.]

Offensive Began Feb. 23

The attack this morning was the fourth on the capital since the enemy offensive began Feb. 23.

In another aspect of the offensive, a spokesman for Premier Tran Van Huong said that he was the target of a Vietcong assassination plot yesterday. The police arrested four men but had not identified them as Vietcong agents.

The most damaging explosion today occured in a densely populated block of houses not far from the city's docks. Eleven bodies were carried out through the narrow footpaths that thread between the houses. Military sources said the rockets all came from the east, as did the three earlier attacks of the offensive.

At the scene of the explosions, firemen uncovered the body of an old woman's husband and carried it out of the wreckage. After her first cry of grief, the woman followed silently behind the litter, her head bowed and her palms pressed together at her forehead in a Buddhist prayer.

A Halting Argument

Nearby, a man started a tearful, halting argument with his dead sister's husband. He belabored his brother-in-law with not being in the house at the time of the blast and with failing to protect his family.

Early reports showed that the enemy fired about 35 mortar and rocket barrages throughout the country last night. Most of the targets were allied military installations, United States Army sources said. Overall damage and casualties in the other attacks were reported to have been light.

In other action in South Vietnam, American infantry forces fought North Vietnamese regulars early yesterday morning 10 hours after ending an all-day fight with the same enemy force.

The fight took place 5 miles northeast of Trangbang and 29 miles northwest of Saigon, in an area beset by enemy troops.

The infantrymen fought the

Continued on Page 15, Column 1

APOLLO 9 MODULE PASSES KEY TEST

But Schweickart Suffers 2 Attacks of Nausea—'Walk' in Space Today Canceled

By JOHN NOBLE WILFORD
Special to The New York Times

HOUSTON, March 5—The squat spacecraft designed to land men on the moon passed its first manned flight test today and was declared in good shape—which was more than could be said for one of the Apollo 9 astronauts.

Col. James A. McDivitt of the Air Force and Russell L. Scheickart, a civilian, squeezed through a connecting tunnel from the main spacecraft into the attached lunar module. They successfully fired one of the lunar module's main rockets.

But Mr. Schweickart was hit twice by severe attacks of nausea that forced the cancellation of his two-hour space "walk," which had been scheduled for tomorrow afternoon. He vomited once before leaving the main spacecraft and once while in the lunar module.

Everything But 'Walk'

Before settling down for the night, he reported that he was feeling better, but was "not completely up to par." At that Colonel McDivitt, the Apollo 9 commander, recommended calling off the "walk," and flight controllers here agreed.

Instead, the astronauts will go through all the preparations for a "walk"—called extravehicular activity, or EVA—including cracking open the hatches of both of the linked vehicles.

Mr. Schweickart may stand up in the hatch, but will not venture out, as previously planned, to cross over from the lunar module to the Apollo command ship. A live telecast is scheduled to be transmitted sometime during the preparations.

Christopher C. Kraft, director of flight operations, said that failure to carry out EVA would not necessarily jeopardize the

Continued on Page 18, Column 1

MARCHI IS BACKED BY G.O.P. IN BRONX

Ribustello, Leader, Charges Lindsay Betrayed Pledges Made in 1965 Campaign

By THOMAS P. RONAN

State Senator John J. Marchi's candidacy for the Republican nomination for Mayor was given a major lift yesterday when the Bronx Republican organization announced its support for him.

The 47-year-old conservative Republican already has the backing of his own county leader, Richard H. Bolton of Staten Island. Mr. Bolton predicted yesterday that his executive committee would unanimously endorse Mr. Marchi when it meets next week.

Mr. Marchi also has considerable backing in Queens, where five of the six state legislators are for him. But Sidney Hein, the county leader, has to take a stand.

Vincent F. Albano Jr., the Manhattan leader, and John R. Crews, the Brooklyn leader, have expressed strong support for the renomination and reelection of Mayor Lindsay if he decides to seek a second term. Their executive committees have yet to give their views on the mayoral nomination.

No Comment at City Hall

With the present line-up, some Republican leaders think Mr. Marchi has a good chance of upsetting Mr. Lindsay in the primary on June 17, but they are not making any firm predictions.

"I really don't know," a prominent Republican said when asked about Mr. Marchi's primary prospects. "That's just what I am trying to find out."

At City Hall, an aide to Mr. Lindsay said the Mayor would have no comment on the development in the Bronx.

In announcing the Bronx organization's position at an Albany news conference, Councilman at Large A. Joseph Ribustello, the county leader, accused Mr. Lindsay of "betraying the pledges on which he campaigned for Mayor four years ago."

"Republicans should have

Continued on Page 48, Column 6

The Vietnam Policy Reversal of 1968

This is the first of two articles written by Hedrick Smith in collaboration with William Beecher, and incorporating reports by Peter Grose, John W. Finney, E. W. Kenworthy, Roy Reed, Benjamin Welles, Edwin L. Dale Jr. and Max Frankel.

Special to The New York Times

WASHINGTON, March 5—On the cold and cheerless early morning of Feb. 28, 1968, the Chairman of the Joint Chiefs of Staff, Gen. Earle G. Wheeler, landed at Andrews Air Force Base after an urgent mission to Saigon. Pausing only to change into a fresh uniform, he hurried through the rain to the White House to deliver a report and make a request.

The report was designed to encourage an anxious President and his beleaguered advisers, but it served only to shock them into extended debate.

The request — for more troops—was designed to bring military victory at last in the eight-year American military effort, but it led instead to a fateful series of decisions that stand in retrospect as one of the most remarkable turnabouts in United States foreign policy.

The month of March, 1968, became a watershed for a nation and a Government in turmoil. The Johnson Administration, by pulling back from the brink of deeper commitments and moving toward disengagement, set a course that affects the daily decisions of the Nixon Administration.

Many of the ingredients of

Continued on Page 14, Column 1

Procaccino Sees a Smear In Investigation Reports

By RICHARD REEVES

Controller Mario A. Procaccino — angrily shaking his fists at unnamed "tinhorns and power brokers who are smearing me" — spent almost an hour yesterday denying that investigations had uncovered more than one isolated case of mismanagement or corruption in his office.

Mr. Procaccino called a news conference to discuss published reports of investigations into the mortgage investments of city pension funds and of a grand jury investigation of his personal activities.

He began by calling account of the grand jury action a "vicious and malicious lie" and quoted a city report clearing him of personal wrongdoing in a past grand jury case. He confirmed, however, that the city's Department of Investigation and District Attorney Frank S. Hogan were investigating his Mortgage Investment Division.

"They won't find anything wrong either," he said. "This is the greatest office in the world."

"There was no hanky panky in the mortgage division," said Eugene L. Sugarman, a former third deputy controller who supervised the division until his resignation last Jan. 31. Mr

Continued on Page 34, Column 1

NIXON RESTRAINT PLEASES CAPITOL

Congressional Leaders of Both Parties Praise Calm Attitude Toward Crises

By PETER GROSE
Special to The New York Times

WASHINGTON, March 5—President Nixon drew praise from Congressional leaders of both parties today for what was regarded as his restrained attitude toward international crises from Vietnam to Berlin.

Maintaining the cautious tone set at last night's news conference, the White House declined tonight to comment on first reports of a new serious rocket attack on Saigon. A spokesman simply reiterated Mr. Nixon's warning to North Vietnam that "the fact that we have shown patience and forbearance should not be considered as a sign of weakness."

Gerald L. Warren, deputy press secretary, noted that Defense Secretary Melvin R. Laird was on his way to Saigon, accompanied by the Chairman of the Joint Chiefs of Staff, Gen. Earle G. Wheeler, on a fact-finding mission.

The President said at his news conference last night that Mr. Laird's report would be considered in deciding on an "appropriate response" to the

Continued on Page 15, Column 4

OCEAN HILL BOARD TO BE REINSTATED

Allen Recommendation Due for Approval Tomorrow

By BILL KOVACH
Special to The New York Times

ALBANY, March 5—State Education Commissioner James E. Allen Jr. has asked the New York City Board of Education to reinstate immediately the Ocean Hill-Brownsville governing board, which has been suspended since Oct. 6.

Dr. Allen said today he had made the recommendation to the city board on the advice of Wilbur R. Nordos, who has served as state trustee for the district.

The city board, at a late afternoon meeting today, informally agreed to accept Dr. Allen's recommendation. A board spokesman said the members would formally act on the matter at a special public meeting Friday morning.

Dr. Allen told the central school board his trustee had advised him "that the schools of the district have been functioning in an orderly manner for the past several weeks, and that in his judgment the governance of the district may properly be returned to the local board."

He also sent to the city board a copy of a letter to the Rev. C. Herbert Oliver, chairman of the Ocean Hill board,

Continued on Page 31, Column 3

Donovan to Quit as School Head; Denies Acting Under Pressure

By LEONARD BUDER

The New York Times

Dr. Bernard E. Donovan

Dr. Bernard E. Donovan announced yesterday that he would step down as Superintendent of Schools on Aug. 31.

The 58-year-old administrator, who has headed the city system for four turbulent years, denied that he was leaving because of a recent attack on him by the Rev. Milton A. Galamison, vice president of the Board of Education.

"It is just my personal desire to do something in education without all the restrictions that are on me as a Superintendent," Dr. Donovan said. "After 40 years in the system, I think I ought to put my experience to other use in the field of education."

Dr. Donovan, who will go on terminal leave Sept. 1 and will retire officially next Feb. 1, said he had not yet specifically decided what he would do after he left the school system here.

In a statement submitted to the Board of Education yesterday, he said:

"My original intent was to

Continued on Page 30, Column 1

Woman on F.B.I.'s Wanted List Is Seized in Georgia Kidnapping

By The Associated Press

WASHINGTON, March 5—Ruth Eisemann-Schier, accused in the kidnapping of the daughter of a wealthy Florida real estate developer, was arrested today in Norman, Okla., by agents of the Federal Bureau of Investigation.

J. Edgar Hoover, director of the bureau, said that Miss Schier, 26 years old, the first woman ever placed on the bureau's list of "10 most wanted" fugitives, had been taken into custody at a restaurant where she had been working as a car hop.

Miss Schier is charged, along with Gary Steven Krist, 23, with abducting Barbara Jane Mackle from a Decatur, Ga., motel last Dec. 17.

Eighty hours after Miss Mackle had been kidnapped she was found alive buried in a box about 20 miles northeast of Atlanta.

The arrest today culminated a search of more than two months. Mr. Hoover said that agents had been led to the Norman area after the woman applied for a nursing position Feb. 27 at a Norman hospital.

Her application required fin-

Continued on Page 22, Column 3

NEWS INDEX

Viet Cong guerrillas often operated out of the thick foliage surrounding Vietnam's rivers. Here, Vietnamese troops patrol the Duong Keo River.

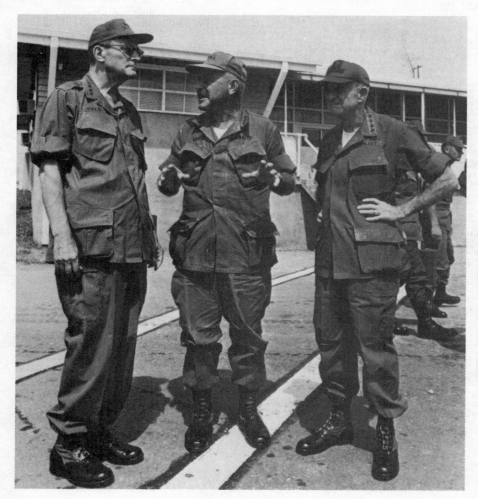

General Creighton W. Abrams, Commander of the U.S. forces in Vietnam, confers with General Earle G. Wheeler (L), Chairman of the Joint Chief of Staff and Admiral John S. McCain (R) Commander in Chief of the Pacific Command during a tour of Da Nang.

"All the News
That's Fit to Print"

The New York Times

LATE CITY EDITION

Weather: Partly sunny and mild today. Fair tonight and tomorrow. Temp. range: today 60-44. Saturday 64-50. Ful U.S. report on Page 71.

SECTION ONE

VOL. CXVIII..No. 40,615

© 1969 The New York Times Company.

NEW YORK, SUNDAY, APRIL 6, 1969

60c beyond 50-mile zone from New York City, except Long Island. 75c beyond 200-mile radius. Higher in air delivery cities.

50 CENTS

BRODERICK TO RUN FOR CONTROLLER ON SCHEUER SLATE

Ex-Commissioner of Police Unable to Raise Funds to Seek Mayoralty

COUNCIL CHIEF IN DOUBT

Negro Is Sought for Ticket —Procaccino Said to Bar Wagner's Plea to Quit

By RICHARD REEVES

Representative James H. Scheuer, the first of the seven announced Democratic candidates for Mayor, has selected former Police Commissioner Vincent L. Broderick as his running mate for Controller. He hopes to find a Negro to run on his ticket for City Council President.

Mr. Broderick, who three times scheduled dates to announce his own candidacy for Mayor, decided to join Mr. Scheuer when he was unable to raise enough money for an independent campaign.

The formal announcement of the Scheuer-Broderick alliance is scheduled for Tuesday, although Mr. Broderick informed his small band of supporters of his decision at a meeting yesterday.

Decision Is Resisted

Some of those supporters had argued bitterly against teaming up with Mr. Scheuer, and had urged Mr. Broderick to accept an offer to run with another candidate, Borough President Herman Badillo of the Bronx, whom they considered more liberal.

The private talks between Mr. Broderick and the candidates seeking his support were among dozens of conversations that have been going on among Democrats in the last few days.

At the same time, former Mayor Robert F. Wagner was reported to have asked Contoller Mario A. Procaccino if he would withdraw as a candidate if Mr. Wagner entered the race. Mr. Procaccino was reported to have said, "No."

The Controller was negotiating with Jack Fuchsberg, a Manhattan lawyer, who may run for Controller on the Procaccino ticket.

In one of the few public discussions, Representative Hugh L. Carey confirmed yesterday that he would announce his candidacy for Mayor tomorrow and present his running mates, Councilman Robert A. Low for City Council President, and Louis J. Laurino, president of the Queens Chamber of Commerce, for Controller.

Mr. Carey, who has the support of the Brooklyn Democratic organization, said during

Continued on Page 31, Column 1

Soviet Assails Tito Press; Prague Scores Newsmen

Moscow Paper Charges Yugoslavs Print Hostile Material on Russia

By BERNARD GWERTZMAN
Special to The New York Times

MOSCOW, April 5 — A Soviet newspaper today leveled against Yugoslavia some of the strongest criticism seen here in more than a decade.

An article in Sovetskaya Rossiya, an organ of the Communist party's Central Committee, was ostensibly an attack on Yugoslavia's press for publishing anti-Soviet material. But it was interpreted by Yugoslav diplomats as a direct rebuke to the Government of President Tito.

Sovetskaya Rossiya, which is the party's newspaper for the Russian Republic, largest in the Soviet Union, has been in the forefront of a campaign for ideological purity in the Communist press.

The publication of today's article suggested that relations with Yugoslavia might be as bad now as those that existed in the fall of 1956, following the Soviet quashing of the Hungarian revolt, when Imre Nagy, leader of the revolt, took refuge in the Yugoslav Embassy in Budapest.

Mr. Nagy was arrested and

Continued on Page 27, Column 1

Czechoslovak Journals Criticized for Balking at New Censorship

By ALVIN SHUSTER
Special to The New York Times

PRAGUE, April 5—The Executive Committee of the Communist party's Presidium issued a scathing attack on the mass media today for balking at the restoration of tight censorship.

The ruling eight-member committee accused journalists in the press, radio and television of insincerity, protection of "antisocialist forces," defiance of party policy and irresponsibility.

Stressing earlier charges by the 21-member Presidium that journalists had helped stir up anti-Soviet feelings to a point of crisis in recent weeks, the committee made clear that the party would not brook any sign of resistance to the decision, made under Soviet pressure, to reimpose prepublication censorship.

The angry declaration was touched off by a response to the party's decision by the Czechoslovak Union of Journalists. The union's statement indicated opposition to prepublication censorship and said journalists preferred to con-

Continued on Page 28, Column 1

Thousands March Here to Demand Withdrawal From Vietnam by U.S.

The New York Times (by Robert Walker)

Demonstrators marching up the Avenue of the Americas yesterday on their way to the antiwar rally in Central Park

By MURRAY SCHUMACH

Thousands of antiwar demonstrators thronged the Avenue of the Americas yesterday as they marched from Bryant Park to Central Park for a rally in a downpour demanding United States withdrawal from Vietnam. With loud chants of "End the war in Vietnam," "Bring the troops home" and "Free speech for G.I.'s" as they strode through the midtown area, they attracted thousands of Easter visitors to the sidewalks. The parade began a weekend of antiwar demonstrations here and in Chicago, Los Angeles, San Francisco, Seattle, Atlanta and elsewhere. The demonstrations are the first since President Nixon took office. Eventually the drive, according to its organizers, is to spread to 43 cities. At the local mass demonstration, hundreds of policemen, many with electronic megaphones, were under heavy pressure to maintain vehicular traffic and at the same time prevent small groups hostile to the marchers from interfering with the parade. Though the bulk of the marchers seemed to be teen-agers and young

Continued on Page 3, Column 3

NIXON HAS BEGUN PROGRAM TO END WAR IN VIETNAM

Secret Talks and Increased South Vietnamese Effort Called Parts of Plan

'VICTORY' DOWNGRADED

Shift in Tactics Would Cut U.S. Casualties and Allow Pullout of Some Troops

By MAX FRANKEL
Special to The New York Times

WASHINGTON, April 5—The Nixon Administration has set in motion an essentially secret program of diplomatic and military measures designed to extricate the United States from Vietnam.

Officials here confirm the adoption of a new approach to the war but refuse to discuss its details. They predict, however, that their approach will become evident by the end of 1969, presumably through a decline in the rate of American casualties and the recall of some American troops.

The current and partly known efforts to arrange secret talks in Paris and to turn over more combat assignments to South Vietnamese units in the war zone are said to be part of the Administration's program, but only a part.

Speak of Gradual Change

Informed officials here also talk about a gradual change of military tactics to reduce casualties while providing greater security for some of South Vietnam's major population centers.

As described here, this change would confirm Washington's readiness to settle for something less than military victory, but it would also buy time for negotiations and the evolution of new political processes in South Vietnam before the final American pullout.

It is still not clear here how much progress has been made in recent days to arrange secret talks, both between Washington and Hanoi and between the Saigon Government and the National Liberation Front, or Vietcong.

All Parts of Maneuvering

However, senior officials contend that every conversation in Paris, many consultations with Moscow and the course of the battle itself are now an essential part of the maneuvering by both sides.

They also contend that American military measures are now geared to diplomatic objectives and that "negotiations" in the largest sense are therefore under way.

It is not clear either whether the announced 10 per cent cutback in B-52 bombing raids in South Vietnam had a clear diplomatic purpose as a part of this program. Defense Secretary Melvin R. Laird represented the

Continued on Page 2, Column 3

Nixon Names 5 to Weigh Executive Branch Change

By WALTER RUGABER
Special to The New York Times

MIAMI, April 5—President Nixon returned today to one of his favorite subjects: the organizational aspects of government administration. He appointed a five-member advisory council to recommend changes.

It was also disclosed today that a review of substantive domestic issues, for which leading advisers flew to the President's vacation home on nearby Key Biscayne yesterday, ended after two hours.

Ronald L. Ziegler, the White House press secretary, reported that yesterday's session had included "a very full discussion" and that the President had made "some preliminary decisions." These were not announced.

The President's Advisory Council on Executive Organization is expected to "undertake a thorough review of the organization of the executive branch," a White House statement said.

Roy L. Ash, one of Mr. Nixon's old friends who is president of Litton Industries, Inc., of Beverly Hills, Calif., was selected as chairman of the group, which will hold its first meeting in Washington on Thursday.

Mr. Ash, who has been president of Litton Industries since 1961, worked for the President on government organization during the transition period between the Johnson and Nixon Administrations. He is highly regarded by Mr. Nixon and there were discussions about bringing him into the Administration.

At one point, the Californian was reported to have been assigned an office in the west wing of the White House. Apparently, however, Mr. Ash was reluctant to sacrifice his large financial holdings to avoid conflict-of-interest problems.

Litton is one of the nation's largest defense contractors. The Administration believes, however, that Mr. Ash will avoid the question of conflicts as a commission member.

The White House statement said that the council would "provide over-all and specific recommendations for improved effectiveness" and would "deal with both immediate and long-range needs for organizational changes to make the executive branch a more effective instrument of public policy."

Further, the statement said, the council will take up three general topics. These were described as follows:

¶"The organization of the

Continued on Page 30, Column 2

Turnpike Gunman Kills 3 and Himself Near Harrisburg

By United Press International

HARRISBURG, Pa., April 5—A man went on a shooting spree with a high-powered rifle on the Pennsylvania Turnpike today, killing two persons and wounding 15 others.

He then shot and killed his wife and himself.

The gunman was identified as Donald Lambright, 31 years old, with addresses in Philadelphia, St. Louis and Cleveland. He was the son of the comedian Stepin Fetchit.

The gunman's father, reached in a Louisville, Ky., hotel, said that he had not seen his son in about three years. The father, whose real name is Lincoln Perry, said that he was no longer married to Lambright's mother.

Six motorists and a truck driver reported that their vehicles had been fired upon by the gunman, who entered the Turnpike at its eastern gate.

For an hour he fired a 30-

Continued on Page 45, Column 3

MILLIONS IN CHINA STREAM TO FARMS

City People 'Sent Down' to Rural Areas for Work and Political Re-education

By CHARLES MOHR
Special to The New York Times

HONG KONG, April 5—One of the largest mass movements of population in history is continuing in Communist China as students and other city dwellers are sent to rural areas to do manual labor.

A Western political analyst in Hong Kong estimates that 25 million people—or 15 per cent of China's urban population—have been or soon will be "sent down," as the Chinese press phrases it.

The Chinese press has given no official figure for the total of those who are going to the countryside to be "re-educated" politically, but the press does indicate that the number is very high.

The radio station of Kiangsi Province, in eastern China, said Sunday that 780,000 residents of Kiangsi urban areas had been sent to rural areas in the province. It is likely that others were sent outside the province to sparsely populated border regions such as Inner Mongolia and Sinkiang.

Earlier this week the Peking radio said that "large numbers of young people are leaving Shanghai for settlement in rural areas." On Saturday it said that in recent days "youths have gone to the countryside in Kirin,

Continued on Page 7, Column 1

4 Britons at North Pole After 407-Day Sled Trek

Special to The New York Times

LONDON, Sunday, April 6—A four-man British expedition reached the North Pole yesterday after a 14-month, 1,300-mile trek by dog sledge, The Sunday Times reported today.

The newspaper, one of the sponsors of the trans-Arctic crossing, said the team arrived at the Pole at 7 A.M., Greenwich mean time (2 A.M., New York time).

The expedition set off from Point Barrow, the northernmost point in Alaska, 407 days ago and traveled by dead reckoning, using only dog sledges to haul the food and equipment.

The men made two long stops, one for two months last summer and one for a five-month winter camp beginning in October when they lived in total darkness. The expedition was supplied by occasional air drops of food, medical supplies and mail.

Second Surface Crossing

The expedition is the second in history to make a surface crossing to the North Pole and the first, according to The Sunday Times, "to do it the hard way, by trekking the 1,300 miles from the north coast of Alaska."

The arrival, made in temperatures of minus 50 degrees Fahrenheit, came almost 60 years to the day of the first successful journey on the surface to the North Pole by the American explorer, Adm. Robert E. Peary.

Admiral Peary, known as the discoverer of the North Pole, reached it on April 6, 1909, after several unsuccessful attempts. He traveled over the ice from Ellesmere Island, northwest of Greenland.

The New York Times April 6, 1969

Expedition left from Point Barrow (1) for North Pole (2) and Spitsbergen (3).

The Sunday Times reported that the British expedition's leader, Wally Herbert, 34 years old, had radioed to Point Barrow that his companions were "in good spirits and good health." The other members of the team are Allan Gill, 38; Maj. Kenneth Hedges, 34, and Dr. Roy Koerner, 36.

Mr. Herbert said in a message to Queen Elizabeth II, and organizations that have supported the trip, that he was "hopeful that by forced marches and a measure of good fortune the expedition will reach Spitsbergen by Midsummer's Day [June 24] of this year, thus concluding in the name of our country the first surface crossing of the Arctic Ocean."

Spitsbergen is an archipelago in the Arctic Ocean belonging to Norway.

The planting of the Union

Continued on Page 19, Column 1

Catholic Schools May Drop 2 Million Pupils

By GENE CURRIVAN

A spokesman for the nation's Roman Catholic bishops has warned that the church's elementary schools will close their doors to almost two million pupils—about half the enrollment—unless there is a vast upsurge in public support for Catholic education over the next six years.

This means that many of the 10,000 elementary schools in the nation may close despite aid expected from state governments. The message to the Catholic laity, in substance, is that it must pay more if it wants to maintain quality parochial education.

The warning came from Msgr. James C. Donoghue, director of the Division of Elementary and Secondary Education of the United States Catholic Conference in Washington, which represents the nation's Catholic bishops. He said the impact on the high schools would not be as great because they are largely self-supporting.

Monsignor Donoghue made the declaration in a recent interview while pondering a constant flow of reports from around the nation on school closings, decreasing enrollments, dwindling finances and a scarcity of teaching nuns.

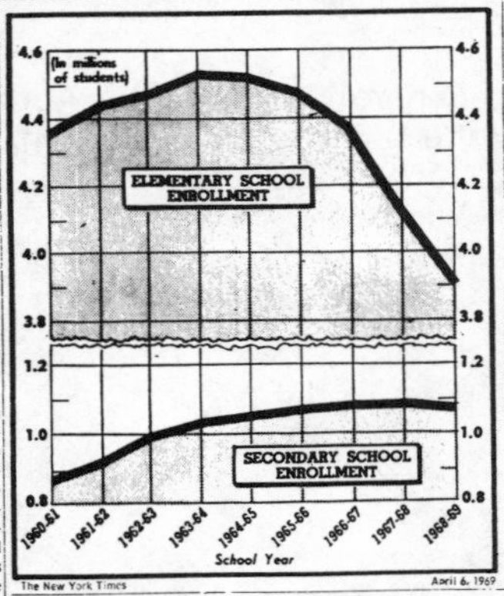

The New York Times April 6, 1969

These problems will receive close attention at a meeting of the Catholic Educational Association, which opens today in Detroit.

In 1968, 360 Catholic elementary schools and 125 high schools were closed, and reports indicate many more closings will follow. Enrollment in elementary and secondary schools has dropped to 4,982,927 in the current school year from 5,600,519 four years ago.

The decline of parochial education has implications for non-Catholics because a steady rise in the flow of students from church to public schools seems likely to jam some already overcrowded urban schools without any compensating rise in school revenues.

Although the church makes public no over-all figures on costs and revenue, officials say the financial crisis stems from steadily mounting operating costs and decreasing revenues in the $1.7-billion-a-year operation.

They say Catholic parents, who already support public schools through taxes, are rebelling against increased tuitions, averaging $338 a year, and are sending their children to public schools.

While the preponderance of school closings so far has been in rural areas, the trend is showing signs of moving into the large cities as well.

The New York archdiocese has closed 17 schools since 1963, mostly in rural areas, but will close four this year in the inner city.

The Milwaukee archdiocese has announced that 18 elementary schools, mostly in rural areas, will close. Later, it said that three inner city schools originally scheduled for closing would continue as nondenomi-

Continued on Page 50, Column 4

Eisenhower Opposed a Nixon Recount

By FELIX BELAIR Jr.
Special to The New York Times

WASHINGTON, April 5—President Eisenhower advised Richard M. Nixon not to demand a recount of 1960 election returns in two states in an effort to win the Presidential race against John F. Kennedy.

General Eisenhower's advice to his Vice President is one of a number of reminiscences coming to light among old associates of the five-star general, who was buried Wednesday at Abilene, Kan.

The associates also recalled that after his second election President Eisenhower toyed with the idea of starting a "suprapartisan" third-party movement because of his great plurality over other candidates on the Republican ticket for Congressional, state and municipal offices.

The unpublished anecdotes were recounted after his death in fond recollection of the man who disliked "politics" in the narrow partisan sense because he said he had no "feel" for the art, but who succeeded at it because he epitomized the simple virtues of American life and enjoyed an unparalleled popularity.

One remembered incident involved a remark made by General Eisenhower several years after he left the White House.

He described Mr. Nixon as the one man best qualified by experience to be President but one who might lack sufficient popularity to be elected to that office. General Eisenhower was quoted in this context as having said:

"There is no question in my mind that Dick Nixon is best qualified of any of the available candidates to be President of the United States. But it's a funny thing about Dick. Almost everywhere I go people tell me they don't like him. I just don't understand it."

General Eisenhower's recollection of his telephone conversation with Mr. Nixon the

Continued on Page 32, Column 1

Today's Sections

Index to Subjects

"FREEDOM AIRLIFT" Jews from Russia: [illegible]

HARVARD ALUMNI—ELECT HENRY NORR '65 TO BOARD OF OVERSEERS.—Advt.

JOBS FOR LIBRARIANS AND TEACHERS Announcements of openings plus listings of individual librarians and teachers seeking new connections appear today in The New York Times. See Section 4.—Advt.

"All the News
That's Fit to Print"

The New York Times

LATE CITY EDITION

Weather: Variable cloudiness today; fair tonight. Sunny, cool tomorrow. Temp. range: today 68-55; Tuesday 69-48. Full U.S. report on Page 94.

VOL. CXVIII ... No. 40,653 — NEW YORK, WEDNESDAY, MAY 14, 1969 — 10 CENTS

BATTISTA TO RUN ON MARCHI SLATE IN G.O.P. PRIMARY

Ends Mayoral Bid to Make Controller Race in a New Challenge to Lindsay

'BUY-OUT,' AURELIO SAYS

Mayor's Aide Charges Joint Conservative Opposition With Party-Wrecking

By BILL KOVACH

State Senator John J. Marchi and Assemblyman Vito P. Battista merged their separate campaigns for Mayor yesterday to present a single conservative challenge to Mayor Lindsay in the Republican primary.

In a move that radically alters the political picture for the June 17 primary, Mr. Battista agreed to abandon his own campaign for the mayoral nomination and run for Controller on a ticket headed by Mr. Marchi.

J. Daniel Mahoney, state chairman of the Conservative party, which has already nominated Senator Marchi for Mayor, interrupted the news conference called to announce the Marchi-Battista alliance to predict that Mr. Battista would be the Conservative nominee for Controller by unanimous consent.

Mayor Lindsay, who now finds himself facing a united challenge from conservative Republicans rather than splintered opposition within the party, refused to comment on the new development.

8 in Democratic Race

Last midnight was the deadline for filing petitions for contestants in primary fights. Eight aspirants submitted petitions seeking the Democratic nomination for Mayor.

They included former Mayor Robert F. Wagner, who topped the list with 59,320 signatures, followed by Controller Mario A. Procaccino with 50,968, as well as Representative Adam Clayton Powell and a surprise entry, John W. Seder, Staten Island investment broker.

The Mayor has the nomination of the Liberal party and both he and Senator Marchi have pledged to carry the nominations they have already gained into the November election regardless of the choice made by Republican voters in the primary.

The Marchi-Battista alliance, though expected by the Lindsay camp, was something of a surprise announcement yesterday. A news conference at the Overseas Press Club, 54 West

Continued on Page 28, Column 1

The New York Times (by Robert Walker)

CONSERVATIVE CHALLENGE: Assemblyman Vito P. Battista, left, and State Senator John J. Marchi announcing that Mr. Battista will run for Controller on Mr. Marchi's ticket.

20 Indicted in Brooklyn College Arson; Columbia's Trustees Abolish R.O.T.C.

Students Arrested Here

By EMANUEL PERLMUTTER

Seventeen Negro and Puerto Rican students at Brooklyn College were arrested at their homes early yesterday on a 23-count indictment charging arson conspiracing to commit arson, and other criminal acts on the college's Flatbush campus.

Although the indictment, handed up Monday night by a Kings County grand jury, named 20 defendants, three have not yet been apprehended. One was not identified.

The Brooklyn school has been plagued by student disorders, disruptions and vandalism in recent weeks. At the request of the college administration, helmeted policemen have been guarding the grounds and buildings since last Friday.

Other Developments

There were these other campus developments in the nation yesterday:

¶At Southern University in Baton Rouge, La., the police fired tear gas and shotguns at students who were throwing firebombs, rocks and bottles. Thirty persons were injured, including eight with gunshot wounds.

¶About 40 students took over the Interfaith Lounge on the campus of Northeastern University in Boston in a protest against the Reserve Officers Training Corps.

¶Tension rose at Cornell University with the impending arrest of several students involved in the armed occupation of the student center four weeks ago. The Tompkins County grand jury handed up 21 sealed indictments.

¶In San Francisco, the trustees of Stanford University decided to sever ties between the university and its affiliated Stanford Research Institute. The action followed demonstrations over war-related research.

If found guilty on all 23

Continued on Page 30, Column 1

Senate Is Approved

By MICHAEL T. KAUFMAN

Columbia University's trustees voted last night to phase out the school's Naval Reserve Officers Training Corps program.

At the same time, the trustees approved the creation of a university senate, with student representation, that will be the central governing body of the university.

Under the formula passed by the trustees in a four-and-a-half-hour meeting, the R.O.T.C. will be abolished at Columbia by June, 1971. In the meantime, no new students will enroll in the program and those now in it will fulfill their requirements at an accelerated pace.

At a campus news conference that followed the trustees' decision, Dr. Andrew W. Cordier, Columbia's acting president, announced:

"For a long period of time there was a feeling that the type of program represented by R.O.T.C. did not fit into the scheme of an academic department."

This feeling, he said, was engendered because the program "was operated by an outside agency."

Dr. Cordier explained that Columbia had originally planned to maintain the R.O.T.C. program as an extracurricular activity but that Federal statutes provided that the program must have aca-

Continued on Page 30, Column 5

New Impasse at C.C.N.Y.

By SYLVAN FOX

Attempts to bring black and Puerto Rican students to the bargaining table at City College reached a new impasse yesterday as Dr. Joseph J. Copeland, the college's acting president, rejected a faculty resolution calling for the removal of the police from the troubled campus.

In a stern speech to the college's 87-member Faculty Senate, Dr. Copeland declared that the police would be kept on the campus as long as there existed a "real and substantial danger of disorders and maltreatment of property, vandalism, arson and the like."

"The police will remain on the campus," he said, "until in fact we have returned to normal." The campus has been closed by disorders from time to time in the last three weeks.

Dr. Copeland said normal classes would be held at the 20,000-student college for the rest of the week unless Negro and Puerto Rican student protesters agreed to resume negotiations under a tight set of conditions he laid down yesterday.

"As of now," he said, "I have no assurance that they will sit down and negotiate."

There have been no direct negotiations between college officials and the black and Puerto Rican student protesters since discussions of the student demands broke down on

Continued on Page 30, Column 4

STONY BROOK RAID LEADS TO A MELEE

Students Smash Windows and Set Fires in Protest

By AGIS SALPUKAS
Special to The New York Times

STONY BROOK, L. I., May 13—Bands of students burned security police cars, smashed windows and set fires on the campus of the State University here early this morning in a melee protesting a narcotics raid at the school.

This afternoon, university officials and student leaders worked to ease the tensions created by the raid and its violent aftermath.

The raid was the latest of several college narcotics raids in the New York area recently, including arrests at C. W. Post College in Brookville, L. I., and Bard College in Annandale-on-Hudson, N. Y.

The university's president, Dr. John S. Toll, today agreed to a proposal endorsed by the student government, the faculty members and graduate students to let each student decide whether he would like to postpone final examinations and not

Continued on Page 31, Column 1

Donegan to Retire As Bishop in 1972

By LACEY FOSBURGH

The Right Rev. Horace W. B. Donegan announced yesterday that he would retire in 1972 as Episcopal Bishop of New York. He called for the immediate election of his successor.

Standing in flowing scarlet robes before 750 clergy and laymen assembled in Synod House of the Cathedral Church of St. John the Divine for the diocese's annual convention, the 68-year-old Bishop told the startled group:

"Canon law allows me to remain in office until 1972, but I feel I should at this time prepare for an orderly transferal of authority."

Because 72 is the mandatory retirement age for bishops, that aspect of his announcement

Continued on Page 16, Column 1

City to Shuffle 2,200 in Brooklyn High Schools

By LEONARD BUDER

Twenty-two hundred high school students—most of them Negro and Puerto Rican—who would normally attend schools in northern Brooklyn and in Queens will be shifted next fall to predominantly white and integrated schools in South Brooklyn.

The zoning changes, which will affect only those who are entering high school, are intended primarily to improve school utilization. Another benefit, according to officials at Board of Education headquarters, is that it would somewhat improve the ethnic distribution of students in the borough's high schools.

But many principals of schools that will receive additional students are unhappy with the rezoning plan.

One said yesterday that although it would take youngsters out of overcrowded schools in one part of the borough, it would send them to schools that are nearly as crowded in another part.

Another principal said that compelling the students to travel across the borough to go to school would work a hardship on them and tend to reduce their interest in education.

Still another official pointed

The New York Times

2,200 students who would normally attend underlined high schools will be shifted to schools in southern Brooklyn.

to the effect that the rezoning plan already has had on his predominantly white community.

"Information about this has spread to the parents," he said. "They are greatly concerned about students coming to our school from an area where children's minds have been painted with instruction from racists."

Under the zoning changes, Franklin K. Lane High School on the Brooklyn-Queens border, which was the scene of serious disorders last winter, will lose 451 incoming students. Many of these are Negroes and Puerto Ricans from the Ocean Hill-Brownsville demonstration district.

Next fall many of the Ocean

Continued on Page 55, Column 1

LODGE RETURNING FOR INSTRUCTIONS ON PARIS PARLEY

He Is Due in Capital Today —Nixon's Speech Tonight Will Have 'New Material'

Special to The New York Times

WASHINGTON, May 13—The White House announced today that Henry Cabot Lodge would return home tomorrow to receive new instructions regarding the allied bargaining posture in Paris. The announcement came as interest grew here in the address on Vietnam President Nixon is to make to the nation tomorrow night at 10 P.M. over television and radio.

Mr. Lodge, chief of the United States negotiating team at the peace talks, is scheduled to arrive tomorrow afternoon.

Mr. Lodge probably will not confer with the President until early Thursday morning. Then, according to the White House, he will give a briefing at a joint meeting of the National Security Council and the Cabinet. He will return to Paris immediately after.

Policy Clarification Foreseen

The White House did not spell out what Mr. Lodge's "new instructions" would be, but officials suggested that Mr. Nixon's address would give some indication of the direction United States policy may be taking.

Responding to questions this morning, the President's press secretary, Ronald L. Ziegler, said Mr. Lodge had been asked to return to consult on "how to proceed in the Paris talks in the light of the President's speech."

Mr. Ziegler also asserted that the speech would contain "new material." When asked whether he would rule out the prospect of "dramatic" new disclosures, he replied: "No, sir, I would not say that."

First Report to Public

The press secretary's mention of new material and his refusal to foreclose the possibility of new announcements represented the first official indication that the speech, which will be President Nixon's first direct report to the public on the war, may amount to more than a general review of the military and diplomatic situation. White House aides used far more modest language yesterday to characterize the address.

At the same time, White House officials stressed again that Mr. Nixon did not plan to announce troop withdrawals in his speech—although they said he might well discuss the possibility of withdrawals in general terms. They reiterated that he did not plan to reveal any "major breakthrough" in the

Continued on Page 9, Column 1

NIXON ASKS DRAFT LOTTERY WITH 19-YEAR-OLDS FIRST; ORDERS DEFERMENT STUDY

Tydings Declares Fortas Must Resign Immediately

Ex-Backer Issues Call

By FRED P. GRAHAM
Special to The New York Times

WASHINGTON, May 13—Senator Joseph D. Tydings, a leader last summer in the effort to win confirmation for Abe Fortas as Chief Justice, called upon him today to resign from the Supreme Court.

"The confidence of our citizenry in the Federal judiciary must be preserved," the Maryland Democrat said at a Capitol Hill news conference this afternoon. "Mr. Justice Fortas must resign. He must resign immediately."

Meanwhile, reports continued to circulate in official circles that Justice Fortas's resignanation was imminent and perhaps would come tomorrow.

These reports were given additional credence when he canceled at the last minute and without explanation this afternoon a scheduled speech before a meeting of Federala judges in New Hampshire.

Until today, Justice Fortas

Continued on Page 33, Column 1

Jurist Under Pressure

By MAX FRANKEL
Special to The New York Times

WASHINGTON, May 13—Justice Abe Fortas faced enormous pressure today to decide whether to resign from the Supreme Court or to try, tenaciously and almost alone, to rescue a brilliant legal career.

There were strong indications this evening that the Justice would yield to the proddings of his colleagues, the Nixon Administration and even of those who were His most fervent supporters in Congress last year, when he almost became Chief Justice. They want him to quit in a final service to the integrity of the nation's judiciary.

But there were still a few personal associates who felt that Mr. Fortas had not yet reached a final decision. They said he might, because of the great pressure upon him, feel compelled to stand fast and virtually dare his detractors to

Continued on Page 32, Column 3

EQUITY IS THE GOAL

Period of Liability to Induction Would Be Reduced to Year

Text of the draft message is printed on Page 20.

By ROBERT B. SEMPLE Jr.
Special to The New York Times

WASHINGTON, May 13—A major reorganization of the draft, altering the methods of selection, was proposed today by President Nixon.

In a message to Congress, the President asked for authority to replace the existing system of selecting draftees with a lottery.

The proposal would reverse the order of induction, and 19-year-olds would be subjected to the first call. At present, the oldest in the draftable 19-to-26 age group are chosen first.

Period of Uncertainty

The proposal would also reduce the period of draft liabilty from seven years to one. A man would be draftable only during a single 12-month period — from sometime after his 19th birthday to sometime after 20th birthday—or, if he receives a college deferment, for the first 12-month period after graduating or dropping out of college.

The principal purpose of the message, White House officials explained, is to reduce the period of uncertainty for draft-age men from seven years to one.

"For almost two million men who reach the age of military service each year—and for their families, the draft is one of the most important facts of life," Mr. Nixon declared. "It is my conviction that the disruptive impact of the military draft on individual lives should be minimized as much as possible, consistent with the national security."

'Equitable and Reasonable'

Mr. Nixon stressed that his plan represented only a way-station on the road to his promised elimination of the draft and its replacement by an all-volunteer Army.

"I am hopeful that we can soon restore the principle of no draft in peacetime," the President declared. "But until we do, let us be sure that the operation of the Selective Serv-

Continued on Page 21, Column 1

Germany Outlines Measures to Fight Domestic Inflation

By DAVID BINDER
Special to The New York Times

BONN, May 13—Chancellor Kurt Georg Kiesinger's "economic cabinet" outlined five measures today to meet the threat of domestic inflation caused by his refusal to revalue upward the mark last Friday.

An emergency meeting, held 24 hours ahead of schedule, was attended by Economics Minister Karl Schiller and members of the central bank. They had recommended in vain last week that the Government revalue the mark upward as the only practicable means of protecting West Germany from "the import of inflation" from other Western countries where prices are steadily rising.

The chief Government spokesman, Günter Diehl, indicated to a news conference this evening that Mr. Schiller and the bank officials had more or less acceded to the measures discussed in the economic cabinet.

Kiesinger in Chair

Mr. Diehl exuded confidence about West Germany's monetary situation, saying that the $4-billion of "fast money" deposited here last week in speculation on a revaluation of the mark was "in the process of flowing out." He implied that the economic cabinet was of the same opinion, although there was no way of checking this immediately.

Continued on Page 69, Column 3

Job Corps Test Won By Nixon in Senate

By United Press International

WASHINGTON, May 13 — The Nixon Administration won its first partisan skirmish in the Senate today when Republicans gained enough Southern Democratic support to kill a Democratic-sponsored resolution urging the President to postpone his decision to close 59 Job Corps centers pending a review by Congress.

On the final roll-call vote of 52 to 40, there were 12 Democrats — all but two of them from the South — who joined 40 Republicans in opposing the resolution, which was offered by Senator Alan Cranston, Democrat of California. Forty Democrats voted for the measure.

After the final vote was announced, Senator Russell B.

Continued on Page 18, Column 3

WILSON DEMOTES CALLAGHAN IN RIFT

Dismisses Him From Inner Cabinet in Dispute Over Union Reform Bill

By ANTHONY LEWIS
Special to The New York Times

LONDON, May 13 — Prime Minister Wilson today brusquely dismissed James Callaghan, the Home Secretary, from his inner Cabinet.

There is a good chance that Mr. Callaghan, who has been sympathetic toward those opposed to the Labor Government's labor-reform bill, will be out of the Government entirely before long.

The Prime Minister's sudden move was seen as an urgent attempt to shore up his personal authority in the face of grim financial and political news.

Figures published today showed that Britain's trading deficit grew worse in April. It stood at $141.6-million. The deficit in March was $124.8-million.

The figure for April virtually killed hopes of bringing the country's international payments into surplus in 1969, as promised. Even worse, it suggested that the whole economic strategy since the devaluation of the sterling 18 months ago had failed.

Bad Slide in Stock Market

The stock market took its worst slide since devaluation. In the City of London, the financial district, there was anxious talk about further restrictive economic measures.

Reports from Washington that Britain was seeking a new loan from the International Monetary Fund, and that the I.M.F. was imposing stringent conditions, brought angry outcries by Members of the House of Commons.

Conservatives suggested that Britain was a bankrupt taking orders from her creditors. Harold Lever, Financial Secretary to the Treasury, answered for the Government:

"One: the Government is not a defaulter. Two: it is not

Continued on Page 13, Column 1

EVERS CAPTURES MISSISSIPPI RACE

The New York Times

Charles Evers after balloting in Fayette yesterday.

By JAMES T. WOOTEN
Special to The New York Times

JACKSON, Miss., May 13—Charles Evers, the Negro civil rights leader, today won his bid to become Mayor of the drowsy little town of Fayette, Miss., a significant achievement in this citadel of white supremacy.

His victory in today's Democratic primary assures his succession to the $50-a-month job held for the last 20 years by his white opponent, 77-year-old R. J. Allen.

As counting ended at the red

Continued on Page 43, Column 1

NEWS INDEX

	Page		Page
Books	44-45	Music	34-41
Bridge	44	Obituaries	47
Business	70	Real Estate	72
Buyers	70	Society	50
Crossword	45	Sports	51-57
Editorials	46	Theaters	34-41
Fashions	42	Transportation	94
Financial	59-70	TV and Radio	95
Food	42	U. N. Proceedings	5
Man in the News	6	Wash. Proceedings	43
Movies	34-41	Weather	94

News Summary and Index, Page 49

As the American policy of Vietnamization intensified, partly because of growing national antagonism to the Vietnam conflict, more and more Vietnamese were trained and armed for combat. Here, South Vietnamese Marines prepare to set out for an operation in the Mekong Delta in 1969.

A wounded soldier is carried to safety by his fellow soldiers during a Communist attack on Bien Hoa.

The New York Times

VOL. CXVIII...No. 40,679 © 1969 The New York Times Company   NEW YORK, MONDAY, JUNE 9, 1969   10 CENTS

LATE CITY EDITION
Weather: Cloudy, chance of showers today. Fair tonight and tomorrow. Temp. range: today 72-82; Sunday 82-63. Temp.-Hum. Index yesterday 73. Complete U.S. report on Page 94.

PLAN WOULD HELP BIG STOCKHOLDERS TAKE HIGH OFFICE

Sales of Shares to Treasury Aimed at Removing Link to Conflict of Interest

SENATORS PREPARE BILL

McIntyre's Proposal Gives Appointee Chance to Serve Without Financial Loss

By WARREN WEAVER Jr.
Special to The New York Times

WASHINGTON, June 8 — A novel plan that would permit millionaire stockholders to serve in high Federal office without risking conflict of interest or financial loss is being drafted in the Senate.

The plan is designed to meet the situation that arose when President Nixon named David Packard Deputy Secretary of Defense. He held $300-million worth of stock in an electronics concern that does about a third of its business with the Pentagon.

Mr. Packard, answering Senate criticism, set up a charitable trust for 3,550,150 shares of Hewlett-Packard Corporation stock with the Bank of America as trustee.

Under the new plan, an appointee would sell his stock to the Treasury, which, in turn, would gradually resell it in small pieces.

Bipartisan Backing

The legislative proposal, developed by Senator Thomas J. McIntyre, Democrat of New Hampshire, has bipartisan backing among leaders of the Senate Banking and Currency Committee. Senators William Proxmire, Democrat of Wisconsin, and Edward W. Brooke, Republican of Massachusetts, have endorsed the measure.

Senator McIntyre's idea has been submitted to several of President Nixon's top domestic advisers in the White House, and they were sufficiently interested in it to schedule a personal presentation to the President shortly.

If the plan wins the approval of Congress and the President, its first beneficiary may be Ray Watt, a California builder who was in line for appointment as the Federal Housing Administrator. He has been plagued by serious conflict-of-interest problems.

Mr. Watt and Mr. Packard both owned large blocks of stock in corporations doing major business with the Federal Government.

Continued on Page 27, Column 1

ROBERT TAYLOR, 57, IS DEAD OF CANCER

Robert Taylor
Associated Press

Special to The New York Times

SANTA MONICA, Calif., June 8 — Robert Taylor, a Hollywood star for more than 30 years, died this morning of lung cancer at St. John's Hospital. He was 57 years old. With him was his wife, the German actress Ursula Thiess.

Hollywood's studio-sponsored star system created one of its most durable luminaries in Robert Taylor, who in 70 feature films, personalized the glamorous leading man adored by movie fans between the two World Wars.

Despite a shock of black, wavy hair, complete with an eye-catching widow's peak, a

Continued on Page 47, Column 2

PREPARING FOR DEBATE: A studio technician adjusts Mayor Lindsay's chest microphone before the start of the program. In foreground is State Senator John J. Marchi.
The New York Times by William E. Sauro

New School Board Warns Of 'Disaster' in Budget Cut

By LEONARD BUDER

The new interim Board of Education, in its first public statement, warned yesterday that the city school system faced "major disaster" next fall because of insufficient operating funds.

The five-member board, which took office two weeks ago, said the indicated city expense budget for the fiscal year starting July 1 would force the system to reduce current services by $96-million.

"We are shocked at the dire prospects facing our schools in the next school year because of the most drastic budget cut ever received by the city school system," the board said.

The budget reduction, which has already stirred an outcry from school, parent and community groups, would have the following impact, according to school officials:

¶The elimination of 4,427 needed teaching and supervisory positions.

¶An expected increase in class sizes in many schools by an average of two pupils for each class.

¶A one-third reduction in the free lunch program for poor children.

¶A cutback in pupil transportation services.

"Even at this late date," the board said, "we hope earnestly that the city, state and Federal Government can help restore the budget at least to the point that will enable our schools to

Continued on Page 87, Column 4

POLICE IN U.S. SEEK TO EASE HOSTILITY

Survey Finds That a Rise in Efforts to Reduce Racial Tension Sometimes Fails

By JOHN HERBERS
Special to The New York Times

WASHINGTON, June 8 — In cities across the nation, white policemen and black militant leaders have been holding "confrontation sessions" in which they probe each other's motivations and prejudices in an effort to lower the level of hostility between the two groups.

Many police departments have opened storefront centers in the slums, at which residents can voice complaints against the police or other public employees to policemen who have a reasonably sympathetic ear.

Virtually every department has stepped up efforts to hire more Negro policemen, and there have been a number of new community relations efforts, such as Operation Handshake, in which a new patrolman must spend several days in the community making friends before he begins enforcing the law.

An Explosive Issue

Despite these efforts, however, the hostility between the police and the Negro community has been worsened in some cities and in others remains the most explosive issue in race relations.

This information is based on a New York Times survey of 13 cities and on interviews with national leaders familiar with the situation. The cities surveyed were Boston, New York, Philadelphia, Chicago, Detroit, Pittsburgh, St. Louis, Houston, Miami, Kansas City, Mo.; Los Angeles, San Francisco and Oakland, Calif.

In the last year, the police departments have made efforts to institute new community relations programs, many of them following the recommen-

Continued on Page 27, Column 1

LINDSAY, MARCHI CLASH IN DEBATE

Senator Charges Ineptness by Mayor, Who Says Rival Helped Deny City Funds

Mayor Lindsay was accused in debate yesterday with State Senator John J. Marchi of being unwilling to deal properly with crime and charged in turn that Mr. Marchi had helped to deny the city the money it needed to solve its problems.

The charges and counter-charges occurred as the two Republican mayoral candidates, standing in three-sided television booths that looked a bit like witness stands, debated some of the issues for the first time. Each found the other inadequate to the task of governing the city.

The half-hour special live telecast on WCBS-TV began with Mr. Lindsay, who had won a coin toss.

In the two minutes allotted for opening remarks, the Mayor said his administration, while not without its setbacks, had "started to do what has to be done." His years in office, he said, proved that the city "can be governed."

Mr. Lindsay, who is the mayoral candidate of the Liberal party, pointed to the addition of men to the police force, new subway construction, a balanced budget for four years running and an improve-

Continued on Page 88, Column 7

NIXON TO REDUCE VIETNAM FORCE, PULLING OUT 25,000 G.I.'S BY AUG. 31; HE AND THIEU STRESS THEIR UNITY

VAGUE ON ISSUES

Statement Is Believed Unlikely to Dispel Saigon's Unease

By TERENCE SMITH
Special to The New York Times

MIDWAY ISLAND, June 8 — President Nguyen Van Thieu departed for Saigon today armed with a joint communiqué that appeared to do little to relieve the widespread uneasiness that prevails in South Vietnam over coming the war.

The 1,200-word joint statement issued by the two Presidents at the conclusion of their five-hour conference appeared too general to be of much use in dispelling the concern that has grown up in political and military circles in South Vietnam about the American plan to negotiate a settlement of the war.

In a brief speech delivered in conjunction with the release of the communiqué, the South Vietnamese leader sought to quell speculation that there were significant differences between his country's position on the peace talks and that of the United States.

Denial of Differences

"It is not true," he said, "that I had to come here to dissipate or discuss those differences." Later, he added: "We have had close consultation before and we have a very close understanding."

Speaking from the stage of the theater at the naval station here, Mr. Thieu also spoke of the "constant duty of the Vietnamese people to take over more responsibility and to alleviate the burden of the United States people to support us and defend freedom in Vietnam."

Expressing his country's gratitude for American sacrifices, Mr. Thieu said, "We never forget that the blood and human life are precious to anyone, to any people, at any time."

The communiqué was most notable for its omissions, particularly of items that Mr. Thieu had come to this Pacific island to obtain, such as a pledge that the United States would stand behind the present Government in Saigon and support the current South Vietnamese Constitution.

As it turned out, the statement included no references to the Constitution, to special elections, or to any of the other questions that have caused concern in Saigon since President Nixon unveiled his eight-point

Continued on Page 17, Column 1

MEET AT MIDWAY: President Nixon and President Nguyen Van Thieu of South Vietnam after their arrival.
Associated Press

Aid to Vietnam Delayed To Force Inflation Control

By B. DRUMMOND AYRES Jr.
Special to The New York Times

SAIGON, South Vietnam, June 8 — The United States has been applying economic pressure on the South Vietnamese Government to convince it of the need to control inflation.

According to American officials, $40-million in United States aid was withheld from Saigon during much of April and May while intense discussions were under way over means to halt price increases and to decrease deficits.

At the end of May, the South Vietnamese agreed to take steps against inflation, and the money was released.

In the last three months prices in South Vietnamese stores and market places have risen about 10 per cent. Prices have risen about 30 per cent every 12 months for several years.

Within a few days recently, the price of a glass of sugar-cane juice doubled, from 5 piasters to 10. A bag of rice that cost 270 piasters one month ago now costs 300 piasters. The official exchange rate is 118 piasters to the dollar. The black market rate is about 180 piasters to the dollar.

The South Vietnamese have agreed to reduce imports of such luxuries as television sets and dried fruits, and to increase imports of such essentials as machinery and fertiliz-

Continued on Page 14, Column 1

SOVIET GAIN SEEN IN MIRV PROGRAM

Pentagon Analysis of Tests Bolsters U.S. Advocates of Continued Testing

By WILLIAM BEECHER
Special to The New York Times

WASHINGTON, June 8 — A new analysis of Soviet missile tests in the Pacific is reinforcing arguments of those within the Administration who favor continuation of United States tests of multiple warheads.

The analysis, by intelligence experts in the Pentagon primarily, suggests that multiple warheads now being tested by the Russians may be capable of being guided to three scattered targets and powerful enough to destroy hardened missile silos.

Until now, United States specialists had believed the Russians were testing a three-part multiple warhead all three elements of which landed in a fairly tight, predictable pattern near one another, attacking only a single target.

Thus the new intelligence information, reliable sources say, suggests the Russians are farther along than previously thought toward development of

Continued on Page 25, Column 1

A MIDWAY ACCORD

Leaders Agree First Cutbacks Will Begin Within 30 Days

Text of the joint communiqué is printed on Page 16.

By HEDRICK SMITH
Special to The New York Times

MIDWAY ISLAND, June 8 — President Nixon met with President Nguyen Van Thieu of South Vietnam today and announced that 25,000 American soldiers would be withdrawn from Vietnam before the end of August.

After the first two hours of five hours of talks on this mid-Pacific island, Mr. Nixon emerged to declare that the Presidents had agreed that troop withdrawals would begin within 30 days.

And with Mr. Thieu standing at his side, Mr. Nixon held out the hope of further reductions in the 540,000-man American force when this first phase was completed.

Replacements Available

He said that the equivalent of a combat division could leave Vietnam because of progress in the training and equipping of South Vietnam's Army.

Both President Nixon and President Thieu underscored the point that the American force being withdrawn would be replaced in the field by South Vietnamese forces.

Mr. Nixon termed the withdrawal a "significant step forward" toward a lasting peace in Vietnam. At the end of the five-hour conference, Mr. Thieu said that the step was "good news for the American people and South Vietnamese combat forces."

Both in announcing the troop withdrawal and in presenting a joint statement to the press at the end of their meeting, the two leaders sought to emphasize their solidarity.

Differences Not Mentioned

Their joint communiqué made no allusion to differences in approach to the Paris negotiations, and President Thieu remarked afterward that it was "not ... ue" that he had come to Midway to thresh out differences with the new American Administration. But little was noted in the public statements of either man that might quiet Saigon's fears about the ultimate intentions of the United States leadership.

Although the announcement of the troop withdrawal was aimed at placating domestic critics of the war and putting pressure on North Vietnam and the Vietcong to negotiate more seriously in Paris by seeking to demonstrate South Vietnam's growing strength, Mr. Nixon mentioned neither American war critics nor the enemy.

As if pleading for more patience from the American pub-

Continued on Page 16, Column 2

Men of Dartmouth Are Troubled By Lingering Echoes of Protest

By MICHAEL STERN
Special to The New York Times

HANOVER, N.H., June 8 — In any other year, the deep green and gold New England summer that is settling in here would be casting a sweet somnolent spell over the hearts and minds of Dartmouth men.

But this year, many of those hearts and minds are deeply troubled by still-fresh memories of chaotic springtime protests over R.O.T.C. on campus and the calling in of 90 state troopers last month to arrest students who had occupied Parkhurst Hall, the college administration building.

Vivid reminders of those events showed up here last week when 36 students—several with jailhouse haircuts—returned to the campus after having served 26 days of 30-day sentences for having defied

a court order to leave the administration building. They got time off for good behavior.

Four others, whose trials had been delayed, left the campus this last week to begin their 30-day sentences and will not be released until July.

Still to come, beginning tomorrow, are hearings before the College Committee on Standing and Conduct, hearings that some condemn as a double jeopardy for the arrested students. The hearings are to determine what penalties will be imposed on those who overstepped Dartmouth's ground rules on free expression and dissent.

"Now is when the agony begins," said Prof. W. W. Ballard, chairman of the committee, as

Continued on Page 87, Column 2

FLEE BATTLE IN TAYNINH: Refugees jamming road near the provincial capital 60 miles northwest of Saigon as allied troops sought to oust several hundred North Vietnamese who had taken a nearby hamlet. Article is on Page 17.
United Press International

President Richard M. Nixon greets the troops stationed at Di An, Vietnam, during his tour of the country in July 1969.

"All the News That's Fit to Print"

The New York Times

LATE CITY EDITION

Weather: Fair, cool today; fair tonight. Partly cloudy tomorrow. Temp. range: today 80-61; Tuesday 80-62. Temp.-Hum. Index yesterday 71. Complete U.S. report on Page 86.

VOL. CXVIII ... No. 40,709 · NEW YORK, WEDNESDAY, JULY 9, 1969 · 10 CENTS

LINDSAY TO BACK SOME DEMOCRATS IN NEW STRATEGY

Fusion Tactics Designed to Discourage Mayoral Bid by a 4th Candidate

REP. CAREY BOWS OUT

Mayor Promises to Set Up 3-Party Advisory Council on City Government

By RICHARD REEVES

Mayor Lindsay will begin moving further away from the Republican party in the next few weeks by campaigning for Democratic City Council candidates and bringing prominent Democrats into the highest level of his own campaign staff.

Mr. Lindsay, who has sometimes refused to support Republicans but has never endorsed a Democrat, discussed his re-election strategy in broad terms at a news conference yesterday. He has discussed it in greater detail at private meetings with potential Democratic supporters.

The new Lindsay strategy, made necessary when he lost the Republican mayoral primary to State Senator John J. Marchi, is designed to attract enough liberal Democrats to his side to discourage any Democrats who may be considering running because they are dissatisfied with the Democratic mayoral candidate, Mario A. Procaccino.

Carey Withdraws

The possibility of a fourth candidate in the race diminished somewhat yesterday when Representative Hugh L. Carey announced he was withdrawing indefinitely from active politics because of the death of two of his sons in an automobile accident last week.

Mr. Lindsay, who is still the Liberal party candidate for Mayor and plans to be the candidate of an as yet unnamed independent party, has made these public and private commitments to Democrats:

¶He will create a Fusion Advisory Council, composed of liberal Republicans, Democrats and Liberals, which will have "a very significant role in governmental policy."

¶He will endorse several Democratic City Council can-

Continued on Page 36, Column 1

Israelis Report 7 MIG's Downed in Syrian Clash

They Assert No Mirages Were Lost in Air Battle in the Golan Area

By JAMES FERON
Special to The New York Times

JERUSALEM, July 8—The Israeli Air Force downed seven Syrian MIG-21's today in a series of dogfights, Israeli defense officials reported. The Israelis said all their planes had returned safely.

The spectacular dogfights took place in midafternoon between Damascus, the Syrian capital, and El Quneitra in the Israeli-held Golan heights, 35 miles to the southwest, the Israelis said.

[A military spokesman in Damascus said that the Syrians had shot down four Israeli aircraft in the clashes while three Syrian aircraft were lost, Reuters reported.]

The official Israeli communiqué said that the Syrian planes "made an attempt to penetrate the Quneitra sector" at about 3:30 P.M.

The Israeli jets, which were probably in the air at the time, engaged them at altitudes of 10,000 to 30,000 feet. Wit-

Continued on Page 12, Column 1

Egyptians Report Troops Crossed Canal, Killed 30 of the Enemy

By RAYMOND H. ANDERSON
Special to The New York Times

CAIRO, July 8—A further intensification of the conflict along the Suez Canal by the United Arab Republic was underlined today in a communiqué reporting that a large-scale assault on a concentration of Israeli troops north of Lake Timsah was carried out last night by regular infantry.

Egyptian forays across the canal have been by volunteer "special units," with the exception of a raid last month in which some regular troops were said to have accompanied commandos.

Cairo reported in a later communiqué that its artillery had destroyed an Israeli vessel and damaged another as they attempted to approach the Egyptian shore of the canal, an area of several Israeli commando raids.

The gunners also shot down an Israeli helicopter trying to rescue the crew of the destroyed vessel, the report said.

A military spokesman said

Continued on Page 13, Column 1

ABM DEBATE AIMS AT TEN SENATORS STILL UNDECIDED

Chamber Closely Divided as Both Sides Maneuver and Stennis Begins Oratory

By JOHN W. FINNEY
Special to The New York Times

WASHINGTON, July 8—A narrowly divided Senate opened the antiballistic missile debate today in an oratorical exercise aimed at influencing about 10 wavering Senators who hold the balance of power.

The first round on the Senate floor was a routine prologue to what is expected to be a prolonged, increasingly bitter debate on the proposed deployment of the $10.8-billion Safeguard ABM system.

As chairman of the Senate Armed Services Committee, Senator John Stennis of Mississippi, a sonorous Southern orator, led off with an explanation of how the committee had included $759-million in a military authorization bill as the first installment on the deployment of two stations in the Safeguard system.

Storm Warning Sounded

A taste of the fight to come was provided when Mr. Stennis, upon the conclusion of his hour-long speech, was blocked in a move to have the Senate go into one of its infrequent secret sessions.

Senator Stennis said he wanted to discuss secret intelligence information about the Soviet military threat unrelated to the missile issue.

Senator Stuart Symington, Democrat of Missouri, and Senator Albert Gore, Democrat of Tennessee, two leading opponents of the antimissile system, immediately objected, saying they would insist on discussing the ABM. With this rare rebuff to a committee chairman, the secret session was put off until tomorrow.

For the moment, however, the debate on the floor was but a backdrop to the intensive maneuvering behind the scenes as each side sought to solidify its shaky position.

Notably absent during the first part of the Stennis speech were the opposition Senators and their aides, who were huddled in cloakroom and hideaway offices in the Capitol planning their strategy against the Administration proposal.

Last night, in a meeting arranged by the Council for a Livable World, an antimissile lobby group, nearly 50 Senatorial aides were given a final "chalk talk" by such leading scientific critics of the Safeguard system as Dr. Jerome B. Wiesner and Dr. George W. Rathjens of the Massachusetts Institute of Technology, and Dr. Herbert F. York of the University of California, San Diego, as well as by former officials of the Arms Control and

Continued on Page 15, Column 3

Nation Greets the First Troops Withdrawn by Nixon

Associated Press

Soldiers back from Vietnam stand near plane that brought them. In foreground are Gen. William C. Westmoreland, Army Chief of Staff, left, and Brig. Gen. A. W. Cruikshank, 62d Military Airlift Wing commander. General Westmoreland was commander in Vietnam.

By United Press International

McCHORD AIR FORCE BASE, Wash., July 8—The first American troops withdrawn from Vietnam by President Nixon arrived home today to a welcome from Gen. William C. Westmoreland, cheering friends and relatives and a brass band. While a military band played "Hands Across the Seas" and "The Caissons Go Rolling Along," the first of four huge C-141 jet transports rolled to a stop at McChord Air Force Base near Tacoma at 3:20 P.M. "You men can stand tall and be proud," said General Westmoreland, Army Chief of Staff and former Vietnam commander. "You can look any man in the eye knowing that you have served your country when you were called." The 94 men aboard were the first of more than 800 being airlifted from Viet-

Continued on Page 3, Column 1

SENATE HEARINGS ON TAX REFORMS WILL DELAY BILL

Long of Finance Committee Bids Colleagues Submit Proposals by July 18

AN APPEAL BY TREASURY

Secretary Kennedy Calls for Early Surtax Extension—Stresses Inflation Peril

By EDWIN L. DALE Jr.
Special to The New York Times

WASHINGTON, July 8—Senator Russell B. Long announced today a wide-open set of hearings on tax reforms to be tied to the income tax surcharge, thus creating the likelihood that no final tax legislation would be enacted until autumn.

The Louisiana Democrat, chairman of the Finance Committee, made his announcement just before David M. Kennedy, the Secretary of the Treasury, gave the committee an urgent appeal for the opposite procedure — early passage of the surcharge, with reforms later.

Mr. Kennedy also cautioned again that if the present 10 per cent surcharge was not extended and the Government's efforts to curb inflation failed, "we would have to consider other alternatives," including wage and price controls and controls allocating credit.

The Secretary, who was repeating a view he expressed on

Stock Market Plunges

The stock market reacted to the statement regarding wage and price controls by producing its biggest decline since mid-February. The Dow-Jones industrial average fell 12.86 points, to 870.35.

June 11, emphasized, however, that he was strongly opposed to such controls.

Senator Long invited all Senators to submit by July 18 any reforms they wanted considered. He pledged hearings on all the proposals, to give taxpayers "an opportunity to state their side of the question."

The hearings on reform will begin July 21 and, though Senator Long said he hoped to have a bill approved by Aug. 1, the prospect was that no floor debate could begin until after the summer recess, which begins Aug. 13 and ends Sept. 3.

Even if Senator Long should decide to separate the surcharge and tax reform legislation, Senator Mike Mansfield, the majority leader, said today he would not call the surtax to the floor before a tax reform package was ready for action.

Mr. Long made clear that to avoid administrative chaos he

Continued on Page 19, Column 2

CITY TURNS DOWN LANDLORDS' CODE

Lindsay Issues Ultimatum on Revising Rent Plan—Council Gives Warning

By MAURICE CARROLL

The city rejected yesterday the rules proposed by the real estate industry to stabilize rents in some 400,000 New York apartments.

Mayor Lindsay called the landlords' code "totally unacceptable" and said in a statement distributed at City Hall that the industry must submit a new code by Friday.

The code was proposed by the landlords under the "self-regulation" concept of the complicated stabilization law, by which the city set the over-all limits of landlord conduct and the real estate industry was charged with spelling out the ground rules.

The Mayor's ultimatum followed a four-and-three-quarter-hour City Hall hearing at which more than 40 persons denounced the landlords' code and a key City Councilman threatened that if the industry could not refashion the code, the Council would write the rules itself.

"What that means," said Councilman Donald R. Manes, Queens Democrat and chairman of the Special Committee on Rental Programs that drew up the stabilization law, "is that either they'll rewrite the rules,

Continued on Page 66, Column 4

Jersey Power Loss Stops Penn Central During Rush Hour

By EMANUEL PERLMUTTER

All commuter and long-distance train service on the Penn Central from New York southward through New Jersey was halted last night by a power failure.

About 16,000 commuters and several thousand long-distance passengers were affected by the power failure, which occurred shortly before 5 o'clock in the railroad's overhead wires near North Elizabeth.

At midnight a Penn Central spokesman said all service was back to normal and the railroad was in "great shape" for this morning's rush hour.

Partial service was restored at 7:10 P.M., and full outbound service by 9 P.M. Incoming trains were stranded between here and Trenton and at many points along the Jersey shore, until about 9:15.

At that time a track was opened, and the Admiral from Chicago pulled in at 9:35, more than seven hours late.

Earlier, hundreds of sweltering commuters milled around in Pennsylvania Station, many berating the railroad. Many lined up by telephones waiting to call home.

"Every time I come to New York," said Marion Powers, a Washington lawyer, "something like this happens. I'm part of every train crisis."

Several thousand commuters, following advice broadcast by railroad personnel over loud-

Continued on Page 66, Column 2

SOVIET AND CHINA CLASH ON BORDER

Both Sides Charge Incursion Over a Disputed Island on the Amur Frontier

By CHARLES MOHR
Special to The New York Times

HONG KONG, July 8—Communist China charged today that Soviet gunboats, troops and aircraft had intruded across the Amur River frontier between the two countries and provoked an "armed conflict."

The incident took place near the Soviet city of Khabarovsk, where a Chinese-Soviet commission on problems of navigation in boundary rivers has been meeting since June 18 in an attempt to ease border tensions that erupted in March.

The Chinese said the latest incident began when Soviet frontier troops aboard two river boats had intruded into Pacha Island, which Peking said was on the Chinese side of the main channel of the Amur River.

[A Soviet statement, referring to the disputed island as Goldinsky, said Chinese hiding on the Soviet part of the island had opened fire on river workers who had come to repair navigation markers on the island.]

A Chinese protest note given

Continued on Page 17, Column 1

TV Industry Panel Offers Plan to End Cigarette Ads by '73

By JOHN D. MORRIS
Special to The New York Times

WASHINGTON, July 8—The television broadcasting industry's self-regulatory agency called today for a gradual elimination of cigarette advertising starting next January.

By Sept. 1, 1973, all cigarette advertising would be barred from the three major television networks and 399 stations that subscribe to the Television Code of the National Association of Broadcasters.

The plan was proposed by the association's nine-member Television Code review board at a meeting at N.A.B. headquarters here. It is subject to ratification by the association's television board of directors. The 15 directors will be polled by mail.

Radio Panel Meets Today

The association's Radio Code board will consider similar action at a meeting tomorrow.

The Television Code board's decision was widely applauded by antismoking forces as a significant breakthrough in the long struggle against what they consider to be the depiction of cigarette smoking as a desirable habit, rather than as a health hazard.

A major purpose of the self-regulatory move was to ward off mandatory Federal controls.

A regulation pending before the Federal Communications Commission would bar all cigarette advertising from radio and television.

A different regulation pending before the Federal Trade Commission would require a

Continued on Page 86, Column 6

WATERBURY FACES SEGREGATION SUIT

Justice Department Seeks Better School Balance—Files 4 Actions in South

By CHRISTOPHER LYDON
Special to The New York Times

WASHINGTON, July 8—The Justice Department told the school board of Waterbury, Conn., today that it must take immediate action to correct racial imbalance or face the first school desegregation suit ever filed by the Government in the northeastern states.

[In Waterbury, Mayor George P. Harlamon said that steps were being taken to eliminate de facto segregation. Page 20.]

Continuing its sudden burst of civil rights activity, the department also filed four new school suits in Tennessee, South Carolina and Louisiana.

With two school suits filed yesterday and several more ready for filing in the next few days, the Justice Department will have taken more school desegregation action in this one week than in the Nixon Administration's preceding five months.

Policy and Progress

Last Friday, Administration officials indicated that they would consider individual exceptions to the general deadline, set for this September, by which school systems must start integration. The new flurry of legal actions appeared to confirm, however, an Administration commitment to immediate progress in the great majority of school districts.

The Justice Department's letter to Waterbury's Board of Education charged that the city's "district lines, bus routes and transfer policies have been drawn so as to insure that predominantly white schools remain 'white' and predominantly nonwhite schools remain nonwhite.'"

The letter — to the board's president, Salvatore Terenzo — stated that Negro teachers in the Waterbury system had been assigned "on the basis of race" to the predominantly Negro

Continued on Page 20, Column 5

ALBANO REBUKED ON TIE TO MARCUS

U.S. Court Critical as It Upholds Conviction of 3

By EDWARD RANZAL

The Republican county chairman in Manhattan and one of his key lieutenants were criticized yesterday by the United States Court of Appeals for having exerted influence in the awarding of contracts by James L. Marcus when he was Water Commissioner.

The criticism was made in the court's 59-page opinion upholding the conviction of a Mafia figure, a labor official and a contractor in the Marcus bribe conspiracy case.

Vincent F. Albano Jr., the chairman of the Republican County Committee, and Joseph Ruggiero, chairman of the Manhattan group's law committee, were named by the court as party officials who suggested favored contractors to Marcus.

The two Republican leaders could not be reached for comment.

In a summary of "the sorry story of the corruption of a public official," Judge Harold R. Medina, who wrote the opinion of the Court of Appeals

Continued on Page 28, Column 5

Reputed Mafia Leaders Take the Stand as Jersey Opens Inquiry

By CHARLES GRUTZNER
Special to The New York Times

TRENTON, July 8—The State Commission of Investigation today questioned three reputed members of the Mafia family headed by Simone Rizzo (Sam the Plumber) DeCavalcante about organized crime and official corruption in Long Branch and other Monmouth County shore areas.

Behind closed doors of a fourth-floor courtroom in the State House Annex, examination was begun of Frank (Big Frank) Cocchiaro, who was alleged to have succeeded Anthony (Little Pussy) Russo as rackets boss of Monmouth; Robert (Bobby Basile) Occhipinti, DeCavalcante's cousin and partner in air-conditioning and contracting businesses, and John Riggi, a reputed capo regima, or captain.

The witnesses are among 14 alleged Mafiosi or business associates of DeCavalcante who have been summoned in the first sweeping investigation by the commission, which was created by the 1968 Legislature and organized six months ago.

William F. Hyland, the com-

Continued on Page 28, Column 1

The New York Times

John Riggi, left, Simone Rizzo (Sam the Plumber) DeCavalcante, center, and Frank (Big Frank) Cocchiaro arriving yesterday for the State Commission of Investigation hearing.

Space Monkey Dies; Autopsy Is Planned

By United Press International

HONOLULU, July 8—Bonny the space monkey died today less than 12 hours after an emergency splashdown in the Pacific three weeks ahead of schedule. Investigators said the space capsule may have been affected by cold.

The 14-pound pigtail monkey was brought down near here at 1 P.M. yesterday and rushed to an intensive care unit at Hickam Air Force Base, where scientists at first said he was "responding favorably." But shortly after midnight Bonny died.

Officials said that an extensive autopsy would be performed on the monkey at Hickam, but they did not know when it would begin.

Dr. W. Roth Adey, principal

Continued on Page 29, Column 4

Mets Beat Cubs in 9th

Ed Kranepool's single with two out in the ninth inning scored the run that gave the New York Mets a 4-3 victory over the Chicago Cubs yesterday at Shea Stadium. A crowd of 55,096 saw the Mets move to within four games of the first-place Cubs in the Eastern Division of the National League. Details are on Page 47.

ANGLICANS REJECT METHODIST UNION

Churches Vote and Split on 14-Year-Old Proposal

By JOHN M. LEE
Special to The New York Times

BIRMINGHAM, England, July 8—A 14-year effort at church unity collapsed tonight when bishops and priests of the Church of England defeated a proposal for reunification with the Methodist Church. The Methodists, at a separate conference, approved the plan.

The outcome, which was in doubt until the votes, was regarded as an acute setback not only for leaders of the two churches, who had advocated reunion, but also for the world-wide ecumenical movement and for advocates of dozens of church unification plans throughout the world.

The Archbishop of Canterbury, the Most Rev. Arthur Michael Ramsey, said he was "sad and disappointed" and he expressed fear that lack of agreement between the churches would disillusion

Continued on Page 9, Column 1

NEWS INDEX

"All the News That's Fit to Print"

The New York Times

LATE CITY EDITION

Weather: Chance of showers today, tonight. Cloudy tomorrow. Temp. range: today 76-65; Wed. 74-68. Temp.-Hum. Index yesterday 71. Complete U.S. report Page 93.

VOL. CXVIII . . No. 40,766

NEW YORK, THURSDAY, SEPTEMBER 4, 1969

10 CENTS

STENNIS CHARGES ARMS FUND CUTS ENDANGER NATION

Answers Pentagon Critics as Senate Resumes Its Debate After Recess

FEARS 2D RATE STATUS

Senator's Defense of New Giant Transport Plane Challenged by Proxmire

By WARREN WEAVER Jr.
Special to The New York Times

WASHINGTON, Sept. 3 — Senate defenders of the Pentagon opened a strong counterattack today on the bipartisan bloc that has been successfully trimming the defense budget and is now questioning the necessity of major new weapons.

Senator John C. Stennis, chairman of the Armed Services Committee, charged that "the safety of the American people will be placed in jeopardy" if a series of moves to limit tank, carrier and aircraft development wins Senate approval over the next few weeks of debate.

In the prepared text of his remarks, he also declared that approval of the anti-Pentagon amendments would be "tantamount to a partial unilateral disarmament," but he dropped this paragraph in delivery.

Praised by Thurmond

The accusation will show up in the record anyway, for a few moments later Senator Strom Thurmond of South Carolina rose to congratulate Senator Stennis and singled out the "unilateral disarmament" charge for particular praise.

Reopening of the two-month Senate debate on the $20-billion military authorization bill was the principal activity on Capitol Hill as Congress returned from a three-week summer vacation to face an imposing accumulation of unprocessed legislation.

In the week before the Senate recessed Aug. 13, a coalition of liberal critics of the Pentagon and economizers succeeded in passing a series of restrictive amendments to the military bill or, alternatively, forcing its sponsors to accept compromises.

Senator Stennis, trying to halt the momentum of the military critics, maintained that if their pending proposals were approved "we will be a second-rate nation by 1975, and this fact shall become well known long before that time."

"I do not want this Senate to be in the position of saying to these young men [in the armed services] that this Gov-

Continued on Page 19, Column 1

Marine Commandant Acts To Ease Racial Tensions

Associated Press

Gen. Leonard F. Chapman Jr. at Washington news session

By WILLIAM BEECHER
Special to The New York Times

WASHINGTON, Sept. 3—The Marine Corps commandant issued an order today calling for an end to racial violence in the corps and outlining steps to eliminate discrimination against Negroes.

The commandant, Gen. Leonard F. Chapman Jr., appeared willing to bend traditional Marine rules a bit in an effort to be conciliatory toward the attitudes of some black marines.

Text of General Chapman's statement is on Page 39.

For example, he said that the Afro haircut would be permitted if it conformed with Marine regulations—that is, if it was neatly trimmed on the sides and in back and stood no more than three inches high on top.

General Chapman's order came in the wake of racial incidents at Camp Lejeune, N.C., and other marine garrisons in

Continued on Page 39, Column 1

Episcopal Leaders Vote $200,000 in 'Reparations'

By SETH S. KING
Special to The New York Times

SOUTH BEND, Ind., Sept. 3—After two days of emotional debate, the Episcopal Church indirectly allocated today $200,000 for the Black Economic Development Conference.

The Episcopalians thus became the first major denomination to offer money or recognition to the Negro group that promulgated the Black Manifesto.

The House of Deputies reversed its previous ban and voted this morning to provide the $200,000 demanded by the group, organized under the leadership of James Forman. This was to be the Episcopal Church's share of $500-million in "reparations" Mr. Forman demanded from the nation's churches and synagogues for their "racist oppression" of Negroes.

Both Houses Pass Measure

The House of Bishops, which shares the responsibility of directing the Episcopal Church, endorsed the House of Deputies' decision tonight.

The 600-man House of Deputies, consisting of clergymen and laymen, declared that it rejected much of the ideology expressed in the Black Manifesto. But it recognized the Black Economic Development Conference as a movement for organizing the "self-determination" of the black community.

The funds would not go directly to the Forman group. Instead they would be allocated to the interdenominational National Committee of Black Churchmen.

"But we expect the Black Economic Development Conference to be the ultimate recipient," said the Rev. Robert P. Varley, chairman of the committee that produced the

Continued on Page 38, Column 7

N.A.A.C.P. IS SUING ON BUILDING JOBS

Asks Halt in Construction Financed by Government Unless Negroes Are Hired

By DAMON STETSON

The National Association for the Advancement of Colored People announced yesterday a series of legal actions aimed at stopping work on Government-financed construction unless qualified Negroes were employed on the projects.

The legal moves are part of a stepped-up national drive to eliminate discrimination in building trades unions and to insure compliance on public construction with Federal laws.

At a news conference here, Roy Wilkins, executive director of the association, described the building trades unions as the "last bastion against employment of Negro workers as a policy" and asserted that the blacks of the nation wanted a just share of the $80-billion budgeted for construction this year by the building industry.

Asked about the effect of the 75 per cent cutbacks in Federal construction reportedly planned by the Nixon Administration, Mr. Wilkins replied that such a move would make things

Continued on Page 40, Column 4

HARTFORD POLICE MAINTAIN CURFEW

71 Are Arrested as Heavy Guard Patrols Streets

By JOHN DARNTON
Special to The New York Times

HARTFORD, Sept. 3—Overseeing a citywide curfew, the state and local police arrested at least 71 persons here tonight, but there was no repetition of the widespread racial disorders that swept this city's predominantly Negro and Puerto Rican North End for two successive days.

Most of tonight's arrest were for violations of the curfew. As heavy contingents of policemen patrolled the streets of the North End, they encountered only a few instances of bottle- and firecracker-throwing and one or two firebombs.

On one occasion, the police fired four tear gas canisters onto the roof of a four-story tenement in the North End where they said they had seen a man hurling bottles. Within seconds, seven patrol cars had rushed to the scene from all directions, but the man on the roof escaped.

The police described the situation in the 40-block riot area as quiet, despite large crowds drawn earlier in the day on

Continued on Page 38, Column 1

Con Edison Cable Failure Halts Stock Trading for Half an Hour

By PETER MILLONES

The New York Stock Exchange suspended trading for 30 minutes yesterday after a Consolidated Edison electric cable failed and the exchange's computers were knocked out of service.

Shouts of "power failure" echoed across the floor of the exchange at 12:28 P.M. when light bulbs flickered and the stock ticker, its tape projected on screens there and in brokerage houses, came to an abrupt halt.

The lights remained on, however, and many traders, undaunted, continued to buy and sell until the hastily convened floor governors of the exchange rang a bell signaling the suspension of trading at 12:35.

Trading and the ticker resumed at 1:05 P.M. and the interruption—allowing a few traders to snatch sandwiches—had no apparent effect on stock prices, which had been lower and remained so. The Dow-Jones industrial average, a barometer of blue chip stocks, closed 2.11 points lower at 835.67, in slightly heavier trading than the previous day.

Con Edison at $28.50 a share, only a few dimes above its 11-year low, was not affected by this latest problem in what has been a long hot summer of difficulties for the giant utility.

Faced almost daily with complaints from some of its three million customers, Con Edison contended that if the New York Exchange had had a better safety device on its computers, yesterday's problem would not have been serious.

An Exchange spokesman

Continued on Page 45, Column 3

WATER POLLUTERS WHO FAIL TO ACT FACE FEDERAL SUIT

Hickel Orders New Drive by Government to Identify and Prosecute Violators

Special to The New York Times

WASHINGTON, Sept. 3—The Interior Department plans to speed up its drive against water pollution by suing individual polluters if necessary.

Announcing a Government drive to "prosecute those who pollute," Interior Secretary Walter J. Hickel today ordered hearings before the Federal Water Pollution Control Administration. The City of Toledo, Ohio, four steel companies and a mining company have been charged by the Government with pollution, and their representatives will appear at the hearings.

The steel companies are the United States Steel Corporation, the Republic Steel Corporation, the Interlake Steel Company, and Jones & Laughlin Steel Company. The mining company is Eagle-Picher Industries, Inc., of Baxter Springs, Kan.

Those charged with water pollution are not required to attend the hearings, but they were sent official notification of the charges yesterday, according to an Interior Department official. If they are found guilty of the charges, and fail to take steps to eliminate pollution within 180 days, the Interior Department plans to bring suit.

Until today, states have had the responsibility for initiating court action against water polluters. Interior officials, however, feel that state court actions have been too slow in coming. The new drive at the Interior Department is designed to accelerate the cleaning up of the nation's waterways.

Act of 1965 Cited

In a statement, Secretary Hickel said: "This is just a beginning. We intend to continue the identification of polluters for prompt cleanup and pollution elimination."

Carl L. Klein, Assistant Secretary for water quality and research, said in a telephone interview that the Government for the first time would use the "abatement proceedings" provision of the Federal Water Pollution Control Act of 1965, which defined water pollution standards in various bodies of water.

Mr. Klein said the Interior Department's campaign procedure started with "fact finding" by scientists and engineers and called for voluntary hearings involving companies, municipalities or others charged with pollution.

Mr. Klein stressed that those found to be polluting water-

Continued on Page 24, Column 3

U.S. WOULD ALTER CURRENCY ABROAD LITTLE BUT OFTEN

Reform in Global Monetary System Deemed Necessary —Dollar to Stay Fixed

By EDWIN L. DALE Jr.
Special to The New York Times

WASHINGTON, Sept. 3 — The United States Government has concluded at the highest level that the international monetary system needs reform to provide more flexibility in exchange rates among currencies.

The method of flexibility favored is some version of a "crawling peg," under which exchange rates would make small but frequent changes, up or down. The change need not be universal but could be adopted only for a limited number of currencies, though that question is still left open.

The dollar would not be affected. Its exchange rate—expressed in terms of gold at $35 an ounce—would remain the "fixed star" of the system. Other currencies would move up or down against the dollar.

The United States will not make a formal proposal for introduction of this major reform at the International Monetary Fund's annual meeting later this month, according to authoritative sources.

Suggestion Likely

However, it is probable that the Secretary of the Treasury, David M. Kennedy, will suggest that the matter be formally studied by the I.M.F. or by the Group of Ten major financial powers or by both.

Even this would be a major step. It would signal to the world that the United States now looks sympathetically upon the next step in monetary reform, widely advocated outside Government circles, and it could lead to the placing of exchange-rate flexibility formally on an international agenda for the first time—a necessary first step in any reform.

The decision to back reform emerged from months of study by a group of high officials that began shortly after the Nixon Administration took office.

The reason for the United States decision is growing awareness of a flaw in the otherwise highly successful 25-year-old postwar monetary system. The keystone of the system has been fixed exchange rates, supported by government intervention in daily trading in the foreign-exchange markets.

The system always allowed for changes in exchange rates—devaluations or upward revaluations—for cases when a nation's economy, its rate of inflation or its foreign trade drift

Continued on Page 10, Column 4

Burns Moves Into City Campaign To Coordinate Procaccino's Race

By CLAYTON KNOWLES

John J. Burns, the Democratic state chairman, quietly moved this week into Mario A. Procaccino's headquarters to coordinate personally the Controller's mayoral campaign.

The move, which political observers said was without precedent in the city's modern political history, was acknowledged yesterday both by Controller Procaccino and by Mr. Burns.

Just where the impetus for the arrangement developed was uncertain—each man credited the other with initiating it—but the two agreed they were "very happy" with the setup.

"When John told me what he wanted to do, I was delighted and told him to move right in," Mr. Procaccino said. "He'll coordinate the party organization effort in the five boroughs."

In Democratic circles, Mr. Burns's decision to associate himself so closely with the campaign was generally taken as an indication that he believed Mr. Procaccino was well ahead and that harmonizing the operation of the five borough organizations would pay dividends in the 1970 election.

Next year voters will elect

The New York Times

John J. Burns

a new state administration and a United States Senator. A long string of Republican victories at the state level, broken only by the late Robert F. Kennedy's Senate victory in 1964, can be attributed largely to the Democrats' poor Election Day showing in New York City, rather than upstate.

Each of New York City's five boroughs is coincident with a county (thus Manhattan is New

Continued on Page 42, Column 3

HO CHI MINH DEAD AT 79; NORTH VIETNAM EXPECTED TO HOLD TO WAR POLICIES

Camera Press-Pix

Ho Chi Minh

HAS HEART ATTACK

He Won Independence for Nation and Led War Against U.S.

Text of Hanoi announcement of Ho's death, Page 16.

By TILLMAN DURDIN
Special to The New York Times

HONG KONG, Thursday, Sept. 4—President Ho Chi Minh of North Vietnam died yesterday morning in Hanoi at the age of 79.

A Hanoi radio report at 7 A.M. this morning announced that he succumbed at 9:47 A.M. Hanoi time yesterday "after a very sudden, serious heart attack."

The radio disclosed only at 4 A.M. yesterday that President Ho had been gravely ill for several weeks and was under emergency treatment day and night by "a collective of professors and medical doctors."

There was no explanation for the delay of almost 24 hours in announcing the President's death.

White House Silent

Under the North Vietnamese Constitution, the Vice President take over if the President dies or is incapacitated, pending a new election. The Vice President is an obscure figure, Ton Duc Thang, 81.

[In San Clemente, Calif., the Western White House said that President Nixon would have no comment on Mr. Ho's death.]

The Hanoi announcement, in the form of a communiqué issued in the name of the Central Committee of the Vietnam Workers (Communist) party, the Standing Committee of the National Assembly and the Council of Ministers, said:

"We feel boundless grief in informing the entire party and the entire Vietnamese people that Comrade Ho Chi Minh, President of the Central Committee of the Vietnam Workers party and President of the Democratic Republic of Vietnam, passed away at 9:47, Sept. 3, 1969, after a very sudden, serious heart attack at the age of 79.

"Everybody has done his best, determined to cure the President at all costs. But due to his advanced age President Ho Chi Minh has departed from us." After the first announce-

Continued on Page 16, Column 1

FRANCE INVOKING MORE AUSTERITY

Government Exhorts Public to Help Save the Franc—Cuts Budget Sharply

By HENRY GINIGER
Special to The New York Times

PARIS, Sept. 3 — The French Government adopted new austerity measures today and appealed to the country to join in a battle to save the franc.

The battle plan includes major cuts in public spending this year, a balanced budget in 1970, immediate tax relief for low income groups only, restrictions on credit and prices, and spurs to savings.

After the Cabinet had adopted the economic-recovery program for the rest of this year and 1970, its details were presented by Premier Jacques Chaban-Delmas and the Finance Minister, Valéry Giscard d'Estaing.

'Our Fates Are Linked'

The state, the individual and the corporation were all enlisted in the fight.

"In this battle our fates are linked," Mr. Giscard d'Estaing declared at a news conference.

"It is not the ambition of the Government on one side and the well-being of Frenchmen on the other. The stake is the same for all."

The Finance Minister outlined the measures to the Finance Committee of the National Assembly, which has been called into special session for Sept. 16. Then, under hot floodlights at the Ministry of Finance, in a wing of the Louvre Palace, he spoke to several hundred reporters and, by radio and television, to the nation.

Tonight Premier Chaban-Del-

Continued on Page 6, Column 1

NO EFFECT IS SEEN ON TALKS IN PARIS

U.S. Officials Say Death of Mystical Leader Won't Alter Peace Outlook

By RICHARD HALLORAN
Special to The New York Times

WASHINGTON, Sept. 3 — United States officials said here tonight that the death of Ho Chi Minh meant the loss of an almost mystical leader but that it was not likely to change the course of the war in South Vietnam or to affect the prospects of reaching a settlement in the peace negotiations in Paris.

Sources close to the Vietnam situation said here that the most immediate impact would be the loss of leadership that has been embodied in Ho Chi Minh, the nationalist, the fighter for Vietnamese independence and the poetic revolutionary.

He has been such a figure for many of the Vietnamese for a half-century since he appeared at the Versailles Peace Conference in 1919 to seek more rights for his countrymen, who were then living under French colonial rule.

No Outstanding Figure

In the North, no other member of the inner circle of Communist leaders, some of whom have served with him for more than 30 years, enjoys anything like the stature of President Ho.

His quality of leadership cannot be passed on, it is thought here, and thus the future cohesion of North Vietnamese leadership is in some doubt. It is thought probable that a collective leadership, as in the Soviet Union after the death of Stalin, will emerge.

In the South, it is thought, the National Liberation Front,

Continued on Page 18, Column 1

City Calls on the Realty Industry To Curb Commercial Rent Rises

By DAVID K. SHIPLER

Reports of rent increases of up to 200 per cent in small stores and other commercial space have prompted the Lindsay administration to ask the real estate industry to police itself.

At the Mayor's direction, Richard Lewisohn, the city's Economic Development Administrator, met Aug. 20 with Rexford E. Tompkins, president of the Real Estate Board of New York, and Lewis Rudin, a major builder and manager, to describe the problem and ask for industry action.

"They were very sympathetic," Mr. Lewisohn said yesterday. "They were aware of the problem, and they said they would get back with a possible procedure."

But Mr. Tompkins said he had never acknowledged the existence of a problem, and added, "We're not volunteering any kind of procedure at this point."

"We said we would take the complaints they had," Mr. Tompkins continued, "and look into them and see what the problem is. We're curious to know who are the complainants and whether they fall into categories and how many they

Continued on Page 53, Column 1

NEWS INDEX

U.S. TELLS KOREANS IT WILL APOLOGIZE

But Pyongyang Rejects Plan to Free 3 on Copter

Special to The New York Times

PANMUNJOM, Korea, Thursday, Sept. 4—The American-led United Nations Command told North Korea today that it was prepared to submit a document of apology admitting that it had violated North Korean airspace if North Korea would, at the same time, release the three crewmen of an American OH-23 helicopter shot down over North Korea on Aug. 17.

The North Korean delegation at the Military Armistice Commission meeting here rejected the proposal.

Maj. Gen. Arthur H. Adams, the senior delegate of the United Nations Command, said that the proposed document would say that the helicopter "was on a military mission, it became lost and therefore flew into your territory."

He added that the document "would contain an expression of regret and statement that measures will be taken to prevent recurrences of an incident of this kind. It is preposterous to think that a three-man, unarmed helicopter would have

Continued on Page 19, Column 1

Poised for action, A U.S. Navy ship patrols the Bo De River.

Masked against a cloud of tear gas dropped on nearby enemy positions, a U.S. trooper prepares to guide a helicopter into the Landing Zone at An Khe Pass during Operation Surprise.

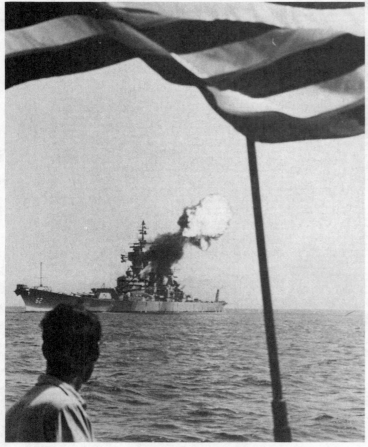

The "Big Guns" that make the U.S.S. *New Jersey* such a lethal battleship pound away at targets in North Vietnam.

"All the News That's Fit to Print"

The New York Times

LATE CITY EDITION

Weather: Fair, cool today. Partly cloudy and cool through tomorrow. Temp. range: today 65-47; Wed. 64-46. Full U.S. report on Page 94.

VOL. CXIX .. No. 40,808 © 1969 The New York Times Company. NEW YORK, THURSDAY, OCTOBER 16, 1969 10 CENTS

VIETNAM MORATORIUM OBSERVED NATIONWIDE BY FOES OF THE WAR; RALLIES HERE CROWDED, ORDERLY

The New York Times (by William E. Sauro)

OBSERVING MORATORIUM: Senator Eugene J. McCarthy, Minnesota Democrat, addressing crowds in Bryant Park

METS TRIUMPH, 2-1, ON ERROR IN 10TH; LEAD SERIES BY 3-1

Wild Throw Following Bunt by Martin Lets In Run—Orioles Gain Tie in 9th

SEAVER IS THE WINNER

Brilliant Catch by Swoboda Helps — Clendenon Hits Homer in 2d Inning

By JOSEPH DURSO

The New York Mets moved to within one victory of the pot of gold yesterday when they defeated the Baltimore Orioles, 2-1, in 10 innings and took a lead of three games to one in the World Series.

The victory was the third straight for the underdog Mets over the champions of the American League and it was laced with potent doses of the "magic" that has marked their fantastic surge to the top in 1969.

They led, 1-0, going into the ninth inning behind the three-hit pitching of Tom Seaver. Then they were caught when the Orioles tied the game, but were saved from losing it by a tumbling backhand catch by Ron Swoboda.

One Step Closer

Finally, an inning later, they scored the winning run with the help of the sun's glare, a 10-foot bunt and a wild throw to first base on an illegal play detected by neither the Orioles nor the umpires (Details on Page 59).

The Mets' latest adventure was witnessed by 57,367 persons, a record paying crowd for Shea Stadium, and it left them in a commanding position to win the championship of baseball one year after they had "advanced" to ninth place.

They will try to nail down the title this afternoon at 1 o'clock, with Jerry Koosman pitching against Dave McNally of the Orioles. If they don't, the Series will return to Baltimore for the final game or games this weekend.

The Mets' astounding success was matched by a series of unlikely upsets for the Orioles, who won their divisional championship by 19 games and were ranked as one of the most powerful teams of modern times:

¶Until the Orioles scored in the ninth inning, they had been shut out for 19 straight innings—and this was a team that had been held scoreless only eight times in 162 games this season

¶Even after they teased home a run in the ninth, they still had crossed home plate only twice in their last 32 innings

Continued on Page 58, Column 2

Bishop Sheen, 74, Resigns Post in Rochester Diocese

Will Return to New York for TV and Other Work —Successor Is Named

By JOSEPH LELYVELD
Special to The New York Times

ROCHESTER, Oct. 15 — The Most Rev. Fulton J. Sheen resigned today as Bishop of Rochester after a three-year tenure and was immediately succeeded by Msgr. Joseph L. Hogan, whose appointment was announced by Pope Paul VI in Rome.

"I am resigning the diocese," said Bishop Sheen who is 74 years old. "I am not resigning work. I am not retiring, I am regenerating." The Vatican announced his appointment as titular archbishop of Newport, England, which now exists as a diocese only on paper.

The New York Times

Bishop Fulton J. Sheen at news conference yesterday.

Bishop Sheen, who presented his successor at a news conference here this morning, ended his tenure on a general note of frustration and disappointment for himself and his flock.

Bishop Sheen said he could recite a "long litany" of his failures here. He said it was up to others to cite any successes he may have had, but he mentioned specifically the certified auditing of the diocese's finances, consultation with his priests on new appointments and the purchase of homes for 14 indigent slum families.

"I move too fast," he said, alluding to his concern with the conditions of slum blacks. "I'm a little too progressive."

A proselytizer used to reaching a mass audience of millions by means of television, Bishop Sheen was widely criticized in his upstate diocese for failing to communicate with ordinary parishioners.

"He stirred the whole dio-

Continued on Page 50, Column 5

A MIDDLE COURSE IS URGED BY COOKE AT BISHOPS' SYNOD

He Stresses Need for Both Papal Supremacy and the Principle of Collegiality

By ROBERT C. DOTY
Special to The New York Times

ROME, Oct. 15 — Cardinal Cooke, Archbishop of New York, urged the Roman Catholic Synod of Bishops today to consider the present period of "stress and strain" in the church "frankly and positively, with great charity."

The 48-year-old New York prelate, first from the United States to speak at the meeting here, made what most observers construed as a middle-of-the-road approach to the issue of balance between papal power and the collegial power of the bishops as a whole.

He spoke on the third day of the synod, which seems to be moving toward consensus on the idea that the Roman Pontiff, whatever his right to rule alone, should, as a practical matter, seek and follow the advice of the bishops on major problems affecting the entire church.

Birth Control Dissent Cited

At least three prelates have cited the storm of dissent that followed issuance of the renewed ban on birth control by Pope Paul VI in July, 1968, as the consequence of failure to associate the bishops with the decision-making process.

Cardinal Cooke limited himself today to describing the nature of the questions to be resolved without suggesting answers beyond a general proposal for "closer cooperative activity and improved communications" between the Vatican and the bishops.

Cardinal Cooke said that both the principle of supreme power of the Pope, declared by a church council a century ago, and that of "collegiality," rule of the church by the Pope with the bishops, were essential to a church in a time of transition.

Sharing of Power Stressed

Sharing of power by the bishops was important, he said, to a world increasingly conscious of the worth of the individual and increasingly suspicious of decisions made unilaterally, of adherence to tradition and of unity for its own sake.

On the other hand, he said, in an age of "socialization" and interdependence, papal authority provides the essential coordination of effort. An age of pluralism would threaten to become chaotic unless there were someone "to discern the truth and indicate what is essential to the faith," he said.

Cardinal Cooke went on to list the problems: the role of the bishops in guiding the church with the Pope, the role of the local bishop, and the proper interaction between the Pope and the bishops in delineating doctrine more clearly.

He suggested that the new international commission of theologians might help find the answers to these questions.

This was the solution proposed forcefully by Julius Cardinal Döpfner, Archbishop of

Continued on Page 4, Column 1

POLICEMAN SLAYS SOMALI PRESIDENT

Assassin Seized After Shot Kills Shermarke Instantly —Curfew in Mogadiscio

By Reuters

MOGADISCIO, Somalia, Oct. 15—President Abdirashid Ali Shermarke of Somalia was assassinated today by a member of the police force, an official announcement said here.

The announcement said that a man had been arrested and accused of the murder at Las Anod in northern Somalia, where the President was touring an area stricken by drought. No reason for the assassination was suggested.

Authorities imposed a dusk-to-dawn curfew in Mogadiscio, the capital of the East African country, which became a republic in 1960.

The President, who would have been 50 years old tomorrow, was said to have died instantly. His body was being flown to Mogadiscio as the Somali Council of Ministers was called into emergency session.

Acting Premier Yassin Nur Hassan, speaking for the Council of Ministers in the absence of Premier Mohammed Ibrahim

Continued on Page 6, Column 1

Senate Unit Drops Two Oil Reforms From the Tax Bill

By EILEEN SHANAHAN
Special to The New York Times

WASHINGTON, Oct. 15—The Senate Finance Committee dropped from the tax reform bill today two sections that would have increased the Treasury's annual collections from oil companies by about $65-million.

The provisions that were dropped from the bill, which has been passed by the House of Representatives, involved the credit that American companies may take on their United States tax returns for taxes paid to a foreign government.

The decision to eliminate the two sections was made, according to committee officials, by a "rather decisive" margin.

Corporations other than oil companies are affected by the provisions, but to a much lesser degree.

The decision on the foreign tax credit is the first that the committee has reached in its work on the reform bill that involves the oil industry. It has not yet considered the question of lowering the 27½ per cent depletion allowance — or other reforms in the House bill that would raise the oil industry's taxes.

In other actions today, the

Continued on Page 40, Column 3

The New York Times (by Patrick A. Burns)

THE WINNING PLAY: J. C. Martin of Mets (9) racing to first base after laying down a bunt in the tenth inning. The throw from Pete Richert (24), Orioles' pitcher, hit Martin and bounced away, allowing Rod Gaspar to score from second. The umpire is Lou DiMuro.

Eisenhower Dollar Voted by Congress

By PETER GROSE
Special to The New York Times

WASHINGTON, Oct. 15 — Congress voted today to coin a new dollar that would honor former President Dwight D. Eisenhower, but the Senate and House of Representatives differed on whether it should be a silver dollar.

Flourishing a letter from Mrs. Eisenhower, a group of Western legislators got the Senate to override the Administration's proposal to produce a copper and nickel coin. A similar effort, backed by the same letter, failed in the House, which opted for the Administration's non-silver dollar.

Mrs. Eisenhower's letter disclosed that the former President had loved to collect and distribute silver dollars as

Continued on Page 24, Column 4

DISSENSION IN CITY

Lindsay Leads Protest and Is Met by Jeers as Well as Cheers

By HOMER BIGART

Peace rallies drew throngs to the city's streets, parks, campuses and churches yesterday in an outpouring of protest against the Vietnam war.

The Times Square area was hit by a colossal traffic jam during the evening rush hour as tens of thousands of demonstrators marched to the culminating event of the day—a rally in Bryant Park, west of the New York Public Library.

The park was saturated with people, many of them unable to see the speaker's stand or hear the denunciations of war by Mayor Lindsay and Senators Charles E. Goodell, Jacob K. Javits and Eugene J. McCarthy.

Mayor Lindsay had decreed a day of mourning. His involvement was bitterly assailed by his political opponents and by many who felt that the nationwide demonstrations were not only embarrassing President Nixon's efforts to negotiate an honorable peace but were giving aid and comfort to the enemy as well.

Flag Dispute at Shea

The Mayor encountered cheers and jeers as he led the protest in the city. State Senator John J. Marchi, his Republican-Conservative rival in the mayoral race, saw the demonstrations as "a strike against America" and "a New York version of Dunkirk."

The dissension even reached World Series level. At Shea Stadium, just before the start of the fourth series game between the Mets and the Orioles, an impasse threatened the pregame flag-raising ceremony.

The Mayor had directed that flags on all city properties be flown at half-staff. Shea Stadium is owned by the city.

But just before the ceremony, the military color guard and 225 wounded Vietnam war veterans announced they would not participate unless the flag was flown full-staff.

Baseball Commissioner Bowie

Continued on Page 20, Column 2

Protests Staged in Capital As Nixon and Aides Meet

Thousands Mark Day

By E. W. KENWORTHY
Special to The New York Times

WASHINGTON, Oct. 15 — President Nixon discussed Latin America, inflation and domestic hunger with his advisers today while thousands of Government workers, students businessmen, lawyers, and housewives in the nation's capital petitioned him to pursue peace in Vietnam.

Tonight the capital's Vietnam Moratorium was brought to the gates of the White House itself, when tens of thousands of persons marched to the President's mansion.

The day's culminating demonstration began with a rally on the grounds of the Washington Monument, where Mrs. Martin Luther King Jr. addressed a throng estimated by the park police at 22,000. From there a solemn procession began, led by Mrs. King, and it soon stretched from the monument grounds to the White House, where Mrs. King paused and lit a candle on a glass-globed stand and then moved on.

It was a quite, almost funereal march, but here and there could be heard soft singing and chants. It was predominantly young, predominantly white, but here and there could be seen the middle-aged and, throughout, a scattering of blacks, their candles flickering against a light, chill wind.

For more than two hours, the throng filed by threes out of the monument grounds and

Continued on Page 18, Column 2

A Pledge by Humphrey

By SETH S. KING
Special to The New York Times

MINNEAPOLIS, Oct. 15 — Former Vice President Hubert H. Humphrey said today he had promised President Nixon that, as the leader of the Democratic party, he would never say, "You are the man who lost the war."

"As head of the Democratic party—and, by God, I am the leader of the party—I didn't want him to worry about me stabbing him in the back later," Mr. Humphrey declared.

The former Vice President met with Mr. Nixon on Friday at the White House. After the meeting, Mr. Humphrey said that he believed Mr. Nixon was on the right path toward ending the Vietnam war and that he would support the President long as he stayed on this path.

"I told him that if he takes the steps that are needed to end the war, he can depend on Hubert H. Humphrey to support him, and I said I would put that in a letter if he wanted it and sign it," Mr. Humphrey said.

The former Vice President said he was astounded that the President had not offered the North Vietnamese a cease-fire He said it could be assumed that this had been discussed in Mr. Nixon's presence.

"I encouraged the President to speak to the nation about the war, and I hope that he will have something to say to us in the speech he had scheduled for

Continued on Page 18, Column 3

OPPONENTS REACT

Many Show Support for Nixon by Flying Flags Full-Staff

By JOHN HERBERS

Protests ranging from noisy street rallies to silent prayer vigils and involving a broad spectrum of the population were held across the nation yesterday in an effort to demonstrate the growing public opposition to the war in Vietnam.

Only scattered incidents of violence marred the outpourings of small and vast crowds in which the black armband was the standard symbol.

The Vietnam Moratorium—which began as a national protest by college students and spilled over to include such groups as the United Automobile Workers union and the Pittsburgh City Council—was termed an overwhelming success by its planners, the youthful members of the Vietnam Moratorium Committee.

But it also demonstrated the great divisions in American society created by the prolonged American involvement in Southeast Asia. The demonstrations generated counter protests in some areas, and some supporters of the war who had been quiet for months spoke out in anger.

Largest Protest So Far

It was the largest public protest of the many that have been held against the Vietnam war. Historians in the Library of Congress said that as a nationally coordinated antiwar demonstration it was unique.

There was no way to estimate immediately the total numbers involved, but counting the demonstrators, the children who stayed out of school, the workers who did not report for their jobs, those who did and wore armbands and those who prayed in homes and churches, possibly millions were involved.

The demonstrations drew largely on students and other youths, the middle class and professional groups. Blue-collar workers and Negroes did not participate in great numbers, even though unions such as the United Auto Workers and the United Shoeworkers of American endorsed the moratorium. In a number of communities blue-collar workers made up the active opposition to the moratorium.

The Pentagon's civil disturbance command post termed the

Continued on Page 18, Column 6

Pacification in Rural Vietnam Making Big but Fragile Gains

By TERENCE SMITH
Special to The New York Times

SAIGON, South Vietnam, Oct. 15—The road that runs south from Saigon to Cantho is clogged these days with trucks and cars that rattle along with careless abandon.

Sixteen months ago, in the wake of the Lunar New Year offensive, a drive along the stretch between Mytho and Cantho was a perilous adventure. Vietcong guerrillas regularly planted mines under the pavement and floated explosives under the bridges. In the evening and early morning snipers fired at passing cars from the trees lining the road.

Today, as an extensive auto trip has confirmed, the only danger along Route 4 is the traffic, which is dreadful, and the potholes, which can shatter an axle.

The improved security along the road is one of the more visible examples of the progress achieved over the last year by the allied pacification program. While the enemy has concentrated his attacks on military targets, the $600-million-a-year effort to secure and develop the South Vietnamese countryside has proceeded almost without opposition.

The gains during the period have been striking. Rural security has been greatly increased—although American officials concede that it is still fragile—and the Saigon Government's control now reaches deeper into the countryside than it has for at least two years.

The expanded security in the

Continued on Page 12, Column 1

NEWS INDEX

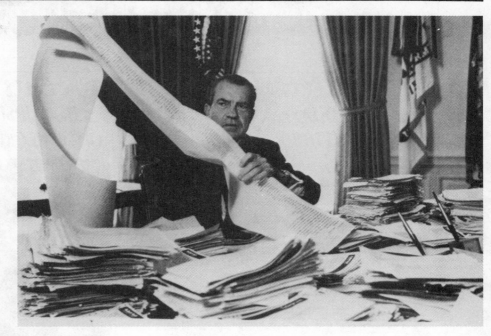

President Nixon shows off a wire he received in November 1969 containing 20,066 signatures demonstrating support and solidarity for his policies in Southeast Asia.

United Press International

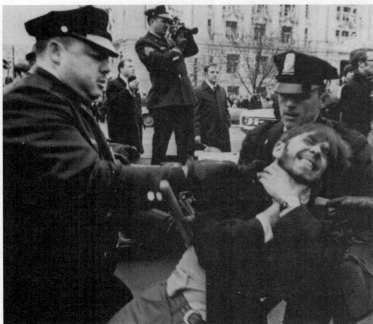

A demonstrator is restrained by the police during a "counter-Inaugural" parade protesting Richard Nixon's re-election and Inauguration on January 20, 1969.

United Press International

Activist priest James Groppi and protestor Rennie Davis (left) were among the antiwar demonstrators arrested in October 1971 for attempting to block traffic during an antiwar protest. Father Groppi and Davis carry their hands behind their heads in a gesture of sympathy for prisoners of war.

United Press International

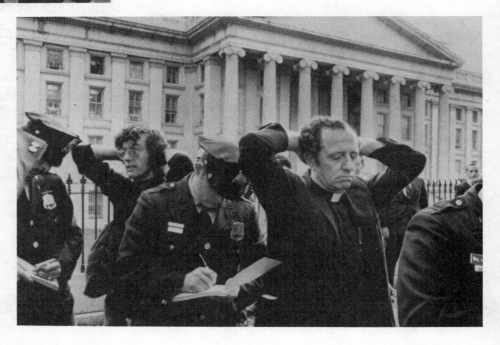

"All the News That's Fit to Print"

The New York Times

LATE CITY EDITION

Weather: Chance of showers today and tonight. Fair, mild tomorrow. Temp. range: today 60-55; Monday 67-57. Full U.S. report on Page 88.

VOL. CXIX..No. 40,827 — © 1969 The New York Times Company. — NEW YORK, TUESDAY, NOVEMBER 4, 1969 — 10 CENTS

CITY WILL ELECT A MAYOR TODAY; PARTIES DIVIDED

2,500,000 TO VOTE

Long Campaign That Broke Traditions Ends Quietly

By RICHARD REEVES

About 2.5 million city voters will elect a Mayor today after an 11-month campaign that has shattered New York's traditional political patterns and ripped apart both the Democratic and Republican parties.

Most poll takers and politicians were predicting that as a result Mayor Lindsay would win a second term without the support of either major party.

A 2.5-million vote would be about normal for a mayoral election. The weather forecast is for cloudy skies with a chance of rain in the afternoon and evening.

Mr. Lindsay, Controller Mario A. Procaccino and State Senator John J. Marchi ended their campaigns rather quietly yesterday after almost a year of speeches and walking tours by two dozen men who at one time or another hoped to move into Gracie Mansion on Jan. 1.

Polls Open at 6 A.M.

The three-way race that began after primary elections last June 17 will be decided today, when polls in the city's 5,293 election districts will be open from 6 A.M. to 9 P.M.

A total of 3,323,200 persons, 2,138,210 of them registered Democrats, are eligible to vote. But Mr. Procaccino, the Democratic and Non-Partisan candidate, who began as a strong favorite on June 18, is generally considered to be trailing Mr. Lindsay, the Liberal-Independent nominee.

The voters here will also choose a City Council President, a Controller, five Borough Presidents, 37 City Councilmen and dozens of judges.

Governors will be elected in Virginia and in New Jersey—where former Gov. Robert B. Meyner, Democrat, and Representative William T. Cahill, Republican, are in a close contest—and Mayors will be chosen in many other cities including Detroit, Cleveland, Pittsburgh and Paterson, N. J.

New York politicians who

Continued on Page 36, Column 1

Meyner Again Says Cahill Injects Bias Into Jersey Voting

By RONALD SULLIVAN
Special to The New York Times

TRENTON, Nov. 3—New Jersey's election for Governor, a bitter campaign that was dominated by repeated conflict-of-interest charges, concluded tonight in more controversy as a result of former Gov. Robert B. Meyner's charges of religious bigotry.

Mr. Meyner, the Democratic candidate, renewed his charge that Representative William T. Cahill, the Republican candidate, had injected religious bigotry into the election by his appeal for Roman Catholic votes.

Mr. Cahill promised in ads placed in Catholic newspapers last week that he would, if elected, attempt to get Catholic parochial school students the same aid that the state now gives the public school students.

On one of four television appearances throughout the day on WOR-TV in New York City, Mr. Meyner said that

Continued on Page 37, Column 1

PHONE REPAIRERS CHARGE LOCKOUT

Union Says Picket Lines Will Be Set Up Today—Overtime an Issue

Union repairmen for the New York Telephone Company walked off the job here last night, on the eve of Election Day, charging the company with "locking out" union members in an overtime dispute.

An official of Local 1101 of the Communications Workers of America said it was likely that all 30,000 union workers in the state would be off the job by this morning as a result of the company's action.

A spokesman for the company insisted there was no lockout.

He said the union had "made no effort whatever" to comply with a restraining order handed down yesterday in Federal District Court, Brooklyn, ordering union workers to perform assigned overtime.

Union men began leaving the job last night when they saw management personnel carrying tool kits walk in at job sites to do repairing and installation.

About 25 pickets appeared at 1 A.M. outside the company's central office building at 435 West 50th Street, according to

Continued on Page 90, Column 1

BLACK UNITY DAY SHUTS 2 SCHOOLS

Some Hospitals Here Also Plagued by Absences

By THOMAS A. JOHNSON

Attendance at heavily Negro schools dropped sharply yesterday and some hospital work had to be rescheduled because of a "day of absence" staged by black New Yorkers to mark the first Black Solidarity Day.

Officials said absences among black teachers and students in heavily Negro schools ran from 70 to 90 per cent, with two schools forced to close. The absences of Negro workers in city hospitals varied. Harlem Hospital operated normally, but Queens General Hospital had to cancel nonemergency surgery.

However, no emergencies were reported as a result of absences from work by black workers. Spokesmen for large private and governmental employers of Negroes—the Post Office, Bell Telephone Company and Transit Authority — said they noticed no large-scale absences because of Black Solidarity Day.

Sponsors of the one-day demonstration, which aimed at a display of unity in opposition to discrimination, had requested that Negroes absent themselves from work or school or wear armbands if they could

Continued on Page 57, Column 1

Lane High School Consolidating Sessions to Tighten Security

By PAUL L. MONTGOMERY

The administration of Franklin K. Lane High School in Brooklyn agreed with teachers yesterday to tighten security at the crowded, racially tense school by consolidating classes in a single session.

About 100 uniformed and plainclothes policemen patrolled the school yesterday, but only 325 students showed up for classes. They were dismissed at 11 A.M.

The school was closed Friday after a melee in the cafeteria between the police and students.

The school, built for 4,000 students in 1937, now has an enrollment of 4,875. It was put on a single session rather than staggered classes last January after three black youths set fire to a teacher in a hallway at the height of a series of disorders.

However, a Federal court overturned the plan in May on the grounds that the plan involved excluding 678 students from the school and that these 678 students' constitutional rights to equal education had been violated.

The plan adopted yesterday after consultations at the school among teachers, an aide of Mayor Lindsay and school officials would not involve the transfer of students.

Details have yet to be worked out, but Morton H. Selub, the principal, said the plan would be implemented "as soon as possible."

Until today the school was on two overlapping sessions between 8 A.M. and 4 P.M. This was to reduce crowding and make classrooms available over a longer period of time.

However, a number of students—"hundreds," according to Mr. Selub—are habitual truants who are carried on the rolls but do not attend classes.

Continued on Page 50, Column 1

POPULATION HERE PUT AT 7,964,200, DECLINE FROM '66

Census Estimates Indicate Brooklyn and Manhattan Showed Main Decrease

By PETER KIHSS

New York City's population has resumed a downward trend again after reaching a peak of 8,019,100 as of July 1, 1966, estimates obtained from the United States Census Bureau indicated yesterday.

The bureau's latest study estimated a decline of 35,200 people in the next year to 7,983,900 as of July 1, 1967, and a further decrease of 19,700 to 7,964,200 as of July 1, 1968.

Other census data indicated that substantial migration out of Manhattan and Brooklyn had been a major influence in the city's population changes.

Manhattan was estimated to have had 196,900 more people moving out than in between 1960 and 1966, the latest years available, and Brooklyn's net outward flow was put at 99,300.

Net Inward Total

For the city as a whole, there were 185,900 more people moving out than in from 1960 to 1966, even though the Bronx, Queens and Staten Island showed a net migration on the plus side.

During the period there were 990,400 births and 567,500 deaths in the city. This represented an increase in population of 422,900. But subtracting the net migration from the city reduced the net rise in population to 237,000 between the 1960 census and the 1966 peak, before the new decline began.

During the decade of the nineteen-fifties, the city witnessed a falling-off in population—down 109,973 from 7,891,957 in 1950 to 7,781,984 in 1960. This was a decade when the city appeared to be losing heavily as middle-income residents moved to the suburbs.

No Reasons Offered

The Census Bureau published its latest figures without attempting to interpret the reasons for the changes. The population study covers the country's 100 largest metropolitan areas for 1967 and 1968.

Earlier year-by-year estimates for New York City were made available at the bureau's headquarters in Suitland, Md. The changes in migration, births and deaths were estimated in a study last summer covering all counties in the United States.

For New York, the bureau said it used population data by boroughs derived from 1965 and 1968 housing and vacancy surveys conducted for the city administration.

These were combined with two methods used in the nationwide estimates. One, the so-called Component Method II, employs birth and death statistics to measure natural increases and school-enrollment data to estimate net migration.

The other is the Housing

Continued on Page 42, Column 1

LEBANESE ACCORD SAID TO ENDORSE COMMANDO HAVEN

Pact, Reached in Cairo, Is Also Reported to Require Coordination With Army

By DANA ADAMS SCHMIDT
Special to The New York Times

BEIRUT, Lebanon, Nov. 3—Lebanese and Palestinian commando negotiators announced tonight that they had reached "full agreement" on an accord to end fighting and discord between their forces in Lebanon.

Under the agreement, announced in Cairo, Lebanon was reported to have formally endorsed the presence of Palestinian commandos on her territory in return for a pledge by the commandos to "cooperate" with the Lebanese Army.

[In Jerusalem, Premier Golda Meir met late into the night with her advisers to discuss the accord's possible consequences for Israel. Page 2.]

The terms of the agreement, which was reached by the Lebanese Army's commander in chief, Maj. Gen. Emile Bustani, and the commandos' chief, Yasir Arafat, were not made public. But authoritative sources said that the acknowledgment and pledge constituted the essential provision.

Link to Syria Involved

The main points in the agreement, the authoritative source here said, included the following:

First, from their stronghold in the Arkoub region where their presence now is admitted and permitted, the commandos can openly maintain the line of communications with Syria by road north to the regular border point in Massnaa. This route has been labeled the "new Arafat trail."

Second, from the Arkoub region the commandos can without fear of Lebanese Army interference operate across the Lebanese border to Israel. When, where, how often, and how much are questions that apparently would be covered by the term "cooperation" with the Lebanese Army.

But the commandos would not be allowed to establish bases outside the Arkoub region, according to the authoritative report on the accord. This is what they especially wanted, and abandoning this objective would be a large concession.

The agreement followed a 13-day military test between Lebanon and Al Fatah comman-

Continued on Page 3, Column 1

VIOLENCE BARRED AT M.I.T. PROTEST

Order Is Issued by Court Against Antiwar Groups

Text of the M.I.T. statement appears on Page 34.

By JOHN H. FENTON
Special to The New York Times

CAMBRIDGE, Mass., Nov. 3—The Massachusetts Institute of Technology obtained a court order today banning members of the November Action Coalition from violence or the threat of violence during planned demonstrations tomorrow against defense research at the institute.

The coalition, a loose organization of about 30 antiwar groups, wants the research halted. The court order, a temporary restrainer, was issued by Judge Thomas J. Spring of Middlesex Superior Court.

Howard W. Johnson, who signed the petition to the court as president of the institute, said that he decided last night that that was the "most reasonable" step he could take. At a special meeting this morning, the faculty voted 344 to 43 to endorse his action.

The petition for court protection was believed to be the first taken by any college or university in anticipation of dis-

Continued on Page 34, Column 3

NIXON CALLS FOR PUBLIC SUPPORT AS HE PURSUES HIS VIETNAM PLAN ON A SECRET PULLOUT TIMETABLE

POLICY UNCHANGED

President Says Hasty Withdrawal Would Be a 'Disaster'

The text of the Nixon speech is printed on Page 16.

By MAX FRANKEL
Special to The New York Times

WASHINGTON, Nov. 3—President Nixon pleaded tonight for domestic support as he persisted in his effort to find peace in Vietnam and as he unfolded what he said was a plan to bring home all United States ground combat forces on an orderly but secret timetable.

It was the first time Mr. Nixon had spoken of a plan to recall "all" combat infantry units, though he set no deadline, and the first time he had referred to a private timetable, though he did not commit himself to a definite pace.

He made clear that his policies on Vietnam remained the same as the ones he outlined last May, the only difference being that a recent enemy restraint on the battlefield had rendered the withdrawal timetable "more optimistic."

Hasty Withdrawal Rejected

Delivering his long-awaited report on Vietnam policy by television and radio from the White House, Mr. Nixon rejected a "precipitate withdrawal," which he said would be a prescription for "a disaster of immense magnitude."

He said the enemy alone bore responsibility for the deadlock in the peace negotiations and offered in evidence some of his hitherto private diplomatic initiatives, including an exchange of letters with the late President of North Vietnam, Ho Chi Minh.

If a settlement cannot be negotiated, Mr. Nixon reiterated, then the nation's responsibility to its allies and to the peace of the world requires a measured pace of disengagement. That pace, the President said again, will be geared to the ability of the South Vietnamese forces to take over combat duties and to the level of combat imposed by the enemy.

Critics' Advice Resisted

Though the emphasis on a deliberate plan to find a lasting peace was clearly addressed to impatient critics of his tactics in Congress and around the country, the President resisted most of the critics' advice for a bold new initiative or announcement, such as a unilateral cease-fire or a public timetable for withdrawal.

In fact, the President placed some of the burden for success of his plan on the cooperation of his critics.

"I pledged in my campaign for the Presidency to end the war in a way that we could win the peace," he said. "I have initiated a plan of action which will enable me to keep that pledge.

"The more support I can have from the American people, the sooner that pledge can be redeemed, for the more divided we are at home, the less likely the enemy is to negotiate in Paris.

"Let us be united for peace. Let us also be united against

Continued on Page 17, Column 1

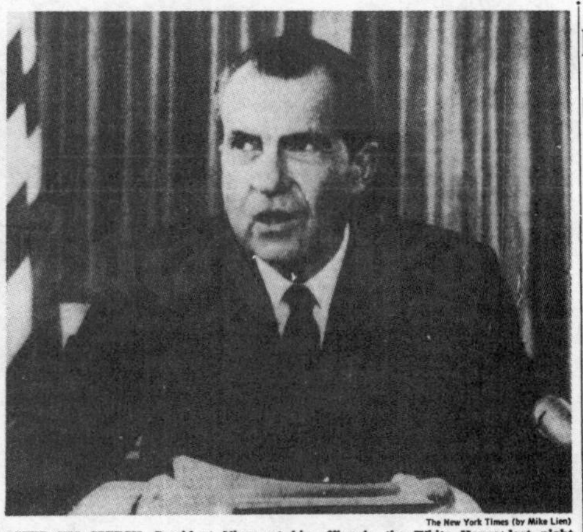

The New York Times (by Mike Lien)

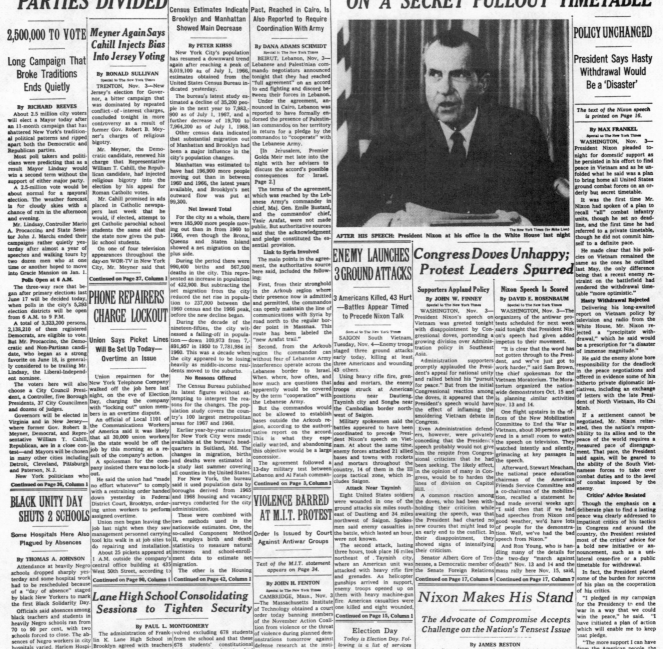

AFTER HIS SPEECH: President Nixon at his office in the White House last night

ENEMY LAUNCHES 3 GROUND ATTACKS

3 Americans Killed, 43 Hurt—Battles Appear Timed to Precede Nixon Talk

Special to The New York Times

SAIGON South Vietnam, Tuesday, Nov. 4—Enemy troops staged three ground attacks early today, killing at least three Americans and wounding 43 others.

Using heavy rifle fire, grenades and mortars, the enemy troops struck at American positions near Dautieng, Tayninh city and Songbe near the Cambodian border northwest of Saigon.

Military spokesmen said the battles appeared to have been coordinated to precede President Nixon's speech on Vietnam. At about the same time, enemy forces attacked 21 allied bases and towns with rockets and mortars throughout the country, 14 of them in the III corps tactical zone, which includes Saigon.

Attack Near Tayninh

Eight United States soldiers were wounded in one of the ground attacks six miles southeast of Dautieng and 34 miles northwest of Saigon. Spokesmen said enemy casualties in the battle, which lasted an hour, were not known.

The second attack, lasting three hours, took place 16 miles northeast of Tayninh city, where an American unit was attacked with heavy rifle fire and grenades. As helicopter gunships arrived in support, enemy troops opened up on them with heavy machine-gun fire. American casualties were one killed and eight wounded,

Continued on Page 15, Column 1

Election Day

Today is Election Day. Following is a list of services that are affected:

Public and Parochial Schools—Closed.

Parking—Alternate side regulations suspended.

Post Office—Mail will be delivered.

Stores—Most open.

Liquor Stores—Closed, along with bars, during voting hours, 6 A.M. to 9 P.M.

Banks—Closed.

Stock Exchanges—Open.

Sanitation—No regular refuse collection.

Libraries—Main reading room, information division and central circulation of the library at Fifth Avenue and 42d Street open from 9 A.M. to 10 P.M.; all branches closed except the Nathan Strauss Young Adult Library, 20 West 53d Street, open from noon to 10 P.M.

Congress Doves Unhappy; Protest Leaders Spurred

Supporters Applaud Policy

By JOHN W. FINNEY
Special to The New York Times

WASHINGTON, Nov. 3—President Nixon's speech on Vietnam was greeted tonight with disappointment by Congressional doves, portending a growing division over Administration policy in Southeast Asia.

Administration supporters promptly applauded the President's appeal for national unity and rallied behind his "pursuit for peace." But from the initial Congressional reaction among the doves, it appeared that the President's speech would have the effect of inflaming the smoldering Vietnam debate in Congress.

Even Administration defenders, however, were privately conceding that the President's speech probably would not give him the respite from Congressional criticism that he had been seeking. The likely effect, in the opinion of many in Congress, would be to harden the lines of division on Capitol Hill.

A common reaction among the doves, who had been withholding their criticism while awaiting the speech, was that the President had charted no new courses that might lead to an early end to the conflict. In their disappointment, they showed signs of intensifying their criticism.

Senator Albert Gore of Tennessee, a Democratic member of the Senate Foreign Relations

Continued on Page 17, Column 6

Nixon Speech Is Scored

By DAVID E. ROSENBAUM
Special to The New York Times

WASHINGTON, Nov. 3—The organizers of the antiwar protests scheduled for next week said tonight that President Nixon's speech had given added impetus to their movement.

"It is clear that the word has not gotten through to the President, and we've just got to work harder," said Sam Brown, the chief spokesman for the Vietnam Moratorium. The Moratorium organized the nationwide demonstrators Oct. 15 and is planning similar activities Nov. 13 and 14.

One flight upstairs in the offices of the New Mobilization Committee to End the War in Vietnam, about 30 persons gathered in a small room to watch the speech on television. They watched intently and silently, grimacing at key passages in the speech.

Afterward, Stewart Meacham, the national peace education chairman of the American Friends Service Committee and a co-chairman of the mobilization, recalled a statement he had made several weeks ago: "I said then that if we had bad speeches from Nixon and good weather, we'd have lots of people for the demonstration. Well, we've had the bad speech from Nixon."

And Ron Young, who is handling many of the details for the two-day "march against death" Nov. 13 and 14 and the mass rally here Nov. 15, said,

Continued on Page 17, Column 7

Nixon Makes His Stand

The Advocate of Compromise Accepts Challenge on the Nation's Tensest Issue

By JAMES RESTON

News Analysis

In the first nine months of his Administration, President Nixon has emphasized compromise, moderation and unity in the nation, but last night he drew the line against his Vietnam critics.

He asserted that he had a plan that "would end the war and serve the cause of peace—not just in Vietnam but in the Pacific and in the world." His was "the right way," he insisted, and he appealed to the "silent majority" of the nation to support him and his plan.

"Let us be united for peace," he said. "Let us also be united against defeat. Because let us understand — North Vietnam cannot defeat or humiliate the United States. Only Americans can do that."

So after the long debate on the war, the President has made his decision. He has been faithful to his promise not to be influenced by the peace-marchers. He supported last night the views of the Joint Chiefs of Staff. He assumed that the "majority" of the American people were with him in his plan, that not only was it right but also would succeed, if only he could get visible support at home.

In short, the President has done on Vietnam precisely what he has opposed on other policies since he came to the White House. He has raised his voice and accepted the challenge of confrontation on the most emotional issue before the nation.

When President Nixon announced his speech last month

Continued on Page 17, Column 3

NEWS INDEX

While the rallies and moratoriums against the war were raging in the United States, the war went on as usual in Vietnam. Here, an American Gunner's Mate works alongside a Vietnamese soldier aboard a river patrol boat.

Vietnamese troops wade through Vietnam's notorious mud to board a U.S. Navy patrol boat following a sweep on the Ca Mau Peninsula.

"All the News That's Fit to Print"

The New York Times

LATE CITY EDITION

Weather: Fair and continued cold today, tonight. Fair tomorrow. Temp. range: today 41-26; Saturday 47-34. Full U.S. report on Page 95.

SECTION ONE

VOL.CXIX.No.40,839
© 1969 The New York Times Company.
NEW YORK, SUNDAY, NOVEMBER 16, 1969

60¢ beyond 50-mile zone from New York City, except Long Island. 75¢ beyond 200-mile radius. Higher in air delivery cities.

50 CENTS

250,000 WAR PROTESTERS STAGE PEACEFUL RALLY IN WASHINGTON; MILITANTS STIR CLASHES LATER

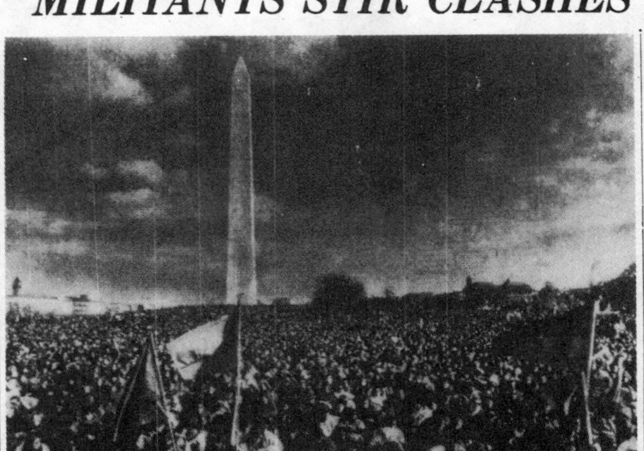

The New York Times (by Barton Silverman)

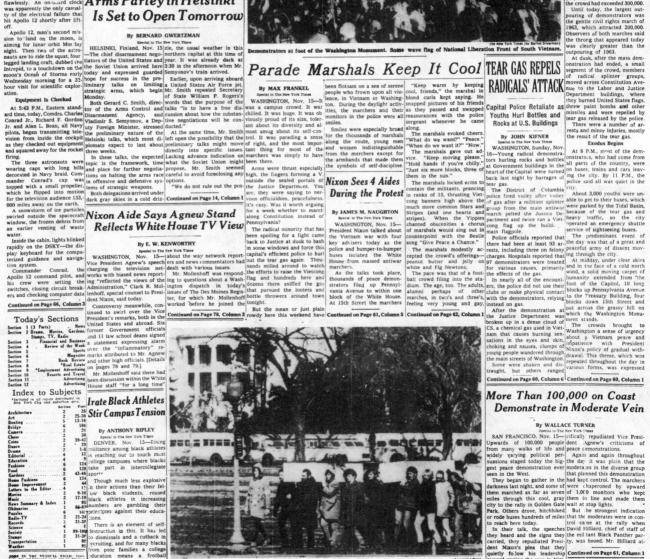

Demonstrators at foot of the Washington Monument. Some wave flag of National Liberation Front of South Vietnam.

A RECORD THRONG

Young Marchers Ask Rapid Withdrawal From Vietnam

By JOHN HERBERS

Special to The New York Times

WASHINGTON, Nov. 15—A vast throng of Americans, predominantly youthful and constituting the largest mass march in the nation's capital, demonstrated peacefully in the heart of the city today, demanding a rapid withdrawal of United States troops from Vietnam.

The District of Columbia Police Chief, Jerry Wilson, said a "moderate" estimate was that 250,000 had paraded on Pennsylvania Avenue and had attended an antiwar rally at the Washington Monument. Other city officials said aerial photographs would later show that the crowd had exceeded 300,000.

Until today, the largest outpouring of demonstrators was the gentle civil rights march of 1963, which attracted 200,000. Observers of both marches said the throng that appeared today was clearly greater than the outpouring of 1963.

At dusk, after the mass demonstration had ended, a small segment of the crowd, members of radical splinter groups, moved across Constitution Avenue to the Labor and Justice Department buildings, where they burned United States flags, threw paint bombs and other missiles and were repelled by tear gas released by the police.

There were a number of arrests and minor injuries, mostly the result of the tear gas.

Exodus Begins

At 8 P.M., most of the demonstrators, who had come from all parts of the country, were on buses, trains and cars leaving the city. By 11 P.M., the police said all was quiet in the city.

About 3,000 youths were unable to get to their buses, which were parked by the Tidal Basin, because of the tear gas and heavy traffic, so the city operated an emergency shuttle service of sightseeing buses.

The predominant event of the day was that of a great and peaceful army of dissent moving through the city.

At midday, under clear skies and in the face of a cold north wind, a solid moving carpet of humanity extended from the foot of the Capitol, 10 long blocks up Pennsylvania Avenue to the Treasury Building, four blocks down 15th Street and out across the grassy hill on which the Washington Monument stands.

The crowds brought to Washington a sense of urgency about a Vietnam peace and impatience with President Nixon's policy of gradual withdrawal. This theme, which was repeated throughout the day in various forms, was expressed

Continued on Page 60, Column 1

Parade Marshals Keep It Cool

By MAX FRANKEL

Special to The New York Times

WASHINGTON, Nov. 15—It was a campus crowd. It was chilled. It was huge. It was obviously proud of its size, tolerant about its diversity and almost smug about its self-control. It was parading a sense of right, and the most important thing for most of the marchers was simply to have been there.

Arms were thrust especially high, the fingers forming a V, outside the sealed portals of the Justice Department. You see, they were saying to nervous officialdom, peacefulness, it's easy. Was it worth arguing for a week whether to march along Constitution instead of Pennsylvania?

The radical minority that has been spoiling for a fight came back to Justice at dusk to bash in some windows and force this capital's efficient police to hurl out the tear gas again. Thousands milled around to watch the efforts to raise the Vietcong flag and hundreds here and dozens there sniffed the gas that pursued the looters and bottle throwers around town tonight.

But the mean or just plain rowdy here this weekend have been flotsam on a sea of serene people who frown upon all violence, in Vietnam or Washington. During the daylight activities, the marchers and their monitors in the police were all smiles.

Smiles were especially broad for the thousands of marshals along the route, young men and women indistinguishable from the marchers except for the armbands that made them the symbols of self-discipline.

"Keep warm by keeping cool, friends," the marshal in blond curls kept saying. He snapped pictures of his friends as they passed and swapped reassurances with the police sergeant whenever he came along.

The marshals evoked cheers. "What do we want?" "Peace." "When do we want it?" "Now."

The marshals gave out advice. "Keep moving please." "Hold hands if you're chilly." "Just six more blocks, three of them in the sun."

The marshals locked arms to contain the militants, prancing in ranks of 15, thrusting Vietcong banners high above the much more common Stars and Stripes (and one hearts and stripes). When the Yippies chanted obscenities a chorus of marshals would sing out in counterpoint with the Beatle song "Give Peace a Chance."

The marshals modestly accepted the crowd's offerings—peanut butter and jelly on white and Fig Newtons.

The pace was that of a football crowd filing into the stadium. The age, too. The adults, alumni perhaps of other marches, in two's and three's, feeling very young and gay,

Continued on Page 62, Column 1

Nixon Sees 4 Aides During the Protest

By JAMES M. NAUGHTON

Special to The New York Times

WASHINGTON, Nov. 15—President Nixon talked about the Vietnam war with four key advisers today as the police and bumper-to-bumper buses isolated the White House from massed antiwar marchers.

As the talks took place, thousands of peace demonstrators filed up Pennsylvania Avenue to within one block of the White House. At 15th Street the marchers

Continued on Page 61, Column 5

TEAR GAS REPELS RADICALS' ATTACK

Capital Police Retaliate as Youths Hurl Bottles and Rocks at U.S. Buildings

By JOHN KIFNER

Special to The New York Times

WASHINGTON, Sunday, Nov. 16—Young radical demonstrators hurling rocks and bottles at Government buildings in the heart of the Capital were turned back last night by barrages of tear gas.

The District of Columbia police fired volley after volley of gas after a militant splinter group from the main antiwar march pelted the Justice Department and twice ran a Vietcong flag up the building's main flagpole.

Police officials reported that there had been at least 93 arrests, including three on felony charges. Hospitals reported that 97 demonstrators were treated for various causes, primarily the effects of the gas.

In nearly all of the encounters, the police did not use their clubs or make physical contact with the demonstrators, relying instead on gas.

After the demonstration at the Justice Department was broken up in a dense cloud of CS, a chemical gas used in Vietnam that causes burning sensations in the eyes and skin, choking and nausea, clumps of young people wandered through the main streets of Washington.

Some were shaken and distraught, but others ranged

Continued on Page 60, Column 6

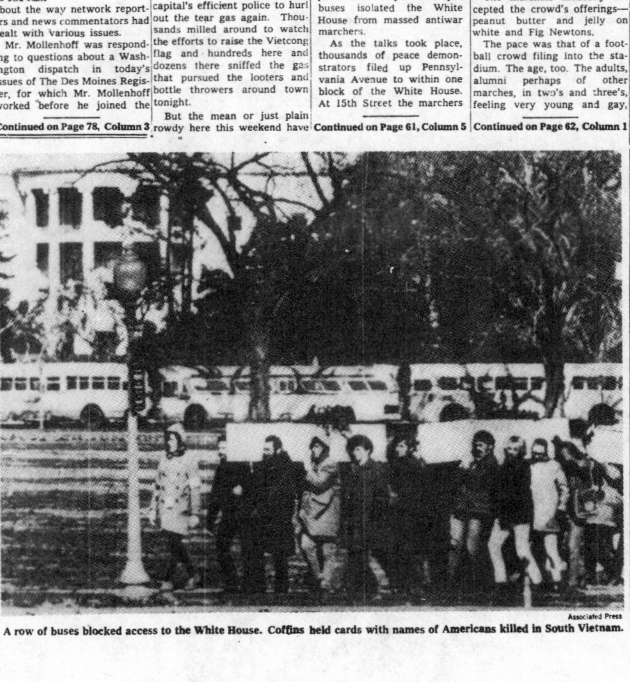

Associated Press

A row of buses blocked access to the White House. Coffins held cards with names of Americans killed in South Vietnam.

More Than 100,000 on Coast Demonstrate in Moderate Vein

By WALLACE TURNER

Special to The New York Times

SAN FRANCISCO, Nov. 15—Upwards of 100,000 people from many walks of life and widely varying political persuasions staged today the biggest peace demonstration ever seen in the West.

They began to gather in the darkness last night, and some of them marched as far as seven miles through this cool, gray city to the rally in Golden Gate Park. Others drove, hitchhiked or rode buses hundreds of miles to reach here today.

In their talk, the speeches they heard and the signs they carried, they repudiated President Nixon's plea that they quietly follow his leadership toward ending the war in Vietnam. Many of them also specifically repudiated Vice President Agnew's criticisms of peace demonstrations.

Again and again throughout the day it was plain that the moderates in the diverse group that planned this demonstration had kept control. The marchers were chaperoned by upward of 1,000 monitors who kept them in line and made them wait at stop lights.

But the strongest indication that the moderates were in control came at the rally when David Hilliard, chief of staff of the militant Black Panther party, was booed. Mr. Hilliard at-

Continued on Page 61, Column 1

PARK AVE. — Midtown. Luxury terraced 6 rm Co-op Rent or Sale 684-1672 ...

APOLLO 12 SWINGS ONTO A WIDER PATH TOWARD THE MOON

Course Correction Is Made to Fulfill Requirements for Landing Wednesday

CRAFT PASSES MIDPOINT

Color TV Beamed to Earth —Clock Only Casualty of Power Lapse in Lift-Off

By JOHN NOBLE WILFORD

Special to The New York Times

HOUSTON, Nov. 15—With a short blast of its rocket, the Apollo 12 spacecraft swung out tonight on a wider, slower and somewhat riskier course toward the moon.

The three moonbound astronauts moved smoothly beyond the midpoint in their outward journey, transmitting a color telecast to the earth, checking out spacecraft systems and generally relaxing after their tense, rain-soaked launching yesterday at Cape Kennedy, Fla.

Flight controllers here reported that the 96,000-pound spacecraft was functioning almost flawlessly. An on-board clock was apparently the only casualty of the electrical failure that hit Apollo 12 shortly after lift-off.

Apollo 12, man's second mission to land on the moon, is aiming for lunar orbit Monday night. Then two of the astronauts are to ride the squat, four legged landing craft, dubbed the Intrepid, to a touchdown on the moon's Ocean of Storms early Wednesday morning for a 32-hour visit for scientific exploration.

Equipment Is Checked

At 5:43 P.M., Eastern standard time, today, Comdrs. Charles Conrad Jr., Richard F. Gordon Jr. and Alan L. Bean, all Navy pilots, began transmitting television from inside the cockpit as they checked out equipment and squared away for the rocket firing.

The three astronauts were wearing caps with long bills decorated in Navy braid. Commander Conrad's cap was topped with a small propeller, which he flipped into motion for the television audience 133,000 miles away on the earth.

A snowstorm of ice particles swirled outside the spacecraft window, the frozen debris from an earlier venting of waste water.

Inside the cabin, lights blinked rapidly on the DSKY—the display keyboard for the computerized guidance and navigation system.

Commander Conrad, the Apollo 12 command pilot, and his crew were setting the switches, closing circuit breakers and checking computer data

Continued on Page 66, Column 3

City's New Master Plan Calls Middle Class Vital

Asserts 'Crucial Challenge' Is to Keep Whites While Improving the Lot of Poor Blacks and Puerto Ricans

The "crucial challenge" facing the city is its ability to retain its largely white middle class, while elevating low-income blacks and Puerto Ricans, according to the first volume of the long-awaited Master Plan for New York.

The 90,000-word installment of the "Plan for New York City," made public yesterday by the City Planning Commission, proposes the strengthening of the city's role as a national center with a goal of "several hundred thousand more office workers in the business districts in the next 10 years."

Donald H. Elliott, the chairman of the City Planning Commission, described the nonbinding Master Plan as a "realistic and pragmatic" guide to urban policy for "the next five or ten years."

The comprehensive document discusses a broad range of city problems and attempts to outline a development strategy for dealing with them.

It envisions a city in which electrically powered taxicabs operate, private cars are restricted from some business streets, more recreational facilities are built to join housing and piers on the waterfront, and a new rail tunnel runs under the Hudson.

It urges more training and jobs for the underemployed, classes for 3-year-olds, a network of neighborhood medical services and mixed residential and industrial buildings.

The plan, much revised from portions of a first draft obtained by The New York Times last February, voices hope on some problems, pessimism on others.

For example, the plan states: "The plain fact is that no one yet knows how to make a ghetto school work." It also warns that the city's parochial schools are in "serious financial difficulties," and maintains that the city must choose between subsidizing them or ex-

Continued on Page 84, Column 3

Arms Parley in Helsinki Is Set to Open Tomorrow

By BERNARD GWERTZMAN

Special to The New York Times

HELSINKI, Finland, Nov. 15—The chief disarmament negotiators of the United States and the Soviet Union arrived here today and expressed guarded hope for success in the preliminary talks on limiting strategic arms, which begin Monday.

Both Gerard C. Smith, director of the Arms Control and Disarmament Agency, and Vladimir S. Semyonov, a Deputy Foreign Minister, stressed the preliminary nature of the Helsinki talks, which most diplomats expect to last about three weeks.

In these talks, the expected topic is the framework, time and place for further negotiations on halting the arms race in offensive and defensive systems of strategic weapons.

Both delegations arrived under dark gray skies in a cold drizzle, the usual weather in this northern capital at this time of year. It was already dark at 3:30 in the afternoon when Mr. Semyonov's train arrived.

Earlier, upon arriving aboard a United States Air Force jet, Mr. Smith repeated Secretary of State William P. Rogers's words that the purpose of the talks "is to have a free discussion about how the substantive negotiations will be conducted."

At the same time, Mr. Smith left open the possibility that the preliminary talks might move directly into specific issues. Lacking advance indication on what the Soviet Union might propose, Mr. Smith seemed careful to avoid foreclosing any options.

"We do not rule out the pos-

Continued on Page 14, Column 1

Nixon Aide Says Agnew Stand Reflects White House TV View

By E. W. KENWORTHY

Special to The New York Times

WASHINGTON, Nov. 15—Vice President Agnew's speech charging the television networks with biased news reporting "reflected the views of the Administration," Clark R. Mollenhoff, special counsel to President Nixon, said today.

Controversy meanwhile, continued to swirl over the Vice President's remarks, both in the United States and abroad. Six former Government officials and 11 law school deans signed a statement expressing alarm over the "inflammatory" remarks attributed to Mr. Agnew and other high officials. [Details on pages 78 and 79.]

Mr. Mollenhoff said there had been discussion within the White House staff "for a long time" about the way network reporters and news commentators had dealt with various issues.

Mr. Mollenhoff was responding to questions about a Washington dispatch in today's issues of The Des Moines Register, for which Mr. Mollenhoff worked before he joined the

Continued on Page 78, Column 3

Irate Black Athletes Stir Campus Tension

By ANTHONY RIPLEY

Special to The New York Times

DENVER, Nov. 15—Rising militancy among black athletes is reaching out to touch most college campuses where blacks take part in intercollegiate sports.

Though much less explosive in their actions than their fellow black students, roused black athletes in increasing numbers are gambling their principles against their educations.

There is an element of self-destruction in this. It has led to dismissals and a cutback in recruiting, and for many blacks from poor families a college education means a football

Continued on Page 85, Column 1

Today's Sections

Index to Subjects

*Included in all copies distributed in New York City and suburban area.

JOBS IN THE MEDICAL FIELD. Openings for professional and non-professional workers appear today in The New York Times. See Section 4 and 9 (Section 9 distributed in New York and vicinity.)

"All the News That's Fit to Print"

The New York Times

LATE CITY EDITION

Weather: Cloudy with drizzle today; cloudy tonight. Rain tomorrow. Temp. range: today 38-32; Wed. 41-34. Full U.S. report on Page 94.

VOL. CXIX..No. 40,962 — © 1970 The New York Times Company. — NEW YORK, THURSDAY, MARCH 19, 1970 — 10 CENTS

SIHANOUK REPORTED OUT IN A COUP BY HIS PREMIER; CAMBODIA AIRPORTS SHUT

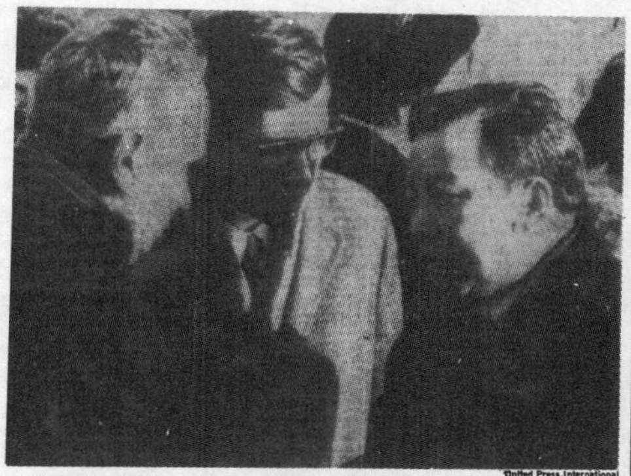

United Press International

Soviet Premier Aleksei N. Kosygin bidding good-by to Prince Norodom Sihanouk, Cambodian Chief of State, who ended a five-day visit to Moscow and was on way to Peking.

PRINCE IS ABROAD

He Hints At Forming An Exile Regime—Reaches Peking

By HENRY KAMM

Special to The New York Times

BANGKOK, Thailand, March 18—Prince Norodom Sihanouk, Chief of State of Cambodia, was overthrown today in his absence, the Pnompenh radio announced.

The Southeast Asian country was cut off from the world, except for the broadcasts. The nation's two commercial airports were closed to all traffic.

Power has apparently been seized by Lieut. Gen. Lon Nol, the Premier and Defense Minister, and the First Deputy Premier, Prince Sisowath Sirik Matak, a cousin of Prince Sihanouk.

Cheng Heng, President of the National Assembly, has been designated as interim Chief of State, pending elections, the radio announced. Informed Pnompenh sources considered him a figure of negligible political stature.

Leaves Moscow

When the announcement of his overthrow was made Prince Sihanouk, who is 47, was in Moscow where he had arrived from Paris five days ago, and was preparing to depart for Peking.

[Prince Sihanouk arrived in Peking Thursday morning from Moscow. In the Soviet capital, the Prince acted as if he were still Chief of State but spoke of the possibility of forming a government in exile. Page 16.]

The announcement came after a week of anti-Communist rioting, reportedly officially inspired, in which the embassies

Continued on Page 16, Column 3

Coup Surprises U.S.; War Spread Feared

By MAX FRANKEL

Special to The New York Times

WASHINGTON, March 18 — The United States Government appears to have been surprised by the overthrow of Prince Norodom Sihanouk. It is not yet prepared to write him off as a force in Cambodian politics, and has not yet decided how the reported coup d'état may relate to other fast-moving developments in Indochina.

With the continuing threat of a North Vietnamese military advance across Laos, there is great concern about any further expansion of the Vietnam war in Cambodian territory.

Although the organizers of the coup, led by Lieut. Gen. Lon Nol, are regarded as friendly to the United States, their accession to complete power

Continued on Page 17, Column 1

Soviet Troops and Missiles Reported to Be in Egypt

A large number of Soviet troops and modern SAM-3 antiaircraft missiles have arrived in the United Arab Republic in the last week, according to information reaching here from reliable diplomatic sources in Cairo.

The missiles, designed to cope with low-flying enemy aircraft, are rapidly being put into position at the port city of Alexandria, at an air base west of Cairo and elsewhere in Egypt, it was reported.

Soviet soldiers have been observed driving trucks bearing the missiles on the desert highway linking Cairo with Alexandria.

For the last week, according to the diplomatic sources, the highway has been closed to foreigners at intervals, and there have been rumors that it may be closed indefinitely to Western residents in the United Arab Republic.

The number of Soviet troops arriving in Egypt with the missiles, estimated from 1,500 upward, suggested to diplomatic observers that the Russians would operate the antiaircraft weapons and the complex radar support facilities.

Concern has been voiced about Soviet reaction if Israeli aircraft attacked the new missile sites, killing or wounding Russians. The Soviet Union might then feel compelled, it has been said, to send fighter

Continued on Page 3, Column 1

SONGMY DATA LAG LAID TO 2 GROUPS

Failure to Report Attributed to Division and Advisers

By WILLIAM BEECHER

Special to The New York Times

WASHINGTON, March 18—The Pentagon investigation into the alleged mass killing of South Vietnamese civilians at Songmy has indicated an apparent failure of two separate Army command channels to provide any word of the incident, highly placed sources said today.

The charges brought yesterday against 14 Army officers are based on allegations that key officers in the Americal Division, whose units participated in the Songmy operation two years ago, failed to report the killings to higher headquarters. But they are also based on allegations that two other American officers, advisers to the South Vietnamese and in no way connected with the division, failed to notify their superiors of a Vietnamese report about the same event.

The latter report, made more than three weeks after American troops swept the

Continued on Page 5, Column 3

U.N. COUNCIL, 14-0, ASSAILS RHODESIA

Resolution Drops Demand for Use of Force That Led to Earlier Veto by U.S.

By SAM POPE BREWER

Special to The New York Times

UNITED NATIONS, N. Y., March 18—The Security Council today approved, 14 to 0, a compromise resolution condemning the white-minority Government of Rhodesia.

The compromise — adopted after a stronger resolution was defeated last night by vetoes of the United States and Britain—strengthens earlier United Nations sanctions against the regime of Ian D. Smith, which declared Rhodesia's independence from Britain in 1965.

It demands that all member nations "immediately sever all diplomatic, consular, trade, military and other relations" with the regime, "terminate any representation that they may maintain" and "immediately interrupt any means of transportation to and from Southern Rhodesia."

The compromise document — prepared by Max Jakobson of Finland and revised in conference with Lord Caradon of Britain and the five African and Asian sponsors of last night's resolution — abandoned the two key points that had led to the vetoes.

It dropped the demand for

Continued on Page 8, Column 1

Evacuation Started At Key Laotian Base

By The Associated Press

VIENTIANE, Laos, March 18—A limited withdrawal of civilians and soldiers from army headquarters at Long Tieng began today after the United States-supported base nearby at Sam Thong fell to 2,000 North Vietnamese troops.

Informed sources saw the advance on Sam Thong as the first significant North Vietnamese push south of the Plaine des Jarres since the Geneva agreement in 1962 set up Laos as a neutral state.

[In Washington, a State Department spokesman said the United States considered the situation "serious."]

Sam Thong, 90 miles north of Vientiane, is 15 miles southwest of the Plaine des Jarres, which was recaptured by the

Continued on Page 18, Column 4

ABORTION REFORM APPROVED, 31-26, BY STATE SENATE

Bill Removes All Restrictions —Prospect for Passage in Assembly Called Good

By BILL KOVACH

Special to The New York Times

ALBANY, March 18—The State Senate, after five straight hours of emotional debate, today voted 31-to-26 to replace the state's 19th-century abortion law with one of the most liberal measures in the country.

The bill, which would allow a pregnant woman and her doctor to decide the question of abortion, now goes to the Assembly, where it is expected to be debated next week.

The measure contained no time limits on when abortions could be performed, no residency requirements or restrictions on how many times a woman could obtain an abortion—all points that had been raised by opponents of the bill.

Assembly supporters, many of whom crowded into the Senate chamber jammed with spectators for the debate, which was described as "one of the most historic" of the Senate's history, are optimistic of its chances in that chamber.

Reformers in the Assembly have carried the battle unsuccessfully for the last five years and believe passage by the Senate—which is normally the more conservative house—is the key to final success.

Signature Likely

Governor Rockefeller has repeatedly called for reform and is considered likely to sign the bill should it reach his desk.

[In Maryland, the House of Delegates approved a bill to repeal the state's laws regulating abortions. The measure now goes to the State Senate. Page 38.]

The present New York State law, one of the most restrictive in the country, permits abortions only to save the mother's life and reformers have argued that it favors the rich who can obtain psychiatric reports to support a legal abortion, and forces the poor to resort to "butchers who illegally ply the trade" of abortions.

Senate galleries were packed with spectators and a wall of staff members—mostly women—circled the Senate floor, pressing against the backs of the rear row of Senate seats through the long hours of debate.

The glaring lights of television—permitted to record the debate under a waiver of Senate rules barring photographers—filtered through clouds of smoke, but the stuffy chamber was orderly through the long

Continued on Page 39, Column 1

Traffic Ban on Two City Streets Set in April 22 Pollution Protest

By DAVID BIRD

Mayor Lindsay said yesterday that as part of a nationwide effort on April 22 to dramatize damage to the environment all traffic would be banned from noon to midnight on 14th Street from Second Avenue to Seventh Avenue and from noon to 2 P.M. on Fifth Avenue between 59th Street and 14th Street.

Even crossing the two streets will be banned, which means that during the two-hour ban on Fifth Avenue, traffic crossing Manhattan will have to use streets north of 59th and south of 14th.

During the 12-hour ban on 14th Street, no north-south traffic will be able to cross that street between Second and Seventh Avenues.

The Mayor announced the plan at a crowded City Hall news conference.

As word of it spread, many business groups expressed dismay and shock, but the idea was welcomed as a "major victory for the people" by the Environmental Action Coalition, a group that is coordinating efforts to protect the environment. The coalition had requested street closings.

The closing of the streets on a Wednesday is designed partly

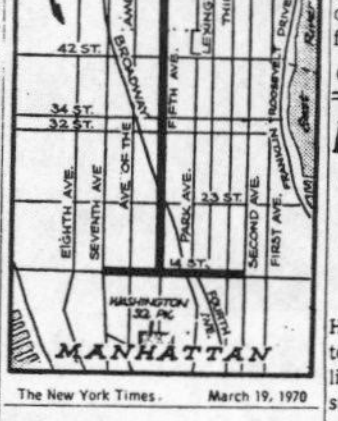

The New York Times — March 19, 1970

to show what the city would be like without automotive traffic, which is said to account for more than half the city's air pollution. It will also give the Environmental Action Coalition a traffic-free space to present demonstrations against other environmental problems from power plants to excess packaging that creates a garbage problem.

For some time the city administration had been uncertain how closely it should be involved with the April 22 environment demonstration,

Continued on Page 95, Column 3

MAIL SERVICE HERE IS PARALYZED BY POSTAL SYSTEM'S FIRST STRIKE; BUSINESS BEGINNING TO FEEL PINCH

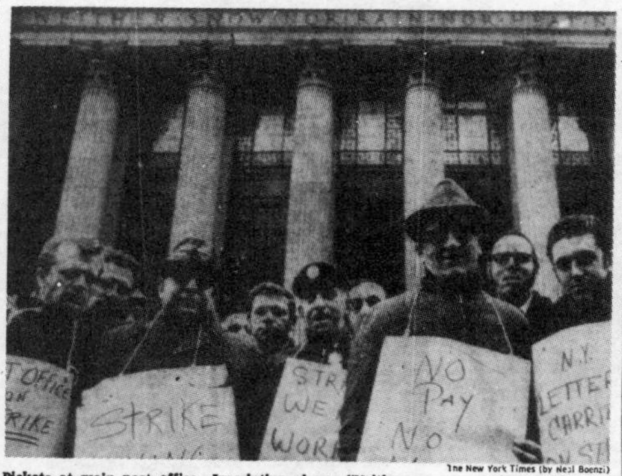

The New York Times (by Neal Boenzi)

Pickets at main post office. Inscription above: "Neither snow nor rain nor heat nor gloom of night stays these couriers from the swift completion of their appointed rounds."

INJUNCTION DEFIED

Tie-Up Is Spreading—L.I., Connecticut and Jersey Are Affected

By HOMER BIGART

Mail service in the metropolitan area was paralyzed yesterday by a strike of postal employes seeking higher wages.

The strike, the first in the history of the national postal system, was in defiance of a Federal Court injunction.

The area affected by the strike was growing last night as other locals joined those in New York City and on Long Island, the first to walk out.

By midnight, locals of the National Association of Letter Carriers had voted to strike in Paterson, Jersey City, North Bergen, Hackensack and Passaic, all in New Jersey; in parts of Westchester County; all of Rockland County and part of Orange County, and in Stamford, Conn.

Walk Out Tomorrow

The Hackensack strike will not begin until tomorrow, however, according to William Taggart, president of the local there.

In Passaic, John Alfieri resigned as president of the local after the vote to strike today. He said he had asked the carriers not to strike, and when they voted to go out anyway, he resigned.

A number of other locals in the area are scheduled to take strike votes today.

To prevent an avalanche of mail from piling up in unmanned post offices here, the Government ordered an embargo on all mail for the affected area.

Some locals said they would honor the Federal Court injunction, but there were strong indications that the majority of the striking workers would stay out despite the court order and that the tie-up would continue for several days at least.

Mail Not Collected

"The men will defy any injunction—they'll stay out until hell freezes over," said Herman Sandbank, executive vice president of the striking union.

Bills, dividend checks, income-tax returns, advertising brochures, credit cards, bank statements, sales flyers and personal mail lay uncollected in thousands of mail drops as letter carriers struck for the first time in the system's 195-year history.

The pay for carriers now ranges from $6,176 to a maximum of $8,442 after 21 years. Postal union leaders have estimated that 7 per cent of their members here are receiving welfare aid.

The embargo once the strike went into effect was ordered

Continued on Page 52, Column 7

U.S. JUDGES TOLD TO DISCLOSE FEES

Public Reports of Gifts Also Required in a New Policy Adopted by Conference

By FRED P. GRAHAM

Special to The New York Times

WASHINGTON, March 18—Federal judges will be required to make semiannual public reports of fees for outside services, gifts and other possible conflicts of interest.

The new reporting system was adopted yesterday by the Judicial Conference of the United States and announced today by its chairman, Chief Justice Warren E. Burger.

Under the new system, the more than 500 Federal judges below Supreme Court level will be required to file their first disclosures June 30. The reports will be placed on public file in the court where each judge sits, in the office of his judicial circuit and in Washington.

The procedure replaces a plan adopted last June at the urging of Chief Justice Earl Warren after Associate Justice Abe Fortas resigned under criticism for having accepted a $20,000 fee from the Wolfson Family Foundation.

Under the earlier procedure, the judges would have been re-

Continued on Page 29, Column 4

Burns Indicates Reserve Is Easing Curb on Money

By EDWIN L. DALE Jr.

Special to The New York Times

WASHINGTON, March 18—Arthur F. Burns, chairman of the Federal Reserve Board, disclosed to Congress today that the Reserve had already moved to relax somewhat its extremely restrictive monetary policy and to permit a resumption of growth in the nation's money supply.

Mr. Burns said it was his view that present circumstances called for a growth in money—currency and demand deposits—of at least 2 per cent, though he disclosed no details of exactly what the Reserve had decided to aim for in this or other monetary measures. Until the last few weeks, there had been no growth at all in the money supply since last June.

Testifying before the Senate Banking and Currency Committee, Mr. Burns presented what he called a "cautiously optimistic" assessment of the economy. After examining individual sectors from automobiles to defense spending, he concluded that, "while a sluggish pace of economic activity may continue a while longer, it seems reasonable to expect a resumption of economic growth in th relatively near future."

No Doubt on Point

He also concluded that, "while there is little basis fo expecting an end to inflation this year, there is reason to expect substantial progress in slowing the rate of price increase."

Mr. Burns's disclosure that the restrictive monetary policy pursued for a year had been relaxed somewhat followed only a day after President Nixon announced a modest switch in the Government's fiscal, or budget, policy in the form of a release of $1.5-billion in construction funds, previously frozen. The

Continued on Page 69 Column 1

Liberals Win Study Of House Seniority

By MARJORIE HUNTER

Special to The New York Times

WASHINGTON, March 18 — House Democrats yielded today to demands of reform-minded liberals and agreed upon a study of the 60-year-old Congressional seniority system.

However, liberals pressing for prompt changes in what they term "the aging establishment" suffered a setback when the party caucus voted to delay the deadline for the study findings until after the Congressional elections in November.

The more militant reformers protested that the delay had "torpedoed the chances for reform." Some of them threatened to seek reform by other routes, possibly even by deserting their own leadership and helping

Continued on Page 20, Column 1

CITY'S ECONOMY SAPPED BY STRIKE

Brokers, Bankers, Lawyers and Others Are Hard Hit by the Postal Tie-Up

By ROBERT J. COLE

The city's economic vitality was slowly sapped yesterday as the impact of the postal strike was felt in brokerage houses, banks, law offices, department stores and thousands of other businesses.

Businesses of every variety, from retail stores to airlines, were already feeling the strike's effects and worrying seriously about the situation that would develop if the mail tie-up persisted.

At Macy's New York, David L. Yunich, the president, said that "nondelivery of the mails seriously affects every aspect of business," and called the strike a "severe hardship."

Gimbels controller, Ralph Waite, said the tie-up would create "an alarming jam" for the store.

Abraham & Straus said, through a spokesman: "We've never been faced with any problem like this. We don't exactly know what to do."

Store Shipments Hurt

The cut-off of mail delivery affects not only the stores' mail-order business but the ability to fill customers' demands for merchandise that is shipped to the stores by mail. The J. C. Penney Company said that the strike would hamper the company in replenishing its stock but would not, thus far, affect its catalog business, which is operated in Atlanta and Milwaukee.

Even at Tiffany & Co. the possible effects of the strike were being considered yesterday by executives of the concern. Walter Hoving, president of the company, which usually receives about 500 mail orders and $300,000 daily in checks, said: 'This is going to tie us up very seriously if it lasts

Continued on Page 52, Column 4

Abram Enters Race For Seat in Senate

By CLAYTON KNOWLES

Morris B. Abram entered the United States Senate race in New York yesterday with a pledge to "dare to dream and plan" for a better America.

The former president of Brandeis University became the 10th Democrat to declare his candidacy for statewide office. But most of the party's attention was focused on a man who may become the 11th—Arthur J. Goldberg.

Mr. Goldberg continued his discussions with party leaders, but said in an interview late last night that he had no statement to make about a possible candidacy for Governor or Senator.

Mr. Abram pictured Americans as part of "a society in peril" and promised to devote

Continued on Page 30, Column 1

NEWS INDEX

"All the News That's Fit to Print"

The New York Times

LATE CITY EDITION

Weather: Fair today; increasing cloudiness tonight. Rain tomorrow. Temp. range: today 55-38; Saturday 56-41. Full U.S. report on Page 91.

SECTION ONE

VOL. CXIX . . No. 40,979 NEW YORK, SUNDAY, APRIL 5, 1970

60¢ beyond 50-mile zone from New York City, except Long Island. 75¢ beyond 200-mile radius. Higher in air delivery cities.

50 CENTS

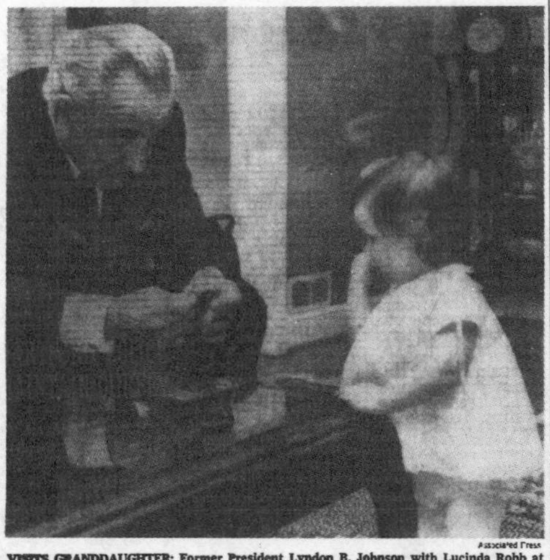

Associated Press

VISITS GRANDDAUGHTER: Former President Lyndon B. Johnson with Lucinda Robb at her Arlington, Va., home yesterday. He and Mrs. Johnson are in Washington to attend a wedding and are scheduled to go to church at White House with President Nixon today.

EXTENSIVE DELAYS ARE FEARED TODAY IN AIRPORT TIE-UP

Volpe Sees 'Breakthrough' as 40 Controllers Return to Work in Cleveland

By EDWARD HUDSON

Aviation officials warned air travelers yesterday of probable extensive delays today—the end of the Easter holiday period—as a result of the continuing 12-day work stoppage by "sick" air traffic controllers.

In Washington, Secretary of Transportation John A. Volpe said last night that 40 controllers who had been absent during the walkout returned to work at the Cleveland air traffic center for the 4 P.M.-to-midnight shift yesterday.

Mr. Volpe called their return a "significant breakthrough" in the dispute. A Federal District Court judge in Cleveland was said to have threatened stiff fines against controllers who did not report yesterday.

A spokesman for the Federal Aviation Administration's Eastern Regional office here said that airlines were expected to operate at near-maximum schedules to accommodate college students returning to school and other vacationers.

Delays are expected as a result of F.A.A. restrictions on air traffic flow at peak hours—a temporary measure designed to ease the demand on air traffic control centers and airport towers.

Heavy Volume Expected

"Sunday afternoon and evening should see extensive delays in and out of New York airports," the official said.

A spokesman for Eastern Airlines said a heavy volume of travelers returning to New York from Florida and Caribbean resorts was expected and that the line planned to run flights from these areas into the early hours tomorrow if necessary to accommodate those who had reserved seats.

There were delays of up to an hour on outbound flights in the morning yesterday at major airports in the metropolitan area. Inbound flights were delayed 15 minutes. The F.A.A. reported few delays by midafternoon. Saturday is normally a relatively light day for air travel.

The absent controllers, members of the Professional Air Traffic Controllers Organization, have tied up much of the country's air transport network

Continued on Page 66, Column 4

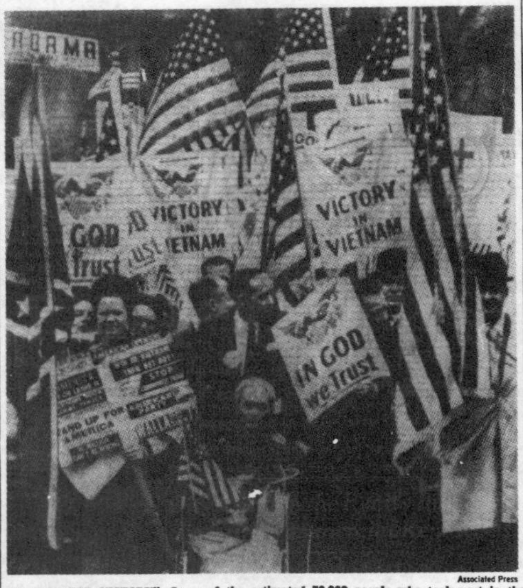

Associated Press

"MARCH FOR VICTORY": Some of the estimated 50,000 people who took part in the parade advocating victory in Vietnam as they assembled in Washington yesterday.

HEAVIEST CLASH SINCE NOVEMBER REPORTED AT DMZ

South Vietnamese Forces on Full Alert at Reports Danang Faces Attacks

SAIGON'S LOSSES HIGH

Number of Dead Put at 319 During 4 Days of Battles —U.S. Deaths Are 88

By The Associated Press

SAIGON, South Vietnam, Sunday, April 5—The allied commands reported yesterday the heaviest fighting involving American troops along the demilitarized zone in nearly five months and new clashes near the Cambodian border.

South Vietnamese forces in and around Danang, South Vietnam's second largest city, were reported on full alert, and officials said United States forces had "heightened their vigilance." These actions were taken following a report in Danang that Hanoi radio had broadcast threats of an impending attack on the city.

It was disclosed too that the nationwide enemy attacks launched four days ago had dealt a much sharper blow to South Vietnamese forces than to those of the United States.

Losses Twice as Great

Government losses have been more than double the American casualties, and several South Vietnamese units have suffered serious setbacks.

Allied communiqués listed 319 Government troops as having been killed and 931 wounded, compared with 88 Americans killed and 469 wounded. About 200 Vietnamese civilians are said to have died in the wave of shellings and ground attacks.

The fighting along the demilitarized zone was centered four miles southwest of Conthien and a mile south of the 17th Parallel, which divides North Vietnam and South Vietnam. Reports were that six Americans had been killed and 40 wounded in one eight-hour battle.

This was the heaviest fighting in the region since last Nov. 14, when 197 North Vietnamese troops and 14 Americans were killed in a day-long clash, the United States command said.

Battle Near Cambodia

South Vietnamese armored cavalry troops clashed with North Vietnamese forces along the foot of Coto Mountain, also called Superstition Mountain, in the Seven Mountains region of Chaudoc Province near the Cambodian border.

The Government forces, backed by allied bombers and artillery, asserted they had killed 23 enemy soldiers. South Vietnamese losses were put at 16 killed and 35 wounded.

In another area of the province, where the attacks began three days before they escalated to national scale, heavy shelling of the Government's Chilang training camp was said

Continued on Page 9, Column 1

Atlantic Avenue Renewal Stirs Dispute in Brooklyn

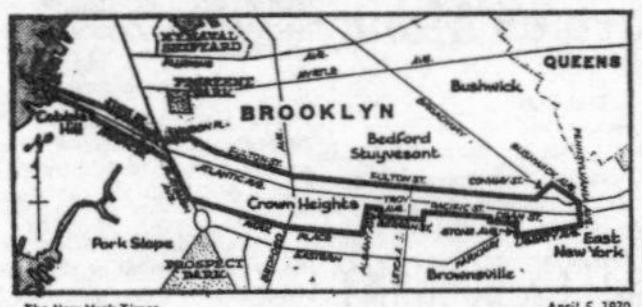

The New York Times April 5, 1970

Area involved in proposed Atlantic Avenue Authority

By PAUL L. MONTGOMERY

An obscure bill for the rehabilitation of Atlantic Avenue that went through the State Senate last week with barely a ripple had residents and legislators from Brooklyn Heights and surrounding communities on the battlements yesterday.

The bill, sponsored by legislators from Bedford-Stuyvesant with technical help from Governor Rockefeller, seeks to create an Atlantic Avenue Development Authority under community control. Its main purpose, the sponsors say, is to attract mortgage investments for deteriorating housing in the area.

However, residents in the landmark areas at the western end of the avenue fear that the plan is a mask for building a cross-Brooklyn expressway through their homes. Community groups from Brooklyn Heights, Cobble Hill, Boerum Hill and Park Slope say they were not consulted about the plan, nor was the City planning Commission or the Landmarks Preservation Commission.

As originally drafted, the bill would have created a 29-member authority having exclusive control over demolition, construction, rehabilitation and transportation access in a five-mile swath across Brooklyn from New York Harbor to the Interboro Parkway.

Among the authority's prerogatives as originally proposed were powers to condemn any building, purchase any property or relocate any public facility it desired in the designated area.

When community groups outside the Bedford-Stuyvesant, Crown Heights and Brownsville areas of the project learned of the bill after its passage by the State Senate on Tuesday, an immediate outcry arose.

To these groups, the proposed area of the authority looked suspiciously like a superhighway route. Many recalled the two-year battle with city and state officials over the proposed Cross-Brooklyn Expressway and Linear City from Long Island to the Verrazano Narrows Bridge. That plan was dropped last year in the face of widespread community opposition.

State Senator Waldaba Stewart, Democrat of Bedford-

Continued on Page 67, Column 1

CARSWELL BACKED BY 57 U.S. JUDGES

But 8 in His Circuit Do Not Sign Telegram—Senate Will Vote Tomorrow

By JAMES T. WOOTEN

Special to The New York Times

ATLANTA, April 4 — Fifty-seven United States District judges in the South have formally endorsed President Nixon's nomination of G. Harrold Carswell to the United States Supreme Court.

Their brief telegram describing Judge Carswell as "well qualified" was released in Washington by the White House today. It has been the subject of speculation here in the South for the last week.

Informed sources said an endorsement campaign in the United States Fifth Judicial Circuit was organized by District Judge Daniel H. Thomas, of Mobile, Ala., a judge of conservative persuasions with a record of numerous reversals in civil rights cases.

The telegram was signed by 50 of the 58 active, sitting district judges in the circuit in which Judge Carswell serves,

Continued on Page 29, Column 1

Hijacked Airliner Returns To Tokyo With 4 Aboard

By TAKASHI OKA

Special to The New York Times

TOKYO, Sunday, April 5—Yodo, the Japan Air Line jet that was hijacked to North Korea, came home this morning. The Boeing 727 stopped at Gate 18 at Haneda Airport here at 9:09 A.M., 121 hours and 34 minutes after it had been hijacked by nine leftist students on a routine flight from here to Fukuoka.

Aboard the plane this morning were three crew members and Shinjiro Yamamura, Japan's Deputy Minister of Transportation, who boarded the plane in Seoul, South Korea, as a hostage in place of the 99 passengers and four stewardesses released by the hijackers Friday afternoon.

At the controls was 47-year-old Capt. Shinji Ishida, who has been in charge of the plane since the hijacking.

After the plane left Pyongyang, North Korea, at 7:11 A.M., Captain Ishida established radio contact with Fukuoka, and the Japan Air Lines' operation center asked him: "Are you feeling all right?"

"I'm young so I'm feeling fine," he replied.

Others aboard the plane were Teiichi Ezaki, the co-pilot, and Toshio Aihara, the flight engineer.

Left behind in North Korea were the nine young men, mostly students, who hijacked the Yodo Tuesday morning by brandishing swords and pistols.

Officials Greet Yamamura

Mr. Yamamura was the first off the plane. He waved, smiled, and then shook hands with Foreign Minister Kiichi Aichi and other officials. Mr. Yamamura went to the microphone and said:

"I have done only what is natural. I am glad we were able to save the lives of some 100 passengers and even more glad to be coming home now with the plane and its crewmen."

Asked what had happened after he had boarded the plane in Seoul Friday to accompany the nine hijackers to Pyongyang. Mr. Yamamura replied

Continued on Page 14, Column 3

50,000 IN CAPITAL SUPPORT THE WAR

Parade and Rally Are Marked by Hymns and Pleas for Bible Reading in School

Special to The New York Times

WASHINGTON, April 4—About 50,000 people marched up Pennsylvania Avenue to a rally at the Washington Monument today to advocate "victory in Vietnam."

Their signs and chants were quotations from Scripture and pleas for Bible reading in the schools. They sang the "Battle Hymn of the Republic" and "Onward Christian Soldiers."

There were distinct right-wing and segregationist elements. A group from South Carolina carried a wide banner reading "No Busing Our Children." Others said "Freedom of Choice in School."

'Let's Segregate!'

Against a background of rebel yells and Confederate flags were shouts of "Let's segregate!"

The march was organized and led by the Rev. Carl McIntire, a fundamentalist right-wing preacher from the Bible Presbyterian Church in Collingwood, N.J. Dr. McIntire, in a prayer over a loudspeaker before the march, proclaimed a "holy crusade." He said: "May this be the great turning point in the worldwide crusade against Communism."

The police-estimated turnout was much smaller than the 250,000 who demanded an immediate and total withdrawal from Vietnam here last November. But it was larger than many Washington observers had expected.

The crowd today included

Continued on Page 4, Column 1

Today's Sections

Index to Subjects

Nonviolence Making Quiet Gains in U.S. Despite Disorders

By JOHN HERBERS

Special to The New York Times

HAVERFORD, Pa., April 3—Two years after the death of the Rev. Dr. Martin Luther King Jr., nonviolence as a technique for social change, although widely rejected, is making quiet gains across the nation.

When Dr. King was assassinated in Memphis on April 4, 1968, the nonviolent movement he had led in civil rights was in decline and disarray as civic disorders erupted in hundreds of cities.

Since then, the trend to violence as a means of protest has continued both in the Negro revolution and among alienated white youths.

The nonviolent movement, nevertheless, has survived and in some respects is now undergoing a revival, largely in the intellectual community. This is seen by the following developments:

¶About 75 colleges are of-

Continued on Page 30, Column 4

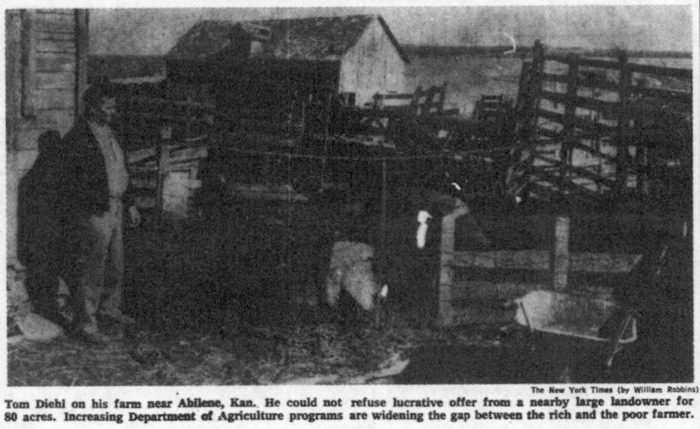

The New York Times (by William Robbins)

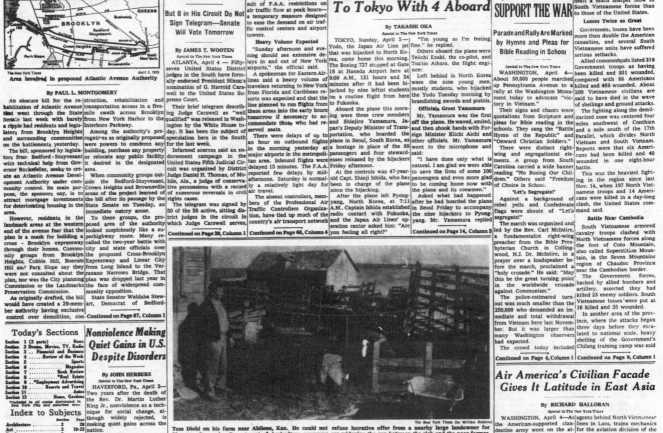

Tom Diehl on his farm near Abilene, Kan. He could not refuse lucrative offer from a nearby large landowner for 80 acres. Increasing Department of Agriculture programs are widening the gap between the rich and the poor farmer.

Farm Policy Helps Make the Rural Rich Richer

By WILLIAM ROBBINS

Special to The New York Times

WASHINGTON, April 4—Young Fred Salyer swung his little red and white monoplane through a bright California sky, looking down on the flat expanse of the San Joaquiin Valley. His father had faced bankruptcy there in the early thirties. Now the land supports a thriving farm, with operations so extensive that only in an airplane can they all be checked in one day.

Three thousand miles away, on a muddy road leading to a sagging house in South Carolina, Thomas Washington looked out over his 67 sandy acres and summed up the result of a year's work. "Mister," he said, "there wasn't nothing left."

Both men are wards of the Department of Agriculture, but both get widely different benefits. The department pays the Salyer family nearly $1.7-million a year in subsidies; it pays Mr. Washington slightly more than $300.

Trips to the major agricultural regions of the United States, interviews with economists and Government officials and examination of official Government budgets and documents over several months show that the stories of Mr. Salyer and Mr. Washington are not unusual.

After three and a half decades and costs of billions of dollars, the Department of Agriculture's farm programs continue to widen the gap between the rich and the poor.

"They have helped create a class of wealthy landowners while bypassing the rural poor—and that means 40 per cent of the poor people in this country," Dr. C. E. Bishop, agricultural economist and vice president of the University of South Carolina, said recently.

Meanwhile, the problems of the rural poor have spilled over into the cities, which are trying to cope with millions of displaced farmers and farm workers. But the records show that the Govern-

Continued on Page 56, Column 1

Air America's Civilian Facade Gives It Latitude in East Asia

By RICHARD HALLORAN

Special to The New York Times

WASHINGTON, April 4—As the American-supported clandestine army went on the attack in Laos again this week, pilots of a flamboyant airline called Air America took to the skies once again to move troops, provide supplies and evacuate wounded.

Air America is a flight charter company that, like the clandestine army, is widely considered to be the servant of the United States Central Intelligence Agency.

With its assorted fleet of 167 aircraft, Air America performs diverse missions across East Asia from Korea to Indonesia. It is believed to be a major link for the C.I.A's extensive activities throughout Asia.

Air America parachutes Meo tribesmen and other secret agents behind North Vietnamese lines in Laos, trains mechanics for the aviation division of the national police in Thailand, hauls American aid cargo for the Agency for International Development in South Vietnam, ferries United States Air Force men from Okinawa to Japan and South Korea, and dispatches intelligence flights from Taiwan along the coast of Communist China.

The company also transports helicopters from France and Italy for assembly in Southeast Asia, flies prospectors looking for copper and geologists searching for oil in Indonesia,

Continued on Page 22, Column 3

A U.S. Air Force F-4 Phantom attacks an enemy camp in the Se San area of Cambodia as part of the air support for Allied ground forces.

A U.S. Army helicopter delivers equipment to Republic of Korea troops who were serving in a support capacity during the Cambodian incursion.

Communist Party guerrillas patrol the Cambodian border against U.S. or South Vietnamese troops.

"All the News
That's Fit to Print"

The New York Times

LATE CITY EDITION
Weather: Mostly sunny today; fair
tonight. Sunny and warm tomorrow.
Temp. range: today 70-53; Wed.
79-60. Full U.S. report on Page 70.

VOL. CXIX..No. 41,004   © 1970 The New York Times Company.   NEW YORK, THURSDAY, APRIL 30, 1970   10 CENTS

Kennedy Veracity Questioned By Judge in Kopechne Inquest

Report Says Senator May Have Driven Car Negligently

By JOSEPH LELYVELD
Special to The New York Times

BOSTON, April 29—The judge at the inquest into the death of Mary Jo Kopechne reported that he could not accept as the truth key elements of Senator Edward M. Kennedy's sworn testimony at the hearing.

Judge James A. Boyle of the Dukes County District Court found neither "responsible" nor "probable" these assertions by

Judge James A. Boyle

United Press International
Senator Edward M. Kennedy in Washington yesterday.

*Kennedy excerpts, Page 30;
Boyle excerpts, Page 31.*

the Senator about the drowning of Miss Kopechne last July:

¶The Senator's testimony that he and Miss Kopechne had left a party at a cottage on Chappaquiddick Island with the intention of catching a ferry back to Martha's Vineyard.

¶His testimony that it was a wrong turn that took him onto a dirt road that led to a narrow, unmarked bridge on Chappaquiddick.

Judge Boyle, who conducted the inquest six months after the Senator's car plunged off the wooden bridge, also took note of testimony showing that both Mr. Kennedy and Miss Kopechne had been driven over the same bridge earlier on the day of the accident.

From this he concluded that there was "probable cause" to believe that the Senator had

Continued on Page 31, Column 1

Kennedy Statement Rejects Findings as 'Not Justified'

By WARREN WEAVER Jr.
Special to The New York Times

WASHINGTON, April 29 — Senator Edward M. Kennedy rejected as "not justified" today a Massachusetts judge's report that the Senator may have driven negligently and contributed to the death of Mary Jo Kopechne at Chappaquiddick Island last July.

In a statement issued by his office, Mr. Kennedy said:

"At the inquest I truthfully answered all questions asked of me. In my personal view, the inference and ultimate findings of the judge's report are not justified.

"Even though the legal procedures resulting from last summer's accident have, come to a close, the tragedy of that event will never really end—for the Kopechne family, for my family and myself. We must all live with the loss of Mary Jo and the pain that this has inflicted upon us.

"The facts of this incident are now fully public, and eventual judgment and understanding rests where it belongs. I plan no further statement on this tragic matter. Both our families have suffered enough from public utterances and speculations."

A few moments after the public statement was issued, however, reporters found Sen-

Continued on Page 31, Column 4

PRESIDENT ORDERS STUDY OF AIR ROLE OF SOVIET IN U.A.R.

His Call for Prompt Action Reflects Growing Alarm in Capital on Mideast

*Text of the Israeli statement
on Russians, Page 8.*

By ROBERT B. SEMPLE Jr.
Special to The New York Times

WASHINGTON, April 29—Reflecting the growing sense of alarm here over the Middle East, President Nixon today ordered an "immediate and full" evaluation of reports that the Soviet Union had assumed a substantially larger role in the defense of The United Arab Republic.

The reports yesterday indicated that over the last two weeks Soviet pilots have been flying combat formations over central Egypt for defense against raids by the Israeli Air Force. The State Department announced later that it had acquired independent information confirming these reports.

[In Jerusalem, Israeli leaders considered the use of Soviet pilots in the Egyptian Air Force as the most serious development in the Middle East since the 1967 Arab-Israeli war.]

U. S. Anxiety Unconcealed

The United States Administration did not conceal its anxiety. There was general agreement in official quarters that Soviet action had probably disturbed the balance of power in the Middle East and had raised at least the possibility that the Administration would reconsider its earlier decision, announced March 23, not to sell 125 jets to Israel for the time being.

The White House Press Secretary, Ronald L. Ziegler, described the evidence of increased Soviet involvement as a matter for serious concern, and pointedly reminded newsmen that the March 23 decision had been only an "interim decision," subject to continuing evaluation of "the military balance in the Middle East."

Potential Danger Seen

At the State Department, the press officer, Robert J. McCloskey, said: "We regard this as a serious development and potentially dangerous," and added that the United States would promptly ask the Soviet Union to explain its purposes.

And in New York, Under Secretary of State Elliot L. Richardson—in a passage hastily written into a speech about the possibilities of Soviet-American cooperation—warned the Soviet Union against "stirring up a

Continued on Page 9, Column 3

U.S. AIDS SAIGON PUSH IN CAMBODIA WITH PLANES, ARTILLERY, ADVISERS; MOVE STIRS OPPOSITION IN SENATE

SENATORS ANGRY

Some Seek to Cut Off Funds for Widened Military Action

By JOHN W. FINNEY
Special to The New York Times

WASHINGTON, April 29—The Administration's decision to support a South Vietnamese military operation in Cambodia set off moves by leading Senators in both parties today to cut off funds for American military operation in Cambodia

The moves, which could lead to a constitutional confrontation with the White House—were indicative of a widespread, angry and frustrated reaction in the Senate.

Some Senators, however, such as John Stennis of Mississippi, chairman of the Armed Services Committee, and Robert P. Griffin of Michigan, the assistant Republican leader, described the operation as a limited one designed to destroy North Vietnamese and Vietcong sanctuaries in Cambodia near the border of South Vietnam.

'Could Be a Turning Point'

Senator Stennis said that the destruction of the enemy sanctuaries in Cambodia was "essential" if the United States was to continue withdrawing troops from South Vietnam. While supporting the Administration action, Senator Stennis made it clear that he was opposed to providing any "extensive" military aid to the Cambodian Government.

"This could be a turning point in the war for us for the good," he said. "I do not believe in itself it is an escalation—not yet, not yet."

The critical reaction to the Administration move was strongest among members of the Senate Foreign Relations Committee.

Two of its members—Senator John Sherman Cooper, Republican of Kentucky, and Senator Frank Church, Democrat of Idaho—announced that they were drafting an amendment that would preclude the use of any funds appropriated by Congress for military assistance or operations in Cambodia. The amendment would be attached to a military sales bill now before the Committee.

Mike Mansfield of Montana,

Continued on Page 3, Column 1

The New York Times   April 30, 1970
THRUST INTO CAMBODIA: The U.S.-backed Saigon force took to Bavet (1) in a Vietcong stronghold. Communist troops took Memot (2) in Cambodia and drove into Attopeu (3) in Laos in an apparently related action. Dotted line shows Cambodian area (4) where foe continued raids.

RISING PERIL SEEN

Nixon to Speak on TV Tonight—Action Is Termed Limited

*Statements issued in Saigon
and Washington, Page 2.*

By WILLIAM BEECHER
Special to The New York Times

WASHINGTON, April 29—The United States announced today that it was providing combat advisers, tactical air support, medical evacuation teams and some supplies to South Vietnamese troops attacking Communist bases in Cambodia.

The South Vietnamese offensive, involving thousands of troops, began this morning.

Announcing an expansion of the nine-year-old active United States involvement in Indochina, Daniel Z. Henkin, Assistant Secretary of Defense for Public Affairs, said that North Vietnamese and Vietcong troops operating from Cambodia had "posed an increasing threat" to American and allied troops in South Vietnam.

Move Is Unexpected

The Nixon Administration's unexpected move, which brought an immediate outcry in Congress, is to be discussed by the President in a televised address to the nation at 9 P.M. tomorrow.

The decision came after six weeks of intensive debate over the risks and opportunities of alternative courses of action against the Communist sanctuaries in Cambodia. The issue arose following the ouster of the neutralist Chief of State, Prince Norodom Sihanouk, on March 18, and the decision of the new Government to attempt to end the Communist forces' use of Cambodian territory.

It was primarily an American decision that the offensive into Cambodia be staged, officials said privately, even though public statements stressed the South Vietnamese initiative.

Numbers Undisclosed

While Administration officials declined to say how many Americans would be involved or how long the South Vietnamese offensive might take, some sources stressed in private the limited nature of the decision, estimating that the number of Americans would be "in the low hundreds."

They also said that the South Vietnamese troops and their American advisers were expected to stay on Cambodian soil only until enemy arms depots and bases could be destroyed, perhaps in a week or two.

A statement issued by the United States command in Saigon reported that Americans were also providing helicopters and artillery support.

The officials declined, in an-

Continued on Page 2, Column 4

Big Allied Sweep Aimed At Enemy's Sanctuaries

By TERENCE SMITH
Special to The New York Times

SAIGON, South Vietnam, Thursday, April 30—South Vietnamese forces supported by United States warplanes and artillery and accompanied by United States advisers swept across the border into Cambodia yesterday in a big operation against North Vietnamese and Vietcong sanctuaries inside Cambodia.

The operation, which involves thousands of troops backed up by armor and heavy artillery, was announced last night in a statement issued here by the South Vietnamese Ministry of Defense and confirmed later by the United States command.

First Announced Operation

It was the first time that either the South Vietnamese or American military commands openly reported operations across the Cambodian border, although at least six such sweeps are known to have been carried out since the overthrow of Prince Norodom Sihanouk as Cambodian Chief of State six weeks ago.

United States officials said the American assistance was in the form of "advisers, tactical air strikes, medical evacuation and some logistics assistance."

A brief statement issued early this morning by the United States military command elaborated slightly, saying that Americans were also providing helicopters and artillery support for the operation.

The current operation appears to be much the largest yet undertaken. It is also the first in which American support has been provided openly. Reliable South Vietnamese sources

Continued on Page 4, Column 4

CATHOLIC CHURCH WARNS RHODESIA

Bishops Say They Will Shut Schools and Hospitals if Segregation Law Stands

Special to The New York Times

SALISBURY, Rhodesia, April 29—A rebellion by Christian churches in Rhodesia against the country's new Land Tenure Act was taken a step further today when the Roman Catholic Bishops presented an ultimatum to the Government.

They threatened that if the provisions of the act that bar interracial worship and interracial association for religious work, are not declared null, the bishops would order the closing of all the church's schools, hospitals, orphanages, homes for the aged and other social welfare institutions in the country.

Copies of a statement, signed by the Archbishop of Salisbury, the Most Rev. Francis Markall, and the bishops of the four other Catholic dioceses, were sent last night to each member of Prime Minister Ian D. Smith's Cabinet. The statement contained the text of the Catholic leaders' decision, made "after months of agonizing consideration and consultations."

They told the Government that the Land Tenure Act, which is part of Rhodesia's Constitution as a republic and which came into effect March 2, made it impossible for the church to carry on its work. The act, which is complex, essentially divides Rhodesia into white areas totaling 44.9 million acres and black areas totaling 45.2 million acres and forbids "occupation" of one area by the other race.

In some circumstances, the Government is apparently empowered to rule that attend-

Continued on Page 16, Column 1

Technical Recovery Lifts Stock Prices

Prices on the New York Stock Exchange staged a sharp technical rally yesterday after the market had declined because of the news about Cambodia. The Dow-Jones industrial average rose 13.06 points to 737.39, with most of its gain coming in the final hour.

Volume on the Big Board climbed to 15.8 million shares, the heaviest in more than a month. For the first time in 20 trading sessions, advancing issues outnumbered declines.

Prices also rose sharply on the American Stock Exchange, where the turnover of 5.67 million shares was the heaviest of this year.

On Tuesday, the Dow indicator had dropped to its lowest level since November, 1963.

Details on Page 51.

City Hospitals to Perform Abortions for All Who Ask

By JOHN SIBLEY

City hospital officials pledged every effort yesterday to perform medically sound abortions on all New York City women who requested the operation after the new reform law became effective on July 1.

The official statement went beyond mere compliance with the state's new abortion reform law. It promised to "make the availability of this service widely known among the women of New York City."

The city has not determined, however, how it will handle pregnant women from outside the state who come here to take advantage of New York's liberalized abortion procedures. The new law does not require that women establish residence for any period before seeking abortions.

JERSEY MAY LIST TENANTS BY RACE

Civil Rights Unit to Require Landlords to File Reports —Court Fight Expected

By RONALD SULLIVAN
Special to The New York Times

NEWARK, April 29 — The New Jersey Division on Civil Rights announced today that it was formulating a state regulation that would require the landlords of apartment houses with 25 or more units to file annual lists designating the race of their tenants.

The lists would be used as evidence in court if systematic patterns of discrimination were found.

A spokesman for the division said the regulation would be the first of its kind by any state and perhaps any city in the nation. He said it would take effect before the beginning of the summer and probably would affect at least half of the more than one million apartments in New Jersey.

Authority to Regulate

Under existing law, the division, which is an agency under the State Attorney General, has the power to promulgate regulations it deems necessary to fight discrimination in the state. The proposed regulation was revealed today at a public hearing conducted by the division at the Rutgers University Law School here.

The proposed rule is similar to existing Federal regulations that require companies with 25 or more employes to file reports with the Equal Employment Opportunity Commission statements on the racial composition of their work forces.

Officials of the Jersey Division on Civil Rights said they expected bitter opposition from landlord groups and, most likely, a court test of the regulation's constitutionality.

The proposal is a result of

Continued on Page 28, Column 5

FIRE UNION WARNS CITY ON PAY RISES

Maye Says U.F.A. Expects Parity to Be Retained if Police Get Increase

By EMANUEL PERLMUTTER

The city firemen served notice yesterday that if policemen received the $1,200 annual raise they were demanding, the firefighters would expect an equal increase.

Michael J. Maye, president of the 12,000-member United Firefighters Association, warned also that if the city should call in the National Guard to break a threatened work stoppage by 20,000 patrolmen "it had better be prepared to call in troops to do firefighting as well."

In substantiation of his contention that the firemen would be entitled to a raise similar to that of the patrolmen, Mr. Maye said the firefighters' contract stated that they were to have wage parity with the policemen, parity they have had for 81 years.

Another warning to the city came from the Uniformed Fire Officers Association. Lieut. Richard E. Kelly, president of the group, said it "insists on the sanctity of the contracts that have already been negotiated."

Continued on Page 26, Column 1

Senators, Friendly to Blackmun, Complete Hearing in Single Day

By FRED P. GRAHAM
Special to The New York Times

WASHINGTON, April 29—The Senate Judiciary Committee completed its hearings today on the Supreme Court nomination of Judge Harry A. Blackmun in a friendly, one-day session that produced no opposition to his confirmation.

The committee will meet in closed session at 10:30 A.M. tomorrow. If no member exercises his right to demand a one-week delay, the committee vote will be taken at that meeting.

An early confirmation of Judge Blackmun seemed likely after today's hearing, which was in sharp contrast to the long, acrimonious sessions that took place over President Nixon's two previous nominations to the same seat.

"President Nixon has this time selected from among the best," said Senator Philip A. Hart of Michigan, a Democrat who opposed the two prior nominees, Clement F. Haynsworth Jr. and G. Harrold Carswell.

Judge Blackmun was praised by liberals as well as conservatives on the committee. Conservatives complimented him for being a "strict constructionist" and liberals who had opposed the earlier nominees remarked that their efforts had borne fruit in the nomination of a superior jurist.

Among his statements were these:

¶If he is confirmed to the Supreme Court he expects to sell all of his corporate securities in order to avoid any possible conflicts of interest with

Continued on Page 18, Column 1

The only sign of lingering bitterness from the earlier nominations came from Senator Strom Thurmond, a South Carolina Republican, who observed that Judge Blackmun was "a man of high ethical conduct, able South Vietnamese sources."

But he said that the forces that defeated the earlier nominees no longer had the "gall to engage in another round of defamation of character."

"They have vented their spleen and I predict that you will be confirmed forthwith," he said. "I support your nomination."

Judge Blackmun's three hours of cross-examination before the seventeen-man committee drew obvious approval from the committee members. The 61-year-old Minnesotan spoke in a clear, precise voice, rarely attempting to avoid answers and commenting more freely on sensitive public issues than most Supreme Court nominees have done in recent years.

Yale Student Petition Supports Brewster's Stand on Panthers

Special to The New York Times

NEW HAVEN, April 29—Yale students closed ranks today behind their embattled president, Kingman Brewster Jr., whose ouster has been proposed by Vice President Agnew.

More than 3,000 of the 9,300 enrolled students signed a petition supporting Mr. Brewster's leadership and his controversial statement expressing skepticism that Black Panthers could get a fair trial in the United States.

Mr. Brewster was cheered by students when he appeared on the steps of Woodbridge Hall, the administration building, to receive the petition. He made no comment on the Agnew attack, nor did he mention Gov. John N. Dempsey, who described himself as "shocked" by Mr. Brewster's criticism of the judicial system.

Mr. Brewster simply thanked the students for having "poured out such energy, common sense and goodwill, not just to protect the university, but to try to improve it."

If that attitude can be maintained through the coming crucial weekend, when New Haven will be the scene of a massive May Day demonstration against the Black Panther trial here, "then we can hopefully respond constructively to the ideas that have been generated," Mr. Brewster said.

The students, who have been on strike since April 21, have presented demands that Yale seek an end to alleged political repression and police bias against the Black Panthers and endeavor to improve its rela-

Continued on Page 28, Column 5

7 Shot, Guard Called In Ohio State U. Riot

Special to The New York Times

COLUMBUS, Ohio, Thursday, April 30—Seven persons were injured, one of them seriously, by shotgun pellets, as student rioting disrupted the Ohio State University campus yesterday. Gov. James A. Rhodes ordered 1,500 National Guardsmen onto the campus.

A police spokesman said that "to his knowledge," none of the more than 300 policemen at the scene had fired anything other than tear gas canisters at the rioting students, but he conceded the possibility that the shots could have been fired by the police.

Observers estimated that 30 policemen, 20 students and seven nonstudents had suffered injuries. More than 60 persons

Continued on Page 36, Column 1

"All the News That's Fit to Print"

The New York Times

LATE CITY EDITION

Weather: Partly sunny today; fair tonight. Partly sunny tomorrow. Temp. range: today 70-51; Thurs. 57-49. Full U.S. report on Page 69.

VOL. CXIX ... No. 41,005 NEW YORK, FRIDAY, MAY 1, 1970 — 10 CENTS

NIXON SENDS COMBAT FORCES TO CAMBODIA TO DRIVE COMMUNISTS FROM STAGING ZONE

U.S. Troops Flown In for Panther Rally; New Haven Braces for Protest by 20,000

4,000 Will Be on Duty in New England Today—Dempsey Asks Aid

By HOMER BIGART
Special to The New York Times

NEW HAVEN, April 30—Federal troops were flown to New England today to stand by in the event of violence at a massive demonstration planned for here tomorrow to protest the murder trial of the Black Panther national chairman, Bobby Seale.

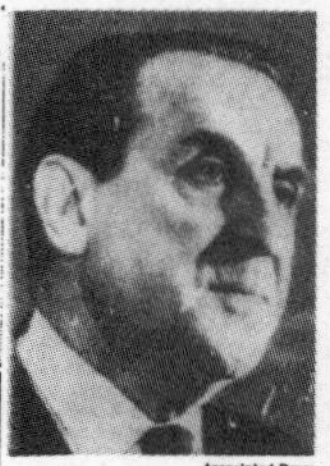

Associated Press
Gov. John N. Dempsey

The troops were requested by Gov. John N. Dempsey, who told Attorney General John N. Mitchell of a "strong possibility" that weekend violence in this tense city could not be contained by National Guard units and state and local policemen.

Mr. Mitchell responded to the Governor's telephone plea by telling Mr. Dempsey to put it in writing. Mr. Dempsey then sent a telegram to Mr. Mitchell and Mr. Mitchell obtained from the Pentagon 4,000 Army paratroopers and marines.

On the eve of a May Day weekend protest that the police say may attract more than 20,000 demonstrators to the New Haven Green, parts of the city assumed an air of siege.

National Guard units with nine armored personnel carriers were deployed in armories on the outskirts of the city. Many merchants were boarding up their windows and planning to stay closed until Monday.

Store Windows Boarded Up—Yale Moves Its Files From Campus

There was evident sympathy for the demonstration in the Yale community; in fact, the university's president, Kingman Brewster Jr., had expressed "skepticism" that black radicals could be assured of a fair trial anywhere in the United States. Nevertheless the university took the precaution of removing important files from the campus.

The Federal paratroopers assigned for possible action here were of the Second Brigade, 82d Airborne Division, from Fort Bragg, N. C. They were

Continued on Page 40, Column 1

HOUSE BARS MOVE TO REDUCE FUNDS FOR ABM SYSTEM

Rejects, 131-85, Amendment to Remove $660.4-Million in Bill for Procurement

By ROBERT M. SMITH
Special to The New York Times

WASHINGTON, April 30—In sometimes emotional debate, the House rejected today efforts to cut funds for the Safeguard antimissile system.

Rejection of the proposed cut was among a series of amendments beaten back in consideration of the $20.2-billion defense authorization bill.

The House then put off until next Wednesday further action on the bill after it became embroiled in a controversy over President Nixon's sending military aid to Cambodia.

Representative Ogden R. Reid Republican of Westchester, introduced an amendment that would prohibit any money from being spent for support of American ground troops in Cambodia.

Among the amendments rejected were two sponsored by Representative Robert L. Leggett, Democrat of California. The first would have chopped $660.4-million from the bill, all the funds for Safeguard procurement. It was rejected, 131 to 85.

Similar Move Last Year

The second amendment would have cut $203-million in procurement funds for the second phase of the Safeguard system. This was rejected, 126 to 86.

The second phase includes a third Safeguard site at Whiteman Air Force Base in Missouri and planning work for five other sites across the country.

Last year the House rejected a similar attempt to cut ABM procurement authorization. It rejected a motion to recommit the then pending bill to the Armed Services Committee with instructions to delete $345.5-million for procurement and $400.9-million for research. The vote then was 270 to 93.

The group of liberals who supported the various amendments argued that the United States had a large enough nuclear arsenal now to allow national economic priorities to be shifted to domestic needs. They said, too, that there had been waste and mismanagement in the Department of Defense.

Supporters of the authorization reported out by the Armed

Continued on Page 23, Column 1

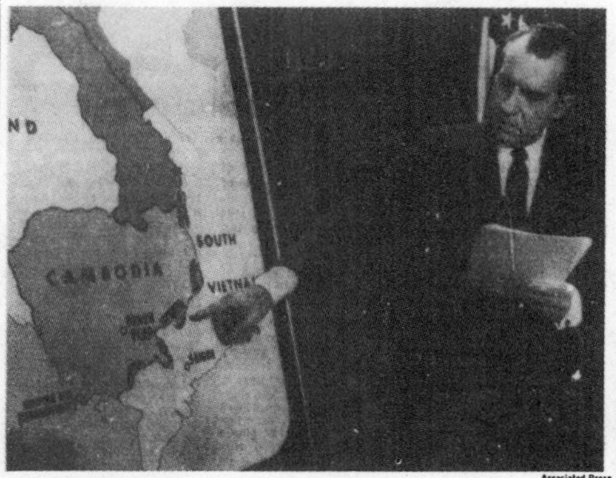

Associated Press
The President points to Fishhook area of Cambodia. Dark areas are enemy strongholds.

'NOT AN INVASION'

President Calls Step an Extension of War to Save G.I. Lives

The text of Nixon's speech Is printed on Page 2.

By ROBERT B. SEMPLE Jr.
Special to The New York Times

WASHINGTON, April 30—In a sharp departure from the previous conduct of war in Southeast Asia, President Nixon announced tonight that he was sending United States combat troops into Cambodia for the first time.

Even as the President was addressing the nation on television, several thousand American soldiers were moving across the border from South Vietnam to Cambodia to attack what Mr. Nixon described as "the headquarters for the entire Communist military operation in South Vietnam."

The area was described by sources here as the Fishhook area of Cambodia, some 50 miles northwest of Saigon.

White House sources said they expected tonight's operation to be concluded in six to eight weeks. They said its primary objective was not to kill enemy soldiers but to destroy their supplies and drive them from their sanctuaries.

Aimed at Staging Aresa

"Our purpose is not to occupy the areas," the President declared. "Once enemy forces are driven out of these sanctuaries and their military supplies destroyed, we will withdraw."

The President described the action as "not an invasion of Cambodia" but a necessary extension of the Vietnam war designed to eliminate a major Communist staging and communications area. Thus it is intended to protect the lives of American troops and shorten the war, he asserted.

The President further described the action as "indispensable" for the continued success of his program of Vietnamization—under which he has been withdrawing American ground combat troops as the burden of fighting is gradually shifted to the South Vietnamese.

The President's rhetoric was tough—probably the toughest of his tenure in office—and was reminiscent of some of the speeches of Lyndon B. Johnson during the last years of his term as President.

Nixon Appears Grim

The President appeared grim as he delivered his address while sitting at his desk in the Oval Office of the White House. Occasionally he used a nearby map to point out the Communist-held sanctuaries, which were shaded in red. But no gesture could match the solemnity of his words.

He portrayed his decision as a difficult one taken without regard to his political future, which he said was "nothing compared to the lives" of American soldiers.

Discussing this future, Mr. Nixon said: "I would rather be a one-term President and do what I believe is right than to be a two-term President at the cost of seeing America become a second-rate power and to see this nation accept the first defeat in its proud 190-year history."

He added that he regarded the recent actions of the North Vietnamese as a test of Ameri-

Continued on Page 2, Column 1

Court Bars Police Tie-Up; P.B.A. Ponders Its Reply

By RICHARD PHALON

The city was granted a preliminary injunction yesterday against a threatened police work stoppage in a salary dispute, but the president of the Patrolmen's Benevolent Association declined to say whether the union would observe the court order.

Asked if the P.B.A. intended to honor the injunction banning widespread absences of men calling in sick—a "job action" scheduled to begin at 12:01 A.M. tomorrow — the P.B.A. head, Edward J. Kiernan, said: "I have no idea."

The question, he told reporters, is to be put before a P.B.A. delegate assembly meeting scheduled for 11 A.M. today in the New Yorker Hotel.

Justice Grants Writ

The injunction was granted in State Supreme Court by Justice Joseph A. Sarafite, who also turned down a police union request for a judgment ordering the city to give an immediate pay increase to patrolmen.

Mr. Kiernan and officials of three other service unions drawn into the police dispute with the city over the ratio between patrolmen's and sergeants' salaries met with Mayor Lindsay yesterday for about half an hour.

Noting that there were inconsistencies in the union contracts on the parity issue, Mr. Lindsay asked the four line organizations to take their problems to the "impartial forum" of the city's Office of Collective Bargaining.

In a statement he read at a news conference at which questions were barred, the Mayor said he had "asked the leadership of the four unions to consider this proposal carefully and to meet again with me at City Hall" at 9 A.M. today.

Apart from the P.B.A., the

Continued on Page 71, Column 4

CITY STUDY BACKS INCREASE IN RENTS

But Sternlieb Report Adds That Money Alone Will Not Stem Decay in Housing

By DAVID K. SHIPLER

A massive, detailed study of the economics of the city's housing—a study on which the Lindsay administration plans to base its revisions of rent control—has concluded that higher rents are "necessary but not sufficient" to stem the flood of decayed and abandoned apartments here.

The two-and-a-half-year, $250,000 investigation of a sample of 963 buildings throughout the city was undertaken by Prof. George Sternlieb of Rutgers University. Professor Steinlieb's report was released yesterday.

Professor Sternlieb refrained from recommending courses of action for the city. But his 1,100 pages, bound into a volume the length, width and thickness of the Manhattan telephone book, depicted the powerful, tangled forces that the city faces in its efforts to preserve the existing stock of 1.3 million rent-controlled apartments.

Entitied "The Urban Housing Dilemma," the report attributes housing deterioration not only to insufficient rents, but also to

Continued on Page 46, Column 1

NEW CLASH ERUPTS AT OHIO STATE U.

100 Seized, 13 Wounded and 73 Hurt—Guardsmen Use Gas Against Students

By JERRY M. FLINT
Special to The New York Times

COLUMBUS, Ohio, April 30 — National Guardsmen and police repeatedly scattered crowds of students on the campus of Ohio State University today, firing hundreds of rounds of tear gas and pepper gas, and discharging shotguns at the youths.

Thirteen students were reported wounded, 73 injured and nearly 100 arrested. Seven persons were shot in yesterday's rioting. The two-day arrest total is about 400.

Today's fighting was touched off by the National Guard and police forces as students began gathering to hold a rally to protest yesterday's violence.

A university vice president explained that only 500 or 550 guardsmen were on hand on the campus this morning instead of the 1,200 to 1,400 promised yesterday by Gov. James A. Rhodes.

The guardsmen and policemen, the university official said, decided on a strategy of scattering the students gathered on a campus mall with tear gas to prevent them from forming any

Continued on Page 38, Column 2

EBAN ASKS U.S. AID TO OFFSET SOVIET

Says Use of Pilots Alters U.A.R. Situation—Rogers Seeks Moscow Meeting

By RICHARD EDER
Special to The New York Times

JERUSALEM, April 30—Foreign Minister Abba Eban said today that the use of Soviet pilots in the United Arab Republic was "an almost revolutionary change" in the military situation and called for quick international assistance to Israel to compensate for it.

The call was directed mainly to the United States, which last month announced that it was holding in abeyance Israel's request for additional jet fighters. Mr. Eban said that the condition set forth by the United States for producing such aid—a shift in the balance against Israel—had now been fulfilled.

[In Washington, Secretary of State William P. Rogers instructed the United States Ambassador in Moscow to seek a high-level meeting with Soviet officials over the reports of Soviet involvement in Egyptian air defenses.]

The last 72 hours had shown, Mr. Eban said, that the new Soviet role in flying protective cover over major centers and military installations in central Egypt was, in fact, an offensive and not a defensive move. Its effect, he asserted was "to enable, nay, to encourage Egyptian forces to develop a stronger attacking role" against Israeli positions on the eastern bank of the Suez Canal.

Mr. Eban's appeal for aid,

Continued on Page 10, Column 1

G.I.'s and Bombers Begin Drive on Foe's Sanctuary

By The Associated Press

SAIGON, South Vietnam, Friday, May 1—The United States sent troops and B-52 bombers inside Cambodia early today in the first strike of an attempt to crush the sanctuary there of the North Vietnamese and Vietcong forces.

Details of the drive, joining a South Vietnamese offensive in its second day, became available here shortly after President Nixon announced that he had committed American combat forces to the new action.

It was learned that about 2,000 American air cavalrymen took part in the action, moving on foot across the border after B-52's, air cavalry, helicopter gunships and artillery had softened up the enemy positions along the allies' route.

Sources here said that helicopter-borne troops from the United States First Cavalry Division (Airmobile) and South Vietnamese troopers had penetrated 20 miles inside Cambodia to attack the headquarters of the Central Office for South Vietnam—the Communist high command, which directs the war in South Vietnam.

The headquarters is a complex of heavy concrete emplacements with underground caverns hidden in heavy tangled underbrush.

Two battalions of North Vietnamese and Vietcong troops—perhaps 1,000 men—are reported to normally provide security for the headquarters.

This headquarters is just

Continued on Page 3, Column 3

Key Congressmen Briefed; Reaction Called Favorable

By JOHN W. FINNEY
Special to The New York Times

WASHINGTON, April 30 — President Nixon was reported tonight to have received a generally favorable reaction from Congressional leaders to his decision to send American ground combat troops into Cambodia to destroy Communist sanctuaries in that country.

Before his speech this evening, the President briefed some 40 Congressional leaders and committee chairmen on his policy decisions in Cambodia. After the speech, Secretary of Defense Melvin R. Laird and Gen. Earle G. Wheeler, Chairman of the Joint Chiefs of Staff, answered questions from the members of Congress.

One Democratic leader who has been critical of the Nixon Administration's policy reported afterward that the President drew "a surprisingly favorable reaction."

"Most everybody seemed quite impressed," he said. "Most felt that something had to be done to eliminate the Communist sanctuaries."

By the decision ... announced tonight the President seemed to risk worsening the already widespread opposition in Congress, particularly in the Senate, to an American military involvement in Cambodia.

This was reflected in a statement of the Senate Foreign Relations Committee, adopted unanimously hours before the

Continued on Page 5, Column 1

Friends of Miss Kopechne Said They Were Told She Was Safe

By JOSEPH LELYVELD
Special to The New York Times

BOSTON, April 30 — Joseph F. Gargan, a cousin of Edward M. Kennedy's who was with him immediately after his July accident on Chappaquiddick Island, told three of Mary Jo Kopechne's friends that night that she had returned to Martha's Vineyard alone in the Senator's Oldsmobile, according to the friends' testimony at the inquest into Miss Kopechne's death.

Mr. Gargan offered this assurance, the testimony indicates, after he and another companion of the Senator's, Paul Markham, had spent 45 minutes diving to rescue her body from the Senator's submerged car.

The car had overturned in a tidal inlet after plunging off a wooden bridge.

The inquest transcripts were released here yesterday along with a report from the presiding judge at the hearing, James A. Boyle. The judge questioned elements of the Senator's testimony and concluded that negligent driving might have been responsible for Miss Kopechne's death.

Mr. Gargan and Mr. Markham testified that, having watched Mr. Kennedy dive into the narrow channel that separates Chappaquiddick from

Continued on Page 23, Column 1

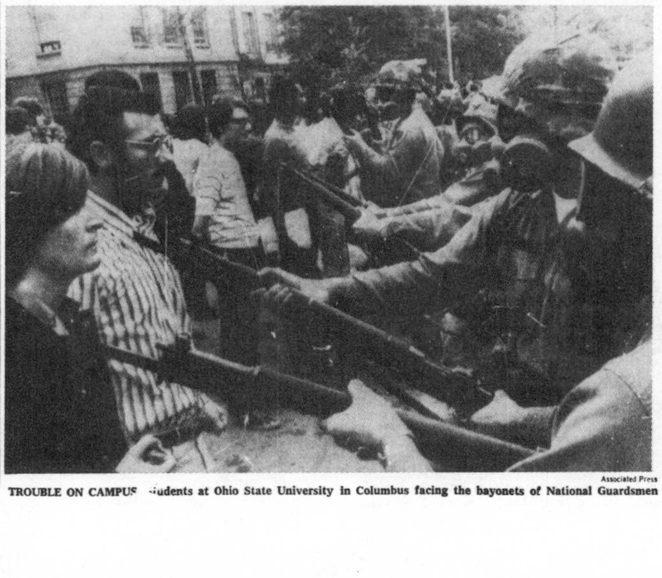

Associated Press
TROUBLE ON CAMPUS: Students at Ohio State University in Columbus facing the bayonets of National Guardsmen

Welfare Plan Stirs Job Rules Dispute

By WARREN WEAVER Jr.
Special to The New York Times

WASHINGTON, April 30—The Senate Finance Committee was startled to learn today that President Nixon's new welfare program would involve less total assistance, in some cases, for poor people who worked than for those who did not.

Figures for welfare families in four American cities were prepared by the Department of Health, Education and Welfare at the request of Senator John J. Williams of Delaware, the ranking Republican on the committee, and made public at a hearing this morning.

Secretary Robert H. Finch of

Continued on Page 13, Column 1

NEWS INDEX

	Page		Page
Art	44	Obituaries	35
Books	33	Society	51
Bridge	32	Sports	24-27
Business	53, 60-61	Theaters	41-49
Crossword	33	Transportation	69
Editorials	34	TV and Radio	71
Financial	52-61	U. N. Proceedings	10
Man in the News	8	Washington Record	21
Movies	41-49	Weather	69
Music	41-49	Women's News	50

News Summary and Index, Page 37

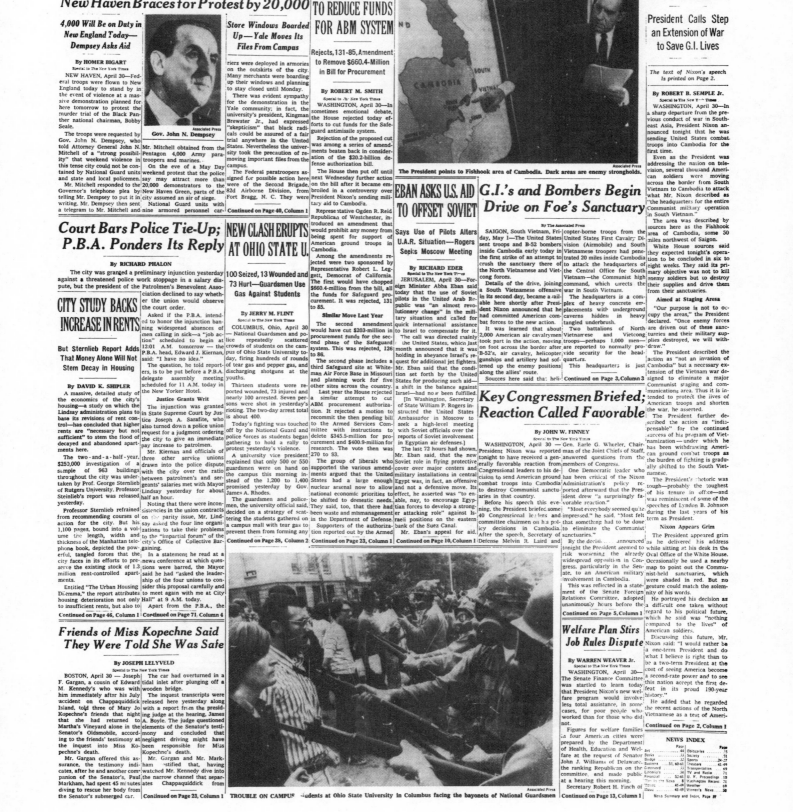

"All the News That's Fit to Print"

The New York Times

LATE CITY EDITION

Weather: Rain ending later today; clear tonight. Partly sunny tomorrow. Temp. range: today 59-56; Saturday 80-62. Full U.S. report on Page 95.

SECTION ONE

VOL. CXIX—No. 41,007 · © 1970 The New York Times Company. · NEW YORK, SUNDAY, MAY 3, 1970 · 60c beyond 50-mile zone from New York City, except Long Island. 75c beyond 200-mile radius. Higher in air delivery cities. · 50 CENTS

NEW HAVEN RALLY ENDS A DAY EARLY; ATTENDANCE DOWN

Protesters Call for a Strike by the Nation's Students Against War in Asia

ADJOURNMENT IS ABRUPT

A Small Group of Radicals Provokes Police Into 2d Tear-Gas Attack

By HOMER BIGART

Special to The New York Times

NEW HAVEN, May 2—Massive demonstrations in support of the Black Panthers ended today with a call for a nationwide student strike, but a small group of white radicals stayed behind and tonight provoked the police into the second tear-gas attack of the generally peaceful protest weekend.

Pelted with bottles, the police, who were aided by a Black Panther sound truck, urged the radicals to leave the New Haven Green, where they had gathered. Backed up by National Guardsmen with fixed bayonets, they gradually forced the bulk of the crowd of 200 into Phelps Gate on the Old Yale campus.

But some youths refused to be dislodged from the green, eluding the police and Yale student marshals, and throwing some rocks and bottles at the police and guardsmen.

Spirits Seemed to Flag

The rally had been adjourned abruptly before tonight's disturbance. It was to have continued tomorrow with a rock music festival, but youthful spirits seemed to be flagging. Attendance today was less than half of the 12,000 to 15,000 who thronged the green on Friday.

The thousands who had gathered here to protest the impending trial of Bobby Seale, the Panther national chairman, and eight other Panthers on murder and kidnapping charges, cheered the proposal for the student strike, which was called

Continued on Page 40, Column 1

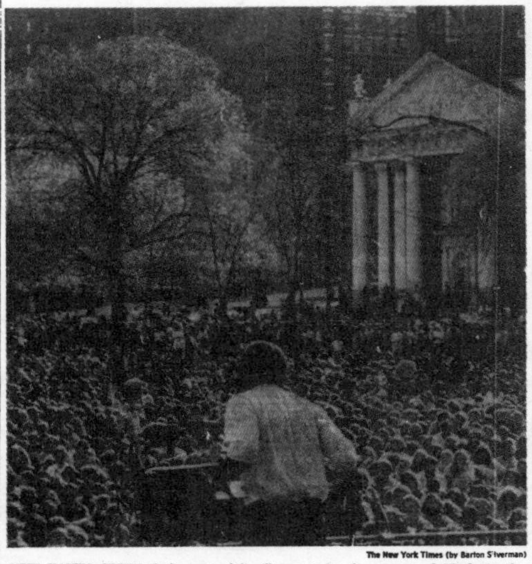

The New York Times (by Barton Silverman)

NEW HAVEN GREEN during peaceful rally yesterday in support of Black Panther defendants. Massive demonstrations ended with call for nationwide student strike.

40 of 63 on New York Jet Safe in Caribbean Ditching

A DC-9 jet on a flight from New York to the Caribbean was ditched off St. Croix yesterday with 63 persons aboard. The Coast Guard reported 40 persons rescued last night, seven dead and at least 16 others missing.

The plane was nearly out of fuel when it hit the water about 30 miles east of St. Croix at 3:48 P.M. New York time. The jet left Kennedy International Airport at 11 A.M. and was due at St. Martin, which lies about 150 miles southeast of San Juan, P. R., at 4 P.M.

Flight 980 of the Dutch Antillean Airlines (ALM) ran into a heavy tropical storm The pilot tried repeatedly to land but was unable to do so. With his fuel gauge almost at zero, he ditched into turbulent waters east of St. Croix.

Most of the passengers were from the New York area, a spokesman for the airline based in Curacao said here last night. There were 55 passengers, 2 infants and 6 crew members on board. The names of those on the flight were withheld pending a determination of the number of fatalities and notification of next of kin.

The Coast Guard reported that seven of those rescued had been injured, at least two seriously. The impact of the ditching shattered the aircraft.

Coast Guard and Navy helicopters dropped life rafts to passengers bobbing in the water, then picked up the survivors.

The helicopters were guided to the rescue site by a Pan American Airways plane, whose pilot reported the ditching by radio, then circled the scene until help came.

Pan American flight 454 from Guadeloupe to San Juan, piloted by Capt. William Prash of Miami, heard the DC-9 report it was low on fuel and about to ditch.

At San Juan, the Federal

Continued on Page 9, Column 1

JOHNSON ACCUSES SOME OF '63 STAFF

On TV, He Asserts Kennedy Holdovers 'Undermined' Him Early in Term

By WARREN WEAVER Jr.

Special to The New York Times

WASHINGTON, May 2—Former President Lyndon B. Johnson has accused some holdover officials of undermining his Administration in the weeks and months after the assassination of President Kennedy.

In a television interview that ranged over the death of President Kennedy and the early disappointments of his own Presidency, Mr. Johnson said that some of the men he inherited from his predecessor in 1963 "did not share either the desire or the hopes that I had for the country and for the Government."

"They, in effect, undermined the Administration and bored from within to create problems for us and leaked information that was slanted, and things of that nature," he continued.

"A good many of them re-

Continued on Page 79, Column 1

LOCAL BOARDS DUE FOR MORE POWER IN SCHOOL AFFAIRS

City Is Taking Steps to Give Community Units Voice in Contract Talks

By LEONARD BUDER

The Board of Education is taking steps to give the city's locally elected community school boards a voice in collective bargaining matters, including the current negotiations with the teacher-aides, and in other school issues.

At the same time, the central board is also planning to grant certain powers to the new local boards to enable them to prepare for a full assumption of duties on July 1, when the city system shifts to a decentralized operation.

The city board's plans, which have been discussed in executive sessions and informally approved, envision the following actions:

¶Establishing a council, composed of one representative from each of the city's 31 community school boards, that would serve in a consultative capacity to the central board and the Chancellor — the post that is to replace Superintendent of Schools — in collective bargaining matters. This would be in line with a provision of the decentralization law.

¶Establishing another council or committee, also composed of 31 local board representatives, that would advise the central board on matters of broad educational policy that would affect the community districts. Although the functions of this council have not yet been defined, a purpose would be to assure close liaison and effective communication between the central and local boards.

¶Granting the new local boards authority to organize, elect officers and formulate their bylaws and to select and even hire district superintendents in advance of July 1. If a new local board hires a superintendent other than the incumbent, this could mean that some districts will have two superintendents for a short period—the outgoing administrator and the incoming official.

¶Operating a training program for the new local board members, as provided by the

Continued on Page 63, Column 1

128 U.S. PLANES CARRY OUT ATTACK IN NORTH VIETNAM; SUPPLY LINES ARE TARGETS

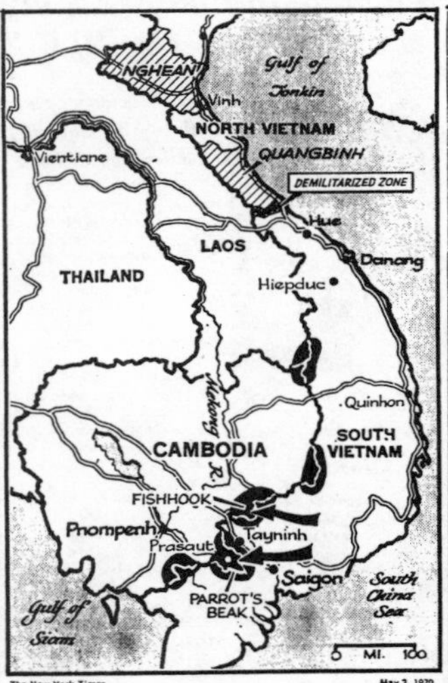

The New York Times · May 3, 1970

Sites of U.S. raid were given by Hanoi as two provinces (diagonal shading) north of the DMZ. Defense Secretary Melvin R. Laird identified principal enemy sanctuaries (dark shading) across the Cambodian border. Arrows show the two allied ground offensives in Cambodia.

HANOI CAUTIONED

Laird Declares an End to Foe's Sanctuary in Cambodia

By WILLIAM BEECHER

Special to The New York Times

WASHINGTON, May 2 — The United States has carried c.i a heavy bombing raid against supply dumps and other targets north of the demilitarized zone in North Vietnam, well-placed Administration sources said today.

The raid was said to be different in both scope and character from any conducted since November, 1968, when the United States announced the end of most bombing of North Vietnam. Since then, the Government has acknowledged only occasional incidents of "suppressive fire" by small numbers of planes against antiaircraft installations threatening American reconnaissance craft.

The latest raid — conducted yesterday or today—was said to have been carried out by 128 fighter-bombers striking at targets not authorized for attack over the last 18 months. Sources said the supply lines were near the entrance to passes leading into Laos.

Nixon Approval Reported

President Nixon was said to have authorized at least one such raid after his television address Thursday night announcing the attack by American ground troops against enemy installations in Cambodia.

Information about the air raid was obtained here today after a Hanoi radio broadcast charged that more than 100 American planes struck "yesterday and today" in Quangbinh and Nghean Provinces in North Vietnam, killing or wounding "many civilians, including 20 children." It also said two American planes had been shot down.

Official spokesmen here openly acknowledged that there had been a raid in that region, but described it as a reinforced mission of "protective reaction" against antiaircraft guns to protect unarmed reconnaissance aircraft. They refused to discuss the number of planes involved and said they knew nothing about casualties.

Policy Change Denied

The indications here were that the Administration intended to make no special announcement of the raid and hoped it would not attract unusual notice.

Officials did not deny the more detailed information supplied by other reliable sources, but they contended that there was no change in the policy on bombing North Vietnam.

Elsewhere in the Administration, however, the raid was portrayed as a significant departure from past practice, although the sources refused to

Continued on Page 2, Column 5

Allied Search in Cambodia Yields Few Signs of Foe

By TERENCE SMITH

Special to The New York Times

SAIGON, South Vietnam, Sunday, May 3—United States and South Vietnamese soldiers have begun a painstaking search of the Fishhook area of Cambodia amid increasing indications that many enemy troops fled in advance of the allied forces' arrival.

The task force discovered several recently evacuated enemy base areas—but no significant numbers of troops—as the allies began to close a giant ring around the suspected location of the Communist military headquarters for operations in South Vietnam.

Enemy resistance to the allied sweep remained light and scattered. This morning, the United States command reported that eight American soldiers had been killed and 32 wounded—a low number for an operation of such size. A total of about 10,000 South Vietnamese and United States soldiers, including 5,000 American infantrymen, are participating.

Enemy losses were listed as 476 killed, of which 161 were said to be victims of tactical air strikes and assaults by helicopter gunships. In addition, 118 persons were detained, but some of these appeared to be Cambodian civilians.

Some Enemy Bases Found

In an effort to find the enemy, the reconnaissance area of the operation was extended 20 miles deeper into Cambodia yesterday, according to reliable military sources. Teams of low-flying helicopters crisscrossed the area north and west of the Fishhook section throughout the day, searching for signs of enemy troop concentrations.

There was no immediate indication whether the United States command would extend the operation still farther into Cambodia if the task force failed to find significant enemy forces in the Fishhook area.

The battalion-size enemy

Continued on Page 2, Column 3

Conservative Beats Yarborough In Democratic Primary in Texas

By MARTIN WALDRON

Special to The New York Times

HOUSTON, Sunday, May 3—A millionaire businessman from Houston, using President Nixon's "Southern strategy" in a Democratic primary, yesterday defeated Senator Ralph W. Yarborough, the Texas maverick liberal who was bidding for a third term in the Senate.

Lloyd M. Bentsen Jr., a former Representative from the Rio Grande Valley who quit Congress in 1955 to enter business in Houston, charged in a whirlwind campaign from one end of the state to the other that Senator Yarborough had betrayed 10 million Texans with his liberal positions.

Unofficial returns early today from 250 of the state's 254 counties gave these figures:

Bentsen 768,937
Yarborough 678,629

One of Mr. Bentsen's major issues in the campaign against Senator Yarborough, who had long been at odds with the conservatives who have dominated the Democratic party since World War II, was that Senator Yarborough had voted against President Nixon's latest two appointees to the Supreme Court.

Mr. Bentsen also accused the Senator of dividing Texas by speaking out against the Vietnam war and by supporting antiwar demonstrators.

In attempting to overcome the effects of Mr. Bentsen's well financed campaign, which cost an estimated total of $750,000 or more, the Senator had tried to weld together once more the coalition of liberals plus Negroes and Mexican-Americans. But the coalition failed as many voters failed to go to the polls.

Mr. Bentsen claimed victory on the basis of unofficial re-

Continued on Page 44, Column 4

Today's Sections

Index to Subjects

15-to-1 Shot Wins Derby

Dust Commander, a 15-1 shot, won the 96th running of the Kentucky Derby at Churchill Downs yesterday by five lengths. With 17 horses running, the race was worth a record $170,300 and the winner earned $127,800. He paid $32.60 for $2 to win. My Dad George finished second and High Echelon was third. Details in Section 5.

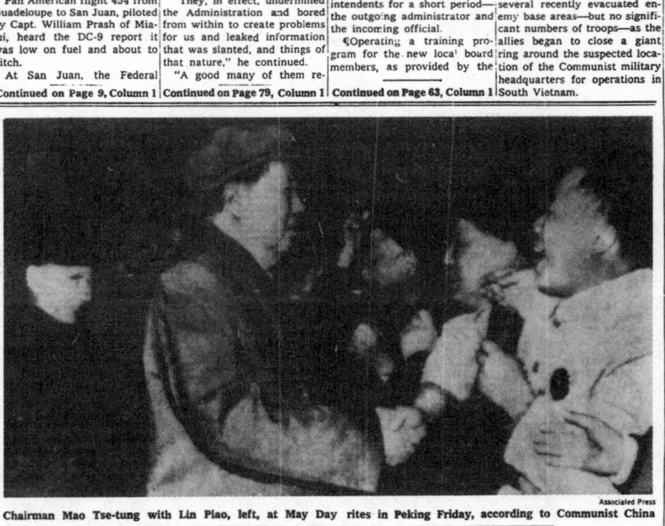

Associated Press

Chairman Mao Tse-tung with Lin Piao, left, at May Day rites in Peking Friday, according to Communist China

Peril to Chinese-Soviet Talks Is Seen in Diatribes

By HARRISON E. SALISBURY

Soviet-Chinese border talks in Peking—and possibly even formal Soviet-Chinese relations—have been imperiled, in the opinion of diplomatic specialists, by new and violent propaganda exchanges.

The Chinese attack on Moscow was in the form of a joint editorial by Peking's three major publications. It attacked Leonid I. Brezhnev, the Soviet party chief, as a "new Hitler" and charged that the Soviet Union had become a "Nazi-type" state, pursuing a racist policy similar to Hitler's "master-race theory" and was planning to conduct a blitzkrieg against China.

The Russians have replied with a special broadcast beamed to China in Mandarin, containing a vituperative attack on Chairman Mao Tse-Tung, charging him with personal responsibility in the death of his first wife, Yang Kai-hui, who was shot by the Chinese Nationalists in 1930, and also, indirectly, for the allegedly mysterious death of his eldest son, Mao An-ying, during the Korean war.

The text of the 6,500 word Chinese declaration, issued April 22 to mark the 100th anniversary of Lenin's birth, is now available in the United States. Like all major pronouncements, it is being given worldwide distribution by the Chinese. The Soviet broadcast was made three days after the editorial was published.

The broadcast accuses Chairman Mao, the Chinese party leader, of "cruelty, selfishness and lust for high position." It charges that he was unfaithful to his second wife, Ho Tzechen, and that he abandoned his first wife "to her fate."

Diplomatic assessors believed that a blow, conceivably fatal, had been dealt the Soviet-Chinese talks in Peking by the exchanges. They noted that Deputy Foreign Minister Vasily V. Kuznetsov, head of the Soviet delegation, had left Peking for Moscow and doubted that he would return.

The Soviet and Chinese embassies, whose personnel have been sharply reduced, are headed at present by relatively low-ranking diplomats. Recently, Moscow named Vladimir I.

Continued on Page 16, Column 6

Greek Warriors' Bones Found At Site of Battle of Marathon

Special to The New York Times

MARATHON, Greece, May 2—The burial place of Greek warriors who fell in the epoch-making Battle of Marathon, defending Athenian civilization from Persian conquest in 490 B. C., has been discovered by Greek archeologists on this ancient battlefield.

The announcement of the discovery was made on the site today by Prof. Spyridon Marinatos, inspector general of Greek antiquities, as he stood on the edge of the mass grave containing the skeletons of some young soldiers slain in the battle between East and West 2,460 years ago.

The professor told a throng of newsmen that the grave had been identified "beyond any reasonable doubt" as the tomb of the Plataeans, who had volunteered to help the Athenian Army under the leadership of Miltiades fight the Persian invaders, though heavily outnumbered by the enemy.

The mass grave lay under a carefully built stone tumulus, or burial mound, 10 feet high and 50 feet in diameter, its edge marked by hewn stones, on a plain 26 miles northeast of Athens.

Only part of the burial trench has been excavated so far, revealing five perfectly preserved skeletons. According to experts they belong to young soldiers

Continued on Page 14, Column 2

"All the News That's Fit to Print"

The New York Times

LATE CITY EDITION

Weather: Rain ending early today; clearing tonight. Fair tomorrow. Temp. range: today 66-49; Monday 62-53. Full U.S. report on Page 90.

VOL. CXIX . . No. 41,009 — NEW YORK, TUESDAY, MAY 5, 1970 — 10 CENTS

4 Kent State Students Killed by Troops

8 Hurt as Shooting Follows Reported Sniping at Rally

By JOHN KIFNER

Special to The New York Times

KENT, Ohio, May 4—Four students at Kent State University, two of them women, were shot to death this afternoon by a volley of National Guard gunfire. At least 8 other students were wounded.

The burst of gunfire came about 20 minutes after the guardsmen broke up a noon rally on the Commons, a grassy campus gathering spot, by lobbing tear gas at a crowd of about 1,000 young people.

In Washington, President Nixon deplored the deaths of the four students in the following statement:

"This should remind us all once again that when dissent turns to violence it invites tragedy. It is my hope that this tragic and unfortunate incident will strengthen the determination of all the nation's campuses, administrators, faculty and students alike to stand firmly for the right which exists in this country of peaceful dissent and just as strongly against the resort to violence as a means of such expression."

In Columbus, Sylvester Del Corso, Adjutant General of the Ohio National Guard, said in a statement that the guardsmen had been forced to shoot after a sniper opened fire against the troops from a nearby rooftop and the crowd began to move to encircle the guardsmen.

Frederick P. Wenger, the Assistant Adjutant General, said the troops had opened fire after they were shot at by a sniper.

"They were under standing orders to take cover and return any fire," he said.

This reporter, who was with the group of students, did not see any indication of sniper fire, nor was the sound of any gunfire audible before the Guard volley. Students, conceding that rocks had been thrown, heatedly denied that there was any sniper.

Gov. James A. Rhodes called on J. Edgar Hoover, director of the Federal Bureau of Investigation, to aid in looking into the campus violence. A Justice Department spokesman said no decision had been made to investigate.

At 2:10 this afternoon, after the shootings, the university president, Robert I. White, ordered the university closed for an indefinite time, and officials were making plans to evacuate the dormitories and bus out-of-state students to nearby cities.

Robinson Memorial Hospital identified the dead students as Allison Krause, 19 years old, of

Continued on Page 17, Column 1

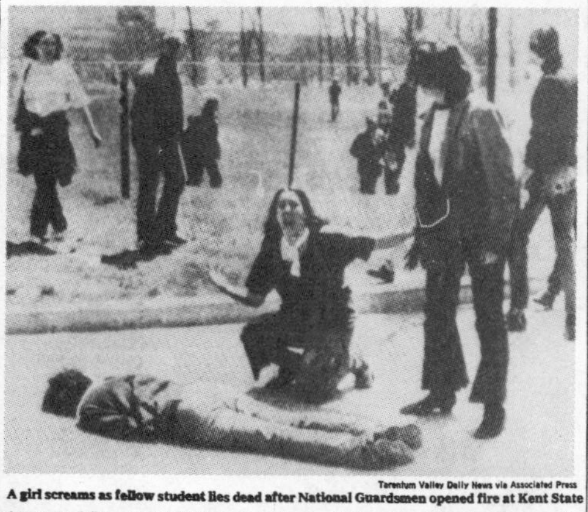

Tarentum Valley Daily News via Associated Press

A girl screams as fellow student lies dead after National Guardsmen opened fire at Kent State

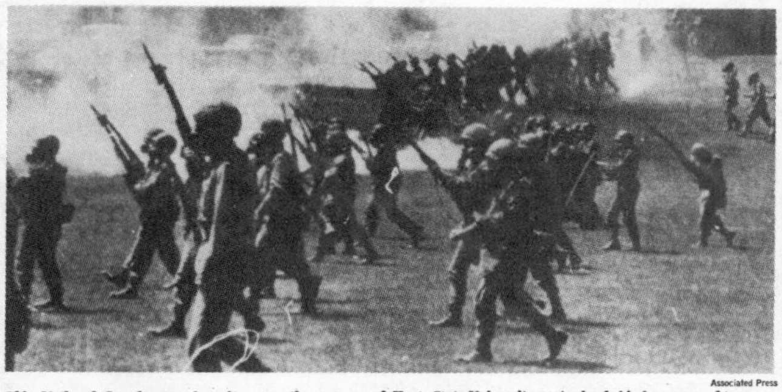

Associated Press

Ohio National Guardsmen advancing over the campus of Kent State University yesterday behind a screen of tear gas

HIGH COURT BACKS CHURCHES' RIGHT TO TAX EXEMPTION

Holds, 7 to 1, That Law Does Not Violate Ban on State Support of Religion

DOUGLAS CASTS DISSENT

Majority Rejects Plea of a Bronx Lawyer Over His Plot on Staten Island

By FRED P. GRAHAM

Special to The New York Times

WASHINGTON, May 4 — The Supreme Court ruled 7 to 1 today that laws that exempt church property from taxation do not violate the Constitution's prohibition against state support of religion.

The opinion was written by Chief Justice Warren E. Burger and was disputed only by Justice William O. Douglas. In it the Court upheld the constitutionality of New York State's exemption from real estate taxes of church property used solely for religious purposes.

The law had been challenged by Frederick Walz, a lawyer from the Bronx who purchased a 22-by-29-foot, weed-choked plot on Staten Island in 1967 and promptly sued the City Tax Commission over his $5.24 tax bill for a year.

'Establishment' Is Seen

Mr. Walz, who described himself as a "religious person, not a member of any religious organization," said that tax exemptions granted to church property raised his own tax bill and forced him to contribute to religious groups against his will.

He asserted that the result was an indirect state subsidy to churches, in violation of the First Amendment's prohibition against any "establishment of religion" by the Government.

The Supreme Court rejected that argument today, partly on the ground that no particular religion is singled out for favorable treatment and partly on the historical ground that church tax exemptions have been accepted almost without challenge in all states for most of the nation's history.

Chief Justice Burger's opinion conceded that the church exemption "necessarily operates to afford an indirect economic benefit." But he reasoned that the state might be less neutral toward churches if it taxed them and that it was faced with the delicate matter of deciding on each church's proper assessment.

Surprise and Concern

He concluded that some contact between churches and the state was inevitable and that it would be unfair to deny tax exemptions to religious groups while granting exemptions to nonsectarian charities that do similar good works.

The Supreme Court's decision to review Mr. Walz's appeal prompted widespread puzzlement in legal circles and concern among churchmen. The constitutionality of church tax exemptions was considered so well settled that the New York courts brushed off the challenge with brief orders declaring that it had no merit.

The American Civil Liberties Union backed Mr. Walz, and

Continued on Page 40, Column 5

3 in Bombing Plot Plead Guilty Here

By ARNOLD H. LUBASCH

Samuel J. Melville, Jane L. Alpert and John D. Hughey 3d pleaded guilty yesterday as the self-styled revolutionaries were about to stand trial on charges of conspiring to bomb Federal buildings here last fall.

After the case was convened amid stringent security measures in Federal Court, Judge Milton Pollack asked the bearded 34-year-old Melville why he wanted to plead guilty to three charges against him.

"I plead guilty to count one because I did conspire with others to destroy Federal property," Melville replied as he stood erectly in blue jeans and

Continued on Page 34, Column 1

WAR AND ECONOMY SPUR STOCK DROPS

Administration Economist Voices Apprehension as Market Falls 19.07

By TERRY ROBARDS

Uneasiness over the United States involvement in Cambodia and the bombing of North Vietnam, plus continuing uncertainty about the nation's business outlook, created a mood of deep pessimism on Wall Street yesterday and sent the securities markets into a tailspin.

Stock and bond prices fell sharply in response to selling by discouraged investors. The Dow-Jones industrial average, a gauge of price action on the New York Stock Exchange, plunged 19.07 points in its worst decline since the loss of 21.16 points Nov. 22, 1963, the day President Kennedy was assassinated.

In Washington, a leading Nixon Administration economist expressed apprehension about the situation. "The Administration is obviously concerned," he said, declining to be publicly identified.

"An emotional reaction triggered by the stock market decline may mislead people concerning the basic strength of the economy and its favorable prospects," he asserted, adding that "the facts in the economic sense are pretty good."

His statements represented the first clear indication of anxiety by the Nixon Administration with respect to the stock market's behavior. They were issued before the close of trading and before it was clear that yesterday's nosedive would be

Continued on Page 69, Column 2

Report of Songmy Incident Wins a Pulitzer for Hersh

By PETER KIHSS

A report on the alleged Songmy massacre of Vietnamese civilians by United States soldiers won the 1970 Pulitzer prize in international reporting yesterday for Seymour Hersh, a free-lance reporter whose article was circulated through the Dispatch News Service.

A black playwright, Charles Gordone, won the drama prize for an Off Broadway play, "No Place to Be Somebody"—the first Off Broadway production so honored.

A musical composition on an electronic synthesizer won the music prize for the first time, the award going to "Time's Encomium," by Charles Wuorinen.

Ada Louise Huxtable, architecture critic of The New York Times, became the winner of the first Pulitzer prize for distinguished criticism. This was a new category, set up for criticism or commentary, and was divided in the judging, with Marquis W. Childs of The St. Louis Post-Dispatch taking the award for distinguished commentary.

The gold medal for meritorious public service went to Newsday of Garden City, L. I., for a three-year investigation and exposé of secret land deals and zoning manipulations by public and political party officeholders.

With 17 individuals named Pulitzer prize-winners in the 54th year of the awards, the laurels for history were carried off by former Secretary of

Continued on Page 48, Column 1

Study of LSD Spurs Suspicions Of Drug's Link to Birth Defects

By SANDRA BLAKESLEE

The first extensive, long-term study comparing the incidence of birth defects with parental use of LSD has concluded that the drug "must be seriously considered as a possible mutagen"—an agent that produces genetic changes in cells.

"Although we cannot rush in and say we have unequivocal evidence at this time that LSD use causes birth defects, we are on firmer ground, more suspicious, than ever before," said Dr. Cheston M. Berlin, a principal investigator in the study.

Dr. Berlin, a pediatrician at George Washington University School of Medicine, where the study was conducted, presented his findings at two recent scientific meetings. He elaborated on the results in an interview yesterday.

The issue of whether LSD (shorthand for lysergic acid diethylamide) is a mutagenic agent has not yet been resolved, Dr. Berlin said.

Such agents, or changers, act in some way to alter the normal configuration of the genetic material within the cells of an organism, often causing the organism to reproduce itself abnormally, producing birth defects.

If LSD is a mutagenic agent, Dr. Berlin said, evidence of its cellular interference might turn

Continued on Page 23, Column 1

37 COLLEGE CHIEFS URGE NIXON MOVE FOR PROMPT PEACE

Warn Invasion of Cambodia Poses New Alienation Peril —Student Strikes Begin

By ROBERT D. McFADDEN

The presidents of 37 colleges and universities urged President Nixon yesterday to "demonstrate unequivocally your determination" to end promptly the United States military involvement in Southeast Asia.

In a letter to Mr. Nixon, the presidents said that "the American invasion of Cambodia" and the weekend bombing of North Vietnam had generated "severe and widespread apprehensions on our campuses."

"We share these apprehensions," the presidents said, adding:

"We implore you to consider the incalculable dangers of an unprecedented alienation of America's youth and to take immediate action to demonstrate unequivocally your determination to end the war quickly."

The signers, representing many of the nation's leading academic institutions, "urgently" requested a meeting with Mr. Nixon.

The letter was drafted by Dr. James M. Hester, the president of New York University, and bore the signatures, among others, of the presidents of Princeton University, Columbia University, the University of Notre Dame, Dartmouth College, the University of Pennsylvania and Johns Hopkins University.

Nationwide Strike Urged

In Washington, the leaders of the National Student Association and the former Vietnam Moratorium Committee called for a nationwide university strike of indefinite duration, starting today, to protest the war and to mobilize public opinion for a withdrawal of United States forces from Indochina. It would involve students, faculty members and administrators.

Antiwar groups at dozens of colleges and universities across the nation, meanwhile, began demonstrations and rallies to protest the Administration's policies.

There were strike pledges from at least 100 colleges and universities, and at some schools the strike began yesterday. Support for the strike was expressed in the editorials of many campus newspapers, along with a condemnation of what some called President Nixon's "illegitimate" decision to send troops into Cambodia.

At many schools, the strike was officially approved by college administrations. Most of

Continued on Page 18, Column 6

ISRAELIS REPORT KILLING 21 ARABS

Toll in Guerrilla Battle at Jordan River Is Termed Largest Since '67 War

By RICHARD EDER

Special to The New York Times

JERUSALEM, May 4—Israeli military authorities announced today that an Israeli patrol surprised and killed 21 armed Palestinian infiltrators shortly after they crossed the Jordan River into Israeli-controlled territory last night.

At the same time the Israelis reported some tentative signs that intensive air strikes on Egyptian artillery positions west of the Suez Canal were beginning to ease the recent pressure on Israeli troops on the east bank.

Last night's encounter with the guerrillas involved the largest death toll reported by Israeli forces since the start of the struggle with Arabs infiltrating into territories occupied by Israel after the 1967 war.

According to the account provided by Israeli military authorities, the infiltrators, members of Al Fatah guerrilla organization, were pinned down by fire from the Israeli patrol just before midnight, not far from the banks of the Jordan River.

The infiltrators tried to take shelter in scrub and thornbushes, the account continued. Apart from firing one bazooka shot, it went on, they made no move to answer the Israeli fire, which went on heavily but intermittently all night and which, by sunup, had killed all but six of them.

When it began to grow light,

Continued on Page 8, Column 4

President Assailed By Fulbright Panel

By JOHN W. FINNEY

Special to The New York Times

WASHINGTON, May 4—The Senate Foreign Relations Committee complained today that the Nixon Administration, by sending American troops into Cambodia "without the consent or knowledge of Congress," was usurping the war-making powers of Congress.

The committee, which is headed by Senator J. W. Fulbright, also charged that over the years the executive branch had been "conducting a constitutionally unauthorized, Presidential war in Indochina." The charge was promptly rejected by the White House, which contended that President Nixon was relying upon his constitutional powers as Commander in Chief.

"The action which the

Continued on Page 4, Column 4

U.S. SAYS BIG RAIDS IN NORTH ARE OVER

Officials Stress That There May Be Smaller Strikes if Flights Are Periled

By WILLIAM BEECHER

Special to The New York Times

WASHINGTON, May 4—The Defense Department announced today it had "terminated" large-scale air raids mounted in recent days against three areas of North Vietnam.

But Pentagon officials stressed that smaller air strikes might be conducted in the future if American reconnaissance flights over North Vietnam were attacked.

For the first time, the Pentagon acknowledged that the raids north of the demilitarized zone over the weekend had been larger in scope than any since the bombing halt in November, 1968, and that so-called "logistics support" facilities for air defense had been struck in addition to antiaircraft gun and missile sites.

3 Areas Attacked

The Defense Department said that from 50 to more than 100 planes had been employed in each of the strikes near Barthelemy Pass, Bankarai Pass and in another area immediately north of the demilitarized zone. Barthelemy Pass, about 240 miles north of the demilitarized zone, is believed to be the farthest point north raided by American aircraft since November, 1968.

All three areas, officials said, are key conduits for the flow of men and matériel to enemy military units throughout Indo-

Continued on Page 15, Column 1

U.S. Officials in Saigon Reduce Their Hopes in Cambodia Drive

Red Leaders Elude Sweep

By TERENCE SMITH

Special to The New York Times

SAIGON, South Vietnam, May 4—Senior United States military and civilian officials here are beginning to scale down their definitions of success for the four-day-old American-South Vietnamese sweep into the Fishhook area of Cambodia.

One of their preliminary conclusions is that the success or failure of the sweep will have to be measured in terms of supplies captured and facilities destroyed, since the top enemy command and the vast majority of the 7,000 Communist soldiers who were believed to have been in the area appear to have fled.

Another preliminary conclusion is that additional forays into other parts of eastern Cambodia are virtually inevitable if lasting damage is to be inflicted on the North Vietnamese supply system. Strikes into eastern Laos, the officials say, are not to be ruled out.

The officials consider that substantial withdrawals of United States combat troops from Vietnam will almost certainly have to be deferred to

Continued on Page 16, Column 3

Big Base Area Discovered

Special to The New York Times

LANDING ZONE NORTH ONE, Cambodia, May 4—Soldiers from this northernmost American outpost in the drive against enemy sanctuaries in Cambodia today reached the site of what is believed to be the largest North Vietnamese base area discovered in the operation, which began last Friday.

The base area, referred to on tactical maps as "The City," is situated in rolling hills and jungles near the northwestern tip of Binhlong Province of South Vietnam. The area is about two miles south of this outpost, which was hastily set up yesterday as a blocking position 20 miles north of where American tanks first plunged into Cambodia along the southern edge of the Fishhook area.

[As the American soldiers advanced, North Vietnamese and Vietcong troops increased their pressure against Pnompenh by cutting the Pnompenh-Saigon highway 29 miles from the Cambodian capital. Page 16.]

A company of soldiers from this base camp was waiting tonight for reinforcements and

Continued on Page 16, Column 3

KOSYGIN ATTACKS NIXON FOR MOVING G.I.'S TO CAMBODIA

He Tells News Conference Action Raises Doubts on Bids for Negotiations

WARNS ON ARMS PARLEY

China Pledges Support to Indochinese People — U.S. in New Drive

Excerpts from Kosygin's text and Q. and A., Page 2.

By BERNARD GWERTZMAN

Special to The New York Times

MOSCOW, May 4—Premier Aleksei N. Kosygin today assailed President Nixon for having sent American forces into Cambodia. He warned that the action might lead to a "further complication" in the international scene and a worsening of Soviet-American relations.

[Communist China also denounced the United States on Cambodia and pledged support to the people of Indochina in their "patriotic struggle" against American forces. Page 3.]

[The Associated Press reported that thousands of American and South Vietnamese troops launched a new offensive into northeast Cambodia Tuesday, according to an announcement by the United States command The command said the attack was launched from a base 50 miles west of Pleiku, in the Central Highlands, near the Laotian border.]

Reading from a statement at the start of his first news conference in the Soviet Union in more than five years in office, Mr. Kosygin said the Cambodia intervention raised doubts about Mr. Nixon's sincerity in seeking an "era of negotiation."

He Sees Contradictions

"Is it possible to speak seriously," Mr. Kosygin said, "about the desire of the United States President for fruitful negotiations to solve pressing international problems while the United States is grossly flouting the Geneva Agreements of 1954 and 1962 to which it is a party, and undertaking one new act after another undermining the foundations of international security?

"What is the value of international agreements which the United States is or intends to be a party to if it so ununceremoniously violates its obligations? It is impossible not to give serious thoughts to the fact that President Nixon's practical steps in the field of foreign policy are fundamentally at variance with those declarations and assurances that he repeatedly made both before assuming the Presidency and when he was already in the White House."

Attack Shocks Envoys

Western diplomats, who had expected a Soviet Government statement against the Cambodian action, were surprised that it was delivered by Mr. Kosygin in person, and were shocked by the personal attack on Mr. Nixon. Although Mr. Kosygin spoke in calm tones, the diplomats were taken aback by his characterization of President Nixon as a man whose words could not be trusted.

This seemed to indicate to the diplomats that a violent campaign would be started to enlist world opinion against Mr. Nixon.

Although the news conference was called to discuss Cambodia, in answer to a question on the Middle East, Mr. Kosygin said that Soviet military advisers were attached to the armed forces of the United Arab Republic to combat Israeli "aggression" and had certain

Continued on Page 3, Column 1

NEWS INDEX

"All the News That's Fit to Print"

The New York Times

LATE CITY EDITION

Weather: Partly sunny, mild today; fair tonight. Cloudy tomorrow. Temp. range: today 78-53; Friday 72-50. Full U.S. report on Page 48.

VOL. CXIX . No. 41,013

NEW YORK, SATURDAY, MAY 9, 1970

10 CENTS

NIXON DEFENDS CAMBODIA DRIVE AS AIDING STUDENTS' PEACE AIM; SAYS PULLOUT WILL BEGIN SOON

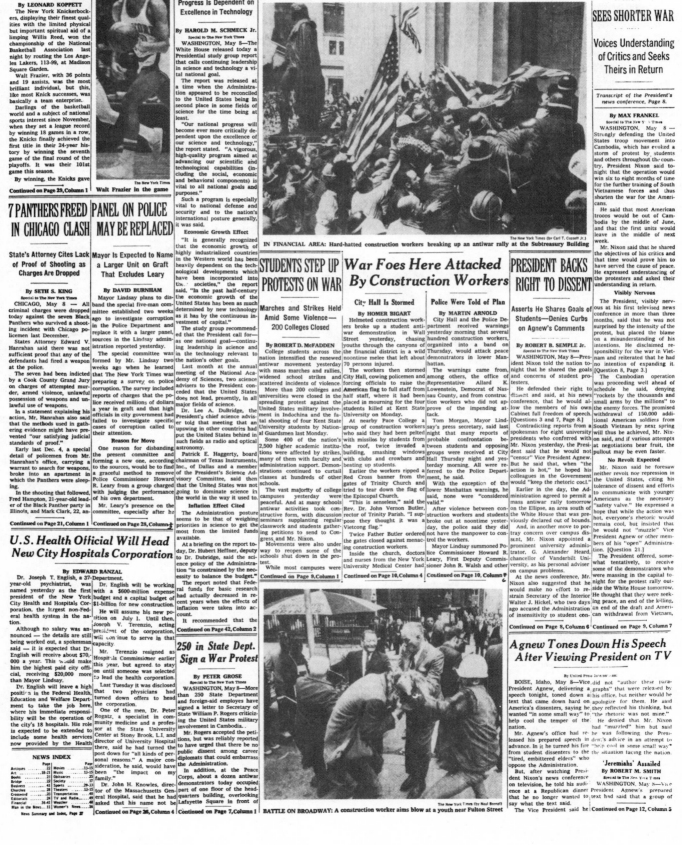

Knicks Take First Title, Beating Lakers, 113 to 99

Frazier Scores 36 Points, Reed Excels on Defense Despite Ailing Knee

By LEONARD KOPPETT

The New York Knickerbockers, displaying their finest qualities with the limited physical but important spiritual aid of a limping Willis Reed, won the championship of the National Basketball Association last night by routing the Los Angeles Lakers, 113-99, at Madison Square Garden.

Walt Frazier, with 36 points and 19 assists, was the most brilliant individual, but this, like most Knick successes, was basically a team enterprise.

Darlings of the basketball world and a subject of national sports interest since November, when they set a league record by winning 18 games in a row, the Knicks finally achieved the first title in their 24-year history by winning the seventh game of the final round of the playoffs. It was their 101st game this season.

By winning, the Knicks gave

Continued on Page 29, Column 1

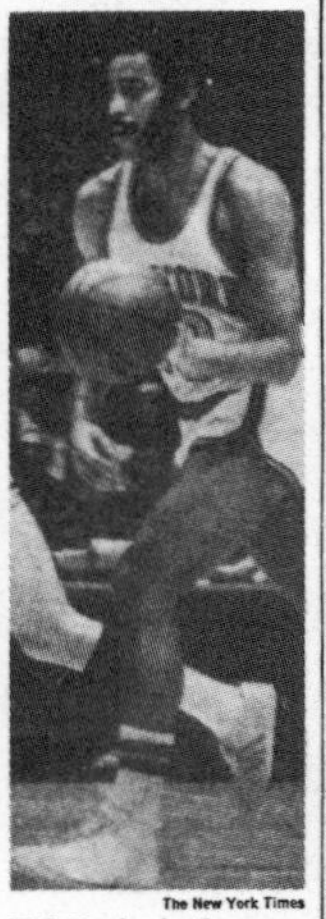

The New York Times

Walt Frazier in the game

NATION IS WARNED TO RETAIN ITS LEAD IN SCIENCE FIELDS

Study Group Contends U.S. Progress Is Dependent on Excellence in Technology

By HAROLD M. SCHMECK Jr.

Special to The New York Times

WASHINGTON, May 8—The White House released today a Presidential study group report that calls continuing leadership in science and technology a vital national goal.

The report was released at a time when the Administration appeared to be reconciled to the United States being in second place in some fields of science for the time being at least.

"Our national progress will become ever more critically dependent upon the excellence of our science and technology," the report stated. "A vigorous, high-quality program aimed at advancing our scientific and technological capabilities (including the social, economic and behavioral components) is vital to all national goals and purposes."

Such a program is especially vital to national defense and security and to the nation's international posture generally, it was said.

Economic Growth Effect

"It is generally recognized that the economic growth of highly industrialized countries in the Western world has been heavily dependent on the technological developments which have been incorporated into the: societies," the report said. "In the past half-century the economic growth of the United States has been as much determined by new technology as it has by the continuous investment of capital."

The study group recommended that the President call for—as one national goal—continuing leadership in science and in the technology relevant to the nation's other goals.

Last month at the annual meeting of the National Academy of Sciences, two science advisers to the President conceded that the United States does not lead, presently, in all major fields of science.

Dr. Lee A. DuBridge, the President's chief science adviser told that meeting that an upswing in other countries had put the United States behind in such fields as radio and optical astronomy.

Patrick E. Haggerty, board chairman of Texas Instruments, Inc., of Dallas and a member of the President's Science Advisory Committee, said then that the United States was not going to dominate science in the world in the way it used to.

Inflation Effect Cited

The Administration posture seems to be that of weighing priorities in science to get the most from the limited funds available.

At a briefing on the report today, Dr. Hubert Heffner, deputy to Dr. Dubridge, said the science policy of the Administration "is constrained by the necessity to balance the budget."

The report noted that Federal funds for basic research had actually decreased in recent years when the effects of inflation were taken into account.

It recommended that the

Continued on Page 42, Column 2

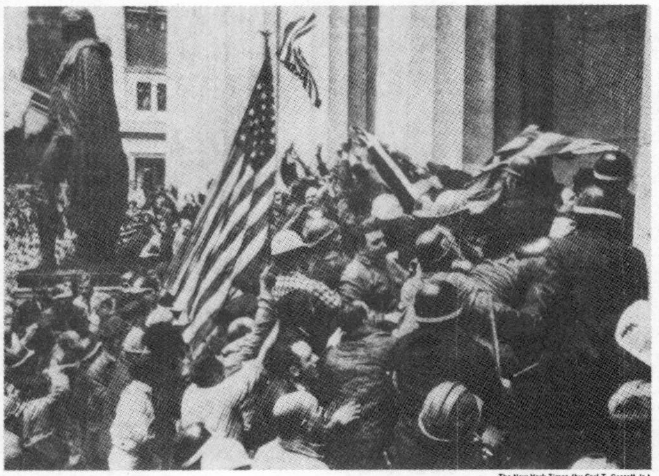

The New York Times (by Carl T. Gossett Jr.)

IN FINANCIAL AREA: Hard-hatted construction workers breaking up an antiwar rally at the Subtreasury Building

SEES SHORTER WAR

Voices Understanding of Critics and Seeks Theirs in Return

Transcript of the President's news conference, Page 8.

By MAX FRANKEL

Special to The New York Times

WASHINGTON, May 8 — Strongly defending the United States troop movement into Cambodia, which has evoked a storm of protest by students and others throughout the country, President Nixon said tonight that the operation would win six to eight months of time for the further training of South Vietnamese forces and thus shorten the war for the Americans.

He said that most American troops would be out of Cambodia by the middle of June, and that the first units would leave in the middle of next week.

Mr. Nixon said that he shared the objectives of his critics and that time would prove him to have served the cause of peace. He expressed understanding of the protesters and asked their understanding in return.

Visibly Nervous

The President, visibly nervous at his first televised news conference in more than three months, said that he was not surprised by the intensity of the protest, but placed the blame on a misunderstanding of his intentions. He disclaimed responsibility for the war in Vietnam and reiterated that he had no intention of expanding it. [Question 8, Page 3.]

The Cambodian operation was proceeding well ahead of schedule he said, denying "rockets by the thousands and small arms by the millions" to the enemy forces. The promised withdrawal of 150,000 additional American soldiers from South Vietnam by next spring will thus be achieved, Mr. Nixon said, and if various attempts at negotiations bear fruit, the pullout may be even faster.

No Revolt Expected

Mr. Nixon said he foresaw neither revolt nor repression in the United States, citing his tolerance of dissent and efforts to communicate with younger Americans as the necessary "safety valve." He expressed a hope that while the action was hot, everyone's rhetoric would remain cool, but insisted that he would not "muzzle" Vice President Agnew or other members of his "open" Administration. [Question 21.]

The President offered, somewhat tentatively, to receive some of the demonstrators who were massing in the capital tonight for the protest rally outside the White House tomorrow. He thought that they were seeking peace, an end of the killing, an end of the draft and American withdrawal from Vietnam,

Continued on Page 9, Column 7

STUDENTS STEP UP PROTESTS ON WAR

Marches and Strikes Held Amid Some Violence—200 Colleges Closed

By ROBERT D. McFADDEN

College students across the nation intensified the renewed antiwar movement yesterday with mass marches and rallies, widened school strikes and scattered incidents of violence.

More than 200 colleges and universities were closed in the spreading protest against the United States military involvement in Indochina and the fatal shooting of four Kent State University students by National Guardsmen last Monday.

Some 400 of the nation's 2,500 higher academic institutions were affected by strikes, many of them with faculty and administration support. Demonstrations continued to curtail classes at hundreds of other schools.

The vast majority of college campuses yesterday were peaceful. And at many schools antiwar activities took constructive form, with discussion seminars supplanting regular classwork and students gathering petitions to send to Congress and Mr. Nixon.

Movements were also under way to reopen some of the schools shut down in the protest.

While most campuses were

Continued on Page 9, Column 1

War Foes Here Attacked By Construction Workers

City Hall Is Stormed

By HOMER BIGART

Helmeted construction workers broke up a student antiwar demonstration in Wall Street yesterday, chasing youths through the canyons of the financial district in a wild noontime melee that left about 70 persons injured.

The workers then stormed City Hall, cowing policemen and forcing officials to raise the American flag to full staff from half staff, where it had been placed in mourning for the four students killed at Kent State University on Monday.

At nearby Pace College a group of construction workers who said they had been pelted with missiles by students from the roof, twice invaded a building, smashing windows with clubs and crowbars and beating up students.

Earlier the workers ripped a Red Cross banner from the gates of Trinity Church and tried to tear down the flag of the Episcopal Church.

"This is senseless," said the Rev. Dr. John Vernon Butler, rector of Trinity Parish. "I suppose they thought it was a Vietcong flag."

Twice Father Butler ordered the gates closed against menacing construction workers.

Inside the church, doctors and nurses from the New York University Medical Center had

Continued on Page 10, Column 4

Police Were Told of Plan

By MARTIN ARNOLD

City Hall and the Police Department received warnings yesterday morning that several hundred construction workers, organized into a band on Thursday, would attack peace demonstrators in lower Manhattan.

The warnings came from, among others, the office of Representative Allard K. Lowenstein, Democrat of Nassau County, and from construction workers who did not approve of the impending attack.

Tom Morgan, Mayor Lindsay's press secretary, said last night that many reports of probable confrontation between students and opposing groups were received at City Hall Thursday night and yesterday morning. All were referred to the Police Department, he said.

With the exception of the lower Manhattan warnings, he said, none were "considered valid."

After violence between construction workers and students broke out at noontime yesterday, the police said they did not have the manpower to control the workers.

Mayor Lindsay summoned Police Commissioner Howard R. Leary, First Deputy Commissioner John R. Walsh and other

Continued on Page 10, Column 6

PRESIDENT BACKS RIGHT TO DISSENT

Asserts He Shares Goals of Students—Denies Curbs on Agnew's Comments

By ROBERT B. SEMPLE Jr.

Special to The New York Times

WASHINGTON, May 8—President Nixon told the nation tonight that he shared the goals and concerns of student protesters.

He defended their right to dissent and said, at his news conference, that he would allow the members of his own Cabinet full freedom of speech. [Questions 3 and 7, Page 8.]

Contradicting reports from a spokesman for eight university presidents who conferred with Mr. Nixon yesterday, the President said that he would not "censcr" Vice President Agnew. But he said that, when "the action is hot," he hoped his colleagues in the Government would "keep the rhetoric cocl."

Earlier in the day, the Administration agreed to permit a mass antiwar rally tomorrow on the Ellipse, an area south of the White House that was previously declared out of bounds.

And, in another move to portray concern over campus dissent, Mr. Nixon appointed a prominent university administrator, G. Alexander Heard, chancellor of Vanderbilt University, as his personal adviser on campus problems.

At the news conference, Mr. Nixon also suggested that he would make no effort to restrain Secretary of the Interior Walter J. Hickel, who two days ago accused the Administration of insensitivity to student con-

Continued on Page 8, Column 6

Agnew Tones Down His Speech After Viewing President on TV

By United Press International

BOISE, Idaho, May 8—Vice President Agnew, delivering a speech tonight, toned down a text that came down hard on America's dissenters, saying he wanted "in some small way" to help cool the temper of the nation.

Mr. Agnew's office had released his prepared speech in advance. In it he turned his fire from student dissenters to the "tired, embittered elders" who oppose the Administration.

But, after watching President Nixon's news conference on television, he told his audience at a Republican dinner that he no longer wanted to say what the text said.

The Vice President said he did not "author these paragraphs" that were released by his office, but neither would he apologize for them. He said they reflected his thinking, but "the rhetoric was not mine."

He denied that Mr. Nixon had "muzzled" him but said he was following the President's advice in an attempt to "help cool in some small way" the situation facing the nation.

'Jeremiahs' Assailed

By ROBERT M. SMITH

Special to The New York Times

WASHINGTON, May 8—Vice President Agnew's prepared text had said that a group of

Continued on Page 12, Column 5

7 PANTHERS FREED IN CHICAGO CLASH

State's Attorney Cites Lack of Proof of Shooting as Charges Are Dropped

By SETH S. KING

Special to The New York Times

CHICAGO, May 8 — All criminal charges were dropped today against the seven Black Panthers who survived a shooting incident with Chicago policemen last December.

States Attorney Edward V. Hanrahan said there was not sufficient proof that any of the defendants had fired a weapon at the police.

The seven had been indicted by a Cook County Grand Jury on charges of attempted murder, armed violence, unlawful possession of weapons and unlawful use of weapons.

In a statement explaining his action, Mr. Hanrahan also said that the methods used in gathering evidence might have prevented "our satisfying judicial standards of proof."

Early last Dec. 4, a special detail of policemen from Mr. Hanrahan's office, carrying a warrant to search for weapons, broke into an apartment in which the Panthers were sleeping.

In the shooting that followed, Fred Hampton, 21-year-old leader of the Black Panther party in Illinois, and Mark Clark, 22, an-

Continued on Page 21, Column 1

PANEL ON POLICE MAY BE REPLACED

Mayor Is Expected to Name a Larger Unit on Graft That Excludes Leary

By DAVID BURNHAM

Mayor Lindsay plans to disband the special five-man committee established two weeks ago to investigate corruption in the Police Department and replace it with a larger panel, sources in the Lindsay administration reported yesterday.

The special committee was formed by Mr. Lindsay two weeks ago when he learned that The New York Times was preparing a survey on police corruption. The survey included reports of charges that the police received millions of dollars a year in graft and that high officials in city government had failed to investigate specific cases of corruption called to their attention.

Reason for Move

One reason for disbanding the present committee and forming a new one, according to the sources, would be to find a graceful method to remove Police Commissioner Howard R. Leary from a group charged with judging the performance of his own department.

Mr. Leary's presence on the committee, especially after he

Continued on Page 28, Column 2

U.S. Health Official Will Head New City Hospitals Corporation

By EDWARD RANZAL

Dr. Joseph T. English, a 37-year-old psychiatrist, was named yesterday as the first president of the New York City Health and Hospitals Corporation, the largest non-Federal health system in the nation.

Although no salary was announced — the details are still being worked out, a spokesman said — it is expected that Dr. English will receive about $70,000 a year. This would make him the highest paid city official, receiving $20,000 more than Mayor Lindsay.

Dr. English will leave a high position in the Federal Health, Education and Welfare Department to take the job here, where his immediate responsibility will be the operation of the city's 18 hospitals. His role is expected to be extended to include some health services now provided by the Health Department.

Dr. English will be working with a $600-million expense budget and a capital budget of $1-billion for new construction.

He will assume his new position on July 1. Until then, Joseph V. Terenzio, acting president of the corporation, will continue to serve in that capacity.

Mr. Terenzio resigned as Hospitals Commissioner earlier this year, but agreed to stay on until someone was selected to lead the health corporation.

Last Tuesday it was disclosed that two physicians had turned down offers to head the corporation.

One of the men, Dr. Peter Rogatz, a specialist in community medicine and a professor at the State University Center at Stony Brook, L.I. and director of University Hospital there, said he had turned the post down for "all kinds of personal reasons." A major consideration, he said, would have been "the impact on my family."

Dr. John H. Knowles, director of the Massachusetts General Hospital, said that he had asked that his name not be

Continued on Page 26, Column 4

250 in State Dept. Sign a War Protest

By PETER GROSE

Special to The New York Times

WASHINGTON, May 8—More than 250 State Department and foreign-aid employes have signed a letter to Secretary of State William P. Rogers criticizing the United States military involvement in Cambodia..

Mr. Rogers accepted the petitions, but was reliably reported to have urged that there be no public dissent among career diplomats that could embarrass the Administration.

In addition, at the Peace Corps, about a dozen antiwar demonstrators today occupied part of one floor of the headquarters building, overlooking Lafayette Square in front of

Continued on Page 7, Column 1

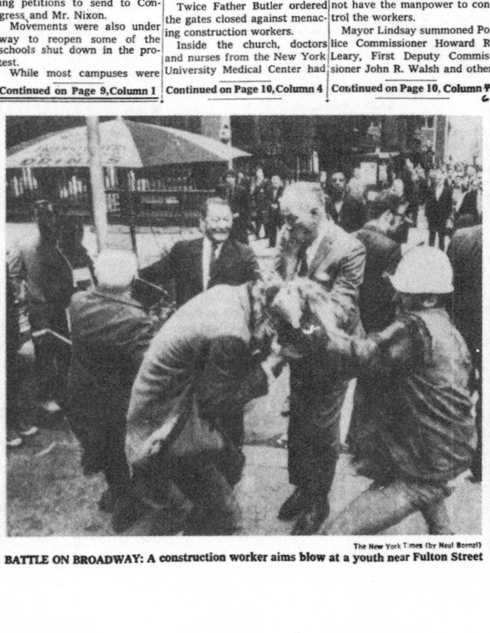

The New York Times (by Neal Boenzi)

BATTLE ON BROADWAY: A construction worker aims blow at a youth near Fulton Street

NEWS INDEX

Members of the ARVN wait to be flown into Laos. The Laotian encursion and subsequent battles were said to be the most brutal and difficult of the war.

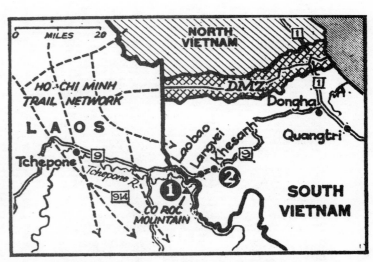

At the end of March 1971, the South Vietnamese ended their drive in Laos but 500 marines were left on a mountain (1) inside Laos to help in the defense of Khe Sanh.

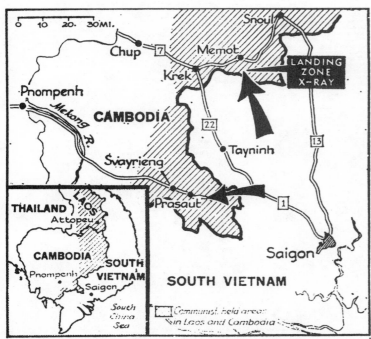

As American actions against Laos were escalated, an Allied task force swept into Cambodia to Landing Zone X-Ray, while a South Vietnamese force reached Prasaut in May 1970.

"All the News That's Fit to Print"

The New York Times

LATE CITY EDITION

Weather: Partly sunny, warm today. Partly cloudy tonight, tomorrow. Temp. range: today 84-58; Saturday 90-56. Full U.S. report on Page 87.

SECTION ONE

VOL. CXIX . No. 41,014 © 1970 The New York Times Company. NEW YORK, SUNDAY, MAY 10, 1970 60c beyond 50-mile zone from New York City, except Long Island. 75c beyond 200-mile radius. Higher in air delivery cities. 50 CENTS

LINDSAY DRAFTING A 2-STEP REVISION OF RENT CONTROLS

City Hall Expected to Offer Plan This Week Ordering Immediate Increases

15% RISES MENTIONED

2d Part, Intended for 1971, Provides for Annual Shifts Reflecting the Economy

By DAVID K. SHIPLER

Mayor Lindsay is expected to propose a two-step revision of the city's 27-year-old rent control law this week, with the first phase mandating immediate rent increases for thousands of tenants.

The second step — effective July 1, 1971—would create a complex formula of rentals based on fluctuating costs of operating and maintaining various classes of housing.

City officials spent two days last week briefing landlords and politicians on the basic structure of the upcoming recommendations. But no specific percentages or dollar amounts were mentioned. The figures to be inserted into the formulas will reportedly be decided upon tonight.

Even after the Mayor proposes exact rent increases, the Democratic leaders in the City Council are said to be planning slight trims in the figures in response to pressure from their constituents and some tenant-oriented junior Councilmen.

Amount Undecided

The first phase of the Lindsay package is expected to recommend immediate increases in rents for apartments that have had no increases since 1953. A rise of 15 per cent has been mentioned for the 200,000 flats in this category, although lower percentages are being considered.

Some sources close to the administration said last week that smaller rent increases might also be asked for apartments that have had only one of two rises since 1953.

Beginning in July, 1971, the city would use data from a study by Prof. George Sternlieb of Rutgers to set rent levels adequate for proper maintenance and operation in eight classes of housing.

The sources said the rents would vary from class to class, and would be based to a certain extent on the "assessed equalization," or market value, of each building.

Tenants paying less than these levels would have their rents increased annually, but probably by no more than 15 per cent every two years, until

Continued on Page 42, Column 4

Police Assailed by Mayor On Laxity at Peace Rally

Leary and His 2 Top Aides Summoned to Gracie Mansion—Lindsay Orders 'Prompt Disciplinary Action'

By MAURICE CARROLL

While Police Commissioner Howard R. Leary sat grim-faced at his left, Mayor Lindsay charged yesterday that New Yorkers had "witnessed a breakdown of the police as the barrier between them and wanton violence" on Friday.

He ordered Mr. Leary to conduct a "thorough investigation" of what he called "failures of police performance" when a band led by helmeted construction workers roamed lower Manhattan on Friday, beating antiwar demonstrators and storming City Hall, forcing officials to lift the United States flag atop the building to full staff. Seventy persons, including four policemen, were injured in the disorders.

The Mayor — angry over charges that the police had failed to marshal enough force to meet the mobs and that some policemen had been slow in guarding youngsters from the construction men — summoned the city's three top police officials to Gracie Mansion yesterday.

Joined by Deputy Mayor Richard R. Aurelio, he met privately for more than three hours with Mr. Leary, First Deputy Commissioner John F. Walsh and Chief Inspector George P. McManus.

Then reporters were called in and Mayor Lindsay read a statement saying that the violence by "marauding bands of construction workers" had been "appalling" and that the police had failed to contain it.

He ordered the following:

¶A "thorough investigation to fix responsibility at the command level" and "prompt dis-

Continued on Page 25, Column 2

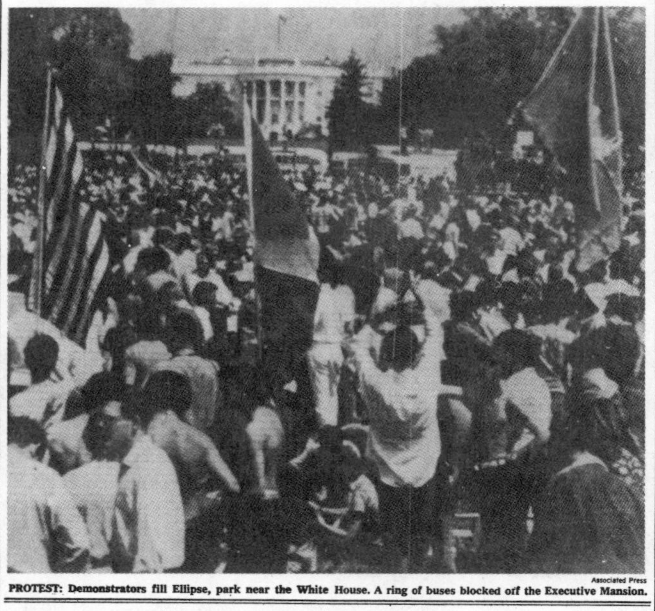

PROTEST: Demonstrators fill Ellipse, park near the White House. A ring of buses blocked off the Executive Mansion. Associated Press

BIG CAPITAL RALLY ASKS U.S. PULLOUT IN SOUTHEAST ASIA

Protesters and Police Clash —Guard Building Bombed —300 Reported Detained

MAJORITY ARE PEACEFUL

Speeches Show Resentment Against Cambodia Action and Killing of Students

By JOHN HERBERS
Special to The New York Times

WASHINGTON, Sunday, May 10—A great crowd of youths, most from the troubled college campuses across the country, demonstrated peaceably yesterday at the rear of a barricaded White House, demanding the withdrawal of United States military forces from Cambodia, Laos and Vietnam.

Afterwards, a few hundred militants in small groups spread through the surrounding streets, crashing the barricades, disrupting traffic, hurling rocks and bottles and breaking windows. The police broke up the most threatening crowds with tear gas.

Blast at Guard Building

Early this morning, a bomb blew out the glass facade of the National Guard building. No one was reported injured.

At about 2 A. M., the police began routing demonstrators from the grounds of the Washington Monument and the Ellipse after an argument between a demonstrator and a Federal park policeman escalated into a rock-throwing melee. About 300 had been arrested in disturbances yesterday and early today.

An at George Washington University nearby, a rally of militant students was broken up by policemen using tear gas.

At midday, under a hot sun, the throng filled the Ellipse, the tree-lined park of several grassy acres just south of the Presidential mansion.

Mayor Walter E. Washington and the District of Columbia police estimated the crowd at between 75,000 and 100,000.

A moatlike ring of 59 city buses, parked bumper to bumper along Executive Avenue, separated the protesters from the White House and President Nixon, who remained inside after making an early morning trip to the Lincoln Memorial and talking to a group of youths.

Only a portion of the crowd could see the White House, but there was constant communication across the buses. Members of the White House staff mingled with the crowd and the White House press room was open to editors of student newspapers.

90 in the Shade

The worst problem was the heat. Several hundred demonstrators were treated by volunteer medics for heat prostration.

When the antiwar program got under way at 1 P.M., the temperature was 90 degrees in the shade and the crowd, as a result, was somewhat languid. Some of the demonstrators splashed in the fountain and two youths were arrested for removing all their clothing.

But the scene created the

Continued on Page 24, Column 2

Crime Jury in Jersey City Calls Whelan and Aides

By RONALD SULLIVAN
Special to The New York Times

JERSEY CITY, May 9—Mayor Thomas J. Whelan, seven leading officials of his administration and one county official have been subpoenaed by a Federal grand jury that is investigating crime and alleged corruption in Hudson County.

Mayor Whelan, who was given a subpoena at his home late last night, said he welcomed the investigation and promised his "full cooperation."

"At long last," the Mayor said, "the cloud that some people insinuate hangs over our city may be disposed of once and for all.",

The Mayor, a Democrat, and city officials were ordered to give the jury all records and memorandums on city construction contracts exceeding $100,000.

State Prepares Indictments

The Federal move in Hudson County was disclosed as state officials reported in Trenton that the state grand jury that was also investigating organized crime and corruption in Hudson County was preparing indictments against a number of political figures here—both Democratic and Republican.

The Federal and state investigations are independent. A high state official said this afternoon he had no prior knowledge of the Federal inquiry until he heard of the subpoenaes.

The subpoenaes for Mayor Whelan and his associates were signed by Frederick B. Lacey, the United States Attorney who obtained Federal indictments last January against Mayor Hugh J. Addonizio of Newark and four Newark city councilmen.

Mr. Addonizio and the other

Continued on Page 41, Column 1

REUTHER BELIEVED DEAD IN AIR CRASH

U.A.W. Leader and Wife Are Reported Among 6 Killed in Fog in Michigan

By The Associated Press

PELLSTON, Mich., May 9—A small jet plane chartered by the United Auto Workers union crashed tonight in a heavy fog near Pellston. The dispatcher for the charter plane service said in Detroit that Walter P. Reuther, United Auto Workers president, was aboard.

Clarence Tatro, the Pellston airport manager, said all six persons aboard the Lear jet plane had been killed when it crashed 1½ miles from the airport in this northern Lower Michigan community.

Larry Hopkins, the midnight dispatcher at Butler Aviation, which routaes planes at Detroit Metropolitan Airport, said that Mr. Reuther and his wife had boarded the plane.

Mr. Tatro said that a U.A.W. driver had been waiting at the airport to take the occupants to the unions nearby family education center near Onoway.

The state police did not immediately release the names of the victims. Union officials declined immediate comment.

At the center, L. W. Woodward, the deskman, said that the union's president, Walter P. Reuther, "was due in this evening around 11."

Mr. Tatro said that the flight was on the way from Detroit to Pellston, a scenic area. He said he understood that the pilot had been in contact with the airport while coming in for a

Continued on Page 84, Column 5

30 U.S. Ships Join Push Into Cambodia On Mekong River

By RALPH BLUMENTHAL
Special to The New York Times

SAIGON, South Vietnam, May 9—Thirty American gunboats joined with a South Vietnamese flotilla today in a thrust into Cambodia on the Mekong River.

The operation and the American involvement were announced tonight by the United States command here. In the last several days the Navy's spokesman in Saigon had denied speculation and unofficial reports that American boats would participate.

The timing of the announcement tonight, after the operation began this morning, indicated that the allied attacking force had already crossed into Cambodia by nightfall.

[A South Vietnamese general said Sunday, according to Reuters, that Saigon's troops in the flotilla operation had captured the strategic Mekong River ferry crossing at Neak Luong. The officer, Maj. Gen. Ngo Dzu, was quoted as having said tehat the soldiers would join up with Cambodian forces later in the day.]

The American command also announced two new ground operations across the border into Cambodia. These added several thousand men to the 12,000 combat soldiers already engaged in the sweeps against Vietnamese Communist forces in Cambodian territory.

It had been reported in the

Continued on Page 22, Column 5

DRIVE IN CAMBODIA TERMED A SUCCESS

White House Says Foe Lost Four Months' Worth of Ammunition In Drive

By TAD SZULC
Special to The New York Times

WASHINGTON, May 9 — Asserting that success in the first nine days of the allied military sweep in Cambodia exceeded all expectations, the White House said today that American and South Vietnamese forces had already captured more enemy ammunition than the North Vietnamese and Vietcong had fired in Vietnam in the first four months of this year.

In making the report, the White House issued a detailed list of allied and enemy casualties and of captured and destroyed enemy matériel, installations and supplies. Administration officials went further than President Nixon did at his news conference last night to express belief that the operations need not foreclose peace talks with Hanoi and broader disarmament negotiations with the Soviet Union.

The move into Cambodia by allied forces last week was aimed, according to the Administration, at destroying a complex of enemy bases and preventing North Vietnam and the Vietcong from expanding their activities in South Vietnam.

President Nixon said at his

Continued on Page 23, Column 1

Nixon, in Pre-Dawn Tour, Talks to War Protesters

By ROBERT B. SEMPLE Jr.
Special to The New York Times

WASHINGTON, May 9—President Nixon left the White House shortly before dawn this morning, drove to the Lincoln Memorial and spent an hour chatting with young people who had come to protest his war policies.

The extraordinary visit, which caught his staff unawares and left the Secret Service "petrified," was Mr. Nixon's first direct exchange with students massed here for a weekend of protest.

As he stood on the steps of the Memorial and talked, the crowd around him grew from eight to 30 to 50, and near the end of what appears to have been more monologue than dialogue, he asked the students "to try to understand what we are doing."

Breakfast at Hotel

Afterwards he drove to the Capitol, ate breakfast at the Mayflower Hotel—his first visit to a restaurant here since his inauguration—then returned to the White House. Then he spent the rest of the day with his family, protected from the demonstrators on the Ellipse but within earshot of their cheers, chants and taunts.

His excursion was brief, lasting three and one-half hours. But it provided a revealing glimpse of a man who has been under exceptional strain for the last few weeks, who has been forced to improvise rapidly to

Continued on Page 24, Column 7

FINCH CRITICIZES AGNEW REMARKS

But H.E.W. Secretary Later Issues a Statement That Softens His Comments

By JAMES T. NAUGHTON
Special to The New York Times

WASHINGTON, May 9—Robert H. Finch, Secretary of Health, Education and Welfare, told student demonstrators today that the public rhetoric of Vice President Agnew and Gov. Ronald Reagan of California had "contributed to heating up the climate in which the Kent State students were killed."

Mr. Finch made the remark to 40 young people on a grassy mall across Independence Avenue from his department's headquarters.

One student asked the Secretary if he saw any connection betwen the shooting of the four Kent State students by Ohio National Guard troops last Monday and Governor Reagan's remark last month that "if it takes a bloodbath" to deal with campus demonstrations "let's get it over with."

Mr. Finch replied that there had been "a whole series of casual relationships, including some of the Agnew rhetoric."

The student asked whether the Vice President's rhetoric had contributed to the deaths.

"It contributed to heating up

Continued on Page 24, Column 3

Lindsay Asks 25c As S.I. Ferry Fare

Mayor Lindsay has proposed a fivefold increase in one of the last things of value that a nickel will buy—a ride on the Staten Island ferry.

The Mayor has made "several overtures" to City Council leaders in an effort to reach agreement on raising the fare, which has been a nickel for more than 70 years, to 25 cents, City Hall sources said.

Spokesmen for the Mayor declined to comment on a report that a deal had been worked out between the Mayor and Council leaders, but a Council spokesman denied the report.

The Council spokesman "denied flatly that there has been

Continued on Page 48, Column 1

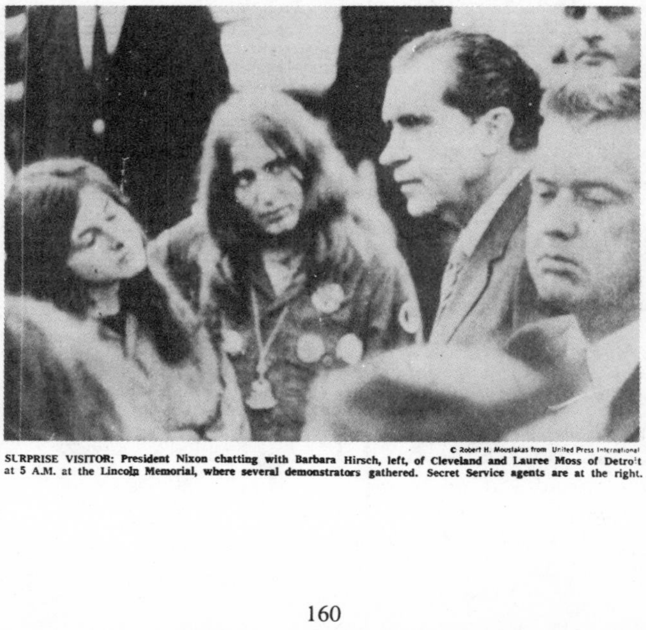

© Robert H. Moustakas from United Press International

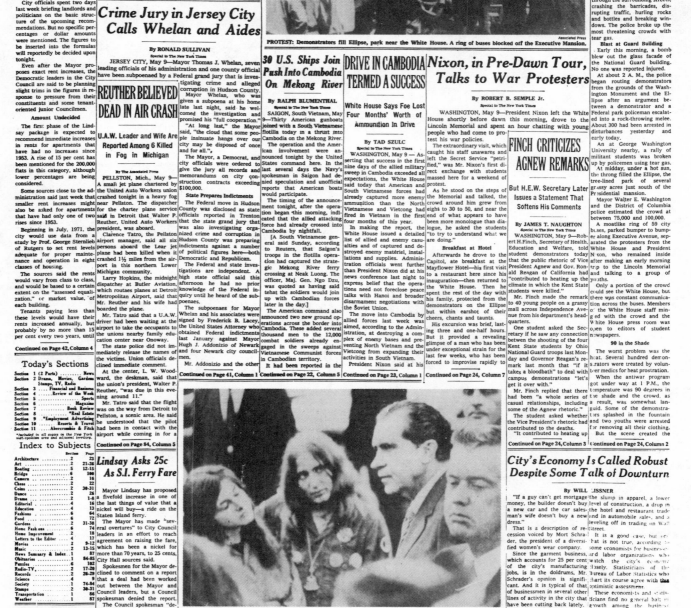

SURPRISE VISITOR: President Nixon chatting with Barbara Hirsch, left, of Cleveland and Lauree Moss of Detroit at 5 A.M. at the Lincoln Memorial, where several demonstrators gathered. Secret Service agents are at the right.

City's Economy Is Called Robust Despite Some Talk of Downturn

By WILL LISSNER

"If a guy can't get mortgage money, the builder doesn't buy a new car and the car salesman's wife doesn't buy a new dress."

That is a description of recession voiced by Mort Schrader, the president of a diversified women's wear company.

Since the garment business, which accounts for 25 per cent of the city's manufacturing jobs, is in the doldrums, Mr. Schrader's opinion is significant. And it is typical of that of businessmen in several other lines of activity in the city that have been cutting back lately.

Is the city's economy about to enter a recession? Some make a case that it is, citing the slump in apparel, a lower level of construction, a drop in the hotel and restaurant trade and in automobile sales, and a leveling off in trading on Wall Street.

It is a good case, but one that is not true, according to some economists for businesses and labor organizations who watch the city's economy closely. Statisticians of the Bureau of Labor Statistics who chart its course agree with this optimistic assessment.

These economists and statisticians find no general halt in growth among the business establishments here, of which

Continued on Page 70, Column 4

Today's Sections

Index to Subjects

"All the News That's Fit to Print"

The New York Times

LATE CITY EDITION

Weather: Partly sunny, cooler today; clear tonight. Fair, cool tomorrow. Temp. range: today 78-63; Thurs. 91-67. Temp.-Hum. Index yesterday 80. Full U.S. report on Page 77.

VOL. CXIX ... No. 41,047

NEW YORK, FRIDAY, JUNE 12, 1970

15 CENTS

NIXON AIDES WEIGH RESHAPING A.E.C. FOR A WIDER ROLE

A New Agency Would Deal With All Energy Forms, but Not With Weaponry

POWER SHIFTS STUDIED

Pentagon Would Take Over Military Programs—Fight in Congress Foreseen

By ANTHONY RIPLEY
Special to The New York Times

WASHINGTON, June 11 — The Nixon Administration is seriously considering a plan to break up the Atomic Energy Commission and remake it into an agency dealing with all forms of energy.

Administration sources said the proposal would shift the commission's military programs to the Department of Defense and many of its research activities to the National Science Foundation.

The A.E.C. would then be broadened into an over-all energy agency. One problem it would deal with is the electric power shortage, which threatens much of the East with power brownouts this summer.

The full dimensions of the reorganization plan, which is still under study, are not clear. Oil, gas and coal are now the provinces of the Department of the Interior, while electric power regulation is under the jurisdiction of the Federal Power Commission.

Coming of Age

Administration sources have made it clear that they believe atomic energy has come of age and should be considered on a competitive basis with other energy sources.

The A.E.C. reorganization, if proposed by the President, would be sure to touch off a major political battle in Congress. The commission is one of the most influential Federal agencies, with strong support on Capitol Hill.

The Presidential study comes at a time when the commission is under attack by environmentalists, the State of Minnesota, peace groups and even some of its own scientists.

The proposal under study is believed to be a recommenda-

Continued on Page 22, Column 2

President Asks End Of 20 Oil Contracts Off Santa Barbara

By E. W. KENWORTHY
Special to The New York Times

WASHINGTON, June 11—President Nixon asked Congress today to approve legislation canceling 20 Federal oil leases in the Santa Barbara Channel, where a blow-out in January, 1969, polluted miles of beaches and destroyed much marine life.

The bill would establish a Federal marine sancutary, approximately 18 miles long, paralleling the shore and extending 20 miles seaward to Santa Cruz Island.

This rough square, totaling 198,200 acres, would be seaward of the Santa Barbara state oil sancutary, extending from the shore to the three-mile limit, which California created in 1955 to protect the scenic coastline.

Oil drilling was banned in the state sanctuary and it will be banned, under the proposed bill, in the larger Federal sanctuary, unless exigencies of national interest require that its reserves be

Continued on Page 23, Column 2

NAMING OF SHULTZ HAILED IN CAPITAL

Agency Officials Glad That an Expert in Economics Will Be Close to Nixon

By EILEEN SHANAHAN
Special to The New York Times

WASHINGTON, June 11—The appointment of George P. Shultz to head the Government's reorganized and expanded budget and management operation has been greeted with enthusiasm by Federal officials responsible for national economic policy.

Their pleasure at the appointment does not reflect any belief that Mr. Shultz will, necessarily, advocate fundamental changes in present economic policies.

He is thought to be in general agreement with those policies, which are aimed at ending inflation without triggering an outright recession, even though the policies have recently come under increasing criticism as unsucoessful on both counts.

The personnel change, rather, is applauded as one that places a man with comprehensive knowledge of economics in a newly created dual position: a key spot on the White House staff and also as the head of a major operating agency.

In the words of one official in a major economic agency:

"I'm pleased not so much because Shultz may bring a change in the political complexion on the White House staff, though he may, as because now there will be some-

Continued on Page 20, Column 1

HUSSEIN ACCEPTS GUERRILLA TERMS; OUSTS 2 GENERALS

King Takes Over Command of the Jordanian Army—Fighting in 5th Day

By DANA ADAMS SCHMIDT
Special to The New York Times

AMMAN, Jordan, June 11—After five days of the bloodiest fighting ever between Arab guerrillas and the Jordanian Army, King Hussein yielded tonight to the two principal commando demands by removing his uncle as Commander in Chief and dismissing the commander of the Third Armored Division, which surrounds the capital.

The 34-year-old monarch announced that he was taking personal command of the army.

The commandos had accused the two ousted officials, Maj. Gen. Nasser Ben-Jamil, the Commander in Chief, and Maj. Gen. Zaid Ben-Shaker, the commander of the armored unit, of plotting with the United States Government against the Palestinian cause.

However, the King was understood to have rejected a commando demand that these and two other men be deported. The two others were Mohammed Rasoul al-Kallani, the former chief of security, and Wasfi Tal, a former premier.

Appeal By U.S. Aide

The King's action came after critical negotiations tonight between a top palace aide and a representative of Yasir Arafat, the over-all commando leader.

The commando groups are demanding the right to conduct unrestricted operations across the border into Israel, but the Jordanian Government is reluctant to allow this, in part out of fear for its own security and in part out of fear of Israeli reprisals.

The critical nature of the talks and the deterioration of security in the capital were underlined by an appeal tonight by the United States chargé d'affaires, Harry Odell, to take measures to protect the lives and property of Americans in Jordan.

Bands Steal Cars

The appeal was made after roving bands, asserting that they were commandos, roamed through residential areas stealing cars. The United States Embassy, had reports of 35 cases of stolen vehicles, some belonging to Americans.

Yesterday, Maj. Robert P. Perry, a United States military attaché, was killed at his home in Amman.

In several cases today, an Embassy spokesman said, American women were roughed up by men who came to the doors of their homes and demanded the keys to cars. "We have advised Americans faced

Continued on Page 2, Column 4

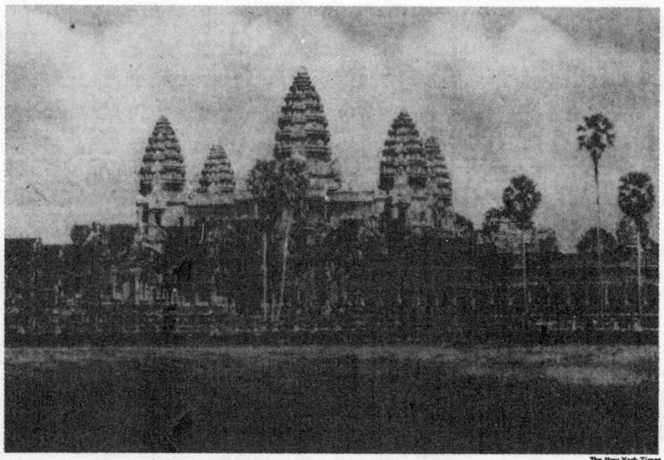

The New York Times

TEMPLES OF CAMBODIA: A view of the ancient structures at Angkor. Communist troops have been reported in area.

Nixon Heads Effort To Free Americans Detained in Amman

By TAD SZULC
Special to The New York Times

WASHINGTON, June 11—President Nixon assumed the direction of urgent efforts today to assure the safety of about 24 Americans held hostage by Palestinian guerrillas in two Amman hotels and of other Americans in Jordan.

The President acted on reports from the United States Embassy in Jordan that the situation was rapidly worsening.

Mr. Nixon met for an hour with Henry A. Kissinger, his national security adviser, to decide what civilian or military rescue operations might be undertaken to protect the estimated 535 Americans in Jordan.

The White House press secretary, Ronald L. Ziegler, said that the Washington Special Action Group—the top-level emergency policy-making team of the Administration—met throughout the day to "consider implications of the Jordanian conflict."

The group is headed by Mr. Kissinger and includes Under Secretary of State Elliot L. Richardson and David Packard, Deputy Secretary of Defense.

The situation was said to have held the President at his desk here much longer than planned.

"The overriding concern is United States citizens in the area," Mr. Ziegler said at a White House briefing.

Officials said that fragmentary reports from the embassy in Amman told of the looting of the homes of Americans in Amman.

State Department officials said that according to the em-

Continued on Page 2, Column 4

SOVIET WIDENS AID TO NORTH VIETNAM

Says Accord Is in Response to Broader Indochina War —Podgorny Assails U.S.

By BERNARD GWERTZMAN
Special to The New York Times

MOSCOW, June 11—The Soviet Union announced today that it was increasing its military and economic aid to North Vietnam as a result of intensified fighting in Indochina.

The new assistance, supplementing an aid agreement signed last October, was announced by Tass, the Soviet press agency, while President Nikolai V. Podgorny was telling the Soviet people that relations with the United States were "in a frozen state" because of Washington's "aggressive course."

Tass published excerpts from a Soviet-North Vietnamese communiqué that said "the Soviet Union is giving additional assistance to Vietnam at a time when American imperialists are intensifying the aggressive war in South Vietnam, when they are bombing some areas of the Democratic Republic of [North] Vietnam, carrying out military escalation in Laos and waging

Continued on Page 14, Column 1

Temple Ruins at Angkor Reported in Foe's Hands

By SYDNEY H. SCHANBERG
Special to The New York Times

PNOMPENH, Cambodia, June 11—Communist troops were reported today to have seized control of the area of the renowned temple ruins at Angkor in northwest Cambodia. Communist forces reportedly also opened a new attack on Siemreap, a provincial capital only four miles from the edge of the huge temple complex.

The Government's military spokesman, Maj. Am Rong, told newsmen of the Siemreap attack and later said enemy troops were believed to be inside the temple complex itself.

[French refugees who fled the fighting said on arrival in Pnompenh that 200 to 300 North Vietnamese troops had set up bases in the temple area and were using the ruins as sanctuaries, Reuters reported.]

Asserting that planes could not be used against the enemy there "because the temples are our patrimony," Major Am Rong made "an appeal to international opinion" for help to save them.

Asked specifically what the Pnompenh Government was appealing for, he said, "All kinds of arms and equipment—not

Continued on Page 15, Column 1

70 CIVILIANS DEAD IN A VIETCONG RAID

Toll in Attack at Hamlet in South Vietnam Is Termed Highest Since Tet Drive

By Reuters

SAIGON, South Vietnam, June 11—Vietcong guerrillas shot their way through a South Vietnamese hamlet early today, killing 70 civilians in their homes, a United States military spokesman said.

He reported that 31 civilians had been wounded and that the death toll had been the highest in any single attack by the enemy since the Tet offensive of 1968.

The spokesman said that the guerrillas had fled before reinforcements for the local militiamen could arrive.

Near Main Road

The hamlet, Baren, is 17 miles southeast of Danang in northern Quangnam Province and only a few hundred yards from Route 1, South Vietnam's main north-south road.

Militiamen guarding a small but important bridge nearby were hit by mortars and assaulted by an undetermined number of Vietcong soldiers only 15 minutes before the hamlet was attacked, the military spokesman said. [The Associated Press reported that United States marines had also been guarding the bridge.]

Baren was the third settlement in the northern coastal lowlands to report heavy casualties in the last week.

The military spokesman gave this account of the raid, which started before dawn:

The defenders of the small bridge, 350 miles north-north-

Continued on Page 14, Column 5

NIXON IS REBUFFED BY SENATE, 52-47, ON CAMBODIA ISSUE

It Rejects Byrd's Proposal to Modify Effort to Curb New Military Forays

A COOPER-CHURCH GAIN

Amendment's Backers Add Clause Denying Aim Is to Cut President's Power

By JOHN W. FINNEY
Special to The New York Times

WASHINGTON, June 11—In a rebuff to President Nixon, the Senate refused today to modify proposed legislative restrictions on future American military operations in Cambodia.

By a vote of 52 to 47, the Senate rejected a proposal to declare that the President, under his authority as Commander in Chief, could retain troops in Cambodia if he thought such action necessary to protect the safety of American forces in Vietnam. The proposal had been offered by Senator Robert C. Byrd, Democrat of West Virginia, and endorsed by Mr. Nixon.

The vote provided the clearest test of the sentiment in the Senate for imposing legislative restrictions on the President's authority to involve the nation in military action in Cambodia without the consent of Congress.

July 1 Deadline Proposed

Such restrictions are embodied in the pending amendment offered by Senators John Sherman Cooper and Frank Church to a bill on foreign sales of weapons.

The amendment would prohibit the President, in the absence of Congressional approval, from spending any funds after July 1 for retaining United States forces in Cambodia, for providing military advisers or combat air support to the Cambodian forces or for financing the pay of forces from third countries going to the aid of the Cambodian Government.

The effect of the vote today was to reinforce expectations that the Senate, trying to reassert Congress's war-making powers under the Constitution, would eventually approve the bipartisan Cooper-Church draft. Mr. Cooper is a Kentucky Republican and Mr. Church an Idaho Democrat.

Provision Added to Bill

Throughout the four-week debate, the discussion has focused on whether the amendment would infringe upon the President's constitutional powers as Commander in Chief.

In an attempt to clarify the issue—as well as to obtain support in a close vote—the Cooper-Church forces added a provision today specifying that nothing in the amendment "shall be deemed to impugn the constitutional powers of the President as Commander in Chief."

The provision, offered by Senator Mike Mansfield, the majority leader, was adopted by a vote of 91 to 0.

The unanimous vote made it

Continued on Page 12, Column 1

REPUTED MAFIOSI SEIZED IN RAIDS

Among 35 Arrested After Contempt Indictments

By LAWRENCE VAN GELDER

Thirty-five reputed underworld figures were arrested yesterday in eight counties in and around New York City as District Attorney Eugene Gold of Kings County announced their indictment on charges of criminal contempt.

Eleven other men whose indictments were also announced were still being sought on the same charges.

The charges resulted from the defendants' alleged refusal to answer questions put to them after they were granted immunity from prosecution by a Kings County grand jury investigating the infiltration of legitimate businesses by organized crime and a series of shootings.

Among those seized in raids carried out as early as 6 A.M. by nearly 100 men from Mr. Gold's office and the Police Department were reputed members of the Mafia "families" of Carlo Gambino and Joseph Colombo and one formerly headed by Joseph Bonanno.

Mr. Gold said the arrests indicated that "we are going to pursue the lawless conduct of organized crime relentlessly." No one, he said, "has the right to flout the authority of a grand jury."

Mr. Gold said he believed the arrests were the most at any one time involving organized crime since 1957, when 62 un-

Continued on Page 16, Column 3

Alexander Kerensky Dies Here at 89

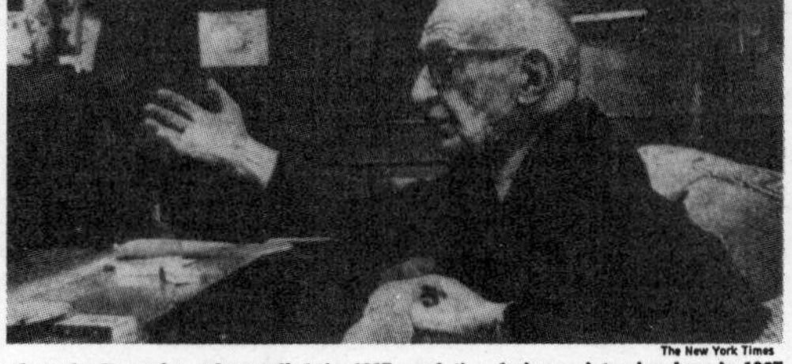

The New York Times

Alexander Kerensky as he recalled the 1917 revolution during an interview here in 1967

By ALDEN WHITMAN

Alexander Kerensky, who led the first phase of the Russian Revolution in 1917 until he was overthrown in the Bolshevik coup, died yesterday of arteriosclerotic heart disease at St. Luke's Hospital. He was 89 years of age.

The former Premier entered the hospital April 24 to recover from a broken elbow and pelvis sustained in a fall, according to Countess Sira Ilinska, a longtime confidante.

For a brief and meteoric moment Alexander Fyodorovich Kerensky, 36 years old and a lawyer, was at the vortex of the Russian Revolution, the greatest social, political and economic convulsion since the French Revolution. The complex forces that generated that event overwhelmed him, and the power he exercised for little more than four months dribbled from his grasp to be picked up and held onto by the Communists. For the remainder of his life he was the epitome of failure in a revolution, a man derided by the victors, an exile from his country who was a curiosity in his adopted land and who passed his time in fulminations against the Soviet State and attempts to justify his actions in the Provisional Government of 1917.

Fortuitously involved in the drama of the revolution, Kerensky (pronounced KAY-ren-ski) seemed to some, in perspective, to deserve Leon Trotsky's verdict: "Kerensky was

Continued on Page 26, Column 1

U.S. Methadone Plan Proposed To Guide Wider Use and Study

By HAROLD M. SCHMECK Jr.
Special to The New York Times

WASHINGTON, June 11—The Federal Government took major steps today toward regulating the use of methadone and gathering proof of its value in rehabilitating narcotics addicts.

New proposed regulations, announced today at a news conference, are expected to drive out of operation some of the groups using the heroin substitute in programs for addicts. Other groups may find it easier to get a legal start. Over-all, methadone use is expected to increase significantly under the new regulations.

Methadone is a narcotic that does not produce the euphoric effect addicts seek in heroin. While taking regular doses of methadone, however, the addict can give up heroin without the painful and sometimes dangerous symptoms of withdrawal that make it difficult for an addict to stop using drugs.

The addict might thus escape the dangerous spiral of increasing heroin use while being maintained on a moderate and level dose of methadone.

In maintenance programs of this sort, however, the addict continues to use methadone indefinitely. Some specialists have objected to this on the ground that it only substitutes one narcotic for another.

"The data which have thus far been collected suggest that the drug, used in the proper fashion, may offer some promise in the treatment and rehabilitation of certain narcotic addicts," said John E. Ingersoll, director of the Justice Department's Bureau of Narcotics and Dangerous Drugs.

Accordingly, he said, the new regulations are intended to allow new research along these

Continued on Page 23, Column 4

Terrorists in Brazil Kidnap Bonn Envoy

Special to The New York Times

RIO DE JANEIRO, June 11—The West Germany Ambassador, Ehrenfried von Holleben, was kidnapped by terrorists tonight as he was being driven home from the embassy.

One of his Brazilian security guards was killed and two others wounded by five terrorists who opened fire after they blocked the ambassador's car. One of the five was reportedly a woman.

This was the second abduction of a West German Ambassador in Latin America this year. The Ambassador to Guatemala, Count Karl von Spreti, was shot to death there on

Continued on Page 6, Column 1

NEWS INDEX

U.S. Troop Cut in South Korea Reported Sought to Save Funds

By WILLIAM BEECHER
Special to The New York Times

WASHINGTON, June 11—A leading Defense Department official said today that strong budgetary pressures were forcing the Administration to seek agreement for the removal of a large part of America's 64,000-man military force from South Korea over two or three years, starting next year.

To that end, secret negotiations are to begin in Seoul within the next several weeks to work out a withdrawal schedule, senior military and diplomatic sources disclosed.

To compensate for the projected reduction, Administration officials say they are prepared to seek a special Congressional outlay of about $1-billion, spread over five years, to modernize the Korean Army.

This expenditure of $200-million annually would be in addition to the $140-million now spent in military aid to maintain the South Korean armed forces, officials say.

Administration officials at the highest levels are known to be worried about whether Congress would be willing to authorize such a heavy expenditure.

But one source, stating a position that will probably be offered to Congress, declared that the cost could be more

Continued on Page 9, Column 1

"All the News
That's Fit to Print"

The New York Times

LATE CITY EDITION

Weather: Partly cloudy today and tonight. Chance of rain tomorrow. Temp. range: today 80-64; Tuesday 86-68. Temp.-Hum. Index yesterday 77. Full U.S. report on Page 90.

VOL. CXIX... No. 41,066 © 1970 The New York Times Company. NEW YORK, WEDNESDAY, JULY 1, 1970 15 CENTS

NIXON'S VETO OVERRIDDEN ON MEDICAL BUILDING BILL; SENATE'S VOTE IS 76 TO 19

MEASURE NOW LAW

Fund of $2.7-Billion Cleared to Construct and Aid Hospitals

By HAROLD M. SCHMECK Jr.
Special to The New York Times

WASHINGTON, June 30—The Senate voted 76 to 19 today to override President Nixon's veto of the three-year, $2.79-billion authorization bill extending the Hill-Burton program of construction and modernization of medical facilities.

The 76 votes were 12 more than the number needed to override the veto—two-thirds of those present and voting.

Last Thursday night the House voted to override the veto, 279 to 98. Thus, the measure becomes law.

This is the first time since July 1, 1960, that Congress has overridden a Presidential veto. On that date the House and Senate passed a Federal pay bill over President Eisenhower's objection to the pay rises it entailed.

Reasons for Veto

The majority today was made up of 53 Democrats and 23 Republicans. All 19 Senators supporting the President were Republicans. The action came on the day the Hill-Burton authorizations were due to expire.

The President objected to the bill on several grounds. He said that it authorized direct grants that were more than $350-million in excess of those in his proposed budget for the fiscal year 1971 which starts tomorrow. Furthermore, it required him to spend any money that Congress appropriated for public health service programs through the 1973 fiscal year. That was the provision to which the President objected most strongly.

In his veto message on June 22 he called the bill a "long step down the road of fiscal irresponsibility" and declared it would significantly restrict his options in managing Federal spending.

Cited Ceiling Measure

President Nixon said a Federal spending ceiling, voted by the House and expected to pass the Senate, would aggravate this restriction. The House has voted for a base ceiling for the next fiscal year of $200.8-billion, which does not include so-called "uncontrollables" such as interest on the national debt.

Several Senators of both parties spoke today in favor of the hospital measure. They stressed the urgency of the nation's health problems. In voting with the majority, Senator Jacob K. Javits, Republican of New York, said he was doing so because passage would tend to exempt health programs from an over-all spending ceiling.

There was disagreement among Senators as to whether Mr. Nixon would actually be forced to spend any health

Continued on Page 28, Column 1

N.A.A.C.P. Charge Called Unfair by the White House

By JACK ROSENTHAL
Special to The New York Times

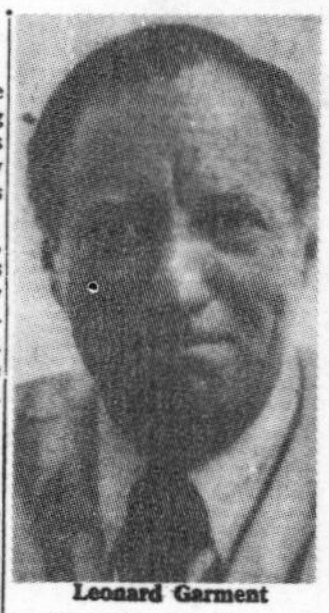

Leonard Garment

WASHINGTON, June 30—The Nixon Administration, stung by an accusation that it was anti-Negro, responded sharply today, labeling the charge as unfair and disheartening.

Such an accusation, it said, paints a false picture, rallies every fear, reinforces every anxiety and makes a just society more difficult to achieve.

The accusation was made last night by Bishop Stephen G.

Text of Garment's telegram will be found on Page 34.

Spottswood, chairman of the board of the National Association for the Advancement of Colored People, who was the keynote speaker at its annual convention in Cincinnati.

The response today came in the form of a long telegram to Bishop Spottswood from the White House. The response declared, "The President and the Administration are committed to achieving equal opportunity for every American, and are determined to maintain their efforts to reach that goal."

Bishop Spottswood, in Cincinnati, said he had not yet received the telegram and had no comment.

The telegram was signed by Leonard Garment, President Nixon's chief liaison with civil rights groups. But it is known to echo the near-despair of other White House moderates.

"It's a calamity," one said

Continued on Page 34, Column 1

SENATE APPROVES POSTAL BILL, 76-10

Votes Retroactive Pay Rise —Right to Work Provision Rejected in Long Session

By MARJORIE HUNTER
Special to The New York Times

WASHINGTON, Wednesday, July 1—A weary Senate voted early today to revamp the nation's postal system and give postal workers an 8 per cent pay rise, retroactive to April 16.

Passage of the sweeping postal reform bill by a vote of 76 to 10 came at the end of a 14-hour session in which the Senate disposed of two other issues — a limitation on the President's power to act in Cambodia and an overriding of the President's veto of a hospital construction bill.

In pushing ahead on postal reform, the Senate sought to avoid a postal walkout such as the one that tied up much of the nation's mail in April.

Postal workers in New York had threatened another walkout this month if Congress refused to grant retroactive pay in-

Continued on Page 26, Column 3

Deficit in '71 Budget Is Expected to Soar By Over $7-Billion

By EDWIN L. DALE Jr.
Special to The New York Times

WASHINGTON, June 30—Congressional action and inaction are threatening to add more than $7-billion to the budget deficit for the fiscal year that begins tomorrow, a new official tally disclosed today.

The tally was compiled by an arm of Congress itself, the Joint Committee on Reduction of Federal Expenditures.

While most members of Congress, supported by many economists, believe that a budget close to balance is appropriate for the new fiscal year—the President has projected a small deficit of $1.3-billion—the collective actions and inactions of Congress and its committees now seem highly likely to produce a deficit between $5-billion and $10-billion.

This is so even though few, if any, members of Congress are seeking that result.

These are some of the major items:

¶Failure to raise postal

Continued on Page 8, Column 3

HOSPITALS UNION REJECTS 2 OFFERS; STRIKE TODAY SEEN

Emergency Plans Are Made for the 6 A.M. Shift by 33 Private Institutions

By DAMON STETSON

The city's private nonprofit hospitals made two new pay offers to their 25,000 nonprofessional employes yesterday, but the union representing the workers rejected both offers as inadequate.

Although spokesmen for the hospitals and the employes agreed that a strike would be a tragedy for the city, both were pessimistic about the prospects of averting one today.

The hospitals made emergency plans for a strike starting with the 6 A.M. shift.

Vincent D. McDonnell, chairman of the State Mediation Board, shuttled back and forth between the two sides during the day, last night and early this morning attempting to establish a basis for settlement.

Minimum Now $100

The workers, represented by Local 1199 of the Hospital and Drug Union, have had a $100-a-week minimum, and have asked to have that increased to $139.71, the figure that the Labor Department lists as the minimum necessary for the support of a family of four in New York City.

The workers have also asked for an across-the-board increase of 30 per cent—but no less than $40 a week—for all full-time employes now on hospital payrolls. The union represents service, maintenance, laundry and technical workers in the hospitals.

The hospitals, represented by the League of Voluntary Hospitals and Homes of New York, made a new offer at a joint morning session that would have given the workers a 6 per cent pay increase each year of a proposed three-year pact.

Proposal Assailed

Leon Davis, president of Local 1199, described the proposal as "totally inadequate." He added:

"It's not enough for breakfast for the workers, let alone lunch."

At a joint session late in the afternoon, the hospitals improved their proposal, reducing it to a two-year contract with an 8 per cent pay increase the first year and a 7 per cent increase in the second.

Other items in the hospitals' offer included making Martin Luther King's birthday a paid holiday, but with the total number of holidays remaining at 11; an additional ½ per cent contribution to the union's welfare fund and improved vacations, effective in the second year. The union also rejected this proposal.

Most of the 33 institutions

Continued on Page 36, Column 1

PRESIDENT HAILS CAMBODIA DRIVE, CALLS ON HANOI FOR SERIOUS TALK; SENATE PASSES WAR POWERS CURB

LONG DEBATE ENDS

Cooper-Church Limits on Cambodia Action Adopted, 58-37

Text of the Cooper-Church amendment is on Page 13.

By JOHN W. FINNEY
Special to The New York Times

WASHINGTON, June 30 — The Senate, moving to reassert the war-making powers of Congress, today adopted the long-debated Cooper-Church amendment to limit Presidential action in Cambodia.

By a vote of 58 to 37, after 34 days of debate, the amendment was made part of the pending foreign military sales bill. The action was viewed as a victory for antiwar forces in the Senate, though it can take effect only if a similar measure passes the House, where the issue now goes. Considerable resistance is expected there.

Restrictions Are Detailed

The Senate's action represents the first time legislative restrictions on the President's powers as Commander in Chief have been voted during a shooting war. If it became law, the amendment—with an effective date of July 1—would bar the President from spending any funds without Congressional consent for the following purposes:

¶To "retain" American forces in Cambodia.

¶To send military advisers to instruct Cambodian forces.

¶To provide air combat support to Cambodian forces.

¶To provide financial assistance to advisers or troops of other countries that go to the assistance of Cambodia. This was known as the "anti-mercenary" provision designed to prevent the Administration, without the knowledge and consent of Congress, from following the example set in South Vietnam, where the United States has provided extra pay allowances for Thai, South Korean and Philippine troops supporting the Saigon Government's fight.

Military Sales Bill Approved

With the Cooper - Church amendment finally adopted after 288 speeches, the Senate went on to pass the foreign military sales bill by a 75 to 20 vote. The bill authorizes $300-million in credit sales of arms in the current and coming fiscal years and imposes new restrictions, opposed by the Pentagon, on the disposal of surplus weapons to other countries. The current fiscal year ends at midnight tonight.

The amendment was co-sponsored by Senator John Sherman Cooper, Republican of Kentucky, and Senator Frank Church, Democrat of Idaho.

As the protracted, often slow-moving and confused debate

Continued on Page 13, Column 1

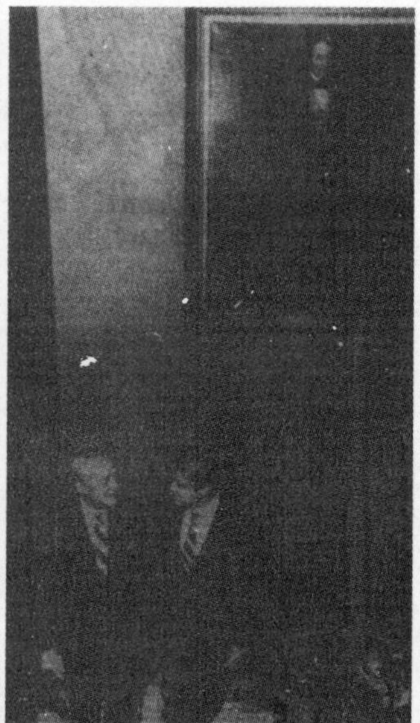

[illegible]

NEW ROLE BARRED

Nixon Says Army Will Not Return—Use of Planes Indicated

Text of the President's report is on Pages 16 and 17.

By ROBERT B. SEMPLE Jr.
Special to The New York Times

SAN CLEMENTE, Calif., June 30—President Nixon today announced the "successful" completion of the American incursion in Cambodia, ruled out the use of American troops there in the future and suggested that the country's defense would be left largely to the Cambodians and their Asian allies.

Mr. Nixon renewed earlier appeals to North Vietnam to begin serious peace negotiations and pledged to accept any solution arrived at by the South Vietnamese themselves. He also acknowledged—as he had before—that any "fair solution" would require a division of postwar power reflecting "the existing relationship of political forces."

Advisers Are Prohibited

The President, in a report, declared that "there will be no U.S. ground personnel in Cambodia except the regular staff of our embassy in Pnompenn" and that the prohibition covered not only fighting men but advisers to the Cambodian and South Vietnamese forces.

At the same time he left himself latitude on the use of American air power. He said he would not provide air or logistical support for South Vietnamese units operating in Cambodia but forecast continued bombing of enemy personnel concentrations and supply targets "with the approval of the Cambodian Government."

In the 7,000-word written report issued at the Western White House, Mr. Nixon devoted himself largely to a familiar if elaborate detailed recital of the accomplishments of the two-month mission—including his feeling that it had assured the continued withdrawal of American troops from Vietnam.

A Test of Doctrine

By suggestion if not by direct statement, Mr. Nixon made clear his conviction that Cambodia, now without United States troops, would become a clear test of the Nixon doctrine of transferring com- responsibilities from American to Asian forces. He called on Cambodia's allies to assist her and said he would help subsidize the efforts of "third countries who wish to furnish Cambodia with troops or material."

Mr. Nixon's stated intention of providing some forms of air support, as well as his offer to help subsidize the military operations of other countries, appeared to constitute a direct challenge to the Cooper-Church

Continued on Page 17, Column 1

Britain and 3 Others Offer Cases to Common Market

By CLYDE H. FARNSWORTH
Special to The New York Times

LUXEMBOURG, June 30—A process that could alter the structure of Europe began today as Britain, Ireland, Denmark and Norway opened negotiations to join the European Economic Community.

All parties presented their toughest bargaining positions at the businesslike opening of the talks in this, the smallest of the six Common Market member states, where two decades ago the first experiment in European unification started with the pooling of the French and West German coal and steel industries.

Anthony Barber, second-ranking official in the British Foreign Office and the man in charge of "entering Europe," wasted little time getting to the crux of the problem for his country—the cost of accepting the market's financial regulations in agriculture.

Four times in a 15-minute address to the ministers, he spoke of a need to find a "fair" solution that would not put an excessive burden on either the British budget or British consumers.

His remarks, coming a few minutes after a tough statement of the principles the market will be guided by in the negotiations, later prompted a Luxembourg official to say, "The battle has begun."

The Dutch Foreign Minister, Joseph M. A. H. Luns, said the negotiations "should succeed" if only because a new failure would put an end to the common goal to unit Europe economically and politically.

Asked if the French, who have vetoed Britain's efforts to join twice in the last seven years, shared his view, Mr. Luns replied: "The French have many qualities and one of them is realism. The French will have to play the game, or as the

Continued on Page 10, Column 3

Picture-Telephone Service Is Started in Pittsburgh

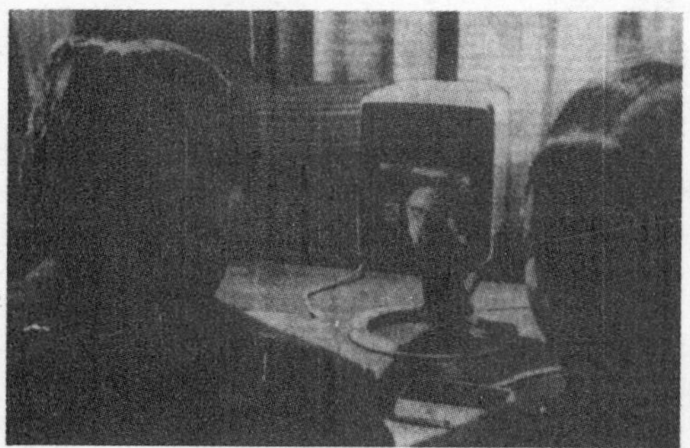

Harry Cabluck, A.P., for The New York Times

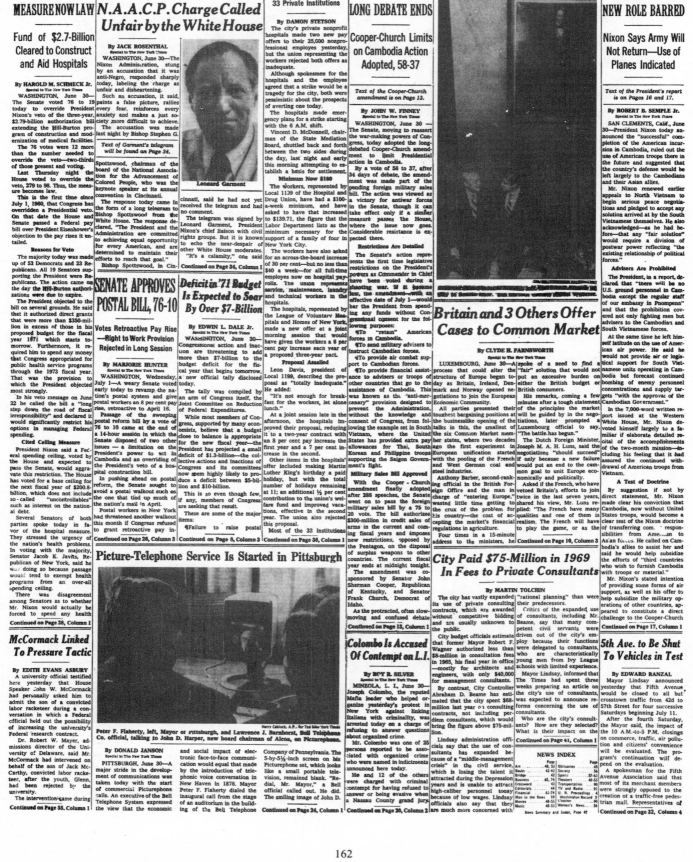

Peter F. Flaherty, left, Mayor of Pittsburgh, and Lawrence J. Barnhorst, Bell Telephone Co. official, talking to John D. Harper, new board chairman of Alcoa, on Picturephone.

By DONALD JANSON
Special to The New York Times

PITTSBURGH, June 30—A major stride in the development of communications was taken today with the start of commercial Picturephone calls. An executive of the Bell Telephone System expressed the view that the economic and social impact of electronic face-to-face communication would equal that made by the introduction of telephonic voice conversation in New Haven in 1878. Mayor Peter F. Flaherty dialed the inaugural call from the stage of an auditorium in the building of the Bell Telephone Company of Pennsylvania. The 5-by-5½-inch screen on his Picturephone set, which looks like a small portable television, remained blank. "Redial, Mr. Mayor," a Bell official called out. He did. The smiling image of John D.

Continued on Page 24, Column 1

McCormack Linked To Pressure Tactic

By EDITH EVANS ASBURY

A university official testified here yesterday that House Speaker John W. McCormack had personally asked him to admit the son of a convicted labor racketeer during a conversation in which a Federal official held out the possibility of increasing the university's Federal research contract.

Dr. Robert W. Mayer, admissions director of the University of Delaware, said Mr. McCormack had intervened on behalf of the son of Jack McCarthy, convicted labor racketeer, after the youth, Glenn, had been rejected by the university.

The intervention came during

Continued on Page 55, Column 1

Colombo Is Accused Of Contempt on L.I.

By ROY R. SILVER
Special to The New York Times

MINEOLA, L. I., June 30—Joseph Colombo, the reputed Mafia leader who helped organize yesterday's protest in New York against linking Italians with criminality, was arrested today on a charge of refusing to answer questions about organized crime.

Mr. Colombo was one of 25 persons reported to be associated with organized crime who were named in indictments announced here today.

He and 12 of the others were charged with criminal contempt for having refused to answer or being evasive when a Nassau County grand jury

Continued on Page 20, Column 2

City Paid $75-Million in 1969 In Fees to Private Consultants

By MARTIN TOLCHIN

The city has vastly expanded its use of private consulting contracts, which are awarded without competitive bidding and are usually unknown to the public.

City budget officials estimate that former Mayor Robert F. Wagner authorized less than $8-million in consultation fees in 1965, his final year in office —mostly for architects and engineers, with only $40,000 for management consultants.

By contrast, City Controller Abraham D. Beame has estimated that the city spent $68-million last year on consulting contracts, not including per-diem consultants, which would bring the figure above $75-million.

Lindsay administration officials say that the use of consultants has expanded because of a "middle-management crisis" in the civil service, which is losing the talent it attracted during the Depression years and is unable to attract high-caliber personnel today because of low wages. Lindsay officials also say that they are much more concerned with "rational planning" than were their predecessors.

Critics of the expanded use of consultants, including Mr. Beame, say that many competent civil servants were driven out of the city's employ because their functions were delegated to consultants, who are characteristically young men from Ivy League schools with limited experience.

Mayor Lindsay, informed that The Times had spent three weeks preparing an article on the city's use of consultants, was expected to announce reforms concerning the use of consultants.

Who are the city's consultants? How are they selected? What is their impact on the

Continued on Page 41, Column 1

NEWS INDEX

5th Ave. to Be Shut To Vehicles in Test

By EDWARD RANZAL

Mayor Lindsay announced yesterday that Fifth Avenue would be closed to all but crosstown traffic from 42d to 57th Street for four successive Saturdays beginning July 11.

After the fourth Saturday, the Mayor said, the impact of the 10 A.M.-to-5 P.M. closings on commerce, traffic, air pollution and citizens' convenience will be evaluated. The program's continuation will depend on the evaluation.

A spokesman for the Fifth Avenue Association said that most of its merchant members were strongly opposed to the creation of a traffic-free pedestrian mall. Representatives of

Continued on Page 32, Column 4

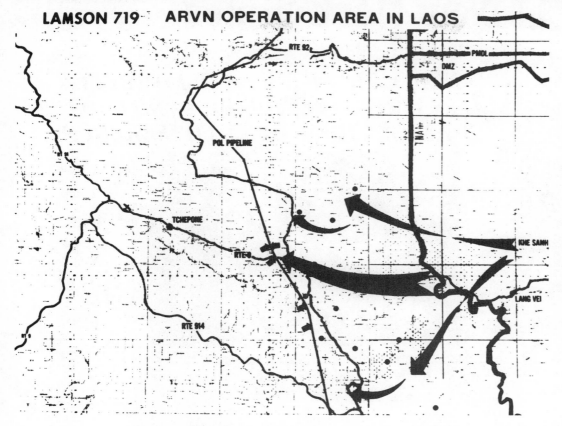

LAMSON 719 ARVN OPERATION AREA IN LAOS

The South Vietnamese invaded Laos for the first time in early 1971 with Operation Lam Son 710. In the first phase of the operation, a South Vietnamese armored column moved along Route 9 to the junction with Route 92, cutting traffic along these two key arteries. The dots indicate a series of landing strips and temporary firebases used during the operation. In later phases, South Vietnamese troops also captured Tchepone, a major objective of the operation, and established positions on Route 914, another principal artery.

Vietnamese troops board helicopters which will carry them across the border into Laos.

The New York Times

LATE CITY EDITION
Weather: Sunny, hazy, warm today; fair and milder tonight, tomorrow. Temp. range: today 81-61; Wed. 79-58. Full U.S. report on Page 93.

VOL.CXX..No.41,165 © 1970 The New York Times Company. NEW YORK, THURSDAY, OCTOBER 8, 1970 15 CENTS

U.S.-Israeli Military Action On Jordan Was Envisioned

Step-by-Step Reconstruction Shows How Plan Would Have Been Used if Tanks From Syria Had Not Been Halted

By BENJAMIN WELLES
Special to The New York Times

WASHINGTON, Oct. 7—The tense diplomatic and military United States and Israel were activity as the crisis approaching preparing to take coordinated proached its climax. As the military action in the recent United States-Israeli agreement Jordanian crisis, according to was being negotiated here it American and Israeli sources. was transmitted, step by step, to the unified military commands overseas and major striking forces — notably the This plan envisioned an Israeli attack on the Syrian tank forces that had entered Jordan Sixth Fleet—thus committing if it appeared that King Hussein's army was incapable of stopping them. In this event, the United States would have used Sixth Fleet and other units to safeguard Israel's rear and flanks from Egyptian or Soviet attacks from the Suez Canal area.

American power to a contingency plan whose outcome was obscure.

The bond between the United States and Israel in this crisis was their joint determination that King Hussein must not be overthrown by outside intervention in Jordan because they assumed he would be replaced by a regime closely linked to Moscow.

The plan was not put into effect because the Syrian tanks, harassed by King Hussein's jets and armor, began retreating into Syria. Informed sources here believe that it was the combination of Israel's troop build-up plus American military alerts—both well publicized— that deterred the Syrians and the Soviet Union.

In fact, an urgent message from King Hussein asking the United States and Britain to consider what military support they could provide him gave impetus to the American plan. Strong force for quick action

President Nixon assumed personal direction of the in-

Continued on Page 12, Column 1

Sadat Tells Cairo Deputies He'll Follow Nasser Policy

By RAYMOND H. ANDERSON
Special to The New York Times

CAIRO, Oct. 7—Anwar Sadat, nominated unanimously tonight by the National Assembly to succeed Gamal Abdel Nasser as President, pledged to follow Mr. Nasser's objectives of struggling to liberate all Arab lands occupied by Israel in the war of 1967 and to achieve a settlement for the Palestinian refugees.

In a speech to the Assembly, however, Acting President Sadat emphasized a frequent remark by President Nasser, that Egypt "does not want war for the sake of war."

The nomination of Mr. Sadat is to be submitted to a national referendum on Oct. 15. An overwhelming yes vote is expected.

Speaking in a soft, slow voice, the Acting President outlined a program to be followed in the coming period.

Cites Nasser's Legacy

Besides the vow to recover the occupied lands, he said that Mr. Nasser's legacy required adherence to these goals:

¶The dream of Mr. Nasser to unite the Arab countries.

¶Defining "the enemies of our nation."

¶Maintaining a position of nonalignment between the major world power blocs.

¶Supporting the national liberation movement.

¶Defending the socialist gains of Egypt.

"I have come to you along the path of Gamal Abdel Nasser," Mr. Sadat said, "and I believe that your nomination of me to assume the responsibilities of the presidency is a nomination for us to continue on the path of Nasser."

Despite the blow of Mr. Nasser's death, Mr. Sadat continued, the Egyptian people should be guided by "what Nasser would have wanted: 'Don't grieve; continue forward to the

Continued on Page 11, Column 1

LEFTIST ASSUMES POWER IN BOLIVIA

General Torres Proclaims Himself President After Air Force Chief Backs Him

By The Associated Press

LA PAZ, Bolivia, Oct. 7 — A leftist general, Juan José Torres, took power today as President of Bolivia with a show of force that toppled his rightist military opponents.

After taking the oath, he gave a speech to cheering crowds from the balcony of the Presidential Palace, promising to give Bolivia "a popular-nationalist government" resting on four pillars — the peasant farmers, the workers, the students and the armed forces. All will be invited into the new regime, he said.

Gen. Rogelio Miranda, the conservative army chief of staff who forced President Alfredo Ovando Candia to resign yesterday, was said to have taken refuge in a foreign embassy. Two members of the three-man junta named yesterday to succeed President Ovando were said to have gone with him.

The Torres takeover in La Paz was bloodless, although some planes flown by air force men backing him bombed the Presidential Palace yesterday in a raid that caused little damage.

The takeover was assured

Continued on Page 5, Column 1

City Labor Council Will Set Up Centers to Aid Addicts in Unions

By BARBARA CAMPBELL

The New York City Central Labor Council voted yesterday to establish addict - referral centers in local union offices and to push for union contracts that include healthinsurance coverage for union members who need medical assistance to break the drug habit.

Michael Sampson, chairman of the labor council's community services committee, said that a "dramatic" increase in drug abuse among union members and their families had led the organization to take action.

The resolutions just adopted unanimously by 95 local union representatives summoned by the council to par-

ticipate in a drug seminar will come to a vote on the issue at the Amalgamated Clothing Workers of America Building, 111 East 15th Street. The Central Labor Council represents more than a million workers in unions affiliated with the American Federation of Labor-Congress of Industrial Organizations.

Milton Luger, chairman of the New York State Narcotic Addiction Control Commission, who attended the seminar to answer questions, said the state would provide money for the referral centers as soon as a proposal was submitted by the

Continued on Page 31, Column 2

CURBS ON CRIME AND DRUG ABUSE GAIN IN CONGRESS

The House and Senate Move Quickly to Vote Measures Requested by President

By MARJORIE HUNTER
Special to The New York Times

WASHINGTON, Oct. 7—Congress moved swiftly today to give President Nixon legislation he has sought to control organized crime, campus bombings and narcotics use and traffic.

Action on the President's "law and order" proposals came first in the House, which passed, 341 to 26, a bill to combat organized crime and permit Federal agents to investigate campus bombings.

Several hours later, the Senate approved, 54 to 9, a bill designed to crack down on narcotics traffic and abuse but reducing penalties for lesser drug violations.

Objections Brushed Aside

Final Congressional clearance of the two bills, however, rests on the ability of Senate and House conferees to resolve differences in the versions passed by the two bodies.

In the House, a small band of Democratic liberals protested to the end that many provisions of the anticrime bill were unconstitutional.

But their objections were brushed aside as the Democratic-controlled House moved to erase charges by the Nixon Administration that the Democrats are "soft on crime."

Somewhat similar legislation cleared the Senate last January, but the House added a number of new provisions, including the death penalty for those convicted of fatal bombings and permission for Federal agents to investigate campus bombings and arson.

Provision for Research

Just last week the House approved drug control legislation, but the Senate today added new provisions that may, or may not, meet with quick House approval.

For example, the Senate voted, 44 to 23, to add to the House-passed bill a broad new program of drug education, research and rehabilitation.

Proposed by Senator Harold E. Hughes, Democrat of Iowa, the amendment would establish a national institute for the prevention and treatment of drug dependence within the National Institutes of Health and would authorize $190-million in Federal grants over three years to states, localities and projects for rehabilitation and treatment of drug users.

The Senate also wrote into the bill provisions to tighten up on the manufacturing and distribution of amphetamines and amphetamine-like drugs, commonly called "pep pills." The House had rejected the proposal. However, one possible

Continued on Page 31, Column 1

NIXON URGES SUPERVISED TRUCE IN VIETNAM, CAMBODIA AND LAOS AND A WIDER PEACE CONFERENCE

President Nixon with Melvin R. Laird, right, Defense Secretary, and William P. Rogers, Secretary of State, before speech
The New York Times (by Mike Lien)

STANDSTILL ASKED

President Says Offer Has No Conditions— Two Elements New

Transcript of Nixon's address is printed on Page 18.

By ROBERT B. SEMPLE Jr.
Special to The New York Times

WASHINGTON, Oct. 7—President Nixon asked Hanoi and the Vietcong tonight to join the allies in a standstill cease-fire throughout Indochina. He also called for an Indochina peace conference to negotiate an end to the fighting in Laos and Cambodia as well as South Vietnam.

Addressing a nationwide television audience from his oval office in the White House, Mr. Nixon conceded that an internationally supervised ceasefire "in place" might be difficult to arrange and even harder to sustain.

He said, however, "An unconventional war may require an unconventional truce; our side is ready to stand still and cease firing."

He said that successful negotiations leading to such a cease-fire might well be a prelude to a large political and military settlement of the conflict and would at the very least bring "an end to the killing."

Allies Reportedly Approved

In his proposal for expanded talks, Mr. Nixon said that the Paris peace conference would remain "our primary forum" for reaching a settlement until such time as a broader arrangement began producing "serious negotiations." He added:

"This war in Indochina has proved to be of one piece; it cannot be cured by treating only one of its areas of outbreak."

The composition and location proposed by Mr. Nixon remained unclear, but Administration officials suggested that it might include not only the present parties in Paris — the United States, North Vietnam, the Vietcong, and South Vietnam — but also Laos, Cambodia, the Soviet Union and Communist China. These officials also said, as Mr. Nixon did yesterday, that Cambodia, Laos and South Vietnam had all approved the proposals.

Two New Elements

Administration officials portrayed the . . . . . . speech as a fresh set of proposals designed to replace Mr. Nixon's original eight-point peace initiative of May 14, 1969. But they said the United States stood by some of the original proposals, such as its endorsement of internationally supervised free elections to determine the composition of a South Vietnamese government.

The only really new elements in tonight's initiative were the standstill cease-fire and the proposal for expanded peace talks. On two crucial questions that have been dividing both sides—troop withdrawals and the composition of the Saigon leadership—Mr. Nixon essentially restated earlier positions, which the North Vietnamese have routinely rejected.

On the subject of troops, Mr. Nixon proposed the eventual withdrawal of all United States forces on a timetable to be worked out in negotiations. He did not, for the first time, call for mutual withdrawals, but

Continued on Page 18, Column 4

Panel Urges Curbs On Ocean Dumping; Nixon Hails Report

By ROBERT M. SMITH
Special to The New York Times

WASHINGTON, Oct. 7 — The Council on Environmental Quality recommended today a national policy to limit the dumping of waste into the oceans and the Great Lakes.

President Nixon welcomed the council's recommendations, congratulated it for "acting rather than reacting to prevent pollution" and forwarded the proposals to Congress. The President said he would submit legislation implementing the recommendations to the next Congress.

The council, headed by Russell E. Train, called basically for laws to ban the unregulated dumping of all materials into the oceans and to prevent or limit the dumping of harmful materials.

It proposed that waste be dumped only after permits are obtained from the administrator of the Environmental Protection Agency, that punishments be established and that the Coast Guard be given the task of enforcement.

In a 40-page study, the council concludes that ocean dumping of waste "is not a serious, nationwide problem now, but the decisions made by municipalities and industries for the next few years could lead to dramatic increases in the level of dumping."

"Once these decisions were made," the council warns, "and the facilities built, communities and industries are likely to turn to them for many years."

Continued on Page 35, Column 1

CITY IS OVERRULED IN BUILDING STRIKE

Court Says It Had No Right to Hire the Employes and Pay Them an Increase

By ROBERT E. TOMASSON

State Supreme Court Justice Thomas C. Chimera ruled yesterday that the city had far exceeded its authority in hiring striking apartment-house workers in the Bronx. He ordered the city to stop the practice, under which the city has been paying the strikers to perform their duties in the buildings.

"In the court's opinion, this was an unauthorized and unwarranted taking of possession of private property and an unauthorized interference in a lawful labor dispute, however well-motivated and regardless of any inconvenience to a segment of the general public in Bronx County," Justice Chimera held.

"Whether so intended or not, it has the effect of destroying the economic counterbalance which both parties to the collective-bargaining process have a right to enjoy without outside interference."

The ruling will have no effect for at least a few days, pending the submitting of additional legal papers by the city and the landlords.

One week ago Justice Chimera ruled in the same labor

Continued on Page 52, Column 2

U.S.-Soviet Space Docking Is Said to Be Under Study

By WALTER SULLIVAN

CONSTANCE, West Germany, Oct. 7—After years of holding at arm's length United States overtures toward closer cooperation in space, Soviet officials are understood to have agreed to explore ways to enable the spacecraft of the two nations to dock with one another.

This development, which many here consider a historic turning point in the exploration of space, is chiefly aimed at making it possible for either nation to rescue the other's astronauts.

[The National Aeronautics and Space Administration confirmed Wednesday that arrangements were being made for a possible meeting of Soviet and American space engineers to discuss ways of implementing cooperation between the two nations in space.]

This month, four Soviet astronauts are to go to Houston for a meeting of the American Institute of Aeronautics and Astronautics. It is possible that they will visit the Manned Spacecraft Center there to be briefed on the American docking system and discuss what measures would be needed to enable spacecraft of the nations to help one another.

However, it is not yet certain they will do so. Accustomed informed sources here differ in this respect and it appears that the question of reciprocity, whereby the Russians would be expected to expose details of their own spacecraft with equal candor, may still be an inhibiting factor.

At present, the manned spacecraft systems of the two countries are so different that international space rescue would be virtually impossible. Even communication between

Continued on Page 32, Column 3

TOP STATE COURT UPHOLDS BADILLO

Rejects Need for a Rerun in Primary — Conservation Party Ruled Off Ballot

Special to The New York Times

ALBANY, Oct. 7—In a series of major election rulings today, the state's highest court rejected the necessity for a Congressional primary rerun for Herman Badillo, restricted Richard L. Ottinger to one line on the November ballot and dismissed nominating petition rules.

In its separate opinions, the Court of Appeals virtually assured the election to Congress next month of Mr. Badillo, the former Bronx Borough President, whose Democratic primary election victory on June 23 had been challenged by one of his five opponents.

The court rejected unanimously a challenge to the validity of the votes, which was brought by Peter F. Vallone, who had finished second to Mr. Badillo in the contest in the new 21st Congressional District.

A new primary had been ordered for tomorrow by State Supreme Court Justice John J. Leahy, but Justice Leahy's ruling was reversed two weeks ago by the Appellate Division, which held that the irregularities cited by Mr. Vallone were not sufficiently large to alter

Continued on Page 43, Column 1

U.S. Aide Says Population Rise Slows

By JACK ROSENTHAL
Special to The New York Times

WASHINGTON, Oct. 7 — The "population bomb" in the United States is being defused, George H. Brown, director of the Census Bureau, said today.

The American woman is having fewer children — and may have still fewer in the future, he said. The probable result, he said, is that the total population will fall significantly short of some earlier estimates.

The nation's future problems are thus more likely to stem from the changed nature of the population than from its explosive growth, he suggested.

In a speech entitled "1985," the text of which was made available here in advance, Mr. Brown gave the Downtown Economists Club in New York this portrait of the future:

¶The population could approach a zero growth rate, but this would not be a panacea for social problems as some have suggested. In a stationary population, the average age would rise from 28 to 37. "There is concern," Mr. Brown said, "that an older, stationary population would be more resistant to change."

¶The next 15 years is the

George H. Brown
United Press International

"era of the young married." By 1985, the number of people in their 20's, 30's and early 40's is expected to increase by 28 million. The number of people between 45 and 64, however, will barely change. The growth among young adults will mean a massive market for housing. The possible shortage of experienced older men, Mr. Brown

said, could create unprecedented opportunities in government and business for younger leaders.

¶If current trends continue, the nation is heading into "a society of an affluent majority." By 1985, average family income is expected to jump from $8,600 to $15,000, as measured in constant purchasing power.

¶By 1985, at present rates, almost half the population will live in suburbs, compared with about a third now. Meanwhile, the black proportion of central city population is likely to grow to about one-third from one-fifth.

¶Elementary and high school enrollment is likely to change little, but the number of college students is expected to surge from 7.5 million to 11.5 million by 1985. Half of this estimated growth is attributed to population growth, half to steady increases in the proportion of young people who go to college.

Mr. Brown's underlying theme was the substantial drop in the national fertility rate. In the 1950's, women

Continued on Page 34, Column 3

Mayor Studies Payless Paydays To Offset Losses in City Revenue

By MARTIN TOLCHIN

Mayor Lindsay said yesterday that his administration was considering "payless paydays," pay cuts and some layoffs by Mayor Fiorello H. La-Guardia during the Depression — to offset anticipated revenue losses caused by the recession.

These proposals, promptly denounced as "absurd" and illegal by several municipal union leaders, were made as the Mayor imposed a job freeze on all city agencies except the Sanitation Department.

"Despite the severity of the job freeze, I fear it is only a first step," the Mayor said in a statement released at City Hall late yesterday afternoon. "There are no indications that our present revenue shortfalls will decrease. If these projections hold, the next steps will become progressively deeper and have even wider impact.

"At present, I see no alternative."

Last month the Mayor and his fiscal aides predicted a revenue loss of $100-million to $150-million because of declines in revenues from the stock transfer tax, the personal income tax and the business tax.

The proposal for payless paydays for the city's 300,000 employes was one of the alternatives suggested by the Budget

Continued on Page 55, Column 1

"All the News That's Fit to Print"

The New York Times

LATE CITY EDITION

Weather: Cloudy today; colder with showers likely tonight, tomorrow. Temp. range: today 54-43; Saturday 54-45. Full U.S. report on Page 91.

SECTION ONE

VOL. CXX . No. 41,210 — NEW YORK, SUNDAY, NOVEMBER 22, 1970 — 50 CENTS

75¢ beyond 50-mile zone from New York City, except Long Island. Higher in air delivery cities.

ROCKEFELLER SEEKS LOCAL-LEVEL HELP TO OBTAIN U.S. AID

Separate Meetings Are Set With Mayors, County Chiefs and Education Boards

WASHINGTON TALKS DUE

State Congressmen Slated to Discuss Fiscal Crisis With Governor Tomorrow

By WILLIAM E. FARRELL

Governor Rockefeller scheduled meetings with the state's mayors, county executives and school boards yesterday to seek their support in his drive to ease the state's fiscal crisis by obtaining more funds from Washington.

Mr. Rockefeller will meet with the county executives on Nov. 30, with the mayors on Dec. 7 and with representatives of school boards Dec. 8 and 9.

Since his re-election to a fourth term, the Governor has all but confined his public comments to dire utterances about "destruction" of the state's economic stability if it is forced next year to raise taxes again because it cannot get more Federal funds.

To Meet Representatives

Tomorrow night he will meet in Washington with the New York Congressional delegation in an attempt to convince the members of the need for goading Congress into sharing more Federal funds with the state.

Mr. Rockefeller says the state sends $23.5-billion in taxes to Washington while receiving only $2.5-billion in return. He has added that $500-million to $1-billion more was needed from the Government just "to hold the line at present levels of activity."

The state's fiscal crisis will dominate the Republican-controlled Legislature when it convenes in Albany on Jan. 6 in a session that is expected to be enlivened by attempts to modify the newly liberalized abortion law, to increase aid to parochial schools and to curb the power of the Liberal and Conservative parties.

Thousands of Bills Due

Thousands of bills will come across the desks of New York's 150 Assemblymen and 57 Senators during the 194th annual legislative session.

But the flood of bills will be overshadowed by the issue of money and where to get it to balance a record state budget that, according to some legislative sources, is expected to rise from its present $7.2-billion to about $8-billion if the state is, at least partially, to respond to the ever-increasing demands of localities for funds, particular-

Continued on Page 60, Column 4

Today's Sections

Index to Subjects

United Press International

CHARGE POLITICAL INTERFERENCE: Terry F. Lenzner, right, former director of Federal poverty law program, and Frank N. Jones, ex-deputy director, hold news conference in Washington to comment on their sudden dismissal. Details appear on Page 46.

For H.R.A., New Approach at the Top

By FRANCIS X. CLINES

After a busy, clamorous fledgling period that emphasized the antipoverty commitment, the Human Resources Administration has been taken in hand by a new group of executives who are emphasizing the quiet art of business management.

Four months ago, Jule M. Sugarman was appointed administrator of the controversial superagency that oversees the city's huge welfare program and smaller antipoverty efforts.

"It happened to be Bastille Day," Mr. Sugarman likes to say with a small smile.

Since then he has assembled a group of chief assistants with backgrounds ranging from Pentagon cost-cutting to black politicking. And together these half dozen executives offer, with a general tone of understatement, an initial perspective on a task that includes the following:

¶The prospect of a budget of more than $2-billion for the next fiscal year because of increased welfare needs as well as a more direct hand in running the welfare bureau with the resignation of Commissioner Jack R. Goldberg.

¶A delicate campaign to get enough City Council votes to establish the H.R.A. as a permanent arm of government rather than a temporary superagency.

¶A continuing effort to clean up a backlog of auditing records to H.R.A.'s founding five years ago.

¶A difficult readjustment of the city's manpower program to shift an emphasis that has given three-fourths of the jobs to women.

¶A greater commitment, symbolized by Mr. Sugarman's dogged executive style, to strengthen administrative, planning and budgeting procedures.

The new management team was brought in after months of controversy over charges of administrative and fiscal mismanagement, theft and fraud against the H.R.A. Several indictments and convictions against employes were obtained, including that of Mrs. Helynn R. Lewis, the

Continued on Page 56, Column 4

City Acts to Cut Spending For 'Frills and Excesses'

By MAURICE CARROLL

A new step in the city's austerity campaign — pressure on agency heads to "expose some frills and some excesses" — was pledged yesterday by Deputy Mayor Richard R. Aurelio.

The administration made public a memorandum to Mayor Lindsay's super-cabinet requiring that reports on possible savings be made to a new productivity panel consisting of Mr. Aurelio, Deputy Mayor Timothy W. Costello and Budget Director Edward K. Hamilton.

Then Mr. Aurelio, sitting in his office next door to the Mayor's, explained that an agency-by-agency review of programs that could be curbed during "this period of austerity" had already started.

Steps that have already been scrutinized, he said, included the following:

¶A study showing that it would be cheaper to stop the "graveyard" shift on the Staten Island ferry and to carry that handful of passengers by taxicab over the Verrazano bridge during the early morning hours.

¶A review of newsletters published by one unnamed city agency. "They serve a purpose but it is a question whether we really need them now," he said.

Yesterday's was the fourth movement in what many persons familiar with the city's finances agree is an orchestrated economic lament. It began early in the week with Mayor Lindsay's announcement that, because of an anticipated deficit of some $300-million in the $7.7-billion city budget for the current fiscal year, 500 provisional employees were to be dismissed.

Then the city's Budget Director warned of possible new

Continued on Page 60, Column 4

Ohio State Defeats Michigan by 20-9; Notre Dame Wins

Ohio State downed Michigan yesterday, 20-9, and won the Big Ten football championship and a berth in the Rose Bowl. Notre Dame beat Louisiana State, 3-0, on a last-period field goal and Harvard upset Yale, 14-12.

Other leading scores:

Arkansas	24	Texas Tech	10
Bost. Col.	21	Mass.	10
Brown	17	Columbia	12
California	22	Stanford	14
Colorado	49	Air Force	19
Cornell	6	Princeton	3
Dartmouth	28	Penn	0
Fla. St.	33	Kan. St.	7
Lafayette	31	Lehigh	28
Missouri	28	Kansas	17
Nebraska	28	Oklahoma	21
No. Car.	59	Duke	34
N'western	23	Mich. St.	20
Ore. St.	24	Oregon	9
Penn. St.	35	Pittsburgh	15
Purdue	40	Indiana	0
Rutgers	30	Colgate	14
Syracuse	56	Miami, Fla.	16
Tenn.	45	Kentucky	0

Details in Section 5.

Graduates Look to Small Businesses

By ROBERT REINHOLD

Special to The New York Times

CAMBRIDGE, Mass., Nov. 21—Groups of business students at Harvard and Stanford, reluctant to become trapped in the big-corporation lockstep, have dipped into their own pockets to start "reverse recruiting" drives to convince small businesses that they can find executive talent at the management schools.

The major graduate schools of business have traditionally served as training grounds for the corporate giants. Harvard, in particular, has educated the managerial élite of companies throughout the world and most of its students have had only to wait for lucrative job offers to roll in.

But a growing number of students with masters degrees in business administration, appear to be seeking the freedom and opportunity offered by small- and medium-sized enterprises.

"There is a myth that business students are not interested in small firms, that the Harvard education is not suited for it and that Harvard students don't want to dirty their hands," said Mitchel M. Diamond of Brooklyn, an organizer of the Harvard drive.

150 Have Contributed

As a result, the students have been compelled to seek out the small companies. At Harvard, to date, 150 students have contributed a total of about $2,600 to a student organization called Small Business Opportunities International for direct mailing and personal visits to company executives. The school graduates 750 a year.

At Stanford, a separate year-long drive by the Stanford Small Business Association has netted about $1,200 from 125 of the school's 600 students for similar purposes. They place advertisements in The Wall Street Journal and publish brochures urging small-business men to consider hiring them.

Although the two groups are independent, they strike a similar note. "We are trying to stay away from the corporate structure and the bureaucracy of large corporations," said Bill Poland, co-chairman of the Stanford group, who added that small businesses offer more responsibility faster.

Similarly, the Harvard group sends out slick brochures informing businessmen that Harvard will soon graduate many men "who do not want to work for the 'Fortune 500.'" The brochure adds:

"We want experience and exposure. We want to get our hands dirty; to work to

Continued on Page 39, Column 1

MITCHELL IS SAID TO ADVISE ROMNEY TO TAKE NEW POST

Dispute on Housing Policy Reported — Move Denied by the Attorney General

By JOHN HERBERS

Special to The New York Times

WASHINGTON, Nov. 21—Attorney General John N. Mitchell has advised George Romney, Secretary of Housing and Urban Development, to take another job in the Administration, according to highly placed sources.

Mr. Mitchell, a close and trusted associate of President Nixon, was reported to have told Mr. Romney that the reason for the suggestion was that Mr. Romney had been acting counter to the Administration's housing policy.

A spokesman for the Attorney General said the report was "absolutely false." A spokesman for Mr. Romney, who was attending a conference in Mexico and could not be reached, had no comment.

According to a high official in the Administration, the two Cabinet officials met a few days ago, and afterward Mr. Romney was considerably upset.

Move Suggested

The official, who is in neither the Department of Housing and Urban Development nor the Justice Department, said there was never any suggestion that Mr. Romney leave the Administration, only that he take a position away from the housing department.

When told that he, as the Administration's chief housing officer, was acting in opposition to the Administration's policy in this area, Mr. Romney, according to the official, asked, "What the hell is the Administration policy? It changes from day to day and hour to hour."

The official did not specify what aspect of housing policy was in question. There has been, however, considerable controversy over policy and plans being made in the housing department to open suburban communities to the central city poor.

'Basic Conflict' Charged

Kevin P. Phillips, a former assistant to Mr. Mitchell, who is now a syndicated columnist, wrote in a recent column that the department's "blueprints and objectives stand in basic conflict with the Nixon Administration's announced support of neighborhood schools and its opposition to the idea that desegregation requires ethnic or racial balance."

Mr. Romney has expressed a different interpretation of what

Continued on Page 40, Column 1

NORTH VIETNAM HIT AGAIN; WAR MATERIALS REPORTED AMONG TARGETS; RAIDS END

The New York Times — Nov. 22, 1970

Hanoi said U.S. bombers struck provinces that are shaded. Secretary Laird says targets were only below 19th parallel.

Report From Hanoi Says U.S. Bombs Shake City

By Agence France-Presse

HANOI, North Vietnam, Nov. 21—Hanoi shook today from the blast of bombs only 25 miles away as United States aircraft carried out raids starting at 2:30 A.M.

Reports told of dead and wounded from the raids, which hit several towns around Hanoi, but there was no official announcement on the extent of casualties.

Tonight, the Foreign Ministry warned that the bombing raids were a "serious threat" to the peace talks in Paris. The statement closely paralleled a declaration made earlier by a spokesman in Paris. The Ministry called the new raids "extremely grave acts of war."

No Mention of Pilots

The North Vietnam news agency said the attacks were aimed at the port of Haiphong or the Red River Estuary, the Quangninh mine complex and the Hatay and Hoabinh areas, causing casualties among the civilian population.

The agency said that a prisoner-of-war camp, containing captured Americans, had been hit by strafing planes and a number of prisoners were wounded.

The agency also said that three United States aircraft and one helicopter had been shot down.

The army high command here also reported the downing of United States aircraft, but did not mention the capture of any pilots and crewmen.

North Vietnamese antiaircraft fire, seen from the city, was dense. The pounding of guns and the clatter of automatic weapons echoed through the quiet Hanoi streets, deserted after the local population took to air raid shelters.

Time to Go to Shelters

Loudspeakers blared reports that United States planes were operating within 30 miles of the city. They warned the population to be on full alert.

By mid-morning, Hanoi seemed back to normal, the streets busy with innumerable bicycles and small trucks, and children, holding hands, walking to school as usual.

In the past, Hanoi authorities have ordered a full alert when enemy aircraft are within 30 miles of the city. This is done to get old people and children into the shelters and to alert antiaircraft positions.

Sirens are sounded when planes come to within 12 miles and appear to be heading for the city.

Observers here viewed this morning's raid as the start of a United States operation aimed at dissuading Hanoi from keep-

Continued on Page 2, Column 3

NEW U.S. POSITION

Laird Asserts Strikes Protect Fliers Over Ho Chi Minh Trail

By WILLIAM BEECHER

Special to The New York Times

WASHINGTON, Nov. 21—The United States continued heavy bombing of North Vietnam today. The announced purpose of the raids was to suppress antiaircraft installations, but there were strong indications that a principal aim was the destruction of war stocks.

Defense Department officials said the bombing ended at about 6 o'clock tonight, Washington time, as scheduled. This was about 28 hours after the bombing began. The raids were first announced by the Hanoi radio and then confirmed at 2:55 A.M. by Secretary of Defense Melvin R. Laird.

Congressional reaction to the renewed bombing ranged from support to shock. Senator Peter H. Dominick, Republican of Colorado, said that the raids had sought "to show North Vietnam they can't use our unarmed planes for target practice." On the other hand, Senator Edmund S. Muskie, Democrat of Maine, said that he deplored the "renewed reliance on military pressure." [Page 4.]

Follows Attack on U.S. Jet

Secretary Laird, in a statement at noon, said that the strikes were being conducted against missile and antiaircraft sites in retaliation for the downing of an American reconnaissance plane nine days ago. The two-man crew is believed to have died in the crash.

"I want to state that we will continue to take protective reaction as necessary to protect the pilots of our unarmed reconnaissance planes," Mr. Laird said.

There have been more than 60 incidents involving United States planes since the halt of regular bombings of North Vietnam in November, 1968. The last major American retaliation strikes took place on May 2.

However, the Defense Secretary, apparently defining a new position today, said the retaliatory raids were also designed to protect pilots who are interdicting the flow of supplies southward along the Ho Chi Minh Trail.

Hanoi Is Contradicted

His statements in effect disputed reports from North Vietnam that raids were being conducted as far north as the Hanoi-Haiphong area. However, well-placed sources said that a major purpose of the strikes was to destroy weapon and fuel stocks waiting to be transported over the Ho Chi Minh Trail in Laos to Cambodia and South Vietnam.

One high-ranking official, who would not be identified for publication, said:

"Heavy rains and B-52 strikes along the Ho Chi Minh Trail system in Laos have prevented the North Vietnamese from moving much of these supplies south. They have been piling up for weeks. If this strike is successful, and I have every confidence it will be, it will present quite a setback to the enemy."

Largest Since May

Pentagon sources said plans for the raids, the largest since May, were approved shortly after the recent downing of the reconnaissance plane. But the strikes had to await a break in cloud cover over the target area, which Mr. Laird described as south of the 19th parallel, well south of the Hanoi-Haiphong area.

Knowledgeable officials said the raids were intended to back up warnings to North Vietnam

Continued on Page 2, Column 5

RUBY KEELER RETURNS TO B'WAY. See Section 2, [illegible]

College-Level Vocational Schools Boom

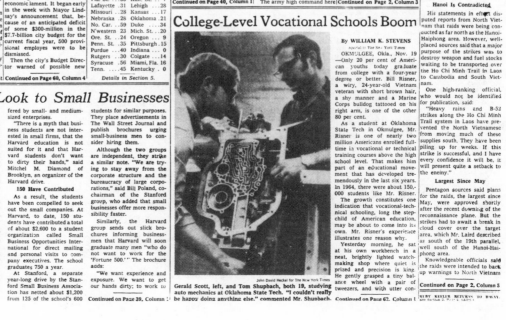

John David Heckel for The New York Times

Gerald Scott, left, and Tom Shupbach, both 19, studying auto mechanics at Oklahoma State Tech. "I couldn't really be happy doing anything else." commented Mr. Shupbach.

By WILLIAM K. STEVENS

Special to The New York Times

OKMULGEE, Okla., Nov. 19—Only 20 per cent of American youths today graduate from college with a four-year degree or better. Bill Risner, a wiry, 24-year-old Vietnam veteran with short brown hair, a shy manner and a Marine Corps bulldog tattooed on his right arm, is one of the other 80 per cent.

As a student at Oklahoma State Tech in Okmulgee, Mr. Risner is one of nearly two million Americans enrolled full-time in vocational or technical training courses above the high school level. That makes him part of an educational movement that has developed tremendously in the last six years. In 1964, there were about 150,000 students like Mr. Risner.

The growth constitutes one indication that vocational-technical schooling, long the stepchild of American education, may be about to come into its own. Mr. Risner's experience illustrates one reason why.

Yesterday morning, he sat at his own workbench in a neat, brightly lighted watchmaking shop where quiet is prized and precision is king. He gently grasped a tiny balance wheel with a pair of tweezers, and with utter con-

Continued on Page 62, Column 1

"All the News That's Fit to Print"

The New York Times

LATE CITY EDITION

Weather: Partly sunny, cold today; clear, cold tonight. Fair tomorrow. Temp. range: today 34-23; Monday 56-31. Full U.S. report on Page 81.

VOL. CXX ... No. 41,212 · NEW YORK, TUESDAY, NOVEMBER 24, 1970 · 15 CENTS

U.S. RESCUE FORCE LANDED WITHIN 23 MILES OF HANOI, BUT IT FOUND P.O.W.'S GONE

Associated Press

Arthur D. Simons, the Army colonel who led the raid, with Defense Secretary Melvin R. Laird at the conference.

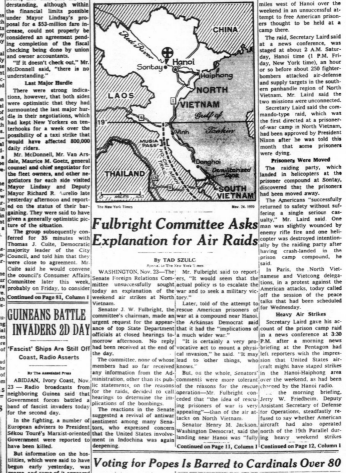

The New York Times · Nov. 24, 1970

ACCOUNT BY LAIRD

He Says a Copter Was Lost, but All Men Returned Safely

Text of Laird's statement is printed on Page 12.

By WILLIAM BEECHER
Special to The New York Times

WASHINGTON, Nov. 23 — Secretary of Defense Melvin R Laird disclosed today that a small task force of Army and Air Force men landed about 23 miles west of Hanoi over the weekend in an unsuccessful attempt to free American prisoners thought to be held at a camp there.

The raid, Secretary Laird said at a news conference, was staged at about 2 A.M. Saturday, Hanoi time (1 P.M. Friday, New York time), an hour or so before about 250 fighter-bombers attacked air-defense and supply targets in the southern panhandle region of North Vietnam. Mr. Laird said the two missions were unconnected.

Secretary Laird said the commando-type raid, which was the first directed at a prisoner-of-war camp in North Vietnam, had been approved by President Nixon after he was told this month that some prisoners were dying.

Prisoners Were Moved

The raiding party, which landed in helicopters at the prisoner compound at Sontay, discovered that the prisoners had been moved away.

The Americans "successfully returned to safety without suffering a single serious casualty," Mr. Laird said. One man was slightly wounded by enemy rifle fire and one helicopter was destroyed intentionally by the raiding party after having crash-landed in the prison camp compound, he said.

In Paris, the North Vietnamese and Vietcong delegations, in a protest against the American attacks, today called off the session of the peace talks that had been scheduled for Wednesday.

Heavy Air Strikes

Secretary Laird gave his account of the prison camp raid in a news conference at 3:30 P.M. after a morning news briefing at the Pentagon had left reporters with the impression that United States aircraft might have staged strikes in the Hanoi-Haiphong area over the weekend, as had been charged by the Hanoi radio.

... the morning briefing, Jerry W. Friedheim, Deputy Assistant Secretary of Defense for Operations, steadfastly refused to say whether American aircraft had also operated north of the 19th Parallel during heavy weekend strikes

Continued on Page 12, Column 1

Fulbright Committee Asks Explanation for Air Raids

By TAD SZULC
Special to The New York Times

WASHINGTON, Nov. 23—The Senate Foreign Relations Committee unsuccessfully sought today an explanation of the weekend air strikes at North Vietnam.

Senator J. W. Fulbright, the committee's chairman, made an urgent request for the appearance of top State Department officials at closed hearings tomorrow afternoon. No reply had been received at the end of the day.

The committee, none of whose members had so far received any information from the Administration, other than its public statements, on the reasons for the raids, decided to call hearings to determine the implications of the bombings.

The reactions in the Senate suggested a revival of antiwar sentiment among many Senators, who expressed concern that the United States involvement in Indochina was again deepening.

Mr. Fulbright said to reporters, "It would seem that the actual policy is to escalate the war and to seek a military victory."

Later, told of the attempt to rescue American prisoners of war at a compound near Hanoi, the Arkansas Democrat said that it had the "implications of a much wider war."

"It is certainly a very provocative act to mount a physical invasion," he said. "It may lead to other things, who knows."

But, on the whole, Senators' comments were more tolerant of the reasons for the rescue operation—Mr. Fulbright conceded that "the idea of rescuing prisoners of war is very appealing"—than of the air attacks on North Vietnam.

Senator Henry M. Jackson, Washington Democrat, said the landing near Hanoi was "fully

Continued on Page 11, Column 1

SENATE SUSTAINS VETO OF FUND CURB ON TV CAMPAIGNS

Bid to Override Nixon Fails by Four Votes as Five in G.O.P. Change Position

PRESIDENT IS PLEASED

O'Brien Calls Result 'Tragic' —Scott Pledges to Seek Wider Bill Next Year

By WARREN WEAVER Jr.
Special to The New York Times

WASHINGTON, Nov. 23 — The bill to limit spending for television and radio time in political campaigns died today when the Senate failed to muster enough votes to override President Nixon's veto.

The vote was 58 to 34 in favor of overriding, four votes short of the required two-thirds majority.

Six Democrats sided with 28 of the 37 Republicans in support of Mr. Nixon. Had they voted with their party colleagues, the veto would have been overridden. Five Republicans who supported the measure earlier this fall voted today to sustain the veto.

"The President is always pleased when decisions he makes are upheld," said Ronald L. Ziegler, the White House press secretary. "We felt we had clearly stated the reasoning behind the veto, and we're pleased that this was agreed to." Mr. Nixon vetoed the bill six weeks ago.

Scott Plans Effort

Senator Hugh Scott of Pennsylvania, the Republican minority leader, who voted against overriding, promised to help draft a more comprehensive substitute bill next year.

The Senate vote came after three hours of debate, in which supporters of the television spending measure conceded that it was an imperfect solution to the problem and critics of the bill almost uniformly conceded that something similar had to be passed soon.

The bill would have limited spending for radio and television time in the 1972 election to $5.1-million for each national ticket, based on 7 cents for each vote cast in the last Presidential contest. In 1968, the Republicans spent about

Continued on Page 21, Column 1

CORRUPTION JURY INDICTS GAMBLER

Mulligan Is Arrested After Refusing to Testify

By ARNOLD H. LUBASCH

Hugh Mulligan, described by authorities as a major bookmaker and key corrupter of policemen, was arrested here yesterday on a 19-count indictment that charged him with criminal contempt for refusing to answer questions in a grand-jury investigation that focused on gambling and corruption.

Mulligan was accused of failing to answer questions on numerous criminal activities that included loansharking, union racketeering and conspiracy to commit murder, in addition to organized gambling and police corruption.

The stocky, gray-haired, 59-year-old defendant refused to answer 19 questions before the grand jury on Oct. 15 although he had been extended immunity from prosecution, according to Alfred J. Scotti, chief assistant district attorney of Manhattan.

Mulligan, who lives in a modest home at 90-09 220th Street in Queens Village, was arraigned in the criminal part of State Supreme Court, where Justice George Postel released him on $5,000 bail and scheduled Dec. 3 as the date for the defendant to plead to the contempt charges.

The first count of the indictment against Mulligan, who is a convicted gambler, cited him for refusing to reply to the following question:

"Mr. Mulligan, have you

Continued on Page 37, Column 1

Wage-and-Price Guidance Urged by Business Group

A New Government Agency Is Proposed to Seek Noninflationary Behavior but Without 'Arm Twisting'

By EDWIN L. DALE Jr.
Special to The New York Times

WASHINGTON, Nov. 23—A sizable majority of a study group composed mainly of prominent present and former businessmen concluded today that the time has come for the Government to try to influence private price and wage decisions, though not by mandatory controls.

A policy statement by the Committee for Economic Development proposed a mechanism for such influence, but it ruled out "arm twisting" of individual firms and unions.

The suggested mechanism would include development by a new Government body of "broad norms of appropriate noninflationary wage and price behavior that would give some guidance to business and labor groups" and public reports on those cases where behavior "deviates substantially from such broad norms."

The various comments of reservation or outright dissent demonstrated clearly that there is no such thing as a monolithic "business" opinion on this delicate and controversial subject. Yet, out of 57 men who voted, only six voted to reject the statement entirely. Fifteen more entered reservations of various kinds—including a few who thought an even stronger policy of Government intervention is needed.

The Nixon Administration has consistently resisted any formal "guideposts" or other system of influencing private wage and price behavior.

The Committee for Economic

Continued on Page 63, Column 1

College Degree Reforms Asked in Carnegie Report

By ANDREW H. MALCOLM

The Carnegie Commission on Higher Education recommended yesterday a series of sweeping reforms that would liberalize the traditional degree structure of American colleges and universities.

Included in the proposals, which were drawn up to give students greater flexibility in designing their college careers, were recommendations to reduce the period of undergraduate education from four years to three years and to extend greatly the opportunities for education throughout life after high school.

Also included were proposals to reduce both the large number of different degrees available and society's emphasis on certification of ability through formal higher education.

Time and Resources

Such reforms, the report said would provide "more effective utilization" both of the time a person devotes to education and the limited resources of financially hard-pressed schools.

The commission said the changes would also "be the most significant undertaken since the modern system of higher education emerged from the classical college beginning a century ago.

It continued:

"Formal higher education would absorb less of the time of students and less of the resources of society and it would, at the same time, serve better both the interests of the students and the needs of society.

"We need more paths and more rates of progress to individual self-fulfillment and to service to society."

The special report, a 55-page

Continued on Page 28, Column 2

BIAS UNIT TO STUDY HIRING IN SCHOOLS

City's Rights Panel Planning Public Hearing in January on Board Practices Here

By LACEY FOSBURGH

The City Commission on Human Rights announced yesterday that it would hold full-scale public hearings in January to investigate the employment practices of the Board of Education.

It said the practices had allowed a lower percentage of professionals from minority groups to enter the school system here than in any other large city in the country.

Eleanor Holmes Norton, chairman of the commission, said the hearings would examine the current methods of recruitment, appointment, examination and promotion of members of minority groups in order to outline constructive proposals for "immediate change and improvement in the way blacks and Puerto Ricans are treated by the education system."

Demands by community and parent groups for a black principal led to a boycott, a sit-in and the temporary closing earlier this fall of Benjamin

Continued on Page 32, Column 1

CITY PLANS TO END WELFARE ABUSES INVOLVING HOTELS

Lindsay Proposes to Curb Squalor and High Rents— Will Seek Other Housing

By MURRAY SCHUMACH

Mayor Lindsay yesterday announced reforms designed to stamp out safety hazards and squalid conditions in hotels occupied by welfare families and to reduce huge rents paid to the hotels by the city.

At the same time, he proposed a long-range plan to acquire leases on apartments and to invest public-assistance funds in nonprofit low-income housing for welfare families, the aged and the helpless.

To get this housing, calculated to bring a virtual end to the use of hotels for welfare families, the Mayor said he would sponsor new legislation in Albany.

'Obsolete' Rules Blamed

In outlining the actions against "welfare hotels," which he said were based on reports forwarded to him last week by key subordinates, Mr. Lindsay said:

"Obsolete state and Federal regulations made it completely impossible for the city to use the millions of dollars spent each year on housing public-assistance clients in any kind of creative way."

To enforce the crackdown on the welfare hotels, special teams from the Department of Social Services will be placed in seven hotels here, each with more than 50 welfare families. In addition all welfare hotels—there are about 40 with a total of 1,000 families—will be rigidly inspected at least once a week by joint teams from the Fire, Buildings and Health Departments, the Mayor said.

He strongly criticized the welfare hotels, which were described in an article in The New York Times yesterday. The article reported the squalor in which welfare families live in hotels and the city's payment of rentals of up to $1,200 a month for individual families.

'Notorious Sore Spots'

The Mayor said in his statement, which had been in preparation before the Times article was printed:

"These hotels have become notorious sore spots in our city. Their rental costs are exorbitant and exploitive. Physical conditions and health standards within many are deplorable and illegal.

"They have created community tensions and deteriorating conditions in many residential areas. The children of families living in these facilities, more often than not, are out of school."

Mr. Lindsay, who said he had ordered an investigation of the hotels last October, said five of them had been stricken from

Continued on Page 32, Column 5

CAB TALKS REACH 'UNDERSTANDING'; STRIKE PERIL EBBS

Union and Owners Express Optimism—Pact Depends on Financial Analysis

By DAMON STETSON

The city's taxi drivers and fleet owners appeared last night to have reached a general understanding for resolving their contract dispute, but both sides refrained from saying they had a full agreement.

Harry Van Arsdale Jr., president of Local 3036 of the Taxi Drivers Union, would say only that "we're close to agreement," adding that union accountants were seeking to verify that "what's been said is so."

But the threat of a citywide taxi strike seemed to be in at least temporary abeyance.

Vincent D. McDonnell, chairman of the State Mediation Board, also said that the understanding, although within the financial limits possible under Mayor Lindsay's proposal for a $53-million fare increase, could not properly be considered an agreement pending completion of the fiscal checking being done by union and owner accountants.

"If it doesn't check out," Mr. McDonnell said, "there is no understanding."

Last Major Hurdle

There were strong indications, however, that both sides were optimistic that they had surmounted the last major hurdle in their negotiations, which had kept New Yorkers on tenterhooks for a week over the possibility of a taxi strike that would have affected 800,000 daily riders.

Mr. McDonnell, Mr. Van Arsdale, Maurice M. Goetz, general counsel and chief negotiator for the fleet owners, and other negotiators for each side visited Mayor Lindsay and Deputy Mayor Richard R. Aurelio late yesterday afternoon and reported on the status of their bargaining. They were said to have given a generally optimistic picture of the situation.

The group subsequently conferred for 35 minutes with Thomas J. Cuite, Democratic majority leader of the City Council, and told him that they were close to agreement. Mr. Cuite said he would convene the council's Consumer Affairs Committee later this week, probably on Friday, to consider

Continued on Page 81, Column 1

GUINEANS BATTLE INVADERS 2D DAY

'Fascist' Ships Are Still Off Coast, Radio Asserts

By The Associated Press

ABIDJAN, Ivory Coast, Nov. 23 — Radio broadcasts from neighboring Guinea said that Government forces battled a band of fascist invaders today for the second day.

In the fighting, a number of European advisers to President Sékou Touré's Marxist-oriented Government were reported to have been killed.

But information on the hostilities, which were said to have begun early yesterday, was sparse, and some of it appeared to be conflicting. Most of the reports came from the Conakry radio, the official voice of the Touré Government, which broadcast communiqués periodically through the day.

The radio repeated the Government's contention that the invaders were mercenaries dispatched by Portugal—a contention that Lisbon has officially denied. At midday, the radio said the ships of the "fascist enemy" were still in Guinean territorial waters.

However, travelers arriving here by air from Conakry later in the day said that the ships had left their moorings yesterday, and they expressed belief that the fighting was over.

Tonight, the Conakry radio called on all workers to go to work tomorrow as usual but to keep their weapons on hand.

The size of the invading group that clashed with the Guinean

Continued on Page 7, Column 1

A City of 200,000 Is Envisioned in Jersey Meadows

Clusters of buildings planned by the Hackensack Meadowlands Development Commission

By RONALD SULLIVAN
Special to The New York Times

RUTHERFORD, N. J., Nov. 23—A plan that would create New Jersey's third largest urban complex was made public here today by the Hackensack Meadowlands Development Commission.

The plan, which would take 30 years to complete on a 19,000-acre tract within sight of the Manhattan skyline, envisions an ultimate residential population of nearly 200,000, with most of the people housed in high-rise, island apartment clusters rising on steel piles along the Hackensack River.

Under the plan, huge commercial, shopping, cultural and transportation centers would also be built that would serve the entire northern New Jersey-New York metropolitan area.

Officials of the development commission, whose chairman is Edmund T. Hume, Commissioner of the State Department of Community Affairs, said that they could not estimate the cost of the

Continued on Page 45, Column 2

Voting for Popes Is Barred to Cardinals Over 80

By PAUL HOFMANN
Special to The New York Times

ROME, Nov. 23—Pope Paul VI ruled today that Cardinals who had reached the age of 80 years could not take part in the election of a new Pope.

The reform, which goes into effect Jan. 1, increases the chances for the next Pope to be non-Italian and, possibly, a progressive.

The rule eliminated 25 Cardinals who on Jan. 1 will be at least 80 from any conclave convened after that date to choose a new head of the Roman Catholic Church.

Eleven of those Cardinals are Italians. Most of these and of the 14 non-Italian Cardinals in the group are noted conservatives.

The only octogenarian among the nine United States Cardinals is Francis Cardinal McIntire of Los Angeles, who is 84 and known for his conservative views.

The Sacred College of Cardinals is at present composed of 127 members, 38 of whom are Italian. After Jan. 1, those eligible to elect a new Pontiff will number 102, including 27 Italians. A two-thirds majority of Cardinals present at the secret conclave is required for the elevation of a new Pope.

Pope Paul also ordered today that on reaching their 80th birthday Cardinals would cease to be members of administrative departments and other permanent institutions of the Vatican.

Cardinals in charge of departments of the Roman Curia—the Vatican's administrative machinery—and of other permanent central church institutions today were "requested to submit their resignation voluntarily" when they reach 75 years of age.

The new rules stated that it was up to the Pope to decide after considering each case individually whether to accept the resignation immediately.

Today's reform heralded a shuffle in the Curia, in which 43 Cardinals—many of whom are older than 75 years—now hold functions.

It is widely expected that Pope Paul will soon call a Consistory to name new Cardinals.

Churchmen here discussed privately today whether the new regulations were indicative of any plans the Pope may have concerning his own future. Asked about this point,

Continued on Page 6, Column 1

NEWS INDEX

South Vietnamese troops about to be airlifted from Laos as Operation Lam Son 719 draws to a close.

The North Vietnamese put up the strongest air defense of the war during Operation Lam Son 719.

South Vietnamese infantrymen search for enemy supply depots and bunkers along the Ho Chi Minh Trail.

"All the News That's Fit to Print"

The New York Times

LATE CITY EDITION
Weather: Sunny and cold today; fair and cold tonight. Cloudy tomorrow. Temp. range: today 25-38; Wed. 28-37. Full U.S. report on Page 78.

VOL. CXX. No. 41,333   © 1971 The New York Times Company.   NEW YORK, THURSDAY, MARCH 25, 1971   15 CENTS

SAIGON DRIVE IN LAOS ENDS AS 1,500 LEAVE LAST BASE; ENEMY KEEPS UP PRESSURE

44-DAY OPERATION

500 Left Behind to Aid Defense of Khesanh, Bombarded Daily

By CRAIG R. WHITNEY
Special to The New York Times

SAIGON, South Vietnam, Thursday, March 25 — The South Vietnamese drive against enemy supply lines in Laos ended yesterday, 44 days after it began.

About 500 South Vietnamese marines were left behind to man a mountain position two miles from the border, but their mission was to help in the defense of the rear base at nearby Khesanh, in northwestern South Vietnam. The marines, on Co Roc Mountain in Laos just south of Route 9, were expected to be withdrawn within two days.

About 1,500 other marines withdrew from the last South Vietnamese fire base in Laos, Dong Da, about six miles from the South Vietnamese border, the Saigon command said. They pulled out along with other units that had formed a protective rear guard for the retreat.

G.I.'s at Khesanh Shelled

North Vietnamese troops also continued to put heavy pressure yesterday on allied positions inside South Vietnam.

American artillery units were digging in at Khesanh, which has been pounded daily by enemy gunners since early last week. Early yesterday 82 enemy rockets and artillery shells reportedly landed around the American helicopter airstrip there, and other shells fell sporadically through the day on South Vietnamese forward command posts nearby.

The last major unit to leave Laos was a column of tanks and armored personnel carriers that fought its way out yesterday, with North Vietnamese tanks close behind.

Enemy Tanks Are Attacked

Twenty-one Soviet-made PT-76 tanks were attacked by American fighter-bombers on a trail only a mile southwest of the border crossing point of Lao-bao, and seven of them were destroyed, the military command in Saigon said. Three other tanks were attacked by helicopter gunships half a mile closer to the border, and one was reported destroyed and two damaged.

At the height of the drive against the Ho Chi Minh Trail network, the South Vietnamese had more than 20,000 troops in Laos. They raided supply and ammunition caches and occupied parts of the trail complex as far west as the road junction of Tchepone, 25 miles inside Laos. The withdrawal eastward began two weeks ago under in-

Continued on Page 5, Column 4

Thieu Said to Have Curbed Offensive to Reduce Loss

By WILLIAM BEECHER
Special to The New York Times

WASHINGTON, March 24 — Well-placed Pentagon planners say that President Nguyen Van Thieu decided to curtail South Vietnam's offensive in Laos despite suggestions from some senior American militarymen that he send in replacements and try to stay on for a few more weeks.

With unseasonably bad weather both in southern Laos and at the key American supply base at Khesanh, they reported, President Thieu decided against running the risk of seeing some of his units trapped and battered with insufficient air support.

The informants say that Mr. Thieu felt that his forces, in more than six weeks of bitter fighting, had already accomplished a good deal.

Senior Defense Department planners hinted, however, that before the onset of monsoon rains in early May, commando-style raids might be staged by small South Vietnamese units up and down the extensive Ho Chi Minh Trail network in southern Laos.

If President Thieu approves such operations, the planners said, raiding parties of 500 to 1,000 men might swoop down in helicopters, attack ammunition caches, truck parks and communications facilities, plant mines and booby traps and then depart before large North Vietnamese reaction forces could reach the site.

There are scores of such targets along the trail network,

Continued on Page 8, Column 1

U.A.R. SAID TO GET NEW SOVIET ARMS

Reported Delivery Coincides With Measures to Prepare Egyptian Public for War

By RAYMOND H. ANDERSON
Special to The New York Times

CAIRO, March 24 — A new wave of weapons and military equipment deliveries from the Soviet Union has reached the United Arab Republic in the last few weeks, according to reliable Western sources, coinciding with stepped-up, widely publicized measures by the Egyptian leadership to prepare the country for war.

The deliveries are reported to include antiaircraft missiles, vehicles, guns and crates with unidentified equipment. They are believed to be part of the periodic Soviet arms shipments to Egypt.

The Egyptians continue to emphasize that they would greatly prefer a political solution that would get the Israeli troops out of the Sinai Peninsula, but there is increasing talk that this is an illusory hope and that military action will be required.

Seek to Deter Israelis

The air-defense build-up is clearly intended to deter the Israelis from leapfrogging the Suez Canal combat zone and conducting retaliatory air strikes deep inside Egypt, as they did during the earlier "war of attrition" along the waterway.

There is general agreement that any new ground fighting would initially be limited to the canal area and would be an intensified version of the war

Continued on Page 12, Column 3

Democratic Council Backs Funds Cutoff For the War by '72

By R. W. APPLE Jr.
Special to The New York Times

WASHINGTON, March 24 — The Democratic party's Policy Council voted unanimously today to support a Congressional cutoff of all funds for American military operations in Indochina after Dec. 31.

Although it endorsed no specific bill, the 100-member council adopted a statement that spoke of "legislation such as" the proposed Vietnam Disengagement Act of 1971."

The resolution also registered opposition to "any expansion of the war by American or South Vietnamese forces in Cambodia, Laos or North Vietnam or by the bombing of North Vietnam."

On Feb. 9, 1970, the council adopted a resolution urging a total withdrawal from Vietnam within 18 months — in other words, by Aug. 9 of this year, but at that time it said nothing about Congressional action to cut off funds.

Last year's action was not taken unanimously. The final resolution was adopted only after associates of former President Lyndon B. Johnson failed in attempts to soften it.

At the meeting today, according to participants, council members generally regarded as

Continued on Page 32, Column 1

STATE BILL VOTED TO LET GOVERNOR FILL WELFARE JOB

Legislature Approves Plan to Strip Board of Power to Name Commissioner

By WILLIAM E. FARRELL
Special to The New York Times

ALBANY, March 24 — Acting with unusual speed, the Senate and the Assembly passed a bill today to strip the State Board of Social Welfare of its power to appoint the Commissioner of Social Services.

The measure, which has been widely interpreted as an attempt to oust Commissioner George K. Wyman from the position that he has held since 1962, now goes to Governor Rockefeller, who is expected to sign it.

Mr. Wyman's term expires on June 30.

Called 'Scapegoat'

Several dissenting Democrats chided their colleagues for using Mr. Wyman as "a scapegoat" for the ills of the state's welfare system, contending that the bill was a superficial way of placating taxpayers angry over welfare costs and the specter of increased taxes.

The bill, which would allow the Governor to appoint the Commissioner of Social Services with the advice and consent of the Senate, passed the Assembly by a vote of 119 to 29 and the Senate by 33 to 20.

The bill had a brief history before being voted upon. It was introduced last week by Republican majority members who were buoyed by recent remarks by the Governor reflecting disaffection with the Commissioner.

Budget Cuts at Issue

The big issue here is finding ways of trimming the Governor's $8.45-billion proposed budget for the new state fiscal year that starts April 1 to avert Mr. Rockefeller's proposed tax increase package of $1.1-billion. One of the most vulnerable areas is welfare, which last year cost the state $1,056-billion and cost localities $902-million.

Key legislators say that many of the problems in the welfare system come from sloppy administration. As head of the vast welfare apparatus, Mr. Wyman looms as an easy target for political and public antipathy.

Quite a few lawmakers who voted for the bill did so after noting for the record that their stand was in no way a reflection on the Commissioner's competence.

"It's like Pontius Pilate washing his hands," one observer said.

Assemblyman Lawrence E. Corbett Jr., an upstate Republi-

Continued on Page 34, Column 3

SENATE BARS FUNDS FOR SST, 51-46; NIXON CALLS VOTE 'SEVERE BLOW'; BOEING SAYS IT WILL END PROJECT

WARNED OF LAYOFFS: Workers in Boeing Company plant in Seattle being told of Senate vote that killed project

United Press International

Hospitals Here Face Financial Emergency

Municipal Squeeze

By JOHN SIBLEY

The city's public hospitals are sure to run out of cash before the fiscal year ends June 30 and will be forced to borrow to keep going.

Forecasts of the deficit range from Controller Abraham D. Beame's $10-million estimate to an acknowledgement from the system itself that the shortage could run to more than $40-million.

No Closings Foreseen

The municipal hospitals' current operating budget is $617.8-million.

Unlike the city schools — which were accused of bringing on a fiscal crisis by spending too much too quickly — the 18 municipal hospitals are running into trouble because they have received less revenue than they had expected.

The deficit does not portend any action so drastic as the closing of a hospital. When their funds are exhausted, hospital officials say, they will simply be forced to borrow again from the city in anticipation of future income. Mr. Beame's office agrees that is the way the immediate problem will be solved.

"We absolutely are not going

Continued on Page 43, Column 2

State Help Sought

By PETER KIHSS

The city has told the state that it cannot keep helping 22 voluntary—private, nonprofit—hospitals to meet their deficits for the next three months, and has asked $4-million in interim state emergency aid. But legislators are talking about slashing such state aid.

Involved are outpatient deficits under the so-called Ghetto Medicine Program, in which the state and city have split the costs since December, 1969, for hospital deficits running about $1.3-million a month.

Outpatient Situation

A memorandum by the city's legislative representative in Albany, Richard A. Brown, has told the Legislature that unless the state takes over the full aid for the three months starting April 1, "some hospitals will close their outpatient departments and the medically needy persons served by them will be deprived abruptly of essential services."

In the Ghetto Medicine Program, the city's Health Department and local departments up-state contract with voluntary hospitals to pay outpatient deficits for poor neighborhoods. The state then pays half the

Continued on Page 43, Column 3

Aircraft Company Is Swept by Gloom; 7,000 Jobs to End

By WALLACE TURNER
Special to The New York Times

SEATTLE, March 24 — The mock-up of the supersonic transport plane, 298 feet long and 53 feet high, dominated the big shop.

With its movable needle nose in a drooped position, it looked a little like a dejected sea monster.

The men stood in little groups, their faces gray with the impact of the news that the Senate had voted not to provide funds for the development of the plane beyond next Wednesday.

That vote will cost about 7,000 people their jobs, L. P. Mikelwaite, a Boeing Company vice president, announced at a news conference. He was overheard by the employes.

"Everybody expected this, but it's a disappointment," said Clair Baumgardner, who has worked for Boeing since 1941. "It's a hardship for a lot of people. There's just no place to go."

Unemployment Heavy

This is a community with an unemployment list that makes a man with a job count his blessings. Since July, 1968, Boeing has cut its work force from 101,000 to 44,000, and the loss of this $500-million payroll has hurt other parts of the economy here.

Moreover, the men who clustered around the mock-up this afternoon had gone as far as they could expect to go in using their seniority to bump shorter-term employes. Most of the men on the mock-up crew have more than 20 years' seniority.

Ed Clayton, 43 years old, a

Continued on Page 24, Column 6

West Coast Chain To Buy Bergdorf's

By LEONARD SLOANE

Bergdorf Goodman, the Fifth Avenue specialty store, has signed an agreement in principle to be acquired by Broadway-Hale Stores, Inc., the largest department store organization in the West and one of the 50 largest retailers in the United States.

The proposed purchase of Bergdorf's, a 70-year-old establishment that has become a household word for fashion merchandise, was announced by Broadway-Hale after its board of directors met yesterday afternoon in San Francisco.

Andrew Goodman, president of Bergdorf's, elaborated on the rationale for selling the store owned by his family in an interview here and in meetings

Continued on Page 59, Column 1

ROLL-CALL TENSE

New Senators Divide 7-4 in Opposition to the Plane

By CHRISTOPHER LYDON
Special to The New York Times

WASHINGTON, March 24 — The Senate voted, 51 to 46, today to end further funding of the supersonic transport aircraft.

President Nixon said in a statement that the vote was "distressing and disappointing." He called it "a severe blow" to the aerospace industry and to United States leadership, but said he was "determined" not to let it halt American technological leadership.

The Boeing Company, prime contractor for the craft's airframe, indicated that it would terminate the eight-year-old program immediately.

"It's the end of the SST," said H. W. Withington, a Boeing vice president, who heard the tense roll-call from the gallery. There is no private financing to replace the Government's support, he said. Lay-offs of as many as 7,000 Boeing employes in Seattle were expected.

Nixon's Efforts Fail

The Senate vote came after weeks of intense lobbying and direct efforts by Mr. Nixon to save the plane in the last 24 hours. The Senate voted, 52 to 41, against the project last Dec. 3.

The House, which kept the project alive through the winter, voted last week to cancel Government funding as of March 31. The Senate, in rejecting an Appropriations Committee amendment that would have restored the House cuts, destroyed the last chance of a compromise extension.

Decisive elements in the defeat of the plane appeared to be that the President did not convert Republicans who opposed the project and that freshman Senators split 7 to 4 against the plane.

Among the new opponents were three Southern Democrats: Senators Lloyd Bentsen of Texas, David H. Gambrell of Georgia and Lawton Chiles of Florida, and two Republicans, William V. Roth Jr. of Delaware and Lowell P. Weicker of Connecticut. Mr. Nixon had counted on all five

Continued on Page 24, Column 1

NEWS INDEX

	Page		Page
Books	37	Obituaries	42
Bridge	36	Op-Ed	39
Business	55, 65-66	Society	51
Chess	36	Sports	48-52
Crossword	37	Theaters	43-47
Editorials	38	Transportation	78
Financial	55-66	TV and Radio	75
Letters	38	U. N. Proceedings	9
Man in the News	14	Washington Record	24
Movies	43-47	Weather	78
Music	43-47	Women's News	51

News Summary and Index, Page 41

Cahill Says the Giants May Move to Jersey

By RONALD SULLIVAN
Special to The New York Times

TRENTON, March 24 — Gov. William T. Cahill announced today that he had a verbal commitment from the New York Giants football club to leave Yankee Stadium and play in a new sports complex in the Hackensack River meadowlands.

The Governor said at a news conference here that he would propose a bill in the State Legislature that would create a five-man state sports authority to oversee the financing and construction of an open stadium on a site that would also accommodate a horse-racing track and indoor facilities for hockey, basketball and conventions, as well as a large hotel.

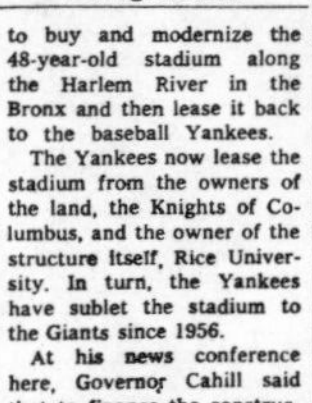

The Governor estimated that the completed project could cost from $100-million to $200-million and could be completed in time for the football season's kickoff in 1973.

Reached in Palm Beach, where he is attending the annual conference of the National Football League, Wellington Mara, the president of the New York Giants, said: "If the Governor makes it possible to take better care of our fans, we would certainly be prepared to enter into serious discussions about leaving the facility."

Later, just as he was leaving the State House here this evening, Mr. Cahill said, "I translate Mr. Mara's statement as saying if we do what we told him we would do, they're coming to New Jersey."

"I'm convinced of their good faith and I think they are convinced of ours," Mr. Cahill said. He also said he had a verbal commitment from Mr. Mara, with whom he said, he had extensive private negotiations.

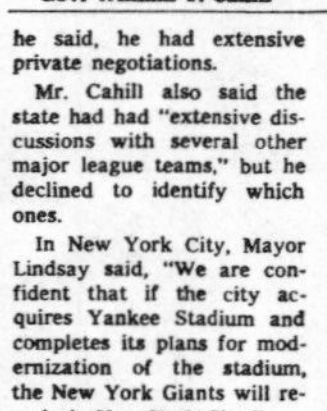

Mr. Cahill also said the state had had "extensive discussions with several other major league teams," but he declined to identify which ones.

In New York City, Mayor Lindsay said, "We are confident that if the city acquires Yankee Stadium and completes its plans for modernization of the stadium, the New York Giants will remain in New York City."

Mr. Lindsay announced three weeks ago that the city planned to spend $24-million to buy and modernize the 48-year-old stadium along the Harlem River in the Bronx and then lease it back to the baseball Yankees.

The Yankees now lease the stadium from the owners of the land, the Knights of Columbus, and the owner of the structure itself, Rice University. In turn, the Yankees have sublet the stadium to the Giants since 1956.

At his news conference here, Governor Cahill said that to finance the construction of the sports complex, the State's Sports Authority

Continued on Page 47, Column 1

Gov. William T. Cahill
United Press International

Wellington Mara
The New York Times

F.B.I. Files Tell of Surveillance Of Students, Blacks, War Foes

By FRED P. GRAHAM
Special to The New York Times

WASHINGTON, March 24 — Copies of Federal Bureau of Investigation documents that have been mailed anonymously to several newspapers and individuals indicate that the agency is engaged in active surveillance of student, Negro and peace groups.

The F.B.I. acknowledged today the authenticity of the documents and said they had been stolen from the two-man bureau office in Media, Pa., near Philadelphia, on March 8.

The documents suggest that F.B.I. surveillance of dissenters on the political left has been far more extensive than is generally known. They also show that the subjects of inquiries include obscure persons marginally suspected of illegal activity.

The disclosures come at a time of mounting controversy over reports of widespread Government surveillance.

A Justice Department source said that a distorted picture of the bureau activities had been given because the thieves had thus far circulated only 14 F.B.I. documents—relating to investigations of students, blacks and New Left groups—out of more than 800 documents that were stolen.

Surveillance discussed in the documents that have been put into circulation ranges from an order by the bureau director, J. Edgar Hoover, to investigate all student groups "organized to project the demands of black students," to a paper

Continued on Page 32, Column 1

NEW JERSEY — Hackensack; Lyndhurst; Jersey City; NEW YORK; BROOKLYN; STATEN I.
Proposed stadium (cross)
The New York Times March 25, 1971

Lieutenant William Calley was implicated in the My Lai massacre affair. He is shown here opening some of the enthusiastic fan mail he received before being brought to trial.

Victims of the My Lai massacre lie huddled in a ditch.

"All the News That's Fit to Print"

The New York Times

LATE CITY EDITION

Weather: Partly cloudy, mild today; chance of rain tonight, tomorrow. Temp. range: today 37-52; Wed. 33-51. Full U.S. report on Page 82.

VOL. CXX . No. 41,340 NEW YORK, THURSDAY, APRIL 1, 1971 — 15 CENTS

CALLEY SENTENCED TO LIFE FOR MURDERS AT MYLAI 4; LENGTHY REVIEW TO BEGIN

Associated Press

Lieut. William L. Calley Jr. after sentencing yesterday

OUSTER ORDERED

But He Will Keep His Rank Till Sentence Is Reconsidered

By HOMER BIGART
Special to The New York Times

FORT BENNING, Ga., March 31—First Lieut. William L. Calley Jr. was sentenced to life imprisonment today for slaying at least 22 South Vietnamese civilians three years ago at the hamlet of Mylai 4.

The military jury also ordered his dismissal from the Army and the forfeiture of his pay and allowances, although he will retain his officer's status and continue to be paid until his case is reviewed by another command.

His sentence could be overturned during the automatic military appeal process, and the term could be shortened at any time by the exercise of clemency by the President or the Secretary of the Army.

If the sentence is allowed to stand, Lieutenant Calley will be eligible for parole after serving 10 years.

Longest Court-Martial

The longest court-martial in history ended at 2:35 P.M., when the short, stocky platoon leader, convicted Monday of premeditated murder, marched up to the jury box with two of his lawyers.

His face, normally pink, was pale and taut. He knew that the six career officers on the jury could have consigned him to the gallows. The mandatory penalty was death or life imprisonment.

Standing at rigid attention, Lieutenant Calley exchanged salutes with the president of the court, Col. Clifford H. Ford, then braced himself.

Colonel Ford, a 53-year-old veteran of World War II and Korea, read the sentence:

"First Lieut. William L. Calley, it is my duty as president of this court to inform you that the court in closed session and upon secret written ballot, three-fourths of the members present at the time the vote was taken concurring, sentences you:

"To be confined at hard labor for the length of your natural life.

"To be dismissed from the

Continued on Page 18, Column 3

G.O.P. DEFERS VOTE ON STATE BUDGET; SHY OF SUPPORT

Leaders Hope to Round Up the Final Backing to Pass $7-Billion Budget Today

'72 FISCAL YEAR BEGINS

Holdout Republicans Fight Any New Taxes—Demand Further Spending Cuts

By WILLIAM E. FARRELL
Special to The New York Times

ALBANY, March 31 — The Republican majority leaders recessed the Legislature late tonight, the eve of the start of the 1972 state fiscal year, after an anxious but fruitless day of searching the G.O.P. ranks for the votes to pass a $7.7-billion budget.

The decision to recess the Senate and the Assembly until tomorrow morning was announced by Senator Majority Leader Earl W. Brydges, Republican of Niagara Falls.

He said he had the concurrence of Assembly Speaker Perry B. Duryea, Republican of Montauk, L. I., because "it got to be pretty late" and there were "loose ends" in the delicate negotiations to obtain the needed votes.

Both houses recessed shortly after 9 P.M.—less than three hours before the start of the new fiscal year. Mr. Brydges said, however, that the state could operate without a budget at least until the first payday of the new year next week.

Sales Tax Rise Planned

While both houses held desultory sessions today, interspersed with long recesses, Mr. Duryea and Mr. Brydges spent long hours trying to change the minds of reluctant Republicans who are fighting any increases in state taxes.

The leaders contend that Governor Rockefeller's original proposed budget of $8.45-billion, containing a record tax increase of $1.1-billion, has been irreducibly pruned.

The latest proposal by the Republican leadership was disclosed yesterday. It contains a $448-million package of state tax increases that relies heavily on a cent-on-the-dollar rise in the state sales tax. The present state sales levy is 3 cents on the dollar.

Asked tonight if there were any moves afoot to revamp this latest tax proposal significantly, Mr. Brydges replied that there "could be some variation there, but I doubt it very much."

He said that the idea of in-

Continued on Page 52, Column 1

Firemen Begin Slowdown To Prod City on Demands

Strict Adherence to Rule Book Designed to Get Movement on Contract Talks—No Delays on Alarms Reported

By DAMON STETSON

City firemen said last night that they were beginning a rule-book slowdown as a pressure tactic aimed at getting further movement in their contract negotiations.

A spokesman for the Uniformed Firefighters Association said that men responding to alarms were stopping for red lights, "stop" signs and "yield" signs in accordance with department regulations. Usually, fire trucks answering alarms do not come to a full stop at such signals or signs.

The spokesman said that the union was making "absolutely no attempt to keep track" of how effective the slowdown was, "except that we have heard it's widespread."

However, a spokesman for the Fire Department said last night, "as far as I can tell as of this moment, there has been no change, no delays" in responding to fires.

But the spokesman, Paul O'Brien, said that department officials could not tell whether engines responding to fires were stopping at traffic signals. "There were no delays reported in responding and we don't have anyone following the engines," he said.

A fireman of Ladder Company 32 in the Bronx said last night that his unit had observed the job action while proceeding to Engine Company 79's house, to fill in for No. 79, as the latter was responding to a fire that killed three elderly persons at 2483 University Avenue, near West 190th Street.

But John Clancy, 19th Battalion Chief, said units with which he went to the fire scene did not stop for traffic signals.

Shortly before the rule-book action began at 6 P.M., Fire Commissioner Robert O. Lowery

Continued on Page 45, Column 2

CON EDISON SEEKS A 14.2% INCREASE IN ELECTRIC RATE

Request, Filed With P.S.C., Would Bring Average Bill Up to $12.61 a Month

By WILL LISSNER

Consolidated Edison asked the state yesterday for electricity rate increases of 11.4 to 15.3 per cent from all three million of its residential and commercial customers in the city and Westchester County.

The increases would push the bill of the average city family using 250 kilowatt hours a month up from $11.04 to $12.61, a rise of 14.2 per cent. The rises would range from 21 cents to $2.70 a month.

The request, filed with the Public Service Commission, is aimed at bringing a 14.9 per cent increase in the company's annual revenues. Con Edison's vice president for public affairs, Robert O. Lehrman, said the revenue increase was needed to improve the utility's rate of return to attract financing for a $2.2-billion construction program at an economical level.

Adding Power Facilities

The program includes eight million kilowatts of new power facilities in various stages of construction.

"Right now we are practically certain to have brownouts—drops in voltage—this summer and we are doing all we can to avoid load-shedding which would interrupt service to some of our customers, as happened to 1 per cent for 90 minutes last year," he said.

"This construction program will lead us out of our present capacity shortage. But we cannot attract the investors needed to carry out the program without rate relief to increase the return on our investment in the near future."

Return of 8.01 Per Cent

The company's actual rate of return for 1970, as a result of the rate increase in September, was 5.85 per cent, or with extraordinary costs removed, 6.38 per cent, he said.

"The Public Service Commission found in our 1970 electric rate case that a fair rate of return was 7.28 per cent," said Mr. Lehrman. The judgment was based on 1968-69, not 1970, costs.

Asked what rate of return on total investment was sought by the new increases, he said, "on total investment, 8.01 per cent." He added that on equity capital, the portion of the investment provided by security owners, "the return will work out around 12 per cent."

The increases sought would yield $142.8-million a year on

Continued on Page 30, Column 4

CASUALTIES HEAVY AS ENEMY BURNS TOWN IN VIETNAM

District Capital Is Struck in Second Major Attack This Week South of Danang

By The Associated Press

SAIGON, South Vietnam, Thursday, April 1 — Enemy troops have attacked and burned most of a district capital in the northern part of South Vietnam, reportedly inflicting heavy casualties on civilians and their militia.

The attack, which began with a mortar barrage on Sunday and ended with the enemy's withdrawal from the town yesterday, was the second heavy enemy blow this week in the area south of Danang.

Meanwhile, a new South Vietnamese attack on North Vietnamese supply lines in Laos was completed today by about 200 to 300 men, flown across the border yesterday by American helicopters. The results of the raid were not disclosed. But reports indicated that the raiders had made contact with the enemy.

200 Casualties Reported

The objective was believed to be along Route 922, which runs east from the main Ho Chi Minh Trail routes to the Ashau Valley of South Vietnam, northwest of Danang.

According to a captured North Vietnamese soldier, the attack on the town of Ducduc, 25 miles southwest of Danang, followed a three-day forced march from the trail network in Laos.

Reports from the field said 200 South Vietnamese civilians had been killed or wounded in the assault, reportedly staged by two battalions of North Vietnamese troops. If at full strength, these could contain up to 1,200 men.

Eighteen regional militiamen were reported killed and 36 were reported wounded.

Heavy Attack Sunday

Reports from the area said that about 1,000 houses had been burned but that the North Vietnamese had failed to penetrate the compound of the United States district advisory team. However, they were reported to have blown up the team's house and a senior adviser's bunker outside. One American was reported wounded slightly.

An American who flew over Ducduc yesterday said it was a blackened area.

Last Sunday, when the attack on Ducduc began, enemy demolition men attacked an American artillery base 40 miles south of Danang, killing 33 and

Continued on Page 8, Column 1

Jobless Rate Rose by 41% In New York Area in 1970

By JAMES F. CLARITY

The unemployment rate in the New York-New Jersey metropolitan area increased 41 per cent in 1970, while the increase for the city alone was 33 per cent. The increases, reported yesterday by the United States Labor Department, necessitated sharp rises in unemployment payments in the city and in four suburban counties in New York and eight in northern New Jersey.

The report said that in the 17-county New York-Northeastern New Jersey area, an average of 4.5 per cent of labor force of 6.6 million was unemployed last year, compared to 3.2 in 1969.

The average number of unemployed persons in the area, the report said, was 300,000, of whom 159,000 were New York City residents. The city labor force was estimated at 3.3 million.

City Rate Rises to 4.8

The increase in the unemployment rate in the city, 3.6 in 1969 to 4.8 in the last year compared with national averages of 3.5 to 4.9 for the same period.

The extent of joblessness was not the worst in the city's history. In 1966, for example, the number of unemployed was 174,000 and in 1958 it was 251,000.

The report, issued by Herbert Bienstock, regional direc-

Continued on Page 26, Column 3

PRESIDENT BACKS CAMPAIGN CEILING

In a Reversal, He Supports Democratic Position on Limitation on Spending

By WARREN WEAVER Jr.
Special to The New York Times

WASHINGTON, March 31 — The Nixon Administration, in a major reversal of position, endorsed today most of the key provisions of Democratic-sponsored legislation designed to reduce spending in election campaigns.

Deputy Attorney General Richard G. Kleindienst called for a "workable and realistic" ceiling on the amount candidates could spend for all communications media, including radio, television, newspapers and billboards. He testified before the Senate Communications Subcommittee, which had reopened hearings at his request.

Scott Bill Dismissed

The only limit that Mr. Kleindienst opposed was on the size of individual campaign contributions. He said that current attempts to impose such ceilings had proved "unrealistic and incapable of enforcement."

The Justice Department official thus effectively dismissed what had previously been the unofficial Administration bill, sponsored by Senator Hugh Scott of Pennsylvania, the minority floor leader. That bill omits any limits on spending but would prohibit contributions

Continued on Page 21, Column 5

Thieu Terms Laos Drive Saigon's 'Biggest Victory'

Special to The New York Times

DONGHA, South Vietnam, March 31—President Nguyen Van Thieu declared today that his troops' recent thrust into Laos had attained "the biggest victory ever" for the armed forces of South Vietnam.

In a news conference of nearly two hours, held under a blazing sun in a cemetery at the South Vietnamese Army base here, Mr. Thieu insisted that the operation had achieved its objectives of disrupting supply lines, destroying stockpiles of war supplies and preventing any "significant" Communist offensives this year in the northern provinces of South Vietnam.

The news conference was Mr. Thieu's first in more than a year.

Seeks to Offset Report

It was clearly called in an effort to offset the widespread belief that the South Vietnamese had been defeated in their 45-day major campaign, that they had been forced to retreat by heavy Communist counterattacks, that their morale was shaken and that frictions had developed between the American and South Vietnamese commands. The President denied all such assumptions.

"I have learned," he said, "through some articles, through some periodic magazines, from daily magazines, which said that the United States said that the Vietnamese did not commit enough troops, that Vietnamese say that the United States had not provided enough support and that the redeployment of the Vietnamese troops from Laos is a defeat—disorder, disaster. I believe that is not true and is completely wrong."

The whole tone and manner of the President, as he spoke in English to reporters and addressed assembled airborne troops, was one of confidence that whatever the price paid by the South Vietnamese in

Continued on Page 12, Column 1

HOUSE DEMOCRATS ASK PULLOUT BY '73

Caucus Vote Is 138 to 62 on Indochina Withdrawal —Action Is Compromise

By MARJORIE HUNTER
Special to The New York Times

WASHINGTON, March 31 — House Democrats called today for an end to United States involvement in Indochina by the start of 1973.

The action was almost identical to that taken by Senate Democrats a month ago. It was the first time that the House Democratic majority had spoken out on the issue.

A resolution, approved by a vote of 138 to 62, went further than some Democratic Representatives, including Carl Albert, the Speaker, had originally wanted.

Statement a Compromise

At the same time, it fell short of demands of the leading doves, who had pushed for total troop withdrawals from Southeast Asia by the end of this year.

Some indication of the sharp division within Democratic ranks was expressed by Representative Teno Roncalio of Wyoming as he emerged from the three-hour closed caucus.

"There is a feeling of togetherness in there," he said wryly. "Everyone is reasonably unhappy."

As finally adopted, the resolution represented a compromise hammered out in recent

Continued on Page 11, Column 1

CLINIC HERE PLANS ABORTIONS FOR $80

Planned Parenthood to Open Center on Second Avenue

By JOHN SIBLEY

A clinic able to perform more than 10,000 abortions a year for an average fee of $80 will be opened here this summer by Planned Parenthood of New York City.

The center is also being designed to serve 10,000 to 12,000 people a year seeking help with contraception. It will occupy the entire fourth floor at 380 Second Avenue, at 22d Street.

The clinic, if the organization's hopes are realized, will handle a significant number of the abortions done here. The total number performed in the city since legalization last July 1 has just passed the 100,000 mark. About half the women were New Yorkers and half were from out of the state.

The clinic's back-up hospital, which is required by the city Health Code, will be the Berth Israel Medical Center. The code requires that in case of emergency an abortion patient can be taken to a hospital in less than 10 minutes.

Alfred F. Moran, executive vice president of Planned Parenthood, predicts that the

Continued on Page 83, Column 3

Hoffa's Parole Bid Is Denied Until '72

By RICHARD HALLORAN
Special to The New York Times

WASHINGTON, March 31—James R. Hoffa, the imprisoned president of the International Brotherhood of Teamsters, was denied parole today.

The United States Board of Parole, in rejecting the union leader's application, also ruled that it would not consider any application for his parole again until June, 1972.

Hoffa was notified of the decision in the Lewisburg, Pa., Federal Prison where he is serving two consecutive terms totaling 13 years for mail fraud and tampering with a jury.

The major impact of the parole denial most likely will be on the internal politics of the union. A struggle for power could break out while Hoffa

Continued on Page 28, Column 1

Nixon Transfers 6 Miles of U.S. Beach to California

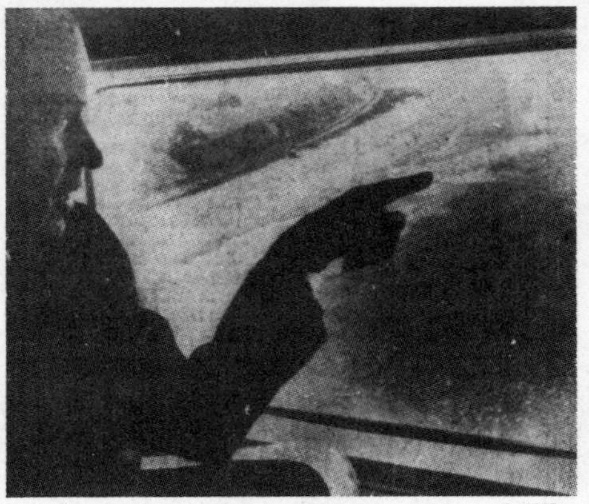

Associated Press

President Nixon viewing Camp Pendleton beach, near Western White House, from copter

By ROBERT B. SEMPLE Jr.
Special to The New York Times

SAN CLEMENTE, Calif., March 31 — President Nixon today asked the Senate and House Armed Services Committees to approve the first in a series of nationwide moves to transfer billions of dollars worth of federally owned land to state and local governments for recreational and other public uses. He announced he had directed Secretary of Defense Melvin R. Laird to offer six miles of California's most valuable beachfront, now part of the Marine base at Camp Pendleton, to the state of California.

In the planned series of nationwide moves, state and local governments will be given the first chance to acquire such lands free. Those lands not taken will then be offered for sale to commercial or industrial bidders. The pro-

Continued on Page 25, Column 3

Parliament in India Condemns Pakistani 'Massacre' in East

By SYDNEY H. SCHANBERG
Special to The New York Times

NEW DELHI, March 3—The Indian Parliament accused Pakistan today of a "massacre of defenseless people" in East Pakistan that "amounts to genocide."

Parliament also assured the East Pakistanis "that their struggle and sacrifices will receive the wholehearted sympathy and support of the people of India."

[According to Reuters, a Pakistan radio broadcast monitored in New Delhi today said that the Pakistani Government had accused India of infiltrating armed troops into border areas of East Pakistan.]

The Indian condemnation of the Pakistani Government, based in West Pakistan, and the expression of solidarity with the Bengali people of East Pakistan came in a resolution introduced by Prime Minister Indira Gandhi and adopted unanimously in both houses to applause, cheers and thumping of benches.

Sitting in the diplomatic gallery in the lower house was Mrs. Sajjad Haider, wife of the Pakistani High Commissioner in New Delhi. India and the two wings of Pakistan, all once British India, are members of the Commonwealth and maintain high commissioners rather than ambassadors in each others' countries.

Meanwhile, the picture of the fighting in East Pakistan remained confused, with all nor-

Continued on Page 6, Column 4

DRUGS WILL CARRY LABELS ON WORTH

U.S. to Require Ratings on Products' Effectiveness

By HAROLD M. SCHMECK Jr.
Special to The New York Times

DENVER, March 31 — The Food and Drug Administration plans soon to require printed ratings on drug labels and advertising to tell the doctor whether there is good evidence that the drug he wants to use is effective.

The move, which could have a major impact on drug use, was disclosed here today by Dr. Henry E. Simmons, director of the agency's Bureau of Drugs.

The target of the plan is a large group of drug products, comprising about 80 per cent of those on the market today, which were originally authorized for use simply on evidence that they were safe. When these drugs were first marketed, between 1938 and

Continued on Page 19, Column 1

NEWS INDEX

In April 1971, about 1,000 Vietnam veterans staged a week-long demonstration against U.S. involvement in Indochina.
United Press International

A survivor of the My Lai massacre points to one of the six tombstones marking the names of Vietnamese victims of the brutal assault.
United Press International

"All the News That's Fit to Print"

The New York Times

LATE CITY EDITION

Weather: Sunny, cool today; clear tonight. Sunny, milder tomorrow. Temp. range: today 37-52; Wed. 36-57. Full U.S. report on Page 82.

VOL. CXX .. No. 41,347 — NEW YORK, THURSDAY, APRIL 8, 1971 — 15 CENTS

NIXON PROMISES VIETNAM PULLOUT OF 100,000 MORE G.I.'S BY DECEMBER; PLEDGES TO END U.S. ROLE IN WAR

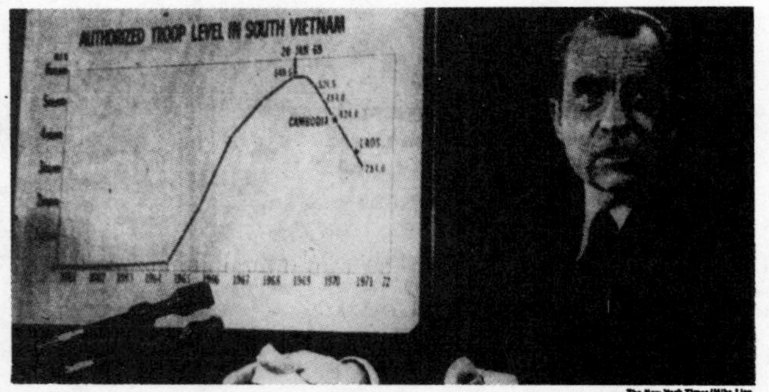

The New York Times/Mike Lien

President Nixon during telecast last night. Chart shows authorized troop levels in South Vietnam from 1961 to present.

LAOS PUSH UPHELD

President Says It Hurt Foe Even More Than Cambodia Action

Transcript of Nixon speech appears on Page 6.

By MAX FRANKEL
Special to The New York Times

WASHINGTON, April 7—President Nixon scheduled tonight a withdrawal of 100,000 more American soldiers from South Vietnam by Dec. 1.

The seven-month goal will leave 184,000 American troops in the war zone 11 months before the 1972 Presidential election. Mr. Nixon asked to be held accountable in that election if he failed in his further goal of ending the American involvement in the war.

Addressing the nation on television and radio at a time of widespread restlessness about his war policy, the President said that the invasion of Laos had proved even more damaging to North Vietnam's offensive capacities than the move into Cambodia a year ago.

Increasing the Rate

"Consequently, tonight I can report that Vietnamization has succeeded," Mr. Nixon said.

[The speech was greeted with praise among Republicans in Congress and with criticism by Democratic doves. Page 7.]

Working with charts that portrayed his scheduled withdrawal of a total of 365,000 of the 540,000 men that he found in Vietnam w... he took office, Mr. Nixon pointed with pride to the fact that he was increasing the rate of reductions.

The withdrawals announced tonight represent a rate of about 14,300 a month between May and November. This compares with an average rate of 12,500 over the last year; the rate in early 1970 was more than 14,000.

The President said the figures should make it clear that the American involvement was coming to an end and that the day when the South Vietnamese could fully handle their own defense was in sight."

Final Date Ruled Out

But he refused to accede to demands that he set a date for that final disengagement, saying it would throw away an American bargaining counter and allow the enemy to plan his attacks for a time of greatest vulnerability.

Obviously sensitive to the public anxieties about the invasion of Laos, about the rate of American disengagement, about the substantiation of atrocities in the Calley trial and about the credibility of his Administration, Mr. Nixon touched on all those points during a vigorous defense of his objectives and tactics.

The objective remains hanging on long enough, he said, to give the South Vietnamese "a

Continued on Page 6, Column 7

ROCKEFELLER SIGNS BILLS REFORMING WELFARE SYSTEM

10-Measure Series Passed in Last Albany Session Before 12-Day Holiday

WORK PROGRAM BACKED

Jobs Incentive Plan Evokes Protests From Democrats, but Is Approved, 110-33

By FRANCIS X. CLINES
Special to The New York Times

ALBANY, April 7—A series of 10 bills that gives Governor Rockefeller closer control over the welfare rolls and seeks stern job incentives for recipients received final legislative approval today.

The Republican-controlled Assembly acted on the bills with sizable support from minority Democrats. The bills were a sweeping attempt at welfare reform hurriedly conceived by the Governor's staff in the last three weeks.

By 2:45 P.M., moments after the final vote, members had begun a 12-day holiday recess, but more than 40 of the big green swivel chairs in the 150-member chamber were empty an hour before that.

Blumenthal Objects

Governor Rockefeller signed the measures into law soon after passage, according to a spokesman. Most of the measures take effect by July 1.

The most controversial measure mandates that an employable adult on home relief or dependent-family aid accept public works jobs. The worker could earn no more than the amount of his welfare check, according to the sponsor, Charles A. Jerabek, Conservative-Republican of Suffolk. The bill passed by 110 to 33.

"God forbid he should earn a full pay check," Albert H. Blumenthal, the assistant Democratic minority leader from Manhattan, declared derisively in leading opposition to the proposal.

Mr. Blumenthal contended that the public works measure, with its limit on the amount of work a recipient might do so that he would not exceed the relief payment, was a "press-release" program to soothe taxpayers. Other critics argued

Continued on Page 37, Column 1

House Rejects Increases In Funding for Education

It Blocks a Move to Add $728.6-Million to Requests by the Administration—$5-Billion Bill Sent to the Senate

By MARJORIE HUNTER
Special to The New York Times

WASHINGTON, April 7—Faced with the threat of another Presidential veto, the House rejected today a move that would have increased education appropriations $728.6-million above the Nixon Administration's requests.

The setback for the potent education lobby came as the House passed, 354 to 7, and sent to the Senate a bill appropriating $5-billion for education programs in the fiscal year starting July 1.

Twice in the last two years, President Nixon has vetoed education money bills because they far exceeded his requests. The House sustained the first veto in 1969 but overrode the second veto last year.

The move today to add $728.6-million to the education appropriations bill failed on a recorded teller vote, 191 to 187, as school superintendents and other education lobbyists watched from the galleries.

Voting for the additional funds were 173 Democrats and 14 Republicans. Voting against were 149 Republicans and 42 Democrats.

Sponsors of the move for higher education funding attributed their defeat to a lack of time to gather support and to absenteeism before a 12-day Easter recess.

The House and the Senate both adjourned today for the holiday recess. The House will return April 19; the Senate resumes proceedings next Wednesday.

The House also rejected efforts to strike from the bill two

Continued on Page 27, Column 5

Kleindienst Assails Boggs; Invites Inquiry Into F.B.I.

By ROBERT M. SMITH
Special to The New York Times

WASHINGTON, April 7—Richard G. Kleindienst, Deputy Attorney General, asserted today that Representative Hale Boggs of Louisiana was "either sick or not in possession of his faculties" when he charged that the Federal Bureau of Investigation had tapped Congressmen's telephones and called for the resignation of J. Edgar Hoover.

Mr. Kleindienst said he would "welcome an investigation by the responsible members of Congress" of the allegations made on the House floor Monday by Mr. Boggs, the Democratic whip.

"Unless that is done or Mr. Boggs retracts his statements," Mr. Kleindienst said, "you have hanging in the air the charge itself — wiretapping the telephones of members of Congress."

Mrs. Abzug Seeks Inquiry

Representative Bella S. Abzug, Democrat of Manhattan, filed a resolution in the House today calling on the Judiciary Committee to conduct "a full and complete investigation of the Federal Bureau of Investigation" that would include "investigation of the ability of the director," Mr. Hoover.

Representative Emanuel Celler, Democrat of Brooklyn, chairman of the Judiciary Committee, said that he would consult with members of the committee about the possibility of holding hearings.

Mrs. Abzug said: "Recent events have made it starkly evident that the F.B.I., busy in-

Continued on Page 23, Column 2

SCHOOL CONTRACT UPSET IN NEWARK

Board Rejects 2-Year Pact as Blacks Cheer — Union Vows, 'Strike Goes On'

By C. GERALD FRASER
Special to The New York Times

NEWARK, April 7 — The Board of Education in a surprise move tonight rejected a contract that would have ended a 10-week-old strike by the Newark Teachers Union.

The union's chief negotiator, Vincent Russell, said immediately, "The strike goes on."

The 5-4 vote rejecting a two-year contract was followed by wild cheering from the predominantly black audience of 400 people in Symphony Hall here.

The meeting was emotional but orderly, although there were four arrests. Newark City Councilman Dennis Westbrook was arrested for sitting in the aisle during the meeting. After the session, two men, Dr. E. Wyman Garrett, 37 years old, a former member of the school board, and Roosevelt Gilbert, 31, were arrested on charges

Continued on Page 50, Column 1

U.S. IS PLANNING STEP-UP IN ARMS FOR JORDANIANS

Tanks and Possibly Planes in a Program Outlined by Laird in Reply to King

By TAD SZULC
Special to The New York Times

WASHINGTON, April 7 — The United States intends to increase substantially its military aid to Jordan, including additional modern tanks and possibly four-engine transport planes, Administration officials disclosed today.

These plans were outlined by Secretary of Defense Melvin R. Laird in his reply to a letter from King Hussein presenting Jordan's long-range military assistance needs.

At the same time, other officials here said that the Administration would ask Congress for a $45-million grant in military assistance for Jordan in the fiscal year beginning July 1. The figure for the current fiscal year is $30-million.

Details Under Study

But officials said that details of the program to be submitted to Congress were still under study. A United States military team surveyed the situation in Jordan last November, and a Jordanian team is expected here later in the spring.

Expanded military aid to Jordan, begun last year, is in line with the Administration's policy to assure King Hussein's survival in his continuing confrontation with the Palestinian guerrillas and to discourage a repetition of Syria's movement of tanks into Jordan during the civil war last September between the King's forces and the guerrillas.

Officials said that the Administration's policy had the tacit approval of Israel, which is known to believe that Middle East stability would be enhanced by the elimination of the guerrilla threat. During the September crisis, Israel allowed United States aircraft to fly over her territory to deliver arms and munitions to the King's troops.

$5-million Still Left

Under a supplemental appropriation voted by Congress in December, Israel was assigned $500-million in military credit and most of it has already been used up. Jordan received $30-million under this appropriation with $5-million still left to be disbursed.

In his reply to King Hussein, Mr. Laird said that the Jordanian request for additional M-60-A-1 tanks, and M-16-A-1 rifles could be met in part immediately from funds already appropriated. The tanks are the most modern in the United States arsenal, and the rifles are the most up-to-date small weapons available here. Reply-

Continued on Page 18, Column 5

ALL MUJIB'S AIDES REPORTED SEIZED

Observer in Dacca During March Tells of Roundup —U.S. Calls for Peace

Pakistani forces have succeeded in rounding up the entire top leadership of the East Pakistani independence movement, according to first-hand information reaching New York.

The source of the information was a prominent man, in a high-level position, from a Western country who spent the last three weeks of March in Dacca, the East Pakistani capital, where the army moved to reassert the military Government's control on March 25. His exceptional opportunities to follow developments there included contacts with the leaders of the Awami League, headed by Sheik Mujibur Rahman.

As evidence of Sheik Mujib's arrest, the Western source cited the fact that his voice had not been heard on the broadcasts of transmitters identifying themselves as voices of liberation. In any event, he added, there is no doubt that Sheik Mujib's associates in the leadership, about 100 in all, disappeared in the early stages of the crackdown.

Points to Passions

It is impossible to say, he went on, whether these leaders have been executed. Earlier this week, Sheik Mujib was reported to be held in West Pakistan.

In Washington, the State Department disclosed that the United States had urged the Pakistani Government to take "every feasible step" to end the conflict in East Pakistan and to achieve "a peaceful accommodation." This appeal, whose tone seemed sterner than previous expressions of concern and of hope for peace, followed the completion of an airlift of about 500 private American and United States employes from East Pakistan. [Page 3.]

In the view of the Western

Continued on Page 2, Column 4

President's Calley Move Arouses Political Debate

By JOHN W. FINNEY
Special to The New York Times

WASHINGTON, April 7—The increasingly political debate over the court-martial of First Lieut. William L. Calley Jr. took a new tack today as Democrats and Republicans clashed over whether President Nixon had improperly intervened in the case.

Senator Birch Bayh, an Indiana Democrat with Presidential aspirations, accused President Nixon of playing politics and failing to provide "moral leadership" in the Calley case.

Senator Robert Taft Jr., an Ohio Republican, defended Mr. Nixon's intervention, contending such action was necessary to reassure the public and restore morale in the armed forces.

From the conflicting statements of the two Senators, it was apparent that the Calley case had taken on a new, controversial dimension, largely as a result of a letter from Capt. Aubrey M. Daniel 3d, the prosecutor in the Calley court-martial, to Mr. Nixon.

Captain Daniel complained in the letter, disclosed yesterday, that the President's intervention had weakened military justice and enhanced the image of a convicted murderer "as a national hero."

The question of Lieutenant Calley's guilt or innocence was becoming intertwined with the issue of whether the President had acted improperly in announcing he would make the final determination on the case and in ordering the convicted officer freed from the stockade while his conviction is reviewed.

The White House refused to

Continued on Page 20, Column 3

U.S. Table Tennis Team To Visit China for Week

15 Invited by Peking

By TAKASHI OKA
Special to The New York Times

NAGOYA, Japan, April 7—The first sizable group of Americans to visit Communist China since the middle nineteen-fifties will be a table tennis team.

Graham B. Steenhoven, president of the United States Table Tennis Association, announced his group's acceptance of a Chinese invitation at a news conference today. The Americans, who have been participating in the 31st world table tennis championships here, received the invitation last night from representatives of the Chinese Table Tennis Association.

Fifteen persons will make the trip to Peking, for seven days starting Saturday.

Throughout the 10-day tour-

Continued on Page 16, Column 3

Washington Pleased

By TERENCE SMITH
Special to The New York Times

WASHINGTON, April 7—The State Department today described the Chinese invitation to an American table tennis team to visit Communist China as an "encouraging development" and said it would welcome reciprocal visits by Chinese athletic teams to this country.

The department spokesman, Charles W. Bray 3d, said the United States would "envisage no difficulties" in granting visas to a Chinese team.

The Chinese invitation, he said, is "clearly consistent with the hopes expressed by the President and Secretary of State that there could be greater contact between the American and Chinese peoples."

Privately, ranking State De-

Continued on Page 16, Column 6

Victorious Radicals in Berkeley See Wider Gains

By EARL CALDWELL
Special to The New York Times

BERKELEY, Calif., April 7—**Three seats on the eight-member City Council were won yesterday by young candidates who are described as radicals, and a black who is allied with them was elected Mayor, late returns showed today.**

The so-called radicals contended they had won a significant measure of control and promised, "In two years, we'll take over the whole city government."

The post of Mayor, who also sits on the Council, was won by Warren Widener, a 33-year-old black Councilman, whose seat will now become vacant, creating a 4-to-4 tie. The new Council will fill the vacant seat.

A controversial proposal to split Berkeley's police force into black, white and campus departments was defeated, 22,712 to 16,142.

Before the election the radicals' strength was widely questioned, but by this morning there was little doubt as to the power of the coalition they had put together.

Mr. Widener, who won a 56-vote victory over Wilmont Sweeney, was considered the radical candidate although he did not have the formal endorsement of the coalition that sponsored the others. Mr. Sweeney, who is also black, ran as a moderate and had the backing of the outgoing Mayor, Wallace Johnson.

In a nine-man race, Mr. Widener polled 21,921 votes to Mr. Sweeney's 21,865.

In the Council races, 33 candidates sought the four seats that were up for election.

Edward E. Kallgren, a moderate, was the top vote-getter, but the so-called radical slate captured the three other seats.

Their successful candidates were Mrs. Ilona Hancock, a 30-year-old housewife who has been involved in the women's liberation movement, and two black lawyers—D'Army Bailey,

Continued on Page 26, Column 2

NEWS INDEX

	Page		Page
Art	34-35	Obituaries	44
Books	39	Op-Ed	41
Bridge	38	Society	50
Business	57, 71	Sports	51-55
Chess	38	Theaters	32-37
Crossword	39	Transportation	82
Editorials	40	TV and Radio	83
Financial	57-72	U. N. Proceedings	5
Man in the News	70	Washington Record	7
Movies	32-37	Weather	82
Music	32-37	Women's News	49

News Summary and Index, Page 4

COLUMBIA DENIED USE OF REACTOR

A.E.C. Unit Bars Operation of Nuclear Device Here

By RICHARD D. LYONS

WASHINGTON, April 7—The Atomic Safety and Licensing Board announced today that it had denied Columbia University permission to operate a small nuclear reactor on Morningside Heights.

The decision followed seven years of legal wrangling between Columbia and local citizens' groups.

Members of the board, who are private citizens appointed by the Atomic Energy Commission, said in effect that they did not have enough information about the potential hazards to the local residents that the reactor posed to justify its operation. The board did not specifically state that it believed that the reactor was unsafe.

The denial was the first time that the licensing board had refused to grant an operating license for any reactor in the United States. Nearly 100 small research reactors, such as the one Columbia has built, and larger nuclear power stations are in operation in the country.

Ironically, the National Science Foundation and the A.E.C. itself have over the last 11 years given Columbia $671,000 in Federal funds to construct the reactor, auxiliary equipment

Continued on Page 72, Column 2

Associated Press

CHAMPION IN SOUTH CAROLINA'S CAPITOL: Joe Frazier, heavyweight titleholder, who had lived in state, addressing joint legislative meeting in Columbia. Details, Page 51.

"All the News That's Fit to Print"

The New York Times

LATE CITY EDITION

Weather: Partly sunny, windy today; cool, clear tonight. Fair tomorrow. Temp. range: today 40-58; Saturday 47-68. Full U.S. report on Page 107.

SECTION ONE

VOL. CXX..No. 41,364 · © 1971 The New York Times Company. · NEW YORK, SUNDAY, APRIL 25, 1971 · 75¢ beyond 50-mile zone from New York City, except Long Island. Higher in air delivery cities. BQLI · 50 CENTS

200,000 Rally in Capital to End War

The New York Times/Mike Lien

Demonstrators protesting against the war in Indochina marching yesterday on Pennsylvania Ave. toward Capitol

By JAMES M. NAUGHTON

Special to The New York Times

WASHINGTON, April 24—Antiwar marchers massed today at a new rallying point, the Capitol, to urge Congress to assume the leadership they seek to bring the Indochina war to an immediate end.

A huge crowd, predominantly young, was peaceful as it gathered behind the White House—the focal point of other peace rallies—and strolled for three hours down Pennsylvania Avenue to the grounds of the Capitol.

The authorities estimated that the number of protesters was about 200,000—double what they had expected—and the rally's leaders set the turnout at half a million.

Across the country, in San Francisco, the police estimated that 156,000 persons participated in a demonstration that featured a march of seven miles from the waterfront to Golden Gate Park.

In Washington, the crowd stood or sat on the rolling, green grounds of Capitol Hill, under budding trees and amid pink and white azalea blossoms, as labor leaders, a few Congressmen and a variety of protest spokesmen exhorted Congress to stop a war that, they said, President Nixon had failed to end.

"We would like for the whole world to know why we are meeting here—to appeal to the members of the House of Representatives and the Senate, and to say to them, 'Under the Constitution, you can end the war,'" said David Livingston, president of District 65 of the National Retail Distributive Workers Union.

The theme was picked up by Representatives Bella S. Abzug of Manhattan and Herman Badillo of the Bronx, both Democrats. "You have come to the right place," Mr. Badillo declared.

There were also expressions of dissatisfaction with the way the President was conducting domestic affairs and the impact the war was having on people in the United States. But the essence of the rally's plea was contained on blue and white placards that could be seen all through the crowd: "Enough—out now."

And former Senator Ernest Gruening, an Alaska Democrat, said to the audience: "There's no hope in the White House."

Mrs. Abzug said: "Your presence here today means that you're going to force the Congress to undeclare this war."

At the White House, the shouts and speeches could not be heard. President Nixon was at his retreat in Camp David,

Continued on Page 58, Column 6

2 RUSSIAN CRAFT LINK UP IN ORBIT AND SOYUZ LANDS

Tass Reports 3 Astronauts Tested Improved Systems During 5½-Hour Docking

By THEODORE SHABAD

Special to The New York Times

MOSCOW, Sunday, April 25—The Soviet Union's three-man spacecraft Soyuz 10 made an unexpectedly early return to earth during the night after having docked and flown jointly with the unmanned orbital laboratory Salyut for a period of five and a half hours yesterday.

The landing of the manned craft after a relatively brief two-day flight confounded wide expectations that the latest Soviet space mission would be more ambitious and would include a boarding of the unmanned scientific workshop.

Tass, the Soviet press agency, announced this morning that the mission's objectives had been fulfilled and that these had involved basically the checking out of improved systems for mutual search, rendezvous, docking and separation of the manned Soyuz and the unmanned Salyut.

On the surface this experiment was similar to several carried out by United States astronauts as early as 1966 when manned Gemini spacecraft docked several times with unmanned target vehicles, which in the American case were the last stage of an Agena rocket equipped with a docking adapter.

Workshop Not Ready

The Soviet manned spacecraft carried out its maneuvers with what has been described as an orbital laboratory and may well be the core vehicle of a future manned workshop to be supplemented by Soyuz craft. But it is now clear that the Russians were not yet ready to assemble such a workshop and man it, at least for a relatively short period of time.

If they had achieved such a mission, they would have beaten by two years a similar United States effort to construct the Skylab, a proposed three-man workshop to be orbited in 1973.

The Soyuz 10 craft, carrying Col. Vladimir A. Shatalov, the commander, and Aleksei S. Yeliseyev and Nikolai N. Rukavishnikov, civilian engineers,

Continued on Page 33, Column 1

Pact Said to Let Atom Arms Stay Temporarily in Japan

But Both State Department and Tokyo's Embassy Deny Accord for Visits by Craft With Nuclear Weapons

By RICHARD HALLORAN

Special to The New York Times

WASHINGTON, April 24—United States officials and foreign diplomatic sources have disclosed that for years a secret agreement with the Japanese Government has permitted the United States to move nuclear weapons temporarily into Japan.

Although the exact form or date of the agreement could not be learned, the sources referred to it as a "transit agreement." Both the State Department and the Japanese Embassy here denied the existence of any such agreement. [A Foreign Ministry spokesman in Tokyo said there was no such secret agreement, oral or written.]

But Congressional sources said that members of the Senate Foreign Relations Committee were aware of the agreement.

The frequent visits of American warships and the landings of military aircraft in Japan have led many Japanese and foreign observers in Japan to believe that the United States was bringing nuclear weapons into Japan.

The agreement has been kept secret because there is no more touchy question in Japan than that of nuclear arms. A large majority of the Japanese people have what has been called a "nuclear allergy" that remains from the atomic bombings of Hiroshima and Nagasaki during the closing days of World War II.

In response to inquiries, a State Department spokesman flatly denied the existence of such an agreement, "secret or otherwise, written or oral." A spokesman for the Japanese Embassy here said "there is no such agreement between the two countries."

But other authoritative sources said that the agreement allowed American naval vessels, including nuclear-powered submarines and surface ships, to call at Japanese ports while armed with nuclear warheads.

The agreement further provides that American aircraft carrying nuclear bombs may land in Japan while on patrol,

Continued on Page 8, Column 1

ROCKEFELLER TELLS MAYOR NEW TAXES CAN DESTROY CITY

Asserts Added Levies Could Also Go Long Way Toward 'Pulling Down the State'

'DISCIPLINE' SUGGESTED

He Says in Reply to Lindsay That Albany Faced Up to Own 'Harsh Realities'

Text of the Rockefeller letter to Lindsay is on Page 69.

By THOMAS P. RONAN

Special to The New York Times

ALBANY, April 24—Governor Rockefeller warned Mayor Lindsay today that the new city taxes the Mayor had proposed, coming on top of the new state taxes recently approved by the Legislature, "could well destroy the economy of the city of New York and go a long way toward pulling down the state as a whole."

He assured the Mayor in a letter that the ramifications" of all the proposals the Mayor had made for new city taxes and state aid were being carefully considered. But the tone of the letter made it clear the Mayor would get far less than he would like.

Both Mr. Lindsay, the man who has asked new taxes, and Mr. Rockefeller, the man who warned today of their impact, have stressed in previous comments the danger that, should New York's tax burden get too far out of line with the tax pattern of neighboring states, businesses and residents might flee to those lower-tax areas.

Earlier Pruning

"Just as the state found it necessary to face the harsh realities, so must every other unit of government in the state—from the smallest school district to the largest urban center—exercise a comparable discipline in the light of the present fiscal crisis," the Governor asserted.

This was a reference to the Republican-controlled Legislature's sharp pruning of the Governor's own requests for new taxes when it approved the state's 1971-72 budget earlier this month.

While the Governor had presented a budget of $8.45-billion and a tax package of more than $1-billion, the Legislature approved a budget of $7.7-billion and tax increases of about $500-million, mostly from a one-cent-on-the-dollar increase in

Continued on Page 69, Column 1

Ceylon's Police and Army Fight Rebels With Terror

By JAMES P. STERBA

Special to The New York Times

COLOMBO, Ceylon, April 24—Ceylon's outnumbered and unprepared police force and army have resorted to mass arrests, torture, executions and other terror tactics in attempting to put down young, well-organized armed insurgents who attacked more than 100 police posts three weeks ago and continue to hold dozens of villages and sizable portions of the countryside.

This dispatch was transmitted from Singapore by a New York Times correspondent on his arrival yesterday from Ceylon, where news is censored.

Bodies of young men presumably killed by policemen and soldiers have been seen floating down rivers in groups of twos and threes toward the sea near Colombo for the last week. Some of them were decapitated and others were riddled with bullets, their wrists bound behind their backs.

This reporter saw bodies floating down the Kalami River on two successive days as villagers gathered on the automobile bridge across the river to watch them float by.

At two crossroads between villages about 50 miles south of Colombo, the bodies of two young men wearing blue trousers, whom the police have linked to the insurgents, were nailed through the wrists to the road signs. Villagers nearby said the police had brought them in trucks to serve as a warning against cooperation with the rebels.

Thousands of young men and

Continued on Page 2, Column 3

Crimmins 'Confession' in '68 Reported

By EMANUEL PERLMUTTER

An alleged confession by Mrs. Alice Crimmins that she had killed her two young children—made while under the influence of a nerve-soothing drug—was ruled inadmissible as evidence by the judge in her recent trial, it was disclosed yesterday by sources close to the case.

Mrs. Crimmins was found guilty Friday by a State Supreme Court jury in Queens of first-degree murder in the death of her 5-year-old son, Edmund Jr., and of first-degree manslaughter in the death of her daughter, Alice Marie, 4. Both deaths occurred in July, 1965.

The disputed confession was alleged to have been made by Mrs. Crimmins in the prison ward of Elmhurst City Hospital on the morning of May 28, 1968, shortly after a jury in her first trial had found her guilty of manslaughter in the death of her daughter.

The statement attributed to Mrs. Crimmins was said to have been in these words:

"Why did I do it? Why did I do it? They were my children. I didn't want to do it."

Drug Given by Doctor

The drug—believed to be sodium pentathol—was said to have been administered by Dr. Lester Samuels, a Queens physician, because she was in a highly distraught condition.

The drug is sometimes used as truth serum, but is not considered reliable in that respect and is therefore customarily not accepted as legal evidence.

The disclosure of the alleged confession set off a controversy yesterday, with Herbert A. Lyon, chief defense lawyer in the second trial, charging that the story had been "leaked" by District Attorney Thomas A. Mackell to prejudice an appeal of her conviction.

Mr. Mackell declined comment. Dr. Samuels was unavailable for a statement.

It was learned that the matter had been discussed in a whispered conversation at the trial by Assistant District Attorneys Thomas Demakos and Vincent Nicolosi and Mr. Lyon with Judge George J. Balbach.

In declining to permit the

Continued on Page 34, Column 1

TOBIN INSTRUCTED TO STRESS TRANSIT

Commissioners Rebuke Head of Port Authority—Ronan Foresees a New Course

By FRANK J. PRIAL

The Commissioners of the Port of New York Authority—12 men long viewed as passive approvers of professional staff decisions—convened a meeting recently with the authority's executive director, Austin J. Tobin, and, according to some who were there, took their subordinate to task.

After ordering Mr. Tobin's aides out of the room, they told him they were tired of staff "negativism." They told him they did not want to hear reasons why the authority could not get into mass transportation. Instead, they said they wanted to hear the reasons in favor, and they instructed Mr. Tobin firmly to involve the agency more fully in mass transit.

Criticism Has Grown

The huge two-state agency, which celebrates its 50th anniversary this month, has been in recent months under a state of virtual siege, its long record of achievement overshadowed by growing criticism of its role in mass transit.

And there are indications that the Port Authority's 50th year may mark the beginning of significant change for the operator of docks, bridges, airports, tunnels and terminals.

"You're going to see a different kind of agency emerge in the years ahead," Dr. William J. Ronan, head of the Metropolitan Transportation Authority in New York as well as a Port Authority Commissioner, said recently.

In addition, one high New York official predicted flatly that both New York and New Jersey would enact legislation forcing the Port Authority into mass-transit projects it has hitherto refused even to consider.

Some of the present Commissioners, including Dr. Ronan and Andrew C. Axtell of New Jersey, have criticized the Port Authority openly for its

Continued on Page 70, Column 4

Many Rank City With Worst Slumlords

By STEVEN R. WEISMAN

The City of New York is gaining a reputation in slum communities and among some of its own housing officials as a careless, indifferent landlord—worse than profiteering slumlords.

In an unusual letter sent last month to Housing and Development Administrator Albert A. Walsh, several urban-renewal project directors said the city's management of property it owns at urban-renewal sites was causing thousands of tenants "severe and unwarranted hardships."

The letter likened the city's practices to those "perpetrated by New York's worst slumlords." It added:

"We can take you into any of our urban-renewal areas and introduce you to tenants who are frequently without heat or hot water in the middle of wintertime, live in fear of fire because electrical wiring isn't repaired and find it impossible to get a broken toilet fixed or broken windows replaced."

41 Urban Renewal Areas

About 11,000 families live in New York's 41 active urban-renewal areas in property that the city acquired by condemnation to make way for new construction. But while construction is postponed, because of administrative delays or lack of funds, the families live in the condemned property as they await relocation.

For 10,000 families, the property is managed by a nonprofit, independent concern, the City Urban Renewal Management Corporation, known as CURMCO (pronounced kerm-koh). A thousand more live in the Central Brooklyn and South Bronx Model Cities areas in property managed on contract by the City Housing Authority, which runs the city's public housing.

Both CURMCO and the Housing Authority have come under attack. The letter from urban-renewal project directors to Mr. Walsh urged that the corporation be replaced. Tenant groups have sat in at local offices and have complained to the courts, the Board of Estimate, the City Planning Commission, and the Federal Government, which assists most of the projects.

Some of the groups applauded a two-month-old Federal embargo on money for the acquisition of new slum property until the city finds "decent, safe and sanitary" housing for its present tenants.

Housing officials, in several recent interviews, expressed fear that this controversy over property management was jeopardizing the city's relationship with community groups, relations that are already strained because of the history of frustrating delays in the production of more housing.

Officials have acknowledged all along that city-owned property in urban renewal areas is

Continued on Page 67, Column 1

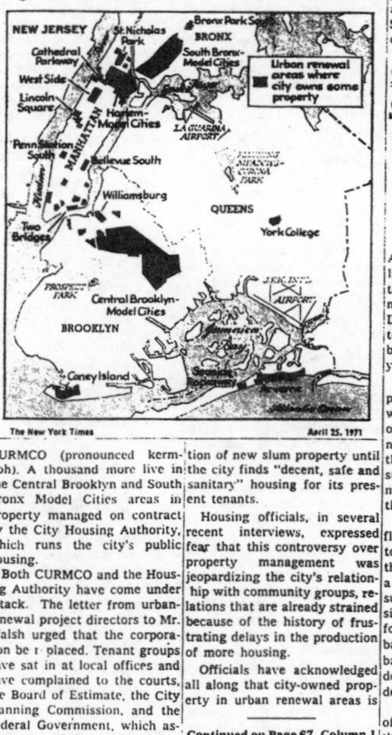

The New York Times · April 25, 1971

Subatomic Tests Suggest A New Layer of Matter

By WALTER SULLIVAN

A number of physicists believe that, through a variety of atomic experiments, they have begun opening the door to the innermost sanctum of matter.

In the first, and probably most important, of these experiments, conducted at the Stanford Linear Accelerator in Menlo Park, Calif., evidence has been found of internal components within the proton and neutron—once considered indivisible building blocks of the universe.

Dr. Wolfgang K. H. Panovsky, director of the center, and his staff recently declared jointly that the results "appear to have uncovered another layer of matter."

Specifically these findings suggest the presence, in proton and neutrons, of points of electric charge that, in several respects, resemble the elusive and long-sought quarks.

In 1964 Dr. Murray Gell-Mann of the California Institute of Technology pointed out that characteristics of the multitude of heavier subatomic particles, discovered in atom-smashing experiments, could be explained in terms of smaller building blocks that he called quarks.

An intensive discussion is under way, here and abroad, as to the meaning of the new observations. But there is widespread belief that a new level, within the atom, has been penetrated. And some scientists hope the new findings will lead to an understanding of the basic forces within atomic nuclei and, perhaps, within the nuclear particles themselves.

Such forces would dwarf any

Continued on Page 59, Column 1

Clocks Set Ahead For Daylight Time

Daylight saving time took effect today at 2 A.M.

To conform, clocks should be set forward one hour.

The system of providing an extra hour of daylight, technically known as advanced time, will be in effect until a return to standard time next Oct. 31 in all states except Arizona, Hawaii, Michigan and Indiana.

These states have enacted laws exempting themselves from the Federal Uniform Time Act of 1966, which mandates the annual change on the last Sunday in April to daylight time.

Sudden Panic Grips Duvalier Mourners In Funeral March

By HOMER BIGART

Special to The New York Times

PORT-AU-PRINCE, Haiti, April 24—With pomp and liturgy and a few touches of terror, Haiti today buried its national leader, Dr. François Duvalier, the enigmatic dictator who ruled this impoverished black republic for 13 and a half years.

The religious service at the palace had been completed without incident and the head of the long procession of mourners was entering the gates of the national cemetery when a sudden panic seized marching mourners and the crowds along the streets.

It began inexplicably on the flower-strewn avenue leading to the cemetery one mile from the palace. It began not with a volley of shots or even a sudden scream. The city lay silent in the midday heat except for the dolorous music of the bands and the distant sullen banging of "cannons of condolence" in the Heroes of Independence Square.

No one, not even the officers of the regular armed forces, the police nor the scowling Tontons Macoutes—Duvalier's

Continued on Page 14, Column 1

Today's Sections

Index to Subjects

News and features of special interest in Brooklyn, Queens and Long Island, Pages 83 to 106.

"All the News That's Fit to Print"

The New York Times

LATE CITY EDITION

Weather: Mostly sunny and pleasant today; fair tonight and tomorrow. Temp. range: today 66-80; Tuesday 72-87. Temp.-Hum. Index yesterday 77. Full U.S. report on Page 90.

VOL. CXX . . . No. 41,423 — NEW YORK, WEDNESDAY, JUNE 23, 1971 — 15 CENTS

SENATE BACKS A VIETNAM PULLOUT IN 9 MONTHS IF P.O.W.'S ARE FREED

VOTE IS 57 TO 42

Amendment a Defeat for Administration—It Goes to House

Text of Mansfield amendment will be found on Page 10.

By JOHN W. FINNEY

Special to The New York Times

WASHINGTON, June 22 — The Senate adopted today an amendment calling for the withdrawal of all American forces from Indochina within nine months if American prisoners of war are released.

Over Administration opposition, the Senate by a vote of 57 to 42 accepted the troop-withdrawal amendment to the Selective Service Bill that was offered by Senator Mike Mansfield of Montana, the Senate majority leader.

The Mansfield amendment must still be passed upon by the House once the Senate completes action on the bill extending Selective Service for two more years. Whether the amendment would be accepted by the more hawkish House was questionable.

Opposition Is Certain

In a House-Senate conference, the amendment was certain to be opposed by conferees from the House Armed Services Committee. But a shift of some Southern conservatives in the Senate to support the Mansfield amendment raised the possibility that in a floor fight a similar shift might occur in the House.

The immediate White House reaction was that the Mansfield amendment, even if enacted, was "not binding" and that the President would "continue the policy which he has set forth of withdrawal of forces from South Vietnam and our efforts to get the other side to enter into serious negotiations."

The White House press secretary, Ronald L. Ziegler, reiterated Nixon's belief that establishment of a withdrawal deadline would "inhibit negotiations" in Paris.

Not View of Whole Congress

Mr. Ziegler added that the amendment "states what 57 Senators think our policy should be. It is not the view of Congress as a whole."

First with the House and then with the White House, the Senate will have some significant leverage, growing out of the fact that it has attached the amendment to the draft-extension bill. Should the amendment be rejected by the House-Senate Conference Committee, then the bill could face a filibuster in the Senate, thus jeopardizing extension of the draft, which expires at the end of this month.

Victory for War Critics

Adoption of the Mansfield amendment represented the first major victory of critics of the Vietnam War in months of attempting to find some legislative formula to end the war.

The amendment would establish the policy that the United States should "terminate at the earliest practicable date all military operations" in Indochina and undertake "prompt and orderly withdrawal" of all American forces within nine months after enactment of the amendment. The withdrawal would be made conditional upon the release of all American prisoners of war held by North Vietnam.

In line with this policy, the amendment calls upon the President to establish a final date for troop withdrawal. to

Continued on Page 11, Column 1

$8.56-Billion City Budget Is Adopted; No Immediate Layoffs Are Involved

The New York Times/Neal Boenzi

City Council President Sanford D. Garelik, left, Mayor Lindsay and Controller Abraham D. Beame at Board of Estimate hearing on the budget held yesterday at City Hall.

An $8.56-billion city budget—half a billion dollars short of what Mayor Lindsay had called a "survival budget" — was adopted last night.

The budget, for the fiscal year that starts July 1, was voted first by the Board of Estimate and then by the City Council.

In the board, the only vote against the budget was cast by Mr. Lindsay. In the Council, the vote was 34 to 1 with 2 abstentions.

The budget provides for no immediate layoffs and avoids imposing half a dozen taxes authorized by Albany. But other taxes—the authorization for which had been wrung from the Legislature by Mr. Lindsay—were imposed.

The largest of these was an increase in the city income tax designed to bring in an extra $225-million a year. Among the others were a tax on the tar and nicotine content in cigarettes and a tax on plastic containers; an increase in the corporation tax and an extension of the unincorporated business tax to self-employed professionals, an extension of the city and state combined 7 per cent sales tax to restaurant meals under a dollar (the "hot-dog" tax), and an increase in the real-property transfer tax.

As the Board of Estimate was acting on the budget, Board of Education officials disclosed that, as an economy measure, they would cut back summer school programs and activities. As a result, city high school students will not be able to take advance work this summer to hasten their graduation, though students will still be able to make up courses they have failed. Other reductions, affecting regular school-year operations, have yet to be announced.

The Board of Estimate and City Council apparently agreed to make comparatively minor cuts in Mr. Lindsay's spending

Continued on Page 49, Column 4

HOUSE APPROVES WELFARE REFORM BY 288-132 VOTE

Senate Gets Measure That Sets Up U.S. Control and Basic Family Income

By WARREN WEAVER Jr.

Special to The New York Times

WASHINGTON, June 22—The House approved tonight a sweeping revision of the nation's much-criticized welfare system that will bring most of it under Federal control and establish for the first time a national income for poor families.

On a vote of 288 to 132, a bipartisan coalition passed a 687-page omnibus bill that included major changes in the Social Security, Medicare and Medicaid programs as well as an extensive reshaping of the welfare laws.

The measure now goes to the Senate where its future remains uncertain. Last year a similar, somewhat less ambitious measure was passed by the House but died in the Senate Finance Committee. This year, Senate backers of the program are more optimistic.

Victory for President

The House action represented a victory for President Nixon, who originally proposed the welfare reform plan in August, 1969, and for Representative Wilbur D. Mills, the House Ways and Means chairman, who revised its extensively during four months of committee consideration.

In a statement tonight, Mr. Nixon hailed the House action as "a major legislative milestone" and told the members who voted for the bill they had his "personal and sincere thanks for their careful and responsible action."

Clearly aware of potential opposition and delay in the Senate, the President said it was his "deeply felt hope that the Senate will move with dispatch now that welfare reform has passed the House."

Nixon Warns of Delay

"We cannot afford," he continued, "to delay any longer in our efforts to remedy the failures of the nation's welfare programs and establish in their place an equitable and uniform system designed to build people up, rather than pull them down."

On the key vote before final passage, supporters of the Family Assistance Plan defeated a motion to strike it from the omnibus bill by a 234-to-187 vote. Then they defeated by a 221-to-158 vote a motion to send the entire package back to committee.

The Family Assistance Plan, the heart of the new welfare proposal, would guarantee a family of four an annual income of $2,400 and continue

Continued on Page 26, Column 1

Times Case Heard, Restraint Extended; U.S. Action Halts a Boston Globe Series

By FRED P. GRAHAM

The United States Court of Appeals here heard arguments yesterday on the Government's effort to enjoin The New York Times from publishing secret information on the Vietnam war. A prompt decision was promised.

The Court continued in effect the temporary restraining order that has blocked further publication of material drawn from a Pentagon study of how the United States became involved in Vietnam.

At about the same time the Federal Court of Appeals in Washington heard arguments in a similar suit by the Justice Department to enjoin The Washington Post from publishing articles based on parts of the Pentagon study. Pending decision the court continued the temporary restraining order that had been issued against The Post.

Meanwhile, the Justice Department's efforts to suppress publication of the secret material spread to Boston, where a Federal District Judge issued a temporary restraining order against The Boston Globe. The newspaper published articles based on the Pentagon study yesterday morning and was sued within hours.

The Globe said it would accede to the order.

Later in the evening, The Chicago Sun-Times published in today's issue an article based, it said, in part on material from the same Pentagon report. A spokesman for the Justice Department said last night that if the Chicago paper had the same documents, he expected the Government would move against it also.

In New York, Chief Judge Henry J. Friendly of the Court of Appeals for the Second Circuit announced after arguments in the case involving The Times that a decision would be made "very promptly"—"surely in the next few days" in any event.

The announcement of the decision is expected to touch off a rush to the Supreme Court by lawyers for the losing side. The Court holds its last scheduled session of the current term next Monday. Lawyers involved with the case expect both Courts of Appeal to decide in time for the cases to reach the high court before the end of this week.

The New York Times series, which included the publication of documents accompanying the Pentagon study, appeared on June 13, 14 and 15, before it was halted by Federal District Judge Murray I. Gurfein pending a final decision on the Government's suit.

At the argument yesterday before the full eight-judge bench of the Second Circuit,

Continued on Page 22, Column 1

REVIEW OF REPORT PROPOSED BY U.S.

Federal Aides Say Survey Could Lead to Release of Parts of Secret Study

By DAVID E. ROSENBAUM

Special to The New York Times

WASHINGTON, June 22—The Government offered today to begin an interagency review of the secret Pentagon study of American involvement in Vietnam to determine how much of it could be declassified.

The offer was made by Federal lawyers in appellate courts here and in New York where the Government is contesting lower court decisions upholding the right of The Washington Post and The New York Times to continue to publish information based on the classified study.

Meanwhile, Secretary of Defense Melvin R. Laird told reporters that he had already ordered a review of the Pentagon documents to see which of them could be publicly released.

At the White House, Ronald L. Ziegler, the press secretary, said that Mr. Laird was responding to a Presidential directive of Jan. 15 that instructed Government agencies to study existing classification procedures. Mr. Ziegler said that the purpose of the directive was to "enlarge the American people's right to know by making more

Continued on Page 23, Column 5

Chicago and Boston Papers Publish Accounts of Study

The New York Times is restrained by Federal court order from publishing further articles in its Vietnam series. These dispatches are based on articles in The Chicago Sun-Times and The Boston Globe and were distributed by The Associated Press and United Press International to all their newspaper, radio, and television subscribers.

Sun-Times Tells of Ouster

CHICAGO, June 22 (AP)—The Chicago Sun-Times said today that it had obtained top-secret State Department documents showing that high-ranking Kennedy Administration officials had advance knowledge of the coup d'état that toppled President Ngo Dinh Diem of South Vietnam in 1963.

The paper, in a copyright article appearing in its second edition dated tomorrow, also printed excerpts from a memorandum from Roger Hilsman, Assistant Secretary of State, to Secretary of State Dean Rusk on Aug. 30, 1963. The memorandum, The Sun-Times said, recommended the United States encourage and assist a coup against Mr. Diem.

The paper said that the documents had been turned over to The Sun-Times by the Citizens Commission of Inquiry Into U.S. War Crimes in Vietnam.

Warning to Rusk Reported

James F. Hoge Jr., the paper's editor, said that part of the material used in the article came from the same Pentagon report, parts of which The New York Times, The Washington Post and The Boston Globe have published.

Late tonight Mr. Hoge said that no representative of the Justice Department had been in contact wtih him or any official

Continued on Page 23, Column 6

Globe Relates '68 Decision

BOSTON, June 22 (UPI)—The Boston Globe reported today that the concluding part of the classified Pentagon study on the Vietnam war says that President Lyndon B. Johnson had decided to support South Vietnam but to reduce American troops in a policy that President Nixon later termed Vietnamization.

The decision was made just before Mr. Johnson announced on March 31, 1968, that he would not seek another term, The Globe said.

The Globe added that sections of the study, which The New York Times and The Washington Post temporarily have been restrained by Federal courts from publishing, came to it Monday. It did not mention the source.

General's Request Reported

The Globe said that the Pentagon study included the following:

¶A recommendation to President Kennedy from Gen. Maxwell D. Taylor that 8,000 United States ground combat troops be sent to South Vietnam under the pretext of flood control. General Taylor said that this might increase world tensions and widen the war. The Globe said that Mr. Kennedy did not approve General Taylor's request for ground combat troops.

¶A request to the Soviet Union in May, 1965, asking it

Continued on Page 23, Column 2

MARKET REACHES PACT WITH BRITAIN

Accord in Luxembourg Ends 10-Year London Effort—Parliament Must Act

By CLYDE H. FANSWORTH

Special to The New York Times

LUXEMBOURG, Wednesday, June 23—Britain and the European Economic Community agreed early today on the terms for British membership in the six-nation trade bloc.

The accord, which came at the end of a troubled two-day meeting in Luxembourg's 23-story European Center, marks the end of Part One of the saga that began 10 years ago when Prime Minister Harold Macmillan filed Britain's first application.

Part Two will now begin as Prime Minister Heath seeks to convince the British parliament and public opinion that membership will be good for Britain.

About 60 per cent of the British public is recorded in opinion polls against joining. But 70 per cent believe membership will come anyway.

The agreement, at 5 A.M., came with a "package deal" resolving the two most important final problems—access for New Zealand butter and cheese in the British market and the

Continued on Page 3, Column 1

Nixon Assails Liberal Plan For National Health Care

By RICHARD D. LYONS

Special to The New York Times

ATLANTIC CITY, June 22—President Nixon for the first time today strongly attacked a bipartisan liberal proposal for national health insurance, telling the American Medical Association that it "would tear apart" the present health care system.

Mr. Nixon told an approving audience of several thousand doctors and guests that a national health insurance plan like that proposed by Senator Edward M. Kennedy would cost too much and would burden the doctor "with the dead weight of more bureaucracy, more forms, more red tape."

The President did not refer specifically to the Kennedy proposal, which the Massachusetts Democrat has introduced into Congress with bipartisan liberal support as well as that of organized labor. A White House spokesman later made it clear, however, that Mr. Nixon had been speaking of the Kennedy plan when he said:

"I believe that the most expensive plan that has been offered in the current discussion on health care in America — a plan for nationalized compulsory health insurance — is the plan that would actually do the most to hurt American health care."

Mr. Nixon referred to his own health legislation, which is aimed at solving what he has called a "massive crisis in health care," but he did not comment on the A.M.A.'s own proposal.

The President's program would rely heavily on private enterprise by mandating that every employed American and his family members be given a private health insurance policy whose premium costs would be shared by the employer and employe. In addition, a family health insurance program would use Federal funds to buy policies for the poor. About 15 million people who are neither employed nor poor would not be covered.

The A.M.A. proposal would have a similar plan for the poor but would give income tax credits for the purchase of private health policies.

The Kennedy plan—the most comprehensive of all proposals to date—would pay almost all the costs of medical services and would cover everyone. It would be operated by the Federal Government and financed

Continued on Page 28, Column 1

Adoptive Parents Awarded Baby Lenore

Special to The New York Times

MIAMI, June 22—The custody of Baby Lenore was awarded here today to her adoptive parents, Mr. and Mrs. Nicholas DeMartino, who fled with the child to Florida after New York courts ordered them to surrender the child.

The action by Circuit Court Judge Ralph O. Cullen denied the 13-month-old girl to her natural mother, Miss Olga Scarpetta, who had filed a writ of habeas corpus in an effort to recover the baby she surrendered for adoption last year.

Shortly after today's decision, Miss Scarpetta's Miami lawyer, Stanley Rosenblatt, announced that Judge Cullen's ruling would be appealed "within one or two weeks" in the Third District Court of Appeals, a state court here.

The battle for custody of Baby Lenore, who was surrendered for adoption on June 18, 1970, and given to the DeMartinos when she was 31 days old, has occupied the attention of the courts of two states and has aroused public sympathy and controversy over the principals.

Five days after she surrendered her child, Miss Scarpetta changed her mind and sought to regain custody of Lenore.

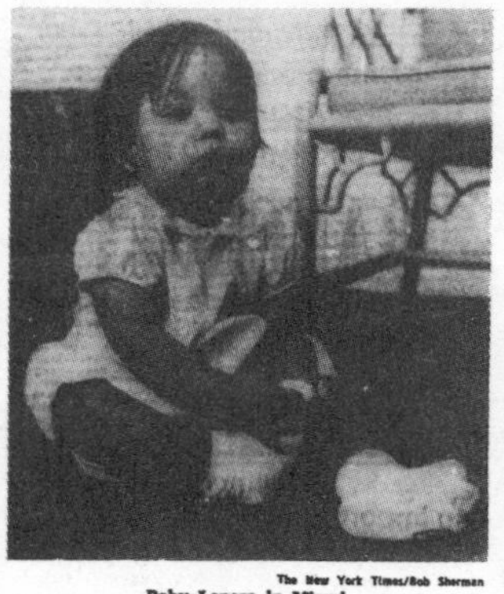

The New York Times/Bob Sherman

Baby Lenore in Miami

The adoption agency refused and the mother started legal action, which held up formal adoption in New York.

Miss Scarpetta, visibly shaken by the adverse ruling today, was nonetheless more composed than the DeMartinos, who sobbed when Judge Cullen ended the day-long hearing with the words: "The petition is denied."

Stating that "no case is more

Continued on Page 54, Column 5

Critics Assert A.S.P.C.A. Here Is Guilty of Cruelty to Animals

By DEIRDRE CARMODY

The American Society for the Prevention of Cruelty to Animals, the primary caretaker for stray animals in the city for more than 100 years, has become the target of mounting criticism, demonstrations and even proposed legal action from members of humane organizations who charge that some of the society's practices are inhumane and some of its employes are cruel to animals.

At the center of the controversy is the A.S.P.C.A.'s method of destroying unclaimed and unadopted strays. These animals are put into carts and wheeled into decompression tanks that look like oversized washing machines. The doors are shut, valves are turned on, and the air is sucked from the tanks until the animals die from lack of oxygen.

The A.S.P.C.A., which last year destroyed 122,839 animals in New York City, contends that the decompression chamber is the "quickest, safest and most humane method for any institution dealing with the number of animals we must handle."

According to Dr. John E. Whitehead, director of the A.S.P.C.A.'s Henry Bergh Memorial Hospital, the animals suffer no pain and they lose consciousness within 20 to 45 seconds. They are dead within approximately three minutes, although the chamber—which is 4 feet 7 inches deep, 2 feet 4 inches wide and 2 feet 10 inches high—is kept running for about 20 minutes to assure that they have all been killed.

But critics and former

Continued on Page 54, Column 1

Chou Says U.S. Shield at Taiwan Is a Main Bar to Diplomatic Ties

By SEYMOUR TOPPING

Special to The New York Times

PEKING, June 21 — Premier Chou En-lai said tonight that the security screen the United States had erected around the island of Taiwan, now ruled by the Government of Chiang Kai-shek, was a key obstacle to the establishment of diplomatic ties with the United States.

The Chinese leader, urging settlement of the Taiwan issue, said that no vengeful action would be taken against the people of Taiwan if the island yielded to Peking's control.

Premier Chou also said that he had received a Soviet proposal for a five-power disarmament conference and that his Government would discuss it, but he indicated personal reservations.

The 73-year-old leader made his remarks at a small dinner in the Great Hall of the People for William Attwood, publisher of Newsday; Robert L. Keatley, Washington reporter for The Wall Street Journal, this correspondent, who is assistant managing editor of The New York Times, and their wives.

Mr. Chou, in a jovial mood, noted that it was the first time in 25 years that he had such a dinner meeting with American newsmen. He added that reciprocal contacts would gradually develop between the peoples of China and the United States and that his Government would consider a request by American businessmen to

Continued on Page 2, Column 4

NEWS INDEX

The South Vietnamese forces encountered much Soviet armor during the incursion into Laos.

Communist engineers rush to repair a part of the Ho Chi Minh Trail that was knocked out by U.S. aircraft.

"All the News That's Fit to Print"

The New York Times

LATE CITY EDITION

Weather: Chance of showers today, tonight. Partly sunny tomorrow. Temp. range: today 74-94; Wed. 72-91. Temp. Hum. Index yesterday 82. Full U.S. report on Page 94.

VOL. CXX... No. 41,431 NEW YORK, THURSDAY, JULY 1, 1971 — 15 CENTS

SUPREME COURT, 6-3, UPHOLDS NEWSPAPERS ON PUBLICATION OF THE PENTAGON REPORT; TIMES RESUMES ITS SERIES, HALTED 15 DAYS

Nixon Says Turks Agree To Ban the Opium Poppy

By JOHN HERBERS

Special to The New York Times

WASHINGTON, June 30—President Nixon announced today that Turkey had agreed to eliminate within a year her production of opium poppies, which account for about two-thirds of the illegal heroin reaching the United States.

Mr. Nixon, in a brief announcement delivered in the White House press room, said that as a result of negotiations between the United States and Turkish Governments, Premier Nihat Erim had agreed to ban altogether the cultivation of opium poppies by June, 1972.

He said the joint announcement, made simultaneously in Washington and Ankara, "represents by far the most significant breakthrough that has been achieved in stopping the source of supply of heroin in our worldwide offensive against dangerous drugs."

Two weeks ago, Mr. Nixon sent a message to William J. Handley, the United States Ambassador in Turkey, saying that the time for talk had passed and the United States must have action by the Turkish Government in ending poppy cultivation.

Today, the President praised Premier Erim for "courageous, statesmanlike action" and said the United States would provide money and technical assistance in helping Turkish farmers shift to other crops.

Officials would not say how much American money would be involved, but the United States has made a $3-million commitment to Turkey on the heroin problem.

Secretary of State William P. Rogers, who helped work

Continued on Page 22, Column 1

PRESIDENT CALLS STEEL AND LABOR TO WHITE HOUSE

He Asks Both Sides to Meet With Him Tuesday Before Contract Talks Start

By PHILIP SHABECOFF

Special to The New York Times

WASHINGTON, June 30 — President Nixon has called negotiators of the steel companies and steelworkers union to meet with him next Tuesday before they sit down to begin contract negotiations, a White House spokesman announced today.

It will be the first time that the President will have met with labor and management in any industry prior to nationwide contract negotiations, according to Ronald L. Ziegler, the White House press secretary.

Discussion Issues Listed

Mr. Ziegler said that the President had called the meeting to discuss general economic developments and trends in the world steel markets.

Earlier today, the chairman of the Federal Reserve Board, Arthur F. Burns, told a Congressional committee that the "first priority" should be given to a new Government move to try to moderate price and wage increases and expressed his concern over the spread of "inflationary psychology" in this country.

The Administration has repeatedly warned that excessive increases in steel wages and prices would severely retard efforts to control inflation. Hints have been dropped that import quotas that protect domestic steel from foreign competition will be eased or lifted if prices go too high.

President Nixon has been in-

Continued on Page 38, Column 1

Pentagon Papers: Study Reports Kennedy Made 'Gamble' Into a 'Broad Commitment'

By HEDRICK SMITH

The Pentagon's study of the Vietnam war concludes that President John F. Kennedy transformed the "limited-risk gamble" of the Eisenhower Administration into a "broad commitment" to prevent Communist domination of South Vietnam.

Although Mr. Kennedy resisted pressures for putting American ground-combat units into South Vietnam, the Pentagon analysts say, he took a series of actions that significantly expanded the American military and political involvement in Vietnam but nonetheless left President Lyndon B. Johnson with as bad a situation as Mr. Kennedy inherited.

"The dilemma of the U.S. involvement dating from the Kennedy era," the Pentagon study observes, was to use "only limited means to achieve excessive ends."

Moreover, according to the study, prepared in 1967-68 by Government analysts, the Kennedy tactics deepened the American involvement in Vietnam piecemeal, with each step minimizing public recognition that the American role was growing.

The expansion of that role, over three decades, is traced in the 3,000 pages of the Pentagon's study, which is accompanied by 4,000 pages of documents on the Vietnam era. Previous articles in The Times's presentation of this material have recounted President Johnson's movement to war in 1964 and 1965.

President Kennedy made his first fresh commitments to Vietnam secretly. The Pentagon study discloses that in the spring of 1961 the President ordered 400 Special Forces troops and 100 other American military advisers sent to South Vietnam. No publicity was given to either move.

Small as the numbers seem in retrospect, the Pentagon study comments that even the first such expansion "signaled a willingness to go beyond the 685-man limit on the size of the U.S. [military] mission in Saigon, which, if it were done openly, would be the first formal breach of the Geneva agreement." Under the interpretation of that agreement in effect since 1956, the United States was limited to 685 military advisers in Vietnam. Washington, while it did not sign the accord, pledged not to undermine it.

On May 11, 1961, the day on which President Kennedy decided to send the Special Forces, he also ordered the start of a campaign of clandestine warfare against North Vietnam, to be conducted by South Vietnamese agents directed and trained by the Central Intelligence Agency and some American Special Forces troops. [See text, action memorandum, May 11, 1961, Page 3.]

The President's instructions, as quoted in the documents, were, "In North Vietnam . . . [to] form networks of resistance, covert bases and teams for

Continued on Page 6, Column 1

The Times today resumes its series of articles on the Pentagon's secret study of the Vietnam war. The study was obtained through the investigative reporting of Neil Sheehan, and the articles were researched and written over three months by Mr. Sheehan and other staff members. The fourth and fifth articles, both by Hedrick Smith, are published today and form an account of decisions in the Kennedy Administration.

Three pages of documentary material covering the Kennedy policy begin on Page 3, and documents on the 1963 coup begin on Page 9. A summary of the three earlier articles, covering the Johnson Administration, appears on Page 15.

BURGER DISSENTS

First Amendment Rule Held to Block Most Prior Restraints

Decision, concurring opinions, dissents start on Page 17.

By FRED P. GRAHAM

Special to The New York Times

WASHINGTON, June 30 — The Supreme Court freed The New York Times and The Washington Post today to resume immediate publication of articles based on the secret Pentagon papers on the origins of the Vietnam war.

By a vote of 6 to 3 the Court held that any attempt by the Government to block news articles prior to pubiication bears "a heavy burden of presumption against its constitutionality."

In a historic test of that principle — the first effort by the Government to enioin publication on the ground of national security — the Court declared that "the Government has not met that burden."

The brief judgment was read to a hushed courtroom by Chief Justice Warren E. Burger at 2:30 P.M. at a special session called three hours before.

Old Tradition Observed

The Chief Justice was one of the dissenters, along with Associate Justices Harry A. Blackmun and John M. Harlan, but because the decision was rendered in an unsigned opinion, the Chief Justice read it in court in accordance with long-standing custom.

In New York Arthur Ochs Sulzberger, president and publisher of The Times, said at a news conference that he had "never really doubted that this day would come and that we'd win." His reaction, he said, was "complete joy and delight."

The case had been expected to produce a landmark ruling on the circumstances under which prior restraint could be imposed upon the press, but because no opinion by a single Justice commanded the support of a majority, only the unsigned decision will serve as precedent.

Uncertainty Over Outcome

Because it came on the 15th day after The Times had been restrained from publishing further articles in its series mined from the 7,000 pages of material—the first such restraint in the name of "national security" in the history of the United States—there was some uncertainty whether the press had scored a strong victory or whether a precedent for some degree of restraint had been set.

Alexander M. Bickel, the Yale law professor who had argued for The Times in the case, said in a telephone interview that the ruling placed the press in a "stronger position." He maintained that no Federal District Judge would henceforth temporarily restrain a newspaper on the Justice Department's complaint that "this is what they have printed and we don't like it" and that a direct threat of irreparable harm would have to be alleged.

However, the United States Solicitor General, Erwin N. Griswold, turned to another lawyer shortly after the Justices filed from the courtroom and remarked: "Maybe the newspapers will show a little

Continued on Page 15, Column 1

Soviet Starts an Inquiry Into 3 Astronauts' Deaths

By BERNARD GWERTZMAN

Special to The New York Times

MOSCOW, June 30—The Soviet authorities appointed a special commission tonight to investigate the deaths of their three astronauts who perished this morning when their Soyuz 11 craft was returning to earth after the longest manned space flight in history.

News of the astronauts' deaths shocked many Soviet people. And Western specialists predicted that their deaths would retard development of the Salyut space station program. The three astronauts had spent more than three weeks working and exercising aboard the Salyut craft, described as the world's first space laboratory.

[In the United States, American officials said the Soviet space disaster had probably been caused by a failure in the oxygen supply. They also said the accident should not delay United States space flights. Articles on Page 30.]

Tonight, the Soviet people seemed caught up in the human aspects of the disaster and the mystery of what caused the deaths of Lieut. Col. Georgi T. Dobrovolsky, the flight commander; Vladislav N. Volkov, the flight engineer, and Viktor I. Patsayev, the test engineer.

Were their deaths caused by the weakened state of their bodies after nearly 24 days of weightlessness? Were they

Continued on Page 30, Column 3

U.S. and Diem's Overthrow: Step by Step

The Pentagon's secret study of the Vietnam war discloses that President Kennedy knew and approved of plans for the military coup d'état that overthrew President Ngo Dinh Diem in 1963.

"Our complicity in his overthrow heightened our responsibilities and our commitment" in Vietnam, the study finds.

In August and October of 1963, the narrative recounts, the United States gave its support to a cabal of army generals bent on removing the controversial leader, whose rise to power Mr. Kennedy had backed in speeches in the middle nineteen-fifties and who had been the anchor of American policy in Vietnam for nine years.

The coup, one of the most dramatic episodes in the history of the American involvement in Vietnam, was a watershed. As the Pentagon study observes, it was a time when Washington—with the Diem regime gone—could have reconsidered its entire commitment to South Vietnam and decided to disengage.

At least two Administration officials advocated disengagement but, according to the Pentagon study, it "was never seriously considered a policy alternative because of the assumption that an independent, non-Communist SVN was too important a strategic interest to abandon."

The effect, according to this account, was that the United States, discovering after the coup that the war against the Vietcong had been going much worse than officials previously thought, felt compelled to do more—rather than less—for Saigon. By supporting the anti-Diem coup, the analyst asserts, "the U.S. inadvertently deepened its involvement. The inadvertence is the key factor."

According to the Pentagon account of the 1963 events in Saigon, Washington did not originate the anti-Diem coup, nor did American forces intervene in any way, even to try to prevent the assassinations of Mr. Diem and his brother Ngo Dinh Nhu, who, as the chief Diem political adviser, had accumulated immense power. Popular discontent with the Diem regime focused on Mr. Nhu and his wife.

But for weeks—and with the White House informed every step of the way—the American mission in Saigon maintained secret contacts with the plotting generals through one of the Central Intelligence Agency's most experienced and versatile operatives, an Indochina veteran, Lieut. Col. Lucien Conein. The colonel, who is now in retirement, first landed in Vietnam in 1944 by parachute for the Office of Strategic Services, the wartime forerunner of the C.I.A.

So trusted by the Vietnamese generals was Colonel Conein that he was in their midst at Vietnamese General Staff headquarters as they launched the coup. Indeed, on Oct. 25, a week earlier, in a cable to McGeorge Bundy, the President's special assistant for national security, Ambassador Lodge had occasion to describe Colonel Conein of the C.I.A.—referring to the agency, in code terminology, as C.A.S.—as the indispensable man:

"C.A.S. has been punctilious in carrying out my instructions. I have personally approved each meeting between General Don [one of three main plotters] and Conein who has carried out my

Continued on Page 12, Column 1

CHOU TIES U.N. SEAT TO TAIPEI'S OUSTER

Also Says Peking Must Have Permanent Council Post if It Is to Be Member

By TAKASHI OKA

Special to The New York Times

TOKYO, June 30 — Premier Chou En-lai of China said in an interview published here today that for his country to join the United Nations it was necessary not only that all membership rights be "restored," including a permanent seat on the Security Council, but that the Nationalists be ousted from the United Nations.

Mr. Chou made the comment in a meeting with Yoshikatsu Takeiri, chairman of Komeito, the Clean Government party, who is visiting Peking with eight of his followers. The Premier's comments were published today in the party newspaper Komei Shimbun as well as in other major Japanese newspapers.

'What Steps Are Necessary?'

Mr. Chou's comments, which are consistent with the line Peking has taken on prospective United Nations membership, apparently weakened attempts by the United States, Japan and other interested members of the United Nations to safeguard at least a General Assembly seat for the Nationalists while admitting the Chinese Communists to the Security Council as well as the Assembly.

"What steps do you think are necessary in order to get China back into the United Nations?" Mr. Chou was asked,

Continued on Page 32, Column 4

Jim Garrison Is Arrested; U.S. Says He Took Bribes

By ROY REED

Special to The New York Times

NEW ORLEANS, June 30—District Attorney Jim Garrison was arrested by Federal agents today and charged with taking bribes to protect illegal pinball gambling in New Orleans.

The Justice Department said that the last payment, $1,000, was delivered to Mr. Garrison at his home last night in marked $50 bills. The payment, the department said, was handed to him by a once-trusted confidant who had secretly gone to work for the Government's agents.

Mr. Garrison, 50 years old, who attempted to prove a conspiracy in the 1963 assassination of President Kennedy, was taken into custody at his home. He was fingerprinted and placed under $5,000 bond by a Federal magistrate.

The Justice Department said that Mr. Garrison had taken up to $1,500 a month in bribes.

According to the Government, Mr. Garrison had received the bribes from pinball operators since 1962.

"I've never accepted a dollar in my life," the District Attorney told reporters as he walked into the French Quarter Courthouse to face the magistrate.

Mr. Garrison was one of 10 men arrested. The others in-

Continued on Page 55, Column 3

Cousin Asserts Jerome Johnson Told of Job With Italian League

By BARBARA CAMPBELL

A cousin of Jerome A. Johnson, who was shot to death at the site of a rally in Columbus Circle after allegedly firing three bullets into Joseph A. Colombo Sr., said yesterday that Johnson told him "several months ago" he was working for the Italian-American Civil Rights League as a photographer.

This was corroborated by a close friend of Johnson's, who said the 24-year-old slain man had also told him on a May 15 visit to California that he was working for the league.

About three months before the shooting, Johnson gave his cousin a telephone number where he could be reached, and a check by The New York Times disclosed yesterday that the number had been recently changed. The operator said the number had been switched to a new number, that of the Italian-American League.

This latest development raised a series of questions for investigators. If Johnson was working for the league, was he known there? Was he an employe or a hanger-on, perhaps a temporary called in on occasions?

Chief of Detectives Albert A. Seedman said last night only that the telephone-number switch, if true, "certainly puts

Continued on Page 53, Column 1

THE STATES RATIFY FULL VOTE AT 18

Ohio Becomes 38th to Back the 26th Amendment

By R. W. APPLE Jr.

Special to The New York Times

WASHINGTON, June 30—The 26th Amendment to the Constitution, lowering to 18 years the minimum voting age in local and state as well as Federal elections, was ratified tonight.

Ohio became the 38th state to approve the Amendment when the state's House of Representatives, meeting in extraordinary evening session, gave its assent, 81 to 9. The Ohio Senate had approved the measure yesterday, 30 to 2.

The ratification of at least 38 states, or three-quarters of the total, is required for constitutional amendments.

An atmosphere of near-panic attended Ohio's climactic vote. The Republican Speaker of the House, Charles F. Kurfess, had planned to let a number of members, both Republicans and Democrats, speak on the issue before calling for a vote.

But after only three short speeches, the Republican floor leader, Robert E. Leavitt, interrupted to warn:

"I've just been informed that the Legislature of Oklahoma

Continued on Page 43, Column 1

Conferees Cut Military Pay Rise As Authority to Draft Runs Out

By DAVID E. ROSENBAUM

Special to The New York Times

WASHINGTON, June 30 — The Nixon Administration won a major budgetary victory today in the House-Senate conference on the draft extension bill.

The conference agreement also appeared to represent a setback for supporters of an all-volunteer Army, who had sought larger pay increases than those cleared by the conferees.

The conferees accepted a figure for military pay and allowances that was more than $900-million below what both the Senate and House had approved. The raises voted by the conferees would cost about $1.8-billion in the fiscal year starting tomorrow and would go into effect Oct. 1.

The figure approved by the conference was still $800-million above what President Nixon sought in his budget, but the House and Senate had passed increases of about $1.7-billion over the budget.

The Nixon Administration had argued that so large an increase would force severe and possibly dangerous reductions in other parts of the defense budget.

The Government's basic authority to draft men into the military expires at midnight tonight.

The conferees completed action on all provisions of the draft bill today except the Senate-passed amendment that calls for the withdrawal of United States troops from Indochina within nine months if prisoners of war are first

Continued on Page 29, Column 1

False Advertising Laid to H&R Block

By JOHN D. MORRIS

Special to The New York Times

WASHINGTON, June 30 — H & R Block, Inc., which says it prepares income tax returns for eight million American annually, was accused by the Federal Trade Commission today of false advertising and illegally using confidential information supplied by customers.

The commission published similar but separate citations against H & R Block and the Beneficial Corporation, which offers income tax services on a smaller scale through a subsidiary, the Beneficial Management Corporation. In radio and television advertisements, the name

Continued on Page 57, Column 2

ACTION BY GRAVEL VEXES SENATORS

But No Disciplinary Action Against Him Is Expected

By JOHN W. FINNEY

Special to The New York Times

WASHINGTON, June 30—Many Senators privately expressed dismay, shock and chagrin today at Senator Mike Gravel's release of parts of the Pentagon's secret study of the Vietnam war. But it appeared that no disciplinary action would be taken against the Alaska Democrat.

Last night Senator Gravel tried to read the documents to the Senate in an all-night speech and, when he was blocked for lack of a quorum, proceeded to call an impromptu meeting of his Senate Public Works subcommittee. He read from the study for three and one-half hours, with his voice sometimes breaking into sobs, and tears occasionally rolling down his face.

His action incurred the displeasure of many of his colleagues, who felt that it reflected on the dignity and composure of the Senate. But in the clublike atmosphere of the Senate, there was a widespread reluctance, extending down from the leadership, to take any formal disciplinary

Continued on Page 16, Column 2

NEWS INDEX

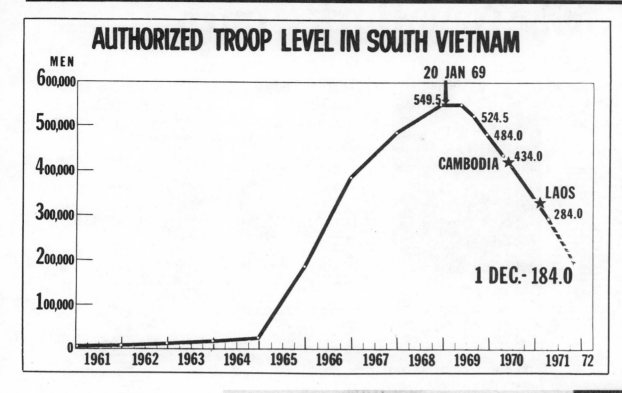

AUTHORIZED TROOP LEVEL IN SOUTH VIETNAM

MEN

600,000

500,000

400,000

300,000

200,000

100,000

20 JAN 69

549.5

524.5

484.0

CAMBODIA   434.0

LAOS

284.0

1 DEC.- 184.0

1961 1962 1963 1964 1965 1966 1967 1968 1969 1970 1971 72

U.S. troop strength in South Vietnam from 1961 projected through 1972.

While hundreds of thousands demonstrated against the war, President Nixon's policies in Southeast Asia were supported and defended by groups such as this one demonstrating for a military victory against the Communists in Vietnam in May 1971.

United Press International

"All the News That's Fit to Print"

The New York Times

LATE CITY EDITION

Weather: Showers likely today; cloudy tonight. Fair tomorrow. Temp. range: today 66-68; Saturday 67-73. Full U.S. report on Page 95.

SECTION ONE

VOL.CXXI..No.41,525 · NEW YORK, SUNDAY, OCTOBER 3, 1971 · 75¢ beyond 50-mile zone from New York City, except Long Island. Higher in air delivery cities. · BQLI · 50 CENTS

Poff Withdraws His Name As Potential Court Choice

Acts to Avoid Long Battle in Senate On Confirmation

Special to The New York Times

WASHINGTON, Oct. 2—Representative Richard H. Poff of Virginia, who had reportedly been President Nixon's first choice to fill the vacant "Southern seat" on the Supreme Court, abruptly withdrew his name from consideration today as a potential candidate.

Four hours after an American Bar Association committee met in New York to evaluate the legal community's opinion of his qualifications, Mr. Poff—who had once said that he would rather be a Supreme Court Justice than President—announced that he had asked Mr. Nixon not to nominate him.

In a statement delivered to The Associated Press and United Press International here, Mr. Poff said that his decision had been prompted by the possibility of a Senate battle if he were nominated.

"I have asked the President not to consider my name for nomination to the Supreme Court," he said. "It appears that the confirmation process would be protracted and controversial."

Rights Record Scored

When Mr. Poff's name appeared at the top of the list of those mentioned in Supreme Court speculation, civil rights, labor and feminist groups began an effort to head off his nomination. They focused their criticism on the civil rights record of the 10-term Republican Representative from southwest Virginia.

It was argued that Mr. Poff had voted against every major civil rights bill and that he had signed both "Southern manifestos" of 1956—one deploring school desegregation and the other opposing pending civil rights legislation.

In Key Biscayne, Fla., where President Nixon is spending the weekend, the White House press secretary, Ronald L. Ziegler, said that Mr. Poff's decision had been "entirely his own." He said that Mr. Poff had been in touch with Attorney General John N. Mitchell, who is in California, and that Mr. Mitchell had been in contact with the A.B.A. committee.

Mr. Ziegler said that after Mr. Poff informed Mr. Mitchell by telephone this morning of his decision, Mr. Mitchell told the President.

"Congressman Poff was under consideration with a number of other people," Mr. Ziegler said. He said that at least a dozen candidates were still being considered for the

Continued on Page 33, Column 1

Justices Face New Issues Tomorrow As Term Opens

By FRED P. GRAHAM

Special to The New York Times

WASHINGTON, Oct. 2—With two empty seats as a reminder of the changes that are overtaking the Supreme Court, the Justices will meet Monday to begin a new Court term that will raise a wide range of new constitutional issues.

Even as President Nixon ponders the selection of "strict constructionist" nominees to carry out his campaign pledge to change the liberal doctrines of the Warren Court, the Burger Court will begin to grapple with a docket laden with new issues that the Warren Court did not consider.

The Justices will meet briefly at 10 A.M. Chief Justice Warren E. Burger will deliver brief tributes to the late Justice Hugo L. Black and Justice John M. Harlan, who retired. Then the Justices will leave the bench for a week of secret conferences on the business of the upcoming term.

'Private Law' on Docket

For the first time in almost a decade, the Court's docket is not dominated by the criminal law issues that led the Warren Court to expand the safeguards of defendants. It was primarily those rulings that prompted Mr. Nixon's pledge to appoint strict constructionists, and he has tended to select nominees with strong law-and-order leanings—some of whom have taken liberal positions on other issues during their careers.

There are still some important criminal questions to be settled—capital punishment is the most obvious—but the variety of new issues to be confronted this term indicates that a Nixon Court, handpicked to take a law-and-order approach to crime, may make its mark in unpredictable ways

Continued on Page 34, Column 1

Baseball Playoffs Start

The National League baseball pennant playoff began yesterday as the Giants beat the Pittsburgh Pirates at San Francisco, 5-4. The American League series opener between the Orioles and Oakland Athletics was rained out at Baltimore. After completing the three-of-five-game series, the winners will meet in the World Series starting Saturday in Baltimore or Oakland. (Details in Section 5.)

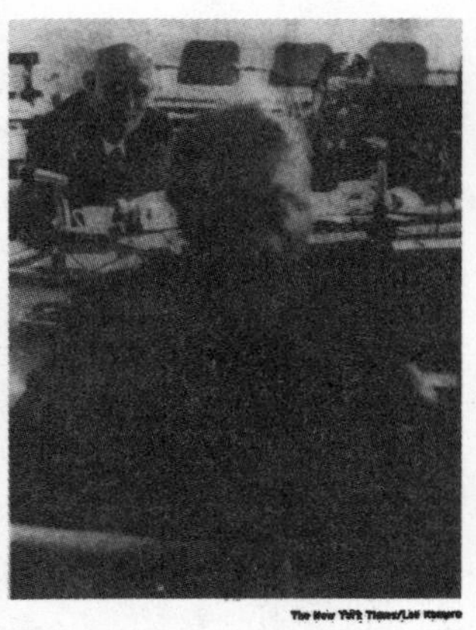

The New York Times/Lee Romero

DISCUSSING CHINA: Secretary of State Rogers, back to camera, with Sir James Plimsoll, left, Australian Ambassador to U.S., and Nigel H. Bowen, foreign minister.

TO OUR READERS

Every Sunday The New York Times includes a separate section, 1-A, on Brooklyn, Queens and Long Island. It contains news and features of interest in these areas and appears in copies distributed in Brooklyn, Queens and Nassau and Suffolk Counties.

Birth Rate Declines Here, Reversing a 3-Year Trend

By MICHAEL STERN

A downturn in the number of births and in the birth rate is being recorded by the city's Health Department this year, reversing a trend of annual increases that began in 1968.

A similar phenomenon, though less sharply defined, is being recorded nationally.

Though Health Department officials here warn that it is too early to call the downturn a new trend, they say they are studying the figures carefully because the decline runs counter to their expectations.

National Birth Drop

In addition, the drop comes at a time when the birth potential of the city's population—that is, the number of women of childbearing age—is substantially higher than it was a decade ago.

Commenting on the figures, Dr. Jean Pakter, director of the department's Maternity Services Bureau, said:

"We expected another boom in births as children born in the post-World War II baby boom reached the peak childbearing ages, but it just isn't happening."

For the nation as a whole, data compiled by the National Center for Health Statistics of the Department of Health, Education and Welfare show that the number of births and the birth rate rose in 1969 and 1970 but began to decline this year.

Many Explanations

Comparison of the center's figures for the first six months of this year and the same months of 1970 show increases in the number of births during February and March, and declines in January, April, May and June.

By June, the rate had dropped to 16.8 births for each 1,000 of population, down significantly from the rate of 18.3 the previous June and lower than in any month in the previous two and a half years.

Though it is clear that fewer babie are being born this year both nationally and in the city, it is not at all clear what the decline means and why it is happening.

Demographers, health officials and sociologists offer a variety of explanations for the downturn in births. Among the

Continued on Page 78, Column 2

ROGERS EXPRESSES CONCERN ON MOVES REPORTED IN CHINA

Says Administration Hopes Nixon's Trip to Peking Won't Be Affected

By TAD SZULC

In the first official expression of the Administration's concern over events in China, Secretary of State William P. Rogers said yesterday that the United States hoped they would not affect President Nixon's plans to visit Peking.

Secretary Rogers's statement, made during a meeting with newsmen after a long discussion of Chinese affairs here with Australian and New Zealand Cabinet ministers, for the first time attached a question to plans for the Presidential trip.

There has been worldwide speculation since the middle of last month that a major political crisis may be under way in China. The speculation included the possibility that the Communist party chairman, Mao Tse-tung, was dead, with a power struggle over succession erupting.

Officials Drop From Sight

The speculation was based on the sudden cancellation of the annual Oct. 1 parade and the traditional speech delivered by Premier Chou En-lai.

Many leading Chinese officials dropped from sight and most military and civilian aircraft flights over China were reported suspended for nearly two weeks after Sept. 12.

Mr. Nixon announced July 15 that he would fly to Peking before May, 1972. Until recent-day, the Administration has refused to comment publicly on

Continued on Page 10, Column 1

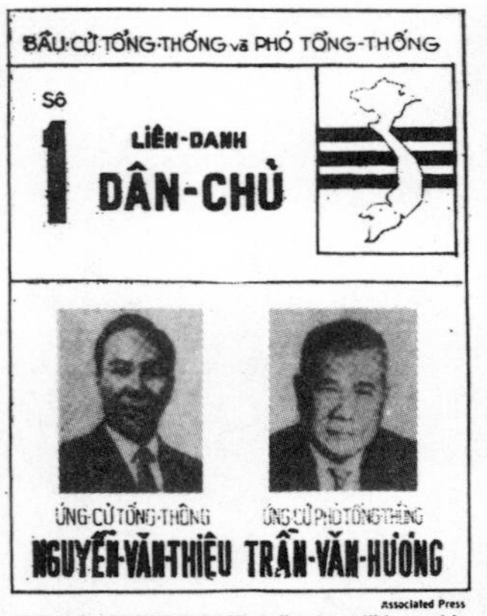
BẦU-CỬ TỔNG-THỐNG và PHÓ TỔNG-THỐNG
Số
1
LIÊN-DANH
DÂN-CHỦ
ỨNG-CỬ TỔNG-THỐNG
NGUYỄN-VĂN-THIỆU
ỨNG-CỬ PHÓ TỔNG-THỐNG
TRẦN-VĂN-HƯƠNG

Associated Press

THE ONLY TICKET IN RACE: Ballot that will be used in today's election in South Vietnam identifies the "Democratic Slate" candidates, Nguyen Van Thieu for President and Tran Van Huong for Vice President. A map of all of Vietnam is superimposed on the South Vietnamese flag, at top right. Opponents of the Thieu candidacy can tear ballot before placing it in box or deposit empty envelope.

Survey Indicates Increase In Espionage by the Soviet

By BENJAMIN WELLES

Special to The New York Times

WASHINGTON, Oct. 2—Soviet espionage appears to be growing around the world—particularly in the West—while Western and Soviet officials negotiate about reducing tensions.

This is indicated in a survey conducted by New York Times correspondents in 20 capitals, plus extensive interviews here with American security officials. The survey was prompted by recent disclosures of persistent, large and expanding Soviet espionage in Britain.

In a countermove that Western security experts here had been expecting, the Soviet Government amplified charges today against the British intelligence service.

Pravda, the Communist party newspaper, asserted that the British had sent agents to Moscow disguised as businessmen, tourists, journalists and scientists. Some businessmen and tourists were identified, but not journalists or scientists.

Last week, Prime Minister Heath, in a crack-down unprecedented in peacetime for its severity and speed, ordered 90 Soviet diplomats and other officials of a total of 550 in Britain expelled. He also refused re-entry permits for 15 others. All were accused of espionage.

Officials Are Heartened

Since 1960, the State Department says, the United States has expelled 11 Soviet officials attached to the Embassy here and 11 others attached to the United Nations in New York on espionage charges.

The British action has heartened Western security officials, particulary Americans—some of whom have feared in recent years that wide publicized efforts at détente between East and West would lead, also, to lower security standards.

"The British showed guts," one said recently. "I sometimes wish we could be as porky about this sort of thing as the British."

The United States reportedly remains the main target of Soviet espionage. Since the mid-1950's, when the K.G.B., the Soviet state security agency and chief espionage arm, had a

Continued on Page 27, Column 1

MILLIONS VOTING IN ONE-MAN RACE IN SOUTH VIETNAM

Rockets Kill 3 and Wound 5 in Saigon Before Balloting —3 Other Cities Struck

PRESIDENT TOURS POLLS

Opposition Urges a Boycott but Thieu Says All Have Duty to Participate

By ALVIN SHUSTER

Special to The New York Times

SAIGON, South Vietnam, Sunday, Oct. 3—Millions of South Vietnamese are voting today to re-elect Prsident Nguyen Van Thieu, the only candidate in an election that has brought embarrassment to American officials and distress to many Vietnamese.

Enemy elements marked the occasion by sending three rockets into Saigon early this morning, the first such attack since December. Three civilians were reported killed and five wounded.

About the same time, shortly before 5 A.M., rockets fell on at least three other cities, Cantho, to the south in the Mekong Delta, Bienhoa to the northeast, and Tayninh to the northwest. In all, about 30 civilians were killed or wounded. [Details of fighting on Page 4.]

Thieu Casts Ballot

Voting for himself this morning at City Hall in Saigon, President Thieu said that scattered rocket incidents were insignificant and that "the Communists have failed in their plans to disrupt the elections."

At an impromptu news conference in City Hall, Mr. Thieu insisted that just because he was the only candidate, it did not mean there was an absence of democracy in South Vietnam. He said the people have a right to stay home or cast invalid ballots to show dissent.

Mr. Thieu, smiling and confident, made a tour of several of Saigon's polling stations and reported that the voting was going well. He said that the turnout in some places was higher than in any other election.

Opponents Urge Boycott

Up to the eve of the election, opposition groups continued to call on the voters to boycott the polls to show their contempt for the one-man race, but Mr. Thieu countered in a television speech last night, telling the Vietnamese it was "their right and duty" to vote. He also said that newspaper reports here and abroad on the extent of the opposition were "exaggerated."

Denouncing the recent protests by students, veterans, anti-Government Buddhists and others, the President said such activities were designed to sabotage the election. He said

Continued on Page 2, Column 3

All 63 on British Airliner Killed in Crash in Belgium

By United Press International

GHENT, Belgium, Oct. 2—A British European Airways plane crashed near here today, killing all 63 persons aboard. Six of the dead were reported to be Americans.

The Vanguard airliner lost a wing when an engine exploded and fell on pasture land, six miles from here, police said.

Airline officials said that the plane carried 55 passengers and a crew of 8— [37 Britons, 8 Austrians and four Japanese in addition to the Americans. The airline said the names of the victims would not be made public until next of kin had been notified.

The 10-year-old Vanguard, en route from London to Salzburg, Austria, went out of control after one of its four turboprop engines exploded, according to a farmer, Walter Maertens, who saw the crash.

"It sloped down, managed to avoid a row of trees, shot up in the air pretty steeply, and then crashed," Mr. Maertens said.

"The cause of the crash is tonight a complete and utter mystery," an airline spokesman said.

The crash occurred on the land of George Bollaert. Mrs. Bollaert said: "We saw what looked like a ball of fire coming down over our fields."

A police spokesman said re-

Continued on Page 12, Column 1

Many Farm Labor Offices Favor Growers

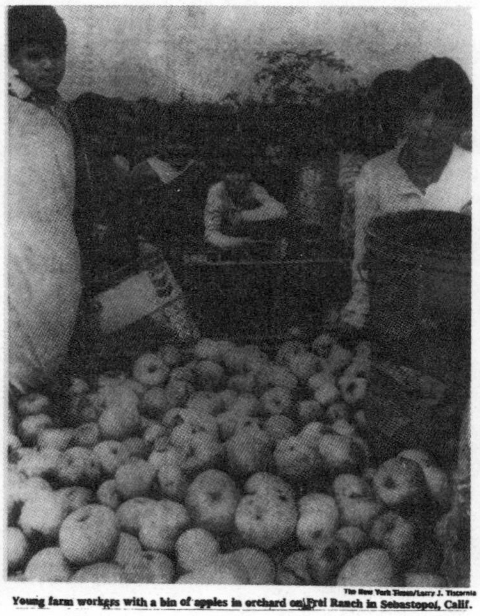

The New York Times/Larry J. Yscornia

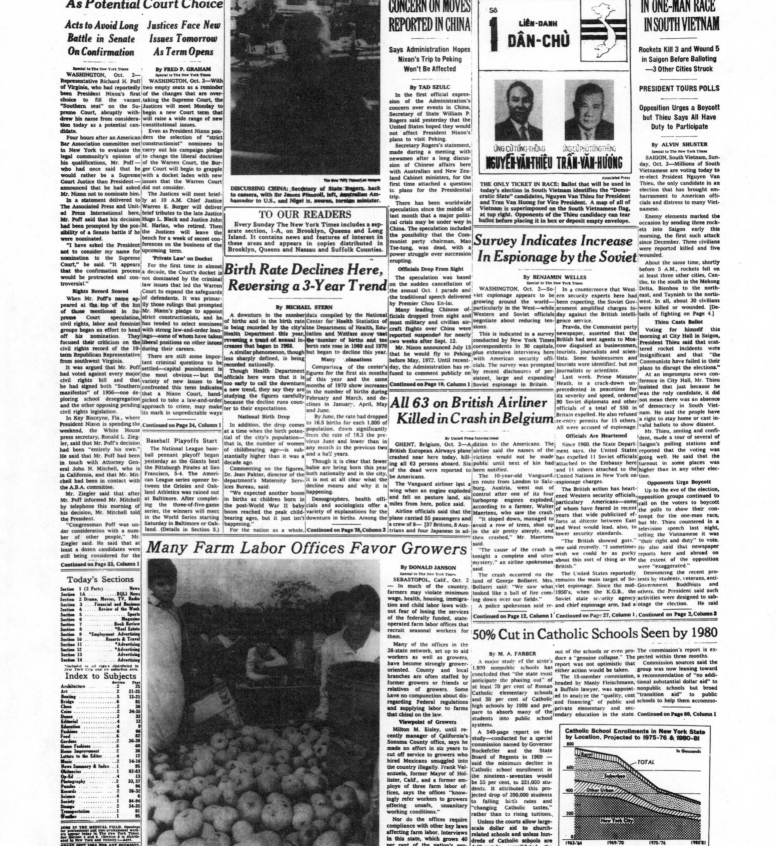

Young farm workers with a bin of apples in orchard on Frei Ranch in Sebastopol, Calif.

By DONALD JANSON

Special to The New York Times

SEBASTOPOL, Calif., Oct. 2 — In much of the country, farmers may violate minimum wage, health, housing, immigration and child labor laws without fear of losing the services of the federally funded, state-operated farm labor offices that recruit seasonal workers for them.

Many of the offices in the 38-state network, set up to aid workers as well as growers, have become strongly grower-oriented. County and local branches are often staffed by former growers or friends or relatives of growers. Some have no compunction about disregarding Federal regulations and supplying labor to farms that chisel on the law.

Viewpoint of Growers

Milton M. Eisley, until recently manager of California's Sonoma County office, says he made no effort in six years to cut off service to growers who hired Mexicans smuggled into the country illegally. Frank Valenzuela, former Mayor of Hollister, Calif., and a former employe of three farm labor offices, says the offices "knowingly refer workers to growers offering unsafe, unsanitary working conditions."

Nor do the offices require compliance with other key laws affecting farm labor. Interviews in this state, which grows 40 per cent of the nation's pro-

Continued on Page 76, Column 1

50% Cut in Catholic Schools Seen by 1980

By M. A. FARBER

A major study of the state's 1,900 nonpublic schools has concluded that "the state must anticipate the phasing out" of at least 70 per cent of Roman Catholic elementary schools and 50 per cent of Catholic high schools by 1980 and prepare to absorb many of the students into public school systems.

A 540-page report on the study—conducted for a special commission named by Governor Rockefeller and the State Board of Regents in 1969 — said the minimum decline in Catholic school enrollment in the nineteen-seventies would be 55 per cent, to 321,000 students. It attributed this projected drop of 390,000 students to falling birth rates and "changing Catholic tastes," rather than to rising tuitions.

Unless the courts allow large-scale dollar aid to church-related schools and unless hundreds of Catholic schools are deliberately consolidated, the report said, the decline could require the wholesale phasing out of the schools or even produce a "genuine collapse." The report was not optimistic that either action would be taken.

The 18-member commission, headed by Manly Fleischmann, a Buffalo lawyer, was appointed to analyze the "quality, cost and financing" of public and private elementary and secondary education in the state. The commission's report is expected within three months.

Commission sources said the group was now leaning toward a recommendation of "no additional substantial dollar aid" to nonpublic schools but broad "transition aid" to public schools to help them accommo-

Continued on Page 80, Column 1

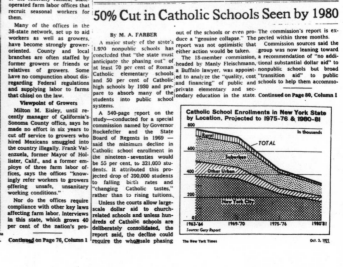

Catholic School Enrollments in New York State by Location, Projected to 1975-76 & 1980-81

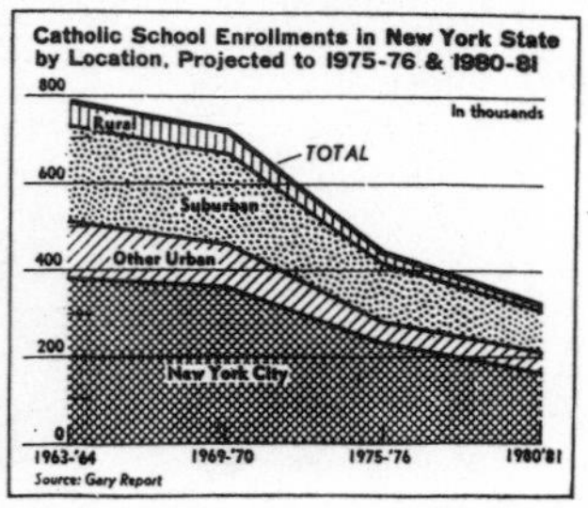
800
600
400
200
0
In thousands
Rural
TOTAL
Suburban
Other Urban
New York City
1963-'64
1969-'70
1975-'76
1980'81

Source: Gary Report

The New York Times · Oct. 3, 1971

Today's Sections

Index to Subjects

"All the News That's Fit to Print"

The New York Times

LATE CITY EDITION

Weather: Mostly sunny, cold today; cloudy and cold tonight, tomorrow. Temp. range: today 20-30; Tuesday 31-56. Full U.S. report on Page 73.

VOL. CXXI . . No. 41,640 © 1972 The New York Times Company NEW YORK, WEDNESDAY, JANUARY 26, 1972 15 CENTS

NIXON DISCLOSES A PEACE PLAN INCLUDING NEW SAIGON ELECTION; SAYS NORTH VIETNAM IGNORED IT

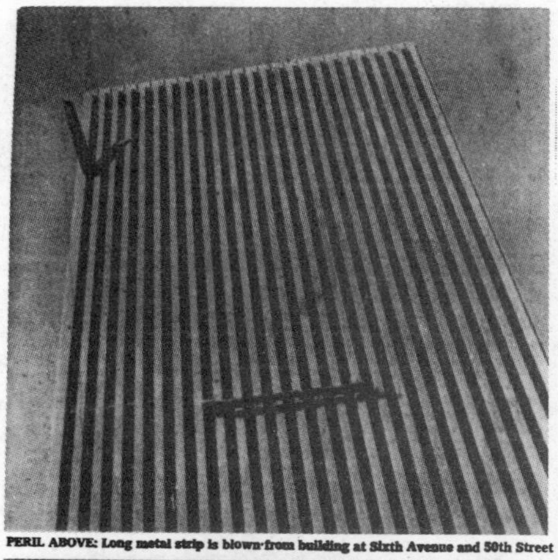

PERIL ABOVE: Long metal strip is blown from building at Sixth Avenue and 50th Street

Photographs for The New York Times by MEYER LIEBOWITZ

LOOKING OUT BELOW: People taking shelter in Rockefeller Center from flying objects

Four Die as Gale Winds Buffet City; Buildings Damaged, Utility Lines Felled

By LAWRENCE VAN GELDER

Winds of gale force savaged the metropolitan area yesterday in a fury of destruction that caused at least four deaths and untold thousands of dollars in property damage.

Gusts of more than 60 miles an hour raked and howled at skyscrapers, buffeted pedestrians and overturned vehicles, uprooted trees and whipped down utility wires, whirled debris and tore away signs, shattered windows and shot stinging bursts of grit and rubble at faces.

The high winds, born of a storm system 300 miles north of Montreal, raged destructively across the eastern part of Canada and across the United States eastward from the Great Lakes and as far south as Maryland.

The National Weather Service office here said the winds, which caused scores of injuries, would gradually diminish by this morning. At 1 A.M., gusts of up to 29 miles an hour were reported. Today's weather is also expected to be colder.

Throughout the day yesterday, the police and firemen were kept busy coping with injuries and damage from wind gusts that swayed tall buildings punched out windows and rained debris from new construction sites onto nearby streets.

Around 1 P.M., the police ordered pedestrians off Fifth Avenue, the Avenue of the Americas and Seventh Avenue between 45th and 51st Streets because of wind-related danger. Part of Times Square was closed off at about the same time, as debris rained from the Arlen Construction Company's multicolored building rising between 43d and 44th Streets.

Early today, the police reported at least three blocks still closed to traffic: 43d Street from the Avenue of the Americas to Times Square, 49th Street from the Avenue of the Americas to Seventh Avenue, and 61st Sttreet from Central Park West to Broadway.

From around the city came reports like these: objects falling from the upper floors of the World Trade Center, a wall collapse at 36th Street and First Avenue, a traffic light blown loose and dangling at Worth and Lafayette Streets, a skylight blown off a roof on 23d Street, a sign blown off a building on East 126th Street, a section of a penthouse blown away at 200 East 78th Street, a trailer truck overturned on the Clearview Expressway in Queens, a tree blown down across utility wires in the New Brighton section of Staten Island, 90 Consolidated Edison wires down in Queens, 12 poles snapped or hit by falling trees in Brooklyn.

Just before noon, a decorative steel and tin beam from the nearby Gulf & Western Building

Continued on Page 42, Column 3

The New York Times/Barton Silverman

IN LOWER MANHATTAN, just as elsewhere in the area, the wind made the going hard

PAY BOARD BACKS RAIL RAISES TIED TO COST CUTTING

Approves 10% for 180,000 Trainmen if Work Rules Changes Take Effect

By WALTER RUGABER

Special to The New York Times

WASHINGTON, Jan. 25—The Pay Board said today that it would approve wage increases of 10 per cent for 180,000 railroad trainmen later this year if a series of cost-cutting work rules were put into effect.

The board, in a compromise ruling on a tangled prefreeze settlement, also specifically endorsed the retroactive payment of two 1971 raises, an April 1 step-up of 4 per cent and an Oct. 1 increment of 5 per cent.

But two smaller increases scheduled for 1973—3 per cent on Jan. 1 and 2 per cent on April 1—were not mentioned in the board's announcement. The trainmen have demanded authorization of all the pay advances.

May Act Today

The United Transportation Union has withheld formal ratification of the contract pending board action. A spokesman said a decision on whether the agency's action was satisfactory would not be reached until tomorrow.

The union president, Al H. Chesser, and the former president, Charles Luna, indicated last week that without full board approval they would move to reopen negotiations or hold a new vote among the members on the contract.

The union, whose members include conductors, brakemen and firemen, reached agreement with the nation's railroads on Aug. 2, but when the freeze was imposed on Aug. 15 it was reluctant to accept the rules changes without assurances that the wage increases would not be blocked.

The pay raises themselves were apparently in no great

Continued on Page 73, Column 6

U.S. JUDGE STAYS RENT RAISES HERE

Acts Pending His Ruling on Suit for Full Review

By EDWARD HUDSON

A Federal judge temporarily restrained housing officials here yesterday from permitting rent increases retroactive to Jan. 1 in 800,000 controlled apartments.

The order, by Judge Lloyd F. MacMahon, prohibits the city from sending out notices of the increases, ranging up to 7.5 per cent, pending his review of a suit brought by tenants organized by Representative Bella S. Abzug, Manhattan Democrat.

The Abzug group filed suit Jan. 15. It sought to bar the sending out of such notices and to require a full review of the increases by the Federal Price Commission.

On Nov. 22, the Price Commission ruled that rents under local control were exempt from Phase Two guidelines. In New York City the ruling applies not only to rent-controlled apartments, but also to those under the rent-stabilization program.

Judge MacMahon made his temporary stay effective until Feb. 4 "unless further extended" by the court. Without the stay, he said, "immediate and irreparable injury, loss and damage" could be inflicted on tenants while he considered the case.

Benjamin Altman, the city's Commissioner of Rent and Housing Maintenance, said his agency had planned to begin

Continued on Page 42, Column 7

REACTION IS MIXED

Backers of President Praise His Offer—Critics Skeptical

By JOHN W. FINNEY

Special to The New York Times

WASHINGTON, Jan. 25—President Nixon's eight-point peace proposal was applauded tonight by Congressional supporters of the Administration, but was greeted with a mixture of skepticism and surprise by critics of the Vietnam War.

To the Administration's supporters, the President's disclosure of the secret negotiations and the American offer was taken as evidence that Mr. Nixon had done everything possible to achieve a negotiated settlement of the war.

Among the critics there was doubt that the President had gone far enough or that his proposal would be acceptable to North Vietnam.

Termed Fair and Just

Senator John Sherman Cooper, Republican of Kentucky, who in the past has teamed with Senator Church in offering Vietnam withdrawal amendments, described the President's offer as "fair and just."

"It ought to be accepted but I doubt that it will be," he said. "If not accepted, I still think we should move out."

Senator J. W. Fulbright, the Chairman of the Senate Foreign Relations Committee and one of the harshest critics of the Administration's Vietnam policies, said that the President had offered what would be considered in Western eyes a "fair and generous" proposal.

"But what looks generous to us may not look generous to North Vietnam," Senator Fulbright said. "We may have to do more" to get a favorable response from North Vietnam."

The "sticking point," he said, remains the question of whether the United States is "willing to get out and leave the Thieu Government to its own devices."

Unity Doubtful

From the initial Congressional reaction, it did not appear that the President, in disclosing his peace initiatives, would achieve one of his stated goals of unifying the American people and the Congress behind his position.

There were expressions of support, such as from Senator John Stennis, Chairman of the Senate Armed Services Committee, and Representative F. Edward Hébert, chairman of the House Armed Services Committee.

Senator Stennis said, "This shows that the President has repeatedly done all that he could reasonably and honorably do as the chief executive of our nation."

Mr. Hébert said that "tonight in the cause of peace the President had his finest hour."

"He demonstrated beyond

Continued on Page 11, Column 1

Text of the Joint Proposal

Special to The New York Times

WASHINGTON, Jan. 25—Following is the text of a proposal by the Governments of the United States and South Vietnam for a negotiated settlement of the Indochina conflict, as released by the White House tonight:

1. There will be a total withdrawal from South Vietnam of all U. S. forces and other foreign forces allied with the Government of South Vietnam within six months of an agreement.

2. The release of all military men and innocent civilians captured throughout Indochina will be carried out in parallel with the troop withdrawals mentioned in Point 1. Both sides will present a complete list of military men and innocent civilians held throughout Indochina on the day the agreement is signed. The release will begin on the same day as the troop withdrawals and will be completed when they are completed.

3. The following principles will govern the political future of South Vietnam:

The political future of South Vietnam will be left for the South Vietnamese people to decide for themselves, free from outside interference.

There will be a free and democratic presidential election in South Vietnam within six months of an agreement. This election will be organized and run by an independent body representing all political forces in South Vietnam which will assume its responsibilities on the date of the agreement. This body will, among other responsibilities, determine the qualification of candidates. All political forces in South Vietnam can participate in the election and present candidates. There will be international supervision of this election.

One month before the presidential election takes place, the incumbent President and Vice President of South Vietnam will resign. The chairman of the Senate, as caretaker head of the Government, will assume administrative responsibilities except for those pertaining to the election, which will remain with the independent election body.

The United States, for its part, declares that it:

¶Will support no candidate and will remain completely neutral in the election.

¶Will abide by the outcome of this election and any other political processes shaped by the South Vietnamese people themselves.

¶Is prepared to define its military and economic assistance relationship with any government that exists in South Vietnam.

Both sides agree that:

¶South Vietnam, together with the other countries of Indochina, should adopt a foreign policy consistent with the military provisions of the 1954 Geneva accords.

¶Reunification of Vietnam should be decided on the basis of discussions and agreements between North and South Vietnam without constraint and annexation from either party, and without foreign interference.

4. Both sides will respect the 1954 Geneva agreements on Indochina and those of 1962 on Laos. There will be no foreign intervention in the Indochinese countries, and the Indochinese peoples will be left to settle their own affairs by themselves.

5. The problems existing among the Indochinese countries will be settled by the Indochinese parties on the basis of mutual respect for independence, sovereignty, territorial integrity and noninterference in each other's affairs. Among the problems that will be settled is the implementation of the principle that all armed forces of the countries of Indochina must remain within their national frontiers.

6. There will be a general cease-fire throughout Indochina, to begin when the agreement is signed. As part of the cease-fire, there will be no further infiltration of outside forces into any of the countries of Indochina.

7. There will be international supervision of the military aspects of this agreement, including the cease-fire in its provisions, the release of prisoners of war and innocent civilians, the withdrawal of outside forces from Indochina and the implementation of the principle that all armed forces of the countries of Indochina must remain within their national frontiers.

8. There will be an international guarantee for the fundamental national rights of the Indochinese peoples, the status of all the countries of Indochina and lasting peace in this region.

Both sides express their willingness to participate in an international conference for this and other appropriate purposes.

SECRECY IS BROKEN

Kissinger Visited Paris —Thieu Would Quit Under Proposal

Transcript of Nixon address is printed on Page 10.

By ROBERT B. SEMPLE Jr.

Special to The New York Times

WASHINGTON, Jan. 25 — President Nixon disclosed to the American public tonight a proposal to end the war in Indochina that he said had been offered in secret channels three months ago but ignored by the North Vietnamese.

The major new element of the plan would be a new presidential election in South Vietnam, with President Nguyen Van Thieu resigning one month before the election. This and other parts of the plan, Mr. Nixon said, were fully endorsed by Mr. Thieu when the proposal was set before the Communists in October.

[In Saigon, President Thieu, speaking on the radio Wednesday, offered to hold new presidential elections in which the Vietcong could participate, Reuters reported. Page 11.]

An 'Accounting' to People

President Nixon also disclosed a series of 12 secret meetings in Paris between Henry A. Kissinger, his adviser on national security, and senior North Vietnamese diplomats. The meetings ended before Mr. Kissinger was able to present the new proposals personally, but they had been sent to the North Vietnamese negotiating team in a private communication from the President.

Mr. Nixon said he had decided to disclose the peace plan, as well as the private talks surrounding it, to give the American people an "accounting" of why negotiations to end the war had been disappointing, to put to rest charges that the Administration had not made its best efforts, and to demonstrate publicly "what we have long been demonstrating privately—that America has taken the initiative not only to end our participation in this war, but to end the war itself."

Other elements of the plan had been offered by Mr. Nixon in one form or another before, and were aimed at resolving both the military and po itical

Continued on Page 10, Column 1

All Wives Ruled Equal In U.S. Foreign Service

By BENJAMIN WELLES

Special to The New York Times

WASHINGTON, Jan. 25—Young American diplomatic wives overseas need no longer do laundry for the ambassador's wife, pack or unpack her personal effects or help prepare sandwiches for embassy receptions.

With a nod in the direction of women's liberation, the State Department has freed young Foreign Service wives at diplomatic posts abroad from the whims and dictates of the wives of the ambassadors or other senior officers.

The wife of a Foreign Service employe who has accompanied her husband to a foreign post is a "private" person and "not a Government employe," the department declared in an order just sent to all foreign missions. "The Foreign Service, therefore, has no right to levy any duties upon her," the order said.

It can only require that she "comport herself in a manner which will not reflect discredit on the United States."

The rank and precedence inherent in any diplomatic community, the order states, "does not grant to any wife authority over, or responsibility for, the wives of other employes."

Furthermore, it adds, comments on wives' participation "or lack thereof" in embassy-sponsored clubs, social

Continued on Page 27, Column 1

A Fiscal Revolution At Trinity Parish

By EDWARD B. FISKE

Trinity Parish, which was chartered by King William III of England in 1697 and has functioned like an ecclesiastical kingdom unto itself ever since, has quietly decreed a revolution.

The 275-year-old Episcopal parish, whose assets include some of the choicest real estate in lower Manhattan, has reversed a policy, begun while it was heavily in debt during the Depression, of saving a large part of its annual income. The parish will now spend all $5-million of it on religious programs.

"The estate is now secure," said Warren H. Turner Jr., deputy for parish administration. "It's time for Trinity once again to become a significant

Continued on Page 41, Column 3

NEW HAT IN RING: MRS. CHISHOLM'S

Representative Is Seeking Presidency as Democrat

By FRANK LYNN

Representative Shirley Chisholm announced her candidacy yesterday for the Democratic Presidential nomination — the first black woman to seek a major-party Presidential nomination.

The Brooklyn Democrat picked an unusual setting to announce her candidacy — a Bedford-Stuyvesant parochial school auditorium—declaring that she sought "to repudiate the ridiculous notion that the American people will not vote for a qualified candidate simply because he is not white or because she is not a male."

However, even some of Mrs. Chisholm's admirers conceded privately that she had at least two strikes—her sex and her

Continued on Page 16, Column 6

NEWS INDEX

"All the News That's Fit to Print"

The New York Times

LATE CITY EDITION

Weather: Cloudy and cooler today; clearing tonight. Fair tomorrow. Temp. range: today 42-48; Saturday 41-57. Full U.S. report on Page 71.

News of special interest to readers in New Jersey will be found on pages 55 to 70.

VOL. CXXI . No. 41,707 © 1972 The New York Times Company NEW YORK, SUNDAY, APRIL 2, 1972 75¢ beyond 50-mile zone from New York City, except Long Island. Higher in air delivery cities. NJ 50 CENTS

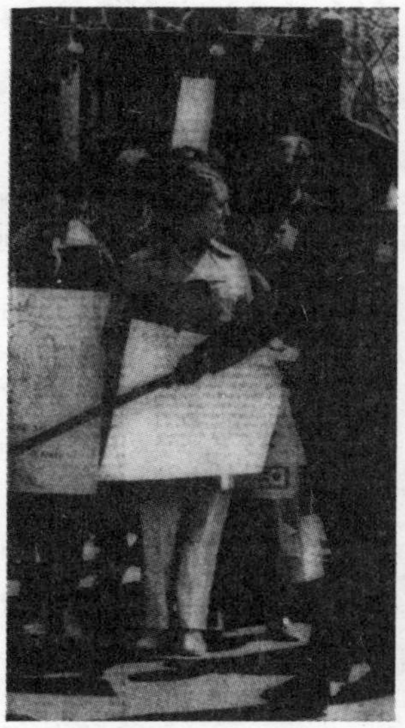

The New York Times/Michael Evans

STRIKE AFFECTS MENTAL INSTITUTION: Picket lines formed outside Willowbrook State School, Staten Island. There was no violence. Inside, a reduced number of staff workers and volunteers took care of the patients.

Strike Beginning to Disrupt State Services

By ROBERT D. McFADDEN

The union representing three-quarters of the state's 185,000 employes mounted the first major public-employe strike against the state yesterday, disrupting services at a dozen mental hospitals, schools for the retarded, prisons and other facilities.

In defiance of a court injunction and the state's Taylor Law, which bans public-employe strikes, picket lines of the Civil Service Employes Association were thrown up at some 40 facilities across the state.

Because most agencies were closed for the weekend, the strike had limited impact and there were no reports of serious hardships. Union officials warned of widespread disruptions with the reopening of state offices tomorrow. They said workers would be called out at the Motor Vehicles Department, the Department of Social Services, the Law and Tax Departments and other agencies

"We are building up to a crescendo," said William Farrell, the union's regional field supervisor here. "By Monday or Tuesday, the state will be tied up as tight as a whistle."

Manpower shortages delayed meals for more than 5,000 retarded children at the Willowbrook State School on Staten Island, generated appeals for volunteers at various mental institutions and forced some parents to take their retarded children home. Picket-line disputes led to at least four arrests.

Negotiators for the union and the state resumed talks that had been broken off in Albany, but there were no signs of a breakthrough in the dispute over wages and other benefits for 140,000 employes represented by the union. Their contracts

Continued on Page 46, Column 6

Employment is Rising...
Millions of persons seasonally adjusted
85
75
65
1966 1967 1968 1969 1970 1971 1972
But Unemployment Rate Stays High
Per cent of civilian labor force
6
5
4
3
2
1966 1967 1968 1969 1970 1971 1972 Feb.

The New York Times/April 2, 1972

Most Business Analysts Discern Upturn, But Economy Is Still Key Election Issue

By H. ERICH HEINEMANN

As the second quarter of 1972 begins, the national economy is gathering momentum. But its performance—and President Nixon's radical policy departures last August to deal with its shortfalls—is still at the center of a swirling controversy in this election year.

The Democratic majority of the Joint Economic Committee in Congress has characterized business as "sluggish," the Phase Two wage and price control program as "ill-conceived and poorly managed," and at the same time charged that little was being done to "meet our most pressing economic problem, which is the need to reduce unemployment."

On the other hand, the preponderant view among professional business forecasters—who, whatever their personal political biases, make their livings on the quality of their advice—appears to be quite the contrary in some major respects.

Alan Greenspan, president of Townsend-Greenspan & Co., Inc., a leading economic consulting concern, says, "the pace of the economy is clearly quickening."

Mr. Greenspan's outlook is consistent with the composite prediction of a large group of forecasters whose opinions are tabulated regularly by the American Statistical Association and the National Bureau of Economic Research. This foresees a marked acceleration in business, coupled with reduced unemployment and somewhat lower inflation.

Interviews with, and a culling of reports from, a large number of business forecasters in recent days disclosed substantial, though far from unanimous, agreement on the following points:

¶A marked acceleration in economic growth is likely this year, in line with the Administration's forecast of a $100-billion increase in gross national product.

¶There is a high probability of a Federal tax increase in 1973—most likely in the form of a value-added tax—to moderate the huge Federal budget deficits that now appear to be in prospect at least through mid-1975.

¶Substantial, though probably erratic, progress is expected in reducing unemployment below last year's average of just under 5 million people, or 5.9 per cent of the civilian labor force.

¶There is wide concern about the possibility of a significant shortfall from the Administra-

Continued on Page 32, Column 1

Mixed-Housing Proposal Stirs Suburb in Jersey

By RONALD SULLIVAN

Special to The New York Times

READINGTON TOWNSHIP, N. J., April 1—A racially and economically mixed 2,000-unit housing development that would nearly double the population of this rural Hunterdon County community will be formally proposed to the Township Committee this month.

The proposed community was described by its principal sponsor, Suburban Action Institute, as the largest housing project to include minority races and persons with limited income ever undertaken in the outlying suburban region surrounding the New York metropolitan area.

Because of the project's magnitude and because it would introduce large numbers of black residents into a region where there are very few of them now, it is expected to generate considerable controversy here and throughout New Jersey.

Reports of the proposed development have already created a stormy reaction in the community. "Let them go some place else," was one reply. "Good Lord, it's happening here" was another.

Already, some local officials have warily begun to compare the proposed development with the controversial plan to build a public housing project for low-income persons in Forest

Continued on Page 48, Column 5

NEW CITY VOTERS FAVOR DEMOCRATS

63.9% of Those Aged 18 to 20 Register With Party

By PETER KIHSS

The first disclosure of party preferences among 18- to 20-year-olds who have registered as voters in New York City showed yesterday that 63.9 per cent of the 127,440 registrants had enrolled as Democrats.

The Republican party attracted 10.9 per cent, the Liberal party 6.8 and the Conservative party 2.6.

The figures confirmed Democratic hopes and Republican fears about the political inclinations of young people, and were in line with the scattered results that have been reported around the country in the wake of court rulings and the ratification of the 26th Amendment to the Constitution, allowing 18-year-olds to vote.

On the other hand, the new voters may also be more open than other registrants to development of their political

Continued on Page 31, Column 1

Baseball Strike On

The first mass strike in major league baseball history caused the cancellation of yesterday's exhibition games. A meeting between Marvin Miller, the players' association executive director, and John J. Gaherin, the owners' counsel, failed to resolve the dispute, which involves owners' contributions to the pension fund. Details, Section 5.

CANDIDATES SPUR WISCONSIN RACE AS VOTING NEARS

McGovern and Humphrey in Close Battle for Lead in Primary Tuesday

CROSSOVER VOTE IS SEEN

G.O.P. Ballots for Wallace Expected—Lindsay Urges Debate With 5 Rivals

By DOUGLAS E. KNEELAND

Special to The New York Times

MILWAUKEE, April 1—The Democratic Presidential primary election here Tuesday appeared today to be shaping up as a close battle for first place between Senator George McGovern of South Dakota and Senator Hubert H. Humphrey of Minnesota.

In the last few days, Senator McGovern has been freely predicting that he will win. No other candidate has been quite as optimistic recently. Senator Humphrey said in a television interview today that he still hoped to win, but that a second-place finish would not hurt his chances in future primaries.

Complicating the race for the two apparent front-runners as well as for the three other active candidates was the unpredictable effect of a large Republican crossover vote that is expected to benefit Gov. George C. Wallace of Alabama.

Meanwhile, a study indicated

Primaries This Month

Wisconsin	Tuesday
Massachusetts	25th
Pennsylvania	25th

that Governor Wallace seemed likely to go to the Democratic National Convention with about 250 delegate votes out of a total of 3,016, probably not enough to cause the confusion feared by some Democrats.

In another development, Senator Henry M. Jackson's Wisconsin campaign has been actively aided by a Boeing Company official who has used company traveler's checks to buy newspaper advertisements. Corporate campaign contributions are prohibited by Federal law, and both Boeing and Senator Jackson said that the official's activities were unauthorized. [Details on Page 40.]

As the clock ran down rapidly on their efforts to gather voter support, all the contenders scrambled frantically around Wisconsin today, trying to develop issues that would swing backers to their side or hold on to the strength they have.

Mayor Lindsay of New York, who is widely regarded as trailing his five rivals, sent telegrams to them today urging an election eve debate in Madison, the state capital. While the Mayor has suggested a debate before, this was his first formal proposal. Since it usually takes days for opponents to agree on ground rules for such a forum, there seemed little likelihood that it would materialize.

Senator Edmund S. Muskie of Maine, the early front-runner whose fortunes have sagged in

Continued on Page 41, Column 1

FOE SWEEPS ACROSS DMZ; SAIGON TROOPS FALL BACK; CLOUDS BLOCK U.S. PLANES

Hanoi
NORTH VIETNAM
Gulf of Tonkin
NORTH VIETNAM
ZONE
ALPHA 2
ALPHA 4
DEMILITARIZED
Giolinh
CHARLIE 2
CHARLIE 4
FULLER
Dongha
CAMP CARROLL
Camlo
Quangtri
NUIBAHO
MAILOC
SARGE
HOLCOMB
Khesanh
SOUTH VIETNAM
Donghoi
Bankarai Pass
Tchepone
Hue
Danang
South China Sea
LAOS
Mekong
HO CHI MINH TRAIL
Kontum
SOUTH VIETNAM
KONTUM PROVINCE
CAMBODIA
CENTRAL HIGHLANDS

The New York Times/April 2, 1972

Offensive in area of fire bases (indicated by squares) was posing a serious threat to Quangtri city (cross).

ADVISERS UNEASY

See a Possible Threat to Hue and Danang if Push Continues

By CRAIG R. WHITNEY

Special to The New York Times

SAIGON, South Vietnam, Sunday, April 2—Thousands of North Vietnamese and Vietcong troops have driven past South Vietnam's northern line of defenses below the demilitarized zone and are pushing South Vietnamese forces in disarray toward their rear bases, United States military sources in Danang said yesterday.

The assault, reportedly by elements of one North Vietnamese main force division, the 304th, with additional artillery and other units equal to another division, followed three days of what was called the most intense enemy artillery and rocket bombardment of the war. A North Vietnamese division at full strength has about 10,000 men.

American sources said that they feared the enemy objective was to take Quangtri, the capital of South Vietnam's northernmost province, and hold it if they could, which would pose a serious threat to the city of Hue farther south and, eventually perhaps, to Danang, the largest city in the north.

Move Under Cloud Cover

The sources said that enemy troops were moving in the open, without their usual careful attempts to conceal themselves, under cover of cloudy skies that have made effective South Vietnamese and American air attacks impossible.

The clouds have also prevented retaliation against the long-range rockets and artillery pieces in and above the buffer zone that reportedly have rained more than 7,000 rounds on South Vietnamese positions since Thursday.

Lieut. Gen. Hoang Xuan Lam, the commander of Military Region I, covering the northern provinces, conferred at his headquarters in Danang with Gen. Frederick C. Weyand, the deputy commander of United States forces in Vietnam, and later General Lam issued a statement saying that "the Communist North Vietnamese are crossing the demilitarized zone to invade Quangtri Province."

His statement said that three artillery regiments and anti-

Continued on Page 16, Column 1

U.S. Officials Say Hanoi Seeks a Show of Strength

By BENJAMIN WELLES

Special to The New York Times

WASHINGTON, April 1—United States Government analysts said today that they saw three principal objectives behind the enemy offensive in the northern part of South Vietnam.

First, the officials said, Hanoi is determined to impress Moscow, Peking, the Communist world and particularly the North Vietnamese people with its determination to fight on.

North Vietnam is thought to be especially concerned that President Nixon's visit to Moscow in May, following his recent visit to Peking, might result in an outside settlement to end the Vietnam war along lines favored by the great powers but not necessarily by Hanoi.

Second, the officials said, Hanoi appears to be seeking to revive antiwar sentiment in the United States and, incidentally, to jeopardize insofar as possible President Nixon's chances of re-election next November.

Finally, they said, Hanoi appears determined to disrupt Mr. Nixon's "Vietnamization" program, inflict as much damage as possible on the South Vietnamese ground forces and, simultaneously, imperil the stability of the Government headed by President Nguyen Van Thieu.

"We've seen the enemy build-up for many weeks," a senior official said. "They're trying to

Continued on Page 18, Column 4

Accord With Soviet in Sight On a Joint Space Mission

By JOHN NOBLE WILFORD

Special to The New York Times

MOSCOW, April 1—The Soviet Union is apparently ready to approve technical plans for a joint earth-orbiting mission by Soviet and American astronauts that could come as early as 1975.

Soviet endorsement of the basic technical arrangements for the joint flight will probably be made known to American space officials in meetings scheduled here in Moscow next week.

Such approval between officials of the Soviet Academy of Sciences and the United States National Aeronautics and Space Administration is expected to clear the way for a formal agreement between the two

Continued on Page 44, Column 3

Associated Press

Dr. Boris N. Petrov, the director of Intercosmos.

U.S. Widens Ties to African Whites

By TERENCE SMITH

Special to The New York Times

WASHINGTON, April 1—The Nixon Administration is quietly pursuing a policy of deliberately expanded contacts and communication with the white governments of southern Africa.

Although this appears to have been Administration policy for the last two years, it is only in recent months that its implementation has become evident.

In practical terms, the policy has resulted in a number of concrete developments, ranging from major new economic undertakings, such as the recent Azores agreement with Portugal, to the authorization of previously forbidden sales of jet aircraft to Portugal and South Africa.

In contrast with the Kennedy and Johnson Administrations, which sought to ostracize the white governments because of their racial policies, President Nixon has taken a series of steps to improve political and economic contacts with South Africa and with Portugal, which controls Mozambique and Angola.

Protests Increasing

In recent months, as the outlines of the Nixon policy have emerged, there has been a growing vocal protest from civil rights, church and academic groups interested in Africa, and there has been criticism in Congress. Every indication is that this current of opposition is likely to gain impetus.

At the same time the policy has had another result: It has generated unconcealed delight among corporate and other interests that make up the powerful Rhodesian and South African lobbies here.

Neither result was the intention of the Administration's policy makers. Rather, the new policy was the end-product of an exhaustive and critical review of the Kennedy and Johnson policies toward southern Africa.

The unpublicized review, begun at the President's direction in April, 1969, was completed and put before the National Security Council at the end of that year.

It contained, according to authoritative sources, three basic options:

¶The "Dean Acheson" option, which the former Secretary of State had often urged in public and in his writing. This proposed the treatment of South Africa as any sovereign,

Continued on Page 14, Column 1

Today's Sections

Index to Subjects

"All the News That's Fit to Print"

The New York Times

LATE CITY EDITION

Weather: Partly sunny today; clear tonight. Sunny and mild tomorrow. Temp. range: today 47-63; Sunday 46-60. Full U.S. report on Page 65.

VOL. CXXI . . No. 41,722 © 1972 The New York Times Company NEW YORK, MONDAY, APRIL 17, 1972 15 CENTS

APOLLO LAUNCHED; LANDING ON MOON SET FOR THURSDAY

LIFT-OFF SMOOTH

But Peeling Insulation on Lander Leads to Momentary Worry

By JOHN NOBLE WILFORD
Special to The New York Times

CAPE KENNEDY, Fla., Monday, April 17—The Apollo 16 astronauts embarked yesterday on the nation's next-to-last mission to the moon in this decade, but soon ran into potential trouble when insulation material was seen peeling and shedding off their lunar landing craft.

The source of the problem remained a mystery today, even after a careful inspection of the vehicle's systems by the astronauts. The crew, however, was in no danger and the flight, aimed at exploring for the first time the moon's volcano-like mountains, continued on course.

When it was determined that there were no holes or fuel leaks in the lunar lander—either of which would have ruled out the planned landing—both the astronauts and Mission Control in Houston appeared to relax.

Two Anxious Hours

But for two anxious hours, they had feared for the mission' success. One possible cause of the trouble, according to the space agency, was that a control thruster on the command ship was firing excessively or at a skewed angle. This could have scorched the metallicized plastic covering on the attached lunar module, producing the peeling that one astronaut likened to "shredded wheat."

Flight controllers continued to study the situation as the astronauts settled down for the coasting flight to the moon, which shone across 230,000 miles of space from the earth.

The planned 12-day mission for Capt. John W. Young and Lieut. Comdr. Thomas K. Mattingly 2d of the Navy and Lieut. Col. Charles M. Duke Jr. of the Air Force got under way at 12:54 P.M. yesterday within milli-seconds of the schedule that should result in a moon landing Thursday and a walk several hours later.

The Earth Shakes

Orange flames spread from the base of the mammoth Saturn 5 rocket. The 36-story moonship rose ponderously off the launching pad. The earth shook for miles around, and thunderclaps of sound rolled across the sandy plain.

The sky was so clear and blue that the rocket's fiery exhaust could be seen with the unaided eye for several minutes after lift-off, first as a glowing ball of flame, then as a red arrow with a vapor trail and finally as a tiny star over the Atlantic Ocean.

Like many of the hundreds of thousands of spectators here, Vice President Agnew said the launching was "one of the finest" he had ever seen. Others out for the spectacle view on a warm Sunday afternoon included the King of Jordan and

Continued on Page 24, Column 1

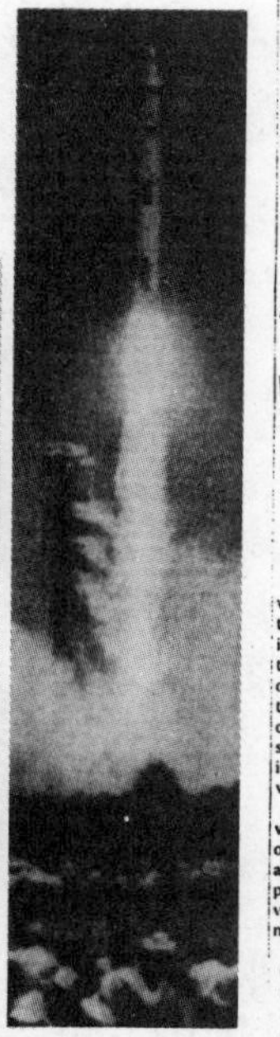

NASA and Associated Press

Astronauts at pre-flight meal are, from top, Capt. John W. Young, Lieut. Col. Charles M. Duke Jr., and Lieut. Comdr. Thomas K. Mattingly 2d. Lift-off was exactly on schedule.

Legislature Begins Push on Major Bills So It Can Adjourn

By WILLIAM E. FARRELL
Special to The New York Times

ALBANY, April 16—Like a grizzly bear stirring from its winter hibernation, the current session of the Legislature—which almost everybody here agrees has been unmatched in recent years for sheer tedium—begins this week to take up major legislation so far ignored.

Evidence that a push for production — and adjournment—is on began late last week and will continue this week, with lawmakers eager to return home to begin campaigning for re-election.

Major legislation that has been consistently deferred during more than three months of foot-dragging, plodding sessions, includes bills on aid to parochial schools, some form of no-fault automobile insurance and enabling legislation affecting New York City's proposed budget of almost $10-billion.

The Republican majority leaders, Senator Earl W. Brydges of Niagara Falls and Assembly Speaker Perry B. Duryea of Montauk, have let it be known that they want to end

Continued on Page 22, Column 3

Yanks Lose Opener

The New York Yankees were beaten by the Orioles, 3-1, at Baltimore in their opening game. In Chicago, Burt Hooton, a rookie, pitched a no-hitter as the Cubs defeated Philadelphia, 4-0. Details on Page 39.

ROCKEFELLER ASKS MORE PRISON AID

$12-Million Is Sought From Legislature to 'Reform and Improve' Penal System

By JAMES F. CLARITY
Special to The New York Times

ALBANY, April 16—Governor Rockefeller today asked the Legislature to authorize $12-million more for "reforms and improvements" in the state prison system.

The Governor said that $1.3-million would be used to create a "special program facility." This is the "maximum program, maximum security" facility that the Correction Department plans to create from an existing prison in the state. Prisoners are scheduled to be moved into the facility beginning May 1. The site has not yet been disclosed.

Slightly more than half of the $12-million requested by the Governor would be used to increase and train the Correction Department staff. The rest would be for services and programs for the prisoners.

Correction Commissioner Russell G. Oswald asserted in February that $22-million had been sliced from his request in the Governor's 1972-73 budget. The budget, approved by the Legislature last month, included $101-million for Mr. Oswald's department.

The concern for prison reform stirred in the Legislature by the uprising at the Attica Correctional Facility last year

Continued on Page 20, Column 1

3 British Soldiers Killed in Upsurge Of I.R.A. Violence

Special to The New York Times

BELFAST, Northern Ireland, April 16—Three British soldiers were killed today in Londonderry and Belfast and two others wounded in an upsurge of Irish Republican Army violence following the death of a senior officer of the illegal group.

Rioting has continued almost nonstop in the two cities since soldiers shot Joseph McCann, a popular community leader. Mr. McCann, a battalion commander of the Marxist-oriented Official wing of the I.R.A., was killed as he fled from a British Army patrol yesterday.

The rioting in Roman Catholic areas dashed hopes, at least temporarily, that the Catholics were about to disown I.R.A. violence. There had been movement in that direction since the imposition of direct rule from London and the suspension of Northern Ireland's parliament more than three weeks ago.

The ferocity of the I.R.A.'s

Continued on Page 3, Column 5

U.S. PREPARED TO EXTEND NORTH VIETNAM BOMBING; MOSCOW PROTESTS RAIDS

A SOVIET WARNING

Wording Is Viewed as a Veiled Threat to Nixon's Visit

By HEDRICK SMITH
Special to The New York Times

MOSCOW, April 16—The Soviet Union made a formal protest to the United States today in reaction to the bombing of the North Vietnamese port city of Haiphong and warned that the expansion of the air war could aggravate not only the situation in Indochina but "the international situation as a whole."

This was taken as a veiled warning that further pursuit of the heavy-bombing campaign against North Vietnam could put President Nixon's scheduled visit to the Soviet Union next month in jeopardy.

[Premier Chou En-lai of China condemned the raids, declaring that the United States had "embarked again on the old track of war escalation," the official press agency reported. Page 10.]

American officials in Moscow said that the Soviet Government did not mention Mr. Nixon's visit in making the protest, evidently an indication that the Kremlin still wanted to go ahead with the meeting and the important round of negotiations that it would involve.

Seen as First Reaction

But well-placed sources suggested that the protest today represented only the first reaction, coming while Kremlin leaders were away for the weekend. The sources emphasized Moscow's acute embarrassment, since it sharply criticized China for receiving Mr. Nixon in February during a heavy air campaign against the North Vietnamese and now was faced with an even sharper intensification.

Ambassador Jacob D. Beam of the United States was summoned to the Foreign Ministry at 10:30 P.M. to hear an oral protest from Anatoly G. Kovalev, a Deputy Foreign Minister, who also gave the envoy the text of the protest.

The contents of the protest were not made public. But while Mr. Beam was at the Foreign Ministry, the Soviet press agency Tass issued an authorized statement condemning the bombing raids and demanding that they be halted.

Although the private protest

Continued on Page 10, Column 5

The New York Times/April 17, 1972

Among target areas struck by American warplanes were Hanoi, Haiphong, Vinh and Baithuong (underlined).

Behind Nixon's Decision: More Than Military Issues

By MAX FRANKEL
Special to The New York Times

WASHINGTON, April 16—President Nixon has kept silent this weekend on his new bombing policy in Vietnam to avoid overt challenge to the Soviet Union, which he still hopes to visit next month, and to avoid further inflammation of public opinion at home.

But it is acknowledged here that more than military considerations lay behind the decision to resume air strikes against North Vietnam's major cities. Specifically, it is said that the President's demonstration of resolve is aimed both at Moscow and at the American electorate, as well as at the Governments in Hanoi and Saigon.

As far as can be determined from secondary sources here, the important elements of Mr. Nixon's calculations are as follows:

¶The President is portrayed as deeply disturbed by the apparently indirect but nonetheless vital Soviet support for the extensive North Vietnamese attack on South Vietnam. The timing of the offensive, though probably not determined by Moscow, had the effect of making the United States appear weak and failing in Indochina at the very moment when Mr. Nixon was heading for the Soviet Union to conclude new agreements on arms control, trade and credits, and European security.

¶If, despite the atmosphere of summitry, the Soviet leaders insist on giving maximum support to their ally in North Vietnam, the President, it is said, is convinced that he can do no less for his ally in the South. The extended bombing may chill the mood of the

Continued on Page 12, Column 4

HANOI ATTACKED

Aides Say Nixon Must Authorize Strikes on Sensitive Areas

By WILLIAM BEECHER
Special to The New York Times

WASHINGTON, April 16 — Administration officials declared today that the United States was prepared to bomb military targets almost anywhere in North Vietnam.

The statement followed weekend air raids on Haiphong and Hanoi by waves of fighter-bombers and eight-engine B-52 bombers. The attacks were the first against those cities since the end of March, 1968, and marked the first time that B-52's had been used against Haiphong or Hanoi.

In a terse statement today, the United States command in Saigon said that at Haiphong the planes had struck fuel dumps, warehouses, truck parks, "and other activities which are supporting the invasion of South Vietnam by the North Vietnamese forces."

[In Saigon, the United States command announced Monday that Hanoi as well as Haiphong had been bombed, and that two American warplanes had been shot down. The command said United States jets shot down three North Vietnamese MIG-21 jets. Page 10.]

Sensitive Areas Cited

In discussing the raids, officials in Washington emphasized that President Nixon must personally authorize future raids in areas that are considered politically sensitive.

In this regard, they said that no consideration was being given "at this time" to hitting targets near North Vietnam's border with China and that the attacks made on Haiphong by B-52's and fighter-bombers did not involve the docks or harbor.

This statement followed a report by the Hanoi radio that a Soviet freighter in the harbor had been damaged and one of the ship's officers injured when bomb fragments and 20-mm. shells from American planes struck the vessel.

Spokesmen for the White House, the State Department and the Pentagon declined to offer a rationale for the raids into the heartland of North Vietnam.

Objectives Listed

But senior military and diplomatic sources said that the rapidly expanding air campaign against the North sought, among other things, the following objectives:

¶To disrupt the flow of war supplies and reinforcements toward North Vietnamese units pressing offensives throughout South Vietnam.

¶To warn Hanoi that if it planned to conduct weeks or even months of heavy fighting in the South, it would face mounting raids in the North.

¶To persuade the Soviet Union to use its influence— partic-

Continued on Page 10, Column 5

Foe Has Been Driven Out Of Anloc, Saigon Reports

By MALCOLM W. BROWNE
Special to The New York Times

SAIGON, South Vietnam, Monday, April 17—South Vietnamese official spokesmen said yesterday that all North Vietnamese troops and tanks had been driven out of Anloc, the provincial capital 60 miles north of Saigon that has been under siege for more than a week.

The only road to the town, Route 13 running north from Saigon, remained cut, however, with powerful enemy forces hemming in and harassing a South Vietnamese relief column.

The United States command announced that an American Army medical evacuation helicopter was struck by ground fire and made a forced landing in Anloc yesterday morning. The white-painted helicopter had picked up a wounded American soldier there just before it was attacked. He and the crew of the rescue craft were plucked out of the besieged town by another American helicopter.

Intelligence sources reported last night that strong North Vietnamese reinforcements had been sighted heading for the battle area from Cambodia.

There was apparently little over-all change in the ground situation yesterday. These were among the highlights of the fighting:

¶In Quangtri Province, four miles from the district capital of Dongha, at a point where Hanoi originally launched its general attack on the South, Saigon claimed a victory.

According to a spokesman, South Vietnamese ranger and tank units fought two engagements near Dongha on Saturday, killing 109 of the enemy, while suffering only one fatality.

¶The besieged South Vietnamese base called Bastogne, 19 miles southwest of Hue, where 500 Government troops are dangerously short of sup-

Continued on Page 10, Column 4

Lincoln Center Proposes Wider Youth Involvement

By PAUL L. MONTGOMERY

Lincoln Center is in the midst of a critical re-examination of its performing arts program for young people, which has reached nearly six million students in the metropolitan area in the last 11 years.

The center's director of education, Mark Schubart, has concluded after leading a year's study of its own and similar programs that the only satisfactory way of making the arts relevant to the young is to begin new community organizations specifically for them, rather than as afterthoughts to the adult schedule.

"Basically, there is no room for young people in the concert hall, the theater, the opera house," says Mr. Schubart's report, to be released today. "The youth is a welcome guest in a grown-up house, but a guest nonetheless. There is no place to talk to him, to find out what is on his mind, to show him things, to let him explore on his own. Is it surprising that he is a reluctant and infrequent visitor?"

In the proposal, entitled "The Hunting of the Squiggle," there would be de-emphasis of presentation of recognized works in a formal setting, which now makes up the bulk of what passes for youth programs. Instead, there would be smaller informal projects, involving artists, which would attempt

Continued on Page 46, Column 1

Tim Kantor

Mark Schubart

Integration Lags in State Police Units

By SETH S. KING

When Douglas DeLeaver first donned the brown and tan uniform of the Maryland State Police a few years ago, he remembers noticing that people stared at him when he walked by.

"It was like I was something strange," he recalls. "One woman told me she'd never seen a black trooper before and didn't know there was such a thing."

Trooper DeLeaver's experience is not unusual. Among the many previously all-white professions that blacks have finally begun entering, none remains more tightly segregated than state police forces.

A Federal court order directing Alabama to enroll blacks in its all-white force pointed to the almost total absence of blacks in Southern state police units. But virtually every other state—North and South—has a racial imbalance similar to Alabama's.

In the nation as a whole, 98 out of every 100 uniformed state troopers are white, the Race Relations Information Center found in a 1970 study.

A more recent check by The New York Times shows that only five states—California, Illinois, Maryland, New Jersey and Pennsylvania—have more than 10 blacks in their uniformed police forces. At least 10 states have no blacks at all on their forces, and many have no more than two. Under the Federal court order in Alabama, that state recently hired its first three black troopers, and the names of more than 100 others were placed on the eligibility list.

Even in those states with more than a handful of blacks on the force, the percentage is minute.

California, where a state law forbids identifying a state employe by race, has at least 80 black troopers. But this number represents slightly more than 1.5 per cent of California's 5,200-man force.

Illinois appears to have the largest percentage of black state policemen in the nation. But its total of 28 blacks—including four special investigators, a supervisor of special agents and a trooper captain

Continued on Page 18, Column 3

NEWS INDEX

Kawabata, Japanese Novelist Who Won Nobel Prize, a Suicide

By JOHN M. LEE
Special to The New York Times

TOKYO, Monday, April 17—Yasunari Kawabata, Japan's only winner of the Nobel Prize for Literature, was found dead last night with a gas hose in his mouth. He was 72 years old and had been in poor health.

His suicide followed that of his protégé, the novelist Yukio Mishima, who, in a spectacular act that shocked the nation, committed ritual hara-kiri in November, 1970, after an unsuccessful attempt to incite a rightist protest movement. Mr. Mishima was 45.

The two men, although

Continued on Page 36, Column 1

Magnum/Burt Glinn

Yasunari Kawabata

The New York Times

LATE CITY EDITION

Weather: Cool, chance of rain today, tonight. Partly cloudy tomorrow. Temp. range: today 50-73; Wed. 53-86. Full U.S. report on Page 90.

VOL. CXXI .. No. 41,725   © 1972 The New York Times Company   **NEW YORK, THURSDAY, APRIL 20, 1972**   15 CENTS

Apollo 16 Rockets Into a Moon Orbit; Fifth Lunar Landing Is Set for Today

By JOHN NOBLE WILFORD
Special to The New York Times

HOUSTON, April 19—Apollo 16 rocketed into an orbit of the moon today and was in position to attempt man's fifth lunar landing tomorrow afternoon.

"Hello, Houston, Sweet 16 has arrived," Capt. John W. Young of the Navy, the Apollo 16 commander, radioed to Mission Control as the spaceship emerged from behind the moon after going into orbit.

A six-minute-15-second firing of the main rocket slowed the spaceship by 1,900 miles an hour until it was captured by lunar gravity. The maneuver began at 3.23 P.M. Eastern standard time, while Apollo 16 was behind the moon and out of communication with the earth.

After a journey of three days and all the worry of peeling paint, communications

'Sweet 16 Has Arrived,' Captain Young Radios to Control in Houston

bugs and guidance quirks, the normally laconic Captain Young greeted the spectacle of the lunar mountains and craters and broad plains with the exclamation:

"Boy, this has got to be the neatest way to make a living anybody's ever invented!"

The 41-year-old Captain Young became the first man to go into lunar orbit twice. The first time was as a pilot in 1969 on Apollo 10, the path-finding mission for the first lunar landing flight of Apollo 11.

It was an entirely new experience for the two other astronauts of Apollo 16 — Lieut. Comdr. Thomas K.

Mattingly 2d of the Navy and Lieut. Col. Charles M. Duke Jr. of the Air Force.

For more than four hours, the astronauts circled the moon in an orbit ranging from 67 miles in altitude behind the moon to 195 miles high over the visible face of the moon. Then, at 7:28 P.M., Apollo 16's main rocket re-fired for 25 seconds and the craft swooped in closer to the surface with a new orbit of 12 miles to 69 miles.

From that orbit, Captain Young and Colonel Duke plan to enter tomorrow the attached lunar landing craft, Orion, and descend to the lunar surface north of the Descartes Crater. The two men are scheduled to cast off from the command ship, Casper, at 1:08 P.M. and complete the landing at 3:41 P.M.

Continued on Page 40, Column 1

Londonderry Clash Study Absolves Troops in Deaths

By ALVIN SHUSTER
Special to The New York Times

LONDON, April 19—An official inquiry absolved the British Army today of gross misconduct in the killing of 13 Roman Catholics in Londonderry. Northern Ireland, on Jan. 30.

The report by Lord Widgery, the Lord Chief Justice of England, questioned some of the tactics of the troops, but

Excerpts from Widgery report will be found on Page 16.

concluded that the first shot came from gunmen of the Irish Republican Army. The findings of the inquiry also blamed the organizers of the illegal march for creating a "highly dangerous situation."

Lord Widgery said that the army was not without some blame. He stated that the firing by some troops "bordered on the reckless." And he concluded that if the army had not launched a "large scale operation to arrest hooligans, the day might have passed off without serious incident."

Major charges from the Londonderry Catholic community were rejected. Lord Widgery insisted that there was no break-

Continued on Page 16. Column 4

Lord Widgery in London yesterday with report.
Associated Press

CITY'S HOSPITALS HIT BY JOB ACTION

3,500 Nonprofessionals Say They Are 'Sick'—10,000 Turned Away at Clinics

By JOHN SIBLEY

Nearly 10,000 clinic patients missed scheduled appointments in municipal hospitals and bed patients had to be transferred from one of the city's 18 hospitals after 3,500 nonprofessional hospital workers telephoned yesterday to say they were too "sick" to come to work.

The job action took place after the Health and Hospitals Corporation tried to resolve a thorny problem of union representation that has plagued the city hospital system since the early days of the hospital affiliation program a decade ago.

Pay Rise Reflected

There are flaws in this indicator of inflation. For example, one full percentage point simply represented a pay raise for Federal Government workers. An index economists consider more accurate, called the private G.N.P. chain price index, showed an inflation rate of 4.6 per cent in the first quarter, compared with 1.7 per cent in the fourth quarter.

Secretary of Commerce Peter G. Peterson, commenting on today's figures, said the inflation problem "continues to be an important challenge" but he expressed confidence "that that number is going to come down in subsequent quarters." Like other officials, he termed the post-freeze price increases a "bulge."

In another report, the Commerce Department said personal income in March rose by

Continued on Page 65, Column 1

Coney Island Situation

As it became clear early in the day that the walkout would be widespread, outpatient departments were switched to holiday schedules. Despite efforts to staff some posts with nonunion personnel, many areas were left with too few people even to offer explanations and to reschedule appointments.

This happened at virtually all city hospitals. But at Coney Island Hospital the situation became even more desperate. Too few workers were left there to care even for bed patients. Some had to be transferred by ambulance to Kings County Hospital, where there weren't enough workers to provide adequate care.

Physicians and nurses played

Continued on Page 23, Column 1

PRODUCTION RISES IN FIRST QUARTER; INFLATION UP, TOO

Higher Prices Make Up Half of Near-Record Increase in Total U.S. Output

By EDWIN L. DALE Jr.
Special to The New York Times

WASHINGTON, April 19 — The nation's economy expanded strongly in the first quarter of this year, but the inflation rate worsened following the wage-price freeze, the Commerce Department reported today.

The gross national product, the total output of goods and services, rose by a near-record amount of $30.3-billion to $1,103.2-billion. But slightly more than half of the increase simply represented higher prices — already indicated by previous reports on consumer and wholesale prices.

The "real" growth of the G.N.P. was at a rate of 5.3 per cent, less than the 5.8 per cent of the final quarter of 1971. But this slight slowdown was almost entirely accounted for by an unusually small growth in business inventories. The rest of the economy, in real terms, did better in the first quarter than in the fourth.

The price index for the entire gross national product rose at an annual rate of 6.2 per cent, a far higher rate of inflation than the 1.7 per cent of the fourth quarter, which reflected the freeze.

9 COLLEGE HEADS DEPLORE BOMBING

Presidents of 8 Ivy League Schools and M.I.T. Back Orderly Forms of Protest

By MARTIN ARNOLD

In an action aimed at heading off more campus disturbances, the presidents of the eight Ivy League universities and the Massachusetts Institute of Technology issued a joint statement yesterday deploring the recent heavy bombing of North Vietnam.

However, minor outbreaks

Text of the joint statement is printed on Page 22.

again erupted at Columbia University and a number of other campuses across the nation.

The presidents said that they supported demonstrations against the war "as long as they are not at the expense of the rights of others or at the expense of the continuation of constructive educational and scholarly activity of universities and colleges."

But even as the statement was issued Columbia obtained a court order restraining striking students from forcibly visiting

Continued on Page 22, Column 1

86° and Lovely

Alluring and summer - like weather, with a record temperature of 86 degrees, graced the metropolitan region yesterday. The result was an epidemic of spring fever. Details, Page 90.

ATTACK BY MIG'S ON U.S. WARSHIPS IN THE GULF OF TONKIN REPORTED; SOUTH VIETNAMESE TOWN OVERRUN

BUILDING ANLOC'S FORCES: Tank is moved up as South Vietnamese soldier watches
United Press International

Opening of Enemy Drive In Highlands Area Seen

Special to The New York Times

SAIGON, South Vietnam, Thursday, April 20—North Vietnamese and Vietcong troops overran the town of Hoaian in South Vietnam's central coastal region yesterday, forcing the Government battalion defending it to withdraw and reportedly causing heavy casualties.

Senior military officials at headquarters in Pleiku, 70 miles to the southwest, said the attack, staged by elements of the enemy's main force, apparently signaled the beginning of the long-expected major military action in the Central Highlands region.

The heavy fighting at Hoaian coincided with enemy attacks on other towns in Binhdinh Province, the most heavily populated on the central coast, where enemy troops have cut the strategic Route 19 at the Ankhe pass between the coastal city of Quinhon and Pleiku in the last 10 days.

The senior American adviser of the region, John Paul Vann, said in Pleiku that the North Vietnamese 20th Division, which infiltrated south along the Ho Chi Minh Trail to Kontum Province in February, had now moved east to Binhdinh Province, and that other North Vietnamese units in the mountains would possibly begin to

Continued on Page 20, Column 1

NORTH IS HIT AGAIN

Enemy Said to Lose One Plane and Two Patrol Boats

By CRAIG R. WHITNEY
Special to The New York Times

SAIGON, South Vietnam, Thursday, April 20 — The United States command announced that American warships bombarding the coast of North Vietnam yesterday came under attack by MIG fighter planes and patrol boats in the Gulf of Tonkin.

The command said that, according to first reports from the American ships, one MIG was shot down and two of the attacking boats were sunk. At least three North Vietnamese MIG's were said to have attacked the ships, which were reported firing at targets in the southern panhandle area of North Vietnam, 20 to 30 miles north of the demilitarized zone.

The reported air-sea action came as the United States command resumed the strategic bombing campaign against North Vietnam with more than 125 strikes, all in the southern panhandle below the 20th Parallel, according to informed officers. The resumption followed two days in which only a handful of bombing missions were flown in North Vietnam.

Report Is Preliminary

The command emphasized that its announcement on the MIG attacks was preliminary and "subject to modification."

It said that one Navy destroyer, the Higbee, had been damaged, apparently by an enemy MIG, and that four American sailors had been wounded. The command said that the extent of damage was still unknown.

The command said that the attack by at least three MIG's came at about 5 P.M. yesterday when an unspecified number of ships of the United States Seventh Fleet were bombarding shore targets in the panhandle.

The command said that one of the ships, the guided missile frigate Sterett, started firing at "several high-speed surface contacts" shown on the vessel's radar. It said the contacts "posed a threat to U.S. ships in the area."

One MIG Reported Down

"Preliminary reports indicate that one MIG aircraft was destroyed and two enemy surface craft were believed sunk by the Sterett," the announcement said. "These reports indicate some damage to one U.S. ship, not the Sterett. Four U.S. Navy men were reported wounded."

This was believed to be the first time in the war that North

Continued on Page 20, Column 3

GOLDWATER MOVE ON WAR THWARTED

Resolution Backing Nixon Is Delayed by Democrats — Party Lines Re-emerge

By JOHN W. FINNEY
Special to The New York Times

WASHINGTON, April 19 — The Democratic leadership of the Senate thwarted an attempt by a group of Republican conservatives today to rush through a resolution condemning the North Vietnamese as aggressors and endorsing United States policies in Vietnam.

The maneuvering over the resolution, which was introduced by Senator Barry Goldwater, Republican of Arizona, underscored the increasingly partisan division developing in both the Senate and House of Representatives over the Administration's Vietnam policies in the wake of the renewed heavy bombing of North Vietnam.

In both houses, the Administration now faces the task of beating back Democratic-supported amendments to set by legislation a termination date for American involvement in the Vietnam war.

In the past, the Administration has relied upon the lower House to block such amendments passed by the Senate, but now there are indications

Continued on Page 21, Column 2

City's Wage Scale Is Up, But Its Job Total Is Down

By RALPH BLUMENTHAL

New Yorkers got some good news and some bad news yesterday from the Federal Bureau of Labor Statistics at an economic - evaluation conference called "Is New York City Necessary?" Participants agreed it was.

The good news: The city moved up in the last 10 years from 30th to 23d place in wage scales among 46 leading metropolitan areas, and the gap between city workers' earnings and the national average narrowed. Women, blacks and, particularly, black women scored some limited, but impressive, gains.

The bad news: The city suffered a net loss over the last two years of 184,000 jobs—about 80,000 more than had been reported earlier—including one out of every seven manufacturing jobs. At the same time the nation as a whole gained 600,000 jobs.

The items were part of a broad, statistical economic portrait of the city that was presented to 115 businessmen, economists and officials in the gilded Great Hall of the New York Chamber of Commerce, 65 Liberty Street. The presentation was at the invitation of the New York City Council on Economic Education.

Only Cleveland, according to the portrait painted by the

Bureau of Labor Statistics, suffered a greater percentage job loss than New York out of 10 major metropolitan areas.

Among the other economic facts presented were the following:

¶The city's shift from a manufacturing to a service economy is accelerating, opening up opportunities for women that the Federal agency described as "further feminization" of the job market.

¶One indication of the service-economy trend is the loss in the last 10 years of 29,447 of the city's approximately

Continued on Page 37, Column 1

Ex-Parkway Chief Indicted in Jersey

By RONALD SULLIVAN
Special to The New York Times

NEWARK, April 19—D. Louis Tonti, the former operating head of the Garden State Parkway and an unsuccessful candidate for the Democratic nomination for Governor of New Jersey in 1969, was indicted by a Federal grand jury today on charges of bribery, income tax evasion and extortion.

United States Attorney Herbert J. Stern also announced that two other men had been indicted with Mr. Tonti. They were Philip May, the chief engineer of the New Jersey Highway Authority, the agency that operates the parkway, and Giovanni Paolini, a businessman from Rome.

The 47-count indictment charged that the three men had conspired from 1965 to 1971 to

Continued on Page 33, Column 8

China's Table Tennis Team Visits City, Plays at U.N.

[image spans center of page]

Ho Tsu-pin of China and George Braithwaite of United States during exhibition match at the U.N. yesterday
The New York Times/Barton Silverman

By MURRAY SCHUMACH
Special to The New York Times

UNITED NATIONS, N. Y., April 19 — Table tennis replaced speeches tonight at the United Nations as the visiting team from China wound up the first day of its visit to New York with an exhibition that induced many seats in cheers and applause.

The table tennis performance, which lasted about an hour, was not only for the benefit of international friendship, but also to raise money for the United Nations International School here, with tickets selling at prices from $10 to $50 each.

Symptomatic of the goodwill of the Chinese team members was their acceptance of a makeshift playing area that was set up in 24 hours in the Trusteeship Council chamber of the United Nations.

The visitors, in red T-shirts and dark shorts, played members of a blue-clad United Nations team, but the most sustained applause and loudest shouts of admiration were during the games the Chinese

played against one another.

The table tennis performance, which lasted about an hour, was not only for the benefit of international friendship, but also to raise money for the United Nations International School here, with tickets selling at prices from $10 to $50 each.

tour of the building, when the players first walked onto the sawdust-smelling boards and made tentative leaps to test resiliency, one of the players talked briefly, through an interpreter, to C. V. Narasimhan, Under Secretary General, who was acting as guide.

"He said," the Under Secretary recalled later, "that the court is too small. I told him it was the best we could do, and that we even covered some steps below to make it bigger. He was willing to make the best of the situation."

The match came as a climax to the team's first visit to New York after a tour of Canada and several other cities in the United States. Tomorrow at 2:30 P.M. the Chinese are scheduled to play an American team at the Nassau Coliseum in Uniondale, L. I.

The exuberance and speed of the game was in startling contrast to the paneled, almost sculptured, two-story chamber. At times the Chinese players, in their wide-ranging style, went back al-

Continued on Page 38, Column 7

F.T.C. Assails Pain-Killer Ads; Says They Mislead the Public

By JOHN D. MORRIS
Special to The New York Times

WASHINGTON, April 19—The Federal Trade Commission, contending that one nonprescription pain killer is about as effective as another, accused the manufacturers of Anacin, Bayer Aspirin, Bufferin and Excedrin today of deceptive advertising.

The commission published proposed complaints and cease-and-desist orders against the country's three leading producers of such pain killers, called analgesics, and their advertising agencies.

The commission said that the manufacturers had misled the public by advertising their respective products as significantly superior to others.

Aspirin is the main ingredient of all the products, and there is no significant difference be-

tween brands of aspirin, according to the commission.

Also challenged as deceptive were advertisements depicting analgesics as effective in relieving stress and tension.

The Food and Drug Administration, meanwhile, published findings by the National Academy of Sciences on effectiveness claims made by 14 analgesics and 18 antacid drugs. The report, commissioned by the F.D.A., cast doubt on the validity of a number of the claims.

Continued on Page 28, Column 4

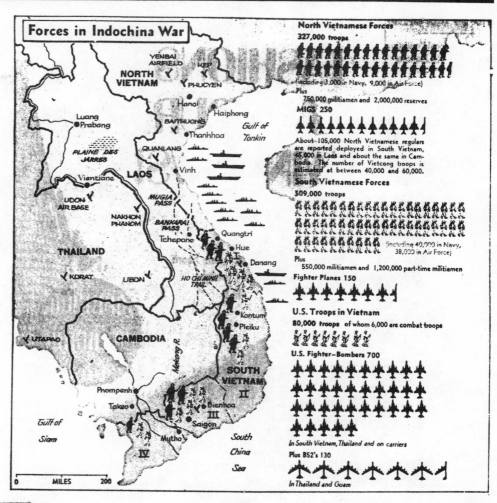

Half of the 6,000 American combat troops still in South Vietnam were west and northwest of Da Nang. Others were in Bien Hoa, northeast of Saigon. Besides its four carriers, the U.S. had more than 20 ships shelling targets north and south of the DMZ. About 50 B-52s were at U-Tapao in Thailand and 80 to 100 on Guam. On the Communist side, forces in Laos were said to include more than 20,000 local men, with several thousand in Cambodian forces.

In April 1972, U.S. warships were reportedly attacked by Migs and patrol boats near the buffer zone (1) U.S. jets resumed heavy raids on North Vietnam's panhandle (2) Fighting flared near Quang Tri and (3) and Hoaian (4) was overrun by enemy forces. On the military front north of Saigon, Laikhe (5) came under attack. In Cambodia, enemy units cut the key Route 1 (6).

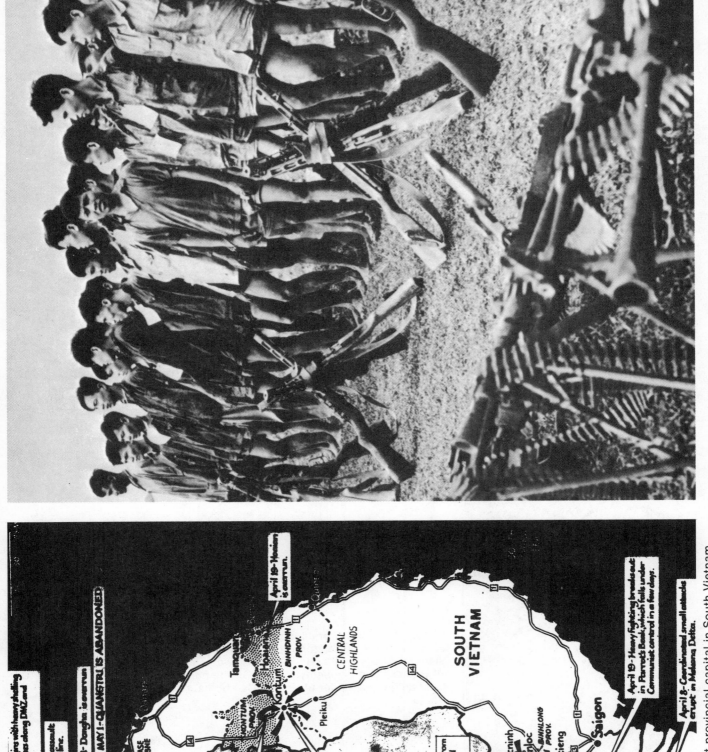

Captured Communists are seen with their arms after South Vietnam stemmed a Communist invasion.

Quang Tri City was the first provincial capital in South Vietnam lost as a result of an enemy offensive. This map details the course of the Communist offensive that began in March 1972 and ended with the fall of Quang Tri on May 1.

184

"All the News That's Fit to Print"

The New York Times

LATE CITY EDITION

Weather: Sunny, cool today; clear and cool tonight. Milder tomorrow. Temp. range: today 37-59; Wed. 38-58. Full U.S. report on Page 85.

VOL. CXXI . . No. 41,732 — © 1972 The New York Times Company — NEW YORK, THURSDAY, APRIL 27, 1972 — 15 CENTS

MUSKIE REPORTED READY TO END ACTIVE CANDIDACY; LIKELY TO FREE DELEGATES

The New York Times/Mike Lien

DECISION-MAKING TIME: Senator Edmund S. Muskie peering from the doorway of his home near Washington yesterday after Mrs. Muskie said good-by to former Defense Secretary Clark Clifford, left, and former Senator Albert Gore of Tennessee.

CANCELS OHIO TRIP

Aides Are Unanimous in Urging Senator to Pull Out Now

By JAMES M. NAUGHTON
Special to The New York Times

WASHINGTON, April 26—Senator Edmund S. Muskie will reportedly withdraw tomorrow from an active campaign for the Democratic Presidential nomination.

The Senator from Maine decided this afternoon, according to distressed architects of his candidacy, that he should pull out of the race and release delegates who are pledged to support him at the Democratic National Convention.

The decision followed the unanimous recommendation of Mr. Muskie's national campaign staff that he withdraw and hold himself out as a possible compromise nominee at a deadlocked convention.

Poor Primary Showings

This was regarded as the only remaining route to an objective that had slipped farther from Mr. Muskie's reach with each of the six state primaries held so far.

The recommendation, based upon Mr. Muskie's poor showings in primaries yesterday in Pennsylvania and Massachusetts, was relayed to the Senator at a meeting with senior staff members and close personal advisers at his home in suburban Bethesda, Md.

Mr. Muskie canceled a scheduled trip tonight to Toledo, where he was to have opened a week-long attempt to revive his candidacy in the Ohio primary next Tuesday.

He Will Stay on Ballot

Even if he withdraws, he will remain on the ballot in that state and in any others where he has entered primaries.

Richard H. Stewart, the Senator's press secretary, issued a statement in which he said Mr. Muskie was "presently evaluating the political situation" and announced that the Senator would hold a news conference tomorrow in the Capitol.

"He has been consulting with his family and his friends and supporters throughout the day and he will continue to do so throughout the evening," Mr. Stewart said.

Later, Mr. Stewart said, "I categorically deny any statements that he's decided to withdraw."

But the word of Mr. Mus-

Continued on Page 32, Column 5

Humphrey Plurality Solid In Pennsylvania Delegates

By DONALD JANSON
Special to The New York Times

PHILADELPHIA, April 26—Senator Hubert H. Humphrey of Minnesota won not only the popularity poll in Pennsylvania's Democratic Presidential primary yesterday but also a solid plurality of the state's elected delegates to the party's national convention, nearly complete returns showed today.

However, the double-barreled Humphrey triumph, while vital to the former Vice President's viability as a candidate, was not so surprising as the strength shown by Gov. George C. Wallace of Alabama, who finished second, and Senator George McGovern of South Dakota, or the extent of the collapse of Senator Edmund S. Muskie of Maine, who concentrated on Pennsylvania for three weeks.

The delegate count, completed this afternoon, gave Mr. Humphrey 57, Senator McGovern 37, Senator Muskie 29 and Governor Wallace 2.

Leads in Delegates

In Massachusetts, Senator McGovern's sweeping primary victory approached an avalanche. He captured 52 per cent of the popularity poll, carried every Congressional district and won all of the state's 102 first-ballot votes at the national convention. [Details on Page 32.]

Senator McGovern also took the lead in committed delegates nationally. According to a compilation by The New York Times, he now has 232.5, against 134.5 for Senator Muskie and 77 each for Senator Humphrey and Governor Wallace. It will take 1,509 delegate votes to win the nomination in Miami Beach in July.

In Pennsylvania, 12 of the 137 newly elected delegates are uncommitted, but some of these favor Mr. Humphrey. And his delegate lead in Pennsylvania will be further extended next

Continued on Page 32, Column 1

SURVEY CONTRASTS 2 FRONT-RUNNERS

In Times Study, Humphrey and McGovern Are Found to Differ in Appeal

By JACK ROSENTHAL

Senators Hubert H. Humphrey and George McGovern, now the two front-runners for the Democratic Presidential nomination, came out of the Pennsylvania primary Tuesday with strongly different constituencies and with their contrasting public images even more sharply drawn.

A New York Times survey of voters disclosed significant, often striking contrasts between supporters of the two men with respect to age, race, residence, religion, ideology and issues.

Compared with Senator McGovern, Senator Humphrey did considerably better Tuesday in the cities, among more conservative Democrats and among blacks, older adults, blue-collar workers and voters impressed by governmental experience.

Senator McGovern, by contrast, did considerably better in suburbs and small towns, among liberals, women and young first-time voters and among those concerned over issues, notably the Vietnam war and business influence on government.

The survey strongly suggested that, after a campaign

Continued on Page 32, Column 5

Hogan Weighs Perjury Charge Against Kriegel for Knapp Data

By DAVID BURNHAM

The office of Manhattan District Attorney Frank S. Hogan decided last week to press perjury charges against Jay L. Kriegel, a mayoral assistant, but then suspended its decision pending receipt of a final legal memorandum from Mr. Kriegel's lawyer.

Mr. Hogan, in response to an inquiry, confirmed yesterday that he was awaiting the memorandum on Mr. Kriegel, one of Mayor Lindsay's closest advisers.

According to law enforcement sources, the prosecutor's office, after months of internal debate, had decided to present to a grand jury the question whether the conflicts in Mr. Kriegel's testimony to the Knapp Commission during its investigation of alleged police corruption constituted perjury.

The key conflict centers on whether Mr. Kriegel told Mr. Lindsay that two policemen had informed him that they believed their department had closed its eyes to a serious allegation of police corruption.

But at the last moment, the sources said, Mr. Kriegel's lawyer requested time to submit a memorandum on some of the factual and legal questions involved in the possible prosecution, and the District Attorney's office agreed to hold up its

Continued on Page 24, Column 1

FORD EARNINGS UP 49% IN QUARTER; CAR PRICE CUT $13

Reduction Made to Put '72 Profit Margin Within the Guideline of U.S. Panel

Special to The New York Times

DETROIT, April 26—Ford Motor Company announced today record earnings of $252-million in the first three months of 1972, up 49 per cent from the January-March period last year. It also said that it was cutting car and truck prices an average of $13 per unit.

The company chairman, Henry Ford 2d, and the president, Lee A. Iacocca, said that a high sales volume and management efficiencies "have substantially improved our profitability."

They said that this "had led us to reduce prices to assure that our 1972 profit margin will be within Price Commission guidelines."

The announcements came two days after the Federal Price Commission in Washington had rejected a Ford request for an increase on some industrial products. The company said that the increase would have added $2-million to annual sales.

New Productivity Rule

In Washington, meanwhile, C. Jackson Grayson Jr., chairman of the Price Commission, said that a new rule on productivity would go into effect on Monday, and that, as a result, permitted price increases would be smaller. [Details on Page 14.]

Ford reported earnings in the first quarter of 1972 of $2.44 a share. Last year, earnings were $169-million, or $1.57 a share. The company said that a strike against Ford of Britain last year reduced the earnings figure by 38 cents a share. [Details on Page 59.]

The company said that the price reductions on the 1972 models would be effective tomorrow and would include units now in dealers' stock.

A company spokesman said that while the cuts average $13 a unit, or 0.3 per cent, only high-volume car lines were affected. He said that the cuts involved 31 of the company's 79 series of cars.

A spokesman said that the cars being cut in price accounted for 48.8 per cent of the company's domestic car sales last year.

The reductions included $16 on four series of regular-size Ford cars—the Custom, Custom 500, LTD and LTD Brougham—and two series in the full-sized Mercury line—the Monterey and Monterey Custom.

The reductions equal $33 on

Continued on Page 15, Column 1

Splashdown Today

Apollo 16 was on course for a scheduled splashdown today at 2:44 P.M., Eastern standard time, in the Pacific Ocean. Details, Page 29.

NIXON TO WITHDRAW 20,000 MORE; EXPRESSES OPTIMISM ON VIETNAM; FOE BEGINS NEW QUANGTRI DRIVE

Associated Press

TAKING REFUGE: South Vietnamese soldier and family, on motorcycle, at checkpoint at entrance to Kontum, hard-pressed Central Highlands capital. Many fled area.

SPEECH TO NATION

President Is Expecting Progress in Paris—Air Raids to Go On

By ROBERT B. SEMPLE Jr.
Special to The New York Times

WASHINGTON, April 26 President Nixon said tonight that he was continuing his troop withdrawal program despite the heavy enemy offensive in South Vietnam.

In a nationwide television and radio address, Mr. Nixon

Transcript of Nixon speech appears on Page 20.

announced that 20,000 more troops would be withdrawn from South Vietnam by July 1, a move that would reduce authorized American troop strength to 49,000.

While sober and earnest in his presentation before the cameras, the President sounded a generally optimistic note about the military situation in Vietnam, and while not going into detail, he also said he was approaching the resumption of the Paris peace talks tomorrow with considerable hope. In Paris earlier, the Vietnamese Communists had agreed to attend. [Page 21.]

Evaluation by Abrams

Mr. Nixon said that he had received this morning an evaluation of the fighting from his commander in Vietnam—Gen. Creighton W. Abrams—and that the general was convinced that despite four weeks of bitter fighting the South Vietnamese could contain the invasion "if we continue to provide air and sea support."

The President pledged to continue such support and to persist with air and naval attacks on enemy installations in North Vietnam "until the North Vietnamese stop their offensive in South Vietnam."

On the diplomatic front, Mr. Nixon offered no new negotiating proposals, asserting that the United States had already offered generous terms for peace. But he said that despite the enemy's refusal to accept these terms, or even talk seriously about them, "we are resuming the Paris talks with the firm expectation that productive talks leading to rapid progress will follow through all available channels."

Although the address was advertised in advance as a speech on troop levels and an evaluation of the military conditions in the field, Mr. Nixon

Continued on Page 20, Column 1

City in Northern Region Reported Under Attack

By JOSEPH B. TREASTER
Special to The New York Times

SAIGON, South Vietnam, Thursday, April 27—North Vietnamese troops were reported advancing on Quangtri city this morning from the west and southwest in what some military officers said might be a renewed attempt to take the provincial capital.

The number of North Vietnamese involved in the attack was not immediately known, but one officer said it appeared to be a "pretty good size" force.

He said the North Vietnamese had paved the way for their advance with artillery fire, and he added that tanks had been sighted a few miles west of Quangtri.

The weather, he said, was "not all that good," suggesting that American and South Vietnamese planes might be hampered in attempts to blunt the North Vietnamese move, which has been expected since the fighting was stalemated there three weeks ago.

Also today, military officers reported that two heavy battles had broken out in the vicinity of Dautieng, 40 miles northwest of Saigon. There were no details immediately available.

Meanwhile, the North Vietnamese appeared to be continuing their efforts to cut South Vietnam in two, having overrun another fire base near the coast in Binhdinh Province, edging closer to the Central Highlands capital of Kontum.

A South Vietnamese spokes-

Continued on Page 21, Column 4

KONTUM IS FACING DO-OR-DIE BATTLE

20 Battalions in Highlands City Expect Encirclement by Enemy Armor Soon

By MALCOLM W. BROWNE
Special to The New York Times

KONTUM, South Vietnam, April 26—With Saigon's military leadership in the Central Highlands seemingly close to paralysis as a result of recent defeats, South Vietnamese troops and their American advisers are preparing to make a do-or-die stand at this key city.

Heavy Soviet-made rockets fired from the heights ringing Kontum have made its airstrip unusable. The hulks of two transport planes lie skewed across a taxiway.

Enemy forces, including many tanks, are expected to surround the picturesque city soon, and emergency defenses against tanks are being prepared. Soldiers are being given quick courses in tank fighting and are being issued great numbers of new American-made armor-piercing rockets.

The remnants of shattered units are drifting into Kontum, sometimes in twos and threes, sometimes a hundred at a time. The American advisers are trying to help reorganize them into some semblance of fighting units.

Military men say there are about 20 battalions here for

Continued on Page 21, Column 6

POLLUTION BONDS GET ALBANY START

Senate Passes Bill to Create $1.15-Billion Issue for Environmental Needs

By ALFONSO A. NARVAEZ
Special to The New York Times

ALBANY, April 26—The Senate today unanimously approved a bill authorizing the state to create a $1.15-billion environmental conservation bond issue to provide funds for air, water and land environmental projects across the state during the next five years.

The bill now goes to the Assembly, where passage is expected. It provides for spending $650-million for cleaning up state waterways, $150-million to combat air pollution and $350-million for land preservation and improvement projects.

A measure providing deferred tuition loans to students in both public and private colleges throughout the state, which won final approval in the Assembly yesterday, is expected to be signed by Governor Rockefeller. The bill is believed to be the first of its kind enacted by any state.

The question of the bond issue will be presented to the voters in a referendum in the November election, if it is signed into law as expected.

The bill, introduced by Senator Bernard C. Smith, Republican of Northport, L. I., would

Continued on Page 35, Column 2

The New York Times/Nancy Moran

LONDONDERRY VIGILANTE: Hooded member of Irish Republican Army guarding a street in Bogside, one of the Roman Catholic areas of Northern Ireland town. Vigilantes control traffic, stopping strangers. Hoods are worn normally for duty. Details, Page 3.

Sweig Gets Parole; Ginzburg Loses Bid

Special to The New York Times

WASHINGTON, April 26—The United States Board of Parole granted today paroles to Dr. Martin Sweig, a 50-year-old former administrative assistant to former House Speaker John W. McCormack, Democrat of Massachusetts, and to Anthony De Angelis, the key figure in a $150-million salad-oil swindle.

The board denied parole to Ralph Ginzburg, the former publisher of Eros magazine, who was convicted of sending pornographic material through the mail.

Sweig's parole is effective July 17. He is now at the Fed-

Continued on Page 18, Column 4

Brezhnev Initiative Is Said to Have Led To Kissinger Visit

By BERNARD GWERTZMAN
Special to The New York Times

WASHINGTON, April 26 — Leonid I. Brezhnev, the Soviet Communist party leader, personally initiated Henry A. Kissinger's secret weekend trip to Moscow, a well-placed Administration source said today. Mr. Brezhnev and Mr. Kissinger discussed the Vietnam situation and other issues sure to arise during President Nixon's visit to the Soviet Union next month.

The official said that Mr. Brezhnev's suggestion that a trusted aide of Mr. Nixon come to Moscow was made recently in a letter to the President. Mr. Nixon, after consulting with Mr. Kissinger, his adviser on national security, and with Secretary of State William P. Rogers, decided to send Mr. Kissinger to have his views made known as clearly as possible to Mr. Brezhnev.

At a briefing for newsmen tonight, before Mr. Nixon's Vietnam speech, Mr. Kissinger

Continued on Page 21, Column 1

NEWS INDEX

News Summary and Index, Page 45

"All the News That's Fit to Print"

The New York Times

LATE CITY EDITION

Weather: Cooler, rain likely today, tonight. Cloudy, milder tomorrow. Temp. range: today 55-63; Monday 58-74. Full U.S. report on Page 86.

VOL. CXXI . . No. 41,737 © 1972 The New York Times Company NEW YORK, TUESDAY, MAY 2, 1972 15 CENTS

ADMINISTRATION EXEMPTS ONE-QUARTER OF ECONOMY FROM PAY-PRICE CONTROLS

SMALL UNITS FREE

Employers With Work Forces of Up to 60 Affected by Move

By PHILIP SHABECOFF
Special to The New York Times

WASHINGTON, May 1—The Administration exempted millions of small businesses and local governments from wage and price controls today, effectively freeing more than a quarter of the nation's total work force and sales from compliance with its economic stabilization program.

The Cost of Living Council announced that all businesses or government units with 60 or fewer employes need no longer comply with wage and price regulations.

The decision affects five million small concerns and about $500-billion in annual sales, or 28 per cent of the nation's total annual sales.

19 Million Exempt

It also means that 19 million workers, or 26 per cent of all payroll employment, will be exempt from wage controls. Some of these had already been exempted as low-wage workers earning $1.90 an hour or less.

Meanwhile, Herbert Stein, chairman of the President's Council of Economic Advisers, sought to allay business fears that the Administration was seeking to put a harsh limit on corporate profits.

In a speech to the Economic Club in New York, he said that there was "reasonable" limits on profit margins, but added that "for business to become frightened at this moment would not only be entirely without foundation but could also precipitate controversy which would really undermine the [controls] system and impede recovery." [Page 57.]

Donald Rumsfeld, director of the Cost of Living Council, said the new exemptions "are not a step toward decontrol or Phase Three."

'Logical Next Steps'

"They are the logical next steps in the refinement of the economic stabilization program," he said.

The decision to exempt small business and government, Mr. Rumsfeld said, will "eliminate unnecessary red tape" from administration and enforcement of the stabilization program and will allow better allocation of the program's limited resources.

The chairman of the Price Commission, C. Jackson Grayson Jr., along with other commissioners, did not concur with the decision to exempt the small businesses, commission staff officials said today.

The commission reportedly believed that, while the decision would have no adverse economic impact, the timing of it might

Continued on Page 14, Column 3

U.M.W. Election of Boyle Is Upset by Federal Judge

By JUAN M. VASQUEZ
Special to The New York Times

WASHINGTON, May 1 — A United States District Court judge here set aside today the election of W. A. Boyle as president of the 200,000-member United Mine Workers of America.

In a 33-page decision, Judge William B. Bryant found that the evidence of wrongdoing by Mr. Boyle and other incumbents in the 1969 election was "too strong to resist." He instructed the Department of Justice to prepare an appropriate order by Monday formally declaring the election results void.

The decision cited violations of Federal law by the union leadership that affected the outcome of the election in many ways. The leaders were fighting an insurgent slate headed by Joseph A. Yablonski, who was slain, along with his wife and daughter, at their home in Clarksville, Pa., on Dec. 31, 1969, three weeks after the election.

Associated Press

W. A. Boyle

Judge Bryant found, for example, that there had been an improper use of the union newspaper to promote Mr. Boyle, improper campaign expenditures and failure to provide adequate safeguards for a fair election.

His findings were the culmination of a six-month trial following the filing of a civil

Continued on Page 28, Column 1

U.S. Indicts G.M. and Ford For Car Fleet Price-Fixing

By JERRY M. FLINT
Special to The New York Times

DETROIT, May 1 — The nation's two largest auto makers, the General Motors Corporation and the Ford Motor Company, were charged today by a Federal grand jury with violating antitrust laws by conspiring to refuse to cut car prices to fleet buyers.

The case stems from a price war, started by the Chrysler Corporation, to win over fleet customers — rental and leasing companies, governmental units and other companies that buy many vehicles. Chrysler cut prices for these customers. General Motors and Ford followed. Then G.M. and Ford stopped the discounts.

State and local governments began suing G.M. and Ford on antitrust grounds. An 18-month grand jury investigation followed and ended in today's indictment.

Ironically, Chrysler is also being sued, by dealers who charge that the two-price system—lower prices for fleet customers and higher prices

Continued on Page 11, Column 1

Beame, in Albany, Says the City Needs Less Than It Asks

By ALFONSO A. NARVAEZ
Special to The New York Times

ALBANY, May 1—New York City's Controller, Abraham D. Beame, told Democratic legislative leaders today that the city needed only $40-million in new state aid, not the $227-million the Lindsay administration has asked for, to meet an anticipated budget gap for the next fiscal year.

The Controller said that the city would not have to impose the full $141-million in nuisance taxes authorized by the Legislature last year and not acted upon by the City Council. Nor, he said, would there be a need for the two-week furlough of city employes as proposed by the Mayor.

Mr. Beame said that implementation of the Mayor's budget plan—with the exception of the $141-million in nuisance taxes—would leave a gap of $368-million. Under the Mayor's plan, this figure would be made up by the $227-million being requested as new state aid and the $141-million in taxes.

The $368-million, Mr. Beame said, could be raised by imposi-

Continued on Page 33, Column 5

U.S. VOICES HOPE OF EXPANDED PACT ON LIMITING ARMS

It Suggests That Exchanges by Nixon and Brezhnev May Have Broken Impasse

By ROBERT B. SEMPLE Jr.
Special to The New York Times

WASHINGTON, May 1—The White House said today that private exchanges between President Nixon and Leonid I. Brezhnev, the Soviet Communist party leader, had advanced the prospect for a significant broadening of the scope of an agreement limiting strategic arms.

A White House spokesman provided no further details, but hinted strongly that a key issue that had stalemated the arms talks might be near resolution. That issue has been an American demand for inclusion of submarine-launched missiles in any first-stage arms accord.

In an announcement late this afternoon, Ronald L. Ziegler, the White House press secretary, said that President Nixon, on the basis of a series of "confidential exchanges" with Mr. Brezhnev, had concluded that the "possibility of reaching an agreement has substantially improved." Mr. Nixon is scheduled to go to Moscow May 22 for talks with Soviet leaders.

'New Instructions' Given

Mr. Ziegler also said that the President had directed the chief United States negotiator, Gerard C. Smith, to return to the conference at Helsinki with "new instructions." The press secretary said that these, together with new instructions Mr. Nixon was "confident the Soviet representative will receive from his Government, can lead to an agreement which is mutually acceptable to both sides."

Mr. Ziegler spoke to newsmen after an afternoon meeting held by the President with Mr. Smith and other key advisers on national security policy. Mr. Smith planned to leave later for Helsinki, the site of the current round of the talks.

Early Accord Sought

Asked directly whether there had been an agreement in principle to resolve the submarine issue, Mr. Ziegler replied that he was not prepared "to discuss details."

"But I would say that what I'm referring to is a major advance and relates to a broadening of the scope of an offensive freeze," he added.

The press secretary said that Mr. Nixon had engaged in confidential exchanges with Mr. Brezhnev in an effort "to see whether major remaining issues

Continued on Page 5, Column 4

SOUTH VIETNAMESE QUIT QUANGTRI; 80 AMERICAN ADVISERS FLOWN OUT; ENEMY IS WITHIN 15 MILES OF HUE

United Press International

U.S. advisers waiting yesterday in landing zone at Quangtri before copter flew them out

PROVINCE IS LOST

Victory Foe's Biggest Since Month-Old Invasion Began

By SYDNEY H. SCHANBERG
Special to The New York Times

HUE, South Vietnam, Tuesday, May 2—The South Vietnamese abandoned Quangtri, their northernmost province capital, yesterday, giving the advancing North Vietnamese their biggest prize so far in their month-old invasion.

The city, the first province capital to be lost since the offensive began March 30, was abandoned by Government forces yesterday afternoon after three days of shelling during which the enemy moved troops and tanks to the edge of the city.

The loss of Quangtri city gave the North Vietnamese control of the entire northern province of the same name.

B-52's Covered Retreat

About 80 American advisers, the commander of the South Vietnamese Third Division and his staff were evacuated in the afternoon in four big rescue helicopters that flew through heavy enemy ground fire to get the men out.

United States B-52's reportedly bombed areas as close as one mile to the northeast of Quangtri city between noon yesterday and 6 A.M. today in efforts first to beat off the enemy attack and then to cover the retreat of the Government forces. One of the 14 missions was nine miles south of Quangtri.

Meanwhile, South Vietnamese units retreated southward toward the even more important city of Hue, Vietnam's ancient imperial capital, in Thuathien Province. They were accompanied by 10 American advisers who had decided to stay with them.

Steady Push by Foe

Hue, with a population that has swollen to more than 300,000 by fleeing refugees, is now directly threatened. The North Vietnamese have reportedly moved to within less than 15 miles of the city on the west and about 25 miles on the north.

[On other fronts, North Vietnamese troops reportedly continued their advance in northern Binhdinh Province on the central coast and tightened their siege of the province capital of Kontum to the west. On the front closer to Saigon, Anloc, the besieged province capital that has been nearly flattened by enemy fire, was subjected anew to intense artillery bombardment.]

Reports reaching Hue indicated that Quangtri had been abandoned without much of a fight by Government troops.

Describing the situation,

Continued on Page 20, Column 1

The Times Wins a Pulitzer For the Pentagon Papers

By PETER KIHSS

The 1972 Pulitzer Prize for meritorious public service in journalism was awarded yesterday to The New York Times for publication of the Pentagon Papers — documents showing how the United States became involved in the Vietnam war.

Jack Anderson, the syndicated columnist, won the Pulitzer Prize for national reporting for his disclosures of Nixon Administration policymaking during the India-Pakistan war.

But for what was believed to be the first time in the 56-year history of the prizes, the Columbia University board of trustees, who officially award them, issued a statement saying a board majority "had deep reservations about the timeliness and suitability of certain of the journalism awards."

While the trustees said they had accepted all the recommendations made by the advisory board on the Pulitzer Prizes, largely because they had done so in the past, they added that "had the selections been those of the trustees alone, certain of the recipients would not have been chosen."

Although none of the members of the 23-man board of trustees who could be reached would be quoted on which awards were opposed, it was learned that the controversy involved the prizes for Mr. Anderson and The Times. In both instances, there was argument over the way that official Government documents had fallen into journalistic hands.

In addition to 11 prizes in journalism, there were six awards in letters and one for music. For the first time since 1968, no award was made for drama.

The cultural awards were as follows:

General Nonfiction — "Stilwell and the American Experience in China, 1911-1945," by Barbara W. Tuchman, her second Pulitzer Prize following her 1963 award for "The Guns of August."

Biography — "Eleanor and Franklin," by Joseph P. Lash, the private and public lives of President and Mrs. Franklin D. Roosevelt.

Fiction—"Angle of Repose," by Wallace Stegner, who directs the writing program at Stanford University.

History—"Neither Black Nor

Continued on Page 37, Column 2

ALLIED PROGRAM FAILS A KEY TEST

Vietnamization Hope Dashed in Coastal Province as Foe Overruns 3 Districts

By CRAIG R. WHITNEY
Special to The New York Times

QUINHON, South Vietnam, May 1—In Binhdinh Province, here on the coast of Central Vietnam, three county-size districts with a combined population of 200,000 have fallen to Communist attacks in two weeks with little real resistance.

Several years' work on pacification programs has been lost and Vietnamization has failed one of its most crucial tests. And the failure is readily conceded by both South Vietnamese and American officials in Quinhon, the provincial capital.

A regiment of South Vietnam's army, reduced to a quarter of its 3,000-man strength largely through desertions, is under attack near here. Few American advisers or South Vietnamese officials believe that it will pull through.

The unit—the 40th Regiment, fighting at a nearby landing zone named English—has reportedly failed every test it has faced in the last two weeks.

Since the fall of the Hoaian district on April 19, said a high-ranking South Vietnamese official who asked that his name not be disclosed, "the 40th Regiment has only 25 per cent of its strength—30 per cent were casualties and 40 per cent or so deserted."

"We lost Hoainhon after that because the local militia troops were demoralized," the official said.

"They thought the regular army had let them down," he

Continued on Page 20, Column 6

NASA via United Press International

AT LUNAR CRATER'S EDGE: Lieut. Col. Charles M. Duke Jr. carries scooper to pick up samples near the Apollo 16 landing site. At rear is lunar rover. Capt. John W. Young took photo, issued yesterday. Another photo is on Page 28.

Halpern to Forgo House Race; Only City G.O.P. Congressman

By FRANK LYNN

Representative Seymour Halpern, New York City's only Republican Congressman, has told Republican leaders that he will not seek re-election to an eighth term in the House this year.

In conversations with G.O.P. leaders in Queens and Nassau Counties and members of the Rockefeller administration, the 58-year-old Congressman, who had tripartisan endorsement in his Queens district two years ago, has cited his health and the stiff contest he faces with a Democratic incumbent, Representative Lester L. Wolff, as his reasons for quitting. The two incumbents have been reapportioned into the same district.

Mr. Wolff, who lives in Great Neck, L.I., intended to make a major issue of charges dating from 1969 that Mr. Halpern had run up debts of more than $100,000 to several banks while he was a member of the House Banking and Currency Committee. Mr. Halpern also had outstanding hotel, restaurant, telephone and credit-card bills.

Mr. Halpern acknowledged that he had a number of unspecified loans and debts but denied any conflict with his duties on the banking committee. He was cleared by the House Ethics Committee but was reassigned last year from the banking committee, where he was the third-ranking Republican, and the Veterans Af-

Continued on Page 24, Column 4

Legislature Backs Formation Of Siting Unit for Power Plants

By FRANCIS X. CLINES
Special to The New York Times

ALBANY, May 1—The Legislature approved today the creation of a power plant siting board that would have full authority to overrule local zoning regulations and settle controversies involving utility, environmental and community factions.

The need for such a panel with the power and responsibility to say yes or no has been cited repeatedly by the Governor as the only way to break the logjam of power plant controversies that has been growing with the public's concern for the environmental issue.

Meanwhile, with the Legislature moving toward adjournment, the Governor was reported to have agreed with the leaders on a bill creating an 11-member state commission to revise New York City's Charter.

[Details on Page 46.]

In the Assembly, most of the debate was on bills that would make homeowner's mortgages more expensive. One measure, which would have increased the insurance premiums of homes

Continued on Page 32, Column 3

NEWS INDEX

"All the News That's Fit to Print"

The New York Times

LATE CITY EDITION

Weather: Showers likely today and tonight. Partly cloudy tomorrow. Temp. range: today 63-75; Tuesday 60-75. Full U.S. report on Page 94.

VOL. CXXI . No. 41,738 NEW YORK, WEDNESDAY, MAY 3, 1972 15 CENTS

Story of Joe Gallo's Murder: 5 in Colombo Gang Implicated

Informant, in Fear, Goes to the F.B.I.

By NICHOLAS GAGE

An associate of the Mafia family of Joseph A. Colombo Sr. has turned himself in to the Federal Bureau of Investigation and said that he and four other men carried out the killing of Joseph Gallo on April 7, according to law-enforcement officials.

An investigation by The New York Times has established that the informant, who is now in police custody, is Joseph Luparelli, a close associate of Joseph Yacovelli, now the acting head of the Colombo family and the man who officials believe sanctioned the Gallo murder.

The New York Times

Joseph Yacovelli after he appeared in the Brooklyn Federal Court last year.

The officials said that over the last three weeks Luparelli had given Federal authorities and the New York police the following account of the events surrounding the shooting of Gallo, a Colombo rival, at Umberto's Clam House on Mulberry Street:

At about 4:30 A.M. on April 7, Luparelli happened to be sitting at the clam bar in Umberto's with a friend. Ten minutes later Joseph Gallo, who was celebrating his 43d birthday, entered with a jovial group—his bride of three weeks, her 10-year-old daughter, Gallo's sister, his bodyguard Peter Diapoulas, 42, and the latter's date.

When he saw Gallo, who for several months had been marked for execution by the Colombo family, Luparelli dropped his spoon and hurried out of the restaurant.

He walked two blocks to another restaurant nearby frequented by Colombo men. Luparelli asked for Yacovelli, acting head of the family since Colombo was gravely wounded last year at a Columbus Circle rally of the Italian-American Civil Rights League. He was told that Yacovelli was not around.

Suspects Abandon Hideout in Nyack

Then Luparelli related what he had seen to Philip Gambino, a Colombo man, and Carmine Di Biase, a former member of the family of the late Vito Genovese who had reportedly shifted to the Colombo group.

The two of them telephoned Yacovelli and were told to arm themselves, according to Luparelli. Gambino and Di Biase left the restaurant briefly and returned about 5:15 with several guns.

Luparelli, two men believed to be brothers whom Luparelli has not as yet identified, Gambino and Di Biase then drove two cars down Mulberry Street and parked not far from Umberto's. One of the cars was to serve as a "crash" car to intercept any car that tried to thwart the getaway.

All but one of the five entered Umberto's through the back door. Luparelli says he stayed at the wheel of one of the cars.

As the four gunmen casually

Continued on Page 39, Column 1

Yoichi Okamoto/Rapho Guillumette

J. Edgar Hoover

J. Edgar Hoover, 77, Dies; Will Lie in State in Capitol

By FRED P. GRAHAM

Special to The New York Times

WASHINGTON, May 2—J. Edgar Hoover, who directed the Federal Bureau of Investigation for 48 years and built it into a dominant and controversial force in American law enforcement, died during the night from the effects of high blood pressure.

Mr. Hoover, who at 77 years of age still held the F.B.I. firmly within his control, died in his bedroom after working a full day in his office yesterday. He was found by his housekeeper at 8:30 this morning, slumped on the floor beside his bed.

His home is near Rock Creek Park in the northwest section of Washington.

Dr. James L. Luke, Washington's Medical Examiner, attributed the death to "hypertensive cardio-vascular disease." He said that Mr. Hoover had been suffering from a heart ailment for some time but gave no details.

He said that death could have been caused by heart failure associated with high blood pressure, but that no autopsy would be performed because the death was known to be due to natural causes.

Acting Attorney General Richard G. Kleindienst announced the death at 11 A.M., after F.B.I. offices around the world had been given the news and reports of it began to circulate here. Congress promptly voted its permission for his body to lie in state in the Capitol Rotunda—an honor accorded to only 21 persons before, of whom eight were Presidents or former Presidents.

Mr. Hoover's body will be taken to the Rotunda tomorrow morning and will lie in state until shortly before the funeral Thursday. Arrangements for the funeral were incomplete today, but it was learned that President Nixon would deliver the eulogy at 11 A.M. Thursday at the National Presbyterian

Continued on Page 53, Column 1

BASES NEAR HUE ATTACKED; SOUTH VIETNAMESE TROOPS FLEE QUANGTRI IN DISORDER

Retreat Leaves Small Unit Of Marines Facing Enemy

By SYDNEY H. SCHANBERG

Special to The New York Times

HUE, South Vietnam, May 2—Thousands of panicking South Vietnamese soldiers—most of whom did not appear to have made much contact with the advancing North Vietnamese—fled in confusion from Quangtri Province today, streaming south down Route 1 like a rabble out of control.

Commandeering civilian vehicles at rifle point, feigning nonexistent injuries, carrying away C rations but not their ammunition, and hurling rocks at Western news photographers taking pictures of their flight, the Government troops of the Third Infantry Division ran from the fighting in one of the biggest retreats of the war.

No one tried to stop them: their officers were running too.

The battlefront north of Hue was thus left solely to a brigade of a few thousand South Vietnamese marines.

The Third Division had fallen back before, at the beginning of the enemy offensive a month ago, but the commander, Brig. Gen. Vu Van Giai, had managed to scrape it together again and put it back on the line around Quangtri until yesterday.

But today, according to American advisers, virtually the entire division—about 10,000 infantrymen plus 1,000 rangers—was in rout, not even stopping at the checkpoints where military policemen were supposed to halt runaways and turn them around.

It was the force that was supposed to have defended the city of Quangtri, which was abandoned yesterday and which had been the northernmost town held by the Government.

There does not seem to be much now between the North Vietnamese and their next and and more important objective,

Continued on Page 20, Column 4

NEW ASSAULT DUE

U.S. General Expects Enemy Step-Up in Next Few Days

By HENRY KAMM

Special to The New York Times

SAIGON, South Vietnam, Wednesday, May 3—With the city of Quangtri lost, two South Vietnamese fire bases on the approaches to the former imperial capital of Hue were reported under enemy attack yesterday.

Hue itself, 32 miles southeast of the fallen capital of Quangtri Province, was bracing for a North Vietnamese onslaught.

Serious attacks could be expected in the next few days, newsmen in Hue were told last night by Brig. Gen. Thomas W. Bowen, senior adviser to the regional commander. United States intelligence sources estimated that it would take the enemy forces six to eight days to prepare for the assault.

Artillery Batters Base

United States military sources said last night that Fire Base Nancy, the northernmost position held by the South Vietnamese and their last one in Quangtri Province, was battered by enemy artillery. [United Press International, quoting officers in the field, said enemy soldiers attacking with the support of tanks had seized part of the outpost.]

The base, which is 20 miles northwest of Hue, lies a little west of Route 1, South Vietnam's main north-south highway, and on the boundary between Quangtri and Thuathien Provinces. Hue is the capital of Thuathien Province.

Heightening the threat to Hue, North Vietnamese troops nearing the city from the southwest reportedly struck at Fire Base Birmingham, 13 miles from the city. The base was subjected to heavy artillery fire.

[Meanwhile, the United States aircraft carrier Midway arrived off Vietnam to help support South Vietnamese forces, The Associated Press reported. With her arrival, the United States had five carriers operating in the area for the first time in the war.]

In the center of South Vietnam, Landing Zone English, the last Government position in the northern part of the coastal province of Binhdinh, was reportedly abandoned last night after several days of heavy enemy pressure. American advisers were evacuated from the base Monday, indicating that the base had been effectively written off.

American military sources reported that South Vietnam's 40th Infantry Regiment pulled out of Landing Zone English, north of the fallen district town

Continued on Page 20, Column 1

Pessimism in Saigon

Army's Inability to Defend the South Puts Government in a Perilous Stage

By CRAIG R. WHITNEY

Special to The New York Times

SAIGON, South Vietnam, May 2—The loss of South Vietnam's northernmost province and the collapse of two of its combat divisions in the last week have brought the Government of President Nguyen Van Thieu to a perilous stage.

News Analysis

Both American and Vietnamese officials here and elsewhere are deeply pessimistic — for the first time in years — about the country's prospects of pulling through.

The growing consensus among Americans here is that the South Vietnamese armed forces, in their country's hour of greatest danger, have unexpectedly proved unequal to the task of defending it. The principal reason is that the commanders, never before tested so rigorously, are not spurring the troops to resist the three-front North Vietnamese onslaught with the vigor and determination that would be required to repel rather than stalemate it.

Vietnamese observers in Hue described the scene in the former imperial capital today as "an agony," with the streets full of soldiers running aimlessly about.

The road from Hue south to Danang, Vietnam's second largest city, is jammed with refugees and with soldiers who appear to be deserters, trying to make their way to safety.

A senior American official in Danang said tonight that the

Continued on Page 21, Column 3

Washington Aides, Discouraged, Hint At Wider Bombings

By WILLIAM BEECHER

Special to The New York Times

WASHINGTON, May 2 — Administration officials tried publicly today to put a brave face on their reaction to news of the battle in South Vietnam, but throughout the Government there were widespread signs of growing pessimism.

Well-placed sources in the Nixon Administration hinted that unless the promise of positive results emerged later this week from public or secret peace talks, the United States would soon resume heavy bombing in the Hanoi and Haiphong areas of North Vietnam.

As officials at the White House, the State Department and the Defense Department studied reports of enemy advances in the south, there were these developments:

¶Pentagon officials said American field commanders were being given increasing latitude in conducting air strikes in the southern part of North Vietnam.

¶Diplomatic and Government

Continued on Page 20, Column 7

Humphrey Indiana Victor; Jackson Quits Primaries

Wallace Defeat Narrow

By SETH S. KING

Special to The New York Times

INDIANAPOLIS, May 2—Senator Hubert H. Humphrey of Minnesota won a narrow victory tonight over Gov. George C. Wallace of Alabama in the Indiana Presidential primary.

The Senator's edge in the statewide total, plus a lead in five Congressional Districts, indicated that he would have 49 of Indiana's 76 first-ballot votes at the Democratic National Convention. Mr. Wallace was leading in six districts, which would give him 27 delegates.

With 88 per cent of 4,480 precincts reporting, the tally was:

Humphrey	286,850 (47%)
Wallace	255,593 (41%)
Muskie	74,307 (12%)

In the Alabama primary today, Governor Wallace appeared to be assured of winning the majority of the state's 29 delegates. In the District of Columbia, a favorite-son slate pledged to the Rev. Walter E. Fauntroy won at least 13 of the district's 15 Democratic delegate votes [Details, Page 32.]

In Indiana, the Alabama Governor's percentage of the total

Continued on Page 32, Column 1

Race in Ohio Is Close

By DOUGLAS E. KNEELAND

Special to The New York Times

COLUMBUS, Ohio, Wednesday, May 3—Senators Hubert H. Humphrey of Minnesota and George McGovern of South Dakota were locked in a tight race early today in the Ohio Presidential primary.

Senator Henry M. Jackson of Washington, who was trailing badly, announced shortly before midnight that, while he would remain a candidate, he would campaign in no more primaries. [Details on Page 32.]

There was no Presidential preference vote as such, but 38 of the 153 Democratic delegates were selected at large, providing a measure of popular sentiment statewide. The voter turnout was large.

With 5,592 of the 12,648 precincts reporting, the tally on at-large slates was:

Humphrey	188,467 (41%)
McGovern	174,589 (38%)
Muskie	45,796 (10%)
Jackson	37,789 (8%)
McCarthy	10,950 (2%)

Far behind were Senator Edmund S. Muskie of Maine, who had withdrawn from active campaigning, and former Senator Eugene J. McCarthy of

Continued on Page 32, Column 4

24 POLICE INDICTED IN A BRIBERY CASE

Accused of Taking $250,000 Annually in Brooklyn to Protect Gamblers

By MORRIS KAPLAN

Three police sergeants, 20 patrolmen and one patrolwoman were arrested and suspended from the Police Department yesterday after they were indicted and accused of taking a quarter of a million dollars annually in payoffs to protect gamblers linked to the Mafia.

The arrests under what was called the largest single indictment ever handed up here against members of the police force followed by a day the suicide of a police lieutenant who was also under investigation in the case. He shot himself in the head in a rented hotel room.

The lieutenant, Fletcher Hueston, had been second in command of the Public Morals Squad of the 13th Division in Brooklyn — the unit to which each of the individuals named in the indictment had been assigned during some portion of the last 18 months.

Deputy Police Commissioner William P. McCarthy indicated that additional investigations were being made in several of the 17 other public morals units. At least two policemen and possibly some gamblers were used as undercover agents in the investigation, police sources said.

The Knapp Commission's

Continued on Page 51, Column 1

Canada Announces Plans To Curb Foreign Business

By JAY WALZ

Special to The New York Times

OTTAWA, May 2—Canada announced her long-awaited plans today to tighten controls over take-overs of Canadian businesses by foreign interests. Under proposed legislation, which is expected to pass, the Government would screen take-overs involving Canadian businesses worth $250,000 or more and whose annual revenues exceeded $3-million.

A prospective buyer would be judged on the basis of Cabinet-level findings that his purchase "will result in significant benefit to Canada."

Text of minister's statement is printed on Page 74.

"Our policy," Revenue Minister Herbert E. Gray told the House of Commons "is designed to insure that this country continues to develop as rapidly as possible in a way which is consistent with Canadian needs and aspirations and which safeguards our vital interests."

Mr. Gray's statement summarized the Government's decision to hold a closer rein on the country's industrial development. Over the last 40 years industry has fallen increasingly into the hands of foreign investors and managers, mostly Americans.

Attending legislation was immediately criticized by the Government's Political Opponents. They maintained that a plan to oversee foreign take-overs was not enough to meet the challenge to Canada's control of her economy.

Jean-Luc Pepin; Industry Minister who would administer the program under the proposed law, said at a news conference that the plan should be considered in the context of existing laws—on taxation, investment and Canadian-content. The proposal, he suggest-

Continued on Page 74, Column 2

Bill to Stop Forest Hills Project Gets Final Passage in Assembly

By ALFONSO A. NARVAEZ

Special to The New York Times

ALBANY, May 2—The Assembly gave final passage today to a bill designed to kill the controversial Forest Hills low-income housing project.

The bill, passed by a vote of 101 to 35, provides that where projects planned by a housing authority have not progressed beyond the foundation stage within five years of the approval by the local legislative body they would have to be resubmitted for review and further determination as to their approval or disapproval.

The bill takes effect immediately. However, it provides that it is deemed to have been in effect since Sept. 1, 1971. The Forest Hills project was approved in the latter part of 1966, putting it within the five-year provision of the bill.

If the Forest Hills issue comes before the Board of Estimate the board is expected to vote it down and kill the plan for three 24-story buildings on the site in the middle-class community.

In other action, the Senate voted to amend the State Constitution to permit the legalization of new forms of gambling that are now illicit. The measure now goes to the Assembly, where the sponsors are hopeful of passage.

In another action, the Assembly Codes Committee released a bill to repeal the state's liberalized abortion law, even though Governor Rockefeller has said he would veto it. (Details on Page 18.)

The housing bill now goes to the Governor, who has not indicated what action he will take. However, during a news conference in March he noted that he was against scatter-site housing, which places low-income projects in the heart of middle income areas. The Governor said that he favored rehabilitating deteriorating communities to provide areas where integrated living could be accomplished.

"I think myself for the long pull that you would avoid exactly the kind of conflict which exists now," the Governor said at that time. "The community is faced with a very unfortunate, intense situation and I can't believe this is going

Continued on Page 17, Column 1

5 Dead, 77 Missing In Idaho Mine Fire

By The Associated Press

KELLOGG, Idaho, May 2 — Fire swept through the nation's deepest and richest silver mine today, killing at least five miners and leaving 77 unaccounted for in the rugged hills of northern Idaho.

Wallace Wilson, vice president of the Sunshine Silver Mine, said only five bodies had been counted and that company officials did not know the condition of the 77 missing men. He said 108 men were brought from the mine after the fire started.

Mr. Wilson held out hope for the missing miners. "There is fresh air as well as smoke-filled areas," he said.

Officials said an electrical failure may have been the cause of the fire.

Miners from other mines in

Continued on Page 22, Column 1

NEWS INDEX

	Page		Page
Art	38	Music	34-38
Books	44-45	Obituaries	50
Bridge	44	Op-Ed	47
Business	63, 65, 75	Society	42
Crossword	45	Sports	55-58
Editorials	46	Theaters	34-38
Family/Style	40	Transportation	94
Financial	62-76	TV and Radio	95
Going Out Guide	36	U. N. Proceedings	5
Man in the News	26	Washington Record	7
Movies	34-38	Weather	94

News Summary and Index, Page 48

Associated Press

FORCED OUT OF QUANGTRI: South Vietnamese soldiers nearing friendly lines near Hue, to the south, yesterday

"All the News That's Fit to Print"

The New York Times

LATE CITY EDITION

Weather: Rain ending, then clearing today; fair tonight and tomorrow. Temp. range: today 60-69; Wed. 50-71. Full U.S. report on Page 90.

VOL. CXXI ... No. 41,739

NEW YORK, THURSDAY, MAY 4, 1972

15 CENTS

THIEU SHAKES UP ARMY COMMAND; OUTPOST ABOVE HUE IS ABANDONED; DESERTERS LOOT CITY, 150,000 FLEE

United Press International

AT BURNED-OUT MARKET IN HUE: Two children among ruins of an area set afire during disorders in the city

PRICE PANEL BARS 1,500 COMPANIES FROM ANY RISES

Cites Major Concerns That Failed to Submit Required Profit Reports on Time

A NEW DEADLINE IS SET

Civil Penalties to Be Sought if Data Are Not Provided Within 5 Working Days

By PHILIP SHABECOFF
Special to The New York Times

WASHINGTON, May 3 — The Price Commission announced today that it was suspending all price increases for about 1,500 major corporations that had failed to submit required profit margin reports on time.

The ban applies to pending increases already approved by the commission, said C. Jackson Grayson Jr., the commission chairman.

The commission is notifying the delinquent companies that they have five working days to submit their quarterly earnings reports. Those that fail to do so, Mr. Grayson said, will be ordered to roll back any price increases that have been approved by the commission, and the Internal Revenue Service and the Justice Department will be asked to impose civil penalties.

Future Requests Ruled Out

The commission also said it would not consider future requests for increases by companies that had failed to submit "acceptable profit margin reports."

Each company with annual sales of $50-million or more is required to file either a quarterly or an annual earnings report or a certificate of no price increase.

The commission noted today that all companies that had not filed at least one such report by May 1 were in violation of the commission's regulations. It added that some companies that had filed would be submitting a second report by May 15.

Mr. Grayson also announced today that the commission had decided not to take any explicit action to control food prices, saying that there had been "a sufficient easing of food prices."

However, Mr. Grayson add-

Continued on Page 9, Column 1

7 Die in Steam-Pipe Blast In Wall St. Area Building

Some Victims Are Found Sitting at Desks 'Like Mannequins,' Fireman Says — 4,000 Evacuated From 80 Pine St.

By LAURIE JOHNSTON

Seven persons were killed yesterday when a high-pressure steam riser pipe exploded in the 36th-floor offices of General Public Utilities Corporation at 80 Pine Street, a 12-year-old building in the heart of the financial district.

Dr. Milton Helpern, the city's Chief Medical Examiner, who went to the scene, said the four women and three men had probably been killed instantly by "a combination of blast impact and 500-degree live steam."

The dead included the corporate secretary of General Public Utilities, a holding company; two assistant secretaries and two visiting auditors working in the office for the day.

Fire officials said the 16-inch pipe that had exploded carried steam, at a pressure of 155 pounds a square inch, to turbocompression air-conditioners on the roof.

In a statement later, Joseph Stein, Commissioner of the Department of Buildings, said an expansion joint of the steam line had ruptured.

"At this time we do not know the cause of this unusual failure," he said.

The effects of the explosion, which occurred about 11:15 A.M., were confined to four rooms. Its impact was so quick that some victims were found upright at their desks, with paper cups of coffee before them.

"They looked like mannequins," said Fireman Charles Cavagnaro of Engine Company 10. "One woman looked like she was still on the telephone."

The corporate secretary,

Continued on Page 90, Column 1

NIXON NAMES AIDE AS CHIEF OF F.B.I. UNTIL ELECTIONS

Gray, an Assistant Attorney General, Chosen in a Move to Bar 'Partisan' Fight

By ROBERT M. SMITH
Special to The New York Times

WASHINGTON, May 3 — President Nixon today appointed L. Patrick Gray 3d, an Assistant Attorney General and long-time personal friend, as acting director of the Federal Bureau of Investigation.

Mr. Gray will serve until after Nov. 7, according to the White House, because the President does not want the appointment to become "involved in partisan politics in an election year."

There were immediate indications of displeasure from Senate Democrats. One staff aide said that Senators had expected to have a chance to confirm the new director. "They are going to have some doubts about this guy's serving eight or nine months," he said.

Mr. Gray temporarily replaces J. Edgar Hoover, who was found dead in his home yesterday morning. The body of Mr. Hoover was moved to the Capitol Rotunda today to lie in state, pending funeral services at 11 A.M. tomorrow.

Pleas for Dismissal

An Administration source said today that President Nixon's chief policy advisers had urged him to dismiss Mr. Hoover last year.

According to this source, the advisers counseled Mr. Nixon to relieve Mr. Hoover, in a dignified fashion, on three occasions last year. The President refused each time.

Mr. Hoover came under criticism last year for a variety of reasons. One was his announcement to a Congressional committee about an alleged plot to kidnap Henry A. Kissinger, the President's national security adviser. Another was the disclosure that the F.B.I. had conducted surveillance of black, student and peace groups. Still another was a series of personnel shifts within the F.B.I. that included the forced resignation of William C. Sullivan, assistant to the director.

During the first two meetings last year, the Administration source reported, only two of Mr. Nixon's policy advisers agreed with the President that Mr. Hoover should stay.

At the last meeting, which took place on a Saturday morning last fall, all but one of the aides present reportedly urged the President to discharge Mr. Hoover by the end of the year. The President refused again, saying he had been in touch repeatedly—by telephone and in personal meetings—with Mr. Hoover. Mr. Nixon reportedly lectured those present on the

Continued on Page 19, Column 1

Humphrey Chief Gainer In 4 Races for Delegates

By R. W. APPLE Jr.
Special to The New York Times

COLUMBUS, Ohio, Thursday, May 4—Senator Hubert H. Humphrey of Minnesota won the most delegates in the four Presidential primaries Tuesday, late returns indicated this morning. He also appeared to have won the closely fought Ohio contest, the centerpiece in the day's events.

But his chief rival for the Democratic Presidential nomination, Sentor George McGovern of South Dakota, did so well in Ohio that he appeared to have lost little ground.

Gov. George C. Wallace of Alabama, the outsider whom the professionals give no chance of winning the nomination, may have picked up the most momentum.

The results were clouded by the agonizingly slow count in Ohio. But 76 delegates pledged to Mr. Humphrey were leading here, and a substantial number of these seemed likely to win, barring a radical reversal in the tabulating trends. The Minnesotan also won 55 delegates in Indiana, and six possibly receptive to him won in Alabama.

Mr. McGovern, who retained the lead in the national delegate count, seemed certain to pick up a sizable block in Ohio, where his supporters were leading for 64 slots. He won none in the other states.

A precise national delegate tabulation was impossible, not only because the Ohio situation remained in flux, but also because there was no accurate count of the delegate defections from Senator Edmund S. Muskie of Maine since he abandoned his active candidacy

Continued on Page 31, Column 1

CONFESSION GIVEN IN YABLONSKI CASE

Huddleston Changes Plea—His Statement Implicates Mine Union Officials

By BEN A. FRANKLIN
Special to The New York Times

WASHINGTON, Pa., May 3—Silous Huddleston, a Tennessee local president of the United Mine Workers of America, confessed today that he had directed, and handled the payoff for, the murder of Joseph A. Yablonksi with what "I believe" was union money.

He said the money was channeled to him by two U.M.W. officials, including Albert Pass, a member of the union's international executive board.

Mine union spokesmen at the union's headquarters in Washington, D.C., said there would be no comment until they had seen the Huddleston confession.

Huddleston, one of seven persons who have been charged in the 1969 slaying of Mr. Yablonski, a U.M.W. insurgent leader and executive board member, changed his not guilty plea today to guilty

Continued on Page 36, Column 4

BUSING BAN GOES TO ROCKEFELLER

Bill to Impose Moratorium Passed by Senate, 40 to 16

By FRANCIS X. CLINES
Special to The New York Times

ALBANY, May 3—The Senate voted final approval by a wide margin tonight of a bill to impose a moratorium on the compulsory assignment of schoolchildren for the sake of racial balance.

The bill, approved 40 to 16, contains no specific reference to busing and includes broad language that critics warned could suspend all attempts at racial adjustments in the schools, including the redrawing of district lines and even the placement of new schools.

Essentially it is the same bill already passed by the Assembly—a moratorium on busing—even though the language in the Senate measure does not use the word busing.

In other legislative actions today, the Assembly passed a bill that would require physicians to issue prescriptions for dangerous drugs in triplicate, with one copy going to the state for a check on abusers.

The Assembly also ratified the proposed Federal Constitution amendment guaranteeing equal rights for women. The action, which followed previous Senate approval, made New York State the 17th state to ratify the amendment.

The school measure became an added starter to this year's

Continued on Page 32, Column 3

The New York Times/George Tames

EULOGY FOR HOOVER: Chief Justice Warren E. Burger speaks near coffin of J. Edgar Hoover in Capitol Rotunda

ABRAMS REPORTS ON DANGER AREA

Fears Drive to Cut Vietnam In Central Region—Laird Sends Aides to Saigon

By TAD SZULC
Special to The New York Times

WASHINGTON, May 3 — Gen. Creighton W. Abrams, the commander of United States forces in South Vietnam, is reported to have advised Washington that the most critical military situation was developing in the central region, where three enemy divisions are said to be trying to cut the country in two.

High Administration officials said today that General Abrams's daily report, covering action yesterday, had expressed the opinion that if Kontum, a key city in the Central Highlands, could hold out for a "few days" it might not fall to the enemy.

The Pentagon said Defense Secretary Melvin R. Laird had decided yesterday afternoon to send a six-man mission to South Vietnam for a week to 10 days to study the needs of the South Vietnamese Army. The group, headed by Barry Shillito, Assistant Secretary of Defense for Installations and Logistics, left today.

Administration officials said

Continued on Page 20, Column 3

'It's Everyone for Himself' As Troops Rampage in Hue

By SYDNEY H. SCHANBERG
Special to The New York Times

HUE, South Vietnam, May 3—The fabric of Hue is disintegrating today, with at least 150,000 panic-stricken people fleeing south on foot, by truck and in flotillas of leaking sampans as the North Vietnamese push ever closer.

The government of Thuathien Province, of which Hue is the capital, is in the process of collapsing, and signs of anarchy began to permeate the city today.

South Vietnamese Army runaways from the scattered Third Division, which abandoned the northern city of Quangtri to North Vietnamese forces on Monday without a fight, were roaming through Hue today like armed gangsters—looting, intimidating and firing on those who displeased them.

Sniper fire and bursts from automatic weapons crackled all day, as rival factions of Third Division deserters clashed with one another.

Deserters Heavily Armed

Neither the city police nor the military police were doing much to try to stem the rampage, for the soldiers, with their automatic rifles and grenades, are much more heavily armed.

"Right now, it's everyone for himself," said a despondent Hue student.

"We are trying desperately to dampen the panic," said an American adviser, "trying to get the local government to form an emergency committee to keep essential services going—police, health, feeding the refugees. I've got my fingers in the dike, but I've got more holes than dike."

Of the deserters, he said: "They ought to shoot them."

Last night, a group of the deserters, who apparently number in the thousands, set fire to the city's sprawling central market place during

Continued on Page 20, Column 3

U.S. DENIES RUMOR OF PEACE ACCORD

Report of Impending Truce Is Ascribed to Communist Informants in Paris

By TERENCE SMITH
Special to The New York Times

WASHINGTON, May 3—Reports that the United States and North Vietnam were approaching agreement on a broad peace settlement circulated throughout world capitals today but drew strenuous denials from the Nixon Administration.

The rumors were stimulated by an account in the French newspaper France-Soir that the United States had proposed a seven-day truce in secret negotiations that the newspaper said were under way in Paris.

Vietnamese Communist sources in Paris reportedly confirmed the account, which was believed to have originated with other sources on the Communist side. This account said that the two sides had agreed in principle on a mutual withdrawal of American and North Vietnamese forces, the exchange of prisoners and the resignation of President Nguyen Van Thieu.

Regime Reported Topic

Henry A. Kissinger, President Nixon's national security adviser, and Le Duc Tho, a member of the North Vietnamese Politburo, were said by the Communist sources to be in Paris negotiating the make-up of the government that would take over in Saigon after the resignation of Mr. Thieu.

Despite the Administration denials of an imminent agreement, it was authoritatively reported in Washington today that Mr. Kissinger had made another secret trip to Paris.

Continued on Page 21, Column 1

1968 HERO SENT IN

U.S. Is Rushing Tanks and Artillery to Replace Losses

By FOX BUTTERFIELD
Special to The New York Times

SAIGON, South Vietnam, Thursday, May 4 — President Nguyen Van Thieu ordered a shake-up in the army command last night in the wake of the loss of South Vietnam's northernmost province, Quangtri, to the North Vietnamese.

Lieut. Gen. Hoang Xuan Lam, commander of the northern military region, was replaced by Maj. Gen. Ngo Quang Truong, who had been serving as commander in the Mekong Delta, south of Saigon. General Truong, the hero of Hue's defense during the Communists' Tet offensive of 1968, is widely regarded as one of South Vietnam's ablest generals.

At the same time, Brig. Gen. Vu Van Giai was relieved as commander of the South Vietnamese Third Division, which was routed at Quangtri. It was announced that he was under investigation.

General 'Overwhelmed'

The view of one United States official in Saigon was that General Giai, who had been promoted from a colonel commanding a regiment last year to head the division then newly formed, was "just overwhelmed by the problems he faced in the invasion."

On the northern front, Government marines yesterday abandoned Fire Base Nancy, about 25 miles northwest of Hue, and pulled back a few miles.

The marines, who have been the only sizable and effective force between Hue and the Communists advancing from Quangtri, moved out of the out-

Continued on Page 20, Column 1

2 Are Found Guilty In L.I. Murder Plot

By ROBERT HANLEY
Special to The New York Times

MINEOLA, L. I., May 3—A former principal of a public school in Brooklyn and one of his fourth-grade teachers were convicted today of conspiring to murder the principal's wife in August, 1970.

Howard Holder and Mrs. Lynnor Gershenson, whose romance blossomed while they were at Public School 57 in the Williamsburg section, heard the verdict rendered less than a minute after they had been ushered into State Supreme Court in mid-morning.

"This court finds that the people have established their

Continued on Page 25, Column 1

General Says Men Disobeyed Orders

By JOSEPH B. TREASTER
Special to The New York Times

DANANG, South Vietnam, May 3—The newly replaced commander of the northern military region of South Vietname said tonight that his troops had disobeyed his orders to stand and protect Quangtri and that some "high-ranking" officers would be brought before a tribunal.

In Saigon, a communiqué from President Nguyen Van Thieu's office said the President had dismissed the commander, Lieut. Gen. Hoang Xuan Lam. But in an emotional interview the general insisted that he had resigned—because his troops gave up the province

Continued on Page 21, Column 1

NEWS INDEX

News Summary and Index, Page 42

U.S. Air Force F-4 fighter-bombers downed the western span of the famed Thanh Hoa railroad and highway bridge in May, 1972. The bridge was a key link in the major North Vietnamese supply line from the Hanoi-Haiphong area to the DMZ.

U.S. tactical jet aircraft strike targets in Haiphong Harbor which house supplies being used to support the North Vietnamese invasion into South Vietnam via the DMZ.

"All the News That's Fit to Print"

The New York Times

LATE CITY EDITION

Weather: Mostly sunny today; cloud and cool tonight. Sunny tomorrow. Temp. range: today 49-67; Thursday 57-65. Full U.S. report on Page 82.

VOL. CXXI ... No. 41,740 | © 1972 The New York Times Company | NEW YORK, FRIDAY, MAY 5, 1972 | 15 CENTS

U.S. HALTS PEACE TALKS IN PARIS; SENDS MORE PLANES TO VIETNAM; ENEMY SETS UP A QUANGTRI REGIME

F.D.A. ACTS TO END POLICY OF SECRECY AND OPEN ITS FILES

90% of Documents on Food and Drug Testing Would Be Available to the Public

A COMPLETE REVERSAL

60 Days Set for Comments on Proposal Before Final Statement Is Published

By HAROLD M. SCHMECK Jr.

Special to The New York Times

WASHINGTON, May 4—Reversing long-standing policy, the Food and Drug Administration announced plans today to make available to the public most of its voluminous data, which have always been held confidential.

Under the new policy, data would be available on the safety and efficacy of thousands of products, on adverse reactions to drugs and on the results of factory and food plant inspections. Even letters to the F.D.A. from businessmen and members of Congress would no longer be held confidential.

In effect, the agency would be transformed from one of the most secretive of Federal civilian agencies to one of the most open.

In a briefing for reporters, Peter Hutt, the agency's general counsel, said that prior policy gave more than 90 per cent of the agency's documents confidential status. Under the new policy all but roughly 10 per cent would be considered open to public inspection.

General Rule Reversed

"In the past, release was the exception, confidentiality was the general rule," he said. The agency's intention is to reverse this in the future.

The new policy is in the form of a proposal to be published tomorrow in the Federal Register. Interested persons will have 60 days to comment before a final policy statement is published.

The final statement will have the force of F.D.A. regulation. It will set out in detail the rules the agency wants to follow in compliance with the Freedom of Information Act.

The agency has been under considerable pressure recently from the news media and consumer advocates to liberalize its disclosure policies.

To some extent the agency has already started implementing its new philosophy of disclosure. For example, it made public several weeks ago its master list of permissible food

Continued on Page 6, Column 1

The New York Times/Mike Lien

AFTER EULOGY: President Nixon returning to his pew after brief ceremony at the National Presbyterian Church. He said Mr. Hoover's bureau would be his real memorial.

U.S. JURY INDICTS 7 IN ATLANTIC CITY

Mayor and Ex-Mayor Among Those Accused of Bribery, Extortion, Conspiracy

Special to The New York Times

NEWARK, May 4 — Seven present and former Atlantic City officials were indicted today by a Federal grand jury on charges of conspiracy, extortion and bribery.

United States Attorney Herbert J. Stern announced the 26-count indictment, which charges the defendants, including the present Mayor and a former Mayor, conspired to shake down contractors, suppliers and businessmen at various times between 1960 and the date of the indictment.

The indictment specifically mentions payoffs totaling $28,421 that were allegedly squeezed out of six companies between 1968 and 1971, but charges that unspecified "sums of United States currency" were extorted from three other concerns over longer periods.

The defendants include Mayor William T. Somers, 55 years old; former Mayor Richard S. Jackson, 64, who is now executive director of the Atlantic City Expressway Authority; Arthur W. Ponzio, 48, the city's Public Works Director; Karlos R. LaSane, 39, Director of Parks and Public Property; Robert Glass, 62, Supervisor of Airport, Parks and Recreation Areas; Germaine Fisher, secretary to Mr. Ponzio, and Florence Clark, 71, former assistant city purchasing agent.

The incumbent Republican

Continued on Page 11, Column 1

New Director Says Nixon Wants Nonpolitical F.B.I.

Gray Discusses Agency

By ROBERT M. SMITH

Special to The New York Times

WASHINGTON, May 4 — L. Patrick Gray 3d, named yesterday acting director of the Federal Bureau of Investigation, said today that he had been instructed by President Nixon to operate the F.B.I. in a totally nonpolitical way.

Mr. Gray said the President had made that point to him very strongly. As a matter of fact, he added, Mr. Nixon had told his wife, Beatrice, that she would have to stop working for the Committee to Re-Elect the President.

In a telephone interview, Mr. Gray disclosed that he had already taken the following actions regarding the F.B.I.:

¶Received and accepted the resignation, for reasons of ill health, of 71-year-old Clyde A. Tolson, the associate director of the bureau and a long-time friend and colleague of the late J. Edgar Hoover.

¶Satisfied himself that the files of the F.B.I. are safeguarded. "My main concern,"

Continued on Page 14, Column 3

President Lauds Hoover

By NAN ROBERTSON

Special to The New York Times

WASHINGTON, May 4 — President Nixon paid the nation's final tribute to J. Edgar Hoover today, calling him a giant, a "legend" during much of his long life and an American institution.

The President, delivering the funeral oration at services held at the National Presbyterian Church for the director of the Federal Bureau of Investigation, said that the "bureau he built to last" over 48 years would be his real memorial.

Mr. Hoover, found dead in his home Tuesday at the age of 77, was buried in historic Congressional Cemetery beside the graves of his parents and a sister who died in infancy. It is only a few blocks from where he was born on Capitol Hill.

The American flag that had covered Mr. Hoover's coffin while he lay in state in the Capitol Rotunda was given to Clyde A. Tolson, his closest friend. Mr. Tolson, 71 years old, who resigned yesterday as

Continued on Page 15, Column 1

BROADCAST BY FOE

Vietcong Urge Troops and Police in City to Turn Themselves In

By TERENCE SMITH

Special to The New York Times

WASHINGTON, May 4—The Vietcong announced the establishment of a "provisional revolutionary administration" in Quangtri city today, three days after the capture of that South Vietnamese provincial capital by North Vietnamese forces.

The new administration was described officially as the

Text of Vietcong broadcast appears on Page 20.

"Quangtri Provincial Capital Provisional People's Revolutionary Committee," which specialists here interpreted to be a provincewide apparatus. Intelligence analysts here said it was the first time in the war that the Communists had succeeded in setting up a government on the provincial level in South Vietnam.

The city and the surrounding Quangtri Province, which lie just south of the demilitarized zone along the border dividing North and South Vietnam, were overrun Monday. Roughly half the province's population of 300,000 fled before the attack.

Warns Against Flight

The announcement of the formation of the Quangtri "revolutionary administration" was broadcast in Vietnamese by the Vietcong's clandestine radio early this morning. It was monitored and translated here by the Foreign Broadcast Information Service of the Central Intelligence Agency.

In its initial statement, the organization called on all officers and men of the South Vietnamese Army, police and administrative apparatus to turn themselves and their weapons in. If they do so, it said, they will be "welcomed," but it added that "anyone who tries to escape to continue to operate for the enemy will be severely punished."

It also called on the people to "eliminate" the South Vietnamese administration and organizations, to refrain from stealing the weapons and equipment left by the retreating South Vietnamese and to protect private property.

In the opinion of intelligence specialists here, the formation of the new administration in Quangtri indicates that the North Vietnamese have entered the expected "political phase" of their offensive.

The specialists noted that similar provisional administrations had been established in the villages and towns of northern Quangtri Province in recent days in the wake of the Communist drive south from the demilitarized zone.

The specialists said that, if

Continued on Page 20, Column 6

Shifts to Bring Total Force To 1,000 Combat Aircraft

Sixth Carrier in War Zone

By WILLIAM BEECHER

Special to The New York Times

WASHINGTON, May 4—The Nixon Administration ordered more than 50 additional fighter-bombers to the Vietnam theater today and decided that, for the first time in the war, six aircraft carriers would operate off Vietnam. This will increase the American air strength in Indochina to nearly 1,000 combat aircraft.

The additional fighter-bombers, three to four more squadrons of F-4's, 54 to 72 aircraft, were ordered from the United States to Thailand.

The carrier Saratoga, with about 75 combat aircraft aboard, soon will join five carriers off Vietnam, Pentagon sources said. Although she was to replace a carrier on line for some months, sources said all six carriers would remain in action for a limited period in an effort to turn back the enemy offensive in South Vietnam.

The orders for air reinforcement came amid strong indications that raids would be

Continued on Page 21, Column 3

Raids on North Planned

By CRAIG R. WHITNEY

Special to The New York Times

SAIGON, South Vietnam, Friday, May 5—American military commanders and senior civilian officials here are preparing plans for drastically intensified bombing of North Vietnam if enemy forces continue their push on the city of Hue, according to authoritative informants.

"We are reviewing all options, and some very serious things are being considered," one official said.

With enemy attacks at the lowest level since the offensive began at the end of March, the new South Vietnamese commander in the northern region, Lieut. Gen. Ngo Quang Truong, toured the front around Hue with President Nguyen Van Thieu yesterday. [Page 21.]

The South Vietnamese are trying to take advantage of the pause to regroup their shattered forces to defend the largely depopulated city before the enemy forces regroup after the capture of Quangtri Province

Continued on Page 21, Column 1

BREAK INDEFINITE

Porter Implies Secret Sessions Are Also in a Deadlock

By JOHN L. HESS

Special to The New York Times

PARIS, May 4—The United States and South Vietnam declared an indefinite halt in the Paris peace conference today.

The American delegate, William J. Porter, said the decision was a result of "a complete lack of progress in every available channel." The clear implication was that secret negotiations were as deadlocked as are the open ones.

Excerpts from Paris statements are printed on Page 20.

Mr. Porter, talking with newsmen after the formal session, said the United States and South Vietnam had told the other side that "we would not agree to set a date for the next meeting."

The Communists described the breakoff as the prelude to new escalation by the United States.

[In Washington, United States officials made a point of suggesting that they had been misled by assurances—presumably from Moscow—of Hanoi's readiness for "serious" talks. The State Department said the latest round in Paris seemed "to have gotten nowhere." Page 20.]

'Intimidation' Termed Useless

As Mrs. Nguyen Thi Binh, foreign minister of the Communist-led provisional revolutionary government of South Vietnam, left the conference hall in Paris, she declared: "If the Nixon Administration thinks it can use intimidation and force to subjugate the Vietnamese people, it is mistaken."

Some Communist officials indicated during interviews that heavy air attacks on North Vietnam were expected imminently in response to the intensifying ground war. One source suggested that the vast network of dikes along the Red River Valley northwest of Hanoi would be a target and added:

"As Vietnamese, we foresee the worst. We are ready to cope with any situation. Last year there was the biggest flood in 55 years in North Vietnam—and we overcame it."

There have been reports

Continued on Page 20, Column 1

Refugees Choking Danang As Threat to Hue Mounts

By JOSEPH B. TREASTER

Special to The New York Times

DANANG, South Vietnam, May 4—Thousands of refugees continued to pour into this bedraggled port city today as fears of an all-out attack on the former imperial capital of Hue mounted.

By early evening, allied officials estimated that more than 200,000 displaced persons had jammed into Danang, which with a population of 440,000 had already been badly overcrowded.

The city's streets were choked with bumper-to-bumper traffic as more and more packed buses, trucks and automobiles arrived from Hue and other smaller communities to the north in the path of the advancing North Vietnamese forces. American officials who flew over Route 1 between Hue and Danang today estimated that there were up to 30,000 people in vehicles creeping south through the steep and winding Haivan Pass and that 20,000 others were heading toward Danang on foot.

Because of the heavy traffic, the 45-mile motor trip from Hue to Danang now takes up to 10 hours, compared with the usual two and a half hours. Some drivers are reportedly charging as much as $100 for a ride from Hue to Danang. Throughout the day, Government helicopters, huge transport planes and coastal barges also ferried people south.

The allies have stockpiled food, blankets and medicine for 500,000 people, but one American official said there could be as many as a million refugees.

Americans returning from Hue say that at least half that city's population has fled and that it is rapidly becoming a ghost town. In contrast, Danang is taking on the appearance of a boom town.

Several stalls offering soft drinks, coconuts and melons have sprung up on the banks of the Han River, which runs

Continued on Page 21, Column 3

AGE-18 MAJORITY GAINS IN JERSEY

Assembly Also Votes for Extension of Turnpike

By RONALD SULLIVAN

Special to The New York Times

TRENTON, May 4—The Assembly voted overwhelmingly today to lower the legal age of majority in New Jersey from 21 years to 18.

The measure—which would, among other things, permit 18-year-olds to marry without parental consent and to sign contracts and file lawsuits—went to the Senate, where its prospects are considered good.

In other legislative actions, the Assembly reversed itself, approving a plan to build a $275-million New Jersey Turnpike extension from South Brunswick to Toms River, in Ocean County, and the Senate rejected a move to restore capital punishment.

Senator Joseph Azzolina, a Monmouth County Republican who was the principal sponsor of the bill to restore the death penalty, said he would seek to bring it to a vote again.

"The only way killers should come out of prison is in a box," he said.

The State Supreme Court struck down capital punishment in January on constitutional grounds. The United

Continued on Page 19, Column 1

Suspect in Slaying Of Gallo Arrested

By NICHOLAS GAGE

Philip Gambino, one of the five men an alleged Mafia informant, Joseph Luparelli, has said participated in the killing of Joseph Gallo, has been arrested, but not in connection with the Gallo murder.

Gambino was arrested near his home late Wednesday and charged with violating the conditions of his parole by associating with known criminals.

Gambino, who is on parole on a sentence for robbery, can be held on the charges until a determination is made on his case, putting him temporarily in custody while the police proceed with their investigation of the killing of Gallo, the leader of a Brooklyn Mafia group.

The New York Times also

Continued on Page 24, Column 1

Humphrey Victor in Ohio Vote; Wallace Wins Tennessee Race

By DOUGLAS E. KNEELAND

Special to The New York Times

COLUMBUS, Ohio, May 4—Senator Hubert H. Humphrey of Minnesota emerged today with a slender victory in Ohio's Democratic Presidential primary, but just how much he had won was still not clear.

With unofficial results of the Tuesday election finally nearing completion, Mr. Humphrey's slate of 38 delegates at large to the Democratic National Convention had defeated the slate pledged to Senator George McGovern of South Dakota by a narrow margin.

In Tennessee, Gov. George C. Wallace of Alabama, aided by an absence of organized opposition and by heavy sentiment against school busing, won his second Democratic Presidential primary today. Senator Humphrey was a distant second.

Mr. Wallace won the legal commitment of Tennessee's 49 convention delegates, but some may nonetheless defect to Mr. Humphrey, Mr. McGovern or Representative Shirley Chisholm of Brooklyn. [Details on Page 27.]

Because there was no Presidential preference contest as such in Ohio, the balloting for the at-large delegates here was the only measure of the candidates' popularity among Democratic voters throughout the state. One hundred fifteen other delegates were chosen from the 23 Congressional districts.

Several of the district races were so close that final official results could tip them to either Senator Humphrey or Senator McGovern.

Delegates listed as being for Senators Edmund S. Muskie of Maine and Henry M. Jackson of Washington and former Senator Eugene J. McCarthy of Minnesota ran far behind. Senator Muskie withdrew from active campaigning last week and Senator Jackson followed suit Tuesday night.

With 99 per cent of the 12,648 precincts reporting, the tally for at-large delegates was:

Humphrey	467,523	(41.5%)
McGovern	441,895	(39.3%)
Muskie	100,152	(9 %)
Jackson	90,911	(7.9%)
McCarthy	25,501	(2.3%)

As the results from the seemingly interminable counting of the long paper ballots continued

Continued on Page 26, Column 7

NEWS INDEX

Forest Hills Project Is Upheld on Appeal

By MURRAY SCHUMACH

The Appellate Division ruled unanimously yesterday that work on the controversial low-income city housing project in Forest Hills, Queens, could "be carried to completion."

The decision by five justices, reversing a ruling by State Supreme Court Justice Irving H. Saypol, said plans for the project need not be resubmitted to the City Planning Commission and the Board of Estimate, because the changes made in the project since these bodies approved it in 1966 were "not substantial."

Justice Saypol asserted in his decision on Feb. 16 that the project should be resubmitted because the plan under construction "is but a metamorphosis of the original, in no

Continued on Page 28, Column 3

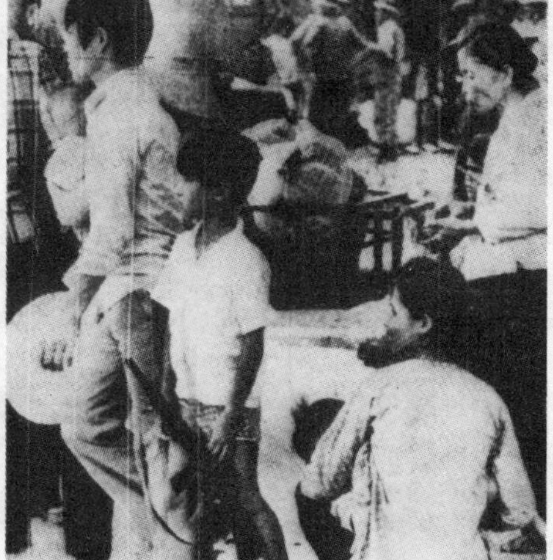

United Press International

PRIZED TOY GUN is held by boy, one of refugees awaiting evacuation from Phubai

"All the News That's Fit to Print"

The New York Times

LATE CITY EDITION

Weather: Rain today; mostly cloudy tonight. Fair and milder tomorrow. Temp. range: today 51-55; Monday 53-66. Full U.S. report on Page 82.

VOL. CXXI . . No. 41,744 NEW YORK, TUESDAY, MAY 9, 1972 — 15 CENTS

NIXON ORDERS ENEMY'S PORTS MINED; SAYS MATERIEL WILL BE DENIED HANOI UNTIL IT FREES P.O.W.'S AND HALTS WAR

Governor Reported Irked By Nixon's Abortion Views

Rockefeller Indicates Plan to Veto Bill Stands Despite President's Support for Repeal of Present State Law

By JAMES F. CLARITY

Special to The New York Times

ALBANY, May 8 — Governor Rockefeller was reliably reported today to be angered by President Nixon's intervention in the issue of elective abortions, now pending in the Legislature.

One of the highest elected Republican officials in the state described Mr. Rockefeller as "very upset" about the President's action.

The Governor's office said that despite the President's announced support for repeal of the state's liberal abortion law, Mr. Rockefeller would veto the repeal if it was approved by the Legislature. Relations between the Governor and the President, which had improved greatly in the last several months, with Mr. Rockefeller agreeing to serve as the President's campaign manager in the state, now seem strained, at least on this one issue.

The Assembly was expected to debate the repeal legislation tomorrow.

Evidence of the Governor's pique was clear in the statement his office issued in response to requests for comments on the President's action: "We are referring all calls to the White House on this."

Mr. Nixon intervened in the state issue in a letter to Cardinal Cooke. The letter, made public Saturday, made clear the President's support for repeal of the New York law, which permits elective abortions through the 24th week of pregnancy.

The day before the letter was made public, Mr. Nixon had rejected recommendations for lib-

Continued on Page 26, Column 2

PAY BOARD TRIMS EAST COAST RAISE OF LONGSHOREMEN

Votes, 6-1, to Permit Rises of 9.8 to 12% Instead of 15 —Fitzsimmons Dissents

By EDWARD COWAN

Special to The New York Times

WASHINGTON, May 8—The Pay Board directed East and Gulf Coast shippers and longshoremen tonight to roll back their agreed wage increase of 70 cents an hour to 55 cents.

About 49,000 longshoremen will be allowed increases ranging from 9.8 per cent to 12 per cent under the decision, which scaled back an agreement that had contemplated an increase calculated by the board at 15 per cent.

George H. Boldt, chairman of the seven-member board, said that he expected the International Longshoremen's Association "to look it over, be disappointed and go along with what's now the law of the land."

Boldt Declines to Predict

However, Judge Boldt, in a brief corridor meeting with newsmen, declined to prognosticate when asked if he thought the dock workers would strike.

Judge Boldt issued a brief summary of the decision after a difficult four-hour board meeting that ended with a vote of 6 to 1. The dissenter was Frank E. Fitzsimmons, president of the International Brotherhood of Teamsters, who is the only labor leader still on the board.

Four other union leaders quit the board in March after it scaled back the longshore settlement on the West Coast to 14.9 per cent from a proposed 20.9 per cent. Only Mr. Fitzsimmons remained.

President Nixon then reconstituted what had been a 15-member tripartite group as a panel of seven public members.

In New York, Thomas G. Gleason, president of the Inter-

Continued on Page 17, Column 1

Associated Press

VIETNAM ADDRESS: President Nixon speaking last night

The New York Times/May 9, 1972

NEW TARGETS: Ports (underlined), rail lines from China

SPEAKS TO NATION

He Gives the Ships of Other Countries 3 Days to Leave

By ROBERT B. SEMPLE Jr.

Special to The New York Times

WASHINGTON, May 8 — President Nixon announced tonight that he had ordered the mining of all North Vietnamese ports and other measures to prevent the flow of arms and other military supplies to the enemy.

Mr. Nixon told a nationwide television and radio audience

The text of Nixon's speech is printed on Page 18.

that his orders were being executed as he spoke.

From the President's somber and stern speech and from explanations by other Administration officials, the following picture of the American action emerged:

¶All major North Vietnamese ports would be mined, ships of other countries in the harbors, most of which are Russian, would have three "daylight periods" in which to leave. After that the mines will become active and ships coming or going will move at their own peril.

¶United States naval vessels will not search or seize ships of other countries entering or leaving North Vietnamese ports, thus avoiding a direct confrontation with the Russians.

¶American and South Vietnamese ships and planes would take "appropriate measures" to stop North Vietnam from unloading matériel on beaches from unmined waters.

¶United States and South Vietnamese forces would interdict, presumably by bombing, the movement of matériel in North Vietnam over rail lines originating in China.

There was much confusion tonight about whether the United States and South Vietnam had proclaimed a blockade. The President did not use the word and Pentagon spokesmen denied that a blockade existed in the technical sense. But some observers felt that the practical effect on North Vietnam of the President's actions would be the same as a blockade.

[In Saigon, the United States command announced Tuesday that Navy planes had completed the initial phases of the mining operations in North Vietnamese harbors ordered by President Nixon.]

Two Basic Conditions

Mr. Nixon said the mining, the attacks on the rail lines within North Vietnam, and the efforts to interdict the movement of supplies by water would cease the moment the enemy agreed to two basic conditions: the return of American prisoners of war, and an internationally supervised cease-fire.

"Then," he said, "we will stop all acts of force throughout Indochina and proceed with the complete withdrawal of all forces within four months."

The White House would not say tonight whether, in these words, Mr. Nixon was in effect making the North Vietnamese a new peace proposal.

But observers here noted that he mentioned no political requirements for American withdrawal. Until now he has always insisted on some form of

Continued on Page 18, Column 5

HIGH MEAT PRICES LAID TO RACKETS

City Consumers Squeezed by 15% Inflation of Costs, Law Officials Report

By LACEY FOSBURGH

The infiltration of organized crime into key positions in the New York City meat industry has artificially inflated the retail prices for fresh meat in supermarkets by 15 per cent, according to information developed by the Manhattan District Attorney's Office and other law-enforcement agencies here and in Washington.

Consumers buying meat in the New York-New Jersey area, they say, are putting at least a million dollars a week directly into the coffers of organized crime.

Years of Collusion Alleged

Racketeers — both in the industry and in the unions that service it — have reportedly been in collusion for at least two years "systematically" extorting "week by week, month by month," as one source put it, "vast sums of money" from the supermarket chains and the wholesale suppliers.

"This is the price they pay to stay in business," another source said, "the price of labor peace."

This picture of extortion, bribery and the ultimate victimization of the consumer

Continued on Page 66, Column 1

State Senate Votes To Liberalize Curbs In Rape Testimony

By ALFONSO A. NARVAEZ

Special to The New York Times

ALBANY, May 8—The Senate gave overwhelming approval today to a bill modifying the extent to which a rape victim's testimony must be corroborated to convict an alleged attacker.

The measure, which passed by a vote of 56 to 1, removes the need for testimony corroborating the identity of the alleged assailant and the fact that penetration actually took place. The bill, passed with no debate, now goes to the Governor, who is expected to sign it.

In other action today as the Legislature continued its push for adjournment:

¶Three city officials—Controller Abraham D. Beame, City Council Majority Leader Thomas J. Cuite and the Council's finance chairman, Mario Merola—met here with state budget officials on legislation affecting the city's proposed $9.9-billion budget. The meet-

Continued on Page 27, Column 1

Ruling Party Leads In Italian Election; Neo-Fascists Gain

By PAUL HOFMANN

Special to The New York Times

ROME, Tuesday, May 9—The governing Christian Democrats achieved a remarkable comeback in Italy's general elections Sunday and yesterday, receiving a clear mandate to continue leading the Government as they have been doing since 1945.

At the same time, however, the neo-Fascists advanced and the Communists won gains in the Chamber of Deputies and suffered losses in the Senate. With most of the votes counted early today, increasing polarization between left and right in Italian politics became apparent.

The Christian Democrats apparently raised their share of the total popular vote close to 40 per cent again and were confirmed once more as the nation's strongest political force.

But no party was anywhere near winning a majority in the 630-seat Chamber or among the 315 elected members of the Senate. The prospects, therefore, appeared to be for another period of coalition governments and, possibly, protracted instability.

Italian commentators attributed the rightist gains and

Continued on Page 3, Column 1

CONGRESS IS SPLIT ON NIXON'S ACTION

Republicans Acclaim His Leadership—Democrats Call Him Reckless

By JOHN W. FINNEY

Special to The New York Times

WASHINGTON, May 8—President Nixon was alternately praised tonight by members of Congress for his firm leadership and accused of setting the nation on a dangerous confrontation with the Soviet Union that could lead to world war.

Republicans praised him on both political and military grounds for his decision to mine North Vietnam's harbors.

Representative Gerald R. Ford, the House Republican leader, described Mr. Nixon as "generous in his bid for peace but firm in his determination that we will not surrender."

"The only way left to end the Vietnam war is to deprive the enemy of the supplies he needs to continue the invasion," Mr. Ford said.

Senator Robert P. Griffin of Michigan, the assistant Republican leader in the Senate, said "it was strong medicine but necessary."

Democrats, however, used

Continued on Page 19, Column 1

President Urges Soviet To Avoid Confrontation

By BERNARD GWERTZMAN

Special to The New York Times

WASHINGTON, May 8—President Nixon's speech tonight appealed to the Soviet Union not to let its support of Hanoi lead it to a confrontation with the United States over his decision to try to cut off supplies to North Vietnam.

In carefully chosen language, Mr. Nixon appeared anxious to avoid turning the Vietnam war into a direct Soviet-American clash.

But some diplomats feel the mining of North Vietnam's ports has raised the possibility of cancellation of Mr. Nixon's scheduled trip to Moscow two weeks from today and even of a military confrontation if Soviet naval forces try to thwart Mr. Nixon's actions.

Dobrynin Informed

Officially, the Nixon Administration said tonight that plans for Mr. Nixon's visit to the Soviet Union were still going ahead. But a high official added that the chances that it would take place had sharply lessened because of the tensions sure to be raised as the result of the effort to prevent supplies from arriving in North Vietnam.

Anatoly F. Dobrynin, the Soviet Ambassador to the United States, was informed of Mr. Nixon's speech about an hour beforehand at a White House meeting with Henry A. Kissinger, President Nixon's adviser on national security.

Mr. Dobrynin was also the Soviet envoy in October, 1962, when President John F. Kennedy ordered a quarantine of offensive Soviet weapons being shipped to Cuba. This led to the so-called Cuban missile crisis,

Continued on Page 19, Column 5

HANOI SAYS RAIDS STRUCK AT DIKES

But U.S. Asserts Military Installations Were Hit in Attacks on North

By CRAIG R. WHITNEY

Special to The New York Times

SAIGON, South Vietnam, Tuesday, May 9—United States Navy fighter-bombers struck at North Vietnamese storage facilities, barracks and training facilities in an area about 15 miles west of Hanoi yesterday in the closest strikes to the North Vietnamese capital since April 16, the American command announced.

The command's announcement said the planes attacked "military heartland targets" that "are helping to support the Communist invasion" of South Vietnam.

The Hanoi radio, in a broadcast at noon, said American planes "deliberately struck at the dike system in Namha Province" southeast of Hanoi.

[The United States command denied that American jets had bombed the dikes, United Press International reported.]

The dikes support an elaborate system of irrigation and

Continued on Page 19, Column 7

New Vega Recall

The General Motors Corporation yesterday recalled 350,000 of its 1971 and 1972 Vegas to correct a safety defect. It was the second major recall of Vegas in a month. Details on Page 16.

Local School Units Defended by Mayor

By LEONARD BUDER

Mayor Lindsay declared yesterday that the city's decentralized school boards had brought "a new vigor to the whole process of achieving quality public education."

Mr. Lindsay said that while it is "much too soon to make a final judgment on decentralization" he felt that "the community school boards have made important advances since the inception of decentralization a little less than two years ago."

The Mayor made the statement in commenting on the assertion Sunday by Dr. Kenneth B. Clark, a member of the State Board of Regents, that school

Continued on Page 53, Column 5

The New York Times/William E. Sauro

CITY OFFICIALS IN ALBANY: Foreground, from left: Controller Abraham D. Beame and Councilmen Thomas J. Cuite, majority leader, and Mario Merola, finance committee chairman. City budget was topic. Rear, from right, State Senator John J. Marchi, Assemblyman Alexander Chananau, almost hidden; Senator Warren M. Anderson.

4 Armed Arab Hijackers Hold Jet and 101 Hostages in Israel

By The Associated Press

TEL AVIV, May 8—Despite a tip-off and a security search, four armed Arabs hijacked an Israel-bound Belgian Sabena jetliner carrying 101 persons today.

After landing in Tel Aviv, they threatened to blow up the plane and its passengers unless Israel freed 300 Palestinian guerrilla prisoners and flew them to Cairo. A senior Israeli Army officer told the hijackers that freeing hundreds of prisoners within a few hours was impossible.

The Israelis, speaking to the hijackers by radio, were reported to have offered to free 15 or 20 military prisoners of war "as a gesture of goodwill."

The gunmen, who seized the plane after it left Vienna, set a deadline of 10 P.M. Tel Aviv time to make a deal, but the deadline passed with no explosion or other evident action.

As negotiations were being carried on by radio, the pilot, Captain Reginald Levy, said that the plane was unfit to take off. The hijackers said that it must be made ready to leave at 5:30 A.M. or that it would be blown up. They later extended the deadline again but stipulated no time.

The Arabs also demanded to talk with a representative of the International Committee of the Red Cross.

"If the plane is not refueled I think they will blow it up," Captain Levy said by radio. "They are serious."

The police in Brussels said that they had been told by tele-

Continued on Page 7, Column 1

NEWS INDEX

"All the News That's Fit to Print"

The New York Times

LATE CITY EDITION

Weather: Mostly sunny, cool today; clear and cool tonight, tomorrow. Temp. range: today 44-58; Tuesday 46-48. Full U.S. report on Page 94.

VOL. CXXI .. No. 41,745 · NEW YORK, WEDNESDAY, MAY 10, 1972 · 15 CENTS

NIXON HOPES HIS VIETNAM MOVE WON'T PREVENT TRIP TO MOSCOW; HANOI AIDES REJECT 'ULTIMATUM'

U.S. IN WIDE RAIDS

200 Planes Hit Rail and Road Links and Attack the Ports

By CRAIG R. WHITNEY

Special to The New York Times

SAIGON, South Vietnam, Wednesday, May 10—Two hundred United States fighter-bombers ranged over North Vietnam yesterday from the demilitarized zone to Hanoi in a heavy bombing and mine-laying campaign aimed at cutting road and rail links with China and blocking the ports.

The air operations were challenged by North Vietnamese MIG's and one was shot down, the United States command reported, but it divulged no further details.

[The Hanoi radio said that 14 United States aircraft had been shot down over North Vietnam Wednesday and that three pilots had been captured, Reuters reported. A Hanoi broadcast Tuesday said two American destroyers had been set afire by coastal guns while shelling Haiphong, the Associated Press reported. There was no United States confirmation of either report.]

Mining Began at 9 A.M.

The mining began at 9 A.M. yesterday, Saigon time, just as President Nixon, speaking on radio and television from the White House in Washington, was announcing new measures to prevent the flow of military supplies to the North Vietnamese.

The mines, set to arm themselves at 6 P.M. Thursday [6 A.M. Thursday, New York time], were dropped by Navy planes at the entrances to the principal North Vietnamese ports. Mr. Nixon had said ships of other countries in the harbors, most of them Russian, would have three daylight periods in which to leave safely.

Haiphong, 60 miles southeast of Hanoi, is the main North Vietnamese port. Others are Thanhhoa, Hongai, Campha, Vinh, Donghoi and Quangkhe.

The United States command

Continued on Page 21, Column 1

The New York Times/May 10, 1972

Underlining marks mined ports in North Vietnam. In the south, foe overran post at Poleikleng (1 on inset) and stormed into Benhet (2). U.S. jets pounded enemy units near Hue (3). Besiegers of Anloc (4) attacked relief column. Cambodian troops lost two towns near Takeo (5).

FOE'S STATEMENT

President's Course Is Termed 'Challenge to Entire World'

By JOHN L. HESS

Special to The New York Times

PARIS, May 9—North Vietnam declared today that "the Vietnamese people will never accept Mr. Nixon's ultimatum."

An official commentary by Hanoi's delegation to the Paris conference said that the President, by mining the port of Haiphong and stepping up the air war, had taken "the gravest step in escalation of the war to date and thrown down an insolent challenge to the Vietnamese people, to the socialist countries, to all peace-loving nations, to the American people and to peoples the world over."

Text of the North Vietnamese commentary is on Page 20.

The North Vietnamese accused the United States of violating the 1954 Geneva agreements and its 1968 pledge to end air attacks and of spurning "all reasonable proposals."

'Colonialist Aggressor'

"Both in the plenary sessions and during private contacts, the American side has always maintained its position of a colonialist aggressor," the statement said.

The statement concluded that the Vietnamese people, while "profoundly attached to peace," would never accept Mr. Nixon's stand.

"As long as the Nixon Administration continues its aggression in Vietnam, continues its policy of Vietnamization of the war and escalation of the war," it said, "all the Vietnamese people, united as ever, will resolutely continue their resistance struggle until they reach their fundamental objectives, namely, independence, freedom and peace."

Condemnation in East Bloc

LONDON, May 9 (Reuters)—Radio stations in Eastern Europe were unanimous today in condemning President Nixon's new moves in Vietnam, and

Continued on Page 20, Column 2

RISKS ARE NOTED

Kissinger Discusses Threat to Relations With Russians

By BERNARD GWERTZMAN

Special to The New York Times

WASHINGTON, May 9—The Nixon Administration acknowledged today that the President's decision to seal off North Vietnam's harbors had caused a serious problem for Soviet policy-makers and endangered the course of Soviet-American relations, but said it still hoped that Mr. Nixon could go ahead with his trip to Moscow, as planned, 13 days from now.

Henry A. Kissinger, the President's national security adviser, said at a White House news conference that the decision announced last night by Mr. Nixon was "very painful and difficult" but had to be made because "no honorable alternative was available."

Excerpts from the Kissinger news conference, Page 18.

Risks Recognized

Mr. Nixon and his chief adviser recognized, Mr. Kissinger said, that the action "involves some risks" and poses "short-term difficulties" for Soviet leaders because of the Soviet Union's close ties to North Vietnam and its heavy maritime traffic there.

But after careful analysis, Mr. Kissinger said, the Administration reached the judgment that the action to cut off North Vietnam's supplies "did not involve an unacceptable risk" to the United States.

This was an allusion to the Administration's conclusion that a Soviet-American military showdown was unlikely to develop as a result of the President's decision. But many Administration officials have strong doubts that Moscow will permit the leaders' meeting to proceed as planned. Mr. Kissinger said he thought it would be a day or two before Soviet leaders made a decision.

But he said that "we are

Continued on Page 18, Column 1

Assembly Votes to Repeal Liberalized Abortion Law

Measure Passes 79 to 68 —Bill Now Faces Action by Senate

By WILLIAM E. FARRELL

Special to The New York Times

ALBANY, May 9—After nearly six arduous hours of speeches, the Assembly voted tonight, 79 to 68, to repeal the liberalized abortion law it barely passed in agonizing debate two years ago.

The bill would replace the present law, which permits a woman to have an abortion on demand up until the 24th week of pregnancy, with the former statute allowing an abortion only when the woman's life was imperiled.

The New York Times

Edward F. Crawford, the repeal bill's sponsor, as he addressed Assembly.

The vote came after several weeks of intense lobbying by so-called "right to life" groups and amid charges that it was let out of committee in an election-year attempt to appeal to voters on a highly charged and emotional issue.

Numerous references were made by opponents of the repeal measure about "politics," particularly about President Nixon's letter to Cardinal Cooke saying he favored abolishing the liberalized law.

The bill now goes to the Senate. A spokesman for the Senate majority leader, Earl W. Brydges, Republican of Niagara Falls, said the bill would be debated there even though Governor Rockefeller has repeatedly said in recent weeks that he

Continued on Page 51, Column 3

M'GOVERN VICTOR OVER HUMPHREY IN NEBRASKA VOTE

Dakotan's Margin Narrow —Minnesotan Easily Tops Wallace in West Virginia

By ANTHONY RIPLEY

Special to The New York Times

OMAHA, Wednesday, May 10—Senator George McGovern of South Dakota, withstanding a hard 10-day campaign challenge from Senator Hubert H. Humphrey of Minnesota, emerged today as the winner of yesterday's Nebraska Presidential preference primary.

In the West Virginia preference contest, Senator Humphrey overwhelmingly defeated Gov. George C. Wallace of Alabama. [Page 36.]

Governor Wallace, who had not campaigned in Nebraska, placed third in a field of 11 in that state.

With 64 per cent of 2,031 precincts reporting, the tally was:

McGovern 46,257 (39%)
Humphrey 42,151 (36%)
Wallace 15,771 (13%)

Nixon Wins in Vote

In the Republican preferential primary, President Nixon was winning 93 per cent of the vote against two opponents. With 34 per cent of the precincts counted, he had 52,872 votes to 2,704, or 5 per cent, for Representative Paul N. McCloskey Jr. of California and 1,498, or 2 per cent, for Representative John M. Ashbrook of Ohio.

There were no early returns in the separate contest for 22 delegates to the Democratic National Convention. They were elected in the state's three Congressional districts.

The eight other Democratic candidates on the ballot were running at 3 per cent or below. They were Senators Edmund S. Muskie of Maine, Henry M. Jackson of Washington, and Vance Hartke of Indiana; former Senator Eugene J. McCarthy of Minnesota; Representative Shirley Chisholm of Brooklyn and Wilbur D. Mills of Arkansas; Mayor Lindsay of New York and Mayor Sam Yorty of Los Angeles.

Curtis Defeats Rivals

Senator Carl T. Curtis, a Republican, easily outdistanced two opponents for re-nomination. He has served in the Senate 18 years.

On the Democratic side, a long-time State Senator, 74-year-old Terry M. Carpenter of Scottsbluff, was leading Wallace C. Peterson, chairman of the economics department at the University of Nebraska, for the Senate nomination. Four other candidates trailed.

Senator McGovern, speaking from Washington last night in an amplified telephone call to his supporters in the ballroom of the Omaha Hilton Hotel, said he had a "strong and growing hunch" of victory.

"I'm going to be prepared in the future primaries and in the general election, to defend my position. I'm not going to be diverted by these distortions and smears," the Senator said.

In Washington, he thanked 250 campaign workers at his

Continued on Page 36, Column 1

A NO-FAULT BILL LOSES IN SENATE

Gordon Measure Defeated, 33-22—Laverne Proposal Is Later Approved

By FRANCIS X. CLINES

Special to The New York Times

ALBANY, May 9—The modified "no fault" auto-insurance bill sought by Governor Rockefeller was defeated in the Senate late tonight after the opposition denounced it as designed more for the insurance industry than for the consumer.

The vote was 22 in favor and 33 opposed, seven votes short of passage.

As a gallery filled with anxious negligence lawyers looked on until nearly midnight, the Senate then approved, 42 to 13, a second measure that would introduce comparative negligence into court actions and would offer a no-fault option that has been denounced as a sham by many consumer groups and state officials.

Repeatedly in the debate on the two bills, Senators took umbrage at the Governor's caution that the numerous lawyer-legislators were oriented toward self-interest on the issue. Mr.

Continued on Page 56, Column 3

2 Miners, Trapped For Week, Rescued; Idaho Toll Now 47

By STEVEN V. ROBERTS

Special to The New York Times

KELLOGG, Idaho, May 9—Two men returned alive tonight from the fireswept Sunshine Mine, a week after the conflagration broke out.

The two miners, Ron Flory, 28 years old, and Tom Wilkinson, 29, were found in good health by a rescue crew that had made a daring descent into the mine in a torpedo-like capsule.

The miners reported that seven other men had died near them on the 4,800-foot level of the smoke-and-gas-choked mine, bringing the total known dead to 47. Forty-four are still missing.

An almost audible wave of joy raced through this grief-stricken community when word was flashed that some survivors had been found. Carloads of relatives crowded the narrow road leading to the mine, the nation's largest producer of silver.

Three young men wearing badges with the name "Wilkinson" on them ran through the parking lot and into the compound where anxious relatives have kept a lonely vigil for

Continued on Page 34, Column 3

Israelis Kill 2 Hijackers And Free 100 on Airliner

Associated Press

Woman hijacker being led from Sabena jet at Lydda Airport in Israel after soldiers overpowered the hijackers.

By MOSHE BRILLIANT

Special to The New York Times

TEL AVIV, May 9—About a dozen Israeli paratroops wearing the white overalls of El Al maintenance crews burst into a hijacked Belgian airliner parked at Lydda Airport this afternoon and rescued 90 passengers and 10 crewmen.

In a 10-second exchange of fire, the Israeli troops shot dead two Arab guerrillas and captured two women hijackers. One was wounded and the other, who was carrying a grenade, surrendered.

Five passengers were hospitalized with wounds resulting from the assault. The Arabs had taken over the plane 23 hours earlier during a flight from Vienna to Lydda airport with the intention of exchanging the passengers for 317 Palestinian guerrillas in Israeli prisons.

The guerrillas presented their demands last night in radio exchanges between the Belgian Sabena airliner's cockpit and

Continued on Page 2, Column 4

City Judge Cleared In Vote Fund Case

By ARNOLD H. LUBASCH

Civil Court Judge Bernard Klieger won acquittal in Federal Court here yesterday on charges of perjury and conspiracy involving political contributions in the 1965 mayoral campaign.

"I'll be back on the bench tomorrow morning at 10 o'clock—if my doctors allow it," Judge Klieger said after the verdict. "I've been waiting a long time to get back there."

The 46-year-old Brooklyn judge, who went on leave from Civil Court when he was indicted last fall, served as a key official in the 1965 campaign of Abraham D. Beame for Mayor, Frank D. O'Connor for City Council President and Mario A. Procaccino for Controller.

Judge Klieger was accused

Continued on Page 13, Column 1

STOCKS DECLINE ON NIXON SPEECH

Commodity Markets Slip—Gold Hits Record High

By TERRY ROBARDS

The nation's securities and commodities markets weakened yesterday in response to President Nixon's announcement of new military initiatives in North Vietnam.

The stock market sold off sharply in heavy trading in the morning, tried to rally, then plunged again in the afternoon. The Dow-Jones industrial average closed at 925.12, down 12.72 points in its biggest one-day slide in more than six months.

Commodities prices generally slipped lower, although the price of gold in London shot up to a postwar high of $54 an ounce at one point. Gold is the traditional haven for frightened investors in times of crisis.

The selling in the stock market appeared to be largely emotional. Volume on the New York Stock Exchange totaled a massive 7.14 million shares in the first hour of trading, representing orders that had ac-

Continued on Page 23, Column 1

NEWS INDEX

Tass Assails U.S. Action; 2 Ships Hit, Peking Says

No Mention Made of Trip

By HEDRICK SMITH

Special to The New York Times

MOSCOW, May 9—Tass, the Soviet press agency, today criticized President Nixon's decision to mine North Vietnamese ports as a violation of international law, but gave no indication whether the move would force the cancellation of Mr. Nixon's scheduled trip to Moscow in two weeks.

The initial Soviet reaction came in the form of a dispatch from Washington summarizing Mr. Nixon's speech last night on new measures against North Vietnam.

Pravda, the authoritative Communist party newspaper, carried the Tass dispatch without any other commentary to signal Moscow's intentions.

American Embassy officials said late tonight that a 20-man White House team, which arrived Sunday evening to begin final preparations for the Nixon visit, was still planning to hold its first meeting with Soviet officials tomorrow morn-

Continued on Page 20, Column 2

Statement Accuses U.S.

By Reuters

PEKING, May 9 — China charged today that United States ships and planes attacked Chinese freighters in North Vietnamese waters over the weekend.

A Foreign Ministry statement said that Chinese crew members and Vietnamese civilians were wounded when the ships Hong Chi 152 and Hong Chi 160 were shelled by United States warships on Saturday and bombed and strafed by American planes on Sunday and again yesterday.

The freighters, which were said to have been badly damaged, were anchored off Hon Ngu island in North Vietnam's Nghean Province at the time, the ministry said.

Although the Foreign Ministry made what it said was a "strong protest" and reserved the right to demand compensation, observers here said the statement was unusually muted for such an occasion. Since President Nixon visited Peking

Continued on Page 19, Column 2

President Took Nearly a Week To Reach His Vietnam Decision

By ROBERT B. SEMPLE Jr.

Special to The New York Times

WASHINGTON, May 9—Even though he began to move nearly a week ago toward his decision to mine the harbors of North Vietnam, President Nixon did not give the final signal to the military to execute the plan until nearly 2 P.M. yesterday—seven hours before his speech to the nation and minutes after a final, sober private talk with the two men who were closest to him during his deliberations.

They were John B. Connally, the Secretary of the Treasury, and Henry A. Kissinger, the President's national security adviser. Earlier that morning, they had attended a meeting of the National Security Council, and when they returned to their offices after noon they found on a summons to return to the Oval Office.

It was a brief meeting, but it said much about Mr. Nixon's moods and his troubles. It was understood that he had already made up his mind to take stern action to stem the flow of supplies to the North Vietnamese.

He had made the decision in privacy and he had drafted the speech, by himself, at Camp David over the weekend. The council meeting that morning had been a formality.

But what he wanted to do in those brief moments with his two advisers was run through it all again, to talk about the impact on the Soviet Union and on the American people before giving the final irretrievable order.

As such, this brief session

Continued on Page 19, Column 3

Other War Developments

APPEAL BY THIEU—President Nguyen Van Thieu, declaring that South Vietnam was in danger, appealed for national unity and a moratorium on politics and requested that he be invested with emergency powers. He vowed in a television address that territory lost because of enemy pressure and mistakes by Saigon commanders would be retaken. [Page 20.]

EMPHASIS ON U.N.—Secretary General Waldheim said in a statement that "the full machinery of the United Nations should be used" to halt the war and arrive at a settlement. He singled out the Security Council as the body charged with maintaining peace. [Page 16.]

EXPLANATION BY KISSINGER—Henry A. Kissinger, the President's adviser, described the peace proposal outlined by Mr. Nixon as a modification of previous American offers and expressed the hope that North Vietnam might accept it because of its improved position on the battlefield. He said in a news conference that the offer to withdraw all United States troops within four months of a return of American prisoners by Hanoi and an internationally supervised cease-fire would leave "the determination of Vietnam's political future to the Vietnamese." [Page 19.]

PROTEST IN WASHINGTON—Senate Democrats, in a caucus, adopted a resolution "disapproving the escalation of the war in Vietnam." The vote was 29 to 14 [Page 22.]

PROTESTS AROUND U.S.—Thousands of antiwar protestors staged mass marches, rallies, window-smashing sprees and traffic-blocking demonstrations in various parts of the country. Most demonstrations began on college campuses, and many were peaceful. But some, as in Albuquerque, N. M., where two students from the University of New Mexico were wounded by buckshot during the ejection of a crowd of 300 demonstrators from a highway, involved violence and confrontations with the police. For the second night, students from Columbia University clashed with the police. [Page 22.]

REGRET IN EUROPE—Most comment, official and unofficial, in Western Europe on the President's decision was unfavorable, with regret expressed that he had chosen to open a new phase of military action. A major exception was the British Government. A Foreign Office statement said "countermeasures by the United States were, in the circumstances, inevitable." [Page 20.]

"All the News That's Fit to Print"

The New York Times

LATE CITY EDITION
Weather: Rain today and tonight. Variably cloudy, mild tomorrow. Temp. range: today 60-66; Saturday 57-79. Full U.S. report on Page 111.

News of special interest to readers in New Jersey will be found on pages 75 to 110.

VOL. CXXI . No. 41,749 — NEW YORK, SUNDAY, MAY 14, 1972 — 75¢ beyond 50-mile zone from New York City, except Long Island. Higher in air delivery cities. — NJ — 50 CENTS

SAIGON'S MARINES ATTACK IN QUANGTRI WITH U.S. AID; 8 RUSSIAN SHIPS EN ROUTE

CARGO FOR NORTH

Moscow Says Vessels Are Loaded With Civilian Goods

By HEDRICK SMITH
Special to The New York Times

MOSCOW, May 13—The Moscow radio said tonight that eight Soviet freighters were on their way from Black Sea ports to Haiphong, the principal North Vietnamese harbor mined by the United States.

The broadcast quoted Nikolai I. Kovalev, head of the eastern department of the Black Sea shipping lines, as saying that the vessels "will deliver mineral fertilizers, agricultural machines, food, clothing and medicine to the D.R.V. [Democratic Republic of Vietnam] and are now crossing the Atlantic and Indian Oceans."

He explained that the ships were "running significantly ahead of schedule." But he did not say when they would reach the Haiphong area. Normally it would take them at least several days from the Indian Ocean or two or three weeks from the Atlantic, depending on their positions.

At the same time, information reaching Western circles through normally reliable Soviet channels reported that the Soviet leadership had considered tough action, including a convoy, to run the American "blockade" of the North Vietnamese coast.

Radiograms from Seamen

In a related development, the newspaper of the Ministry of Merchant Marine, Vodny Transport, carried radiograms from crews of Soviet vessels reportedly still in port at Haiphong, declaring that the American military actions "will not stop ships under the Soviet flag" and that the Soviet ships "will proceed along their course set by the Motherland."

This report was not carried in the central press, which had several reports of workers' protest against the American actions at factories in Baku, Len-

Continued on Page 28, Column 3

Mines Said to Hold Device for Shutoff Before Nixon Trip

By BENJAMIN WELLES
Special to The New York Times

WASHINGTON, May 13—The mines recently sown by United States aircraft in Haiphong and six other North Vietnamese ports are designed to deactivate themselves before President Nixon's planned trip to Moscow on May 22, responsible informants said today.

The sources said that the different types of magnetic mines now in place are capable of turning themselves on and off automatically in an irregular sequence deliberately timed to make detection and countermeasures more difficult.

The mines are also designed to turn themselves off permanently and harmlessly, the sources added. They declined on grounds of military security to discuss the cutoff schedule, but they strongly hinted that if President Nixon so decided he could order an end to the bombing and mining of North Vietnamese ports when he visited Moscow.

"The mines we're using turn themselves off permanently after so many days," said one qualified source. "If the President wants to resume mining we just have aircraft drop more mines in—no problem."

The Administration decided to lay magnetic, rather than acoustical or pressure mines,

Continued on Page 28, Column 5

War Protests

Peaceful antiwar marches and rallies were held in New York, Washington and other cities across the country yesterday. At the same time, disorders subsided on some college campuses that have been the scene of student-police clashes the past few days. Details, Page 30.

FOE IS SURPRISED

Carrier's Helicopters Lift 1,000 Behind Enemy's Lines

By JOSEPH B. TREASTER
Special to The New York Times

DANANG, South Vietnam, Sunday, May 14—About 1,000 South Vietnamese Marines made a surprise attack yesterday in enemy-held territory southeast of Quangtri city, which the North Vietnamese captured 14 days ago.

The South Vietnamese were lifted by 17 American Marine Corps helicopters from the carrier Okinawa after being picked up at a fire base north of Hue. The South Vietnamese were accompanied by six American Marine advisers and naval gunfire liaison officers.

[North Vietnamese tanks and troops launched the battle for Kontum early Sunday, but initial reports indicated that the first attack had been beaten back with heavy enemy losses. In the air war, American military sources reported that United States planes made 150 raids on North Vietnam Saturday. Page 28.]

Civilians Rescued

The move near Quangtri was the first serious offensive effort by the South Vietnamese in the northern military region since the North Vietnamese offensive began more than six weeks ago.

Simultaneously, about 500 marines moved northward from the present front line on the Mychanh River north of Hue to serve as a blocking force for the assault troops.

A Saigon Government spokesman said that this force had rescued "a number of civilians from enemy-held territory and had brought them back behind

Continued on Page 28, Column 7

SOUTH VIETNAMESE board a copter for Quangtri as . . .

Associated Press

. . . U.S. pilots flying them in counteroffensive observe

GOVERNOR VETOES ABORTION REPEAL AS NOT JUSTIFIED

Tells Legislature He Finds No Cause for 'Condemning' Women to 'the Dark Age'

'COERCION' IS DECRIED

Rockefeller Denounces Way Backers of Bill Exerted Election-Year Pressure

By WILLIAM E. FARRELL
Special to The New York Times

ALBANY, May 13—In a strong denunciation of the "personal vilification and political coercion" that surrounded the issue, Governor Rockefeller fulfilled a pledge today and vetoed the Legislature's repeal of the state's liberalized abortion law.

The Governor's action meant that the current abortion law, passed in 1970, which permits a woman to have an abortion on demand until the 24th week of pregnancy, remains intact at least until next year.

In dooming the bill that would have abolished the current law and restored the

Text of Governor's message is printed on Page 62.

state's previous abortion statute, which allowed an abortion only when a mother's life was jeopardized, Mr. Rockefeller said:

"I can see no justification now for repealing this reform and thus condemning hundreds of thousands of women to the dark age once again."

The Legislature, which adjourned last night, was under heavy election-year pressure in recent weeks from the Roman Catholic Church and "right to life" groups around the state to abolish the present law.

As the momentum to let a repeal bill be debated built up, Mr. Rockefeller attempted to head off the effort by announcing that he would veto a repealer, but would sign a bill that modified the present law and permitted elective abortions until the 18th week of pregnancy.

Governor Is Disturbed

But the antiabortion groups were not assuaged by this move and said that it was "a numbers game" and that the only measure they endorsed was legislation restoring the old statute.

Those who favored revocation of the current law received support last week when the Archdiocese of New York released the text of a letter President Nixon had sent Cardinal Cooke. In the letter the President allied himself with opponents of the liberalized state law.

Mr. Nixon said in the letter to the Cardinal that "I would personally like to associate myself with the convictions you

Continued on Page 62, Column 1

Associated Press

KENTUCKY
VIRGINIA
Bean Station
Kingsport
Morristown
TENNESSEE
Knoxville
Asheville
NORTH CAROLINA

The New York Times/May 14, 1972

14 DIE IN BUS CRASH: Wreckage of a Greyhound bus that collided with tractor-trailer northeast of Knoxville, Tenn., at dawn yesterday. Fifteen of the passengers were hurt; both drivers were killed. Details are on Page 19.

Rockefeller Vetoes a Bill To Kill Forest Hills Plan

By ALFONSO A. NARVAEZ
Special to The New York Times

ALBANY, May 13—Governor Rockefeller today vetoed a bill that would have killed the controversial low-income housing project in Forest Hills.

The Governor's action means that construction of the project can go ahead in some form. Earlier this month Mayor Lindsay said he was willing to compromise on the housing complex of three 24-story towers containing 840 apartments, and today he praised the Governor's action.

Opponents of the low-income project are appealing an appellate court decision that held that the changes in the design of the complex that have taken place since it was first approved by the Board of Estimate were "not substantial" and that the project "could be carried to completion."

The bill vetoed by the Governor would have required that plans for any public housing project be resubmitted to the local governing body if five years after the initial approval the work had not progressed beyond the foundation stage.

The bill would have made this requirement retroactive to Sept. 1, 1971, bringing the Forest Hills project on which site preparation work has started, under its provisions. Members of the Board of Estimate had indicated that they would disapprove the controversial project if it were resubmitted to them.

The proposal stirred a bitter controversy in the middle- and high-income section, where opponents charged that it would strain already overcrowded schools and increase crime. They said the introduction of low-income families into the area would destroy middle-class values and turn the one-family and two-family area into a slum.

Supporters of the project argued that these fears were exaggerated and that while

Continued on Page 62, Column 5

No Big Layoff by City Seen Despite Major Budget Gap

United Press International

Perry B. Duryea, Assembly Speaker, brings down gavel ending 1972 session.

By MARTIN TOLCHIN

There will be no massive layoffs of city employes despite a remaining budget gap of $540-million, David A. Grossman, the city's Budget Director, said yesterday.

In one of its last acts before adjourning Friday, the Legislature approved a $100-million program of additional borrowing for the city, substantially less than the city had sought to balance its proposed $9.988-billion budget.

The city had warned that failure to fill the gap would lead to massive layoffs, but Mr. Grossman said in an interview yesterday only that "it will be difficult, if not impossible, to avoid some layoffs."

"Catastrophic layoffs should be able to be avoided," Mr. Grossman said, "although it's quite clear that the people in Albany wanted there to be layoffs. It was a blood lust."

Mr. Grossman's office said that the 1,067 city employes

Continued on Page 62, Column 4

NIXON SAID TO BAR TAX REFORM IN '72

Aide Cites Fear of Emotion in Election Year, But Vows Changes in a 2d Term

By ROBERT B. SEMPLE Jr.
Special to The New York Times

WASHINGTON, May 13—A senior White House official said today that the Nixon Administration would not propose any major reforms in the individual and corporate income tax structure this year. But he added that President Nixon, if re-elected, would ask for such reforms in his second term.

In a briefing for newsmen at the White House, John D. Ehrlichman, the President's principal assistant for domestic affairs, said that Mr. Nixon had decided that "it was not in the national interest nor was it in the interest of the average taxpayer to attempt to consider and adopt major changes in the Internal Revenue Code" in the emotion-charged atmosphere of a political year.

Criticizes Democrats

Mr. Ehrlichman also criticized contenders for the Democratic Presidential nomination, whom he did not identify, for circulating what he called "a number of phony tax facts" in the primary campaigns. This was an apparent reference to charges by some candidates in particular Senator George McGovern, Democrat of South Dakota, that taxes in middle-income ranges are too burdensome while those of the rich and of business are too light.

To some observers here, Mr. Ehrlichman's appearance to state the Administration's opposition to tax reform at this time was as important and suggestive itself as what he said.

His appearance before newsmen represented the first time that Mr. Nixon has lent the prestige of his office to the Administration's attempt to counter the growing cry for tax reform.

It also reflected a widespread belief within the President's senior staff that the Administration had not explained its case against tax reform with sufficient force or clarity, as well as a fear among his political advisers that the Demo-

Continued on Page 40, Column 2

Wallace Campaign Is Expected to Peak In Tuesday's Races

By R. W. APPLE Jr.
Special to The New York Times

CAMBRIDGE, Md., May 13—The climax of Gov. George C. Wallace's powerful insurgent campaign for the Democratic Presidential nomination appears likely to come next Tuesday in the Michigan and Maryland primaries.

Regular politicians in both states have abandoned their earlier brave words about beat-

Primaries This Month	
Maryland, Michigan	Tuesday
Oregon, Rhode Island	May 23

ing the belligerent, outspoken Alabama Governor. They now concede that he will probably win the preferential balloting in both and take a substantial share of Maryland's 53 and Michigan's 132 convention votes.

High Point of Campaign

Winning a Northern industrial state and a Border state—something he has never done before—would constitute the high point of a campaign that has already brought Mr. Wallace triumphs in three Southern primaries (Florida, Tennessee and North Carolina) and strong second places in three Northern ones (Wisconsin, Indiana and Pennsylvania).

But Tuesday will almost certainly mark the end of the primary trail for Mr. Wallace, with the exception of a write-in campaign in California. He will have run out of target states.

Moreover, party regulars are

Continued on Page 59, Column 1

50,000-Man Draft Limit Announced for All of '72

By DAVID E. ROSENBAUM
Special to The New York Times

WASHINGTON, May 13—Defense Secretary Melvin R. Laird announced today that no more than 50,000 men would be drafted this year.

If this many men are drafted—and they probably will be—men with lottery numbers below 60 will almost certainly be inducted.

Selective Service System officials, as is their policy, refused to speculate today on what the top lottery number reached in the year would be. But private experts said that the ceiling might go as high as No. 100 if the remaining inductions were concentrated in the summer months.

Speaking to a group of civic leaders, Mr. Laird said that a maximum of 35,000 men would be drafted in the last six months of 1972. By the end of June, 15,000 men will have been inducted, and the top lottery number reached is expected to be 35.

A call of 50,000 men would be the lowest for a year since 1949, just before the Korean war, when about 10,000 men were drafted.

Draft calls reached a peak of 364,000 men in the Vietnam build-up in 1966. In 1970, the first year of the lottery system, 163,500 men were drafted, and the top lottery number reached was 195.

Last year, 98,000 men were conscripted, and the highest lottery number was 125.

Officials at the Selective Service System estimate that in the first six months of this year every lottery number brings about 400 men into the service. Thus, through June, about 35 numbers will be needed to get 15,000 men.

Over the summer, when men who have graduated from college begin to lose their student deferments and enter the pool of eligible men, one lottery

Continued on Page 30, Column 1

118 Killed in Japan In a Nightclub Fire

By Reuters

OSAKA, Japan, Sunday, May 14—At least 118 persons died in a fire that swept through a department store building here last night.

The dead were trapped in the Playtown Cabaret, a nightclub on the top floor of the seven-story Sennichi department store building in the center of Osaka, about 300 miles southwest of Tokyo.

Witnesses reported having seen many persons killed in desperate leaps as flames swept through the building. The fire apparently started on the third floor.

About 20 persons died when an emergency escape chute collapsed, plunging them to the

Continued on Page 3, Column 3

Estate Taxes Drive Farmers Off Land

By DAVID A. ANDELMAN

Thousands of American farmers are being driven off their lands—forced to sell their farms to real estate speculators, some of them say, because of the method used by the Internal Revenue Service to assess inheritance taxes.

Such taxes are assessed on what the land could be sold for, rather than what it is worth as farmland. Thus, many people who have inherited farms have had to sell them to developers simply to pay the taxes.

As a result, the revenue service is being termed partly responsible for destroying a segment of American agriculture and, at the same time, accelerating the spread of the suburbs to the rural areas of the United States.

Over the last decade, the value of agricultural lands in wide sections of the nation within easy access to metropolitan areas has skyrocketed as land speculators have bought up every available piece of property. The value of this land for agriculture, however, has largely remained constant or has declined.

The Internal Revenue Service insists on assessing all agricultural land at the "price at which property would change hands between a willing buyer and a willing seller."

The result has been that farmers holding property whose value for development is five to 10 times its agricultural worth have been forced to sell their property to the waiting speculators simply to pay their inheritance taxes, which run as high as 25 per cent. Children who would have remained on the land are being forced off.

Most of this pressure has been focused on the spreading areas on the fringes of the suburbs where metropolitan America is pushing out to meet rural America—areas such as the farther reaches of Suffolk County, L. I.; suburban Phoenix, Ariz.; the extreme northwestern part of Cook County in Illinois, and the Sierra Foothills region of California.

"Once farmland is given to the speculators, that's the final step as far as agriculture is concerned," said James E. Cross, a farmer in semirural Cutchogue, L. I. "You're taking land that took 25,000 years to develop, an amazing land that is rich and fertile, and overnight you bring in bulldozers and sock

Continued on Page 45, Column 1

Today's Sections

Index to Subjects

"All the News That's Fit to Print"

The New York Times

LATE CITY EDITION
Weather: Partly sunny, mild today; fair tonight. Cloudy tomorrow. Temp. range: today 67-82; Saturday 66-79. Full U.S. report on Page 87N.

News of special interest to readers in New Jersey will be found on pages 67 to 86.

VOL. CXXI ... No. 41,840 — © 1972 The New York Times Company — NEW YORK, SUNDAY, AUGUST 13, 1972 — 75¢ beyond 50-mile zone from New York City, except Long Island. Higher in air delivery cities. — NJ — 50 CENTS

The New York Times/Lee Romero

Marie Liguori peering from her position supporting the tail of the eight-legged dragon that ran loose on the grounds of the Cloisters during the medieval festival.

...And a Dragon Said No to St. George

By MURRAY SCHUMACH

There was this dragon in Fort Tryon Park yesterday that wanted to eat St. George instead of submitting to his sword. And there was the creature that was to have been a horse but became a unicorn-dragon. And a costumed madrigal singer wearing sunglasses, and a knight with a camera.

All of this, plus a jousting tournament, happened at a medieval festival staged under the auspices of the Cloisters, the Metropolitan Museum of Art, Community Environments and neighborhood groups from Washington Heights, Inwood and Marble Hill.

The plea for social justice by the dragon began in the courtyard of the Cloisters, just before the procession of costumed children — and some adults—began winding among a few thousand spectators, mostly parents.

"We don't want to die," said Jimmy Fitzpatrick, the head of the four-youngster handmade dragon. "We want to eat St. George."

"I'm St. George," growled Jeff Hordath from behind his silvered paper helmet, "and I kill you." And he flailed his handmade sword.

Marie Liguori objected to being the tail of the dragon. She wanted to be the head.

"You're too small," said Jimmy.

"I am not," she retorted. "I'm 4 feet 2."

"You'd make the dragon look like a hunchback," said Jimmy, who is at least 5 feet tall.

Eventually, however, the four youngsters behaved like

Continued on Page 58, Column 1

DEMOCRATS PRAISE CHOICE OF WAGNER AS START OF UNITY

McGovern to Visit Johnson and Daley—Wins Backing of State Liberal Party

By THOMAS P. RONAN

A broad cross section of New York State Democrats yesterday welcomed Senator George McGovern's appointment of former Mayor Robert F. Wagner as state chairman of his Presidential campaign.

They called it an opportunity to unite their diverse elements and get the state campaign rolling.

In Woodstock, N. Y., Senator McGovern and his wife, Eleanor, were spending a restful day at the summer home of friends.

The Senator's effort to unify the party on the national scene as well was highlighted in his schedule for the next two weeks.

According to the schedule, the Democratic Presidential nominee will meet with Mayor Richard Daley in Chicago on Wednesday, and both he and the Vice-Presidential candidate, Sargent Shriver, will visit former President Lyndon B. Johnson at Mr. Johnson's Texas ranch on Aug. 22.

Delayed by Protesters

In another development yesterday, the South Dakota Democrat easily won the state Liberal party nomination for President as expected at the party's meeting at the Roosevelt Hotel.

The endorsement was delayed, however, when two dozen persons demonstrating against the British presence in Northern Ireland attempted to get into the meeting room.

Among the local leaders who have pledged to do everything they can to help Mr. Wagner mount a campaign in the city was Meade H. Esposito, the Brooklyn Democratic county leader.

Previously, he had made no secret of his bitterness at the failure of the McGovern forces to name him a delegate to the National Convention last month in Miami.

"Wagner is an old pro and he's an old friend of mine and he's well respected in the party," Mr. Esposito told an interviewer. "He will have every cooperation from me."

Last month Mr. Esposito said that the South Dakota Senator could not carry Brooklyn without the help of the political "pros," and that he would have to mend his fences with them.

Asked again if Mr. McGovern

Continued on Page 30, Column 4

Associated Press

Sgt. Maj. George R. Green of the 3d Battalion, 21st Infantry, furling the colors held by Lieut. Col. Rocco Negris, in stand down ceremony at Danang yesterday.

Last G.I. Combat Troops Leave Quietly

By JOSEPH B. TREASTER
Special to The New York Times

SAIGON, South Vietnam, Aug. 12—In Danang this morning there were no flourishes, not even a parade, as the Third Battalion of the 21st Infantry and other components of what had been Task Force Gimlet said good-by to the war. Maj. Gen. H. H. Cooksey said a few words, pinned on some ribbons and then, for all practical purposes, the last American ground troops were gone.

Remaining in South Vietnam are about 43,500 men—mainly service personnel—in administrative and supply jobs, but also several hundred advisers and the pilots and crews of about 600 helicopters and 200 other combat planes.

As President Nixon has scaled down the American forces in South Vietnam itself, he has assembled an armada of more than 60 warships and 39,000 sailors and pilots off shore and has increased the American military strength in Thailand to about 50,000 men. All together, on three aircraft carriers and more than half a dozen bases in Thailand, there are more than 900 combat planes. Additional B-52's are based on Guam and other support troops are on Okinawa and elsewhere in the Pacific.

While it is sometimes possible for newsmen to arrange visits to the aircraft carriers, they are prohibited from entering the American bases in Thailand. Thus, a large part of the American military effort in Vietnam is in fact kept secret.

It is widely conceded that American air power saved the South Vietnamese Army from collapse under the pressure of the North Vietnamese offensive

Continued on Page 4, Column 1

AIR UNITS REPORT HEAVIEST ATTACK BY B-52'S IN NORTH

13 Missions Flown Within 63 Miles of Donghoi in Panhandle Region

SUPPLIES ARE TARGETS

Northern Provinces and the Delta Are Also Bombed—Plane Crash Kills 13

By MALCOLM W. BROWNE
Special to The New York Times

SAIGON, South Vietnam, Aug. 12—In the last 24 hours B-52 bombers carried out what a spokesman described as "probably their heaviest raids ever" over North Vietnam.

An Air Force announcement said the bombers flew 13 missions, which consist of from one to three planes, against supply points within 63 miles of the city of Donghoi in the southern panhandle.

The strikes evidently were intended to hamper efforts to supply North Vietnamese forces in the northern part of South Vietnam. Other targets were hit by smaller American jets in addition to the B-52 raids.

American bombing in South Vietnam was concentrated mainly in the northernmost provinces of Quangtri and Thuathien, where enemy ground forces have been attempting to close a pincers on Hue from the north and the southwest.

U.S. Plane Crashes

Air activity was also heavy over the Mekong Delta south of Saigon, where commanders believe the Communists may be opening a "second front."

An air accident at the delta town of Soctrang killed six Americans and seven South Vietnamese. An American spokesman said a four-engine C-130 Hercules transport plane crashed shortly after take-off, apparently as the result of mechanical failure.

Investigators said that there had been 38 passengers aboard the C-130, which normally carries a crew of six. The spokesman said the number of Vietnamese injured had not been determined. Five Americans were among the injured.

Heavy ground fighting and artillery duels continued in and around the northern town of Quangtri and along the western flank of Government lines southeast to Danang.

Effective Concealment

Among the hundreds of enemy shells landing on Government positions in the Quangtri region, many reportedly were fired by big 130-mm. guns, whose range is 17 miles.

"It is evident the Communists are moving their heavy guns very skillfully, often concealing them in caves and otherwise keeping them out of the way of our air strikes," a high military source said.

Heavy shelling was also reported in the mountainous corridor that extends from enemy

Continued on Page 5, Column 1

GOLAR GIVES PLAN FOR FOREST HILLS

Housing Head Suggests a 3d of Controversial Project Be Built as Mid-Income Units

By PETER KIHSS

Simeon Golar, chairman of the City Housing Authority, has proposed continuing the construction of all three 24-story buildings in the controversial Forest Hills low-income housing project—but then to sell one building to house middle-income families.

The first such known compromise bid by Mr. Golar would be conditioned on a proposal that the lost low-income units —280 out of the project's 840— be replaced by an equal or larger number of low-income units on scatter-sites elsewhere in Queens.

A largely similar proposal has been voted by the often-influential Citizens Housing and Planning Council, which would also complete all three 24-story buildings at 108th Street and 62d Drive but then turn them all into a Mitchell-Lama project.

The Mitchell-Lama program under state law provides middle-income housing through a sponsoring company that can arrange financing through the city's Housing and Development Administration.

30% for the Poor

Roger Starr, the council's executive director, said yesterday that the council proposal would then reserve 30 per cent of the units—mathematically, this would mean 252—for low-income families as in some other Mitchell-Lama ventures.

The council resolution would call for a city commitment to build enough other Mitchell-Lama or public housing in Queens to wind up with a total of at least the 840 low-income units originally scheduled for Forest Hills.

Mayor Lindsay's office reported he was still engaged in "active study" of the compromise proposed by his special mediator, Mario M. Cuomo, which recommended halving the project to three 12-story buildings with only 432 units.

A Housing Authority spokes-

Continued on Page 29, Column 1

New Hawaiian Economy Causes Minority Unrest

By WALLACE TURNER
Special to The New York Times

HONOLULU, Aug. 3 — Oblivious to the glory of life around him, Levi Kaupu's ears were deaf to the sea bird cries above the whisper of the waves on the lava beach and the snuffling of pigs in the pen across the road. Nor could he see the stunning colors of the tropical sunset.

His Polynesian soul was torn by the need to leave the village of Milolii where he was born in the house that he pointed to "there on the hill." The world had failed to open a place for him when he graduated from high school last spring, so frustration and disruption are his lot at the age of 17.

He had just come from telling his girl friend that he will enlist in the Army. The reason? "Nothing to do," the young man said, and when he brought up his glance from the beached outrigger hull, his dark Hawaiian eyes were full of agony and sorrow and shame.

His is one measure of the problems of social unrest that now shake the foundations of society in these islands. He is the young Hawaiian, descendant of the Polynesians who once

Continued on Page 36, Column 1

Harriman and Vance Back Shriver's Charge on War

By E. W. KENWORTHY
Special to The New York Times

WASHINGTON, Aug. 12 — W. Averell Harriman and Cyrus R. Vance supported today the assertion of Sargent Shriver, the Democratic Vice-Presidential nominee, that President Nixon, at the outset of his Administration, "blew" an opportunity for a negotiated peace in Vietnam.

Mr. Harriman was in charge of preliminary discussions on negotiations with the North Vietnamese in Paris in the spring of 1968, following President Johnson's decision not to seek re-election and his suspension of the bombing of North Vietnam.

Mr. Vance was Mr. Harriman's deputy at the time, and later was his successor as the head of the United States delegation. After Mr. Nixon's inauguration, Mr. Vance remained in the post for about a month at Mr. Nixon's request until the Nixon Cabinet was installed and operating.

In a joint statement released here today, Mr. Harriman and Mr. Vance said:

"We support completely Sargent Shriver's view that President Nixon lost an opportunity for a negotiated settlement in Vietnam when he took office.

"At that time North Vietnam

Continued on Page 31, Column 1

SAIGON TORTURE IN JAILS REPORTED

Documents and Interviews Indicate Wide Abuse of Political Prisoners

By SYDNEY H. SCHANBERG
Special to The New York Times

SAIGON, South Vietnam, Aug. 12—Documents smuggled out of South Vietnamese prisons and extensive interviews with former prisoners paint a picture of widespread torture of people jailed by the Saigon Government since the North Vietnamese offensive started four and a half months ago.

Here is a sampling of the prisoners' accounts:

¶"Nguyen Thi Yen was beaten unconscious with a wooden rod. Later, when she revived, she was forced to stand naked before about 10 torturers, who burned her breasts with lighted cigarettes."

¶"Trinh Dinh Ban was beaten so badly in the face that the swelling shut and infected his eyes. The police drove needles through his fingertips and battered him on the chest and soles of his feet until he was unable to move."

¶"Vo Thi Bach Tuyet was beaten and hung by her feet under a blazing light. Later, they put her in a tiny room half flooded with water and let mice and insects run over her body."

Stories Are Typical

These particular accounts are said to describe the torture of three student leaders still being held in South Vietnamese jails on suspicion of being Communist sympathizers. The accounts in these documents and many others obtained by this correspondent were purportedly written by prisoners —and in some cases by sympathetic guards — and then smuggled out.

The three accounts are typical of the stories told in the other documents and in the interviews about the treatment of the thousands of students, workers, peasants, women and children arrested by the national police and military authorities in the "pre-emptive sweeps" made in the search for Communist sympathizers and agents since the North Vietnamese Army began its offensive.

Some of the documents

Continued on Page 3, Column 1

A Rapid Transit System of the Future Will Serve California Now

By ROBERT LINDSEY
Special to The New York Times

SAN FRANCISCO — The nation's first new regional rapid-transit system in 50 years is ready to open next month after 15 years of planning and eight years of construction.

It is a stunning showcase of modern transit concepts that urban planners and transportation leaders will be watching for years for answers to this question: Can fast, clean, air-conditioned transit trains lure an automobile-oriented society away from the car.

The $1.4-billion Bay Area Rapid Transit system, known as BART, will attempt to do what virtually no other major urban transit system in the world has done in recent years—operate without a deficit, through labor-saving automation methods.

BART trains, whose aerodynamic shape makes them look more like blunt-nosed rocket re-entry vehicles than trains—are now making regular test runs over the 75-mile network of subways, tunnels and elevated and surface lines that link San Francisco and Oakland and two suburban counties north and south of Oakland.

Meanwhile, engineering teams are at work in an effort to solve several remaining technical bugs to get

Continued on Page 56, Column 5

The New York Times/Teresa Zabala

One of the new BART trains during a test run on an elevated track. In the background is downtown Oakland.

Today's Sections

Index to Subjects

A U.S. Standard Arm Missile in flight over Haiphong Harbor, North Vietnam.

Carrying two Sidewinder missiles, A U.S. F-105 is refueled in the air.

RAILROAD SECTION

BREAK IN SPAN

SECTIONS OF ROAD IN THE RED RIVER

The Paul Doumer Bridge in Hanoi, a vital link in the North Vietnamese rail and highway system was destroyed by U.S. Air Force F-4s in May 1972.

"All the News That's Fit to Print"

The New York Times

LATE CITY EDITION
Weather: Partly sunny, cold today; fair and cold tonight and tomorrow. Temp. range: today 18-29; Saturday 25-35. Full U.S. report on Page 79.

SECTION ONE

VOL. CXXII . . . No. 41,966 | © 1972 The New York Times Company | NEW YORK, SUNDAY, DECEMBER 17, 1972 | 75c beyond 50-mile zone from New York City, except Long Island. Higher in air delivery cities. | 50 CENTS

KISSINGER SAYS TALKS HAVE NOT REACHED 'JUST AND FAIR' AGREEMENT; BLAMES HANOI

The New York Times

SEASONAL SIGNS: While Senator Edward M. Kennedy and Mrs. Robert F. Kennedy escort one of 120 children from Bedford-Stuyvesant around the Rockefeller Center rink, left, a boy on Fifth Avenue takes a look at Santa, and a youth hurries along East 116th Street with presents.

APOLLO ROCKETS FROM LUNAR ORBIT FOR TRIP TO EARTH

Splashdown Set for Tuesday —Scientists Assert Data Hint Moon Still Lives

By JOHN NOBLE WILFORD
Special to The New York Times

HOUSTON, Dec. 16—The astronauts of Apollo 17 began their three-day voyage back to earth tonight as scientists praised the mission's achievements and suggested that the moon might not be an altogether dead world.

Capt. Eugene A. Cernan and Comdr. Ronald E. Evans of the Navy and Dr. Harrison H. Schmitt, a civilian geologist, rocketed out of lunar orbit at 6:35 P.M., Eastern standard time, accelerating their spaceship by some 2,000 miles an hour to break out of the embrace of lunar gravity.

The rocket firing, which aimed the spacecraft for a splashdown at 2:24 P.M. Tuesday in the Pacific Ocean, lasted about two and a half minutes. It occurred while Apollo 17, on its 75th revolution, was behind the moon and out of radio contact with Mission Control at the Manned Spacecraft Center here.

'On Our Way'

When the command ship America swung around from behind the moon, Captain Cernan employed nautical language to report:

"America has found fair winds and following seas, and we're on our way home."

For about 45 minutes, Apollo 17 transmitted a color telecast of the moon as the craft climbed away at a rate of 195,000 feet a minute.

There were clear views of the Crater Tsiolkovsky, with its blocky central peak, a lunar feature that cannot be seen from the earth. And there was the broad plain of the Sea of Tranquility, the place where men first landed on the moon in July, 1969.

Today was the last time for no one knows how long that men would be so close to the moon, departing after walking and working on its cratered surface.

"It is a beginning," Captain Cernan said. "I don't think

Continued on Page 42, Column 1

United Press International

Henry A. Kissinger speaking at White House yesterday

HE DEFENDS STAND

Also Says Washington Won't Allow Thieu to Veto a Pact

By BERNARD GWERTZMAN
Special to The New York Times

WASHINGTON, Dec. 16—Henry A. Kissinger said today that the negotiations between the United States and North Vietnam had so far failed to reach what President Nixon regarded as "a just and fair agreement" to end the Vietnam war.

Breaking the Administration's silence on his just-completed talks in Paris with Hanoi's chief negotiator, Le Duc Tho, Mr. Kissinger acknowledged that South Vietnam's objections to

Excerpts from transcript of Kissinger remarks, Page 34.

an agreement were serious—adding that the United States would not allow South Vietnam to veto an American decision to sign—but insisted that Hanoi must accept the largest share of blame for the failure to reach an accord.

Won't Be 'Blackmailed'

He gave no indication of when talks might be resumed. He said the two sides would remain "in contact through messages," adding: "We can then decide whether, or when, to meet again."

"We will not be blackmailed into an agreement," Mr. Kissinger said in a news conference. "We will not be stampeded into an agreement. And if I may say so, we will not be charmed into an agreement, until its conditions are right."

Mr. Kissinger seemed anxious to justify his statement on Oct. 26 that "peace is at hand," and he defended the American proposals made in the latest round of talks. which apparently brought counterproposals from Hanoi that Mr. Kissinger said had often been "frivolous."

Broke Secrecy Pledge

Mr. Kissinger said that there had been an agreement with Mr. Tho not to discuss the negotiations, but that Mr. Nixon had decided to break it because it was important not to maintain a "charade" in front of the American people.

This was an apparent reference to the mood of expectation that had been created by the Administration's oft-stated optimism of the last seven weeks.

Mr. Kissinger said the negotiations were now at "a curious point." On the one hand, he said, "we have an agreement that is 99 per cent completed," but on the other, he said, solution of the remaining 1 per cent requires a major decision by Hanoi.

Mr. Kissinger, President Nix-

Continued on Page 35, Column 1

Kissinger Charges Untrue, Hanoi Aide in Paris Says

By The Associated Press

PARIS, Sunday, Dec. 17—The North Vietnamese delegation to the Paris peace talks today termed "completely untrue" charges by Henry A. Kissinger that the Communists had demanded changes in the Vietnam cease-fire agreement.

Nguyen Thanh Le, spokesman for the North Vietnamese delegation, said in a statement issued early today:

"We feel it regrettable that the United States side has once again acted at variance with the agreement that both parties shall not publicly comment on the substance of the private talks between the Democratic Republic of Vietnam and the United States.

"Moreover the U.S. side has deliberately distorted the facts, claiming that the DRVN [Democratic Republic of Vietnam] side had demanded changes to many questions and it had thus created obstacles to the conclusion of the agreement. This is completely untrue."

The statement said that if the United States really wants to settle the Vietnam war peacefully and insure the return of captured servicemen, "it should sign the agreement agreed upon without delay and without any change."

"For its part the DRVN side will strictly respect the entire text of the agreement and is prepared to sign it with the U.S. side; the sooner the better," the statement said.

Before the statement was issued, North Vietnamese sources in Paris said Mr. Kissinger's remarks yesterday in Washington on the status of negotiations showed that it was the United States that had gone back on the draft agreement announced Oct. 20.

The sources disputed Mr. Kissinger's statements about the difficulties he said he had encountered in negotiating with the North Vietnamese. They said Le Duc Tho, Hanoi's repre-

Continued on Page 36, Column 1

Legislation Urged to Avert Drug Thefts From Police

By EMANUEL PERLMUTTER

Two District Attorneys and a judge yesterday urged legislation that would enable the Police Department to destroy contraband narcotics quickly and thus avoid a repetition of the recently disclosed thefts of 81 pounds of heroin from the police property clerk's office.

Police Commissioner Patrick V. Murphy responded to the suggestion by saying that "any legislation in this area would be helpful and be welcomed." But, pending such legislation, he said, such methods as sampling contraband narcotics and retaining only a minimum necessary to establish a court case could ease the problem.

Inquiry Continues

The suggestions for the destruction of seized narcotics were made in separate interviews with District Attorney Frank S. Hogan of Manhattan and District Attorney Eugene Gold and State Supreme Court Justice Irwin Brownstein of Brooklyn.

Meanwhile, top officials continued their efforts to discover who was responsible for the theft of the 81 pounds of heroin that had been impounded during the celebrated "French Connection" case of 1962.

A police spokesman said the department was "conducting an across-the-board investigation of anyone who had anything to do with the stolen heroin, whether they are still in the department or out."

The missing heroin, valued at $15-million to $17-million, was part of the 97 pounds confiscated. The heroin had been held for the last decade because authorities considered the affair an open case since some defendants had not been apprehended. A white powder resembling heroin had been substituted for about 47 pounds of the stolen drug.

The suggestion for quick destruction of contraband narcotics was made initially yesterday by District Attorney Hogan.

"There is no reason why seized heroin cannot be merely analyzed and photographed and then burned," he said. "These records could be used as secondary evidence. I am sure that

Continued on Page 27, Column 1

Truman's Condition

Former President Harry S. Truman remained in "very serious" condition in a Kansas City hospital yesterday, suffering from lung congestion, heart irregularity, kidney malfunction and inability to absorb food. Page 60.

SEYMOUR ASKS AID ON BUSINESS CRIME

Issues Booklet Listing Steps to Be Followed to Fight Illegal Procedures

By ARNOLD H. LUBASCH

A special booklet telling businessmen how to uncover and crack down on white-collar crime was issued here yesterday by United States Attorney Whitney North Seymour Jr.

The 64-page booklet was prepared by Mr. Seymour's staff to advise businessmen on the steps they should take to combat consumer frauds, securities violations, tax evasions, price fixing, commercial bribery, kickbacks, embezzlement and the misuse of foreign bank accounts, among other crimes.

"Businessmen have an obligation to make themselves aware of the extent of white-collar crime," Mr. Seymour said in a statement announcing distribution of the booklet. "They must realize the damage they do when they condone corruption and fraud at any level.

"The only way to stop business crimes is for businessmen to express strong disapproval

Continued on Page 68, Column 1

Scientists to Utilize Computers to Detect Environment Perils

By LAWRENCE K. ALTMAN

Scientists of the World Health Organization are expanding their use of computers to develop an "early warning system" to detect environmental health hazards, with the ultimate aim of building a world-wide monitoring and surveillance system to avoid major dangers.

Such a system would keep watch on the physical, chemical, biological and social factors that affect health, such as disease-spreading insects and malnutrition, the health organization said in a report.

One means of detecting environmental hazards more quickly, the report says, would be computer analysis of the frequency with which babies are born with minor birth defects, such as extra fingers and toes. A higher than normal frequency might suggest that some environmental condition was causing the defects.

More than 100 scientists from 15 countries contributed to the report, which draws together in a concise form "what is and what is not known about environmental hazards to human health, thus revealing important

Continued on Page 48, Column 1

Freed P.O.W.'s Carry Psychic Scars of War

By STEVEN V. ROBERTS
Special to The New York Times

SAN DIEGO, Dec. 16—When Lieut. David Matheny drove home for lunch the other day, he saw that his wife's car was gone. He turned around and left without even going in.

Lieutenant Matheny was a prisoner of war in North Vietnam for about six months. Most of that time was spent in solitary confinement, and since he was released four years ago he has tried to avoid empty houses.

Douglas Hegdahl was also a P.O.W., and spent more than seven straight months in solitary. Back in this country, he found so many people "zooming around in a mad dash" that he sought relief by driving to the desert and camping out. Alone.

More than 500 American prisoners are now held by North Vietnam or by Vietcong guerrillas. What will their lives be like when they return? What problems will they face? What changes have been wrought by such prolonged captivity?

David Matheny and Douglas Hegdahl are two of only 12 prisoners released by Hanoi since the war began. Their reactions to solitary confinement illustrate two important points. Each prisoner has endured a searing experience that will affect, in some way, the rest of

Continued on Page 51, Column 1

$25-Million N.Y.U. Library Is Dedicated

The New York Times/Edward Hausner

Mr. and Mrs. Elmer Holmes Bobst, left, at dedication ceremonies with Mrs. David Eisenhower, who read message from President Nixon, and James M. Hester, N.Y.U. head.

By ROBERT D. McFADDEN

After years of controversy, delay, planning, promotion and construction, New York University yesterday formally dedicated its Elmer Holmes Bobst Library and Study Center, a $25-million edifice of Medici magnificence overlooking Washington Square Park.

The first major research center built in New York City since Columbia University's Butler Library opened 35 years ago, the new library is scheduled to open next September and to become within a few years one of the nation's largest open-stack reference libraries.

In dedication ceremonies marking the library's birth yesterday afternoon, the university also commemorated the 88th birthday of its principal benefactor, Elmer Holmes Bobst, the honorary chairman of the Warner-Lambert Pharmaceutical Company, who gave $11-million for the project.

The ceremonies and speeches—a well-orchestrated blend of solemnity, wit and tribute—unfolded before 1,100 scholars, civic and religious leaders, political figures and other guests, including a few who had once been stanch opponents of the construction, in the block-

Continued on Page 66, Column 3

United Press International and The New York Times

Lieut. David Matheny, left, Douglas Hegdahl and Lieut. Comdr. Robert F. Frishman

Today's Sections

Index to Subjects

A Vigilante Photo Reconnaissance Aircraft prepares to conduct a photographic reconnaissance mission over South Vietnam.

Attack aircraft wait aboard the battleship, U.S.S. *Constellation*, to be launched on air strikes in the Haiphong Harbor area.

The U.S. destroyer, U.S.S. *Higbee* suffered extensive damage after being struck by a 250-pound-bomb dropped by a North Vietnamese Mig.

"All the News That's Fit to Print"

The New York Times

LATE CITY EDITION

Weather: Cloudy, rain likely today and tonight. Rain ending tomorrow. Temp. range: today 35-44; Wed. 38-44. Full U.S. report on Page 70.

VOL. CXXII . . . No. 41,970 | NEW YORK, THURSDAY, DECEMBER 21, 1972 | 15 CENTS

U.S. INDICTS EIGHT IN SALE OF STOCK IN NURSING HOMES

$200-Million Fraud Charged to 3 Officers of Concern That Went Bankrupt

BROKERAGE AIDES NAMED

2 Former Vice Presidents of Walston & Co. Cited With 3 Accountants

By ARNOLD H. LUBASCH

Federal charges of a massive stock fraud that allegedly cost investors $200-million were filed yesterday against top officials of a bankrupt nursing-home corporation, officers of a major brokerage company and partners in a national accounting firm.

The charges came in a 65-count indictment in Federal Court here as a result of a 10-month investigation into the collapse of the Four Seasons Nursing Centers of America, Inc., whose stock soared from $11 to more than $100 a share in the late nineteen-sixties before it plunged into bankruptcy.

The eight defendants in the indictment are three officials of Four Seasons, two former vice presidents of the brokerage-banking house of Walston & Co., Inc., two partners in the accounting firm of Arthur Andersen & Co., and an Andersen accountant. Arthur Andersen & Co. itself was not named as a defendant, nor was Walston & Co.

Seymour Sees a First

United States Attorney Whitney North Seymour Jr. said that "this white-collar crime indictment" represented the nation's largest stock-fraud case in his memory.

The financial loss attributed to the Four Seasons case overshadowed the $150-million allegedly lost in the soybean-oil scandal involving Anthony De-Angelis, the $47-million in the accounting fraud case of Harold Roth, the $24-million in the fertilizer-tank scheme of Billy Sol Estes and the $15-million in the Charles Ponzi swindle more than a generation ago.

"This indictment is the first criminal fraud charge ever filed against high officers of a major Wall Street investment banking concern and only the second such indictment ever filed against partners of a national accounting firm," Mr. Seymour said.

In 1968, he added, three partners in the national accounting firm of Lybrand, Ross Bros. & Montgomery were convicted of mail fraud.

Declaring that the public lost "hundreds of millions of dollars" when Four Seasons went bankrupt in 1970, Mr. Seymour said that the bankruptcy trustee estimated in court proceedings that investors had

Continued on Page 62, Column 1

219 Pounds More of Seized Narcotics Found Stolen From Police Department

The 'Worst' Corruption So Far, Murphy Says

By DAVID BURNHAM

Eighty-eight pounds more of heroin and 131 pounds of cocaine have been stolen from the Police Department, a high source in the city administration disclosed yesterday.

This is in addition to the 81 pounds of heroin whose disappearance was disclosed last week by Police Commissioner Patrick V. Murphy.

The size of the newly discovered thefts was made known by the administration source as Mr. Murphy called a news conference to announce that there was evidence now that "the problem is well beyond the scope of my original announcement."

He also said that Maurice H. Nadjari, the state's special anticorruption prosecutor, had "entered this investigation with our full cooperation and support."

In his original announcement last Thursday, Mr. Murphy disclosed that 57 pounds of heroin —originally seized in the 1962 investigation that inspired the book and film "The French Connection"—had been stolen from the department.

The next day the department issued a brief statement that 24 more pounds of heroin from

The New York Times

Patrick V. Murphy at his news session yesterday.

the same case—in which 97 pounds are believed to have been seized—also had been stolen. The missing heroin had a street value estimated at $15-million to $18-million.

At yesterday's news conference Mr. Murphy did not disclose the poundage of the missing contraband—the disappearance that led him to say the problem had gone well beyond what he outlined in his initial statement.

But he did announce the setting up of a special 200-man

Nadjari Enters Inquiry—Inventory Unit Set Up

team of patrolmen and detectives, which he said would make a complete inventory of all the contraband narcotics now in the possession of the police.

"This is, without doubt, the worst instance of police corruption I have uncovered," Mr. Murphy said at his news conference. "I will not stand for it. I am determined not to rest until the last vestiges of this problem have been rooted out."

The high official source said the initial evidence gathered by police investigators suggested that the newly stolen contraband—the 88 pounds of heroin and 131 pounds of cocaine —probably was taken much more recently than the heroin involved in Mr. Murphy's original statement.

The source said the indications were that the recent thefts might have taken place around last January— more than a year ago after Mr. Murphy's appointment as Police Commissioner. He also indicated that the evidence suggested the material was stolen by the substitution of dummy material for the real drugs.

Tho Commissioner said

Continued on Page 62, Column 5

C.B.S. and Strikers Reach Tentative Pact in 6th Week

By ALBIN KREBS

The Federal Mediation and Conciliation Service announced late last night that negotiators for the Columbia Broadcasting System and its striking technicians' union had reached tentative agreement on a new contract.

The agreement, subject to ratification by the 1,200 members of the union, would end a strike that has gone on almost seven weeks. The tentative settlement was announced by the mediation service in Washington.

Spokesmen for both C.B.S. and the striking union were unable immediately to say on what terms the proopsed settlement had been made. It could not be determined when a ratification vote was likely to be held. One union spokesman, reached in Washington, said, "I am personally not sure it's a final settlement," but he declined to elaborate.

A spokesman for the service said the pact had been reached after talks that began Dec. 8 and continued eight days, then recessed over last weekend so that the negotiators could rest.

The strike, which began Nov. 3, was called by Local 1212 of the Radio and Broadcast Engineers Union, International

Continued on Page 71, Column 2

9 KILLED AS JETS COLLIDE AT O'HARE

North Central DC-9 Hits Delta Plane on Take-Off at Foggy Chicago Field

Special to The New York Times

CHICAGO, Dec. 20—A North Central Airlines DC-9 jet, taking off in heavy fog, hit a Delta Air Lines Convair 880 tonight at Chicago's O'Hare International Airport.

Fire Department officials said that at least nine persons —six women and three men, all believed to have been aboard the North Central plane—were known dead.

But firemen continued to search for more bodies in the smoldering wreckage of the twin-engine North Central plane, Flight 575, which had been bound for Duluth, Minn., with a stop in Madison, Wis.

Sixteen persons, including two from the Delta flight, were reported injured and were taken to the nearby Resurrection and Lutheran General Hospitals.

Twenty-two persons aboard the North Central plane and 100 aboard the Delta flight were reported uninjured. The crash was the second in Chicago in 12 days.

Witnesses said the North Central plane, which had been de-

Continued on Page 26, Column 5

LABOR CHIEFS HINT SHIFT ON CONTROLS

Group Led by Meany Is Said to Offer to End Opposition if More 'Equity' Is Won

By PHILIP SHABECOFF

Special to The New York Times

WASHINGTON, Dec. 20—A group of labor leaders, headed by George Meany, gave President Nixon today a conditional offer of cooperation in an extended program of wage and price controls, a labor source close to the participants reported.

Mr. Meany, who is president of the American Federation of Labor and Congress of Industrial Organizations, and other labor members of the National Productivity Commission met at the White House with George P. Shultz, Secretary of the Treasury. Mr. Shultz, chairman of the Cost of Living Council, which oversees the controls, sought their views on how to make the economic stabilization program more effective.

Mr. Meany, acting as spokesman for the group, reportedly said that labor would not oppose an extension of the Economic Stabilization Act beyond

Continued on Page 24, Column 3

2 Airport Guards Shot

A Vietnam veteran who had been confined for mental illness shot and wounded two Federal security officers yesterday at Kennedy International Airport before being captured, the police said. Details on Page 70.

State Investigating Charge By Deposed Shubert Heir

By MURRAY SCHUMACH

Lawrence Shubert Lawrence, deposed head of the Shubert empire, has filed a complaint with Attorney General Louis J. Lefkowitz, challenging the right of his successors to remain in power over the Shubert Foundation and the 23 corporations it owns.

In a virtual declaration of war against the triumvirate that ousted him five months ago, the last of the Shubert family in the business accused his successors of "acting invalidly," of conflicts of interest and of excessive largesse in distributing foundation funds to favorite charities.

Mr. Lefkowitz, who confirmed that the complaint had been filed, declined to give details, but he said he had opened an investigation into all aspects of the charges.

"I am investigating the Shubert Foundation, the accounting of the estate of the late J. J. Shubert and will look into every point raised," he said.

"Since my office has the authority to supervise the operations of foundations, I can request resignations of foundation officers if I find serious irregularities."

Mr. Lefkowitz declined to say if any allegations of crime were contained in the complaint by Mr. Lawrence, who for 10 years was president and chief executive officer of the Shubert domain.

"If we find any evidence of crime," Mr. Lefkowtz said, "we will turn it over to the office of District Attorney [Frank S.] Hogan."

The three men accused of infractions by Mr. Lawrence are Irving Goldman, Bernard Jacobs and Gerald Schoenfeld, who make up the executive committee that now rules the Shubert Foundation and corporations valued at $60-million to $100-million.

When the three members of the executive committee were told of the complaint by a reporter, they said it was the first they had heard of it. They then made the following comment:

"We had no prior comment of this matter. The first information that we received came from The New York Times. Based upon what The New York Times told us, the complaint is utterly groundless. If we are apprised of the details, we may have a further statement."

The lawyer for Mr. Law-

Continued on Page 31, Column 1

Newark Council Rejects Kerr As First Black Police Director

Special to The New York Times

NEWARK, Thursday, Dec. 21—Newark's City Council, voting 5 to 3 along racial lines, early today rejected Lieut. Edward L. Kerr as Newark's first black police director in a tumultuous five-and-a-half-hour meeting.

When the vote was announced, the 400 persons jammed into City Hall chambers jumped to their feet and demanded the recall of the five white councilmen who voted no.

Lieutenant Kerr had been proposed by Mayor Kenneth A. Gibson to replace John L. Redden, who had resigned effective Jan. 1 because of his dissatisfaction over the administration's handling of the Kawaida Towers housing dispute in the city's North Ward.

Lieutenant Kerr will serve as acting police director for 90 days while Mayor Gibson considers a new appointment or resubmits his name.

Early in the meeting, which began at 8 P.M., speaker after speaker urged the council to approve Lieutenant Kerr's appointment. They argued that as a black man he is sensitive to the needs of blacks, who make up 60 per cent of the city's population.

Only four of the more than 50 speakers were white, including the Rev. Jan Van Arsdale, who endorsed Lieutenant Kerr. Two of the white speakers said they represented Italian-American groups that are starting recall drives of Mayor Gibson.

The speakers said the Mayor

Continued on Page 43, Column 4

ENVIRONMENT JOB WILL BE RETAINED BY RUCKELSHAUS

He Says He Agreed to Stay After Pledge by Nixon on Decision-Making Power

Special to The New York Times

WASHINGTON, Dec. 20—William D. Ruckelshaus, who has sometimes differed vigorously with other Nixon Administration officials on environmental questions, will stay on as administrator of the Environmental Protection Agency, the White House announced today.

The announcement, which followed speculation that Mr. Ruckelshaus might resign his post, perhaps to take over as head of the Central Intelligence Agency, was made at a White House news briefing by Ronald L. Ziegler, President Nixon's press secretary.

Mr. Ziegler said that the President considered the environmental agency "one of the most important new agencies in government," and that he believed it had achieved "a very active and effective record in" the two years that Mr. Ruckelshaus has been its head.

Sees a Commitment

At a separate news conference, held shortly after his reappointment was made public, Mr. Ruckelshaus said that, before agreeing to remain, he had sought and received assurance from President Nixon that he would continue to have "the authority to exercise the decision-making power given to the administrator of this agency by law."

Mr. Nixon, he said, "expressed his full support of this concept," and he added, "I believe I have a very strong commitment from the White House."

Mr. Ruckelshaus noted what he called "considerable speculation in the media that what the [Nixon Administration] organizers have in mind is controlling many of the departments and agencies of Government out of a centralized base."

There are, he said, "memos floating around this Government involving everything from the Atomic Energy Commission to the national egg board," and said that he had seen some "suggestions that the Environmental Protection Agency be included in a larger department of national resources."

No Threat, He Says

But he is confident, he said, that "the President and others at the White House understand the need for a strong and independent Environmental Protection Agency," and that he "accepted with great enthusiasm the President's suggestion" that he remain as its head.

"There was no threat on my part," he added. "I simply needed to have an understanding about what the future of this agency was."

Mr. Ruckelshaus said that although "there are not going to be any massive personnel changes" at the agency, "there may be two or three." He said that he had been assured by "the White House personnel operation" that he would be given the opportunity to make recommendations before any

Continued on Page 8, Column 3

PENTAGON SAYS BOMBINGS WRECK MILITARY TARGETS; IT DENIES 'TERROR' RAIDS

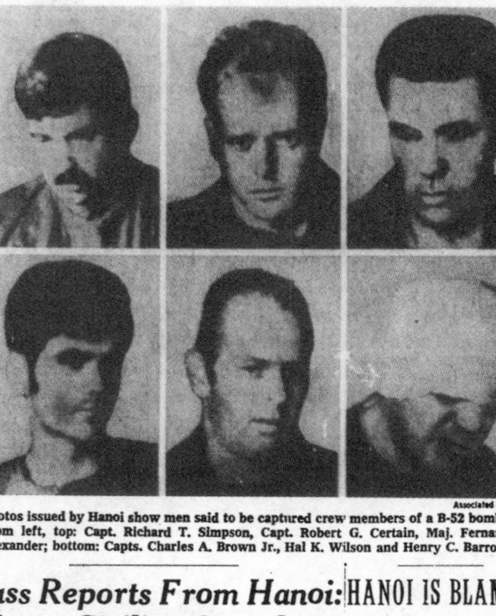

Associated Press

Photos issued by Hanoi show men said to be captured crew members of a B-52 bomber. From left, top: Capt. Richard T. Simpson, Capt. Robert G. Certain, Maj. Fernando Alexander; bottom: Capts. Charles A. Brown Jr., Hal K. Wilson and Henry C. Barrows.

Tass Reports From Hanoi: 'Heavy Civilian Casualties'

Special to The New York Times

MOSCOW, Dec. 20—Tass, the Soviet press agency, reported from Hanoi today that the latest American air raids there had caused "heavy civilian casualties" and destroyed "thousands of homes."

In one dispatch, Tass also said that a Polish vessel, the Jozef Conrad, had suffered a direct hit in the port of Haiphong. The ship was set afire and, seriously damaged, was left listing heavily, Tass said.

[In Warsaw, the Polish press agency said that the freighter had been sunk and three seamen killed. It added that Poland had officially protested to the United States.]

Two dispatches from Aleksandr Mineyev, a Tass correspondent, asserted that the American raids last night and tonight had destroyed or severely damaged blocks of workers' housing, a hospital building, a movie theater, a student village at the Hanoi Technical Institute, among other places in Hanoi.

The Tass report gave no precise estimates of casualties, although one dispatch specifically said "several students" had been found dead under the wreckage at the Polytechnical Institute. [The Hanoi radio reported 215 killed and 326

Continued on Page 16, Column 6

Concessions by Both Sides Reported Urged by Nixon

By Reuters

SAIGON, South Vietnam, Thursday, Dec. 21—Official South Vietnamese sources said today that President Nixon had urged both North Vietnam and South Vietnam to make concessions toward a peace settlement.

But a senior Government official said that reports that the request included an ultimatum to South Vietnam threatening to cut off military and economic aid was "poor speculation." He added that "no such ultimatum was made."

The officials were giving the first reports today on a visit here of Gen. Alexander M. Haig Jr., President Nixon's envoy.

The general, who is the deputy adviser to the President on national security, under Henry A. Kissinger, is reported to have brought a confidential letter from President Nixon.

Details of the letter have not been made public, but the sources said that the United States was bringing pressure to bear on both North and South to make concessions.

Military pressure is being put on North Vietnam with a severe bombing campaign over the North's main cities of Hanoi and Haiphong.

The sources did not spell out what pressure was being brought to bear on South Vietnam, although the possibility of

Continued on Page 14, Column 3

Associated Press

The Jozef Conrad, a Polish ship, was said in Warsaw last night to have been sunk, and three seamen killed, in U.S. bombing of Haiphong, North Vietnam. Photo from files.

HANOI IS BLAMED

Lack of Seriousness at Paris Talks Charged —4th B-52 Lost

By JOHN W. FINNEY

Special to The New York Times

WASHINGTON, Dec. 20—The Defense Department said today that the intensive American bombing of North Vietnam in the last two days had caused "very significant damage" to a broad range of military targets.

The department insisted that civilian targets were not being struck, as asserted by Hanoi, and dismissed suggestions that the United States was engaged in "terror bombing."

Other Administration officials, meanwhile, insisted that the United States had resumed heavy bombing because of what they described as North Vietnam's lack of seriousness at the Paris negotiations, and they said that Hanoi was entirely to blame for the breakdown of the talks. [Details on Page 16.]

[In Paris, the North Vietnamese announced the postponement of scheduled lower-level discussions on the technical details of a Vietnam cease-fire. Page 15.]

Destroyer Is Hit

As the heavy bombing, which began Monday, went into its fourth day, the Defense Department and the United States military command in Saigon announced the loss of two more American planes, including a third B-52 bomber. [Thursday in Saigon, the loss of a fourth B-52 was announced.]

The Hanoi radio, however, asserted in a broadcast today that two other B-52's and four more fighter-bombers had also gone down. [A broadcast Thursday said that as the raids continued through the night the North Vietnamese shot down 13 more American planes, among them seven B-52's and an F-111 swing-wing fighter-bomber, Reuters reported.]

In their reports during the third day of bombing, the Defense Department and the United States command in Saigon announced that enemy shore batteries in the Thanh Hoa area had hit the guided-missile destroyer Goldsborough, killing

Continued on Page 16, Column 2

NEWS INDEX

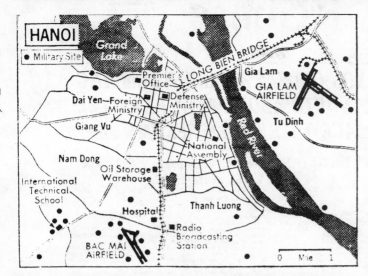

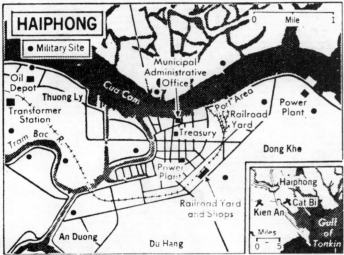

Detailed maps of Hanoi and Haiphong

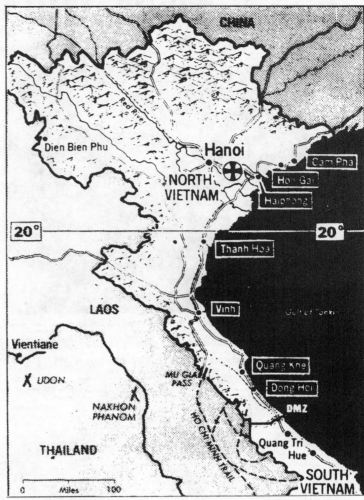

U.S. planes resumed bombing of the key Hanoi-Haiphong areas in December of 1972. The mined ports are shown with their names outlined in white.

Communist troops marching south to attack across the Demilitarized Zone in March 1972.

"All the News That's Fit to Print"

The New York Times

LATE CITY EDITION
Weather: Very mild today, tonight with some showers. Mild tomorrow. Temp. range: today 37-53; Saturday 31-40. Full U.S. report on Page 46.

SECTION ONE

VOL. CXXII . . No. 41,980

NEW YORK, SUNDAY, DECEMBER 31, 1972

75¢ beyond 50-mile zone from New York City except Long Island. Higher in air delivery cities.

50 CENTS

NIXON ORDERS A HALT IN BOMBING OF NORTH ABOVE 20TH PARALLEL; PEACE TALKS WILL RESUME JAN. 8

HANOI'S REACTION

Aide in Paris Denies Yielding to Pressure From Washington

By HENRY GINIGER
Special to The New York Times

PARIS, Dec. 30—North Vietnam sought tonight to dispel the idea that it had yielded to military pressure in agreeing to further peace talks with the United States.

"The resumption of the bombings, while negotiations were proceeding, did not succeed in subjugating the Vietnamese people," a statement by the North Vietnamese delegation to the formal peace talks here said. The delegation pointed instead to the "heavy losses" suffered in American planes shot down and to the severe condemnation of the attacks by "wide sectors of world opinion."

The Hanoi delegation's spokesman, Nguyen Thanh Le, said that the United States had halted its attacks above the 20th Parallel, which North Vietnam had insisted on all week, as of 7 P.M., Washington time yesterday. The corresponding time in Hanoi was 7 A.M. today.

Schumann Expresses Hope

The North Vietnamese reference to the timing of the halt in the bombing suggested that an agreement had been reached yesterday. France's Foreign Minister, Maurice Schumann, who had been active in trying to get the two sides together again, declared: "Hope is reborn. I am starting to think that our constant efforts will not have been in vain."

The North Vietnamese said that Le Duc Tho, the Politburo member charged with the private talks, would return to Paris to join Xuan Thuy, nominal head of their delegation, in the negotiations with Henry A. Kissinger, President Nixon's adviser on national security.

Formal Talks Not Mentioned

They also confirmed the resumption of technical talks at the expert level, to which the United States is sending William H. Sullivan, a Deputy Assistant Secretary of State for East Asian and Pacific Affairs. Mr. Thuy has represented the North Vietnamese in past technical sessions. One such session proposed by the United States for last Wednesday had been rejected by Hanoi.

No reference was made by Hanoi to the formal sessions of the four delegations. The United States has proposed a meeting for Thursday. The Vietcong delegation said of that

Continued on Page 3, Column 2

U.S. Aides Differ Sharply Over Value of the Raids

By SEYMOUR M. HERSH
Special to The New York Times

WASHINGTON, Dec. 30 — Official Washington seemed unsure today whether the heavy bombing of North Vietnam, which was ordered halted this morning, had helped or hindered the United States in getting the Paris negotiations reopened.

Interviews with military and civilian intelligence officials after this morning's announcement by Gerald L. Warren, deputy White House press secretary, produced sharp divisions over the value of the bombing of North Vietnam — a dispute that has been waged since the first air strikes over the North in the mid-nineteen-sixties.

One high-ranking military man said that the recent bombing of the heavily populated Hanoi area was primarily aimed at coercing further concessions at the peace talks, which are to resume Jan. 8.

"There is a business of coercion in there and that's the business of war," the officer said. "So what's new?"

'Isn't Just Coercion'

"But it isn't just coercion," the officer added. "Even without successful negotiations, we're preparing the way so that we can have the ally over there stand on his own without our help. Even if the bombs don't coerce the enemy into successful peace talks, they're destroying his will to fight."

But there were many other government officials who — citing the heavy United States air losses, the growing international outcry and the mounting Congressional unrest — believe that the bombing has been extremely counterproductive.

"Personally, I don't think we're doing the right thing," said one official who generally has taken a hard-line approach to the Vietnam issue. "Is bombing going to be effective? I can't see any reason in the world why it would be."

"All they've got to do is hang on," the official said of the North Vietnamese. "How long can we keep it up? What with our losses and international opinion against us, the key question is: Can we force them to do something by bombing?"

Up-to-date statistics on the number of bombing raids and

Continued on Page 4, Column 1

United Press International
Gerald L. Warren, who announced the move.

ACTION IS SUDDEN

Kissinger Will Renew His Efforts With Tho, White House Says

By BERNARD GWERTZMAN
Special to The New York Times

WASHINGTON, Dec. 30—The White House announced today that President Nixon had ordered a halt to the bombing of North Vietnam above the 20th Parallel and that Henry A. Kissinger would resume negotiations for a Vietnam settlement with Le Duc Tho in Paris on Jan. 8.

The announcement of the renewed efforts to seek a nego-

Text of White House news conference, Page 3.

tiated settlement, ending nearly two weeks of heavy bombing of Hanoi and Haiphong, also said that the technical talks of lower-level American and North Vietnamese experts would resume on Tuesday in Paris.

Gerald L. Warren, a deputy White House press secretary, said in answer to a question at a White House briefing for newsmen that "as soon as it was clear that serious negotiations could be resumed at both the technical level and between the principals, the President ordered that all bombing be discontinued above the 20th Parallel."

Cause Is Unclear

It was unclear whether the impetus for the new round of negotiations had come from Hanoi, reeling under B-52 raids, or from Washington, which was possibly looking for an excuse to suspend the latest raids because of increasing foreign and domestic pressure.

News of the renewal of the peace efforts came without much advance warning. The White House telephoned newsmen at home shortly after 9 A.M. and told them that there would be a special briefing at 9:45.

There already had been some news reports from Saigon suggesting that a halt in the bombing had been ordered, but those reports did not make clear whether it was a temporary halt—just for the New Year's

Continued on Page 3, Column 1

Associated Press
Parts of the fuselage of the Eastern jetliner dot the swamp near Miami Airport. The tail section is visible at center.

89 Die, 80 Survive and 8 Are Missing In Florida Crash of Jet From New York

By JON NORDHEIMER
Special to The New York Times

MIAMI, Dec. 30 — Eighty men, women and children were rescued in the predawn darkness of the Florida Everglades today after a jumbo jetliner from New York with 177 persons aboard crashed late last night while on an approach to Miami International Airport.

The Eastern Airlines L-1011 TriStar shattered on impact in the mud and mire of the swamp about 17 miles west of the airport. An airline official said that the bodies of 89 persons had been recovered and that eight other passengers were missing and presumed dead.

It was the first air disaster involving a wide-bodied commercial airliner, and Federal investigators at the scene expressed hope that the high survival rate was an indication that the big jets offered an extra measure of protection against the shock of impact in a crash.

A number of passengers walked away from the wreckage with only minor injuries. Most of the survivors, however, suffered broken bones and more serious physical injuries as the three-engine jet, which has been in domestic service since last spring, disintegrated in a quarter-mile-long trail of twisted aluminum and steel.

The TriStar, a $19-million aircraft that has a seating capacity of 226, left Kennedy International Airport in New York last night, bound for Miami with holiday travelers. It was in a routine approach pattern to the Miami Airport in clear weather when it vanished from the field's radar control scanners at 11:42 P.M. without warning, investigators said.

Helicopters Used

A Coast Guard helicopter located the wreckage about 25 minutes later in a section of the Everglades where furrows of sand and water and sawgrass give the terrain a washboard pattern. A wide rescue effort was mounted, with military and municipal disaster rescue teams evacuating the injured and dying in helicopters and propeller-driven airboats. The crash scene was inaccessible by road.

There was no immediate clue to the cause of the crash, the third major domestic airline accident this month. Three jets were involved in two separate accidents at Chicago airports earlier in December.

"There was no warning," said one of the surviving passengers, Martin Siminerio, a 22-year-old accountant from Lynbrook, L.I. "We had gotten the O.K. to land when the nose of the plane moved up a bit, and suddenly there was a crunch. The next thing I knew I could see the sky above me, and I was out in a field holding my briefcase."

Two men were hunting frogs nearby in the Everglades aboard an airboat when the crash occurred.

"We saw the plane go over real low," said Ray Dickens of

Continued on Page 34, Column 5

ISRAELI JETS RAID SYRIAN ARMY BASE

Shelling of Occupied Golan Heights Brings Retaliation —No Planes Lost

By The Associated Press

TEL AVIV, Sunday, Dec. 31 —Syria shelled Israeli settlements in occupied territory yesterday, and Israeli planes retaliated with their second attack in four days, bombing an army camp north of Damascus.

The Damascus radio said the shelling, near the cease-fire line where heavy fighting flared last month, was a reprisal for an air raid Wednesday by Israel. The Israeli command said Syrian artillery fired an hour-long barrage into the northern Golan Heights section and then shelled the southern section.

The Israeli command reported that its planes flew into Syria late last night and bombed the army camp at Nebk, 120 miles inside the border.

Planes Return Safely

The air attack, an Israeli communiqué said, was "in retaliation to Syrian artillery shelling directed at civilian settlements and positions on the Golan heights." It said the planes returned safely. The Damascus radio said one plane was damaged but did not say to what extent.

The Israelis reported no casualties in the Syrian shelling, and gave no estimates of bomb damage or Arab casualties from the air attack. Israel captured the Golan Heights in the 1967 war.

The night bombing raid, ordered under Israel's new "strike fast" policy of hitting the Arabs even after minor provocations, came less than

Continued on Page 16, Column 5

A Fresh Nationalism Is Sweeping Australia

By ROBERT TRUMBULL
Special to The New York Times

SYDNEY, Australia, Dec. 30—From the traffic-choked cities along the shore to the vast open spaces of the Outback, where cattlemen casually fly their own planes 100 miles or more for a drink with the nearest neighbor, there is a feeling that Australia has turned a corner.

A fresh breeze of nationalism is sweeping across this normally placid country under the new Government of Prime Minister Gough Whitlam, whose moderately socialist Labor party came to power in a resounding electoral victory over the old conservative coalition that had governed for 23 years.

The new mood has followed a series of ego-building steps by Mr. Whitlam, a tall, 56-year-old former lawyer. His most dramatic actions abruptly ended the military draft, brought the last Australian soldiers in Vietnam home ahead of schedule, opened diplomatic relations with China and East Germany and upgraded the Australian dollar as compared with American and other currencies.

"That should jolly well show the Yanks," said a woman in a supermarket, commenting on the developments.

"Bloody Poms, too," she added, using the common Australian epithet for the British. (The origin of the term Pom, or Pommie, is a mystery, but "bloody" goes with it like the traditional Southerner's "damn" in "damn Yankee.")

If the mass of Australians walk a little taller because of Mr. Whitlam's new "independ-

Continued on Page 2, Column 3

Employment Falls in City For 3d Consecutive Year

By PETER KIHSS

Employment in New York City has declined for the third consecutive year, although the decrease was less than that in 1971, the Federal Bureau of Labor Statistics reported yesterday.

In a year-end review, Herbert Bienstock, the bureau's regional director, said the city lost 73,300 jobs this year, a 2 per cent decline, based on averages for the first 10 months as against the same period a year ago. This contrasted with a national gain of two million jobs—a 2.8 per cent rise—and an increase of 19,000 in the nearby suburbs in Nassau, Suffolk, Rockland and Westchester Counties.

Mr. Bienstock described "weaknesses in all of New York City's major employment sectors," including those that had had significant growth during the last half of the nineteen-sixties. For instance, services (such as health facilities, dry-cleaning establishments and filling stations) were down 12,200 jobs; state and local government work, down 1,500, and financial, insurance and real estate employment, down 3,900.

On the other hand, the annual review said many workers who did have jobs experienced gains in purchasing power—up 3.4 per cent for factory production workers when earnings changes were adjusted for changes in Federal income and Social Security taxes and consumer prices.

This followed a 1.9 per cent increase in such "real after-tax pay" in 1971, following an actual decline of net spendable earnings in real terms in 1969

Continued on Page 21, Column 1

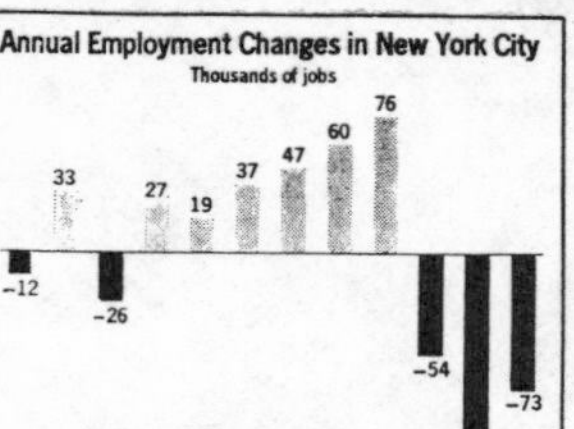

The New York Times/Dec. 31, 1972

KEY JOBS OFFERED TO LABOR BY NIXON

President Reported Willing to Name Union Men to All Federal Departments

By PHILIP SHABECOFF
Special to The New York Times

WASHINGTON, Dec. 30 — President Nixon has offered to put a labor union representative at a high level in every Federal Government department, a well-informed White House official has disclosed.

The offer, said to be unparalleld in labor history, was made to union members on the National Productivity Commission, including George Meany, president of the A.F.L.-C.I.O., and Frank E. Fitzsimmons, president of the International Brotherhood of Teamsters, at a White House meeting last week.

The White House is now awaiting recommendations from Mr. Meany and Mr. Fitzsimmons on whether the President's offer is to be accepted and, if so, how it will be implemented.

The White House official was not specific about what sort of posts would be offered to trade union representatives. However, labor sources said they understood the proposal included an offer to place union men at the assistant secretary level in all relevant Government agencies.

Mr. Nixon is reported to have told the union leaders that he wants a labor "input" in every part of his Government. He also wants to demonstrate

Continued on Page 19, Column 1

St. John's Captures Final in Basketball

St. John's won the Holiday Festival basketball tournament at Madison Square Garden yesterday by upsetting South Carolina, 86-79.

In college football, Auburn gained a 24-3 Gator Bowl victory over Colorado. North Carolina beat Texas Tech in the Sun Bowl, 32-28. Tennessee beat Louisiana State, 24-17, in The Astro-Bluebonnet Bowl.

Pro football's representatives for the Super Bowl Jan. 14 will be decided today in playoffs at Pittsburgh and Washington. At Pittsburgh, the Steelers meet the Miami Dolphins at noon for the American Conference title. The Redskins play the Dallas Cowboys at 3 P.M. for the National Conference crown.

Details in Section 5.

The New York Times/Lee Romero
ANSWERING AN APPEAL: Scene at the Red Cross Building here yesterday as donors gathered to give blood in drive to increase area's blood supplies. Details, Page 36.

To Our Readers

Because of changes in production schedules for the holiday weekend, the Week in Review (Section 4) was printed early. As a result, it was not possible to include news or editorial comment on the Vietnam bombing halt ordered yesterday by President Nixon.

Today's Sections

Index to Subjects

"All the News That's Fit to Print"

The New York Times

LATE CITY EDITION

Weather: Mostly sunny, mild today; fair and milder tonight, tomorrow. Temp. range: today 32-49; Monday 34-44. Full U.S. report on Page 77.

VOL. CXXII . . . No. 41,996 · © 1973 The New York Times Company · NEW YORK, TUESDAY, JANUARY 16, 1973 · 15 CENTS

PRESIDENT HALTS ALL BOMBING, MINING AND SHELLING OF NORTH; POINTS TO 'PROGRESS' IN TALKS

4 MORE ADMIT GUILT AS SPIES IN WATERGATE

Bernard L. Barker, left, and Virgilio R. Gonzalez arriving at U.S. District Court in Washington.

2 STILL ON TRIAL

Judge Dubious About Defendants' Replies to His Questions

By WALTER RUGABER

Special to The New York Times

WASHINGTON, Jan. 15—Four of the six remaining defendants in the Watergate trial pleaded guilty today in Federal Court to spying on the Democrats during last year's campaign.

They pleaded guilty to all seven counts of an indictment charging them with conspiracy, second-degree burglary and wiretapping. The action subjects them to a maximum of 55 years in prison.

The four are Bernard L. Barker, a Miami real estate agent, and three of his associates—Frank A. Sturgis, Eugenio Rolando Martinez and Virgilio R. Gonzalez.

Last Thursday, E. Howard Hunt Jr., a former White House consultant, pleaded guilty to all six charges against him.

United Press International

Frank A. Sturgis at the courthouse.

Associated Press

Eugenio R. Martinez on his way to the trial.

2 Insist on Innocence

Chief Judge John J. Sirica of the United States District Court here questioned the four defendants, who changed their pleas from not guilty, about their motives for spying and about the possible involvement of others, and then sent them to jail in lieu of $100,000 surety bonds each, to await sentencing.

Testimony in the case resumed immediately with the remaining defendants, both officials of President Nixon's political organization when the spying charges arose, maintaining their innocence.

When the defendants who pleaded guilty answered Judge Sirica's questions, the replies were not directly illuminating. The four men appeared confident and even bland in their exchanges with the judge, and they confined their answers as much as possible to the allegations against them.

Judge Sirica was openly dubious about a number of their responses. At one point, after all the men said they were uncertain about the source of the money that had been supplied to them, he said, "Well, I'm sorry, but I don't believe you."

The judge did not pursue some lines of questioning in the face of limited replies, but it was later pointed out by legal observers that he was not strictly entitled to force answers on some points.

The four men were arrested inside the offices of the Democratic National Committee on June 17. They admitted today that they had gone there to install wiretaps and bugging equipment and to rifle the party's files.

Arrested with them was one

Continued on Page 18, Column 1

Stock Prices Plummet

Stock prices registered their fourth largest decline yesterday in more than two years. Traders' fears were attributed to prospects of renewed inflation and uncertainty about President Nixon's Phase 3 economic plans. The Dow-Jones industrial averaged slumped 13.77 points to close at 1,025.59. Earlier in the day, prices had climbed on Vietnam peace hopes. Details on Page 51.

I.B.M. TO SELL UNIT TO CONTROL DATA IN SETTLING SUITS

$16-Million Will Be Paid for Subsidiary—Effect of Pact on U.S. Case a Question

By WILLIAM D. SMITH

The Control Data Corporation and the International Business Machines Corporation announced yesterday settlement of Control Data's antitrust suit against the computer giant, and I.B.M.'s subsequent counterclaims.

The agreement calls for I.B.M. to sell its Service Bureau Corporation subsidiary to Control Data for $16-million in cash. It also provides for payment over the next 10 years by I.B.M. to Control Data of about $60-million for various expenses and services.

Control Data, based in Minneapolis, is the nation's fifth largest manufacturer of computers and is responsible for about 4.5 per cent of the installed value of data processing equipment in the United States, mostly in the large-scale segment of the market. The company was established in 1957.

Suit Was Filed in 1968

Control Data's suit against I.B.M. was filed in March 1968, 10 months before the Government's antitrust suit against I.B.M. Control Data charged I.B.M. with violation of antitrust laws during the mid-1960's with regard to marketing large-scale computers, and I.B.M's counterclaims accused Control Data of similar violations.

A trial date of Nov. 5, 1973, had been set for the case in a Federal court in Minnesota.

Yesterday's settlement came as a surprise to many industry observers, partly because of the vigorous opposition to I.B.M.'s dominance that William C. Norris, Control Data's chairman and president, has often stated.

Important Trust Action

A major question now is what effect the Control Data settlement will have on the Department of Justice's antitrust suit against I.B.M. The Government's suit was filed in January of 1969 and has relied heavily on information obtained by Control Data.

The Justice Department's suit is considered one of the most important antitrust actions because of the size and importance of the computer industry.

The Department of Justice declined yesterday to comment on the Control Data Settlement.

In a letter to shareholders yesterday, Mr. Norris commented:

"The decision to file a lawsuit in 1968, although difficult at the time, has now proved

Continued on Page 59, Column 1

ENLARGED COUNCIL VETOED BY MAYOR

Bill Would Have Created 6 Minority Seats—Lindsay Cites Insufficient Debate

By EDWARD RANZAL

Mayor Lindsay vetoed a bill yesterday that would have created six City Council districts to increase black and Puerto Rican representation on the Council, contending that there had not been sufficient notice, awareness and debate by the public on the bill.

The bill would have raised the number of Councilmen to 43 from 37. Mr. Lindsay said that many community leaders had complained that they had not had sufficient time to obtain and study maps and hold community-level talks prior to the public hearings.

A spokesman for the Council leadership termed the Mayor's position "much nonsense" and said that there were sufficient votes to override the veto. The spokesman said that the Council would probably act next week. To override the veto would require 25 votes, or two-thirds of the Council.

The bill was passed 28-7 on Dec. 22. The Council acted on a mandate of the State Legislature to create the districts by Feb. 1.

New Lines Feared

If the Council is unable to override the veto, its leaders acknowledge, there will not be enough time before the Feb. 1 deadline to draw up a new bill.

The matter would then be returned to the Legislature where, Council leaders said, they fear new Councilmanic lines would be drawn along State Senatorial district lines, with the possibility of the Council membership being reduced by three, rather than a gain of six.

There now are 27 Councilmen and 10 Councilmen-at-large. There are 24 Senatorial districts wholly within the city. If these Senate districts were also to be construed as Councilmanic districts, there would be a loss of three seats on the Council.

A realignment might also change the political make-up of the Council, which is now 32 Democrats, three Republicans and two Liberals. Two of the Democrats were Liberals

Continued on Page 31, Column 2

Mrs. Meir Confers With Pope in Vatican

By PAUL HOFMANN

Special to The New York Times

ROME, Jan. 15 — Premier Golda Meir of Israel and Pope Paul VI met in the Vatican for an hour today and discussed peace efforts for the Middle East, the status of Jerusalem and the question of Palestinian refugees.

In the first encounter at the Vatican between a head of the Roman Catholic Church and an Israeli Government chief, Mrs. Meir also raised the problem of Arab terrorism and the condition of Jews in the Soviet Union.

Before broaching specific issues in his talk with the Premier, Pope Paul recalled "the history and the sufferings of the Jewish people," a Vatican statement said later.

However, the Vatican took pains to stress, through a spokesman, that Mrs. Meir's audience with the Pope had not been a "preferential or exclusive gesture" and did not mean or imply any change, however slight, in "the attitude of the Holy See concerning the Holy Land."

Mrs. Meir said at a crowded news conference tonight: "It isn't once a week that a representative of Israel has the opportunity to meet the Pope and discuss our problems with him; I'm very happy that the audience took place."

"Anybody with historic perspective cannot possibly refuse to see there is historic value in it," she said, and added, "I was very, very gratified when the Pope expressed his appreciation of the way Israel is taking care of the holy places."

The Vatican indicated through its spokesman that its views on the future of Jerusalem remained quite different from Israel's plans Is-

Continued on Page 16, Column 3

Associated Press

Premier Golda Meir after audience with Pope Paul VI

PARIS SESSION DUE

Ziegler Says Kissinger Will Return There in 'Near Future'

By JOHN HERBERS

Special to The New York Times

KEY BISCAYNE, Fla., Jan. 15—President Nixon, citing "progress" made in the cease-fire negotiations in Paris, suspended bombing, mining, shelling and all other offensive action throughout North Vietnam today.

Ronald L. Ziegler, the White House press secretary, announced the suspension this

Transcript of Ziegler news conference is on Page 12.

morning after several hours of consultations between the President and his chief negotiator, Henry A. Kissinger.

This was the first time that a spokesman for Mr. Nixon has said publicly that progress had been made in the latest round of Paris negotiations. But, while acknowledging reports in a number of world capitals that an agreement had been reached between the United States and North Vietnam, Mr. Ziegler said he could not confirm the existence of an agreement for a cease-fire.

Agreement Cited

"We have made it very clear we have a mutual agreement with the North Vietnamese that we will in no way discuss the substance of the negotiations in Paris" as long as they are under way, Mr. Ziegler said.

He said Mr. Kissinger would return to Paris in the "relatively near future" as the negotiations proceed. Mr. Kissinger flew from Paris Saturday after six days of talks and conferred with President Nixon in three meetings yesterday. Last night, Mr. Nixon sent Gen. Alexander M. Haig Jr., who has been one of the chief participants in the negotiations, to Saigon to "consult" with President Nguyen Van Thieu about what Mr. Kissinger and Le Duc Tho had done in Paris.

[General Haig arrived in Saigon Tuesday morning and, accompanied by Ambassador Ellsworth Bunker, went to the presidential palace to begin talks with President Thieu. Page 12.]

'All Offensive Action'

Today, in announcing the halt of offensive action, Mr. Ziegler said, "Because of the progress made in the negotiations between Dr. Kissinger and special adviser Le Duc Tho, President Nixon has directed that the bombing, shelling and any further mining of North Vietnam be suspended. This order went into effect at 10 A.M. today, Jan. 15, Washington time."

"The directive which I have referred to by the President applied to action north of the 17th Parallel, the entire area of North Vietnam," Mr. Ziegler said. This includes "all offensive action" in North Vietnam, he added later, but reconnaissance action continues.

The order, Mr. Ziegler said, does not apply to military activity in South Vietnam and other countries.

Thus Mr. Nixon restricted American military activity against North Vietnamese forces to its lowest level since last spring before American offensive action in North Viet-

Continued on Page 12, Column 3

P.S.C. PLAN OFFERS PHONE-AID CHARGE

Bids Company Allow a Drop of $12-Million Basic Rates in Return for Revenue Gain

By GRACE LICHTENSTEIN

Special to The New York Times

ALBANY, Jan. 15—A Public Service Commission representative recommended today that the New York Telephone Company be allowed to charge for local information calls if the number requested was in the local directory. In return, he suggested, the company should reduce the basic monthly charge.

Richard S. Hesser of the Public Service Commission's communications division estimated that charging for directory assistance would net the company $20-million more a year in revenue.

The reduction in the basic charge—which would cost the company $12-million a year—would cut the average New York City resident's bill about 16 cents a month.

A decision by the full Public Service Commission is not likely for several months, because both sides must still submit more testimony and a report must be written by the P.S.C. hearing examiner, Thomas R. Matias.

Mr. Hesser's plan was presented here at the latest hear-

Continued on Page 48, Column 3

Strict Auto Curb on Coast Doubted by Ruckelshaus

By GLADWIN HILL

Special to The New York Times

LOS ANGELES, Jan. 15—Although its administrator indicated he did not expect such a measure to be put into effect, the Environmental Protection Agency formally proposed today an 80 per cent reduction in auto travel in the Los Angeles basin, to be made effective through gasoline rationing.

The administrator, William D. Ruckelshaus, said the proposal had been promulgated in conformance with a Federal court order, with "grave reservations" about its feasibility. He said it was subject to modification at forthcoming public hearings and that if the Federal requirements ultimately proved impossibly stringent, people have the remedy of "the political process."

'Transportation Strategies'

The stringent action was proposed as the only certain way the Los Angeles basin could comply with Federal air quality standards by the legal deadline of 1977.

The proposal, which would cripple economic and social life in one of the world's most motorized areas, was the most sweeping to emerge in two years of implementation of the Clean Air Act of 1970.

Mr. Ruckelshaus said Los Angeles was unique in the severity of its problem, but that some other cities might have to employ some traffic restriction to meet Federal air quality standards.

He said he did not know what the outlook was for New York City. All states except California have until Feb. 15 to file "transportation strategies" where necessary as part of "implementation plans" to comply with the Clean Air Act.

Under the act, the E.P.A. set

Continued on Page 21, Column 1

U.S. Hijacking Case Ends in a Mistrial

By ROBERT LINDSEY

Federal District Judge George Rosling in Brooklyn declared a mistrial yesterday in the trial of Garrett B. Trapnell, who had admitted hijacking a Trans World Airlines jet last Jan. 29, but contended he was insane at the time.

The jury was split 11 to 1 for conviction as the five-week trial ended—as it had been since deliberations begin last Thursday morning. The lone holdout, Gertrude Hass, a middle-aged, unemployed psychiatric therapist, was bitterly criticized by fellow jurors. Through a lawyer for the New York Civil Liberties Union, she issued a statement defending her posi-

Continued on Page 78, Column 3

Patient and His Doctor: Quandary for Medicine

By JANE E. BRODY

Fifteen years ago Milton Blackstone was clearly at the top among entertainment publicists. A clever, personable man whom friends called "a genius," Mr. Blackstone guided Eddie Fisher to stardom and was the acknowledged man-behind-the-scenes whose ideas converted Grossinger's from a small summer hotel in the Catskills to an international year-round resort.

Today, the once wealthy Milton Blackstone is in debt and living in a fourth-rate hotel on Manhattan's West Side, the sole occupant of a 20-bed dormitory adjoining a steam room. His friends say that in recent years he has undergone a dramatic personality change, becoming increasingly withdrawn, occasionally paranoid and, at times, severely emaciated.

The causes of his condition are not clear, but Mr. Blackstone's two brothers said they believed it is connected with the treatment he has been receiving for 20 years from Dr. Max Jacobson, the 72-year-old Manhattan practitioner recently described in The New York Times as physician to a long list of celebrities and others. Dr. Jacobson treats his patients by injections that he says contain vitamins, hormones and often amphetamines.

The story of Milton Blackstone—as told to The Times by his brothers—underscores the serious difficulties involved in the ability of medicine to regulate itself. It points particularly to the apparent impotence of the local medical society and the extreme reluctance of physicians to report what they believe to be the questionable practices of their colleagues.

Many of Dr. Jacobson's patients have had high praise for the care he has given them, including Milton Blackstone who, while refusing to discuss details of his relationship with the doctor, said that the doctor "saved my life" and is "more than a friend."

However, a few of Dr. Jacobson's former patients have complained of bad reactions to the injections, including excessive talkativeness, severe weight loss, paranoia and a dependence on the shots.

After the article was published in The Times, a number of Dr. Jacobson's former patients, and in some cases their relatives, told The Times of

Continued on Page 22, Column 1

Garden Track Meet Will Drop U.S. Anthem to Avoid Incidents

By GERALD ESKENAZI

Amid growing controversy over whether it should be played at sports events, the national anthem has been dropped from the Olympic Invitational track and field meet at Madison Square Garden.

The playing of "The Star-Spangled Banner" is not obligatory, since "its purpose and relevance to sports events has never been established," Jesse Abramson, the meet director, said yesterday.

The meet will be staged Feb. 16. A Garden official said it would be the first time that a sports event would be held at the world's most famous indoor arena without the anthem being played. The new Garden will be 5 years old next month, and has housed more than 500 athletic contests, from the roller derby to wrestling. It was traditional since World War II to play the anthem at the old Garden.

The action on the anthem came two days after the Eastern Michigan track team had been disqualified for not standing during the playing of the anthem at the Nassau Coliseum in Uniondale, L. I., where the Knights of Columbus meet was held.

Three members of the mile-relay team, all blacks, went through stretching exercises during the traditional playing. Some fans hooted and cursed and, after a delay, Jim Foley, the meet referee, summoned the games committee to the floor and a decision was made to disqualify the team.

However, the chairman of

Continued on Page 45, Column 1

Gangs Spread Terror in the South Bronx

This is the second of four articles on the South Bronx.

By MARTIN TOLCHIN

A 37-year-old drug pusher is fatally struck by six bullets that shape a cross on his body. A bus is invaded and its driver held at gunpoint while passengers are relieved of wallets, watches and other valuables, Wild West style. A runaway girl is crippled after being beaten with belts and chains.

These acts of violence, all committed last month, were among more than 800 reported examples of violent crimes last year that have been linked by the police to the youth gangs that have been proliferating in the South Bronx.

Police Inspector Robert H. Johnson, who is in charge of the 90-man youth gang task force in the Bronx, says the 130 gangs in the South Bronx last year accounted for more than 30 murders, 22 attempted homicides, 300 assaults, 10 rapes and 124 armed robberies. In all, some 1,500 gang arests were made

The police believe that the largest number of youth-gang homicides in any one previous year was 12 for the entire city, in 1962.

A National Problem

The resurgence of street-gang warfare became a national problem last year. But many police observers believe that the growth began in the rubble-strewn, graffiti-splattered, disease-ridden streets of the South Bronx. Many South Bronx gangs now have "divisions" in other parts of the city.

Street gangs had terrorized slum areas, including the South Bronx, during the nineteen-fifties and early sixties. Many experts say these gangs broke up after their members became addicted to heroin and in their drug-induced torpor dropped out. But now, specialists at Lincoln Hospital and other health and community officials in the South Bronx say they have observed a marked increase in youth violence that has accompanied a marked decrease in overdose cases and other indicators of narcotics use.

There are those in the South Bronx who credit the gangs with routing drug pushers and restoring a feeling of pride. But others contend that few gangs are drug-free and that some of them are used by drug dealers as armies to consolidate their power.

Many residents also complain that the gangs have unleashed a reign of terror on their neighbors, menacing merchants, assaulting students in virtually all of the borough's

Continued on Page 28, Column 1

NEWS INDEX

"All the News That's Fit to Print"

The New York Times

LATE CITY EDITION

Weather: Partly sunny, mild today; cold tonight. Fair, mild tomorrow. Temp. range: today 36-49; Tuesday 45-58. Full U.S. report on Page 81.

VOL. CXXII . . No. 42,004 — NEW YORK, WEDNESDAY, JANUARY 24, 1973 — 15 CENTS

VIETNAM ACCORD IS REACHED; CEASE-FIRE BEGINS SATURDAY; P.O.W.'S TO BE FREE IN 60 DAYS

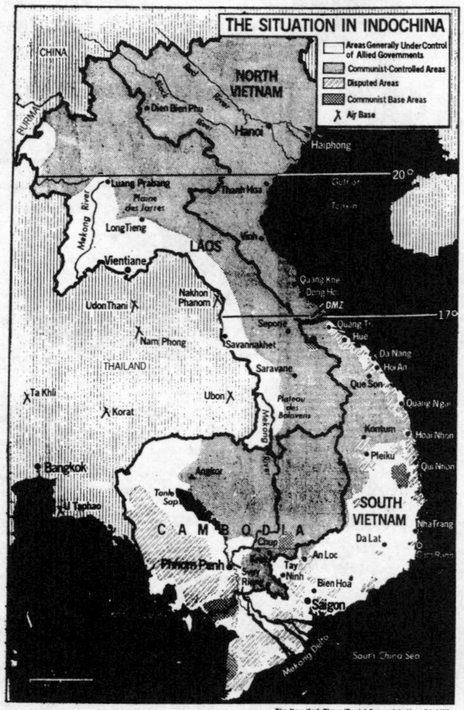

The New York Times/Daniel Brownstein/Jan. 24, 1973

Map shows approximate areas held by Communist and Government forces in South Vietnam, Laos and Cambodia. While Communists control large regions, population concentrations are mostly in Government-dominated areas.

THIEU IS CAUTIOUS

Says the Agreement Doesn't Guarantee Lasting Peace

By SYLVAN FOX

Special to The New York Times

SAIGON, South Vietnam, Wednesday, Jan. 24—President Nguyen Van Thieu, joining in announcing the Paris accord on Vietnam, declared today that he considered it only as a cease-fire and not as a guarantee of "a stable, long-lasting peace."

While contending the agreement demonstrated that Communist aggression against the South had "been smashed," President Thieu said:

"Let me say frankly of the peace accord to be signed in three days that I consider it only as a cease-fire agreement. As to whether or not we will have real peace, we must wait and see.

Excerpts from Thieu speech are printed on Page 16.

'Not More or Less'

"I say this is only a cease-fire agreement, not more or less. In the days to come, we'll sée if the Communists will observe the agreement."

President Thieu made his declarations in a 40-minute speech broadcast to the South Vietnamese people this morning. The beginning of his speech was timed to coincide with the radio and television address by President Nixon, which was broadcast on the armed forces radio here, but Mr. Thieu continued long after Mr. Nixon had finished his talk.

Like President Nixon, Mr. Thieu announced that a cease-fire would go into effect throughout South Vietnam at 8 A.M. Sunday Saigon time.

Mr. Thieu did not indicate whether his Government had signed or would sign the peace

Continued on Page 16, Column 5

Transcript of the Speech by President on Vietnam

Following is a transcript of President Nixon's televised address to the nation last night on the Vietnam war, as recorded by The New York Times:

Good evening. I have asked for this radio and television time tonight for the purpose of announcing that we today have concluded an agreement to end the war and bring peace with honor in Vietnam and Southeast Asia.

The following statement is being issued at this moment in Washington and Hanoi:

"At 12:30 Paris time today, Jan. 23, 1973, the agreement on ending the war and restoring peace in Vietnam was initialed by Dr. Henry Kissinger on behalf of the United States and Special Adviser Le Duc Tho on behalf of the Democratic Republic of Vietnam.

"The agreement will be formally signed by the parties participating in the Paris Conference on Vietnam on Jan. 27, 1973, at the International Conference Center in Paris. The cease-fire will take effect at 2400 Greenwich mean time, Jan. 27, 1973. The United States and the Democratic Republic of Vietnam express the hope that this agreement will insure stable peace in Vietnam and contribute to the preservation of lasting peace in Indochina and Southeast Asia."

Essential Conditions 'Have Been Met'

That concludes the formal statement.

Throughout the years of negotiations, we have insisted on peace with honor.

In my addresses to the nation from this room on Jan. 25 and May 8, I set forth the goals that we considered essential for peace with honor. In the settlement that has now been agreed to, all the conditions that I laid down then nave been met—a cease-fire internationally supervised will begin at 7 P.M. this Saturday, Jan. 27, Washington time. Within 60 days from this Saturday all Americans held prisoners of war throughout Indochina will be released.

There will be the fullest possible accounting for all of those who are missing in action.

During the same 60-day period all American forces will be withdrawn from South Vietnam.

The people of South Vietnam have been guaranteed the right to determine their own future without outside interference.

By joint agreement, the full text of the agreement and the protocols to carry it out will be issued tomorrow.

Throughout these negotiations we have been in the closest consultation with President Thieu and other representatives of the Republic of Vietnam.

This settlement meets the goals and has the full support of President Thieu and the Government of the Republic of Vietnam as well as that of our other allies who are affected.

The United States will continue to recognize the Gov-

Continued on Page 16, Column 3

C.B.S. News

President Nixon during his White House speech.

TROOPS TO LEAVE

On TV, Nixon Asserts 'Peace With Honor' Is Aim of Pact

By BERNARD GWERTZMAN

Special to The New York Times

WASHINGTON, Jan. 23—President Nixon said tonight that Henry A. Kissinger and North Vietnam's chief negotiator, Le Duc Tho, had initialed an agreement in Paris today "to end the war and bring peace with honor in Vietnam and Southeast Asia."

In a televised report to the nation, a few hours after Mr. Kissinger returned to Washington, Mr. Nixon said a cease-fire in Vietnam would go into effect on Saturday at 7 P.M., Eastern standard time.

Simultaneous announcements were made in Hanoi and Saigon.

Mr. Nixon said that under the terms of the accord—which will be formally signed on Saturday—all American prisoners of war would be released and the remaining 23,700-man American force in South Vietnam would be withdrawn within 60 days.

Wider Peace Indicated

He referred to "peace" in Southeast Asia, suggesting that the accord extended to Laos and Cambodia, which have also been engaged in the war. But there was no direct mention of those two nations today, and it is not known if the cease-fire extends to them as well.

Obviously pleased by the long-awaited development, ending the longest war in American history, Mr. Nixon said the Hanoi-Washington agreement "meets the goals" and has the "full support" of President Nguyen Van Thieu of South Vietnam.

Earlier Mr. Thieu had expressed strong reservations about the draft agreement worked out by Mr. Kissinger and Mr. Tho in October.

Tonight Mr. Nixon sketched only the outline of the accord. The full text of the agreement and accompanying protocols will be issued tomorrow by joint agreement with Hanoi, he said.

It was not possible, for instance, to determine from Mr. Nixon's 10-minute address what changes had been made in the agreement since October.

In his brief description of the accord, Mr. Nixon said that the cease-fire would be "internationally supervised," a refer-

Continued on Page 16, Column 1

CONGRESS UNITED IN VOICING RELIEF

Some Worry Is Expressed on Permanence of Peace by Critics of War

By JAMES M. NAUGHTON

Special to The New York Times

WASHINGTON, Jan. 23—Members of Congress, after years of bitter debate over the war in Vietnam, united tonight in voicing relief and gratitude that the conflict appeared to be at an end.

At the same time, however, some supporters and critics of the Vietnam policies of two Administrations sought to draw from President Nixon's announcement fresh justification for their opposite viewpoints in the long dispute that divided Congress and the nation.

"Peace has come, may peace remain," said Hugh Scott of Pennsylvania, the Senate Republican leader and one of those who had steadfastly defended Mr. Nixon's four-year search for a negotiated truce.

"This is a day for which each of us should be thankful to the Lord," he said.

Senator Edward W. Brooke, a Massachusetts Republican who had been among leaders of an unsuccessful attempt to legislate a United States withdrawal from Indochina, expressed elation that "in four days, a decade of death and destruction will end."

But Mr. Brooke said that the nation had "waited so long for this day that, instead of joy,

Continued on Page 17, Column 7

MITCHELL LINKED TO $199,000 FUND

Watergate Witness Asserts He and Stans Approved of Payments to Liddy

By WALTER RUGABER

Special to The New York Times

WASHINGTON, Jan. 23—A witness said today that $199,000 was paid to a defendant in the Watergate trial during last year's campaign with the approval of former Attorney General John N. Mitchell and former Commerce Secretary Maurice H. Stans.

The money was said to have gone to G. Gordon Liddy, an attorney for President Nixon's campaign organization last year who had been assigned to establish what another witness described as "an intelligence gathering operation."

For the second consecutive day, Chief Judge John J. Sirica indicated dissatisfaction with the prosecution's examination of a witness, excused the jury, and posed a series of questions himself.

It was the United States District Court judge who elicited from Hugh W. Sloan Jr., former treasurer of the Finance Committee to Re-elect the President, the names of Mr. Nixon's two former Cabinet officers.

Mr. Sloan told Judge Sirica

Continued on Page 15, Column 1

Thousands at Johnson Bier

By ROY REED

Special to The New York Times

AUSTIN, Tex., Wednesday, Jan. 24—Thousands of persons of all ages and from all walks of life filed past the coffin of former President Lyndon B. Johnson yesterday and throughout the night as his body lay in state in the huge library bearing his name at the University of Texas.

The flag-draped coffin of Mr. Johnson, who died Monday, had been brought from the Weed Corley Funeral Home here to the library at noon. It was placed at the top of a long stairway in front of a long metal wall etched with scenes of Mr. Johnson's life.

His widow, Lady Bird, and their two daughters and sons-in-law, Mr. and Mrs. Charles S. Robb and Mr. and Mrs. Patrick J. Nugent, arrived with the coffin. Mrs. Johnson was escorted by Brig. Gen. James Cross, retired, pilot of the Presidential plane while Mr. Johnson was President.

Once during a brief service around the coffin, Mrs. Johnson glanced at a group of reporters nearby and beckoned to Norma Milligan of Newsweek's Washington bureau, whom she had known in Washington. The two women embraced, both with moist eyes, and after a few words of consolation Mrs. Johnson smiled and said, "Oh, but didn't he live well!"

The former President's body

Continued on Page 22, Column 6

Trinity's Bells Ring Out News of Accord

As soon as President Nixon ended his Vietnam peace announcement last night, Larry King, the organist at Trinity Church, went to an octave-and-a-half keyboard in the sanctuary and began pealing the 10 bells in the tower of the historic church at Broadway and Wall Street.

Mr. King was one of many persons in New York and its environs who were moved, in one way or another, to express their joy, their relief—and some their cynicism—at the official word from the President that peace in Vietnam had been tentatively agreed upon.

For 15 minutes the sound of Trinity's bells, which weigh up to 3,000 pounds apiece and include the oldest bells still in use in New York City, resounded off the walls of the skyscrapers in the financial district. Mr. King called the bell-ringing "a symbolic gesture of the gratitude all of us at Trinity Church feel that this war is being ended."

By the Episcopal church's original charter given by King William III of England in 1697, the bells can be rung only by the specific direction of the rector. The current rector, the Rev. Robert R. Parks, said that other than normal use preceding and following services, they are rung only on "great occasions," such as the conclu-

Continued on Page 17, Column 1

Associated Press

Mrs. Lyndon B. Johnson near coffin of the former President as a clergyman delivered a eulogy. With her at the Johnson Library in Austin, Tex., are her elder daughter, Mrs. Charles S. Robb and Mr. Robb, left.

Envoy Held Captive

The United States Ambassador to Haiti, Clinton E. Knox, was being held at gunpoint early today by at least two men in his residence in Port-au-Prince. Details on Page 8.

War Leaves Deep Mark on U.S.

By JAMES RESTON

Special to The New York Times

News Analysis

WASHINGTON, Jan. 23—America is moving out of Vietnam after the longest and most divisive conflict since the War Between the States. But Vietnam is not moving out of America, for the impact of the war there is likely to influence American life for many years to come. Though it is probably too early to distinguish between the temporary and the enduring consequences, one thing is fairly clear: There has been a sharp decline in respect for authority in the United States as a result of the war—a decline in respect not only for the civil authority of government but also for the moral authority of the schools, the universities, the press, the church and even the family.

There was no cease-fire on this front. Vietnam did not start the challenge to authority, but it weakened respect for the executives who got the nation involved in the war in the first place, for the Congress that let it go on for more than a decade and for the democratic process of debate, which failed to influence the course of battle for years and which finally declined into physical combat and sporadic anarchy.

Even after a cease-fire, there will still be considerable contention in the country over whether the challenges to authority are good or bad.

Many Americans have maintained that it was precisely the dissent and the defiance that forced social reform at home and a settlement abroad.

Others have argued that the war produced a whole new revolutionary climate in America, which encouraged the Communists to prolong the conflict and disrupted the nation's unity and the previously accepted attitudes, standards and restraints in American public and private conduct. But few Americans challenge the proposition that for good or bad, something has happened to American life—something not yet understood or agreed upon, something that is different, important and probably enduring.

Even at the moment of the Vietnam compromise, for example, there was a rash of teacher strikes in several of the great cities of the nation; one-time members of the Central Intelligence Agency, some of them

Continued on Page 17, Column 3

NEWS INDEX

	Page		Page
Art	34	Movies	33-37
Books	39	Music	33-37
Bridge	38	Obituaries	44, 47
Business	48-63	Op-Ed	41
Crossword	39	Sports	27-30
Editorials	40	Theaters	33-37
Family/Style	46	Transportation	81
Financial	48-63	TV and Radio	82-83
Going Out Guide	34	U. N. Proceedings	2
Man in the News	18	Weather	81

News Summary and Index, Page 43

"All the News That's Fit to Print"

The New York Times

LATE CITY EDITION
Weather: Sunny and milder today; fair and mild tonight, tomorrow. Temp. range: today 30-46; Wed. 37-44. Full U.S. report on Page 77.

VOL. CXXII . . . No. 42,005 | NEW YORK, THURSDAY, JANUARY 25, 1973 | 15 CENTS

U.S. EXPECTS TRUCE IN LAOS AND CAMBODIA; P.O.W. AIRLIFT FROM HANOI TO START SOON; KISSINGER AND THO GIVE DETAILS OF ACCORD

Photo issued yesterday shows Paris scene as Henry A. Kissinger, seated to left, and Le Duc Tho initialed the agreement. In foreground are George H. Aldrich, left, and William H. Sullivan, of State Department. North Vietnamese officials are, from left, Luu Van Loi, Xuan Thuy and protocol aide: Nguyen Co Thach is at right.

THO IS JUBILANT

Says, in Paris, Pact Is 'Basically the Same' as October Draft

Special to The New York Times

PARIS, Jan. 24 — Le Duc Tho, North Vietnam's chief representative at the negotiations on a cease-fire, declared today that the agreement initialed yesterday was "basically the same" as the draft reached in October, before the talks collapsed.

The agreement is a "great victory for the Vietnamese people," a jubilant Mr. Tho said

Transcript of news conference by Tho is on Page 22.

at a crowded press conference at the former Hotel Majestic on the Avenue Kléber, where formal negotiations had been going on since 1968 and where he and Henry A. Kissinger initialed the documents.

He waved in a gesture of triumph as he entered the room, and in the Communist manner joined in the applause that broke out for him in the hall.

'A Moment of Joy'

"It is a moment of joy," Mr. Tho said, "a joy that is shared."

The "victory," he said, "crowned a valiant combat conducted in unity by the army and the people of Vietnam on all fronts at the cost of innumerable sacrifices and privations."

In a prepared statement, Mr. Tho went on to claim "very great victory for the Vietnamese people," "for the solidarity in combat of the three Indochinese people," "for the Socialist countries, the oppressed and all the peace-loving peoples of the world, including the American people who displayed their solidarity and gave devoted support to the just struggle of our people."

Only on a few points did Mr. Tho specify what had been a compromise and how it had been reached.

He spoke warmly of the American people more than once, and specificaliy thanked those "in many countries" who made "sacrifices" for the Vietnam peace movement. The tri-

Continued on Page 22, Column 5

Highlights of Agreement

Special to The New York Times

WASHINGTON, Jan. 24—Following are highlights of the Vietnam agreement, as set out in the text and in a news conference today by Henry A. Kissinger:

CEASE-FIRE—A cease-fire throughout North Vietnam and South Vietnam will go into effect on Jan. 27 at 7 P.M., Eastern standard time. Mr. Kissinger, the principal American negotiator, said that he expected a cease-fire in Laos to take effect "within a short period of time" and also expected a "de facto" cease-fire to come eventually in Cambodia. The United States will begin removing or deactivating mines off the coast of Vietnam Saturday.

TROOP WITHDRAWAL—All Americans, military and civilian, involved in combat will be withdrawn from Vietnam within 60 days of the signing. Economic advisers and technicians, some of whom may be in the military, can remain. North Vietnamese troops can stay in the South, but there can be no troop replacements. Foreign troops are to be withdrawn from Laos and Cambodia, although no deadline is set. Bases are prohibited in these countries, and the movement of troops and supplies through Laos and Cambodia is forbidden.

PRISONERS—A list of all American prisoners of war is to be given to the United States on Saturday. The prisoners will be turned over to American authorities within 60 days. The first prisoners will be released within 15 days, and the rest in equal installments at intervals of about 15 days. The status of imprisoned Vietnamese civilians is to be negotiated over three months.

TRUCE SUPERVISION—An international commission, with a 1,160-man force, is to supervise the release of prisoners, troop withdrawals, elections and other aspects of the agreement. The force will consist of troops from Canada, Hungary, Indonesia and Poland and will be based throughout South Vietnam, including at border crossing points. A joint military commission, at first with forces from the United States, South Vietnam, the National Liberation Front and North Vietnam, is to conduct preliminary investigations of violations and report to the international commission. The United States and North Vietnam will withdraw from the joint commission within 60 days. An international conference, including the Soviet Union and China, is to be convened within 30 days.

VIETNAM GOVERNMENT—The United States and North Vietnam agree to respect "the South Vietnamese people's right to self-determination." The present Government of President Nguyen Van Thieu will remain in office pending an election, for which no date has been set. The election is to be supervised by a National Council of National Reconciliation and Concord, made up of members from the South Vietnamese Government, Communists and neutralists. All sides agree to respect the demilitarized zone, and there is to be no military movement across the zone. The use of force to bring about the reunification of North Vietnam and South Vietnam is prohibited.

CAPITAL BRIEFING

Goals 'Substantially Achieved,' Kissinger Says of Efforts

By BERNARD GWERTZMAN
Special to The New York Times

WASHINGTON, Jan. 24—Henry A. Kissinger said today that the United States had "a firm expectation" that the Vietnam cease-fire that goes into effect on Saturday would soon extend to both Laos and Cambodia as well.

Speaking at a 90-minute news conference, following the release

Text of accord, Pages 15 to 17; Kissinger news conference is printed on Pages 19 to 21.

of the text and the four protocols, or annexes, of the Vietnam accord he initialed in Paris yesterday, Mr. Kissinger said that the United States had "substantially achieved" the negotiating goals it had set for an "honorable agreement."

Mr. Kissinger, who was personally involved throughout the four years of what he called the "peaks and valleys" of negotiations, presented the Administration's argument that it had secured a "fair and just" settlement, one that he said could not have been achieved four years ago.

[In Saigon, President Nguyen Van Thieu's closest adviser said the South Vietnamese Government was prepared to meet with the National Liberation Front 24 hours after the cease-fire agreement was signed to discuss the political future of the country.]

Series of Key Points

Besides revealing that the United States had indications from Hanoi to expect a formal cease-fire in Laos and an informal, de facto halt to the fighting in Cambodia, Mr. Kissinger made the following major points at his news conference:

¶As part of the provision for the release of American prisoners within 60 days, North Vietnam has agreed to allow United States Air Force medical evacuation planes to land at Hanoi to pick up prisoners who were confined in North Vietnam and Laos. The first release of prisoners was expected no later than 15 days after the formal signing Saturday. Prisoners in South Vietnam will be released there. North Vietnam said no Americans were prisoners in Cambodia. [Page 17.]

¶The agreement makes it clear "that there is an entity called South Vietnam," and that any unification of North Vietnam and South Vietnam will be decided only by negotiations and not by military force—an issue of some importance to Saigon.

¶The demilitarized zone was recognized in the accord at American insistence to enforce the provision against the infiltration of men and equipment from North Vietnam into South Vietnam.

¶North Vietnam was not obliged by the accord to remove its troops—estimated at 145,000—from South Vietnam, a goal sought by Saigon, but provisions of the accord bar any replacement or reinforcement of those forces. Thus, the United States expects North

Continued on Page 19, Column 1

U.S. ENVOY IN HAITI FREED BY CAPTORS

Is Exchanged for $70,000 and Release of 12 Held by the Government

By The Associated Press

PORT-AU-PRINCE, Haiti, Jan. 24—The United States Ambassador, Clinton E. Knox, was released unharmed today after being held at gunpoint for nearly 20 hours in his residence.

Two gunmen and a woman freed the Ambassador and Consul General Ward L. Christenscn in exchange for the release of 12 Haitian prisoners, safe conduct to Mexico and a ransom of $70,000.

[A Haitian plane carrying the three kidnappers and the 12 released prisoners arrived safely in Mexico City, United Press International reported.]

In Washington, the State Department said that at one point the gunmen had demanded $500,000 in ransom from the United States and that the reply was "flatly negative" from Secretary of State William P. Rogers.

Charles W. Bray 3d, the State Department spokesman, said he did not know where the ransom came from but that "I know it did not come from the

Continued on Page 7, Column 1

U.S. Foreign Trade Deficit Topped $6-Billion in 1972

By EDWIN L. DALE Jr.
Special to The New York Times

WASHINGTON, Jan. 24—The United States deficit in foreign trade—only the second in this century—soared to $6.4-billion last year, the Commerce Department reported today.

The deficit for 1971, the first, was only $2-bililon. Prior to that the nation had consistently exported more than it imported. Last year saw a good growth in exports but a much larger increase in imports, which have shown explosive growth in recent years.

Today's report said the trade deficit in December, at $563.2-mililon, was the highest since June. However, the second half of the year showed a somewhat smaller deficit than the first half.

Jump in Imports Value

Last year's results reflected chiefly an enormous jump in the dollar value of imports, partly reflecting the reduced valuation of the dollar against other major currencies at the end of 1971 and partly reflecting the pickup in United States economic activity.

The change in currency valuations meant that any given volume of imports cost more in dollar terms, and the economic expansion meant pressure for more imports.

Imports last year totaled $55.56-billion, up 22 per cent from 1971. This far outpaced the growth in exports of 13 per cent to $49.12-billion—an export increase that would normally be regarded as fairly good.

For December alone imports were at a record level of $5.03-billion, the second month in a row that the $5-billion mark was exceeded. Exports were $4.47-billion—like imports, little changed from November.

The Commerce Department said that the initial effect of the dollar devaluation "was to induce a prompt increase in dollar import prices without an immediate accompanying reduction in volume."

The agency said preliminary figures, through November, sug-

Continued on Page 63, Column 3

Stocks Tumble Despite Accord

The nation's financial markets moved sharply lower yesterday following President Nixon's disclosure Tuesday night that a cease-fire agreement had been initialed. Investors were said to be focusing on the outlook for inflation, tight money and high interest rates under Phase 3—instead of on the approaching cease-fire. Wall Street had been anticipating an end to the Vietnam war.

The Dow-Jones average of industrial stocks plunged 14.07 points to 1,004.59 in its biggest decline in almost 18 months.

Bond prices rose slightly in early trading but later declined. [All in Page 55.]

Leading members of the business and financial community said the cease-fire would have no dramatic short-term impact on the national economy. [Page 24.]

Some Leaders in Congress Fear a Short-Lived Truce

By JAMES M. NAUGHTON
Special to The New York Times

WASHINGTON, Jan. 24 — Congressional leaders, including some prominent opponents of the Indochina war, gave President Nixon a standing ovation after a lengthy White House briefing this morning on the negotiated truce in Vietnam.

But several members of Congress expressed concern that the peace might prove short-lived. One of them, Senator Frank Church, Democrat of Idaho, said that he would introduce legislation Friday to bar "re-entry" of American combat forces, including air forces, should the truce be broken.

The dominant reaction on Capitol Hill, as Senators and Representatives learned—a few at the White House, most by watching television—of the details of the agreement, appeared to be one of gratitude at American disengagement, but no more than frail hope that the war itself was over.

According to several accounts of the private 2-hour-20-minute meeting between Mr. Nixon and the Congressional leaders, the President also alluded to the

Continued on Page 24, Column 4

Johnson Lies in State in Capitol Rotunda

By JAMES T. WOOTEN
Special to The New York Times

WASHINGTON, Jan. 24 — The body of Lyndon Baines Johnson lay in state here today after thousands had quietly watched it borne in solemn procession to the Capitol.

As the second day of tribute to the 36th President ended, tens of thousands of mourners had filed slowly past his flag-draped coffin in the Rotounda, and other lines waited outside, swelling the number of Americans who have joined in a final farewell to him since his death in Texas on Monday.

President Nixon, Vice President Agnew and a number of Mr. Johnson's personal and political friends joined his family for a brief ceremony at the Capitol during which he was eulogized as "President for the people" and praised as a man "whose honesty was as deep and strong as his devotion to his country."

Then Mr. Nixon placed a wreath at the base of the black catafalque on which have rested the coffins of eight other Presidents, and the Rotunda was opened to the first public mourners.

Tomorrow has been declared

Continued on Page 34, Column 6

Associated Press

President Nixon, bareheaded in wind, with Mrs. Johnson as her husband's coffin was carried to the Capitol.

Metropolitan Listing Discloses Sale of 5 More Major Paintings

By JOHN L. HESS

A list of sales by the Metropolitan Museum of Art last year reveals the previously undisclosed disposal of five important paintings.

Further, it develops that the museum disposed of a group of six modern French masters at far less than their value, as appraised for the museum by a leading New York gallery.

Both disclosures emerge from an examination of documents provided to The New York Times in a modification of the institution's long-standing policy of secrecy on art dealings. The museum declined to reveal prices paid and obtained or to list works "deaccessioned" for sale but withdrawn from the market. It did, however, accede to requests for a list of all objects disposed of in the last two years, and for the appraisals consulted in the disposal of the six French masters.

The list showed sales last year of 50 paintings from the bequest of the late Adelaide Milton de Groot, whose will requested that the Metropolitan give to other museums any pictures it did not want.

Of these, 45 had been reported previously in The Times. The five others were Renoir's "In the Garden at Cagnes" and Boudin's "Market in Brittany,"

Continued on Page 52, Column 1

In Maspeth, the Memory Of War's Cost Mutes Joy

By GEORGE VECSEY

In Wally's Bar in Maspeth, Queens, where the construction men stop to drink on their way home from work, there is a "Support Our P.O.W.'s" banner pasted on the telephone booth and a bartender who talks of killing during his tour in Vietnam.

But yesterday, the day after a peace agreement was announced, the two dozen men in Wally's said that they were glad the war was over and that they could not recall a single good reason for fighting there.

"I only know four people who liked the war—Nixon, Johnson, Kennedy and Eisenhower," said Herbie Ehmann, having an afternoon drink in this neighborhood of factories and attached houses, railroad tracks and elevated highways. The area voted for President Nixon last fall.

"It's a funny neighborhood," said Tommy Gross, who spent 23 months as a marine in Vietnam. "You come in this place on Friday night but you'd better bring a helmet," he said. "Guys get going on this topic of Vietnam—they really get hot."

This may be the case on Friday night with the war going on, but not on Wednesday afternoon with the end

Continued on Page 25, Column 5

NEWS INDEX

HANOI

A composite photograph of the Hanoi area taken in January 1973 upon the completion of the Linebacker Operations. The photograph demonstrates that all areas targeted for strikes during the operations were military and that there was no indiscriminate carpet bombing of Hanoi as alleged by the Viet Cong.

Military Target Areas

1. Gia Lam R. R. Yard and Shops
2. Hanoi Thermal Power Plant
3. Hanoi/Gia Lam Airfield
4. Hanoi R. R. Station Yard and Shops
5. Hanoi Barge Yard D
6. Hanoi Port (Areas A, C, E)
7. Hanoi Depot Army No. 1
8. Hanoi Tank Truck Conversion Facility
9. Hanoi RADCOM Station No. 11 South
10. Hanoi Military Vehicle Repair Area South
11. Hanoi Storage Area Quinh Lai
12. Hanoi/Bac Mai Airfield
13. Hanoi Storage Area Bac Mai

Accidental Damage Areas

14. An Duong/Nghia Dung Area
15. Cuban Chancellery Compound
16. Kham Thien Area
17. Bac Mai Hospital
18. Hanoi Textile Plant

Landmark Not Damaged

19. Hanoi Hilton (Ha Lo PW Camp)

Military target areas are outlined in black, areas of accidental damage in white.

"All the News That's Fit to Print"

The New York Times

LATE CITY EDITION

Weather: Cold today, rain ending by midday; cold tonight, tomorrow. Temp. range: today 28-42; Sunday 36-41. Full U.S. report on Page 57.

VOL. CXXII . . . No. 42,069 NEW YORK, MONDAY, JANUARY 29, 1973 15 CENTS

CEASE-FIRE GENERALLY WORKING; U.S. BOMBS SUPPLY LINES IN LAOS; HANOI LISTS 555 WAR PRISONERS

Nixon Urges Public To Seek Budget Lid

Appeals for Pressure on Congressmen—Will Submit Fiscal Plan Today

By ROBERT H. PHELPS

Special to The New York Times

MIAMI, Jan. 28—President Nixon disclosed today plans for cuts in long-standing programs of aid to hospitals, schools and urban areas in appealing to the nation to put pressure on Congress to hold down Federal spending.

In an 11-minute radio address taped in Washington before the President came South for a long weekend in the sun, Mr. Nixon also disclosed proposals for shifting some of the savings to programs to control

The text of Nixon speech is printed on Page 18.

pollution, fight crime and drug abuse and step up research on cancer and heart disease.

The President also repeated his determination to avoid a tax increase.

The President gave no dollar figures on the amounts of the proposed cuts or increases or when he wanted them to take effect. Those details, as well as other proposed reductions and increases, will be released tomorrow when he sends to Congress his budget for the fiscal year 1974, which begins July 1 this year.

Recognizing that some leaders of the Democratic-controlled Congress disagree with him over how Federal funds should be allocated, the President used most of his radio time to give his argument for holding spending to $268.7-billion, the budget total he disclosed Friday, and to justify "sharp reductions" in programs that have become "sacred cows."

The address ended with an appeal to the people to support those in Congress "who have the courage to vote against higher spending."

The President began his speech by noting that the cost of Government had "skyrocketed" over the last few decades.

"For every $1 we were spending in 1952, we are spending nearly $4 today," he said. "If the budget continues to double every 10 years, it will be over a trillion dollars by the nineteen-nineties—20 years from now—or as big as our entire economy is now."

Mr. Nixon offered three reasons for resisting this trend.

The first was to prevent a tax increase. Asserting that taxes by all levels of government take more than 20 per cent of family budgets, he said, "This growing burden works to dull individual incentive and discourage responsibility. As government takes more from people, people can do less for themselves."

'Could Be Our Best Year'

The second reason the President gave for holding down spending was to prevent inflation. "Nineteen seventy-three could be our best year ever, ushering in a new era of prolonged and growing prosperity," the President said. "The greatest threat to our new prosperity is excessive Government spending."

The third argument the President made for his budget was to curb growth of Government. "The bigger Government became, the more clumsy it became, until its attempt to help

Continued on Page 18, Column 3

EXTRA DUTY TOURS FOR POLICE SET UP AFTER 2D AMBUSH

6 Sought in Police Attacks Said to Be Members of Black Liberation Army

By EMANUEL PERLMUTTER

Extra tours of duty for all policemen were authorized last night by Police Commissioner Patrick V. Murphy, who said six alleged members of the Black Liberation Army were being sought in the wounding of four policemen in two ambushes here in less than 72 hours.

Mr. Murphy acted after two policemen in a radio car were ambushed early yesterday while they were stopped at a traffic light at Baisley and Farmers Boulevards in Jamaica, Queens. On Thursday, two other patrolmen were ambushed in similar fashion at Newport Avenue and Sackman Street in the Brownsville section of Brooklyn.

All four policemen were wounded, though not seriously. In both incidents, the assailants were identified as black men who used high-powered weapons and escaped in automobiles.

Suspects Named

The six suspects were identified as Joanne Chesimard, 25 years old; Andrew Jackson, also known as Harvey Mitchell, 26; Avon White, also known as George, 22; Fred Hilton, also known as Fred Jamal, 19; Melvin Kearney, also known as Omar, 27; and Twymon Myers, 22.

Miss Chesimard and Jackson have been sought as suspects in the murders of Patrolmen Gregory Foster and Rocco Laurie in the East Village last year. Jackson is also being sought as a suspect in the fatal shooting in May, 1971, of Patrolmen Waverly Jones and Joseph Piagentini in a Harlem housing project. After the Harlem shooting, news media received letters in which the Black Liberation Army said it was responsible for the killings.

The two policemen ambushed yesterday were Patrolman Michael O'Reilly, 37 years old, and Patrolman Roy R. Pollina, 36, both attached to the 105th precinct, and both nine-year veterans of the force.

Both Satisfactory

They were both reported in satisfactory condition last night at Mary Immaculate Hospital—Patrolman O'Reilly with a shoulder wound and Patrolman Pollina with a bullet graze of the forehead. Both policemen are married and live in Holbrook, L. I.

The policemen who were shot in Brooklyn Thursday night were Patrolmen Carlo Imperato, 28, and his brother, Vincent, 32, both of whom suffered minor wounds.

As a result of Thursday's ambush, Commissioner Murphy announced Friday that he had authorized 1,000 extra tours of duty for policemen in 11 pre-

Continued on Page 57, Column 1

100-PLANE STRIKE

Attacks Expected to Continue Until Laos Truce Is Reached

By JOHN W. FINNEY

Special to The New York Times

WASHINGTON, Jan. 28—About 100 American planes, including B-52 bombers, attacked suspected Communist positions and supply lines in Laos after the Vietnam cease-fire went into effect, Administration officials said today.

This afternoon, the Defense Department, on orders from the White House and State Department, declined to comment on the bombing operations, refusing to confirm or deny that American planes based in Thailand were continuing missions over Laos. But late in the day the Pentagon spokesman, Jerry W. Friedheim, confirmed the raids.

Indirect confirmation of the operations came earlier from State Department officials and from William H. Sullivan, Deputy Assistant Secretary of State for East Asian and Pacific Affairs, who indicated that American bombing would continue in Laos until a cease-fire was reached there.

Appearing on the National Broadcasting Company television program "Meet the Press," Mr. Sullivan, a former Ambas-

Continued on Page 12, Column 6

The New York Times/Mike Lien

Mrs. Carroll E. Flora Jr. celebrating in her home in Walkersville, Md., with children, Dwayne, 6, and Teresa, 14. With her are Sgt. 1st Cl. Flora's grandmother, Mrs. Lucille Anders, and mother, Mrs. Frances Flora. Other relatives were on hand, also.

Long Wait Over for 1,925 U.S. Families

By STEVEN V. ROBERTS

Jo Anne Flora has been waiting for six years. Her husband, Sgt. 1st Cl. Carroll E. Flora Jr., was listed as missing after he fell from a medical evacuation helicopter near the Demilitarized Zone and disappeared.

Mrs. Flora had never heard a word from him. Saturday night at her home in Walkersville, Md., a casualty assistance officer came to her door at about 11 and asked her whether she had anything in the house to drink.

"Why?" she asked. "Do I have something to celebrate?" "You sure do," replied the officer, "Eddie is on the list."

A listing of war prisoners will be found on Page 16.

He was referring to the list of 555 American military prisoners in North and South Vietnam who will be released in the next two months. The list, which was handed over Saturday to United States officials in Paris by the North Vietnamese and the Vietcong, was gradually made public yesterday as next of kin were notified.

Dramas were played out in the metropolitan area and across the country over the weekend as 1,925 families learned whether their husbands, fathers and sons were identified captives or were still lost somewhere in the jungles of Indochina.

Thousands of miles away from Mrs. Flora's home, in Azusa, Calif., Patty Hardy had been waiting even longer for a phone call, and Saturday night she got it.

Her husband, Capt. John K. Hardy, has been listed as miss-

Continued on Page 14, Column 3

FIGHTING DECLINES

Saigon Charges Many Minor Violations by Communists

By SYLVAN FOX

Special to The New York Times

SAIGON, South Vietnam, Monday, Jan. 29 — The South Vietnamese Government said today that the Communists committed hundreds of cease-fire violations during the first 22 hours of the formal truce but indicated that almost all of them were minor.

Earlier, South Vietnamese military spokesmen had said that the cease-fire appeared to be gradually taking hold and the intense fighting that had marked its early hours was waning.

They had reported that only "minor ground action" was continuing.

The South Vietnamese reports of waning combat came at the same time that the American command announced that the United States had ended all military operations in Vietnam at 8 A.M. yesterday (7 P.M. Saturday, Eastern standard time), the hour that the cease-fire started.

An American spokesman refused, however, to comment on whether United States air operations were continuing in Laos or Cambodia.

2 U.S. Planes Downed

But he said that in the 24 hours preceding the cease-fire two American planes were shot down. Their four crewmen are missing, he said.

In a report issued today and covering the period from the start of the cease-fire until 6 A.M. today, the South Vietnamese said that 426 cease-fire violations had been committed by Communist troops.

The most serious appeared to be an attempt by the Communists last night to cut Route 14 north of Pleiku.

According to initial reports by the South Vietnamese, 200 enemy soldiers were killed in that engagement, which lasted six hours. The South Vietnamese said that five of their soldiers had been killed and 14 wounded.

In another battle, the South Vietnamese said, Communist troops yesterday afternoon attacked a hamlet five miles southeast of Hoa Vang, a district capital in Quang Nam Province, south of Da Nang.

The South Vietnamese said that in repelling the assault they had killed 32 enemy soldiers and captured eight, while two of their own men had been killed and 1[illegible] wounded.

Yesterday South Vietnamese military officials had said that

Continued on Page 12, Column 1

Fighting Rages Along Route 1 After Truce

Associated Press

South Vietnamese soldier wounded yesterday in fighting at Trang Bang, near Saigon, being helped from field

By CHARLES MOHR

Special to The New York Times

TRANG BANG, South Vietnam, Jan. 28—At exactly 8 A.M. today the American Armed Forces Radio began reading President Nixon's proclamation of thanksgiving for "the end of the war in Vietnam" and the "beginning of a new era of world peace."

As the announcer's voice came over a portable radio, a 500-pound bomb dropped from a South Vienamese fighter plane and exploded with a shattering crash 250 yards up the highway. It was followed by many more bombs.

As the cease-fire officially came into effect, a day-long battle began between a large force of South Vietnamese troops and Communist soldiers along Route 1 about 31 miles northwest of Saigon.

There were many similar incidents in the area around Saigon.

The blame for the continued fighting will undoubtedly become a matter of dispute. The sequence of events indicated that the difficulty lay in interpretation of the cease-fire agreement.

Before dawn yesterday Communist forces, possibly North Vietnamese, had closed the highway to the provincial capital of Tay Ninh by moving into Gia Loc, a hamlet about one and a half miles west of Trang Bang. Government troops could not break through the roadblock yesterday.

This morning armored cars

Continued on Page 12, Column 3

Cahill Budget Would Keep Taxes at Present Levels

By RONALD SULLIVAN

Special to The New York Times

TRENTON, Jan. 28 — Governor Cahill will recommend to the New Jersey Legislature tomorrow an election year state budget of $2.4-billion that avoids new or increased taxes, thus precluding any major new programs that would require much in additional state funds.

The big exception is a $90-million increase in state aid to local education. The major share of this increase will be met with New Jersey's first installment of the new Federal revenue-sharing funds.

The Governor said he had been able to bring about a balanced spending program for the fiscal year beginning July 1 largely because of the new Federal funds, an expanding economy in the state and ways he had found to achieve savings.

At a briefing here Friday afternoon, Mr. Cahill, a Republican, conceded that he and his budget officials were not unmindful of its political impact in a year when he and the Legislature were up for election.

"This no-tax budget," he said, was "dramatic evidence that the state can get along without an income tax." Mr. Cahill said that the 403-page document was a testament to the message he and other politicians were receiving from New Jersey's voters and taxpayers.

"They want relief from the relentless cycle of new and rising taxes at all levels of government," the Governor declared.

But despite the fiscal restraints imposed by the lack of new revenues, Mr. Cahill said he had succeeded in submitting a budget "without cutting any necessary services."

"In fact," he said, "we are able to expand many programs which have valid high priori-

Continued on Page 33, Column 3

Nixon Aide Reported Being Forced Out

Dwight L. Chapin

By SEYMOUR M. HERSH

Special to The New York Times

WASHINGTON, Jan. 28—Dwight L. Chapin, President Nixon's appointments secretary, who has been linked to political espionage activities of the Republican re-election committee, has reportedly decided to leave the White House staff.

One high-ranking Administration official told The New York Times that Mr. Chapin was being forced to leave as a result of newspaper disclosures naming him as the White House contact with Donald H. Segretti, a California lawyer who has said he played a key role in what he describes as widespread Republican efforts to disrupt the Democratic primaries and harass Democratic Presidential candidates.

A former White House associate of Mr. Chapin subsequently also said, "Dwight's going to be leaving." He said that he, too, had heard that Mr. Chapin was being forced out.

Friends of Mr. Chapin, who is 32 years old, say that he has already rejected or discouraged offers from defense industries for $70,000 a year or more, far above his current salary, because the positions would have involved lobbying.

Mr. Chapin's office said that he was unavailable to comment on the report, but Gerald L. Warren, deputy White House press secretary, later pointed out that the White House announced after the November elections "that Dwight Chapin had been asked to stay on and we have previously denied any involvement on his part in the Watergate."

Mr. Warren said that he had not discussed The Times's information with Mr. Chapin.

According to one of The Times's sources, Mr. Chapin was initially asked to quit his job by his immediate superior, H. R. Haldeman, the White

Continued on Page 10, Column 1

NEWS INDEX

Associated Press

Lieut. Col. William B. Nolde of Mount Pleasant, Mich.

An Army Colonel From Michigan Is Last American to Die in War

By JERRY M. FLINT

Special to The New York Times

DETROIT, Jan. 28—Lieut. Col. William B. Nolde, 43, of Mount Pleasant, Mich., was identified by the Pentagon today as the last American to die in the Vietnam war.

His death from an artillery shell at An Loc made the unofficial toll of United States personnel killed in the war 45,997, although hundreds of men are still listed as missing and unaccounted for.

Colonel Nolde died just 11 hours before the truce took effect.

"I knew he wasn't coming back. I knew it the other night," his wife, Joyce, said.

"I had a dream," Mrs. Nolde said today in a telephone interview from Onaway, Mich. "A rocket came in."

There was reason for some worry. Her husband had written that a captured prisoner had told of a big push to come just before the expected truce. Mrs. Nolde said that in the dream, "he said, 'Don't worry honey, I'm all right,' and turned, and there was an explosion."

She said she had told the children to be prepared because she had a feeling "Dad's gone." Last evening an Army officer went to Mount Pleasant, where Mrs. Nolde and her five children live, and told them that

Continued on Page 13, Column 4

Other News About Indochina

COMMUNIST TEAMS—An advance party of North Vietnamese and Vietcong representatives arrived in Saigon but refused to leave the aircraft until South Vietnamese dropped a requirement that they fill out landing cards. Two American planes flew to Hanoi to pick up about 150 military men who will help supervise the truce. [Page 13.]

TRUCE OBSERVERS—Hungarian, Polish, Indonesian and Canadian soldiers and political officers arrived in Saigon. [Page 13.]

NORTH VIETNAM—Hundreds of thousands of people thronged the streets of Hanoi to hear the announcement that hostilities had officially ended. [Page 13.]

CAMBODIA—President Lon Nol called on North Vietnamese and Vietcong forces in Cambodia to stop fighting and leave. [Page 13.]

"All the News That's Fit to Print"

The New York Times

LATE CITY EDITION

Weather: Sunny, cold today; cloudy, cold tonight. Not as cold tomorrow. Temp. range: today 18-30; Monday 14-29. Full U.S. report on Page 74.

VOL. CXXII ... No. 42,010 | NEW YORK, TUESDAY, JANUARY 30, 1973 | 15 CENTS

© 1973 The New York Times Company

SAIGON AND THE VIETCONG CHARGE FIGHTING GOES ON; U.S. AIDES TERM IT 'LIGHT'

VIOLATIONS LISTED

Combat Described as on Downward Trend and Indecisive

By SYLVAN FOX

Special to The New York Times

SAIGON, South Vietnam, Tuesday, Jan. 30—The South Vietnamese Government and the Communists accused each other of scores of additional cease-fire violations yesterday, but American analysts described the fighting that continued around the country as "scattered light activity" that was gradually diminishing in intensity.

South Vietnamese military spokesmen said that the Communists committed 257 additional cease-fire violations between noon yesterday and 6 A.M. today, bringing the total since the cease-fire began to 737 alleged Communist violations.

The South Vietnamese did not report any cease-fire violations by their own troops although information from the field indicated that such violations were occurring.

Saigon Is Accused

The Vietcong command, in a North Vietnam press agency transmission monitored in Hong Kong, accused Saigon Government troops of violating the cease-fire repeatedly and said that Vietcong units were "scrupulously" adhering to the terms of the Paris accord.

A high American official said: "The fighting is definitely on a downward trend, more noticeably in some areas than in others. There are no major units fighting. Nothing decisive is happening."

He said that despite high casualties, the fighting was "inconsequential" and that he expected it to subside substantially "in a day or two more."

No knowledgeable analysts had expected the fighting to end precisely at the moment when the cease-fire went into effect Sunday, the official said.

"I never thought this messy

Continued on Page 10, Column 7

A South Vietnamese soldier wounded in fighting along Route 13 north of Saigon gets aid. Another, top, waits.

Associated Press

At another point near the same highway, South Vietnamese pass near the body of a Vietcong soldier.

United Press International

A North Vietnamese captain, center, posing with a South Vietnamese soldier, left, and a Vietcong soldier yesterday. The three met privately in a graveyard at Cai Lay.

Saigon Troops Selectively Ignore Truce

By CHARLES MOHR

Special to The New York Times

CAM LONG, South Vietnam, Jan. 29—South Vietnamese forces were openly ignoring the cease-fire agreement in the area northwest of Saigon today, but on a relatively small scale and selectively.

Government spokesmen in Saigon were charging that there had been hundreds of Vietcong and North Vietnamese violations of the cease-fire since it supposedly began at 8 A.M. Sunday. But to a foreign observer touring Routes 1 and 22 in an area 30 to 45 miles northwest of Saigon for the last two days, there was no clear evidence.

What was happening was that Saigon forces were trying, with considerable success, to drive away Communist forces that had blocked roads and occupied hamlets in a last-minute offensive shortly before the cease-fire.

The sounds of an American B-52 bombing raid could also be heard faintly from Cambodia, a few miles away.

American sources said that Communist troops in a few cases were moving about in South Vietnamese uniforms.

There was no full-scale resumption of the Vietnam war. Instead, there was an attempt to win semantic arguments with bombs and bullets in isolated areas.

The Saigon Government clearly seemed to have made a decision that it would not tolerate Communists' successful efforts to block key roads and lines of communications just before the cease-fire. On a much smaller scale, Government artillery was also shelling the fringes of hamlets that were under military pressure from Vietcong and North Vietnamese infantrymen.

For instance, at this little hamlet about 10 miles southeast of the provincial capital of Tay Ninh, the road to Saigon was closed because of the presence of an undetermined number of Communist soldiers in the northern part of the hamlet, about 45 miles from Saigon.

Late this morning and into early afternoon Government troops were throwing grenades and firing weapons sporadically but at times furiously. The sound of occasional return fire from AK-47 automatic rifles could also be heard.

Earlier, in the morning, two South Vietnamese propeller-driven Skyraiders and two South Vietnamese jets dropped

Continued on Page 10, Column 2

DIVINE consciousness in man can be asleep. ARICA Institute 419-7430—(Advt.)

EL COCA-COLA GRANDE broke all records Americana Hotel, Huixtla, Guatemala. Advt.

LINDSAY ORDERS POLICE TO SPEED RECRUIT TRAINING

Reinforced Patrols Search for 6 Militants Suspected in Ambush Shootings

By MURRAY SCHUMACH

Spurred by the ambush shootings of four policemen in less than a week, Mayor Lindsay yesterday ordered a drastic speed-up in the training of police recruits.

The acceleration, to be accomplished without lowering training standards, will require double or perhaps triple sessions at the Police Academy. Armories and college space may have to be used to cut as much as a year from the two-year program to add 3,150 recruits to the force.

"The attacks on the force, planned as ambush, make the crime crisis in the city greater than before," the Mayor said.

As the Mayor spoke, hundreds of patrolmen and detectives, working on overtime in police cars, in unmarked cars and on foot, joined the regularly assigned policemen, crisscrossing hundreds of streets in Brooklyn and Queens, seeking six black militants suspected of the ambush-shootings of the four policemen.

Cost Put at $13-Million

The Mayor and Police Commissioner Patrick V. Murphy made public the plan, which will cost an additional $13-million, at the Police Academy, before 196 recruits, seven of them women. The class was the first since Feb-ˑary, 1970, when the Mayor, …r economy reasons, imposed a job freeze on the uniformed forces. He ended the freeze last Oct. 31.

At present, the police force totals 29,571. It was as high as 32,000 about two and a half years ago. Besides the recruit program, the city will hire 2,300 skilled civilians to relieve policemen now doing inside work so they can do patrol duties.

"The academy may burst at the seams," the Mayor said shortly after the recruits, standing in a second-floor auditorium, were sworn in. "I want the public to see as many police officers on the street as can possibly be cranked out."

Sense of Danger

Though Commissioner Murphy's speech was low-keyed, it was threaded with the sense of danger that has spread through the department with the ambush-shooting attributed to the Black Liberation Army, which the Commissioner believes to be small and unorganized.

Toughness, compassion, self-restraint and courage, beyond

Continued on Page 43, Column 1

10 Die in Rest Home Fire; Arson Is Laid to a Resident

By DONALD JANSON

Special to The New York Times

PLEASANTVILLE, Jan. 29—Ten of the 16 elderly residents of a rest home, including a 106-year-old woman, died early this morning when fire swept the two-story, wood-frame building. Late tonight a 22-year-old man described as having lived in the home was arrested and charged with arson by the state police.

When the fire broke out shortly before 1 A.M. at Street's Rest Home on California Avenue in this community seven miles west of Atlantic City, the first alarm was given by a passing policeman, Sgt. James Mong of the Absecon force.

Seeing two men on the roof of the building, through which flames were spreading rapidly, Sergeant Mong drove his squad car up to one side of the house. He helped the two down to the car and to safety. The rescued men were Joseph Postick, 90 years old, and Harry F. Kemp, 22, said to be roommates in the home.

It was Mr. Kemp who was later arrested on the arson charge.

Mr. Kemp, previously of Baltimore, was held under guard at Shire Memorial Hospital in Somers Point where he had been taken for treatment for smoke inhalation. Others among the surviving residents of the rest home were taken to Atlantic City for treatment.

Before tonight's arrest, authorities had suspected arson but had been uncertain as to where the blaze originated. Mrs. Minor Pierce, 67 years old, one of two night attendants on duty who escaped along with the six residents, heard a fire alarm go off at 12:45 A.M. She said she saw flames shooting from a linen closet.

Gary Wilson, the other employe, said he believed the flames had come from the basement beneath the closet. Mrs. Pierce and Mr. Wilson aroused four first-floor occupants, one of them blind, and led them out a back door.

Fire Chief Elwood Dix of

Continued on Page 41, Column 3

NEWS INDEX

NIXON BUDGET LISTS 100 PROGRAMS THAT WOULD BE LIMITED OR ENDED TO ATTAIN A 'SAFE' SPENDING LEVEL

LARGE SOCIAL CUTS

Reductions Are Aimed at Big Poverty and Education Efforts

By JACK ROSENTHAL

Special to The New York Times

WASHINGTON, Jan. 29—The Nixon Administration's new budget proposes a sharp pruning of Federal social programs that, in effect, calls for the repeal of major initiatives of the Truman, Eisenhower, Kennedy and Johnson Administrations.

Among the proposed targets are the Community Action Program, the heart of President Johnson's war on poverty; the Depressed Areas Program begun by the Kennedy Administration, and a group of education measures, some of which date back to the late nineteen-fifties.

Total social spending in the new budget is higher than last year's. Income security programs — Social Security, welfare, and unemployment insurance — would rise 8 per cent, to $82-billion. Antihunger spending would continue at high levels. Substantial increases are proposed in fields ranging from drug abuse control to heart and cancer research.

Stress on Social Programs

But the most consistent theme is the elimination or reduction of social programs. Scores of such cuts dominate a list that alone occupies seven and a half pages of small type in the new budget.

The combination, one high official acknowledged, is the most sweeping structural realignment proposed in any budget at least since the Korean war.

The budget documents offer a series of practical or philosophical reasons for the proposed cuts. But the proposals are likely nonetheless to prompt extended Congressional debate.

Among the abolitions, suspensions and revisions proposed are the following:

¶Dissolution of the Office of Economic Opportunity, the antipoverty program. Some components are to be dispersed among other agencies, but the keystone segment, the Community Action Program, is to be killed.

¶Savings of almost $600-mil-

Continued on Page 22, Column 1

Highlights of the Budget

Special to The New York Times

WASHINGTON, Jan. 29—Following are highlights of President Nixon's budget for the fiscal year 1974:

MILITARY—President Nixon wants to spend $79-billion for defense in the first post-Vietnam war fiscal year, an increase of $4.2-billion over this year. The "peace dividend" resulting from an end to United States involvement in Indochina will be consumed by pay rises and by inflation, according to defense officials. A substantial increase is also sought for research and development of strategic and conventional weapons.

HEALTH—The Administration plans to ask for legislation that would require Medicare patients to pay more than twice as much as they now pay for the average hospital stay. Together with other suggested changes, the Government would make about $1.6-billion less in Medicare payments. Aside from Medicare, the health budget would be increased slightly, but some old programs, like those for hospital construction, would be eliminated.

EDUCATION—The Administration would like to dismantle most elementary and secondary education programs and replace them with $2.5-billion in education revenue-sharing. The total education budget would rise slightly, but it is not clear how much would be spent if revenue-sharing is not enacted. Nearly $1-billion is to be spent on a new scholarship program for college students, but there is no money for direct aid to colleges and universities.

RESEARCH—The prospect is for severe belt-tightening in the main Federal research agencies. The emphasis in the budget is on the achievement of practical short-term results and not on the traditional role of expanding the sum of human scientific knowledge.

CIVIL RIGHTS—Money is to be concentrated on programs to assist minority businessmen and to implement new laws against sex discrimination rather than on the traditional areas of civil rights enforcement.

SOCIAL PROGRAMS—The Office of Economic Opportunity would be dissolved and its keystone segment, the community action program, killed. The Administration hopes to save $600-million by eliminating ineligible welfare recipients and overpayments in this area. Many urban development programs, including urban renewal, model cities and public service jobs, would be phased out.

ENVIRONMENT—The Administration wants to spend a little more than $1-billion more for the Environmental Protection Agency than is now being spent. But, while the request is the largest ever submitted, it falls far short of such Congressional programs as sewage treatment plants.

AGRICULTURE—Spending by the Department of Agriculture would be severely trimmed, with deep cuts in rural housing subsidies, price-support operations, rural environmental assistance and the special school milk program.

Budget Plan Would Raise Hospital Costs of Elderly

By RICHARD D. LYONS

Special to The New York Times

WASHINGTON, Jan. 29—The Nixon Administration plans to seek legislation that would require the elderly to pay a sharply increased share of their hospital costs, a change that seems sure to trigger opposition from senior citizens and to lead to a fight in Congress.

The planned change in Medicare charges, which is disclosed in President Nixon's Budget Message for the fiscal year 1974, would require the 23 million Americans eligible for Medicare benefits to pay an additional $1-billion a year in hospitalization costs.

Put another way, the cost to the patient of the average Medicare-financed stay in a hospital, now about 13 days, would rise from the present $72 to almost $200, if the planned legislation goes into effect next January.

Two other Medicare changes that would also need Congressional approval would increase charges to the 22.5 million people enrolled in the supplementary insurance feature of Medicare, also known as Part B.

The net result of the three proposals would be a reduction in payments by Medicare of an estimated total of $1.6-billion in their first full year of operation.

Some knowledgeable officials here complain privately that the changes are a disguised at-

Continued on Page 22, Column 5

F.B.I. Did No Full Study Of Reported G.O.P. Spy

By SEYMOUR M. HERSH

Special to The New York Times

WASHINGTON, Jan. 29—The Federal Bureau of Investigation has made no attempt to investigate fully the political espionage and sabotage activities allegedly conducted last year by Donald H. Segretti, a California lawyer, who reportedly acted under the direction of the White House and Republican re-election officials.

The disclosure came as both sides rested today in the trial of the two remaining defendants in the Watergate case.

Well-placed Administration sources have said that Justice Department officials learned of some of Mr. Segretti's activities within weeks after the Watergate arrests last June 17, but decided on the basis of preliminary interviews with Mr. Segretti that his activities were legal and therefore beyond the scope of an extensive F.B.I. inquiry.

That decision was reaffirmed last October, the source said, after newspaper accounts indicated the full scope of Mr. Segretti's activities, which were said to have involved sabotage attempts against Democratic candidates during the primary election campaigns.

It was further learned that Mr. Segretti began his operations, apparently on behalf of some White House officials, as early as September, 1971, at about the same time E. Howard Hunt, then a White House consultant, reportedly began organ-

Continued on Page 30, Column 1

DEFICIT IS HALVED

President Says Trims Will Hold Outlays to $268.7-Billion

By EDWIN L. DALE Jr.

Special to The New York Times

WASHINGTON, Jan. 29—President Nixon presented Congress today with a budget containing a list of more than 100 cutbacks or outright terminations of Government programs and said he could accomplish the great majority of these himself without Congressional action or concurrence.

As previously disclosed, the budget estimated spending at $268.7-billion in the new fiscal year 1974, beginning July 1,

> **Slip-Out Section**
> Additional budget articles and excerpts from Nixon message are printed on Pages 19, 20, 21, 22.

with the deficit approximately cut in half to $12.7-billion. The latest outlay estimate for the current year, following a number of decisions to hold back Congressionally approved spending, was $249.8-billion with a deficit of $24.8-billion.

The budget contained a major innovation, apart from its sweeping list of cuts. For the first time the President told Congress in advance what the "safe" outer limit on spending would be a year from now in his next budget for the fiscal year 1975—$288-billion—and said this figure would swell to $312-billion unless the cuts announced now were carried out.

'Alternative' Cited

There was even a breakdown by agency and function of probable spending in the fiscal year 1975—all designed to show the "momentum" of the budget and how decisions made now would affect spending two and a half years in the future.

For the fiscal year 1974, Mr. Nixon said, the budget would have risen to $288-billion if not for his cutbacks.

The President said the "only responsible alternative" to the reductions he announced would be a tax increase. But he added: "If the recommendations presented in this budget are followed, and if this disciplined approach to Federal spending is firmly adhered to in the years ahead, it will be possible for

Continued on Page 22, Column 7

PROSECUTOR AND 2 GUILTY OF BRIBERY

Mackell Aide Is Convicted With Co-Defendants

By ARNOLD H. LUBASCH

An assistant district attorney and two confederates were convicted last night of taking a $15,000 bribe to fix a criminal case in Queens.

The principal defendant was Norman D. Archer, a 52-year-old prosecutor who headed the Queens County indictment bureu last year when he became involved in a case with the elements of a gangster film.

A special agent posing as a Mafia mobster provided the crucial evidence by tape-recording bribery talks with Archer's ‘wo co-defendants—Frank R. Kleir, an influential lawyer, and Leon Wasserberger, an associate of bail bondsmen.

Since being indicted last July 25, Archer has been suspended from his $24,500-a-year position as chief assistant district attorney in the office of Thomas J. Mackell, the Queens District Attorney.

Richard Ben-Veniste, the prosecutor in the Federal Court trial here, told the jury that "this case involves a charge

Continued on Page 23, Column 1

PLAN your next vacation at

"All the News
That's Fit to Print"

The New York Times

LATE CITY EDITION

Weather: Sunny and cold today; fair, cold tonight and tomorrow. Temp. range: today 10-29; Sunday 12-26. Full U.S. report on Page 53.

VOL. CXXII . No. 42,023 NEW YORK, MONDAY, FEBRUARY 12, 1973 15 CENTS

FIRST WAR PRISONERS RELEASED TO U.S. IN CEREMONIES AT HANOI; DISPUTE DELAYS GROUP IN SOUTH

Associated Press

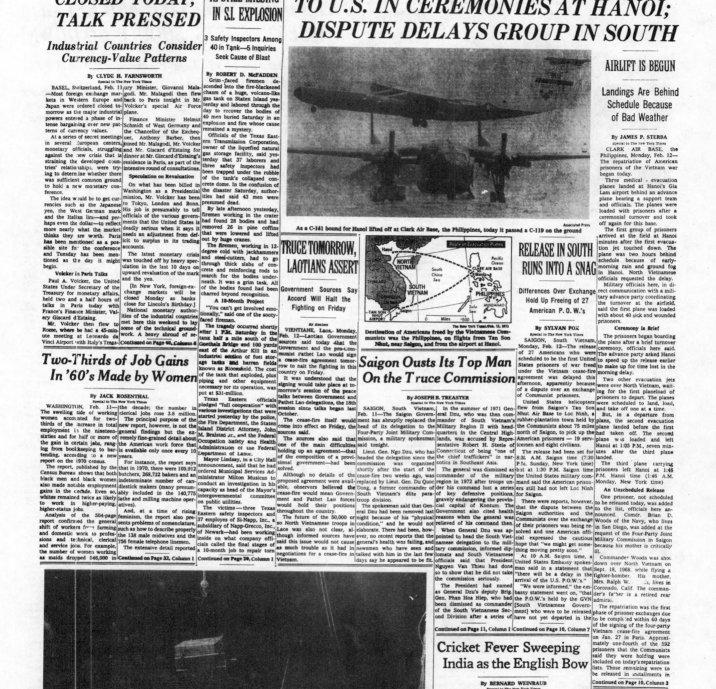

As a C-141 bound for Hanoi lifted off at Clark Air Base, the Philippines, today it passed a C-119 on the ground

AIRLIFT IS BEGUN

Landings Are Behind Schedule Because of Bad Weather

By JAMES P. STERBA

Special to The New York Times

CLARK AIR BASE, the Philippines, Monday, Feb. 12—The repatriation of American prisoners of the Vietnam war began today.

Three medical - evacuation planes landed at Hanoi's Gia Lam airport behind an advance plane bearing a support team and officials. The planes were loaded with prisoners after a ceremonial turnover and took off again for this base.

The first group of prisoners arrived at the field at Hanoi minutes after the first evacuation jet touched down. The plane was two hours behind schedule because of early-morning rain and ground fog in Hanoi. North Vietnamese officials requested the delay.

Military officials here, in direct communication with a military advance party coordinating the turnover at the airfield, said the first plane was loaded with about 40 sick and wounded prisoners.

Ceremony Is Brief

The prisoners began boarding the plane after a brief turnover ceremony, officials here said. The advance party asked Hanoi to speed up the release earlier to make up for time lost in the morning delay.

Two other evacuation jets were over North Vietnam, waiting for the first planeload of prisoners to depart. The planes were scheduled to land, load, and take off one at a time.

But, in a departure from plans, the second evacuation plane landed before the first had taken off. The second plane was loaded and left Hanoi at 1:05 P.M., seven minutes after the third plane landed.

The third plane carrying prisoners left Hanoi at 1:46 P.M. Hanoi time (1:46 A.M. Monday, New York time)

An Unscheduled Release

One prisoner, not scheduled to be released today, was added to the list, officials here announced. Comdr. Brian D. Woods of the Navy, who lives in San Diego, was added at the request of the Four-Party Joint Military Commission in Saigon because his mother is critically ill.

Commander Woods was shot down over North Vietnam on Sept. 18, 1968. while flying a fighter-bomber. His mother, Mrs. Ralph W[illegible]s, lives in Coronado, Calif. The commander's father is a retired rear admiral.

The repatriation was the first phase of prisoner exchanges due to be completed within 60 days of the signing of the four-party Vietnam cease-fire agreement on Jan. 27 in Paris. Approximately one-fourth of the 592 prisoners that the Communists said they were holding were included on today's repatriation lists. Those remaining were to be released in installments in

Continued on Page 10, Column 3

MONEY MARTS CLOSED TODAY; TALK PRESSED

Industrial Countries Consider Currency-Value Patterns

By CLYDE H. FARNSWORTH

Special to The New York Times

BASEL, Switzerland, Feb. 11—Most foreign exchange markets in Western Europe and Japan were ordered closed tomorrow as the major industrial powers entered a phase of intense bargaining over new patterns of currency values.

At a series of secret meetings in several European centers, monetary officials, struggling against the new crisis that is straining the developed countries' relationships, were trying to determine whether there was sufficient common ground to hold a new monetary conference.

The idea would be to get currencies such as the Japanese yen, the West German mark and the Italian lira—and perhaps even the dollar—to reflect more nearly what the market thinks they are worth. Paris has been mentioned as a possible site for the conference and Tuesday has been mentioned as the day it might begin.

Volcker in Paris Talks

Paul A. Volcker, the United States Under Secretary of the Treasury for monetary affairs, held two and a half hours of talks in Paris today with France's Finance Minister, Valery Giscard d'Estaing.

Mr. Volcker then flew to Rome, where he had a 45-minute meeting at Leonardo da Vinci Airport with Italy's Treasury Minister, Giovanni Malagodi. Mr. Malagodi then flew back to Paris tonight in Mr. Volcker's special Air Force plane.

Finance Minister Helmut Schmidt of West Germany and the Chancellor of the Exchequer, Anthony Barber, then joined Mr. Malagodi, Mr. Volcker and Mr. Giscard d'Estaing for dinner at Mr. Giscard d'Estaing's residence in Paris, as part of the intensive round of consultations.

Speculation on Revaluation

On what has been billed in Washington as a Presidential mission, Mr. Volcker has been to Tokyo, London and Bonn. His job is presumably to tell officials of the various governments that the United States is deadly serious when it says it needs an adjustment from deficit to surplus in its trading accounts.

The latest monetary crisis was touched off by heavy speculation in the last 10 days on upward revaluation of the mark and the yen.

[In New York, foreign-exchange markets will be closed Monday as banks close for Lincoln's Birthday.]

National monetary authorities of the industrial countries met here this weekend to lay some of the technical groundwork. A heavy shroud of se-

Continued on Page 40, Column 6

28 VICTIMS FOUND, 12 STILL MISSING IN S.I. EXPLOSION

3 Safety Inspectors Among 40 in Tank—5 Inquiries Seek Cause of Blast

By ROBERT D. McFADDEN

Grim-faced firemen descended into the fire-blackened chasm of a huge, volcano-like gas tank on Staten Island yesterday and labored through the day to recover the bodies of 40 men buried Saturday in an explosion and fire whose cause remained a mystery.

Officials of the Texas Eastern Transmission Corporation, owner of the liquefied natural gas storage facility, said yesterday that 37 laborers and three safety inspectors had been trapped under the rubble of the tank's collapsed concrete dome. In the confusion of the disaster Saturday, authorities had said 43 men were presumed dead.

By late afternoon yesterday, firemen working in the crater had found 28 bodies and had removed 26 in pine coffins that were lowered and lifted out by huge cranes.

The firemen, working in 12-degree cold with jackhammers and steel-cutters, had to go through thick slabs of concrete and reinforcing rods to search for the bodies underneath. It was a grim task. All of the bodies found had been charred beyond recognition.

A 10-Month Project

"You can't get involved emotionally," said one of the sooty-faced fireman.

The tragedy occurred shortly after 1 P.M. Saturday in the tank half a mile south of the Goethals Bridge and 100 yards east of the Arthur Kill in an industrial section of fuel storage tanks and barren fields known as Bloomfield. The cost of the tank that exploded, plus piping and other equipment necessary for its operation, was put at $31-million.

Texas Eastern officials pledged "full cooperation" with various investigations that were started yesterday by the police, the Fire Department, the Staten Island District Attorney, John M. Braisted Jr., and the Federal Occupation Safety and Health Administration of the Federal Department of Labor.

Mayor Lindsay, in a City Hall announcement, said that he had ordered Municipal Services Administrator Milton Musicus to conduct an investigation in his capacity as head of the Mayor's intergovernmental committee on public utilities.

The victims—three Texas Eastern safety inspectors and 37 employes of Si-Napp, Inc., a subsidiary of Napp-Grecco, Inc., of Newark—had been working inside on what company officials called the final stages of a 10-month job to repair torn

Continued on Page 20, Column 1

TRUCE TOMORROW, LAOTIANS ASSERT

Government Sources Say Accord Will Halt the Fighting on Friday

By Reuters

VIENTIANE, Laos, Monday, Feb. 12—Laotian Government sources said today that the Government and the pro-Communist Pathet Lao would sign a cease-fire agreement tomorrow to halt the fighting in this country on Friday.

It was understood that the signing would take place at tomorrow's session of the peace talks between Government and Pathet Lao delegations, the 18th session since talks began last October.

The cease-fire itself would come into effect on Friday, the sources said.

The sources also said that one of the main difficulties holding up an agreement—that of the composition of a provisional government—had been solved.

Although no details of the proposed agreement were available, observers believed the cease-fire would mean Government and Pathet Lao forces would hold their positions throughout the country.

The future of the 50,000 or so North Vietnamese troops in Laos was also not clear, although informed sources have said this issue would not cause as much trouble as it had in negotiations for a cease-fire in Vietnam.

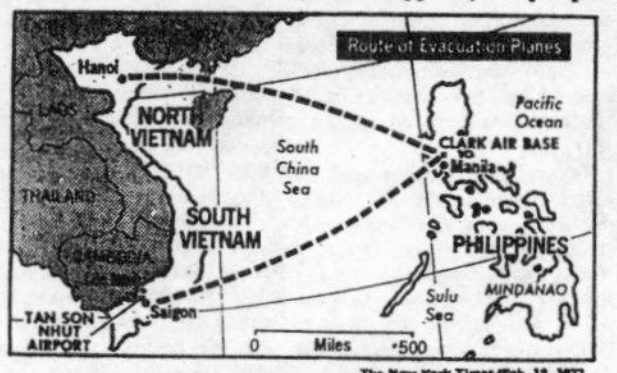

The New York Times/Feb. 12, 1973

Destination of Americans freed by the Vietnamese Communists was the Philippines, on flights from Tan Son Nhut, near Saigon, and from the airport at Hanoi.

RELEASE IN SOUTH RUNS INTO A SNAG

Differences Over Exchange Hold Up Freeing of 27 American P.O.W.'s

By SYLVAN FOX

Special to The New York Times

SAIGON, South Vietnam, Monday, Feb. 12—The release of 27 Americans who were scheduled to be the first United States prisoners of war freed under the Vietnam cease-fire agreement was delayed this afternoon, apparently because of a dispute over an exchange of Communist prisoners.

United States helicopters flew from Saigon's Tan Son Nhut Air Base to Loc Ninh, a rubber-plantation town held by the Communists about 75 miles north of Saigon, to pick up the American prisoners — 19 servicemen and eight civilians.

The release had been set for 8:30 A.M. Saigon time (7:30 P.M. Sunday, New York time) but at 1:30 P.M. Saigon time the United States military command said the American prisoners still had not left Loc Ninh for Saigon.

There were reports, however, that the dispute between the Saigon authorities and the Communists over the exchange of their prisoners was being resolved and one American official expressed the cautious hope that "we might get something moving pretty soon."

At 10 A.M. Saigon time, a United States Embassy spokesman said in a statement that "there will be a delay in the arrival of the U.S. P.O.W.'s."

"We were informed," the embassy statement went on, "that the P.O.W.'s held by the GVN [South Vietnamese Government] who were to be released have not yet departed in the

Continued on Page 10, Column 7

Saigon Ousts Its Top Man On the Truce Commission

By JOSEPH B. TREASTER

Special to The New York Times

SAIGON, South Vietnam, Feb. 11—The Saigon Government has abruptly replaced the head of its delegation to the Four-Party Joint Military Commission, a military spokesman said tonight.

Lieut. Gen. Ngo Dzu, who has headed the delegation since the commission was organized shortly after the start of the cease-fire two weeks ago, was replaced by Lieut. Gen. Du Quoc Dong, a former commander of South Vietnam's élite paratroop division.

The spokesman said that General Dzu had been removed last night because of his "physical condition," and he would not elaborate. There had been, however, no recent reports that the general's health was failing, and newsmen who have seen and talked with him in the last few days say he appeared to be fit.

In the summer of 1971 General Dzu, who was then commander of South Vietnam's Military Region II with headquarters in the Central Highlands, was accused by Representative Robert H. Steele of Connecticut of being "one of the chief traffickers" in narcotics in Southeast Asia.

The general was dismissed as commander of the military region in 1972 after troops under his command lost a series of key defensive positions, gravely endangering the provincial capital of Kontum. The Government also cited health reasons when the general was relieved of his command then.

When General Dzu was appointed to head the South Vietnamese delegation to the military commission, informed diplomats and South Vietnamese officials said that President Nguyen Van Thieu had done so to show that he did not take the commission seriously.

The President had named as General Dzu's deputy Brig. Gen. Phan Hoa Hiep, who had been dismissed as commander of the South Vietnamese Second Division after a series of

Continued on Page 11, Column 1

Two-Thirds of Job Gains In '60's Made by Women

By JACK ROSENTHAL

Special to The New York Times

WASHINGTON, Feb. 11—The swelling tide of working women accounted for two-thirds of the increase in total employment in the nineteen-sixties and for half or more of the gain in certain jobs, ranging from bookkeeping to bartending, according to a new report on the 1970 census.

The report, published by the Census Bureau shows that both black men and black women also made notable employment gains in the decade. Even so, whites remained twice as likely to work in higher-paying, higher-status jobs.

Analysis of the 504-page report confirmed the general shift of workers from farming and domestic work to professions and technical, clerical and service jobs. For example, the number of women working as maids dropped 546,000 in the decade; the number in clerical jobs rose 3.8 million.

The principal purpose of the new report, however, is not the general findings but the extremely fine-grained detail about the American work force that is available only once every 10 years.

For instance, the report says that in 1970, there were 109,912 butchers, 268,732 bakers and an indeterminate number of candlestick makers (many presumably included in the 140,775 lathe and milling machine operatives).

And, at a time of rising feminism, the report also presents problems of nomenclature, such as how to describe properly the 138 male midwives and the 756 female telephone linemen.

The extensive detail reported

Continued on Page 32, Column 1

The New York Times/William E. Sauro

At the bottom of the burned-out gas storage tank on Staten Island, firemen prepared the coffins of some of the workmen killed in the disaster to be lifted out by a crane. The search for victims continued through last night and into the morning.

Cricket Fever Sweeping India as the English Bow

By BERNARD WEINRAUB

Special to The New York Times

NEW DELHI, Feb. 11 — Youngsters scampered through the markets of New Delhi tonight shrieking the news. Old men on Connaught Circus, in the center of the city, whispered and broke into grins. Crowds in coffee shops, hovering around transistor radios, clapped excitedly.

After more than three tense weeks, India had humbled England in cricket, the sport that epitomized the British raj and a popular legacy of colonial domination. The final five-day test match in Bombay — with overtones of a pupil upstaging the teacher—ended late this afternoon before 50,000 people when India won the "rubber," the trophy that goes to the winner of the five tests, or matches, and is the equivalent of the world championship.

Some Indians said that the victory over England was the most ebullient national occasion since December, 1971, when the Indian Army defeated Pakistan and helped create Bangladesh from what had been East Pakistan. Then—as in the last week—Indians virtually stopped work in shops, bazaars, Government offices, banks and homes to listen to the bulletins over their transitor radios.

Although India had won a "rubber" in a 1971 series in

Continued on Page 35, Column 1

David Lawrence Dies

David Lawrence, founder of U.S. News & World Report magazine and a conservative syndicated columnist for more than half a century, died yesterday at 84 in Sarasota, Fla. His columns appeared in more than 300 newspapers. Details, Page 30.

NEWS INDEX

"All the News That's Fit to Print"

The New York Times

LATE CITY EDITION

Weather: Mostly cloudy, seasonably mild today, tonight and tomorrow. Temp. range: today 42-56; Thursday 36-54. Full U.S. report on Page 78.

VOL. CXXII . . . No. 42,069 | NEW YORK, FRIDAY, MARCH 30, 1973 | 15 CENTS

U.S. Forces Out of Vietnam; Hanoi Frees the Last P.O.W.

United Press International

SAIGON: M. Sgt. Vincent Jacobucci of New York, one of last American servicemen to leave South Vietnam yesterday, proposing a farewell toast at Tân Son Nhut Airport.

War Role Is Ended After Decade of Controversy

By JOSEPH B. TREASTER

Special to The New York Times

SAIGON, South Vietnam, March 29—The last American troops left South Vietnam today, leaving behind an unfinished war that has deeply scarred this country and the United States.

There was little emotion or joy as they brought to a close almost a decade of American military intervention.

Texts of Weyand speeches appear on Page 17.

Remaining after the final jet transport lifted off from Tan Son Nhut air base at 5:53 P.M. were about 800 Americans on the truce observation force who will leave tomorrow and Saturday. A contingent of 159 Marine guards and about 50 military attachés also stayed behind.

The fighting men were gone, but United States involvement in South Vietnam was far from ended.

When Gen. Frederick C. Weyand presided over the furling of the colors of the United States Military Assistance Command, Vietnam, this afternoon, he told a handful of American servicemen, "You can hold your heads up high for having been a part of this selfless effort."

In a second address later in the afternoon, delivered in halting Vietnamese, General Weyand declared: "Our mission has been accomplished. I depart with a strong feeling of pride in what we have achieved, and in what our achievement represents."

As the last American commander in Vietnam said goodby to the huge white tropical building that was sometimes called Pentagon East, a force of 7,200 American civilians employed by the Department of Defense was standing under the eaves.

A majority of these civilians are technicians who are already at work with the South Vietnamese armed forces, trying to fill the gap in special skills that the Vietnamization program has been unable to provide. Many are repairing helicopters, jet fighter-bombers, radar systems and computers, and some are instructing the Vietnamese in these tasks.

This afternoon at Tan Son Nhut, while waiting for his plane to take off, Col. Einar Himma, a naturalized American from Estonia, talked of his two tours in Vietnam. He had

Continued on Page 17, Column 1

Thousands Watch 67 Prisoners Depart

Associated Press

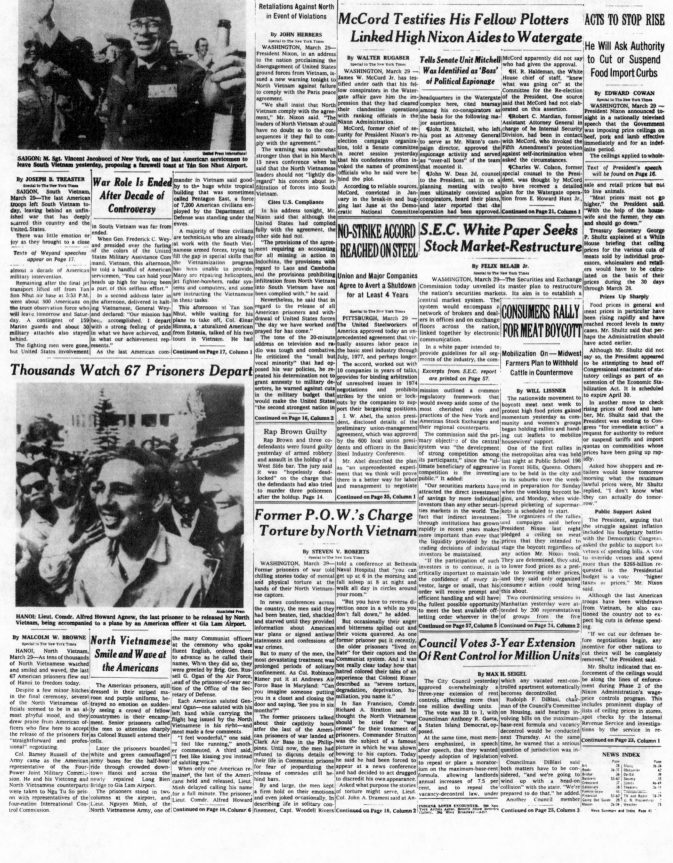

HANOI: Lieut. Comdr. Alfred Howard Agnew, the last prisoner to be released by North Vietnam, being accompanied to a plane by an American officer at Gia Lam Airport.

North Vietnamese Smile and Wave at the Americans

By MALCOLM W. BROWNE

Special to The New York Times

HANOI, North Vietnam, March 29—As tens of thousands of North Vietnamese watched and smiled and waved, the last 67 American prisoners flew out of Hanoi to freedom today.

Despite a few minor hitches in the final ceremony, several of the North Vietnamese officials seemed to be in an almost playful mood, and they drew praise from American officers who flew here to accept the release of the prisoners for "straightforward and professional" negotiating.

Col. Barney Russell of the Army came as the American representative of the Four-Power Joint Military Commission. He and his Vietcong and North Vietnamese counterparts were taken to Nga Tu So prison with representatives of the four-nation International Control Commission.

The American prisoners, still dressed in their striped maroon and purple uniforms, betrayed no emotion on suddenly seeing a crowd of fellow countrymen in their encampment. Senior prisoners called the men to attention sharply as Colonel Russell entered their cells.

Later the prisoners boarded white and green camouflaged army buses for the half-hour ride through crowded downtown Hanoi and across the newly repaired Long Bien Bridge to Gia Lam Airport.

The prisoners stood in two columns at the airport, and Lieut. Nguyen Minh, of the North Vietnamese Army, one of the many Communist officers at the ceremony who spoke fluent English, ordered them to advance as he called their names. When they did so, they were greeted by Brig. Gen. Russell G. Ogan of the Air Force, head of the prisoner-of-war section of the Office of the Secretary of Defense.

Each American saluted General Ogan—one saluted with his left hand while carrying the flight bag issued by the North Vietnamese in his right—and most made a few comments.

"I feel wonderful," one said. "I feel like running," another commented. A third said, "I feel like kissing you instead of saluting you."

When only one American remained, the last of the Americans held and released, Lieut. Minh delayed calling his name for a full minute. The prisoner, Lieut. Comdr. Alfred Howard

Continued on Page 18, Column 6

PRESIDENT WARNS HANOI TO COMPLY WITH TRUCE PACT

Holds Out the Threat of U.S. Retaliations Against North in Event of Violations

By JOHN HERBERS

Special to The New York Times

WASHINGTON, March 29—President Nixon, in an address to the nation proclaiming the disengagement of United States ground forces from Vietnam, issued a new warning tonight to North Vietnam against failure to comply with the Paris peace agreement.

"We shall insist that North Vietnam comply with the agreement," Mr. Nixon said. "The leaders of North Vietnam should have no doubt as to the consequences if they fail to comply with the agreement."

The warning was somewhat stronger than that in his March 15 news conference when he said that the North Vietnamese leaders should not "lightly disregard" his concern about infiltration of forces into South Vietnam.

Cites U.S. Compliance

In his address tonight, Mr. Nixon said that although the United States had complied fully with the agreement, the other side had not.

"The provisions of the agreement requiring an accounting for all missing in action in Indochina, the provisions with regard to Laos and Cambodia and the provisions prohibiting infiltration from North Vietnam into South Vietnam have not been complied with," he said.

Nevertheless, he said that in regard to the release of all American prisoners and withdrawal of United States forces "the day we have worked and prayed for has come."

The tone of the 20-minute address on television and radio was tough and combative. He criticized the "small but vocal minority" that had opposed his war policies, he repeated his determination not to grant amnesty to military deserters, he warned against cuts in the military budget that would make the United States "the second strongest nation in

Continued on Page 16, Column 2

Rap Brown Guilty

Rap Brown and three codefendants were found guilty yesterday of armed robbery and assault in the holdup of a West Side bar. The jury said it was "hopelessly deadlocked" on the charge that the defendants had also tried to murder three policemen after the holdup. Page 14.

NIXON SETS MEAT PRICE CEILINGS AT BOTH WHOLESALE AND RETAIL; ASSERTS COSTS 'SHOULD GO DOWN'

ACTS TO STOP RISE

He Will Ask Authority to Cut or Suspend Food Import Curbs

By EDWARD COWAN

Special to The New York Times

WASHINGTON, March 29—President Nixon announced tonight in a nationally televised speech that the Government was imposing price ceilings on beef, pork and lamb effective immediately and for an indefinite period.

The ceilings applied to wholesale and retail prices but not to live animals.

Text of President's speech will be found on Page 16.

"Meat prices must not go higher," the President said. "With the help of the housewife and the farmer, they can and should go down."

Treasury Secretary George P. Shultz explained at a White House briefing that ceiling prices for the various cuts of meats sold by individual processors, wholesalers and retailers would have to be calculated on the basis of their prices during the 30 days through March 28.

Prices Up Sharply

Food prices in general and meat prices in particular have been rising rapidly and have reached record levels in many cases. Mr. Shultz said that perhaps the Administration should have acted earlier.

Although Mr. Shultz did not say so, the President appeared to be attempting to head off Congressional enactment of statutory ceilings as part of an extension of the Economic Stabilization Act. It is scheduled to expire April 30.

In another move to check rising prices of food and lumber, Mr. Shultz said that the President was sending to Congress "for immediate action" a request for authority to reduce or suspend tariffs and import quotas on commodities whose prices have been going up rapidly.

Asked how shoppers and retailers would know tomorrow morning what the maximum lawful prices were, Mr Shultz replied, "I don't know what they can actually do tomorrow."

Public Support Asked

The President, arguing that the struggle against inflation included his budgetary battles with the Democratic Congress, asked the public to support his vetoes of spending bills. A vote to override vetoes and spend more than the $268-billion requested in the Presidential budget is a vote "higher taxes or prices," Mr. Nixon said.

Although the last American troops have been withdrawn from Vietnam, he also cautioned the country not to expect big cuts in defense spending.

"If we cut our defenses before negotiations begin, any incentive for other nations to cut theirs will be completely removed," the President said.

Mr. Shultz indicated that enforcement of the ceilings would be along the lines of enforcement during Phase 2 of the Nixon Administration's wage-price controls program. This includes prominent display of lists of ceiling prices in stores, spot checks by the Internal Revenue Service and investigations by the service in re-

Continued on Page 23, Column 1

McCord Testifies His Fellow Plotters Linked High Nixon Aides to Watergate

Tells Senate Unit Mitchell Was Identified as 'Boss' of Political Espionage

By WALTER RUGABER

Special to The New York Times

WASHINGTON, March 29—James W. McCord Jr. has testified under oath that his fellow conspirators in the Watergate affair gave him the impression that they had cleared their clandestine operations with ranking officials in the Nixon Administration.

McCord, former chief of security for President Nixon's re-election campaign organization, told a Senate committee in secret session yesterday that his confederates often invoked the names of prominent officials who he said were behind the plot.

According to reliable sources, McCord, convicted in January in the break-in and bugging last June at the Democratic National Committee headquarters in the Watergate complex here, cited hearsay among his co-conspirators as the basis for the following major assertions.

¶John N. Mitchell, who left his post as Attorney General to serve as Mr. Nixon's campaign director, approved the espionage activity and served as "over-all boss" of the team that mounted it.

¶John W. Dean 3d, counsel to the President, sat in on a planning meeting with two men ultimately convicted as conspirators, heard their plans, and later reported that the operation had been approved. McCord apparently did not say who had given the approval.

¶H. R. Haldeman, the White House chief of staff, "knew what was going on" at the Committee for the Re-election of the President. One source said that McCord had not elaborated on this assertion.

¶Robert C. Mardian, former Assistant Attorney General in charge of he Internal Security Division, had been in contact with McCord, who invoked the Fifth Amendment's protection against self-incrimination when asked the circumstances.

¶Charles W. Colson, former special counsel to the President, was thought by McCord to have received a detailed plan for the Watergate operation from E. Howard Hunt Jr.,

Continued on Page 21, Column 1

NO-STRIKE ACCORD REACHED ON STEEL

Union and Major Companies Agree to Avert a Shutdown for at Least 4 Years

Special to The New York Times

PITTSBURGH, March 29—The United Steelworkers of America approved today an unprecedented agreement that virtually assures labor peace in the basic steel industry through July, 1977, and perhaps longer.

The accord, worked out with 10 companies in years of talks, provides for binding arbitration of unresolved issues in 1974 negotiations and prohibits strikes by the union or lockouts by the companies to support their bargaining positions.

I. W. Abel, the union president, disclosed details of the preliminary union-management agreement, which was approved by the 600 local union presidents and officers in the Basic Steel Industry Conference.

Mr. Abel described the plan as "an unprecedented experiment that we think will prove there is a better way for labor and management to negotiate

Continued on Page 35, Column 1

S.E.C. White Paper Seeks Stock Market-Restructure

By FELIX BELAIR Jr.

Special to The New York Times

WASHINGTON, March 29—The Securities and Exchange Commission today unveiled its master plan to restructure the nation's securities markets. Its aim is to establish a central market system. The system would encompass a network of brokers and dealers in offices and on exchange floors across the nation, linked together by electronic communication.

In a white paper intended to provide guidelines for all segments of the industry, the commission outlined a common regulatory framework that would sweep aside some of the most cherished rules and practices of the New York and American Stock Exchanges and their regional counterparts.

Excerpts from S.E.C. report are printed on Page 57.

The commission said the primary objective of the central system was "the development of strong competition among its participants," since the "ultimate beneficiary of aggressive competition is the investing public." It added:

"Our securities markets have attracted the direct investment of savings by more individual investors than any other securities markets in the world. The fact that indirect investment through institutions has grown rapidly in recent years makes more important than ever that the liquidity provided by the trading decisions of individual investors be maintained.

"If the participation of such investors is to continue, it is critically important to maintain the confidence of every investor, large or small, that his order will receive prompt and efficient handling and will have the fullest possible opportunity to meet the best available offsetting order wherever in the

Continued on Page 57, Column 5

CONSUMERS RALLY FOR MEAT BOYCOTT

Mobilization On—Midwest Farmers Plan to Withhold Cattle in Countermove

By WILL LISSNER

The nationwide movement to boycott meat next week to protest high food prices gained momentum yesterday as community and women's groups began holding rallies and handing cut leaflets to mobilize housewives' support.

One of the first rallies in the metropolitan area was held last night at Public School 196 in Forest Hills, Queens. Others are to be held in the city and in its suburbs over the weekend in preparation for Sunday when the weeklong boycott begins, and Monday, when widespread picketing of supermarkets is scheduled to start.

The organizers of the rallies and campaigns said before President Nixon last night pledged a ceiling on meat prices that they intended to stage the boycott regardless of any action Mr. Nixon took. They are determined, they said, to lower food prices as a prelude to lowering other prices, and they said only organized consumer action could bring this about.

Two coordinating sessions in Manhattan yesterday were attended by 200 representatives of groups from the five

Continued on Page 24, Column 2

Former P.O.W.'s Charge Torture by North Vietnam

By STEVEN V. ROBERTS

Special to The New York Times

WASHINGTON, March 29—Former prisoners of war told chilling stories today of mental and physical torture at the hands of their North Vietnamese captors.

In news conferences across the country, the men said they had been beaten, tied, shackled and starved until they provided information about American war plans or signed antiwar statements and confessions of war crimes.

But to many of the men, the most devastating treatment was prolonged periods of solitary confinement. As Col. Robinson Risner put it at Andrews Air Force Base in Maryland: "Can you imagine someone putting you in a closet and closing the door and saying, 'See you in six months'?"

The former prisoners talked about their captivity hours atfer the last of the American prisoners of war landed at Clark Air Base in the Philippines. Until now, the men had refused to discuss details of their life in Communist prisons for fear of jeopardizing the release of comrades still behind bars.

By and large, the men kept a firm hold on their emotions and even joked occasionally. In describing life in solitary confinement, Capt. Wendell Rivers told a conference at Bethesda Naval Hospital that "you can get up at 6 in the morning and fall asleep at 8 at night and walk all day in circles around your room."

"But you have to reverse direction once in a while so you don't fall down," he added.

But occasionally their anger and bitterness spilled out and their voices quavered. As one former prisoner put it recently, the older prisoners "lived on hate" for their captors and the Communist system. And it was not really clear today how that hatred colored their tales of an experience that Colonel Risner described as "severe torture, degradation, deprivation, humiliation, you name it."

In San Francisco, Comdr. Richard A. Stratton said he thought the North Vietnamese should be tried for "war crimes" for their treatment of prisoners. Commander Stratton was the subject of a famous picture in which he was shown bowing to his captors. Today he said he had been forced to appear at a news conference and had decided to act drugged to discredit his own appearance.

Asked what purpose the stories of torture might serve, Lieut. Col. John A. Dramesi said at An-

Continued on Page 18, Column 2

Council Votes 3-Year Extension Of Rent Control for Million Units

By MAX H. SEIGEL

The City Council yesterday approved overwhelmingly a three-year extension of rent controls affecting more than one million dwelling units.

The vote was 33 to 1, with Councilman Anthony R. Gaeta, a Staten Island Democrat, opposed.

At the same time, most members emphasized, in speech after speech, that they wanted speedy adoption of legislation to repeal or place a moratorium on the maximum-base-rent formula, allowing landlords annual increases of 7.5 per cent, and to repeal the vacancy-decontrol law, under which any vacated rent-controlled apartment automatically becomes decontrolled.

Rudolph F. DiBlasi, chairman of the Council's Committee on Housing, said hearings involving bills on the maximum-base-rent formula and vacancy decontrol would be conducted next Thursday. At the same time, he warned that a serious question of jurisdiction was involved.

Councilman DiBlasi said both matters have to be considered, "and we're going to wind up with a head-on collision" with the state. "We're prepared to do that," he added.

Another Council member

Continued on Page 25, Column 3

NEWS INDEX

	Page		Page
Art	28	Music	26-34
Books	36-37	Obituaries	42
Bridge	36	Op-Ed	39
Business	53-62	Society	35
Crossword	37	Sports	46-49
Editorials	38	Theaters	26-31
Family/Style	44	Transportation	[illegible]
Financial	53-62	TV and Radio	78-79
Going Out Guide	28	U. N. Proceedings	[illegible]
Movies	26-34	Weather	78

News Summary and Index, Page 41

American POWs about to be released from North Vietnam prepare to embark on their long-awaited trips home.

Two returned prisoners from North Vietnam arrive to a hero's welcome at Clark Air Base in the Philippines.

Returned POW, Everett Alvarez, Jr. is reunited with his family for the first time in eight and a half years.

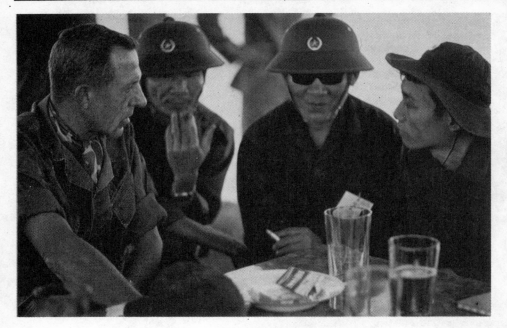

U.S. and North Vietnamese officials delicately negotiate the terms for the release and exchange of POWs.

The cease-fire agreement between North Vietnam and the United States was initialed in Paris, on January 23, 1973 by Henry Kissinger and Le Duc Tho.

War-disabled North Vietnamese soldiers released from captivity in South Vietnam.

"All the News That's Fit to Print"

The New York Times

LATE CITY EDITION

Weather: Cooler, rain today; cloudy tonight. Fair and warmer tomorrow. Temp. range: today 71-74; Tuesday 68-82. Temp.-Hum. Index yesterday 76. Full U.S. report on Page 74.

VOL. CXXII... No. 42,207 © 1973 The New York Times Company NEW YORK, WEDNESDAY, AUGUST 15, 1973 15 CENTS

BOMBING OF CAMBODIA STOPPED, MARKING THE OFFICIAL U.S. END OF COMBAT IN SOUTHEAST ASIA

The New York Times/Denis Cameron

Refugees in motorcycle-drawn carts pass a bomb crater along Route 1 in Cambodia

CAPITAL AREA HIT

Final Hours Intense —Phnom Penh Life Seems Unruffled

By United Press International

PHNOM PENH, Cambodia, Wednesday, Aug. 15 — American warplanes carried out intense bombing yesterday around this beleaguered capital in the last hours before the official end of more than a decade of United States combat involvement in Southeast Asia.

The bombing officially ended at 11 A.M. today (midnight Tuesday, New York time), leaving the Cambodian Government dependent on its army of 250,000 men, women and teen-agers and on a tiny unsophisticated air force. The cessation marked the end of 160 consecutive days of intense American bombing throughout the country.

American planes bombed Cambodia intermittently for four and a half years, at first secretly, and in the last six months have dropped more than 240,000 tons of bombs—50 per cent more than the conventional explosives dropped on Japan in World War II.

Fierce 11th-Hour Bombing

Phnom Penh was rocked by fierce 11th-hour bombing as air controllers called in strike after strike against some 10,000 rebel forces on the city's defense perimeter. B-52 bombers, F-111 jet fighter-bombers and tactical aircraft carried out the strikes. Flares lit the night sky around Phnom Penh searching out rebel concentrations. With daylight, air activity became intense on the outskirts, rattling windows and doors in the capital.

Residents in Phnom Penh went about their work apparently unruffled despite the impending bombing halt, which is a result of Congressional action.

The Cambodian Army will now depend on air support from a fleet of about 100 aircraft that have none of the advanced equipment of American warplanes.

100 Planes Available

The American Embassy — with about 200 personnel, the largest in the capital—said it would remain in operation despite a warning Sunday from the deposed Cambodian Chief of State, Prince Norodom Sihanouk, that victory by his rebel forces was "already practically achieved" and that all foreigners should leave.

More than 200 foreign newsmen, television cameramen and

Continued on Page 14, Column 2

SUPPORT PLEDGED

American Planes Will Remain on Station in Guam and Thailand

By BERNARD GWERTZMAN
Special to The New York Times

WASHINGTON, Wednesday, Aug. 15—American bombing in Cambodia officially ended last midnight with the Nixon Administration still pledging to do everything possible within the law to support the Government of President Lon Nol.

The cessation of all bombing activity, voted by Congress on June 30, and accepted by President Nixon with "grave personal reservations," marks the official end to America's dozen years of combat activity in Southeast Asia. Some 46,000 American lives have been lost—most of them in South Vietnam — since the first American casualties in 1961.

The Vietnam cease-fire agreement, signed on Jan. 27 in Paris, ended the American combat role in North and South Vietnam, and the Laotian agreement a month later ended the American role there.

Fighting Goes On

The Cambodian fighting, however, has not stopped, and it is unclear what the effect the end of American bombing will have on the Cambodian belligerents.

But even as B-52 strategic bombers and F-4 fighter-bombers carried out their last missions, the Pentagon stressed that American planes would remain on station in Thailand and in Guam, prepared to resume their raids if Congress authorized them—something viewed as unlikely unless North Vietnam launched a vast invasion of South Vietnam.

Although the end to American bombing was a historic landmark in the long, controversial Indochina war, the Administration chose virtually to ignore it. Neither the White House, nor the Pentagon nor the State Department volunteered any statement on the occasion.

Berrigans Arrested

On the final day of United States bombing, 60 persons, including the antiwar activists Daniel J. Berrigan and his brother Jerome were arrested as they knelt and prayed at the White House in a protest against the raids. [Page 14.]

At the Defense Department, officials said the end of the bombing was being treated routinely.

The Pentagon, in answer to questions, supplied statistics on the latest Cambodian phase of the bombing, betw[illegible] Jan 28, the day following the Vietnam cease-fire agreement, and Aug. 11, the last day for which figures were available. During that period, 35,410 sorties, or flights, were carried out, cost-

Continued on Page 14, Column 1

Agnew Offers to Answer Any Questions in Inquiry

Will Open His Records to U.S. Attorney Checking Maryland Kickback Charges —but He Avoids Constitutional Issue

By ANTHONY RIPLEY
Special to The New York Times

BALTIMORE, Aug. 14—Vice President Agnew offered today to answer questions personally and open his records to the United States Attorney here who is investigating allegations of extortion, bribery, tax fraud and conspiracy that allegedly took place when Mr. Agnew was Governor of Maryland.

"I have done nothing wrong. I have nothing to hide. And I have no desire save that justice be done speedily and efficiently," Mr. Agnew said in a letter hand-delivered late today to George Beall, the United States Attorney.

Letter from Vice President is printed on Page 16.

On Aug. 1, Mr. Beall had written the Vice President's lawyer, Judah Best, asking for personal financial records and stating that Mr. Agnew was under investigation.

In his reply today, Mr. Agnew said the records had been assembled and that "you and any of your assistants may inspect them there [at his offices] at any time you may desire."

He stressed that by making the records available "I do not acknowledge that you or any grand jury have any right to the records of the Vice President. Nor do I acknowledge the propriety of any grand jury investigation of possible wrongdoing on the part of the Vice President so long as he occupies that office."

Difficult Questions

"These are difficult constitutional questions which need not at this moment be confronted," he wrote.

But Mr. Agnew went one step beyond Mr. Beall's request by offering to submit to questions personally. Mr. Beall had requested bank statements, check stubs, canceled checks, check vouchers, check books, and deposit tickets and savings account books along with income tax returns.

The Vice President said his "desire to cooperate" in the investigation did not stop with only turning over records.

"I am eager to be of any help I can," he wrote. "Specifically, should you wish, I shall be glad to meet with you and your colleagues for a personal interview so that I may answer any questions you may have."

The letter was delivered by

Continued on Page 16, Column 3

MORE PRICE RISES SET BY COMPANIES ON KEY PRODUCTS

Phone Rates Up in 6 States —G.M., Ford and U.S. Steel Plan Increases

By MICHAEL C. JENSEN

The trickle of price increases that began Monday when the Nixon Administration's price freeze gave way to Phase 4 swelled to a steady stream yesterday.

Increases were announced, and in some cases put into effect, for such diverse items as airline tickets, telephone calls, automobiles, steel, macaroni and baseballs.

Internal Revenue Service offices in such cities as New York, Pittsburgh, Detroit and Chicago said they had received a number of prenotifications of price increases by large corporations.

Ford Seeks $106 Increase

In one of the most important price moves the General Motors Corporation and the Ford Motor Company joined the Chrysler Corporation in asking for permission to raise prices of 1974 model cars and trucks. Ford asked for an average increase of $106, and General Motors asked for $102. Chrysler asked for an average increase of $71 Monday.

Separately, the United States Steel Corporation, by far the nation's largest steelmaker, asked for an increase of almost 5 per cent on the steel used in home appliances and automobiles, making the request virtually industrywide.

The American Telephone and Telegraph Company, which as a regulated industry is not subject to approval by the I.R.S., said Bell System companies in six states were implementing rate increases of almost a quarter of a billion dollars annually.

Rises Held Up by Freeze

The increases, already approved by state authorities, had been held up by the 60-day price freeze that ended Monday. They are taking place in Massachusetts, Rhode Island, Oregon, Florida, Ohio and Texas, and affect the prices of telephone service within each state, but not interstate calls.

The I.R.S. office in Manhattan said two dozen to three dozen companies filed for price increases yesterday. Michael J. Greco, chief of stabilization, said almost all the local retail department-store chains had filed special forms required in their industry, either locally or in their home cities, and would

Continued on Page 52, Column 1

Dollar Value Climbs

The value of the dollar jumped to its highest level in six weeks in Europe yesterday. The price of gold fell $7 an ounce to $95, its lowest level in three months. Prices on the New York Stock Exchange dropped sharply for the third day. Page 47.

NIXON WILL SPEAK TO NATION TONIGHT

Address on Watergate Set for 9 O'Clock—Poll Finds Popularity at New Low

Special to The New York Times

WASHINGTON, Aug. 14 — President Nixon will address the nation on the Watergate case over television and radio at 9 P.M. tomorrow, the White House announced today.

The speech will be Mr. Nixon's first comment since May 22 on the scandal that has resulted in resignations and nearly paralyzed the White House staff and has led to a tense confrontation, perhaps a constitutional crisis, with Senate investigators and the special Watergate prosecutor.

The speech was announced after the Gallup Poll disclosed that Mr. Nixon's popularity had fallen to the lowest point for an American President in 20 years. The poll found that 31 per cent of those interviewed approved the way he was handling his job, a decline of 9 percentage points in four weeks. [Details on Page 19.]

Gerald L. Warren, the deputy White House press secretary, said that the speech would last 20 to 30 minutes and that a separate 4,000-word statement on the Watergate case would

Continued on Page 19, Column 1

7 Hurt, 2 Missing In Lodi Explosion At Chemical Plant

By FRANK J. PRIAL
Special to The New York Times

LODI, N. J., Aug. 14—Seven men were injured and at least two others were missing after an explosion rocked a chemical plant near busy Route 46 here today. Five of the injured were in critical condition at Hackensack Hospital last night, but all were expected to live.

As flames swept over the wreckage and black plumes of smoke hung in the windless, moist air, neighborhood residents clustered on street corners and front stoops, some complaining about the danger of accidents in chemical plants in the community.

The explosion rocked the Washine Division of the Mallinckrodt Chemical Company at about 7:50 A.M. It twisted heavy iron window frames and reduced windows in nearby stores to shards.

Some residents were evacuated from their homes, but injuries were confined to the area of the plant, which covers a square block near Main Street.

Firemen said the blast might have taken place in a reactor likened by a worker to a big pressure cooker. The reactor is used to "cook" chemical compounds.

For a time, officials feared

Continued on Page 41, Column 2

Chuck Zanlunghi

Firemen fighting blaze that followed explosion at Mallinckrodt Chemical Company plant in Lodi, N.J., yesterday

NARCOTICS THEFT REPORTED SOLVED

Nadjari Says More Proof Is Awaited for Arrests in Police Loss of Drugs

By CHRISTOPHER S. WREN

Maurice H. Nadjari, the special state prosecutor, said yesterday that authorities investigating the theft of more than $70-million worth of narcotics from Police Department custody now "know exactly how it was done and who did it" but had not yet gathered enough evidence for arrests.

He indicated that the "well-staged conspiracy" included an undisclosed number of police officers below the rank of inspector, some still on duty.

The disclosure came as Mr. Nadjari announced the indictment of Vincent C. Papa, who has been described as a key narcotics dealer, on eight counts of first-degree criminal contempt for having refused to answer questions before a special grand jury in Manhattan that has been looking into police complicity in the case.

Papa's indictment was the

Continued on Page 42, Column 1

Confusion in Cambodia

People Mystified as Direct U.S. Role Ends at a Time of Military Adversity

The writer of the following article has frequently reported from Cambodia for The New York Times since February, 1970, just before Prince Norodom Sihanouk's ouster.

By HENRY KAMM

As the orders went out to stop the American bombing of Cambodia, the end of direct United States military involvement there—like the beginning—was wrapped in controversy and confusion.

News Analysis

The President began the United States role, and Congress ended it. Domestic American considerations dictated the halt in the bombing, for the military situation has not changed in favor of the Phnom Penh Government since the final bombing campaign began in February.

Why the United States, having intervened, ended its intervention now, at a date that seems arbitrary, leaves the Cambodians confounded. But the Cambodian Government and most of the people of what had until this decade been a singularly placid country have believed all along that their fate would be decided by remote powers over which they have no control.

No Influence on U. S. Policy

With few exceptions Cambodians do not understand the controversy between President Nixon and Congress, which resulted in the halt in the bombing, because they believe that the President is the chief and senators and representatives are his employes.

The end—the United States acting out of reasons unconnected with Cambodia, and the Cambodians left uncomprehending—was characteristic of the relationship between the two countries since the overthrow of Prince Norodom Sihanouk on March 18, 1970, drew Cambodia into the Indochina war and made the United States the ally of the Government in Phnom Penh.

For nearly three and a half years President Nixon and President Lon Nol have made war together without meeting. In all that time the Cambodian leader has depended on the United States for the survival of his Government while remaining mystified by the course and rationale of American policy. It cannot be said that he has influenced it.

From the beginning of Marshal Lon Nol's Government, relations between the two countries have been rooted in a fundamental misconception.

Marshal Lon Nol, then a lieutenant general and Prince Sihanouk's appointee as Premier, counted on the same American support against the Vietnamese Communists that South Vietnam and Laos were receiving. Moreover, despite the ex-

Continued on Page 14, Column 6

State Court Upsets Civil Obscenity Law

By C. GERALD FRASER

The state's civil statute on obscenity was ruled unconstitutional yesterday by Justice Abraham J. Gellinoff of the State Supreme Court in Manhattan.

The effect of the ruling is to allow the sale, distribution, display and exhibition of films, books and pictures without interference from law enforcement agencies.

The judge ruled in what has been regarded as a critical test case following the United States Supreme Court's significant obscenity decisions of two months ago.

Norman Redlich, the city's Corporation Counsel, said that he and the other plaintiff, District Attorney Frank S. Hogan of Manhattan, would appeal the

Continued on Page 43, Column 2

NEWS INDEX

	Page		Page
Books	35	Music	22-27
Bridge	34	Obituaries	40
Business	46-57	Op-Ed	37
Crossword	35	Society	43
Editorials	36	Sports	28-34
Family/Style	44	Theaters	22-27
Financial	46-57	Transportation	74
Going Out Guide	22	TV and Radio	75
Letters	32	U.N. Proceedings	7
Movies	22-27	Weather	74

News Summary and Index, Page 39

Israel's Interception of Airliner Is Deplored by U.S. at the U.N.

By ROBERT ALDEN
Special to The New York Times

UNITED NATIONS, N.Y., Aug. 14—The United States warned Israel today in the Security Council that while national and international efforts to control terrorism must go forward, they must do so "within and not outside the law."

John A. Scali, the United States representative, told the Council that the United States deplored the violation of Lebanese sovereignty that occurred when Israeli aircraft on Friday intercepted an airliner that had just taken off from Beirut and forced it to fly to Israel.

"We deplore this violation of the United Nations Charter and of the rule of law in international civil aviation," Mr. Scali said. "It is high time to call a full stop to all such acts and related acts and threats of violence." The meeting had been called by Lebanon to protest the interception of the plane, an Iraqi Airlines charter flight with 82 people aboard, while on its way to Baghdad.

"National and international efforts to control terrorism must go forward," Mr. Scali said. "They must go forward, however, within and not outside the law. The commitment to the rule of law in international affairs, including the field of international civil aviation, imposes certain restraints on the methods governments can use to protect themselves against those who operate outside the law.

"My Government believes ac-

Continued on Page 7, Column 1

"All the News That's Fit to Print"

The New York Times

LATE CITY EDITION

Weather: Sunny and pleasant today; partly cloudy tonight, tomorrow. Temp. range: today 57-75; Monday range 50-75. Details on Page 67.

VOL.CXXIII..No.42,605   © 1974 The New York Times Company   NEW YORK, TUESDAY, SEPTEMBER 17, 1974   Higher in air delivery cities.   20 CENTS

President Publicly Backs Clandestine C.I.A. Activity

Confirms Chilean Involvement but Not in Coup—Senate Contempt Charge Urged for Helms and 3 Others

Special to The New York Times

WASHINGTON, Sept. 16—President Ford tonight publicly declared his support for the clandestine use of the Central Intelligence Agency "to help implement foreign policy and protect national security," but he denied that the C.I.A. had been involved in the Chilean coup d'etat last year.

In his televised news conference, the President bluntly acknowledged that the C.I.A. activities in Chile had been authorized because "there was an effort being made by the Allende Government to destroy opposition news media, both the writing press as well as the electronic press, and to destroy opposition political parties." He said the C.I.A. operations were "in the best interest of the people of Chile." [Question 7, Page 22.]

In a related development, The New York Times learned earlier that the staff of a Senate For-

eign Relations subcommittee had recommended that the tempt of Congress charges be placed against Richard Helms, former C.I.A. director, and three retired Nixon Administration officials because of their misleading Senate testimony last year on the clandestine activities in Chile. [Details on Page 10.]

Mr. Ford's defense of covert C.I.A. operations came amid a growing protest in Congress and newspaper editorials stemming from published reports last week that the intelligence agency had been authorized to spend more than $8-million between 1970 and 1973 in an effort to make it impossible for President Salvador Allende Gossens to govern Chile.

Until today, the Nixon and Ford Administrations had repeatedly insisted that the United States had not inter-

Continued on Page 11, Column 1

City to Restudy Rent Rise On 400,000 Apartments

The head of the city's Rent Guidelines Board said yesterday that the board would meet soon to consider whether rent-rise limits it recently announced for 400,000 apartments were too high.

NEW YORK WINS LOTTERY GO-AHEAD

Justice Department Clears Program of Violating Any Criminal Law

Special to The New York Times

WASHINGTON, Sept. 16—The Justice Department today gave the New York State Lottery a clean bill of health, and exempted the lottery from a planned Federal crackdown.

"They do not appear to have violated any Federal criminal statutes," said Marvin R. Loewy, deputy chief of the Organized Crime and Racketeering Section. "They appear not to include any use of U.S. mails or any use of interstate facilities."

Mr. Loewy said that no such determination had been made in the cases of New Jersey, Connecticut or any of the 10 other states that conduct lotteries.

He was interviewed after a 60-minute meeting with Ronald Maiorana, New York State's director of the lottery and offtrack betting.

"I am most gratified with the recognition by the Attorney General's office of the propriety of New York's lottery," Mr. Maiorana said. "The meeting today was an important step in restoring public confidence and dispelling any inadvertent inference that the New York lottery was in danger of being shut down by the Federal Government because of illegal practices."

Mr. Maiorana said that his office had been besieged with

Continued on Page 67, Column 5

TOP BUSINESSMEN CALL FOR EASING OF MONEY POLICY

40 at Meeting Sponsored by White House Also Advise Cuts in Federal Spending

By MARYLIN BENDER

Special to The New York Times

PITTSBURGH, Sept. 16—A Forty of the nation's business leaders attending a White House-sponsored conference on inflation strongly expressed support today for the Administration's call for balanced budgets and cuts in Federal spending.

But the businessmen recommended an easing of tight monetary policy, concurring with the opinions of economists, housing experts and labor leaders at similar conferences earlier this month.

"Because the risk of major recession is so high, the time has come for a moderate easing of monetary policy which has depressed the stock market and made difficult expanded capital investment," said Frank T. Cary, chairman of the International Business Machines Corporation.

The high cost of money evidenced by record interest rates has contributed to inflation by becoming a fixed cost of business, some said.

Shortages of capital and high interest rates have shrunken allotments for research and development and plans for technological improvement, the representatives said repeatedly.

Rogers C. B. Morton, Secretary of the Interior, said today in Dallas at another White House-sponsored conference that the Government might have to keep price controls on domestic crude oil for "two years or more." [Page 56.]

Edgar B. Speer, chairman of the United States Steel Corporation, indicated that his company could establish a plant that would reduce energy consumption by 35 to 40 per cent but he added, "we haven't been able to formulate the capital to take advantage of it."

The businessmen asked for

Continued on Page 56, Column 2

2 Freed as Judge Scores U.S. Wounded Knee Case

By MARTIN WALDRON

Special to The New York Times

ST. PAUL, Sept. 16—A Federal judge tongue-lashed the prosecution, the Justice Department and particularly the Federal Bureau of Investigation today and then dismissed the charges against the two men who led last year's Indian take-over of the community of Wounded Knee, S.D.

United States District Judge Fred J. Nichol said that the Justice Department, by refusing to let 11 members of the jury decide the case after the 12th became ill, appeared to be more interested in convicting the Indians than in justice.

Judge Nichol also accused the chief prosecutor, R. D. Hurd, of

deliberately deceiving the court and said that the F.B.I. had "stooped to a new low."

The judge asked that the function of the Justice Department and Government prosecutors was not to convict defendants but rather to seek justice. If the department had been interested in justice, he said, it would have let the 11 jurors decide the case instead of insisting on a mistrial.

Doctors reported today that the ill juror, Mrs. Therese Cherrier, 53 years old, had suffered a stroke and would not be able to rejoin the jury. Over the weekend, Mr. Hurd had said

Continued on Page 12, Column 1

FORD OFFERS AMNESTY PROGRAM REQUIRING 2 YEARS PUBLIC WORK; DEFENDS HIS PARDON OF NIXON

ANY 'DEAL' DENIED

President Asserts His Major Reason Was 'To Heal Nation'

By PHILIP SHABECOFF

Special to The New York Times

WASHINGTON, Sept. 16—President Ford said emphatically tonight that he had made "no deal" with former President Richard M. Nixon and insisted that the major reason for his decision to pardon him was "to heal the nation."

At a news conference in the White House, his second since taking office, Mr. Ford conceded that he had been surprised by the "antagonism" that his decision to grant a full, unconditional pardon to his predecessor had created.

But under a barrage of questions, he strongly defended his act.

"I'm still convinced, despite the public reaction so far, that the decision I made was the right one," he said. [Question 8, Page 22.]

He said that a number of factors entered into the decision, including accounts he had received about Mr. Nixon's health.

"But the major reason for the action I took related to the effort to reconcile divisions in our country and to heal the wounds that had festered far too long," he said. [Question 2.]

He said that Mr. Nixon had been "shamed and disgraced" by his resignation.

Questions about the pardon dominated tonight's news conference, but the President did

Continued on Page 22, Column 1

President Ford during his news conference at the White House last night
The New York Times/Mike Lien

Haig Plea on Nixon Health Linked to Ford's Reversal

By EVERETT R. HOLLES

Special to The New York Times

SAN CLEMENTE, Calif., Sept. 16—The White House chief of staff, Gen. Alexander M. Haig Jr., after being advised of the "alarming state" of Richard M. Nixon's health, was reliably reported today to have persuaded President Ford to reverse his publicly stated position and grant an immediate pardon to the former President.

A longtime friend of Mr. Nixon identified General Haig as the person "primarily responsible" for the surprise pardon announced on Sept. 8 by President Ford. This friend, who is a former member of the Presidential staff, is in daily touch with affairs inside the Nixons' heavily guarded Casa Pacifica estate here.

Warns of Tragedy

General Haig, he said, warned Mr. Ford on Aug. 29 that unless he moved quickly in announcing a full, unconditional pardon, instead of waiting for legal action to be taken, it might be too late to avert what he called "a possible personal and national tragedy" of Mr. Nixon's complete physical and mental collapse.

Only the day before, the President had told newsmen he would not act on a pardon until legal action had been brought against Mr. Nixon for his role in the Watergate case or other Federal offenses related to that scandal.

The four-star general, a hold-over from the Nixon Adminis-

tration, who was named today commander of NATO forces, was reported to have initiated the highly secret pardon discussions after receiving accounts of Mr. Nixon's deteriorating physical and emotional health from the Nixon daughters, Julie Eisenhower and Tricia Cox.

He is said to have immediately discussed the reports at length in telephone conversations with Ronald L. Ziegler, the former White House press secretary, who is now Mr. Nixon's closest confidant.

In a news conference tonight, Mr. Ford said that before he decided to pardon Mr. Nixon, he had no "specific information" about his predecessor's health beyond what had been reported in the media, except for the observations of a

Continued on Page 23, Column 1

Courageous Wins 3d: Title Bout Postponed

Courageous, the United States defender, defeated Southern Cross of Australia for the third straight race yesterday off Newport, R.I., and can clinch the America's Cup today.

George Foreman's world heavyweight title defense against Muhammad Ali was postponed at least a week when Foreman was cut over his right eye in training. Details on Page 29.

GEN. HAIG NAMED NATO COMMANDER

Appointment Is Approved by Allied Unit in Brussels— No Word on Successor

Special to The New York Times

WASHINGTON, Sept. 16—President Ford announced today the appointment of Gen. Alexander M. Haig Jr., the White House chief of staff, as Supreme Allied Commander in Europe.

The appointment, which had been reported in recent weeks to be imminent, was approved today in Brussels by the defense planning committee of the North Atlantic Treaty Organization. It becomes effective Dec. 15.

President Ford also named General Haig as commander of United States Forces in Europe, effective Nov. 1. The general is expected to leave the White House before then for a vacation.

There had been some objection to General Haig's NATO appointment, particularly from the Government of The Netherlands. But the United States overcame the opposition and the appointment was accepted.

General Haig, who had also served President Nixon as chief of staff and was the highest ranking holdover from the Nixon White House, has been the focus of controversy in recent weeks.

"Al Haig has been the lightning rod for almost all of the criticism the White House has taken since President Ford took over," a White House official said friendly to the general said today.

Asked about a successor to General Haig, an official in the

Continued on Page 24, Column 2

A 'RE-ENTRY' PLAN

Goodell Named Head of Clemency Unit— Hesburgh Included

By MARJORIE HUNTER

Special to The New York Times

WASHINGTON, Sept. 16—President Ford offered conditional amnesty today to thousands of Vietnam era draft evaders and military deserters who agree to work for up to two years in public service jobs.

"My sincere hope," he said in a statement, "is that this is a constructive step toward calmer and cooler appreciation of our individual rights and re-

Texts of the Ford statement and proclamation, Page 24.

sponsibilities and our common purpose as a nation whose future is always more important than its past."

In announcing his "earned reentry" program, the President also established a nine-member Presidential clemency board to review the cases of those already convicted by courts of desertion or draft evasion.

Mr. Ford designated Charles E. Goodell, a former Republican Senator from New York and an early critic of United States involvement in the Vietnam war, as chairman of the clemency board.

Among others named to the clemency board was the Rev. Theodore M. Hesburgh, president of the University of Notre Dame, who has called for unconditional amnesty.

Effectively Immediately

The amnesty program became effective immediately when President Ford signed a Presidential proclamation and two Executive orders just before noon in the Cabinet Room of the White House. Earlier, he explained details of the program to Congressional leaders of both parties. No Congressional action is needed.

In his proclamation, the President declared that "desertion in time of war is a major, serious offense," and that draft evasion "is also a serious offense." Such actions, he said, need not "be condoned."

"Yet," he continued, "reconciliation calls for an act of mercy to bind the nation's wounds and to heal the scars of divisiveness."

President Ford denied tonight at his news conference that the amnesty plan was in any substantial way linked to his unconditional pardon of former President Richard M. Nixon on Sept. 8—action that has created widespread controversy throughout the nation. [Question 13, Page 22.]

Asked at his news conference tonight why he had granted a conditional amnesty to draft evaders while granting a full pardon to Mr. Nixon, the President replied:

"Well, the only connection

Continued on Page 23, Column 5

Ford Offer Greeted Coolly By U.S. Exiles in Canada

By WILLIAM BORDERS

Special to The New York Times

MONTREAL, Sept. 16—President Ford's offer of conditional amnesty was reacted to coolly today by American draft evaders and deserters in Canada, the country that attracted the largest number of them over the years.

Some of the young exiles said that they would consider Mr. Ford's offer of "earned reentry." But others, in interviews across Canada, reiterated opposition to any kind of involuntary service carrying implications that they have something to atone for.

"The American people have come to accept the judgment

that was made about the Vietnam war when we refused to fight in it," said Stanley J. Pietlock, a 31-year-old draft evader who now lives in Toronto. "The only thing we were guilty of was premature morality."

Urging that the clemency

Continued on Page 23, Column 6

Grand Jury to Get Report On Police Killing of Boy

By MARY BREASTED

The fatal shooting of a 14-year-old Brownsville boy by a police officer who had been called to check out a reported burglary in the Brooklyn neighborhood late Sunday evening was under investigation by the Brooklyn District Attorney's office yesterday.

Eugene Gold, the District Attorney, said through a spokesman that the results of this investigation would be presented to a grand jury soon.

The shooting, brought about by what the 73d Precinct's commanding officer said was the mistaking a small saw with a pistol grip, for a gun in the hand of the boy, has become the focus of community reaction.

Claude Reese, the dead boy, was black. The officer who shot him, 24-year-old Frank Bosco, a three-year veteran of the force, is white, and the killing aroused bitterness among residents in the community, who milled about during the day in front of the Powell Street tenements behind which the boy was shot.

Last night, more than 200 persons gathered in front of the 73d Precinct station at East New York Avenue and Rockaway Avenue. The crowd was mostly peaceful until around 10:15 when several dozen youths broke away and ran down Rockaway Avenue, toss-

Continued on Page 70, Column 1

STALEMATE AT THE HAGUE: A Japanese terrorist, left, pulling up a package of food into the French Embassy yesterday. Above: the two women hostages being escorted to the U.S. Embassy after being released. Negotiations appear to have stalled. Story on Page 3.
Associated Press

CREDIT CARD reservations at the Met Opera: 799-3125. See today's ad.

"All the News That's Fit to Print"

The New York Times

LATE CITY EDITION

SECTION ONE

Weather: Partly sunny today and tonight. Cloudy skies tomorrow. Temperature range: today 32-44; Saturday 38-42. Details on Page 39.

VOL. CXXIV ... No. 42,701 NEW YORK, SUNDAY, DECEMBER 22, 1974 — $1.00 beyond 50-mile zone from New York City, except Long Island. Higher in air delivery cities. — 60 CENTS

The New York Times/George Tames

Vice President Rockefeller and President Ford conferring yesterday at the White House

ROCKEFELLER GETS KEY JOB GUIDING DOMESTIC COUNCIL

Ford Gives Him Major Role 'Explaining' Domestic and Foreign Programs

2 MEET AT WHITE HOUSE

Vice President Will Study System of Presidential Scientific Advisers

By LINDA CHARLTON

Special to The New York Times

WASHINGTON, Dec. 21—The White House announced today that President Ford was appointing Vice President Rockefeller vice chairman of the Domestic Council and expected him to play a major role in "explaining" the President's domestic and foreign programs "throughout the country."

The first official announcement about Mr. Rockefeller's role was made by the White House press secretary, Ron Nessen, after Mr. Rockefeller and the President met, both alone and with members of both of their staffs, for about 90 minutes late this afternoon.

Earlier, the President held a meeting with a group of his economic advisers to receive final recommendations for a new attack on inflation and recession, with a limited tax cut reportedly under consideration.

Although today's announcement outlined, at least for the moment, Mr. Rockefeller's official duties and responsibilities, they gave little hint of how much actual power he would have.

Day-to-Day Administrator

Mr. Ford is ex officio chairman of the Domestic Council and, as Mr. Nessen pointed out, the executive director's job is a day-to-day administrative post. This could mean, then, that the real power in the Domestic Council could be Mr. Rockefeller's.

Mr. Nessen, at a 6:30 P.M. news briefing, also announced the following duties for the new Vice President, who was sworn in Thursday night:

¶Mr. Rockefeller will assume the post of vice chairman of the National Security Council.

¶As vice chairman of the Domestic Council, of which Mr. Ford is the chairman, there will be a strong emphasis on his helping the White House find a new director to replace Kenneth R. Cole Jr., who has announced his resignation.

¶At his own request, he will have a "special interest in handling the Domestic Council role in coordinating activities

Continued on Page 27, Column 1

HUGE C.I.A. OPERATION REPORTED IN U.S. AGAINST ANTIWAR FORCES, OTHER DISSIDENTS IN NIXON YEARS

Richard Helms

James R. Schlesinger

The New York Times

William E. Colby

FILES ON CITIZENS

Helms Reportedly Got Surveillance Data in Charter Violation

By SEYMOUR M. HERSH

Special to The New York Times

WASHINGTON, Dec. 21—The Central Intelligence Agency, directly violating its charter, conducted a massive, illegal domestic intelligence operation during the Nixon Administration against the antiwar movement and other dissident groups in the United States, according to well-placed Government sources.

An extensive investigation by The New York Times has established that intelligence files on at least 10,000 American citizens were maintained by a special unit of the C.I.A. that was reporting directly to Richard Helms, then the Director of Central Intelligence and now the Ambassador to Iran.

In addition, the sources said, a check of the C.I.A.'s domestic files ordered last year by Mr. Helms's successor, James R. Schlesinger, produced evidence of dozens of other illegal activities by members of the C.I.A. inside the United States, beginning in the nineteen-fifties, including break-ins, wiretapping and the surreptitious inspection of mail.

A Different Category

Mr. Schlesinger was succeeded at the C.I.A. by William E. Colby in September, 1973.

Those other alleged operations, in the fifties, while also prohibited by law, were not targeted at dissident American citizens, the sources said, but were a different category of domestic activities that were secretly carried out as part of operations aimed at suspected foreign intelligence agents operating in the United States.

Under the 1947 act setting up the C.I.A., the agency was forbidden to have "police, subpoena, law enforcement powers or internal security functions" inside the United States. Those responsibilities fall to the F.B.I., which maintains a special internal security unit to deal with foreign intelligence threats.

Helms Unavailable

Mr. Helms, who became head of the C.I.A. in 1966 and left the agency in February, 1973, for his new post in Teheran, could not be reached despite telephone calls there yesterday and today.

Charles Cline, a duty officer at the American Embassy in Teheran, said today that a note informing Mr. Helms of the request by The Times for comment had been delivered to Mr. Helms's quarters this morning. By late evening Mr. Helms had not returned the call.

The information about the

Continued on Page 26, Column 1

Shah Bids Americans Push For Big Contracts in Iran

By SEYMOUR TOPPING

Special to The New York Times

TEHERAN, Iran, Dec. 21 — Shah Mohammed Riza Pahlevi challenged American businessmen today to become "more aggressive and dynamic" in competing for Iranian development contracts worth billions of dollars.

The Shah in an interview also invited thousands of Americans to come to Iran to alleviate the critical manpower shortage in this country's development program. He suggested that American companies advertise to encourage engineers, teachers, nurses, technicians and skilled workers to apply for jobs.

The 55-year-old Iranian ruler, wearing a dark lounge suit and white polka-dot tie, was interviewed in the large, chandeliered audience chamber in the modern Niavaran Palace on a snow-covered northern height overlooking Teheran. He had flown by helicopter to the palace an hour earlier from a residence on Kish Island in the Persian Gulf where he and Empress Farah celebrated their 15th wedding anniversary.

Struggle for Contracts

The Shah issued his invitation to Americans at a time when American, Japanese and European companies are locked in a struggle for Iranian development contracts worth many billions of dollars. Some billion-dollar contracts already have been signed but others are being negotiated through letters of intent because of delays caused by shortages of manpower, housing and other facilities.

"In our current five-year plan we shall be spending $80-billion to $90-billion on the purchase of capital goods and services to complete planned projects," the Shah said. Iran's five-year plan is now in its second year and is being financed by oil revenues that the Government says will bring in $25-

Continued on Page 7, Column 1

2D LONDON STORE IN 3 DAYS BOMBED

Harrods Gets Shoppers Out and Police Begin Search for 2 More Explosives

Special to The New York Times

LONDON, Dec. 21—A bomb exploded today in Harrods, one of London's most exclusive department stores, and set fire to part of the third floor.

There was one minor casualty, according to Comdr. Robert Huntley, head of Scotland Yard's bomb squad. He said the almost simultaneous discovery of the explosive by a Harrods staff member and a telephoned warning allowed 10 minutes for Christmas shoppers and the store staff to be evacuated.

There were unofficial reports that the blast came during the evacuation. The police sought two more bombs.

The bombing, the second such incident in London in three days, came a day after the militant Provisional wing of the Irish Republican Army announced a Christmas cease-fire in Britain and Northern Ireland, to start at midnight Sunday.

The bomb, in a bag on a display shelf of the motor-accessory department of Harrods, was spotted by a staff member

Continued on Page 2, Column 3

INFLATION CURBS CHRISTMAS SALES

Shorter Shopping Season Also Cited by Stores as Buyers Stretch Funds

By ISADORE BARMASH

Inflation, unemployment, layoffs and concern over what the national economy holds next year have produced generally disappointing Christmas sales so far for merchants across the country.

With only three shopping days left, the nation's consumers have apparently approached their Christmas gift-giving in a sober, even somber mood. They are paring their shopping lists, keeping a tight rein on buying by using cash more than credit and by purchasing fewer holiday decorations.

"I'm spending less because of the inflated prices," Mrs. Diane Yemano, the mother of two young children, said in a Los Angeles shopping center, "and I'm only spending a certain amount for each person."

Many retailers hope they can

Continued on Page 24, Column 3

Extensive Abuses Found In Court-Hiring Practices

By RALPH BLUMENTHAL

The role of political patronage in the appointment of state-court aides and employes has come under official investigation in connection with the indictments of five law secretaries.

Alleged abuses cited by the State Bar Association and law-enforcement authorities include the appointment of political party officials and leaders and their relatives as $26,000-a-year law secretaries, the selection of law secretaries without law degrees, and the naming of no-show jobholders who spend most of their time away from court.

Discretion Limited

The inquiry into criminal aspects of such abuses is being conducted by Special Prosecutor Maurice H. Nadjari, whose job it is to ferret out corruption in the state's justice system.

An informal check by The New York Times of a dozen State Supreme Court justices and a dozen law secretaries—close to 10 per cent of the city's total—has indicated that law secretaries are routinely screened and designated, or "recommended," as judges preferred to say, by the local party organization before being hired by the judges.

Usually, the judge's only discretion is to reject his prospective employe. In such cases, the organization then provides him with another choice or several choices, the survey showed.

In many of the cases checked, the law secretaries were known prior to the survey to have had a history of Democratic or Republican political activities on a club or county level. At least three were identified as district leaders and two as county committeemen.

The survey also found that seven of the law secretaries checked had private law practices listed in the telephone directory. Law secretaries here are supposed to work full-time and are barred from working privately on any case under litigation in any court.

However, with the permission of the Appellate Division, they may work on uncontested matters in Surrogate and Supreme

Continued on Page 32, Column 4

93d Congress Set Historic Precedents

By DAVID E. ROSENBAUM

Special to The New York Times

WASHINGTON, Dec. 21—The last two years were tumultuous ones politically, and the 93d Congress, which adjourned last night, was in the center of the storm.

It will go down in history as the Congress that helped expose and depose a President and, in the process, set precedents for investigation and impeachment that will outlive the members of the Congress themselves.

History will also record that it was the 93d Congress that first used the procedures of the 25th Amendment to the Constitution — to confirm Gerald R. Ford and then Nelson A. Rockefeller as Vice President.

Because of the political turmoil, the legislative accomplishments of the last two years received less attention than they might have otherwise. But Congressional leaders believe that some of the laws that were enacted may also prove to be historic.

For example, while the nation's attention was focused on Richard M. Nixon's resignation and Mr. Ford's ascension to the Presidency, Congress cleared legislation last August setting strict standards for private pension plans.

There are 30 million Americans who are members of such plans, and many experts believe the Congressional action was as important as was the enactment of Medicare a decade ago in protecting the welfare of the elderly.

In the area of foreign affairs, the 93d Congress passed legislation limiting the power of the President to commit United States armed forces to foreign hostilities without Congressional approval.

The law, enacted over Mr. Nixon's veto, was designed to prevent "another Vietnam."

Moreover, by using its power to withhold funds, Congress forced Mr. Nixon to accept a compromise and end the bombing of Cambodia in August, 1973.

Congress also took steps to improve its own machinery for dealing with the Federal budget and enacted legislation that alters the traditional method of financing political campaigns through large private contributions.

Also of importance to long-

Continued on Page 27, Column 1

Recycling of Waste Is Recession Victim

By DAVID BIRD

Recycling, the idea nurtured by environmental awareness that brought millions of Americans into collection centers with their carefully separated newspapers, glass and cans, has been hit hard by the recession.

The market for waste materials—especially old newspapers, a staple to many of the collection drives—has dropped so severely that some centers have had to close. They are choked with paper that once provided the income to keep them going and that now they cannot even give away.

The depressed state of recycling has begun to worry environmentalists. They fear that people may become disillusioned with the concept of respecting land by not throw-

Continued on Page 32, Column 1

Today's Sections

Index to Subjects

Associated Press

Firetrucks and ambulances on the scene outside Harrods, at rear, where a bomb exploded. A warning enabled the London department store to evacuate Christmas shoppers in time.

State Studying Klan

A teacher at an upstate state prison who allegedly identified himself as a local Ku Klux Klan leader, has been suspended in an investigation into alleged Klan activities by some prison employes, including guards. Details on Page 14.

Raiders, Vikings Victors In Pro Football Playoffs

The Oakland Raiders defeated the Miami Dolphins, 28-26, and the Minnesota Vikings beat the St. Louis Cardinals, 30-14, yesterday in the opening games of the National Football League playoffs.

The Raiders' victory ended the Dolphins' two-year reign as league champions. An 8-yard touchdown pass from Ken Stabler to Clarence Davis with 26 seconds left provided the winning touchdown in an exciting game. The Raiders led, 21-19, late in the fourth quarter following a 72-yard scoring play on a pass from Stabler to Cliff Branch. Then Miami came back and scored on a 22-yard run by Ben Malone, giving the Dolphins a 26-21 lead with two minutes remaining. It was enough time for the Raiders to accomplish their comeback.

The Dolphins had led most of the game, starting with the opening kickoff that Nat Moore returned 89 yards for a touchdown. But Stabler's touchdown pass to Davis at the end gave the Raiders the victory and a berth in the championship final of the American Conference. They will play for the conference title against the winner of today's game between the Pittsburgh Steelers and Buffalo Bills.

Minnesota advanced to the National Conference final against the winner of the Washington Redskins-Los Angeles Rams game today.

Details in Section 5.

"All the News That's Fit to Print"

The New York Times

LATE CITY EDITION

Weather: Sunny today; cold tonight. Chance of showers later tomorrow. Temperature range: today 35-52; Monday 41-55. Details on Page 74.

VOL. CXXIV ... No. 42,787

NEW YORK, TUESDAY, MARCH 18, 1975

Price higher in air delivery cities.

20 CENTS

SUPREME COURT GIVES U.S. ATLANTIC SHELF OIL TITLE, DENYING 13 STATES' CLAIM

A UNANIMOUS VOTE

Ruling Clears Way for Leasing of Tracts for Exploration

By E. W. KENWORTHY
Special to The New York Times

WASHINGTON, March 17—The Supreme Court ruled unanimously today that the Federal Government has exclusive rights to any oil and gas resources on the Atlantic Outer Continental Shelf beyond the three-mile limit.

Thirteen Atlantic states had contended that their original royal charters had given them title to seabed resources out to 100 miles; that they had not surrendered ownership of these resources to the National Government upon entering the union, and that Supreme Court decisions in 1947 and 1950 conferring title in the Federal Government were in error and should be overturned.

In the 8-to-0 opinion today, written by Justice Byron R. White, the Court reaffirmed its earlier rulings as recommended by a special master, Albert M. Maris, last August. The court said further that its decision was in accordance with the Submerged Lands Act and the Outer Continental Shelf Lands Act, both enacted in 1953.

Early Action Foreseen

Justice William O. Douglas did not participate in the decision.

The ruling will clear the way for the Department of the Interior to proceed with its announced intention of exploiting undiscovered oil and gas deposits in so-called frontier areas off the Atlantic Coast, Southern California and Alaska in an effort to make the nation more nearly independent of imports.

More immediately, it will open the way for the department to lease tracts in the Baltimore Canyon of the Atlantic Outer Continental Shelf for exploration and production by oil companies.

The leasing had been held up pending today's decision, issued in a suit brought by the Federal Government challenging claims of the Atlantic coastal states to ownership of

Contined on Page 25, Column 1

Associated Press

The Rev. Theodore M. Hesburgh, head of the University of Notre Dame, gives honorary degree to President Ford.

President Scans C.I.A. Tie To Any Death Plot Abroad

By RICHARD L. MADDEN
Special to The New York Times

WASHINGTON, March 17—President Ford, declaring that he condemned any involvement by the Central Intelligence Agency in alleged assassination plots against foreign leaders, said tonight that he was "personally analyzing" such charges.

The President, speaking at a regional news conference on the

Transcript of news conference will be found on Page 22.

campus of the University of Notre Dame at South Bend, Ind., acknowledged that he discussed the matter last week with Vice President Rockefeller, who heads a Presidential commission investigating domestic activities of the C.I.A. [Question 5, Page 22.]

White House sources disclosed over the weekend that the commission would investigate reports that the agency had been implicated in assassination plots against foreign leaders as an outgrowth of the commission's domestic investigation.

Mr. Ford said he had asked his staff to bring him information on all the charges of alleged assassination plots and added that he would determine "in the next few days" the best way for the executive branch to handle the matter appropriately.

"This Administration does not condone under any circumstances any assassination attempts," he said.

When the question was raised again a few moments later, he said, "I condemn any C.I.A. involvement" in any "assassination planning."

The President, in response to other questions, also expressed strong personal and political support for Mr. Rockefeller, who has been under criticism from conservative Republicans. [Question 12.]

He said that if he had equivocated in the past on whether he wanted Mr. Rockefeller as his running-mate in 1976, as a questioner seemed to imply, he was not aware of it. He praised Mr. Rockefeller as an "active and able Vice President" and added, "I see no reason whatsoever why that team should not be together in 1976."

On other matters, the Presi-

Continued on Page 22, Column 5

21 HOSPITALS HERE HIT BY A WALKOUT OF HOUSE DOCTORS

Residents and Internes on Picket Line, but Service Is Generally Maintained

By PETER KIHSS

In the country's first major work stoppage by doctors, 21 of the city's 91 voluntary and municipal hospitals were struck yesterday by a union of 3,000 internes and resident physicians seeking a reduction in long hours.

But canvasses indicated that medical services were generally being maintained by senior attending physicians, with minor adjustments in services and with incoming patients diverted in some cases to hospitals that were not affected.

The walkout by the union, the Committee of Internes and Residents, began at 7 A.M., when negotiations with the League of Voluntary Hospitals broke down. The union had demanded an 80-hour work week instead of schedules it said ran to 100 hours a week, including at times more than 50 consecutive hours.

The league had made an offer at 1:15 A.M. for the establishment of a committee at each hospital, made up of equal numbers of union and hospital appointees, to tackle the work schedules.

Arbitration Request

Dr. Richard A. Knutson, the union president, said the offer failed to provide "firm guarantees" for reduced schedules. He said at a news conference later that "the strike would stop immediately if the league agreed to arbitration" of the dispute over hours and what was called "out-of-title work" that doctors had to do.

"We went out with a heavy heart," Dr. Ramesh Tandon, a senior resident, said on the picket line outside the Hospital for Joint Diseases. "Every minute we are waiting to hear. We miss our patients."

Outside the Queens Hospital Center in Jamaica, Dr. James Rossi, a resident, said, "Oh, I want to go back to work." He said he had just learned that a bone-marrow analysis he had requested had confirmed a suspicion that a patient with hitherto undiagnosed weight loss and aching bones had cancer.

The striking physicians made no attempt to prevent others from entering or working in the hospitals. But a threat of difficulties came during the day when Leon J. Davis, president of District 1199, National Union of Hospital and Health Care Employes, representing hospital

Continued on Page 50, Column 3

Pickets outside an entrance to a clinic at Mount Sinai Hospital yesterday as internes and residents struck

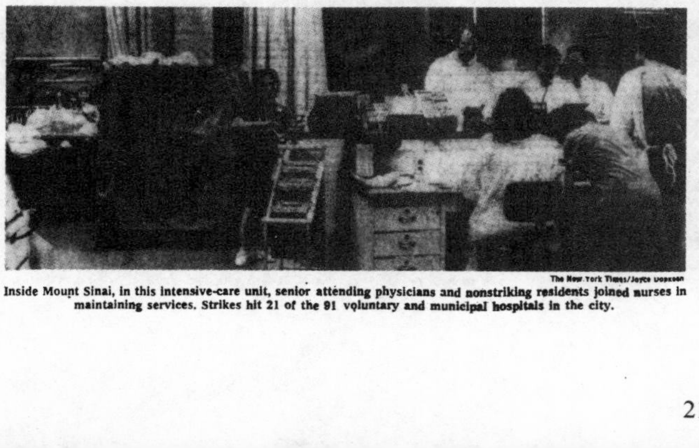

The New York Times/Joyce Dopkeen

Inside Mount Sinai, in this intensive-care unit, senior attending physicians and nonstriking residents joined nurses in maintaining services. Strikes hit 21 of the 91 voluntary and municipal hospitals in the city.

SOUTH VIETNAM REPORTED YIELDING MOST OF CENTRAL HIGHLANDS AREA; MAIN EVACUATION ROUTES CUT OFF

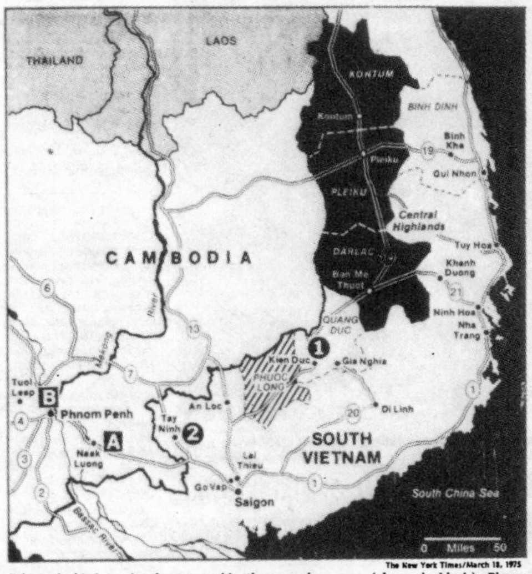

The New York Times/March 18, 1975

Saigon decided to abandon a roughly three-province area (shown in black). Phuoc Long Province (diagonally shaded) was previously lost. Kien Duc (1) was target of Communist drive, and heavy fighting was reported near Tay Ninh (2). In Cambodia, airstrip of Neak Luong (A) was attacked by rebels. Pressure was kept on capital (B).

A MAJOR PULLOUT

Saigon Takes Action After Two Weeks of Sharp Reverses

By JAMES M. MARKHAM
Special to The New York Times

SAIGON, South Vietnam, Tuesday, March 18—The Saigon Government has decided to abandon most of the Central Highlands of South Vietnam because the area has become militarily indefensible, well-placed Western sources said today.

The decision, one of the most momentous of the long Vietnam war, was made after 14 days of sharp military reverses in the vast, rolling highlands. It was certain to have important political reverberations.

The area to be abandoned was reported to include the pivotal border provinces of Darlac, Pleiku and Kontum. South Vietnam has 44 provinces but these three are among the largest. They were the cradle of American involvement in the war and cover most — but not all—of the high, mountain-studded plains that are commonly regarded as making up the Central Highlands.

Defensibility Considered

These provinces are divided along administrative lines, however, while the Saigon military command's decision could be expected to follow lines of military defensibility, perhaps leaving parts of the three provinces still within its new line of defense and consigning parts of adjoining highlands provinces to the other side.

The Government might try to hold certain sections of the highlands either as staging areas for further withdrawal or as staging points for future actions. One informant indicated that the Government might even attempt to retake the city of Ban Me Thuot, giving itself an anchor in the southern highlands, but the sources doubted that such an attempt would be made.

It could not be learned how swiftly the movement of Government forces from the highlands—and particularly the important cities of Pleiku and Kontum—was unfolding.

According to some accounts, Government units were trekking down little used paths and provincial roads because the two main routes leading out of the region, 19 and 21, are cut.

Speedy Action Taken

"I think it can be said that the Vietnamese moved very quickly," one W[illegible]rn analyst said this morning, "and that once the decision was made it was carried out with considerable speed."

The well-placed Western sources said that, with the civilian populations alerted to the pullout, airports had become a difficult withdrawal route and that most of the troops—and civilians who wanted to leave—might have to fight their way out.

The decision to abandon the area was reportedly made sometimes after Friday when President Nguyen Van Thieu flew to the coastal city of Nha Trang to confer with Maj. Gen. Pham Van Phu, commander of Military Region II, which includes a stretch of the central coast as well.

Starting late last week, after the North Vietnamese seized the important highlands town

Continued on Page 18, Column 1

FORD SEES PROOF OF DOMINO THEORY

Cites Cambodia as Evidence That Other Nations May Drop From U.S. Camp

By PHILIP SHABECOFF
Special to The New York Times

SOUTH BEND, Ind., March 17—President Ford said here today that events in Southeast Asia tended to validate the so-called domino theory and that the existence of a non-Communist government in Cambodia was vital to American security.

Answering questions at a news conference at the University of Notre Dame, Mr. Ford indicated that the "very serious" military situation in Cambodia might be linked to recent moves in Thailand and the Philippines to review their relationship with the United States.

The Ford Administration has asked for emergency military aid for Phnom Penh, but the request has run into opposition in Congress.

[The Senate Foreign Relations Committee on Monday approved $82.5-million in aid, but with the provision that all military assistance be terminated on June 30. A similar proposal was rejected last week in a House committee. Page 19.]

President Ford said a "potential request" from Thailand for the withdrawal of United States

Continued on Page 18, Column 7

U.S. Starting to Evacuate Relief Aides in Cambodia

By SYDNEY H. SCHANBERG
Special to The New York Times

PHNOM PENH, Cambodia, March 17—The United States Embassy today began to evacuate international relief personnel from Cambodia as the battlefront news continued to be discouraging for the American-backed Government of Marshal Lon Nol.

The Embassy insisted that the evacuation was only a temporary measure "until the situation clarifies a bit," but it took place against a backdrop of other evacuation activity by foreigners — including the packing and shipping of household effects by American Embassy personnel.

Pressure on Neak Luong

The move came on the eve of the fifth anniversary of the Government's coming to power; on March 18, 1970, Marshal Lon Nol and several colleagues deposed Prince Norodom Sihanouk. The Prince, now in exile in Peking, is the nominal head of the Cambodian insurgent government, whose Communist-led army has encircled Phnom Penh and is trying to bring down the Lon Nol regime

In the southeast, the crucial town of Neak Luong, the Government's last remaining major post on the Mekong River, is being choked by the rebels, who have advanced to the airstrip on the southern edge of town.

Shelling of the town from all sides, including the opposite bank of the Mekong, has become so intense that not a single Government helicopter

Continued on Page 19, Column 2

U.S. WITHDRAWAL SOUGHT BY THAIS

Premier Proposes Pullout of Troops in a Year in Bid for Leftist Support

By The Associated Press

BANGKOK, Thailand, March 17 — Premier Kukrit Pramoj said in a policy statement today that his coalition would seek the complete withdrawal of the 25,000 American troops and 350 aircraft from Thailand within a year.

The statement, issued after his seven-party civilian coalition was confirmed by King Phumiphol Aduldet, also said the Government would seek to establish diplomatic relations with China and would try to open talks with North Vietnam. The new Cabinet faces a confidence vote in the lower house of Parliament Wednesday.

The previous cabinet, headed by Mr. Kukrit's brother. Seni Pramoj, was confirmed Feb. 22 and resigned eight days later when it lost a confidence vote.

Short of Majority

Mr. Kukrit's coalition has 124 of the 269 seats in the house, 11 short of a majority. His policy statement was aimed at winning the support of left-wing parties that have demanded the American withdrawal.

He said, however, that the withdrawal must be completed within a year only if "the political and military situation in this region permits." His brother had called for withdrawal in 18 months and failed to win the leftists' support:

"Withdrawing the American forces doesn't mean that we don't like America," Mr. Kukrit told reporters today. "Our good relations must continue."

The United States carried out bombing missions in Indochina from air bases in Thailand for eight years.

Mr. Kukrit's moderate Social Action party ran fifth among the 22 parties represented in

Continued on Page 9, Column 1

Garelik Is Transit Police Chief; Declares Safety 'No. 1 Priority'

By SHAWN G. KENNEDY

Sanford D. Garelik, former City Council President and former chief inspector of the city's police force, took over as chief of the Transit Authority Police Department yesterday and pledged to make safety on the city's subways his "No. 1 priority."

Mr. Garelik replaced Robert H. Rapp, who was removed as head of the department this month after he admitted that he had lied about payoffs to the Transit Authority police and about condoning falsification of subway-crime statistics.

Noting the recent state grand jury investigation of Transit Authority patrolmen and officials, Mr. Garelik said: "We do have problems and I intend to make a thorough study of the department, but my No. 1 priority is to provide security for the people of New York, to make the subways safe to ride."

David L. Yunich, chairman of the Metropolitan Transportation Authority, announced the appointment of Mr. Garelik as chief of the 3,700-member police force at a news conference at the agency's headquarters at 1700 Broadway.

In his announcement, Mr. Yunich said that Mr. Garelik had been chosen by an 11-member board from a field of seven candidates. Among them, he said, were policemen and former members of the Federal Bureau of Investigation.

Mr. Garelik, who rose in 29 years from patrolman to the

Continued on Page 28, Column 3

"All the News That's Fit to Print"

The New York Times

LATE CITY EDITION

Weather: Chance of showers today; fair and cooler tonight, tomorrow. Temperature range today 45-53; Wednesday 39-56. Details, Page 78.

VOL. CXXIV..No. 42,789 © 1975 The New York Times Company NEW YORK, THURSDAY, MARCH 20, 1975 Price higher in air delivery cities. 20 CENTS

SAIGON REPORTED ABANDONING TWO-THIRDS OF SOUTH VIETNAM; QUANG TRI FALLS, HUE IN PERIL

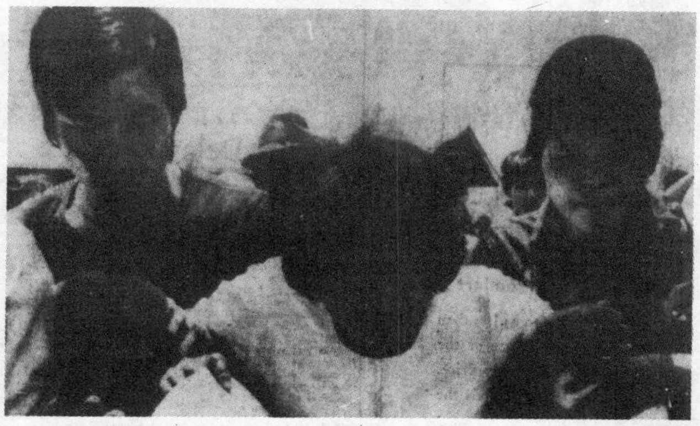

Associated Press

A refugee from South Vietnam's Central Highlands being aided as she entered town of Tuy Hoa yesterday

CIVILIANS FLEEING

Communist Foes Said to Be Assisting the Troop Pullout

By MALCOLM W. BROWNE
Special to The New York Times

SAIGON, South Vietnam, Thursday, March 20 — South Vietnamese forces have begun rapidly withdrawing from the northernmost part of the country, and according to well-placed military sources they are being assisted in their evacuation by Communist troops.

By late this morning, a military source said, all of Quang Tri Province had been occupied by the North Vietnamese.

Sources close to the South Vietnamese command said today that President Nguyen Van Thieu had decided that 10 or more provinces, including most of the northern two-thirds of the country, must be sacrificed if necessary to save the rest.

Troops Give Up Quang Tri

A Vietnamese military source reported that a company of 100 South Vietnamese soldiers guarding the smashed remains of the citadel of Quang Tri had been ordered to withdraw toward Hue.

As they moved out, North Vietnamese military units approached, but did not open fire, using the strong headlights of their tanks to light the way for the Government troops.

Quang Tri was one of the main centers of fighting in 1972 and was completely destroyed.

Evacuation of Hue

A source close to the South Vietnamese command said that the former imperial city of Hue, along with the rest of Thua Thien Province, was being evacuated this morning, and that by late today Hue itself would be in Comunist hands.

In addition to the military evacuation, tens of thousands of refugees have started an exodus southward. Earlier this week many thousands more began fleeing the central Highlands after a series of Government reverses.

By some estimates, as many as half a million people were now fleeing their homes in five provinces.

Two days ago, airborne troops in the north were withdrawn to the Saigon area, and today the marine brigades near Hue the other principal defense force in the area, was said to have moved to Huong Dien on the nearby seacoast for evacuation both by road and sea.

Harassment Avoided

It appears clear that the Communists have been well informed as to developments, and have been avoiding any form of harassment or causing casualties.

Throughout South Vietnam, ordinary people as well as officials were preparing for any eventuality as events moved swiftly.

It was announced at noon that the curfew in Saigon starting tonight will go into effect at 10 P.M. instead of midnight, an indication of concern about a possible attack on the capital itself.

Several Western Embassies, including that of the United States, reportedly were completing details on their long-standing evacuation plans.

President Thieu's decision possibly to sacrifice 10 provinces was reportedly made last week, and some Government forces immediately began leaving the areas. As units moved out, there has been civilian

Continued on Page 18, Column 6

Record Payments Deficit Set in 4th Quarter of '74

Big Outflow of Long-Term Capital Puts Figure at $5.87-Billion—Oil Rises Lift Year's Total to Near a High

By EDWIN L. DALE Jr.
Special to The New York Times

WASHINGTON, March 19—A big increase in the net outflow of private long-term capital threw the nation's basic balance of payments into a record deficit of $5.87-billion in the last quarter of 1974, the Commerce Department reported today.

For 1974 as a whole, a combination of larger payments for imported oil and a rise in capital outflows produced a near-record deficit of $10.58-billion in the basic balance, formally known as the balance of current account and long-term capital. The deficit in 1973 was only $1.03-billion. The record deficit was $11.2-billion in 1972.

Nearly every nation that imports oil showed a worsening in its balance of payments last year. In addition, in a world of floating exchange rates, balance-of-payments deficits and surpluses do not mean what they used to mean.

Entirely because of higher payments for oil, the nation's trade balance worsened last year by $6.35-billion to a deficit of $5.88-billion, as measured in the balance-of-payments accounts.

But this deterioration in current transactions was largely offset by a big jump of $4.39-billion, to $9.68-billion, in the return of income to the United States from corporate and other investments abroad.

The result was that the "balance on goods and services" in 1974 showed a surplus of $3.19-billion, down only a little from the surplus of $4.33-billion in 1973.

The balance on current account, influenced by an essentially artificial accounting convention affecting government foreign aid transactions, showed a deficit of $4.03-billion.

Special transactions with India, Israel and Vietnam produced an outflow of Government aid on current account, offset by a matching capital inflow, with no effect on the basic balance.

Apart from the impact of oil on the trade balance, the main feature of the balance of payments in 1974 was a worsening of $7.66-billion in the long-term capital account. This reflected two main influences:

¶The end of controls on capital outflows at the beginning of the year was a factor in large increases in outflows for direct corporate investment abroad, long-term bank lending abroad and Americans' purchases of foreign securities.

¶The weak United States stock market was a factor in a

Continued on Page 59, Column 4

THRUWAY PLANS 15% RISE IN TOLLS BEFORE MID-JUNE

Increase, First Since 1970, Would Offset $12-Million Decline in Revenue

By FRANK LYNN

The New York State Thruway Authority plans to raise its tolls about 15 per cent across the board by mid-June, authority officials disclosed yesterday.

Gerald Cummins, the newly designated chairman of the Thruway Authority, and Edwin Fehrenbach, a Republican holdover and the acting chairman, said in interviews that an increase was necessary because of declining revenues resulting from energy conservation and expected gasoline tax increases.

The disclosure came only a day after the New Jersey Turnpike Authority announced an average increase of 19 per cent in its tolls — 4 percentage points more than the planned New York increase. The New Jersey increases, to go into effect 6:30 A.M. Sunday, will range as high as 50 per cent.

Delay in Application

The actual New York rise is being held up by political considerations. The two present Republican members of the Authority—Mr. Fehrenbach, a former Assemblyman from Nassau County, and Charles T. Lanigan, former Republican state chairman—will not formally authorize the toll increase until Mr. Cummins, who was Governor Carey's campaign manager, is confirmed by the State Senate. The two Republicans want to share the responsibility for the toll increase with Mr. Cummins, a Democrat.

Mr. Fehrenbach said he hoped that the increase, which would produce about $12-million a year, would go into effect in time for the summer tourist season, when thruway travel is at its height.

The toll increase would be the first since 1959 for automobiles and since 1970 for commercial vehicles. Annual permits for regular users have been increased several times. The 559-mile thruway, the longest toll road in the country, was completed in 1960; its first section opened in 1954.

The 15 per cent increase would, for example, raise the New York-to-Albany toll on the

Continued on Page 78, Column 5

3 Panels in Congress Plan Inquiries Into Sub Salvage

By SEYMOUR M. HERSH
Special to The New York Times

WASHINGTON, March 19—The White House, the Pentagon and the Central Intelligence Agency firmly refused today to discuss any aspects of the C.I.A.'s reported attempt to salvage a sunken Soviet submarine last year, but three Congressional committee chairmen said they planned to investigate the project.

Members of the Senate and the House, meanwhile, disagreed over the intelligence value of the multimillion-dollar recovery operation.

The New York Times and other newspapers reported today that, according to high Government officials, the C.I.A. had secretly spent more than $350-million to construct a salvage vessel that recovered one-third of the Soviet submarine but failed to recover the prime objectives—the ship's nuclear missiles and its code room. The submarine sank northwest of Hawaii in 1968.

The salvage vessel was built under cover for the C.I.A. by Howard R. Hughes, the billionaire industrialist, according to the officials.

High-level Government officials said today that the sunken Soviet submarine was not nuclear-powered, as some officials had indicated prior to publication of the salvage articles, but instead was a 1958 diesel-powered ballistic missile submarine of the Soviet "G" class. As such, the submarine's potential intelligence value in terms of salvage was far less than if she had been nuclear-powered. The United States, for example, has not constructed diesel-powered submarines since 1958.

The G-class vessel carried three nuclear missiles with ranges of up to 650 miles. She also was reported to have been carrying nuclear-tipped torpedoes. The ship's normal crew was 12 officers and 74 men.

There was no official reaction today from the Foreign Ministry in Moscow, and it could not be learned what information about the recovery operation, known as Project

Continued on Page 30, Column 5

Goldman Is Taking Leave of Absence From Shubert Post

By LAWRENCE VAN GELDER

Irving Goldman asked for and received a leave of absence yesterday from all activities of the Shubert Foundation, in another action prompted by his indictment last week on bribery, grand larceny, conspiracy and perjury charges.

At the same time, Mr. Goldman, who is president of the foundation, which has extensive real-estate and theatrical interests, resigned as an officer and director of all corporations controlled by the foundation.

On March 13, Mayor Beame, a longtime friend, granted Mr. Goldman a voluntary leave of absence from his post as the city's $1-a-year Commissioner of Cultural Affairs.

The 65-year-old Mr. Goldman, the first Commissioner in the Beame administration indicted, was the target of a six-month inquiry by Maurice

Continued on Page 48, Column 4

CAMBODIAN REBELS NEAR NAVAL BASE

Insurgents Break Through Government Lines Only 2 Miles From Capital

By DAVID A. ANDELMAN
Special to The New York Times

PHNOM PENH, March 19—Communist-led insurgents early today broke through Government lines to the east bank of the Mekong River across from Phnom Penh's naval base and about two miles east of the capital.

Artillery, air strikes and ground attacks failed to dislodge the insurgents, who were apparently seeking to improve their position for mortar attacks on the base, which is separated from the capital itself by a peninsula and another river, the Tonle Sap.

Insurgent forces penetrated to the position earlier in this offensive but were driven back. In recent weeks they have been firing rockets at the Chrui Changwar naval base from further north and inland and are now believed to be seeking to improve their position for such attacks.

Push From Tuol Leap

The new advance, however, does not give the insurgents the opportunity to move across the river against the capital itself.

West of the capital, Government forces began pushing out from Tuol Leap. The insurgent force that had pinned them in the town has apparently retreated north to defend the rocket positions from which it has been firing missiles at Pochentong Airport, which is Phnom Penh's only supply link to the outside world.

Western military observers said that these Government forces had still not been able to advance closer than a half mile from the nearest of the

Continued on Page 18, Column 2

Gen. Brown Calls Aid Cut A Key to Saigon Pullback

By JOHN W. FINNEY
Special to The New York Times

WASHINGTON, March 19—Gen. George S. Brown, chairman of the Joint Chiefs of Staff, said today that South Vietnamese "backs are against the wall" partly because of the lack of military aid from the United States.

General Brown said Saigon was being "forced into an increasingly defensive position in the face of the current major series of attacks by the North Vietnamese" unless the United States provided more aid.

"The principal difficulty of the South Vietnamese armed forces today is the lack of support," he said in a speech prepared for delivery before a Navy League meeting in San Diego. A copy of the speech was made available here by the Pentagon.

The speech reflected a new effort to link the withdrawal of Saigon forces from the Central Highlands to Congressional cutbacks in military aid. For the present fiscal year, ending June 30, Congress originally provided $700-million, half the amount requested. The Administration has now asked Congress to provide $300-million in addition for the last three months of the fiscal year.

Because of the cutbacks, General Brown said, aid has been limited largely to ammunition and fuel. The United States, he said, has not replaced losses in aircraft, tanks or armored personnel carriers. For lack of spare parts and maintenance, he continued, Saigon has not been able to keep large numbers of transport aircraft and helicopters in the air.

As a consequence, he said, district capitals are falling to the Communists and Saigon must "make the tough decision which province capitals can still be saved."

"How can we now terminate our aid and leave these people helpless in the face of this Communist offensive?" he said.

"To cut off aid now would be viewed by much of the world as a fundamental lack of resolve on our part—or even worse, a suggestion that aggression pays."

The White House press secretary, Ron Nessen, said President Ford was watching developments in South Vietnam "closely and with considerable concern."

Mr. Nessen said the President believed the additional aid was urgently needed. Without the aid, he said, Saigon is forced to conserve ammunition and the United States is unable to replace damaged weapons.

At the State Department,

Continued on Page 18, Column 2

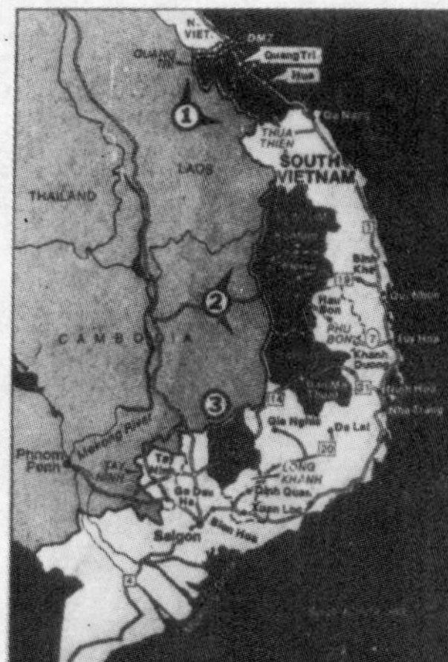

The New York Times/March 20, 1975

Flight from northernmost provinces (1) was spurred as Saigon's forces abandoned them. Central area (2) was given up earlier this week, and Phuoc Long (3) was lost to the Communist forces in January.

Justices Back Widowers' Equal Rights

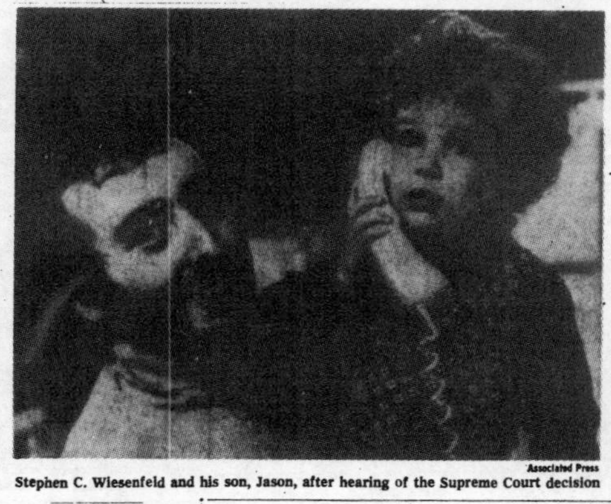

Associated Press

Stephen C. Wiesenfeld and his son, Jason, after hearing of the Supreme Court decision

By WARREN WEAVER Jr
Special to The New York Times

WASHINGTON, March 19—The Supreme Court struck down today as unconstitutional a 36-year-old provision of the Social Security law that authorizes survivors' benefits for the widow of a deceased worker with children but denies them to a widower in the same position.

The Justices ruled unanimously that the Constitution "forbids the gender-based differentiation that results in the efforts of women workers, required to pay Social Security taxes, producing less protection for their families than is produced by the efforts of men."

Although men stood to gain directly from the decision, it represented a major victory for supporters of equal rights for women, with the high court taking its strongest stand to date against discrimination based on sex and setting aside virtually all reservations voiced in contrary rulings in 1973 and 1974.

It was the first time the Court had insisted on equal treatment in a sex discrimination case when such a ruling would be very expensive to the Government. In 1974, according to Social Security estimates, an expanded benefit program covering widowers would have cost $20-million extra.

The case (No. 73-1892, Weinberger v. Wiesenfeld) involved a New Jersey couple, Stephen C. Wiesenfeld and Paula Polatschek, who were married in 1970. She continued to work as a teacher, earning about $10,000 a year, while his income as a self-employed consultant ran from $2,000 to $3,000 a year.

In 1972 Mrs. Wiesenfeld died in childbirth, leaving her husband to care for their infant son, Jason. He applied for Social Security survivors' benefits for himself and the child. He was given the latter but told that only widows were entitled to such benefits for themselves.

Mr. Wiesenfeld filed suit in

Continued on Page 29, Column 1

State Court Asks Removal of Judge

By MARY BREASTED

Justice Wilfred A. Waltemade of State Supreme Court was accused yesterday of 46 instances of improper rudeness to witnesses, litigants and lawyers in a report by the State Court on the Judiciary. It concluded that he should be removed from the bench.

The court's charges against the 65-year-old judge — assigned to the First Department, Manhattan and the Bronx—do not officially remove him. Accusing him of "oppressive and arbitrary" behavior and "reckless disregard of the rights of litigants," the document is similar to an indictment in a criminal case. Its conclusions

Continued on Page 45, Column 5

A New Safety Rule Set for Jumbo Jets

By RICHARD WITKIN

The Government told the nation's aviation industry yesterday that it had decided to put forward a program for major modification of all jumbo-jet airliners to reduce exposure to the type of hazard that led to the DC-10 crash last year in which 346 died.

It is estimated the changes would cost at least $250,000 a plane, or a total of more than $130-million if made on all 530 American-made jumbos now operating around the globe.

The Government action will be in the form of a proposed rule of the Federal Aviation Administration. Government sources said the announcement

Continued on Page 78, Column 6

NEWS INDEX

"All the News That's Fit to Print"

The New York Times

LATE CITY EDITION

Weather: Periods of rain today and tonight. Cloudy, warmer tomorrow. Temperature range: today 36-49; Friday 23-52. Details on Page 44.

VOL. CXXIV ... No. 4?,798 · NEW YORK, SATURDAY, MARCH 29, 1975 · Price higher in air delivery cities. · 20 CENTS

DA NANG COMES UNDER SHELLFIRE; DISINTEGRATION OF ARMY FEARED; A BILLION IN WEAPONS ABANDONED

COURT OVERTURNS 1974 CONVICTIONS OF MACKELL AND 2

Voids Conspiracy Indictment of Ex-Queens Prosecutor, Son-in-Law and an Aide

LACK OF EVIDENCE CITED

Nadjari Scored for Neglect of 'Basic Rules'—Murtagh Chastised—Appeal Set

By MARCIA CHAMBERS

A state appeals court yesterday unanimously reversed the conspiracy convictions of Thomas J. Mackell, the former Queens District Attorney, and two chief aides, and dismissed their indictments on the ground of insufficient evidence.

The reversal, by the Supreme Court's Appellate Division, Second Department, was based on both the law and the facts.

Appellate Division's decision is excerpted on Page 32.

Prosecutors familiar with the case privately viewed the decision as a stunning defeat for Maurice H. Nadjari, the special state prosecutor, who considered the Mackell conviction the major victory of his first two and a half years of office. The misdemeanor trial was deemed so important that Mr. Nadjari led the prosecution himself.

'Disregard of Rules' Cited

The opinion came from the same appeals court that has, in the past, denounced Mr. Nadjari as being overzealous in his prosecutions. It did so again in its 21-page Mackell opinion, saying that had it not dismissed the indictment it would have granted the defendants a new trial because the prosecutor "was guilty of constant and patent disregard of the basic rules of evidence."

Moreover, the five-man panel said, "it requires a tortured logic unsupported by the facts to find that Mackell was proceeding in furtherance of a conspiracy." The opinion was written by Justice M. Henry Martuscello.

Supreme Court Justice John M. Murtagh, who presides over Mr. Nadjari's special anticorruption cases, was also chastised by the appeals court—for giving the impression that he "unduly favored the prosecutor and his cause."

Nadjari Plans Appeal

Mr. Nadjari said yesterday that he planned to appeal the dismissal of the indictment. Other than that, he refused comment on the decision, although he sounded bitter.

In Douglaston, Queens, a boisterous victory party got under way as friends, neighbors and relatives flocked to the Mackell home as news of the reversal spread.

"This is the end of the nightmare that began for us on April 12, 1973," Mr. Mackell said, referring to the date Mr. Nadjari announced the indictment. "I never should have been indicted in the first place, and this unanimous opinion confirms my confidence in the judicial system." Mr. Mackell also expressed eagerness to return to politics.

Mr. Mackell, James D. Rob-

Continued on Page 32, Column 3

The New York Times/Robert Walker

Thomas J. Mackell celebrating the reversal of his conviction at his home in Queens

National's No-Frills Flights At 35% Saving Approved

By RICHARD WITKIN

The Civil Aeronautics Board gave National Airlines the go-ahead yesterday for a "no frills" service that will slash many fares 35 per cent for passengers willing to forgo meals and liquor, fly on weekdays, and buy tickets a week in advance.

The plan, proposed by four other airlines with variations, will go into effect April 14 on National, and on the other lines too if the expected C.A.B. approval is forthcoming.

The fare from New York to Miami will drop to $61 from the current $98 and $75 for coach and night coach. A one-way flight from Miami to Los Angeles will cost $103.70, under the no frills scheme, instead of $169.44.

The new austerity service is probably the most innovative of a growing number of marketing approaches devised to try to reverse the sharpest dip in air travel in this country since World War II. It counters a pricing trend that, under pressure from soaring fuel costs in particular, has brought a 20 per cent rise in domestic air fares in the last 16 months.

Still awaiting C.A.B. decisions are proposals to revive the domestic youth fare (trans-Atlantic youth fares were reinstated Thursday), to bring back family fares, and to offer a cut-rate fare for older people.

The hope is that all the discounts will help fill up the rows and rows of seats now flying empty, rather than divert travelers from higher-fare sections.

As a National executive put it when the plan was proposed: "We believe that those passengers who traditionally seek the inflight amenities of first-class and coach will continue to do so. But there's a large market out there which shows signs of responding to no frills, rock bottom air fares."

The airlines that have proposed similar plans are generally not nearly so enthusiastic or optimistic. But the view in the industry is that they had to come up with matching schemes if they were not to lose a lot of business to National.

National will use its plan primarily on Boeing 747 and DC-10 jumbo jets serving 32 markets. But the same prices will be available on five other runs from Fort Lauderdale, Fla., westward—markets not served by these wide-body craft.

The no frills passengers will

Continued on Page 45, Column 3

FORD TO ANNOUNCE TAX PLAN TONIGHT

Broadcast Address Slated—Advisers Said to Be in Conflict on Veto

By PHILIP SHABECOFF
Special to The New York Times

WASHINGTON, March 28 — President Ford will announce in a speech tomorrow evening his decision on whether to veto or sign the $22.8-billion tax-cutting bill passed by Congress earlier this week, Ron Nessen, the White House press secretary, announced today.

Mr. Nessen gave no clue as to what the decision would be.

By all accounts from White House aides today, the President was having an extremely difficult time making up his mind about the crucial legislation. He reportedly has received sharply conflicting advice from his economic and political advisers.

One White House official who is close to the President recalled Mr. Ford's remark on the tax bill yesterday of, "It's a tough call."

After seeing Mr. Ford this evening, Mr. Nessen said that

Continued on Page 21, Column 4

Saudis See Planning in the Assassination

By JUAN de ONIS
Special to The New York Times

RIYADH, Saudi Arabia, March 28—A security investigation into the assassination of King Faisal of Saudi Arabia has uncovered evidence that the killing was carefully planned and was not the unreasoned act of a lunatic, according to official sources.

Some evidence points to a political motive on the part of the accused killer, Prince Faisal ibn Musad Abdel Aziz, a young, American-educated member of the royal family who had a record of mental illness and drug use.

Sheik Fahd al-Sudairi, Deputy Minister of Information, said that Prince Faisal, who is under detention in a secret place, would be tried under the law of the Koran. If he is judged to have been sane when he killed the King, he could be sentenced to death.

Official sources said that the Prince, under questioning, had made a statement acknowledging responsibility for the assassination, which took place Tuesday in King Faisal's offices in the presence of several persons.

No evidence has been found to indicate a plot involving other people, according to these sources.

There is no public political opposition in this absolute monarchy, but the assassination seemed to contain a confused element of political antagonisms toward the Saudi system, symbolized by the austere King.

"He was not so deranged

Continued on Page 7, Column 2

Associated Press

Mourners visiting the grave of King Faisal of Saudi Arabia on the outskirts of Riyadh, the national capital

ARMS LEFT BY U.S.

Loss by Saigon Force Called Catastrophic

By BERNARD WEINRAUB
Special to The New York Times

SAIGON, South Vietnam, March 28—The South Vietnamese have lost more than $1-billion in American military weapons and other equipment over the last two weeks, according to qualified Vietnamese sources.

The abandonment of hundreds of artillery pieces, trucks, planes, mortars, tanks, armored personnel carriers, rifles and ammunition—coupled with the rapid retreat of army units—is viewed by Vietnamese and Western sources as a stunning and, quite possibly irreversible military and psychological blow for South Vietnam.

A senior Western official, who has spent more than a decade in South Vietnam, said today: "These losses are very, very, very considerable. It's a catastrophic loss."

Another informed Western source said: "We've made no attempt to quantify the loss, but it's staggering. The equip-

Continued on Page 2, Column 5

U.S. Beginning an Airlift Of Military Aid to Saigon

Special to The New York Times

SAIGON, South Vietnam, Saturday, March 29—The United States Embassy announced today that an airlift of "urgently needed military and medical supplies" had begun to Vietnam. The first plane loads reportedly began landing by noon today.

The announcement came in an embassy statement.

The statement noted that Gen. Frederick C. Weyand, United States Army Chief of Staff, had arrived here yesterday to determine how the United States "can best assist the South Vietnamese people." The statement said the American commander would make further recommendations to President Ford on his return to the United States.

Evacuation Role Weighed

Special to The New York Times

WASHINGTON, March 28—The Ford Administration was trying today to decide how far the United States could and should go in evacuating civilian refugees and possibly troops of refugees.

If the United States is involved in a large-scale evacuation effort, officials say, there is an eventual possibility that President Ford might have to decide whether to send in troops for protection and order as the refugees are withdrawn.

If American troops are used, even if only for what was described as humanitarian purposes, it is the consensus of officials that the President would have to obtain Congressional permission in the light of legislation prohibiting "the involvement of United States military forces in hostilities."

It was largely because of this Congressional restriction, according to officials, that the Administration devised at least outwardly a civilian sealift and airlift to start getting refugees out of Da Nang.

Under the procedures worked out by the Administration, the Agency for International Development, which administers foreign aid abroad, will provide the money. But it will depend upon the Pentagon's Military Sealift Command and Military Airlift Command to work out the contracts chartering civilian ships and planes. The explanation offered by a Pentagon

Continued on Page 4, Column 3

CITY NOW IN CHAOS

Situation in Northern Enclave Described as 'Very Serious'

By FOX BUTTERFIELD
Special to The New York Times

SAIGON, South Vietnam, Saturday, March 29 — North Vietnamese troops, closing in on the northern city of Da Nang, have now seized a provincial capital only 15 miles away, a Saigon Government spokesman said early today.

With evidence increasing that large segments of the Government's army were fast disintegrating, the spokesman termed the situation in the Da Nang enclave, Saigon's last remaining territory in the northern part of the country, "very serious." He said both the city and its principal airport came under shelling early this morning.

But communications with the area were uncertain, and it could not be determined whether the North Vietnamese had already driven closer than Hoi An, the nearby city they had just overrun. Hoi An, capital of the province in which Da Nang is situated, was the 13th provisional seat to fall to the Communists.

Bao Loc Falls

The 12th, it had been reported only hours earlier, had fallen early yesterday here in the southern part of the country, 93 miles northeast of Saigon. North Vietnamese soldiers, arriving in trucks, took over Bao Loc, capital of Lam Dong Province. The defenders of the city, a ramshackle community of 49,000 people, were said to have fled.

All through yesterday, Da Nang, swollen with half a million refugees or more, was reported in chaos. Efforts to evacuate some of them by air had to be suspended as thousands swarmed over the city's two airfields.

Violators to Be Shot

Government troops were commanded to restore order in 48 hours and to shoot violators at sight.

In this chaotic situation, it could not be determined how extensive the shelling reported by the Saigon spokesman was or even who was doing the firing. It appeared possible that Saigon artillery units themselves were in action against other Saigon units.

However, the Saigon spokesman was able to confirm that North Vietnamese troops had occupied Ho[illegible] a city 15 miles southeast of Da Nang on Route 1.

Among other developments that stirred alarm here in Saigon were the following:

¶North Vietnamese troops appeared to be continuing an advance along the central coastal plain that began Thursday. An outpost in Binh Dinh Province was reported overrun, two district capitals were shelled and many residents of Qui Nhon, a major port city, were said to be moving southward to Nha Trang.

¶A Saigon military spokesman, reporting on action 40 miles north of the capital, said Government troops had repulsed a North Vietnamese infantry and tank assault on Chon Thanh, a district capital on the northern boundary of Saigon's defense perimeter. He said that the Communist attacks there were viewed as the possible start of a much larger campaign to seize the capital.

¶South Vietnamese sources estimated that the Saigon

Continued on Page 2, Column 1

United Press International

Gen. Frederick C. Weyand calling on President Nguyen Van Thieu yesterday in Saigon

Isle Is Vital to Da Nang Refugees

By MALCOLM W. BROWNE
Special to The New York Times

RE ISLAND, South Vietnam, March 28—With the collapse of Government authority in the city of Da Nang, this volcanic isle in the South China Sea has become the last place in the vicinity of central Vietnam where American helicopters and small airplanes can land safely.

The island, three miles long and a mile wide, is dominated by an extinct volcano, around which farmers have cultivated fields and tended fleets of fishing sampans over the centuries, with little regular contact with the mainland.

Re Island, lying 70 miles southeast of Da Nang and 15 miles from the nearest land, has suddenly assumed vital importance to American pilots and to Saigon's officials who had been maintaining a tenuous hold in Da Nang.

Though the city, with perhaps a million people, including tens of thousands of refugees, in its area, has been surrounded for nearly a week by powerful North Vietnamese units and though the forces defending it have been shedding their uniforms and fleeing, no systematic plans were made to evacuate it by air until it was too late.

The South Vietnamese Air Force did nothing to establish an airlift; the Government airline flew its regularly scheduled flights, nothing more.

American officials and other foreigners who were left in Da Nang counted until the last minute on a handful of World

Continued on Page 3, Column 1

Mortgage Money Is Plentiful, But Home Sales Fail to Revive

By ROBERT LINDSEY
Special to The New York Times

LOS ANGELES, March 28—Many of the nation's banks and savings institutions are suddenly trumpeting an unfamiliar message to potential middle-income home buyers: There's money for mortgages again.

But, for the most part, the potential buyers aren't buying yet.

Continuing anxieties over the nation's economy, lofty price tags on many of the available homes, and inflation-squeezed family budgets are continuing to impede a broad turnaround in the country's construction industry that some industry leaders hoped would accompany a loosening of mortgage funds.

Mortgage money—which was all but unavailable a few months ago and often cost upwards of 10 per cent in annual interest charges when it was available—is now plentiful, and it is getting cheaper to borrow.

Largely because of a record inflow of savings to lending institutions, which began last October and which has accelerated since, interest rates in many parts of the nation are edging close to 8.5 per cent. Some bankers expect the rate to drop to as little as 8 per cent or even lower by May or June.

In New York, state law limits the mortgage rate to 8.5 per cent, so New Yorkers have been spared some of the higher rates paid elsewhere. Recently there has been a softening of the requirements for mortgages in New York in many cases, according to bankers.

Real estate brokers and builders interviewed in Los Angeles and 10 other cities across the country this week said the sale of new and previously occupied homes had picked up measurably—but not substantially—in recent weeks, largely as a result of the greater availability of lower priced mortgage money as well as the usual surge

Continued on Page 31, Column 1

SNIPER IN JERSEY SLAYS 2 OFFICERS

Holds Off Police for Hours From Mount Holly Home

By ROBERT HANLEY

A sniper spraying gunfire from the attic bedroom window of his home killed two policemen and wounded two others in Mount Holly, N.J., last night before the man was shot by the police and seized in the house, authorities said.

The four policemen were all struck in the first volleys of shooting from the small third-floor room where the man barricaded himself with at least two rifles and several handguns and survived withering barrages of gunfire from scores of police from 7 until 10 P.M.

The three-hour siege ended when about a dozen police officers wearing gas masks and portable oxygen tanks on their backs rushed through clouds of tear gas outside the home, entered the building, and fired several shots through the sec-

Continued on Page 21, Column 1

NEWS INDEX

"All the News That's Fit to Print"

The New York Times

LATE CITY EDITION

Weather: Rain today; partly cloudy tonight. Sunny and cool tomorrow. Temperature range: today 38-48; Wednesday 37-54. Details, Page 74.

VOL. CXXIV . No. 42,803

NEW YORK, THURSDAY, APRIL 3, 1975

Price higher in air delivery cities.

20 CENTS

COMBAT ERUPTS CLOSER TO SAIGON AS MORE COAST TOWNS ARE LOST; VIETCONG CALL FOR THIEU OUSTER

STANDARD & POOR DROPS 'A' RATING FOR CITY'S BONDS

Suspension Further Clouds Prospects for Note Sale —May Be 'Temporary'

BEAME ASSAILS ACTION

'We Have Never Defaulted,' Mayor Says, Promising to Balance the Budget

By JOHN DARNTON

Standard & Poor's, one of the two foremost credit-rating agencies in the country, announced yesterday that it had "suspended" its "A" rating of New York City bonds—an action that was seen as a severe setback in the city's battle to remain solvent.

The move is expected to erode further the confidence of investors in city securities, thereby raising interest rates and worsening the already bad prospects for a $450-million note sale, probably to be held next week.

Mayor Beame immediately denounced the action by Standard & Poor's, which 16 months ago raised its rating one notch, from "BBB" to "A," meaning that it upgraded the city's obligations from a medium-grade investment to a good investment.

'Unwarranted Statement'

Leaving his City Hall corner office, into which he had hurriedly retreated for a conference when the news of the rating came, Mr. Beame said with evident irritation:

"All I can say is it's an unwarranted statement. We will meet all of our obligations on time. We have never defaulted, and we will have a balanced budget."

"All I can say is they're wrong," the Mayor added, buttoning his black raincoat.

In a statement, Controller Harrison J. Goldin also condemned the rating agency as irresponsible and injudicious. He said its action was "unfair" and "strikes the city a cruel blow at the very time we are exerting every effort to overcome immediate problems and achieve a much sounder fiscal condition in the future."

The suspension of a rating—as opposed to a change in rating—was so unusual that many fiscal experts, including the Mayor and the Controller, had never heard of it.

Hopeful of Restoration

In its announcement, Standard & Poor's said it was "hopeful" that the suspension "will only be temporary" and that "we will be able to restore a rating on the city's obligations quickly."

It continued: "New York City's rapidly deteriorating ability to raise money in the capital markets places unusual strains on its cash position for the immediate future."

The agency cited the possible "inability or unwillingness of the major underwriting banks to continue to purchase the city's notes and bonds" as a primary reason for the suspension.

"Until we can more clearly discern what the receptivity of these banks will be toward the city's offerings, we are faced with a situation that defies

Continued on Page 11, Column 1

The New York Times/Meyer Liebowitz

Charles F. Luce, Consolidated Edison chairman, telling of the company's bid for a 21.7 per cent rate increase.

CON EDISON SEEKS INCREASE OF 21.7% IN ELECTRIC RATES

Asks P.S.C. for 2-Part Rise Adding $4 to $5 a Month to Home Bills in City

By RICHARD SEVERO

The Consolidated Edison Company asked the State Public Service Commission yesterday for the largest electric rate increase in the commission's history — a 21.7 percent rise. It would add $4 to $5 a month to the utility bills of most city residents and give Con Edison $456-million in additional revenue.

The utility estimated that a New Yorker who now used 250 kilowatt-hours a month and paid $22.44 would pay $27.41 for the same service in 1976. In Westchester County, where most residential customers use twice as much electricity and now pay $40.98 a month, the bill would go to $49.78 in 1976.

The proposed increase includes provision for a summer surcharge that would cost the same New Yorker 50 cents a month and his Westchester counterpart $1, for bills between May 15 and Oct. 15. The surcharge, Con Edison said, "is designed to recover extra costs of providing service during the peak summer demand period." Con Edison serves about nine million people.

Regret Voiced

The request comes less than five months after the Public Service Commission had granted the utility its largest previous increase in electricity rates, a rise designed to bring the company more than $300-million in additional revenues each year.

Yesterday's request was outlined by Charles F. Luce, the Con Edison chairman, in a news conference at the company's headquarters at 4 Irving Place.

"We regret that we must file this request at a time when our customers are fighting twin battles against inflation and recession," Mr. Luce said, "but to defer it would result in a progressive deterioration of electric service and reliability in New York City and Westchester."

Mr. Luce conceded that approval of the proposed increase would mean "the customer is going to get hurt," but said that in its rate application Con Edison sought the creation of an "energy stamp program" that would enable low-income customers to obtain a subsidy for their energy consumption. The subsidy would be administered through the Federal Food Stamp program.

"We know that our rates

Continued on Page 7, Column 1

U.S. Charges 'Footprints' Of Payoff Led to Connally

By JAMES M. NAUGHTON
Special to The New York Times

WASHINGTON, April 2—A Government prosecutor told the jury today in the bribery trial of John B. Connally that there was documentary evidence to prove that the former Secretary of the Treasury had solicited and received a $10,000 payoff for helping the dairy industry.

"Unlike most cash, this money left a trail of footprints," the assistant Watergate special prosecutor, Jon A. Sale, declared as he outlined the Government's case in United States District Court here. And the footprints, he said, led to Mr. Connally.

But Edward Bennett Williams, the chief defense attorney, told the jurors that he would show that Jake Jacobsen, the key prosecution witness on whose testimony the documents would bear, was an inveterate perjurer who "embezzled" the funds that allegedly went to Mr. Connally in 1971.

The 58-year-old former Cabinet member and former Governor of Texas sat, his face flushed, as the prosecution and defense took turns describing the case that they would make to a jury of seven women and five men impaneled this morning.

Mr. Connally stared at the prosecutor and shook his head, as if to say "no," when Mr. Sale described the $10,000 as a dairy industry "thank you" for Mr. Connally's part in a

Continued on Page 27, Column 1

Ford Reported Undecided On Tax Cut Bill Until End

By PHILIP SHABECOFF
Special to The New York Times

WASHINGTON, April 2 — President Ford was reportedly so undecided about the big antirecession tax cut bill passed by Congress last week that he had two speeches prepared before he announced his decision Saturday night—one for use with a veto and the other for signing the legislation.

He finally signed the bill, although he did not like it, after he was urged to do so by a majority of his closest advisers, most of whom did not like it either.

As described by high-ranking Administration officials close to the President, Mr. Ford was more secretive than usual about which way he was leaning on the tax bill. A day before signing the $22.8-billion tax cut, some of his closest advisers did not know what he would do.

Before reaching his decision, Mr. Ford asked all his top aides, both economic and political, to submit their recommendations in writing. After reading them he also asked some of the advisers for additional oral comments.

As reported privately by Administration insiders, only two high-ranking advisers strongly urged the President to veto the tax bill—Arthur F. Burns, the chairman of the Federal Reserve Board, and William E. Simon, the Secretary of the Treasury.

Dr. Burns reportedly made

Continued on Page 9, Column 1

5 Slain in Buffalo

Five elderly men and women were murdered in Buffalo and left in a burning slum building after the suspected robbery of $1,000 in their welfare money. Page 33.

PEACE-TALK OFFER

Reds' Aides in Paris Seek Parley With a New Regime

By FLORA LEWIS
Special to The New York Times

PARIS, April 2—Vietcong officials issued a series of statements here today calling for an uprising against the Saigon Government of President Nguyen Van Thieu and a negotiated end of the fighting.

Nguyen Thi Binh, the Vietcong Foreign Minister who negotiated the Paris agreements on Vietnam in 1973, was back here for the first time, smiling and eyes alight. She said in an airport statement that the Vietcong were prepared to start talks immediately with a new Saigon Government.

Text of Vietcong statement is printed on Page 17.

While the Vietcong side, which calls itself the Provisional Revolutionary Government of South Vietnam, has called for an alternative government in Saigon in the past, the timing of today's announcement was significant because of the current pressure on President Thieu to step down.

Seven-Point Statement

One of the Vietcong statements distributed here was a seven-point policy declaration calling on all South Vietnamese to join the Vietcong cause. While the statement made no threats against those who refused to join, neither did it offer a general amnesty similar to one proposed by the Cambodian insurgents.

Dinh Ba Thi, the chief Vietcong delegate here, said in answer to a question that members of the "third force" were being given positions of responsibility in areas taken over in the current drive. "Third force" is the term given to those who are neither Communists nor supporters of the Thieu Government.

Both Mr. Thi and Mrs. Binh, the Foreign Minister, said Vietcong policy was to put the 1973 Paris cease-fire accord into effect. Article 12 of the agreement called for talks between Saigon and the Vietcong to establish a National Council of National Reconciliation and Concord, consisting of Vietcong, Saigon and third-force delegates in three equal segments.

Earlier today, in Algiers,

Continued on Page 17, Column 2

The New York Times/April 3, 1975

Government forces reportedly lost coastal enclaves of Tuy Hoa, Nha Trang and Cam Ranh. Saigon command confirmed loss of Da Lat, Phan Rang and Phan Thiet. Fighting was reported in provinces ringing Saigon.

A Fear-Swept Saigon Is on Brink of Chaos

By BERNARD WEINRAUB
Special to The New York Times

SAIGON, South Vietnam, April 2—This capital is on the brink of chaos. The streets are humid and eerily silent at night as soldiers cluster on street corners or sprawl on the pavement and sleep beneath tamarind trees.

By day, fear and rumor breed among the capital's two million people. The airport is packed. Foreigners are rapidly shipping home their ceramic elephants and furniture and stereo sets. Vietnamese men stand in small groups reading the afternoon newspapers then quickly walk home.

"C'est fini, c'est fini," a Vietnamese Roman Catholic priest repeated over and over at the airport. A Vietnamese man, with tears in his eyes, said good-by to an American and whispered hoarsely: "We will survive in Vietnam. Another million people may die perhaps, but we will survive and be proud."

A Sense of Doom

There is a sense of doom now in Saigon, a sense of engulfing darkness in a capital that seems terrified. A Vietnamese woman burst into tears the other day at a restaurant. "What's going to happen to us?" she asked companions. "Will they shoot us? Will they shoot my family? What's going to happen?"

In a small apartment near downtown Saigon, the 23-year-old widow of a soldier, with two small children, trembled and bit her lip. "Where is there to go after Saigon?" she asked. "What is here to do? Wait, wait, wait."

An American in his office at the embassy shrugged and said: "I asked my wife to leave, I begged her to, and she said no, she wants to stay with me until the end." He smiled and said: "It's the end of the line, isn't it? It's going so fast I can't believe it."

President Nguyen Van Thieu's abrupt decision to abandon most of the northern two-thirds of the nation

Continued on Page 17, Column 6

U.S. Staff Starting To Leave Cambodia

By DAVID A. ANDELMAN
Special to The New York Times

PHNOM PENH, Cambodia, April 2—The United States Embassy announced today that it would begin evacuating diplomatic and other personnel from the Cambodian capital tomorrow and would also take members of other allied missions.

Meanwhile, with the loss of Neak Luong, the vital Mekong River town, 12 small river boats docked at the capital with all that the Government had been able to salvage there and at another outpost. [Page 12].

The initial American evacua-

Continued on Page 13, Column 1

TROOPS EXHORTED

Thieu's Generals Try to Prevent Complete Collapse of Army

By MALCOLM W. BROWNE
Special to The New York Times

SAIGON, South Vietnam, Thursday, April 3—The number of coastal towns reported abandoned to Communist forces without resistance by collapsing Government troops continued to swell yesterday.

The coastal enclaves of Tuy Hoa, Nha Trang and Cam Ranh, the huge military base and deep-water port, were reported lost, and this morning the Saigon military command confirmed that Da Lat in the Central Highlands, and Phan Rang and Phan Thiet along the coast were also gone.

Saigon's armed forces appeared to be falling apart rapidly, although little actual fighting was reported in the northern provinces. There was fighting in the provinces ringing the capital, however, even in Go Cong in the south, which had been quiet for years.

Appeals by Generals

Against a background of deepening crisis, the Government seemed powerless. Generals exhorted the people and their troops to stand fast and the vanguard of what promised to be a host of refugees began to flow into Saigon.

Communist demolition units and infantry divisions supported by tanks, were reported drawing closer to the capital.

The South Vietnamese Senate overwhelmingly approved a resolution calling for the formation of a "government of national union" to end the war. It did not seem likely that the resolution, which has no legal force without President Nguyen Van Thieu's approval, would bring about any change here. [Page 17.]

Losses Acknowledged

Last night, for the first time in the history of the Vietnam war, the Saigon command issued a military communiqué without reference to Military Regions I and II—the northern part of the country. The communiqué thus acknowledged their loss, although pockets of Government troops were undoubtedly scattered through the region.

The apparent loss of Nha Trang deprives the Government of its last major port city on the South China Sea. A spokesman said radio contact with the city was lost Tuesday.

Although Da Lat had been abandoned, it was not known last night whether Communist forces had yet reached that city. In any event, it was theirs if they chose to occupy it.

In Saigon, sound trucks cruised the streets broadcasting recordings of machine guns and artillery, playing martial music and exhorting the people to fight the Communists with determination.

In a two-minute address on

Continued on Page 16, Column 7

Planeload of Vietnamese Orphans Arrives in U.S.

By The Associated Press

OAKLAND, Calif., April 2— A plane carrying 57 orphaned Vietnamese children to new homes in the United States landed here tonight after leaving Saigon without official clearance.

The children were greeted by doctors, nurses and numerous well-wishers as they landed at Oakland International Airport. They ranged in age from 3 months up, and in most cases were already spoken for by adoptive parents. They were loaded onto a World Airways DC-8 jet in almost total darkness because Tan Son Nhut Airport in Saigon was on full military alert.

[A much larger airlift, of 2.000 Vietnamese orphans, was announced Wednesday night by the head of the United States Agency for International Development. Page 16. Adoption agencies in the United States are being swamped with calls from people eager to care for Vietnamese orphans. Page 32.]

The orphans traveled on the blanketed cabin floor of the cargo plane, each with a pillow. Some were chattering with excitement in Vietnamese.

A few minutes after the chil-

Continued on Page 16, Column 3

Associated Press

Orphans from South Vietnam aboard World Airways DC-8 that left Saigon with them last night. They are shown as the jet stopped to refuel in Japan on way to the U.S.

Federal Aid Gets 20,000 Jobs Here

By PETER KIHSS

Accelerated hiring for federally financed public-service jobs for city agencies led Lucille Rose, Commissioner of Employment, to forecast yesterday that 20,000 formerly jobless people would be at work by April 30. This could double the number working under the program at the end of March.

The temporary jobs come at a time when regular city-paid workers have had to be laid off.

In addition to the temporary jobs, most of the 18,312 persons scheduled to start training programs by June 30 have been

Continued on Page 10, Column 1

Waldheim Bars U.N. Plea on Refugees

By PAUL HOFMANN
Special to The New York Times

ROME, April 2—Secretary General Waldheim said today that the fate of Vietnamese refugees in areas occupied by Communist forces was "a very controversial political problem" that the United Nations should avoid.

In an interview here, Mr. Waldheim explained why he rejected yesterday a United States request that he appeal to the Communist authorities in Vietnam not to interfere with the evacuation of refugees.

"There is a war going on and one side has occupied a part of the territory and does not want to cooperate and this creates a political problem," the Secretary General said. "It is not in the interest of the United Nations to get involved in this political aspect."

Mr. Wadheim said he was maintaining contact with the Vietcong through its new liaison office in Geneva, and with North Vietnam through private channels by way of Paris.

He made it clear that he believed a public appeal by him to the Communists in Vietnam to allow refugees to leave would be "counterproductive."

The Secretary General said he had received assurances from North Vietnam and the Provisional Revolutionary Government of the Vietcong that they would "do everything" to feed and aid displaced people in areas under their control.

According to Mr. Waldheim, the Communist authorities estimated the total of displaced people in the territories they have recently gained as four million. South Vietnam and the United States have mentioned figures of 1.2 million to 1.5 million refugees to be evacuated.

The Secretary General said

Continued on Page 14, Column 4

NEWS INDEX

"All the News That's Fit to Print"

The New York Times

LATE CITY EDITION

Fair and cool today and tonight; Mostly sunny, milder tomorrow. Temperature range: today 33-50; Saturday 36-51. Details on Page 67.

SECTION ONE

VOL. CXXIV. . No. 42,813 NEW YORK, SUNDAY, APRIL 13, 1975 — $1.00 beyond 50-mile zone from New York City, except Long Island. Higher in air delivery cities. — 60 CENTS

MILITARY TAKING OVER IN CAMBODIA AS LAST AMERICANS ARE EVACUATED; SIHANOUK SAYS U.S. WANTS HIM BACK

AN F.B.I. INFORMER ASSERTS SHE SPIED ON ATTICA DEFENSE

Says She Gave Reports on Strategy for Ex-Inmates —Bureau Issues Denial

KUNSTLER ASKS HEARING

Governor Orders Lefkowitz to Name Aide to Evaluate State's Investigation

By MICHAEL T. KAUFMAN

A 26-year-old Buffalo woman said yesterday that she had infiltrated the Attica defense camp and reported back to the Federal Bureau of Investigation on legal strategy surrounding the trials of former inmates under indictment for crimes stemming from the 1971 prison rebellion.

The assertion came shortly before Governor Carey announced that a lawyer "of outstanding integrity, ability and reputation" would soon be appointed to evaluate the conduct of the state's investigation and prosecution of crimes arising from the Attica revolt. [Details on Page 50.]

Discuss Charge

The announcement followed a week of meetings involving top state officials—including the Governor, Attorney General Louis J. Lefkowitz, the state's chief judge and Mr. Carey's legal counsel—to discuss a charge by a former key Attica prosecutor, Malcolm H. Bell, that the chief prosecutor had covered up possible crimes by law enforcement officers who put down the prison rebellion in 1971.

In Washington, a spokesman for the F.B.I. acknowledged that the woman, Mary Jo Cook, "has furnished information to the bureau on a confidential basis for which she was paid." The spokesman added, however, that "at no time had she furnished to the F.B.I. information on the Attica defense."

Miss Cook told of her involvement with the F.B.I. during a

Continued on Page 50, Column 4

Sadat Declares That U.S. Must Order Israeli Pullout

In an Interview, Egyptian President Says That Mediation No Longer Is Enough —Vows to Continue Reform Policy

By HENRY TANNER
Special to The New York Times

CAIRO, April 12—President Anwar el-Sadat said in effect today that United States mediation in the Middle East was no longer enough and that the American administration must state clearly that it wants Israel to withdraw to the borders that prevailed before the 1967 war.

"It is time for the United States to declare to the whole world and not only to Israel whether it is protecting Israel within its borders or whether it is protecting Israel's occupation of the land of other states as well," the President said.

The issue of peace and war hangs in the balance, he said.

In a lengthy interview, Mr. Sadat also said that Israeli behavior during Secretary of State Kissinger's mission last month "humiliated the United States in the area."

He vowed that despite an increased danger of war, he would continue his policy of economic and political liberalization at home.

"This policy is irreversible," he said.

The pledge took on added significance because he is understood to be preparing major changes in the Government in the next few days and because Foreign Minister Ismail Fahmy is due to fly to Moscow next Saturday.

The Soviet leaders have bitterly criticized Mr. Sadat's domestic liberalism.

President Sadat confirmed that the Soviet Union resumed

Continued on Page 4, Column 1

Arson Increasing Rapidly; Recession Called a Factor

By WILLIAM K. STEVENS
Special to The New York Times

DETROIT, April 12—Seattle bans topless dancing in go-go bars, the clientele drops off, and immediately some of the bars burn down—suspiciously so in some cases, according to the fire department.

Two elderly New York sisters, 66 and 73 years old, are accused of hiring professional "torches" to set hundreds of fires in Queens and Nassau Counties to collect millions in insurance payments.

A multimillion-dollar arson-for-profit racket involving home repairs and insurance fraud is uncovered here, where 222 fires were set last year with Molotov cocktails, which are easier and cheaper to get than guns.

Arson. It is the shadowy preserve not only of the pyromaniac and the professional torch but also of some everyday citizens. It is said to be the fastest growing major crime in the country, one of the most costly, the hardest to detect, the most overlooked by both the public and law-enforcement agencies.

Known losses from arson are expected to surpass $1-billion this year for the first time, and are estimated to be increasing by 10 to 15 per cent annually.

A prominent factor in the rise during this time of economic recession, according to arson investigators, is that desperate businessmen — from clothing contractors in the South to auto-parts makers in the North to restaurant and bar owners everywhere — are seeking a time-tested way out: Insure and burn.

Recession-inspired fires are expected to help increase the incidence of arson by 20 per

Continued on Page 43, Column 1

SAIGON REPORTING GAINS AT XUAN LOC AND ON A KEY ROAD

But Some Communist Units May Have Bypassed Town to Continue Advance

VIETCONG GIVE WARNING

Say 'Uprising' Is Imminent in Capital Unless Thieu Resigns Immediately

By MALCOLM W. BROWNE
Special to The New York Times

SAIGON, South Vietnam, Sunday, April 13—The Saigon Government said last night that its forces had fought off Communist troops at Xuan Loc, 38 miles northeast of here, and on a key road 21 miles southwest of the capital.

But it appeared that some Communist units had bypassed Xuan Loc, on both the northern and southern flanks of Route 1, moving westward toward Bien Hoa and Saigon.

Indications were growing, however, that an attack on Saigon itself, regarded by military analysts as imminent, might start from within the city. Many Communist demolition units are believed to be here already, awaiting a signal to begin the type of attacks that characterized the 1968 Tet offensive, when the American Embassy compound was among the targets.

Warning of 'Uprising'

A warning that an "uprising" in Saigon was imminent unless President Nguyen Van Thieu resigns immediately and the Americans leave was made at Tan Son Nhut airport yesterday morning by Col. Vo Dong Giang, deputy chief of the military delegation of the Vietcong's Provisional Revolutionary Government. [Page 18.]

A Saigon Government spokesman said last night that in the battle of Xuan Loc, the capital of Long Khanh Province, more than 1,000 Communist troops had been killed in and around the city, which is now in ruins. He put Government casualties at 18 killed and 100 wounded.

New Attacks Reported

Communist pressure on Xuan Loc continued today, however.

A Government spokesman said that before dawn today the Communists began an artillery attack with 100-mm. guns and that at 4:50 A.M. Communist infantry and tanks attacked the northern part of the town.

The results of the new attacks were not immediately known here.

Communist troops and tanks penetrated the city last Wednesday and for a time held nearly half of it. According to the Saigon spokesman, 20 Communist tanks and many

Continued on Page 18, Column 1

Cambodian civilians about to leave Phnom Penh walk to an evacuation helicopter. A U.S. marine stands guard.

Associated Press

John Gunther Dean, U.S. Ambassador to Cambodia, arriving at the U Taphao air base in Thailand after flight from Phnom Penh. He carries flag that flew over the embassy.

LONG BORET STAYS

Premier Pledges Fight Will Continue Until Peace Is Gained

The writer of the following dispatch, who has reported from Cambodia for The New York Times over the last five years, decided to remain in Phnom Penh when the American airlift removed embassy and other personnel.

By SYDNEY H. SCHANBERG
Special to The New York Times

PHNOM PENH, Cambodia, April 12—Premier Long Boret announced tonight that a "summit committee" dominated by generals had been formed to run the Government and continue the fight against the insurgents until peace can be achieved.

This announcement, made in a radio broadcast, came several hours after the American Embassy had been closed and Ambassador John Gunther Dean together with the last remaining staff members were evacuated by helicopter. [They flew to U Taphao air base in Thailand.]

Other Cambodians Leave

Fleeing the country on the Ambassador's helicopter was Lieut. Gen. Saukham Khoy, who had been acting president of Cambodia since Marshal Lon Nol went int[illegible]ile on April 1.

Also evacuated with the remaining 50 or so embassy staff members and some Cambodian employes were a number of other Cambodian military officers and Government officials who had been closely identified with the Americans and now feared for their lives.

In his broadcast, the Premier said the new governing committee had been given full powers for three months. He appealed to the people "to remain calm and cooperate with the military."

"We and the army are determined to stand by you to obtain peace for our country," the Premier added.

No Longer Recognized

Mr. Long Boret said that General Saukham Khoy had left the country without telling anyone about his plans and that therefore the Government no longer recognized him as acting president.

To fill this "leadership vacuum," the Premier said, he called together today the main generals and political leaders as well as the Cabinet and other key Cambodian figures.

In a two-hour meeting, he said, it was decided to form the military-dominated "supreme committee" and to ask Parliament to give it full

Continued on Page 20, Column 7

40 School Buildings to Shut Here

By LEONARD BUDER

Prompted by declining enrollments and a need to cut costs, the Board of Education is planning to close as many as 40 school buildings by June, 1976, and take other measures to use its buildings more efficiently.

The expected school closings will mark the first time within memory of headquarters personnel that the city system will be giving up so many buildings because of diminishing numbers of pupils.

Dr. Bernard R. Gifford, deputy school chancellor, said yesterday that the system hoped to close—at least as far as regular pupils were concerned —10 schools by the end of the current term in June, and 30 others by the end of the 1975-76 term. He declined to identify the schools that might be closed.

Some buildings no longer needed for regular classes may be used for other school-related purposes, such as for administrative offices that now occupy rented outside space. Other buildings will be given back to the city and then will probably be returned to the tax rolls. The school system now occupies more than 950 school buildings.

In some instances, the system is expected to cut across local district boundaries to consolidate schools now under-used. As a result, some elementary and junior high school pupils from one district may have

Continued on Page 33, Column 1

Knicks Eliminated

The New York Knickerbockers lost yesterday to the Houston Rockets, 118-86, and were eliminated from the National Basketball Association playoffs. Details, Section 5.

U.S. Aides in Saigon Fear Disorder May Hamper Exit

By FOX BUTTERFIELD
Special to The New York Times

SAIGON, South Vietnam, April 12—There is widespread concern here that in an evacuation many Americans and almost all Vietnamese who have worked for Americans will be trapped in Saigon.

Officials familiar with the United States Embassy's planning say the 6,000 or more Americans still in Saigon could be evacuated only if Government soldiers and police remain friendly.

But some qualified officials doubt that, if fighting did spread to the capital, the Government forces could be counted on to refrain from disorder or violence against the remaining foreigners. When Da Nang and Nha Trang collapsed two weeks ago, Government troops fought their way aboard planes and rioted in the streets, endangering the evacuation of even the small number of Americans.

Such problems would be magnified in Saigon, a city of two million, which has tens of thousands of police and soldiers. Even the city's Tan Son Nhut Airport, three and a half miles from the embassy, may not be usable in an emergency, United States sources believe.

Only 150 in Pnom Penh

The evacuation of American officials and newsmen from Phnom Penh did not change this assessment. One diplomat said it only increased the fear of Vietnamese that the United States would abandon them.

Moreover, there were only 150 Americans to be evacuated from Phnon Penh, and most of them were concentrated in two downtown hotels.

Whatever the difficulties of getting Americans out of South Vietnam, United States officials say it will be even more difficult to evacuate the hundreds of thousands of Vietnamese

Continued on Page 19, Column 1

CAMBODIAN PRINCE SAYS HE DECLINED

He Reports Offer by Chief of American Liaison Office in Chinese Capital

By BERNARD GWERTZMAN
Special to The New York Times

WASHINGTON, April 12—Prince Norodom Sihanouk, the former ruler of Cambodia, said today in Peking that the United States had informed him that "everyone in Phnom Penh" wanted him to return there to head a new government and help work out a cease-fire with the Communist forces encircling the city.

In a statement that he made public, Prince Sihanouk said that he had declined the offer, which he said had come in a letter last night from George Bush, the chief of the American liaison office in Peking.

Power Play Suggested

But Prince Sihanouk added that he had advised the Americans, in a return note, to evacuate their embassy in Phnom Penh, and a few hours later Mr. Bush had called him to say that that had been done.

State Department officials—and Mr. Bush, in Peking—declined to comment on the exchanges. But a ranking official said that it was possible that the exiled leader might be trying to take credit for last night's evacuation of 276 Americans, Cambodians and others to improve his own chances of taking power in Phnom Penh.

For about six months, the United States has been trying privately to persuade Prince Sihanouk to loosen his ties with the Cambodian Communists, or

Continued on Page 20, Column 6

Today's Sections

Index to Subjects

Josephine Baker Dies

Josephine Baker, the American dancer and singer who became one of France's most famous music-hall stars, died in Paris at 68. Page 60.

United Press International

South Vietnamese civilians fleeing from Xuan Loc to Saigon run past the body of a man killed by rocket fire

The New York Times

LATE CITY EDITION
Weather: Clear and cold today and tonight. Fair and warmer tomorrow.
Temperature range: today 28-42; Friday 30-37. Details on Page 58.

VOL. CXXIV . No. 42,805   © 1975 The New York Times Company   NEW YORK, SATURDAY, APRIL 5, 1975   Price higher in air delivery cities.   20 CENTS

JOBLESS RATE UP TO 8.7% IN MARCH, HIGHEST SINCE '41

Total Unemployment Is Put at 8 Million—1.1 Million Out of Labor Force

ONE NOTE OF OPTIMISM

Figures on Persons Working Show Smallest Loss Since Recession Hit Hard

By EDWIN L. DALE Jr.
Special to The New York Times

WASHINGTON, April 4—Unemployment rose substantially in March to 8.7 per cent of the labor force, and the number of "discouraged workers" who have dropped out of the labor force altogether reached a record of 1.1 million, the Labor Department reported today.

The number of unemployed was eight million, the highest total in 35 years, since 8.1 million were listed as unemployed in 1940, at the end of the Great Depression. The unemployment rate was the highest since 1941, when it reached 9.9 per cent.

The March unemployment rate was up 0.5 per cent, from 8.2 per cent, in February. The number unemployed was up 500,000, on a seasonally adjusted basis, from 7.5 million in February.

Loss of Jobs Slows

The figures for March contained one potentially hopeful sign. The two separate measures of total employment—one based on a sample of households and one on payroll reports—both showed the smallest monthly loss of jobs since the recession began to hit with full force last September.

Julius Shishkin, Commissioner of Labor Statistics, told the Congressional Joint Economic Committee, "For what it is worth, the limited evidence provided by the March employment figures may be suggesting a weakening of the forces of recession." But Mr. Shishkin stressed that "the unemployment situation is extremely serious."

Earnings Index

George Meany, president of the American Federation of Labor and Congress of Industrial Organizations, called the situation "appalling." He said that adding the officially unemployed and the "discouraged workers" produced an "actual" rate of unemployment of "at least 9.8 per cent."

Calling the big tax reduction bill just signed by the President "obviously not enough," Mr. Meany said, "the job-creating bills now pending in Congress must be passed immediately despite any implied threat of a Presidential veto."

Surprisingly, in light of the widespread unemployment, the

Continued on Page 20, Column 6

Ford Acts to Extend to '77 Aid Plan for Unemployed

Will Submit Emergency-Help Bill When Congress Returns — Names Former Wyoming Governor to Interior Post

By JOHN HERBERS
Special to The New York Times

SAN FRANCISCO, April 4—President Ford, responding to the news that unemployment reached 8.7 per cent of the work force in March, said today that he would recommend an extension until the end of 1976 of the emergency benefits program for the unemployed.

He made the announcement in a speech tonight before the San Francisco Bay Area Council, a business and civic group that promotes the interests of this region.

In a separate statement, Mr. Ford announced the appointment of a former Wyoming Governor, Stanley K. Hathaway, to be Secretary of the Interior. Mr. Hathaway, if confirmed by the Senate, will succeed Rogers C. B. Morton, who has been appointed Secretary of Commerce.

The appointment of Mr. Hathaway, which had been expected, was a controversial one, more so than any of the four other Cabinet appointments

Mr. Ford has made since he became President last August. Mr. Hathaway is expected to be opposed in his confirmation hearings by environmental groups that have charged he favored business interests over environmental concerns when he was Governor.

Mr. Ford said that when Congress returned from its Easter recess, he would propose legislation that would extend the benefits under two emergency programs designed to help the unemployed.

At the same time, he said that the economy was "starting to show tentative signs that the worst may be behind us after too long a period of recession and inflation."

"I frankly expect a restructuring of our tolls to be authorized in the near future, designed to discourage the one-passenger use of automobiles for commuting purposes."

¶Extend for an additional 13

Continued on Page 20, Column 2

Democrats Decide to Push For State-Operated Bank

By MAURICE CARROLL
Special to The New York Times

ALBANY, April 4—Formation of a state bank to compete with commercial banks—a suggestion that was thought to be no more than a tactical threat when state officials believed that banks were too slow in helping the Urban Development Corporation—will be pressed by Democrats in the Legislature.

The bank, built on $3-billion or so in government deposits now scattered in commercial banks around the state, would be a profit-seeking venture, as well as a governmental "yardstick" to measure the performance of commercial banks.

"It's got No. 1 priority," said William Haddad, a special assistant to Assembly Speaker Stanley Steingut, who first made the state-bank suggestion.

Hearings Scheduled

Hearings on the bank plan—which could prove irritating to commercial bankers, who have lost some of their goodwill in Albany in the aftermath of the struggle to rescue the U.D.C. from bankruptcy — are to be held toward the end of the month.

The Speaker himself will be the lead-off witness.

As Mr. Haddad describes it, the Government bank theory is simmering in academic and government circles around the nation and is about to emerge here and there; there is one such institution—small and not really comparable to the New

Continued on Page 21, Column 5

LISBON'S LEADERS OUTLINE CHARTER

All Essential Power Is Given to Military Council for 3-to-5-Year Period

By HENRY GINIGER
Special to The New York Times

LISBON, April 4—Portugal's armed forces virtually imposed a constitution on the country today, with all essential power reserved for their governing body, the High Council of the Revolution, exclusively a military body of 28 officers.

A 14-page document outlining the new constitution was accepted by all the major political parties that are campaigning for the election of a constituent assembly on April 25.

With a pact of sorts concluded today between the parties and the armed forces, the elections were in effect turned into a plebiscite for the armed forces' plan to run Portugal for a provisional period of three to five years and place the country "irreversibly on the road that will lead it to Portuguese socialism."

The document was handed to the parties on Wednesday. They gave their answer this afternoon and the plan is expected to be published next week.

The Communist party, faithful to its policy of support for the armed forces, backed the plan without reservation.

Continued on Page 2, Column 3

---

3 Held in Slayings

The police arrested three teen-agers yesterday who they said had collectively murdered an elderly man, blinded an elderly woman in one eye and robbed two other elderly men in Brooklyn. Details on Page 14.

---

10 Subway Stations Evacuated After Suspect Warns of Bombs

Ten major Manhattan subway stations were evacuated and hundreds of thousands of riders were delayed for an hour in the homebound rush last night by the bomb threats of an alleged bank-extortionist who had set off a device earlier as authorities seized him on a crowded corner at Herald Square.

City and Transit Authority policemen began herding crowds out of the stations in midtown and lower Manhattan at 5:40 P.M., and police bomb experts searched platforms, tracks, lockers and lavatories for time bombs that the suspect had said were set to go off at 6 P.M.

About 45 minutes after that deadline, the alert was called off and straphangers poured back into the stations, which had been bypassed by trains during the bogus emergency.

The police later said the bomb threats had been made by a man who identified himself as Edward Williams, 26 years old of 317 Jones Drive, Paterson, N.J. He was taken into custody outside Macy's at 34th Street and Broadway shortly after 1 P.M. by Federal and city law-enforcement officers posing as bankers with a payoff.

As he was seized, the suspect hurled a suitcase that contained gunpowder packed in a mayonnaise jar. It exploded, inflicting second-degree and third-degree burns on the face of Bruce Brotman, a Federal Bureau of Investigation agent, and slightly injuring several other law-enforcement officers.

Authorities said the suspect earlier had walked into two branches of the Bankers Trust

Continued on Page 58, Column 7

RONAN TOLL PLAN WOULD PROMOTE USE OF CAR POOLS

Proposal Is to Ban 50c Rate if Autos Have Less Than 3 Riders at Jersey Points

By EDWARD C. BURKS

Commuters driving their cars between New Jersey and New York City each day will probably have to pay higher bridge and tunnel tolls soon unless they participate in car pools, Dr. William J. Ronan said yesterday.

Dr. Ronan, chairman of the Port Authority of New York and New Jersey, which operates the six toll crossings, including the Holland and Lincoln Tunnels and the George Washington Bridge, told a New York State legislative panel here yesterday:

"I frankly expect a restructuring of our tolls to be authorized in the near future, designed to discourage the one-passenger use of automobiles for commuting purposes."

84,000 Books a Month

Commuters can now buy reduced-rate coupon books permitting a round trip for 50 cents instead of the regular rate of $1. The proposed new system would withhold this discount unless there are at least three people in the vehicle.

Port Authority spokesmen said 84,000 half-rate coupon books were sold to commuters each month. They added that no increase in the basic $1 round-trip rate was contemplated at the moment and said further that trucks, tractor-trailers and buses would not be affected by any changes.

Tolls have never been raised at the Port Authority toll facilities, where traffic last year amounted to 158.6 million vehicles. Critics for years have acted on emphasis on motor-vehicle facilities and neglecting mass transit.

Proposals Listed

Testifying before a combined Senate and Assembly panel studying the possible revamping of public authorities to make them more responsive to public needs, Dr. Ronan made the following points:

¶The authority's area of activity, within a 25-mile radius of the Statue of Liberty, should be expanded to perhaps 50 miles.

¶As part of its mandate to develop transportation and other facilities of commerce, it is looking into the role that it can play in attracting and

Continued on Page 58, Column 2

Move on Phnom Penh

Part of the Cambodian insurgent force that had captured the Mekong River town of Neak Luong earlier this week was reported to be moving toward Phnom Penh, the capital. Details on Page 10.

OVER 100 VIETNAM ORPHANS KILLED WITH 25 ADULTS IN SAIGON CRASH; HANOI SAID TO SEND MORE TROOPS

Grief-stricken women taking tiny survivors of the crash of a C-5A plane to a hospital in Saigon yesterday
Associated Press

---

4 U.S. CARRIERS SET FOR RESCUE ROLE

But Ford Has Not Ordered Ships to Vietnam Waters to Evacuate Americans

By LESLIE H. GELB
Special to The New York Times

WASHINGTON, April 4—Four United States Navy aircraft carriers are standing by in the Western Pacific to evacuate American citizens and some Vietnamese from South Vietnam, but President Ford has not issued orders for these carriers to proceed to Vietnam waters, according to Administration officials.

The carriers earmarked for the evacuation operation are the Coral Sea, now in port in the Philippines; the Midway, at sea near Japan; the Enterprise, about half way between the Philippines and Indochina, and the Hancock, nearing Subic Bay in the Philippines en route to the Indochina area. The Pentagon had announced the Hancock's orders several weeks ago in connection with the deteriorating situation in Cambodia.

Already on station in the Gulf of Siam is the helicopter carrier Okinawa.

Also being discussed by the Administration is the question of additional military aid to Saigon. The Pentagon is argu-

Continued on Page 10, Column 5

Communist Units Probe Defenses Around Saigon

Special to The New York Times

SAIGON, South Vietnam, Saturday, April 5—A vast southward movement of North Vietnamese troops was reported yesterday as Communist units carried out probing actions along the Government's defense lines in an arc around Saigon.

But no major battles or further Government military reverses were reported. In fact, a military spokesman announced that the Government had now re-established contact with the coastal cities of Nha Trang, Phan Rang and Phan Thiet, which had previously been reported abandoned to the Communists without a fight.

According to some Western officials, the Saigon Government assumed that the cities were lost when commanders, soldiers and refugees fled.

At Nha Trang, the most important of the three and the reported scene of looting by Government troops Tuesday and Wednesday, the commander of a small artillery unit retreating through the city reportedly called Saigon by radio and asked permission to assume command.

This surprising request was granted, and the South Vietnamese Air Force sent small teams to each of the three places yesterday to reopen communications facilities. But how long the isolated troops there could hold out against the large Communist forces nearby appeared uncertain.

Western intelligence officials, meanwhile, were reporting that North Vietnam was now believed to be moving all but one of its eight reserve divisions into South Vietnam.

The commitment of almost all of Hanoi's troops to the South, these analysts say, appears particularly ominous because it comes at a time when the balance of power has al-

Continued on Page 9, Column 7

Thieu Shifts Cabinet And Criticizes U.S.

Special to The New York Times

SAIGON, South Vietnam, April 4—President Nguyen Van Thieu named a new Premier tonight to head a "government of war and national union" and said that that Government in order to defend the country's remaining territory against the Communists.

Speaking over television and radio, Mr. Thieu called upon the United States "to meet its commitments to South Vietnam."

"The American people as well as the American Congress must see now that they have got to do something for the people of South Vietnam to keep from

Continued on Page 9, Column 1

---

305 ABOARD PLANE

Huge Air Force Craft Was Flying Children to Refuge in U.S.

By FOX BUTTERFIELD
Special to The New York Times

SAIGON, South Vietnam, Saturday, April 5—An American Air Force transport carrying 243 Vietnamese orphans to refuge in the United States crashed and burned shortly after take-off here yesterday. More than 100 of the children and at least 25 of the adults accompanying them were believed to have been killed.

Rescue work was still going on in the mud of rice paddies about five miles northeast of Tan Son Nhut air base. Bodies of the children, some of whom were as young as 8 months, were buried in the mud. Debris—a baby bottle, blankets, a Donald Duck comic book—was scattered over the scene.

The rescue effort for the orphans of the war was the first of an airlift series announced by the United States Government Wednesday to take about 2,000 children to safe homes away from the fighting.

More Than 100 Survive

There were 305 people aboard the Galaxy C-5A jet—the 243 orphans, 44 women volunteers acting as escorts, 16 crewmen and two flight nurses. About 100 of the children and 15 to 20 adults were known to have survived.

According to a preliminary report by the pilot, Capt. Dennis Traynor, the accident began when a sudden depressurization in the four-engine jet, the world's biggest, blew out the rear door "and struck the tail."

After that, Captain Traynor reported, he was able only to "maintain limited control," and tried to bring the plane back to Tan Son Nhut. Mr. Traynor's report was made public by the United States Embassy this morning.

The crash flattened the cargo hold, where about 50 children had been strapped in. "Some of us got through a chute from the top of the plane, but the children at the bottom of the plane didn't have a chance," one survivor said.

The orphans were to be taken to Travis Air Force Base in California. They were to be adopted by American families

Continued on Page 8, Column I

---

3 Orphans Land Here Amid Grief Over Saigon Crash

By JAMES FERON

Months of anxious waiting ended early today at La Guardia Airport as three orphaned Vietnamese girls were embraced by their new American families.

It was an emotional scene, made more poignant because of earlier reports that a C-5A Galaxy carrying hundreds of other orphans had crashed outside Saigon, killing more than 100.

One of the new mothers, Adell Kolinsky, wept when she heard the news. For Ronnie Starr, who had waited two years for her child, anxiety briefly turned to sorrow "for those children and those people waiting for them."

A few hours later, as Mrs. Kolinsky embraced Nguyen Thi My Huong, whom she renamed Robyn Lan, she murmured: "We love her so. It's so good to save one."

The children blinked and gazed from face to face as they were carried from the plane, an Eastern Airlines flight from Los Angeles. The youngsters seemed confused and weary after a series of flights that began in Qui Nhon and Diem Phuc and ended in Spring Valley and

Continued on Page 8, Column 6

At La Guardia Airport, Adell Kolinsky of Spring Valley, N.Y., greeted child she and her husband are adopting.
The New York Times/Meyer Liebowitz

In Saigon, a survivor of the crash in which orphans were killed grieved as she saw a victim taken to a hospital.
United Press International

Shortly after the American troops were withdrawn from Vietnam, desperate South Vietnamese like these refugees crowding the decks of a U.S. merchant ship, struggled to escape the invading North Vietnamese.

A helpful marine gives a hand to a young Vietnamese refugee boarding a ship which will take him to a safer area.

Hopeful Vietnamese refugees look toward a brighter future as a U.S. cargo ship takes them away from their war-torn country.

"All the News That's Fit to Print"

The New York Times

LATE CITY EDITION

Weather: Partly sunny today; cold tonight. Sunny, cooler tomorrow. Temperature range: today 35-49; Thursday 32-58. Details on Page 69.

VOL. CXXIV . . No. 42,811
© 1975 The New York Times Company
NEW YORK, FRIDAY, APRIL 11, 1975

Price higher in air delivery cities.

20 CENTS

FORD ASKS $972-MILLION IN AID FOR SAIGON AND RIGHT TO USE TROOPS FOR EVACUATION; FEARS IT IS 'TOO LATE' TO HELP CAMBODIA

SENATE APPROVES CEILING ON PRICES FOR DOMESTIC OIL

Measure Is Opposed by Ford as Congress Acts to Set National Energy Policy

By DAVID E. ROSENBAUM

Special to The New York Times

WASHINGTON, April 10—The Senate passed today, by a vote of 60 to 25, legislation that would place a price ceiling on all oil produced in the United States.

The measure is sharply opposed by President Ford, who wants to remove price controls on oil, believing that consumption will decrease as the price rises.

It was the first formal action in what is expected to be a year-long effort by the Democratic-controlled Congress to develop a national energy policy.

Conservation Measures

The legislation would permit the President to take a broad range of actions to conserve energy, but an order installing gasoline rationing would be subject to disapproval by either house of Congress.

A companion bill is being prepared by the House Commerce Committee. In addition, the House Ways and Means Committee is drafting legislation that would sharply increase the Federal tax on gasoline and impose other selected taxes in an effort to reduce energy consumption.

Since 1973, the price of domestic oil has been based on a two-tiered system.

The price of "old" oil—generally, oil produced from any property up to the level produced from that property in 1972—has been set at $5.25 a barrel.

'New' Oil Is $12

The price of "new" oil—production from new wells or from old wells in excess of the 1972 level—is not controlled now and has risen to more than $12 a barrel.

The bill passed today would give Congress the chance to disapprove any Presidential action raising the price ceiling on old oil.

The price of new oil would be rolled back to the prevailing price of last Jan. 31, which was $11.25 a barrel.

If the price-rollback were to be enacted, according to Congressional experts, the price of gasoline could be expected to drop by about a penny a gallon.

About one-third of the oil

Continued on Page 13, Column 1

Walker Evans Dies

Walker Evans, the photographer noted for his bleak portraits of American life, died yesterday. He was 71 years old. Page 40.

Port Authority Increases Tolls at Crossings by 50%

By EDWARD C. BURKS

The Port Authority of New York and New Jersey yesterday raised basic automobile toll rates to $1.50 from $1 a round trip at the George Washington Bridge, Lincoln and Holland Tunnels and three other bridges, effective May 5.

At the same time, however, the agency announced a new rate of 50 cents a round trip for motorists who form car pools consisting of three persons or more in one automobile. Reduced-rate ticket books for car pools will be put on sale.

The 50 per cent increase in basic rates is the first in the history of the toll crossings between New Jersey and New York and also applies to trucks.

The three other crossings affected are the Bayonne and Goethals Bridges and the Outerbridge Crossing, all between New Jersey and Staten Island.

More than 158 million vehicles used the six crossings last year, including 138 million automobiles. Nearly half of the business was at the George Washington Bridge, where 75.8 million vehicles were counted.

Existing reduced-rate ticket books will be phased out. They will be honored until their expiration dates, but no new ones will be issued. The new car-pool books will contain 60 tickets valid for six months and will cost $30.

Dr. William J. Ronan, the Port Authority chairman, described the toll increases as evidence of the agency's commitment to several major mass-transit improvements in the area. The added tolls are expected to bring in $39-million in addition to the $80-million now being collected.

Buses will not be assessed additional tolls. The existing round-trip rate of $1.80 will not be changed.

As the 12 Commissioners from the two states voted to ratify the new toll schedules yesterday afternoon, Dr. Ronan explained that the schedules would automatically be subject to review by the United States Department of Transportation

Continued on Page 70, Column 3

Ex-Attica Prosecutor Says Evidence Was Denied Him

By M. A. FARBER

Malcolm H. Bell, the former Attica prosecutor who has charged his superior with covering up possible crimes by law enforcement officers, told Governor Carey in his confidential report that he had been blocked from obtaining audiotapes and pictures of the assault on the prison in 1971.

This was one of a number of major items in the 160-page report that came to light for the first time yesterday as the controversy over Mr. Bell's charge continued to develop.

The Governor's counsel met for an hour yesterday with Charles D. Breitel, the state's chief judge, to discuss whether any action was warranted by the state's judiciary to resolve the allegation of a cover-up.

A spokesman for Mr. Carey said it would be "inappropriate" to disclose the conversation between Judge Breitel and Judah Gribetz, the Governor's counsel.

Mr. Carey rescheduled to Monday a meeting on the charge of a cover-up with Attorney General Louis J. Lefkowitz. The session, according to the Gov-

Continued on Page 44, Column 3

2 Legislative Units To Examine Charge Of Prison Cover-Up

By SELWYN RAAB

The chairmen of two legislative committees yesterday announced investigations into charges that officials of the State Commission of Correction covered up prison irregularities and spied on a critic.

In a major move to reorganize the watchdog prison agency, the chairmen—State Senator Ralph J. Marino and Assemblyman Stanley Fink—also proposed separately that the seven part-time commissioners who now head the commission be replaced by a smaller, full-time executive body.

Governor Carey, through a spokesman, said the reports of "questionable activities" by the commission were "extremely disturbing." Robert Laird, Mr. Carey's press secretary, said that "the matter is under review by the Governor and the results of that review will be announced shortly."

The New York Times reported yesterday that staff members, including the former head of the commission's special inves-

Continued on Page 44, Column 6

REACTION IS COOL

But Many in Congress Support Request for Humanitarian Aid

By RICHARD L. MADDEN

Special to The New York Times

WASHINGTON, April 10 — Leading members of Congress reacted quickly and overwhelmingly negatively tonight to President Ford's request for $722-million in additional military aid to South Vietnam.

But there appeared to be support in Congress for the President's request for $250-million for economic and humanitarian aid for South Vietnam as well as for authority for the use of United States military forces for the limited purpose of insuring the possible evacuation of American citizens from Vietnam.

Senators and Representatives sat silently as the President somberly described the situation in South Vietnam and Cambodia and requested additional aid.

A Few Democrats Walk Out

The first time he mentioned the $722-million military-aid figure, a hiss was heard from the Democratic side. A few Democrats walked out of the chamber as Mr. Ford continued his speech.

"I can't conceive of this Congress voting $722-million in military aid for South Vietnam," said Representative Thomas P. O'Neill Jr. of Massachusetts, the House Democratic majority leader.

"There would have to be a complete turnaround in the opinion of the American public, as I read it talking with members when they came back from the Easter recess, to support such aid," he said. He added, however, that there was "no question" that there was a moral obligation to make sure American citizens got out of Vietnam safely.

Jackson Is Opposed

"It's dead," said Senator Henry M. Jackson, Democrat of Washington, of the requested military aid. Mr. Jackson, who is a candidate for the Democratic Presidential nomination, added: "I oppose it. I don't know of any on the Democratic side who will support it."

Senator John J. McClellan, Democrat of Arkansas and chairman of the Senate Appropriations Committee, which would have to approve the mili-

Continued on Page 11, Column 7

The New York Times/Mike Lien

President Ford addressing Congress last night. At rear is Vice President Rockefeller.

Life Under Vietcong: A Portrait by Refugees

By FOX BUTTERFIELD

Special to The New York Times

SAIGON, South Vietnam, April 10—Refugees who fled from areas of South Vietnam lost by the Saigon Government in the last month report that the Communists have moved quickly to round up all ranking South Vietnamese Army and Government officers. But the refugees add that they know of only a few executions of Government officials.

According to the refugees, the Communists often appeared surprised by the speed of the local governmental collapse and, in many cases, were not prepared to assume the tasks of local administration fully.

But the Communists, usually led by small numbers of teen-aged North Vietnamese soldiers, have generally succeeded in restoring order, getting water and electricity running again and taking a census. In addition, the refugees say, students in occupied areas have been ordered to go back to school, take poltical-indoctrination courses and report to the Vietcong authorities on family members or neighbors who worked for the local Saigon Government structure.

This picture of life in the two-thirds of South Vietnam that has been yielded to the Communists since March 8 was pieced together from accounts of refugees who fled from such cities as Hue and Quang Ngai in the north, Tuy Hoa and Nha Trang on the central coast and Ban Me Thuot and Pleiku in the Central Highlands.

In almost every case, the refugees related, local people long associated with the Vietcong have been appointed to new jobs in Communist civil administrations, but the troops in charge are North Vietnamese. The refugees' accounts also suggested that the Communists were able to set up new governments most quickly where they had long had strong local sympathy and organized guerrilla movements.

For example, a functioning Provisional Revolutionary Gov-

Continued on Page 8, Column 7

FIGHTING IS HEAVY IN SOUTH VIETNAM

Battle for Xuan Loc Is Seen as Test of Regime's Will to Defend the Capital

By ANDREW H. MALCOLM

Special to The New York Times

SAIGON, South Vietnam, Friday, April 11 — Communist forces, bolstered by tanks and heavy artillery, maintained their pressure on Saigon today with more heavy fighting in and around Xuan Loc, a key provincial city 38 miles northeast of here. Control of the area was uncertain in a fluid battle situation.

Reports from the area said that the defenders were not abandoning territory as Saigon troops had done in the last few weeks in retreating from northern parts of the country. Airborne troops at Xuan Loc were fighting, but Communist soldiers were said to be slipping past them on both sides, chopping at their flanks and moving closer to Saigon.

Government spokesmen said that South Vietnamese fighter-bombers struck enemy positions in the Xuan Loc area and that there was destruction or damage to 25 trucks and two tanks. The battle, now in its third day, and fighting along the road west toward Bien Hoa, are considered a critical test of how determined the South Vietnamese are to defend

Continued on Page 8, Column 1

EARLY VOTE URGED

A Big Sum Said to Be Needed to Rescue Up to 200,000

By BERNARD GWERTZMAN

Special to The New York Times

WASHINGTON, April 10—President Ford appealed to Congress tonight to approve "without delay" nearly a billion dollars in military and humanitarian aid for Saigon to give South Vietnam a chance to "save itself" as a country and make possible a large-cale evacuation of Americans and South Vietnamese "should the worst come to pass."

In a nationally televised address to a joint session, Mr. Ford painted a gloomy picture of the situation in South Vietnam.

Transcript of Ford's speech is printed on Page 10.

Faced with various options, Mr. Ford said, he decided to ask for $722-million in military aid—more than twice the $300-million sought earlier—and $250-million in economic and humanitarian aid for Saigon.

Purpose of Aid Stated

Mr. Ford stressed that this large request, which he asked to be acted on by April 19—a week from Saturday—was meant not only to keep Saigon from a military collapse, but to buy time for allowing the United States to try to arrange a political solution between Hanoi and Saigon.

This would also allow the orderly withdrawal, if necessary, of 6,000 Americans and of tens of thousands of Vietnamese, or a total estimated by some as high as 200,000.

The President also asked Congress for clear authority to use troops for the possible evacuation, and officials disclosed that the American embassy in Saigon, which had been resisting evacuation, had been ordered to begin a reduction of the number of United States Government employes still in the city. [Details on Page 11.]

A Plea on the C.I.A.

Late in the speech, the President made an impassioned plea to Congress not to allow its investigations of the intelligence community to destroy national security or harm the effectiveness of the Central Intelligence Agency. [Page 11.]

As to Cambodia, Mr. Ford seemed to acknowledge that Phnom Penh was on the verge of collapse. Without even repeating his old aid proposal for $222-million, he asserted that aid for the Cambodians may be "too late."

His point was underscored tonight when an Administration official said the fate of Phnom Penh would probably be decided in the next few days.

The President said he planned

Continued on Page 11, Column 3

Computerized Chrysler Engine Planned to Save Fuel in '76 Car

By RICHARD WITKIN

Special to The New York Times

DETROIT, April 10 — The Chrysler Corporation has ordered into production for 1976 cars a radically modified computerized engine that does away with the catalytic converter and improves fuel consumption, company officials said today.

The so-called "lean burn" engine will be installed in at least 200,000 standard-size Chryslers, Dodges and Plymouths to be marketed in late fall. The innovation will not increase the price of the cars, and eventually, when production gets into full swing, it is expected to bring price savings, the company officials said.

Keys to the new system are, first, a pair of very small computers mounted under the hood, and, second, the resulting ability to accomplish combustion of "lean" air-fuel mixtures. These are mixtures where the ratio of air to fuel is 18 or more to 1 instead of the conventional 15 or 16 to 1.

"This lean burning," said Charles M. Heinen, director of the project, "will give us a 5 per cent or more improvement in fuel consumption, a less cluttered engine compartment, lower costs, a peppier car and just as good driveability."

The Chrysler move represented one of the largest changes in engine technology made in

Continued on Page 71, Column 4

GOLD! The fabulous Scythian Gold from the U.S.S.R.. April 19. Metropolitan Museum of Art.—ADVT.

Pictorial Parade

Communist troops entering Da Nang, one of the South Vietnamese coastal cities they have occupied recently

Phnom Penh Defense Weakens; Rebels Within 3 Miles of Airport

By SYDNEY H. SCHANBERG

Special to The New York Times

PHNOM PENH, Cambodia, April 10—The weary and thinly stretched army defending this encircled city fell back at several points today, leaving large gaps in its defense.

Government commanders were making frantic but poorly coordinated efforts to plug the holes, which put the insurgents less than three miles from the airport, Phnom Penh's last link with the outside world.

The Communist-led Cambodian insurgents have been shelling the airport daily with artillery and rockets. But now they are close enough to fire their even more accurate mortars. This morning the American airlift that keeps this Government alive was interrupted briefly by a barrage that killed and wounded several Cambodian cargo handlers.

As yet, no large concentrations of insurgent troops have poured through the defense gaps directly north of the airport, but as one pessimistic military source put it tonight, "The stage is set."

Other developments added to

Continued on Page 8, Column 5

NEWS INDEX

"All the News That's Fit to Print"

The New York Times

LATE CITY EDITION

Weather: Showers today; periods of rain tonight and tomorrow. Temp. range: today 45-56; Monday 39-56. Full U.S. report on Page 81.

VOL. CXXIV. No. 42,817 · © 1975 The New York Times Company · NEW YORK, THURSDAY, APRIL 17, 1975 · Price higher in air delivery cities. · 20 CENTS

PHNOM PENH SURRENDERS TO REBEL FORCES AFTER OFFER OF A CEASE-FIRE IS REJECTED

Saigon Peril Grows as Troops Near Xuan Loc Fall Back

S.E.C. Says Northrop Kept $30-Million Secret Fund

By EILEEN SHANAHAN
Special to The New York Times

WASHINGTON, April 16 — The Securities and Exchange Commission filed suit today accusing the Northrop Corporation of maintaining a secret fund of $30-million for political and other purposes, at least some of them illegal.

The company immediately announced that it had agreed to settlement of the suit.

The alleged fund was the largest that any company has so far been accused of maintaining for such purposes and far exceeded the $1.2-million that Northrop had previously admitted maintaining as an illegal fund from which political contributions were made.

Northrop, a relatively small company in the aerospace industry, has specialized in making jet fighters. Its F-5 has been used in as many as 17 air forces. In 1972 its total assets were some $409.9-million. The industry's leader, Boeing Company, has assets of more than $2-billion.

The suit, similar to ones filed recently by the S.E.C. against such companies as the Gulf Oil Corporation, the United Brands Company and the Phillips Petroleum Company, formally accused Northrop only of statutory violations over which the S.E.C. has jurisdiction. These are confined to charges that the companies failed to make proper disclosure in their reports to stockholders and to the Government of what they were doing with significant sums of money.

Northrop, Thomas V. Jones, its board chairman, and James Allen, former vice president and board member who retired in December, were all named as defendants in the suit filed in United States District Court here.

The S.E.C.'s complaint al-

Continued on Page 56, Column 1

BIEN HOA POUNDED

South Vietnam Force Abandons Port City of Phan Rang

By MALCOLM W. BROWNE
Special to The New York Times

SAIGON, South Vietnam, Thursday, April 17 — Government units holding the approaches to the devastated city of Xuan Loc, 38 miles northeast of here, were falling back yesterday as the military situation for Saigon appeared to worsen.

A thousand shells again fell on Xuan Loc, where resistance continued, but many Government troops were also pulling back with crowds of refugees from the fighting.

Communist gunners firing at Bien Hoa air base, 15 miles northeast of Saigon, seriously disrupted fighter-bomber traffic.

In a further blow to Saigon, the enclave held by Government forces at the port city of Phan Rang, 170 miles northeast of the capital, was abandoned.

Enemy Reinforcements Sent

Thus the military situation for the Government appeared markedly worse tonight than at any time since the central part of the country was yielded to the Communist forces two weeks ago.

The North Vietnamese have been rushing fresh divisions from central Vietnam to the fighting northeast of Saigon, and there are indications that some of these forces are now in combat.

Several days ago, long-barrelled 122-mm. artillery with a range of 15 miles, about equal to that of the Communists' 130-mm. gun, was brought to bear on Bien Hoa as well as on Xuan Loc and the surrounding area.

In barrages yesterday, about 60 shells fell on or near the Bien Hoa air base. A Government spokesman, reporting that two persons had been killed, conceded that air traffic had been hampered by damage from the shelling and from the explosion two nights ago of a large bomb storage dump. That blast apparently was set off by a commando attack.

The Bien Hoa air base is the main remaining center of Government air operations against the Communists.

The Communists' 122-mm. guns and other heavy artillery

Continued on Page 20, Column 1

Associated Press

Insurgents manning a 105-mm. howitzer in an attack on Cambodian Government forces in positions around Phnom Penh, according to the caption with this photograph. It was radioed from Peking and relayed from Warsaw.

REPORT IS ON RADIO

Government Soldiers Are Directed to Cease Combat

By United Press International

The Cambodian Government surrendered to insurgent forces today, the Cambodian radio announced. The Phnom Penh Government ordered all its troops to stop firing and lay down their arms.

Brig. Gen. Mey Sichan, chief of operations for the Cambodian Government Army, went on the radio and said

Text of cease-fire proposal is printed on Page 18.

soldiers and functionaries should cease all combat and invite the rebels to take power. This announcement was monitored in Saigon.

After his speech a "representative of the liberation forces" told all Government officers to report to the Information Ministry, site of the radio station, under a white flag of surrender.

"We enter Phnom Penh as conquerors," the insurgents' representative said. "We order the surrender of all officers and officials of the Phnom puppet regime under a white flag."

The rebels' representative said the final victory for the insurgents had come at 9 A.M. (10 P.M., Wednesday, New York time) when insurgent troops seized the Information Ministry. The ministry and its third-story broadcasting studio are in the center of Phnom Penh about 200 yards from the Phnom Hotel.

There was no initial word on the fate of the foreigners sequestered at the hotel. These included newsmen, a few diplomats and representatives of the International Red Cross and the United Nations.

Truce Was Sought

By SYDNEY H. SCHANBERG
Special to The New York Times

PHNOM PENH, Cambodia, Thursday, April 17 — The Cambodian military Government asked yesterday for an immediate cease-fire from the Cambodian insurgents, who were attacking Phnom Penh from all sides. The Government said it would turn over power to them.

Several hours later, reports from Peking said that Prince Norodom Sihanouk, the nominal leader of the insurgents who is in exile there, had rejected the cease-fire proposal as unacceptable.

The Phnom Penh Government's proposal, which might be described as conditional surrender, had called for a complete transfer of power to the insurgent side under the supervision of the United Nations and representatives of the International Committee of the Red Cross who are now in Phnom Penh.

A second major point among the five in the proposal was a demand for assurances that there would be no reprisals against persons or organizations for their activities during the five-year war.

The cease-fire proposal, which was transmitted through the Red Cross delegation here, came as this suffering city of more than two million, relatively calm until now, began to show signs of collapse.

Throughout the day, the Com-

Continued on Page 18, Column 1

EXTRA TAX SOUGHT TO AID DOWNTOWN

Business Group Backs City Plan to Assess Area for Civic Improvements

By PAUL GOLDBERGER

The Downtown-Lower Manhattan Association, an influential organization of businessmen and civic leaders, has approved a city plan for a special real estate tax in lower Manhattan to pay for such urban amenities as pedestrian malls and park areas and to raise planning funds for new projects, such as the now-stalled Manhattan Landing.

The special assessment, which would raise the tax by approximately $1.25 per $1,000 of assessed valuation, would be limited to a five-year period and would apply in a district from river to river bordered on the north by either Chambers Street or Canal Street. It is expected to yield $3-million to $4-million annually.

The plan, developed by the city's Office of Lower Manhattan Planning, was called a "persuasive vote of confidence in lower Manhattan" yesterday by Mayor Beame, who said he "strongly supports this imaginative and sound approach."

Mr. Beame said that the

Continued on Page 30, Column 3

Business Leaders Assert Recession Nears a Low Point

By MICHAEL C. JENSEN

Even as the nation suffers from some of the grimmest economic conditions since the nineteen-forties, a number of industrialists and businessmen across the country say they are convinced that the current recession is reaching its low point.

"The worst that can happen already has," said Malcolm Baldridge, chairman of the Scovill Manufacturing Company in Waterbury, Conn. "Most businessmen are still very concerned with the present recession, but we've seen the beginning of the end."

In Washington yesterday the Department of Commerce, reporting on new home-building and individual income levels in March, found that the pace of the business downturn was slowing but disclosed no indication of an upturn. [Page 57.]

Reginald H. Jones, chairman of the General Electric Company, agreed that the rate of decline in the economy had clearly slackened. "We should reach bottom by the end of the second quarter, or the early part of the third quarter," he added.

The businessmen's views were sought in a canvass of a dozen executives in major

Continued on Page 63, Column 3

Radhakrishnan Dies

Sarvepalli Radhakrishnan, the philosopher and former President of India, died in Madras at 86. Page 42.

FORD ASSERTS U.S. HAS FAILED SAIGON

Says Commitments on Aid Were Not Met, Creating a 'Tragic Situation'

By PHILIP SHABECOFF
Special to The New York Times

WASHINGTON, April 16 — President Ford said today that the failure of the United States to meet its commitments to Saigon had created "this present tragic situation" in South Vietnam.

Responding to questions at the annual convention of the American Society of Newspaper Editors, the President compared the United States behavior toward its South Vietnamese ally unfavorably with what he characterized as the fidelity of Moscow and Peking to Hanoi.

He said that this country had promised Saigon when the Paris peace accords were signed in January, 1973, that it would supply replacement war matériel to South Vietnam. He said he assumed that the Soviet Union and China had made similar commitments to North Vietnam.

"It appears that they have maintained that commitment," the President said. "Unfortunately the United States did not carry out its commitment in the supplying of military

Continued on Page 20, Column 4

Reporter's Notebook: Cambodia

The following dispatch by Sydney H. Schanberg accompanied his account of the battle for Phnom Penh.

Special to The New York Times

PHNOM PENH, Cambodia, April 16 — Last night, with this city facing imminent capture by the insurgents who surround it, the National Bank of Cambodia sent a cablegram to the Irving Trust Company in New York, asking the American bank, where it presumably has dollar credits, to confirm that it was carrying out an earlier order to pay $1-million to Marshal Lon Nol. The earlier order was sent by letter on April 1, the day that the marshal, Cambodia's former President, went into exile under American prodding.

Perhaps the marshal was worried that if Phnom Penh fell to the insurgents before the transaction was confirmed, he would never get the money.

How did the marshal come by the money? It was always rumored here that he was deeply corrupt and had used American aid to build large bank accounts abroad. But no one could ever pin it down. Maybe Irving Trust can shed some light now.

In any case, it was only one of the many peculiar things that have happened here in the last few days as the insurgents closed in. Here are a few of them.

•

It is possible that people in the outside world imagine us hunkered down in bunkers, praying as shells fall all around us. Sometimes, near a front line, things do get hairy, and even in Phnom Penh, as this is being written, the sounds of shelling are fierce just outside the southern gates of the city. But there have always been oases. Two nights ago, near the hotel's

Continued on Page 18, Column 5

U.S. Considers Corridor To Evacuate Vietnamese

By DAVID E. ROSENBAUM
Special to The New York Times

WASHINGTON, April 16 — Gen. Frederick C. Weyand, the Army Chief of Staff, told a Senate committee today that the Pentagon was considering establishing a corridor from Saigon to the sea to evacuate tens of thousands of Vietnamese.

Creation of such a corridor, one of several evacuation plans being considered, could involve a major commitment of American forces.

Pentagon officials said that, under hostile conditions, at least one Marine division — about 20,000 men — plus air power from Navy carriers would be required to protect the corridor.

At the same time, State Department officials said that the United States was expected to announce tomorrow that 980 Cambodian refugees would be admitted as temporary residents. [Page 18.]

Meanwhile, the rift between President Ford and Congress over aid to South Vietnam and the evacuation of Americans widened.

The President rejected as inadequate a Congressional plan that would give him $200-million for emergency assistance and restricted authority to use troops for evacuation purposes.

Members of the Senate Foreign Relations Committee said they had been misled about the rate at which Americans were being evacuated and put off, at least until tomorrow, further action on legislation.

An accommodation over the amount of money to be made available still appeared pos-

Continued on Page 20, Column 6

VIETCONG DEMAND FULL U.S. PULLOUT

Charge American Military Has 25,000 in Vietnam Disguised as Civilians

By FLORA LEWIS
Special to The New York Times

PARIS, April 16 — The representative of the Vietcong's Provisional Revolutionary Government issued a call here today for "immediate and permanent" withdrawal of what he said were 25,000 American military personnel "disguised as civilians" in South Vietnam.

In a series of statements and at a press conference, he said there would be "no difficulty, no obstacle" placed in the way of their departure.

"If the U.S. really wants to save their lives," a statement said, "it should withdraw them totally and immediately."

But Dinh Ba Thi, interim head of the government's mission here, would not respond to efforts by reporters to determine exactly what would happen to Americans and other foreigners if they remained in areas that fell under Vietcong control. He referred only to a previous statement saying their lives and property would be protected if they obeyed "the policy of the revolutionary power."

The statements accused the Ford Administration of advancing plans for evacuations from Vietnam only as a "pretext for renewed American military intervention."

The warning by Defense Secretary James R. Schlesinger that the lives of 200,000 South Vietnamese would be endangered if they remained in their country was denounced as "a pure fabrication" and a "cal-

Continued on Page 20, Column 7

Soviet Politburo Drops Shelepin, Formerly a Contender for Power

By CHRISTOPHER S. WREN
Special to The New York Times

MOSCOW, April 16 — Aleksandr N. Shelepin, who once figured as a prominent contender for the authority assumed by Leonid I. Brezhnev, was removed from the Communist party's ruling Politburo today.

The departure of the 56-year-old trade union chief was viewed here as strengthening Mr. Brezhnev's hand by eliminating a long-standing and younger rival in anticipation of the 25th congress of the Communist party.

The meeting of the Central Committee that eliminated Mr. Shelepin today scheduled the congress for Feb. 24, 1976. The congress, which lays down long-term policies, is convened every five years.

Mr. Shelepin, who headed the secret police under Nikita S. Khrushchev, attracted Western attention two weeks ago when he was hounded by demonstrators during an official visit to Britain and returned home early. Some Soviet insiders have suggested that Mr. Shelepin was sent to Britain with the knowledge that he would be embarrassed and thus provide a pretext for removal.

While the official press agency Tass, in a one-sentence reference, reported only that

Continued on Page 2, Column 4

Associated Press

FUNERAL OF CHIANG KAI-SHEK IS HELD: Members of the family of President Chiang Kai-shek, who died on April 5, beside his coffin as it was closed during the service yesterday on Taiwan. From left: Chiang Hsiao-wu, grandson; Premier Chiang Ching-kuo, son; Mrs. Chiang and Gen. Chiang Wei-kou, younger son. Page 42.

NEWS INDEX

GOLD! Fabulous Scythian Gold from the USSR Apr. 19. Metropolitan Museum.—Advt.

"All the News That's Fit to Print"

The New York Times

LATE CITY EDITION

Weather: Mostly sunny today; cool tonight. Fair and mild tomorrow. Temperature range: today 36-58; Monday 42-54. Details on Page 70.

VOL. CXXIV... No. 42,822 · © 1975 The New York Times Company · NEW YORK, TUESDAY, APRIL 22, 1975 · Price higher in air delivery cities. · 20 CENTS

THIEU RESIGNS, CALLS U.S. UNTRUSTWORTHY; APPOINTS SUCCESSOR TO SEEK NEGOTIATIONS; EVACUATION OF ALL AMERICANS CONSIDERED

HOUSE SUPPORTS ROAD FUNDS PLAN FOR 150,000 JOBS

Would Alter Ecology Laws to Spur Projects Here and in 2 Other States

By RICHARD D. LYONS
Special to The New York Times

WASHINGTON, April 21—In this Congressional session's first major confrontation between employment and environment priorities, the House of Representatives voted today for jobs.

The issue involves changing Federal environmental protection laws to end legal snarls that have halted about 130 highway construction projects in New York, Connecticut and Vermont. The projects, worth about $2.3-billion, would employ about 150,000 workers.

Should the legislation be enacted into law, legal objections to the projects would be dropped and construction could start. Funds for the projects have already been appropriated.

Congressional passage and Presidential approval seem likely, in view of the size of the House vote margins on two bills involved—257 to 99 and 370 to 5—and Ford Administration support.

Appeals Court Ruling

In New York City, the major projects involved are an approach to Kennedy International Airport and reconstruction of portions of the West Side Highway.

The House action today would nullify a ruling by the United States Court of Appeals for the Second Circuit in New York that held that the Federal Government had not played an adequate role in the preparation and review of environmental impact statements for the highway projects. Such statements are necessary under the National Environmental Policy Act of 1969.

The act has usually been interpreted to require substantial but not exclusive Federal involvement in the preparation of the impact statements, thus allowing state involvement. But in December the Court of Appeals ruled that the Department of Transportation must

Continued on Page 10, Column 4

Port Authority Trims Rise In Its Commuter-Rate Plan

By RALPH BLUMENTHAL

The Port Authority of New York and New Jersey, at the insistence of the Governors of both states, yesterday modified its scheduled toll increase for Hudson River crossings by agreeing to retain monthly discount tickets, but at a higher rate.

Under the compromise approved by the Governors, the round-trip toll for ticket-holding commuters riding alone in their cars would go as of May 5 to $1—double the current commuter toll but 50 cents cheaper than the new standard cash toll.

Yesterday's unexpected modification—voted at a brief meeting of 8 of the 12 Port Authority Commissioners — won the endorsements of Governor Byrne of New Jersey and Governor Carey of New York, who had agreed at a meeting Friday to demand the change on threat of a veto of the increase. Their agreement virtually assured imposition of the new toll schedule, revenues of which are earmarked for mass transit.

However, the Automobile Club of New York, among other motorist groups, vowed to continue its opposition. In response, the Federal Highway Administration said it was preparing to send a team of investigators here to review Port Authority figures on the need for the toll increase.

Hailing the compromise, the Port Authority chairman, Dr. William J. Ronan, thanked the Governors for "this historic revision of the Port Authority revenues to make possible new mass-transit projects."

In its original, controversial decision on April 10 to raise the tolls for the George Washington Bridge, Lincoln and Holland Tunnels, the Bayonne and Goethals Bridges and the Outerbridge Crossing between New Jersey and Staten Island, the Port Authority ordered a new flat tariff of $1.50 a round trip—eliminating a 25-year-old policy of half-price discounts for commuters with monthly tickets.

The exception — which remained unaffected by yesterday's modification—was for those riding in car-pools of

Continued on Page 59, Column 1

FEAR IN PENTAGON

Kissinger Opposes Call for an Immediate Pullout by U.S.

By JOHN W. FINNEY
Special to The New York Times

WASHINGTON, April 21 — Defense Department officials concluded today that the situation in South Vietnam was deteriorating so rapidly that the United States must plan on the immediate evacuation of all Americans and their dependents.

The issue was under urgent consideration at the White House during the day, officials said, with Secretary of State Kissinger opposing proposals for complete evacuation of the 2,800 Americans and 1,200 Vietnamese dependents still in Saigon.

Mr. Kissinger's basic argument is that any overt move toward evacuation — a word that he has ordered not to be used in any Government announcement—could cause panic in the already unstable situation in Saigon.

Evacuation Airlift On

Meanwhile, an evacuation airlift from Saigon continued, and reports from the Philippines, where the planes were landing, said hundreds of Vietnamese, some present and former military officers, were aboard with Americans. [Page 14.]

There was no immediate indication whether a decision on a total evacuation had been reached by President Ford.

This evening, in a CBS television interview, Mr. Ford said there was "no problem" about his authority to use United States troops to evacuate American citizens, if necessary, from South Vietnam.

But the President said that if there was resistance from either North Vietnam or South Vietnam, it would be "virtually impossible" to withdraw large numbers of South Vietnamese citizens without a "sizable military involvement" of American troops "on a short-term basis." [Page 16.]

On Capitol Hill, Gen. Frederick C. Weyand, the army chief of staff, testified before the House Appropriations Committee that the North Vietnamese divisions now encircling Saigon "have the capability to overwhelm South Vietnam if they want to," and he expressed doubt that the situation could

Continued on Page 15, Column 1

United Press International

Nguyen Van Thieu announcing his resignation as President on TV in Saigon yesterday

The New York Times/George Tames

Gen. Frederick C. Weyand, Army Chief of Staff, with Secretary of State Kissinger before they testified before the House Appropriations Committee on South Vietnam.

10-YEAR RULE ENDS

Vice President Huong, 71 Years Old, Takes Office in Saigon

By MALCOLM W. BROWNE
Special to The New York Times

SAIGON, South Vietnam, April 21—President Nguyen Van Thieu, denouncing the United States as untrustworthy, resigned tonight after 10 years in office.

He immediately appointed his Vice President, the 71-year-old Tran Van Huong, to replace him.

He said that President Huong would immediately press the enemy to cease all acts of

Excerpts from Thieu's speech of resignation, Page 14.

war and enter into peace negotiations. The Vietcong have said repeatedly that they would not negotiate while Mr. Thieu held office.

[A spokesman for the Vietcong delegation in Saigon said Tuesday the resignation of President Thieu "decidedly cannot change the situation," Reuters reported.]

Accuses the U.S.

In an impassioned address to the nation, President Thieu defended his character and the accomplishments of his regime while chronicling its collapse. He called for peace, but also said the successor government would fight on.

Speaking before assembled members of his Government and National Assembly at the Presidential Palace, President Thieu accused the United States of breaking its promises to support an anti-Communist Government in Saigon.

Mr. Thieu said that he had objected in October, 1972, to Secretary of State Kissinger's "acceptance of the continued presence of North Vietnamese troops in South Vietnam."

Pledge by Nixon

Mr. Thieu added that South Vietnam would fight on to defend the territory left to it. The armed forces chief of staff, Gen. Cao Van Vien, also spoke briefly, to say that his troops would continue fighting to "defend the homeland against the communist aggressors."

"I resign but I do not desert," President Thieu said in concluding his one-and-a-half-hour address. "From this minute I will put myself at the disposal of the President and people. I will continue to stay close to you all in the coming task of national defense. Good-by to you all."

His voice taut with emotion, President Thieu devoted most

Continued on Page 14, Column 1

State Agrees to Transfer 2,650 Out of Willowbrook

By PETER KIHSS

Governor Carey announced an agreement yesterday to settle a three-year court fight over the state's Willowbrook Developmental Center for the mentally retarded. The agreement would reduce the number of patients at the facility—once overcrowded and depicted as a place of horror—from a current 2,900 to 250 in six years.

The plan would set up 200 community places for patients in the next 12 months — hostels, halfway houses, group homes, workshops, day-care training centers — in sites yet to be chosen. The moves would be part of a continuing effort to get away from oversized institutions.

Bruce J. Ennis, counsel for the New York Civil Liberties Union, said the agreement involving the center, which is on Staten Island, "recognizes that retarded persons are capable of physical, intellectual, emotional and social growth." He said it called for specific individualized

Continued on Page 59, Column 1

Sawhill Appointed To Succeed Hester As N.Y.U. President

By EDWARD B. FISKE

John C. Sawhill, former Federal Energy Administrator, was named yesterday to be the 12th president of New York University.

The 38-year-old economist succeeds James M. Hester, who is stepping down after 13 years as head of the 40,000-student university to become the first rector of the newly formed United Nations University, an international research and training institution with headquarters in Tokyo.

The choice was announced at a news conference at the school's new Elmer H. Bobst Library by John M. Schiff, chairman of the board of trustees. He said that a committee of five trustees, working in consultation with faculty members, students and alumni, had examined nearly 400 can-

Continued on Page 70, Column 6

France Urges New Talks To Carry Out '73 Accords

Paris Issues Statement

By FLORA LEWIS
Special to The New York Times

PARIS, April 21—The French Government appealed urgently today for a quick resumption of negotiations to carry out the 1973 Paris agreements on Vietnam, accompanied by a cease-fire covering all South Vietnam.

The statement, issued by the spokesman for President Valéry Giscard d'Estaing, said France was "naturally ready to do all in its power" toward the application of the Paris agreements.

Careful checks in Paris produced no evidence that any direct contacts had yet been made between the Saigon Government and the Vietcong or between the United States and the North Vietnamese.

Nguyen Xuan Phong, who heads the South Vietnamese Embassy here, was asked whether any direct contacts had been made with the Communist side. "Not yet," he re-

Continued on Page 15, Column 5

A Shift in U.S. Policy

By LESLIE H. GELB
Special to The New York Times

WASHINGTON, April 21—Administration sources said today that President Ford two or three weeks ago ordered a "hands off" policy that neither supported nor abandoned President Nguyen Van Thieu of South Vietnam.

Either President Ford or Secretary of State Kissinger—it could not be determined which — specifically instructed Ambassador Graham A. Martin in Saigon to follow this line, the officials said.

This instruction, to the extent that Ambassador Martin carried it out, must have been interpreted by high South Vietnamese officials and military men as a change in American policy, one official said.

The officials speculated that close associates of Mr. Thieu put pressure on him in recent weeks to resign, arguing that

Continued on Page 15, Column 4

VIETNAM FIGHTING VIRTUALLY CEASES

Few Clashes Reported After Resignation—2 Towns Shelled Earlier

Special to The New York Times

SAIGON, South Vietnam, Thursday, April 22—Fighting in South Vietnam virtually ceased after President Nguyen Van Thieu's resignation last night, highly informed military sources reported today.

"There were some incidents but practically no military activity since then," one source said.

The Vietcong radio, while denouncing the new President, Tran Van Huong, spoke mostly in terms of carrying out the Paris peace accord rather than making military threats.

Just before President Thieu resigned the military situation was essentially stable despite continued heavy Communist shelling and probes and clashes in some places.

Among the targets of the shelling were two besieged provincial capitals on the northeastern and eastern approaches to Saigon.

The radio antenna at Xuan Loc, capital of Long Khanh Province 38 miles northeast of

Continued on Page 15, Column 7

Accident Rule Voted

The State Senate gave final approval yesterday to a major change in the tort law. It would permit a person who is partly at fault in an accident to collect damages for the part of the accident that is attributable to the other party. Page 72.

Legacy of Wounded Knee: Hatred, Violence and Fear

By GRACE LICHTENSTEIN
Special to The New York Times

PINE RIDGE, S.D. — The week of April 20-26 has been proclaimed as Law and Order Week on the Pine Ridge Oglala Sioux Reservation.

The designation—announced by the local Roman Catholic Church in conjunction with tribal and Federal officials—is ironic, because, for the last several months, law and order have been virtually nonexistent here.

Since Jan. 1, according to Federal Bureau of Investigation statistics, six people have been killed on this reservation, the site of the original Wounded Knee massacre in 1890 and of the take-over by militant Indians of that landmark in 1973. There have been 67 assaults, including tomahawk and hammer bludgeonings.

On a per-capita basis, the Pine Ridge homicide rate is six times greater than that of the city of Chicago, the assault rate four times greater. Residents are afraid to leave their houses, even in daylight.

Two years after the militant American Indian Movement took over Wounded Knee for 71 days to dramatize a new Indian consciousness, the Pine

Continued on Page 18, Column 1

NEWS INDEX

	Page		Page
Books	33	Movies	40-43
Bridge	32	Music	40-43
Business	45-58	Notes on People	27
Chess	32	Obituaries	38
Crossword	33	Op-Ed	35
Editorials	34	Sports	28-32
Family/Style	26	Theaters	40-43
Financial	45-58	Transportation	70
Going Out Guide	42	TV and Radio	71
Man in the News	14	Weather	70

News Summary and Index, Page 37

FREE—Current issue on Catholic education. Write SIGN, Dept T Union City 07087 or call (212) 279-3578—Advt.

United Press International

A helicopter descending to a field along Route 1 to evacuate South Vietnamese who fled the fighting in Xuan Loc

Drug-Smuggling Logistics Bizarre and Often Fatal

Second of four articles on why Latin America is now the major source of hard drugs entering the United States.

By NICHOLAS GAGE

The rainy season has ended in Chulumani, Bolivia, and on the steeply terraced mountainside, Juan Mamani is crouching in his small plot of coca plants, beginning to strip the tiny green leaves that will be his first crop of the year. He will pack the leaves into bales, called tambors, and sell the 300 pounds he harvests for $250.

In Jackson Heights, Queens, drug dealers are waiting for new supplies of cocaine from South America. The 300 pounds from Juan Mamani's small plot will produce one kilogram of the drug (2.2 pounds). Although he will get $250 for his crop, the kilo of cocaine will bring in at least $75,000 in the New York City retail market.

The huge profit between New York and Latin America, which has become the major source of hard drugs entering the United States, is what makes thousands of men and women willing to take the risks involved in smuggling cocaine into the United States.

The methods they use are imaginative, bizarre and sometimes fatal to the couriers, who have been known to soak their clothes in cocaine or to swallow drugs stuffed in a prophylactic pouch.

Every conceivable container has been used by couriers to secrete drugs coming in from Latin America — false-bottomed wine bottles, frames of paintings, hollow

Continued on Page 24, Column 1

"All the News That's Fit to Print"

The New York Times

LATE CITY EDITION

Weather: Continued mostly cloudy, cool today, tonight and tomorrow. Temperature range: today 46-58; Tuesday 45-53. Details on Page 81.

VOL. CXXIV. . No. 42,830 — NEW YORK, WEDNESDAY, APRIL 30, 1975 — Price higher in air delivery cities. — 20 CENTS

MINH SURRENDERS, VIETCONG IN SAIGON; 1,000 AMERICANS AND 5,500 VIETNAMESE EVACUATED BY COPTER TO U.S. CARRIERS

United Press International

A crewman from an American helicopter helping evacuees to the top of a building in Saigon for flight to a U.S. carrier

FORD UNITY PLEA

President Says That Departure 'Closes a Chapter' for U.S.

By JOHN W. FINNEY
Special to The New York Times

WASHINGTON, April 29—The United States ended two decades of military involvement in Vietnam today with the evacuation of about 1,000 Americans from Saigon as well as more than 5,500 South Vietnamese.

The emergency helicopter evacuation was ordered last night by President Ford after the Saigon airport was closed

Ford statement and excerpts from Kissinger's, Page 17.

because of Communist rocket and artillery fire. The 1,000 Americans were the last contingent of a force that once numbered more than 500,000.

They were carried by a fleet of 81 American helicopters to carriers in the South China Sea.

The helicopters removed the 5,500 South Vietnamese citizens because their lives were presumed to be in danger with a Communist take-over of South Vietnam. Over the last two weeks, a total of about 55,000 South Vietnamese have been removed. Most of them will come to the United States. The helicopter flights ended the United States evacuation of South Vietnamese.

Last Marines Evacuated

The final withdrawal of Americans was completed at 7:52 P.M., about two hours after the White House had announced the evacuation was completed, when 11 marines were taken by helicopter from the roof of the American Embassy in Saigon. Officials said that the marines, the last of a security guard sent in to protect the evacuation, were safely removed although small-arms fire had broken out around the deserted embassy.

President Ford, in a statement issued by the White House, said the evacuation "closes a chapter in the American experience." In a plea for national unity in the post-Vietnam period, the President said:

"I ask all Americans to close ranks, to avoid recrimination about the past, to look ahead to the many goals we share and to work together on the great tasks that remain to be accomplished."

Appeal by Kissinger

At a news conference, Secretary of State Kissinger appealed to North Vietnam not to storm Saigon by force because the United States believed the new South Vietnamese Govern-

Continued on Page 17, Column 1

END OF DEFENSE

Troops Leave Posts in Capital and Turn in Their Weapons

By The Associated Press

SAIGON, South Vietnam, Wednesday, April 30—President Duong Van Minh announced today the unconditional surrender of the Saigon Government and its military forces to the Vietcong.

Columns of South Vietnamese troops pulled out of their defensive positions in the capital and marched to central points to turn in their weapons.

[In Washington, the White House said that President Ford had "no comment" on the surrender of Saigon, but a White House spokesman said the surrender was considered "inevitable." Page 16]

Troops Move In

Within two hours, Communist forces began moving into Saigon, and a jeep flying the Vietcong flag and carrying eight cheering men in civilian

The text of President Minh's statement is on Page 16.

clothes armed with an assortment of weapons could be seen driving near the United States Embassy compound.

The Vietcong flag was raised over the presidential palace at 12:15 P.M. (12:15 A.M. Wednesday, New York time), and soon after a detachment of Communist troops in a jeep arrived at the palace and asked General Minh to accompany them. He drove off with them, but their destination was not immediately disclosed.

Vietcong flags materialized on other buildings as well, and Vietcong soldiers soon walked along the main streets shaking hands with Saigon residents. The red, yellow-starred flag of North Vietnam could also be seen on trucks carrying soldiers in green helmets and uniforms.

Bursts of Fire

Sporadic bursts of firing could be heard, but the only resistance to the Communist take-over was reported to be from marines stationed at the zoo and public gardens.

The take-over followed by hours the ending of the American involvement in Vietnam through the evacuation of most of the approximately 1,000 Americans still here yesterday.

The surrender announcement, made in a broadcast to the nation, signaled the end of three decades of fighting. It came 21 years after the 1954 Geneva accords divided Vietnam into North and South and a little more than two years after the Vietnam cease-fire

Continued on Page 16, Column 1

U.S., GREECE AGREE TO END HOME PORT FOR THE 6TH FLEET

Air Base of Americans at Athens Is Also Closed, but Some Facilities Remain

By United Press International

ATHENS, April 29—United States and Greek officials announced today the termination of the home-port arrangement for Sixth Fleet ships at the port of Eleusis near Athens and the closing of the American air base at Athens airport.

The announcement came in a joint statement at the end of a second round of talks on the status of United States military facilities in Greece.

The Greek Government threatened to close all United States bases and it withdrew from the North Atlantic Treaty Organization's military command after the invasion of Cyprus by Turkey last July.

"Certain United States facilities which contribute to Greek defense needs will continue to operate on the Greek Air Force base at Hellenikon," today's statement said.

The statement said that the second phase of the talks, held April 7 to 29 by the two delegations under the United States Embassy Minister, Monteagle Stearns, and Ambassador Petros Kalogeras of Greece also discussed the status of other facilities.

"Agreement is also expected on the elimination, reduction and conservation of other United States facilities in Greece," it said.

The two delegations said that they made progress on the review of the privileges, immunities and exemptions of American personnel in Greece.

The two Governments said

Continued on Page 4, Column 4

G.M.'s Profits Fall

First-quarter profits of General Motors declined 50.8 per cent from the depressed 1974 quarter. Page 53.

HEAVY USERS FACE CON ED INCREASE

P.S.C. Also Orders Cuts for Smaller Consumers

By WILL LISSNER

The state's Public Service Commission ordered the Consolidated Edison Company yesterday to raise its rates for those customers who accounted for the heaviest summer power demands and to cut the rates for customers whose usage did not create excess power demand.

The change — technically a revision of the rate structure approved last November to give the utility $338.7-million more a year — will not mean any extra revenue for the company. Nor will it affect the rates for the great majority of customers, the 2.5 million small residential and commercial users.

Instead, yesterday's order makes revisions in bills that will take less than $20-million from some customers and give it to others, a relatively small amount compared with its total annual billings for electricity of $2.10-billion. It affected less than 500,000 of its 2.9 million customers in New York City, Westchester County and part of Nassau County.

But the order was significant because it introduced into energy ratemaking the philosophy that the customers who are responsible for excess costs should be required to bear more

Continued on Page 34, Column 5

Abram Offers Bills To Curtail Abuses Of Nursing Homes

By ALFONSO A. NARVAEZ
Special to The New York Times

ALBANY, April 29—Morris B. Abram proposed today a series of changes in the laws governing nursing homes to "deal with the most serious immediate problems" uncovered during his month-long investigation.

The proposals were contained in a package of 11 bills submitted to Governor Carey and legislative leaders by Mr. Abram, head of the Moreland Act Commission investigating the nursing-home industry.

Among other things, they would authorize nursing-home residents to file class-action suits for deprivation of their rights and would entitle them to receive a minimum of 25 per cent of the daily reimbursement rate paid by government regulations for each day of a violation.

[In Washington, Senator Frank Moss, Democrat of Utah and chairman of the long-term care subcommittee of the Special Committee on Aging, introduced a package of 36 bills for nursing home reform. Among them were measures to make long-term care more readily available to all older Americans, improve inspection and enforcement procedures and provide training for nursing-home physicians, nurses,

Continued on Page 81, Column 3

CAMBODIA ORDERS FOREIGNERS OUT

Planned 250-Mile Road Trip to Border Is Protested by Paris as Debilitating

By FLORA LEWIS
Special to The New York Times

PARIS, April 29—The French Government said today that the people who have been isolated in its Phnom Penh embassy since the Cambodian Communists took over two weeks ago had been ordered expelled "in the worst possible conditions."

There are 610 refugees in the embassy. They are to be sent out by truck to the town of Poipet on the Thailand border, beginning tomorrow.

Foreign Minister Jean Sauvagnargues told newsmen after having conferred with President Valéry Giscard d'Estaing:

"We fear these extremely precarious evacuation conditions will be beyond the strength of some whose health is poor."

"We continue to insist that the plane that we have held in Vientiane for evacuation of the ill be allowed to land in Phnom Penh."

However, a Foreign Ministry spokesman said that so far there has been no response to

Continued on Page 17, Column 6

74 Saigon Planes Fly 2,000 to Thailand

By DAVID A. ANDELMAN
Special to The New York Times

BANGKOK, Thailand, April 29—At least 74 South Vietnamese Air Force planes fleeing the country streamed into U Taphao air base in southern Thailand without warning this afternoon.

The pilots and passengers—2,000 people—requested asylum, American and Thai Foreign Ministry officials said.

About 30 of the planes were F-5 jet fighters and there were reports that at least one had crashed on a highway near the base as it was making its approach.

The planes began arriving at the huge naval and air base on the Gulf of Siam at about the time that the American evacuation of South Vietnam was ending and the planes were still landing as night fell.

The aircraft were said to include C-47 transports and the C-130 cargo planes that the American military has been using to ferry refugees from South Vietnam to Guam and the Philippines. However, all the aircraft were understood to be Vietnam Air Force planes, originally supplied by the United States.

A Thai Foreign Ministry spokesman said that American authorities at U Taphao had been asked to turn over the aircraft to the Thai Government, which would return them to "the new South Vietnamese government." The pilots and passengers, the Thai spokesman said, "must leave Thailand."

"They just landed first and asked permission afterwards," said an astounded Thai Foreign Ministry official. Other Government sources said that apparently no efforts were made to prevent the planes from landing and no aircraft went up to intercept the fighters as they roared in.

American Embassy officials in Bangkok declined to comment on the Thai request that the planes be returned and their status was unclear. An unresolved question here appeared to be whether the planes were still American property or belonged to whatever government continued in Saigon. The planes could be worth $200-million, one official said.

No details were available on the status of the refugees or

Continued on Page 16, Column 6

United Press International

President Ford and Secretary of State Kissinger returning to White House to resume talks on Vietnam. They had just said good-by to King Hussein of Jordan after visit.

2d Key Met Museum Aide Quits In Dispute Over Hoving Methods

By GRACE GLUECK

With an attack on Thomas P. F. Hoving's administration at the Metropolitan Museum of Art alleging its inability to function "in any way that creates or preserves trust, confidence and decency," Anthony M. Clark, chairman of the museum's department of European paintings, has resigned.

Mr. Clark's resignation, one of several that have occurred among senior curatorial personnel at the museum in recent years, represents the first open challenge to Mr. Hoving's administration.

The resignation, effective June 30, follows that of John Walsh, the vice chairman and curator of this key department a month ago. Mr. Clark would not speak for Mr. Walsh, who is abroad, but it is understood that their basic grievances are similar.

"I can't work with or for the present administration at the Met," said Mr. Clark, who had been director of the Minneapolis Institute of Arts for 10 years before his appointment to the Metropolitan in 1973. "I believe that its relation to art has become incidental, wrong and even risky. It's also hell on professionals."

In a statement last night, Mr. Hoving said that he was

Continued on Page 24, Column 1

NEWS INDEX

Saigon Copter Lands on Another In Stampede to U.S. Ship's Deck

By The Associated Press

ABOARD U.S.S. BLUE RIDGE, in South China Sea, April 29—Scores of South Vietnamese helicopters filled with military men and civilians fled Saigon today and headed out to sea to search for the carriers of the United States Seventh Fleet.

Seven of the helicopters arrived unexpectedly above this vessel carrying Americans and Vietnamese evacuated from South Vietnam. The seven copters made a dash for the helipad at the rear of the ship.

One pilot dropped his helicopter on the blades of another that had just landed and chunks of metal ripped through the air. The top helicopter, with its load of women and children, nearly toppled into the sea, but they were rescued and there were no injuries.

United States sailors heaved the two damaged choppers overboard to clear the landing pad. For the Vietnamese it was a last-ditch chance to survive.

As other Vietnamese helicopters landed their passengers were pulled free. American sailors ripped the doors off the craft to make them sink and the pilots then jettisoned them in the sea to make room for other arrivals circling overhead. Two small craft rescued the swimming pilots.

The American evacuation was reported orderly, although it was delayed several times because of weather and pilot fatigue.

The Blue Ridge is the command and communications vessel of the 40-ship Seventh Fleet armada waiting off the coast of South Vietnam to evacuate Americans and other foreigners

Continued on Page 17, Column 2

"All the News That's Fit to Print"

The New York Times

LATE CITY EDITION

Weather: Turning cloudy today; cool tonight. Partly sunny tomorrow. Temperaure range: today 46-65; Wednesday 43-64. Details, Page 81.

VOL. CXXIV . . . No. 42,831

NEW YORK, THURSDAY, MAY 1, 1975

Price higher in air delivery cities.

20 CENTS

COMMUNISTS TAKE OVER SAIGON; U.S. RESCUE FLEET IS PICKING UP VIETNAMESE WHO FLED IN BOATS

United Press International

Graham A. Martin, center, the United States Ambassador to South Vietnam, being escorted aboard the U.S.S. Blue Ridge yesterday after his arrival by helicopter. Mr. Martin was one of the last persons to leave his embassy

'HO CHI MINH CITY'

Communications Cut Soon After Raising of Victory Flag

By GEORGE ESPER
The Associated Press

SAIGON, South Vietnam, April 30—Communist troops of North Vietnam and the Provisional Revolutionary Government of South Vietnam poured into Saigon today as a century of Western influence came to an end.

Scores of North Vietnamese tanks, armored vehicles and camouflaged Chinese-built trucks rolled to the presidential palace.

The President of the former non-Communist Government of South Vietnam, Gen. Duong Van Minh, who had gone on radio and television to announce his administration's surrender, was taken to a microphone later by North Vietnamese soldiers for another announcement. He appealed to all Saigon troops to lay down their arms and was taken by the North Vietnamese soldiers to an undisclosed destination.

[Soon after, the Saigon radio fell silent, normal telephone and telegraph communications ceased and The Associated Press said its wire link to the capital was lost at 7 P.M. Wednesday, Saigon time (7 A.M. Wednesday, New York time).

[In Paris, representatives of the Provisional Revolutionary Government announced that Saigon had been renamed Ho Chi Minh City in honor of the late President of North Vietnam. Other representatives said in a broadcast monitored in Thailand that former Government forces in eight provinces south of the capital had not yet surrendered, but no fighting was mentioned.]

The transfer of power was symbolized by the raising of the flag of the National Liberation Front over the presidential palace at 12:15 P.M. today, about two hours after General Minh's surrender broadcast.

Hundreds in Saigon Cheer

Hundreds of Saigon residents cheered and applauded as North Vietnamese military vehicles moved to the palace grounds from which the war against the Communists had been directed by President Nguyen Van Thieu, who resigned April 21, and by President Ngo Dinh Diem, who was killed in a coup in 1963.

Broadcasting today in the

Continued on Page 14, Column 1

A War History

An illustrated review of the long conflict in Vietnam appears on Pages 17 through 20.

Kissinger Says U.S. May Shelter 70,000

By JOHN W. FINNEY
Special to The New York Times

WASHINGTON, April 30—United States Navy ships continued today to pick up South Vietnamese refugees fleeing their country in small boats, the State and Defense Departments reported.

In addition to 6,000 South Vietnamese evacuated by helicopter yesterday from Saigon along with 1,373 Americans, the State Department said, 22,000 South Vietnamese have been picked up by Navy ships waiting off the South Vietnamese coast.

As the flow of refugees continued, Secretary of State Kissinger, who yesterday used a figure of 56,000 refugees, estimated that the United States might have to resettle as many as 70,000 South Vietnamese.

Mr. Kissinger told reporters on Capitol Hill that the Administration would soon ask Congress for funds to handle the resettlement of the refugees. Philip C. Habib, Assistant Secretary of State for East Asia and Pacific Affairs, estimated that as much as $500-million might be required over the next year to take care of the refugees.

The Defense Department declined to say how many ships had been left in position to pick up South Vietnamese who were able to flee by small boat into the South China Sea. As for the legal authority to continue the rescue effort now that Americans have been evacuated from South Vietnam, Joseph Laitin, Assistant Secretary of Defense for Public Affairs, said at a Pentagon briefing: "There is no law that says you can't pick up people in distress on the high seas."

The Defense Department said the ships were remaining in international waters, outside the three-mile territorial limit claimed by the former South Vietnamese Government. There is some question, however, whether this limit still applies, since North Vietnam, and presumably the Provisional Revolutionary Government, which is taking over control in Saigon, claim a 12-mile territorial limit.

Confusion over the territorial limit claimed by North Vietnam was a key element in the Gulf of Tonkin incident in August, 1964, which led to a Congressional resolution authorizing President Lyndon B. Johnson to introduce troops into South Vietnam. The Defense Department at first contended that two destroyers that it said had come under North Vietnamese attack were in international waters but later acknowledged that they had gone within the 12-mile limit claimed by North Vietnam.

The Defense Department declined today to say whether the United States was con-

Continued on Page 15, Column 3

SAIGON REDS LOOK TO NONALIGNMENT

Regime, in Paris Statement, Also Pledges to Protect Lives of Foreigners

By FLORA LEWIS
Special to The New York Times

PARIS, April 30—The war in Vietnam is over, the Provisional Revolutionary Government said here today in a statement hailing "a victory of historic significance for the South Vietnamese population."

The statement, which followed the surrender of Saigon to the Vietnamese Communists

Text of statement issued in Paris is on Page 14.

early today, said the new South Vietnamese regime would follow a foreign policy of "peace and nonalignment," and gave assurances that the lives and property of foreigners in the country would be protected.

The statement was issued by Dinh Ba Thi, the head of the South Vietnamese Communist delegation here that was established under the 1973 Paris agreement to negotiate a political solution with the Government of President Nguyen Van Thieu.

"Henceforth," the statement said, "South Vietnam is free and independent. The sacred testament of our beloved President Ho Chi Minh is realized."

No details were issued here

Continued on Page 14, Column 5

Associated Press

Marines carrying children who were rescued when a copter carrying them from Vietnam crashed on deck of U.S.S. Blue Ridge, command ship, Tuesday. All were saved.

Thieu Aide Discloses Promises Of Force by Nixon to Back Pact

By BERNARD GWERTZMAN
Special to The New York Times

WASHINGTON, April 30—A former Saigon Cabinet official made public today letters from President Richard M. Nixon that promised the Saigon Government in 1972 and 1973 that the United States would "take swift and severe retaliatory action" and would "respond with full force" if North Vietnam violated the Paris cease-fire accords.

This was believed the first disclosure of any such actual

Texts of letters released by former minister, Page 16.

correspondence between Mr. Nixon and former President Nguyen Van Thieu of South Vietnam. The White House conceded earlier this month that there had been letters between the leaders as part of an exchange surrounding the signing of the 1973 cease-fire.

An aide of Secretary of State Kissinger said at that time that in one letter before the signing, Mr. Nixon had promised that the United States would react to a major Communist attack, but that the former President had not been specific.

The contents of the letters made public by Nguyen Tien Hung, former Minister of Planning, seemed more specific about the possible use of American retaliatory military force than the White House indicated initially earlier this month when the matter of secret assurances" to Saigon first became an issue.

Coincidentally with Mr. Hung's disclosures, at a crowded news conference in the Mayflower Hotel, President Ford formally refused to give Con-

Continued on Page 16, Column 1

Ford Delays Oil Fee Rise, But Will End Price Curbs

President Again Prods Congress to Act on Energy—Democrats Expected to Fight 2-Year Phase-Out of Controls

By EDWARD COWAN
Special to The New York Times

WASHINGTON, April 30—In another prod to Congress to enact comprehensive energy legislation, the White House announced today that President Ford was again deferring an increase in the special fee on imported crude oil but that he was starting an administrative process that could end all price controls on domestic crude oil in two years.

The move to phase out the remaining controls on crude oil prices was expected to provoke new frictions between the Republican President and some Democrats in Congress.

However, the White House left open the possibility that Mr. Ford might sign legislation that would extend the decontrol period to three and a half or four years, if Congress wrote such a provision into an energy bill otherwise acceptable to the President. The Administration plan, as outlined at a White House news briefing by Frank G. Zarb, Federal Energy Administrator, is to reduce the volume of price-controlled crude oil by about 4 per cent a month for two years. Presumably, the present average ceiling price on oil still under controls would remain unchanged at $5.25 a barrel.

Mr. Zarb said that this plan might go into effect as early as June 1. It could cause the price of a gallon of gasoline to rise by 1.25 cents every six months, or five cents in two years, Mr. Zarb said.

The White House announcement came at the end of a 60-day truce between Mr. Ford and Congress that began when the President delayed for two

Continued on Page 29, Column 1

Amtrak, at Age of 4, Still Problem-Ridden

By RALPH BLUMENTHAL

Amtrak executives and a Federal judge riding the Metroliner from Washington to New York recently for a hearing on rail passenger problems, including train delays, inadvertently became prime exhibits when they got stuck behind a slow-moving freight train and pulled in 35 minutes late.

A week later, some of the same Amtrak officials taking the Broadway Limited to Chicago for another of the hearings arrived an hour and a half late after a burning coal from the kitchen stove set the dining car afire before the train ever left Penn Station.

As it marks its fourth birthday today, Amtrak, the country's seminationalized rail passenger system, remains plagued by embarrassing mishaps and breakdowns that have embroiled it in controversy with the Interstate Commerce Commission over the quality its service.

Over the last two months, scores of disgruntled Amtrak riders have appeared at I.C.C. hearings around the country to complain about a wide range of problems from broken air-conditioning to vermin infestation to surly train personnel.

The hearings have dismayed and angered Amtrak officials, who have charged the commission with seeking to divert attention from its own critics and complained that the bad publicity has already cost Am-

Continued on Page 37, Column 1

Legislature Votes U.D.C. $228-Million

By LINDA GREENHOUSE
Special to The New York Times

ALBANY, April 30—The Legislature voted tonight to give the Urban Development Corporation $88-million and to lend it $140-million as the state's part of a delicate agreement with the major commercial banks to make it possible for the insolvent agency to repay its debts and finish its building programs.

Tonight's action, which the two houses took with obvious reluctance at the end of a day of partisan wrangling, was the price that the 11 clearing-house banks had set for their willingness to lend the U.D.C. $140-million. That loan is due to be

Continued on Page 44, Column 2

The New York Times/Neal Boenzi

1975 MEETS 18TH CENTURY IN WALL STREET: Frank Malora, dressed as a town crier for re-enactment of Washington's inaugural at Federal Hall National Memorial, preparing to announce the event as a young woman in 20th-century garb passed. A report, Page 45.

FARMERS' PRICES UP 4%, IMPLYING RETAIL RISE SOON

Cattle and Hogs Are Among Main Items That Climbed in Month Ended April 15

By WILLIAM ROBBINS
Special to The New York Times

WASHINGTON, April 30—Prices of farm commodities rose 4 per cent in the month ended April 15, the Agriculture Department reported today. A top departmental economist noted that the increase was focused largely in areas where it would be most quickly reflected at the retail counter.

Increased prices for cattle and hogs were among the main reasons for the rising average. Cotton, soybeans and grains also gained.

"Price changes for cattle and hogs come through to the retail counter pretty fast," C. Kyle Randall, administrator of the Agriculture Department's economic research service, said, but he added that the rise had been expected.

The increase reversed a five-month slide in farmers' prices. The April 15 level was still 8.1 per cent below the average of last October, before the decline began, and 7 per cent below the level of a year ago.

Outlook Unchanged

Mr. Randall said the farm-price rise would not change Agriculture Department economists' assessment of the outlook for food prices.

"Our original forecast was an increase in livestock prices in the second quarter," he said, "but we are standing by our prediction that retail prices from the first to the second quarter won't rise as much as they did from the fourth to the first quarter."

He said retail prices were expected to rise "something less than 2 per cent" in the second quarter. The increase in the first quarter was 2 per cent.

Coincidentally, the turn in farm prices comes at a time when President Ford is expected momentarily to veto a bill to support farm prices and provide income protection for farmers.

Action in Congress

The long slide in farm prices had helped stimulate the movement in Congress for the farm bill, which would increase both "target prices" and price-support loans for cotton and grains and price supports for dairy products.

Target prices set off subsidy payments when market prices fall below the target level. The price-support loans enable farmers to withhold products when market prices are weak.

House farm-bloc leaders have already described the prospects

Continued on Page 56, Column 7

$104,000 Damages And Former Job Won By College Teacher

By WALTER H. WAGGONER
Special to The New York Times

FREEHOLD, N. J., April 30—A judge ordered today that Brookdale Community College reinstate a journalism professor who had criticized the college president, and that the college president and six trustees each pay her $10,000 in punitive damages.

The teacher, Patricia Endress, was awarded a total of $104,000 in damages and lawyers' fees.

"Punitive damages are absolutely necessary to impress people in authority that an employe's constitutional rights cannot be infringed," said Judge Merritt Lane in Superior Court here.

Last June 27, three days before Miss Endress would have gained tenure, the college's board of trustees voted to ter-

Continued on Page 28, Column 4

NEWS INDEX

	Page		Page
Books	39	Music	48-50
Bridge	38	Notes on People	47
Business	56-71	Obituaries	44
Chess	38	Op-Ed	41
Crossword	39	Sports	51-56
Editorials	40	Theaters	48-50
Family/Style	46	Transportation	81
Financial	56-71	TV and Radio	82-83
Going Out Guide	48	U.N. Proceedings	2
Movies	48-50	Weather	81

News Summary and Index, Page 43

"All the News That's Fit to Print"

The New York Times

LATE CITY EDITION

Weather: Becoming cloudy today; rain likely tonight and tomorrow. Temperature range: today 58-73; Wednesday 59-80. Details, Page 86.

VOL. CXXIV . No. 42,845 | NEW YORK, THURSDAY, MAY 15, 1975 | Price higher in air delivery cities. | 20 CENTS

U.S. FREES CAMBODIAN-HELD SHIP AND CREW; MARINES STORM ISLAND, SUFFER CASUALTIES; PLANES HIT AIRFIELD, SINK 3 PATROL BOATS

Ford Rejects a Plea By Beame for Help

President Calls for Reliance on State

By FRED FERRETTI

Special to The New York Times

WASHINGTON, May 14 — President Ford, asserting that a federally guaranteed loan to New York City "would provide no real solution," tonight turned down the city's plea for the $1.5-billion in cash it says it needs for its expenses through June 30.

In a letter that began "Dear Abe," read by an aide over the telephone to Mayor Beame and Governor Carey as they attended the Democratic dinner tonight at the Waldorf-Astoria Hotel and released by the White House shortly before 9 P.M., the President said:

Text of the President's letter appears on Page 38.

"I believe that the proper place for any requests for backing and guarantee is to the State of New York."

Despite the President's decision, Congressional leaders said they would continue to work for some kind of Federal loan guarantee or bond purchase by the Federal Reserve System to help the city avoid having to sell additional securities in an increasingly reluctant commercial money market. But they conditioned support on economies by the city and aid from the state and banks.

Mr. Beame has said repeatedly that he was "optimistically" counting on the Federal

Continued on Page 38, Column 1

Carey and Mayor Express Anger

By FRANK LYNN

Governor Carey and Mayor Beame reacted angrily last night to President Ford's rejection of Federal assistance to New York City, with the Governor declaring that "we didn't even get 30 pieces of silver."

The Governor declared, at a Brooklyn Democratic dinner at the Waldorf-Astoria Hotel, that the President's move showed "a level of arrogance and disregard for New York that rivals the worst days of Richard Nixon and his gang of cutthroats."

"Have they no heart? Have they no understanding of our problems? Must a city riot?" the Governor said before an audience of 2,300 Brooklyn Democrats who had been prepared for a routine political dinner speech.

The Governor and the Mayor had been called out from the dinner to take telephone calls from aides who had been notified by the White House of President Ford's decision.

Mr. Carey, the principal speaker at the dinner, began his speech with the traditional references to his Brooklyn background and the praise of various Brooklyn Democrats, but he soon began a stump-style attack on "this Republican Administration, the Ford and Rockefeller Administration."

"The Mayor and I were not elected to be participants in

Continued on Page 39, Column 3

VIOLENCE IN LAOS

U.S. Offices in 2 Cities Are Ransacked and 3 Americans Seized

By DAVID A. ANDELMAN

Special to The New York Times

VIENTIANE, Laos, May 14—Anti-American demonstrators ransacked United States mission buildings in the cities of Luang Prabang and Savannakhet today, and embassy officials here said that as a result, the evacuation of Americans scheduled to leave later in the year would begin at once.

At Savannakhet, in central Laos, three American employes of the United States Agency for International Development were reportedly seized during the demonstrations and held in the home of the provincial governor.

[The Americans happened to be in the governor's home and were taken by rioters who burst in, Reuters reported. They were identified as Sanford J. Stone, the agency's director for central Laos; Daniel P. Ster, an economic affairs officer, and Charles R. Pearcy, a property management aide.]

Here in Vientiane, the American chargé d'affaires, Christian A. Chapman, filed a formal protest with the Laotian Government headed by Prince Souvanna Phouma and demanded police protection for Americans and American installations.

Pathet Lao's Gains

The Communist-led Pathet Lao, which shares the coalition Government with Vientiane rightists but has been growing substantially in power in recent weeks, has for some time been calling for the removal of Americans from provincial areas. But the leftists have stopped short of demanding a full pullout of the American aid program, which has amounted to $27-million a year. A.I.D. administers American foreign aid abroad.

According to United States Embassy officials here and to witnesses in the two Laotian cities, the ransacking was done by crowds of students.

In the royal capital of Luang Prabang, in north-central Laos, students entered the Agency for International Development compound and broke windows, smashed desks and threw typewriters out of the building.

In Savannakhet, students marched on that city's A.I.D. compound. As they reached the walls, the mission's radio transmitter failed, cutting off the compound from the outside world. Communications remained cut through the night.

American Embassy officials in Vientiane said it was be-

Continued on Page 17, Column 1

Associated Press

President Ford sitting between Carl Albert of Oklahoma, left, Speaker of the House, and Mike Mansfield of Montana, Senate majority leader, at a meeting with a Congressional delegation on the dispute with Cambodia. The meeting was held at the White House.

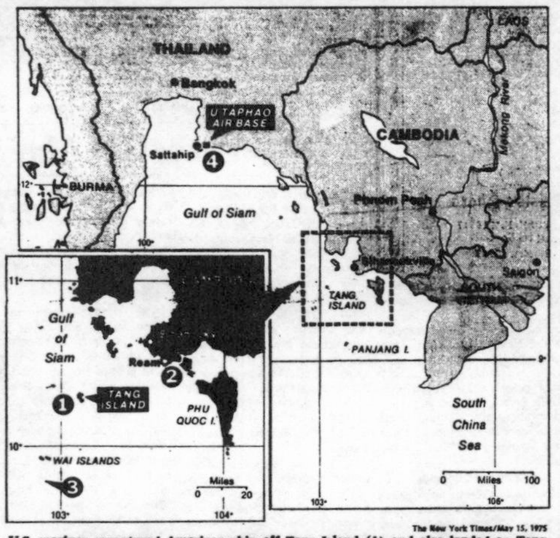

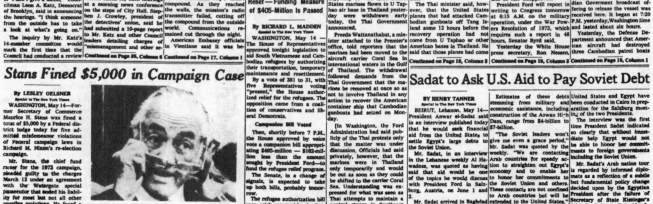

The New York Times/May 15, 1975

U.S. marines recaptured American ship off Tang Island (1) and also landed on Tang. American planes attacked airfield at Ream (2). U.S. ship had been seized off Wai (3). Marines flown by U.S. to Thai base (4) were removed to a carrier.

FORD IS BACKED

Senate Unit Endorses His Right to Order Military Action

By PHILIP SHABECOFF

Special to The New York Times

WASHINGTON, May 14—The White House said tonight that President Ford had consulted with Congressional leaders both before ordering the recapture of the merchant vessel Mayagüez and before ordering the sinking earlier today of Cambodian patrol boats.

At least some of the leaders later insisted, however, that they had not been consulted but merely informed of Presidential decisions already taken.

However, members of Congress generally expressed approval of the President's action and the Senate Foreign Relations Committee adopted a strong resolution of support this evening acknowledging the President's constitutional right to order military operations.

After a meeting at the White House tonight between the President and a bipartisan delegation of Congressional leaders, Robert C. Byrd of West Virginia, the Senate Democratic whip, reported that the President had been criticized by some of the leaders for his handling of the consultation process.

Senator Byrd said: "I certainly approve of the effort to take the ship and to land marines on the island."

Some Concern Voiced

There were "some expressions of concern" voiced by some of the leaders over the President's handling of the decision-making process, including the fact that the leadership of Congress had not been brought in on the process, Mr. Byrd told reporters. He said he shared in that concern.

Senator Byrd said that the concern was over what he characterized as "the failure to ask at least some of the leaders to participate in the decision-making process," even though the President was not required to take such action.

Late tonight, the White House reported that immediate public response to today's military action, including the marine assault, was overwhelmingly in support of the President. The White House said that by 10:30 P.M. 778 telephone calls approved the President's actions and 98 had disapproved.

President Ford will report in writing to Congress tomorrow at 6:15 A.M. on the military operation, under the War Powers Resolution of 1973, which requires such a report in 48 hours, Senator Byrd said.

Yesterday the White House press secretary, Ron Nessen,

Continued on Page 18, Column 3

3 COPTERS LOST

President, on TV After Midnight, Hails Valor of Servicemen

By JOHN W. FINNEY

Special to The New York Times

WASHINGTON, Thursday, May 15—U.S. forces have recaptured the American merchant vessel Mayagüez, which the Cambodian Communists seized Monday, President Ford announced early today.

He said all 39 crew members had been rescued.

The President, who said he had ordered the operation last night, announced its results in a brief statement shortly after midnight. He praised the valor of the sailors and marines who took part. He said that some were still "under hostile fire" and indicated that they would be withdrawn from combat shortly.

Ford's statement on Cambodian rescue, Page 18.

As part of the operation, marines stormed Tang Island, where they suffered what were described as "light" casualties. No deaths were confirmed. Three helicopters were lost on the beaches, a Pentagon spokesman said, either from ground fire or mechanical failure.

Carrier-based fighter-bombers attacked the Ream airfield and a naval base in the area of Sihanoukville on the Cambodian mainland.

Confusion in Capitol

In the confused situation here this morning, it was not clear whether the bomb attack would have taken place had Mr. Ford known that the Cambodian vessel was prepared to turn over 30 of the Mayagüez crewmen.

The President met early last night with Congresional leaders. This morning the White House press secretary, Ron Nessen, said Mr. Ford would formally report to Congress today on the military operations.

Of the 39 crew members, 30 were delivered by a small Cambodian vessel flying a white flag to an American destroyer. How or where the other nine were found could not be learned at once.

The military operation was undertaken, according to American officials, about an hour before word of a Cambodian Goverment broadcast offering to release the vessel was received here. It began at 7:20 P.M. yesterday, Washington time and lasted about six hours.

Yesterday, the Defense Department announced that American aircraft had destroyed three Cambodian patrol boats

Continued on Page 18, Column 1

City Council Plans Inquiry On Effectiveness of Police

By SELWYN RAAB

Disturbed by reports of breakdowns in police administration and poor morale, the chairman of the City Council's Committee on Public Safety announced yesterday that hearings would be held soon on the operations of New York's 30,000-member Police Department.

"There seems to be a growing attitude within the department of 'I don't give a damn,'" Councilman Leon A. Katz, Democrat of Brooklyn, said in announcing the hearings. "I think someone from the outside has to take a look at what's going on."

The inquiry by Mr. Katz's 14-member committee would mark the first time that the Council had conducted a review of the city's police force and its effectiveness. Mr. Katz, who together with a committee staff member has been looking into police procedures for the last month, said he expected the public hearings would be held during the summer.

Union Calls for Inquiry

The councilman's announcement came shortly after the Detectives' Endowment Association called for such hearings at a morning news conference on the steps of City Hall. Stephen J. Crowley, president of the detectives' union, said he had submitted a 10-page report to Mr. Katz and other Council leaders detailing charges of "mismanagement and other se-

Continued on Page 35, Column 6

Stans Fined $5,000 in Campaign Case

By LESLEY OELSNER

Special to The New York Times

WASHINGTON, May 14—Former Secretary of Commerce Maurice H. Stans was fined a total of $5,000 by a Federal district judge today for five admitted misdemeanor violations of Federal campaign laws in Richard M. Nixon's re-election campaign.

Mr. Stans, the chief fund raiser for the 1972 campaign, pleaded guilty to the charges March 12 under an agreement with the Watergate special prosecutor that ended his liability for most but not all other possible violations. He faced a possible maximum term under the arrangement of either two or five years in prison, depending on how the statutes were interpreted.

This morning, in a brief hearing at the United States Courthouse, he pleaded for "understanding and leniency," insisting that he did not "intentionally violate any law."

Judge John Lewis Smith Jr. granted the request, saying that, because of a number of factors, including Mr. Stans's "long public and private career," a "monetary penalty" was punishment enough.

Later, outside the court, Mr. Stans said to reporters that Judge Smith's action showed that the court recognized that his violations of the law had not been intentional.

He contended, too, that he had been "fully exonerated of any improper activities in connection with Watergate and its aftermath," and that with today's proceedings he had

Continued on Page 24, Column 4

Associated Press

Maurice H. Stans leaving court in Washington yesterday

HOUSE APPROVES REFUGEE AID BILLS

Votes 381 to 31 to Authorize Relief — Funding Measure of $405-Million Is Passed

By RICHARD L. MADDEN

Special to The New York Times

WASHINGTON, May 14 — The House of Representatives approved tonight legislation to aid South Vietnamese and Cambodian refugees by authorizing their transportation, temporary maintenance and resettlement.

By a vote of 381 to 31, with five Representatives voting "present," the House authorized relief for the refugees. The opposition came from a coalition of conservatives and liberal Democrats.

Companion Bill Voted

Then, shortly before 7 P.M., the House approved by voice vote a companion bill appropriating $405-million — $102-million less than the amount sought by President Ford—to fund the refugee relief program.

The Senate, in a change of signals, is expected to take up both bills, probably tomorrow.

The refugee authorization bill won quick approval by the Senate Foreign Relations Committee two days ago, but the chairman of a Senate appropriations subcommittee, Senator Daniel K. Inouye, Democrat of Hawaii, proposed yesterday to delay approval of the spending bill until next week to obtain

Continued on Page 15, Column 1

Thais Report Withdrawal Of Marines After Protest

By Reuters

BANGKOK, Thailand, Thursday, May 15—All 1,100 United States marines flown to U Taphao air base in Thailand yesterday were withdrawn early today, the Thai Government announced.

Preeda Wattanathabut, a minister attached to the Premier's office, told reporters that the marines had been moved to the aircraft carrier Coral Sea in international waters in the Gulf of Thailand. The withdrawal followed demands from the Thai Government that the marines be removed at once so as not to involve Thailand in any action to recover the American container ship that Cambodian gunboats had seized on Monday.

[In Washington, the Ford Administration had said publicly of the Thai protests only that the matter was under discussion. Officials had said privately, however, that the marines were in Thailand only temporarily and would be out as soon as they could be shifted to the carrier Coral Sea. Understanding was expressed for what was seen as Thai attempts to maintain a neutral stance in Southeast Asia.]

Participation Uncertain

The announcement that the United States marines had left U Taphao followed the disclosure that American marines had recaptured the cargo ship Mayagüez as it lay at anchor off Tang Island, 30 miles from the Cambodian mainland. It was not known here whether any of the newly departed marines had participated in that operation.

The Thai minister said, however, that the United States planes that had attacked Cambodian gunboats off Tang Island some 12 hours before the recovery operation had not come from U Taphao or other American bases in Thailand. He said that those planes had come

Continued on Page 18, Column 3

Sadat to Ask U.S. Aid to Pay Soviet Debt

BY HENRY TANNER

Special to The New York Times

BEIRUT, Lebanon, May 14—President Anwar el-Sadat said in an interview published today that he would seek financial aid from the United States to settle Egypt's large debts to the Soviet Union.

Mr. Sadat, in an interview in the Lebanese weekly Al Hawadess, was quoted as having said that aid would be one of the topics he would discuss with President Ford in Salzburg, Austria, on June 1 and 2.

Mr. Sadat arrived in Baghdad tonight from Kuwait, where he spent three days in conversations with Emir Sabah al-Salem al-Sabah, the Kuwaiti ruler. Mr. Sadat will visit Jordan and Syria before returning to Cairo early next week.

In the interview, President Sadat reiterated his frequent complaint that the Soviet leaders had refused to agree to requests for a rescheduling of Egypt's debts.

Estimates of these debts stemming from military and economic assistance, including construction of the Aswan High Dam, range from $4-billion to $7-billion.

"The Soviet leaders won't give me even a grace period," Mr. Sadat was quoted by the weekly. "We are contacting Arab countries for speedy action to straighten out Egypt's economy and to enable her to honor her commitments to the Soviet Union and others. These contacts are not confined to Arab countries but will be extended to the United States."

Financial talks between the United States and Egypt have been conducted in Cairo in preparation for the Salzburg meeting of the two Presidents.

The interview was the first time President Sadat indicated so clearly that without immediate help Egypt would not be able to honor her commitments to foreign governments including the Soviet Union.

Mr. Sadat's Arab nation tour is regarded by informed diplomats as a reflection of a subtle but fundamental policy change decided upon by the Egyptian President after the failure of Secretary of State Kissinger's "shuttle diplomacy" in March.

For the last 18 months, since Mr. Kissinger's first visit to Cairo after the war in October, 1973, Mr. Sadat has been acting with deliberate independence as far as other Arab leaders were concerned.

Now, while still relying on the United States as the key to the Middle East conflict, Mr. Sadat has resolved to operate

Continued on Page 4, Column 3

NEWS INDEX

"All the News That's Fit to Print"

The New York Times

LATE CITY EDITION

Weather: Rain ending today; cool tonight. Fair and mild tomorrow. Temperature range: today 58-69; Thursday 62-78. Details on Page 74.

VOL. CXXIV . . . No. 42,846 — © 1975 The New York Times Company — NEW YORK, FRIDAY, MAY 16, 1975 — Price higher in air delivery cities. — 20 CENTS

COPTERS EVACUATE U.S. MARINES AND SHIP-RESCUE MISSION ENDS; TOLL INCLUDES ONE KNOWN DEAD

United Press International from the Department of Defense

U.S. marines moving out on Tang Island after landing by copter yesterday to take the Mayagüez and crew

OPERATION HAILED

Schlesinger Asserts It Affirmed Freedom of the High Seas

By JOHN W. FINNEY

Special to The New York Times

WASHINGTON, May 15 — Under the cover of aerial and naval gunfire, 200 marines were lifted by helicopters today off an island in the Gulf of Siam, completing the military rescue of an American merchant ship and crew that had been seized by Cambodian forces.

Officials at the Pentagon said casualties in the 14-hour operation appeared to have

The text of President's letter is printed on Page 15.

been light, despite the sometimes stiff resistance encountered on Tang Island.

Pentagon sources said one marine and one Air Force man had been killed and eight marines and six Air Force helicopter crewmen were missing. But a Defense Department spokesman said that thus far there had been only one verified casualty—a marine killed by small-arms fire on the island.

Wounded Being Treated

In addition, an unspecified number of wounded were being treated aboard Navy ships.

President Ford's use of military power to rescue the merchant ship Mayagüez and its 39-man crew, which had been seized by Cambodian patrol craft on Monday, drew general praise from members of Congress. There was some criticism that Mr. Ford should have consulted more with Congress before ordering the operation.

Acting in compliance with a provision of the War Powers Resolution that requires the President to report to the Congress within 48 hours of the initial commitment of troops to hostilities, Mr. Ford sent a letter to representatives of Carl Albert, Speaker of the House of Representatives, and James O. Eastland, president pro tempore of the Senate, at about 2:30 A.M. today. Congressional leaders had received White House briefings earlier.

Schlesinger Lauds Move

Defense Secretary James R. Schlesinger, at an early-morning news conference at the Pentagon, described the rescue as "an eminently successful operation incorporating the judicious and effective use of American force for purposes that were necessary for the well-being of this society."

In a statement, Mr. Schlesinger said the operation "represents a much needed and timely reaffirmation of the freedom of the seas."

"Moreover, it represents a firm and measured response to the high-handed and crude use of force," he added. "To countenance such an act would mean the weakening of international order and civilized communication."

Privately, key Administra-

Continued on Page 14, Column 5

CAMBODIANS TELL WHY THEY YIELDED

Official Declares 'Our Weak Country' Could Not Afford Confrontation With U.S.

By Reuters

BANGKOK, Thailand, May 15—The Cambodian Government said today that it had decided to let the American merchant ship Mayagüez go because "our weak country cannot have a confrontation with the U.S.A."

In a broadcast over the Phnom Penh radio, monitored here, Information Minister Hu Nim accused the United States of systematic spying on Cam-

Text of Cambodia communiqué will be found on Page 15.

bodia since the Communists took over on April 17. He said the Mayagüez, which was captured last Monday, was only one of several spy vessels seized in the Gulf of Siam.

The minister asserted that the Cambodians had captured several ships "camouflaged as fishing boats and handled by Thai and Khmer crews" in waters near the port of Sihanoukville and near small Cambodian islands in the Gulf of Siam.

"These crews admitted," the minister said, "that they were agents of the C.I.A. who had to establish contact with other agents in hiding on Cambodian soil."

Mr. Hu Nim said that these vessels had moved to within a mile of the Cambodian mainland and that at times their

Continued on Page 15, Column 5

Praise for the President

Domestic and Foreign Triumph Is Seen As U. S. Reasserts Its Presence Abroad

By JAMES M. NAUGHTON

Special to The New York Times

News Analysis

WASHINGTON, May 15—By nearly every measure President Ford's military venture in the Gulf of Siam was being evaluated here today as a diplomatic and domestic political triumph. The merchant ship Mayagüez, steaming once more through Southeast Asian waters, serves as a visible symbol of United States resolve to remain an influence—and, if necessary, a military presence—abroad despite the recent debacle in Indochina.

Democrats in Congress who expect their party to elect the successor to Mr. Ford in 1976 termed his actions right and accorded him high marks for leadership. Republican conservatives who had begun questioning his capacity declared him, in the words of one, "a man who knows how to act."

The President's decision to use marines, warships and military aircraft to retrieve the crew and recover the Mayagüez from their Cambodian captors was, White House officials acknowledged, a calculated gamble with a broad purpose.

The military operation was mounted without any certainty on the whereabouts of the captive seamen and with no guarantee that the broad goal of demonstrating United States resolve for worried allies or potentially capricious opponents would be buttressed by the rescue. The real test, a White House aide said when the outcome was still in doubt yesterday, would be how many of the 39 crew members were saved.

All were. That the crew was surrendered by a small boat flying a white pennant rather than rescued by the marine landing forces did not diminish the belief here that pluck had been more responsible than luck.

'I'm Glad It Worked'

"It worked," said Senator Robert C. Byrd of West Virginia, the Senate Democratic whip. "I'm glad it worked. It's certainly a plus for the country. It will strengthen our prestige throughout the world."

Administration officials, including Secretary of State Kissinger and Secretary of Defense James R. Schlesinger, were said to have been eager to find some dramatic means of underscoring President Ford's stated intention to "maintain our leadership on a worldwide basis."

The occasion came with the capture of the vessel. While Administration officials emphasized that the first objective of the rescue operation was to save the American crew, they made it clear that they welcomed the opportunity to show that Mr. Ford had the will and the means to use

Continued on Page 15, Column 4

TIMING OF ATTACK RAISES QUESTIONS

Drive Said to Be On at Time Ford Heard Cambodians Would Free the Ship

By R. W. APPLE Jr.

Special to The New York Times

WASHINGTON, May 15—The American attack in the Gulf of Siam was already in progress, according to official accounts, when President Ford received word that the Cambodian Government was willing to release the American merchant vessel Mayagüez and its crew of 39.

But there remains considerable confusion as to the reasons why air strikes were carried out on the Cambodian mainland at almost the moment the crew members were approaching an American destroyer in a small fishing boat.

The sequence of events that unfolded last night and early this morning over and off the coast of Cambodia, and at the White House and Pentagon, was still not completely clear late today.

But a careful reconstruction, based on interviews with American officials, as well as public briefings, yielded the following picture:

Since the capture Monday of the Mayagüez, a container ship, by Cambodian forces, diplomatic initiatives had evoked no response. Indeed, the White House press secretary, Ron Nessen, said this morning, Mr. Ford not only had no idea what

Continued on Page 14, Column 1

White House Photograph/David Hume Kennerly

President Ford, at desk, getting a telephone report from Defense Secretary James R. Schlesinger on action to recapture the Mayagüez. Secretary of State Kissinger, left, listens on extension. Center, Robert McFarland, of the National Security Council staff, talks with Donald H. Rumsfeld, Presidential assistant. Scene is Oval Office.

United Brands Bribe Linked to Honduran

By The Associated Press

A Honduran commission reported last night that former Economics Minister Abraham Bennaton Ramos was the official who received a $1.2-million bribe from the United Brands Company to lower a banana export tax.

Initial reports last month had named the chief of state, Gen. Oswaldo Lopez Arellano, as the recipient of the payoff, and he was subsequently overthrown in a bloodless coup.

In Costa Rica, President Daniel Oduber gave United Brands until noon today to disclose which Costa Rican officials it paid bribes to or lose its banana operations.

The multinational company,

Continued on Page 53, Column 3

G.O.P. in Albany Rejects Beame's 640-Million Plea

United Press International

Governor Carey and Mayor Beame at a news session in Albany yesterday. They urged Warren M. Anderson, Senate Republican leader, to alter stand against aid to city.

Special to The New York Times

ALBANY, May 15—The New York State Senate Republican leaders rejected today a renewed plea by Mayor Beame for a $640-million package of aid and taxes to finance next year's municipal budget.

The Senate majority leader, Warren M. Anderson, said the city's "real problem" was a loss of investor confidence that was the legacy of "trick-or-treat municipal budgetry." To restore that confidence, he said, the city must balance its budgets with existing revenues, cut costs and "stop trying to deliver more services than it can afford to give."

In a joint statement of response, however, Mayor Beame and Governor Carey said the cuts suggested by Mr. Anderson "will seriously jeopardize the social stability of eight million people and will . . . place the safety and health of the citizens at risk."

The New York Times/Ray Hoy

Senator Anderson tells of opposition to aiding city.

And they said the State Senate Republicans and President Ford were "driving a great city into default" by denying it help in meeting its immediate cash-flow problems.

The President had announced last night his rejection of the city's bid for a Federal loan guarantee to let it meet its bills in the next six weeks without having to try to borrow the funds in commercial money markets.

Two groups of banks in New York City said, meanwhile, that they were trying to find investors willing to bid on the $280-million of notes the city has scheduled for sale Monday. Underwriters, however, said they doubted they would bid. [Page 18.]

Senator Anderson delivered his rejection to Mayor Beame in a face-to-face meeting over a glass-topped conference table in the Red Room of the Capitol.

The $640-million package the Mayor had asked for would be "counterproductive," he said, in part because of its effects on the financial community.

Mr. Beame, who hardly ever uses profanity, slammed his

Continued on Page 18, Column 1

Simon Says a City Default Would Not Hurt Economy

By JOHN DARNTON

Secretary of the Treasury William E. Simon said yesterday that he had conducted an "analysis" of what the effects would be if New York City defaulted on its obligations, and concluded that the impact on the national economy would be "negligible."

"There would obviously be a psychological effect," said Mr. Simon. "But it's difficult to judge." He emphasized repeatedly that default was "not the single option open to the city," saying it could instead adopt stern austerity measures and secure financial aid from the state.

In the unsuccessful negotiations with President Ford and Mr. Simon and other Federal monetary officials for $1-billion in assistance to the city, Governor Carey and Mayor Beame have asserted that a default would have disastrous consequences—for the municipal bond market, the major New York banks and the national economy.

Mr. Simon's comments came during a news conference at the Waldorf - Astoria Hotel, where he attended a business group luncheon. He used the occasion to outline the Ford Administration's position in refusing the assistance point by point, as if to refute some of the denunciations delivered the night before by the Mayor and Governor Carey in the ballroom next door.

Governor Carey, for example, told an assembled throng of Brooklyn Democrats on Wednesday that the President's decision showed "a level of ar-

Continued on Page 18, Column 3

2,000 Telephone Workers Face a 4-Day Week Here

By DAMON STETSON

The New York Telephone Company is planning to put 2,000 of its 5,800 telephone operators in the five boroughs on a four-day work week at four days' pay beginning July because of a drop in business.

John Nicholson, an assistant vice president of the company, said the alternative would have been layoffs of 400 operators.

A spokesman for the Telephone Traffic Union, representing the operators, said the union felt a four-day work week, with health and welfare benefits continuing, was preferable to the layoffs.

The company's work volume has been decreasing for some time, Mr. Nicholson said, partly because of the state of the economy and partly because of increased mechanization, with customers doing more of their own dialing.

The number of operators employed in the city has dropped through attrition from 11,500 in 1970 to 5,800 now. The decision to place the 2,000 operators on the four-day week was the first such step taken in recent years by the company.

Continued on Page 21, Column 1

NEWS INDEX

FEDERAL RESERVE CUTS RATE TO 6%; OUTPUT DECLINES

Move Is First Overt Step to Easier Money Since March—Production Drop Slight

Special to The New York Times

WASHINGTON, May 15 — The Federal Reserve Board announced today a reduction in its discount rate to 6 per cent from 6¼ per cent — its first overt move toward easier money since early March.

The announcement came shortly after the board reported that industrial production continued to decline in April, but by a much smaller rate than in the preceding months of deepening recession.

The April decline was only four-tenths of 1 per cent, partly reflecting a temporary revival of automobile production last month. The slackening rate of decline in this key economic indicator was taken by officials as another sign that the recession may be nearing bottom.

Other Rates Cited

The announcement by the Reserve of the discount-rate reduction said, "The action was taken in recognition of declines that have occurred recently in other short-term interest rates and is intended to bring the discount rate into better alignment with short-term rates generally."

Changes in the discount rate — the interest rate at which the Federal Reserve lends to member banks in need of temporary funds — do not necessarily lead to changes in other interest rates. This reduction appears to be one of the many cases where the discount rate follows, rather than leads, in rate trends.

But today's announcement had the effect of "ratifying" earlier, unannounced Federal Reserve actions in the money market that have contributed in the last two weeks to a resumption of the downward trend in short-term interest rates following a period of stability, or even increases. Rates fell sharply from last August to early March and then tended to stabilize until the last two weeks.

A Contributing Factor

Another contributing factor to the recent downward movement in rates was the disclosure by the Treasury that it would need to borrow $5-billion less in the current half year than it had estimated earlier.

The last time the discount rate was as low as 6 per cent was early June, 1973. It reached a peak of 8 per cent in April, 1974, and has been reduced in five steps, starting last December, to its present level.

The report on industrial production put the production index for April, on a preliminary

Continued on Page 47, Column 7

Accord to Resolve Malpractice Issue Reached in Albany

By ALFONSO A. NARVAEZ

Special to The New York Times

ALBANY, May 15—Governor Carey and legislative leaders of both parties announced today that they had reached agreement on legislation designed to resolve the medical malpractice crisis facing physicians and hospitals in the state as a result of a decision by the major insurer to stop offering such coverage after June 30.

The proposal calls for the creation of a Medical Malpractice Underwriting Association consisting of the 300 private insurance companies offering personal liability insurance. This association would offer malpractice insurance and would compete with other insurance companies, including the Medical Liability Mutual Insurance Company now being formed by the State Medical Society.

In the event the assets of the underwriting company are exhausted and insurance is not available from the private sector, the state insurance fund

Continued on Page 11, Column 1

"All the News That's Fit to Print"

The New York Times

LATE CITY EDITION

Weather: Sunny and hot today; mild tonight. Partly sunny tomorrow. Temperature range: today 66-89; Monday 62-89. Details on page 77.

VOL. CXXV ... No. 43,333 | NEW YORK, TUESDAY, SEPTEMBER 14, 1976 | 20 CENTS

25 cents beyond 50-mile zone from New York City, except Long Island. Higher in air delivery cities.

The New York Times/William E. Sauro

Representative Bella S. Abzug and Daniel P. Moynihan, with his daughter, Mora, nearly crossed paths in the garment district as they held Senate campaign's final rallies. Also, in the closing hours of primary eve,

The New York Times/D. Gorton

Ramsey Clark planned to campaign all night winding up at the Fulton Fish Market at dawn. City Council President Paul O'Dwyer met with party backers and Abraham Hirschfeld spent the day at his campaign headquarters.

5 HIJACKERS CHARGED BY U.S. AS AIR PIRATES; MURDER COUNT ADDED

Defendants Queried About Dec. 29 Blast at La Guardia Airport—$1 Million Bail Set for Each

By PETER KIHSS

Four men and a woman who staged a 30-hour trans-Atlantic airliner hijacking to promote Croatian independence were held yesterday in New York in $1 million bail each on Federal air piracy charges and also were confronted with murder charges.

The murder complaint, filed in Criminal Court in Manhattan on orders of District Attorney Robert M. Morgenthau, charged them with "placing a live bomb" in the Grand Central subway station that later exploded at the police bomb range in the Bronx and killed Officer Brian J. Murray.

Questioned by the F.B.I.

And it was learned that the five defendants had been questioned about the La Guardia Airport bombing last Dec. 29 that killed 11 persons and injured 75.

Officials have declined to discuss any of the statements made by the defendants to Federal Bureau of Investigation agents and the New York police since the five hijackers were brought back by French security officials Sunday afternoon.

The explosive device that took the life of Officer Murray and seriously injured three other policemen while they were seeking to deactivate it was understood to have contained dynamite. As late as last month, the police here reported that the La Guardia bomb fragments were still being analyzed to establish the explosive involved.

Threat to Blow Up Plane

The weekend hijacking involved 86 passengers and seven crew members of a Trans World Airlines Boeing 727 that left La Guardia Airport Friday night for Chicago but was seized by the five defendants over Buffalo. The terrorists were armed with what later turned out to be make-believe bombs.

They forced the airliner to head for Montreal, and eventually Keflavik, Iceland; London and Paris, threatening to blow it up with all aboard unless lengthy demands for Croatian freedom were printed by The New York Times and other major newspapers.

A French ultimatum early Sunday ended the hijacking with none of the passengers or crew injured. The pilot, Capt. Richard W. Carey, said on his return to Kennedy Airport that it had been "30 hours of hell."

The hijackers, the 40-year-old pilot

Continued on Page 32, Column 1

United Press International

AFTER SOUTHERN VOTES: Jimmy Carter in Birmingham, Ala., with Gov. George C. Wallace. Page 28.

Bid to Grumman For Nixon Fund In '72 Is Charged

By SEYMOUR M. HERSH

Special to The New York Times

WASHINGTON, Sept. 13—The former head of a Grumman Corporation subsidiary told a Senate subcommittee today that a White House aide urged the company to contribute $1 million to the 1972 Republican re-election campaign in return for President Richard M. Nixon's "assistance" in arranging an aircraft sale to Japan.

Dr. Thomas B. Cheatham, the former president of Grumman International, said that the aide, Richard V. Allen, made the recommendation during a meeting in the Executive Office Building in April 1972, four months before Mr. Nixon held a summit meeting in Honolulu with Japan's Prime Minister, Kakeui Tanaka. At the time, Mr. Allen was deputy assistant to President Nixon for international economic affairs.

Dr. Cheatham, who left Grumman later in 1972 and now is a private consultant, told the Senate Foreign Relations Subcommittee on Multinational Corporations that he subsequently arranged some meetings between Mr. Allen and other Grumman officials. He did not know whether any contributions were, in fact,

Continued on Page 63, Column 1

U.S. DECIDES TO VETO VIETNAM'S REQUEST FOR U.N. MEMBERSHIP

SCRANTON DISCLOSES POSITION

Says Failure of Hanoi to Account for All Missing Americans Shows It Lacks Commitment to Peace

By JAMES M. NAUGHTON

Special to The New York Times

WASHINGTON, Sept. 13—President Ford directed the United States delegation today to veto Vietnam's application for membership in the United Nations.

The decision to block the application, disclosed here by William W. Scranton, the United States representative at the

Vietnamese statement and exchange of diplomatic notes, page 16.

United Nations, provoked an angry response from Vietnamese officials awaiting a meeting tomorrow of the Security Council's admissions committee.

Mr. Scranton said after meeting with the President that Hanoi's continued failure to make a full accounting of Americans still listed as missing in the Vietnam war showed that the Communist Government lacked the commitments to peace and humanitarianism necessary for membership in the General Assembly.

In a statement issued at United Nations headquarters, Vietnamese officials charged that President Ford's "real concern is not on American MIA's and their families but on the vote in this election campaign."

Confidential Notes Made Public

The Vietnamese, accusing the United States of "an arrogant and hostile policy," also made public confidential notes exchanged between Washington and Hanoi in an effort to renew negotiations to normalize diplomatic relations between the two capitals.

A White House spokesman said late today that "the publication of these confidential exchanges raises a question as to whether there was ever a serious willingness to negotiate."

Membership in the world body, requiring unanimous approval of the 15-member Security Council, was blocked last year by the United States when North Vietnam sought entry. The new application by the recently reunited Vietnam was to be considered at a meeting tomorrow of the Council's admissions committee, but the American position appeared to assure its ultimate rejection.

Mr. Scranton told reporters the veto decision was based solely on Hanoi's

Continued on Page 16, Column 1

Scientists Back New Aerosol Curbs To Protect Ozone in Atmosphere

By HAROLD M. SCHMECK Jr.

Special to The New York Times

WASHINGTON, Sept. 13—Some uses of fluorocarbon gases—the propellants commonly used in aerosol spray cans—will almost certainly have to be curtailed because the gases weaken the atmosphere's protective ozone layer, a committee of the National Academy of Sciences reported today.

The committee recommended a waiting period of no more than two years before regulatory action is taken so that some of the many uncertainties concerning the gases' effects can be resolved.

"Selective regulation of fluorocarbon uses and releases is almost certain to be necessary at some time and to some degree of completeness," the committee concluded. "Neither the needed timing nor the needed severity can be reasonably specified today."

The committee said research programs now under way promise to reduce the uncertainties in the near future.

Two Principal Worries

The ozone depletion is expected to occur slowly, because of the slow pace at which the gases find their way to the ozone level, which begins roughly 7 to 12 miles above the earth's surface and extends up to about 30 miles. Some molecules of the gases reach that altitude rapidly, some take a century, according to current estimates. They tend to rise to that level because the molecules are light and earth's atmosphere, both locally and globally, is constantly in motion moving and mixing its constituents.

There are two principal worries concerning the fluorocarbons. The first is that their weakening effect on the high-altitude ozone layer will allow more biologically active ultraviolet light to penetrate to earth's surface. This could increase the incidence of human skin cancer and harm plants and aniamls.

The other concern is that the gases may contribute to a trend toward warming of the earth's atmosphere with as yet unknown effects on climate.

Answering a question at a news conference today, Dr. John W. Tukey, chairman of the academy's Committee on Impacts

Continued on Page 27, Column 1

The New York Times/George Tames

Dr. John W. Tukey, chairman of committee, reviews ozone report.

DEMOCRATS WIND UP 5-WAY SENATE DRIVE

Light Vote Is Expected Today in 111 Races in New York State

By FRANK LYNN

Hours before the New York state primary polls opened, five Democratic contenders for the United States Senate wound up their campaigns last night as they had begun—debating nuances and images rather than substantive differences.

At the same time, on the Republican Senate primary front, Senator James L. Buckley, the Conservative-Republican incumbent, continued to ignore his challenger in the Republican primary, Representative Peter A. Peyser of Irvington, while Mr. Peyser, a liberal Republican, continued to argue that the incumbent's conservative voting record ran counter to the best interests of New Yorkers.

Most in New York City

The contests for the Senate nominations in both parties highlight a primary election in which voters throughout the state will also decide the outcome of 111 primary contests for Congressional, legislative and judicial nominations in the Democratic, Republican and Conservative Parties. All but 20 of the contests involve Democratic nominations, and almost all are in New York City.

New York is one of a dozen states—including Massachusetts, Rhode Island and Vermont—with Congressional and local primaries today. [Page 29.]

The polls will be open from 6 A.M. to 9 P.M. in New York City, and from noon to 9 P.M. outside the city. Only enrolled members of a party are entitled to vote in their party's primary.

An All-Night Effort

A light turnout of 25 percent or less is expected, based on recent primaries. A total of 3.7 million Democrats and 2.8 million Republicans are eligible to vote.

The five Democratic contenders—Representative Bella S. Abzug, Daniel P. Moynihan, Ramsey Clark, City Council President Paul O'Dwyer and Abraham Hirschfeld—essentially ended their campaigns with a 90-minute debate on a statewide public television network, Channel 13 locally.

However, Mr. Clark, in a departure from the usual campaign finales, planned to campaign throughout the night among night workers, winding up at the Fulton Fish Market at dawn.

The debate was one of the most

Continued on Page 30, Column 2

Chance of Averting a Ford Strike, Due at Midnight, Is Put at 1 in 100

By WILLIAM K. STEVENS

Special to The New York Times

DEARBORN, Mich., Sept. 13—It appeared all but certain today that the United Automobile Workers would strike the Ford Motor Company at midnight tomorrow.

Leonard Woodcock, the union president, told newsmen tonight that there was only a "one-in-one-hundred" chance of avoiding a walkout by 165,000 Ford workers in 22 states. He made his assessment after the company revised upward its offer on wages, Supplementary Unemployment Benefits, increased time off for workers and health benefits.

"It's in the ditch," another high union official said today, before the company's new offer was made, in describing the effort to avert a strike. "It would take a major miracle," he said, to reach a settlement by the time the present contract between Ford and the union expires at 11:59 P.M. tomorrow.

After the new Ford proposal was laid on the table at Ford headquarters here this afternoon, Mr. Woodcock said, "We are a long way apart." There is not enough time to reach a settlement by the deadline, he added, because "there's too much of a gap to bridge."

And Sidney F. McKenna, the chief Ford negotiator, said that he was "not particularly optimistic."

Very little has been settled, according to union officials, and many issues are still in dispute. Today's company proposal would allow a worker to start out each year with a "bank" of 20 to 40 hours of time off that he could take, in a block, any time in the following year. Days would be subtracted for absences by the worker, who would be eligible for the plan after three years on the job.

The union rejected the offer, which was made in response to one of its high-priority concerns. Mr. Woodcock called the offer "skimpy" and "essentially unresponsive" to the union's objective of "putting new people into the work force."

The new wage offer would add less than a cent an hour per year to the com-

Continued on Page 18, Column 5

Car Insurance Fees Are Called Inflated

By FRANCES CERRA

The acting Federal Insurance Administrator said yesterday that automobile insurance premiums nationally were unnecessarily inflated, and he predicted that the insurance industry was headed for record profits in 1978.

The administrator, J. Robert Hunter, asserted that the industry had over-reacted to a number of recent events, among them the near-collapse of the Government Employees Insurance Company, general inflation and the industry's own investment losses.

"Things are getting better fast, and you will see underwriting in the black next year, and record profits the following year, but the companies are going on as if they were still at the bottom," he said. "To have these vagaries imposed on the public is an outrage."

Mr. Hunter testified at a hearing of the

Continued on Page 17, Column 1

INSIDE

Vorster on Rhodesia

Prime Minister Vorster of South Africa said he would not try to force Rhodesia to turn over power to blacks against its will. Page 4.

Clubbing Victim Dies

A 22-year-old man, clubbed Wednesday night during a gang attack on blacks and Hispanics in Washington Square Park, has died. Page 14.

First Day of School

New York City's school year began with teachers and pupils trying to adjust to large classes and reductions in services. Page 43.

United Press International

Leaders pay respects to Mao Tse-tung, lying in state in Peking. From left: Prime Minister Hua Kuo-feng, Wang Hung-wen, a deputy party chairman; Yeh Chien-ying, Defense Minister; Chang Chun-chiao, Deputy Prime Minister; Chiang Ching, Mao's widow; Yao Wen-yuan, Shanghai party leader, Li Hsien-nien, a Deputy Prime Minister.

China's Military Now Expected to Play a Bigger Role

By FOX BUTTERFIELD

Special to The New York Times

HONG KONG, Sept. 13—The Chinese armed forces are suddenly being given heightened public attention and could play a key role in any struggle for leadership of China following the death of Chairman Mao Tse-tung, analysts here believe.

Last week, in an unusual move that apparently signals an increased role for the 3.5 million-member People's Liberation Army, the Communist Party's military commission was named along with the party Central Committee and the Government as co-author of the message announcing Mao's death to the Chinese people. Strictly speaking, the military commission is subordinate to the Central Committee.

[In Peking, foreigners were allowed for the first time to pay their respects to Chairman Mao, whose body was newly covered by a glass case. Among those filing by was the former United States Secretary of Defense, James R. Schlesinger. Page 3.]

The army's new prominence began in July after thousands of soldiers were sent to the city of Tangshan, devastated in an earthquake, to lead the relief work and prevent looting. The army had been in some disrepute since 1972 when Lin Piao, then the Minister of Defense, is said to have tried to assassinate Chairman Mao and some senior commanders were implicated. Marshal Lin reportedly died in a plane crash in Mongolia as he was trying to escape.

There have been indications that the

Continued on Page 3, Column 1

"All the News
That's Fit to Print"

The New York Times

LATE CITY EDITION

Weather: Partly cloudy today; very cold tonight. Sunny, cold tomorrow. Temperature range: today 13-25; Tuesday 17-23. Details on page A18.

VOL. CXXVI . . . No. 43,453

NEW YORK, WEDNESDAY, JANUARY 12, 1977

25 cents beyond 50-mile zone from New York City, except Long Island. Higher in air delivery cities.

20 CENTS

FRENCH COURT FREES TERRORIST SUSPECT; HE FLIES TO ALGERIA

ISRAELIS CALL ENVOY HOME

Palestinian Is Released Hurriedly After Ruling Rejects 2 Nations' Requests for Extradition

By JAMES F. CLARITY
Special to The New York Times

PARIS, Jan. 11—After a swift and unexpected judicial hearing, French authorities today freed a prominent Palestinian militant who had been arrested by French intelligence agents on suspicion of having been responsible for the killing of members of the Israeli team at the 1972 Olympics in Munich.

The Palestinian, known as Abu Daoud, was freed and allowed to fly, first class, to Algeria, after the court rejected requests from Israel and West Germany that he be detained pending formal extradition proceedings. The French prosecutor agreed, in effect, with Abu Daoud's lawyers that Israel had no right of extradition and that the West German request for detention had not been properly formulated.

A few hours later, Israel recalled its Ambassador from Paris. Foreign Minister Yigal Allon also summoned the French Ambassador, Jean Herly, to Jerusalem tomorrow to deliver a sharp protest, it was reported from Tel Aviv.

In Bonn, the West German Justice Ministry officially deplored the French court's decision.

The case of Abu Daoud, who was arrested in Paris Friday after he arrived to attend the funeral of a Palestinian ac-

Continued on Page A6, Col. 1

United Press International
Abu Daoud, Palestinian leader, on his arrival in Algiers from Paris.

Vance Says U.S. Erred in Joining War in Vietnam

Gives View at Senate Nomination Hearing

By BERNARD GWERTZMAN
Special to The New York Times

WASHINGTON, Jan. 11—Cyrus R. Vance, who was the No. 2 official in the Defense Department when American involvement expanded in Vietnam, told the Senate Foreign Relations Committee today that in hindsight, "it was a mistake to intervene in Vietnam."

Testifying at the hearing on his nomination as Jimmy Carter's Secretary of State, Mr. Vance said: "We learned a number of lessons in Vietnam and I'm the wiser for that."

His comment on Vietnam came in a friendly three-hour session during which Mr. Vance sought to allay the concern of Senators on a number of subjects.

Meanwhile, Harold Brown, who is Mr. Carter's nominee for Secretary of Defense, told the Senate Armed Services Committee that he believed the United States military spending could be reduced by $5 billion to $7 billion annually through saving, but not until fiscal 1979. [Page A18.]

A Pledge to 'Come Clean'

Mr. Vance told the Foreign Relations Committee that he would "come clean" on everything and would pursue a policy of "openness" wherever possible. He promised to seek arms control and détente with the Soviet Union "aggressively." He also proposed a policy to insure the ability of Congress to influence Mr. Carter in deciding on whether to carry out specific covert activities.

Mr. Vance, who sat alone at the witness table, seemed well briefed on the variety of topics he was asked about by the committee. He answered in a matter-of-fact way, seeking to reassure senators at every opportunity of the closest possible cooperation.

Stress on Economic Problems

After the hearings no voices were heard in opposition to his nomination and he is expected to be confirmed by the full Senate shortly after inauguration. In the period between the Jan. 20 inauguration and his confirmation, Philip C. Habib, Under Secretary of State for Political Affairs, will be acting secretary.

Mr. Vance told the senators that the United States would pursue solutions not only of political issues such as a definition of what détente really means, but of global economic problems that he said would overshadow political questions.

When discussing his recommendations on the handling of covert activities, he said that if they were carried out, and

Continued on Page A8, Col. 4

The New York Times/George Tames
At Senate confirmation hearings in Washington yesterday were these designated members of President-elect Carter's Cabinet: Left, Cyrus R. Vance as Secretary of State; above, Harold Brown as Secretary of Defense; below, Griffin B. Bell as Attorney General.

COURT BACKS ZONING THAT IN EFFECT BARS LOW-INCOME BLACKS

WHITE CHICAGO SUBURB UPHELD

Justices Rule, 5-3, That Such Curbs Are Illegal Only if 'Intent' Is to Keep Out Minority Groups

By LESLEY OELSNER
Special to The New York Times

WASHINGTON, Jan. 11—The Supreme Court ruled 5 to 3 today that it was not inherently unconstitutional for a suburb to refuse to change zoning restrictions whose practical effect is to block construction of racially integrated housing for persons with low and moderate income.

The Court held, in a case involving the nearly all-white Chicago suburb of Arlington Heights, that the refusal of a suburb to rezone is not unconstitutional just because it has a "racially disproportionate impact."

To be unconstitutional, the Court said, there must also be an "intent" or a "purpose" to discriminate. The suburb, in other words, must be shown to have refused the zoning change because it wanted to keep out minority group members.

Some Bias Acceptable

The Court also said, however, in a footnote, that even if the suburb was "motivated in part by a racially discriminatory purpose," its action would not necessarily be unconstitutional.

The footnote, citing a principle that the Court described today in another decision involving First Amendment protections, said that as long as the suburb could prove that it would have refused the rezoning anyway, for other reasons besides the discriminatory one, it would be permissible.

The Court's decision, written by Justice Lewis F. Powell Jr., is a serious blow for those who wish to use the Federal Constitution to force the suburbs to share in solving such problems of the nation's inner cities as housing. In some localities, the issue is being raised successfully on state constitutional grounds.

The decision reverses a ruling by the United States Court of Appeals for the Seventh Circuit, which found that Arlington Heights had violated the 14th Amendment's guarantee of equal protection of the laws when it refused to rezone a parcel of land for would-be developers of a proposed project.

Re-Examination Urged

Justices Byron R. White, William J. Brennan Jr. and Thurgood Marshall dissented and said that the Supreme Court should have let the appeals court re-examine the case.

The appeals court did not find that the village acted with any racially discriminatory intent; it found, however, that the "ultimate effect" was to discriminate against blacks.

The appeals court relied in part on the pattern of residential segregation in the Chicago area. It found that Arlington Heights could not "ignore" the problem just because it had not itself directly caused it.

The Supreme Court refused to take that approach. In broad social terms, it refused to place on the suburbs an affirmative duty to help provide solutions for

Continued on Page B6, Col. 1

BELL DEFENDS ACTS AS GEORGIA ADVISER

Tells Senators He Didn't Defy Law on Desegregation 2 Decades Ago

By ANTHONY MARRO
Special to The New York Times

WASHINGTON, Jan. 11—Griffin B. Bell, whose nomination to be Attorney General is opposed by a number of civil rights groups but whose confirmation nonetheless seems assured, told the Senate Judiciary Committee today that his actions two decades ago as counsel to Gov. Ernest Vandiver of Georgia might have contributed to a delay of school desegregation, but did not defy the law.

"We never had any violence," Mr. Bell, now an Atlanta lawyer, told the committee. "Maybe we delayed [desegregation], but we never defied the law."

Later, during the afternoon session, he added that any delay that resulted was part of an effort to "keep the schools open" at a time when many Georgians were demanding that they be closed rather than integrated.

'Voice of Moderation'

Throughout the day of hearings, Mr. Bell, who was reminded by several senators that his nomination was the most controversial that President-elect Carter has made, sought to portray himself as a man who had been a voice of moderation in "a volatile time." He said that as a counsel to Governor Vandiver he had urged that the court orders should be complied with, and that he had been a "voice of moderation" in his nearly

Continued on Page A14, Col. 4

Henry Ford 2d Quits Foundation, Urges Appreciation for Capitalism

By MAURICE CARROLL

Henry Ford 2d resigned as a trustee of the Ford Foundation yesterday, complaining that the philanthropic agency was spreading itself too thin, was cultivating a "fortress mentality" and had a staff that often failed to appreciate the capitalist system that provided the money the foundation gave away.

The resignation of Mr. Ford, who is chairman of the Ford Motor Company, left the board of the nation's largest tax-exempt foundation without a representative of the family that founded it. Mr. Ford's brother Benson quit last year.

According to aides of Mr. Ford and officials of the foundation, there was no specific event that precipitated either his resignation or his criticism.

"There really wasn't a blow-up," said McGeorge Bundy, the foundation president. "There is neither more nor less to this than meets the eye."

"The letter should speak for itself," a spokesman for Mr. Ford said at the automobile company's offices in Dearborn, Mich.

The spokesman said, in response to a telephone call, that Mr. Ford himself had approved the Ford Foundation press re-

Excerpts from Ford letter, page B6.

lease about his resignation, quoting only two paragraphs of praise for the trustees from his four-page letter.

But in the letter to Alexander Heard, the foundation chairman, the text of which became available yesterday, Mr. Ford wrote:

"I'm not playing the role of the hard-headed tycoon who thinks all philanthropoids are socialists and all university professors are Communists. I'm just suggesting to the trustees and the staff that

Continued on Page B6, Col. 5

Troy Reported Indicted in Queens On Larceny and Perjury Charges

By MURRAY SCHUMACH

A sealed indictment was handed up in Queens yesterday against Matthew J. Troy Jr. reportedly accusing the Queens City Councilman of grand larceny and perjury.

The grand jury allegations against the former Democratic leader of Queens County followed an investigation since last September of charges that he had juggled the funds of estates of his law clients. The details of the indictment could not be obtained last night.

Mr. Troy's latest clash with the law follows his release, on Dec. 16, from a Federal detention center, where he served 55 days after pleading guilty to tax evasion in 1972. The tax case led to the grand jury investigation.

The 47-year-old Councilman is scheduled to be arraigned today in Queens before Justice Bernard Dubin in State Supreme Court. Justice Dubin received the sealed report yesterday in his court from an assistant district attorney, Michael Berne, who presented the case to the grand jurors.

Comment Is Refused

District Attorney John J. Santucci of Queens refused to comment on the indictment, and even declined to call it an indictment.

"It would be improper," he said, "for me to discuss the contents of this sealed report until it is opened in court tomorrow by the judge."

Mr. Troy was said to be in Puerto Rico yesterday. However, according to sources familiar with the case, he was notified on Monday to be available to be in court today.

Mr. Troy's counsel in this case, Marvyn Kornberg, said: "My client is available to the District Attorney's office any time they want him."

This indictment could be more serious for Councilman Troy's political and professional career than was the tax-evasion case. If convicted of grand larceny or perjury, felony charges, he would be ousted as councilman and would not be permitted to run for re-election.

The tax-evasion case, while a felony under Federal law, is a misdemeanor in this state. So, while Mr. Troy, under considerable pressure, resigned his job as chairman of the Council's important Finance Committee on Oct. 10, nearly two weeks after he began his jail term, he

Continued on Page B7, Col. 4

I.M.F. Makes First Vietnam Loan; U.S. Raises No Bar to $35 Million

By CLYDE H. FARNSWORTH
Special to The New York Times

WASHINGTON, Jan. 11—The International Monetary Fund announced today that it had made its first loan to Vietnam, apparently with the consent of the United States, which has twice vetoed admission of the country to the United Nations.

The 129-nation fund said it was lending the equivalent of $35 million to Vietnam under a facility that provides third world countries with compensatory financing to cover shortfalls in their exports.

News of the loan, which would help in the reconstruction of the country, came a week before a five-man mission from the I.M.F.'s sister organization, the World Bank, was to arrive in Hanoi for a month-long study of Vietnam's economic policies, conditions and needs.

That mission is being headed by Edward Hawkins, a British economist and senior official at World Bank headquarters here.

American sources said the United States raised no objections to either the World Bank or fund decisions.

U.S. Raises Technical Points

The United States, a source said, raised some questions only on technical aspects of the proposal to lend money under the compensatory financing facility.

"There was a broad consensus in favor," the source said.

Sam Y. Cross, the American delegate on the I.M.F. executive board, asserted that since Vietnam was now a member, it was "eligible in the same way any other country is for any of the fund's facilities."

Vietnam was officially reunified last July, 15 months after the American withdrawal, and then last September it took up the membership in both the fund and the World Bank that had been held since 1956 by South Vietnam.

The United States had raised questions last September whether Vietnamese membership would be premature, but failing to get much support for this position, it did not press the point.

United Nations membership for Vietnam has been opposed by the United States on the ground that Hanoi has refused to give information about Americans missing in action.

Hanoi has linked supply of the data with American participation in reconstruction efforts.

In 1973 during the Paris peace talks

Continued on Page D7, Col. 1

Ford Mood, 9 Days to Go: Regret and Relief

By JAMES M. NAUGHTON
Special to The New York Times

WASHINGTON, Jan. 11—The gaunt, ravaged look was gone, and in its place was a grin as familiar and bright as the sunlight that glistened on ice-cloaked snow beyond the Oval office window. President Ford seemed at peace with his fate.

Nine days away from elder statesmanship, the President sat before a crackling log fire today and reflected on the burden he never sought but will reluctantly yield next week to President-elect Carter.

"It's a mixed feeling," he said. He spoke of "disappointment" that he would no longer confront the decisions of national leadership. But he conceded something that he never disclosed in his accidental Presidency and his futile campaign for election: "It is a relief to not have that burden."

Mr. Ford still has some chores to perform. Tomorrow, he will deliver his final State of the Union address, a valedictory as much to his 28 years in Washington as to his 29 months in the White House. He will submit a budget to Congress. And even as he met with two visitors, his aides were outlining a proposal for a new Department of Energy.

But there was an air of going through the motions, of paying homage, as Mr. Ford put it, to "the obligation of a President" to function to the end. His plans include a possible book about his experiences.

Mr. Ford, freed of the necessity to weigh his words for political effect, was

Continued on Page A14, Col. 1

President Ford during interview in the White House Oval Office yesterday

INSIDE

Coffee May Reach $4

Economic forces are pushing coffee prices up, and they may reach $4 a pound, industry analysts say. Page D1.

A Chill in East Germany

East Germany's mood is chilly in the wake of a government crackdown on dissidents following protests by artists and writers. Page A3.

Inaugural Funds Sought

President-elect Carter's Inaugural Committee asked corporations, unions and trade groups for $350,000 to help pay for the inaugural celebration. Page A12.

"All the News That's Fit to Print"

The New York Times

LATE CITY EDITION

Weather: Fair, windy today; colder tonight. Turning cloudy tomorrow. Temperature range: today 16-23; Friday 20-26. Details on page 44.

VOL. CXXVI . . . No. 43,463 · NEW YORK, SATURDAY, JANUARY 22, 1977 · 20 CENTS

25 cents beyond 50-mile zone from New York City, except Long Island. Higher in air delivery cities.

CARTER PARDONS DRAFT EVADERS, ORDERS A STUDY OF DESERTERS; VETERANS PROTEST, OTHERS SPLIT

PRESIDENT URGES 65° AS TOP HEAT IN HOMES TO EASE ENERGY CRISIS

CITES UNUSUALLY COLD WINTER

Says Natural Gas Shortage Is Most Acute but Asks Conservation in All Other Forms of Fuel

By EDWARD COWAN
Special to The New York Times

WASHINGTON, Jan. 21—President Carter called on "all Americans" tonight to turn down their thermostats at home "to 65 degrees in the daytime and lower at night" to help cope with what Mr. Carter called an energy "crisis" precipitated by this winter's unusally cold temperatures.

The shortage has been most acute for natural gas but Mr. Carter, in a White House statement, said that the 65-degree standard should be adopted by those who heat with other forms of energy, such as oil or electricity.

Text of President's statement, page 31.

There was no mention in the statement of Federal law or any other form of compulsion and indeed the Government has no way to compel adoption of the standard or punish those who do not follow it.

The 65-degree standard was three degrees lower than the temperature former President Richard M. Nixon asked Americans to adopt in their homes three years ago during an oil shortage caused by an Arab embargo. At that time it was believed that typical indoor winter temperatures were 70 to 72 degrees and that 68 represented a significant reduction.

Reduction in Temperature

Since then, energy analysts believe, there has been some further reduction, making 65 degrees perhaps less of a jolt for some families than it would have been three years ago.

The Presidential statement reflected the strong conservationist views of Mr. Carter and his energy chief, James R. Schlesinger, and was issued after a two-hour meeting between Mr. Schlesinger and more than two dozen executives of natural gas pipelines.

Mr. Carter said that the extremely cold weather and the worsening fuel shortage had thrown more than 200,000 persons out of work. "An equal number of children have been turned out of their schools because of natural gas shortages," he said.

The President said he was "concerned about the growing cost in human suffering that will increase if severe winter continues."

That evidently was a reference to the possibility of interrupted natural gas deliveries to homes, which have the highest priority and would be the last to be cut off.

Mr. Carter said that turning the heat down to 65 degrees or lower would yield "great savings." A Government energy analyst estimated informally that this

Continued on Page 31, Column 4

SUBURBAN HEAT COST FORCING SHIFT TO OIL

Westchester Agency Is Seeking to Convert 115 Electric Apartments

By JAMES FERON
Special to The New York Times

WHITE PLAINS, Jan. 21—The Greenburgh Housing Authority, one of many suburban landlords who have found themselves pinched this winter by increasing heating costs, appeared likely today to recommend a costly switch from electric to oil heating in its 115 subsidized apartments.

Officials said that tenants who earned $3,000 to $8,000 a year and paid monthly rents ranging from $50 to $230 were costing the Housing Authority $200 to $375 a month in electric bills alone. The immediate capital costs of a switchover could be recovered by savings on operating costs over the next decade, officials said.

Greenburgh, a central Westchester town of several villages and large unincorporated areas, appeared to be a victim both of the unexpected rise in electric heating costs that began two years ago with the increase in the cost of oil and of the extremely cold winter this year.

The unusually cold weather has hurt others. Homeowners with more traditional forms of heating have seen their bills double, while apartment owners estimate that a recently mandated rent increase of 3 to 7 percent will be absorbed over the winter season alone.

Barrett G. Kreisberg, chairman of the

Continued on Page 22, Column 1

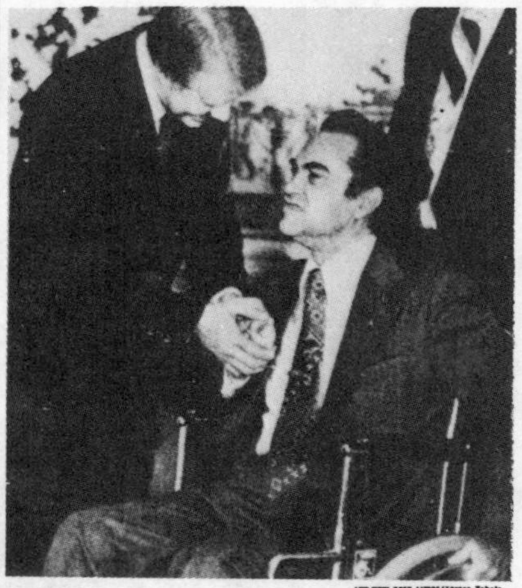

The New York Times/Teresa Zabala
President Carter greeting Gov. George C. Wallace at White House yesterday

The New York Times/George Tames
Vice President Mondale reviewing briefing papers in his office yesterday

Liberalized Abortion Bill in Italy Passes in Chamber, Goes to Senate

By ALVIN SHUSTER
Special to The New York Times

ROME, Jan. 21—Over the objections of the Vatican and the governing Christian Democrats, the Chamber of Deputies tonight approved legislation that would give Italy one of the most liberal abortion laws in Western Europe. The bill, which now goes to the Senate for expected approval, would in effect allow abortion on demand.

It would permit women over age 16 to decide, with or without authorization by a doctor, to terminate pregnancies during the first 90 days. The existing law, which the new one would replace, held that abortion was a "crime against the race."

The governing Christian Democratic Party and the Roman Catholic Church fought vigorously against the liberal abortion bill, and Pope Paul VI spoke out against it several times in recent weeks, noting that the church regarded abortion as the killing of an unborn child.

The bill carried tonight in the Chamber of Deputies by a vote of 310 to 296.

The vote was a result of a long campaign by reformers. Early last year they gathered more than 800,000 signatures on a petition calling for a referendum aimed at repealing the existing law.

The issue became so heated that a bitter debate in Parliament over the legislation brought down the government and forced a general election last June. The election prevented the referendum from taking place, and the reformers, including the small but vocal Radical Party, carried the struggle into the new Parliament.

The passage of the bill once again reflected the declining influence of the Roman Catholic Church in Italian politics. In a defeat for the church hierarchy in May 1974, for instance, Italians voted by a 3-to-2 margin to retain a controversial law permitting divorce in this overwhelmingly Catholic country.

In political terms, too, the Vatican has

Continued on Page 26, Column 3

In Brazil's North, Thousands Die Of Third-World Ills Defying Cure

By JONATHAN KANDELL
Special to The New York Times

RECIFE, Brazil, Jan. 14—For the last three months, António Alves Dos Anjos has lain listlessly on his hospital cot. His legs, feet, liver, spleen and heart are swollen. He is short of breath and looks 10 years older than his 34 years.

Mr. Alves Dos Anjos, a peasant from Brazil's poverty-stricken northeast, will soon be dead, either from Chagas' disease, which brought him to the hospital, or from schistosomiasis, which the doctors detected only after he had been admitted.

Most Americans and Europeans have never heard of either ailment. There is no known cure for Chagas' disease, although eight million South Americans are believed to suffer from it.

There are medicines that cure schistosomiasis, which is thought to afflict four million people in Brazil's northeast and millions elsewhere. But most patients seek treatment only in the final stages of their illness, when the medicines are too dangerous to use. Those who are treated early enough usually go on to contract the disease again.

Throughout the third world, millions of the rural and urban poor are debilitated, crippled and killed by a host of diseases that belie the medical breakthroughs of the 20th-century Western world.

In the most dramatic cases, such as Chagas' disease, no cures have been discovered. Little research is done on them in modern industrialized societies, whose main concerns are heart disease and cancer—illnesses that many third world residents do not live long enough to contract. For other third world diseases, the cures are far less important than the need for widespread sanitation and the teaching of hygiene to prevent outbreaks.

There are also illnesses whose cures are too expensive and others for which

Continued on Page 6, Column 3

Pro-Amnesty Groups Offer Praise But Assert That Plan Is Too Limited

By ROBERT D. McFADDEN

President Carter's pardon for draft resisters drew sharp denunciations yesterday from major veterans' organizations and only qualified praise from pro-amnesty groups, which called it insufficient because of its exclusion of deserters and veterans with less-than-honorable discharges.

Among members of Congress, Democrats generally said the pardon was long overdue, and conservative Republicans said it would undermine military discipline and the rule of law.

Peace, religious and antiwar veterans groups called it a positive step, but said it would cover only a few thousand individuals. They noted, too, that the review ordered by Mr. Carter of the cases of deserters and veterans with qualified discharges would only prolong employment problems and other difficulties confronted by these individuals.

The only unfettered praise came from some of the draft evaders who were pardoned; others, however, expressed gratitude tinged with regret that the pardon was not a universal order.

"We deeply regret and strongly protest the President's action," said William J. Rogers, the national commander of the 2.8-million-member American Legion, which has favored a case-by-case review for all evaders and deserters. He said Mr. Carter's decision would be "more divisive than healing."

"It's a sad day in the history of our nation," said Cooper Holt, the executive director of the Washington office of the Veterans of Foreign Wars, which has 1.8 million members. The President, he said, had "shown a lack of concern for the 30 million living veterans who have served our nation in time of war."

The pardon "extends overdue relief to a small segment of the war resisters of the Vietnam era," the American Civil Liberties Union said in a statement. "But military offenders and veterans with less-than-honorable discharges are more numerous than draft violators by a factor of 100 to 1. They are also, by and large, more likely to be poor, from minority

Continued on Page 10, Column 1

Carter White House, Opening Day: Staff Displays a Down-Home Style

By JAMES T. WOOTEN
Special to The New York Times

WASHINGTON, Jan. 21—With a lopsided smile, Charles Kirbo tried to explain what it was he was doing today in the White House office of Jody Powell, President Carter's press secretary.

"Well," he drawled, brushing a gray cowlick from his florid forehead, "we're just slicing up a melon in here, that's all," a fragment of Georgia vernacular that translates roughly as a relaxed endeavor lacking in specific purpose.

In fact, however, Mr. Kirbo, the laconic lawyer from Atlanta who helped the President win his first election 11 years ago, was putting the finishing touches on Mr. Carter's first official act, the pardon of Vietnam draft resisters. It was the fulfillment of a highly volatile campaign promise and a document of considerable historical significance.

It was only a brief, isolated moment in the early hours of Mr. Carter's residence at 1600 Pennsylvania Avenue, but it provided nevertheless a theme common to the Administration's first full day. It was suggestive, perhaps, of days to come, a Southern motif reflected in Mr. Kirbo's soft modesty, accented by Mr. Powell's maiden appearance before the White House press corps and ubiquitously evident here in the celebration of the last week.

The ultimate impact of the down-home style on Federal substance remains to be seen, of course, but its immediate flavor is striking in a city that John F. Kennedy once said was characterized by "Northern charm and Southern efficiency."

For the time being, at least, the people who came with Mr. Carter from below

Continued on Page 10, Column 4

10,000 AFFECTED NOW

Action Postponed on Nearly 100,000 Who Fled Armed Forces During War

By CHARLES MOHR
Special to The New York Times

WASHINGTON, Jan. 21 — President Carter granted a pardon today to almost all draft evaders of the Vietnam war era, but he left unsettled the status of those who deserted the armed forces in the long Asian conflict.

In effect, the first major act of the new President offered immediate, full legal relief to a relatively small number—estimated by the Justice Department at about 10,000 — of predominantly white, middle-class and upper-class young men who either fled the country or refused to enter military service.

Proclamation and order are on page 10.

For the nearly 100,000 men who entered but then deserted the armed forces, many of whom were black, poor or disadvantaged, Mr. Carter postponed action but said that he would "immediately" initiate a study of a process that might accelerate the review of their cases with a view toward upgrading less-than-honorable discharges.

Protests and Praise

The President's actions drew protests, some of them vehement, from some veterans organizations and from some conservative politicians. There was mild praise from some pro-amnesty groups but also complaint that his decision was too grudging.

Although he holds no official position, Mr. Carter's close friend, Charles Kirbo, played a major role in fashioning the policy announced today in the President's first full day in office and is believed to have helped resist pressures for a more generous package. On Jan. 12, David Berg, a Houston lawyer who drafted the program, spent many hours at the Atlanta law offices of Mr. Kirbo seeking his approval, and Mr. Kirbo was at the White House today.

The pardon was the most important action in a day largely occupied with hours of White House social events to

Continued on Page 10, Column 1

Associated Press
RETURNS TO PRIVATE LIFE: Former President Ford chatting with Arnold Palmer, his golfing partner, in the Bing Crosby Pro-Am tournament at Pebble Beach, Calif., yesterday, his first full day out of office. Details, page 9.

Korean Lobbyist a U.S. Tax Target

By RICHARD HALLORAN
Special to The New York Times

WASHINGTON, Jan 21—The Internal Revenue Service says that Park Tong Sun, a central figure in the alleged bribery of United States Congressmen by Korean figures, owes the United States Government $4.5 million in back income taxes, interest and penalties.

A tax lien against Mr. Park's property filed with the Recorder of Deeds here shows that the revenue service contends that Mr. Park, who is reportedly in London now, owes taxes for 1972 through 1975. These were the years that Mr. Park, also known here as Tongsun Park, was allegedly active in cultivating, entertaining and bribing American Congressmen.

A spokesman for the service said that estimates of Mr. Park's income for those years were not available. However, he is alleged to have spent $500,000 to $1 million each year in that period in Congressional lobbying.

The spokesman for the tax agency also said that the sources of Mr. Park's income and the value of the property against which the liens were filed were not available. Neither was a list of his real property available in the jurisdictions in which the liens were filed. Earlier reports held that Mr. Park had income from rice, oil, shipping, and real estate.

Meanwhile, new information about Mr.

Continued on Page 9, Column 3

INSIDE

Consumer Shows Fictionalized

New York City's Department of Consumer Affairs, which warns people against fraud, has fictionalized many of its daily radio broadcasts. Page 25.

McFeeley Disciplined

Ken McFeeley, the former head of the P.B.A., was assessed $7,500 and placed on a year's probation for staging a one-man strike last fall. Page 26

"All the News That's Fit to Print"

The New York Times

LATE CITY EDITION

Weather: Showers likely today and tonight. Partly sunny tomorrow. Temperature range: today 47-70; Wednesday 47-63. Details, page D25.

VOL. CXXVI . . . No. 43,566 — NEW YORK, THURSDAY, MAY 5, 1977 — 20 CENTS

25 cents beyond 50-mile zone from New York City, except Long Island. Higher in air delivery cities.

U.S. Won't Bar Hanoi From U.N.; Vietnam to Press Hunt for Missing

Progress Toward Normal Ties Is Made as First Round of Paris Talks Concludes

By FLORA LEWIS
Special to The New York Times

PARIS, May 4—The United States and Vietnam made progress today toward normalization of relations, with the United States pledging that it would not veto Vietnam's admission to the United Nations and that it would lift a trade embargo after diplomatic relations had been established.

In turn, the Vietnamese promised to intensify efforts to provide information about Americans listed as missing in action in the Vietnam War.

Text of Vietnamese statement, page A12.

Both sides showed satisfaction with the results of two days of the talks, although it was clear that there were still important problems outstanding. The sides expressed their views with careful reserve. The two delegations said they had agreed to meet here again in about two weeks for a second round of talks.

'Cordiality and Frankness'

The two-day session was held in Vietnam's elaborate but unfinished new embassy. The next session, probably at the same level as the meeting that has just been concluded, is to be held in the United States Embassy.

Deputy Foreign Minister Phan Hien of Vietnam, and its chief negotiator, read a statement to the press in his embassy terming the talks "constructive and useful" and their atmosphere one of "cordiality and frankness." Later, in the United States Embassy, the American spokesman Morton Smith used the same words. There was no joint communiqué and no formal American statement.

Mr. Hien welcomed the American pledge not to obstruct his country's admission to the United Nations, but insisted on an "immediate" end of the trade embargo, separate from further negotiations on aid and relations. The American spokesman said his country's position remained that lifting the embargo had to be part of normalizing of relations.

However, it was learned that the leader of the United States delegation, Richard Holbrooke, the Assistant Secretary of State for Asian Affairs, told the Vietnamese today that the United States promised to end the embargo once relations and embassies were established. It is a nuance of timing, but it was an important change that the United States was now prepared to make the pledge, even though it would rather wait for an agreement.

A U.S. Promise Is Disclosed

On the issue of aid, there were similar subtle differences in public and private positions. Publicly, the Vietnamese maintained that "a contribution to healing the wounds of war and to reconstruct the country" was an American obligation that must be "linked" to establishment of relations.

Mr. Hien said, in answer to a question, that the aid pledged in a letter from President Richard M. Nixon at the time of the 1973 Paris cease-fire agreement amounted to $3.25 billion, plus another billion or billion and a half in what he called "concessional aid," and indicated that Hanoi still demanded that amount.

The Vietnamese negotiator did say, in response to other questions, that the "form" of aid was a matter to be discussed—a hint that loans, credits, private American gifts, and United States contributions through international aid agencies would all be included in calculating

Continued on Page A12, Col. 3

Vance Reports No Arms Progress As Two Sides Prepare for Geneva

BY BERNARD GWERTZMAN
Special to The New York Times

WASHINGTON, May 4—Secretary of State Cyrus R. Vance said today that the United States and Soviet Union were heading for a new round of talks in Geneva without having made any concessions to break the impasse that blocks a new agreement on limiting strategic arms.

In weeks of discussions in Washington with Ambassador Anatoly F. Dobrynin, Mr. Vance said, "we have put no new proposals on the table, nor have they.

"We have merely reviewed the existing proposals," he added.

As to the Geneva talks with Foreign Minister Andrei A. Gromyko starting on May 18, he said that he could not predict the result, but that "any time the parties sit down and start talking to each other, there is always a possibility that something constructive can come out of it."

U.S. Bars Reparations to Vietnam

On other matters, in a wide-ranging news conference, Mr. Vance said:

¶In the talks in Paris with the Vietnamese, the United States said it would pay no war reparations, but would not oppose Vietnam's admission to the United Nations in return for progress made so far on the missing in action. Mr. Vance said Hanoi insisted on economic aid as a condition to normalization of relations, though not necessarily diplomatic recognition.

¶On the Middle East, the United States is preparing suggestions on how to achieve a settlement, and Mr. Vance will go to the Middle East with the American ideas after a new Israeli Government emerges from elections this month and the new prime minister has an opportunity to visit Washington.

¶American policy toward South Africa has taken a new turn. Vice President Mondale intends to ask Prime Minister John Vorster in their meeting on May 19 how South Africa plans to move away from apartheid and deal with its minority problems. The previous United States Government paid little attention to apartheid and put stress on winning South African cooperation on Rhodesia and South-West Africa.

¶On China, Mr. Vance described normalization as a difficult question because of Taiwan and he said he hoped to discuss the issue when he goes to Peking later in the year.

Mr. Vance leaves with President Carter tomorrow for an economic conference in London and will then be on the road for

Continued on Page A10, Col. 1

Associated Press

SILVER JUBILEE ADDRESS: Queen Elizabeth II opening celebration of the 25th year of her reign yesterday with address to both Houses of Parliament in Westminster Hall. Prince Philip is seated at right. Page A8.

ALBANY AGREEMENT REACHED ON EASING MARIJUANA CURBS

Measure's Passage Appears Certain —Some Penalties Would Be Cut to Traffic-Offense Class

By RICHARD J. MEISLIN
Special to The New York Times

ALBANY, May 4—Legislative action to remove the threat of jail for the possession of small amounts of marijuana for personal use was virtually assured tonight when negotiators for the Assembly and Senate announced agreement on such a measure.

The bill, announced by the chairmen of the Senate and Assembly Codes Committees, would make the possession of up to one and one-quarter ounces of marijuana a violation—the same class of offense as a traffic infraction—with fines of up to $100 for a first offense.

A spokesman for Governor Carey tonight reiterated the Governor's stand that he would approve a measure to decriminalize the possession of small amounts of marijuana.

Changing of Laws Debated

The easing of marijuana laws has been a subject of debate in the lay, legal and scientific communities locally and nationally, sharply dividing those who believe that the drug is no more harmless than alcohol and that its illegality engenders disrespect for the law, and those who feel that the use of marijuana is dangerous medically or socially or both.

The measure announced tonight is considerably more stringent than a bill that was reported out of the Codes Committee of the Democratic-controlled Assembly earlier this year and is in some ways even more stringent than the one approved by the Codes Committee of the Republican-controlled Senate.

But it is far more lenient than the current law, which makes possession of less than a quarter of an ounce of marijuana, or 25 marijuana cigarettes, a misdemeanor punishable by up to one year in jail, and possession of more than a quarter of an ounce a felony punishable by up to seven years in prison.

Penalties for possession or sale of hashish—concentrated resin or oil from the cannabis plant, the same one that produces marijuana—would not be changed by the new law, which has now become known as the Marijuana Reform Act of 1977.

Optimism on Quick Passage

Senator H. Douglas Barclay, Republican of Pulaski, and Assemblyman Richard N. Gottfried, Democrat of Manhattan, said in a statement that they were "optimistic that the bill will receive swift passage in the Senate and Assembly."

Mr. Gottfried's proposal to make free transfer—such as the passing of a marijuana cigarette from one person to another—a violation was scrapped in the compromise. Instead, transfer of less than a sixteenth of an ounce or one cigarette would be a Class B misdemeanor, carrying a three-month jail term or $500 fine.

Public use of marijuana would be subject to the same sanctions as transfer, a move designed to discourage its use where children might be present.

The bill also would increase the penal-

Continued on Page B15, Col. 1

NIXON, CONCEDING HE LIED, SAYS 'I LET THE AMERICAN PEOPLE DOWN,' DENIES ANY CRIME ON WATERGATE

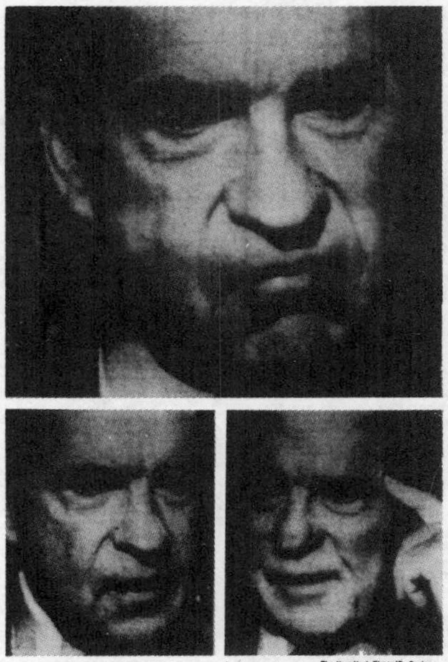

The New York Times/D. Gorton

Former President Richard M. Nixon at the emotional conclusion of his telecast interview when he said that his political career was over.

'IMPEACHED MYSELF'

In TV Interview With Frost Former President Says Motives Were Political

By JAMES M. NAUGHTON
Special to The New York Times

WASHINGTON, May 4—Former President Richard M. Nixon said tonight that he had "let the American people down" by lying, disregarding his constitutional oath and abetting the Watergate cover-up while in the White House.

But the former President insisted, in a nationally televised interview, that he had committed no criminal or impeachable offenses because his deeds sprang, he said, from purely political and humanitarian motives.

Transcript of program, pages B10, B11.

"I brought myself down," Mr. Nixon told David Frost in the emotional peak of an interview videotaped last month. "I have impeached myself," he said, "by resigning."

First Comment Since End

The dramatic apologia, marking Mr. Nixon's first public comment on the Watergate scandal since it cut short his Presidency 999 days ago, nonetheless was more rueful than remorseful.

He refused repeatedly, in long and sometimes sharp exchanges with the British interviewer, to concede that his conduct had amounted to obstruction of justice. The former President offered a personal interpretation of that law that Mr. Frost immediately challenged on the basis of his own reading of the statute just before the interview was taped.

Mr. Nixon specifically denied knowing in advance of the June 17, 1972, burglary at the Democratic Party headquarters in the Watergate office complex here, condoning payment of hush money to the Watergate burglars and coaching White House aides on how to avoid perjury charges.

Seemed on Defensive

In many of these exchanges, Mr. Nixon bristled defensively and, at times, appeared even distraught. Closeups in some of the tougher questioning showed that Mr. Nixon has aged in his 32 months out of the public eye—his hair thinner, his jowls more pronounced than when he left office in August 1974.

In an exchange toward the end of the interview, in which Mr. Frost urged him to apologize to the nation for having put it through two years of trauma, both Mr. Nixon and Mr. Frost seemed on the verge of losing their composure. It was a scene reminiscent of Mr. Nixon's emotional farewell speech on the day he resigned.

Mr. Nixon and Mr. Frost, who spent 11 days together producing "The Nixon Interviews" for private syndication, both stand to realize a substantial profit from this and three subsequent programs. By some estimates, the former President could receive as much as $1 million.

At one point, the former President suggested that Mr. Frost was "making the case" as though for the prosecution and said that he would therefore act, "even if I were not the one who was involved, for the defense."

But after Mr. Frost urged him to admit "wrongdoing" and apologize for it lest he be "haunted for the rest of your life," the 64-year-old former President, his

Continued on Page B12, Col. 1

The Interview vs. the Record

Discrepancies Appear When Broadcast Remarks Of Nixon Are Compared With the Official Data

By DAVID E. ROSENBAUM
Special to The New York Times

News Analysis

WASHINGTON, May 4—About halfway through his interview with David Frost that was broadcast tonight, former President Richard M. Nixon declared, "I know it really better than you do, and I should know it better because I was there." That assertion is not open to challenge, but the Watergate case is extraordinary in that so much of the evidence is on the public record. Foremost, of course, is the fact that virtually every official conversation that Mr. Nixon had in the period in question was tape-recorded, and transcripts of the tapes of the critical discussions have been published.

Major discrepancies become apparent when that official record is compared with remarks made by Mr. Nixon in his interview with Mr. Frost.

Second, nearly all of the other participants have testified in public forums.

Finally, the special prosecutor, the Senate Watergate committee and the House Judiciary Committee made independent evaluations of Mr. Nixon's role in Watergate and expressed their views.

The Watergate prosecution force listed Mr. Nixon in February 1974 as an unindicted co-conspirator in the cover-up case against his former top aides, including John N. Mitchell, H. R. Haldeman and John D. Ehrlichman. Leon A. Jaworski, then the special prosecutor, said that Mr. Nixon was not indicted because there were questions about whether the Constitution permitted the indictment of a sitting President.

Moreover, the evidence against Mr. Nixon was strong enough for the House Judiciary Committee to recommend that he be impeached. Twenty-eight of the 38 members of the panel voted to recommend at least one article of impeachment. At the time, there was no doubt that the full House of Representatives would have voted to impeach Mr. Nixon if he had not resigned, and most Congressional observers felt sure that he would have been convicted in the Senate.

What follows is an examination of how

Continued on Page B12, Col. 1

Carter Says Sacrifices on Energy Will Be Less Than He Expected

By MARTIN TOLCHIN
Special to The New York Times

WASHINGTON, May 4 — President Carter, who urged the American people last month to make sacrifices for an energy program that would be "the moral equivalent of war," reportedly told the House energy committee today that those sacrifices would be less substantial than he had then envisioned.

The President also told the committee, according to representatives who attended the one-hour White House meeting, that the nation would accept a gasoline tax as a symbolic gesture of patriotism, and urged the committee to share with him some of the public disapproval.

The private meeting was held prior to the committee's first public hearing, during which members heard testimony from Secretary of State Cyrus R. Vance and Secretary of Defense Harold Brown.

Both Democrats and Republicans privately expressed surprise that the President seemed to be retreating from his Churchillian summons of last month, although Mr. Carter did not indicate the areas in which public sacrifice would be lessened.

[Sugar subsidies of up to 2 cents a pound for domestic producers have been approved by President Carter. However, he has vetoed tightening of the import quota, according to a White House announcement. Page D-1]

"He said that until a month ago, he honestly felt that some substantial sacrifices were required on the part of the American people," said Representative John Anderson of Illinois, the ranking Republican on the ad hoc select committee on energy.

"He said that now he had changed his

Continued on Page A16, Col. 3

Individuals, Businesses and States Would Benefit From Tax Cut Plan

By CLYDE H. FARNSWORTH
Special to The New York Times

WASHINGTON, May 4—Business enterprises, cities, states and individuals, including 120,000 Americans who work overseas, would all gain from the tax reduction and simplification bill that was approved by House-Senate conferees last night.

The bill, envisaging $2.8 billion in tax cuts in the fiscal year 1977, which ends Sept. 30, and $17.7 billion in cuts in the fiscal year 1978, is expected to be signed by President Carter later this month after formal approval by the Senate and House.

Taxes for low-and middle-income Americans would be reduced. For example, a couple with two children and an income of $10,000 would save $205.

Most of the projected revenue loss comes from extension through 1978 of the individual and corporate tax cuts enacted in 1975 and 1976, which were due to expire at the end of the year. They include the general tax credit—the greater of either $35 per person or 2 percent of the first $9,000 of taxable income—and lower tax rates for small business.

But there are a number of new things in the bill, which would affect all Americans.

One of the most important is not a tax change at all, but an amendment authorizing up to $1 billion of additional countercyclical funds for the current fiscal year and $2.25 billion for the fiscal year 1978.

Under current law such funds are set aside for state and local governments

Continued on Page A18, Col. 3

INSIDE

Ludwig Erhard Dies in Bonn

Ludwig Erhard, architect of West Germany's economic recovery after World War II, died in a Bonn hospital. He was 80 years old. Page D24.

Vote on Excommunication

The Roman Catholic bishops of the United States voted 231 to 8 to drop the penalty of excommunication on those who divorce and rewed. Page A16.

Security Guard Held

A security guard once convicted of child molesting was charged with hurling an 8-year-old boy to his death from an apartment house roof. Page B2.

"All the News That's Fit to Print"

The New York Times

LATE CITY EDITION

Weather: Blustery, colder today; clear tonight. Sunny tomorrow. Temperature range: today 45-31; yesterday 42-36. Details on page 36.

VOL.CXXVIII . . No.44,077

Copyright © 1978 The New York Times

NEW YORK, MONDAY, DECEMBER 25, 1978

25 cents beyond 50-mile zone from New York City. Higher in air delivery cities.

20 CENTS

The New York Times / Fred R. Conrad

WHO SAW WHOM KISSING SANTA CLAUS? Actually, this youngster was just making a last-minute Christmas wish in Herald Square. Page 21.

SOVIET'S RELUCTANCE ON FINAL ARMS PACT LINKED TO CHINA TIE

Vance Aides Say Delay May Mean Moscow Is Concerned About U.S.-Peking Relationship

By BERNARD GWERTZMAN

Special to The New York Times

WASHINGTON, Dec. 24 — A deep-seated Soviet concern over President Carter's sudden decision to normalize relations with China was seen by some American officials today as a major factor in the Soviet Union's reluctance to conclude a strategic arms limitation agreement with the United States in Geneva yesterday.

Secretary of State Cyrus R. Vance came home this afternoon after three days of intensive negotiations with Foreign Minister Andrei A. Gromyko in Geneva and a brief stopover in Brussels for Middle East talks. Mr. Vance said again today that he and Mr. Gromyko had resolved most of the major issues holding up a strategic arms accord and had come "clo.e to the end of the road" in the negotiations.

But to the frustration of most members of the delegation, Mr. Gromyko, after agreeing to solutions of some of the most difficult and persistent issues on Friday, suddenly began to hold firm on Saturday morning on what were regarded by the United States as less crucial matters. The mood of the talks changed, and this blocked both an early conclusion of the accord and an early visit by Leonid I. Brezhnev, the Soviet leader, to Washington.

Brezhnev Visit Still Expected

American officials said toaay that they believe the Russians still want an agreement very much and that Mr. Brezhnev will certainly come to Washington within a few months. But they said the apparent decision by the Soviet leadership to hold off on the arms accoru when it seemed to the Americans to be very close at hand was indicative of problems being raised in the Kremlin about American policy.

The reasons behind the Soviet actions are still unclear, and members of the Vance team disagree about them. But they agree that the Russians were probably unhappy about the impression fostered by American officials, including President Carter, that the Soviet Union

Continued on Page 4, Column 3

Associated Press

Cyrus R. Vance, center, Mustafa Khalil, left, and Moshe Dayan in Brussels

VANCE, IN BRUSSELS, IS UNABLE TO REVIVE ISRAEL-EGYPT TALKS

PARTIES TO MAINTAIN CONTACT

No Indication Is Given That Either Side Is Considering a Further Meeting on Peace Treaty

By FLORA LEWIS

Special to The New York Times

BRUSSELS, Dec. 24 — High officials of the United States, Egypt and Israel met today but failed to arrange a resumption of Middle East peace negotiations. They agreed, however, to maintain contacts and to try to avoid further mutual recriminations.

Secretary of State Cyrus R. Vance appeared in the seasonally decorated lobby of the hotel where the meeting was held and read the only official statement, issued jointly with Egypt's Prime Minister, Mustafa Khalil, and Israel's Foreign Minister, Moshe Dayan, both of whom silently flanked him.

None of the three answered reporters' questions, as part of an agreement to "lower the tone" of what, according to several delegates in private comments later, had become shrill exchanges. Mr. Vance beamed when someone wished him a Merry Christmas, and responded in kind to the crowd of reporters present. Then he hurried off to his plane to return home for Christmas Eve, as he said he had promised his wife. Mr. Khalil and Mr. Dayan also flew home almost immediately.

'Useful and Full Exchange'

The official statement said there had been a "useful and full exchange of views on all the outstanding issues." Each participant, it continued, is to report to his head of Government and "will be in contact and discuss with the Secretary of State their views as to the next steps to be taken."

Later, in a briefing and in private conversations, United States officials emphasized that the agreement was intended to halt arguments in public and to concentrate instead on proposals that could be forwarded through the State Department. There was no sign that Egypt or Israel were considering further con-, tacts, nor that the United States had made any suggestions of its own, even on

Continued on Page 4, Column 5

Interest Groups' Campaign Gifts To House Leaders Doubled in '78

By WARREN WEAVER Jr.

Special to The New York Times

WASHINGTON, Dec. 24 — Political committees representing corporations, unions and controversial causes gave more than twice as much money to House committee chairmen seeking re-election in 1978 as they did in the previous campaign.

In 1976, special interest groups contributed an average of $21,700 to each of the House chairmen, who are among the most influential officials in Washington in determining the outcome of legislation. This year, the groups gave an average of $45,000 each to help these incumbents stay in Congress.

This is one available index of the rapid proliferation and expanding influence of these groups, known as political action committees, since they were formally sanctioned by Congress in 1974 and their powers were defined by the Federal Election Commission in 1975.

Number of Committees on Rise

Not all final reports on the 1978 campaign have reached the election commission yet, and its computer is unable to provide overall figures. But one statistic is firm: The number of political action committees rose from about 450 in 1976 to about 1,900 this year.

The available financial reports indicate how swiftly and extensively these special interest groups have moved into the political process. In 1978, for example, they provided 56 percent of the money that the 22 House chairmen spent on their campaigns.

With this influx of financing, campaign spending by this group of Representatives rose from an average of $36,500 per chairman in 1976 to more than $80,000 this year. The average chairman had $9,300 left over, available for any lawful purpose he chose.

The steep rise in spending cannot be attributed to serious political competition. Of the 28 Democratic House chairmen, only three received less than 55 percent of the vote, the generally accepted dividing line for close contests. And 17 chairmen won by landslide votes of 60 percent or more. All the chairmen who sought re-election in November were returned to office.

The figures, available for only the second year, appeared certain to spur members of Congress to seek legislation providing campaign subsidies for Senate

Continued on Page 17, Column 3

2 Victims of Mao's Purges Honored At Big Memorial Service in Peking

By FOX BUTTERFIELD

Special to The New York Times

CANTON, Dec. 24 — In an extraordinary gesture of atonement, China held a large memorial service in Peking today for two of the most prominent victims of purges by Mao Tse-tung.

The service was dedicated to the memory of Peng Teh-huai, one of the country's greatest military heroes, who was ousted by Mao in 1959 after a bitter quarrel, and Tao Chu, who was the fourth-ranking member of the Communist Party before he was cast into disgrace in 1967. Both men died during the Cultural Revolution, according to eulogies to them read today and broadcast by the Peking radio.

Emphasis on Economic Development

There were earlier indications in the Chinese press that both men had been rehabilitated at an extended Communist Party meeting that began last month. But the memorial service today in Peking, attended by all the senior Communist leaders, underscored an announcement by the party's Central Committee in Peking yesterday that it was now shifting its focus from political struggle to economic development.

A long communiqué issued today, following the completion of a session of the Central Committee, declared that Mao had made "great contributions" to the Chinese revolution that were "immutable."

But the communiqué added that Mao had also made mistakes and that China must now act to sweep away all impediments to the country's economic growth.

Teng Hsiao-ping, the Deputy Prime Minister, who delivered the eulogy at the memorial service for Mr. Peng, said nothing about the late marshal's clash with Mao over the disastrous Great Leap Forward program that led to his purge. Instead, in keeping with the party's current policy, Mr. Teng blamed the country's radicals, or "Gang of Four," who include Mao's widow, Chiang Ching, for Peng's ouster and death.

Yesterday, after the end of the Central Committee meeting, it was disclosed that Chen Yun, another prominent victim of the Cultural Revolution, had been appointed a deputy chairman of the party. Mr. Chen will rank fifth in the party's hierarchy, moving Wang Tung-hsing, the former commander of Mao's bodyguards, down from fifth to sixth place.

Mr. Wang has reportedly been under veiled criticism in recent months because

Continued on Page 3, Column 3

The New York Times / Marilynn K. Yee

Herbert Muhammad, left, and James Clark outside the bakery and grocery store in Harlem from which they were evicted by the Muslim sect.

Indians' Tribal Courts Prepare to Take Over Child Custody Cases

By MOLLY IVINS

Special to The New York Times

DENVER, Dec. 23 — For years, Indian children have been taken from their families and placed in foster care or put up for adoption in such great numbers that Indian leaders, church groups and child welfare experts have been putting increasing pressure on the Federal Government for change.

Congress took a step in that direction last session by passing, over the opposition of government agencies, an Indian Child Welfare Act that will let tribal courts decide custody cases.

Many Indians think the situation will now improve. Thelma Stiffarm, a lawyer with the Native American Rights Fund, said: "If anybody is worried about whether tribal judges can handle such cases, their fear is unfounded. I've worked with tribal courts and Indian judges and I find them better trained than many Anglo judges. The National American Indian Court Judges Association has held seminars and training sessions on all aspects of juvenile and family law."

Publications of the American Academy

Continued on Page 14, Column 3

"THE TREE" IS LIT AT LUCHOW'S FOR THE 96th YEAR. Bring kids (8 to 80) to ooh in awe. 110 E. 14th St. 477-4860—ADVT.

Radical Changes by New Leader Leave Many Muslims Disaffected

By PAUL DELANEY

As the fourth anniversary of the death of Elijah Muhammad approaches, the World Community of Al-Islam of the West, formerly the Black Muslims, is still reeling from the radical changes instituted by Mr. Muhammad's son and successor, Wallace Deen Muhammad.

Interviews with Muslims in a dozen cities — including New York, Chicago, Atlanta, El Paso, Tex.; Washington, and Nashville — found disaffection greater than previously reported, and apparently growing. Every Muslim leader interviewed acknowledged a loss of members who disagreed with the changes. There have been sporadic challenges to the new policies.

Elijah Muhammad made the Black Muslims into a militant, disciplined, feared antiwhite force that, feeling itself abused, misunderstood and threatened, insulated itself from the society outside.

After Mr. Muhammad's death in February 1975, Wallace Muhammad brought the sect full circle, abolishing strict dress codes, changing the policy against admission of white members and lifting the ban on contact with outsiders. Wallace Muhammad also began selling the group's businesses and properties — which had been symbols of Elijah Muhammad's success — to satisfy Federal tax judgments.

Today, the Muslims prefer to be called Bilalians in honor of an Abyssinian, Bilail, who, they say, was the first of the muezzins in the 14th century to call the faithful to prayer, and they are consid-

Continued on Page 16, Column 1

ROTHSCHILDS, Ezra (still intact!) will end your world rule. See ad on Book pages —ADVT

U.S. Embassy Guards In Iran Fire Tear Gas At Student Protesters

By JOHN VINOCUR

Special to The New York Times

TEHERAN, Iran, Dec. 24 — Students ran wildly through stalled traffic today, pounding car roofs with their fists and slipping sheets of paper that said "Death to the Shah" under windshield wipers.

Other groups of students — some shouting "Death to Jimmy Carter!" — gathered in front of the American Embassy, which sits behind a heavy protective fence with chains on its gates. At one point, the Marine guards at the embassy fired tear gas into a crowd near the gates.

An American official said the tear gas was fired when bricks were thrown over the wall around the embassy compound and it appeared that one or two demonstrators were going to try to scale it.

One Person Tried to Enter

A source close to the embassy, who requested that his position not be disclosed, said: "As best I know only one person tried to enter the embassy grounds. Bricks and rocks and other projectiles were thrown. You could say there was an attack, but there was absolutely no attempt to storm the embassy. Iranian

Continued on Page 3, Column 2

DAN MAY-HAPPY BIRTHDAY. LOVE AND RESPECT FROM LOTS AND LOTS OF PEOPLE. ADVT

Cambodia-Vietnam Battles Spur U.S. Concern Over 'Proxy' War

By DAVID BINDER

Special to The New York Times

WASHINGTON, Dec. 24 — The Carter Administration has become more concerned in recent days over increased fighting between Cambodia and Vietnam, which knowledgeable officials now characterize as full-scale war.

The Administration's concern focuses not only on the impact of the fighting on Indochina but also upon its potential for involving the major powers in the rivalry, specifically China on behalf of Cambodia and the Soviet Union for Vietnam.

Murder Called Politically Motivated

In Peking today, Cambodian officials were quoted by Reuters as having said that an attack yesterday on three western visitors to Phnom Penh was politically motivated, designed to show that Cambodia could not protect its friends. A British scholar, Malcolm Caldwell, was killed in that attack. Two American journalists in the same party, which was staying in a government guest house in the Cambodian capital, escaped injury in the attack. [Page 6.]

Diplomats in Peking suggested that the attack on Mr. Caldwell, a London University lecturer, might have been staged by a new insurgency movement, whose establishment was recently announced by Hanoi radio.

It is 11 months since Zbigniew Brzezinski, the President's national-security adviser, described what was then a violent border conflict between Cambodia and Vietnam as a "proxy war," with the respective combatants acting as proxies for China and the Soviet Union. At that time none of the Indochina specialists in the United States' intelligence and defense communities accepted this definition, arguing that the rivalry between the two Indochinese neighbors was much too grave

Associated Press

Malcolm Caldwell

Continued on Page 7, Column 1

INSIDE

Falcons, Oilers Gain in Playoffs

The Atlanta Falcons and the Houston Oilers won wild-card games to advance in the National Football League championship playoffs. Page 23.

8 Children Die in Fire

An apartment fire, apparently started by a short circuit in Christmas tree lights, killed eight children in a New Orleans family. Page 10.

Season's Drinks Changing

Hard liquor seems to be losing ground to wine, but the liquor industry says over all, anything expensive is "in" this holiday season. Page 33.

Because of production requirements, The Times appears today in two sections. Metropolitan Report begins on page 21, SportsMonday on page 23 and Business Day on page 33. The four-section format will resume tomorrow.

"All the News That's Fit to Print"

The New York Times

LATE CITY

Weather: Mostly sunny, clear to cloudy tonight. Snow likely tomorrow. Temperature range: today 5-15; yesterday 4-13. Details on page 41.

VOL.CXXVIII . . . No.44,132 — Copyright © 1979 The New York Times — NEW YORK, SUNDAY, FEBRUARY 18, 1979 — $1.00 beyond 50-mile zone from New York City. Higher in air delivery cities — 85 CENTS

CHINESE TROOPS AND PLANES ATTACK VIETNAM; U.S. URGES WITHDRAWAL, HANOI IN PLEA TO U.N.

Iranian Premier Talks of Resuming Oil Sale to U.S. as Soon as Possible

By NICHOLAS GAGE
Special to The New York Times

TEHERAN, Iran, Feb. 17 — Prime Minister Medhi Bazargan said today that Iran's new revolutionary Government intended to resume oil exports as soon as possible "to all parts of the world, including the United States," and was eager to maintain good relations with Washington.

In an interview, his first since taking office on Monday, Mr. Bazargan asserted that the revolutionary court — which ordered four generals executed late Thursday night — would turn over to his Government the responsibility of punishing corrupt former officials.

Liason Agency/Gamma

Prime Minister Mehdi Bazargan

Mr. Bazargan's Government made another gain today as merchants, shopkeepers, office workers and others responded to an appeal from Ayatollah Ruhollah Khomeini to return to their jobs. The exodus of Americans and other foreigners resumed during the day, with about 800 Americans flying out after they were escorted to the airport by supporters of the Ayatollah. [Details, page 14.]

In the interview, Mr. Bazargan also said that the Komiteh, the group of aides to Ayatollah Ruhollah Khomeini that has been making the major decisions until now, would be dissolved "in one or two weeks" and would transfer its responsibilities to his Government.

New National Guard Planned

He conceded that the country's security forces had been "demolished" in the last 10 days of fighting and said that a new national guard to restore order was being formed out of remnants of the revolutionary militias and the armed forces. On the subject of order, Mr. Bazargan said he deeply regretted the attack on the American Embassy Wednesday.

Leftist groups such as the People's Fedayeen, which have been blamed for many of the attacks this week, including the attack on the embasssy, will be allowed a role in political life, even to the degree of forming a Communist party, he said. "But if they continue to fight and destabilize the country, we're going to crush them," Mr. Bazargan asserted.

The Prime Minister said his Government would move quickly to hold a referendum on the future form of government, but Iranians will not be given a wide selection. Mr. Bazargan said they would be asked to answer yes or no to the question

Continued on Page 14, Column 6

SOVIET IS CAUTIONED

Washington Bids Moscow Take No Military Step to Back Hanoi Ally

By BERNARD GWERTZMAN
Special to The New York Times

WASHINGTON, Feb. 17 — The United States called on China today to withdraw its forces from Vietnam and said it opposed the invasion with the same severity with which it had earlier criticized Vietnam for attacking Cambodia.

Faced with what officials regarded as a major international crisis, the United States also advised the Soviet Union both publicly and privately against retaliating and attacking China in support of Vietnam, an ally of the Russians.

Officially, the United States is neutral in conflicts among the Communist countries in Asia, but the threat of a wider war that could involve Moscow has been a concern here for weeks.

Poss. .ility of Exchange

A senior American official said that he expected the United Nations Security Council to take up China's invasion soon. He said it was possible that Chinese troops might remain in Vietnam to be used in exchange for a withdrawal of Vietnamese forces now in Cambodia.

American intelligence sources reported that 150,000 Chinese troops, backed by air power and armor, were involved in the invasion. A similar number of Vietnamese troops are believed to be in Cambodia.

President Carter and other officials had tried and failed to persuade the Chinese not to attack Vietnam in response to the Vietnamese invasion of Cambodia, an ally of China, in December.

Call by State Department

"We are opposed both to the Vietnamese invasion of Cambodia and the Chinese invasion of Vietnam," Hodding Carter 3d, the State Department spokesman said. "We call for the immediate withdrawal of Vietnamese troops from Cambodia and Chinese troops from Vietnam.

"The United States is critical of any use of force outside one's own territory. The reported Chinese invasion of Vietnam, which we oppose, was preceded by the Vietnamese invasion of Kampuchea," he said, referring to Cambodia.

United States officials regarded the invasion by China as a major military move. But some of them noted hopefully that Hsinhua, the official Chinese press

Continued on Page 10, Column 1

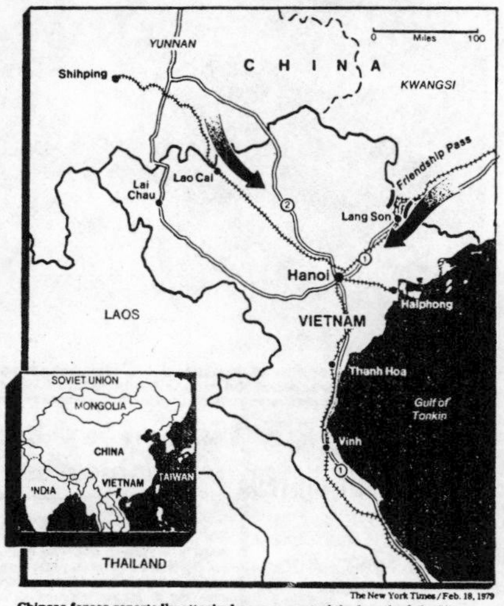
YUNNAN
C H I N A
KWANGSI
Shihping
0 Miles 100
Friendship Pass
Lao Cai
Lai Chau
Lang Son
Hanoi
VIETNAM
Haiphong
LAOS
Thanh Hoa
Gulf of Tonkin
Vinh
SOVIET UNION
MONGOLIA
CHINA
INDIA
VIETNAM
TAIWAN
THAILAND

The New York Times/Feb. 18, 1979

Chinese forces reportedly attacked across most of the length of the Vietnam border. Arrows indicate movements thought to be the main thrusts.

A Classic Military Operation

China's Drive on a Wide Front in Vietnam Leaves Hanoi Guessing About Main Focus and Objective

By DREW MIDDLETON

The Chinese invasion of Vietnam followed, at the outset, the classic pattern of attacks over a wide front — with the defenders left guessing about the principal axis of advance.

Military Analysis

The operations of the Chinese Army developing in the Lao Cai area of Vietnam appeared the most dangerous to the Vietnamese at the close of the first day's fighting. If pushed successfully, the operations would give the Chinese control of the railroad to Hanoi from China and the north.

A second attack, in the Lang Son area, northeast of the capital, also appeared to be gaining momentum. But it was possible that one or both of these might prove to be holding operations and that the main thrust along the front of about 480 miles might come from elsewhere, possibly along the coast.

The most important missing element in the strategic equation is Chinese intentions about the duration of the action. Until very recently, it was thought that in any action against Vietnam, the Chinese Army would follow the pattern of the 1962-63 operation in India.

In the earlier operation, the Chinese made a series of successful attacks, for limited objectives, in India's northern frontier territory. The Chinese consolidated their positions and did not advance further.

Less Freedom of Action Today

The Chinese, experts emphasized, do not possess the same freedom of action today that they had during the invasion into northern India.

By attacking Vietnam, an ally of the Soviet Union, the Chinese may have jeopardized what they concede is a weak military position on the long border with the Soviet Union. The expectation is that the Chinese operations in Vietnam, although delivered with the maximum weight of

Continued on Page 10, Column 1

4 PROVINCES INVADED

Thrust Reported All Along Border — Peking Says Move Is Retaliatory

By FOX BUTTERFIELD
Special to The New York Times

HONG KONG, Sunday, Feb. 18 — The Chinese Government announced last night that its troops had struck against Vietnam along much of their 480-mile border.

The Vietnam News Agency reported yesterday evening that Chinese troops,

Texts of the statements by China and Vietnam are on page 10.

supported by aircraft and artillery, had attacked four Vietnamese border provinces earlier in the day from Quang Ninh in the east to Hoang Lien Son in the west.

There was no immediate word from either Peking or Hanoi on how far the Chinese had pushed into Vietnam. But Hsinhua, the Chinese press agency, called the action counterattacks. In a dispatch with the dateline "Kwangsi and Yunnan Border Fronts," the agency said "fighting is still going on" at the time of the transmission.

China Disavows Territorial Aims

Hsinhua asserted that Peking did "not want a single inch of Vietnamese territory" and that "after counterattacking the Vietnamese aggressors as they deserve, the Chinese frontier troops will strictly keep to defending the border of their own country."

The Chinese attack began at 4 A.M. yesterday Peking time (3 P.M. Friday, New York time). It followed by six weeks the Vietnamese invasion of Cambodia and seizure of its capital, Phnom Penh, and by 15 weeks the Vietnamese signing of a treaty of peace and cooperation with the Soviet Union.

China is still supporting Cambodian forces loyal to Prime Minister Pol Pot, whose regime was routed by the Vietnamese.

Vietnamese Ask Soviet Help

The Vietnamese news agency said last night that "the people and Government of Vietnam "urgently call on the Soviet Union, the fraternal socialist countries" and other friendly countries throughout the world to "support and defend Vietnam." A spokesman for the Vietnamese Foreign Ministry said a letter had been sent to the United Nations Security Council calling on China to cease its "invasion."

[At the United Nations, Vietnam accused China of launching a "war of aggression" and asked the United Nations to take "appropriate measures" to force Peking's troops to withdraw from Vietnam. Page 11.]

China appeared to be trying to limit the repercussions of its actions to prevent a long fight with Vietnam or retaliation by the Soviet Union.

Hsinhua said the Chinese Government proposed that "the two sides speedily hold negotiations at any mutually agreed place" to discuss "the restoration of peace and tranquillity along the border."

The Chinese attack, if Peking cannot bring a quick end to the fighting, could seriously damage China's ambitious drive for economic modernization, di-

Continued on Page 10, Column 1

Carter, Wary of Carey Ambitions, Is Courting Other State Democrats

By STEVEN R. WEISMAN
Special to The New York Times

WASHINGTON, Feb. 17 — President Carter's political aides, expecting Governor Carey to chart an independent course in the 1980 Presidential election, have begun a quiet campaign to strengthen their ties to a variety of different influential Democrats in New York State.

In the last few weeks, Mr. Carter has met at the White House with Assembly Speaker Stanley Fink and the Queens Borough President, Donald R. Manes, who is also the Democratic county leader, for conversations described as a mixture of policy and politics.

In addition, only two days after Mr. Carter held a well-publicized meeting with Mayor Koch and Mr. Carey on the subject of New York City's finances, Stuart E. Eizenstat, the President's chief adviser on domestic policy, met privately with major municipal labor leaders, who have been at odds with Mr. Koch.

Just below the surface of all the activity lies what various aides describe as a certain distance persisting between Mr. Carter and Mr. Carey. The Governor, a late supporter of Mr. Carter in 1976, has been openly critical of the White House staff, and many politicians think he is trying to position himself for a run for the Presidency or the Vice Presidency.

At the very least, politicians say, Mr. Carey is trying to build up his strength nationally so that he might play a key role in the maneuvering of 1980, should Mr. Carter be challenged by other Demo-

Continued on Page 32, Column 1

2 Arrested in Robbery Of Millions at Airport

By LESLIE MAITLAND

Two men were arrested yesterday by the Federal Bureau of Investigation in connection with the Dec. 11 robbery of more than $5 million from the Lufthansa cargo area at Kennedy International Airport.

One of the men was charged with participating in the theft, and the other, a Lufthansa employee, was held as a material witness in the case, believed to have been the largest cash robbery in history. None of the money has been recovered.

According to law-enforcement officials, the suspect charged in the robbery was Angelo J. Sepe, 37 years old, of 107-68 101st Street, Ozone Park, Queens.

The officials identified the Lufthansa employee as Peter Gruenawald, 39, of Levittown, L.I. They said he had been arrested on a material witness order when authorities learned he was planning to leave the country. He was not at the airport the morning that the six or seven

Continued on Page 25, Column 1

The New York Times/John L. Alexandrowicz

Dr. Donald C. Johanson, left, talks with Richard Leakey in a break in the Pittsburgh symposium on human evolution

Rival Anthropologists Divide on 'Pre-Human' Find

By BOYCE RENSBERGER
Special to The New York Times

PITTSBURGH, Feb. 17 — Two well-known anthropologists challenged each other today in what could become a wide-ranging debate over whether a finding last month was indeed a new species of pre-human being ancestral to all other known forms of human and human-like creatures.

Richard Leakey, the Kenya anthropologist, is challenging the announcement last month by two American scientists that they had discovered such a new species. Dr. Donald C. Johanson, one of the Americans, appeared with Mr. Leakey at a symposium here on human evolution and vigorously defended his interpretation.

Wide Implications

The difference between the two views has implications beyond the details. If Dr. Johanson is correct, it would mean that the human species emerged from more primitive ancestors more recently, perhaps only two million years ago.

On the other hand, if Mr. Leakey is correct, mankind appeared on the scene so long ago — more than four million years — that there is no clear evidence of a fossil form that could have been ancestral to human beings.

Although honest differences of opinion are common enough in all sciences, there were overtones of a confrontation between the two anthropologists, each of whom leads a major fossil-hunting expedition in eastern Africa. The two men have often been viewed as rivals.

Although the two lines of argument turn on fine points of interpretation, they provide an unusual glimpse of the ways in which anthropologists think about their

Continued on Page 41, Column 1

Hispanics Lead U.S. Minorities In Growth Rate

By ROBERT LINDSEY
Special to The New York Times

LOS ANGELES, Feb. 17 — In Minneapolis-St. Paul, Mexican-Americans have replaced blacks as the largest minority. In Los Angeles, 35 percent of public school students are of Hispanic descent, but the figure is almost 50 percent for kindergarten pupils. In Seattle, the Hispanic population is growing almost twice as fast as that of non-Hispanic whites.

A tide of immigration unequalled since the turn of the century, coupled with a high birth rate among residents of Hispanic origin, has made Hispanic people this nation's fastest-growing minority, and some demographers expect them to overtake blacks as the nation's predominant minority before 1985.

Population experts say it is too early to appraise precisely the long-term implications of that rapid increase in Hispanic population. But their growing presence is beginning to have a broad impact on the economic, social and cultural life of mainstream America despite a tendency to remain behind a formidable barrier to assimilation — the Spanish language.

The Hispanic presence can be seen in the vivid murals splashed onto buildings by Hispanic artists from Boston to Los Angeles, heard in the peppery beat of Latin-flavored disco music, and tasted in the proliferation of Mexican restaurants that, according to a food industry study, have supplanted Chinese restaurants as

Continued on Page 16, Column 1

Today's Sections

Index to Subjects

"All the News That's Fit to Print"

The New York Times

LATE CITY EDITION

Weather: Partly cloudy, mild today; clear tonight. Cloudy, rain tomorrow. Temperature range: today 42-53; yesterday 50-56. Details on page B6.

VOL.CXXVIII . . . No.44,149 | NEW YORK, WEDNESDAY, MARCH 7, 1979 | 25 cents beyond 50-mile zone from New York City. Higher in air delivery cities. | 20 CENTS

Copyright © 1979 The New York Times.

PRESIDENT REVIVING A REDUCED AID PLAN ON JOBLESS IN CITIES

ASKS $400 MILLION IN 2 YEARS

Proposal, a Turnaround by Carter, Is Sent to Congress, Where It Faces Heavy Opposition

By ROBERT REINHOLD

Special to The New York Times

WASHINGTON, March 6 — President Carter pledged strong support today to the revival of a major program of providing fiscal aid to cities with high unemployment rates, which died in Congress last year.

The bill would channel $400 million to the country's most distressed cities over the next two years, with New York City getting $69 million, or 17 percent, of the money. The funds would be more narrowly concentrated on the most distressed places than under the previous version.

The President's position, laid out in a message to Congress today and in a meeting he held with a score or so of state, county and city officials at the White House, represents a sharp turnaround. The Administration earlier indicated it preferred to drop the measure, the so-called countercyclical revenue-sharing program.

Faces Opposition in Congress

But even with Mr. Carter's support and even though the measure is greatly scaled down from last year's failed version, the bill is expected to face rough sledding in a hostile Congress.

At a press briefing, Stuart E. Eizenstat, the President's chief domestic adviser, said he thought the new bill would have a "broader base of support" in Congress than last year's much more costly one, but he conceded it would be a "difficult fight." He said the President considered it one of his "very highest priorities."

Details on Allocations

The Administration has been under intense pressure from city and county leaders all over the country to restore the program, which they liked because the money came free of the usual restrictions on use that come with most Federal aid. When it died abruptly in the House last October after approval in the Senate, many cities had already built the expected money into their budgets.

While the broad outlines of the proposal had been known, the Administration provided further details today on the allocation formulas and amounts due to each eligible city and county. In all, 1,231 localities would get money, as against 26,600

Continued on Page A17, Column 1

The New York Times/Neal Boenzi

ANOTHER SOGGY DAY IN NEW YORK: With parts of the city starting to look more and more like the watery canals of Venice, these New Yorkers sloshed through ankle-deep puddle. Cloudy skies are expected today. Page B3.

FUEL SHORTAGE CUTS FLIGHTS BY UNITED

429 Departures a Week Canceled for March — Iran Cutoff Cited

By RICHARD WITKIN

United Airlines, the nation's largest air carrier, said yesterday that it was canceling 429 flights a week for the rest of March because of a jet-fuel shortage that it attributed in large measure to the curtailment of oil exports from Iran.

The cancellations, mostly on weekends, will amount to 3.4 percent of the 12,000 trips a week that the airline normally flies.

The planned cutback followed a series of unexpected flight cuts that started last Saturday and represented the most far-reaching airline reaction so far to the fuel shortage.

Last week, Trans World Airlines and National Airlines announced that the shortage was compelling them to cancel a sizable number of flights — mainly those with relatively light demand. Yesterday, Delta Airlines joined United in announcing cutbacks, although Delta's were minor compared with United's. Delta said it would not be flying nine runs in and out of the Chicago area yesterday and today.

The Delta move underscored a statement made by one of its top officials Mon-

Continued on Page D4, Column 1

Vietnam Says It Is Willing to Talk If Chinese Keep Pledge to Pull Out

By HENRY KAMM

Special to The New York Times

BANGKOK, March 6 — The Vietnamese Government said today that it was ready to negotiate with China if China carried out its plan to withdraw all its forces.

But the statement, by a Foreign Ministry spokesman, said Chinese attacks had continued even after yesterday's announcement of the withdrawal plan.

[In Peking, an editorial to be published in People's Daily, the Communist Party newspaper, said Chinese troops were "victoriously returning" from Vietnam after having "exploded the myth of the invincibility" of the Vietnamese Army. There was confusion about the battlefield situation, but the editorial seemed to indicate that China was going ahead with the plan.]

The Vietnamese declaration said the war would continue if Peking was using the announcement of the withdrawal as a subterfuge. The statement said:

"If China really withdraws all of its troops from Vietnam as it has stated, and after all the Chinese forces have been withdrawn to the other side of the historical border that both sides have agreed to respect, then the Vietnamese side will be ready immediately to enter into negotiations with the Chinese side at the deputy foreign ministers' level at a place and date to be agreed upon on the restoration of normal relations."

Diplomatic observers said the declaration seemed to indicate that Vietnam was willing to allow the Chinese troops, estimated at 100,000, to withdraw without harassment. The difficulties of extricating troops in the face of a hostile force might have tempted Vietnam to exploit the withdrawal to gain an advantage. [United Press International reported from Bangkok that Vietnam announced later in a broadcast by Radio Hanoi that its troops would not attack the Chinese force as it withdrew.]

The Vietnamese statement said the Chinese had been forced to announce their withdrawal because of the resistance they had encountered.

Western analysts here said there were only vague indications of a withdrawal, with no troop movements observable.

Continued on Page A4, Column 3

SADAT SAID TO BUOY HOPES FOR ACCORD DURING CARTER TRIP

U.S. Sends Ships To Arabian Sea In Yemen Crisis

Action Is Meant to Warn Soviet and Help Saudis

By RICHARD BURT

Special to The New York Times

WASHINGTON, March 6 — President Carter has ordered a carrier task force into the Arabian Sea to show concern over Southern Yemen's continuing drive into Yemen, to warn the Soviet Union of the risks involved in backing the incursion and to demonstrate support for Yemen's neighbor and backer, Saudi Arabia.

Administration officials said today that the decision had been made at a White House meeting yesterday. According to Defense Department aides, the carrier Constellation and three other ships will leave Subic Bay in the Philippines tomorrow and reach the Arabian Sea in eight days. The Yemens are at the southern end of the Arabian Peninsula on the Gulf of Aden, which leads to the Arabian Sea.

Officials here said that fighting in Yemen had intensified and that Southern Yemeni forces had penetrated more than 30 miles into the country despite the adoption of a peace plan early this morning by foreign ministers of Arab League countries, including both Yemens, at a meeting in Kuwait.

Support for Arab Moderates

After the upheaval in Iran and other crises in the region, Mr. Carter's decision to send a naval force into the Arabian Sea is designed, officials said, to demonstrate American support for Saudi Arabia and other moderate Arab nations that have recently expressed private doubts about the credibility of American commitments.

They said that Saudi Arabia had not specifically requested a carrier but that last weekend Saudi leaders had asked for a show of American concern over the conflict in Yemen. "Now we're giving them one," said a Defense Department aide.

Mr. Carter's decision is a departure in his Administration's use of military force. It is said to reflect his interest in showing American concern for the security of the Persian Gulf and the Middle East.

Late in 1978, as the revolt in Iran reached its peak, Mr. Carter ordered the

Continued on Page A12, Column 1

U.S. REMAINS CAUTIOUS

Egyptian Won't Comment on Specific Proposals Accepted by Israel

By BERNARD GWERTZMAN

Special to The New York Times

WASHINGTON, March 6 — President Anwar el-Sadat of Egypt has informed President Carter that he wants the American leader's Middle East trip to result in a peace treaty between Egypt and Israel but that he is reserving judgment on the latest American compromise proposals until Mr. Carter arrives in Cairo Thursday.

It was stated authoritatively today that Mr. Sadat, in his phone conversation with Mr. Carter yesterday, stressed his intention to help make Mr. Carter's trip a success. But because of Mr. Sadat's desire to withhold comments on the three compromise ideas that Israel accepted yesterday, American officials have also decided to remain cautious about the trip.

The American proposals were conveyed in detail to Mr. Sadat in Cairo today by Zbigniew Brzezinski, the President's national security adviser, and Alfred L. Atherton Jr., the special Middle East negotiator, who flew to Cairo in advance of Mr. Carter's departure tomorrow evening. [Page A11.]

Idea of Target Date Retained

Senior American officials like Secretary of State Cyrus R. Vance, who will accompany Mr. Carter to Cairo, are known to believe that the proposals accepted by the Israelis will also be agreeable to Mr. Sadat. This is because the proposals retain the idea of a target date — one year from now — for completing preparations for elections for Palestinian self-rule in the occupied West Bank and Gaza Strip.

Administration officials said that the United States planned to discuss major increases in military and economic aid with both Israel and Egypt during the trip, but that there was no intention of seeking either American bases or defense treaties with either country.

Defense Secretary Harold Brown, who recently visited the Middle East to discuss bolstering security in the region, will also accompany Mr. Carter, Administra-

Continued on Page A10, Column 3

F.B.I. Is Said to Report Aid to Carter Business Violated Banking Law

By NICHOLAS M. HORROCK

Special to The New York Times

WASHINGTON, March 6 — A preliminary report by the Federal Bureau of Investigation has found technical violations of banking laws in the administration of loans to President Carter's warehouse business, well-placed Administration sources said today.

The Justice Department is studying the matter to determine whether a broader investigation, possibly involving a special prosecutor, is warranted, according to Attorney General Griffin B. Bell.

The Justice Department made its first formal announcement that the report had been completed in the inquiry into the Carter warehouse loans at a meeting with Republican members of the House Judiciary Committee today. The departmental officials did not disclose the contents, but other Administration officials did.

The officials at the meeting, led by Mr. Bell, reported that a 16-month investigation of Bert Lance's banking practices had been completed and that the findings were now under study here. According to well-placed Administration sources, a field team of prosecutors has recommended that Mr. Lance, the former Federal budget director, be indicted on a

Continued on Page A16, Column 3

Minor Changes for New Yorkers Seen in Landmark Alimony Case

By LESLEY OELSNER

The telephones started ringing early in many New York law firms yesterday. The divorced and the soon-to-be-divorced were calling; they wanted to know what the United States Supreme Court's landmark ruling on alimony Monday meant for them.

The answer was, probably not very much — for most of them, at least.

The Supreme Court held that state laws under which only husbands, not wives, could be required to pay alimony were unconstitutional.

New York, like 10 other states, has such a law. The Court's ruling, on its face, seems to make the law unenforceable.

But divorce-law experts here said yesterday that the ruling did not mean that alimony requirements already imposed under the New York law were unenforceable.

Nor does it mean that New York men will be spared alimony requirements in the future, they said.

'A Lot of Fuss and Feathers'

"There's going to be a lot of fuss and feathers," predicted Eleanor Alter, a prominent Manhattan lawyer who specializes in domestic relations. "But in reality it's not going to make much difference as a practical matter. Men should not be jumping for joy."

The Supreme Court ruling did not say whether it was retroactive.

Lawyers such as Mrs. Alter and academic experts such as Henry H. Foster, recently retired as a professor at New York University Law School, said that, in the absence of any statement to the contrary, they assumed that the Court had intended the ruling to be prospective only, not retroactive.

Beyond that, however, the great majority of alimony requirements in New York have been imposed as a result of separation agreements between the spouses, rather than as a result of a judicial decision. In the typical case, the husband and wife agree on a settlement and then have it formalized by a court.

The separation agreements are essentially contracts, and they generally must be enforced regardless of what the divorce laws may or may not say.

There is one exception — one way, a few lawyers suggested, in which a man who is now paying alimony under a separation agreement might be able to get the agreement changed and get his ex-wife to pay him.

The exception arises from the fact that a separation agreement may specify either that the agreement "survives" the court's divorce decree or that it is

Continued on Page B3, Column 2

AGATHA—
MAY YOUR DROPPED BREAD BE BUTTERED ONLY ON THE CRUST.
MANDRAKE—Advt.

"ONLY $16.00 A MONTH"—24 HOUR PHONE ANSWERING SERVICE TOTALLY NEW CONCEPT!! INCREDIBLE!! (712) 779-3670 —ADVT.

Lynn Karlin

MEDICAL LEADER DIES: Dr. John H. Knowles, president of Rockefeller Foundation, died in Boston at 52. Article, page A22.

INSIDE

800 Reported Slain in Chad

More than 800 Moslems in Chad's southern city of Moundou were killed in new strife over the weekend, Government officials reported. Page A3.

11 Indicted in Dock Inquiry

Eleven men, two of them linked to organized crime, were indicted following a Federal investigation of corruption on the New York waterfront. Page B1.

Oil Reserve May Be Tapped

Energy Secretary James R. Schlesinger said the oil shortage may force the nation to dip into its Strategic Petroleum Reserve by next fall. Page D1.

President Anwar el-Sadat of Egypt welcoming Zbigniew Brzezinski to his Cairo residence yesterday

South Africa Strikes Namibian Rebel Bases in Angola

By JOHN F. BURNS

Special to The New York Times

PRETORIA, South Africa, March 6 — South Africa sent troops and warplanes into Angola today on what it described as limited strikes against bases of the South-West Africa People's Organization.

In a speech in Parliament in which he announced the attacks, Prime Minister P. W. Botha also said that the Government had rejected a cease-fire proposal by the United Nations.

The strikes, launched at dawn, continued through the day, according to Gen. Magnus Malan, chief of the South African Defense Force. The general said that the attacks were aimed at guerrilla bases.

Mr. Botha told Parliament that the attacks had been ordered because of a new situation that had arisen after Secretary General Kurt Waldheim's proposal of a cease-fire last week in the United Nations Security Council. Mr. Botha did not describe how the situation had changed, but a statement by General Malan referred to a buildup of guerrillas at bases close to the border. The general indicated that the buildup could have been related to guerrilla plans to increase infiltration into South-West Africa before an armistice.

At midnight, 18 hours after the raids began, defense headquarters here were still withholding details of the operation.

The secrecy implied that the attacks could have been on a scale similar to those mounted against some guerrilla bases in Angola in May, when several hundred people were killed in daylong attacks involving paratroopers, helicopter gunships and fighter-bombers.

In Mr. Botha's address, which lasted more than an hour, he made public a letter to Mr. Waldheim from Foreign Minister Roelof F. Botha. In the letter, which was delivered yesterday, South Africa formally rejected the cease-fire proposals.

A principal objection stated in the let-

Continued on Page A9, Column 1

"Happy Twentieth Anniversary to Sylvia from John, Alison and Amy."—Advt.

GLASER & BLITZ lawyers practicing in medical malpractice products & accident cases. First consult free. (212) 421-4884—ADVT

Appendix

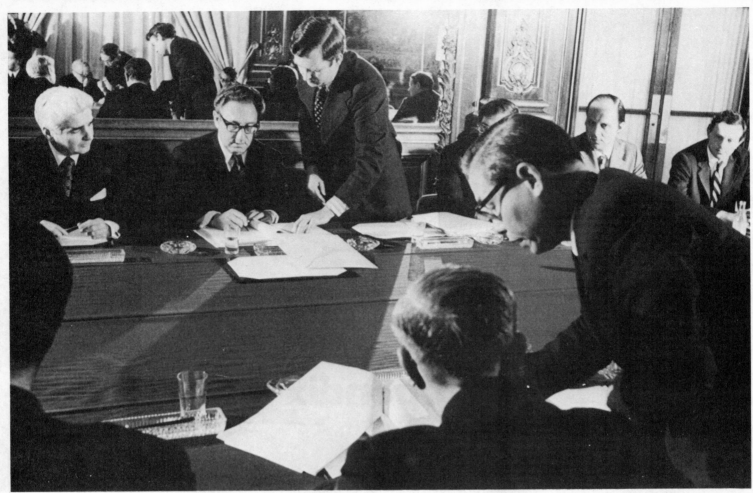

Dr. Henry Kissinger initials the cease-fire agreement that formally ended the Vietnam War in Paris on January 23, 1973. In the foreground is Le Duc Tho, chief negotiator for Hanoi, affixing his signature to the agreement.

Le Duc Tho, Hanoi's representative at the Paris Peace Talks during one of the negotiating sessions.

South Vietnamese President Nguyen Van Thieu approved the cease-fire agreement in principle on January 18, 1973. Thieu's "go-ahead" paved the way for the agreement's signing in Paris five days later by Henry Kissinger and Le Duc Tho.

THE VIETNAM AGREEMENT AND PROTOCOLS

Special to The New York Times

WASHINGTON, Jan. 24—Following, as made public by the White House today, are the texts of the Vietnam cease-fire agreement initialed in Paris yesterday by Henry A. Kissinger and Le Duc Tho, and of the four accompanying protocols detailing means of carrying it out. The accord and three of the protocols have been drafted in two versions. The "four-party" versions will be signed Saturday morning. Because South Vietnam is unwilling to imply recognition of the Vietcong's Provisional Revolutionary Government, "two-party" versions mentioning that Government will be signed in the afternoon only by the United States and North Vietnam.

The Cease-Fire Agreement

Agreement on Ending the War and Restoring Peace in Vietnam

The parties participating in the Paris conference on Vietnam,

With a view to ending the war and restoring peace in Vietnam on the basis of respect for the Vietnamese people's fundamental national rights and the South Vietnamese people's right to self-determination, and to contributing to the consolidation of peace in Asia and the world,

Have agreed on the following provisions and undertake to respect and to implement them:

Chapter I

The Vietnamese People's Fundamental National Rights

ARTICLE 1

The United States and all other countries respect the independence, sovereignty, unity and territorial integrity of Vietnam as recognized by the 1954 Geneva Agreements on Vietnam.

Chapter II

Cessation of Hostilities, Withdrawal of Troops

ARTICLE 2

A cease-fire shall be observed throughout South Vietnam as of 2400 hours G.M.T., on Jan. 27, 1973.

At the same hour, the United States will stop all its military activities against the territory of the Democratic Republic of Vietnam by ground, air and naval forces, wherever they may be based, and end the mining of the territorial waters, ports, harbors and waterways of the Democratic Republic of Vietnam. The United States will remove, permanently deactivate or destroy all the mines in the territorial waters, ports, harbors and waterways of North Vietnam as soon as this agreement goes into effect.

The complete cessation of hostilities mentioned in this article shall be durable and without limit of time.

ARTICLE 3

The parties undertake to maintain the cease-fire and to insure a lasting and stable peace.

As soon as the cease-fire goes into effect:

(a) The United States forces and those of the other foreign countries allied with the United States and the Republic of Vietnam shall remain in place pending the implementation of the plan of troop withdrawal. The Four-Party Joint Military Commission described in Article 16 shall determine the modalities.

(b) The armed forces of the two South Vietnamese parties shall remain in place. The Two-Party Joint Military Commission described in Article 17 shall determine the areas controlled by each party and the modalities of stationing.

(c) The regular forces of all services and arms and the irregular forces of the parties in South Vietnam shall stop all offensive activities against each other and shall strictly abide by the following stipulations:

¶All acts of force on the ground, in the air and on the sea shall be prohibited.

¶All hostile acts, terrorism and reprisals by both sides will be banned.

ARTICLE 4

The United States will not continue its military involvement or intervene in the internal affairs of South Vietnam.

ARTICLE 5

Within 60 days of the signing of this agreement, there will be a total withdrawal from South Vietnam of troops, military personnel, including technical military personnel and military personnel associated with the pacification program, armaments, munitions and war material of the United States and those of the other foreign countries mentioned in Article 3 (a). Advisers from the above-mentioned countries to all paramilitary organizations and the police force will also be withdrawn within the same period of time.

ARTICLE 6

The dismantlement of all military bases in South Vietnam of the United States and of the other foreign countries mentioned in Article 3 (a) shall be completed within 60 days of the signing of this agreement.

ARTICLE 7

From the enforcement of the cease-fire to the formation of the government provided for in Articles 9 (b) and 14 of this agreement, the two South Vietnamese parties shall not accept the introduction of troops, military advisers and military personnel, including technical military personnel, armaments, munitions and war material into South Vietnam.

The two South Vietnamese parties shall be permitted to make periodic replacement of armaments, munitions and war material which have been destroyed, damaged, worn out or used up after the cease-fire, on the basis of piece-for-piece, of the same characteristics and properties, under the supervision of the Joint Military Commission of Control and Supervision.

Chapter III

The Return of Captured Military Personnel and Foreign Civilians, and Captured and Detained Vietnamese Civilian Personnel

ARTICLE 8

(a) The return of captured military personnel and foreign civilians of the parties shall be carried out simultaneously with and completed not later than the same day as the troop withdrawal mentioned in Article 5. The parties shall exchange complete lists of the above-mentioned captured military personnel and foreign civilians on the day of the signing of this agreement.

(b) The parties shall help each other to get information about those military personnel and foreign civilians of the parties missing in action, to determine the location and take care of the graves of the dead so as to facilitate the exhumation and repatriation of the remains, and to take any such other measures as may be required to get information about those still considered missing in action.

(c) The question of the return of Vietnamese civilian personnel captured and detained in South Vietnam will be resolved by the two South Vietnamese parties on the basis of the principles of Article 21 (b) of the Agreement on the Cessation of Hostilities in Vietnam of

July 20, 1954. The two South Vietnamese parties will do so in a spirit of national reconciliation and concord, with a view to ending hatred and enmity, in order to ease suffering and to reunite families. The two South Vietnamese parties will do their utmost to resolve this question within 90 days after the cease-fire comes into effect.

Chapter IV

The Exercise of the South Vietnamese People's Right to Self-Determination

ARTICLE 9

The Government of the United States of America and the Government of the Democratic Republic of Vietnam undertake to respect the following principles for the exercise of the South Vietnamese people's right to self-determination:

(a) The South Vietnamese people's right to self-determination is sacred, inalienable and shall be respected by all countries.

(b) The South Vietnamese people shall decide themselves the political future of South Vietnam through genuinely free and democratic general elections under international supervision.

(c) Foreign countries shall not impose any political tendency or personality on the South Vietnamese people.

ARTICLE 10

The two South Vietnamese parties undertake to respect the cease-fire and maintain peace in South Vietnam, settle all matters of contention through negotiations and avoid all armed conflict.

ARTICLE 11

Immediately after the cease-fire, the two South Vietnamese parties will:

¶Achieve national reconciliation and concord, end hatred and enmity, prohibit all acts of reprisal and discrimination against individuals or organizations that have collaborated with one side or the other.

¶Insure the democratic liberties of the people: personal freedom, freedom of speech, freedom of the press, freedom of meeting, freedom of organization, freedom of political activities, freedom of belief, freedom of movement, freedom of residence, freedom of work, right to property ownership and right to free enterprise.

ARTICLE 12

(a) Immediately after the cease-fire, the two South Vietnamese parties shall hold consultations in a spirit of national reconciliation and concord, mutual respect and mutual nonelimination to set up a National Council of National Reconciliation and Concord of three equal segments. The council shall operate on the principle of unanimity. After the National Council of National Reconciliation and Concord has assumed its functions, the two South Vietnamese parties will consult about the formation of councils at lower levels. The two South Vietnamese parties shall sign an agreement on the internal matters of South Vietnam as soon as possible and do their utmost to accomplish this within 90 days after the cease-fire comes into effect, in keeping with the South Vietnamese people's aspirations for peace, independence and democracy.

(b) The National Council of National Reconciliation and Concord shall have the task of promoting the two South Vietnamese parties' implementation of this agreement, achievement of national reconciliation and concord and insurance of democratic liberties. The National Council of National Reconciliation and Concord will organize the free and democratic general elections provided for in Article 9 (b) and decide the procedures and modalities of these general elections. The institutions for which the general elections are to be held will be agreed upon through consultations between the two South Vietnamese parties. The National Council of National Reconciliation and Concord will also decide the procedures and modalities of such local elections as the two South Vietnamese parties agree upon.

ARTICLE 13

The question of Vietnamese armed forces in South Vietnam shall be settled by the two South Vietnamese parties in a spirit of national reconciliation and concord, equality and mutual respect, without interference, in accordance with the postwar situation. Among the questions to be discussed by the two South Vietnamese parties are steps to reduce their military effectives and to demobilize the troops being reduced. The two South Vietnamese parties will accomplish this as soon as possible.

ARTICLE 14

South Vietnam will pursue a foreign policy of peace and independence. It will be prepared to establish relations with all countries irrespective of their political and social systems on the basis of mutual respect for independence and sovereignty and accept economic and technical aid from any country with no political conditions attached. The acceptance of military aid by South Vietnam in the future shall come under the authority of the government set up after the general elections in South Vietnam provided for in Article 9 (b).

Chapter V

The Reunification of Vietnam and the Relationship Between North and South Vietnam

ARTICLE 15

The reunification of Vietnam shall be carried out step by step through peaceful means on the basis of discussions and agreements betweeen North and South Vietnam, without coercion or annexation by either party, and without foreign interference. The time for reunification will be agreed upon by North and South Vietnam.

Pending reunification:

(a) The military demarcation line between the two zones at the 17th Parallel is only provisional and not a political or territorial boundary, as provided for in paragraph 6 of the Final Declaration of the 1954 Geneva Conference.

(b) North and South Vietnam shall respect the demilitarized zone on either side of the provisional military demarcation line.

(c) North and South Vietnam shall promptly start negotiations with a view to re-establishing normal relations in various fields. Among the questions to

be negotiated are the modalities of civilian movement across the provisional military demarcation line.

(d) North and South Vietnam shall not join any military alliance or military bloc and shall not allow foreign powers to maintain military bases, troops, military advisers and military personnel on their respective territories, as stipulated in the 1954 Geneva Agreements on Vietnam.

Chapter VI

The Joint Military Commissions, The International Commission of Control and Supervision, The International Conference

ARTICLE 16

(a) The parties participating in the Paris conference on Vietnam shall immediately designate representatives to form a Four-Party Joint Military Commission with the task of insuring joint action by the parties in implementing the following provisions of this agreement:

¶The first paragraph of Article 2, regarding the enforcement of the cease-fire throughout South Vietnam.

¶Article 3 (a), regarding the cease-fire by U.S. forces and those of the other foreign countries referred to in that article.

¶Article 3 (c), regarding the cease-fire between all parties in South Vietnam.

¶Article 5, regarding the withdrawal from South Vietnam of U.S. troops and those of the other foreign countries mentioned in Article 3 (a).

¶Article 6, regarding the dismantlement of military bases in South Vietnam of the United States and those of the other foreign countries mentioned in Article 3 (a).

¶Article 8 (a), regarding the return of captured military personnel and foreign civilians of the parties.

¶Article 8 (b), regarding the mutual assistance of the parties in getting information about those military personnel and foreign civilians of the parties missing in action.

(b) The Four-Party Joint Military Commission shall operate in accordance with the principle of consultations and unanimity. Disagreements shall be referred to the International Commission of Control and Supervision.

(c) The Four-Party Military Commission shall begin operating immediately after the signing of this agreement and end its activities in 60 days, after the completion of the withdrawal of U.S. troops and those of the other foreign countries mentioned in Article 3 (a) and the completion of the return of captured military personnel and foreign civilians of the parties.

(d) The four parties shall agree immediately on the organization, the working procedure, means of activity and expenditures of the Four-Party Joint Military Commission.

ARTICLE 17

(a) The two South Vietnamese parties shall immediately designate representatives to form a Two-Party Joint Military Commission with the task of insuring joint action by the two South Vietnamese parties in implementing the following provisions of this agreement:

¶The first paragraph of Article 2, regarding the enforcement of the cease-fire throughout South Vietnam, when the Four-Party Joint Military Commission has ended its activities.

¶Article 3 (b), regarding the cease-fire between the two South Vietnamese parties.

¶Article 3(c), regarding the cease-fire between all parties in South Vietnam, when the Four-Party Joint Military Commission has ended its activities.

¶Article 7, regarding the prohibition of the introduction of troops into South Vietnam and all other provisions of this article.

¶Article 8 (c), regarding the question of the return of Vietnamese civilian personnel captured and detained in South Vietnam;

¶Article 13, regarding the reduction of the military effectives of the two South Vietnamese parties and the demobilization of the troops being reduced.

(b) Disagreements shall be referred to the International Commission of Control and Supervision.

(c) After the signing of this agreement, the Two-Party Joint Military Commission shall agree immediately on the measures and organization aimed at enforcing the cease-fire and preserving peace in South Vietnam.

ARTICLE 18

(a) After the signing of this Agreement, an International Commission of Control and Supervision shall be established immediately.

(b) Until the international conference provided for in Article 19 makes definitive arrangements, the International Commission of Control and Supervision will report to the four parties on matters concerning the control and supervision of the implementation of the following provisions of this agreement:

¶The first paragraph of Article 2, regarding the enforcement of the cease-fire throughout South Vietnam.

¶Article 3 (a), regarding the cease-fire by U.S. forces and those of the other foreign countries referred to in that article.

¶Article 3 (c), regarding the cease-fire between all the parties in South Vietnam.

¶Article 5, regarding the withdrawal from South Vietnam of U.S. troops and those of the other foreign countries mentioned in Article 3 (a).

¶Article 6, regarding the dismantlement of military bases in South Vietnam of the United States and those of the other foreign countries mentioned in Article 3 (a).

¶Article 8 (a), regarding the return of captured military personnel and foreign civilians of the parties.

The International Commission of Control and Supervision shall form control teams for carrying out its tasks. The four parties shall agree immediately on the location and operation of these teams. The parties will facilitate their operation.

(c) Until the international conference makes definitive arrangements, the International Commission of Control and Supervision will report to the two South Vietnamese parties on matters concerning the control and supervision of the implementation of the following provisions of this agreement:

¶The first paragraph of Article 2, regarding the enforcement of the cease-fire throughout South Vietnam, when the Four-Party Joint Military Commission has ended its activities.

¶Article 3 (b), regarding the cease-fire between the two South Vietnamese parties.

¶Article 3 (c), regarding the cease-fire between all parties in South Vietnam, when the Four-Party Joint Military Commission has ended its activities.

¶Article 7, regarding the prohibition of the introduction of troops into South Vietnam and all other provisions of this article.

¶Article 8 (c), regarding the question of the return of Vietnamese civilian personnel captured and detained in South Vietnam.

¶Article 9 (b), regarding the free and democratic general elections in South Vietnam.

¶Article 13, regarding the reduction of the military effectives of the two South Vietnamese parties and the demobilization of the troops being reduced.

The International Commission of Control and Supervision shall form control teams for carrying out its tasks. The two South Vietnamese parties shall agree immdiately on the location and operation of these teams. The two South Vietnamese parties will facilitate their operation.

(d) The International Commission of Control and Supervision shall be composed of representatives of four countries: Canada, Hungary, Indonesia and Poland. The chairmanship of this commission will rotate among the members for specific periods to be determined by the commission.

(e) The International Commission of Control and Supervision shall carry out its tasks in accordance with the principle of respect for the sovereignty of South Vietnam.

(f) The International Commission of Control and Supervision shall operate in accordance with the principle of consultations and unanimity.

(g) The International Commission of Control and Supervision shall begin operating when a cease-fire comes into force in Vietnam. As regards the provisions in Article 18 (b) concerning the four parties, the International Commission of Control and Supervision shall end its activities when the commission's tasks of control and supervision regarding these provisions have been fulfilled. As regards the provisions in Article 18 (c) concerning the two South Vietnamese parties, the International Commission of Control and Supervision shall end its activities on the request of the government formed after the general elections in South Vietnam provided for in Article 9 (b).

(h) The four parties shall agree immediately on the organization, means of activity and expenditures of the International Commission of Control and Supervision. The relationship between the international commission and the international conference will be agreed upon by the International Commission and the International Conference.

ARTICLE 19

The parties agree on the convening of an international conference within 30 days of the signing of this agreement to acknowledge the signed agreements; to guarantee the ending of the war, the maintenance of peace in Vietnam, the respect of the Vietnamese people's fundamental national rights and the South Vietnamese people's right to self-determination; and to contribute to and guarantee peace in Indochina.

The United States and the Democratic Republic of Vietnam, on behalf of the parties participating in the Paris conference on Vietnam, will propose to the following parties that they participate in this international conference: the People's Republic of China, the Republic of France, the Union of Soviet Socialist Republics, the United Kingdom, the four countries of the International Commission of Control and Supervision, and the Secretary General of the United Nations, together with the parties participating in the Paris conference on Vietnam.

Chapter VII

Regarding Cambodia and Laos

ARTICLE 20

(a) The parties participating in the Paris conference on Vietnam shall strictly respect the 1954 Geneva Agreements on Cambodia and the 1962 Geneva Agreements on Laos, which recognized the Cambodian and the Lao peoples' fundamental national rights, i.e., the independence, sovereignty, unity and territorial integrity of these countries. The parties shall respect the neutrality of Cambodia and Laos.

The parties participating in the Paris conference on Vietnam undertake to refrain from using the territory of Cambodia and the territory of Laos to encroach on the sovereignty and security of one another and of other countries.

(b) Foreign countries shall put an end to all military activities in Cambodia and Laos, totally withdraw from and refrain from reintroducing into these two countries troops, military advisers and military personnel, armaments, munitions and war material.

(c) The internal affairs of Cambodia and Laos shall be settled by the people of each of these countries without foreign interference.

(d) The problems existing between the Indochinese countries shall be settled by the Indochinese parties on the basis of respect for each other's independence, sovereignty and territorial integrity, and noninterference in each other's internal affairs.

Chapter VIII

The Relationship Between the United States and the Democratic Republic of Vietnam

ARTICLE 21

The United States anticipates that this agreement will usher in an era of reconciliation with the Democratic Republic of Vietnam as with all the peoples of Indochina. In pursuance of its traditional policy, the United States will contribute to healing the wounds of war and to postwar reconstruction of the Democratic Republic of Vietnam and throughout Indochina.

ARTICLE 22

The ending of the war, the restoration of peace in Vietnam and the strict implementation of this agreement will create conditions for establishing a new, equal and mutually beneficial relationship between the United States and the Democratic Republic of Vietnam on the basis of respect for each other's independence and sovereignty and noninterference in each other's internal affairs. At the same time this will insure stable peace in Vietnam and contribute to the preservation of lasting peace in Indochina and Southeast Asia.

Chapter IX

Other Provisions

ARTICLE 23

This agreement shall enter into force upon signature by plenipotentiary representatives of the parties participating in the Paris Conference on Vietnam. All the parties concerned shall strictly implement this agreement and its protocols.

Done in Paris this 27th day of January, 1973, in Vietnamese and English. The Vietnamese and English texts are official and equally authentic.

For the Government of the United States of America
WILLIAM P. ROGERS
Secretary of State

For the Government of the Republic of Vietnam
TRAN VAN LAM
Minister for Foreign Affairs

For the Government of the Democratic Republic of Vietnam
NGUYEN DUY TRINH
Minister for Foreign Affairs

For the Provisional Revolutionary Government of the Republic of South Vietnam
NGUYEN THI BINH
Minister for Foreign Affairs

2-Party Version

Agreement on Ending the War and Restoring Peace in Vietnam

The Government of the United States of America, with the concurrence of the Government of the Republic of Vietnam,

The Government of the Democratic Republic of Vietnam, with the concurrence of the Provisional Revolutionary Government of the Republic of South Vietnam,

With a view to ending the war and restoring peace in Vietnam on the basis of respect for the Vietnamese people's fundamental national rights and the South Vietnamese people's right to self-determination, and to contributing to the consolidation of peace in Asia and the world,

Have agreed on the following provisions and undertake to respect and to implement them:

[Text of agreement Chapters I-VIII same as above]

Chapter IX

Other Provisions

ARTICLE 23

The Paris agreement on Ending the War and Restoring Peace in Vietnam shall enter into force upon signature of this document by the Secretary of State of the Government of the United States of America and the Minister for Foreign Affairs of the Government of the Democratic Republic of Vietnam, and upon signature of a document in the same terms by the Secretary of State of the Government of the United States of America, the Minister for Foreign Affairs of the Government of the Republic of Vietnam, the Minister for Foreign Affairs of the Government of the Democratic Republic of Vietnam and the Minister for Foreign Affairs of the Provisional Revolutionary Government of the Republic of South Vietnam. The agreement and the protocols to it shall be strictly implemented by all the parties concerned.

Done in Paris this 27th day of January, 1973, in Vietnamese and English. The Vietnamese and English texts are official and equally authentic.

For the Government of the United States of America
WILLIAM P. ROGERS
Secretary of State

For the Government of the Democratic Republic of Vietnam
NGUYEN DUY TRINH
Minister for Foreign Affairs

Protocol on Clearing Sea Mines

Protocol to the Agreement on Ending the War and Restoring Peace in Vietnam Concerning the Removal, Permanent Deactivation or Destruction of Mines in the Territorial Waters, Ports, Harbors and Waterways of the Democratic Republic of Vietnam

The Government of the United States of America,

The Government of the Democratic Republic of Vietnam,

In implementation of the second paragraph of Article 2 of the Agreement on Ending the War and Restoring Peace in Vietnam signed on this date,

Have agreed as follows:

ARTICLE 1

The United States shall clear all mines it has placed in the territorial waters, ports, harbors and waterways of the Democratic Republic of Vietnam. This mine-clearing operation shall be accomplished by rendering the mines harmless through removal, permanent deactivation or destruction.

ARTICLE 2

With a view to insuring lasting safety for the movement of people and watercraft and the protection of important installations, mines shall, on the request of the Democratic Republic of Vietnam, be removed or destroyed in the indicated area; and whenever their removal or destruction is impossible, mines shall be permanently deactivated and their emplacement clearly marked.

ARTICLE 3

The mine-clearing operation shall begin at twenty-four hundred (2400) hours G.M.T. on Jan. 27, 1973. The representatives of the two parties shall consult immediately on relevant factors and agree upon the earliest possible target date for the completion of the work.

ARTICLE 4

The mine-clearing operation shall be conducted in accordance with priorities and timing agreed upon by the two parties. For this purpose, representatives of the two parties shall meet at an early date to reach agreement on a program and a plan of implementation. To this end:

(a) The United States shall provide its plan for mine-clearing operations, including maps of the minefields and information concerning the types, numbers and properties of the mines.

(b) The Democratic Republic of Vietnam shall provide all available maps and hydrographic charts and indicate the mined places and all other potential hazards to the mine-clearing operations that the Democratic Republic of Vietnam is aware of.

(c) The two parties shall agree on the timing of implementation of each segment of the plan and provide timely notice to the public at least 48 hours in advance of the beginning of mine-clearing operations for that segment.

ARTICLE 5

The United States shall be reponsible for the mine clearance on island waterways of the Democratic Republic of Vietnam. The Democratic Republic of Vietnam shall, to the full extent of its capabilities, actively participate in the mine clearance with the means of surveying, removal and destruction, and technical advice supplied by the United States.

ARTICLE 6

With a view to insuring the safe movement of people and watercraft on waterways and at sea, the United States shall in the mine-clearing process supply timely information about the progress of mine clearing in each area, and about the remaining mines to be destroyed. The United States shall issue a communiqué when the operations have been concluded.

ARTICLE 7

In conducting mine-clearing operations, the U.S. personnel engaged in these operations shall respect the sovereignty of the Democratic Republic of Vietnam and shall engage in no activities inconsistent with the Agreement on Ending the War and Restoring Peace in Vietnam and this protocol. The U.S. personnel engaged in the mine-clearing operations shall be immune from the jurisdiction of the Democratic Republic of Vietnam for the duration of the mine-clearing operations.

The Democratic Republic of Vietnam shall insure the safety of the U.S. personnel for the duration of their mine-clearing activities on the territory of the Democratic Republic of Vietnam, and shall provide this personnel with all possible assistance and the means needed in the Democratic Republic of Vietnam that have been agreed upon by the two parties.

ARTICLE 8

This protocol to the Paris Agreement on Ending the War and Restoring Peace in Vietnam shall enter into force upon signature by the Secretary of State of the Government of the United States of America and the Minister for Foreign Affairs of the Government of the Democratic Republic of Vietnam. It shall be strictly implemented by the two parties.

Done in Paris this 27th day of January, 1973, in Vietnamese and English. The Vietnamese and English texts are official and equally authentic.

For the Government of the United States of America
WILLIAM P. ROGERS
Secretary of State

For the Government of the Democratic Republic of Vietnam
NGUYEN DUY TRINH
Minister for Foreign Affairs

Protocol on the Cease-Fire

Protocol to the Agreement on Ending the War and Restoring Peace in Vietnam Concerning the Cease-Fire in South Vietnam and the Joint Military Commissions

The parties participating in the Paris conference on Vietnam.

In implementation of the first paragraph of Article 2, Article 3, Article 5, Article 6, Article 16 and Article 17 of the Agreement on Ending the War and Restoring Peace in Vietnam signed on this date which provides for the cease-fire in South Vietnam and the establishment of a Four-Party Joint Military Commission and a Two-Party Joint Military Commission,

Have agreed as follows:

Cease-Fire in South Vietnam

ARTICLE 1

The high commands of the parties in South Vietnam shall issue prompt and timely orders to all regular and irregular armed forces and the armed police under their command to completely end hostilities throughout South Vietnam, at the exact time stipulated in Article 2 of the Agreement and insure that these armed forces and armed police comply with these orders and respect the cease-fire.

ARTICLE 2

(a) As soon as the cease-fire comes into force and until regulations are issued by the Joint Military Commissions, all ground, river, sea and air combat forces of the parties in South Vietnam shall remain in place; that is, in order to insure a stable cease-fire, there shall be no major redeployments or movements that would extend each party's area of control or would result in contact between opposing armed forces and clashes which might take place.

(b) All regular and irregular armed forces and the armed police of the parties in South Vietnam shall observe the prohibition of the following acts:

(1) Armed patrol in to areas controlled by opposing armed forces and flights by bomber and fighter aircraft of all types, except for unarmed flights for proficiency training and maintenance;

(2) Armed attacks against any person, either military or civilian, by any means whatsoever, including the use of small arms, mortars, artillery, bombing and strafing by airplanes and any other type of weapon or explosive device;

(3) All combat operations on the ground, on rivers, on the sea and in the air;

(4) All hostile acts, terrorism or reprisals; and

(5) All acts endangering lives or public or private property.

ARTICLE 3

(a) The above-mentioned prohibitions shall not hamper or restrict:

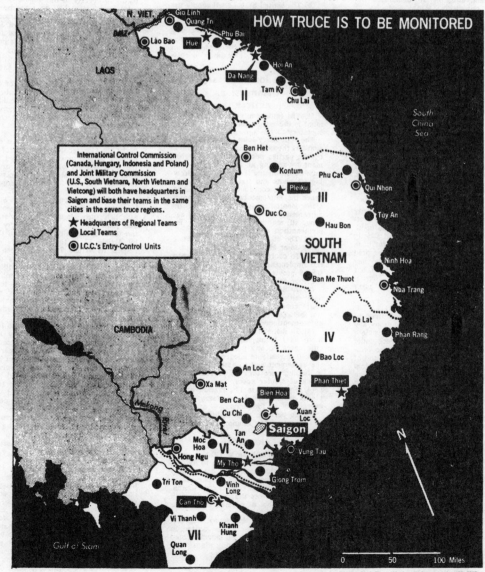

HOW TRUCE IS TO BE MONITORED

International Control Commission (Canada, Hungary, Indonesia and Poland) and **Joint Military Commission** (U.S., South Vietnam, North Vietnam and Vietcong) will both have headquarters in Saigon and base their teams in the same cities in the seven truce regions.

★ Headquarters of Regional Teams
● Local Teams
◎ I.C.C.'s Entry-Control Units

The New York Times/Stephen Hadermayer/Jan. 25, 1973

Map, showing cities where I.C.C. and Joint Military Commission representatives will be based, is drawn from data supplied by the White House. But the White House did not supply official maps referred to in truce protocols.

(1) Civilian supply, freedom of movement, freedom to work and freedom of the people to engage in trade, and civilian communication and transportation between and among all areas in South Vietnam.

(2) The use by each party in areas under its control of military support elements, such as engineer and transportation units, in repair and construction of public facilities and the transportation and supplying of the population.

(3) Normal military proficiency conducted by the parties in the areas under their respective control with due regard for public safety.

(b) The Joint Military Commissions shall immediately agree on corridors, routes and other regulations governing the movement of military transport aircraft, military transport vehicles and military transport vessels of all types of one party going through areas under the control of other parties.

ARTICLE 4

In order to avert conflict and insure normal conditions for those armed forces which are in direct contact, and pending regulation by the Joint Military Commissions, the commanders of the opposing armed forces at those places of direct contact shall meet as soon as the cease-fire comes into force with a view to reaching an agreement on temporary measures to avert conflict and to insure supply and medical care for these armed forces.

ARTICLE 5

(a) Within 15 days after the cease-fire comes into effect, each party shall do its utmost to complete the removal or deactivation of all demolition objects, minefields, traps, obstacles or other dangerous objects placed previously, so as not to hamper the population's movement and work, in the first place on waterways, roads and railroads in South Vietnam. Those mines which cannot be removed or deactivated within that time shall be clearly marked and must be removed or deactivated as soon as possible.

(b) Emplacement of mines is prohibited, except as a defensive measure around the edges of military installations in places where they do not hamper the population's movement and work, and movement on waterways, roads and railroads. Mines and other obstacles already in place at the edges of military installations may remain in place if they are in place where they do not hamper the population's movement and work, and movement on waterways, roads and railroads.

ARTICLE 6

Civilian police and civilian security personnel of the parties in South Vietnam, who are responsible for the maintenance of law and order, shall strictly respect the prohibitions set forth in Article 2 of this protocol. As required by their responsibilities, normally they shall be authorized to carry pistols, but when required by unusual circumstances, they shall be allowed to carry other small individual arms.

ARTICLE 7

(a) The entry into South Vietnam of replacement armaments, munitions and war material permitted under Article 7 of the agreement shall take place under the supervision and control of the Two-Party Joint Military Commission and of the International Commission of Control and Supervision and through such points of entry only as are designated by the two South Vietnamese parties. The two South Vietnamese parties shall agree on these points of entry within 15 days after the entry into force of the cease-fire. The two South Vietnamese parties may select as many as six points of entry which are not included in the list of places where teams of the International Commission of Control and Supervision are to be based contained in Article 4 (d) of the protocol concerning the international commission. At the same time, the two South Vietnamese parties may also select points of entry from the list of places set forth in Article 4 (d) of that protocol.

(b) Each of the designated points of entry shall be available only for that South Vietnamese party which is in control of that point. The two South Vietnamese parties shall have an equal number of points of entry.

ARTICLE 8

(a) In implementation of Article 5 of the agreement, the United States and the other foreign countries referred to in Article 5 of the agreement shall take with them all their armaments, munitions and war material. Transfers of such items which would leave them in South Vietnam shall not be made subsequent to the entry into force of the agreement except for transfers of communications, transport and other noncombat material to the Four-Party Joint Military Commission or the International Commission of Control and Supervision.

(b) Within five days after the entry into force of the cease-fire, the United States shall inform the Four-Party Joint Military Commission and the International Commission of Control and Supervision of the general plans for timing of complete troop withdrawals which shall take place in four phases of 15 days each. It is anticipated that the numbers of troops withdrawn in each phase are not likely to be widely different, although it is not feasible to insure equal numbers. The approximate numbers to be withdrawn in each phase shall be given to the Four-Party Joint Military Commission and the International Commission of Control and Supervision sufficiently in advance of actual withdrawals so that they can properly carry out their tasks in relation thereto.

ARTICLE 9

(a) In implementation of Article 6 of the agreement, the United States and the other foreign countries referred to in that article shall dismantle and remove from South Vietnam or destroy all military bases in South Vietnam of the United States and of the other foreign countries referred to in that article, including weapons, mines and other military equipment at these bases, for the purpose of making them unusable for military purposes.

(b) The United States shall supply the Four-Party Joint Military Commission and the International Commission of Control and Supervision with necessary information on plans for base dismantlement so that those commissions can properly carry out their tasks in relation thereto.

The Joint Military Commissions

ARTICLE 10

(a) The implementation of the agreement is the responsibility of the parties signatory to the agreement.

The Four-Party Joint Military Commission has the task of insuring joint action by the parties implementing the agreement by serving as a channel of communication among the parties, by drawing up plans and fixing the modalities to carry out, coordinate, follow and inspect the implementation of the provisions mentioned in Article 16 of the agreement, and by negotiating and settling all matters concerning the implementation of those provisions.

(b) The concrete tasks of the Four-Party Joint Military Commission are:

(1) To coordinate, follow and inspect the implementation of the above-mentioned provisions of the agreement by the four parties.

(2) To deter and detect violations, to deal with cases of violation, and to settle conflicts and matters of contention between the parties relating to the above-mentioned provisions.

(3) To dispatch without delay one or more joint teams, as required by specific cases, to any part of South Vietnam, to investigate alleged violations of the agreement and to assist the parties in finding measures to prevent recurrence of similar cases.

(4) To engage in observation at the places where this is necessary in the exercise of its functions.

(5) To perform such additional tasks as it may, by unanimous decision, determine.

ARTICLE 11

(a) There shall be a Central Joint Military Commission located in Saigon. Each party shall designate immediately a military delegation of 59 persons to represent it on the central commission. The senior officer designated by each party shall be a general officer, or equivalent.

(b) There shall be seven Regional Joint Military Commissions located in the regions shown on the annexed map and based at the following places:

REGIONS	PLACES
I	Hue
II	Da Nang
III	Pleiku
IV	Phan Thiet
V	Bien Hoa
VI	My Tho
VII	Can Tho

Each party shall designate a military delegation of 16 persons to represent it on each regional commission. The senior officer designated by each party shall be an officer from the rank of lieutenant colonel to colonel, or equivalent.

(c) There shall be a joint military team operating in each of the areas shown on the annexed map and based at each of the following places in South Vietnam:

Region I
Quang Tri
Phu Bai
Region II
Hoi An
Tam Ky
Chu Lai
Region III
Kontum
Hau Bon
Phu Cat
Tuy An
Ninh Hoa
Ban Me Thuot
Region IV
Da Lat
Bao Loc
Phan Rang
Region V
An Loc
Xuan Loc
Ben Cat
Cu Chi
Tan An
Region VI
Moc Hoa
Giong Trom
Region VII
Tri Ton
Vinh Long
Vi Thanh
Khanh Hung
Quan Long

Each party shall provide four qualified persons for each joint military team. The senior person designated by each party shall be an officer from the rank of major to lieutenant colonel, or equivalent.

(d) The Regional Joint Military Commissions shall assist the Central Joint Military Commission in performing its tasks and shall supervise the operations of the military teams. The region of Saigon-Gia Dinh is placed under the responsibility of the central commission, which shall designate joint military teams to operate in this region.

(e) Each party shall be authorized to provide support and guard personnel for its delegations to the Central Joint Military Commission and Regional Joint Military Commissions, and for its members of the joint military teams. The total number of support and guard personnel for each party shall not exceed 550.

(f) The Central Joint Military Commission may establish such joint subcommissions, joint staffs and joint military teams as circumstances may require. The central commission shall determine the numbers of personnel required for any additional subcommissions, staff or teams it establishes, provided that each party shall designate one-fourth of the number of personnel required and that the total number of personnel for the Four-Party Joint Military Commission, to include its staffs, teams and support personnel, shall not exceed 3,300.

(g) The delegations of the two South Vietnamese parties may, by agreement, establish provisional subcommissions and joint military teams to carry out the tasks specifically assigned to them by Article 17 in the agreement. With respect to Article 7 of the agreement, the two South Vietnamese parties' delegations to the Four-Party Joint Military Commission shall establish joint military teams at the points of entry into South Vietnam used for replacement of armaments, munitions and war material which are designated in accordance with Article 7 of this protocol. From the time the cease-fire comes into force to the time when the Two-Party Joint Military Commission becomes operational, the two South Vietnamese parties' delegations to the Four-Party Joint Military Commission shall form a provisional subcommission and provisional joint military teams to carry out its tasks concerning captured and detained Vietnamese civilian personnel. Where necessary for the above purposes, the two parties may agree to assign personnel additional to those assigned to the two South Vietnamese delegations to the Four-Party Joint Military Commission.

ARTICLE 12

(a) In accordance with Article 17 of the agreement, which stipulates that the two South Vietnamese parties shall immediately designate their respective representatives to form the Two-Party Joint Military Commission, 24 hours after the cease-fire comes into force, the two designated South Vietnamese parties' delegations to the Two-Party Joint Military Commission shall meet in Saigon so as to reach an agreement as soon as possible on organization and operation of the Two-Party Joint Commission, as well as the measures and organization aimed at enforcing the cease-fire and preserving peace in South Vietnam.

(b) From the time the cease-fire comes into force to the time when the Two-Party Joint Military Commission becomes operational, the two South Vietnamese parties' delegations to the Four-Party Joint Military Commission at all levels shall simultaneously assume the tasks of the Two-Party Joint Military Commission at all levels, in addition to their functions as delegations to the Four-Party Joint Military Commission.

(c) If, at the time the Four-Party Joint Military Commission ceases its operation in accordance with Article 16 of the agreement, agreement has not been reached on organization of the Two-Party Joint Military Commission, the delegations of the two South Vietnamese parties serving with the Four-Party Joint Military Commission at all levels shall continue temporarily to work together as a provisional two-party joint military commission and to assume the tasks of the Two-Party Joint Military Commission at all levels until the Two-Party Joint Military Commission becomes operational.

ARTICLE 13

In application of the principle of unanimity, the Joint Military Commissions shall have no chairmen, and meetings shall be convened at the request of any representative. The Joint Military Commissions shall adopt working procedures appropriate for the effective discharge of their functions and responsibilities.

ARTICLE 14

The Joint Military Commissions and the International Commission of Control and Supervision shall closely cooperate with and assist each other in carrying out their respective functions. Each Joint Military Commission shall inform the international commission about the implementation of those provisions of the agreement for which that Joint Military Commission has responsibility and which are within the competence of the international commission. Each Joint Military Commission may request the international commission to carry out specific observation activities.

ARTICLE 15

The Central Four-Party Joint Military Commission shall begin operating 24 hours after the cease-fire comes into force. The Regional Four-Party Joint Military Commissions shall begin operating 48 hours after the cease-fire comes into force. The joint military teams based at the places listed in Article 11 (c) of this protocol shall begin operating no later than 15 days after the cease-fire comes into force. The delegations of the two South Vietnamese parties shall simultaneously begin to assume the tasks of the Two-Party Joint Military Commission as provided in Article 12 of this protocol.

ARTICLE 16

(a) The parties shall provide full protection and all necessary assistance and cooperation to the Joint Military Commissions at all levels, in the discharge of their tasks.

(b) The Joint Military Commissions and their personnel, while carrying out their tasks, shall enjoy privileges and immunities equivalent to those accorded diplomatic missions and diplomatic agents.

(c) The personnel of the Joint Military Commissions may carry pistols and wear special insignia decided upon by each Central Joint Military Commission. The personnel of each party while guarding commission installations or equipment may be authorized to carry other individual small arms, as determined by each Central Joint Military Commission.

ARTICLE 17

(a) The delegation of each party to the Four-Party Joint Military Commission and the Two-Party Joint Military Commission shall have its own offices, communication, logistics and transportation means, including aircraft when necessary.

(b) Each party, in its areas of control, shall provide appropriate office and accommodation facilities to the Four-Party Joint Military Commission and the Two-Party Joint Military Commission at all levels.

(c) The parties shall endeavor to provide to the Four-Party Joint Military Commission and the Two-Party Joint Military Commission, by means of loan, lease or gift, the common means of operation, including equipment for communication, supply and transport, including aircraft when necessary. The Joint Military Commissions may purchase from any source necessary facilities, equipment and services which are not supplied by the parties. The Joint Military Commissions shall possess and use these facilities and this equipment.

(d) The facilities and the equipment

for common use mentioned above shall be returned to the parties when the Joint Military Commissions have ended their activities.

ARTICLE 18

The common expenses of the Four-Party Joint Military Commission shall be borne equally by the four parties, and the common expenses of the Two-Party Joint Military Commission in South Vietnam shall be borne equally by these two parties.

ARTICLE 19

This protocol shall enter into force upon signature by plenipotentiary representatives of all the parties participating in the Paris conference on Vietnam. It shall be strictly implemented by all the parties concerned.

Done in Paris this 27th day of January, 1973, in Vietnamese and English. The Vietnamese and English texts are official and equally authentic.

For the Government of the United States of America
WILLIAM P. ROGERS
Secretary of State

For the Government of the Republic of Vietnam
TRAN VAN LAM
Minister for Foreign Affairs

For the Government of the Democratic Republic of Vietnam
NGUYEN DUY TRINH
Minister for Foreign Affairs

For the Provisional Revolutionary Government of the Republic of South Vietnam
NGUYEN THI BINH
Minister for Foreign Affairs

2-Party Version

Protocol to the Agreement on Ending the War and Restoring Peace in Vietnam Concerning the Cease-Fire in South Vietnam and the Joint Military Commissions

The Government of the United States of America, with the concurrence of the Government of the Republic of Vietnam,

The Government of the Democratic Republic of Vietnam, with the concurrence of the Provisional Revolutionary Government of the Republic of South Vietnam,

In implementation of the first paragraph of Article 2, Article 3, Article 5, Article 6, Article 16 and Article 17 of the Agreement on Ending the War and Restoring Peace in Vietnam signed on this date which provide for the cease-fire in South Vietnam and the establishment of a Four-Party Joint Military Commission and a Two-Party Joint Military Commission,

Have agreed as follows:

[Text of protocol Articles 1-18 same as above]

Article 19

The protocol to the Paris Agreement on Ending the War and Restoring Peace in Vietnam Concerning the Cease-fire in South Vietnam and the Joint Military Commissions shall enter into force upon signature of this document by the Secretary of State of the Government of the United States of America and the Minister for Foreign Affairs of the Government of the Democratic Republic of Vietnam, and upon signature of a document in the same terms by the Secretary of State of the Government of the United States of America, the Minister for Foreign Affairs of the Government of the Republic of Vietnam, the Minister for Foreign Affairs of the Democratic Republic of Vietnam and the Minister for Foreign Affairs of the Provisional Revolutionary Government of the Republic of South Vietnam. The protocol shall be strictly implemented by all the parties concerned.

Done in Paris this 27th day of January, 1973, in Vietnamese and English. The Vietnamese and English texts are official and equally authentic.

For the Government of the United States of America
WILLIAM P. ROGERS
Secretary of State

For the Government of the Democratic Republic of Vietnam
NGUYEN DUY TRINH
Minister for Foreign Affairs

Protocol on Control Commission

Protocol to the Agreement on Ending the War and Restoring Peace in Vietnam Concerning The International Commission of Control and Supervision

The parties participating in the Paris conference on Vietnam,

In implementation of Article 18 of the Agreement on Ending the War and Restoring Peace in Vietnam signed on this date providing for the formation of the International Commission of Control and Supervision,

Have agreed as follows:

ARTICLE 1

The implementation of the agreement is the responsibility of the parties signatory to the agreement.

The functions of the international commission are to control and supervise the implementation of the provisions mentioned in Article 18 of the agreement. In carrying out these functions, the international commission shall:

(a) Follow the implementation of the above-mentioned provisions of the agreement through communication with the parties and on-the-spot observation at the places where this is required.

(b) Investigate violations of the provisions which fall under the control and supervision of the commission.

(c) When necessary, cooperate with the Joint Military Commissions in deterring and detecting violations of the above-mentioned provisions.

ARTICLE 2

The international commission shall investigate violations of the provisions described in Article 18 of the agreement on the request of the Four-Party Joint Military Commission, or of the Two-Party Joint Military Commission or of any party, or, with respect to Article 9 (b) of the agreement on general elections, of the National Council of National Reconciliation and Concord, or in any case where the international commission has other adequate grounds for considering that there has been a violation of those provisions. It is understood that, in carrying out this task, the international commission shall function with the concerned parties' assistance and cooperation as required.

ARTICLE 3

(a) When the international commission finds that there is a serious violation in the implementation of the agreement or a threat to peace against which the commission can find no appropriate measure, the commission shall report this to the four parties to the agreement so that they can hold consultations to find a solution.

(b) In accordance with Article 18 (f) of the agreement, the international commission's reports shall be made with the unanimous agreement of the representatives of all the four members. In case no unanimity is reached, the commission shall forward the different views to the four parties in accordance with Article 18 (b) of the agreement, or to the two South Vietnamese parties in accordance with Article 18 (c) of the agreement, but these shall not be considered as reports of the commission.

ARTICLE 4

(a) The headquarters of the international commission shall be at Saigon.

(b) There shall be seven regional teams located in the regions shown on the annexed map and based at the following places:

REGIONS	PLACES
I	Hue
II	Danang
III	Pleiku
IV	Phan Thiet
V	Bien Hoa
VI	My Tho
VII	Can Tho

The international commission shall designate three teams for the region of Saigon-Gia Dinh.

(c) There shall be 26 teams operating in the areas shown on the annexed map and based at the following places in South Vietnam:

Region I
Quang Tri
Phu Bai
Region II
Hoi An
Tam Ky
Chu Lai
Region III
Kontum
Hau Bon
Phu Cat
Tuy An
Tinh Hoa
Ban Me Thuot
Region IV
Da Lat
Bao Loc
Phan Rang
Region V
An Loc
Xuan Loc
Ben Cat
Cu Chi
Tan An
Region VI
Moc Hoa
Giong Trom
Region VI
Tri Ton
Vinh Long
Vi Thanh
Khanh Hung
Quan Long

d) There shall be 12 teams located as shown on the annexed map and based at the following places:

Gio Linh (to cover the area south of the provisional military demarcation line)
Lao Bao
Ben Het
Duc Co
Chu Lai
Qui Nhon
Nha Trang
Vung Tau
Xa Mat
Bien Hoa Airfield
Hong Ngu
Can Tho

(e) There shall be seven teams, six of which shall be available for assignment to the points of entry which are not listed in paragraph (d) above and which the two South Vietnamese parties choose as points for legitimate entry to South Vietnam for replacement of armaments, munitions and war material permitted by Article 7 of the agreement. Any team or teams not needed for the above-mentioned assignment shall be available for other tasks, in keeping with the commission's responsibility for control and supervision.

(f) There shall be seven teams to control and supervise the return of captured and detained personnel of the parties.

ARTICLE 5

(a) To carry out its task concerning the return of the captured military personnel and foreign civilians of the parties as stipulated by Article 8 (a) of the agreement, the international commission shall, during the time of such return, send one control and supervision team to each place in Vietnam where the captured persons are being returned, and to the last detention places from which these persons will be taken to the places of return.

(b) To carry out its tasks concerning the return of the Vietnamese civilian personnel captured and detained in South Vietnam mentioned in Article 8 (c) of the agreement, the international commission shall, during the time of such return, send one control and supervision team to each place in South Vietnam where the above-mentioned captured and detained persons are being returned, and to the last detention places from which these persons shall be taken to the places of return.

ARTICLE 6

To carry out its tasks regarding Article 9 (b) of the agreement on the free and democratic general elections in South Vietnam, the international commission shall organize additional teams, when necessary. The international commission shall discuss this question in advance with the National Council of National Reconciliation and Concord. If additional teams are necessary for this purpose, they shall be formed 30 days before the general elections.

ARTICLE 7

The international commission shall continually keep under review its size, and shall reduce the number of its teams, its representatives or other personnel, or both, when those teams, representatives or personnel have accomplished the tasks assigned to them and are not required for other tasks. At the same time, the expenditures of the international commission shall be reduced correspondingly.

ARTICLE 8

Each member of the international commission shall make available at all times the following numbers of qualified personnel:

(a) One senior representative and 26 others for the headquarters staff.

(b) Five for each of the seven regional teams.

(c) Two for each of the other international control teams, except for the teams at Gio Linh and Vung Tau, each of which shall have three.

(d) One hundred sixteen for the purpose of providing support to the commission headquarters and its teams.

ARTICLE 9

(a) The international commission, and each of its teams, shall act as a single body comprising representatives of all four members.

(b) Each member has the responsibility to insure the presence of its representatives at all levels of the international commission. In case a representative is absent, the member concerned shall immediately designate a replacement.

ARTICLE 10

(a) The parties shall afford full cooperation, assistance and protection to the international commission.

(b) The parties shall at all times maintain regular and continuous liaison with the international commission. During the existence of the Four-Party Joint Military Commission, the delegations of the parties to that commission shall also perform liaison functions with the international commission. After the Four-Party Joint Military Commission has ended its activities, such liaison shall be maintained through the Two-Party Joint Military Commission, liaison missions or other adequate means.

(c) The international commission and the Joint Military Commissions shall closely cooperate with and assist each other in carrying out their respective functions.

(d) Wherever a team is stationed or operating, the concerned party shall designate a liaison officer to the team to cooperate with and assist it in carrying out without hindrance its task of control and supervision. When a team is carrying out an investigation, a liaison officer from each concerned party shall have the opportunity to accompany it, provided the investigation is not thereby delayed.

(e) Each party shall give the international commission reasonable advance notice of all proposed actions concerning those provisions of the agreement that are to be controlled and supervised by the international commission.

(f) The international commission, including its teams, is allowed such movement for observation as is reasonably required for the proper exercise of its functions as stipulated in the agreement. In carrying out these functions, the international commission, including its teams, shall enjoy all necessary assistance and cooperation from the parties concerned.

ARTICLE 11

In supervising the holding of the free and democratic general elections described in Articles 9 (b) and 12 (b) of the agreement in accordance with modalities to be agreed upon between the National Council of National Reconciliation and Concord and the international commission, the latter shall receive full cooperation and assistance from the national council.

ARTICLE 12

The international commission and its personnel who have the nationality of a member state shall, while carrying out their tasks, enjoy privileges and immunities equivalent to those accorded diplomatic missions and diplomatic agents.

ARTICLE 13

The international commission may use the means of communication and transport necessary to perform its functions. Each South Vietnamese party shall make available for rent to the international commission appropriate office and accommodation facilities and shall assist it in obtaining such facilities. The international commission may receive from the parties, on mutually agreeable terms, the necessary means of communication and transport and may purchase from any source necessary equipment and services not obtained from the parties. The international commission shall possess these means.

ARTICLE 14

The expenses for the activities of the international commission shall be borne by the parties and the members of the international commission in accordance with the provisions of this article:

(a) Each member country of the international commission shall pay the salaries and allowances of its personnel.

(b) All other expenses incurred by the international commission shall be met from a fund to which each of the four parties shall contribute twenty-three per cent (23%) and to which each member of the international commission shall contribute two per cent (2%).

(c) Within 30 days of the date of entry into force of this protocol, each of the four parties shall provide the international commission with an initial sum equivalent to four million five hundred thousand (4,500,000) French francs in convertible currency, which sum shall be credited against the amounts due from that party under the first budget.

(d) The international commission shall prepare its own budgets. After the inter-

national commission approves a budget, it shall transmit it to all parties signatory to the agreement for their approval. Only after the budgets have been approved by the four parties to the agreement shall they be obliged to make their contributions. However, in case the parties to the agreement do not agree on a new budget, the international commission shall temporarily base its expenditures on the previous budget, except for the extraordinary, one-time expenditures for installation or for the acquisition of equipment, and the parties shall continue to make their contributions on that basis until a new budget is approved.

ARTICLE 15

(a) The headquarters shall be operational and in place within 24 hours after the cease-fire.

(b) The regional teams shall be operational and in place, and three teams for supervision and control of the return of the captured and detained personnel shall be operational and ready for dispatch within 48 hours after the cease-fire.

(c) Other teams shall be operational and in place within 15 to 30 days after the cease-fire.

ARTICLE 16

Meetings shall be convened at the call of the chairman. The international commission shall adopt other working procedures appropriate for the effective discharge of its functions and consistent with respect for the sovereignty of South Vietnam.

ARTICLE 17

The members of the international commission may accept the obligations of this protocol by sending notes of acceptance to the four parties signatory to the agreement. Should a member of the international commission decide to withdraw from the international commission, it may do so by giving three months' notice by means of notes to the four parties to the agreement, in which case those four parties shall consult among themselves for the purpose of agreeing upon a replacement member.

ARTICLE 18

This protocol shall enter into force upon signature by plenipotentiary representatives of all the parties participating in the Paris conference on Vietnam. It shall be strictly implemented by all the parties concerned.

Done in Paris this 27th day of January, 1973, in Vietnamese and English. The Vietnamese and English texts are officially and equally authentic.

For the Government of the
United States of America
WILLIAM P. ROGERS
Secretary of State

For the Government of the
Republic of Vietnam
TRAN VAN LAM
Minister for Foreign Affairs

For the Government of the
Democratic Republic of Vietnam
NGUYEN DUY TRINH
Minister for Foreign Affairs

For the Provisional
Revolutionary Government of
the Republic of South Vietnam
NGUYEN THI BINH
Minister for Foreign Affairs

2-Party Version

Protocol to the Agreement on Ending the War and Restoring Peace in Vietnam Concerning the International Commission of Control and Supervision

The Government of the United States of America, with the concurrence of the Government of the Republic of Vietnam,

The Government of the Democratic Republic of Vietnam, with the concurrence of the Provisional Revolutionary Government of the Republic of South Vietnam,

In implementation of Article 18 of the Agreement on Ending the War and Restoring Peace in Vietnam signed on this date providing for the formation of the International Commission of Control and Supervision,

Have agreed as follows:

[Text of protocol Articles 1-17 same as above]

ARTICLE 18

The Protocol to the Paris Agreement on Ending the War and Restoring Peace in Vietnam concerning the International Commission of Control and Supervision shall enter into force upon signature of this document by the Secretary of State of the Government of the United States of America and the Minister for Foreign Affairs of the Government of the Democratic Republic of Vietnam, and upon signature of a document in the same terms by the Secretary of State of the Government of the United States of America, the Minister for Foreign Affairs of the Government of the Republic of Vietnam, the Minister for Foreign Affairs of the Government of the Democratic Republic of Vietnam and the Minister for Foreign Affairs of the Provisional Revolutionary Government of the Republic of South Vietnam. The protocol shall be strictly implemented by all the parties concerned.

Done in Paris this 27th day of January, 1973, in Vietnamese and English. The Vietnamese and English texts are official and equally authentic.

For the Government of the
United States of America
WILLIAM P. ROGERS
Secretary of State

For the Government of the
Democratic Republic of Vietnam
NGUYEN DUY TRINH
Minister for Foreign Affairs

Protocol on the Prisoners

Protocol to the Agreement on Ending the War and Restoring Peace in Vietnam Concerning the Return of Captured Military Personnel and Foreign Civilians and Captured and Detained Vietnamese Civilian Personnel

The parties participating in the Paris conference on Vietnam,

In implementation of Article 8 of the Agreement on Ending the War and Restoring Peace in Vietnam signed on this date providing for the return of captured military personnel and foreign civilians, and captured and detained Vietnamese civilian personnel,

Have agreed as follows:

The Return of Captured Military Personnel and Foreign Civilians

ARTICLE 1

The parties signatory to the agreement shall return the captured military personnel of the parties mentioned in Article 8 (a) of the agreement as follows:

¶All captured military personnel of the United States and those of the other foreign countries mentioned in Article 3 (a) of the agreement shall be returned to United States authorities.

¶All captured Vietnamese military personnel, whether belonging to regular or irregular armed forces, shall be returned to the two South Vietnamese parties; they shall be returned to that South Vietnamese party under whose command they served.

ARTICLE 2

All captured civilians who are nationals of the United States or of any other foreign countries mentioned in Article 3 (a) of the agreement shall be returned to United States authorities. All other captured foreign civilians shall be returned to the authorities of their country of nationality by any one of the parties willing and able to do so.

ARTICLE 3

The parties shall today exchange complete lists of captured persons mentioned in Articles 1 and 2 of this protocol.

ARTICLE 4

(a) The return of all captured persons mentioned in Articles 1 and 2 of this protocol shall be completed within 60 days of the signing of the agreement at a rate no slower than the rate of withdrawal from South Vietnam of United States forces and those of the other foreign countries mentioned in Article 5 of the agreement.

(b) Persons who are seriously ill, wounded or maimed, old persons and women shall be returned first. The remainder shall be returned either by returning all from one detention place after another or in order of their dates of capture, beginning with those who have been held the longest.

ARTICLE 5

The return and reception of the persons mentioned in Articles 1 and 2 of this protocol shall be carried out at places convenient to the concerned parties. Places of return shall be agreed upon by the Four-Party Joint Military Commission. The parties shall insure the safety of personnel engaged in the return and reception of those persons.

ARTICLE 6

Each party shall return all captured persons mentioned in Articles 1 and 2 of this protocol without delay and shall facilitate their return and reception. The detaining parties shall not deny or delay their return for any reason, including the fact that captured persons may, on any grounds, have been prosecuted or sentenced.

The Return of Captured and Detained Vietnamese Civilian Personnel

ARTICLE 7

(a) The question of the return of Vietnamese civilian personnel captured and detained in South Vietnam will be resolved by the two South Vietnamese parties on the basis of the principles of Article 21 (b) of the agreement on the Cessation of Hostilities in Vietnam of July 20, 1954, which reads as follows:

"The term 'civilian internees' is understood to mean all persons who, having in any way contributed to the political and armed struggle between the two parties, have been arrested for that reason and have been kept in detention by either party during the period of hostilities."

(b) The two South Vietnamese parties will do so in a spirit of national reconciliation and concord with a view to ending hatred and enmity in order to ease suffering and to reunite families. The two South Vietnamese parties will do their utmost to resolve this question within 90 days after the cease-fire comes into effect.

(c) Within 15 days after the cease-fire comes into effect, the two South Vietnamese parties shall exchange lists of the Vietnamese civilian personnel captured and detained by each party and lists of the places at which they are held.

Treatment of Captured Persons During Detention

ARTICLE 8

(a) All captured military personnel of the parties and captured foreign civilians of the parties shall be treated humanely at all times, and in accordance with international practice.

They shall be protected against all violence to life and person, in particular against murder in any form, mutilation, torture and cruel treatment, and outrages upon personal dignity. These persons shall not be forced to join the armed forces of the detaining party.

They shall be given adequate food, clothing, shelter and the medical attention required for their state of health. They shall be allowed to exchange postcards and letters with their families and receive parcels.

(b) All Vietnamese civilian personnel captured and detained in South Vietnam shall be treated humanely at all times, and in accordance with international practice.

They shall be protected against all violence to life and person, in particular against murder in any form, mutilation, torture and cruel treatment, and outrages against personal dignity. The detaining parties shall not deny or delay their return for any reason including the fact that captured persons may, on any grounds, have been prosecuted or sentenced. These persons shall not be forced to join the armed forces of the detaining party.

They shall be given adequate food, clothing, shelter and the medical attention required for their state of health. They shall be allowed to exchange postcards and letters with their families and receive parcels.

ARTICLE 9

(a) To contribute to improving the living conditions of the captured military personnel of the parties and foreign civilians of the parties, the parties shall, within 15 days after the cease-fire comes into effect, agree upon the designation of two or more national Red Cross societies to visit all places where captured military personnel and foreign civilians are held.

(b) To contribute to improving the living conditions of the captured and detained Vietnamese civilian personnel, the two South Vietnamese parties shall, within 15 days after the cease-fire comes into effect, agree upon the designation of two or more national Red Cross societies to visit all places where the captured and detained Vietnamese civilian personnel are held.

With Regard to Dead and Missing Persons

ARTICLE 10

(a) The Four-Party Joint Military Commission shall insure joint action by the parties in implementing Article 8 (b) of the agreement. When the Four-Party Joint Military Commission has ended its activities, a Four-Party Joint Military Team shall be maintained to carry on this task.

(b) With regard to Vietnamese civilian personnel dead or missing in South Vietnam, the two South Vietnamese parties shall help each other to obtain information about missing persons, determine the location and take care of the graves of the dead, in a spirit of national reconciliation and concord, in keeping with the people's aspirations.

Other Provisions

ARTICLE 11

(a) The Four-Party and Two-Party Joint Military Commissions will have the responsibility of determining immediately the modalities of implementing the provisions of this protocol consistent with their respective responsibilities under Articles 16 (a) and 17 (a) of the agreement. In case the Joint Military Commission, when carrying out their tasks, cannot reach agreement on a matter pertaining to the return of captured personnel they shall refer to the international commission for its assistance.

(b) The Four-Party Joint Military Commission shall form, in addition to the teams established by the protocol concerning the cease-fire in South Vietnam and the Joint Military Commissions, a subcommission on captured persons and, as required, joint military teams on captured persons to assist the commission in its tasks.

(c) From the time the cease-fire comes into force to the time when the Two-Party Joint Military Commission becomes operational, the two South Vietnamese parties' delegations to the Four-Party Joint Military Commission shall form a provisional subcommission and provisional joint military teams to carry out its tasks concerning captured

and detained Vietnamese civilian personnel.

(d) The Four-Party Joint Military Commission shall send joint military teams to observe the return of the persons mentioned in Articles 1 and 2 of this protocol at each place in Vietnam where such persons are being returned, and at the last detention places from which these persons will be taken to the places of return. The Two-Party Joint Military Commission shall send joint military teams to observe the return of Vietnamese civilian personnel captured and detained at each place in South Vietnam where such persons are being captured, and at the last detention places from which these persons will be taken to the places of return.

ARTICLE 12

In implementation of Articles 18 (b) and 18 (c) of the agreement, the International Commission of Control and Supervision shall have the responsibility to control and supervise the observance of Articles 1 through 7 of this protocol through observation of the return of captured military personnel, foreign civilians and captured and detained Vietnamese civilian personnel at each place in Vietnam where these persons are being returned, and at the last detention places from which these persons will be taken to the places of return, the examination of lists and the investigation of violations of the provisions of the above-mentioned articles.

ARTICLE 13

Within five days after signature of this protocal, each party shall publish the text of the protocol and communicate it to all the captured persons covered by the protocol and being detained by that party.

ARTICLE 14

This protocol shall come into force upon signature by plenipotentiary representatives of all the parties participating in the Paris conference on Vietnam. It shall be strictly implemented by all the parties concerned.

Done in Paris this 27th day of January, 1973, in Vietnamese and English. The Vietnamese and English texts are official and equally authentic.

For the Government of the United States of America
WILLIAM P. ROGERS
Secretary of State

For the Government of the Republic of Vietnam
TRAN VAN LAM
Minister for Foreign Affairs
For the Government of the Democratic Republic of Vietnam
NGUYEN DUY TRINH
Minister for Foreign Affairs

For the Provisional Revolutionary Government of the Republic of South Vietnam
NGUYEN THI BINH
Minister for Foreign Affairs

2-Party Version

Protocol to the Agreement on Ending the War and Restoring Peace in Vietnam Concerning the Return of Captured Military Personnel and Foreign Civilians and Captured and Detained Vietnamese Civilian Personnel

The Government of the United States of America, with the concurrence of the Government of the Republic of Vietnam,

The Government of the Democratic Republic of Vietnam, with the concurrence of the Provisional Revolutionary Government of the Republic of South Vietnam,

In implementation of Article 8 of the Agreement on Ending the War and Restoring Peace in Vietnam signed on this date providing for the return of captured military personnel and foreign civilians, and captured and detained Vietnamese civilian personnel,

Have agreed as follows:

[Text of protocol Articles 1-13 same as above]

ARTICLE 14

The protocol to the Paris Agreement on Ending the War and Restoring Peace in Vietnam concerning the Return of Captured Military Personnel and Foreign Civilians and Captured and Detained Vietnamese Civilian Personnel shall enter into force upon signature of this document by the Secretary of State of the Government of the United States of America and the Minister for Foreign Affairs of the Government of the Democratic Republic of Vietnam, and upon signature of a document in the same terms by the Secretary of State of the Government of the United States of America, the Minister for Foreign Affairs of the Government of the Republic of Vietnam, the Minister for Foreign Affairs of the Government of the Democratic Republic of Vietnam and the Minister for Foreign Affairs of the Provisional Revolutionary Government of the Republic of South Vietnam. The protocol shall be strictly implemented by all the parties concerned.

Done in Paris this 27th day of January, 1973, in Vietnamese and English The Vietnamese and English texts are official and equally authentic.

For the Government of the United States of America
WILLIAM P. ROGERS
Secretary of State

For the Government of the Democratic Republic of Vietnam
NGUYEN DUY TRINH
Minister for Foreign Affairs

Transcript of Kissinger's News Briefing to Explain Vietnam Cease-Fire Agreement

Following is a transcript of Henry A. Kissinger's news conference in Washington yesterday on the Vietnam cease-fire accord, as recorded by The New York Times:

Opening Statement

Ladies and gentlemen:

The President last evening presented the outlines of the agreement and by common agreement between us and the North Vietnamese we are today releasing—we have today released—the text and I'm here to explain—to go over briefly—what these texts contain and how we got there, what we have tried to achieve in recent months and where we expect to go from here.

Let me begin by going through the agreement, which you have read.

The agreement, as you know, is in nine chapters. The first affirms the independence, sovereignty, unity and territorial integrity as recognized by the 1954 Geneva Agreements on Vietnam—agreements which established two zones, divided by a military demarcation line.

Chapter II deals with a cease-fire. The cease-fire will go into effect at 7 o'clock Washington time on Saturday night. The principal provisions of Chapter II deal with permitted acts during the cease-fire and with what the obligations of the various parties are with respect to the cease-fire.

Withdrawal of Forces

Chapter II also deals with the withdrawal of American and all other foreign forces from Vietnam within a period of 60 days and it specifies the forces that have to be withdrawn. These are, in effect, all military personnel and all civilian personnel dealing with combat operations. We are permitted to retain economic advisers and civilian technicians serving in certain of the military branches.

Chapter II further deals with the provisions for resupply and for the introduction of outside forces. There is a flat prohibition against the introduction of any military forces into South Vietnam from outside of South Vietnam, which is to say that whatever forces may be in South Vietnam from outside South Vietnam—specifically North Vietnamese forces—cannot receive reinforcement, replacement or any other form or augmentation by any means whatsoever.

With respect to military equipment, both sides are permitted to replace all existing military equipment on a one-to-one basis under international supervision and control.

Return of Prisoners

There will be established, as I will explain when I discuss the protocols, for each side three legitimate points of entry through which all equipment — all replacement equipment — has to move. These legitimate points of entry will be under international supervision.

Chapter III deals with the return of captured military personnel and foreign civilians as well as with the question of civilian detainees within South Vietnam. This, as you know, throughout the negotiations, presented enormous difficulties for us. We insisted throughout that the question of American prisoners of war and of American civilians captured throughout Indochina should be separated from the issue of Vietnamese civilian personnel detainees, partly because of the enormous difficulty of classifying the Vietnamese civilian personnel by categories of who was detained for reasons of the civil war and who was detained for criminal activities.

And secondly, because it was foreseeable that negotiations about the release of civilian detainees would be complex and difficult and because we did not want to have the issue of American personnel mixed up with the issues of civilian personnel in South Vietnam, this turned out to be one of the thorniest issues that was settled at some point and kept reappearing throughout the negotiations.

It was one of the difficulties we had during the December negotiations.

As you can see from the agreement, the return of American military personnel and captured civilians is separated in terms of obligations and in terms of the time frame from the return of Vietnamese civilian personnel. The return of American personnel and the accounting of missing-in-action is unconditional and will take place within the same time frame as the American withdrawals.

3 Months to Negotiate

The issue of Vietnamese civilian personnel will be negotiated between the two Vietnamese parties over a period of three months and, as the agreement says, they will do their utmost to resolve this question within a three-month period.

So I repeat: the issue is separated both in terms of obligations and in terms of the relevant time frame from the return of American prisoners, which is unconditional.

We expect that American prisoners will be released in —at—intervals of two weeks or 15 days in roughly equal installments.

We have been told that no American prisoners are held in Cambodia. American prisoners held in Laos and North Vietnam will be returned to us in Hanoi. They will be received by American medical evacuation teams and flown on American airplanes from Hanoi to places of our own choice, probably Vientiane.

There will be international supervision of both this provision and of the provision for the missing-in-action and all American prisoners will, of course, be released within 60 days of the signing of the agreement. The signing will take place on Jan. 27 in two installments, the significance of which I will explain to you when I have gone through the provisions of the agreement and the associated protocols.

Chapter IV of the agreement deals with the right of the South Vietnamese people to self-determination.

Its first provision contains a joint statement by the United States and North Vietnam in which those two countries jointly recognize the South Vietnamese people's right to self-determination, in which those two countries jointly affirm that the South Vietnamese people shall decide for themselves the political system that they shall choose and jointly affirm that no foreign country shall impose any political solutions on South Vietnamese people.

The other principal provisions of the agreement are that in implementing the South Vietnamese people's right to self-determination, the two South Vietnamese parties will decide — will agree — among each other on free elections for officers to be decided by the two parties at a time to be decided by the two parties.

Will Not Impose Solutions

These elections will be supervised first—and organized first—by an institution which has the title of National Council for National Reconciliation and Concord, whose members will be equally appointed by the two sides, which will operate on the principle of unanimity and which will come into being after negotiations between the two parties, who are obligated by this agreement to do their utmost to bring this institution into being within 90 days.

Leaving aside the technical jargon, the significance of this agreement — of this part of the agreement— is that the United States has consistently maintained that we would not impose any political solutions on the people of South Vietnam.

The United States has consistently maintained that we would not impose a coalition governmment or a disguised coalition government on the people of South Vietnam.

If you examine the provisions of this chapter you will see, first, that the existing government in Saigon can remain in office; secondly, that the political future of South Vietnam depends on agreement between the South Vietnamese parties and not on an agreement that the United States has imposed on these parties.

Thirdly, that the nature of this political evolution, the timing of this political evolution, is left to the South Vietnamese parties and that the organ that is created to see to it that the elections that are organized will be conducted properly is one in which the South Vietnamese parties—each of the South Vietnamese parties—has a view.

The other significant provision of this agreement is the requirement that the South Vietnamese parties will attempt—will bring about—a reduction of the armed forces and that the forces being reduced will be demobilized.

The next chapter deals with the reunification of Vietnam and the relationship between North and South Vietnam.

In the many negotiations that I've conducted over recent weeks not the least arduous was the negotiation conducted for the ladies and gentlemen of the press who constantly raised issues with respect to sovereignty, existence of South Vietnam as a political entity and other matters of this kind.

I will return to this issue at the end when I sum up the agreement. But it is obvious that there is no dispute in the agreement between the parties that there is an entity called South Vietnam and that the future unity of Vietnam as it comes about will be decided by negotiations between North and South Vietnam, that it will not be achieved by military force.

Coercion Ruled Out

Indeed, that the use of military force with respect to bringing about unification or any other form of coercion is impermissible according to the terms of this agreement.

Secondly, there are specific provisions in this chapter with respect to the demilitarized zone. There is a repetition of the agreement of 1954, which makes the demarcation line along the 19—along the 17th parallel—provisional, which means pending reunification.

There's a specific provision that both North and South Vietnam shall respect the demilitarized zone on either side of the provisional military demarcation line.

And there is another provision that indicates that among the subjects that can be negotiated will be modalities of civilian movement

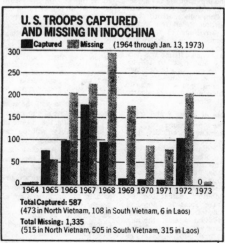

U. S. TROOPS CAPTURED AND MISSING IN INDOCHINA

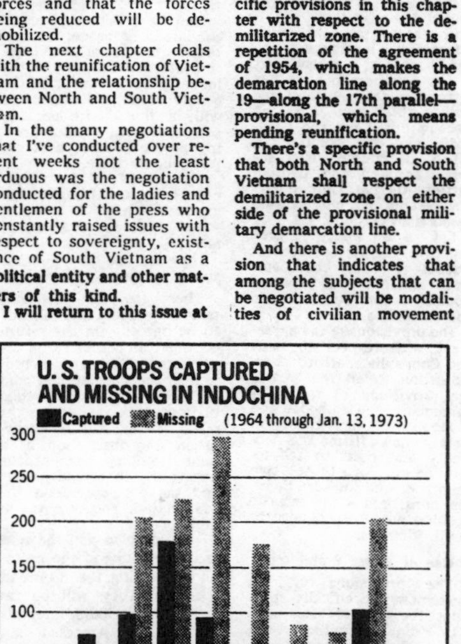
Captured
Missing
(1964 through Jan. 13, 1973)
300
250
200
150
100
50
0
1964 1965 1966 1967 1968 1969 1970 1971 1972 1973

Total Captured: 587
(473 in North Vietnam, 108 in South Vietnam, 6 in Laos)
Total Missing: 1,335
(515 in North Vietnam, 505 in South Vietnam, 315 in Laos)

The New York Times/Jan. 25, 1973

across the demarcation line, which makes it clear that military movement across the demilitarized zone is in all circumstances prohibited.

Issue of the DMZ

Now this may be an appropriate point to explain what our position has been with respect to the DMZ:

There has been a great deal of discussion about the issue of sovereignty and about the issue of legitimacy, which is to say which government is in control of South Vietnam, and finally about why we laid such great stress on the issue of the demilitarized zone.

We had to place stress on the issue of the dimilitarized zone because the provisions of the agreement with respect to infiltration, with respect to replacement, with respect to any of the military provisions would have made no sense whatever if there was not some demarcation line that defined where South Vietnam began.

If we had accepted the proposition, it would have, in effect, eroded the demilitarized zone. Then the provisions of the agreement with respect to restrictions about the introduction of men and matériel into South Vietnam would have been unilateral restrictions applying only to the United States and only to our allies and, therefore, if there was to be any meaning to the separation of military and political issues —if there was to be any permanence to the military provisions that have been negotiated—then it was essential that there was a definition of where the obligations of this agreement began.

And as you can see from the text of the agreement, the principles that we defended were essentially achieved.

Chapter VI deals with the international machinery and we will discuss that when I discuss—when I talk about—the associated protocols of the agreement.

Laos And Cambodia

Chapter VII deals with Laos and Cambodia. Now the problem of Laos and Cambodia has two parts: one part concerns those obligations which can be undertaken by the parties signing the agreement—that is to say the three Vietnamese parties and the United States — those measures that we can take which affect the situation in Laos and Cambodia; a second part of the situation in Laos has to concern the nature of the civil conflict that is taking place within Laos and Cambodia and the solution of which, of course, must involve as well the Laotian parties—the two Laotian parties — and the innumerable Cambodian factions.

Let me talk about the provisions of the agreement with respect to Laos and Cambodia and our firm expectations as to the future in Laos and Cambodia.

The provisions of the agreement with respect to Laos and Cambodia reaffirm as an obligation to all the parties the provisions of the 1954 agreement on Cambodia and of the 1962 agreement on Laos, which affirms the neutrality and right to self-determination of those two countries. And they are therefore consistent with our basic position with respect also to South Vietnam.

Use of Bases Prohibited

The provisions of the agreement specifically prohibit the use of Laos and Cambodia for military and any other operations against any of the signatories of the Paris agreement or against any other country. In other words, there is a flat prohibition against the use of base areas in Laos and Cambodia. There is a flat prohibition against the use of Laos and Cambodia for infiltration into Vietnam or for that matter into any other country.

Finally, there is a requirement that all foreign troops be withdrawn from Laos and Cambodia and it is clearly understood that North Vietnamese troops are considered foreign with respect to Laos and Cambodia.

Now as to the conflict within these countries, which could not be formally settled in an agreement which is not signed by the parties of that conflict. Let me make this plain without elaborating.

It is our firm expectation that within a short period of time there will be a formal cease-fire in Laos, which in turn will lead to a withdrawal of all foreign forces from Laos and, of course, to the end of the use of Laos as a corridor of infiltration.

Change by Force Barred

The situation in Cambodia, as those of you who have studied it will know, is somewhat more complex because there are several parties headquartered in different countries and therefore we can say about Cambodia that it is our expectation that a de facto cease-fire will come into being over a period of time relevant to the execution of this agreement.

Our side will take the appropriate measures to indicate that it will not attempt to change the situation by force.

We have reason to believe that our position is clearly understood by all concerned parties and I will not go beyond this in my statement.

Chapter VIII deals with the relationship between the United States and the Democratic Republic of Vietnam.

As I have said in my briefings on Oct. 26 and on Dec. 16 and as the President affirmed on many occasions—the last time in his speech last evening — the United States is seeking a peace that heals.

We have had many armistices in Indochina. We want a peace that will last. And therefore it is our firm intention in our relationship to the Democratic Republic of Vietnam to move from hostility to normalization and from normalization to conciliation and cooperation.

Protocols Discussed

And we believe that under conditions of peace, we can contribute throughout Indochina to a realization of the humane aspirations of all the people of Indochina and we will in that spirit perform our traditional role of helping people realize these aspirations in peace.

Chapter IX of the agreement is the usual implementing provision.

So much for the agreement.

Now let me say a word about the protocol.

There are four protocols, or implementing instruments, to be agreed—on the return of American prisoners, on the implementation an institution of an international control commission, on the regulations with respect to the cease-fire and the implementation and institution of a joint military commission among the concerned parties and the protocol about the deactivation and removal of mines.

I have given you the relevant provisions of the protocol concerning the return of prisoners. They will be returned at periodic intervals in Hanoi to American authorities and not to American private groups. They will be picked up by American airplanes except for prisoners held in the southern part of South Vietnam which will be released at designated points in the South again to American authorities.

We will receive on Saturday—the day of signing of the agreement—a list of all American prisoners held throughout Indochina and those parties, it is to say—all parties have an obligation to assist each other in obtaining information about the prisoners missing in action and about the location of graves of American personnel throughout Indochina.

The international commission has the right to visit the last place of detention of the prisoners as well as the place from which they are released.

Size of Commission

Now, to the international control commission.

You will remember that one of the reasons for the impasse in December was the difficulty of agreeing with the North Vietnamese about the size of the international commission, its function or the location of its teams.

On this occasion there is no point in reviewing all the differences. It is, however, useful to point out that at that time the proposal of the North Vietnamese was that the international control commission have a membership of 250, no organized logistics or communication, dependent entirely on its authority to move on the party it was supposed to be investigating and on behalf of. Its personnel was supposed to be located in Saigon, which is not the place where most of the infiltration that we were concerned with was likely to take place.

We have distributed to you an outline of the basic structure of this commission.

Briefly stated, its total number is 1,160, drawn from Canada, Hungary, Indonesia and Poland.

Seven Regional Teams

It has a headquarters in Saigon. It has seven regional teams, 26 teams based in localities throughout Vietnam which were chosen either because forces were in contact there or because we estimated that these were the areas where the violations of the cease-fire were most probable.

There are 12 teams at border crossing points. There are seven teams that are set aside for points of entry which have yet to be chosen for the replacement of military equipment. That is for Article 7 of the agreement. There will be three on each side and there will be no legitimate point of entry into South Vietnam other than those three points.

The other border and coastal teams are there simply to make certain that no other entry occurs and any other entry is by definition illegal. There has to be no other demonstration except the fact that it occurred. This leaves one team free for use in particular at the discretion of the commission and, of course, the seven teams that are being used for the return of prisoners can be used at the discretion of the commission after the prisoners are returned.

There is one team — one reinforced team—located at the demilitarized zone and its responsibility extends along the entire demilitarized zone. It is, in fact, a team and a half. It is 50 per cent larger than a normal border team. And it represents one of the many compromises that were made between our insistence on two teams, their insistence on one team and by a brilliant stroke we settled on a team and a half.

With respect to the operation of the international commission, it is supposed to operate on the principle of unanimity, which is to say that its reports—if they are commission reports—have to have the approval of all four members.

However, each member is permitted to submit its own opinion so that as a practical matter any member of the commission can make a finding of a violation and submit a report in the first instance to the parties.

The international commission will report for the time being to the four parties to the agreement.

Institutions Planned

We expect an international conference will take place—we expect at the foreign ministers' level—within a month of signing the agreement. That international conference will establish a relationship between the international commission and itself or any other international body that is mutually agreed upon, so that the international commission is not only reporting to the parties that it is investigating.

For the time being, until the international conference has met, there was no other practical group to which the international commission could report. In addition to this international group there are two other institutions that are supposed to supervise the cease-fire.

There is, first of all, an institution called the four party joint military commission, which is composed of ourselves and the three Vietnamese parties, which is located in the same places as the international commission, charged with roughly the same functions but as a practical matter, it is supposed to conduct the preliminary investigations. Its disagreements are automatically referred to the international commission and moreover any party can request the international commission to conduct an investigation regardless of what the four-party commission does and regardless of whether the four-party commission has completed its investigation or not.

After the United States has completed its withdrawal the four party military commission will be transformed into a two-party commission composed of the two South Vietnamese parties.

The total number of supervisory personnel, therefore, will be in the neighborhood of 4,500 during the period that the four-party commission is in existence and in the neighborhood of about 3,000 after the four-party commission ceases operating and the two-party commission comes into being.

Removal of Mines

Finally, there is a protocol concerning the removal and deactivation of mines which is self-explanatory and simply explains—discusses—the relationship between our efforts and the efforts of the D.R.V. concerning the removal and deactivation of mines, which is one of the obligations we have undertaken in the agreement.

Now let me point out one other problem: on Saturday, Jan. 27, the Secretary of State on behalf of the United States will sign the agreement bringing the cease-fire and all the other provisions of the agreement and the protocols into force. He will sign in the morning a document involving the four parties and in the afternoon a document between us and the Democratic Republic of Vietnam and these documents are identical except that the preamble differs in both cases.

The reason for the somewhat convoluted procedure is that while the agreement provides that the two South Vietnamese parties should settle their disputes in an atmosphere of national reconciliation and concord, I think it is safe to say that they have not yet quite reached that point.

Parties Not Named

Indeed, that they have not yet been prepared to recognize each other's existence. This being the case, it was necessary to devise one document in which neither of the South Vietnamese parties was mentioned by name and therefore no other party could be mentioned by name on the principle of equality.

So the four-party document—the document that will have four signatures — can be read with great care and you will not know until you get to the signature page whom exactly it applies to. It refers only to "the parties participating in the Paris Conference" which are of course well-known to the parties participating in the Paris Conference.

It will be signed on two separate pages — the United States and the GVN is signing on one page and the Democratic Republic of Vietnam and its ally is signing on a separate page. And this procedure has aged us all by several years.

Then there is another document which will be signed by the Secretary of State and the Foreign Minister of the Democratic Republic of Vietnam in the afternoon. That document in its operative provisions is word-for-word the same as the document which will be signed in the morning and which contains the obligations to which the two South Vietnamese parties are obligated. It differs from the document only in the preamble and in its concluding paragraph. And in the preamble it says, "The United States with the concurrence of the Government of the Republic of Vietnam and the D.R.V. with the concurrence of the Provisional Revolutionary Government." And the rest is the same.

And then the concluding paragraph has the same adaptation. That document, of course, is not signed by either Saigon or its opponent and therefore their obligations are derived from the four-party document.

Ceremonies Explained

Now I don't want to take any time in going into the abstruse legalism. I simply wanted to explain to you why there were two different signature ceremonies. That is why, when we handed out the text of the agreement, we appended to the document which contains the legal obligations which apply to everybody — namely the four parties — why we appended another section that contained a different preamble and a different implementing paragraph which is going to be signed by the Secretary of State and the Foreign Minister of the Democratic Republic of Vietnam and this will be true with respect to the agreement and three of the protocols.

The fourth protocol regarding the removal of mines applies only to the United States and the Democratic Republic of Vietnam and therefore we are in the happy position of having to sign only one document.

Now then, let me summarize for you how we got some of the aspects of the agreement that we considered signifcant and then I will answer your questions.

As you know, when I met with this group on Dec. 16, we had to report that the negotiations in Paris seemed to have reached a stalemate.

We had not agreed at that time, though we didn't say so, on the—we could not find a formula to take into account the conflicting views with respect to signing. There were disagreements with respect to the DMZ and with the associated aspects of what identity South Vietnam was to have in the agreement.

There was a total deadlock with respect to the protocols, which I summed up in the Dec. 16 press conference.

'Totally at Variance'

The North Vietnamese approach to international control and ours were so totally at variance that it seemed impossible at that point to come to any satisfactory conclusion. And there began to be even some concern that the separation which we thought we had achieved in October between the release of our prisoners and the question of civilian prisoners in South Vietnam was breaking down.

When we reassembled on Jan. 8, we did not do so in the most cordial atmosphere that I remember. However, by the morning of Jan. 9 it became apparent that both sides were determined to make a serious effort to break the deadlock in negotiations.

And we adopted a mode of procedure by which issues in the agreement and issues of principle with respect to the protocols were discussed at meetings between Special Adviser Le Duc Tho and myself while concurrently an American team headed by Ambassador Sullivan and a Vietnamese team headed by Vice Minister Thach would work on the implementation of the principles as they applied to the protocols.

For example, the special adviser and I might agree on the principle of border control posts and their number. But then the problem of how to locate them, according to what criteria and with what mode of operations, presented enormous difficulties.

And let me on this occasion also point out that these negotiations required the closest cooperation throughout our Government — between the White House and the State Department, between all the elements of our team. And that therefore the usual speculation of who did what to whom is really extraordinarily misplaced. Without a cooperative effort by everybody, we could not have achieved what we have presented last night and this morning.

The special adviser and I then spent the week first on working out the unresolved issues in the agreement and then the unresolved issues with respect to the protocols. And, finally, the surrounding circumstances of schedules and procedures.

Ambassador Sullivan remained behind to draft the implementing provisions of the agreements that had been achieved during the week. The special adviser and I remained in close contact. So by the time we met again yesterday the issues that remained were very few indeed and were settled relatively rapidly.

And I may on this occasion also point out that while the North Vietnamese are the most difficult people to negotiate with that I have ever encountered when they do not want to settle, they are also the most effective that I have to deal with when they finally decide to settle.

So that we have gone through peaks and valleys in these negotiations of extraordinary intensity.

Now then, let me sum up where this agreement has left us. First with respect to what we said we would try to achieve, then with respect to some of its significance and finally with respect to the future.

First, when I met this group on Oct. 26 and delivered myself of some epigrammatic phrases, we obviously did not want to give a complete checklist and we did not want to release the agreement as it then stood, because it did not seem to us desirable to provide a

checklist against which both sides would then have to measure success and failure in terms of their prestige.

At that time, too, we did not say that it had always been foreseen that there would be another three or four days of negotiations after this tentative agreement had been reached. And the reason why we asked for another negotiation was because it seemed to us at that point that for a variety of reasons, which I explained then and again on Dec. 16, those issues could not be settled within the time frame that the North Vietnamese expected.

It is now a matter of history and it is therefore not essential to go into a debate of—on what we based this judgment. But that was the reason why the agreement was not signed on Oct. 30 and not any of the speculations that had been so much in print and on television.

Controls to Be in Place

Now what did we say on Oct. 26 we wanted to achieve?

We said first of all that we wanted to make sure that the control machinery would be in place at the time of the cease-fire. We did this because we had information that there were plans by the other side to mount a major offensive to coincide with the signing of the cease-fire agreement. This objective has been achieved by the fact that the protocols will be signed on the same day as the agreement, by the fact that the international control commission and the four party military commission will meet within 24 hours of the agreement going into effect or no later than Monday morning, Saigon time, that the regional teams of the international control commission will be in place 48 hours thereafter and that all other teams will be in place within 15 and a maximum to 30 days after that.

Second, we said that we wanted to compress the time interval between the cease-fire expected in Laos and Cambodia and the cease-fire in Vietnam. For reasons which I have explained to you we cannot be as specific about the cease-fires in Laos and Cambodia as we can about the agreements that are being signed on Saturday.

But we can say with confidence that the formal cease-fire in Laos will go into effect in a considerably shorter period of time than was envisaged in October, and since the cease-fire in Cambodia depends to some extent on developments in Laos we expect the same to be true there.

Ambiguities Removed

We said that certain linguistic ambiguities should be removed. The linguistic ambiguities were produced by the somewhat extraordinary negotiating procedure whereby a change in the English text did not always produce a correlative change in the Vietnamese text. All the linguistic ambiguities to which we referred in October have in fact been removed. At that time I mentioned only one, and therefore I'm pleased to recall it.

I pointed out that the United States position had consistently been a rejection of the imposition of a coalition government on the people of South Vietnam. I said then that the National Council of Reconciliation was not a coalition government nor was it conceived as a coalition government. The Vietnamese language text, however, permitted an interpretation of the word administrative structure as applied to the National Council of Reconciliation which would have lent itself to the interpretation that it came close or was identical with a coalition government.

You will find that in the text of this agreement the word "administrative structure" does not—no longer exists, and therefore this particular, shall we say, ambiguity has been removed.

I pointed out in October that we had to find a procedure for signing which would be acceptable to all the parties for whom obligations were involved. This has been achieved.

I pointed out on Oct. 26 that we would seek greater precision with respect to certain obligations, particularly without spelling them out as they applied to the demilitarized zone and to the obligations with respect to Laos and Cambodia. That, too, has been achieved.

South's Sovereignty Noted

And I pointed out in December that we were looking for some means which—some expression which would make clear that the two parts of Vietnam would live in peace with each other and that neither side would impose its solution on the other by force. This is now explicitly provided and we have achieved formulations in which in a number of the paragraphs of Article 14, 18 (e) and 20, have specific references to the sovereignty of South Vietnam. There are specific references, moreover to the same thing in Article 6 and Article 11 of the I.C.C.'s protocol. There are specific references to the right of the South Vietnamese people to self-determination and therefore we believe that we have achieved substantial changes that we mentioned on October—or adaptations that we asked for on Oct. 26.

We did not increase our demands after Oct. 26, and we substantially achieved the clarifications which we sought.

Now then, it is obvious that a war that has lasted for 10 years will have many elements that cannot be completely satisfactory to all the parties concerned, and in the two periods the North Vietnamese were working with dedication and seriousness on a conclusion—the period in October and the period after we resumed talks in Jan. 8. It was always clear that a lasting peace could come about only if neither side sought to achieve everything that it had wanted.

Indeed its stability depended on the relative satisfaction and therefore on the relative dissatisfaction of all the parties concerned. And therefore it is also clear that when—whether this agreement brings a lasting peace or not depends not only on its provisions but also on the spirit in which it is implemented. It will be our challenge in the future to move the controversies that could not be stilled by any one document from the level of military conflict to the level of positive human aspirations and to absorb the enormous talents and dedication of the people of Indochina in tasks of construction rather than in tasks of destruction.

We will make a major effort to move to create a framework where we hope in a short time the animosities and the hatred and the suffering of this period will be seen as aspects of the past and where the debates concerned differences of opinion as to how to achieve positive goals.

'Less Brutal Means'

Of course the hatred will not rapidly disappear, and of course people who have fought for 25 years will not easily give up their objectives. But also people who have suffered for 25 years may at last come to know that they can achieve their real satisfaction by other and less brutal means.

The President said yesterday that we have to remain vigilant and so we shall. But we shall also dedicate ourselves to positive efforts, and as for us at home, it should be clear by now that no one in the war has had a monopoly of anguish and that no one in these debates has had a monopoly of moral insight. And now that at last we have achieved an agreement in which the United States did not prescribe the political future to its allies, an agreement which should preserve the dignity and the self-respect of all of the parties. And together with healing the wounds in Indochina, we can begin to heal the wounds in America.

And now I'll be glad to answer your questions.

Questions and Answers

Q. [What supervision] do you envisage over the Ho Chi Minh Trail by an international agency?

A. We expect that the International Control Commission that exists in Laos will be reinstituted. We have also provided for the establishment of border teams—as you can see from the maps—at all the terminal points of the Ho Chi Minh Trail into South Vietnam. And therefore we believe that there will be international supervision of the provisions both within Laos and within South Vietnam. Marvin.

Q. One of the major problems has been the continued presence of North Vietnamese troops in the South. Could you tell us first, so far as you know, how many of these troops are there in the South now, and do you have any understanding or assurance that these troops will be withdrawn?

A. Our estimate of the number of North Vietnamese troops in the South is approximately 145,000. Now, I want to say a number of things with respect to them.

First, nothing in the agreement establishes the right of North Vietnamese troops to be in the South. Secondly, the North Vietnamese have never claimed that they have a right to have troops in the South. And while opinions may differ about the exact accuracy of that statement, from a legal point of view it is important because it maintains the distinction that we too maintain.

Thirdly, if this agreement is implemented, the North Vietnamese troops in the South should over a period of time be subject to considerable reduction. First, there is a flat prohibition against the introduction of any outside forces for any reason whatsoever. So that the normal attrition of personnel cannot be made up by the reinfiltration of outside forces—I'm talking now about the provisions of the agreement.

Secondly, there is a flat prohibition against the presence of foreign forces in Laos and Cambodia and therefore a flat prohibition against the use of the normal infiltration corridors.

Zone Activity Prohibited

Thirdly, as the agreement makes clear, military movement of any kind across the demilitarized zone is prohibited, both in the clause requiring respect for the demilitarized zone, which by definition excludes military personnel, and second, in the clause that says only modalities of civilian movement can be discussed, not of any other movement between North and South Vietnam.

And fifthly, there is a provision requiring the reduction and demobilization of forces on both sides, the major part of which on the South Vietnamese side is believed by all knowledgeable observers to have arrived from outside of South Vietnam.

Therefore, it is our judgment that there is no way that North Vietnam can live up to that agreement without there being a reduction of the North Vietnamese forces in South Vietnam, without this being explicity stated.

Of course, it is not inconceivable that the agreement will not in all respects be lived up to. In that case, adding another clause that will not be lived up to, specifically requiring it, would not change the situation. It is our judgment and our expectation that the agreement will be lived up to and therefore we believe that the problem of these forces will be taken care of by the evolution of events in South Vietnam. Peter.

Clarification on Troops

Q. Can I try to get a clarification of that point? Several times I think you said it is understood that North Vietnamese troops in Laos and Cambodia are considered foreign troops. A. That is right.

Q. Are they so considered? A. I said it was, Peter.

Q. Well, you said it in answer to Marvin's question. But is it so considered in South Vietnam? Is North Vietnam a foreign entity in South Vietnam according to this agreement?

A. This is one of the points on which the bitterest feeling rages. And which it is best not to deal with in a formal and legalistic manner. As I have pointed out, in this agreement there are repeated references to the identity of South Vietnam, to the fact that the South Vietnamese people's right of self-determination is recognized both by the D.R.V. and by the United States, to the fact that North and South Vietnam shall settle their disputes peacefully and through negotiation, and other provisions of a similar kind.

Therefore, it is clear there is no legal way by which North Vietnam can use military force against South Vietnam. Now whether that is due to the fact that there are two zones temporarily divided by a provisional demarcation line or it's because North Vietnam is a foreign country with relation to South Vietnam—that is an issue which we have avoided making explicit in the agreement, and on which opinions—and in which ambiguity has its merits.

Legal Use of Force Is Out

From the point of view of the international position, and from the point of view of the obligations of the agreement, there is no legal way by which North Vietnam can use military force vis-à-vis South Vietnam to achieve its objectives.

Q. By what means was the United States able to convince President Thieu to accept the presence of North Vietnamese troops in South Vietnam?

A. First of all, it is not easy to achieve through negotiations what had not been achieved on the battlefield. And if you look at the settlements that have been made in the postwar period, the lines of demarcation have always, almost always, followed the lines of actual control.

Secondly, we have taken the position throughout that the agreement cannot be analyzed in terms of any of its provisions. But it has to be seen in its totality, and in terms of the evolution that it starts.

Thirdly, we have not asked President Thieu, nor has he accepted the presence of North Vietnamese troops in South Vietnam as a legal right. Nor do we accept that as a legal right. We have since October, 1970, proposed a cease-fire in place. A cease-fire in place always has to be between the forces that exist. The alternative of continued war also would have maintained the forces in the country. Under these conditions, they are cut off from the possibility of renewed infiltration, they are prevented from undertaking military action. Their resupply is severely restricted.

And President Thieu, after examing the totality of the agreement, came to the conclusion that it achieved the essential objectives of South Vietnam of permitting his people to bring about self-determination, and of not posing a security risk that he could not handle with the forces that we have equipped and trained. Mr. Horner?

Q. Dr. Kissinger, because of a news report from Paris this morning that actually there were some 15 or 20 protocols of which only four are being made public, were there any secret protocols agreed to?

A. The only protocols that exist are the protocols that have been made public.

Q. Wait a minute—what about understandings?

A. There are with respect to certain phrases read into the record certain statements as to what they mean. But these have been explained in these briefings and made clear. There are no secret understandings.

Q. It's been widely speculated that the 12-day saturation bombing of the North was the key to achieving the agreement that you found acceptable. Was it? And if not, what was?

A. I was asked in October whether the bombing or mining of May 8 brought about the breakthrough in October. I said then that I did not want to speculate on North Vietnamese motives; I have too much trouble analyzing our own. I will give the same answer to your question.

But I will say that there was a deadlock which was

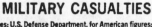

MILITARY CASUALTIES

(Sources: U.S. Defense Department, for American figures; South Vietnamese command, for South Vietnamese figures and North Vietnamese and Vietcong estimates)

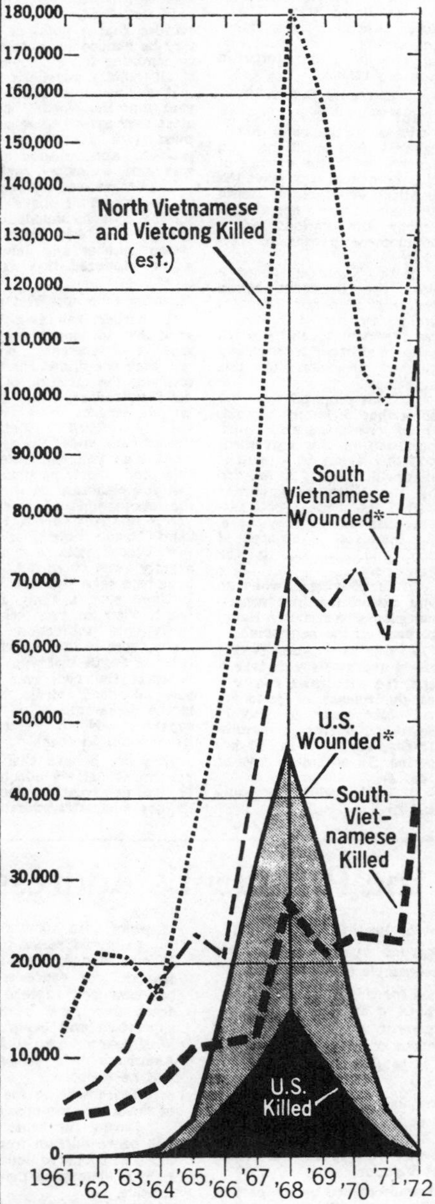

*Requiring hospitalization. U.S. also lists the wounded who do not require hospitalization. South Vietnam does not.

Totals from Jan. 1, 1961 through Jan. 13, 1973:

45,933 Americans killed, 153,300 wounded (303,616, if less seriously wounded are also added)

183,528 South Vietnamese killed, 499,026 wounded

924,048 North Vietnamese and Vietcong killed

The New York Times/Jan. 25, 1973

described in the middle of December, and there was a rapid movement when negotiations resumed on the technical level on Jan. 3, and on the substantive level on Jan. 8. These facts have to be analyzed by each person for himself.

Basis for Confidence

I want to make one point with respect to the question about understanding. It is obvious that when I speak with some confidence about certain developments that happened with respect to Laos and other places, that this must be based on exchanges that have taken place. But for obvious reasons I cannot go further into them. The formal obligations of the parties have all been revealed and there are no secret formal obligations.

Q. [Is there an] amount to which the United States is committed in rebuilding, in the construction you referred to in North Vietnam, in reparations or whatever it's going to be? Any dollar amount?

A. We will discuss the issue of economic reconstruction of all of Indochina, including North Vietnam, only after the signature of the agreements. And after the implementation is well advanced. And the definition of any particular sum will have to await the discussions which will take place after the agreements are in force.

Q. Dr. Kissinger, is there any understanding with the Soviet Union or with Communist China that they will take part in an international conference or will help toward the preservation of the framework of the agreement?

A. Formal invitations to the international conference have not yet been extended. But we expect both the Soviet Union and the People's Republic of China to participate in the international conference which will take place within 30 days of the signature of the agreement.

We have reason to believe that both of these countries will participate in this conference. Now with respect to their willingness to help this agreement become viable, it is, of course, clear that peace in Indochina requires the self-restraint of all of the major countries. And especially of those countries which on all sides have supplied the wherewithal for this conflict.

We on our part are prepared to exercise such restraint.

We believe that the other countries—The Soviet Union and the Peoples Republic of China — can make a very major contribution to peace in Indochina by exercising similar restraint.

Q. If the peace treaty is violated and if the I.C.C. proves ineffective, will the United States ever again send troops into Vietnam?

A. Well I—

Q. What was the question?

A. The question is whether the United States will ever again send troops into Vietnam if the peace treaty is violated and if the international control commission proves ineffective. We don't —I don't want to speculate on hypothetical situations that we don't expect to arise.

Q. What agreement or understanding is there on the— on the role that will be played by the so-called neutralist or third-force groups in Vietnam in the National Council of Reconciliation?

A. The question is what agreement or understanding is there with respect to the so-called neutralist forces that exist in Vietnam in the so-called National Council of Reconciliation. We have taken the position throughout that the future political evolution of South Vietnam should be left to the greatest extent possible to the South Vietnamese themselves and should not be predetermined by the United States. Therefore, there is no understanding in any detail on the role of any particular force in South Vietnam.

Elections Favored

The United States has always taken the view that it favored free elections but, on the whole, the essence of this agreement is to leave the political evolution of South Vietnam to negotiation among the various South Vietnamese parties or factions.

Q. Dr. Kissinger, about a year ago President Nixon outlined a peace proposal which included a provision for President Thieu to resign prior to election. Is there any similar provision in this agreement?

A. That proposal was in a somewhat different context. In any event, there is no such provision in this agreement and this again is a matter that will have to be decided by the Vietnamese parties within the context of whatever negotiation they have. But there's no requirement of any kind like this in the agreement.

Q. Dr. Kissinger, when do you expect the first American planes to arrive in Hanoi to pick up the prisoners?

A. Our expectation is that the withdrawals will take— that the withdrawals as well as the release of prisoners will take place in roughly equal increments of—within 15 days each over the 60-day period. So, within 15 days of Jan. 27.

Q. You've addressed yourself to . . .

A. That's the outside time. It could be faster.

Q. . . . the earliest time, sir.

A. Well, I can't give any earlier time than within 15 days.

Q. You've addressed yourself to this general area before, Doctor, but the question keeps coming up. Would you just review for us briefly how you feel that the agreement that you've reached differs from one that could have been reached, say, four years ago.

A. Four years ago, the North Vietnamese totally refused to separate political and military issues. Four years ago, the North Vietnamese insisted that, as a condition to negotiation, the existing governmental structure in South Vietnam would have to be disbanded and only after this governmental structure had been disbanded and a different one had been installed would they even discuss much less implement any of the other provisions of the agreement. And therefore, until Oct. 8 of this year, all of the various schemes that were constantly being discussed foundered on the one root fact of the situation that the North Vietnamese until Oct. 8 of this year demanded that a political victory be handed to them as a precondition for a discussion of all military questions.

It was not until Oct. 8 this year that the North Vietnamese ever agreed to separate these two aspects of the problem, and as soon as it was done, we moved rapidly.

Then there was the second phase which I have described, which included the changes that were made between October and January which produced this agreement.

Identity of South Vietnam

Q. Earlier you said that as of Dec. 16, there were various disagreements which you then listed, and the first one was the question of the demilitarized zone and associated aspects over what identity South Vietnam should have under the agreement. Can you elaborate on this and most particularly can you elaborate on it from the standpoint of whether you're referring here to President Thieu's objections?

A. I have made clear what exactly was involved. We have here several issues: one, is there such a thing as a South Vietnam even temporarily until unification; secondly, who is the legitimate ruler of South Vietnam. This is what the civil war has been all about; thirdly, what is the demarcation line that separates North Vietnam from South Vietnam.

Now we believe that the agreement defines adequately the demarcation line. It defines adequately what the identity is to which we refer. It leaves open to negotiation among the parties the political evolution of South Vietnam and therefore the definition of what ultimately will be considered by all South Vietnamese the legitimate rule.

The President has made clear yesterday that as far as the United States is concerned, we recognize President Thieu. This is a situation that has existed in other countries and these were the three principal issues involved, of which two have international significance and were settled within the agreement and the third has significance in terms of the political evolution of South Vietnam and that has been left to the self-determination of the South Vietnamese people.

As to the question of President Thieu's objections and comments, and so forth, we said on Oct. 26 that obviously in a war fought in South Vietnam, in a war that has had hundreds of thousands of casualties of South Vietnamese, enormous devastation within South Vietnam, it stands to reason that the views of our allies will have to be considered. There's nothing wrong or immoral for them to have such views.

Second, their perception of the risks has to be different from our perception of the risks. We are 12,000 miles away. If we made a mistake in our assessment of the situation, it will be painful. If they made an assessment—a mistake in the assessment of the situation, it can be fatal, and therefore they have had a somewhat less flexible attitude. Where we in some respects have wanted to—had at some points been content with more ambiguous formulations, they were not.

Nevertheless, it is also obvious from any reader of the Saigon press and of their official communications that we did not accept all of their comments and that we carried out precisely what the President had said and what was said at the various press conferences in which I presented the U.S. Government's view, namely that we would make the final determination as to when the American participation in the war should end.

Those parts of their comments that we thought were reasonable we made our own; those that we did not we did not. And once we had achieved an agreement with the North Vietnamese that we considered fair and just and honorable, we presented it with great energy and conviction in Saigon.

Q. You say you made some of his points your points. What did he get in January that he didn't have in October?

A. I do not want to discuss what he got. I can only point out what the—I pointed out the list of objectives we set ourselves in October and what was achieved. I point out the changes that were achieved between October and January. We believed them to be substantial, and I do not want to make a checklist of saying which originated in Saigon, which originated in Washington. I think somebody in the rear has been very patient.

Q. Did you first feel strength in the negotiations as a result of the saturation bombing?

A. The term "saturation bombing" has certain connotations. We carried out the— what was considered to be necessary at the time in order to make clear that the United States could not stand for an indefinite delay in the negotiations.

My role in the negotiations was to present the American point of view. I can only say that we resumed the negotiations on Jan. 8 and the breakthrough occurred on Jan. 9 and I will let those facts speak for themselves.

Q. What is now the extent and the nature of the American commitment to South Vietnam?

A. The United States, as the President said, will continue economic aid to South Vietnam. It will continue that military aid which is permitted by the agreement. The United States is prepared to gear that military aid to the actions of other countries and not to treat it as an end in itself and the United States expects all countries to live up to the provisions of the agreement.

RONALD ZIEGLER. I think we have time for two more questions.

Q. You say that you —

MR. KISSINGER. If Ron had real courage he wouldn't have recognized you.

Why More Arms?

Q. The two South Vietnamese parties, you say, shall be permitted to make periodic replacements of armaments, munitions and war materials which have been destroyed. Why do we have to put any more war materials in there? Why should they be in there, and will these materials come from the United States or what countries?

A. Well let's separate two things—what is permitted by the agreement and what we shall do. What is permitted by the agreement is that military equipment that is destroyed, worn out, used up or damaged can be replaced. The reason for that provision is that if for any reason the war should start at any level, it would be an unfair restriction on our South Vietnamese allies to prohibit them from replacing their weapons if their enemies are able to do so. The second question is the degree therefore to which these weapons have to be replaced—will depend on the degree to which there is military activity. If there is no military activity in South Vietnam, then the number of weapons that are destroyed, damaged or worn out will of course be substantially less than in other circumstances. Secondly, what will be the United States position?

This depends on the overall situation. If there is no military activity, if other countries do not introduce massive military equipment into Vietnam, we do not consider it an end in itself to give military aid, but we believe that it would be unfair and wrong for one country to be armed by its allies while the other one has no right to do so.

Q. What is the plan for the rather sizable United States military force offshore in warships off South Vietnam and also at B-52 bases in Thailand? Will these forces be red[illegible] and is there an understanding with the North Vietnamese that you have not mentioned to us here that would reduce those forces?

A. There is no restriction on American military forces. That is not mentioned in the agreement. One would expect as time goes on that the deployment of our naval forces will take account of the new situation. As you know, we have kept many of our forces on station for longer than the normal period of time, and we have had more carriers in the area than before. But this is not required by the agreement and this is simply a projection of what might happen.

The same is true with respect to Thailand. There are no restrictions on our forces in Thailand. It has always been part of the Nixon doctrine that the deployment of our forces will be related to the degree of the dangers and has not an abstract quality of its own, so that as a general rule one can say that in the initial of the agreement before one knows how it will be implemented, the deployment will be more geared to the war situation, and as the agreement is being implemented, the conditions of peace will have a major impact on it.

But this is simply a projection of our normal policy and is not an outgrowth required by the agreement.

Q. Thank you, gentlemen. Thank you.

Q. Have you worked yourself out of a job?

Transcript of the President's Address Announcing Agreement to End the War

Following is a transcript of President Nixon's address Tuesday night, as recorded by The New York Times and reprinted from yesterday's late editions:

Good evening. I have asked for this radio and television time tonight for the purpose of announcing that we today have concluded an agreement to end the war and bring peace with honor in Vietnam and Southeast Asia.

The following statement is being issued at this moment in Washington and Hanoi:

"At 12:30 Paris time today, Jan. 23, 1973, the agreement on ending the war and restoring peace in Vietnam was initialed by Dr. Henry Kissinger on behalf of the United States and Special Adviser Le Duc Tho on behalf of the Democratic Republic of Vietnam.

"The agreement will be formally signed by the parties participating in the Paris Conference on Vietnam on Jan. 27, 1973, at the International Conference Center in Paris. The cease-fire will take effect at 2400 Greenwich mean time, Jan. 27, 1973. The United States and the Democratic Republic of Vietnam express the hope that this agreement will insure stable peace in Vietnam and contribute to the preservation of lasting peace in Indochina and Southeast Asia."

Essential Conditions 'Have Been Met'

That concludes the formal statement.

Throughout the years of negotiations, we have insisted on peace with honor.

In my addresses to the nation from this room on Jan. 25 and May 8, I set forth the goals that we considered essential for peace with honor. In the settlement that has now been agreed to, all the conditions that I laid down then have been met—a cease-fire internationally supervised will begin at 7 P.M. this Saturday, Jan. 27, Washington time. Within 60 days from this Saturday all Americans held prisoners of war throughout Indochina will be released.

There will be the fullest possible accounting for all of those who are missing in action.

During the same 60-day period all American forces will be withdrawn from South Vietnam.

The people of South Vietnam have been guaranteed the right to determine their own future without outside interference.

By joint agreement, the full text of the agreement and the protocols to carry it out will be issued tomorrow.

Throughout these negotiations we have been in the closest consultation with President Thieu and other representatives of the Republic of Vietnam.

This settlement meets the goals and has the full support of President Thieu and the Government of the Republic of Vietnam as well as that of our other allies who are affected.

The United States will continue to recognize the Government of the Republic of Vietnam as the sole legitimate government of South Vietnam. We shall continue to aid South Vietnam within the terms of the agreement, and we shall support efforts for the people of South Vietnam to settle their problems peacefully among themselves.

We must recognize that ending the war is only the first step toward building the peace.

All parties must now see to it that this is a peace that lasts and also a peace that heals, and a peace that not only ends the war in Southeast Asia but contributes to the prospects of peace in the whole world. This will mean that the terms of the agreement must be scrupulously adhered to. We shall do everything the agreement requires of us, and we shall expect the other parties to do everything it requires of them. We shall also expect other interested nations to help insure that the agreement is carried out and peace is maintained.

As this long and very difficult war ends I would like to address a few special words to each of those who have been parties in the conflict.

First, to the people and Government of South Vietnam. By your courage, by your sacrifice, you have won the precious right to determine your own future and you have developed the strength to defend that right.

We look forward to working with you in the future, friends in peace as we have been allies in war.

To the leaders of North Vietnam: As we have ended the war through negotiations, let us now build a peace of reconciliation.

For our part, we are prepared to make a major effort to help achieve that goal. But just as reciprocity was needed to end the war, so too will it be needed to build and strengthen the peace.

To the other major powers that have been involved, even indirectly: Now is the time for mutual restraint so that the peace we have achieved can last.

And finally, to all of you who are listening, the American people: Your steadfastness in supporting our insistence on peace with honor has made peace with honor possible.

I know that you would not have wanted that peace jeopardized.

With our secret negotiations at the sensitive stage they were in during this recent period, for me to have discussed publicly our efforts to secure peace would not only have violated our understanding with North Vietnam, it would have seriously harmed and possibly destroyed the chances for peace.

Therefore I know that you now can understand why during these past several weeks I have not made any public statements about those efforts. The important thing was not to talk about peace but to get peace and to get the right kind of peace.

This we have done.

Now that we have achieved an honorable agreement let us be proud that America did not settle for a peace that would have betrayed our allies, that would have abandoned our prisoners of war or that would have ended the war for us but would have continued the war for the 50 million people of Indochina.

Let us be proud of the two and a half million young Americans who served in Vietnam, who served with honor and distinction in one of the most selfless enterprises in the history of nations.

And let us be proud of those who sacrificed, who gave their lives, so that the people of South Vietnam might live in freedom, and so that the world might live in peace.

In particular, I would like to say a word to some of the bravest people I have ever met—the wives, children, the families of our prisoners of war and the missing in action.

Long Vigil by Families Coming to End

When others called on us to settle on any terms, you had the courage to stand for the right kind of peace, so that those who died and those who suffered would not have died and suffered in vain and so that where this generation knew war, the next generation would know peace. Nothing means more to me at this moment than the fact that your long vigil is coming to an end.

Just yesterday, a great American who once occupied this office died. In his life, President Johnson endured the vilification of those who sought to portray him as a man of war, but there was nothing he cared about more deeply than achieving a lasting peace in the world.

I remember the last time I talked with him. It was just the day after New Year's.

He spoke then of his concern with bringing peace, with making it the right kind of peace. And I was grateful that he once again expressed his support for my efforts to gain such a peace.

No one would have welcomed this peace more than he.

And I know he would join me in asking for those who died and for those who live, let us consecrate this moment by resolving together to make the peace we have achieved a peace that will last.

Thank you, and good evening.

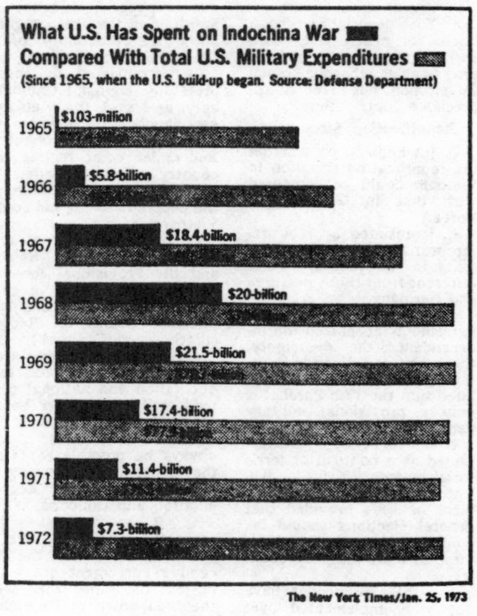
What U.S. Has Spent on Indochina War
Compared With Total U.S. Military Expenditures
(Since 1965, when the U.S. build-up began. Source: Defense Department)
1965
$103-million
1966
$5.8-billion
1967
$18.4-billion
1968
$20-billion
1969
$21.5-billion
1970
$17.4-billion
1971
$11.4-billion
1972
$7.3-billion

The New York Times/Jan. 25, 1973

Transcript of Le Duc Tho's News Conference in Paris on the Vietnam Settlement

PARIS, Jan. 24 (Reuters)—Following, in unofficial translation from the French, is a transcript of Le Duc Tho's news conference today:

Opening Statement

Dear friends, the struggle of the Vietnamese people for independence and liberty has lasted nearly 30 years. In particular, the resistance in the last 13 years with its many trials was the most difficult in the history of our people's struggle against foreign invasion over several centuries.

It is also the most murderous war in the history of the movement of national liberation of the oppressed peoples throughout the world.

Finally, this war has deeply stirred the conscience of mankind.

The negotiations between our Government and the Government of the United States of America for a peaceful settlement of the Vietnamese problem have lasted nearly five years and have gone through many particularly difficult and tense moments.

But we have overcome all obstacles and we have at last reached the agreement on ending the war and restoring peace in Vietnam.

This agreement will be officially signed in Paris in a few days.

The just cause triumphs over the evil cause. The will to live in freedom triumphs over cruelty.

The conclusion of such an agreement represents a very big victory for the Vietnamese people. It is the crowning of a valiant struggle waged in unity by the army and the people of Vietnam on all fronts, at the price of countless sacrifices and privations.

'A Very Big Victory'

It is a very big victory for the fighting solidarity of the peoples of the three countries of Indochina who have always fought side by side against the common enemy for independence and liberty.

It is a very great victory for the Socialist countries, the oppressed peoples and all the peace-loving and justice-loving peoples throughout the world, including the American people, who have demonstrated their solidarity and given devoted assistance to the just struggle of our people.

The return of peace in Vietnam will be greeted with immense joy by our people. At the same time, it will answer the hope which has so long been harbored by the American people and the peace-loving peoples in the world.

With the return of peace, the struggle of the Vietnamese people enters a new period. Our people, lifting high the banner of peace and of national concord, is decided to strictly apply the clauses of the agreement maintaining peace, independence and democracy and heading toward the peaceful reunification of its country.

It will also have to rebuild its war-devastated country and consolidate and develop its friendly relations with all the peoples of the world, including the American people.

Big Tasks Lie Ahead

Heavy tasks still await us in this new period. But the Vietnamese in the North as in the South, at home as abroad, rich in their traditions of unity and perseverance in struggle, following a just policy, strengthened by the close solidarity of the peoples of Laos and Cambodia and benefiting from strong aid from the Socialist countries and all the peace-loving countries of the world, will be able to smooth out all difficulties and victoriously accomplish their tasks.

At a time when peace is dawning on our country, in the name of the Government and people of Vietnam we wish to address our warm thanks to the Socialist countries, to the governments of many countries and to the peoples of the entire world for the sympathy they have shown toward the just struggle of the Vietnamese people and for the active help given in all fields.

In the past years, how many fighters for peace in many countries have known repression and prison, and certainly even sacrificed their lives in the fight they carried out to support the resistance of the Vietnamese people? These noble internationalist feelings and these sublime sacrifices occupy forever a place in our hearts.

The signature of the "Agreement for the Cessation of War and the Reestablishment of Peace in Vietnam" is only a first victory, because the task of strictly applying the agreement is important.

Application of Agreement

Anxious to maintain peace, independence and democracy and heading toward reunification of the country, the Vietnamese people will act in a unified manner to insure the correct and serious application of the clauses of the agreement which will be signed in a few days, and at the same time it will show vigilance towards reactionaries who try to sabotage the agreement.

But we must say that the situation in our country and in the world is developing in an extremely favorable way for the cause of the Vietnamese people.

We have the conviction that the dark designs of the reactionary forces in the country and abroad to obstruct the application of the agreement, or to sabotage it, can only fail.

The Vietnamese people has, therefore, every reason to believe in the victorious accomplishment of its tasks in the new period. No reactionary force will be able to slow down the march forward of the Vietnamese people.

I have finished my statement and I now reserve 20 minutes for questions and replies.

Questions and Answers

Q. I have two questions to put. First, what role did international solidarity in the struggle of the Vietnamese people play in the success of the negotiations? Second, do you think that the Vietnam war will be the last war in the world?

A. The victory of the Vietnamese people is due, above all, to the Vietnamese people's own efforts in its resistance for independence and true freedom. But this victory cannot be separated from the powerful and vigorous help brought by the Socialist countries, by the working class of the whole world and by the oppressed peoples in the whole world.

I will now reply to your second question. I am a Communist, and according to Marxist-Leninist theories so long as imperialism persists in the world there will still be wars.

Q. Where will the scheduled international conference take place? Have the Americans dropped their objections to your proposals to hold it in Paris?

A. As regards the international conference and the location of the conference, the American side and our side are in the process of discussing this question and we have not yet reached a final decision.

Q. Is the January agreement different from the October agreement?

A. Basically, as regards the agreement we reached in the month of October, 1972, and the agreement we reached in the month of January, 1973, the contents are the same.

You can make the comparison in comparing the texts of the agreement of the month of October, 1972, and the agreement of the month of January, 1973.

'No More Problems'

Q. Aside from the conference site, after the signature of the agreements are there other subjects for discussion between you and the United States?

My second question is, I note a difference between the résumé of the agreements of October and those you have shown us and the fact that you talk of negotiations between the concerned South Vietnamese parties. Is there a date fixed for this?

A. After the end of the negotiations, the completion of the agreement and the annex protocols between the American side and our side there are no more problems to be solved. Everything has been completed. That is to say the only thing we will have to discuss will be the site of the conference of international guarantees.

But according to the agreement, the guarantees conference will be called one month after the signature of the agreement. We still have time to solve this question.

After the start of the cease-fire, the South Vietnamese sides will immediately meet to settle the internal questions of South Vietnam. Naturally the two South Vietnamese sides will meet and fix the first dates for the start of their work.

Q. Aside from the four protocols you have just handed to us, are there other protocols which have not been published and are there other tacit annex agreements which have not been published?

A. There is one agreement and four protocols—all the documents which have just been distributed to the press—and these are complete documents covering everything which was negotiated between the two sides.

'What Will Happen?'

Q. You said earlier that the agreement would be initialed by the P.R.C. as a government. President Thieu as well as Mr. Tran Van Lam said yesterday that they would refuse to sign a document on which they found the signature of the P.R.G. as a government. What will happen exactly?

A. The situation in South Vietnam can be characterized in the following manner: There is the existence of two administrations, two armies, two controlled zones and three political forces. No one can deny this truth. Those who deny this truth pass themselves off as blind men. Anyway this truth is well reflected by the agreement which will be signed between the Government of the Democratic Republic of Vietnam and the United States and in the document which will be signed by the four sides at the Paris conference, by the four foreign affairs ministers, on January 27.

Q. Last night President Nixon said the United States continued to admit the Saigon Government as the only true Government of South Vietnam. Does the Government of the DRVN agree with this point of view and if not what will it do?

A. As I answered earlier, the situation in Vietnam is characterized by the existence of two administrations, of two armies, of two differently controlled zones and of three public forces, and this idea is well reflected in the clauses of the agreement and in the course of the negotiations.

You can refer back to the document, the document signed by the two sides, the document signed by the four sides, that is, by the DRVN, the Provisional Revolutionary Government, the Government of the United States, the Government of the Republic of Vietnam, and you will see that this idea is well represented in this agreement.

This idea comes out well in the first paragraph of the agreement on the end of the war and in Article 23 of the agreement signed by the Democratic Republic of Vietnam and the United States of America, the bipartite agreement.

And, besides, you will have the chance of attending in a few days the official signature of the agreement by the four foreign ministers and naturally this will be an event which will concretize this situation existing in South Vietnam.

On Hanoi's Troops

Q. (in English, on the status of North Vietnamese troops in South Vietnam.)

A. [translated into English by interpreter.] Regarding the question of the so-called North Vietnamese forces in South Vietnam, we have been discussing this question for over five years now, and during the scores of private meetings between Dr. Kissinger, Minister Thuy and myself we repeatedly discussed this question.

We have completely rejected the allegation about the so-called North Vietnamese forces in South Vietnam. We have completely rejected this question because, politically speaking, as well as legally speaking, this allegation has no point—is pointless.

And finally, the United States side dropped completely this proposal of theirs. Therefore, in the agreement you can find no word, not a single word implying the presence of the so-called North Vietnamese troops.

Q. The negotiations have been held in France. What do you think of the role of France?

A. The negotiations have lasted for nearly five years and during this period of time I can say that the French Government has made an appreciable contribution.

Reunification Situation

Q. (in English, on whether the reunification situation in Vietnam could be compared with that in Germany or Korea.)

A. [translated by interpreter into English.] The conditions in Vietnam are quite different from those in Korea and Germany.

Moreover, the 1954 Geneva agreement recognized the independence, the sovereignty, the unity and territorial integrity of Vietnam and stipulated that the 17th Parallel is only a provisional military demarcation line.

It can in no way be interpreted as a political or territorial boundary.

Moreover, the Geneva agreement of 1954 provided that general elections should be, would be, organized with a view to reunifying the country.

But these provisions have not been implemented over the past years.

As to the historical causes of this nonimplementation of the general agreement which we repeatedly expounded to you, I think it is unnecessary to repeat here.

Now in the current agreement, there is an explicit provision that the United States, as are other countries, should respect the independence, sovereignty, the unity and the territorial integrity of Vietnam.

The current agreement also stipulates that the 17th Parallel is only a provisional military demarcation line. It is not a political or territorial boundary.

Therefore, it is also stipulated in the agreement that the two zones of Vietnam should consult each other as soon as possible to reunify the country.

Therefore, undoubtedly our people, the Vietnamese people, will advance to the reunification of the country. This is the necessary advance of history. No force can prevent this advance. Moreover, in the agreement there are explicit provisions in this connection.

On Elections in South

Q. [in English.] Despite your hopes, do you really believe that the Thieu Government will allow free and democratic elections in the South. Can the Thieu regime allow the possibility of a Communist Government?

A. [translated by interpreter into English.] Undoubtedly, as I said, the Vietnamese people will advance to reunification of the country. But under what regime the country will be reunited—it depends on the decision of the people in North and South Vietnam.

Q. (on possibility of disagreement between Saigon and the Provisional Revolutionary Government in consultations on setting up National Council of Reconciliation and Concord.)

A. We are firmly convinced that the will for peace, reconciliation and national concord will triumph in South Vietnam. This is why, if there are difficulties, it will always be possible to settle the question of forming a National Council of Reconciliation and Concord.

Q. If, as you have just said, the agreement which you have signed and the December agreement are more or less the same, then why the breakdown in December and why the American bombings?

A. It must be said that, at the time, the negotiations were in the process of developing and I had returned home to report to my Government. The first waves of bombings took place a few hours after my arrival in Hanoi.

And it must be said that these bombings failed completely.

As regards the reaction in the world from the peoples, the organizations, the governments, I believe that you journalists were certainly aware of this reaction.

And naturally these bombings in no way helped the negotiations. On the contrary, they contributed to delay the negotiations. Besides, I already had the opportunity of discussing this subject with you the last time.

But in the end, our side and the American side reached agreement. It is a very great victory for our people.

Vietnamese-American Ties

Q. (on future relations between the United States and North Vietnam and on the October draft agreement.)

A. On this subject, Article 22 states that the cessation of the war, the re-establishment of peace in Vietnam as well as the strict application of the present accord will create conditions for the establishment between the Democratic Republic of Vietnam and the United States of new relations of equality and mutual advantage on the basis of mutual respect, independence, sovereignty and reciprocal noninterference in the internal affairs of each country.

As far as the draft project of October is concerned, we have already given extracts of its main points.

Q. What will be the fate of Saigon's political prisoners?

A. The fate of Saigon's political prisoners is clearly dealt with in Article 8(c) of the agreement. It is certain that the sides should free all political prisoners.

Q. Could you indicate the zones controlled by the Saigon Government and the P.R.G., and the number of residents in them?

A. When the cease-fire becomes effective, there will be very clear indications on this question of the zones controlled by the two parties.

Number of Inhabitants

Q. What is the number of inhabitants of the zones?

A. It is difficult to establish the population in one zone or the other now. There will have to be a control after the cease-fire.

Naturally, one must beware of hazardous forecasts, for example, that such and such a population in such and such a zone follows such and such party, etc. It is difficult to evaluate the exact figure of the population behind such and such a party in a mechanical fashion.

Q. Can you tell us categorically if there are any additional secret understandings or agreements in addition to the published accords and protocols, and if the answer is yes, can you tell us what general subjects might be covered by these additional agreements?

A. (translated into English by interpreter.) The answer to this question has been given.

Q. (on what specific agreements have been reached concerning the amount and form of United States aid for the reconstruction of Vietnam.)

A. (translated into English by interpreter.) The question has been discussed with the U.S. side and it will continue to be discussed with the U.S. side. The United States cannot avoid responsibility for contributing to the healing of the war wounds after so many years of war.

Q. Where will the South Vietnamese parties meet, in Paris or in South Vietnam itself? And, secondly, what provisions have been made for bringing about a cease-fire in Laos and Cambodia?

A. After the cease-fire comes into effect, the two sides of Vietnamese parties will meet to discuss procedural questions and to determine the place of their next meeting. The negotiations between the DRV and the U.S. deal with the question of peace in Vietnam.

As to the question of peace in Laos and Cambodia, it falls within the competence and the sovereignty of the peoples of Laos and Cambodia. As to the international guarantee conference, its aim is to guarantee peace in Vietnam and not for Indochina.

Signing by the Parties

Q. (on whether meetings between the South Vietnamese sides will be based on equality of the two sides and on the procedure for signing the agreement and protocol.)

A. The two South Vietnamese sides will meet on a basis of equality, of mutual respect and reciprocal noneliminataion.

The four ministers of foreign affairs will sign the agreement and three protocols, and the two sides—the Democratic Republic of Vietnam and the United States of America—will sign four protocols, the fourth protocol being a protocol which concerns the U.S.A. and the DRVN only since it is a protocol dealing with minesweeping in North Vietnam.

Q. (on the agreement on the National Council of Reconciliation and Concord.)

A. In the end, we reached an agreement not to use the term "structure of power" or "administrative structure" but to call it directly the National Council of Reconciliation and National Concord, for the importance of the body lies in its way of proceeding in its work. The council has three equal components; therefore, the unanimity principle is indispensable so as not to allow one party to eliminate or bring pressure to bear on another party; therefore, the principle does not at all weaken the power of this council. On the contrary, this principle responds to the very nature of the council.

The 60-Day Period

Q. (concerns the immediate events expected to take place in Vietnam within 60 days.)

A. [translated into English by interpreter.] The 60-day period is determined for the complete withdrawal from South Vietnam of United States forces and of those countries allied with the United States. This is also the trial period for the dismantling of U.S. military bases in South Vietnam, and this is also the trial period for the total release of captured military personnel of the parties. All these things can be done within 60 days.

Q. (on the third force.)

A. The two South Vietnamese parties will start consultation to fix the composition of the National Council of Concord.

Q. Have the four countries of the International Control Commission agreed to participate?

A. [Translated into English by interpreter.] They have accepted to be members of the I.C.C., and the commission begins operating immediately after the cease-fire comes into effect.

Q. Have Canada, Poland, Hungary and Indonesia agreed to participate in that commission?

A. [translated into English by interpreter.] They have.

Q. (on possible difficulties of the talks in October being due to controversy over the number of members of the International Control Commission.)

A. As far as the October difficulties are concerned, there were several reasons, not only the reason concerning the International Commission. Concerning the number of personnel of the International Commission, we have arrived at an agreement—1,160.

Q. (on contacts between Vietcong and Saigon.)

A. At present, Madame Binh is in Paris. Naturally we await the signature by the four foreign ministers. Naturally after the re-establishment of peace, the parties will enter into consultation and there will not be any difficulties about movement.

Q. Has the Provisional Revolutionary Government established a capital in South Vietnam?

A. (translated into English by interpreter.) After the restoration of peace, of course the P.R.G. will have its government machinery and mechanisms and its location in South Vietnam. You will know about that. The reason why we cannot tell you the location of the P.R.G. before is because if it is known then the U.S. will bomb it.

Q. How many U.S. military personnel will be based in North Vietnam to supervise the mining operations in the rivers and estuaries?

A. (translated into English by interpreter.) We have come to an agreement on the removal of mines. The U.S. will play the principal role in this removal of mines and we are now discussing such questions with the United States.

Q. How many will be based in North Vietnam?

A. (translated into English by interpreter.) We have not decided on that question. This question, technical questions, are being discussed now. But in any case, there will be a number of Americans admitted to cooperate with us on the removal of the mines.

Mr. Tho: Thank you to you all. During our long resistance and during the long years of negotiations our journalist friends have closely followed the situation, and I can say you have contributed in part to the re-establishment of peace in Vietnam.

In the name of the Government and the people of Vietnam, I wish to thank you. I have accomplished my task and I will be returning very soon to my country. I wish to take the opportunity to say goodbye and thank you, and since the Vietnamese Tet is close, I wish you a good Vietnamese New Year.

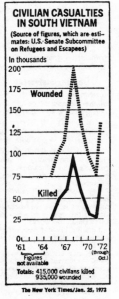

CIVILIAN CASUALTIES IN SOUTH VIETNAM

(Source of figures, which are estimates: U.S. Senate Subcommittee on Refugees and Escapees)

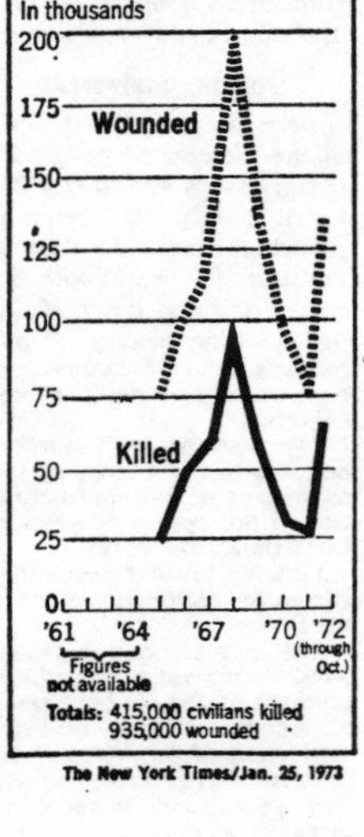

In thousands
200
175
150
125
100
75
50
25
0
Wounded
Killed
'61
'64
'67
'70
'72
(through Oct.)
Figures not available

Totals: 415,000 civilians killed
935,000 wounded

The New York Times/Jan. 25, 1973

Excerpts From Thieu's Talk on Accord

Following, in unofficial translation, are excerpts from President Nguyen Van Thieu's radio speech in Saigon yesterday on the cease-fire agreement. The excerpts appeared in late editions of The New York Times yesterday and are being reprinted to complete the documentary record of the Vietnam peace agreement.

To all my compatriots, soldiers and Government cadres:

You probably remember on Oct. 24 I talked to you for about two hours regarding the signing of a peace in Vietnam. Today my talk will deal with the same thing. My talk goes to all of you —to our religious, political and social leaders, to our soldiers, our police, to all the people in the villages, our civil servants and veterans.

After three months of negotiating between the United States and Hanoi, and after much bombing we finally have results today.

Today, Jan. 24, 1973, an agreement on peace for Vietnam has been reviewed for the last time and will be officially signed between all parties participating in the Paris peace talks on Vietnam on Jan. 27 and a cease-fire will come into effect at 8 A.M. Saigon time on Sunday Jan. 28.

After 18 years of savage fighting the Communists have been forced to stop the conflict because they cannot beat us by force or by violence.

Our people have truly destroyed the Communist troops that have come from the North and we have valiantly fought the forces that are in the South.

Vietnam will remain two zones and will be reunified through peaceful means. The Communists have been forced to recognized two Vietnams.

North Vietnam will respect the sovereignty and independence of South Vietnam. Up to now the Communists have not been successful in carrying out their plans and have been forced to recognize that in the South there is one legal government and that is the legal Government of South Vietnam.

There will not be a two-part government in South Vietnam. The Communists have failed to win their demands for neutralism in the Communist way and to overthrow the President of Vietnam and abolish the legal institutions of Vietnam.

The Communists have failed and will fail in their demand to disband the Vietnamese Army and pull down the structure of Government in Vietnam. They have failed and will fail to make the South Vietnamese people accept a coalition government in South Vietnam.

The Communists demanded that we recognize the Provisional Revolutionary Government of South Vietnam. But they have failed in this respect and no longer pursue this demand because they know we will never accept two governments in South Vietnam.

In South Vietnam there is only one legal government, established and elected by the people of South Vietnam. The Communists have been made to recognize the sovereignty of South Vietnam and that the South Vietnamese people will decide their own fate by elections and through negotiations with the Liberation Front.

As long as there are foreign troops in South Vietnam the sovereignty and independence of South Vietnam cannot be respected.

All these things which the Communists have been made to respect are in the cease-fire agreement.

In regard to the participation of members of the National Liberation Front in the Government of Vietnam — this will be discussed and negotiated between the South Vietnamese Government and the Front.

The signing of the agreement means the beginning of peace. But it does not mean peace.

It is not that we are overly suspicious. It is because we have had plenty of experience with the Communists in this regard and we don't place too much trust in their signature.

Even if there is an agreement between the South Vietnamese Government and the National Liberation Front it remains to be seen if the Front will carrry out the terms of the agreement.

If an election is agreed on by the Republic of Vietnam Government and the Liberation Front, it remains to be seen whether the Front will accept the result of the election.

Although I cannot guarantee there will be a true peace in Vietnam, I shall see to it that peace will come.

This is only the beginning of the end of the Communist aggression by force. Another phase will now come and it is going to be a political phase. This political struggle is inevitable.

The political struggle phase, although not as bloody, will be as tough and dangerous as the military struggle phase.

If South Vietnam still exists after 17 long years of hard struggle then South Vietnam will not be lost to the Communists.

As long as the 17 million people of South Vietnam, as long as the Government, as long as the Constitution, and as long as the people and cadres remain, then the Republic of Vietnam will survive.

We are determined to step into the new phase of the struggle with strength. Only in this way will we win.